1/87

The Encyclopedia of Religion

The Encyclopedia of Religion

Mircea Eliade

EDITOR IN CHIEF

Volume 2

MACMILLAN PUBLISHING COMPANY
New York

Collier Macmillan Publishers
London

MACMILLAN PUBLISHING COMPANY
866 Third Avenue, New York, NY 10022

Collier Macmillan Canada, Inc.

Library of Congress Catalog Card Number: 86-5432

PRINTED IN THE UNITED STATES OF AMERICA

printing number
1 2 3 4 5 6 7 8 9 10

Library of Congress Cataloging-in-Publication Data

The Encyclopedia of religion.

Includes bibliographies and index.
1. Religion—Dictionaries. I. Eliade, Mircea, 1907–1986. II. Adams, Charles J.
BL31.#46 1986 200′.3′21 86-5432
ISBN 0-02-909480-1 (set)
ISBN 0-02-909710-X (v. 2)

Acknowledgments of sources, copyrights, and permissions to use previously published materials are gratefully made in a special listing in volume 16.

Abbreviations and Symbols Used in This Work

abbr. abbreviated; abbreviation
abr. abridged; abridgment
AD *anno Domini,* in the year of the (our) Lord
Afrik. Afrikaans
AH *anno Hegirae,* in the year of the Hijrah
Akk. Akkadian
Ala. Alabama
Alb. Albanian
Am. *Amos*
AM *ante meridiem,* before noon
amend. amended; amendment
annot. annotated; annotation
Ap. *Apocalypse*
Apn. *Apocryphon*
app. appendix
Arab. Arabic
ʿArakh. *ʿArakhin*
Aram. Aramaic
Ariz. Arizona
Ark. Arkansas
Arm. Armenian
art. article (pl., arts.)
AS Anglo-Saxon
Asm. Mos. *Assumption of Moses*
Assyr. Assyrian
A.S.S.R. Autonomous Soviet Socialist Republic
Av. Avestan
ʿA.Z. *ʿAvodah zarah*
b. born
Bab. Babylonian
Ban. Bantu
1 Bar. *1 Baruch*
2 Bar. *2 Baruch*
3 Bar. *3 Baruch*
4 Bar. *4 Baruch*
B.B. *Bava' batra'*
BBC British Broadcasting Corporation
BC before Christ
BCE before the common era
B.D. Bachelor of Divinity
Beits. *Beitsah*
Bekh. *Bekhorot*
Beng. Bengali
Ber. *Berakhot*
Berb. Berber
Bik. *Bikkurim*
bk. book (pl., bks.)
B.M. *Bava' metsiʿa'*
BP before the present
B.Q. *Bava' qamma'*
Brāh. *Brāhmaṇa*
Bret. Breton
B.T. Babylonian Talmud
Bulg. Bulgarian
Burm. Burmese
c. *circa,* about, approximately
Calif. California
Can. Canaanite
Catal. Catalan
CE of the common era
Celt. Celtic
cf. *confer,* compare
Chald. Chaldean
chap. chapter (pl., chaps.)
Chin. Chinese
C.H.M. Community of the Holy Myrrhbearers
1 Chr. *1 Chronicles*
2 Chr. *2 Chronicles*
Ch. Slav. Church Slavic
cm centimeters
col. column (pl., cols.)
Col. *Colossians*
Colo. Colorado
comp. compiler (pl., comps.)
Conn. Connecticut
cont. continued
Copt. Coptic
1 Cor. *1 Corinthians*
2 Cor. *2 Corinthians*
corr. corrected
C.S.P. Congregatio Sancti Pauli, Congregation of Saint Paul (Paulists)
d. died
D Deuteronomic (source of the Pentateuch)
Dan. Danish
D.B. Divinitatis Baccalaureus, Bachelor of Divinity
D.C. District of Columbia
D.D. Divinitatis Doctor, Doctor of Divinity
Del. Delaware
Dem. *Dema'i*
dim. diminutive
diss. dissertation
Dn. *Daniel*
D.Phil. Doctor of Philosophy
Dt. *Deuteronomy*
Du. Dutch
E Elohist (source of the Pentateuch)
Eccl. *Ecclesiastes*
ed. editor (pl., eds.); edition; edited by
ʿEduy. *ʿEduyyot*
e.g. *exempli gratia,* for example
Egyp. Egyptian
1 En. *1 Enoch*
2 En. *2 Enoch*
3 En. *3 Enoch*
Eng. English
enl. enlarged
Eph. *Ephesians*
ʿEruv. *ʿEruvin*
1 Esd. *1 Esdras*
2 Esd. *2 Esdras*
3 Esd. *3 Esdras*
4 Esd. *4 Esdras*
esp. especially
Est. Estonian
Est. *Esther*
et al. *et alii,* and others
etc. *et cetera,* and so forth
Eth. Ethiopic
EV English version
Ex. *Exodus*
exp. expanded
Ez. *Ezekiel*
Ezr. *Ezra*
2 Ezr. *2 Ezra*
4 Ezr. *4 Ezra*
f. feminine; and following (pl., ff.)
fasc. fascicle (pl., fascs.)
fig. figure (pl., figs.)
Finn. Finnish
fl. *floruit,* flourished
Fla. Florida
Fr. French
frag. fragment
ft. feet
Ga. Georgia
Gal. *Galatians*
Gaul. Gaulish
Ger. German
Giṭ. *Giṭṭin*
Gn. *Genesis*
Gr. Greek
Ḥag. *Ḥagigah*
Ḥal. *Ḥallah*
Hau. Hausa
Hb. *Habakkuk*
Heb. Hebrew
Heb. *Hebrews*
Hg. *Haggai*
Hitt. Hittite
Hor. *Horayot*
Hos. *Hosea*
Ḥul. *Ḥullin*
Hung. Hungarian
ibid. *ibidem,* in the same place (as the one immediately preceding)
Icel. Icelandic
i.e. *id est,* that is
IE Indo-European
Ill. Illinois
Ind. Indiana
intro. introduction
Ir. Gael. Irish Gaelic
Iran. Iranian
Is. *Isaiah*
Ital. Italian
J Yahvist (source of the Pentateuch)
Jas. *James*
Jav. Javanese
Jb. *Job*
Jdt. *Judith*
Jer. *Jeremiah*
Jgs. *Judges*
Jl. *Joel*
Jn. *John*
1 Jn. *1 John*
2 Jn. *2 John*
3 Jn. *3 John*
Jon. *Jonah*
Jos. *Joshua*
Jpn. Japanese
JPS Jewish Publication Society translation (1985) of the Hebrew Bible
J.T. Jerusalem Talmud
Jub. *Jubilees*
Kans. Kansas
Kel. *Kelim*

Ker. *Keritot*
Ket. *Ketubbot*
1 Kgs. *1 Kings*
2 Kgs. *2 Kings*
Khois. Khoisan
Kil. *Kil'ayim*
km kilometers
Kor. Korean
Ky. Kentucky
l. line (pl., ll.)
La. Louisiana
Lam. *Lamentations*
Lat. Latin
Latv. Latvian
L. en Th. Licencié en Théologie, Licentiate in Theology
L. ès L. Licencié ès Lettres, Licentiate in Literature
Let. Jer. *Letter of Jeremiah*
lit. literally
Lith. Lithuanian
Lk. *Luke*
LL Late Latin
LL.D. Legum Doctor, Doctor of Laws
Lv. *Leviticus*
m meters
m. masculine
M.A. Master of Arts
Ma'as. *Ma'aserot*
Ma'as. Sh. *Ma'aser sheni*
Mak. *Makkot*
Makh. *Makhshirin*
Mal. *Malachi*
Mar. Marathi
Mass. Massachusetts
1 Mc. *1 Maccabees*
2 Mc. *2 Maccabees*
3 Mc. *3 Maccabees*
4 Mc. *4 Maccabees*
Md. Maryland
M.D. Medicinae Doctor, Doctor of Medicine
ME Middle English
Meg. *Megillah*
Me'il. *Me'ilah*
Men. *Menaḥot*
MHG Middle High German
mi. miles
Mi. *Micah*
Mich. Michigan
Mid. *Middot*
Minn. Minnesota
Miq. *Miqva'ot*
MIran. Middle Iranian
Miss. Mississippi
Mk. *Mark*
Mo. Missouri
Mo'ed Q. *Mo'ed qaṭan*
Mont. Montana
MPers. Middle Persian
MS. *manuscriptum*, manuscript (pl., MSS)
Mt. *Matthew*
MT Masoretic text
n. note
Na. *Nahum*
Nah. Nahuatl
Naz. *Nazir*
N.B. *nota bene*, take careful note
N.C. North Carolina
n.d. no date
N.Dak. North Dakota
NEB New English Bible
Nebr. Nebraska
Ned. *Nedarim*
Neg. *Nega'im*
Neh. *Nehemiah*
Nev. Nevada
N.H. New Hampshire
Nid. *Niddah*
N.J. New Jersey
Nm. *Numbers*
N.Mex. New Mexico
no. number (pl., nos.)
Nor. Norwegian
n.p. no place
n.s. new series
N.Y. New York
Ob. *Obadiah*
O.Cist. Ordo Cisterciencium, Order of Cîteaux (Cistercians)
OCS Old Church Slavonic
OE Old English
O.F.M. Ordo Fratrum Minorum, Order of Friars Minor (Franciscans)
OFr. Old French
Ohal. *Ohalot*
OHG Old High German
OIr. Old Irish
OIran. Old Iranian
Okla. Oklahoma
ON Old Norse
O.P. Ordo Praedicatorum, Order of Preachers (Dominicans)
OPers. Old Persian
op. cit. *opere citato*, in the work cited
OPrus. Old Prussian
Oreg. Oregon
'Orl. *'Orlah*
O.S.B. Ordo Sancti Benedicti, Order of Saint Benedict (Benedictines)
p. page (pl., pp.)
P Priestly (source of the Pentateuch)
Pa. Pennsylvania
Pahl. Pahlavi
Par. *Parah*
para. paragraph (pl., paras.)
Pers. Persian
Pes. *Pesaḥim*
Ph.D. Philosophiae Doctor, Doctor of Philosophy
Phil. *Philippians*
Phlm. *Philemon*
Phoen. Phoenician
pl. plural; plate (pl., pls.)
PM *post meridiem*, after noon
Pol. Polish
pop. population
Port. Portuguese
Prv. *Proverbs*
Ps. *Psalms*
Ps. 151 *Psalm 151*
Ps. Sol. *Psalms of Solomon*
pt. part (pl., pts.)
1 Pt. *1 Peter*
2 Pt. *2 Peter*
Pth. Parthian
Q hypothetical source of the synoptic Gospels
Qid. *Qiddushin*
Qin. *Qinnim*
r. reigned; ruled
Rab. *Rabbah*
rev. revised
R. ha-Sh. *Ro'sh ha-shanah*
R.I. Rhode Island
Rom. Romanian
Rom. *Romans*
R.S.C.J. Societas Sacratissimi Cordis Jesu, Religious of the Sacred Heart
RSV Revised Standard Version of the Bible
Ru. *Ruth*
Rus. Russian
Rv. *Revelation*
Rv. Ezr. *Revelation of Ezra*
San. *Sanhedrin*
S.C. South Carolina
Scot. Gael. Scottish Gaelic
S.Dak. South Dakota
sec. section (pl., secs.)
Sem. Semitic
ser. series
sg. singular
Sg. *Song of Songs*
Sg. of 3 *Prayer of Azariah and the Song of the Three Young Men*
Shab. *Shabbat*
Shav. *Shavu'ot*
Sheq. *Sheqalim*
Sib. Or. *Sibylline Oracles*
Sind. Sindhi
Sinh. Sinhala
Sir. *Ben Sira*
S.J. Societas Jesu, Society of Jesus (Jesuits)
Skt. Sanskrit
1 Sm. *1 Samuel*
2 Sm. *2 Samuel*
Sogd. Sogdian
Soṭ *Soṭah*
sp. species (pl., spp.)
Span. Spanish
sq. square
S.S.R. Soviet Socialist Republic
st. stanza (pl., ss.)
S.T.M. Sacrae Theologiae Magister, Master of Sacred Theology
Suk. *Sukkah*
Sum. Sumerian
supp. supplement; supplementary
Sus. *Susanna*
s.v. *sub verbo*, under the word (pl., s.v.v.)
Swed. Swedish
Syr. Syriac
Syr. Men. *Syriac Menander*
Ta'an. *Ta'anit*
Tam. Tamil
Tam. *Tamid*
Tb. *Tobit*
T.D. *Taishō shinshū daizōkyō*, edited by Takakusu Junjirō et al. (Tokyo, 1922–1934)
Tem. *Temurah*
Tenn. Tennessee
Ter. *Terumot*
Ṭev. Y. *Ṭevul yom*
Tex. Texas
Th.D. Theologicae Doctor, Doctor of Theology
1 Thes. *1 Thessalonians*
2 Thes. *2 Thessalonians*
Thrac. Thracian
Ti. *Titus*
Tib. Tibetan
1 Tm. *1 Timothy*
2 Tm. *2 Timothy*
T. of 12 *Testaments of the Twelve Patriarchs*
Ṭoh. *Ṭohorot*
Tong. Tongan
trans. translator, translators; translated by; translation
Turk. Turkish
Ukr. Ukrainian
Upan. *Upaniṣad*
U.S. United States
U.S.S.R. Union of Soviet Socialist Republics
Uqts. *Uqtsin*
v. verse (pl., vv.)
Va. Virginia
var. variant; variation
Viet. Vietnamese
viz. *videlicet*, namely
vol. volume (pl., vols.)
Vt. Vermont
Wash. Washington
Wel. Welsh
Wis. Wisconsin
Wis. *Wisdom of Solomon*
W.Va. West Virginia
Wyo. Wyoming
Yad. *Yadayim*
Yev. *Yevamot*
Yi. Yiddish
Yor. Yoruba
Zav. *Zavim*
Zec. *Zechariah*
Zep. *Zephaniah*
Zev. *Zevaḥim*

* hypothetical
? uncertain; possibly; perhaps
° degrees
\+ plus
− minus
= equals; is equivalent to
× by; multiplied by
→ yields

A

(CONTINUED)

AUTHORITY is a constant and pervasive phenomenon in the history of religions. One often speaks of traditional authority, scriptural authority, ecclesiastical authority, or imperial authority based on religious claims. As legitimate power to require and receive submission and obedience, it is found in primitive and archaic religions as well as in founded religions wherever the question of order is involved. At different stages of history, a variety of religions have contributed to the creation and maintenance of order by providing the necessary sources of authority. These sources are diverse, but the following may be counted among the major ones: (1) persons, usually classified into various types of religious leadership such as kings, founders of religions, and other leaders of religious communities, (2) sacred writings, (3) traditions, oral and/or written, constituting doctrinal truths and ethical precepts, (4) religious communities with a priesthood and sacramental rites, and (5) personal experience. The question of the legitimacy of this or that authority has been a cause of tension and conflict in and between individual religions, for any authority recognized as legitimate must be respected and placed in proper order, while a rejected authority must be combated.

Authority in Primitive Religions. Among many primitive peoples authority is embodied in orally transmitted traditions of the tribal community. Oral traditions reign supreme, imposing a binding authority on the tribal community in which they are preserved. Especially authoritative are myths, as distinguished from legends and fables. Myth carries authority in primitive society for at least three reasons. First, myth is a "true" story, never a fable, a fiction, or a childish fancy tale. Second, it is a sacred story narrating the acts of the gods and other divine beings that took place in the beginning of mythical time. What occurred—in the words of Mircea Eliade—*in illo tempore* ("at that time") represents for the primitive peoples a reality higher and greater than any kind of historical reality known to them. Myth is authoritative because it reveals the "absolute truth" of the events at the beginning of mythical time. And third, this transhistorical reality that occurred *in illo tempore* serves as the exemplary model for the activities of man in primitive society. According to Bronislaw Malinowski, myth functions as the "charter" of established social facts, including religious beliefs and practices, morality, and everyday rules of conduct.

This divinely sanctioned authoritative tradition is transmitted orally from elders to adolescents during rites of initiation. The candidate for these rites undergoes the process of symbolic death and rebirth, and it is precisely in this process of spiritual regeneration that he receives knowledge about the secrets of the tribal tradition: the myths serve as bearers of traditional authority; they tell of the gods and the origin of the world, the names of the gods, the role and origin of the initiation ceremonies, and, of course, codes of morality and rules of conduct. Thus the initiate comes to obtain gnosis, true authoritative knowledge, essential for his life as a human being, that is, knowledge about the higher and greater reality that sustains the order of the primitive society in which he lives. [*See* Myth.]

Authority in Archaic Religions. The rise of the great civilizations in Mesopotamia, Egypt, India, and China during the third and second millennia BCE marked a significant turning point in history. All these civilizations originated and unfolded along rivers. Irrigation systems had to be worked out in order to control nature and produce a good harvest, and this necessity called for the formation of the efficient administrative organization, which was accompanied by the institution of kingship. A system of writing was a *sine qua non* for this new development.

Under these circumstances, the authority of the oral traditions, which had characterized primitive culture, tended to be replaced by that of written traditions embodied in literary texts. These texts were primarily the creation of royal courts and temples, and those who were engaged in the interpretation and transmission of the texts were scribes and priests. They were professional carriers of the written traditions. In China, for example, government officials were thought to possess magical charisma by virtue of their familiarity with the Confucian classics. These officials made the study, interpretation, and transmission of the words of the master Confucius the focal point of their efforts. Their vision was preeminently political in orientation, and eventually they achieved an extraordinarily stable social order. In India, brahmans occupied the authoritative status in society on account of their esoteric knowledge of the Vedas, the Brāhmaṇas, and the many other sacred writings. Not only in China and India, but also in the ancient Near East, the scribes and priests who served as guardians of the written traditions were the chief religious figures vested with authority. [*See* Scripture.]

It was the king, however, who exercised supreme authority. In archaic civilizations the state functioned as a religious community, as a cosmos, and the king was the person supremely responsible for the maintenance of this cosmic order. Imperial authority was sustained by both the kingship ideology, which was grounded in myths, and the celebration of rituals, especially the New Year festival. The ideology used for the legitimation of imperial authority was different from one region to another; that is, the nature of the king's person and his role in the given cosmic order was variously conceived in different societies, depending on their religious outlook on life and the universe.

In ancient Egypt, for example, the king was believed to be divine in essence. His coronation, usually celebrated at the beginning of a new year, signified not an apotheosis but an epiphany, or self-manifestation, of the god. As long as he ruled, the king was identified with the god Horus; in fact, he was Horus incarnate in his earthly existence, but upon his death he was mystically assimilated to Osiris, the god of rebirth and immortality. Egyptian kingship was also intimately associated with the theme of cosmogony. The dais, for example, on which the new king was seated symbolized the hill of sand, the "first" land, which, according to the Egyptian cosmogonic myth, emerged out of the primeval ocean at the time of beginning. Ascension to the royal throne represented a ritual reenactment of the emergence of a cosmos out of chaos, the primeval waters. Thus, the king repeated the act of creation at his enthronement.

In Mesopotamia, too, the king played a part of vital importance in the well-being of the cosmic order. The *Enuma elish*, the Babylonian epic of creation, was recited and reenacted during the New Year festival. The primary purpose of this recitation and ritual reenactment of the cosmogonic myth was the renewal and regeneration of the cosmos; the king, representing the god Marduk on earth, repeated what took place at the time of absolute beginning, as narrated in the myth. However, the king in ancient Mesopotamia was generally not conceived as a divine being. More properly, he was viewed as divine only while he participated in the ceremonies as representative of Marduk. He was essentially a mortal being, not divine; he represented the gods on earth as their "chosen servant."

The king in ancient China was called the "unique man" as well as the "Son of Heaven" *(t'ien-tzu)*. The Son of Heaven was one who received the mandate of Heaven *(t'ien-ming)*. This notion of the mandate of Heaven implied that imperial authority could not become a permanent possession of the ruler, that Heaven had the complete freedom to confer or withdraw his mandate, just as in ancient Israel God was absolutely free to confer or withdraw his charisma or "gift of grace" from the ruler on earth. The Chinese Son of Heaven obviously had nothing to do with the genealogical concept of kingship, such as in ancient Egypt or Japan, where the king was considered the descendant or incarnation of a certain god; he was simply the earthly representative of Heaven, or heavenly will.

The Chinese king was also conceived as the unique man, one supremely responsible for the maintenance of the cosmic order. He maintained the cosmic order by assisting Heaven in the regulation and harmonization of the *yin* and *yang* principles, as best exemplified by his performance in the ceremonial building, the *ming-t'ang*. This structure was an *imago mundi* ("image of the universe"); it had a square plan symbolizing the earth and was covered by a circular roof, symbolic of the sky. Other features, such as the building's twelve rooms, reflected the cycle of the year. Thus the whole structure was a vast space-and-time diagram, a microcosm. Here the king observed the rituals of worship and sacrifice to Heaven and Earth and myriad spirits in order to secure their favor for the entire universe. When he was to inaugurate the seasons and months, he placed himself in an appropriate room of the building: in the second month of the spring, for example, the king took his position facing east, clothed in green, the color of spring and the east, while in the fall he faced west, clothed in a white ceremonial dress appropriate for the fall and the west. Thus, the king assisted Heaven in guaranteeing the ascendancy of the *yang* principle in spring, while in the fall he helped the rise of the *yin* principle. In essence, the Chinese king was expected to be the harmonizer of the cosmic movement. [*See* Kingship.]

Authority in Founded Religions. The emergence of Buddhism, Christianity, and Islam is an innovation in the history of religions. While in primitive and archaic religions authority is embodied in the sacred kings as well as in oral or written traditions of the tribal community and state, in these founded religions authority is ultimately derived from the founder of a new community of faith, and/or his religious experience. Consequently, the founded religion, whatever it is, develops its own structure of authority and authoritative tradition, which is distinctively different from that in primitive and archaic religions.

Buddhism. The Buddha's authority was grounded in his conviction that he had discovered the Dharma, the universal law of existence, through his personal experience of enlightenment. He himself lived in accordance with it, and on his deathbed he urged his disciples to depend on it as the sole guiding principle of life.

But this truth was not self-evident; it was the truth taught and interpreted by the Buddha that his followers accepted. After his death his closest disciples assumed a new responsibility for the successful realization of the Buddhist ideal. Inevitably, important traditions emerged that were transmitted orally until they were put into writing in the first century BCE. These authoritative oral traditions included the memories and interpretations of the Buddha's own teaching concerning the Dharma and the rules of conduct, the Vinaya, which he had established for the regulation of the *saṃgha,* or Buddhist community.

However, there exists no single canon of scriptures that is universally recognized by all Buddhists. The development of such a canon was impossible because of the decentralized nature of the Buddhist community or the lack of a central ecclesiastical authority to determine orthodoxy. From the beginning of its history, Buddhism allowed its local monastic orders to function as autonomous, self-governing bodies in accordance with the teachings and disciplinary rules that they had inherited. As might be expected, the development of the autonomous monastic orders, or "schools," led to the rise of different versions of the canon without, however, invalidating the importance of the concept of canon or the theoretical unity of the Buddhist community as a whole.

Underneath all this evidence for a virtual absence of the canonical and ecclesiastical authority is the Buddha's insistence on the primacy of self-knowledge, the immediacy of experience, or the personal realization of truth. The canon of scriptures in Buddhism was generally authoritative in concept, but in practice it functioned meaningfully only on the level of particular monastic orders or schools. Moreover, the concept of canonicity itself was often in conflict with the Buddhist belief in the immediacy of the experience of enlightenment. [*See* Buddhist Literature, *article on* Canonization.]

This general trend, away from the traditional scriptures and toward the exploration of new insights, wisdom, and interpretations, is more evident in Mahāyāna Buddhism, which arose in the first century CE, than in Theravāda, that is, Buddhism in more traditional forms, especially regarding the concepts of the Buddha and the Dharma. The concept of the Buddha in Mahāyāna has changed so much that he is no longer simply the person who attained enlightenment in the sixth century BCE, but is regarded as a self-manifestation in history of the *dharmakāya,* a cosmic principle immanent in all beings, the ground of all expressions of the eternal Buddha nature. The Buddha preaching on the Vulture Peak, as he does in Mahāyāna scriptures, is not a human teacher talking to a band of his disciples but a transhistorical being addressing himself to representatives of the whole universe. Mahāyāna scriptures purport to be ever-recurring revelations of the eternal universal principle *(dharmakāya)* and tend to be dissociated from the tradition that is deeply rooted in the particular life of the historical Buddha. A scripture is considered useful insofar as it can lead one to the same religious experience that the Buddha himself had during his life. The implication is that scriptures can ultimately be dispensed with. This implication is most evident in Zen Buddhism, which claims to be based on a "special transmission outside the scriptures" and stresses only the immediate personal experience of *kenshō* ("seeing into one's true nature"), or enlightenment.

Christianity. During his public life of ministry, Jesus of Nazareth rejected the authority of the oral Torah in Judaism, which is often referred to in the New Testament as the "tradition of the fathers." For this he substituted his own authority as interpreter of the written Torah (the Mosaic Law), namely, the authority of the one who proclaimed, in word and deed, God's will as well as the imminent coming of the kingdom of God. Jesus thus presented himself as the ultimate source of the new traditions, which were to become authoritative for the emerging church or community of Christians.

After the resurrection of Jesus, his immediate disciples understood the meaning of his life, suffering, and death in the light of the Hebrew scriptures: Jesus was the Messiah (the Christ) and the fulfillment of God's promise. Naturally, the church assumed responsibility for the creation and transmission of the traditions concerning the words and deeds of Jesus Christ. For the primitive Christian community these traditions were the most appropriate and correct interpretations of the written Torah; they were, in effect, the oral Torah of Christianity. It was especially the apostles and Paul—eyewitnesses to the earthly life and to the resurrection of Jesus Christ—who played a vital role in the interpretation and transmission of the traditions, just as in Judaism scribes and rabbis made essential contributions to the transmission of the oral Torah. Here emerged the authoritative apostolic tradition, which was initially transmitted orally, then written down in the various literary forms, and finally codified by the church as the canon of the New Testament. This New Testament took its place beside the canon of the Old Testament. While Protestantism accords supreme authority to the combined Old and New Testament as the sum total of the apostolic tradition, distinguishing it from the postapostolic tradition, Catholicism asserts the ongoing tradition of the church as having equal authority with the apostolic tradition embodied in the scripture. For Catholics there is no fundamental opposition between scripture and tradition; they are manifestations of one and the same thing, the apostolic tradition.

The essence of the Roman Catholic church lies in its institutional character as the objective organ of salvation, which is embodied in tradition, sacraments (seven in number), and priesthood. The church stands for the eternal presence of Jesus Christ in history, and the papacy is based on the founder's explicit designation of Peter as the foundation rock of the church. Roman Catholics claim a direct succession of papal authority from Peter to the present pope, and this claim to legitimacy, which under the pope's sanction extends to the entire Roman Catholic priesthood, is a vital element in grounding the authority of the church. Sacraments are the objective and tangible channels through which God's grace is communicated to the faithful. The objectivism of Roman Catholicism is best exemplified in its interpretation of the Eucharist, namely, the theory of transubstantiation, officially proclaimed as doctrine in 1215. As to the teaching of the church, it is the *magisterium* (teaching authority) of the church, the pope, who determines the legitimate interpretation of scripture and tradition. From medieval times, membership in the Roman Catholic church has involved submission to papal authority. This is certainly a typical example of institutionalized charisma, and over the centuries it has proved its strength as a source of authority in the lives of its adherents.

Eastern Orthodoxy and Roman Catholicism agree that the church possesses the divinely given infallible authority. Eastern Orthodoxy differs from Roman Catholicism, however, in that its church has no organ of infallibility; the quality of infallibility resides in the mystically conceived church itself, not in any fixed office like that of the Roman Catholic papacy.

The Protestant understanding of authority is inclined more or less toward subjectivism in contrast to the objectivism of medieval Christianity. The Protestant Reformation hinged upon two main principles of complementary importance: justification by faith and the authority of scripture.

The question that most preoccupied Martin Luther was soteriology, that is, the question of personal salvation and its certainty. According to Luther, man is justified before God by faith alone; the church with its priesthood, sacraments, and tradition can by no means guarantee man's salvation. Hence Luther reduced the sacraments to two, baptism and the Lord's Supper. While justification by faith is the "material" principle of the Reformation, scripture alone is its "formal" principle. For Luther, as well as for John Calvin, the Bible, not the church, is the final authority for Christian life. While Calvin in his practice of interpretation seems to accept particular words of the Bible as the revealed word of God, Luther distinguishes between the words of the Bible and the word that God speaks through them: the words of the Bible are the "cradle of Christ." Accordingly, Luther does not support the literal interpretation of the Bible, nor does he find the word of God equally in all its parts, but regards some as inferior in quality. The corollary of the two main principles of the Reformation is the theory concerning the priesthood of all believers: each and every individual is a priest to himself or herself and as such is to serve God by listening to the word of God within the words of the Bible. This emphasis on personal conscience constitutes a great innovation of the Reformation, but it has also opened the way for uncontrolled interpretations of the Bible as well as the proliferation of an ever-increasing number of Protestant denominations and small sects led by conscientious, "inspired" leaders.

Trends away from the Roman Catholic type of objectivism and toward subjectivism are even more evident in many sectarian Protestant communities. They insist on the importance of Bible study, prayer, and the personal experience of salvation and its certainty; and for members of these communities the ideas of sin, salvation, and faith in Jesus Christ assume an intense and vivid personal reality. One of the best examples of this Protestant emphasis is George Fox, the founder of the Society of Friends, also known as the Quakers. Fox organized a community of the faithful without priesthood or sacramental rites. He was convinced that true religion consisted not in the church or in the creeds, but in the personal experience of what he called illumination by the Holy Spirit; the source of final authority for him was the personal experience of the inner light.

Islam. For Muslims the Qur'ān is the immediate and complete revelation of God's message to mankind through Muḥammad. It is the heavenly book of revelation, the word of God *par excellence.* While controversies have raged among Muslims as to the sense in which this is true, that it is true has never been questioned. The Qur'ān for some Muslims is "created," but for the majority it is not a historical creation; just as the Torah in Judaism is of celestial origin, deriving from the time prior to the creation, the Qur'ān, although composed in Arabic, reflects its heavenly archetype. Thus the Qur'ān is "uncreated," not conditioned by time and history. The Qur'ān is unquestionably the supreme source of authority for the *ummah*, or Muslim community.

The Muslim community has also accepted the *ḥadīth* ("tradition," i.e., the record of the words and deeds) of the prophet Muḥammad as the normative authority for its beliefs and practices. While Muslims do not consider him the savior in the Christian sense of the word, they are firmly convinced that Muḥammad was divinely guided in the years after receiving the revelation; he is God's prophet and apostle and the perfect man, the exemplary model and spiritual guide for humanity. For Muslims, everything Muḥammad said and did during his life is worthy of study and imitation.

Still another tradition, which is accepted as authoritative by the orthodox Muslims (Sunnīs), is the *ḥadīth* of the first four caliphs. In his later years, when he was in Medina, Muḥammad attempted to build up a socioreligious community on the basis of Islamic principles, and after his death this ideal was carried on by his four immediate successors (caliphs), known as the ideal rulers. The Muslim community then was in need of detailed rules for ordering both its communal life and the life of its individual members. These rules of life, called *sharī'ah*, or Islamic law, are based on the interpretation of the Qur'ān and the *ḥadīth*s of Muḥammad and the first four caliphs who followed him.

Significantly, the caliph as head of the community had no pontifical or even priestly functions. His task was not to expound or to interpret the faith, but to serve as the guardian of the public order. The task of interpreting the Qur'ān and *ḥadīth*s and applying them to the actual life of the community was carried out by the *'ulamā'*. They were not priests and claimed no priestly power or authority, but, on account of their learning in the Qur'ān and *ḥadīth*s, played an important role quite analogous to that of the Jewish rabbinate.

While the Sunnīs consider the *ḥadīth* concerning the first three caliphs as one of the sources of authority for Islam, the Shī'īs have rejected it as such, because they view the three caliphs as illegal usurpers and recognize instead 'Alī, Muḥammad's cousin and son-in-law, as the first caliph, or, more properly, the first imam. What underlies the Shī'ī contention is the belief that Muḥammad's personal charisma, which he received from God, is transmitted genealogically only in his family tradition. This view is remarkably different from the Sunnī view that Muḥammad's charisma is channeled through the office of caliph regardless of its occupant: while Sunnī orthodoxy is committed to the principle of institutional charisma, the Shī'īs reject it and uphold the principle of hereditary charisma. Accordingly, the Shī'īs have replaced the *ḥadīth* of the first three caliphs with the *ḥadīth* of the twelve imams.

In sharp contrast to the caliph, who has no legal authority, the imam is authorized to interpret the *ḥaqīqah*, or inner mysteries, which are hidden in the Qur'ān and *ḥadīth*s. He is endowed with such a spiritual gift because, through the chain of direct transmission, he has received from Muḥammad a body of gnosis, or esoteric knowledge. Consequently, the imam is charged with a power at once political and religious; he is one who rules the community with mercy and justice but who also interprets Islamic law and its inner meanings. Naturally, the Shī'īs are persuaded that the final authority for Islam is in the hands of the imam himself. According to them, the last, or twelfth, imam, the so-called hidden imam, did not die but entered a prolonged "concealment." One day, so they believe, from that state of concealment he will emerge as the Mahdi ("expected one"), that is, the messiah. Until he comes, a group of leading lawyer-theologians, called *mujtāhid*s, will continue to exercise an extensive authority on matters of religion and law. [*See* Imamate.]

Tension between Religious and Secular Authorities. While tension between religious and secular authorities may be present in primitive and archaic cultures, it arises in its sharpest forms only after the emergence of the founded religion. Then it occurs between rival principles, each claiming universal supremacy, and only under particular cultural and historical circumstances.

Islam has rarely experienced tensions analogous to those between church and state in medieval Western Christendom because the Muslim community has been founded on the principle of theocracy, and a distinct ecclesiastical body powerful enough to challenge secular authorities has never existed.

Buddhism knows of no such tensions either, but for different reasons. While it succeeded in establishing a theocratic state in Tibet, in many other Asian countries it has been placed in a defensive position vis-à-vis the indigenous institution of sacral kingship and its ideology; the Buddhist community has either been headed by the king or indirectly put under control of the state. Consequently, it has been constantly exposed to the temptation of soliciting favor from secular authorities. It may be noted, in this connection, that Buddhism developed a theory for peaceful interdependence between its own community and the state: the ideal of the *ca-*

kravartin, a righteous, universal king. Whereas the Buddha was depicted as a universal king in the spiritual domain, who set in motion of wheel of Dharma, the *cakravartin,* essentially political in nature, was widely expected to appear as a universal king and to turn a wheel of Dharma in the secular domain. The Buddhist community saw in Aśoka, the third emperor of the great Mauryan kingdom, the realization of the *cakravartin* ideal: he converted to Buddhism, supported its community, sent out missionaries, and governed people in accordance with the Dharma. To the eyes of the Buddhists, the two wheels of Dharma, one in the spiritual domain and the other in the secular, should go hand in hand. This theory, a kind of caesaropapism, has exerted enduring influences on Asian countries.

The Christian church in its early centuries had no ambition to stand against the Roman imperial authority. It desired only freedom from persecution. This whole situation was changed by the conversion of Constantine, in the fourth century, and by the subsequent spread of Christianity as the official religion of the Roman empire. What emerged in the arena of church-state relations was caesaropapism. The Byzantine emperors transformed the church of the Eastern Empire into a state church closely dependent on the imperial government; these emperors claimed the right to control the church and decide any disputes that arose in the ecclesiastical sphere, and the prelates of Constantinople accepted their claims.

In the Western Empire the situation was different. All effective imperial power gradually declined during the early Middle Ages, and this resulted in the emergence of the popes as temporal governors of Rome and its surroundings. Moreover, they abandoned their old allegiance to the Byzantine emperors and formed a new alliance with the Frankish kings. The climax of this Frankish-papal alliance occurred with Leo III's coronation of Charlemagne as emperor of the Romans in 800; thus Leo established the precedent, followed through the Middle Ages, that papal coronation is essential to the making of an emperor, and in so doing he implanted the germ of the idea that empire is a gift to be bestowed by the papacy.

The king's office, however, was conceived to be as sacred as the papacy, a view supported by Old Testament texts; kings were regarded as the Lord's anointed, as ministers of God, and were hailed as vicars of Christ. As such, they aspired to supreme power, both spiritual and temporal. It soon became customary throughout Europe for kings to choose bishops; they gave them great fiefs and invested them with the ring and pastoral staff that symbolized episcopal office. This practice proved beneficial for the kings, but it was a radical departure from the sacred tradition of the church. A measure of this imperial power can be illustrated by an incident that occurred in 1046. When Henry III of Germany arrived in Rome for his imperial coronation, he found there three rival candidates for the papal throne, each claiming to be the rightful pope. Henry settled the issue in high-handed manner: he dismissed all three and installed his own choice. It seemed to Henry that he had as much right to appoint a bishop for Rome as for any other diocese in his territory, and as vicar of God he was also very much aware of his duty to appoint the best man available to such an important office.

The clash between papal theocracy and imperial theocracy became inevitable in 1073 when Hildebrand became Pope Gregory VII and asserted the church's independence from, and indeed its domination over, the imperial power embodied in Henry IV of Germany. Henry could not give up the right of appointing bishops without abandoning all hope of welding Germany into a unified monarchy, and Gregory could not acquiesce in the imperial claims, which included a claim to appoint the popes themselves. The Roman pontiff maintained that as God's vicar he possessed a direct authority—not only spiritual but also political—over all men and all their affairs in the *Corpus Christianum.* He even asserted in the *Dictatus Papae,* issued in 1075, that the pope could depose emperors. Henry then appointed a bishop of Milan and strengthened his position by summoning a council of German bishops, which accused Gregory of gross abuse of papal authority. Gregory replied in 1076 with a decree in which he declared Henry excommunicated and deprived of his imperial authority. Rarely has the history of religions witnessed more direct clashes between religious and secular authorities.

[*See also* Truth; Tradition; Canon; *and the entries that deal with problems of religious authority in the modern context:* Politics and Religion; Intellectuals; *and* Bureaucracy. *For a discussion of the topic in Islam, see* Sunnah; *for a treatment of the topic in Christianity, see* Papacy.]

BIBLIOGRAPHY

There are no comprehensive presentations on the theme of authority in the general history of religions based on comparative or typological studies. On the authority of myth in premodern society, see Mircea Eliade's *Myth and Reality* (New York, 1963). This book contains an excellent bibliography. Bronislaw Malinowski has attempted to elucidate the authentic nature and function of myth in primitive society on the basis of his fieldwork among the Trobriand Islanders in New Guinea. See his classic work *Myth in Primitive Psychology* (New York, 1926), which has been reprinted in his *Magic, Science and Religion* (New York, 1948), pp. 93–148.

The best single book on the problem of imperial authority in the ancient Near East remains Henri Frankfort's *Kingship and the Gods: A Study of Ancient Near Eastern Religion as the Integration of Society and Nature* (Chicago, 1948). The eighth International Congress for the History of Religions met in Rome in the spring of 1955 to discuss the theme of kingship. Its proceedings have been published as *The Sacral Kingship* (Leiden, 1959). On imperial authority in ancient China and Japan, see D. Howard Smith's "Divine Kingship in Ancient China," *Numen* 4 (1957): 171–203, and my own "Conceptions of State and Kingship in Early Japan," *Zeitschrift für Religions- und Geistesgeschichte* 28 (1976): 97–112. On the structure of authority in the Buddhist community, there is an excellent discussion in Sukumar Dutt's *The Buddha and Five After-Centuries* (London, 1957).

The sources of authority in Islam are succinctly presented in Sir Hamilton A. R. Gibb's *Mohammedanism*, 2d rev. ed. (New York, 1961), which still remains the best introduction to Islam.

The origins and development of the structure of authority in the early Christian church has been masterfully studied by Hans von Campenhausen in *Kirchliches Amt und geistliche Vollmacht* (Tübingen, 1953), translated by J. A. Baker as *Ecclesiastical Authority and Spiritual Power in the Church of the First Three Centuries* (Stanford, Calif., 1969). On scriptural authority in the modern period, there is much useful material in J. K. S. Reid's *The Authority of Scripture: A Study of the Reformation and Post-Reformation Understanding of the Bible* (London, 1957) and in Georges H. Tavard's *Holy Writ or Holy Church: The Crisis of the Protestant Reformation* (London, 1959). Concerning authority in Eastern Orthodoxy, see Georges Florovsky's *Bible, Church, Tradition: An Eastern Orthodox View* (Belmont, Mass., 1972).

On the manifold relations of church and state, a useful comparative and typological study has been presented by Joachim Wach in his *Sociology of Religion* (1944; Chicago, 1962), pp. 287–330. The standard work on the confrontation between papal and secular authorities in the Middle Ages remains Walter Ullmann's *The Growth of Papal Government in the Middle Ages*, 2d ed. (London, 1962). The primary sources relating to the subject have been skillfully assembled by Brian Tierney in *The Crisis of Church and State, 1050–1300* (Englewood Cliffs, N.J., 1964).

MANABU WAIDA

AUTOBIOGRAPHY. [*This entry discusses the literary genre of autobiography on the basis of Western examples. For discussion, in broad cultural and religious perspective, of notions of personhood, individuality, and self-consciousness, see* Soul *and* Human Body, *article on* Myths and Symbolism. *See* Biography *for discussion of sacred biography.*]

The proliferation of autobiographies in the twentieth century, especially since the end of World War I, obscures the fact that the emergence of the genre as we know it today is a surprisingly recent phenomenon. Autobiography required the coalescence of several factors before it could become the tradition we now recognize: the breakup of the traditional community, increasing sensitivity to change, new forms of self-consciousness and religious awareness, a shift from deductive to inductive modes of thought, the alteration of class structure, and increased literacy. The emergence of autobiography had, in other words, to await the appearance of the "individual"—someone who could imagine himself or herself in a variety of roles, someone whose self-definition rested as much on change as on continuity, and someone whose true self could not be captured by any universal model. The Good Citizen eventually had to give way to Jean-Jacques Rousseau's "myself alone," the latter nonetheless assuming, as much as the former, a relationship to its world.

While scholars of autobiography might place varying emphasis on one or another of these factors in the rise of autobiography, all would probably agree with Karl Joachim Weintraub that it reflects a Western ideology about the nature of selfhood as historically grounded. The belief that the self creates as well as reflects its history is basic to the autobiographical impulse along with the assumption that direction and unity are to be discovered in the examined life.

Augustine of Hippo, 354–430. Despite the overriding scholarly view that autobiography as a genre came on the Western scene no earlier than the Renaissance (and, according to some, as late as the early nineteenth century), there is a general consensus that Augustine's *Confessions*, written between 397 and 401, marks the beginning of the autobiographical tradition. [*See the biography of Augustine.*] Augustine lived during a period of tumultuous change, when the classical world was giving way to a recently christianized culture. He records the effects of those seismic shifts on his own life, exploring in psychological as well as theological depth the wrenching his life underwent and developing a language of introspection that remains influential to this day. It is no wonder that Georg Misch, the early historian of autobiography, called Augustine the first modern.

I begin this necessarily selective discussion of autobiography with the *Confessions* not only because it has influenced and continues to influence the writing of autobiography but especially because it has so fundamentally shaped the very definition of the genre. To root the genre of autobiography in religious confession (and, in this case, in a piece of confessional writing which itself reaches back to the legacy of the Pauline letter and the Hebrew psalm) acknowledges a religious impulse at the heart of autobiography—a religious impulse that informs the self's search for meaning, whether the goal of that search is theistic or worldly. It is only by means of the "Other" that the autobiographical self can make its way back to who and what it is. The Other has had a variety of faces in the autobiographical tradition from Augustine's late fourth-century *Confessions* to Malcolm X's twentieth-century autobiography.

For Augustine, the Other is God—at times, the God of Plato, at times, the God of the Hebrew and Christian scriptures. Although Augustine keeps God at the center of the story he wants to tell, the compelling autobiographical interest of the *Confessions* lies in the nature of the self. Throughout his narrative, Augustine describes himself as "fluttering" and "scattered." He aims to find rest in God, but even in the process of finding out that God has all along been with him, Augustine discovers how much of himself remains a mystery. "Am I not then myself, O Lord my God? and yet there is so much difference betwixt myself and myself." It is precisely in God's presence, Augustine confesses, that he has become such a problem to himself. The knowledge he gains of God exposes the slightness of his self-knowledge, making it all the more obvious how critical is the gathering together of his broken and scattered self that only God can do. "I know less of myself than of Thee; I beseech now, O my God, discover to me myself. . . . [I have no] safe place for my soul, but in Thee, whither my scattered members may be gathered."

What is religiously important in the *Confessions'* contribution to the autobiographical tradition is not so much Augustine's conversion itself as the standpoint that the conversion allows on his narrative past. Looking backward from the redeemed present he now occupies (as the son of Monica, as the bishop of Hippo, as an influential spokesman for orthodoxy, even as a retired—but still dedicated—rhetorician), Augustine finds it possible to gather up the scattered pieces of his past in a narrative that moves simultaneously on two levels: the level of the fallen protagonist (or what he once was), and the level of the saved narrator (or what he has since become). Those levels begin to merge in book 10 when he undertakes his phenomenological analysis of time and memory, the ever-moving repositories of all experience within which he finally finds both God and himself.

Michel de Montaigne, 1533–1592. To move on from the *Confessions* to Montaigne's *Essays* is to leap over nearly twelve hundred years of autobiographical writing that, by and large, lies buried as bits and pieces amidst documents devoted to other subjects or that reflects the monastic dedication to hagiography so popular in the Middle Ages. According to Georg Misch, no more than eight or ten self-contained autobiographies are to be turned up between the years 500 and 1400, among them Peter Abelard's *Story of My Calamities* (1132–1136), Dante Alighieri's *La vita nuova* (c. 1294), and Petrarch's *Secretum* (1342–1343), in the form of three dialogues with Augustine.

Like Augustine, Montaigne has been claimed for membership in the modern autobiographical tradition. About him, Erich Auerbach writes in *Mimesis: The Representation of Reality in Western Literature* (Princeton, 1968): "among all his contemporaries he had the clearest conception of the problem of a man's self-orientation; that is, the task of making oneself at home in existence without fixed points of support. In him for the first time, man's life—the random personal life as a whole—becomes problematic in the modern sense."

Unlike Augustine, Montaigne was unwilling to come to "conclusions"; he claimed only to write essays. Such might not have been the case, he says, had his mind been able to "find a firm footing." But like Augustine, Montaigne lived in a world undergoing profound upheaval—in this case, the Reformation and the religious wars in France. In its shaky transition from the vestiges of feudalism into the modern era, the cultural ground could offer no one a firm footing. Instead of searching, like Augustine, for stability and permanence within a time of dissension, schism, and uncertainty, Montaigne devoted his final years of retirement to Cato's search for a good death and to the task of capturing the phenomenon of life's constant mutability: "I cannot fix my subject. He is always restless, and reels with a natural intoxication. I catch him here, as he is at the moment when I turn my attention to him. I do not portray his being; I portray his passage."

Diversity and variety, not ideal unity—this for Montaigne was the universal quality of existence. Because of life's quixotic character, Montaigne felt the autobiographer's self-portrait had best be painted on the run. What better literary instrument than the essay—the experiment, the rehearsal, the trial—to record the mercurial nature of self-knowledge? Not only did Montaigne produce three books of essays between 1580 and 1588; he undertook the revision of these essays, never by expunging what he had already written but rather by adding copious marginal and interlinear notations, thereby creating a multilayered palimpsest that editorially dramatizes a self in the making.

As a self-described "accidental" philosopher, Montaigne was interested in the practical life of action and ethics, and his famous motto "What do I know?" was meant to rouse to action slothful persons who would otherwise hide under cover of their ignorance of (nonexistent) ultimate answers. That motto stood guard against presumptuousness as well, a presumptuousness evident in current religious controversies in which the Deity was being strained, so Montaigne noted, through doctrinal sieves. By insisting that certain questions be left open, Montaigne earned himself a place on the Roman Catholic church's Index of Forbidden Books in 1676, eighty-four years after he died.

What we have in the *Essays* is the dramatic presentation of a man looking at his world through the lens of what Auerbach calls "creatural realism"—a Christian perspective on the human that was formed during the Middle Ages and that was becoming, by the sixteenth century, a positive valuation of the physical dimension of life. "I, who am a very earthy person, loathe that inhuman teaching which would make us despise and dislike the care of the body," Montaigne wrote. The mortal condition of all human existence is not merely the foundation of the human condition, it is the basis upon which all human achievement rests: "The soul's greatness consists not so much in climbing high and pressing forward as in knowing how to adapt and limit itself." Even as Augustine understood his religious goal as coming to rest in God, Montaigne wanted finally to acknowledge that no matter how high the stilts the creature mounts, it is on his own bottom that he sits. More than any of the accounts that deserve a place in the tradition of religious autobiography, the *Essays* most clearly portrays the comic limits of all autobiographical activity.

John Bunyan, 1628–1688. Another autobiography, which reflects the Protestant Reformation in an even more immediate way, is John Bunyan's *Grace Abounding to the Chief of Sinners* (1666), written during Bunyan's twelve-year imprisonment (1660–1672) for his refusal to stop his unlicensed preaching in the Particular Baptist community of Bedford, England. [*See the biography of Bunyan.*] Bunyan's autobiography, like Augustine's, brings a heightening and polish to a kind of writing that had already been in use for some time. Bunyan's title, for instance, makes use of a phrase, "chief of sinners," that had become conventional in Calvinism and, before that, in the Pauline tradition. Like Paul, Bunyan addresses his words as a distant missionary to his recent converts for their comfort and guidance. Moreover, the autobiography reflects a threefold pattern of development that Calvinist doctrine routinely presented. It begins with the acknowledgment of sin, continues with a search for the faith that the elect soul is expected to have, and concludes with the justification that faith will award.

Three things are of special importance about the place of *Grace Abounding* within the autobiographical tradition. First, it signals the transformation of hagiography into the more modern form of autobiography, where salvation's drama is played out on the stage of individual psychology. Second, it is the confession of an ordinary tinkerer, not of a bishop like Augustine or a nobleman like Montaigne, thus anticipating how democratic a genre autobiography would fast become ("The Confessions of Practically Everybody," as the title of a 1960 book review had it). Third, it marks by its manner of narration a significant change in the Augustinian tradition of confession within which Bunyan wrote his own Calvinistic account. Augustine maintains a noticeable distance between his saved narrator and his fallen protagonist, a distance that establishes two different levels in his narrative and that seems often to express a separation between the experiences of nature and grace. Bunyan, however, occupies a single plane, a plane located somewhere between the City of Destruction and the Celestial City of *The Pilgrim's Progress* (1678), which he would begin writing in 1672. This place-in-between is not only where the chief of sinners confronts both nature and grace, but where he also takes constant note of the multifariousness of life which no ultimate unity can enclose. Bunyan's pilgrim, Christian, will traverse much the same territory in that later allegorization of the Calvinist autobiography.

Jean-Jacques Rousseau, 1712–1778. The Bunyanesque autobiography paved the way to the prismatic and peripatetic autobiography which not only recorded but reformed and created a self—the protean self of Rousseau: philosopher, novelist, social reformer, composer of operas, and (along with Montaigne) inventor of modern autobiography. [*See the biography of Rousseau.*] Rousseau began writing his *Confessions* in 1764, soon after Voltaire's attack against him for presuming to give advice on religion and honor when he, Rousseau, had engaged in years of debauchery, dragging with him from place to place the woman who had mothered the five infants he had given over, one after the other, to an orphanage, thus "abjuring all natural sentiments." Rousseau wrote his autobiography to set the record straight.

This eighteenth-century set of confessions begins, like Augustine's, with an address to God. But instead of asking for divine assistance in confessing his life, Rousseau imagines a scene at the Last Judgment when he will present himself before the "Sovereign Judge," the completed autobiography in hand, in order to receive final approval for the truthful baring of his secret soul. We can assume that the Deity's final judgment will reflect Rousseau's:

> Here is what I have done, and if by chance I have used some immaterial embellishment it has been only to fill a void due to a defect of memory. I may have taken for fact what was no more than probability, but I have never put down as true

> what I knew to be false. I have displayed myself as I was, as vile and despicable when my behaviour was such, as good, generous, and noble when I was so.

A chronicle of his wanderings (from his boyhood in Geneva to Paris where he died) and his dwelling places (the eight years in the country house of Madame de Warens recalled as the most idyllic), the *Confessions* is divided into twelve books. The first six deal with his youth up to age thirty and establish for all subsequent autobiography the importance of childhood; the second six books are an account of how Rousseau became a writer and reformer. Using his own life as a case study of reform, he shows how the misery of life lies in the discrepancy between the self molded by society and the truer self reared by nature. While Rousseau, like Bunyan and Augustine, would lay claim to being chief among sinners, the sin for which he seeks forgiveness is the sin against the true self, not the sin against God.

"I have displayed myself as I was": in this avowal of transparency lies the basis for exoneration (and salvation) Rousseau wants to achieve. He has looked at his subject, himself, steadily and without flinching; he has seen himself as in truth he is and not as he conforms to some general model. To achieve the transparency with which he wanted to display his true self, Rousseau realized that he must present that self in all of its multifaceted and protean quality. It is a Montaignesque self, forever changing, and, in some surprising respects, an Augustinian self—acutely aware that nothing differs more from the self than the self (the "difference betwixt myself and myself," as Augustine put it).

It is to the reader, not to the Deity, that Rousseau wishes to confess himself—a confession that acknowledges, as does Augustine's, that the self is scattered and needs to be gathered together. Rousseau calls upon his reader not only to hear his confession but to assemble and assess the prism of selfhood that the account has reflected.

> I should like in some way to make my soul transparent to the reader's eye, and for that purpose I am trying to present it from all points of view, to show it in all lights, and to contrive that none of its movements shall escape his notice, so that he may judge for himself of the principle which has produced them. . . . His task is to assemble these elements and to assess the being who is made up of them.

Conclusion. The large distance in time between Augustine's autobiography, with which I began, and Rousseau's, with which I now end, shrinks in light of the surprising continuity of effort throughout the autobiographical tradition to lay hold on the self by means of narrative. Basically a temporal form, narrative has been able to accommodate an often illusive, frequently dispersed, and always changing self. The distance between Augustine and Rousseau narrows even further when we find their autobiographical modes being employed together, for example, in the 1964 autobiography of the black American revolutionary Malcolm X. [*See the biography of Malcolm X.*] Like Augustine's account, Malcolm X's is structured by a conversion, in fact, by two conversions—the first to the Black Muslim religion of Elijah Mohammed and the second to the religion of Islam itself after a pilgrimage to Mecca. He looks back on his early life in Augustinian fashion, from a level of enlightenment by means of which he is able to view it not only as a life on the hustle but also as the product of an institutionalized racism of which he was both victim and perpetrator. When Malcolm X comments that his life "never has stayed fixed in one position for very long," he gives expression to the protean selfhood that finds its way into autobiographical writing with Montaigne and continues, more than ever, to characterize contemporary autobiography. Nothing communicates the ever-changing self and circumstances of Malcolm X better than the string of names he holds, from the time he is born as Malcolm Little to his assassination as El-Hajj Malik El-Shabazz. Like Rousseau, Malcolm X wanted to put straight the record of his life to a world that was hostile to him. That he expected a violent end to his life gave a special edge to his autobiography and reminds us that most autobiography, like Montaigne's *Essays*, prepares the way for death.

BIBLIOGRAPHY

Little critical attention has been paid to non-Western autobiography as a genre of writing, partly because the discovery of the autobiographic genre has been so recent and partly, too, because the governing conditions of the genre, growing as they have out of the Western experience, tend to rule out of consideration much of the life-writing of other cultures. While Mohandas Gandhi's autobiography seems to represent an exception, it may well be the influence of the West within the account that eased its way into Western critical attention. That non-Western autobiography has taken a different form and served a different function than Western examples is likely. Such differences will have to be recognized before autobiography as a worldwide genre gets the attention belatedly paid it in the West, with the result that comparative studies may open new ways of looking at the genre as a whole. The following works can be recommended for further reading.

Delany, Paul. *British Autobiography in the Seventeenth Century.* London and New York, 1969. An excellent introductory chapter on the factors giving rise to autobiography in the Renaissance as well as an extended discussion of religious autobiography organized by church and sect membership.

Misch, Georg. *Geschichte der Autobiographie.* 4 vols. Bern, 1949–1950 (vol. 1), and Frankfurt, 1955–1969 (vols. 2–4).

Translated by E. W. Dickes as *A History of Autobiography in Antiquity,* 2 vols. (Cambridge, Mass., 1951). An ambitious history of the genre beginning with Egyptian tomb inscriptions and ending (some 3,800 pages later) with the nineteenth-century writer Theodor Fontane. Influenced by Misch's father-in-law, Wilhelm Dilthey.

Olney, James, ed. *Autobiography: Essays Theoretical and Critical.* Princeton, 1980. An important collection of contemporary essays on the genre, including the watershed essay by Georges Gusdorf, "Conditions and Limits of Autobiography," translated by Olney, whose own extensive work on autobiography reflects his interest in William Butler Yeats and C. G. Jung. Includes an extensive bibliography. Olney cites only five references on non-Western autobiography, including Erik H. Erikson's piece on Gandhi, "Gandhi's Autobiography: The Leader as Child," *American Scholar* 35 (1966): 632–646.

Pascal, Roy. *Design and Truth in Autobiography.* Cambridge, Mass., 1960. An early effort to look at autobiography as a literary genre. For a sense of variety and change in autobiography studies, contrast Pascal's formalist approach with Jeffrey Mehlman's structuralist treatment in *A Structural Study of Autobiography: Proust, Leiris, Sartre, Lévi-Strauss* (Ithaca, N.Y., 1974).

Spengemann, William C. *The Forms of Autobiography: Episodes in the History of the Literary Genre.* New Haven, 1980. Includes a particularly helpful chapter on Augustine's *Confessions,* which Spengemann views as proleptic for the three emerging forms that will define the autobiographical tradition (the historical, the philosophical, and the poetic). Only two references to non-Western autobiography appear in the author's seventy-five page "Bibliographic Essay."

Waghorne, Joanne Punzo. *Images of Dharma: The Epic World of C. Rajagopalachari.* New Delhi, 1985. A recent example of the effort to relate Western autobiographical theory of Eastern materials.

Weintraub, Karl Joachim. *The Value of the Individual: Self and Circumstance in Autobiography.* Chicago, 1978. Continuing the historical interests of Georg Misch, Weintraub traces the idea of individuality in Western civilization through the use of autobiographical writing from classical antiquity through Johann Wolfgang von Goethe, whose *Poetry and Truth (Dichtung und Wahrheit)* represents for Weintraub a high-watermark of the autobiographical tradition. Weintraub's excellent study stands out in turn among increasing treatments of what was called not long ago (1968) "the dark continent of literature"; see Stephen A. Shapiro's "The Dark Continent of Literature: Autobiography," *Comparative Literature Studies* 5 (1968): 421–454.

JANET VARNER GUNN

AVALOKITEŚVARA, a *bodhisattva* especially associated with the principle of compassion, is the most popular figure in the pan-Asian Mahāyāna Buddhist pantheon. Worshiped and invoked in both male and female forms, Avalokiteśvara is considered a potent savior in times of life-threatening dangers, who watches over all beings and heeds their cries of suffering and distress. He responds directly to the pleas of those in great need, while also serving in symbolic manner as the embodiment of the principle of compassion, a fundamental aspect of the Buddhist way of life. In addition to his numerous pan-Asian roles, Avalokiteśvara has played a significant role in distinctive local traditions throughout Buddhist Asia.

The meaning of this *bodhisattva*'s name traditionally has been understood in several ways, emphasizing his sovereignty over the material world and his responsiveness to the calls of suffering humanity. A principal interpretation holds that the name *Avalokiteśvara* is a compound of Sanskrit *avalokita* and *īśvara,* translated variously as "the lord of what is seen, the lord who is seen" or "the lord who surveys, gazing lord." The celebrated seventh-century Chinese monk-scholar Hsüan-tsang upheld this view, translating the *bodhisattva*'s name as *Kuan-tzu-tsai* ("gazing lord").

An alternate spelling of this name—*Avalokitasvara*—also existed, as seen in some fifth-century Sanskrit manuscripts and as noted by learned Chinese exegetes such as Ch'eng-kuan (eighth century). This led to the well-known Chinese translation *Kuan-yin* ("he who has perceived sound"). The frequently seen Chinese translation *Kuan-shih-yin* ("he who perceives the sounds of the world") appears to have a dubious etymological basis, but expresses well the functional quality of the *bodhisattva*: a savior who hears all cries of suffering and responds with potent aid.

Avalokiteśvara has numerous epithets. The most common are *Padmapāṇi* ("lotus bearer") and *Lokeśvara* ("lord of the world"), by which he is best known in Southeast Asia. Many epithets related to his specific saving functions are connected to a dizzying panoply of iconographic forms.

Origins. It generally is agreed that the cult to Avalokiteśvara arose in the northwestern borderlands of India. Much scholarly energy has been devoted to determining the "origins" of the *bodhisattva.* Many of these efforts presuppose a diffusionist model for the formation of the Mahāyāna pantheon; they assume that the pantheon was in some way devised or adapted from the various deities of neighboring religious movements. For example, Mallmann (1948) suggested Iranian antecedents based on Avalokiteśvara's name and functions. Others hold that the pantheon came into being as the deification of early Buddhist principles or of potent moments in the life of Śākyamuni Buddha; for example, Giuseppe Tucci (1948) suggested that Avalokiteśvara is the personification of the compassionate gaze of Śākyamuni. Such views are far distant from the notable intensity of belief in the compassionate lifesaving powers of this deity, as expressed among Buddhist Asians from all levels of society. Mahāyāna scriptural traditions simply hold that Avalokiteśvara is one among many beings having human history whose dedication and spiritual development has led to successful fruition as a *bodhisattva*.

Principal Scriptural Sources. Among the numerous scriptural sources on Avalokiteśvara, three works are especially important: the *Saddharmapuṇḍarīka Sūtra* (Lotus Scripture), various versions of the *Sukhāvatīvyūha Sūtra* (Pure Land Scripture), and the so-called *Amitāyurdhyāna Sūtra* (Contemplation on Amitāyus Scripture). The *Lotus* provides much information on the *bodhisattva*'s lifesaving powers, while the *Pure Land* and the meditation scripture reveal his spiritual kinship to Amitābha Buddha and outline his functions in this context. These aspects both have been essential features of the cult.

The *Lotus* devotes a full chapter to Avalokiteśvara, and this chapter (chapter 25 in Kumārajīva's eloquent fourth-century Chinese translation) not uncommonly has been memorized, recited, and treated as an independent scripture by East Asian devotees. The chapter includes discussion of the *bodhisattva*'s name, the dangers that he can dispel, and the myriad forms in which he may appear to aid devotees.

The *bodhisattva*'s name in this well-known version of the *Lotus* clearly is Avalokitasvara, translated by Kumārajīva as Kuan-shih-yin, or "hearer of the sounds of the world." Śākyamuni Buddha explains in the scripture that this name arises from the *bodhisattva*'s pledge to heed the call of any suffering being who cries out his name and to appear before him in rescue.

The list of dangers and difficulties that the *bodhisattva* can counter is impressive: fire, drowning in a river, being lost at sea, murder, demonic attack, fierce beasts and noxious snakes or insects, legal punishment, attack by bandits, falling from steep precipices, extremes of weather, internecine civil or military unrest, and others. The *bodhisattva* also assists those ensnared by the traditional three poisons of Buddhism: lust, anger, and delusion. Avalokiteśvara also grants children—both male and female—in response to the pleas of barren women. According to the *Lotus*, Avalokiteśvara is a master of skillful means *(upāya)* who is adept at manifesting himself in any suitable form (thirty-three are listed) to convey the deliverance of any being.

The *Pure Land* scriptures, of which several versions are extant in Chinese translation, pair Avalokiteśvara with a *bodhisattva* named Mahāsthāmaprāpta. Both are principal assistants to the Buddha Amitābha, lord of the Western Paradise, a glorious realm free of suffering where diligent questers for enlightenment may be reborn after earthly existence. Among his various functions, Avalokiteśvara guides devotees from earthly deathbed to rebirth in the spirit land. He acts as emissary for the Buddha throughout the various realms of the universe, and he is described as the eventual heir to the throne of this realm. (The *Karuṇāpuṇḍarīka Sūtra*, translated into Chinese in the early fifth century, extends this relationship by explaining that Avalokiteśvara was the first son of Amitābha in an earlier incarnation.)

The meditation scripture provides an extended description of Avalokiteśvara as the focus for one of the stages of a multifaceted visualization practice. Successful accomplishment of this practice leads not only to future rebirth in the Western Paradise, but also to continuous invocation of the principal lords of that land, with the accompanying protection and inspiration they afford. Avalokiteśvara is described as a golden-skinned princely being of enormous stature, wearing a great crown made of wondrous gems within each of which there stands a manifested Buddha. Many-hued rays of light stream forth from his body in a patterned manner; these rays reach into the various realms of existence and send forth manifested Buddhas and *bodhisattvas*, who accomplish his works of compassion. Innumerable rays of soft light extend from his hands, illumining all things, and he is seen to be assisting all beings with these hands.

Paradise. Avalokiteśvara is believed to dwell on a certain mountain from which he attentively hears the rising cries of suffering beings and extends his mystic aid. A version of the *Avataṃsaka Sūtra* (Flower Garland Scripture) identifies this site as Potalaka Mountain, a name that became well known throughout Buddhist Asia. This mountain has been identified with a number of actual geographical sites in Asia. The seventh-century monk-traveler Hsüan-tsang noted that Potalaka could be found on the Malaya coast, although few who sought the *bodhisattva* had been successful in their quest. From at least the tenth century it was identified as an island off the coast of the southern China seaport of Ning-po, which was named P'u-t'o Shan (Potalaka Mountain) and remains an important pilgrimage center to the present day. In Japan, several sites have been identified as Potalaka: at the Nachi Falls within the Kumano Shrine complex near the ocean on the Kii Peninsula, in the mountains at Nikko, and at the Kasuga Shrine in Nara. In Tibet, the seventeenth-century palace of the Dalai Lama, built upon a hill facing Lhasa and constituting one of the world's great architectural treasures, was named the Potala. Thus, the mountain palace was physically made manifest as the residence of the Tibetan ruler, believed to be the physical embodiment of the *bodhisattva*.

Principal Iconographic Forms and Cultic Activity. Numerous forms of Avalokiteśvara are seen in art and described throughout a wide range of ritual texts, meditation manuals, and scriptures. These range from the simplicity of the Water-Moon form, with the princely *bodhisattva* seated upon Mount Potalaka gazing at the evanescent reflection of the full moon upon a still sea, to the complexity of the eleven-headed, thousand-armed, thousand-eyed images, the multiplicity of features expressing the *bodhisattva*'s extraordinary abilities to seek out and respond to the distress of all beings.

Āryāvalokiteśvara ("noble Avalokiteśvara"), sometimes termed "great compassionate one," is a simple form of the *bodhisattva* bearing in his left hand a lotus flower. Often, especially from the ninth century onward, this form wears a crown or headpiece in which the image of his spiritual father Amitābha Buddha is depicted. Closely related to this form is the White-Robed (Paṇḍaravāsinī) Avalokiteśvara, the most frequently seen East Asian type from the tenth or eleventh century to the present. With special emphasis on the motherly compassion of the *bodhisattva*, this form most often is depicted as a female seated in meditation or holding a lotus blossom. Caṇḍī, less commonly seen, is another female form, having three eyes and eighteen arms.

Paintings and sculptures depict some of the specialized abilities of the *bodhisattva*: as savior of those subject to life-threatening dangers such as fire, flood, and attack; as benevolent bestower of sons; as guide of souls, leading them in the journey from deathbed to Amitābha's Western Paradise; as a king of healing, in one form holding both a willow branch (as sign of the ability to ward off disease) and a vase of *amṛta* (the nectar of enlightenment), or in another healing form seated upon a roaring lion. Other important forms include Amoghapāśa ("unfailing rope"), holding out a lasso to assist all beings, or the fiercely protective Hayagrīva, horse-headed with dark flames emanating from his body. Avalokiteśvara is also shown paired with Mahāsthāmaprāpta in attendance on Amitābha, performing various functions in the Western Paradise, and he is seen as one among eight or more *bodhisattvas* in numerous types of assembly scenes throughout Mahāyāna art. This vast array of iconographic forms, only touched upon here, provides a sense of Avalokiteśvara's preeminent popularity throughout the Asian Buddhist populace.

An eleven-headed form of the *bodhisattva* is seen in the art of numerous Buddhist lands. These eleven heads may represent an elaboration of the concept of Avalokiteśvara as an all-seeing lord, encompassing views of the four cardinal and the four intermediate directions, as well as the nadir, center, and zenith. In East Asia, this form was first associated with special confession and repentance rites undertaken by lay and monastic practitioners. According to a text translated from Sanskrit into Chinese in the sixth century, the eleven heads are related to an elevenfold vow made by the *bodhisattva* to aid all sentient beings, including pledges to do such things as relieve beings of illness, misfortune, suffering, and worries, free them of unwholesome intentions, and turn their thoughts toward that which is wholesome. Iconographically, the eleven heads should be depicted in the following manner: three heads in the center with a compassionate expression—suited to devotees with predominantly good karma (Skt., *karman*); three heads on the left with an angry expression—directed towards saving beings with unwholesome qualities; three heads on the right with white tusks protruding from the tops of the mouths—to assist people with good karma to find enlightenment; a single face in back with an expression of violent laughter—to reform evildoers; and a Buddha face on top, preaching the Dharma—for those capable of following the Mahāyāna path.

The development of this *bodhisattva*'s cult is closely related to his function as extender of life and protector from the hardships and dangers of the world, who, as the *Lotus* puts it, "confers the gift of fearlessness" in the midst of terror and trouble. Based on the records of Chinese travelers to India, there was some worship of Avalokiteśvara in the fourth century at Mathurā, and by the seventh century the cult was widespread throughout India; by this time, according to Hsüan-tsang, images of the *bodhisattva* flanked the "diamond seat" of Śākyamuni Buddha's enlightenment at Bodh Gayā, one of the most sacred sites in the Buddhist world.

In all the coastal areas of Mahāyāna Buddhist countries, Avalokiteśvara has been expecially worshiped and invoked for his lifesaving protection of seafarers. This ability, mentioned in the *Lotus Scripture*, is attested to in numerous travel diaries and miracle tales from the fourth century to the present.

As noted above, in East Asia Avalokiteśvara has been the most popular of all Buddhist deities, most especially by virtue of the prominence accorded him in the *Lotus Scripture* traditions. The *Lotus* traditions of the thirty-three types of manifestations of the *bodhisattva* led in Japan to several very important pilgrimage circuits devoted to Kannon (Avalokiteśvara), each having thirty-three stations dedicated to the *bodhisattva*.

Avalokiteśvara (Spyan-ras-gzigs) is one of the key protective deities of Tibet, and the recitation of his six-syllable Sanskrit *mantra*, "Oṃ maṇi padme hūṃ," has been a widespread practice among Tibetans. Tibetan myths hold that Avalokiteśvara was the progenitor of the Tibetan people, and they believe that the founder of the first Tibetan dynasty, Sroṅ-btsan-sgam-po (seventh century), was an incarnation of Avalokiteśvara. Similarly, especially since the seventeenth century, the Dalai Lamas, successive temporal rulers and spiritual leaders of Tibet, have been believed to be human incarnations of Avalokiteśvara.

[*See also* Bodhisattva Path *and* Celestial Buddhas and Bodhisattvas.]

BIBLIOGRAPHY

The most comprehensive Western-language study of Avalokiteśvara is Marie-Thérèse de Mallmann's *Introduction à l'étude d'Avalokiteçvara* (Paris, 1948), which surveys the myriad forms of the *bodhisattva* seen in Indian art. Mallmann's diffusionist views were rejected by Giuseppe Tucci in his "À propos Ava lokiteśvara," *Mélanges chinois et bouddhiques* 9 (1948–1951): 173–220. Another diffusionist, Alexander Coburn Soper, has also made a study of the origins and iconography of the *bodhisattva*, relying on Chinese sources; see "The Triad Amitāyus-Amitābha, Avalokiteśvara, Mahāsthāmaprāpta," in his *Literary Evidence for Early Buddhist Art in China* (Ascona, 1959), pp. 141–167. For a valuable study of Chinese perceptions of Avalokiteśvara written by a learned Buddhist practitioner and devotee of the *bodhisattva*, see C. N. Tay's "Kuan-Yin: The Cult of Half Asia," *History of Religions* 16 (November 1976): 147–177. For the so-called *Avalokiteśvara Sutra*, chapter 25 of the *Lotus*, see *Scripture of the Lotus Blossom of the Fine Dharma*, translated by Leon Hurvitz (New York, 1976). Also helpful is Henri Maspero's discussion in "The Mythology of Modern China," in *Taoism and Chinese Religion*, translated by Frank A. Kierman, Jr. (Amherst, 1981), pp. 166–171.

RAOUL BIRNBAUM

AVATĀRA. The idea of an *avatāra*, a form taken by a deity, is central in Hindu mythology, religion, and philosophy. Literally the term means "a descent" and suggests the idea of a deity coming down from heaven to earth. The literal meaning also implies a certain diminution of the deity when he or she assumes the form of an *avatāra*. *Avatāras* usually are understood to be only partial manifestations of the deity who assumes them.

The *avatāra* idea in Hinduism is associated primarily with the god Viṣṇu. One of the earliest references to the idea is found in the *Bhagavadgītā* (c. 200 BCE), where we find a concise statement concerning Viṣṇu's primary in tention in assuming different forms:

> Whenever righteousness wanes and unrighteousness increases
> I send myself forth.
>
> In order to protect the good and punish the wicked,
> In order to make a firm foundation for righteousness,
> I come into being age after age. (4.7–8)

Theologically an *avatāra* is a specialized form assumed by Viṣṇu for the purpose of maintaining or restoring cosmic order. The form is suited to particular circumstances, which vary greatly, and therefore the different *avatāras* that Viṣṇu assumes also vary greatly. All the *avatāras*, however, perform positive functions vis-à-vis the cosmic order and illustrate Viṣṇu's nature as a deity who is attentive to worldly stability.

Historically the different *avatāras* of Viṣṇu often appear to represent regional, sectarian, or tribal deities who have been subsumed by established Hinduism under the rubric of one of Viṣṇu's many forms. By viewing these regional deities as so many varying forms of one transcendent deity, Hinduism was able to accommodate itself to a great variety of local traditions while maintaining a certain philosophic and religious integrity. This process also obviated unnecessary tension and rivalry among differing religious traditions.

Although the number of Viṣṇu's *avatāras* varies at different periods in the Hindu tradition and in different scriptures, the tradition usually affirms ten *avatāras*. While the sequence in which these *avatāras* is mentioned varies, the following order is common: fish, tortoise, boar, man-lion, dwarf, Rāma the Ax Wielder, Rāma of the *Rāmāyaṇa*, Kṛṣṇa, the Buddha, and Kalki. Traditionally, each *avatāra* appears in order to perform a specific cosmic duty that is necessary to maintain or restore cosmic order. Having performed that task, the *avatāra* then disappears or merges back into Viṣṇu.

Viṣṇu assumed the form of a great fish in order to save Manu Vaivasvata, the progenitor of the human race in this present cosmic age. A great deluge occurred at the beginning of the world, but Manu Vaivasvata was rescued when a giant horned fish appeared in the midst of the waters and bade him tie himself to its great horn. Bearing the seeds of creation for all living species (which the fish had instructed him to collect), the parent of the human race was prevented from drowning.

Viṣṇu appeared in the form of an immense boar when the demon Hiraṇyākṣa took possession of the goddess Pṛthivī (Earth) and carried her away beneath the cosmic waters. Diving into the waters, Viṣṇu battled and defeated Hiraṇyākṣa. Then he placed Pṛthivī on his tusk and lifted her above the waters. In both the fish and boar forms Viṣṇu involves himself dramatically in the cosmic process. He does so in order to preserve an element of order and life in the midst of overwhelming chaos represented by a limitless expanse of water.

Viṣṇu assumed the form of a tortoise when the gods and demons combined their efforts to churn the ocean of milk in order to extract from it the nectar of immortality. Having acquired Mount Meru, the cosmic axis, as a churning stick and Vāsuki, the cosmic serpent, as a churning rope, the gods and demons despaired because they were unable to find a secure base upon which to set the mighty churning stick. At that point, Viṣṇu assumed the form of a gigantic tortoise on whose broad back the gods and demons were able to set the churning stick and thus proceed with their task. In this form Viṣṇu assumes the role of cosmic foundation, that upon which all things securely rest and without which the world would lack stability.

Viṣṇu appeared as a man-lion to uphold the devotion and righteousness of Prahlāda, who was being persecuted by his father, Hiraṇyakaśipu, a demon who was oppressing the world and who violently opposed his son's devotion to Viṣṇu. Because of a special boon that Hiraṇyakaśipu had received, namely, that he would be invulnerable to man and beast, Viṣṇu assumed the form of the man-lion, which was neither man nor beast, and defeated him.

Viṣṇu assumed the form of a dwarf in order to restore the world to the gods. The world had been taken over by Bali, a powerful yet virtuous member of the ordinarily unrighteous race of the *asuras*. Appearing as a dwarf, Viṣṇu asked Bali for a favor, which Bali piously granted. Viṣṇu asked for the territory he could encompass in three strides, and Bali gladly agreed. Then Viṣṇu assumed his cosmic form and traversed the entire universe. He thereby restored the cosmos to the gods.

As Paraśu Rāma (Rāma the Ax Wielder) Viṣṇu chastened the *kṣatriyas*, the warrior class, for the haughty, presumptuous, and overbearing attitudes with which they had oppressed the brahmans. In several bloody campaigns, Paraśu Rāma humbled the *kṣatriyas* and asserted the priority of the brahmans in the social and theological systems.

As Rāma, the hero of the *Rāmāyaṇa* (one of the two great Indian epics), Viṣṇu defeated the demon Rāvaṇa, who had brought the world under his sway. After a long exile and a heroic battle Rāma defeated Rāvaṇa and became ruler of India. He then instituted a reign of virtue, order, and prosperity that has come to assume in the Hindu tradition the place of a golden age. In this *avatāra* Viṣṇu descended to the world to set forth a model of ideal kingship that might serve as an inspiration for all rulers at all times.

As Kṛṣṇa, Viṣṇu descended to the world in order to defeat the demon Kaṃsa, who was oppressing the earth with his wickedness, and to ensure the victory of the Pāṇḍava brothers in their war against their cousins, the Kauravas. The story of this battle is related in the other great Hindu epic, the *Mahābhārata*.

As the Buddha, Viṣṇu acted to delude those who already deserved punishment for their bad deeds. Deceived by the Buddha's false teachings, these individuals renounced the Vedas and traditional Hinduism, thus earning punishment in hell or in inferior births. In a number of later texts, Viṣṇu's Buddha *avatāra* is interpreted positively. He is said to have assumed this form in order to teach nonviolence and gentleness to the world.

Kalki is the form that Viṣṇu will assume at the end of this cosmic age. As Kalki he will appear in human form riding a white horse; he will bring the world to an end, reward the virtuous, and punish the wicked.

So popular did the *avatāras* Rāma and Kṛṣṇa become in medieval Hindu devotion that they assumed for their respective devotees the position of supreme deity. For Kṛṣṇa devotees, Kṛṣṇa is the highest expression of the divine and as such is understood not as an *avatāra* himself but rather as the source of all *avatāras*. In this context, Viṣṇu is understood to be a lesser manifestation of Kṛṣṇa. Similarly, devotees of Rāma regard him as the highest expression of the divine.

The *avatāra* idea also came to be applied to other Hindu deities. Śiva and Durgā, for example, are said in some later scriptures to assume appropriate forms in order to preserve the world or to bless their devotees. Especially in devotional contexts, *avatāras* no longer function primarily to restore cosmic order. Rather, their *raison d'être* is to bless devotees with the presence of the divine, to rescue devotees from peril, or to reward them for heroic devotion or service.

[*See also* Kṛṣṇa; Viṣṇu; *and* Rāma.]

BIBLIOGRAPHY

A convenient summary of the principal Sanskrit texts in which the *avatāra* myths are told is found in *Classical Hindu Mythology: A Reader in the Sanskrit Purāṇas*, edited and translated by Cornelia Dimmitt and J. A. B. van Buitenen (Philadelphia, 1978), pp. 59–146. An abbreviated account of the *avatāra* myths may be found in John Dowson's *A Classical Dictionary of Hindu Mythology and Religion, Geography, History, and Literature* (London, 1878), pp. 33–38. Jan Gonda's *Aspects of Early Viṣṇuism* (Utrecht, 1954) discusses some of the *avatāras* in historical context and shows how the development of the *avatāra* theology developed in the Hindu tradition.

David Kinsley

AVEMPACE. *See* Ibn Bajjah.

AVERROËS. *See* Ibn Rushd.

AVESTA. Only a small part of the Avesta (MPers., Abastāq; the name probably means "the Injunction [of Zarathushtra]"), the collection of sacred books of Zoroastrianism, has come down to us: about three-quarters of the original texts, whose codification dates to the Sasanid period (third to seventh centuries CE), have been lost. The oldest extant manuscript is from the thirteenth century.

The oral tradition that has permitted the transmission of the texts is therefore very long, especially since significant portions of the Avesta go as far back as the first years of the first millennium BCE. This fact, together with the problems connected with the writing system employed (derived from the Pahlavi alphabet, of Aramaic origin) and with the manuscript tradition, means that the study of the Avesta is philologically among the most difficult and complex.

The selection of texts that has survived—first published by their discoverer, Anquetil du Perron, in 1771—was apparently primarily determined by liturgical interests. For the most part, these are the texts that were used for religious services during the period in which the manuscript tradition arose, and they are accompanied by Pahlavi versions. It should be remembered that their language (which, being impossible to locate geographically within the Iranian world beyond a general characterization as eastern Iranian, is simply called Avestan) was no longer understood. Pahlavi versions were, consequently, necessary for an understanding of the text, which was thus strongly influenced by a relatively late exegetical tradition (in any case, not earlier than the Sasanid period). The compilation must have had to meet the requirements of the new Zoroastrian state church to provide—as did the contemporary and rival religions Christianity, Judaism, and Manichaeism—scriptures that would promote the establishment of a solid and rigid orthodoxy. Indeed, the process of selection of the scriptures is mentioned explicitly in the Pahlavi literature.

The surviving texts are highly varied, both in content and in language. Several parts of the *Yasna* are written in a dialect known as Gathic: the *Gāthās,* the five compositions in verse attributed to Zarathushtra (Zoroaster) himself, which constitute chapters 28–34, 43–46, 47–50, 51, and 53; the *Yasna Haptanhāiti,* or Yasna of the Seven Chapters (35–41); the three fundamental prayers of Zoroastrianism, Yenhē Hātam, Ashem Vohu, and Yatha Ahū Vairyō (chap. 27); and the prayer Airyema Ishyō (chap. 55). The other parts of the Avesta are written in a linguistically later Avestan, more or less archaic and also more or less correct. They include the rest of the *Yasna* and the *Nyāyishn,* the *Gāh,* the *Yashts, Sīrōza, Āfrīnagān, Vendidad, Nīrangistān, Hadhōkht Nask, Aogemadaēchā.*

The *Yasna* is the most important section, and not just because the *Gāthās* are inserted in it: these are the seventy-two chapters recited by the priest during the ceremony of the same name (*Yasna,* "sacrifice"). Among these is found the *Hōm Yasht,* the hymn to Haoma (chap. 9–11); the *Fravarānē* ("I profess"), a confession of faith (chap. 12); and the so-called *Bagān Yasht,* a commentary on the three fundamental prayers (chaps. 19–21). But without doubt the most important part of the *Yasna,* and the most beautiful part of the whole Avesta, is the *Gāthās* ("songs") of Zarathushtra. Difficulties of interpretation do not diminish their value: they are the primary source for a knowledge of the doctrines of the prophet. In their literary genre, they are close to the Vedic hymns and testify to the presence in Iran, as elsewhere, of a tradition of Indo-European sacred poetry.

Among the other sections, the *Yashts* (hymns to various divinities) deserve special mention. Several of these hymns or prayers are particularly significant in the history of religions, as they are the most direct evidence of the new faith's adaptation of the older religious tradition. Especially noteworthy are those dedicated to Anāhitā (5); to Tishtrya, the star Sirius (8); to Mithra (10); to the *fravashi*s (13); to Verethraghna (14); to Vāyu (15); and to Khvarenah (19).

The *Vendidad* (*vī-daēvo-dāta,* "the law abjuring *daivas*"), the only section that may be an addition to the text, contains, along with mythological parts like the second chapter dedicated to Yima, the king of the golden age, a detailed body of rules for achieving purity. The *Hadhōkht Nask* and the *Aogemadaēchā* are texts dealing with events after death and funeral rites. The other parts are primarily invocations and prayers for the various forms, articulations, and requirements of worship services.

BIBLIOGRAPHY

Editions and Translations of the Avesta or of Its Sections

Bartholomae, C. *Die Gathas des Avesta: Zarathustra's Verspredigten.* Strassburg, 1905. Translated by J. H. Moulton in *Early Zoroastrianism* (1913; reprint, London, 1972), pp. 343-390.

Darmesteter, James. *The Zend-Avesta,* pt. 2, *The Sirozahs, Yashts and Nyayesh.* Sacred Books of the East, vol. 23. Oxford, 1883; reprint, Delhi, 1965.

Darmesteter, James. *The Zend-Avesta,* pt. 1, *The Vendīdād.* 2d ed. Sacred Books of the East, vol. 4. Oxford, 1895; reprint, Delhi, 1965.

Duchesne-Guillemin, Jacques. *Zoroastre: Étude critique avec une traduction commentée des Gâthâ.* Paris, 1948. Translated by Maria Henning as *The Hymns of Zarathushtra* (London, 1952).
Humbach, Helmut. *Die Gathas des Zarathustra.* 2 vols. Heidelberg, 1959.
Insler, Stanley. *The Gathas of Zarathushtra.* Acta Iranica, 3d ser., vol. 1. Leiden, 1975.
Lommel, Herman. *Die Yäšt's des Awesta.* Göttingen, 1927.
Lommel, Herman. *Die Gathas des Zarathustra.* Edited by Bernfried Schlerath. Basel, 1971.
Mills, L. H. *The Zend-Avesta,* pt. 3, *The Yasna, Visparad, Afrinagan, Gahs and Miscellaneous Fragments.* Sacred Books of the East, vol. 31. Oxford, 1887; reprint, Delhi, 1965.
Smith, Maria W. *Studies in the Syntax of the Gathas of Zarathushtra, Together with Text, Translation and Notes.* Philadelphia, 1929; reprint, Millwood, N.Y., 1966.
Taraporevala, Irach J. S. *The Divine Songs of Zarathushtra.* Bombay, 1951.

Editions and Translations of the Pahlavi Version

Anklesaria, Behramgore Tahmuras, trans. *Pahlavi Vendidâd.* Edited by Dinshah D. Kapadia. Bombay, 1949.
Dhabhar, Bamanji Nasarvanji, ed. *Zand-i Khūrtak Avistāk.* Bombay, 1927.
Dhabhar, Bamanji Nasarvanji, ed. *Pahlavi Yasna and Vispered.* Bombay, 1949.
Jamasp, Hoshang, ed. *Vendidâd.* Bombay, 1907. Avestan text with Pahlavi translation, commentary, and glossary.
Kanga, Ervad Maneck F., ed. *Pahlavi Version of Yašts.* Bombay, 1941.

Studies of the Transmission, Transliteration, and Oral Tradition

Altheim, Franz. *Awestische Textgeschichte.* Halle, 1949.
Bailey, H. W. *Zoroastrian Problems in the Ninth-Century Books* (1943). Reprint, Oxford, 1971.
Henning, W. B. "The Disintegration of the Avestic Studies." *Transactions of the Philological Society* (1942) : 40–56.
Morgenstierne, G. "Orthography and Sound System in the Avesta." *Norsk tidsskrift for sprogvidenskap* 12 (1942): 38–82.
Widengren, Geo. "The Problem of the Sassanid Avesta." In *Holy Book and Holy Tradition,* pp. 36–53. Manchester, 1968.

General Studies

Christensen, Arthur. *Études sur le zoroastrisme de la Perse antique.* Copenhagen, 1928.
Gershevitch, Ilya. "Old Iranian Literature." In *Iranistik-Literatur.* Leiden, 1968.
Hoffmann, Karl. "Das Avesta in der Persis." In *Prolegomena to the Sources on the History of Pre-Islamic Central Asia,* edited by J. Harmatta, pp. 89–93. Budapest, 1979.
Meillet, Antoine. *Trois conférences sur les Gâthâ de l'Avesta.* Paris, 1925.
Schlerath, Bernfried. *Avesta-Wörterbuch.* 2 vols. Wiesbaden, 1968.
Schmidt, Rüdiger, comp. *Indogermanische Dichtersprache.* Darmstadt, 1968.
Wesendonk, O. G. von. *Die religionsgeschichtliche Bedeutung des Yasna Haptanhāti.* Bonn, 1931.

GHERARDO GNOLI
Translated from Italian by Roger DeGaris

AVICENNA. *See* Ibn Sīnā.

AVIDYĀ. The Sanskrit term *avidyā,* which means, literally, "absence of knowledge," or "false belief," has been used in different senses in different systems of Indian philosophy, as in the *hetucakra* of Buddhism or in Patañjali's Yoga philosophy; yet only in the Advaita Vedānta taught by Śaṅkara is the term *avidyā* used in an important technical sense. I shall explain here only the Advaita theory.

In Advaita Vedānta *avidyā* is closely connected with another key concept, *māyā.* In fact, *avidyā* and *māyā* are two aspects of the same ontological principle. Advaita philosophers hold that the ultimate reality is pure, impersonal consciousness beyond all change. The world of change and multiplicity is not real, but neither is it wholly unreal, for a wholly unreal object cannot be perceived while the empirical world is undoubtedly experienced as real. The material cause, "the stuff," of this neither-real-nor-unreal world must itself be neither real nor unreal; *māyā* is this ultimate matter of the world. Just as the world is an appearance, so is the evolution of the world from *māyā* also an appearance. Advaita Vedānta accepts the Sāṃkhya order of evolution of the world from *prakṛti,* rejecting only the metaphysical status of *prakṛti* as a real. The first evolute of *māyā* is, therefore, *buddhi,* the second *ahaṃkāra,* the third *manas,* and so on, until the five gross elements of matter—earth, water, fire, air, and ether—are evolved. These five elements in different combinations constitute the objects of the material world. But this world is a mere appearance, and our perception of it is illusory. Just as *māyā* is the ontological principle underlying the world, *avidyā* is the epistemological principle that vitiates our perceptual experience. Infinite pure consciousness is the only reality, and we ought to know this reality; instead we see the world, and the reality lies hidden behind the world show. Thus *māyā* and *avidyā* are the same principle, the one in its ontological aspect, the other in its epistemological aspect.

Advaita Vedānta explains how *avidyā* functions to produce illusory perception by contrasting it with veridical perception, in particular, veridical perception of sense objects. In veridical perception the finite subject has an idea, a modification of the *antaḥkaraṇa* ("inner sense, ego, mind") that is an evolute of *māyā* caused by an empirically real object. But in illusory perception, for example, when one sees a snake when in fact there is no snake to be seen, the idea of the snake does not depend on the actual existence or presence of a snake. Yet it cannot be denied that illusory perception is nonetheless perception, that is, immediate experience of an object. To regard illusion as somehow a wrong inference is to go against the verdict of experience. Yet the object of illusory perception exists "out there" only so long as the illusion lasts. Thus although the object of illusion cannot be simply identified with a subjective idea, still it cannot be denied that its existence is somehow dependent on perception. In such cases the existence of the object consists in its being perceived. So the function of *avidyā* in such cases is twofold: (1) to produce the idea of the snake that cannot be causally produced by the snake itself and (2) to produce simultaneously the illusory object. The idea of the snake is not an idea of the *antaḥkaraṇa* by means of which the empirical subject perceives the empirically real object; it is a modification of *avidyā (avidyāvṛtti)*. Thus the empirical subject has two epistemologically different sorts of ideas: (1) modifications of *antaḥkaraṇa* caused by objects that are known by means of these ideas and (2) modifications of *avidyā*, the ideas by means of which the empirical subject perceives an object that is not independent of this perception.

From another point of view, *avidyā* has two other types of function to perform in order to produce illusory perception. It is necessary for the real nature of the object (in illusory perception there is always a real object that is mistaken for another and that is thus different from hallucination) to be hidden; and it is also necessary for the illusory object, that is, the empirically unreal object, to be projected out there. These two functions of *avidyā*—concealment of the real nature of the object *(āvaraṇa)* and the projection of the unreal object *(vikṣepa)*—are together sufficient to produce illusory perception.

How is an illusion canceled if it is canceled at all? According to Advaita Vedānta, it is the very nature of illusion to be canceled eventually by veridical perception. It is obvious that illusion gets canceled only by veridical perception; one can be disillusioned only by knowing reality. When I mistake a piece of rope for a snake, my mistake is corrected only when I perceive the piece of rope. But when I perceive the piece of rope, I know not only that there is no snake to be seen now but also that there was no snake even when I perceived it. Thus cancellation of a mistake always has a retrospective effect. Moreover, as all illusion involves modes of *avidyā*, and all veridical perception modes of *antaḥkaraṇa*, cancellation of error is always the destruction of a mode of *avidyā* by a mode of *antaḥkaraṇa*. This principle leads to a more profound theory of Advaita Vedānta.

All veridical perceptions of external objects are by means of ideas, that is, modes of *antaḥkaraṇa*, yet it is obvious that inner states as well as personal identity cannot be known by means of ideas. We know external objects by means of ideas, and if, again, we need ideas to know these ideas, then there will be infinite regress. So according to Advaita Vedānta, inner states as well as personal identity are self-illuminating. This mode of direct knowledge without the mediation of ideas is called "witnessing" *(sākṣin)*. This knowledge is eternally there, there being nothing to stand between the inner states and consciousness, nothing to obstruct this inner vision. But then a question arises: if everyone always is aware of the self-shining consciousness that is the inner reality, how does this knowledge of the self coexist with *avidyā*, which causes the subject to have illusions about external objects and also about himself as an embodied finite creature? To answer this question, Advaita Vedānta formulated its theory of the type of knowledge *(vidyā)* that can cancel *avidyā*. The witnessing consciousness is, of course, consciousness of the inner nature of the self; still it is not by means of any ideas. It is only knowledge by means of ideas, by modes of *antaḥkaraṇa*, that can cancel illusion. So in liberation, which is the final cancellation of *avidyā*, one has to have an ideational representation of the inner self, the mode of *antaḥkaraṇa* that has the form of *brahman*, the absolute reality. When one has this representational cognition of the inner reality behind the world show, the representation itself then vanishes; as the *antaḥkaraṇa* vanishes, the *buddhi* vanishes; the individual vanishes in very much the same manner as the illusory vanishes when one knows the piece of rope. Yet the difference between liberation and bondage is simply the difference between having an ideational knowledge of reality and having the nonideational witnessing consciousness of reality that everyone has all the time.

[*For further discussion of avidyā in Advaita Vedānta, see* Vedānta. *See also* Māyā *and* Prakṛti.]

BIBLIOGRAPHY

Sanskrit Works Translated into English

Dharmarājādhvarīndra. *Vedāntaparibhāṣā*. Edited and translated by S. Suryanarayana Sastri. Adyar, 1942.

Gauḍapāda-Kārikā. Edited and translated by Raghunath Damodar Karmarkar. Poona, 1953.

Nimbārka. *Commentaries on the Brahma-Sūtras*. 3 vols. Translated by Roma Chaudhuri. Calcutta, 1940–1943.

Rāmānuja. *Śrībhāṣya.* Translated by George Thibaut. Sacred Books of the East, vol. 48. Oxford, 1904.

Sadānanda. *Vedāntasāra: A Work on Vedānta Philosophy.* Edited and translated by Mysore Hiriyanna. Poona Oriental Series, no. 14. Poona, 1929.

Vācaspati Miśra. *The Bhāmatī of Vāscapati on Śaṅkara Brahmasūtra (Catuḥsūtrī).* Edited and translated by S. Suryanarayana Sastri and C. Kunhan Raja. Adyar, 1933.

Books and Articles in English

Bhattacharyya, Sibajiban. "Philosophy as Self-Realisation." In *Indian Philosophy Today,* edited by N. K. Devaraja, pp. 54–81. New York, 1975.

Raychaudhuri, Anil Kumar. *The Doctrine of Māyā.* 2d ed. Calcutta, 1950.

Sen, Nani Lal. *A Critique of the Theories of Viparyaya.* Calcutta, 1965.

SIBAJIBAN BHATTACHARYYA

AVRAHAM BEN DAVID OF POSQUIÈRES (c. 1125–1198), known by the acronym Ra'ABaD (Rabbi Avraham ben David). Avraham ben David is best known for his original and versatile contributions to the literature of *halakhah.* He composed commentaries on various types of Talmudic literature: on the Mishnah (e.g., *'Eduyyot* and *Qinnim*); on the Talmud (e.g., *'Avodah Zarah* and *Bava' Qamma'*); and on halakhic midrashim (e.g., *Sifra'*). Further works include *responsa* (Heb., *teshuvot,* decisions concerning the interpretation of application of the law), which reveal his character and method; homiletic discourses (e.g., *Derashah le-Ro'sh ha-Shanah*); codes of rabbinic law; and critical annotations or glosses *(hassagot)* on standard works of rabbinic literature.

The most important and influential of Avraham ben David's codes, which include *Hilkhot lulav* (Laws concerning the Palm Branch), *Ḥibbur harsha'ot* (A Manual on the Laws of Agency), and *Perush yadayim,* is the *Ba'alei ha-nefesh,* a careful presentation of the laws of uncleanness and purity. The last chapter of his *Sha'ar ha-qedushah* (Gate of Holiness) is an ethical-homiletical disquisition that formulates and analyzes the moral norms and religious attitudes that enable one to achieve self-control in sexual matters and attain purity of heart and action.

Avraham ben David is referred to as the *ba'al hassagot* ("author of the glosses") because of the critical scholia and animadversions that he composed toward the end of his life on the *Halakhot* of Yitsḥaq ben Ya'aqov Alfasi, the *Sefer ha-ma'or* of Zeraḥyah ha-Levi, and especially the *Mishneh Torah* of Maimonides. These glosses combine criticism and commentary; they are not exclusively polemical, and their polemical emphasis varies in intensity and acuity. *Hassagot,* a wide-ranging form of writing based on a firm premise and finely honed polemical skill, are refined by Avraham ben David and his Provençal contemporaries into an expressive genre of pointed, precise, and persuasive critique. This genre played an important role in the preservation of the spirit of criticism and intellectual freedom so central to rabbinic literature.

Beyond his literary creations, Avraham ben David contributed significantly to the development of a critical-conceptual approach to Talmudic literature that sought to define with rigor and precision complex concepts discussed fragmentarily in numerous, unrelated sections of the Talmud. Many of his interpretations and innovations were endorsed and transmitted by subsequent generations of Talmudists and incorporated into standard works of Jewish law.

During the lifetime of Avraham ben David the centers of rabbinic learning in southern France provided a home for the transplanted philosophic-scientific-ethical literature of Spanish Jews. At this time, an undercurrent of mystical speculation began to emerge that was to find its expression in medieval qabbalistic literature. Avraham ben David was involved in both these developments. He encouraged and benefited from this newly translated philosophical literature, and his own writing reflects some traces of philosophy and philology in the use of terms, phrases, and concepts from this new literary phenomenon. He is described by later qabbalists (e.g., Yitsḥaq of Acre, Shem Ṭov ben Ga'on, and Menaḥem Recanati, and others from the school of Moses Nahmanides and Shelomoh ben Avraham Adret) as one of the fathers of qabbalistic literature. This is supported by references in the writings of Ra'abad's son, Yitsḥaq the Blind, and Yitsḥaq's nephew, Asher. They depicted him as a mystic who was worthy of receiving special revelations and who actually did receive them. In the absence of explicitly qabbalistic statements in Avraham ben David's own works, our knowledge of his use of doctrines and symbolism of Qabbalah depends on passages quoted by others in his name. These deal with mystical meditations during prayer *(kavvanot)* and the doctrine of the ten *sefirot,* and they reveal an acquaintance with early Heikhalot terminology and its fusion with contemporary philosophic vocabulary.

BIBLIOGRAPHY

Abramson, Sheraga. "Sifrei halakhot shel ha-Ra'abad." *Tarbiz* 36 (December 1966): 158–179.

Gross, H. "R. Abraham b. David aus Posquières." *Monatsschrift für Geschichte und Wissenschaft des Judenthums* 22 (1873):

337–344, 398–407, 446–459; 23 (1874): 19–29, 76–85, 164–182, 275–276.

Twersky, Isadore. *Rabad of Posquières: A Twelfth-Century Talmudist.* Rev. ed. Philadelphia, 1980. Includes a complete bibliography.

ISADORE TWERSKY

AVVAKUM (1620/1–1682), Russian Orthodox archpriest; founding father of the Old Believers; martyr. Avvakum was ordained to the priesthood at the age of twenty-two, serving in the area of Nizhni Novgorod; eight years later he was promoted to be archpriest. By then he had amply demonstrated his zeal as a reformer. Following in the wake of the Muscovite "God-seekers," an influential group of scholarly zealots, he sought to revive liturgical life and public morality. The resentment which this provoked led to his displacement and his first visit to Moscow (1652). There he was welcomed by the leading God-seekers and introduced to the tsar.

The election of Nikon as patriarch of Moscow later that year promised to confirm and revitalize the God-seekers' reforms. However, Nikon proceeded arbitrarily to reform liturgical phraseology and practice, particularly concerning the sign of the cross. Avvakum vociferously objected to these reforms, which he saw as a challenge to the true faith. For if even minor rituals were to change, the whole edifice of related doctrine would be undermined. He was arrested and exiled to Siberia (1653). After many tribulations he was permitted to return to Moscow (1664), but his insistence on the validity and importance of the pre-Nikonian liturgical norms led to renewed exile.

Avvakum and his companions were brought back to Moscow and anathematized at a church council of 1666–1667; he in turn anathematized the council. Thus was confirmed the existence of the Russian church schism, which was to have a decisive influence on the ordering of Russian society over the centuries to come. Avvakum was sent to the arctic outpost of Pustozersk from which he and his companions issued tracts and letters. More important than these was Avvakum's apologetic autobiography composed in 1672 to 1673. It is a masterpiece of Russian literature and one of Europe's great confessional texts.

The accession of a new patriarch of Moscow (Joachim) was probably a decisive factor in taking the state's campaign against the Old Believers a stage further, and Avvakum, together with his three companions, was sent to the stake in April 1682. Avvakum had persuasively presented himself as confessor and prophet in defense of the sacred Orthodox heritage delivered to Moscow, the "third Rome," and he is remembered as a martyr of the old faith.

BIBLIOGRAPHY

Avvakum's autobiography has been reedited from the manuscript by Andrei N. Robinson, *Zhizneopisaniia Avvakuma i Epifaniia* (Moscow, 1963). The most scholarly edition and translation of the text in a Western European language is by Pierre Pascal, *La vie de l'archiprêtre Avvakum écrite par lui-même*, 2d ed. (Paris, 1960). Even so, Robinson utters words of caution about the redaction on which the translation is based. It was also Pascal who provided a magnificent treatment of Avvakum and his times in *Avvakum et les débuts du Raskol: La crise religieuse au dix-septième siècle en Russie*, 2d ed. (Paris, 1963).

SERGEI HACKEL

AXIS MUNDI, the "hub" or "axis" of the universe, is a technical term used in the study of the history of religions. It comprises at least three levels of reference: the images themselves, their function and meaning, and the experiences associated with them.

Vivid images of the axis of the universe vary widely, since they depend on the particular worldview entertained by a specific culture. Foremost among the images designated by the term *axis mundi* is the cosmic mountain, a sacred place deemed to be the highest point of the universe and perhaps identified with the center of the world and the place where creation first began. Well-known examples of the cosmic mountain are Mount Meru of South Asian cosmology, Haraberazaiti of Iranian tradition, and Himingbjör of Scandinavian mythology.

The cosmic tree, at whose top abides the celestial divinity, is another frequent image standing for the axis of the world. The roots of such a tree may sink into the underworlds, while its branches traverse the multiple world planes. At the center of the classical Maya vision of the world stood Yaxche, the "first tree," the "green tree," whose place marked the center of all meaningful directions and colors of the universe.

A cosmic pillar may also serve as an *axis mundi.* Such is the case with the Delaware (Lenape) Indians and other Eastern Woodland peoples of North America. The center post of their ceremonial cult house supports the sky and passes into the very hand of the celestial deity. The Milky Way is often viewed as another form of cosmic pillar that supports the heavens and connects them with earth.

Many other images fall under the designation *axis mundi* because they share in the symbolic meaning represented by a cosmic mountain, tree, or pillar that joins heaven, earth, and underworld. This category includes cities, especially imperial capitals deemed "heavenly" sites by virtue of proximity to the divine realm; palaces or temples that continue the imagery of the cosmic mountain (e.g., the Babylonian ziggurat); vines or ropes that pass from heaven to earth; and sacred ladders such as the seven-rung ladder, described by Origen, that brings the candidate in the cult of Mithra through the seven heavens.

None of these images has a static function. They are all places of active passage and transition. As places of dynamic union where beings of quite different natures come together or pass into one another, the images of *axis mundi* may be associated with the coincidence of opposites—that is, the resolution of contradictions by their progress onto a more spiritual plane.

Because the *axis mundi* serves as the locus where cosmic regions intersect and where the universe of being is accessible in all its dimensions, the hub of the universe is held to be a place sacred above all others. It defines reality, for it marks the place where being is most fully manifest. This connection of the *axis mundi* with the full manifestation of being is often expressed as an association with the supreme being to whom the axis provides access. This *axis mundi* is often traversed and its heights attained in a state of ecstasy brought about by spiritual techniques. Hence the term *axis mundi* implies an intersection of planes through which transcendence to other kinds of being may be achieved.

There is a tendency to replicate the image of the *axis mundi* in multiple forms. Such is the case with the cross—the cosmic tree of Christianity. Recreating the image of the *axis mundi* in the form of village sites, house plans, ritual furnishings, personal ornaments, and even kitchen items tends to identify the universe as a whole with the fullness of being characteristic of action at that sacred place. It ensures that contact with the fullness of reality is everywhere possible. As a result, the meaning and function of the *axis mundi* rest not in abstract and geometrical concepts alone but in everyday gestures that can effect the same transcendence.

All these symbols imply a particular quality of experience. The symbols of *axis mundi* are ambivalent: on the one hand, they connect realms of being but on the other hand they emphasize the distance between such realms. In short, they point to the need for a rupture of planes of existence, for experience of an order quite different from that of the ordinary world.

[*See also* Mountains *and* Trees; *for discussion of symbolization of the* axis mundi *in religious architecture, see* Architecture.]

BIBLIOGRAPHY

For a wide-ranging discussion of the general concept of *axis mundi*, see Mircea Eliade's *Patterns in Comparative Religion* (New York, 1958), pp. 367–387, which concern the "center of the world," and pp. 265–303, which treat the question of the *axis mundi* manifest as cosmic tree. See also Eliade's *The Sacred and the Profane: The Nature of Religion* (New York, 1959), pp. 20–67, and *Images and Symbols: Studies in Religious Symbolism* (New York, 1961), pp. 27–56, which provide bibliographies tracing the history of this concept in scholarly study of religion.

For contemporary studies representing investigations of specific aspects of *axis mundi*, the following may serve as illustrations: for the image of mountain, I. W. Mabbett's "The Symbolism of Mount Meru," *History of Religions* 23 (August 1983): 64–83; for cosmic tree, Y. T. Hosoi's "The Sacred Tree in Japanese Prehistory," *History of Religions* 16 (November 1976): 95–119; as a city, Werner Müller's *Die heilige Stadt* (Stuttgart, 1961) and Paul Wheatley's *The Pivot of the Four Quarters: A Preliminary Enquiry into the Origins and Character of the Ancient Chinese City* (Chicago, 1971), esp. pp. 411–476. For an examination of the temple as place of union of beings and manifestation of sacred presence, see David Dean Shulman's *Tamil Temple Myths* (Princeton, 1980).

For a consideration of the liturgical function of sacred geography and spatial images when seen as expressions of being, see Kees W. Bolle's "Speaking of a Place," in *Myths and Symbols*, edited by Joseph M. Kitagawa and Charles H. Long (Chicago, 1969), pp. 127–140.

LAWRENCE E. SULLIVAN

ĀYURVEDA. The traditional Hindu system of medicine widely practiced in India, Āyurveda is based on authoritative treatises written in Sanskrit over approximately the past two millennia. Three major classical medical systems have flourished on the Indian subcontinent: Āyurveda among Hindus, Yunānī among Muslims, and Siddha among Tamils in South India. Their reliance on elaborate textual traditions distinguish these three systems from the assorted medical practices offered by astrologers, exorcists, priests, snakebite specialists, and kindred healers in the context of diverse folk traditions. In general, folk practices are associated with a magico-religious understanding of illness, whereas Āyurveda is associated with an understanding of illness that refers to the balance of three physiological principles suggestive of, yet distinct from, the Galenic humors. Such boundaries delimiting classical and folk traditions are not absolute, however, and humoral concepts pervade many folk practices just as magico-religious considerations have at times played a significant role in the practice of Āyurveda.

Texts. Major traditions evolving in the context of Hinduism frequently trace their roots to one of the four Vedic Saṃhitās, the earliest canonical texts, and Āyurveda is associated with the *Atharvaveda.* While all four Vedas demonstrate at least a peripheral concern for medical issues, they do so in the context of a decidedly supernatural worldview. At this early stage one finds barely a hint of the later humoral physiology among the charms, prayers, and propitiatory rites suggested for the relief of specified ailments frequently attributed to demons.

The tradition of Āyurveda holds that the medical doctrine was revealed through a series of deities and sages to human physicians who in turn composed the basic texts. According to the *Suśruta Saṃhitā,* the doctrine passed from Indra, chief among the gods, to Dhanvantari, who has come to be regarded as the Hindu god of medicine, and then to Suśruta himself, who composed this treatise. The *Caraka Saṃhitā* states that the doctrine passed to the sage Ātreya Punarvasu, who trained a disciple named Agniveśa, author of the *Agniveśa Tantra* (an Ayurvedic, not a Tantric, text). When this text subsequently fell into disrepair, it was partially restored first by Caraka and later by Dṛḍhabala. Both the *Caraka Saṃhitā,* as revised by Caraka, and the *Suśruta Saṃhitā* are believed to have been written during the first three hundred years CE, and the redaction by Dṛḍhabala is thought to have been made in approximately 500 CE. It is widely accepted that these texts are based on a medical doctrine that was followed for at least several centuries before it was committed to writing, and some scholars claim that the tradition extends back several millennia, although this assertion is disputed by many Indologists. Other major texts include the *Aṣṭāṅgahṛdaya Saṃhitā* of Vāgbhaṭa from approximately 600 CE, *Mādhavanidāna* of Mādhava from approximately 700 CE, and *Bhela Saṃhitā,* which may have been contemporaneous with the *Agniveśa Tantra* and hence is the oldest surviving text. The most often cited of these treatises are *Caraka, Suśruta,* and *Vāgbhaṭa,* collectively known as "the great three" *(bṛhat trayī).*

Theory of Disease and Treatment. According to Āyurveda, most sickness results from an imbalance of one or more of three humors *(tridoṣa):* wind *(vāta),* bile *(pitta),* and phlegm *(kapha).* A patient's illness is determined by the character of the particular disease *(vyādhi),* which is dependent on both the deranged humor and the body substance (*dhātu,* e.g., blood, flesh, fat, bone, etc.) or anatomical part that is affected. Such factors as dietary imbalance, physical and emotional stresses, suppression of natural urges, or the effects of deeds in a previous life *(karmavipāka)* are said to cause the deranged humoral balance in a particular disease or subtype. Although this *tridoṣa* theory has been emphasized, a number of independent external factors are also recognized, including injuries, poisons, and supernatural agencies. Some early Ayurvedic passages employ references to these supernatural agencies as technical terms in order to develop meaningful diagnostic concepts while explicitly denying a supernatural conceptual frame of reference (see, for example, *Caraka Saṃhitā* 2.7.19–23). Other passages refer to demonic possession as it is more popularly understood. Specific classes of demons and deities, generically referred to as *bhūta*s, serve as paradigms for a range of character types and categories of mental disorder based on the well-known traits of *deva*s, *gandharva*s, *rākṣasa*s, *piśāca*s, and others.

Therapy according to Ayurvedic principles is based on the premise that a humoral imbalance must be corrected by either pacifying or eliminating the excited humor. This is accomplished with preparations of herbs, animal products, and heavy metals; decoctions in clarified butter *(ghī);* dietary adjustments; or by other means. One type of treatment described in the early texts that became especially popular in South India is *pañcakarma;* it involves emesis, purgation, sternutation, medicinal enema, and phlebotomy. Surgery is emphasized in the *Suśruta Saṃhitā.* The texts also specify ritual offerings, the recitation of sacred formulas (mantras), and other ritual procedures.

Medical and Soteriological Pluralism. The humoral theory of *tridoṣa* appears to have remained dominant throughout the course of development of the Ayurvedic tradition. In contrast, perhaps due in part to the growing influence of Tantra—the ritualization of otherwise socially unacceptable practices—in the culture at large from the middle of the first millennium CE, later Ayurvedic texts pay increased attention to magico-religious concepts and interventions that resonated with strains not only of Tantric literature but of the mystical aspects of Vedic literature as well. The number of classes of supernatural beings (*bhūta*s) associated with insanity steadily grew from eight in *Caraka* and *Suśruta* to twenty in the thirteenth-century text *Śārṅgadhara Saṃhitā* (1.7.38–39).

To the extent that this conceptual shift from a secular humoral theory toward a supernatural orientation is manifest in the later Ayurvedic compositions, it signifies a reaffirmation of certain aspects of the distinctly different worldview of the *Atharvaveda,* with which the mechanistic physiological theory of *tridoṣa* had made a definite break at an early stage in the development of Āyurveda. In the twentieth century, competition with

Western-styled cosmopolitan medicine may have led some advocates of Āyurveda to ignore magico-religious aspects persisting in the tradition in favor of the systematic principles of the *tridoṣa* doctrine, and at the same time to focus on the issue of clinical efficacy of Ayurvedic therapies rather than the validity of the underlying humoral theory of other theoretical premises.

Hybrid ideologies that have emerged in the medically pluralistic setting of India presently complicate any analysis of the relationship between Āyurveda and other therapeutic options, both Western-styled and indigenous, since each system exerts some influence on the evolving conceptualizations of the others. Historically, Āyurveda has also stood in a complex relationship with coexisting traditions in its cultural context. However, it may be stated generally that healing is emphasized in Āyurveda, whereas other Hindu traditions such as Tantra, Yoga, and Indian alchemy *(rasavidyā)*, which are primarily concerned with spiritual attainments, have overlapping objectives. Anatomical and physiological principles provide a framework in Āyurveda for understanding sickness and health in the physical body, but in Tantra and Yoga provide a framework for understanding the mystical path leading to the attainment of spiritual objectives. Similarly, although Indian alchemy was concerned with the use of preparations of mercury, other heavy metals, and herbs to restore youth and promote health, such motives were secondary to the primary goal of liberation of the spirit.

A number of philosophical concepts are specified in the Ayurvedic texts, referring to ideas more fully developed in the orthodox systems of Hindu philosophy, mainly Sāṃkhya, but also Nyāya-Vaiśeṣika and the rest. Social and ethical issues are also considered. Medical students are instructed to pledge diligence and purity, in accordance with the traditional values guiding students of the Veda, as they commence training under a guru after a prescribed initiation ceremony. Professional standards for physicians are advocated not only in medical treatises but in other Sanskrit treatises as well, especially in the Nītiśāstra and Dharmaśāstra texts on polity and Hindu law.

[*For further discussion of Indian medicine, see* Medicine, *article on* Medicine and Religion in Eastern Cultures. *For a broader discussion of religious and magico-religious concepts of medicine, see* Healing.]

BIBLIOGRAPHY

Primary Sources. Translations of several Ayurvedic classics are available. *The Caraka Saṃhita*, 6 vols., prepared by the Shree Gulabkunverba Ayurvedic Society (Jamnagar, 1949), contains the Sanskrit text, translations into English, Hindi, and Gujarati, and an introductory volume. *Caraka-Saṃhitā: Agniveśa's Treatise Refined and Annotated by Caraka and Redacted by Dṛḍhabala*, 2 vols. (Varanasi, 1981–1983), is a critical edition and translation prepared by R. K. Sharma to facilitate further study of the text and its commentaries. The *Sushruta Samhita*, translated by Kaviraj Kunjalal Bishagratna (Calcutta, 1907–1916) has been reprinted (Varanasi, 1963), but it appears to be based on a Sanskrit text that varies somewhat from current printed editions. While only the first five chapters of *Vāgbhaṭa's Aṣṭāṅgahṛdayasaṁhitā* have been translated into English from the Tibetan version by Claus Vogel (Weisbaden, 1965), printed with the Tibetan and Sanskrit text, there is a complete translation in German by Luise Hilgenberg and Wilibald Kirfel: *Vāgbhaṭa's Aṣṭāṅgahṛdayasaṁhitā: Ein altindisches Lehrbuch der Heilkunde* (Leiden, 1941). The work by G. J. Meulenbeld, *The Mādhavanidāna and Its Chief Commentary: Chapters 1–10* (Leiden, 1974), is the only English translation to provide both an Ayurvedic text and commentary, and it also contains useful appendices. Sanskrit editions of all the major texts are available.

Secondary Sources. The classic survey by Julius Jolly, *Medicin* (Strassburg, 1901), has been translated by C. G. Kashikar as *Indian Medicine*, 2d ed. (Delhi, 1977), and it remains a useful source for access to a range of texts on a given topic. The Ayurvedic tradition with reference to its context in the Vedic literature and its relationship to Greek medicine has been analyzed by Jean Filliozat in *La doctrine classique de la médecine indienne: Ses origines et ses parallèles grecs* (Paris, 1949), translated by Dev Raj Chanana as *The Classical Doctrine of Indian Medicine: Its Origins and Its Greek Parallels* (Delhi, 1964). *Asian Medical Systems: A Comparative Study*, edited by Charles Leslie (Berkeley, 1976), contains several noteworthy articles on various aspects of the Ayurvedic tradition, including A. L. Basham's survey of the social history of medicine during the classical period, "The Practice of Medicine in Ancient and Medieval India," pp. 18–43, and Charles Leslie's essay on the modernization of Ayurvedic institutions through the nineteenth and twentieth centuries, "Ambiguities of Revivalism in Modern India," pp. 356–367. Yoga, Tantra, and Indian alchemy are discussed in contrast to the objectives of "utilitarian medicine" in Mircea Eliade's *Yoga: Immortality and Freedom*, 2d ed. (Princeton, 1969). A comprehensive study of Indian chemistry and its roots in alchemy, tracing its development from pre-Harappan times through Vedic, Ayurvedic, and Tantric epochs, can be found in *History of Chemistry in Ancient and Medieval India*, edited by Priyadaranjan Ray (Calcutta, 1956).

MITCHELL G. WEISS

AZTEC RELIGION developed in the capital city of Tenochtitlán in the Valley of Mexico between the fourteenth and sixteenth centuries CE. The Aztec religious tradition combined and transformed a number of ritual, mythic, and cosmic elements from the heterogeneous cultural groups who inhabited the central plateau of Mesoamerica. Seldom has a capital city fit the category of "center of the world" more completely than Tenochtitlán: the high plateau of Mexico is roughly the center of Mesoamerica; the Valley of Mexico is the heart of that plateau; interconnected lakes formed the center of the valley; and Tenochtitlán was constructed near the center of the lakes.

Mexico's central highlands had been the dominant cultural region of central Mesoamerica since the beginning of the common era, when the great imperial capital of Teotihuacán ("abode of the gods") had been established thirty miles north of where Tenochtitlán would later rise. Like Tenochtitlán, Teotihuacán was organized into four great quarters around a massive ceremonial center. Scholars and archaeologists have theorized that the four-quartered city was a massive spatial symbol for the major cosmological conceptions of Aztec religion. In many respects, the cultural and religious patterns of Teotihuacán laid the groundwork for all later developments in and around the Valley of Mexico. The mythologies of successive cultures—the Toltec and the Aztec most prominent among them—looked back to Teotihuacán as their symbolic place of origin and as the source for the legitimacy of their political authority.

Between 1300 and 1521 all roads of central Mesoamerica led into the lake region of the valley from which the magnificent capital of the Aztec arose. When the Aztec's precursors, the Chichimec ("dog lineage"; lit., "dog rope") migrated into the region in the thirteenth century, the valley was held by warring city-states constantly competing for land and tribute. This fragmented world was partly the result of the twelfth-century collapse of the northern Toltec empire centered at the illustrious capital of Tollan ("place of reeds"). The Toltec collapse brought waves of Chichimec and Toltec remnants into the Valley of Mexico, where they interacted with different city-states and religious traditions.

The basic settlement of central Mexico from Teotihuacán times was the *tlatocayotl,* or city-state, which consisted of a capital city surrounded by dependent communities that worked the agricultural lands, paid tribute, and performed services for the elite classes in the capital according to various ritual calendars and cosmological patterns. Occasionally one city-state would grow to large proportions and establish widespread territorial control and integration into some form of tributary empire. Around 1325, a Chichimec group who called themselves *Méxica* settled Tenochtitlán and within a hundred years had organized a political unit with the power to dominate an expanding number of cities and towns in the central valley.

One of the major problems in the study of Aztec religion is the fragmentary nature of the pictorial, written, and archaeological sources associated with Tenochtitlán. The Spanish military conquest of Mexico was accompanied by a sustained campaign to eliminate Aztec symbols, images, screenfolds, and ceremonial buildings, as well as members of the military and priestly elites. Surprisingly, a counter attitude developed among certain Spanish officials and priests, who collected indigenous documents and organized their reproduction in order to enhance missionary work and inform Spanish officials about native religion and life. The result is a spectrum of sources including art and architecture; pre-Columbian screenfolds depicting the ritual, divinitory, historical, and genealogical traditions of different cities; post-Conquest codices sometimes accompanied by Spanish commentary; prose sources dependent on indigenous pictorial and oral traditions; histories written by descendants of Aztec royalty; Spanish eyewitness accounts; and large histories and ritual descriptions by Spanish priests such as Diego Durán, Toribio Motolinía, and Bernardino de Sahagún, who vigorously researched Aztec religion. It is only through a skillful combination of these sources that the complex character of Aztec religion can be discerned.

Cosmogony and Cosmology. The general attitude toward the Aztec position in the cosmos is made clear in a poetic fragment about the capital that states:

> Proud of Itself
> Is the city of México-Tenochtitlán
> Here no one fears to die in war
> This is our glory
> This is your Command
> Oh Giver of Life
> Have this in mind, oh princes
> Who would conquer Tenochtitlán?
> Who could shake the foundation of heaven?
> (Miguel León-Portilla, *Pre-Columbian Literatures of Mexico,* 1968, p. 87)

The image of the capital city as the foundation of heaven, which the Aztec conceived of as a vertical column of thirteen layers extending above the earth, points to the cosmological conviction underpinning Aztec religion that there existed a profound correspondence between the sacred forces in the universe and the social world of the Aztec empire. This correspondence between the cosmic structure and the political state was anchored in the capital of Tenochtitlán.

In his important summary of religion in pre-Hispanic central Mexico, H. B. Nicholson (1971) outlines the "basic cosmological sequential pattern" of the Aztec cosmogony found in the myths and historical accounts associated with the Méxica. A summary view reveals that Aztec life unfolded in a cosmic setting that was dynamic, unstable, and finally destructive. Even though the cosmic order fluctuated between periods of stability and periods of chaos, the emphasis in many myths and historical accounts is on the destructive forces which repeatedly overcame the ages of the universe, divine society, and the cities of the past.

This dynamic universe appears in the sixteenth-century prose accounts *Historia de los Mexicanos por sus pinturas* and the *Leyenda de los soles*. In the former, the universe is arranged in a rapid, orderly fashion after the dual creative divinity, Ometeotl, dwelling in Omeyocan ("place of duality") at the thirteenth level of heaven, generates four children, the Red Tezcatlipoca ("smoking mirror"), the Black Tezcatlipoca, Quetzalcoatl ("plumed serpent"), and Huitzilopochtli ("hummingbird on the left"). They all exist without movement for six hundred years, whereupon the four children assemble "to arrange what was to be done and to establish the law to be followed." Quetzalcoatl and Huitzilopochtli arrange the universe and create fire, half of the sun ("not fully lighted but a little"), the human race, and the calendar. Then, the four brothers create water and its divine beings.

Following this rapid and full arrangement, the sources focus on a series of mythic events that constitute a sacred history. Throughout this sacred history, the dynamic instability of the Aztec universe is revealed. The universe passes through four eras, called "Suns." Each age was presided over by one of the great gods, and each was named for the day (day number and day name) within the calendrical cycle on which the age began (which is also the name of the force that destroys that Sun). The first four Suns were called, respectively, 4 Jaguar, 4 Wind, 4 Rain (or 4 Rain of Fire), and 4 Water. The name of the fifth (and last) cosmic age, 4 Movement, augured the earthquakes that would inevitably destroy the world.

The creation of this final age, the one in which the Aztec lived, took place around a divine fire in the darkness on the mythical plain of Teotihuacán (to be distinguished from the actual city of that same name). According to the version of this story reported in Fray Bernardino de Sahagún's *Historia general de las cosas de la Nueva España* (compiled 1569–1582; also known as the Florentine Codex), an assembly of gods chose two of their group, Nanahuatzin and Tecuciztecatl, to cast themselves into the fire in order to create the new cosmic age. Following their self-sacrifice, dawn appears in all directions, but the Sun does not rise above the horizon. In confusion, different deities face in various directions in expectation of the sunrise. Quetzalcoatl faces east and from there the Sun blazes forth but sways from side to side without climbing in the sky. In this cosmic crisis, it is decided that all the gods must die at the sacrificial hand of Ecatl, who dispatches them by cutting their throats. Even this massive sacrifice does not move the Sun until the wind god literally blows it into motion. These combined cosmogonic episodes demonstrate the fundamental Aztec conviction that the world is unstable and that it draws its energy from massive sacrifices by the gods. Large-scale sacrifice became a basic pattern in Aztec religion, a ritual means of imposing or maintaining social and cosmological order.

With the creation of the Fifth Sun, the focus of the sacred history shifts from heaven to earth, where agriculture is discovered and human sacrifice is established as the proper ritual response to the requirements of the gods. In one account, Quetzalcoatl, as a black ant, travels to Sustenance Mountain with a red ant where they acquire maize for human beings. Other accounts reveal the divine origins of cotton, sweet potatoes, different types of corn, and the intoxicating drink called pulque. In still others, we learn that warfare was established so that human beings could be captured and sacrificed to nourish the Sun on its heavenly and nocturnal journey. Typically, a god like Mixcoatl creates four hundred human beings to fight among themselves in order for captives to be sacrificed in ceremonial centers to provide the divine food, blood, for the gods who ensure cosmic life.

Finally, a number of accounts of the cosmic history culminate with the establishment of the magnificent kingdom of Tollan where Quetzalcoatl the god and Topiltzin Quetzalcoatl the priest-king organize a ceremonial capital divided into five parts with four pyramids and four sacred mountains surrounding the central temple. This city, Tollan, serves as the heart of an empire. Aztec tradition states that "from Quetzalcoatl flowed all art and knowledge," representing the paradigmatic importance of the Toltec kingdom and its religious founder.

The spatial paradigm of the Aztec cosmos was embodied in the term *cemanahuac*, meaning the "land surrounded by water." At the center of this terrestrial space, called *tlalxico* ("navel of the earth"), stood Tenochtitlán, from which extended the four quadrants called *nauchampa*, meaning "the four directions of the wind." The waters surrounding the inhabited land were called *ilhuicatl*, the celestial water that extended upward to merge with the lowest levels of the thirteen heavens. Below the earth were nine levels of the underworld, conceived of as "hazard stations" for the souls of the dead, who, aided by magical charms buried with the bodies, were assisted in their quests for eternal peace at the lowest level, called Mictlan, the land of the dead.

The Mesoamerican pattern of quadrapartition around a center was a pervasive organizing principle of Aztec religion. It was used in the Aztec conceptions of temporal order as depicted in the famous Calendar Stone, where the four past ages of the universe are arranged in orderly fashion around the fifth or central age. Recent research has shown that this same spatial model was used to organize the celestial order of numerous deity clusters, the architectural design of palatial structures, the collection of economic tribute in the empire, and the ordering of major ceremonial precincts.

The Pantheon. One of the most striking characteristics of the surviving screenfolds, which present ritual and divinatory information, is the incredible array of deities who animated the ancient Mesoamerican world. Likewise, the remaining sculpture and the sixteenth-century prose accounts of Aztec Mexico present us with a pantheon so crowded that H. B. Nicholson's authoritative study of Aztec religion includes a list of more than sixty distinct and interrelated names. Scholarly analysis of these many deities suggests that virtually all aspects of existence were considered inherently sacred and that these deities were expressions of a numinous quality that permeated the "real" world. Aztec references to numinous forces, expressed in the Nahuatl word *teotl,* were always translated by the Spanish as "god," "saint," or "demon." But the Aztec *teotl* signified a sacred power manifested in natural forms (a rainstorm, a tree, a mountain), in persons of high distinction (a king, an ancestor, a warrior), or in mysterious and chaotic places. What the Spanish translated as "god" really referred to a broad spectrum of hierophanies that animated the world. While it does not appear that the Aztec pantheon or pattern of hierophanies was organized as a whole, it is possible to identify clusters of deities organized around the major cult themes of cosmogonic creativity, fertility and regeneration, and war and sacrificial nourishment of the Sun.

Aztec deities were represented pictorially as anthropomorphic beings. Even in cases where the deity took an animal form, as in the case of Xolotl, the divine dog, or the form of a ritual object, as in the case of Itztli, the knife god, he was disguised with human features like arms, torso, legs, face, and so on. Aztec deities dwelt in the different levels of the thirteen-layered celestial sphere or the nine-layered underworld. The general structuring principle for the pantheon, derived from the cosmic pattern of a center and four quarters, resulted in the quadruple or quintuple ordering of gods. For instance in the Codex Borgia's representation of the Tlaloques (rain gods), the rain god, Tlaloc, inhabits the central region of heaven while four other Tlaloques inhabit the four regions of the sky, each dispensing a different kind of rain. While deities were invisible to the human eye, the Aztec saw them in dreams, visions, and in the "deity impersonators" *(teixiptla)* who appeared at the major ceremonies. These costumed impersonators, sometimes human, sometimes effigies of stone, wood, or dough, were elaborately decorated with identifying insignia such as conch shells, masks, weapons, jewelry, mantas, feathers, and a myriad of other items.

As we have seen, Aztec religion was formed by migrating Chichimec who entered the Valley of Mexico and established important political and cultural centers there. This process of migration and urbanization informed and was informed by their concept of deity. An outstanding feature of Aztec religion was the tutelary-patron relations that specific deities had with the particular social groups whom they guided during their peregrinations. These patron deities (or *abogados,* as the Spanish chroniclers called them) were represented in the *tlaquimilolli,* or sacred bundles, that the *teomamas* ("godbearers," or shaman-priests) carried on their backs during the long journeys. The *teomama* passed on to the community the divine commandments communicated to him in visions and dreams. These sacred specialists were considered *hombre-dioses* (Span., "mangods"), whose extraordinary powers of spiritual transformation, derived from their closeness with these numinous forces, enabled them to guide, govern, and organize the tribe during migrations and the settlement of new communities. A familiar pattern in the sacred histories of Mesoamerican tribal groups is the erection of a shrine to the patron deity as the first act of settlement in a new region. This act of founding a settlement around the tribal shrine represented the intimate tie between the deity, the *hombre-dios,* and the integrity of the people. In reverse fashion, conquest of a community was achieved when the patron deity's shrine was burned and the *tlaquimilolli* was carried off as a captive.

This pattern of migration, foundation, and conquest associated with the power of a patron diety is clearly exemplified by the case of Huitzilopochtli, patron of the wandering Méxica. According to Aztec tradition, Huitzilopochtli inspired the Méxica *teomama* to guide the tribe into the Valley of Mexico, where he appeared to them as an eagle on a cactus in the lake. There they constructed a shrine to Huitzilopochtli and built their city around the shrine. This shrine became the Aztec Great Temple, the supreme political and symbolic center of the Aztec empire. It was destroyed in 1521 by the

Spanish, who blew up the temple with cannons and carried the great image of Huitzilopochtli away. This colossal image of the Aztec god has never been found.

Creator Gods. The Aztec high god, Ometeotl ("lord of duality") was the celestial, androgynous, primordial creator of the universe, the omnipotent, omniscient, omnipresent foundation of all things. In some sources he/she appears to merge with a number of his/her offspring, a sign of his/her pervasive power. Ometeotl's male aspects (Ometecuhtli and Tonacatecuhtli) and female aspects (Omecihuatl and Tonacacihuatl) in turn merged with a series of lesser deities associated with generative and destructive male and female qualities. The male aspect was associated with fire and the solar and maize gods. The female aspect merged with earth fertility goddesses and especially corn goddesses. Ometeotl inhabited the thirteenth and highest heaven in the cosmos, which was the place from which the souls of infants descended to be born on earth. Ometeotl was more "being" than "action." Most of the creative effort to organize the universe was acomplished by the divine couple's four offspring: Tezcatlipoca, Quetzalcoatl, Xiuhtecuhtli, and Tlaloc.

Tezcatlipoca ("smoking mirror") was the supreme active creative force of the pantheon. This powerful, virile numen had many appellations and was partially identified with the supreme numinosity of Ometeotl. Tezcatlipoca was also identified with Itztli, the knife and calendar god, and with Tepeyolotl, the jaguar-earth god known as the Heart of the Hill, and he was often pictured as the divine antagonist of Quetzalcoatl. On the social level, Tezcatlipoca was the arch-sorcerer whose smoking obsidian mirror revealed the powers of ultimate transformation associated with darkness, night, jaguars, and shamanic magic.

Another tremendous creative power was Xiuhtecuhtli, the ancient fire god, who influenced every level of society and cosmology. Xiuhtecuhtli was represented by the perpetual "fires of existence" that were kept lighted at certain temples in the ceremonial center at all times. He was manifested in the drilling of new fires that dedicated new ceremonial buildings and ritual stones. Most importantly, Xiuhtecuhtli was the generative force at the New Fire ceremony, also called the Binding of the Years, held every fifty-two years on the Hill of the Star outside of Tenochtitlán. At midnight on the day that a fifty-two-year calendar cycle was exhausted, at the moment when the star cluster we call the Pleiades passed through the zenith, a heart sacrifice of a war captive took place. A new fire was started in the cavity of the victim's chest, symbolizing the rebirth of Xiuhtecuhtli. The new fire was carried to every city, town, and home in the empire, signalling the regeneration of the universe. On the domestic level, Xiuhtecuhtli inhabited the hearth, structuring the daily rituals associated with food, nurturance, and thanksgiving.

Fertility and Regeneration. A pervasive theme in Aztec religion was fertility and the regeneration of agriculture. Aztec society depended on a massive agricultural system of *chinampas* ("floating gardens") that constituted large sections of the city's geographical space. Also, surrounding city-states were required to pay sizable amounts of agricultural goods in tribute to the capital. While many female deities inspired the ritual regeneration of agriculture, the most ancient and widespread fertility-rain god was Tlaloc, who dwelt on the prominent mountain peaks, where rain clouds were thought to emerge from caves to fertilize the land through rain, rivers, pools, and storms. The Aztec held Mount Tlaloc to be the original source of the waters and of vegetation. Tlaloc's supreme importance is reflected in the location of his shrine alongside that of Huitzilopochtli in the Templo Mayor. Surprisingly, the great majority of buried offerings excavated at the temple were dedicated to Tlaloc rather than Huitzilopochtli.

Two other major gods intimately associated with Tlaloc were Chalchihuitlicue, the goddess of water, and Ehécatl, the wind god, an aspect of Quetzalcoatl. Ehécatl was known as *in tlachpancauh in tlaloques* ("road sweeper of the rain gods"), meaning that Ehécatl's forceful presence announced the coming of the fertilizing rains. Other prominent fertility deities included Centeotl, goddess of maize; Xilonen, goddess of the young maize; Ometochtli, goddess of maguay; and Mayahueal, whose four hundred breasts insured an abundant supply of pulque for ritual drinking.

The most powerful group of female fertility deities were the *teteoinnan,* a rich array of earth-mother goddesses, who were representatives of the usually distinct but sometimes combined qualities of terror and beauty, regeneration and destruction. These deities were worshiped in cults concerned with the abundant powers of the earth, women, and fertility. Among the most prominent were Tlazolteotl, Xochiquetzal, and Coatlicue. Tlazolteotl was concerned with sexual powers and passions and the pardoning of sexual transgressions. Xochiquetzal was the goddess of love and sexual desire and was pictured as a nubile maiden associated with flowers, feasting, and pleasure. A ferocious goddess, Coatlicue ("serpent skirt") represented the cosmic mountain that conceived all stellar beings and devoured all beings into her repulsive, lethal, and fascinating form. Her statue is studded with sacrificed hearts, skulls, hands, ferocious claws, and giant snake heads.

A prominent deity who linked agricultural renewal with warfare was Xipe Totec, whose gladiatorial sacrifice renewed vegetation in the spring and celebrated success on the battlefield. Part of his ceremony, called the Feast of the Flaying of Men, included the flaying of the sacrificial victim and the ceremonial wearing of the skin by the sacred specialist. Xipe Totec's insignia, including the pointed cap and rattle staff, was the war costume of the Méxica emperor.

Ceremony and Sacrifice. Another important facet of Aztec religious practice was human sacrifice, usually carried out for the purpose of nourishing or renewing the Sun or other deity (or to otherwise appease it), thus ensuring the stability of the universe. The mythic model for mass human sacrifice was the story of the creation of the fifth age, in which the gods themselves were sacrificed in order to empower the Sun. Tonatiuh, the personification of that Sun (whose visage appears in the center of the Calendar Stone), depended on continued nourishment from human hearts.

Some of the large-scale sacrificial ceremonies re-created other sacred stories. For example, women and masses of captive warriors were sacrificed in front of the shrine of Huitzilopochtli atop the Templo Mayor. Their bodies tumbled down the steps to rest at the bottom with the colossal stone figure of Coyolxauhqui, Huitzilopochtli's dismembered sister, symbolically reenacting the legendary slaughter of the four hundred siblings at Huitzilopochtli's birth. [*See* Huitzilopochtli.]

Cosmology, pantheon, and ritual sacrifice were united and came alive in the exuberant and well-ordered ceremonies carried out in the more than eighty buildings situated in the sacred precinct of the capital and in the hundreds of ceremonial centers throughout the Aztec world. Guided by detailed ritual calendars, Aztec ceremonies varied from town to town but typically involved three stages: days of ritual preparation, death sacrifice, and nourishing the gods. The days of ritual preparation included fasting; offerings of food, flowers, and paper; use of incense and purification techniques; embowering; songs; and processions of deity-impersonators to various temples in ceremonial precincts.

Following these elaborate preparations, blood sacrifices were carried out by priestly orders specially trained to dispatch the victims swiftly. The victims were usually captive warriors or purchased slaves. Though a variety of methods of ritual killing were used, including decapitation, burning, hurling from great heights, strangulation, and arrow sacrifice, the typical ritual involved the dramatic heart sacrifice and the placing of the heart in a ceremonial vessel *(cuauhxicalli)* in order to nourish the gods. Amid the music of drums, conch shell trumpets, rattles, and other musical instruments, which created an atmosphere of dramatic intensity, blood was smeared on the face of the deity's image and the head of the victim was placed on the giant skull rack *(tzompantli)* that held thousands of such trophies.

All of these ceremonies were carried out in relation to two ritual calendars, the 365-day calendar or *tonalpohualli* ("count of day") consisting of eighteen twenty-day months plus a five-day intercalary period and the 260-day calendar consisting of thirteen twenty-day months. More than one-third of these ceremonies were dedicated to Tlaloc and earth fertility goddesses. Beside ceremonies relating to the two calendars, a third type of ceremony related to the many life cycle stages of the individual. In some cases, the entire community was involved in bloodletting.

Aztec religion, as we have seen, was formed during the rise to empire of a minority population who inherited urban traditions and sociopolitical conflicts of great prestige and intensity. This remarkable tradition came to an abrupt end during the military conquest of Tenochtitlán by the Spanish and the subsequent destruction of ceremonial life. But it is important to note that one of the last images we have of the Templo Mayor of Tenochtitlán before it was blown apart by Spanish cannon is the image of Aztec warriors sacrificing captive Spanish soldiers in front of the shrine to Huitzilopochtli.

[*See also* Human Sacrifice; Coatlicue; Quetzalcoatl; Tezcatlipoca; *and* Tlaloc.]

BIBLIOGRAPHY

Broda, Johanna. "El tributo en trajes guerreros y la estructura del sistema tributario Mexica." In *Economia, política e ideología en el México prehispanico.* Edited by Pedro Carrasco and Johanna Broda. Mexico City, 1978. A valuable study of the pattern and structure of tributary payments to Tenochtitlán during the height of its dominance.

Brundage, Burr C. *The Fifth Sun: Aztec Gods, Aztec World.* Austin, 1979. The best English-language monograph introduction to Aztec religion which provides an insightful understanding of the Aztec pantheon and human sacrifice.

Carrasco, Davíd. *Quetzalcoatl and the Irony of Empire: Myths and Prophecies in Aztec Tradition.* Chicago, 1982. Utilizing the history of religions approach, the author focuses on the Quetzalcoatl paradigm to study the history of Mesoamerican religions.

López Austin, Alfredo. *Hombre-Dios: Religión y política en el mundo Nahuatl.* Mexico City, 1973. The best Spanish-language account of the interweaving of myth, history, politics, and religious authority in Mesoamerican history.

Matos Moctezuma, Eduardo. *Una visita al Templo Mayor de Tenochtitlán.* Mexico City, 1981. The chief excavator of the

Aztec Great Temple describes the fascinating treasures found at the heart of the Aztec empire.

Nicholson, H. B. "Religion in Pre-Hispanic Central Mexico." In *Handbook of Middle American Indians*, edited by Robert Wauchope, vol 10. Austin, 1971. The classic description of Mesoamerican religion in the central plateau of Mexico during the decades prior to the Conquest.

Pasztory, Esther. *Aztec Art*. New York, 1983. The finest single-volume description and interpretation of Aztec art and its religious significance. Excellent prose accompanied by magnificent photographs.

Townsend, Richard. *State and Cosmos in the Art of Tenochtitlán*. Washington, D.C., 1979. A concise, brilliant interpretation of the monumental art of the Aztec capital of Tenochtitlán in the light of a good understanding of religious realities.

DAVÍD CARRASCO

B

BAAL, or, more fully, Baal Hadad, was a Canaanite weather and fertility god whose cult was extremely widespread throughout the entire Levant. By itself, *baal* means "lord," and the term can refer to other gods, but when used without qualification it almost invariably refers to Hadad. The name *Hadad* possibly means "the thundering one."

Baal's home was said to be Mount Tsefon, south of Antioch. His sister and consort was the goddess Anat. There seem to be two traditions concerning his lineage: he is alternately the son of El and the son of Dagan. To assume that Baal, Yamm, and Mot were the three vying sons of El seems to fit better the context of the Baal myths. The cult of Baal took particular forms in different locales, and thus there were geographically specialized manifestations of Baal: Baal-Sidon, Baal-Peor, Baal-Gebal, and others. The common Old Testament expression "the baals" meant Baal in the totality of these manifestations.

Baal has long been known from the Old Testament. In *Numbers* 25 the Israelites apostatize to Baal-Peor. *Judges* 6 is the story of Gideon and the altar of Baal. In *1 Kings* 18, Elijah mocks the prophets of Baal (could this particular *baal* be Melqart?) because they can get no response from him: "Perhaps he is musing, or on a journey, or asleep and must be wakened." *Hosea* 2 gives an elaborate description of Baal worship.

The excavation of Canaanite cuneiform tablets from 1929 onward at Ugarit in Syria has provided scholars with a wealth of cultic and mythological material in which Baal is very prominent. In this literature the most common epithets for Baal are "strong one," "rider on the clouds" (a title also given to Yahveh in *Psalms* 68:5; see also the description of Yahveh as a Baal-like weather god in Psalm 18), and "Baal Prince [of the earth]." This last epithet, *ba'al zebul* [*artsi*] in the original, is the source of the Beelzebul of *Matthew* 10:25, 12:24, and parallels; the Beelzebub, "lord of the flies," in *2 Kings* 1 is a contemptuous wordplay. Similarly, in some Old Testament names the element *ba'al* is changed to *boshet* ("shame"); for example, Ishbaal ("man of Baal") becomes Ishbosheth ("man of shame").

Although there is some disagreement among scholars as to how to sequence the relevant texts, the overriding theme of the Ugaritic poems that fit into the so-called Baal cycle is Baal's quest for, and ultimate attainment of, kingship over the gods, especially over his rivals Yamm and Mot. His first encounter is with Yamm ("sea"), a symbol of primeval chaos, whom he conquers. (This motif, reminiscent of the Babylonian god Marduk's triumph over Tiamat, is also applicable to Yahveh in the Old Testament, in *Job* 26:12–13.) In the battle with Yamm and his forces, Baal is aided by Anat, whose fighting is described in characteristically bloody terms.

Achieving victory over chaos, Baal is free to exercise his control over the weather and, therefore, agriculture without challenge. In his new position of ascendancy he demands that he have his own house (or temple) as any king should (cf. *2 Sm.* 7:5–7). At first El, the head of the pantheon, is averse to the idea, but Anat threatens him, and he submits, sending the vulcan god Kothar-wa-Hasis ("crafty and clever") to oversee the construction.

Unfortunately, Baal decides after some hesitation to have a window installed in his house. This allows Mot ("death"), a god whom Baal in his arrogance as victor over Yamm has slighted, to enter his house (cf. *Jer.* 9:21). Baal and his entourage descend into the gullet of Mot, into the belly of the underworld, and the earth is now threatened with sterility because Baal can no longer bring the rains. In a rage, Anat attacks Mot, cuts him up, winnows him, and sows him in the fields. The death of Mot allows Baal to revive and bring back fertility. This encounter between Baal and Mot recurs periodically, thereby mythologically accounting for the agricultural cycles of fertility and sterility.

There are extant numerous iconographic representations of Baal, most notably a stela from Ugarit on which Baal strides to the right with a club over his head in his right hand and a lightning bolt in his left. Small bronze statuettes exhibiting a similar pose have been uncovered throughout the Mediterranean area, and these undoubtedly are images of Baal. Typically, he wears a conical crown with two horns projecting from the front.

[*See also* Dying and Rising Gods.]

BIBLIOGRAPHY

A very readable translation of the Baal texts with a concise commentary can be found in *Stories from Ancient Canaan*, edited and translated by Michael D. Coogan (Philadelphia, 1978). Theodor H. Gaster's *Thespis: Ritual, Myth, and Drama in the Ancient Near East*, rev. ed. (New York, 1961), relates the Baal material to parallel ancient literature and provides a lengthy, provocative interpretation of the themes.

WILLIAM J. FULCO, S.J.

BAʿAL SHEM ṬOV. *See* Besht.

BABA YAGA, known in Russian folklore as a witch and an ogress, is the ancient goddess of death and regeneration of Slavic mythology, with roots in the pre-Indo-European matrilinear pantheon. In Slavic folk tales (mainly Russian), Baba Yaga lives in nocturnal darkness, deep in the woods, far from the world of men. She is variously depicted as an evil old hag who eats humans, especially children, and as a wise, prophetic old woman. In appearance, she is tall, bony-legged, and pestle-headed, with a long nose and disheveled hair. At times she appears as a young woman, at other times as two sisters, one young and one old. Her primary theriomorphic image is that of a bird or a snake, but she can turn instantly into a frog, a toad, a turtle, a mouse, a crab, a vixen, a bee, a mare, a goat, or an inanimate object.

Baba Yaga never walks; she either flies in a fiery mortar or lies in her hut on top of the oven, on a bench, on the floor, or stretched from one end of the hut to the other. The fence around her hut is made of human bones and is topped with human skulls, with eyes intact. The gate is fastened with human legs and arms instead of bolts, and a mouth with sharp teeth serves as a lock. The hut, which is supported on bird's legs and which can turn around on its axis like a spindle, is, in fact, Baba Yaga herself.

Linguistic analysis of Baba Yaga's compound name reveals prehistoric characteristics. *Yaga*, from Proto-Slavic **(y)ęga*, means "disease," "fright," and "wrath" in Old Russian, Serbo-Croatian, and Slovene, respectively, and is related to the Lithuanian verb *engti* ("strangle, press, torture"). The early form may be related to Proto-Samoyed **nga*, meaning "god," or "god or goddess of death." The Slavic etymon *baba* means "grandmother," "woman," "cloud woman" (a mythic being who produces rain), and "pelican." The last points to Baba Yaga's avian nature, comparable to that of the archetypal vulture and owl goddess of European prehistory, who represents death and regeneration. In Russian tales, Baba Yaga eats humans by pecking like a bird.

In East Slavic areas, Baba Yaga has a male counterpart, Koshchei Bessmertnyi, "Koshchei the Immortal." His name, from *kost'* ("bone"), bears the notion of a dying and rising god, that is, a deity who cyclically dies and is reborn. In tales in which Koshchei appears, Baba Yaga is either his mother or his aunt. Another male equivalent of Baba Yaga is Morozko ("frost"). Baba Yaga is also the "mother of winds," analogous to the German Frau Holle. Other relatives in current folklore are the Lithuanian goddess Ragana and the Basque vulture goddess, the "Lady of Amboto."

BIBLIOGRAPHY

Shapiro, Michael. "Baba-Jaga: A Search for Mythopoeic Origins and Affinities." *International Journal of Slavic Linguistics and Poetics* 27 (1983).

Toporov, V. N. "Khettskaia ^{SAL}ŠU: GI i slavianskaia Baba-Iaga." *Kratkie soobshcheniia Instituta slavianovedeniia* (Moscow) 38 (1963) : 28–37.

MARIJA GIMBUTAS

BĀBĪS are the followers of Sayyid ʿAlī Muḥammad, known as the Bāb ("gate"). The idea of a *bāb* or gateway between the living but hidden imam and the believers is very old in Shīʿī Islam. When the last imam went into hiding in Samarra in the tenth century CE, he appointed a man charged with conveying his orders to the distressed Shīʿī community. This man was called the Bāb.

After a succession of four such Bābs, the gateway to the imam was definitively closed, and the so-called greater occultation began.

The Emergence of the Bābīs. In the first half of the nineteenth century, a young merchant of Shiraz declared himself to be the Bāb and began to preach theories that, if enforced, would have ended the power of the numerous mullahs and ayatollahs who were dominant in Iran. Sayyid ʿAlī Muḥammad was born in Shiraz in October 1819; he came from a merchant family of sayyids (supposed descendants of the prophet Muḥammad) who enjoyed special privileges in Iran. Orphaned as a child, he was entrusted to the care of a maternal uncle, Sayyid ʿAlī, and was trained in the same business his father had pursued. Both Bābī and Muslim sources affirm that from a very young age he was extremely pious. During a pilgrimage to Karbala, he became acquainted with Sayyid Kāẓim Rashtī, the leader of the Shaykhī movement.

His subsequent relations with the Shaykhīyah are not clear. In Muslim eyes he became a Shaykhī, that is, a follower of Sayyid Kāẓim Rashtī, while the Bābīs hold that Sayyid ʿAlī Muḥammad enjoyed a special rank in the Shaykhī school. In any event, he accepted many of the theories of the school, which held, among other things, that hints concerning eschatology contained in the Qur'ān and Islamic tradition were to be interpreted symbolically rather than literally. Sayyid Kāẓim Rashtī died in December 1843, but before his death he sent his disciples to all parts of Persia in search of the expected Mahdi, the Ṣāḥib al-Zamān ("master of the age") who, he predicted, would soon manifest himself.

One of these disciples, Mullah Husayn of Bushrūyah, was fascinated by the young Sayyid ʿAlī Muḥammad and became the first to think of him as the "gate" leading to the truth and also as the initiator of a new prophetic cycle. This recognition came on 23 May 1844, when the Bāb satisfactorily answered a number of questions that Mullah Ḥusayn put to him. On this occasion also the Bāb began composing the *Qayyūm al-asmā'*, a long commentary on the surah of Yūsuf (Joseph) in the Qur'ān, which Bābīs and Bahā'īs consider to be his first revealed work. From that year he drew an increasing number of disciples, eighteen of whom he designated as Ḥurūf al-Ḥayy ("letters of the living"). Bābī and Muslim authors alike expressed admiration for the speed with which he wrote and the indescribable charm of his voice. Among his followers, overcome by his charisma although she had never seen him, was the young poet Qurrat al-ʿAyn, who may be considered one of the forerunners of the modern feminist movement.

The Bāb set out on a pilgrimage to Mecca but had a rather bad impression of the journey, which reflects itself in various passages of the *Bayān* (Declaration), the holy book of the Bābīs. In Mecca, according to Bābī tradition, the Bāb publicly declared his mission as Mahdi but with disappointing results. Soon afterward, the disciples of the Bāb began to revolt, and many were arrested. Upon his return from Mecca in the spring of 1845, the Bāb himself was arrested; after short stays in Shiraz and Isfahan, he was imprisoned in the mountain fortress of Māhkū in Azerbaijan. When he managed to convert even the governor of the fortress, ʿAlī Khān, the Bāb was transferred to the inaccessible castle of Chirīq. Following the convention of Badasht in 1848, when the Bābīs publicly withdrew from Islam and the jurisdiction of *sharīʿah* law, a chain of Bābī insurrections broke out and met with violent repression. In July 1850 the Bāb was transported to Tabriz and executed before a firing squad together with one of his followers.

Subsequent Developments. The history of the Bābīs is one of persecution. It falls into two periods, separated by the repression of 1852–1853, which followed an attempt on the life of Nāṣir al-Dīn Shāh and virtually broke the back of the new movement. The Bābīs of the first period were not averse to violence and were responsible for several revolts against the government that were poorly resisted by the Persian troops of the shāh. They displayed great heroism and were so successful that some Orientalists actually predicted that Iran would soon become Bābī.

The activities of the second period may be considered pacifist, although many Bābīs were also killed during that time. One of the victims of the persecutions of 1853 was the poet Qurrat al-ʿAyn. The principal Bābīs, among them Bahā' Allāh (Mīrzā Ḥusayn ʿAlī Nūrī) and his stepbrother Ṣubḥ-i Azal (Mīrzā Yaḥyā Nūrī), were exiled to Iraq. After Bahā' Allāh proclaimed his own prophetic mission in 1864, the movement split into two unequal branches, the Bahā'īs, who followed him, and the Azalīs, who followed Ṣubḥ-i Azal. The Azalīs remained always a minority; even the membership of fifty thousand attributed to them by certain authors seems exaggerated.

The Bāb wrote many works, all of which are considered sacred by his followers; the Arabic and Persian *Bayān*s, containing various laws, are holy books to them, although many are inclined to think that all of the Bāb's writings can be included in the *Bayān*. Their teachings consist principally of a spiritualization of the eschatological doctrines of Islam and expressions of waiting for *man yuẓhiruhu Allāh* ("he whom God shall manifest")—according to the Bahā'īs, none other than Bahā' Allāh, and according to the Azalīs, one who is yet to come.

[*See also* Bahā'īs *and the biography of* Qurrat al-ʿAyn.]

BIBLIOGRAPHY

A rich collection of source material on the Bābīs is available in European languages, including two near-contemporary accounts translated from Persian: Nabīl Zarandī's *Ta'rīkh-i Nabīl,* written in 1887/8 and translated by Shoghi Effendi as *The Dawn-Breakers* (1932; reprint, Wilmette, Ill., 1970), and 'Abbās Effendi's *Maqālah-i shakhṣī sayyāḥ,* translated by E. G. Browne as *A Traveller's Narrative Written to Illustrate the Episode of the Bāb* (1891; reprint, Amsterdam, 1975). Zarandī's editions of the *Bayān* have been translated by A. L. M. Nicolas as *Le Béyan arabe, le livre sacre du Babysme* (Paris, 1905), and *Le Béyan persan,* 4 vols. (Paris, 1911–1914).

Persian, Arabic, and English documents are collected in E. G. Browne's *Materials for the Study of the Bābī Religion* (1918; reprint, Cambridge, 1961). Joseph Arthur (Comte de) Gobineau's *Les religions et les philosophies dans l'Asie Centrale,* 2d ed. (1863; reprint, Paris, 1957), includes a large section on the Bābīs; it was this report that inspired Browne to seek them out in Iran in 1887. Additional Western sources are compiled in *The Bābi and Bahá'í Religions, 1844–1944,* edited by Moojan Momen (Oxford, 1981).

For modern views, see my articles on "Bāb" and "Bābīs" in *The Encyclopaedia of Islam,* new ed. (Leiden, 1960–), which provide extensive bibliography. See also H. M. Balyuzi's biography, *The Bāb* (Oxford, 1973).

ALESSANDRO BAUSANI

BABYLONIAN RELIGION. *See* Mesopotamian Religions.

BACHOFEN, J. J. (1815–1887), Swiss comparative legal historian and mythologist. Johann Jakob Bachofen was born to a prominent Basel family. At the University of Basel in 1833 and at the University of Berlin the next year his interests shifted from philology to law and legal history. His teacher and influence at Berlin was the great German historian of law Friedrich Karl von Savigny, with whom he studied from 1835 to 1837; in 1839 Bachofen took his doctorate of law. In 1841 he was appointed professor of Roman law at Basel; he became a judge in 1842 and a city councillor in 1844. Later that year he resigned as professor and councillor in order to do research. His early publications, from 1840, are devoted to aspects of ancient Roman law and property. From 1859 to 1870 his chief works appeared: *Versuch über die Gräbersymbolik der Alten* (1859); *Das Mutterrecht: Eine Untersuchung über die Gynaikokratie der alten Welt nach ihrer religiösen und rechtlichen Natur* (1860; reprint, Basel, 1948); *Das lykische Volk und seine Bedeutung für die Entwicklung des Altertums* (1862); *Die Sage von Tanaquil: Eine Untersuchung über den Orientalismus in Rom und Italien* (1870). After attracting attention in his later lifetime, his work was neglected. But from 1925, particularly in Germany, interest revived, and new editions and selections appeared. Until then, Bachofen was best known for his work in legal and social history and its implications for religious history. The revival of interest in Bachofen has stressed his somewhat romantic view of symbol and myth.

The whole of Bachofen's work stands in deliberate opposition, on one side, to the philological, nonhistorical approach to religion and myth of such mid-nineteenth-century nature mythologists as F. Max Müller and, on another side, to the "rationalistic" approach of the eminent classical historians Theodor Mommsen and Barthold Niebuhr. Bachofen instead sought a return to institutional history and a romantic access to the depths of ancient meaning. On either side, he attempted to move beyond secondary or derivative phenomena to an underlying or original historical stratum. As he turned from philology to ancient law, so he turned from what myth narrates to its antecedent in the concentering symbol.

Along with his contemporaries Henry Maine and Lewis H. Morgan, Bachofen pioneered use of the massive amount of new data coming from comparative ethnology and kinship studies. Morgan in America examined the kinship relations of living Indian tribes; Bachofen, like the Englishman Maine, focused on ancient custom and law. Far more than these others, however, Bachofen explicitly related the new evidence to religious history, cult, artifact, and myth. In terms of this evidence, he developed the theory for which he is still most widely known. In his *Das Mutterrecht* he presented a new morphology of the earliest social and religious phases. According to this scheme, before the patriarchal societies and pantheons familiar since Homeric antiquity there were two earlier and universal stages. The first was a stage of sexual promiscuity and social anarchy. Here, descent could be reckoned only through the mother. In time, women rebelled against this disorderly life and instituted "mother-right," at once a juridical system, a principle of ideal social order, and a religious view. Now the materfamilias governed human society, the moon and night rather than the sun were worshiped, the chthonic was favored over the heavenly. This gynecocracy was finally overthrown by the patriarchal phase: the Apollonian principle replaces the Dionysian; the ouranic, celestial male gods like Zeus are dominant; and the father and king holds sway in human affairs. Mother-right, before it corrupted into ferocious Amazonism, endorsed piety, communal peacefulness, and the survival of the people and life; the male principal and patriarchate, in contrast, endorsed a much higher spirituality but also outward violence and inward divisiveness.

Bachofen viewed myth as "the exegesis of the symbol." Myth narrates through a series of connected actions what the symbol unifyingly embodies, profoundly although mysteriously: "The symbol awakens intimations; speech can only explain." Using myth as a guide, Bachofen, in his *Gräbersymbolik*, distinguished between *sanctum* (the untouchable, the chthonic powers) and *sacrum* (the consecrated, the heavenly gods) and elaborated these to suggest a symbolic phenomenology that treats the relation between egg and serpent symbolism, man and woman, energy and passivity, and, among other matters, the duality of Roman power as in Romulus and Remus, consul and magistrate. Bachofen also stressed myth as an incomparable expression of the inner life of the nation in light of its religious experience. He explained the similarity between myths in widely separated regions by way of migration or relocation, which can also involve the transformation of religious myth into historical myth. *Die Sage von Tanaquil* explores the instance of the "Asiatic" myth of the feminine origin of supreme power, which was set forth as part of Roman history.

To the turn of the century, there was much interest in a matriarchal phase. Lewis H. Morgan, in his *Ancient Society* (1877), closely adapted Bachofen's views. Friedrich Engels, in turn, adapted Morgan's use of Bachofen to Marxist history of earliest society in his *Origin of the Family, Private Property, and the State* (1884). In another way, Bachofen influenced the portrayal of the primal sexual scene in Sigmund Freud's *Totem and Taboo* (1913). More recent interest in the origin and meaning of Great Goddess or Great Mother cults may be seen as prolonging some of Bachofen's emphases. Bachofen's view of the deep spirituality of symbol and myth has had influence on such students of religion as C. G. Jung, Károly Kerényi, Walter F. Otto, and Leo Frobenius as well as on nationalistic uses of myth.

BIBLIOGRAPHY

Bachofen's work is collected in his *Gesammelte Werke,* 10 vols., edited by Karl Meuli (Basel, 1943–1967). A generous selection of Bachofen's major work in English translation, with helpful notes, glossary, and bibliography, is *Myth, Religion, and Mother Right: Selected Writings of J. J. Bachofen,* translated by Ralph Manheim, with preface by George Boas and introduction by Joseph Campbell (Princeton, 1967). Bachofen's affinities with and influence on other thinkers is examined in Károly Kerényi's *Bachofen und die Zukunft des Humanismus: Mit einem Intermezzo über Nietzsche und Ariadne* (Zurich, 1945) and in Adrien Turel's *Bachofen-Freud: Zur Emanzipation des Mannes vom Reich der Mütter* (Bern, 1939). An assessment of Bachofen as historian of religions is Carl Albrecht Bernoulli's *Johann Jakob Bachofen als Religionsforscher* (Leipzig, 1924).

BURTON FELDMAN

BACON, FRANCIS (1561–1626), Lord Verulam, Viscount St. Albans; English statesman, essayist, and philosopher of science. A major political figure in early Stuart England, Bacon drew a visionary picture of the role and practices of the science of the future. This science was to be experimental, and Bacon advocated setting up public institutions for its pursuit. Written in the conviction that science, properly conducted, would lead to the improvement of the material conditions of life, his major works are at the same time philosophical discourses and recommendations for public policy.

Bacon was born of distinguished parents. His father was lord keeper of the great seal to Elizabeth I, and his mother was the niece of Lord Burghley, Elizabeth's lord treasurer. In 1573 he entered Trinity College, Cambridge, and two years later was enrolled briefly as a law student at Gray's Inn. His father's death in 1579 left Francis, the youngest son, comparatively poor, and he embarked on a career in law and politics. In 1584 he became a member of the House of Commons, where he sat until his elevation to the House of Lords in 1618. Despite wide knowledge, great ability, and influential friends, Bacon never achieved high office under Elizabeth, but after the accession of James I in 1603 he became successively king's counsel, solicitor general, attorney general, lord keeper, and lord chancellor. Then, in 1620, he was found guilty of taking a bribe and was removed from public office. He spent the remainder of his life working on a vast project: to provide both a new foundation for knowledge and a program for its acquisition.

This project had occupied him since he first entered Parliament. An essay written in 1584 has not survived, but from 1594 we have *Discourse in Praise of Knowledge,* a contribution to an entertainment devised for Elizabeth. Its themes, the sterility of traditional Aristotelian philosophy on the one hand and the lack of progress in empirical endeavors like alchemy on the other, reappeared in *The Advancement of Learning* (1605); book 1 of this work contains a defense of learning, and book 2 a catalog of the branches of knowledge, with a commentary showing where each is deficient. An expanded version, in Latin, was published in 1623 as *De augmentis scientarum.* Bacon thought of this version as the first section of his "great instauration" of the sciences, of which the second part, *Novum organum* (The New Organon), had already appeared (1620). Posthumously published, though written in 1610, was *New Atlantis;* here, in the guise of a traveler's tale, Bacon depicts his ideal scientific community. The science he proposed was to be both experimental and systematic: "The men of experiment are like the ant, they only collect and use; the reasoners resemble spiders, who make cobwebs out of their own substance. But the bee takes a middle course: it gathers its material from the flowers of the garden and of the field, but transforms and digests it by a power of its own" (*Novum organum* 95). Similarly, adherence to proper principles of induction would yield scientific knowledge from experimental findings.

Bacon's methodology of science has been criticized for its rejection of those speculative hypotheses that contribute essentially to progress; he is also faulted for his dismissal of the use of mathematics in science. But these criticisms are made with hindsight: when, in 1662, the Royal Society was founded along Baconian lines, its early members, including speculative natural philosophers like Robert Boyle, were lavish in their praise of him.

In his lifetime, however, the works most widely read were *De sapientia veterum* (Of the Wisdom of the Ancients, 1610), which puts forward rational reinterpretations of classical fables and mythology, and his *Essays.* The essays, appearing in several editions between 1597 and 1625, are aphoristic in style and worldly in content; like Machiavelli, whom he admired, Bacon sought to describe the political world as it is rather than as it should be. He described the essays as "recreations of my other studies," but they may also be regarded as supplying material for "civil knowledge," a branch of "human philosophy" in Bacon's scheme.

Bacon's views on religion are problematic. Although the first edition of the *Essays* included his *Meditationes sacrae* (Sacred Meditations), in the essays themselves religion is viewed merely as a useful social cement, contributing to the stability of the state. And, along with Aristotelian philosophy, Bacon rejected the scholastic tradition within theology. Repeatedly he emphasized the necessity of a divorce between the study of science and of religion: the truths of science are revealed in God's works, the truths of morality and religion by God's word, that is, in sacred scripture. Fact and value become apparently dissociated. But those commentators who claim that Bacon's frequent protestations of faith were either politic or ironical must deal with the recurrence of theological elements within his thought. For example, his inductive system rests on a belief that the surface of nature can be made transparent to us, provided we rid ourselves of the misconceptions ("idols," Bacon calls them) that are the product of our fallen state; proper inductive procedures will, at least partially, restore the "commerce between the mind of man and the nature of things" to its original condition, that is, to its condition before the Fall. Again, Bacon's *New Atlantis* is suffused with a mystical Christianity, which, it has been persuasively argued, owes much to the Rosicrucian movement. Of course, such religious elements are open to reinterpretation, as Bacon's own reinterpretation of the myths of antiquity shows. And although certain eighteenth-century religious ideas, like the "argument from design" for God's existence, are prefigured in Bacon's writings, it was his insistence on the autonomy of science, as well as his systematic ordering of its various components, that earned him the admiration of Enlightenment thinkers like Voltaire and d'Alembert. They rightly saw him as among those who made the Enlightenment possible. For good or ill, he was also a herald, not only of the technological age that succeeded it, but also of the compartmentalization of experience characteristic of our culture.

BIBLIOGRAPHY

The standard edition of Bacon's *Works* (London, 1857–1874) was edited by James Spedding, R. L. Ellis, and D. D. Heath; volumes 1–7 contain the works, together with translations of all the major Latin works into English; volumes 8–14 contain a life, letters, and miscellanea. All important works appear in English in *Philosophical Works,* edited by J. M. Robertson (London, 1905). Noteworthy among editions of individual works is a scrupulously annotated edition of *The Advancement of Learning* and *New Atlantis,* 3d ed., edited by Arthur Johnston (Oxford, 1974). Three interesting and previously untranslated minor works appear in Benjamin Farrington's *The Philosophy of Francis Bacon* (Liverpool, 1964), together with a valuable monograph on Bacon's thought. A useful, albeit adulatory, account of Bacon's philosophy is Fulton H. Anderson's *The Philosophy of Francis Bacon* (1948; reprint, Chicago, 1971); more critical is Anthony Quinton's *Francis Bacon* (Oxford, 1980). Paulo Rossi's *Francis Bacon: From Magic to Science* (Chicago, 1968) offers an intriguing study linking Bacon's thought with the hermetic tradition. Other aspects of Bacon scholarship are covered in *Essential Articles for the Study of Francis Bacon,* edited by Brian Vickers (Hamden, Conn., 1968).

R. I. G. HUGHES

BACON, ROGER (c. 1214–c. 1292), philosopher and Franciscan friar. Born in the west of England of a wealthy family, for most of his life Bacon alternated between England and France. His first, if not his only, university education was at Oxford, and soon thereafter he pioneered in lecturing on Aristotle's metaphysics and on natural philosophy at Paris. Several Artistotelian commentaries survive from this period, but Bacon was soon to undergo a profound intellectual reorientation, inspired at least partly by another work that he believed to be by Aristotle, the *Secretum secretorum*, a long letter of advice on kingship supposedly written to Alexander the Great.

Bacon's intellectual universe was peopled with heroes and villains. Aristotle was a particularly great ancient hero, while among the few contemporaries admitted to the pantheon were Robert Grosseteste and Adam Marsh. Grosseteste (whom Bacon may not have known personally) had been a lecturer to the Franciscans at Oxford, and Marsh was a Franciscan himself. These men must have been very important in influencing Bacon's somewhat surprising decision to join the Franciscan order, for he was no model of simple humility. Indeed Bacon could be almost as rude about fellow Franciscan intellectuals as about rival Dominicans, such as Albertus Magnus. His relations with his superiors were probably never easy, and it seems certain that he was at least once put under some form of confinement, although the reasons remain obscure. It has been suggested, notably by Stewart C. Easton, that one of the principal reasons for strained relations was his sympathy for the spirituals, the more austere wing of the order, but this view has not been universally accepted.

Both before and after becoming a Franciscan Bacon developed his new approach to philosophy, and in the 1260s his big chance came. His schemes were brought to the attention of Cardinal Guy de Foulques, who in 1265 became Pope Clement IV. Bacon was ordered to produce his writings, but unfortunately there were as yet none fit for dispatch. Bacon, therefore, began to write in a flurry; the results were not only the famous *Opus majus* but also the *Opus minus* and *Opus tertium*, both of which supplemented and summarized the *Opus majus*. Some if not all of these works reached Rome, but there is no evidence of their having provoked any reaction there, and Clement died in 1268. For the rest of his intellectual life Bacon may not unfairly be described as rewriting the same major work, often with great vehemence at what he saw as the increasing ignorance and corruption of his times. Although he never completed a new grand synthesis, he was still at work in 1292. Tradition places his death in the same year.

A cornerstone of Bacon's mature thought is the postulate that all wisdom is included in the scriptures but is in need of explication by means of canon law and philosophy. Thus, while subordinating philosophy to theology Bacon also accorded it immense importance. Moreover, he did not conceive philosophy narrowly but included in its domain—besides its crowning glory, moral philosophy—the study of languages, mathematics, geography, astrology, optics, and alchemy. His emphasis was often empirical, and this, together with the fact that one part of the *Opus majus* is devoted to "experimental science," has led many to portray Bacon as a harbinger of modern experimental science. There is some truth in this, but it is a view that can all too easily lead to anachronism. For instance, it must be remembered that Bacon emphasized that experience was accessible through both external senses and interior illumination, and that revelation was necessary even for philosophical knowledge. Indeed, in his view the plenitude of philosophy had first been revealed to the ancient patriarchs and prophets. It was then transmitted to posterity, with an inevitable decline in quality accompanying the process, the decline only occasionally being arrested by special illuminations to such men as Pythagoras, Socrates, Plato, and Aristotle. Among other means of reversing the decline, according to Bacon, was the study of languages, which would allow ancient texts to be read in the orignal.

Bacon believed that there were six (although at times he appears to allow seven) principal religions, which were astrologically linked to six of the seven planets. The rise and decline of the religions were also correlated with the heavenly motions, so that, for instance, astrology could indicate that the time of the last religion, that of the Antichrist, was near at hand. Christianity was one of the principal religions, but was unique in that philosophy could provide conviction of its truth.

Bacon saw preaching to the unconverted as a bounden, but in fact neglected, duty of Christians, and he strongly disapproved of the Crusades, which, he held, shed Christian blood unnecessarily while actually hindering the conversion of Muslims. But even with effective preaching there would still be those who obstinately resisted conversion and would need to be physically repulsed. Here again philosophy came into play, for Bacon was a firm advocate of what in modern terms would be called the application of technology in warfare. Among his proposals was the use of huge burning mirrors to destroy enemy encampments and the use of "fascination" (psychic influence), a phenomenon Bacon believed could be explained naturalistically. The Antichrist would be well armed with such weapons, and so it was imperative that Christendom defend itself in similar fashion.

Bacon could often seem suspiciously close to advocating the use of magic. He was very conscious of this, and made strenuous efforts to distinguish philosophy sharply from magic and its appeals to demons. Nevertheless, although some of his "pure scientific" writings had considerable influence (notably those on optics), it is not surprising that he went down to posterity as part of the magical tradition. By the learned he was cited as a defender of what in the Renaissance was called natural magic, but to the public at large he was himself a full-blooded magician who had no compunction about trafficking with spirits. Later this image was transformed into that of a hero of experimental science born centuries before his time; more recent critical scholarship, in its urge to demythologize, has often unjustly muted the individuality and originality of this intellectually turbulent figure.

BIBLIOGRAPHY

The best general introduction to Bacon is Stewart C. Easton's *Roger Bacon and His Search for a Universal Science* (New York, 1952), although Easton perhaps exaggerates Bacon's sympathies for the teachings of Joachim of Fiore. A very useful trilogy for probing the basic structure of Bacon's thought is by Raoul Carton: *L'expérience physique chez Roger Bacon, L'expérience mystique de l'illumination intérieure chez Roger Bacon,* and *La synthèse doctrinale de Roger Bacon* (all, Paris, 1924). *Roger Bacon: Essays,* edited by Andrew G. Little (1914; reprint, New York, 1972), remains of considerable value. A good, up-to-date account of Bacon and his attitude to non-Christians is provided in E. R. Daniel's *The Franciscan Concept of Mission in the High Middle Ages* (Lexington, Ky., 1975).

A. GEORGE MOLLAND

BĀDARĀYAṆA, reputed author of the *Vedānta Sūtra (Brahma Sūtra),* the source text for all subsequent philosophical Vedānta. No biographical information is available; the name may be a convenient surrogate for the process of redaction that eventuated in the present text. Indeed, a recent tradition identifies Bādarāyaṇa with Vyāsa, the eponymous "compiler" of much late Vedic and epic material, including the *Mahābhārata.*

The name *Bādarāyaṇa* occurs in the *Mīmāṃsā Sūtra* (1.5) of Jaimini, there referring to a *ṛṣi* to whose opinion on an important point Jaimini seems to defer. If the *Vedānta Sūtra* is indeed Bādarāyaṇa's, then he also refers to himself in the context of other teachers whose disputations evidently formed the beginnings of early Vedānta speculation (*Vedāntra Sūtra* 4.4.5–7).

Modern discussion of Bādarāyaṇa is focused chiefly on the date of the *sūtra* text, on Bādarāyaṇa's "relations" to other post-Upaniṣadic teachers, notably Jaimini, and on the question of which of his many commentators has been most faithful to his thought. Paul Deussen in general prefers Śaṅkara's monistic version, the oldest extant commentary, but others (George Thibaut, Vinayaka S. Ghate, and, more recently, Louis Renou) have suggested important reservations in this view and have often concluded that Rāmānuja's *bhedābheda* ("difference within unity") more accurately reflects Bādarāyaṇa's original thesis. [*See* Vedānta.] The discussion is made extremely difficult by the fact, universally admitted, that Bādarāyaṇa's *sūtras*, of an extreme brevity and terseness, are often unintelligible without an explanatory commentary.

Bādarāyaṇa's relation to the *ṛṣi* of the other (Pūrva) Mīmāṃsā, Jaimini, is again not easy to decipher. [*See* Mīmāṃsā.] The names appear in the collections attributed to the other teacher, which has led many to suspect that the two may have been close contemporaries. But the doctrines that they espouse in these stray passages do not seem clearly related to the perhaps later massive schism implied by the existence of the separate text collections to which their names were attached. What is clear is that they were preeminent among the many teachers whose names alone survive. The date of Bādarāyaṇa is also closely tied to that of Jaimini but, like all such early Indian dating, is highly speculative and often circularly argued. If, as Renou concludes, Bādarāyaṇa does directly confront the Buddhist Mahāyāna in several *sūtras* (see 2.2.28–32), then his date cannot be much earlier than the third century of our era. But Jaimini's date is sometimes put back as far as the third century BCE (see, e.g., Jacobi, 1911). Bādarāyaṇa's name had of course become associated with the *sūtra* text by the time of Śaṅkara (early eighth century).

The text itself is composed of 555 *sūtras*, grouped in four major chapters (*adhyāyas*), each with four subdivisions (*pādas*). Commentators have further identified various "topics" within each *pāda,* but the number and boundaries of these differ markedly from one commentator to another. In general, the first chapter is fundamental, treating *brahman* as the one source of the world. It argues that the various Upaniṣadic teachings concerning *brahman* present one doctrine. Much of the discussion in the fourth *pāda* appears directed against the Sāṃkhya. The second chapter refutes speculative objections to the Vedānta theses from the Sāṃkhya, Nyāya, and Bauddha schools and discusses certain problems of "realism," notably whether the world is "caused" or not. The third chapter treats the individual soul *(jīva)* and how it "knows" *brahman.* The final chapter, on "fruits," discusses meditation and the condition of the liberated soul before and after death.

BIBLIOGRAPHY

The *Vedānta Sūtra* has been translated by George Thibaut as *The Vedānta Sūtras of Bādarāyaṇa* in "Sacred Books of the East," vols. 34, 38, and 48 (Oxford, 1890–1904). Thibaut's work contains an extensive introduction to the text. Important secondary sources include Paul Deussen's *Das System des Vedānta* (Leipzig, 1883), translated by Charles Johnston as *The System of the Vedānta* (Chicago, 1912); Hermann Jacobi's *Zur Frühgeschichte der indischen Philosophie* (Berlin, 1911); Vinayaka S. Ghate's *Le Vedânta: Études sur les Brahma-Sūtras et leurs cinq commentaires* (Paris, 1918); and Louis Renou and Jean Filliozat's *L'Inde classique,* vol. 2 (Hanoi, 1953).

EDWIN GEROW

BAECK, LEO (1873–1956), rabbi and theologian, representative spokesman of German Jewry during the Nazi era. Born in Lissa, Posen (then in Prussian Germany, now in Poland), a son of the local rabbi, Baeck first pursued his higher education at the university in Breslau and the moderately liberal Jewish Theological Seminary. In order to study with the distinguished scholar of religion Wilhelm Dilthey, Baeck transferred to the university in Berlin, where he earned a doctorate in 1895. Two years later, he was ordained as a rabbi at the Hochschule für die Wissenschaft des Judentums, a leading institution of Liberal Judaism. Baeck then held pulpits in Oppeln (Silesia) and Düsseldorf, and in 1912 he was called to Berlin where, with the exception of a stint as chaplain during World War I, he remained until his deportation to a concentration camp by the Nazis. During his years in Berlin, Baeck assumed a number of increasingly influential positions. In 1913 he joined the faculty of the Hochschule as a docent of Midrash and homiletics. In 1922 he became chairman of the national association of German rabbis, and in 1925 he assumed the presidency of the B'nai B'rith, a fraternal network, in Germany.

When Hitler ascended to the German chancellorship, it was Baeck who had the prescience to declare that "the thousand-year" history of German Jewry had come to an end. Baeck was instrumental in founding the Reichsvertretung der deutschen Juden, an organization that made the most successful attempt in German-Jewish history to unify Jewish defense, welfare, and cultural activities on a nationwide scale. As president of this body, he devoted himself to defending the rights of Jews in Germany, facilitating their emigration, and raising the morale of those still left in Hitler's Reich. A noteworthy example of the last effort was a special prayer composed by Baeck for public recitation on the Day of Atonement (Yom Kippur) in 1935, which included a defiant rejection of Nazi slanders: "In indignation and abhorrence, we express our contempt for the lies concerning us and the defamation of our religion and its testimonies" (*Out of the Whirlwind: A Reader of Holocaust Literature,* ed. Albert Friedlander, New York, 1968, p. 132). Arrested repeatedly by the Nazis for his outspokenness, Baeck persisted in his refusal to flee Germany until every Jew had been rescued. He continued to head the national body of German Jews after it was forcibly reorganized by the government into a council that was accountable to the Nazis. In January 1943 Baeck was deported along with other elderly German Jews to the concentration camp of Theresienstadt (now in Czechoslovakia). In that "model camp" he served as honorary president of the ruling Jewish council and devoted his time to comforting and teaching his fellow inmates. When the camp was liberated, he still refused to leave his flock until he had been assured of their safety.

Baeck immigrated to London after the war. His last years were devoted to work on behalf of the World Union of Progressive Judaism, teaching at the Hebrew Union College (the Reform rabbinical school in Cincinnati), and organizing the surviving remnants of German Jewry. In England, he served as president of the Council of Jews from Germany. And shortly before his death, Baeck helped found an international research institute for the study of central European Jewry that bears his name (the Leo Baeck Institute).

Baeck's writings reflect his lifelong efforts to defend his people and faith. He achieved early fame by rebutting the anti-Jewish claims of Adolf von Harnack, a liberal Protestant theologian who denigrated Judaism in his book *Das Wesen des Christentums* (The Essence of Christianity). Baeck's first book, a polemical work entitled *Vorlesungen über das Wesen des Judentums* (Lectures on the Essence of Judaism; 1905), continued this defense and boldly proclaimed Judaism superior to Christianity, a claim that won Baeck considerable attention as a champion of German Jewry. Employing the approach to religion developed by his mentor, Dilthey, Baeck attempted to penetrate the underlying psychology of Judaism and understand the Jewish religion in its totality *(Gestalt).*

In subsequent essays and reworkings of his first book, Baeck sharpened the contrast between Judaism and Christianity: the latter, he claimed, was a "romantic religion" which exalted feeling, self-indulgence, dogma, and passivity; Judaism, by contrast, is a "classical religion" imbued with ethical concerns. In Judaism, Baeck saw a religion in which God's mystery and commandment exist as polarities. *Dieses Volk* (This People Israel), a book written in Nazi Berlin and the concentration camp of Theresienstadt, explores the meaning of Jewish existence. Written during the bleakest era of Jewish history, it is a work of optimism that expresses Leo Baeck's belief in the eternity of the Jewish people and their ongoing mission. In defiant rejection of Nazi barbarism, Baeck affirmed the messianic role of the people Israel to heed God's ethical command.

BIBLIOGRAPHY

Two of Baeck's most important books have been translated into English: *The Essence of Judaism,* rev. ed. (New York,

1961), and *This People Israel: The Meaning of Jewish Existence*, translated by Albert H. Friedlander (New York, 1965). Several of his major essays appear in *Judaism and Christianity: Essays by Leo Baeck*, translated by Walter Kaufmann (Philadelphia, 1958). There are two book-length studies of Leo Baeck: Friedlander's *Leo Baeck: Teacher of Theresienstadt* (New York, 1968) primarily analyzes Baeck's writings; Leonard Baker's *Days of Sorrow and Pain: Leo Baeck and the Berlin Jews* (New York, 1978), a more popular account, describes, on the basis of extensive interviews, Baeck's communal and wartime activities.

JACK WERTHEIMER

BAHĀ'ĪS are the followers of Mīrzā Ḥusayn ʿAlī Nūrī (1817–1892), known as Bahā' Allāh ("glory of God"). The new religion arose in the second half of the nineteenth century among those Bābīs who recognized in Bahā' Allāh the prophetic figure foretold by their leader, the Bāb: "he whom God shall manifest" *(man yuẓhiruhu Allāh)*. [*See* Bābīs.]

Historical Development. Mīrzā Ḥusayn ʿAlī Nūrī was born into a noble Tehran family that had given several ministers to the Persian court. According to Bahā'ī tradition and his own writings, he never attended school. He was a profoundly religious personality and soon converted to the new Bābī teachings, although he never met the Bāb personally. From his writings it appears that he never read the Bābīs' holy book, the *Bayān* (Declaration), but nevertheless knew it by heart.

In the wave of repression against Bābīs that followed an attempt on the life of Nāṣir al-Dīn Shāh in 1852, he was thrown into the Tehran prison known as Siyāh Chāl ("Black Hole"), where he had the mystical experience that Bahā'īs consider to be the first intimation of his future mission. As he describes this experience in *Lawḥ-i Ibn Dhi'b* (Epistle of the Son of the Wolf), he heard a voice crying, "Verily we will succor you by means of yourself and your pen. Be not afraid . . . you are in security. And soon God will raise up the treasuries of the heart, namely those men who shall succor you for love of you and your name, by which God will bring to life the hearts of the sages." At other times he felt that a great torrent of water was running from the top of his head to his chest "like a powerful river pouring itself out on the earth from the summit of a lofty mountain."

Upon his release from prison in January 1853, his possessions were confiscated and he was banished with his family to Baghdad. There he exerted increasing spiritual influence on the Bābī exiles, while that of his half brother, Mīrzā Yaḥyā (known as Ṣubḥ-i Azal, "dawn of eternity") declined. In 1854 Bahā' Allāh went to Kurdistan, where he lived as a nomadic dervish near Sulaymānīyah. When he returned to Baghdad two years later, his influence upon the Bābī exiles and numerous Persian visitors was such that the Persian consul asked the Ottoman authorities to remove him to Istanbul. Shortly before his departure, on 21 April 1863, in the garden of Najīb Pāshā near Baghdad (called by Bahā'īs Bāgh-i Riẓvān, the "garden of paradise"), Bahā' Allāh declared himself to be "he whom God shall manifest" as promised by the Bāb.

After some months in Istanbul, the exiles were sent to Edirne, and there Bahā' Allāh openly declared his prophetic mission, sending letters (known as *alwāḥ*, "tablets") to various sovereigns, including Pope Pius IX, to invite support for his cause. The majority of the Bābīs accepted him and came to be known as Bahā'īs. A minority, followers of Ṣubḥ-i Azal (hence Azalīs), provoked incidents that impelled the Ottomans to banish the Bahā'īs (with some Azalīs) to Palestine and the Azalīs (with some Bahā'īs) to Cyprus. Bahā' Allāh arrived in Acre with his family in August 1868, and for this reason the Bahā'īs consider Palestine as the Holy Land.

For nine years Bahā' Allāh was imprisoned in the fortress at Acre but was then allowed to move to a country house he had rented at Mazraʿah. Between 1877 and 1884 he occupied himself with writing his fundamental work, *Kitāb al-aqdas* (The Most Holy Book). About 1880 he was allowed to go to Bahjī, near Haifa, where he died twelve years later after a short illness. According to his will *(Kitāb ʿahdī)*, his eldest son, ʿAbbās Effendī (1844–1921), who had faithfully accompanied his father in his travels and his exile, became the infallible interpreter of his father's books and writings and the "center of the covenant" *(markaz-i ʿahd)*. He was known thereafter as ʿAbd al-Bahā' ("servant of the glory [of God]"). Bahā' Allāh's will was contested by his other son, Muḥammad ʿAlī, who set up a rival organization and tried with all his means to compromise his brother in the eyes of the already hostile Ottoman authorities. ʿAbd al-Bahā' was formally released from prison in 1908 under the amnesty granted by the new government of the Young Turks. In 1910 he began his three missionary journeys to the West: to Egypt (1910), to Europe (1911), and to America and Europe (1912–1913); he returned to Palestine in 1913.

The first Bahā'ī group in America was formed as early as 1894, and in December 1898, the first American pilgrims arrived in Acre. Although one of the objects of ʿAbd al-Bahā's trips was to counter the propaganda of his brother's supporters, he also formed Bahā'ī groups in the countries he visited. In 1920 he was knighted by the British government; he died the following year and was buried near the Bāb in the great shrine on Mount Carmel. In his will he appointed Shoghi Effendi Rabbani (1899–1957), the eldest son of his eldest daughter, as "guardian of the cause of God" *(walī-yi amr Allāh)* and infallible interpreter of his writings and those of his father. After studying at Oxford, Shoghi Effendi returned in 1923 to his native Haifa, which became the administrative center of the Bahā'ī faith. In 1936 he married Mary Maxwell, daughter of the Canadian architect responsible for the shrine of the Bāb on Mount Carmel and other Bahā'ī monuments; she took the name Rūḥīyah Khānum. When Shoghi Effendi died without leaving a will, the cause was administered for five years by a Council of the Hands of the Cause residing in Israel; in 1962 the International House of Justice, foretold by Bahā' Allāh in his *Kitāb al-aqdas,* was then selected by an international convention held in Haifa. This body has since been reelected every five years.

The Bahā'ī faith has spread rapidly all over the world; it is practiced in 340 different countries, and its literature has been translated into 700 languages. The king of independent Samoa is Bahā'ī, as are entire villages of Indios in Peru and Bolivia. Precise figures for the total number of Bahā'īs in the world are difficult to supply, since available statistics normally deal only with the number of administrative units, of which there were, in 1985, 143 national spiritual assemblies and 27,887 local assemblies. At that time, the world Bahā'ī population was estimated at 1.5 to 2 million, with about 300,000 members in Iran constituting that country's largest religious minority. In the late twentieth century the Bahā'ī faith showed enormous growth in Africa, the Indian subcontinent, and Vietnam, where they were then counted in the hundreds of thousands.

Beliefs and Practices. The core of Bahā'ī theology can be succinctly expressed as "evolution in time and unity in the present hour." According to Bahā'ī teachings, "Religious truth is not absolute but relative." The inaccessible essence of God manifests itself through the eternal Logos, but while the Logos is one, its manifestations are many. Their task is to create ever-wider unities in the world. Hence Abraham unified a tribe; Moses, a people; and Muḥammad, a nation, while Jesus was to purify the souls of individuals. The task of each manifestation of God has been completely fulfilled: Christianity has not failed, because Christ's task of creating individual sanctity has been achieved. This is not enough, however: collective sanctity of the entire human race is now required. Such was the task of Bahā' Allāh.

But the manifestation of God through the prophets never ceases. While Muslims hold that Muḥammad is the last manifestation of the will of God and that no other is needed, the Bahā'īs insist that people always need a divine manifestation and that even Bahā' Allāh will not be the last. The Bahā'ī faith is the only one that foresees its own eventual abolition, although not before "a thousand years," as it is written in the *Kitāb al-aqdas.* The Bahā'īs recognize the divine mission of Muḥammad and are willing, in fact, to accept him as the *khātam al-nabīyīn* ("seal of the prophets") in the sense that every prophet is the seal of those preceding.

Bahā'ī psychology is more complex than is often perceived. 'Abd al-Bahā' distinguished five types of spirit: animal, vegetable, human, that of faith, and the Holy Spirit. The spirit of faith, which is given by God, is the only one that confers "eternal life" on the human spirit (and this tenet explains why some Orientalists have written that the Bahā'īs do not believe in the immortality of the soul). Faith is essential to Bahā'ī spiritual life. As the first verse of the *Kitāb al-aqdas* proclaims: "The first commandment of God to his servant is knowledge of the dawn of his revelation and the dayspring of his degree [i.e., the prophet, the manifestation of God], who is his appointed representative in the created world. He who has attained this knowledge has attained all good. And he who does not know it is of the world of error even though he performs all good works." Eternity of the soul for the Bahā'īs means a continuation of the voyage toward the unknowable essence of God. Paradise and hell are symbols, the first standing for the believers' journey toward God and the second for the fruitless path toward annihilation followed by those who knowingly reject the faith and perform evil works.

The Bahā'ī religion has no public ritual nor any sacrament or private rites of a sacred character. The sole religious duties of a Bahā'ī are (1) to assemble every nineteen days, on the first day of each Bahā'ī month, for a celebration called the Feast of the Nineteenth Day; (2) to fast for nineteen days from dawn to sunset, following Muslim usage, for the entire month of 'Alā, which concludes with the New Year on 21 March (like the traditional Persian New Year, that of the Bahā'īs falls on the vernal equinox); (3) to abstain completely from alcoholic beverages; and (4) to pray daily. In contrast to Islamic and Christian practice, the obligatory prayers (Pers., *namāz;* Arab., *ṣalāt*) are intended to be performed privately and not, with the exception of a special prayer for the dead, in congregation; likewise, they may be recited in any language rather than in Arabic alone, as is the case with Islam.

Apart from these duties, the *Kitāb al-aqdas* lays down precise rules for the division of inheritance (part going to one's teachers), levies a tax of 19 percent on revenues, and prescribes numerous other rules and laws (penal, civil, and religious), which, by the late twentieth century, were followed only by Bahā'īs living in the East. Men and women are held to be equals, and marriage is monogamous. (Bigamy was permitted in the *Kitāb al-*

aqdas, but that provision was canceled by ʿAbd al-Bahāʾ.) A valid marriage requires the consent of the couple's parents; divorce is allowed but discouraged.

Perhaps the most original aspect of Bahāʾī teaching is the administration of the community, a sort of "democratic theocracy" similar to that of early Islam and considered to be of divine origin. The controlling bodies of the community, pyramidal in structure, are of two types, administrative and instructional. The former include the local and national Spiritual Assemblies and the International House of Justice. Local Spiritual Assemblies, each consisting of nine members elected by universal suffrage, are constituted wherever there are at least that number of Bahāʾīs. Election is considered an act of worship and thus does not imply responsibility on the part of the elected toward the electors, since the latter are considered merely instruments of the will of God. Elections are held yearly during the Riẕvān feast (21 April–2 May). When there is a sufficient number of local Assemblies, a convention, elected by universal suffrage, in turn elects a nine-member national Assembly from the Bahāʾī community at large. Every five years (this period is subject to change), an international convention of all the national Assembly members elects the International House of Justice *(bayt al-ʿadl-i umūmī)*, which functions as the supreme administrative body. It is empowered, when the needs of the time warrant, to abrogate previous laws and to frame new ones not laid down in the *Kitāb al-aqdas* or other writings of the founder.

The instructional pyramid includes the Hands of the Cause (first appointed by Bahāʾ Allāh, then by Shoghi Effendi), the Continental Board, and the Auxiliary Board, whose members nominate their own assistants. All members of the instructional pyramid obey the administrative bodies in their practical work.

Although the Bahāʾīs have no public worship, the *Kitāb al-aqdas* recommends the erection of a temple structure, called Mashriq al-Adhkār (literally "a place where mention of the name of God arises at dawn"), which is a nine-sided building surmounted by a dome of nine sections. It is open to the faithful of every creed. The first such temple, located in ʿIshqābād, now Soviet Turkistan, was built in 1920 but later destroyed by an earthquake. In 1910, ʿAbd al-Bahāʾ laid the first stone of the Mashriq al-Adhkār in Wilmette, Illinois; this building was officially inaugurated in 1953. By the late twentieth century, five others had been completed, in Panama, Australia, Germany, Uganda, and Samoa, and one more was under construction in India. Other significant Bahāʾī monuments include the tomb of Bahāʾ Allāh in Bahjī and those of the Bāb and ʿAbd al-Bahāʾ at the World Center of the Faith in Haifa.

The fact that the World Center is located in Israel (formerly Palestine) has caused the Bahāʾīs to be regarded as something of a fifth column in Muslim countries, and they have suffered great persecution as a result. Particularly cruel measures have been taken against the Bahāʾīs in Iran following the proclamation of the Islamic Republic: all religious and testimonial activities were officially banned in August 1983, and more than 170 Bahāʾīs were said to have been executed in the first five years after the Iranian Revolution.

BIBLIOGRAPHY

Bahāʾ Allāh's *Kitāb al-aqdas*, written in Arabic, has been edited and translated into Russian by A. G. Tumanski as *Kitab akdes*, in "Zapiski *Imp. Akad. Nauk*," Hist.-Phil. Class, ser. 8, vol. 6 (St. Petersburg, 1899). Among the writings of Bahāʾ Allāh that were translated into English by Shoghi Effendi are *Kitāb-i-Íqán: The Book of Certitude* (Wilmette, Ill., 1943), *The Hidden Words* (London, 1944), *Prayers and Meditations* (New York, 1938), and *Selected Writings of Bahá'ulláh* (Wilmette, 1942). Also available in English is *The Seven Valleys and the Four Valleys*, translated by Ali-Kuli Khan assisted by Marzieh Gail, rev. ed. (Wilmette, 1952).

Conversations with ʿAbd al-Bahāʾ in Acre were collected and translated by Laura Clifford Barney as *Some Answered Questions* (1908; reprint, London, 1961). English translations of ʿAbd al-Bahāʾs writings include *The Mysterious Forces of Civilization* (Chicago, 1919), *Selected Writings of ʿAbdu'l Bahá'* (Wilmette, 1942), *Tablets of ʿAbdu'l Bahá'*, 3 vols. (New York, 1930), and *The Wisdom of ʿAbdu'l Bahá'* (New York, 1924). Among the published works of Shoghi Effendi are *Baha'i World Faith* (Wilmette, 1943), *Gleanings from the Writings of Baha'ullah* (New York, 1935), and *God Passes By* (Wilmette, 1945).

For the early history of the Bahāʾīs, see Nabīl Zarandī's *Taʾrīkh-i Nabīl*, translated by Shoghi Effendi as *The Dawn-Breakers* (1932; reprint, Wilmette, 1970). *The Bábí and Bahá'í Religions 1844–1944: Some Contemporary Western Accounts*, edited by Moojan Momen (Oxford, 1981), offers a documentary history compiled from the writings and records of missionaries, travelers, and government officials. Various aspects of Bahāʾī activity in the Middle East, North America, and elsewhere are presented in *Studies in Babi and Baha'i History*, vol. 1, edited by Moojan Momen (Los Angeles, 1982), and the second volume, published as *From Iran East and West*, edited by Juan R. Cole and Moojan Momen (Los Angeles, 1984), both of which include extensive bibliographies. For sources in Persian and Arabic, see my entries "Bahāʾ Allāh" and "Bahāʾīs" in *The Encyclopaedia of Islam*, new ed. (Leiden, 1960–).

ALESSANDRO BAUSANI

BAḤYE IBN PAQUDA (second half of the eleventh century), also known as Baḥya; Jewish moral philosopher. Virtually nothing is known of Baḥye's life, except that he probably lived in Saragossa and served as a *dayyan*, a judge of a Jewish court. His Hebrew poems, only a few examples of which are extant, were highly regarded by at least one medieval critic. All are on religious themes, and most were composed to serve in the liturgy. His two best-known poems, intended for private devotion, are both appended to his *magnum opus*, a treatise on ethics written in Arabic and entitled *Al-hidāyah ilā fara'iḍ al-qulūb* (Right Guidance to the Duties of the Hearts). Composed sometime between 1050 and 1090, this work was disseminated in the Hebrew translation by Yehudah ibn Tibbon under the title *Ḥovot halevavot* (1161), becoming one of the most influential religious treatises in Judaism.

Baḥye was heir to a Judeo-Arabic religious tradition in which the rabbinic Judaism of the Talmud and the geonim had been synthesized with Islamic rationalistic theology *(kalām)*. This synthesis had received its definitive formulation in the writings of Sa'adyah Gaon (882–942), which had become authoritative for the educated elite class of Jews in Arabic-speaking countries such as Spain. To this synthesis, Baḥye contributed a new element: the traditions of Islamic asceticism and mysticism. Although his immediate literary sources in Islamic literature have not been identified—the earlier opinion that he drew on the writings of Abū Ḥāmid al-Ghazālī (d. 1111) is now generally rejected on chronological grounds—his writing is replete with sayings, exempla, and technical terminology derived from the writings of earlier Muslim mystics, ascetics, and moralizers; the very structure of his book has Islamic antecedents. Although many passages in the Bible, rabbinic literature, and the writings of the geonim could be cited in support and elaboration of the thesis that the true function of religious practice is to enable man to develop his inner life toward spiritual perfection and love of God, Baḥye was the first Jewish writer to develop it into a complete spiritual program.

Baḥye's treatise begins with an introduction in which the concept of "duties of the heart" is defined and explained, and continues with ten chapters, each on a different virtue. The distinction between "duties of the limbs" and "duties of the heart," between outward *(ẓāhir)* and inward *(bāṭin)* piety is borrowed from the disciples of the early Muslim mystic Ḥasan al-Baṣrī (d. 728). Reason, the Torah, and the rabbinic tradition all teach that the true worship of God is through the intention that accompanies the observances dictated by religious law. Yet most people feel secure that they fulfill God's will through formal obedience to religious law, and they neglect the spiritual development that is the purpose of the system.

Thus, most Jews believe that they fulfill the obligation to acknowledge God's existence and unity by passive assent and by ritual recitation of the Shema' in their daily prayers. This sort of formal compliance with a religious duty *(taqlīd)* is, in Baḥye's opinion, adequate only for children, the uneducated, and the feebleminded. An adult of normal intellectual capacity is obliged, first, to grasp the meaning of God's unity in its logical and philosophical essence, as far as the human mind is able to grasp it. Accordingly, Baḥye devotes his first chapter to a restatement of the definitions and proofs of God's existence and unity that had been advanced by Sa'adyah and other *kalām* writers.

Second, one must grasp the meaning God's existence and unity has for one's relations both to God and to one's fellow man. Since God is not accessible to direct observation, man can learn about God's relationship to the world only by studying nature, in which God's actions are evident, and by studying man, the microcosm. Thus the study of nature makes man aware of God's work in the world and brings him closer to knowledge of God. It further has the effect of instilling in him a profound gratitude, the attitude that makes for the perfect fulfillment of the duties of the heart.

The constituent elements of man are the body and the soul; as taught by the Neoplatonists, the soul is foreign to the body, being celestial in origin. It was placed in the body by God's will, both as a trial for it and to help the body. For all its yearning to return to its source, the soul is in constant danger of being diverted from its mission because of love of pleasure and love of power. With the help of reason and revelation, however, the soul can purify itself and, after the death of a body, complete its journey.

In order to achieve the soul's desired end, it is necessary to practice certain virtues, to each of which Baḥye devotes a chapter: worship, trust, sincerity, humility, repentance, self-examination, asceticism, and love of God. These virtues flow spontaneously from the gratitude to the creator felt by the thoughtful believer. While the organization of these virtues as a series of degrees of perfection is derived from the writings of such Muslim mystics as Abū Ṭālib al-Makkī (d. 996), Baḥye does not accept their concept of progressive mystic ascension toward illumination. In fact, Baḥye's demands and expectations are quite moderate. Thus, "trust" does not mean that a person should neglect his work and expect God to provide him a living, but that he should pursue his livelihood modestly and conscientiously, knowing that it is not his work that provides his living but God's will. Likewise, "asceticism" does not mean extreme self-abnegation and mortification, and it has no intrinsic value. The closest to "the moderation of the law" are those who are not outwardly distinguishable from other men.

Finally, there is no conception in Baḥye's thought of mystical union with God. The love of God results from the soul's natural yearning to rejoin its source, but while the soul can perfect and purify itself, it cannot fulfill its desire while attached to the body. The "lover" keeps a respectful distance from the "beloved." Baḥye's mysticism is thus fully compatible with rabbinic Judaism.

[*For further discussion of Baḥye's thought, see* Jewish Thought and Philosophy, *article on* Premodern Philosophy.]

BIBLIOGRAPHY

Baḥya ben Yosef ibn Pakuda. *The Book of Direction to the Duties of the Heart.* Edited and translated by Menahem Mansoor with Sara Arenson and Shoshana Dannhauser. London, 1973.

Safran, Bezalel. "Baḥya ibn Paquda's Attitude toward the Courtier Class." In *Studies in Medieval Jewish History and Literature,* edited by Isadore Twersky, pp. 154–197. Cambridge, Mass., 1979.

Sifroni, A. *Sefer ḥovot ha-levavot be-targumo shel R. Yehudah Ibn Tibbon.* Jerusalem, 1927/8.

Vajda, Georges. *La théologie ascétique de Baḥya Ibn Paquda.* Paris, 1947.

Yahuda, A. S., ed. *Al-hidāya 'ila fara'id al-qulūb des Bachja ibn Jōsēf ibn Paqūda, aus Andalusien.* Leiden, 1912.

RAYMOND P. SCHEINDLIN

BAKONGO. *See* Kongo Religion.

BALARĀMA is a Hindu god, the elder brother of the god Kṛṣṇa. He is sometimes considered as the third of the three Rāmas, and thus the eighth *avatāra* of Viṣṇu; at other times he appears as an incarnation of the serpent Śeṣa or Ananta. [*See* Avatāra.] He is also known by the names Baladeva, Balabhadra, Bala, and Halāyudha. Legends of Balarāma are found in the Brahmanical and Jain literature. He is mentioned along with Kṛṣṇa in the *Mahābhārata,* especially in its sequel *Harivamśa,* in the *Bhāgavata Purāṇa,* and other Vaiṣnava Purāṇas.

The birth of Balarāma was extraordinary. When a disembodied voice predicted that the demon Kamsa would be killed by the eighth child of his sister Devakī, Kamsa vowed to kill her male children. Balarāma was conceived as the seventh child of Devakī and was saved from Kamsa when he was transferred to Rohiṇī's womb by the *yogamāyā* (magical power) of Viṣṇu. Balarāma was thus born of Rohiṇī. Another story narrated in the *Mahābhārata* accounts for his white color. Viṣṇu, extracted one of his white hairs and sent it to Devakī's womb; the hair then was born as Balarāma.

Balarama and Kṛṣṇa are always together and are in perfect contrast with each other: Balarāma is white, whereas Kṛṣṇa is black; Balarāma is the all-masculine figure with the powerful plowshare as his weapon, whereas Kṛṣṇa's beauty is described as graceful and feminine, dark in color, and attractive to women.

Once, while intoxicated, Balarāma called the river Yamunā (personified as a goddess) to come to him so that he could bathe. When she did not comply with his wish, he plunged his plowshare into the river, pulling the waters until Yamunā surrended.

Balarāma married the daughter of King Raivata. The king, who thought that his daughter was so beautiful that she could not be wed to a mortal, took her to the world of Brahmā to seek advice. Brahmā advised the king that Balarāma was the most suitable bridegroom for her. The visit with Brahmā took many aeons, and by the time they returned, mankind had grown smaller. Balarāma found Revati so tall that he shortened her with his plowshare before marrying her.

Balarāma was an expert of three weapons, the plow, the mace, and the club. He taught the use of the mace to Duryodhana. Balarāma disapproved of Kṛṣṇa's role in the *Mahābhārata* war and wanted the cousins, the Kauravas and the Paṇḍavas, to make peace. When the cousins were fighting, Balarāma refused to take sides and went on a pilgrimage. He was indignant when in the final mace battle Bhīma hit Duryodhana on his thighs, against all propriety. Balarāma vowed to kill Bhīma and could only be pacified by Kṛṣṇa.

Although addicted to liquor himself, Balarāma prohibited intoxicants in the holy city of Dvārakā. After the battle of Kurukṣetra the Yādavas of Dvārakā were involved in a drunken brawl and killed each other. Balarāma sat in deep meditation and the serpent Śeṣa, of whom Balarāma was an incarnation, came from his mouth and entered the ocean.

According to the Jain *Harivamśa Purāṇa,* Balarāma watched over Kṛṣṇa, and also helped his brother, who was raised by Yaśoda, to visit his real mother, Devakī. When Devakī saw Kṛṣṇa, her breasts spontaneously flowed with milk. In order to protect her identity, Balarāma poured a jar of milk over her.

[*See also* Kṛṣṇa.]

BIBLIOGRAPHY

Further information on Balarāma can be found in *Srimad Bhagavatam,* 2 vols., translated by N. Raghunathan (Madras, 1976).

VELCHERU NARAYANA RAO

BALINESE RELIGION. Eight degrees south of the equator, toward the middle of the belt of islands that form the southern arc of the Indonesian archipelago, lies the island of Bali, home of the last surviving Hindu-Buddhist civilization of Indonesia. A few kilometers to the west of Bali is the island of Java, where major Hindu-Buddhist kingdoms flourished from the time of Borobudur (eighth century) until the end of the sixteenth century, when the last Javanese Hindu kingdom fell to Islam. Just to the east of Bali is the Wallace Line, a deep ocean channel marking the biogeographical frontier between Asia and the Pacific. The Wallace Line is also a cultural frontier: journeying eastward from Bali, one leaves the zone of historical Asian civilizations and enters a region of tribal peoples. Bali is the last stepping-stone from Asia to the Pacific.

The preservation of Hindu-Buddhist kingdoms on Bali centuries after their disappearance elsewhere in the region is largely the result of geography. The island is not only remote but quite small—172 kilometers east-west by 102 kilometers north-south. The fertile valleys that form the heartland of Balinese civilization face southward, toward a largely untraveled sea. Behind them lies an arc of steep jungle-covered mountains, a natural barrier to Java and the busy seas to the north. Balinese kingdoms nestled along the south coast, each of them so tiny that a man could easily ride across an entire "kingdom" in half a day on horseback. The Balinese attitude toward the world beyond their shores is nicely illustrated by the complaints of the first European ambassadors to Bali, who frequently could not even obtain an audience with a Balinese prince—the Balinese were simply too preoccupied with their own affairs!

Sources of Balinese Religion. Evidence for the nature of prehistoric Balinese religion comes from three sources: archaeology, historical linguistics, and comparative ethnography. Linguistically, Balinese belongs to the Malayo-Polynesian language family, itself derived from Proto-Austronesian, which is thought to have been spoken by Southeast Asian peoples around six thousand years ago. Proto-Austronesian-speakers on Bali had words for many religious concepts: nature gods, such as a sky god; ancestral spirits (who were probably thought to inhabit mountaintops); a human soul, or perhaps multiple souls; and shamanistic trance. Such beliefs and practices remain widespread in Indonesia, reflecting the influence of Malayo-Polynesian culture. [*For Bali's megalithic culture and links with Oceania, see* Megalithic Religion, *article on* Historical Cultures.] The vocabulary of Proto-Austronesian reflects a Neolithic culture; the advent of the Metal Age in Bali is marked by a magnificent bronze kettledrum, the "Moon of Pejeng." Stylistically related to similar "Dong-son" drums found over much of eastern Indonesia and Vietnam, the Balinese drum is distinguished by its large size (186 × 150 cm) and splendid ornamentation. The discovery of a casting mold used to make the drum in a nearby village proved that the drum was created by indigenous Balinese metalsmiths, some time between the second century BCE and the second century CE. [*See* Music, *article on* Music and Religion in Southeast Asia.]

Fifty-three stone sarcophagi, tentatively dated to the same era as the "Moon of Pejeng," provide additional evidence for a sophisticated Metal Age culture in Bali with well-developed social ranking and elaborate funerary rituals. Hewn from stone with bronze tools and ornamented with protruding knobs decorated with stylized human heads, they contain human skeletons of both sexes along with bronze arm and foot rings, carnelian beads, and miniature socketed bronze shovels. Even more impressive are the stepped stone pyramids of this era, reminiscent of Polynesian *marae,* which apparently served as temples to the ancestors and nature gods, and perhaps also as monuments for important chiefs. Thus, by the first millennium CE Balinese society was organized into sedentary villages ruled by chiefs. The major economic occupation was wet-rice agriculture, supported by small-scale irrigation. The economy supported craft specialists, such as metalworkers and builders of megaliths.

Sometime in the early first millennium of the common era, Bali came into contact with Indian civilization and thus with the Hindu and Buddhist religions. The nature of this contact and the ensuing process of "indianization" has long been a subject of scholarly debate. At one extreme, J. C. van Leur maintained that "hinduization" was wholly initiated by Southeast Asian rulers who summoned Indian brahmans to their courts, creating merely a "thin and flaking glaze" of Indic culture among the elite (van Leur, 1955). At the other extreme, R. C. Majumdar postulated wholesale colonization of Southeast Asia by Indian exiles. Between these two poles, nearly every conceivable intermediate position has been staked out, and there is as yet no consensus as to which is most likely, although there is no persuasive evidence for large-scale colonization by Indian exiles (Majumdar, 1963).

In Bali, the first clear indication of "indianization" is entirely of a religious nature, consisting of several sorts of physical evidence: stone sculptures, clay seals and ritual apparatus, and a series of stone and copperplate inscriptions. The sculptures closely resemble Central

Javanese sculptures of the same era (both Hindu and Buddhist), while the clay seals contain Mahāyāna formulas duplicated in the eighth-century Javanese temple Candi Kalasan. However, it is important to note that these objects show no evidence of Javanese influence (whether conceptual or stylistic); they are obviously Indian and seem to have appeared in both Java and Bali at about the same time.

The first inscriptions appear in the ninth century CE and are the earliest written texts discovered in Bali. They were written by court scribes in two languages, Sanskrit and Old Balinese, using an Indian alphabet. Inscriptions in Sanskrit proclaim the military triumphs of Balinese rulers, and were addressed to the (Indic) world at large. They are not unique to Bali, for similar inscriptions are found throughout the western archipelago—monuments intended to validate the authority of rulers in the idiom of Indian theories of kingship. Such validation was essential because of the cosmological significance of kings, according to the Hindu and Buddhist medieval traditions. Inscriptions in Old Balinese, by contrast, were addressed very specifically to particular villages or monasteries, and they document the interest of the rulers in supporting a variety of Hindu and Buddhist sects. To explain the process of indianization in Bali, it is tempting to postulate the conversion of a powerful Balinese chief to some Hindu or Buddhist sect, who then zealously promoted the new faith among his subjects—except that the inscriptions clearly reveal patronage for a multitude of sects. No single group was given precedence; all were encouraged, suggesting that a ruler's enthusiasm for Indian ideas went deeper than the doctrinal differences that divide sect from sect. The texts specifically mention Tantric and Mahāyāna Buddhism, the major schools of Śaiva Siddhānta and Vaiṣṇava Hinduism, and the cults of Sūrya and Gaṇeśa. Early sculptures include *dhyāni* Buddhas, Padmapāṇi (Avalokiteśvara) and Amoghapāśa, Viṣṇu on Garuḍa, Viṣṇu as Narasiṃha, and Śiva in many forms including Ardhanāri, quadruplicated as the *catuḥkāyas*, and accompanied by Durgā, Gaṇeśa, and Guru.

Most of the 250 known inscriptions, which date from the ninth through the fourteenth century, direct the inhabitants of particular villages to provide various kinds of assistance to the monks and monasteries, including taxes, hospitality, labor, and military defense against sea raiders. Through the inscriptions we can trace the development of an intricate web of ties linking indianized courts and Hindu and Buddhist monasteries to the villages. As early as 1073 CE, a royal inscription describes the population as divided into the four castes of the Indian *varṇa* system (*brāhmaṇa, kṣatriya, vaiśya,* and *śūdra).* The inscription is significant not as proof that the Balinese had managed to magically re-create the Hindu caste system, but as evidence of the ruler's desire to impose the Indian ideal of caste on his kingdom.

In time, the Balinese came to identify their own sacred mountain, Gunung Agung, with the mythical Mount Meru, center of the "Middle World" of Indic cosmology. The old Balinese nature gods were perhaps not so much nudged aside as reincorporated into the new Indic pantheon. The great earth serpent Anantaboga was symbolically buried in the Balinese earth, his head beneath the crater lake of Batur near the island's center, his tail just touching the sea at Keramas. But the old gods were not entirely eclipsed. The most popular character of contemporary Balinese epics, and star of the shadow play *(wayang),* is the ancient buffoon Twalen, who usually plays the servant of the Hindu gods. Like the Balinese themselves, he is pleased to serve the splendid Hindu gods. But in reality, as everyone knows, Twalen is older and more powerful than all the Hindu gods. From time to time in the stories, when the gods have gone too far astray, he ceases to play the aging buffoon and reveals his true powers as "elder brother" to Siwa (Skt., Śiva), the supreme Hindu god.

Living Traditions. At some time between the fourteenth and nineteenth centuries, the monastic tradition of Bali came to an end, and the various competing sects of Hinduism and Buddhism fused into what is now perceived as a single religion, called Bali Hindu or, more accurately, Āgama Tīrtha, the Religion of Holy Water. There are, as of 1984, approximately two and a quarter million Balinese, the vast majority of whom adhere to this religion. Bali Hindu is officially sanctioned by the Indonesian government, which insists that all of its citizens belong to some recognized religion. Consequently, in recent years there has been some attempt to include tribal religions from other islands such as Sulawesi (Celebes) under the Bali-Hindu umbrella.

The ultimate source of religious knowledge for the Balinese remains ancient Hindu and Buddhist texts, some still written in Sanskrit, the majority in Kawi (Old Javanese) and Balinese. As in India, high priests are invariably brahmans who have studied this literature extensively. Various types of lesser priests are also recognized, belonging to the other castes, most of whom have made at least some study of the written sources for their religion. Some priests and healers do not go through a course of study but are instead "chosen by the gods" directly in trance rituals. Even these priests revere the palm leaf *lontar* manuscripts. All books, and the written word itself, are consecrated to the goddess of wisdom, Sarasvatī. She alone among the gods has no special shrines. Instead, on her festival day all books and libraries are given offerings for her, because they are her temples.

No one knows, as yet, how many manuscripts exist in Balinese libraries, but the number is certainly in the thousands. The entire literature of Classical Javanese, which eventually boasted over two hundred distinct metrical patterns and which flourished for a millennium, would have been lost to the world but for the painstaking efforts of generations of Balinese literati, who had to recopy the entire corpus onto fragile palm-leaf manuscripts about once each century. Western scholars have only begun to examine this vast and rich literary tradition.

In considering the significance of these texts for Balinese religion, it is important to pay attention to the ways in which they are read and used. The Balinese approach to the activity of reading, and the "life of texts in the world," is quite different from that of the modern West. Balinese "reading groups" *(sekehe bebaosan)*, for example, gather to read the ancient texts, either informally or to "embellish" a worthy gathering of people preparing for a ritual or temple festival. A reader intones a line from the text in its original language; if he strays from the correct metrical pattern, the line may have to be repeated. Then another reader will propose a spontaneous translation into modern colloquial Balinese. He pauses, in case anyone cares to suggest a better translation or a different interpretation. Once the meaning has been agreed upon, the first reader will recite the next line. The Balinese words for these "readings" are perhaps best rendered into English as "sounding" the texts, in both senses of turning letters into sounds, and searching for their meaning. "Sounding the texts" brings written order into the world, displaying the *logos* that lies behind mundane reality. Words themselves may have intrinsic power, as is hinted in the poem that begins "Homage to the god . . . who is the essence of written letters . . . concealed in the dust of the poet's pencil."

Ritual Life. It is possible to participate fully in Balinese religion all one's life without reading a single line from a *lontar* manuscript. Moreover, one is never called upon to make a public declaration of faith, either in a particular god or the efficacy of a particular ritual. Religion, for the Balinese, consists in the performance of five related ritual cycles, called *yajña*. Broadly speaking, the five *yajña* are sacrifices, and thus founded on ancient brahmanic theology. However, the details of the *yajña* are unique to Bali. The five *yajña* are

1. *déwa yajña* (sacrifices to the gods)
2. *būta yajña* (sacrifices to the chthonic powers or "elements")
3. *manuṣia yajña* (rites of passage)
4. *pitṛ yajña* (offerings to the dead)
5. *ṛṣi yajña* (consecration of priests)

Déwa yajña. Offerings to the gods *(déwa yajña)* are made in temples. The importance of these temples goes far beyond what we usually think of as religion, for temples provide the basic framework of Balinese economic and social organization. Classical Bali was a civilization without cities, in which important institutions such as irrigation networks, kinship groups, or periodic markets were organized by specialized temple networks. Most of these temple networks continue to function today. For example, consider the "irrigation" or "water temples." Each link in an irrigation system, from the small canal feeding one farmer's fields to the headwaters of a river, has a shrine or temple. The festivals held in these temples determine the schedule of "water openings" (flooding of the fields) for fields downstream. Later festivals mark the major events of the farmer's calendar: planting, transplanting, appearance of the milky grain (panicle), pest control, and so forth. The rituals of water temples synchronize farming activities for farmers using the same irrigation canals, and perhaps more important, allow higher-level temples to stagger cropping cycles to maximize production and minimize pest damage.

In similar ways, the Balinese version of a Hindu caste system was organized through temple networks—to belong to a caste translated into participating in the festivals of "caste temples," from the family shrine for the ancestors, through regional caste "branch temples," to the "origin temples" for whole castes or subcastes. Each Balinese temple has a specific purpose—it is part of an institutional system—and draws its membership exclusively from members of that institution. A Balinese worships only in the temples of the institutions he belongs to, which usually amount to half a dozen or more, including village temples, kinship or caste temples, water temples, and perhaps others as well.

Physically, Balinese temples consist of open rectangular walled courtyards with a row of shrines at one end. This architectural plan owes more to ancient Malayo-Polynesian megalithic shrines than to Indian temple design. Within the temple, space is ordered along a continuum, also Malayo-Polynesian in origin:

seaward ⟷ mountainward (toward the center of Bali)
downstream ⟷ upstream
profane ⟷ sacred
chthonic ⟷ ouranic

The gods are not believed to be continuously present in

the temples but to arrive for only a few days each year as invited guests to temple festivities.

Members of the congregation prepare the temple and bring offerings for the gods, "not merely a fruit and a flower," as Margaret Mead observed, "but hundreds of finely wrought and elaborately conceived offerings made of palm leaf and flowers, twisted, folded, stitched, embroidered, brocaded into myriad traditional forms and fancies" (Belo, 1970, p. 335). Priests invite the gods to descend into their shrines with incense, bells, and prayers in Sanskrit. Worshipers kneel and pray for a few seconds, flicking flower petals toward the shrines of the gods, and are rewarded with a blessing of holy water from a temple priest. The remainder of the festival, which may last for days, is occupied with artistic performances for the amusement both of the gods and the human congregation. It was these performances that led Noel Coward to complain that "It seems that each Balinese native / From the womb to the tomb is creative." Temple festivals adhere to rigid schedules, based on the extremely complex Balinese permutational calendar. The gods must appear on a particular day, and at a given moment they must depart. Since the gods partake only of the essence of their offerings, the end of a temple festival is the beginning of a feast, for each family retrieves its offerings and shares the edible portions with friends and clients.

Būta yajña. Būta, usually translated into English as "demon," actually is the Balinese version of the Sanskrit word for "element of nature" *(bhūta).* It is therefore an oversimplification to describe the rituals of *būta yajña* as "demon offerings." Every important ritual, such as a temple festival, begins with *būta yajña* offerings as a purification or cleansing. Usually, these offerings require some form of blood sacrifice to satisfy the raw appetites of the elemental powers. All Balinese "demons" may take form either in the outer worlds *(buana agung)* or the inner world of the self *(buana alit).* A strong Tantric element in Balinese religion suggests that demons are essentially psychological projections but differs from Western psychology in insisting that "demonic" forces are part of the intrinsic constitution of both inner and outer reality.

Demons *(būta)* are the raw elements from which the higher realities of consciousness and the world are created. If their energy is not contained, they quickly become destructive. The purpose of *būta yajña* may be made clearer by considering the supreme *būta yajña* ceremony, called Eka Dasa Rudra, last held in 1979. The year 1979 marked the beginning of a new century according to the Balinese Icaka calendar. In order for the new century to begin auspiciously, it was felt necessary to complete all unfinished *būta* rituals, such as cremations, and then hold a gigantic ceremony at Bali's supreme temple, Besakih, to transform all of the accumulated demonic energies of the prior century into divine energies, to begin a new cycle of civilization in a phase of growth rather than decline. Nearly all Balinese participated in the yearlong preparations for Eka Dasa Rudra, which climaxed at the moment the old century ended, in a ceremony at Besakih temple involving over one hundred thousand people.

Manuṣia yajña. *Manuṣia yajña* are rites of passage, fitted to the Balinese belief in reincarnation. Twelve days after birth, an infant is given a name, and offerings are made to the four birth spirits *(kanda empat)* who have accompanied him. After three 35-day months, the child and his spirits are given new names, and the child's feet are allowed to touch the earth for the first time, since before this time he is considered still too close to the world of the gods. More offerings are made for the child's 210-day "birthday," at puberty, and finally in the climactic ceremony of tooth filing, which prepares the child for adulthood. The six upper canine teeth and incisors are filed slightly to make them more even, symbolically reducing the six human vices of lust *(kāma),* anger *(krodha),* greed *(lobha),* error *(moha),* intoxication *(mada),* and jealousy *(matsarya).* The *manuṣia yajña* cycle ends with the performance of the marriage ceremony.

Pitṛ yajña. These rituals are the inverse of *manuṣia yajña:* they are the rituals of death and return to the world of the gods, performed by children for their parents. The Balinese believe that people are usually reincarnated into their own families—in effect, as their own descendants—after five or more generations. The rituals of preparing the corpse, preliminary burial, cremation, and purification of the soul ensure that the spirits of one's parents are freed from earthly attachments, are able to enter heaven, and eventually are able to seek rebirth. Cremation is regarded as a major responsibility, costly and emotionally charged since the cremation bier proclaims both the wealth and the caste status of the family of the deceased. After these rituals are completed, the souls of the departed are believed to begin to visit their family shrines, where they must receive regular offerings, so the *pitṛ yajña* ritual cycle is never really finished.

Ṛṣi yajña. While the other four *yajña* involve everyone, the ceremonies of the consecration of priests *yajña)* are the exclusive and esoteric provenance of the various priesthoods. In general, each "caste" has its own priests, although "high priests" *(pedanda)* are invariably brahmans. Buddhist traditions are kept alive by a special sect of high priests called *pedanda bodha*. The greatest of the *ṛṣi yajña* is the ceremony of consecration for a new *pedanda,* during which he must symbolically undergo his own funeral as a human being, to reemerge as a very special kind of being, a Balinese high priest.

[*See also* Southeast Asian Religions, *article on* Insular Cultures.]

BIBLIOGRAPHY

The most influential modern scholar of Balinese religion is Clifford Geertz. Several of his important essays are collected in *The Interpretation of Cultures* (New York, 1973), and his analysis of cosmology and kingship is presented in *Negara: The Theatre State in Nineteenth-Century Bali* (Princeton, 1980). Translations of Balinese texts on religions are provided in the many publications of Christiaan Hooykaas, including *Cosmogony and Creation in Balinese Tradition* (The Hague, 1974) and *Surya-Sevana: The Way to God of a Balinese Siva Priest* (Amsterdam, 1966). Many important essays from the 1930s by scholars such as Margaret Mead and Gregory Bateson are collected in *Traditional Balinese Culture,* edited by Jane Belo (New York, 1970). Belo also provides excellent descriptive accounts in *Bali: Temple Festival* (Locust Valley, N.Y., 1953) and *Trance in Bali* (New York, 1960). Opposing theories on the "indianization" of Bali are presented in J. C. van Leur's *Indonesian Trade and Society: Essays in Asian Social and Economic History* (The Hague, 1955) and in R. C. Majumdar's *Ancient Indian Colonization in South-East Asia* (Calcutta, 1963). Rites of passage are nicely evoked in Katherine Edson Mershon's *Seven Plus Seven: Mysterious Life-Rituals in Bali* (New York, 1971). Many important articles by Dutch scholars of the colonial era have been translated into English in *Bali: Studies in Life, Thought, and Ritual* (The Hague, 1960) and a second volume entitled *Bali: Further Studies in Life, Thought, and Ritual* (The Hague, 1969), both edited by J. L. Swellengrebel.

One of the most delightful books describing the relationship of the performing arts to religion is Beryl de Zoete and Walter Spies's *Dance and Drama in Bali* (1938; reprint, Oxford, 1973). A worthy successor is I. M. Bandem and Frederick De Boer's *Kaja and Kelod: Balinese Dance in Transition* (Oxford, 1981). Urs Ramseyer's survey of *The Art and Culture of Bali* (Oxford, 1977) is a beautifully illustrated encyclopedia of Balinese religious art by a Swiss anthropologist. My *Three Worlds of Bali* (New York, 1983) provides an introduction to the role of religion and art in shaping the evolution of Balinese society.

J. STEPHEN LANSING

BALTIC RELIGION. Latvians, Lithuanians, and Old Prussians constitute the Baltic language and cultural unit. The Old Prussians, who lived in the territory of the present-day German Democratic Republic, were conquered during the period of eastward German expansionism, from the ninth to the eleventh century. They were assimilated progressively and disappeared completely in the seventeenth century. Latvians and Lithuanians have preserved their national identities to this day. At one time or another since the Crusades of the eleventh century, all these peoples have been subject to German, Polish, Russian, and Swedish colonization. This fact is of special significance since it has affected our understanding of the elements of the ancient religious systems that have been preserved. As colonies, the three national groups were subject to extensive political and economic exploitation. Although formally christianized, they continued their traditional ways of religious life despite colonial restrictions.

The Baltic peoples have inhabited their present territory from the middle of the second millennium BCE. At that time, however, their territory extended farther east, to Moscow, and southwest, across the banks of the Vistula. Living on the fringe of eastern Europe, they were virtually unknown to the West, and thus were able to remain relatively untouched by the influence of Christianity up to the seventeenth century. As early as the first millennium BCE, these isolated peoples, untouched by foreign developments, had developed from a hunting and fishing culture to an agrarian one. The structure of agrarian society and its routine determined the development of the belief system and the structure of cultic life.

The Baltic peoples came to the attention of European linguists at the end of the eighteenth century. These linguists were especially interested in the Vedic language of ancient India and its literature. In their attempt to build a bridge to the living European languages, they discovered that the closest European affinity to the Vedic language, both etymologically and to some extent lexically, existed with the Baltic language group, especially Lithuanian. (Contemporary comparative linguists such as Alois Walde, Julius Pakorny, Antoine Meillet, and Hans Krahe have devoted particular attention to the Baltic languages.) Interest in the languages generated interest in the ethnogenesis of the Baltic peoples. This subject fascinated scholars as late as the nineteenth century. It became apparent that the geographic isolation of these peoples had not only allowed but had furthered an unhindered and uninterrupted development free from external influence. But their rather late appearance in the European arena and their previous isolation have fostered a great deal of guesswork about their linguistic and ethnic origins and kinships. Up to recent times there has been great confusion on this subject. The Baltic languages were usually classified as Slavic, although linguists (e.g., Jānis Endzelīns, Wolfgang Schmid, and Vladimir Toporov) had long known that they are no more closely related to the Slavic language group than to the Germanic. That the Baltic languages are related to both Slavic and Germanic language groups can be explained by their common Indo-European base.

Any investigation of the Baltic religion must touch upon the central problem of sources, of which there are three types: archaeological evidence, folklore, and historical documents. The archaeological evidence can easily be surveyed since these peoples have always lived in the same region. Excavations have unearthed artifacts from the second millennium BCE that present a clear picture of material culture, but not of religious life. There is no evidence of gods and their cults. The burial rites and belief systems connected with these rites have been carefully researched by such scholars as Marija Gimbutas and Francis Balodis. Evidence from historical documents is meager. The earliest documents are from the tenth century, when Germans and Danes attacked the eastern shore of the Baltic Sea. There is mention of contact with the Balts but little further information. The situation remained almost unchanged up to the beginning of the seventeenth century, when more elaborate descriptions were written by leading clergymen—Paul Einhorn and certain Jesuit fathers, for example.

Despite the dearth of archaeological evidence and historical documentation, the folklore materials of these peoples is one of the richest in all of Europe. Songs *(dainas)*, stories, tales, proverbs, and beliefs have been recorded. [*See* Dainas.] The diversity of these sources has, however, proved to be a stumbling block, because each type of source has required a particular investigatory method. As a result, objective investigation of Baltic religion was slow to come. At first, there was a tendency to approach the topic ideologically, from both Marxist and Christian points of view; then, during the period of national awakening in the latter half of the nineteenth century, came a tendency to create pseudogods, figments of imagination, and an attempt to raise the national consciousness of the former colonial nations by finding "precedents" in the primary ethnic tradition. Scholarship in recent years (e.g., that of Jonas Balys, Marija Gimbutas, Liene Neulande, and myself) has become more scientifically accurate.

The Sky Gods. Of all the Baltic gods in heaven the most prominent is Dievs. Linguists agree that etymologically the Latvian name *Dievs* (Lith., *Dievas*; OPrus., *Deivas*) is derived from names such as the ancient Indian *Dyaus* and the Greek *Zeus*, which are in turn derived from the Indo-European root **dyeu-* and its derivatives. The meaning of words derived from this root is "the heavens." Older scholarship sought to establish a semantic connection between this root and the daytime sky or light, but this contention lacks proof, and one must therefore assume that the meaning "the heavens" is more precise, as Grace Hopkins (1932) has argued. The original identity of Dievs then becomes clearer from his name. The nature of, and the psychological motives behind, the god's development from a phenomenon of nature to a personification and, later, to a personal god is, however, a source of contention. Despite these uncertainties, it is clear that Dievs is closely connected with the heavens.

Cardinal Valenti in 1604 provided the oldest evidence that the Balts worshiped a god of heaven: "Credono un Dio Supremo, che chiamano Tebo Deves" ("They believe in a high god, called Tebo Deves"). *Tebo Deves* is a corrupted form of *debess dievs* ("sky god"). That same year the Jesuit father Jānis Stribiņš, in his discussion of ancient Latvian religion, noted that the Balts claim "Habemus Deum q[ui] habetet [*sic*] curam coeli" ("We have a god, who in the sky takes care"). Though these documents offer only fragmentary evidence, they do show that the Balts worshiped a god of heaven (Dievs). Folklore materials, which allow one to delve deeper into the essence, function, and attributes of this god, support the claim.

The anthropomorphic character of Dievs has been carefully described and compared to that of other divinities. He is clad in a silver overcoat, gray jacket, and hat. He is girded with a decorated belt and wears mittens. In certain situations he also has a sword, but this is probably a later development. His dress resembles that of a prosperous farmer.

That Dievs has his abode in the heavens is self-evident from his name. The heavens resemble a mountain, and this mountain is his farm. Herein lies one of the peculiarities of Baltic religion. The gods are closely associated with horses, and horses have a special significance in the activities of Dievs: he appears as a horseman and often rides in a chariot down the mountain. It appears that in this association with horses the motifs of very ancient Indo-European myths have been preserved.

The homestead of Dievs consists of several buildings. In addition to the house there are stalls and barns for horses and cows, a threshing barn for drying grain, a storage room, and a sauna. The sources make no mention of castles, which are very common in other religions. From the configuration of the homestead one can conclude that Dievs oversees a large farmstead: the buildings are encircled by large fields, meadows, and forests. Dievs needs the help of the members of his own family, especially his sons, the number of whom varies, to work this farm, but others participate in the labors as well, plowing, harrowing, planting, and reaping the grain and hay. Special attention is devoted to the cultivation of hops and barley, from which beer is brewed. (Beer, the "drink of the gods," is the traditional drink of Baltic sacral feasts.) The inhabitants of the heavenly mountain not only work together, they celebrate feasts, especially marriages, together, and they gather together in the sauna.

Indo-European creator gods are usually so mighty and distant that they retreat to a realm removed from men and turn into a type of god referred to as *deus otiosus* ("god at leisure"). Other gods, whose function is to monitor the daily lives of humans, take their place. This is not, however, the case in the religion of the Balts. Instead, the Baltic gods follow an agricultural way of life that corresponds to that of the Baltic farmer. And this is not only a formal analogy. Dievs, who dwells in heaven, is a neighbor of the farmer on earth. At times of the most important decisions, the farmer meets and consults with Dievs, just as farmers meet and consult among themselves. Dievs rides down on a horse or, more frequently, in his chariot. These visitations coincide with key events in the agricultural calendar.

Dievs usually appears in the spring, at the beginning of the agricultural year. His participation in planting is described in beautiful myths. He accompanies the farmer and advises him so that the field will be evenly sown. When the horses are led out to the first nightwatch, he accompanies the farmer, accepts his due in the sacral feast, and spends the entire night with the farmer, tending the fire and protecting the horses. In many of the planting myths, Dievs leaves the night watchers after sunrise but forgets his mittens. Dievs has an even more significant role in the fall, after the harvest and threshing. Once again a sacral meal is shared and Dievs participates in ecstatic song and dance. At these times the boundary between the transcendental god and the earthbound farmer becomes blurred.

From time to time, Indo-European gods display universal qualities, which are revealed in creation stories and in myths describing the establishment of the world order, including individual and societal norms of morality. The role of Dievs as creator is expressed in the words *laist* ("to give birth to"), *likt* ("to determine fate"), and *dot* ("to provide for"), all of which are words that describe his function. Everything is the creation of Dievs and corresponds to this threefold activity. The act of creation is final and unalterable, and the same is true of the world order. Man is subject to the laws of nature as they were ordained in the act of creation. Dievs, therefore, in his function as creator, is almighty. Man is subject to fate, especially in the realm of morality, but this does not lead to resignation and quietism, although such moods exist as undeniable undercurrents in Baltic religion. Man accepts the moral laws of the universe as set down by Dievs as a framework for his life. Within this framework, however, he is free to determine and order his life in concordance with his moral outlook and practical needs; therefore, he experiences freedom of choice and assumes responsibility for his actions. His morality is practically determined: he must do all to further his well-being, and "the good" is whatever aids him in achieving this goal.

The cult of Dievs is not so formalized as are the cults of gods of heaven in other religions. As we have seen, Dievs actively participates at the most important junctures in the life of the farmer. He even shares in the sacrificial feasts, but there is no evidence that goods were sacrificed to him in order to ensure his benevolence. That can be concluded only indirectly. One can best describe the nature and function of Dievs metaphorically: he is the neighbor of the farmer, the grand farmer living on the mount of heaven.

A second important god of heaven is Saule, the personification of the sun. This name is also derived from an Indo-European root (*sauel-*, and variants). Unlike personifications of the sun in other traditions, Saule is a female deity. The Balts seem to have borrowed this concept from the Vedic tradition of Sūryā, the feminine counterpart to the masculine sun god, although proof for this contention is not conclusive. There could be other explanations for the feminine gender of Saule. She dwells together with the moon god Mēness, who is masculine and who requires a feminine counterpart. In certain situations she is also referred to as Saules Māte ("mother sun") and as Saules Meita ("daughter of the sun").

Descriptions of Saule's appearance are incomplete. A white shawl and one or more silver brooches, which secure the shawl, are mentioned in the sources. Occasionally she wears a wreath. Otherwise she appears in peasant dress. If the texts are vague about Saule's appearance, they do provide insight into her life both on the mount of heaven and in the midst of the farmers during their labors and festivals. She is the personification of gaiety, especially at the betrothal of her daughters, when all the gods of heaven join in her rejoicing. But there are also times of discord. Conflicts with the farmer arise as a result of harm done by the Dieva Dēli ("sons of god") to the Saules Meitas ("daughters of the sun") during play. The most frequent cause of this discord is the destruction of the latter's playthings. More serious conflicts arise between Saule and Dievs when the Dieva Dēli remove the rings of the Saules Meitas. This is part of an ancient betrothal tradition, during which the girl is abducted. Then for three days Saule and Dievs accuse one another of wrongdoing. Saule also has conflicts with other gods of heaven, especially Pērkons ("thunder"). [*See* Pērkons.] She lives the life of an ordinary landlady and oversees her daughters' spinning and weaving, but after her linen has been put in the sun to dry, Pērkons comes and ruins the work with rain, and so Saule has good reason to be angry. Apart from these minor conflicts, harmony reigns on the mount of heaven. Saule provides sunlight and brightness for the others. The gods' harmony in the common labors, in love, and in gaiety can easily be compared to that of the Olympian gods.

Saule and Dievs are neighbors, and both oversee their farmsteads. Saule also has her own horses; in this she is similar to Apollo, who is depicted in frescoes with his chariot and four horses. Sometimes she rides across the sky in her chariot; she also crosses the sea in a boat. The steersman and oarsmen are her servants. She begins her ride in the boat early in the morning, at dawn, and finishes it in the evening, at sundown, when the oars are thrown into the boat and the passengers disembark. At times, however, Saule begins her boat ride in the evening, and rides in the night unseen. This latter myth gives rise to the question of the Baltic conception of the form of the universe. As we have seen, the heavens have the form of a mountain. They are subject to the same laws of nature as the earth is, but only gods may dwell there. The belief that Saule travels by boat as well as by chariot indicates some kind of connection between the sea and the heavens.

The Balts do not appear to be overly concerned about the composition of the world, or at least no trustworthy record of such speculation has been found. The universe, however, is assigned two levels: the heavens and the earth. This becomes evident when one looks closely at several word forms. The word for "world" is *pasaule,* a compound form consisting of *pa* and *saule. Saule,* the substantive, means "the sun"; with the prefix *pa* it means "below the sun." Thus *pasaule* means "everything that is under the sun." The adjectival form is *pasaulīgs,* meaning "profane," or "not sacred." A synonym for *pasaule* is *šīsaule,* a compound that is formed with the demonstrative pronoun *šī* and means "all that can be seen in sunlight." The antithesis of *šīsaule* is *viņasaule,* a compound that is formed with the demonstrative pronoun *viņa* and implies all that is still in the realm of the sun but cannot be seen.

This dualistic worldview is at the base of Baltic religion. The tradition concerning Saule's traveling developed further and is crucial to the Baltic understanding of death. Saule travels by chariot or by boat in the visible world during the day but in the invisible one at night. Similarly, the dead continue to live a life in the invisible world, just as the sun does at night. The land of the dead is located just beyond the horizon, in the place where the sun sets.

In addition to the concepts of the mountain of heaven and the dualistic cosmos there is in the Baltic myths a *saules koks* ("tree of the sun"). It grows on the mount of heaven and is often referred to as an oak, a linden, or an apple tree. The difference between this tree and common trees on earth is symbolized by its gold or silver color. No mortal has ever seen this tree, although many youths have set out to search for it, only to return unsuccessfully in old age. A magical round object, often compared to a pea or an apple, rolls down its branches. The *saules koks* on the mount of heaven is one of the oldest elements of Baltic religion. It seems that this tree is the "center of the world," as Mircea Eliade has pointed out, but it also is the "tree of life." Whether the latter idea developed under the influence of Christianity is hard to determine. It certainly could stem from an older tradition in which Saule is the mother and source of life.

A cult surrounding Saule is not fully described in the sources. A few strands of tradition suggest her begetting and nurturing role. Similar to Dievs, she too comes down from the mountain to aid the farmer: she raises her skirt and inspects his fields. This tradition has caused some scholars to speculate about the existence of a belief that the baring of sexual organs improved fertility. The texts, however, provide inconclusive evidence. Saule could also have raised her skirt to avoid breaking or flattening the stalks. She does, at any rate, promote fertility. The result of her walk across the field is wholesome grain and a plentiful harvest.

The most significant element of the cult of Saule is the celebration of the summer solstice, in which everyone on the farmstead takes part. After the setting of the sun a fire is lit in a bucket and raised on top of a pole. A feast and dancing around the fire follow, and special songs of praise are sung. The major components of the feast are cheese and newly brewed beer. At this time shepherds become the center of attention. This has led August Bielenstein, a prominent linguist and ethnologist, to conclude that the summer solstice festival began as a celebration commemorating the breeding of livestock. The origin of this festival is obscure, but today it is a celebration of the sun. The feast continues through the entire night, lasting until dawn. Those who retire early are believed to be subject to evils and to encounter failure in the next year. This celebration of the sun is a fertility rite of sorts. The authors of Christian chronicles were especially critical of it, accusing celebrants of sexual excesses. Indeed, promiscuity is allowed during the festival and at times even encouraged. A sexual act performed in a field was believed to improve the field's fertility.

Mēness, the moon god, is also among the gods of heaven. The Latvian word for "moon," *mēness* (Lith., *menulis;* OPrus., *menins*), derives from the Indo-European root **me-*, meaning "a measure of time." The measure of time was an apt designation for Mēness, who periodically disappears from the sky and then reappears in it once again. No substantial evidence in Baltic sources proves that Mēness was originally a feminine deity. As a full-standing member of the mount of heaven, he, too, has his own farmstead there, along with his family, sons, servants, and horses. His horses are represented by the morning and evening stars. Like Saule, Mēness travels through the sky by boat and at times even accompanies her. He has close ties to Saule: he is her untiring suitor.

In other religions the moon has a special connection with water and fertility, but this is not true in Baltic religion. Instead, Mēness is the god of war, and the stars are his troops, which, like a true general, he counts and leads. These metaphors reveal Mēness's true function: he is worshiped before battle, and his symbol appears in insignia of war. Although Mēness is frequently mentioned in the sources, his cult, like that of the other gods, is not fully described. Only sparse evidence of it remains, and none proves that offerings were made to him. The cult disappeared completely during the period of christianization.

The two groups identified in Latvian as Dieva Dēli ("sons of god") and Saules Meitas ("daughters of the sun") are among the most interesting of the Baltic gods of heaven. As early as 1875, Wilhelm Mannhardt observed:

> Already Welcker and Preller have pointed to the close similarity between the Greek Dioscuri and the Indian Aśvins. The analogy is even closer with the Latvian *Dieva dēli* found in the sun songs. The Aśvins are sons of Dyaus, heaven, *divo napāta*. . . . One can easily conclude from the Vedic texts that they are personifications of the morning and evening stars, which never appear at the same time.
>
> (Mannhardt, 1875; my trans.)

Although this contention was based on scanty evidence in Mannhardt's time, additional evidence has since been gathered and analyzed. As a result, it can be shown that the Vedic Divo Napāta (i.e., the Aśvins), the Greek Dioskouroi (i.e., the Dioscuri), and the Baltic Dieva Dēli are not only typologically parallel but are also historically connected. They differ only inasmuch as they developed in different cultural settings.

A closer comparison reveals some more unusual parallels. While the discussion about the nature and function of the Vedic and Greek "sons of god" continues to the present day, the Baltic materials provide a clear answer: the Dieva Dēli are the morning and evening stars. Whereas the Vedic and Greek gods represent hypostases of the differentiated functions or traits of the primary gods, this is not true of the Baltic gods. Rather, their social background is stressed, and their functions are expressed in terms of family relationships. Like the Aśvins, the Baltic "sons of god" or "sons of heaven," the Dieva Dēli, are the suitors of the "daughters of the sun," the Saules Meitas, and are their active marriage partners. There is no evidence, however, to prove that the Dieva Dēli are twins, as are the Aśvins.

Just as the function of Dievs is transferred to his sons, so is the function of Saule transferred to her daughters. The Vedic Divo Duhitā ("daughter of heaven"), Sūryasya Duhitā ("daughter of the sun"), and the goddess Sūryā (the feminine aspect of the sun), like the Greek Helen (a daughter of Zeus), and Phoebe and Hilaeria (the Leucippides, daughters of Leucippus), correspond to the Baltic Saules Meitas, although scholars still disagree about their original connection. The designation *Saules meitas* is not original, since *meita* is a rather late loanword from German. The most ancient designation, meaning "daughter of heaven," has been preserved in Lithuanian, *dieva dukryte.* This designation might refer to dawn, as do the names of the Vedic goddess Uṣas and the Greek goddess Ēōs.

Heavenly nuptials are central to Baltic myths about heaven. Dievs, Mēness, or Pērkons may be the bridegroom, and Saule is the bride. For linguistic reasons, in some contexts it is hard to determine who participates in the marriage, Saule or her daughter, for Saule is regarded as a maiden and is sometimes referred to as Saules Meita. However, this circumstance does not alter the marriage procedure. A peculiarity of the event is that all the gods take part, each performing his or her specific role, which can be traced to ancient Baltic marriage traditions. The abduction and auctioning of the bride is an integral part of the ritual. The ceremony concludes with a feast of song and dance on the mount of heaven. Scholars have observed that these elements establish a connection with an old stratum of Indo-European marriage traditions.

The most unusual part of the marriage ceremony is the gathering of the gods in the sauna, which, as mentioned above, is a part of the heavenly farmstead. (Baltic ethnographic traditions reveal that the sauna was a place not only for washing but also for birthing and for sacral feasting. The Baltic sauna had the same status as a holy place or precinct, like a church in the Christian tradition.) Folklore materials reveal the procedure by which gods prepare the sauna: a fire is lit, special birch whisks are brought in, and water is drawn. The gods split up these chores, with lesser gods performing special tasks. The gathering of gods has special significance, since this is not just an occasion for bathing but also the preparation for a wedding. Special attention is paid to the Saules Meitas, who await the Dieva Dēli, their suitors. In the sauna the most fitting partner is chosen. All the gods are guests in the sauna, not owners of it. The matron of the sauna, Pirts Māte ("sauna mother"), is the hostess. Latvian peasants have traditionally prepared offerings to her to guarantee her benevolence at the time of birthing. After the visit to the sauna, members of the farmstead left a whisk and a vessel with clean water so that Pirts Māte could also bathe.

The gods of heaven described above correspond roughly to other Indo-European gods. They are especially similar to the Vedic and Greek gods, but they also have some unique qualities and functions that developed in the Baltic social structure. The primitive world of the Baltic farmer is reflected in the conceptions and functions of his gods.

Gods of Prosperity and Welfare. As one can see from an analysis of the essence and function of the Baltic gods, it is clear that they were an integral part of the daily life cycle. This is especially true of a particular group of gods whose special function was to protect and guarantee the welfare of humans. These gods can be subdivided into two groups: fertility gods and determiners of fate. The most prominent of the second group is Laima, whose name means "fortune." She occupies a central place among the Baltic gods, but unlike the gods of heaven, she is not removed from the realm of human activity; she lives on earth and is involved in the minutest details of everyday life. [*See* Laima.] Kārta, another goddess of fate, fulfills similar functions and has evolved into an independent hypostasis. Her name, derived from the verb *kārt* ("to hang"), is proof of this. Laima's most basic function is to determine and fix the birth of a child, which involved hanging a cradle, as ethnographic traditions show. From this function developed an independent goddess, Kārta, and with her an entire cult. Under the influence of the Christian church her function was assumed by Saint Thecla (Latv., Dēkla).

The major fertility goddess is Zeme (Lith., Žemýna), a very different type of goddess. [*See* Zeme.] Her name means "earth," and she is commonly referred to as Zemēs Māte ("earth mother, mother of the earth"). She plays a variety of roles that, over time, have developed into independent hypostases; tradition has it that she has seventy sisters. Some of them have very special functions, indicated by their descriptive names: *Dārzu māte* ("mother of the garden"), *Lauku māte* ("mother of the fields"), *Meža māte* ("mother of the forest"), and *Linu māte* ("mother of flax"). These descriptive names point to a specific place or plant that is under each mother's protection. The same is true of *Lazdu māte* ("mother of the hazel"), *Sēņu māte* ("mother of mushrooms"), and *Briežu māte* ("mother of elk"). The role of each particular mother is expanded: they are transformed from purely fertility goddesses to protectors in general, as indicated by such names as *Pirts māte* ("mother of the sauna"), *Uguns māte* ("mother of fire"), and *Pieguļas māte* ("mother of the night watch"). Morphologically related are the goddesses designated as *Nāves māte* ("mother of death"), *Kapu māte* ("mother of the grave"), *Smilšu māte* ("mother of sand"), and *Veļu māte* ("mother of the dead"). In many names the word *māte* is used to mean not only "mother" but also "goddess," as in, for example, the names *Saules māte* and *Laimas māte,* designating the mother goddess of the sun and the mother goddess of fortune.

The question of the character and role of these mothers has not been adequately investigated. Two schools of thought are current. One maintains that the development of the mothers is a thoroughly Baltic phenomenon; the other (upheld by Jonas Balys) maintains that it occurred under the influence of the cult of the Virgin Mary. If the mothers are judged by their functions, it must be concluded that they are closely connected with the annual agricultural cycle and that as guarantors of fertility in the fields and for livestock they are an outgrowth of the Christian church. It must be noted, however, that many of the mothers—among them, those designated as *Vēja māte* ("mother of the wind"), *Ziedu māte* ("mother of blossoms"), and *Dzīparu māte* ("mother of colored wool")—are the products of poetic fantasy. These lack any cult and are the products of mythopoetic processes.

The annual reports of the Society of Jesus contain many references to pagan traditions among the Balts against which the Jesuits waged war. One such report from the beginning of the seventeenth century mentions Ceroklis, a god whose name is derived from the verb *cerot,* meaning "to sprout several stalks [*ceri*] from one seed or root." This name, suggestive of grains such as rye and wheat, implies a bountiful harvest. One must assume that from this natural process the god Ceroklis, a fertility god, developed.

A special fertility god is Jumis. The etymological connection between his name and the Vedic stem is not clear. The name could be related to *yama* ("pair, twins") or to *yuti* ("conjunction, connection"). But the differences overshadow the connections between these terms. In Baltic religion the meaning of the word *jumis* is clear: two ears of grain, stalks of flax, or vines or branches bearing fruit that have grown together. Therefore the god with this name is the one who brings a double dose of fertility. After reaping, the final sheaf is completed and designated as Jumis, the god of fertility of the field. If the final sheaf is not reaped, the uncut ears of grain are bound or weighed down by a rock. Whether the sheaf is cut or not, the basic rationale is the same: the sign of fertility is left intact in the field. With this sign thanks are expressed and the next year's grain harvest is guaranteed. Jumis is believed to remain in the field and to hibernate below the sod or underneath a rock. Around him an entire cultic ritual has developed. The abandoning of Jumis in the field is accompanied by song and dance, a cultic feast, and offerings, which continue inside the house when the reapers return home. The final sheaf may also be brought home, and Jumis can be put to rest either in the granary or in the form of a wreath in a central place within the living quarters. The grain of this wreath is mixed with the grain to be planted in the spring. Jumis has many of the same functions as the fertility gods of other religions, and his rituals resemble theirs.

It can be concluded that Baltic religion has two major conceptions of gods. One concerns the gods of heaven and their various functions. They are personifications and deifications of certain processes of nature, but they are also determined by the social structure of the farmstead and the daily life of the farmer. The farmer acquires the foundation for all of his life from the sky god Dievs. The other concept is closely connected with the life cycle and welfare of the individual. The gods associated with this concept determine the fate of humans from birth to death. This aspect is very practically determined: humans regard the gods as their equals, as beings with whom they can discuss problems but whom they can also censure. Nevertheless a total equality is never developed, since humans remain dependent on the gods. The gods do what humans cannot. For this reason the gods become universalized, and moral qualities are attributed to them. At the center of this religious moral system is the idea of the good, described in terms of the social context on a cosmic level.

[*See also* Indo-European Religions, *and, more particularly,* Germanic Religion *and* Slavic Religion.]

BIBLIOGRAPHY

Adamovičs, Ludvigs. "Senlatviešu reliģija." In *Vēstures atziņas un tēlojumi*, pp. 45–115. Riga, 1937. A concise survey of the main traits of Baltic gods but without an analysis of sources.

Bertuleit, Hans. "Das Religionswesen der alten Preussen mit litauisch-lettischen Parallen." *Prussia* 25 (1924).

Biezais, Haralds. *Die Religionsquellen der baltischen Völker und die Ergebnisse der bisherigen Forschungen*. Uppsala, 1954. An annotated bibliography of sources and studies through 1953.

Biezais, Haralds. *Die Hauptgöttinnen der alten Letten*. Uppsala, 1955.

Biezais, Haralds. *Die Gottesgestalt der lettischen Volksreligion*. Uppsala, 1961.

Biezais, Haralds. "Baltische Religion." In *Germanische und baltische Religion*, edited by Åke Ström and Haralds Biezais, pp. 307–391. Stuttgart, 1965.

Biezais, Haralds. *Die himmlische Götterfamilie der alten Letten*. Uppsala, 1972.

Biezais, Haralds. *Lichtgott der alten Letten*. Uppsala, 1976. My works listed here are the only up-to-date surveys of Baltic religion based on critical analyses of the sources.

Bratiņš, Ernests. *Latvju dievadziesmas*. 2d ed. Würzburg, 1947. A selected collection of *dainas* (songs) concerning the sky god Dievs.

Clemen, Carl C., ed. *Fontes historiae religionum primitivarum, praeindogermanicum, indogermanicum minus notarum*. Bonn, 1936. A collection of selected Greek and Roman sources.

Gimbutas, Marija. *The Balts*. London, 1963. See pages 179–204 for a short, popular survey of Baltic religion.

Hopkins, Grace. *Indo-European *Deiwos and Related Words*. Philadelphia, 1932. A valuable etymological and semantic study of names of Indo-European sky gods.

Ivinskis, Zenonas. *Senoves lietuvių religijos bibliografija*. Kaunas, 1938. The best complete bibliography of Baltic religion up to 1938.

Johansons, Andrejs. *Der Schirmherr des Hofes im Volksglauben der Letten*. Stockholm, 1964. Valuable as a collection of material, but the speculative construction of "house god" is false.

Mannhardt, Wilhelm. "Die lettischen Sonnenmythen." *Zeitschrift für Ethnologie* 7 (1875): 73–330. Out of date but still important as a standard study of solar mythology.

Mannhardt, Wilhelm. *Letto-preussische Götterlehre*. Riga, 1936. The best sourcebook on Baltic religion.

Neuland, Lena. *Jumis die Fruchtbarkeitsgottheit der alten Letten*. Stockholm, 1977. A basic study of the fertility cult with extensive analyses of sources and bibliography.

Pisani, Vittore. *Le religioni dei Celti e dei Balto-Slavi nell'Europa precristiana*. Milan, 1950. A brief comparative survey marred by linguistic shortcomings.

Zicāns, Eduards. "Die Hochzeit der Sonne und des Mondes in der lettischen Mythologie." *Studia Theologica* 1 (1935): 171–200. Important as a supplement to Wilhelm Mannhardt's solar mythology.

HARALDS BIEZAIS

BALUBA. *See* Luba Religion.

BAMBARA RELIGION. The Bambara, the most important Mande group, number about 1.5 million people. They are agriculturists who live in the Republic of Mali on both sides of the Niger River, from the capital city of Bamako northeast to Mopti. Bambara agriculture and religion are closely intertwined. For example, the Bambara high god is conceived of as a grain from which three other divine "persons," and finally, the whole of creation, are born. Bambara theology and religion are complex. Deep religious speculations exist among the Bambara sages and are transmitted orally without codification.

The Supreme Being and the Creation. The Bambara believe in one god, Bemba, or Ngala, who is the creator of all things and has, in a way, created himself as a quaternity. This quaternity consists of Bemba himself, Mousso Koroni Koundyé (or Nyale), Faro, and Ndomadyiri; the last three correspond to the four elements—air, fire, water, and earth. Before the creation Bemba was named Koni and was, in a sense, "thought" *(miri)* dwelling in a void; he is also the "void" itself *(lankolo)*. Accordingly, he cannot be perceived by humans using their usual senses. His existence is manifested as a force: a whirlwind, thought, or vibration that contains the signs of all uncreated things.

Bemba realized the creation of the world in three stages, each corresponding to one of the three other divine beings. In the first stage, called *dali folo* ("creation of the beginning"), the naked earth is created. God is known as Pemba in this stage, and he manifests himself in the form of a grain, from which grows an acacia *(Balanza)*. This tree soon withers, falls to the ground, and decays. One oblong beam, however, called Pembélé, survives. An avatar of God, Pembélé kneads the rotten wood with his saliva and forms Mousso Koroni Koundyé ("little old woman with a white head"), who becomes the first woman and his wife. Although she is associated with air, wind, and fire, Mousso Koroni Koundyé engenders plants, animals, and human beings. But because her person is unbalanced, her creations are produced in haste, disorder, and confusion.

The second stage, called *dali flana* ("second creation"), brings order and equilibrium to the previous creation. It is conducted under the authority of the deity Faro, an androgynous being issued from the breath of Bemba and identified with water, light, speech, and life. Faro gives every creature and thing a place in the world, a physical space, as well as a position in relation to other beings and things. He stops short of differentiating between things, however.

Differentiation of creation belongs to Ndomadyiri, the heavenly blacksmith, who is the eponymous ancestor of all blacksmiths. His principal task is to separate and distinguish things from each other, to make, in a sense, a comprehensible "speech" from the thought of creation. He is associated with the earth (from which food originates) and with trees (which produce remedies for ill health).

Thus the supreme being of the Bambara exists first as a sort of repository of energy and then manifests itself as four "persons" who generate the creation by each performing a different phase of activity. In this way the creation proceeds from confusion to clarity, from the unintelligible to the intelligible.

Ancestor Worship and the Dasiri Cult. Only those who led exemplary lives and died in a "natural" way (not due to any sorcery) can become ancestors. An ancestor must have reached an advanced age upon death and lived a life that is beyond reproach ethically, religiously, socially, and intellectually. One generation must separate the living and the dead before the rites of ancestor worship can be celebrated.

Nonfermented foodstuffs (e.g., fresh water, saliva, kola nuts, and mixtures of millet flour and water) are offered to appease the ancestor. These often precede more sophisticated offerings such as sorgo beer and blood. The beer is meant to "excite" the ancestor and to make him shake off his indolence toward living persons. The blood, usually obtained from sacrificed chickens or goats, represents the communion of the living and the dead. The place of worship differs according to the ancestor, but both sides of the entrance door to the hut are a preferred spot.

The founding ancestor is held in higher esteem than all other ancestors. His preeminence appears in the cult of the *dasiri*, a group of *genius loci*, or spiritual places, chosen by the founding ancestor when he created the village. One finds in each agglomeration two sorts of *dasiri:* a fixed one (e.g., tree, rock), which functions as the *axis mundi* of the village; and a mobile one, embodied in a wild or domestic animal (except birds). Offerings are made to the *dasiri* each time a community member encounters difficulties or a significant household event takes place. Sacrificial victims are always white, a color that symbolizes calmness and peace.

Initiatory Societies and Spiritual Life. Bambara religious life is mostly fulfilled during the epiphanies, or ritualistic manifestations, of the six initiatory societies: the N'domo, Komo, Nama, Kono, Tyiwara, and Korè. Together they give their members a complete (according to the Bambara ideal of perfection) intellectual, moral, and religious education.

The N'domo, open exclusively to noncircumcised children, teaches the origin and destiny of human beings. The highlight of the annual N'domo ceremonies is a sacred play featuring an androgynous child dancer who maintains complete silence while he performs. Dressed so that not one part of his body is visible, the dancer wears a wooden mask with human features and horns. The N'domo comprises five classes, each representing one of the five other initiation societies. Passage from one stage to another prefigures the adept's access to the Komo, Nama, Kono, Tyiwara, and Korè. In its structure as well as in its ceremonies, the N'domo attempts to answer, in a symbolic way, the following questions: What is man? Where does he come from? What is his destiny? Its answers are: He is androgynous; he comes from God; his fate is to return to God.

After their initiation into the N'domo, Bambara boys are circumcised. The operation has a double goal: to suppress their femininity (represented by the foreskin) and thus guide them to seek the opposite sex in marriage and to introduce the spirit to knowledge. Once these goals have been met, the boys are entitled to seek entry to the Komo society, whose purpose is to reveal to them the mysteries of knowledge.

Komo initiation societies consist of dances performed by masked individuals and sacrifices offered at the society's various altars. The Komo dance mask represents a hyena. Its jaws emphasize the animal's crushing force, which symbolizes knowledge. It should be noted that knowledge, as presented in the Komo, constitutes an entity in itself, independent and distant from man and "descending" upon him when he acquires it. For this reason, the Komo mask is worn on top of the head, like a helmet, and not on the face.

The Nama teaches its adepts about the union of spirit and body, of male and female, and of good and evil. Initiation ceremonies are particularly concerned with the union of a man and woman in matrimony and with the duality of good and evil (evil is symbolized by sorcery). The third society, the Kono, deals with the problems of human duality in greater depth. It examines the union of thought and body, a union that gives birth to the conscience.

The Tyiwara, the fourth society, is meant to teach its adepts about agriculture and work in the fields. It confers special significance on the relationship between the sun and the nurturing earth. At its annual festival, the growth of edible plants, and of vegetation in general, is ritually mimed by two dancers in a performance invested with cosmic symbolism.

The Korè is the last of the initiation societies. It bestows knowledge of man's spiritualization and divinization; an initiate learns how to resemble God, that is, how to become "immortal." Its vast program of initiation is conducted over several weeks for two consecutive years. The society marks the final attainment of the knowledge that assures salvation. The term *salvation* should not be interpreted here in its Christian sense; salvation, for the Bambara, consists of the ability to return to earth by being reborn within one's own clan lineage. The reincarnations continue as long as one's descendants preserve one's memory and cult. The Korè's ceremonies are held every seven years.

The Bambara believe that by following the exigencies of their religion—by not only assisting at religious ceremonies but also participating in them—they can vanquish death and become equal to God. This kind of immortality, proposed to the faithful by the Korè, exemplifies the spiritual finality of Bambara religion, whose aim is to make the believer participate in the deity's essence. The faithful Bambara is not meant to enjoy the presence of God eternally, however: his destiny is to be continually reincarnated so that he can return to his clan. His postmortem contact with God is like a brief, gentle "touch"; he will not be attached permanently to the creator until all reincarnations within the clan cease.

BIBLIOGRAPHY

To the best of my knowledge, the most complete and current survey of Bambara religion remains my own work *The Bambara,* "Iconography of Religions," sec. 7, fasc. 2 (Leiden, 1974). It not only offers a rich and original analysis of Bambara iconography but also provides a fresh view of the rites and institutions of these people. My *Sociétés d'initiation bambara: Le N'domo, le Korè* (Paris, 1960) is an essential study of two of the Bambara initiatory societies and the mystical life, and my *Antilopes du soleil: Art et rites agraires d'Afrique noire* (Vienna, 1980), which treats the Tyiwara, is a penetrating study of the religious role of the Bambara bestiary. Germaine Dieterlen and Youssouf Cissé's *Les fondements de la société d'initiation du Komo* (Paris, 1972) is a remarkable introduction to the inquiries on the Komo. For brilliant studies of some of the Bambara creation myths, see the following works: Solange de Ganay, "Aspects de mythologie et de symbolique bambara," *Journal de psychologie normale et pathologique* 42 (April–June 1949): 181–201 and "Notes sur la théodicée bambara," *Revue de l'histoire des religions* 135 (1949): 187–213; Solange de Ganay and Dominique Zahan, "Un enseignement donné par le *komo*," in *Systèmes de signes: Textes réunis en hommage à Germaine Dieterlen* (Paris, 1978), pp. 151–185; Germaine Dieterlen, *Essai sur la religion bambara* (Paris, 1951); and also by Dieterlen two articles in the *Journal de la Société des Africanistes*, "Mythe et organisation sociale au Soudan Français," vol. 25, nos. 1–2 (1955): 39–76 and "Mythe et organisation en Afrique occidentale," vol. 29, nos. 1–2 (1959): 119–138.

DOMINIQUE ZAHAN
Translated from French by Eva Zahan

BANARAS. The city of Banaras, also known in India as Vārāṇasī, is one of the most important and ancient of the sacred places of India. Such places are called *tīrthas*, "crossings" or "fords." Many *tīrthas*, like Banaras, are located geographically on the banks of India's rivers and were, indeed, fords where ferries plied the river. As places of pilgrimage, however, such *tīrthas* are seen primarily as spiritual fords, where one might safely cross over to the "far shore."

Banaras is located on the bank of the Ganges River in North India, at a place where the river curves northward, as if pointing back toward its Himalayan source. The river itself is considered holy, having fallen from heaven upon the head of Lord Śiva, who tamed the goddess-river in his tangled ascetic's hair before setting her loose to flow upon the plains of North India. In Banaras great stone steps called *ghāṭs* lead pilgrims from the lanes of the city down to the river's edge to bathe. To the north and south of the city, smaller rivers named the Varaṇā and the Asi, respectively, join the Ganges, thus providing a popular etymology for the city's ancient name Vārāṇasī.

Another of the ancient names of this place is Kāśī, which means "shining, luminous." Kāśī is also the name of one of the North Indian kingdoms that rivaled one another from about the eighth to sixth century BCE. The city of Vārāṇasī seems to have been the capital of the kingdom of Kāśī. Located on the high Rājghāṭ plateau overlooking the Ganges, this city, known as both Vārāṇasī and Kāśī, maintained a degree of importance for many hundreds of years, through the period of the Maurya and Gupta empires. Perhaps the height of its prestige was in the late eleventh and early twelfth centuries, when it was one of the administrative capitals of the Gāhaḍavāla kings of the Ganges Plain. Throughout its long history, however, the political significance of the city and its surrounding kingdom could not compare with its religious importance.

As a place of religious significance, Banaras was not only a "city" but a forest, which stretched beyond the small urban center and attracted sages and seekers to its forest hermitages. It was to these rural envirors of Banaras, to a place called Sarnath, that the Buddha came following his enlightenment at Bodh Gayā. There he encountered his former companions in asceticism and preached his first sermon to them. Until the late twelfth century, much of the area south of the Rājghāṭ plateau, which today is the center of urban Banaras, was still an extensive forest, filled with pools and rivulets, and dotted with temples and shrines. In the Purāṇas, it is called the Ānandavana, the "forest of bliss." Even today, when Banaras brahmans speak of ancient Banaras, they refer to the time when this city was the Ānandavana.

In the time of the Buddha, the most popular form of worship in this part of North India was the worship of what might be called "life-force" deities, such as *yakṣas*, *yakṣīs*, and *nāgas*. [*See also* Nāgas and Yakṣas.] Such deities were propitiated with offerings called *bali*, which often included wine or meat. These deities were known for their strength, which they could use in either harmful or beneficent ways. With the rise of theism, whether Buddhist, Śaiva, or Vaiṣṇava, these life-force deities were gathered into the entourage of the great gods. In Banaras, it was Śiva who rose to preeminence and, according to mythological tradition, attracted the allegiance and even the devotion of many *yakṣas*. They became his *gaṇas* ("flocks, troops") and *gaṇeśas* ("troop leaders") and were appointed to positions of great responsibility within the precincts of Śiva's city.

The mythology of Banaras, including the stories of Śiva's connection to this city, is found in the Purāṇas in a genre of praise literature called *māhātmya*. The most extensive of such *māhātmyas* is the *Kāśī Khaṇḍa*, an entire section of the voluminous *Skanda Purāṇa*. One myth tells of the divine hierophany of Śiva in this place. Here, it is said, Śiva's fiery pillar of light *(jyotirliṅga)* burst from the netherworlds, split the earth, and pierced the sky—a luminous and fathomless sign of Śiva. Kāśī is not only the place where that *liṅga* of light is said to have split the earth, but in a wider sense, Kāśī is also said to be the *liṅga* of light—an enormous geographical *liṅga*, with a radius of five *krośas* (about ten miles). Even today pilgrims circumambulate Kāśī on the Pañcakrośī Road, a five-day pilgrimage circuit around the whole of the city.

There are countless shrines and temples of Śiva in Kāśī, each containing a *liṅga*, which, according to Śaiva theology, is a symbol *(pratīka)* of that fathomless light of Śiva. It is said that in Kāśī there is a *liṅga* at every step; indeed, the very stones of Kāśī are Śiva *liṅgas*. Within this wider array, however, there are several temples that have special fame as sanctuaries of Śiva. The most significant of these *liṅgas* are Oṃkāreśvara, Viśveśvara, and Kedāreśvara, which traditionally centered the three *khaṇḍas*, or "sectors," of Banaras—north, central, and south. Oṃkāreśvara was of great importance in ancient Kāśī, but was damaged during the early Muslim destruction of the city and has never regained its former prominence. Viśveśvara (modern-day Viśvanātha) rose to preeminence and popularity around the twelfth century, and later continued to hold its position and reputation despite repeated Muslim devastation. Finally, Kedāreśvara anchors the southern sector of Kāśī. Its original home and prototype even today is the shrine of Kedār in the Himalayas, but it is one of the many *liṅgas* from elsewhere in India that have an important presence in this sacred center. The three *khaṇḍas* centered by these temples also have traditional circumambulatory routes that take the pilgrim through the most important temples and *tīrthas* of each sector.

In another mythic sequence from the *Kāśī Khaṇḍa,* Śiva populated the city of Vārāṇasī with the entire pantheon of gods. At that time, Śiva dwelt in his barren Himalayan home with his new bride, Pārvatī. He surveyed the entire earth for a suitable abode for the two of them. Seeing the beautiful Kāśī, he set about the task of evicting its ruling king, Divodāsa, so that he could have the city for himself. One by one, Śiva sent the various gods and demigods to Kāśī to find some way to force the king to leave. Not only did each god fail, but all the gods were so entranced with the city itself that they remained there without reporting to Śiva. Finally, with the help of Viṣṇu, Śiva succeeded in evicting King Divodāsa. The city into which he triumphantly entered was full of the gods.

As a sacred center, then, Kāśī is not only the city of Śiva, but also a *maṇḍala* containing the entire divine population of the Hindu pantheon. There are the twelve *ādityas,* "suns"; sixty-four *yoginīs,* "goddesses"; and eight *bhairavas,* the "terrible ones," led by Kāla Bhairava, the divine governor of the city. There are fifty-six *gaṇeśas,* protectively situated around the city in seven concentric circles at the eight compass points. Lord Brahmā and Lord Viṣṇu are there, both of whom have prominent locations within the city.

In addition to assigning a place to each of the gods, the city of Banaras has a place within its precincts for each of the other great *tīrthas* of India. India's twelve *jyotirliṅgas,* its seven sacred cities, and its sacred rivers and lakes all have symbolic locations in Kāśī. Banaras, then, is a microcosm of India's sacred geography.

The intensity of power that comes from the symbolic gathering of gods, *tīrthas,* and sages in this one place has made Banaras India's most widely acclaimed place of pilgrimage. While it is visited for the benefits associated with pilgrimage in this life, Kāśī is most famous as an auspicious place to die; a popular phrase is "Kāśyām maranam muktiḥ" ("Death in Kāśī is liberation"). According to tradition, those who die within the precincts of the holy city are certain to be instructed by Śiva himself at the time of death: in Banaras, Śiva's teaching is said to carry one across the flood of *saṃsāra* to the "far shore" of immortality.

[*See also* Śiva *and* Pilgrimage, *article on* Hindu Pilgrimage.]

BIBLIOGRAPHY

Eck, Diana L. *Banaras: City of Light.* New York, 1982. A study of the city of Banaras, based on its traditional literature in the Sanskrit Purāṇas and its modern sacred geography and patterns of pilgrimage.

Sherring, Matthew A. *The Sacred City of the Hindus: An Account of Benares in Ancient and Modern Times.* London, 1868. A consideration of the temples and legends of Banaras by a nineteenth-century British missionary.

Sukul, Kuber Nath. *Vārānasī down the Ages.* Patna, India, 1974. A study of the religious history and spiritual life of Banaras, including consideration of its saints, fairs, festivals, and arts.

DIANA L. ECK

BANTU RELIGIONS. *For discussion of the religious systems of Bantu-speaking peoples, see* East African Religions, *article on* Northeastern Bantu Religions; Interlacustrine Bantu Religions; Central Bantu Religions; *and* Southern African Religions.

BAPTISM. The word *baptism* comes from the Greek *baptein,* which means to plunge, to immerse, or to wash; it also signifies, from the Homeric period onward, any rite of immersion in water. The frequentative form, *baptizein,* appears much later (Plato, *Euthydemus* 227d; *Symposium* 176b). The baptismal rite is similar to many other ablution rituals found in a number of religions, but it is the symbolic value of baptism and the psychological intent underlying it that provide the true definition of the rite, a rite usually found associated with a religious initiation.

Pre-Christian Religions. The purifying properties of water have been ritually attested to ever since the rise of civilization in the ancient Near East. [*See* Water.] In Babylonia, according to the *Tablets of Maklu,* water was important in the cult of Enki, lord of Eridu. In Egypt, the *Book of Going Forth by Day* (17) contains a treatise on the baptism of newborn children, which is performed to purify them of blemishes acquired in the womb. Water, especially the Nile's cold water, which is believed to have regenerative powers, is used to baptize the dead in a ritual based on the Osiris myth. This ritual both assures the dead of an afterlife and rids them of blemishes that may not be taken into the other world. Baptism of the dead is also found among the Mandaeans (cf., the *Book of John*), and a similar rite is mentioned on Orphic tablets (*Orphicorum fragmenta,* 2d ed., Otto Kern, ed., Berlin, 1963, p. 232).

The property of immortality is also associated with baptism in the Greek world: according to Cretan funeral tablets, it was associated especially with the spring of Mnemosyne (memory). A bath in the sanctuary of Trophonios procured for the initiate a blessed immortality even while in this world (Pausanias, *Description of Greece* 9.39.5). Greek religious sanctions did impose a number of lustral ablution rites for the removal of sins, but these rites were only preliminary to the principal rites of the mysteries. Thus, the bath in the sea with which the initiation rites of the great Eleusinian mysteries began was simply a physical purification, accompanied by the sacrifice of a piglet. This was true as well of the immersion of the followers of the god Men Askaenos, near Antioch in Pisidia, and of the ablutions required of the Corybantes and of the followers of the Thracian goddess Cotyto, who were called *baptai* ("the baptized ones"). In all these cases, baptism was only a preamble, as the *Magic Papyrus* of Paris testifies (43): "Jump into the river with your clothes on. After you have immersed yourself, come out, change your clothes, and depart without looking back." Such a rite marked the beginning of an initiation; this practice was required to put the neophyte in the state of purity necessary for him to receive the god's oracle or an esoteric teaching. [*See* Ablutions.]

In Hellenistic philosophy, as in Egyptian speculation, divine water possessed a real power of transformation. Hermetism offered to man the possibility of being transformed into a spiritual being after immersion in the baptismal crater of the *nous;* this baptism conferred knowledge on man and permitted him to participate in the gnosis and, hence, to know the origins of the soul. Having received baptism, the gnostic "knows why he has come into existence, while others do not know why or whence they are born" (*Corpus Hermeticum* 1.4.4). Egyptian cults also developed the idea of regeneration through water. The bath preceding initiation into the cult of Isis seems to have been more than a simple ritual purification; it was probably intended to represent symbolically the initiate's death to the life of this world by recalling Osiris' drowning in the Nile (Apuleius, *Metamorphoses* 11.23.1).

In the cult of Cybele, a baptism of blood was practiced in the rite of the Taurobolium: the initiate went down into a pit and was completely covered with the blood of a bull, whose throat was cut above him. At first, the goal of this rite seems to have been to provide the initiate with greater physical vitality, but later it acquired more of a spiritual importance. A well-known inscription attests that he who has received baptism of blood is *renatus in aeternum,* that he has received a new birth in eternity (*Corpus inscriptionum Latinarum* 6.510). In other inscriptions associated with the Taurobolium, the word *natalicium* seems to be the exact equivalent of the Christians' *natalis,* suggesting that the day of the baptism of blood is also the day of a new and spiritual birth. However, the fact that this baptism was repeated periodically shows that the idea of complete spiritual regeneration was not originally associated with it. Only under the influences of Christianity and the Mithraic cult does the idea of an atonement for past sins through shed blood appear; henceforth, it was possible to believe that the Taurobolium procured the hope of eternity, and that the Mithraic bull sacrifice was a redeeming act that gave the initiate a new life.

The liturgical use of water was common in the Jewish world. Mosaic law imposes the performance of ablutions before ritual entry into sacred areas; likewise, it describes the chief impurities that water can erase (*Nm.* 19:1–22; *Lv.* 14, 15, 16:24–28). Under Persian influence, rites of immersion multiplied after the exile. Some prophets saw in the requirement of physical purity a sign of the necessity of inner and spiritual purification (*Ez.* 36:25–28). The Essenes linked the pouring forth of the divine life in man to purification by baptism in flowing water. They practiced a baptism of initiation that brought the neophyte into the community at Qumran after a year's probation. However, the rite did not produce any magical effects, for, as the *Manual of Discipline* asserts, a pure heart was necessary for the bath to be effective, and an impure man who receives it merely soils the sanctified water (*Manual of Discipline* 6.16–17, 6.21).

Toward the beginning of the Christian era, the Jews adopted the custom of baptizing proselytes seven days after their circumcision, the rabbis having added the impurity of converted gentiles to the chief impurities enumerated in the Torah. After their baptism, new converts were allowed access to the sacrifices in the Temple. A series of specific interrogations made it possible to judge the real intentions of the candidate who wished to adopt the Jewish religion. After submitting to these interrogations, he was circumcised and later baptized before witnesses. In the baptism, he was immersed naked in a pool of flowing water; when he rose from the pool, he was a true son of Israel. Clearly a rite of unification with the community of believers, this baptism developed under the influence of the school of Hillel and emphasized the importance of a new birth. "Every proselyte," says the Babylonian Talmud, "is like a newborn child" (*Yev.* 22a, 48b, 62a, etc.).

The ministry of John the Baptist in the Jordanian desert was connected with this baptist movement, which symbolically linked immersion in a river of flowing water to the passage from death to a new and supernatural life. To achieve the erasing of sin that is closely tied to inner conversion, John administered a baptism of water, but by doing so in the water of the Jordan itself, not in the ritual water of purified pools, John made a clear departure from official practice. This departure was all the more striking because his baptism appears to be a substitute for the *ḥaṭa't,* the sacrifice for sin, and is not a rite of unification with the Israelite community but rather a sign of divine pardon and of the advent of the messianic era. Not surprisingly, John drew down upon himself the fierce hatred of the scribes and Jewish authorities (Josephus Flavius, *Jewish Antiquities* 18.116–119).

The Mandaeans take their baptismal practice directly from the example of John, whom they consider the perfect gnostic; they administer baptism in the flowing water of a symbolic Jordan. "Be baptized with the flowing water I have brought you from the world of light," says the *Right Ginza* (19.24). Mandaean baptism is followed by a sacred meal where a blessing is given to bread and water mixed with wine, considered the sustenance of divine beings; in addition, the Mandaeans practice baptism of the dead. Johannine and Christian rites of baptism do not, however, have their origin in these practices, as was thought at the beginning of the twentieth century. Rather, Jewish and Christian influences create the numerous ritual similarities found in Mandaean practice, including the white garments with which recipients of Mandaean baptism are clothed. "Clothe yourselves in white, to be like the mystery of this flowing water," says the *Right Ginza*.

The same influences were felt by the Elkesaites, who at the beginning of the second century abolished the fire of the patriarchal sacrifice and substituted for it a baptism by water that both remits sin and brings the neophytes into a new religion. Their baptismal ritual takes place in the flowing water of a brook or river after invocations are addressed to earth, air, oil, and salt. This sort of baptism also becomes a method of physical healing and appears again in numerous Baptist sects of the modern period.

Christian Baptism. John baptized Jesus, like others who came to him, in the waters of the Jordan, but the manifestations of the Father and the Holy Spirit during Jesus' baptism give it a completely new dimension (*Mk.* 1:9–11). Jesus' baptism also inaugurated his public ministry, and he later gave his disciples the mission of baptizing in the name of the trinitarian faith—a mission that they carried out even before their master's death (*Mt.* 28:19, *Jn.* 4:1–2). The apostles continued to practice the baptism of water of the type administered by John; but they emphasized the necessity of an inner conversion preceding the profession of the trinitarian faith, the focus of the new belief.

It was Paul who first defined the theological and symbolic significance of Christian baptism, joining the neophyte's ritual descent into water to Christ's death and rebirth to a new and spiritual life through his resurrection (*Rom.* 6:3–4). Sin is not carried away by the flowing water but by the Lord's death and resurrection; through baptismal immersion, the Christian is able to participate in this new existence (*Col.* 2:12). In *Titus* 3:5, Paul describes baptism as the gift of "a bath of regeneration and renewal"; the baptismal water is at once the water of death in which the old, sinful man is immersed and the water of life from which he emerges renewed. In fact, Paul rediscovers the meaning of a very ancient symbolism of death and resurrection found in archaic initiation rituals a symbolism that has been admirably analyzed by Mircea Eliade (*Images et symbols: Essais sur le symbolisme magico-religieux,* Paris, 1952, pp. 199–212; *Traité d'histoire des religions*, Paris, 1949, pp. 64–65).

Every detail of the Christian ritual is intended to symbolize birth to a new life in Jesus Christ: nudity (at least for men) during immersion; conferral of new names on the neophytes, who are also given new, white garments; imposition of the sign of the cross, understood as the seal *(sphragis),* mentioned in *Revelation;* and the dispensation of a drink of milk and honey to the newly baptized. Ever since the *First Letter of Peter,* new Christians have been compared to little children (*1 Pt.* 2:2), a comparison frequently represented in the early Christian art of the catacombs; in another early symbol, they are likened to "little fish, so named for our great Ichthus, Jesus Christ, who is born in water and remains alive by living there" (Tertullian, *On Baptism* 1.3). Old Testament prototypes of baptism—the Flood, the crossing of the Red Sea, the crossing of the Jordan, and entrance into the Promised Land—are evoked in catechesis even by the first generations of Christians, who recognized in them the passage through the water of life and death (cf. *1 Cor.* 10:1–2). As Chrysostom explained in the fourth century, "Baptism represents death and the sepulcher but also resurrection and life. Just as the old man is buried in the sepulcher, so we immerse our heads in water. At the moment when we come out of the water, the new man appears" (*Homilies* 25.2). Christian representations of baptism were also enriched by other symbols drawn from the Old Testament, notably the deer drinking at the spring, from Psalm 42, and the Good Shepherd surrounded by his sheep, from Psalm 23 (*Ps.* 23, 42:25). Both these psalms were sung during the Easter Vigil by candidates for baptism.

Christian baptismal practice is founded on the commandment of Jesus himself to his disciples (*Mt.* 28:19). Its administration during the first centuries of the church took place at Easter night and Pentecost and was limited to bishops, the heads of the Christian communities. Reception of baptism seems often to have been put off until the moment of death by neophytes who were reluctant to accept the full consequences of inner conversion; and infant baptism, though possible, was probably not practiced in the early period of the church (cf. *Mt.* 19:14, *Acts* 16:33, *1 Tm.* 2:4). As the gateway to the sacraments, baptism opened the way into the church community, and prayers and rites increasingly describe it as the entrance to a holy place, the opening of the different routes offered by the faith.

The church was especially concerned, however, to organize a period of probation during which the catechumens were prepared to receive the sacrament through prayer, fasting, and doctrinal instruction. The *Didache,* in chapter 7, clearly asserts the duty of candidates to live according to evangelical precepts and to renounce evil in all its forms. As a number of patristic texts attest, the baptismal ritual was quickly enriched through such additions as interrogations (like those preceding Jewish baptism), a triple renunciation of the devil (recalling Jesus' triple renunciation during his temptations), a triple immersion (representing the Trinity), the anointing of the neophyte with the holy chrism, and the laying on of hands by the bishop or priest (Tertullian, *Against Praxeas* 26; *On Baptism;* Hippolytus, *Apostolic Tradition*).

Because it was the sacrament that indicated entrance into the life of faith and the community of the church, baptism was also considered a means to inner enlightenment. In the Eastern church, those who were initiated into the Christian mysteries by baptism were called the "enlightened," for, as Gregory of Nazianzus explains, the baptismal rite opens the catechumen's eyes to the light that indicates God's symbolic birth in man (Discourse 40: *On Baptism*). In this view, the bishop theologian merely continues a long tradition begun by Paul. "Awake, sleeper," the apostle writes in *Ephesians,* "and Christ will shine upon you"—an admonition he repeats in the *Letter to the Hebrews* (*Eph.* 5:14, *Heb.* 6:4, 10:32). Writing of baptism in the second century, Justin Martyr speaks of the "bath that is called enlightenment" (*First Apology* 61); in the following century, Clement of Alexandria wrote: "Baptized, we are enlightened; enlightened, we are adopted; adopted, we are made perfect; perfect, we become immortal" (*Pedagogue* 1.6.26). Thus, in the early church, baptism was clearly understood as the initiation required for a man to recognize the divine light and to participate in eternal life while still in this world.

But because it was also the fundamental rite of entry into the church community, baptism was quickly claimed as a prerogative by several rival churches, each of which called itself orthodox and accused the others of heresy and schism. Modifications of baptismal rites by the various sects were inevitable. After the second half of the fourth century, the Anomoeans, exponents of a doctrine akin to Arianism, rejected triple immersion, the symbol of a Trinity equal in all its members, a doctrine they contested; for the same reason, they even modified the baptismal formula that had been fixed by scripture (*Mt.* 28:19). What is more important, from the third century on, the Arians insisted upon the invalidity of a rite of baptism conferred by a heretic or schismatic, a view given great importance by the Donatists. The Arians denied the validity of Catholic baptism, and in Italy (especially in Milan) and Vandal Africa they required rebaptism (cf. Michel Meslin, *Les Ariens d'Occident,* Paris, 1967, pp. 382–390). Arians and Donatists alike did not believe that a person could be brought within the church community by a minister who was personally alien to it and did not share its faith; they held that baptism was valid only if it was accompanied by a pure intention in the person who administered it, who had also to belong to the true church. They refused to accept the Catholic view that the rite of baptism is in itself the canal of an omnipotent divine grace that completely surpasses a channel for qualities of the individual who administers it.

From the sixth century on at the latest, the Catholic church permitted the baptism of children, the engagement to follow the faith being taken in their name by adult Christians. The custom of baptizing infants soon after birth became popular in the tenth or eleventh century and was generally accepted by the thirteenth (Thomas Aquinas, *Summa theologiae* 3.68.3). In the fourteenth century, baptismal ritual was simplified, and a rite of spiritual infusion, in which water is poured on the head of a child held above the baptismal font, replaced baptism by immersion.

After 1517, the questions posed by the practice of the baptism of small children served as a major foundation for dissident Christian movements stemming from the Reformation. To adherents of these movements, an uncompromising interpretation of the doctrine of individual justification by faith alone implied that the rite of entry into the Christian community had to be restricted to adults who were conscious of their salvation through Christ and who asked to be baptized. The dissidents formally denied the validity of baptism given to nonresponsible children and required those who had received such baptism to be rebaptized as adults, thus earning the name Anabaptists *(Wiedertäufer).* Going even further, Thomas Müntzer (1485–1525), one of the "prophets of Zwickau," affirmed that individual inspiration by the Holy Spirit determined a person's conduct and demonstrated the unique rule of faith. Along with this demand for religious discipline, the Anabaptist movement, especially in Germany, developed a revolutionary ideology, preached radical egalitarianism, community of property, and even polygamy, and actively supported the German Peasants' Revolt. Denounced and condemned by Luther, Calvin, and Zwingli, Müntzer was executed at Mülhausen, and the Anabaptists were subjected to a pitiless repression. Nevertheless, their movement survived in northern Europe and expanded during the seventeenth and eighteenth centuries in Holland, where the Mennonites still practice adult baptism by immersion and advocate a policy of nonviolence that denies them participation in public office or military service.

In 1633, a group of English Baptists immigrated to North America, beginning the development in the New World of a number of Baptist sects and churches, whose members founded their belief on the theological baptism of Paul (cf. *Rom.* 6:4, *Col.* 2:12) and insisted upon a return to strict apostolic practice. These sects and churches have in common the practice of baptism by immersion administered in the name of the Trinity only to adults who believe and confess their faith in Jesus Christ; in addition, from their distant Anabaptist origins, a majority retains the doctrine of the freedom of each confessional community to interpret the scriptures and the Christian faith.

[*See also* Purification.]

BIBLIOGRAPHY

Beasley-Murray, G. R. *Baptism in the New Testament.* New York, 1962.

Beirnaert, Louis. "La dimension mythique dans le sacramentalisme chrétien." *Eranos-Jahrbuch* (Zurich) 17 (1949): 255–286.

Drower, Ethel S., trans. *The Canonical Prayerbook of the Mandaeans.* Leiden, 1959.

Gilmore, Alec, ed. *Christian Baptism.* Chicago, 1959.

Lundberg, Per. *La typologie baptismale dans l'ancienne église.* Leipzig, 1942.

Malaise, Michel. *Les conditions de pénétration et de diffusion des cultes égyptiens en Italie.* Leiden, 1972.

Meslin, Michel. "Réalités psychiques et valeurs religieuses dans les cultes orientaux (premier–quatrième siècles)." *Revue historique* 512 (October–December 1974): 289–314.

Payne, Ernest A. *The Fellowship of Believers: Baptist Thought and Practice Yesterday and Today.* 2d ed., enl. London, 1952.

Reitzenstein, Richard. *The Hellenistic Mystery Religions* (1927). Translated by John E. Seeley. Pittsburgh, 1978.

Rudolph, Kurt. *Die Mandäer.* 2 vols. Göttingen, 1960–1961.

Thomas, Jean. *Le mouvement baptiste en Palestine et en Syrie.* Gembloux, 1935.

MICHEL MESLIN

Translated from French by Jeffrey C. Haight and Annie S. Mahler

BAPTIST CHURCHES. As with most denominational names, the name *Baptist* began as a pejorative nickname. It first appeared as *Anabaptist*, or "rebaptizer," since in the sixteenth century, when this group arose in Western Christendom, virtually all persons had already been baptized as infants. These rebaptizers were scandalously denying the validity of that first baptism, setting themselves up as a truer church if not, indeed, the true church. Gradually, as infant baptism became less prevalent and as alternative modes of worship grew more widespread, this still young denomination adopted the shortened form of "Baptist" both as a convenient distinction and a point of honor. (New England churches in the seventeenth and early eighteenth centuries show a gradual progression from simply "the Church of Christ" to "the Church of Christ in Gospel Order" to "the Church of Christ Baptized Upon Profession of Their Faith" to "the Baptized Church of Christ" to, finally, the Baptist Church.) To be sure, the new subject of the baptism (namely the adult, or "believer"), and not originally the mode of baptism (whether by sprinkling, pouring, or immersing), stood out as the most glaring liturgical innovation of this politically powerless, socially suspect group. Although not preserved in the denominational designation, the other feature of the early Baptist movement that most alarmed contemporaries was the Baptists' novel notion that civil government had no responsibility and indeed no right to enforce a religious conformity. As one of their seventeenth-century opponents wrote, Anabaptists "deny Civil Government to be proved of Christ." [*See also* Anabaptism.]

As used by their enemies, the word *Anabaptist* was calculated to have an unnerving effect upon all who believed in a well-ordered society, for the term suggested that English rebaptizers of the seventeenth century were of a piece with the most radical continental rebaptizers of the century before. Thus every fanaticism, every antinomianism, every vagary of the Reformation's bloodiest days could be laid at the doorstep of those English Separatists opposing infant baptism. History, to say nothing of the specific individuals involved, was by this indiscriminate name-calling badly served, for modern Baptists have only the most tenuous connection with the radical reformers of the sixteenth century. (Modern Mennonites may be more accurately seen as lineal descendants of the Reformation's left wing.) English and American Baptists, who in the twentieth century account for nearly 90 percent of all Baptists worldwide, emerged from the Puritan agitations of Elizabethan and Jacobean England.

Sharing many of the Puritan concerns about a Church of England still too "papist," still too engrossed with civil enforcement and ecclesiastical preferment, these separating Puritans early distinguished themselves by insisting that the church be a voluntary society. That voluntarism had two critical components: (1) the insistence that members choose their church rather than be born into it; this voluntary act was testified to by the act of baptism, which was both obedient to Christ's command and declarative of one's personal, uncoerced confession of faith; and, (2) the conviction that the covenant of believers to work and worship together was a private agreement with which the state had nothing to do, for conscience must be left free. As Thomas Helwys, one of that first generation of English Baptists, wrote, "the King is a mortal man and not God, therefore hath no power over the immortal souls of his subjects, to make laws and ordinances for them, and to set spiritual lords over them."

The leadership of Helwys and two others, John Smyth and John Murton, proved decisive in the first two decades of the seventeenth century as the English "General Baptists" (that is, non-Calvinist, affirming an unrestricted or general atonement for mankind) grew from a scarcely visible knot of believers in 1609 to around twenty thousand members by 1660. Despite this impressive showing, however, the major strength of the modern Baptist churches was to come from a somewhat later development of the 1630s: the rise of the Particular Baptists (of Calvinist orientation, affirming a limited or particular redemption for mankind). Under the leadership of John Spilsbury, in the decade following 1633, a single church became mother to six more. By the time seven such churches existed in and around London, these Calvinist Baptists had also reintroduced the ancient Christian practice of baptism by immersion, this mode being preferred as a more suitable symbol of one's burial with Christ followed by one's new birth or resurrection from that death to walk in a wholly new life. One of the members of Spilsbury's group, Mark Lucar, emigrated to America, settling in Newport, Rhode Island. There he introduced the "new baptism" to New England's scattered Anabaptists, as they were still being called. Lucar, arriving sometime before 1648, also helped strengthen ties between American and English Baptists as the two groups, together, labored to make clear the unfairness of the broad application of the "Anabaptist" label. (Anabaptists continued to be legislated against in New England.) In this endeavor, they were much assisted by the moderate, well-reasoned, properly Calvinist London Confession of 1644.

Baptist growth in America lagged behind that of England in the seventeenth and early eighteenth centuries. Roger Williams, it is true, gave the infant denomination both a geographical base and a theological thrust when in 1636, as an exile from Puritan Massachusetts Bay Colony, he made his way on foot to a territory at the head of the Narragansett Bay. After a careful and conscientious purchase of land from the Indians, he named the first settlement Providence in gratitude to God for having delivered him safely from the Puritans, the Indians, and the rigors of his fourteen-week exposure to the New England winter. The colony of Rhode Island, founded on the principle of a "full liberty in religious concernments" as well as on a hot hatred of "The Bloudy Tenent of Persecution" (the title of Williams's 1644 London publication), received into its midst all manner of religious pariahs: Baptists, Quakers, Ranters, Fifth Monarchists, Gortonists, and many others. Yet only in a limited sense did Rhode Island become a Baptist stronghold. By the end of the seventeenth century, Quakers dominated the colony politically, while Baptists had managed to separate into Calvinist, Arminian (Six Principle), and Seventh Day factions. Roger Williams, moreover, had remained within the Baptist fold only briefly; the leadership of the Providence church quickly passed into other hands. In Newport, on the other hand, the more enduring leadership of Dr. John Clarke (assisted by Mark Lucar, Obadiah Holmes, and Joseph Torrey) gave the infant denomination a firm if tiny base in the New World. [*See also the biography of Williams.*]

The great growth of Baptists in North America (and by extension in the world) followed the eighteenth century's Great Awakening, that Calvinist explosion of evangelical zeal and intense religious experience. Even though Baptists were not prime leaders in the movement, they were the prime beneficiaries of it. Churches separating from the Congregational establishments in New England often moved from a halfway house called "Separatist" to a new denominational home called "Baptist." For example, the eminent pastor, theologian, historian, and civil libertarian Isaac Backus followed this path. Moreover, the Awakening, even if it did not make an itinerant ministry respectable, did make such traveling evangelism both popular and pervasive. John Leland, a New Englander transplanted to Virginia, serves as an instructive example of such a ministry: irregular, unauthorized, ill-supported, and enormously effective. The names of Backus and Leland also point to a rhetoric that during the Revolutionary period served to identify Baptists with the cause of liberty, both civil and ecclesiastical. In the South, where the Church of England had for so long enjoyed a legal monopoly, Baptists seized upon the discomfort of a church so swiftly disestablished and so widely under suspicion to make major conquests among farmers, artisans, and even gentry.

After the American Revolution, Baptists also made phenomenal advances among the nation's blacks. Using a persuasive preaching style, an accessible theology, an appealing baptismal ritual, and an ecclesiology that granted freedom from white rule, the Baptist message found ready hearers among both enslaved and free blacks. By the end of the nineteenth century, black Baptists had formed their own national organizations, publishing boards, and mission societies. By the mid-twentieth century, approximately two-thirds of America's black Christians were Baptists. Also, by that time one-third or more of all of America's Baptists were black. Like their white counterparts, however, blacks found it difficult to maintain organizational or theological unity.

The pattern of increasing diversity had been set by the white Baptists. Even before the nineteenth century began, some Baptists, disturbed by the prevailing Calvinist orientation of their denomination, chose to emphasize man's free will; thus, Free Will Baptists maintained a separate identity until early in the twentieth century. Others in the new nation, fearing that Baptists would aspire to national status with all the evils that bureaucracy and hierarchy implied, resisted the creation of national societies and boards, preferring to remain in smaller, more local, more nearly autonomous units. In the bitter conflict over slavery, more specifically over the appointment of a slaveholding missionary, white Baptists split along geographical lines in 1845, and the Southern Baptist Convention was organized in Augusta, Georgia. (A national organization of Baptists dated back only to 1814, so denominational unity in America enjoyed but a brief life.) The Southern Baptist Convention, with its base initially in the states of the southern Confederacy, moved aggressively to the West, to the North, and to "foreign fields" to become the largest single Baptist entity in the world. By the mid-twentieth century it had also become the largest Protestant denomination in the United States. The northern group (originally the Northern Baptist Convention, now the American Baptist Churches, U.S.A.), with about three-fourths the number of churches as the southern group at the time of separation, found itself repeatedly bled in the twentieth century by separations and schisms—most of them related to the conflict between modernists and fundamentalists. As a consequence, by the late twentieth century the Southern Baptist Convention outnumbered its northern counterpart by about ten to one. Although the other major Protestant groups that divided over slavery have reunited—the Methodists in 1939 and the Presbyterians in 1983—the Baptists have shown little sign of returning to a single fold.

In the early 1980s, the northern and southern "halves" had an aggregate membership of around fifteen million, the two oldest black denominations a combined membership of eight to ten million. This leaves uncounted some four or five million Baptists in America who are scattered among a wide variety of other organizations. Most of these groups affirm a strict congregational polity (eschewing any national superstructure or headquarters), a rigid biblical theology (rejecting all critical study of the biblical text itself), and their own special hold on "the faith once delivered to the saints" (opposing all ecumenical ventures, even with other Baptist bodies). The Baptist family in the United States is large, Protestantism's largest by far in the nation, as it approaches thirty million; but, as in many another large family, some members do not speak to other members.

Outside the United States, the Baptist churches are unevenly and often sparsely scattered. One may speak most conveniently in terms of continents rather than individual nations in offering estimates of membership: in Africa and Europe, about one million in each area; in Asia, about 1.5 million; and in Central and South America, something less than one million. In Canada, to which New England Baptists began to migrate in the late eighteenth century, there are between one and two hundred thousand Baptists.

The Soviet Union (counted in the European total) constitutes something of a special case as the Baptist presence there is both highly visible and highly vulnerable; Baptists entered Russia from several points of departure in the late nineteenth century to encounter severe opposition from the czars and the Russian Orthodox church. In the U.S.S.R., that opposition has intensified as Baptists, true to an ancient heritage, have found any interference or regulation by the state intolerable.

In England, the General Baptists of the seventeenth century lost either zeal or identity or both, many of that number merging with the Universalists. The Calvinist, or Particular, Baptists maintained both zeal and identity, but in the face of a powerful and sometimes repressive national church, the numbers of these dissenters never approached that of their co-religionists in the United States. British Baptists in the 1980s numbered about one hundred thousand.

Because of their belief in a threefold immersion (separately in the name of the Father, the Son, and the Holy Spirit), German Baptists received the nickname of Dunkers, or Dunkards. Known officially since 1908 as the Church of the Brethren, these Baptists originated in Germany early in the eighteenth century. Fleeing from persecution there, however, they emigrated virtually *en masse* to America, settling in Pennsylvania, the Virginia backcountry, and the Midwest. Although distinguished by liturgical emphases on the Love Feast and the ceremonial washing of each other's feet, these German Baptists attract most public attention by their consistent witness for peace and their choice of alternative service rather than military enlistment. Their membership in the 1980s neared two hundred thousand. One other sizable group of distinctive ethnic heritage, the (Swedish) Baptist General Conference, dropped its ethnic label in 1945; its membership in the United States exceeds one hundred thousand.

Across nearly four centuries and six continents, the Baptist churches have multiplied in variety nearly as much as in number. Yet it is possible to point to broad features generally characteristic of the entire group. The first broad feature is voluntarism, which places Baptists squarely in the free-church tradition. Membership is by choice; creeds are to emerge from below, not be handed down from above; covenants are ideally arrived at by the local congregation and periodically revised; worship follows no fixed form, without service books or a canon of prayers. That voluntarism also sees its integrity and spontaneity as fatally compromised whenever the state intrudes into the realm of religious conscience. Voluntarism has its weaker side in becoming the passive reflection of a surrounding culture, in surrendering slowly and unthinkingly to what one author has called the "cultural captivity of the churches."

The second broad feature is pietism, which places its first priority on the personal and direct encounter with God. Such individualism protects against an autocratic or coldly impersonal structure, but it can also lead to a chaotic splintering where, as Emerson said, every man is his own church. Pietism ensures a zeal; it does not always carry with it a corresponding bounty of knowledge and public responsibility.

The Baptist movement's third broad feature is evangelism, which in some times and places has been seen as the totality of the Baptist effort. Special classes and techniques in "soul winning" have been developed, and the "revival meeting" became standard fare in most Baptist churches, large or small, urban or rural. This evangelistic emphasis has also been responsible for a heavy investment in missions, both at home and abroad. In the opening of the American West, such men as Isaac McCoy and John Mason Peck played major roles. And in nations abroad, the path cut in the early nineteenth century by Adoniram Judson and Luther Rice was traveled by thousands, male and female, in succeeding decades. Yet there is also a strong antimission strain in Baptist history, this being institutionalized in several "Primitive" Baptist bodies, both black and white.

The fourth broad feature is sectarianism, which has kept most Baptists on the fringes of the ecumenical movement. The transition from "sect" to "denomination" is an uneven and, to some degree, an unpredictable one. A mid-nineteenth-century movement known as Landmarkism represents the sectarian extreme; it held that true Baptist churches have existed from the apostolic age to the present, and only the true local church has a valid ministry, valid sacraments, and biblical authenticity. The American Baptist Association, with about one million members in the 1980s, constitutes the contemporary manifestation of a sectarianism that rejects all ecumenical endeavors, is strongly suspicious of Roman Catholicism, and deeply resents those Baptist churches that behave in a more "denominational" way.

BIBLIOGRAPHY

Two books on English Baptists that provide not only good historical background but excellent insight into contemporary life and thought are H. Wheeler Robinson's *The Life and Faith of the Baptists*, rev. ed. (London, 1946), and Ernest A. Payne's *The Fellowship of Believers: Baptist Thought and Practice Yesterday and Today*, rev. ed. (London, 1952). These two works have been reprinted together under the title *British Baptists* (New York, 1980). A world view is provided in Robert G. Torbet's *A History of the Baptists*, 4th ed., rev. (Valley Forge, Pa., 1975), while Torbet and S. S. Hill, Jr., have reviewed the American scene in *Baptists: North and South* (Valley Forge, Pa., 1964). On the Southern Baptist Convention specifically, see Robert A. Baker's *The Southern Baptist Convention and Its People, 1607–1972* (Nashville, 1974). Two works on Baptist development in early America have made giant historiographical strides over most previous efforts: William G. McLoughlin's *New England Dissent, 1630–1833*, 2 vols. (Cambridge, Mass., 1971), and C. C. Goen's *Revivalism and Separatism in New England, 1740–1800* (New Haven, 1962). Finally, for an informed view of alternative ecclesiological styles among Baptists, see *Baptist Concepts of the Church*, edited by Winthrop S. Hudson (Philadelphia and Chicago, 1959).

EDWIN S. GAUSTAD

BAR AND BAT MITSVAH. *See* Rites of Passage, *article on* Jewish Rites.

BAR-ILAN, ME'IR (1880–1949), born Me'ir Berlin; one of the foremost leaders of the religious Zionist movement Mizraḥi. A native of Volozhin, Russia, he was the son of Naftali Berlin, the head of the famous Volozhin *yeshivah* (rabbinic academy). Bar-Ilan joined the religious Zionist movement and attended many Zionist congresses from 1905 onward. In 1911, he became the secretary of the Mizraḥi movement and moved to Berlin. In 1915, he immigrated to the United States, and in 1925 he settled in Jerusalem, where he remained until his death.

As the Mizraḥi representative, Bar-Ilan held many important positions in the Zionist movement before the creation of the state of Israel. He edited the religious Zionist Hebrew weekly *Ha-'Ivri* from 1910 through 1921 and was editor in chief of the Tel Aviv daily *Ha-tsofeh* from 1938 to 1949.

In both his political activities and his writings, Bar-Ilan tried to create a central role for Orthodox Jews in Jewish nationalism. He rejected the notion of separation of synagogue and state, but he also rejected the more extreme religious arguments against any cooperation with the secular nationalists. He argued for inculcation of traditional religious values through the educational system. He believed that only by education, not by coercion, could the Orthodox win the struggle with the secularists over the final status of religion in the Jewish state. His position can be summed up in the Mizraḥi slogan that he coined: "The Land of Israel for the people of Israel according to the Torah [God's law] of Israel."

Bar-Ilan's position on the relationship between religion and state in Israel remains substantially that of the present religious Zionist party, the Mafdal (National Religious Party). The Bar-Ilan University near Tel Aviv, which was founded in 1955 to wed traditional Jewish learning with modern academic scholarship, was named after him.

[*For further discussion of the relationship between Jewish Orthodoxy and Jewish nationalism, see* Zionism.]

BIBLIOGRAPHY

In addition to Zvi Kaplan's article on Bar-Ilan in *Encyclopaedia Judaica* (Jerusalem, 1971), further biographical information can be found in Moshe Krone's *Ha-Rav Me'ir Bar-Ilan* (Jerusalem, 1954) and in *The Zionist Idea*, edited by Arthur Hertzberg (Philadelphia, 1959), pp. 546–555.

DAVID BIALE

BARLAAM OF CALABRIA (c. 1290–c. 1350), humanist, philologist, and theologian; one of the forerunners of the Renaissance. Barlaam was born in Seminara commune, Calabria, a Greek by ethnic descent and language, and a member of the religious groups that still preserved the memory of their Orthodox Christian past in southern Italy. With the passage of time the inhabitants of the region were obliged to submit to Rome, but they felt themselves to be Orthodox as a result of their long tradition. The religious duality of the Greek communities of southern Italy explains the oscillation in Barlaam's advocacy of the two competing traditions. He was possessed of a sentimental love of Orthodoxy on account of his Greek ancestry, but as a theologian and philosopher, he was influenced by Western Scholasticism.

In 1326, traveling from Italy to the Greek peninsula, Barlaam doffed the clothes of a Western monk and put on Greek monastic dress. He stayed in Thessalonica several years and strengthened his reputation as a philosopher. Barlaam later settled in Constantinople, where he soon gained the confidence of ecclesiastical and political circles, especially of the emperor Andronicus III Palaeologus, who gave him a professorial chair at the university. No one had any doubts about the sincerity of his Orthodox convictions. He was made abbot of the Monastery of Our Savior, and two confidential missions on behalf of the emperor were entrusted to him. During the years 1333–1334, Barlaam undertook to negotiate the union of churches with the representatives of Pope John XXII. For this occasion he wrote twenty-one treatises against the Latins in which he opposed papal primacy and the *filioque* doctrine. In 1379, he was sent to the exiled Pope Benedict XII at Avignon to suggest a crusade against the Turks and to discuss the union of churches, but he was not successful.

A reaction against Barlaam was not late in coming on both the philosophical and theological fronts. In a public discussion with Nikephoros Grigoros, Barlaam was defeated. More serious was his defeat in the area of theology by the spiritual leader Gregory Palamas. Because of his Western theological presuppositions, Barlaam was not able to understand the mystical-ascetical tradition of the East, and therefore he criticized it, with the result that he was condemned in Constantinople at the synod of 1341, and both he and his followers were formally anathematized there at the synods of 1347 and 1351. After his condemnation, he returned to the West and adhered to Roman Catholicism; he was subsequently ordained a bishop by the pope, a fact that was interpreted in the East as a confirmation of the suspect role he had played in the ranks of the Greek church.

Barlaam's theological works include eighteen anti-Latin treatises, antihesychastic writings (*On Light*, *On Knowledge*, and *Against the Messalians*, all of which are lost), and treatises and letters supporting Western theology such as *Advisory Discourse* and the draft of the *Discourse to Pope Benedict XII*. In his antihesychastic works Barlaam held that knowledge of worldly wisdom was necessary for the perfection of the monks and denied the possibility of the vision of the divine life. In addition to theological works, Barlaam also composed philosophical, astronomical, and mathematical works. Among these are his *Ethics According to the Stoics*, a treatise on calculating the eclipses of the sun, six books on arithmetic, and a paraphrase of the second book of Euclid's *Elements*.

A product of both East and West, Barlaam influenced the culture of both. Petrarch and Boccaccio were his pupils, and there is no doubt that he contributed to the strengthening of the current that led to the Italian Renaissance. On the other hand, Barlaam's interest in the hesychast dispute resulted in the development of a lively theological movement in the fourteenth century in Constantinople and Thessalonica. One of its consequences was the formulation of the mystical-ascetical teaching of the Orthodox church by Gregory Palamas.

Barlaam overestimated the significance of philosophy (especially of Greek philosophy) for theology, asserting that only through philosophy could humanity arrive at perfection. He thus denied the renewing power of the Holy Spirit, which makes saints even out of uneducated people, as it made the fishermen apostles. Being a humanist, Barlaam placed emphasis on created means of salvation (e.g., philosophy and knowledge) and reduced the role of the grace of the Holy Spirit.

BIBLIOGRAPHY

Works by Barlaam

Giannelli, Ciro. "Un progetto di Barlaam per l'unione delle chiese." In *Miscellanea Giovanni Mercati,* vol. 3, "Studi e Testi," no. 123. Vatican City, 1946. See pages 157–208 for excerpts from his writings.

Migne, J.-P., ed. *Patrologia Graeca,* vol. 151. Paris, 1857. Includes excerpts from the *Discourse to Pope Benedict XII* and the *Advisory Discourse.*

Schiro, Giuseppe, ed. *Barlaam Calabro: Epistole greche.* Palermo, 1954.

Works about Barlaam

Christou, Panagiotis C., "Barlaam." In *Threskeutikē kai ēthikē enkuklopaideia,* vol. 3, cols. 624–627. Athens, 1963.

Jugie, Martin. "Barlaam de Seminara." In *Dictionnaire d'histoire et de géographie ecclésiastiques,* vol. 6, cols. 817–834. Paris, 1932.

Meyendorff, John. "Un mauvais théologien de l'unité au quatorzième siècle: Barlaam le Calabrais." In *L'église et les églises, 1054–1954,* vol. 2, pp. 47–65. Chevetogne, 1955.

THEODORE ZISSIS
Translated from Greek by Philip M. McGhee

BARTH, KARL (1886–1968), Swiss Reformed theologian, described by Pope Pius XII as the greatest theologian since Thomas Aquinas, and certainly the most influential of the twentieth century. Barth stands as a prophetic voice in the tradition of Athanasius, Augustine, and Calvin, calling the Christian church back to the Bible and to its foundation in Jesus Christ. This message sounded forth powerfully in his first book, *Romans* (especially in the largely rewritten second edition of 1921), which drew widespread attention. Barth later said that in writing this book he was like a man in a dark church tower who accidentally trips, catches hold of the bell rope to steady himself, and alarms the whole countryside. As a result, he was called to university chairs in Göttingen (1921), in Münster (1925), and in Bonn (1930). From this latter post he was dismissed in 1935 because of his refusal to take an oath of loyalty to Hitler and because of his leading role in the *Kirchenkampf,* the struggle against the Nazi attempt to control the German Evangelical church. He returned to his native Switzerland to a professorship in Basel, where he taught for the rest of his long life until his death in 1968, drawing students from all over the world to his classrooms and publishing his lectures in his massive *Church Dogmatics.*

Barth was born in Basel on 10 May 1886, the son of Fritz Barth, a professor of church history and New Testament in Bern. In Bern Barth received his earliest education, and there, on the eve of his confirmation, he "boldly resolved to become a theologian" out of an early eagerness to understand his faith and see its relevance for the twentieth century. He commenced his university studies in Bern, where, while receiving a solid grounding in Reformed theology, he began to study the theoretical and practical philosophy of Immanuel Kant, whose "Copernican revolution" in the theory of knowledge and ethics awakened Barth to an acute awareness of the question of our knowledge and service of God. At the same time he developed his early and lifelong interest in the theologian Friedrich Schleiermacher, whose analysis of religious experience and desire to commend religion to its "cultured despisers" had dominated German theology since his death in 1834. Like Schleiermacher, Barth was later to interpret Christian dogmatics as the function of the Christian church, scrutinizing scientifically the content of the Christian faith, but unlike Schleiermacher he saw, not religious experience in general, but the revelation of God in Jesus Christ, attested in holy scripture, as the criterion of truth.

Barth expressed a desire to study at Marburg with Wilhelm Hermann (1846–1922), the leading Kantian theologian in Europe, but under his father's influence he went first to Berlin to spend a semester under Adolf von Harnack, the most outstanding church historian and liberal theologian of the day, before returning to complete a third year in Bern. In 1907 he enrolled in Tübingen to study under the conservative New Testament theologian Adolf Schlatter, before spending a final year in Marburg. Hermann defined faith in terms of "inner experience" which has its "ground" in the "inner life of Jesus" and is awakened in man's conscience by the influence of Jesus, the so-called Jesus of history of the nineteenth-century liberal quest. Although influenced by Hermann, Barth came to feel that his conception conflicted with the New Testament and Reformed understanding of the Christ of faith and with the church's creeds, and that it was more the product of modern individualistic bourgeois liberal idealism and Kantian philosophy than of sound New Testament scholarship. He also felt that the very nature and possibility of a scientific approach to Christian theology was being called into question by the philosophical and historical presuppositions of the "culture-Protestantism" of the day, wherein theology and relativizing historicism, religion, and culture were fused, obscuring the gospel through "reverence before history" and reducing Christian theology to a branch of the general philosophy of religion.

These questions assumed acute importance for Barth once he was ordained to the pastoral ministry and sought to take seriously the exposition of the Bible and the preaching of the gospel, while also taking full account of critical biblical scholarship. It was during his time as a pastor in Safenwil, Switzerland (1911–1921), that his theological position underwent a drastic change. On the one hand, when World War I broke out, he was deeply disturbed by the "Manifesto of the Intellectuals," "the black day" he called it, when ninety-three scholars and artists, including his own teachers Harnack and Hermann, supported the war policy of Kaiser Wilhelm II, which seemed to him to call into question his colleagues' understanding of the Bible, history, and dogmatics. Was this where the synthesis of (German) culture and religion was leading the Christian church? On the other hand, in his industrial parish, he became acutely aware of the issues of social justice, poor wages, factory legislation, and trade union affairs. In 1915 he became a member of the Social Democratic party, but unlike his Christian Socialist friends, he refused to identify socialism with the kingdom of God.

Throughout his life Barth endeavored to interpret the gospel and examine the church's message in the context of society, the state, war, revolution, totalitarianism, and democracy, over against the pretensions of man to solve the problems of his own destiny, without the judgment of the message of the cross and the resurrection of Jesus Christ. Toward the end of his life he could write, "I decided for theology, because I felt a need to find a better basis for my social action." The fundamental question was how to relate what the Word of God in the Bible says about the sovereignty and transcendence of God, grace, the coming of the Kingdom, the forgiveness of sins, and the resurrection of the dead with human problems. Barth voiced his concern over the bankruptcy of much contemporary religion and theology in his commentary on *Romans* (*Der Römerbrief*, 1919), where the influence of Kierkegaard, Dostoevskii, Franz Overbeck, Johann Christian Blumhardt, and Christoph Blumhardt in their attacks on institutionalized Christianity is evident. In this book, which was described by a Roman Catholic theologian as "a bombshell in the playground of the theologians," Barth seeks to summon the church back to the living God of the Bible, before whom are exposed the pretensions of human religion or piety, the proud sinful attempts to assert oneself without God. Salvation is God's gift, and the Kingdom must break in "vertically from above," summoning humankind to radical response and decision, that God's righteous purposes might be fulfilled in the world.

Barth used Paul's letter to the Romans for a critique of philosophical idealism, romanticism, and religious socialism. If his concern was that the church should listen to the divine word of judgment on our political and intellectual towers of Babel, his concern throughout his life was also to assert "that there is joy with God . . . and that the Kingdom on earth begins with joy." Together with his lifelong friend Éduard Thurneysen (1888–1974), he discovered in the Bible "a strange new world, the world of God," which is the kingdom of God, established by God and not man. Like Luther, he was gripped by the Pauline message of the righteousness of God, which calls into question all human righteousness.

Only by listening to the Word of God and recognizing God's prior righteousness can we regain a proper foundation for culture, morality, state, and church. Theologically this means we must ground Christian dogmatics in the Word of God and seek to interpret God out of God, as he reveals himself in Christ in the scriptures, and not subsume him under our prior generic concepts, categories, and ideologies. The task of theology is to allow revelation to shine in its own light. The inner meaning of the resurrection of Christ, who as creator and redeemer is lord over all, is not just a word of hope for the future, but the action of God in vindicating his righteous purposes in history and giving us a pledge of the triumph of God's righteousness in the world. Far from belittling the need for social action, the resurrection, as God's act in establishing the Kingdom, should be for us a summons to participate in this event and engage in social action with a passion for God's righteousness. There must be no divorce between justification and justice.

There were distinctive stages in Barth's theological development, in each of which he wrestled with the polarities of God and man. Nineteenth-century liberal thought too readily presupposed an inward continuity between the divine and the "highest" and "best" in human culture, positing that knowledge of God is given in the depths of the human spirit in human self-understanding and inward religious experience. Barth rejected this view early in his ministry, saying that we do not talk about God by "talking about man in a loud voice." At first, like Hermann, he identified conscience with the voice of God, but increasingly he argued that the voice of God is heard only in scripture, in encounter with Christ, the living Word. During the period of the so-called dialectical theology or theology of crisis, stemming from the second edition of Barth's *Romans,* and under the influence of Kierkegaard's critique of Hegel, Barth stressed "the infinite qualitative difference between God and man." God meets us in the moment of crisis and decision, creating his own point of contact and summoning us to radical obedience. As he wrote in his preface, "If I have a system, it is limited to a recognition of what Kierkegaard called the 'infinite qualitative distinction' between time and eternity and to my regarding this as possessing negative as well as positive significance: 'God is in heaven, and thou art on earth'" (Barth, 1933, p. 10).

The chasm between God and man can be bridged by God alone, and not by man. The Word of the cross means that God says no to our human sin and pride and pretensions, while in grace God says yes to his own good creatures in a word of forgiveness. If in this early period Barth, like the early Luther, stressed God's "no" (i.e., God's righteousness as God), his later message, like that of the later Luther, became more powerfully a "yes": God's righteousness as a triumph of grace through the vicarious humanity of Jesus Christ. In the manner of the great medieval theologians, Barth saw that there are elements of negation and affirmation in all human knowledge of God, leading him to see an analogy of "relation," but not of "being," between God and man grounded in grace.

In 1927 Barth began writing *Christian Dogmatics,* intending to expound all the main Christian doctrines, by grounding all he had to say on God's self-revelation in Jesus Christ. The first volume was entitled *Christian Doctrine in Outline, Volume I: The Doctrine of the Word of God, Prolegomena to Christian Dogmatics.* In it he argues that possibility of Christian knowledge of God is grounded on the actuality of the revelation in Jesus, as he makes himself known to faith by the Holy Spirit. Such a revelation is trinitarian in character, having a triadic pattern. God makes himself known as Father in Jesus Christ the Son, and to us by the Holy Spirit. The doctrine of the Trinity thus unfolds from the fact that "God reveals himself as the Lord." As such, this doctrine is the starting point and grammar for all Christian knowledge of God, and not merely an appendix, as in Schleiermacher.

Within this self-revelation of the triune God we can distinguish three forms of the one Word of God: the eternal Word incarnate in Jesus Christ, the written Word in the witness of the Bible to that primary Word, and the Word of God as proclaimed in the church. The task of Christian dogmatics is to be faithful to this Word, and therefore to examine the content of the church's preaching by tracing it back to its source in God, by the standard of holy scripture, and under the guidance of its creeds and confessions.

The reviewers of this first volume criticized Barth for so casting the gospel into the language of an immediate timeless encounter with God that he was in danger of dehistoricizing the gospel and transposing theology into a new philosophical mold. Barth took this criticism seriously, having himself seen this development of dialectical theology in Rudolf Bultmann, and gave himself to examining the question of method in theology by a careful study of Anselm's *Proslogion.* In 1931 he published his results in *Fide quaerens intellectum* (Faith Seeking Understanding). From Anselm he had learned that the Word of God has its own rational content in God. The polarity of God and man must be interpreted, not so much in the language of an existential encounter between God and man in the crisis of faith, but primarily in terms of the given unity of God and man in Jesus Christ, the incarnate Lord, in whom God has come—not simply *in* a man, but *as* a man—in a once and for all reconciling act in which we are called to participate through the Holy Spirit.

Barth's approach in the future was to build all theology on the reality of the Word of God in Jesus Christ. This led him to turn from his *Christian Dogmatics* to a new work entitled *Church Dogmatics,* which he began in 1932 and which occupied him for the rest of his life (resulting in thirteen part-volumes). In *Church Dogmatics* he argues that all we know and say about God and about humankind is controlled by our knowledge of Jesus Christ as "true God and true man." From this dogmatic starting point, Barth expounds the four intersecting areas of Christian doctrine: the doctrine of the Word of God (vol. 1), of God (vol. 2), of creation (vol. 3), and of reconciliation (vol. 4). (A fifth volume, dealing with redemption [eschatology], remained unwritten at the time of his death.) Each of these doctrines is expounded in a trinitarian framework in terms of a double movement, a God-manward movement and a man-Godward movement in Jesus Christ, revealing a bipolarity in every doctrine. Fundamental to his whole theology is the axiom by which the ancient church expounded the doctrine of an "ontological Trinity," that what God is toward us in Jesus Christ, he is "eternally and antecedently in himself." By looking at Jesus Christ through the Holy Spirit, we know the heart of the eternal Father. In Jesus Christ we see the inner meaning of creation as well as of redemption, for Christ is the one by whom and for whom all things were created, and in redemption we see brought to fulfillment God's filial purposes for the whole human race. Consequently, our anthropology as well as our theology must be built on this christological foundation, not on any "natural theology," on any independent concept of "orders of creation," or on any purely empirical concept of man.

Barth was concerned to unpack the implications of this Christ-centered perspective in every area of life. It proved highly significant in his outspoken opposition to Hitler, to the persecution of the Jews, and to the so-called German Christians who sought to justify National Socialism and its racist policies by an appeal to the natural orders of creation. Barth felt that this was a betrayal of the Christian understanding of grace by its appeal to sources of revelation other than that given to us in Jesus Christ. God's election of Israel for a vicarious role among the nations finds its fulfillment in Jesus Christ, the Jew in whom God has broken down the barriers between the Jews and all other ethnic groups (the gentiles). Christ as Lord is head over church and state, and to him alone we owe supreme loyalty in both spheres. The state must be interpreted not just in terms of the orders of creation and preservation (as he had earlier thought), but in terms of the orders of redemption. This found explicit formulation in the *Barmen Declaration* of 1934, largely written by Barth. For this stand he was deprived of his university chair in Bonn, but his theological insights and interpretation of the political scene gained him enormous prestige. Barth saw himself standing in the tradition of the ancient fathers of the church like Irenaeus and Athanasius, and of the Protestant reformers like Luther and Calvin, engaging in lifelong dialogue with liberal Protestantism on the left and Roman Catholicism on the right, both of which he felt weakened the emphasis of the Bible that God accepts us by grace alone in Jesus Christ.

BIBLIOGRAPHY

The best and most authoritative biography is Eberhard Busch's *Karl Barth: His Life from Letters and Autobiographical Texts* (London, 1976). On the early period of the so-called dialectical theology, the most influential work was Barth's *The Epistle to the Romans*, translated by Sir Edwyn C. Hoskyns (Oxford, 1933). The significance of this work is discussed in Thomas F. Torrance's *Karl Barth: An Introduction to His Early Theology, 1910–1931* (London, 1962). Barth's *Protestant Theology in the Nineteenth Century*, translated by Brian Cozens and John Bowden (Valley Forge, 1973), is invaluable for understanding his European theological background. The book that marked his transition to the later period of the *Church Dogmatics* is his *Anselm: Fides Quaerens Intellectum; Anselm's Proof of the Existence of God*, translated by I. W. Robertson (Richmond, 1960). In the Gifford Lectures given in Aberdeen, Barth expounded the 1560 Scots Confession in *The Knowledge of God and the Service of God*, translated by J. L. M. Haire and Ian Henderson (London, 1938). His massive exposition of Christian doctrine is set out in *Church Dogmatics*, 4 vols., edited by Geoffrey W. Bromiley and Thomas F. Torrance (Edinburgh, 1956–1969). Very readable is Barth's short *Evangelical Theology*, translated by Grover Foley (New York, 1963).

JAMES B. TORRANCE

BASILICA, CATHEDRAL, AND CHURCH.

[*This entry focuses specifically on Christian houses of worship. For the related buildings of Christian religious communities, see* Monastery.]

Over the centuries Christians have employed different terms to denominate their religious buildings, and *basilica*, *cathedral*, and *church* are but three of many. The word *church*, deriving ultimately from the Greek *kuriakos* ("of the Lord") designates a building belonging to God and, in a sense, God's dwelling. [*See* Architecture and Religion.] A church where the bishop's throne (cathedra) is located is called a cathedral, while *basilica* refers to a class of Roman public buildings predating Christianity, particularly those with royal association. In usage the three terms overlap. During the early centuries of the Christian era, a cathedra was placed in a basilica, and it was not until the eighth century that the word *cathedral* itself became current. From the Middle Ages on, the word *church* has been applied to parish churches, but it is also proper to speak of the Cathedral Church of Saint John the Divine (New York City) or of the Holy and Undivided Trinity Church (Bristol, England). The terms themselves provide no clue to the forms that the edifices may take; rather, they are the result of a host of factors, including the need to provide for certain functions as well as stylistic and aesthetic influences, the availability of materials, patronage, and climatic conditions.

Origins: The House-Church. The first Christians were Jews who quite naturally continued to attend synagogue and, when possible, the Temple in Jerusalem; in addition, they had their own distinctive celebration which took the form of a meal. Jesus had enjoyed table fellowship with his followers during his ministry, at the Last Supper, and, so it was reported, after his resurrection. The Lord's Supper, soon to be called the Eucharist, or thanksgiving, was interpreted as a remembrance and renewal of the communion experienced at these gatherings. The only architectural provision required for such a service was a dining room, so Christians in the apostolic age met in private houses: at Ephesus in the home of Aquila and Prisca, at Laodicea in the home of Nymphas, and at Colossae in the home of Philemon.

The property concerned would vary from single-family buildings up to four stories high, common in the East, to apartments arranged horizontally as in the tenements of Rome.

In the third century the church took the step of acquiring, either by purchase or by gift, houses of its own, and at Dura-Europos on the Euphrates there is an actual example of a house modified for use by a Christian congregation (see figure 1). Built shortly after the year 200, it underwent alteration in 231, when the room across the courtyard opposite the street was enlarged by knocking down a wall, and a dais was inserted, probably for the bishop's chair. West of the atrium there was a chamber, possibly for the use of catechumens, and by the entrance was another chamber for initiation. The alterations did not affect the character of the house as an example of local domestic architecture or the character of the Eucharist as a domestic event within the family of Christians. It is not surprising therefore, that several writers of the period, such as Minucius Felix and Arnobius, asserted, "We have no temples and no altars." The situation was to change dramatically in the early fourth century.

The Nature of the Basilica. The conversion of the Roman emperor Constantine I in the year 313 conferred on Christianity a new role: as the state religion, it was now charged with ensuring the well-being of the empire; its worship, replacing the pagan sacrificial system, was to obtain the divine favor; the preeminence of the ruler was to be recognized and safeguarded; the identity of the populace as citizens of Rome was to be fostered. Christianity, as it were, went public, and the unpretentiousness of the private dining room was out of keeping. Consequently, when Constantine wrote to Bishop Macarius of Jerusalem in 326 or 327 concerning his project of adorning the site of the Holy Sepulcher, he instructed him to build a basilica. This term referred to a type of Roman structure that combined religious overtones with the criteria of an official building; it was a large meeting hall, often containing an effigy of the emperor. The Christian basilica belonged to the same genus: it was a monumental public edifice where devotion to God as emperor of heaven was substituted for the imperial cult.

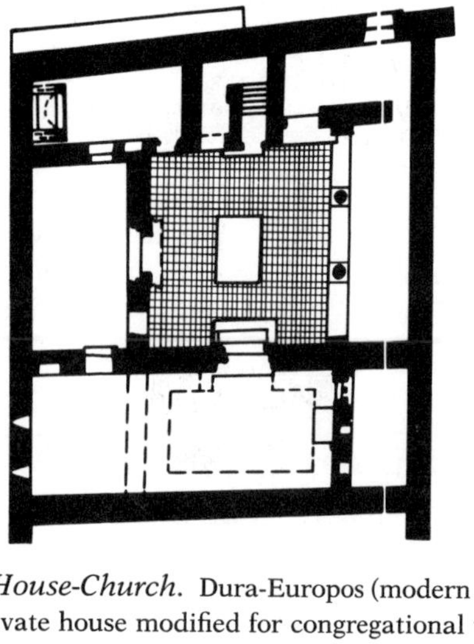

FIGURE 1. *House-Church.* Dura-Europos (modern Salahiyeh, Syria). A private house modified for congregational use.

Initially there was no uniform plan for basilicas, but by the end of the fourth century there were sufficient common features to constitute a recognizable form. Apart from Mesopotamia, where the basilican hall was transverse, one entered through a narrow side into a rectangle, the nave, flanked usually by one aisle on either side. At the opposite end there was a triumphal arch leading to a semicircular apse; at the center back of the apse was the bishop's throne, with seats for the presbyters to the right and left and the altar in front of them framed by a triumphal arch. This interior had all the characteristics of a path. Continuity and directionality were ensured by floor patterns, by the advancing row of columns, and by the succession of windows. The altar at the end of the central axis provided the terminal and goal of what Christians (themselves a pilgrim people) often called the royal highway. Architecturally, then, the Christian basilica was a structure whose walls molded and defined space as a continuum that found its climax in the altar as the center of the eucharistic action. The altar was seen as a symbol of Christ, the mediator between God and man, the meeting place of heaven and earth, so it testified to the historical specificity in time and space of the New Testament revelation.

As centers of the state religion, Christian basilicas replaced the pagan temples and thus acquired the character of holy places that had not been associated with the earlier house-churches. This character was reinforced when, since there was nothing in the New Testament about church buildings, recourse was had to the Old Testament and to the account of the Jerusalem Temple in particular for guidance. Saint Peter's in Rome, for example, would appear to have deliberately followed Solomon's model, not only with part corresponding to part but with the orientation (the apse or Holy of Holies at the west end) and even the proportions identical.

Differences of detail between one basilica and another did not affect the building's essential nature as a sacred area and a path. The apse might protrude, as in the western half of the Mediterranean, or be enclosed to create side chambers, as in the Middle East. The outer walls might be carried up to the level of those of the nave, thus making a clerestory impossible and necessitating windows that opened into the aisles and the apse, as in Asia Minor. A forecourt or atrium was frequent, but it was not indispensable. An external porch might be favored, as in Italy, or incorporated into the structure to create a narthex, where the catechumens had their place, as in Greece. The roof might be steep-pitched, made of wood or stone, even domed. A side chamber for initiation might be provided, as was often the case in North Africa and Palestine, or there could be a detached baptistery adjacent to it, as in France or Austria. No matter what the variations, the basilica met the needs of Christian congregations so well that it was not modified in any important particular for a thousand years and was still the recognizable prototype of the more elaborately planned churches of the later Middle Ages.

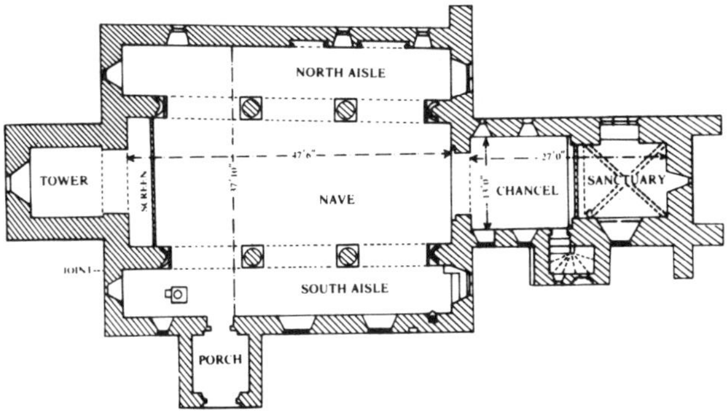

FIGURE 2. *Two-Room Medieval Church.* Church of Saint Nicholas, Compton, Surrey, England. Elaboration of the basic two-room plan separating the sanctuary from the nave.

Churches of the Middle Ages in the West. Two factors above all had striking effects on architecture in the Middle Ages: a growing distinction between priests and laity and the definition of the essential role of the priests to be that of offering the sacrifice of the Mass. During the patristic period up to about 1000 CE, the place of the clergy had been demarcated by low balustrades or chancelli, but by the Middle Ages these had developed into chancel screens that virtually shut the priest off from the congregation. Indeed, by that time many churches consisted of two rooms, as the sanctuary became a chamber separate from the nave (see figure 2). The altar ceased to be freestanding, and the celebrant stood with his back to the body of the church. If there were more than one priest, additional altars and side chapels were introduced: there was no longer one altar, as had been the case in the basilica. For larger churches and cathedrals, there were additional factors at work.

Cathedrals. By the Middle Ages, parish churches ceased to have a bishop's throne, and even cathedrals no longer gave it prominence—as the high altar was no longer freestanding, the cathedra was pushed to one side. A large number of cathedrals were under the direction of monks, for whom a fenced-off choir was fitted into the building for the saying of the divine office. A self-contained unit constituting an independent place was thus inserted into a system of paths. Since many of the religious were ordained, the need for extra altars for each priest to celebrate the daily Mass was more pronounced than in the parish church, and an abundance of small chapels was created. This multiplication of altars was also encouraged by the practice of celebrating votive masses (masses offered with special intentions), culminating in the chantry chapels, which were separate structures endowed for masses on behalf of the dead. Some chapels opened off transepts, others radiated from the ambulatory encircling the east end. This later arrangement, known as the chevet, was also the outcome of two other influences: pilgrimages and the cults of the saints. Attention had to be given to the location and means of housing the sacred relics and to the circulation space necessary for the crowds who came to honor them. Some relics were enshrined within the altars, some in crypts; the ambulatory facilitated movement, as did galleries, and consequently many pilgrimage centers, such as Santiago de Compostela, present a much more complex plan than that of the basilica (see figure 3). In elevation, too, there were differences, largely the outcome of stylistic change.

Romanesque, Gothic, and Renaissance. Although adapted for Christian use, the early Christian basilica is best categorized as an example of Roman architecture,

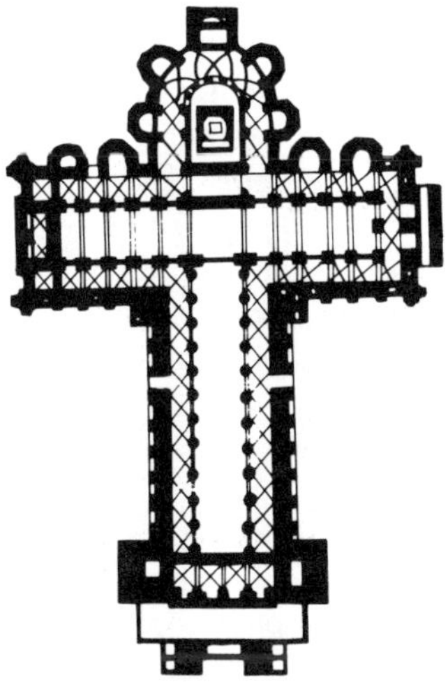

FIGURE 3. *Cruciform Ground Plan.* Cathedral of Santiago de Compostela, Spain. Enshrining of relics, especially in pilgrimage churches, necessitates elaboration of altars and spaces for circulation of congregants.

apart from the virtual neglect of the potentialities of the original Roman vault: the walls and ceiling had a space-shaping function producing a carefully proportioned interior that was an uninterrupted continuum of flowing space. After the year 1000, something essentially new in church design emerged when the vault came into its own. The vault had three effects: it determined the shape and form of the supports, which had to be much larger than the columns of the basilica because the burden was greater; it united ceiling and walls; and it created a series of bays, that is, individual spatial units. This last feature of the Romanesque style attenuated the west-to-east drive. The whole remained a path or system of paths, but it now constituted a place in itself; a focus for gathering with a character of its own. It declared that instead of advancing to meet God—the message of the basilica—the faithful live in God and are embraced by God.

The nature of the Gothic style, which succeeded Romanesque particularly in England, France, and Germany from the mid-twelfth to the early fifteenth century, was similarly determined by the vault, but now the round Roman arch was replaced by a pointed one, derived possibly from mosque architecture, familiar through the Crusades and the reconquest of Spain from the Muslims, and adopted for aesthetic reasons rather than, as nineteenth-century art historians believed, for its structural convenience. The pointed arch and the corresponding crisscrossing ribs turned the vault into a composition of triangles and diamonds; diagonality became prominent. The effect was to turn the supports into two juxtaposed V's, one jutting out into the nave and the other into the aisle, so replacing the flatness of Romanesque with projection. Verticality became the predominating factor, but this heavenward movement was balanced by a horizontal progression in that the bays were no longer independent but interlocked, and the nave became a way from expectancy to fulfillment. Every Gothic church or cathedral corresponded in a sense with one of the greatest literary creations of the age, namely the *Commedia* of Dante, who recounted how he was led ever onward and upward to the beatific vision.

A further stylistic change took place at the beginning of the fifteenth century with a rebirth of classical culture. This development derived from a careful study of the writings and ruins of ancient Rome, coupled with an imaginative re-creation of that past era as a "golden age" in which consolation and refreshment could be sought. The entire Roman architectural vocabulary was pressed into service to articulate the walls and later the three-dimensional shapes of the buildings. There was an overriding concern for proportion and harmony. The intention was to make churches to human scale because human beings are in the image of God, to create an architecture in which they could move naturally (see figure 4). Hence the change from the dominating verticality of the Gothic style to horizontality. There was no longer the propulsion of the early Christian drive to the east or the slow progression of Romanesque bays. In a Renaissance church one is at ease because one is the measure of it all. There is peace and serenity since the whole is a single self-contained hall; there is minimal movement, and the church is best perceived as a place, concentrated in form, reality comprehensible in shape, limited in size, a focus for assembly and quite evidently to be experienced as an interior volume, in contrast to a surrounding exterior. These characteristics of place apply even more precisely to the churches of Eastern Orthodoxy.

The Churches of Eastern Orthodoxy. For the first flowering of the Byzantine style, from which all later Orthodox buildings derive, it is necessary to return to the sixth century, when there was a decisive break with the basilican tradition. Just as later the combination of the Roman groin vault with the basilica was to produce the Romanesque church, under the emperor Justinian (527–565) it was the alternative form of Roman vault, the dome, that became favored in the East. Ideologically the dome was perceived as a symbol of heaven and so was regarded as suitable for tombs, baptisteries, and martyria. When the cult of the saints came to the parish churches, the dome came with it, and preference was given to a centralized plan constructed according to the baldachin principle. A baldachin, or ciborium, is a dome carried on four columns. No load-bearing walls are needed between these four columns, and so the spaces can be perforated, replaced by columnar screens,

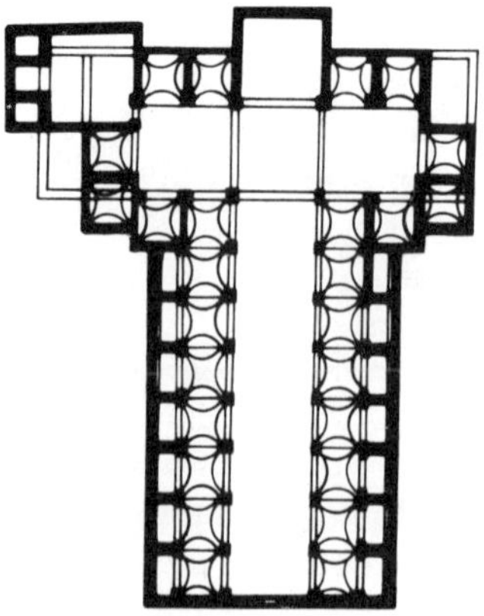

FIGURE 4. *Renaissance Proportion and Harmony.* Church of San Spirito, Florence, Italy. Serenity and comprehensibility of the divine achieved on human scale.

or simply eliminated, reducing the enveloping system to a mere skin stretched on a skeleton. Churches of this type are planned from the top downward, that is, the lower parts exist simply for the dome and would be meaningless without it. The general effect is that of a hanging architecture: the vault has no apparent weight of its own; the columns are conceived not as supports but as pendulous roots; the space radiates downward. Heaven, represented by the dome, condescends to earth, which corresponds to the flat pavement: incarnation is given architectural expression. But this is incarnation understood not in the sense of the divine veiled in human flesh but in the sense of the material transfigured, because in and through it the divine is made visible. The mosaics, which ideally should clothe every surface within a Byzantine church, as in Saint Mark's in Venice, affirm this transfiguration: while remaining themselves, the natural substances become spirit-bearing; the material reality is integrated with the divine life that pours down from above, and glory is made visible.

While the dome was the characteristic feature of such churches, there was some variety in substructure, but the most popular became a quincunx (see figure 5). This is divided into nine bays, with a central large square dominated by the principal dome. This domed square is abutted by four rectangular bays that are usually barrel-vaulted, and at each of the four corners there is a small square, usually domed. To provide for the liturgy, an apse appears at the east end, generally flanked by side chambers, while at the west end there is a porch or narthex; galleries too are common. External decoration

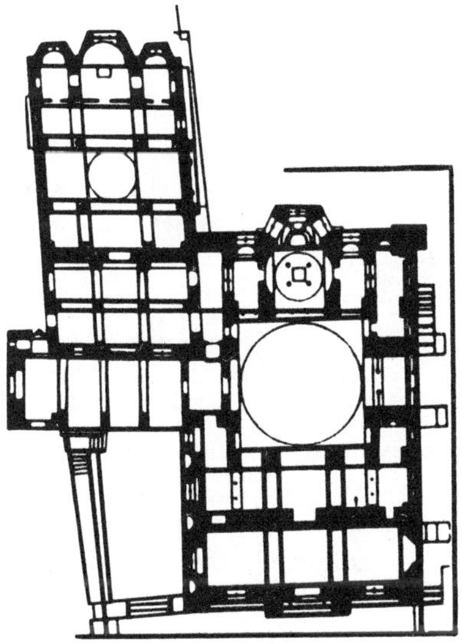

FIGURE 5. *Quicunx.* Church of the Theotokos, Hosios Loukas, Greece. The arrangement of a domed square abutted by four bays focuses assembly.

was much increased, and domes of different sizes and height were juxtaposed, as seen at the Church of Saint Sophia in Novgorod. Beginning in Russia toward the end of the fourteenth century, a solid screen—the iconostasis—covered with pictures of the saints and scenes from the Bible, shuts off the sanctuary, thus entirely blunting any suggestion of a horizontal axis or of a path. These churches then became holy places with all the features they require: union with the divine in wrapt contemplation tends to replace the movement associated with pilgrimage. Gradually this uniform architectural vocabulary began to break down in certain areas such as Bulgaria and Russia. Plans then became more diversified when, for example, a centralized sanctuary was fused with a basilica-type nave.

The Counter-Reformation and Baroque. It was in 1054 that the eastern and western halves of Christendom split in the Great Schism, but even more fragmentation was to come in the sixteenth century with the Protestant Reformation, which had profound effects on churches and cathedrals. First to be noted is the Roman Catholic church reaction to the Protestants—the Counter-Reformation—which found artistic expression in the Baroque style.

With the Counter-Reformation in full spate in the latter half of the sixteenth century, church buildings began to convey ecclesiastical self-assurance and authority. Power and exuberance were embodied in physical structures. Facades acquired a new propaganda function, both proclaiming the confidence of the church in an awe-inspiring manner and seeking to persuade and entice those who regarded them to come inside. The interior was equally designed to impress: the use of the oval plan, combining the centralized effect of a circle with an eastward thrust, produced dynamic tension that allowed no repose. There was a planned movement through space; in the drive to the high altars, the aisles, which might have distracted from the importance of the nave, were reduced to a series of side chapels, and the transepts, likewise, to mere bulges (see figure 6).

On the main altar there was now a tabernacle, or receptacle, for the reserved sacrament. To celebrate this localized presence of the divine, the church borrowed from both the court and the theater. This was the period of the emergence of nation-states, each with its own monarch enjoying magnificent apartments and ceremonial. Since God is the king of kings, his residences were to display even more splendor—all the visual arts being fused to achieve this—while the liturgy became the etiquette of the heavenly ruler. At the same time the Mass became the religious equivalent of the principal artistic creation of the age, namely the opera. The main devotional act was now the exposition of the reserved

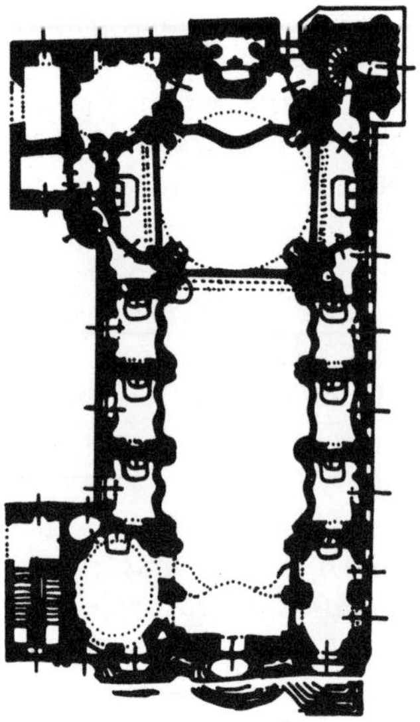

FIGURE 6. *Baroque Exuberance.* Church of Saint Nicholas, Prague, Czechoslovakia. Elaboration of enticing detail engenders the church's message.

sacrament: the displaying, at the end of a magnificent scenographic approach, of the consecrated Host to the assembly.

Within this divine theater, every worshiper was assigned an active role. One was made aware that the earthly interior was in communication with heaven above since the vast illusionistic ceiling paintings denied enclosure and gave access to the throne of God. This was the style that spread throughout the Roman Catholic church, becoming even more decorative than in Italy when it passed to Spain and its colonies in the New World, where miners and slave owners sought to honor God and thank him for the treasures they believed he had bestowed on them.

The Churches of Protestantism. One of the organs of the Counter-Reformation had been the Council of Trent (1545–1563), which reaffirmed many medieval theological ideas, among them the view that the essence of Christian priesthood is to offer the sacrifice of the Mass. Protestants reacted strongly against this position, emphasizing the fellowship aspect of the Eucharist and the importance of preaching while lowering the barrier between clergy and laity. These three factors were to have important results in the building of churches, but in the early decades after the Reformation few new structures were erected; rather, the main architectural activity consisted in adapting those buildings taken over, for example, by the Calvinists and Anglicans. The former destroyed rood screens, brought the pulpit into the midst of the congregation, and similarly advanced the baptismal font. The latter used the nave for the ministry of the word, using the second of the two medieval rooms, the sanctuary, for the ministry of the sacrament.

As time passed and additional churches were planned, Protestants in general tended to favor some kind of centralization to express the idea of the gathered congregation. Lutherans brought table, pulpit, and font together to produce the *Prinzipalstück*, or triple liturgical focus, at the east end. Anglicans approved of the auditory church devised by Christopher Wren (1632–1723): elongated chancels and prominent side aisles were suppressed to produce a single volume of such a size that all present could both hear and see what was taking place. Other denominations adopted plans that were both modest and domestic in character; many an early Quaker meetinghouse, for example, is externally indistinguishable from a private dwelling: in a sense the wheel had come full turn. Stylistically the buildings followed the current fashion, although preference began to be given to the restrained classicism that had been popularized by Wren and which in England represented the influence of the Renaissance as mediated through the Italian architect Andrea Palladio (1518–1580). Baroque, with its implicit triumphalism, did not appeal to the heirs of the Reformation, but most if not all were eventually to succumb to architectural revivalism.

The Gothic Revival in England. Once the task of the architect was conceived to be the reproduction of the styles of a former age, then there appeared to be no reason why any one epoch should be given preference. In Germany, for example, the *Rundbogenstil* (Romanesque style) was favored. In England there is the Church of Saint Mary at Wilton, Wiltshire (1840–1846), complete with freestanding Italianate campanile. It is, however, the Gothic style that most commended itself in the end. The adherents of this late eighteenth-century style rested their case on a number of vigorously argued but largely untenable beliefs. First, they held that national churches should promote whatever is the main national style, and this they identified in Great Britain as Gothic—in ignorance of the fact that it had originated in France. Second, they maintained that every religion produces its own architectural style that best expresses its character; Greek temples, for example, were deemed to embody paganism and therefore to be unsuited for Christianity. Wedded to this consideration was a third conviction that architecture mirrors the spirit of the age in which it is produced and that consequently, the Gothic of the thirteenth century, which was held to be the "age of faith" is to be recognized above all others as the Christian style.

The Gothic revival appealed to many because of a contemporary emphasis on spirituality, on sacramentality, on ritual rather than preaching, and on the visual and decorative elements that went with that emphasis. From 1839 to 1845, the Cambridge Camden Society, with the *Ecclesiologist* as its organ, campaigned all over England for the restoration of existing churches that did not conform to its ecclesiastical canons, and for the designing of new churches with extended chancels, screens, and a clear division of sanctuary from nave. Three-decker pulpits were reduced to a single level; box pews were replaced by benches all facing the altar; the empty space in the architectural choir was filled with a robed singing choir.

Beginning with Anglicanism but soon influencing Roman Catholicism, this movement quickly spread to affect all denominations. Methodism and Congregationalism in particular followed suit, though probably more for social than theological reasons: they wanted their buildings to look like "churches." Inside, however, their arrangement remained more "protestant" in that it featured a central pulpit on a rostrum and galleries, thus laying stress on the word rather than the sacrament and giving the building something of the appearance of an auditorium.

Gothic revivalism was to spread throughout the world—from the United States to Australia, from New Zealand to Iran. Failing to distinguish the gospel from its embodiment in Western cultural forms, Christians rejected indigenous architecture as primitive and even essentially pagan. Hence there appeared in Kuala Lumpur in Malaysia a complete Gothic cathedral, and a similar alien immigrant enshrines the tomb of the apostle Thomas in Madras, India.

Church Buildings in the Twentieth Century. Revivalism continued into the twentieth century, although it was being hotly contested by many architects. Indeed, it was not until the 1920s that the ideals of the modern movement in architecture began to be related to those of the liturgical movement within Roman Catholicism. The technical achievements of the modern movement were first utilized in the reinforced concrete church of Le Raincy near Paris (1923). The principles of the liturgical movement found expression in the hall of the Catholic Youth Movement headquarters at Schloss Rothenfels-am-Main in Germany (1828, see figure 7). This was a large rectangular space devoid of decoration and furnished with a hundred black cubical stools. For a liturgical celebration a provisional altar was set up, the faithful on three sides of it, and the president completed the circle by facing them across the table. This arrangement embodied the principles that the Mass should be the central Christian act of devotion, that it should be intelligible, with a unity of word and sacrament, and that it should be corporate. The space for the altar and

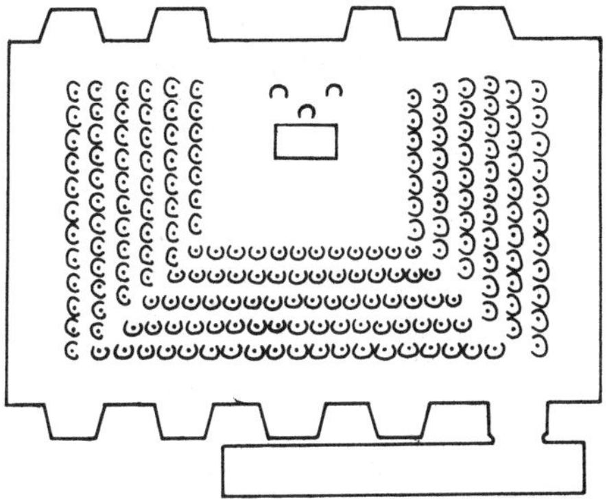

FIGURE 7. *Unified Space.* Main Hall, Schloss Rothenfels, Germany. The Mass as the central act of Christian devotion determines the modification of this hall for liturgical use.

that for the congregation were united in a single volume. When this was translated into parish church terms—for example, in the Church of Corpus Christi in Aachen, Germany (1928–1930), which was to have a potent influence on design throughout the decade before World War II—it resulted in a narrow rectangle with the altar somewhat isolated. Because the fundamental concept was that the building should be planned from the altar outward, this article of furniture was required to be a large, static object that constituted the visual and monumental focus of the entire space. The persistence of this view into the 1960s is evidenced by the chapel of Saint John's Abbey in Collegeville, Minnesota (1963).

The main characteristic of the period prior to Vatican II, in all denominations, was the progressive abandonment of the rectangular plan in favor of a design based on the square, as seen in the Church of Saint James the Fisherman, Cape Cod, Massachusetts, or Saint Paul's Church, Bow Common, London (1960). At the same time, experimentation was at its height, leading to a great variety of shapes and often, under the influence of Le Corbusier's pilgrimage chapel at Ronchamp, northeastern France (1950–1955), to asymmetry. There was, in fact, a temptation for architects to seek to display their individual genius in buildings that were monumental in conception.

The tenets of the liturgical movement, already operative within and outside the Roman communion—they were visibly embodied in the North Christian Church, Columbia City, Indiana (1964)—were fully endorsed by Vatican II, which began its sessions in October 1962. A complete break with the monumental image was now promoted; church buildings were expected to be at the "service" of the congregation. The altar was no longer regarded as the unique pole. To integrate word and sacrament, emphasis was now also placed on the pulpit or lectern and the teaching chair. A growing ecumenical consensus and an acceptance of common principles so influenced church buildings that many could not now be identified in denominational terms. It is possible to visit churches in Switzerland or the United States and be unaware of which belong to the reformed tradition and which to the Roman Catholic. Nevertheless, differences may be detected; Unitarians, for example, generally lay less stress on sacraments than do Episcopalians. As a result, Unitarian churches are likely to limit or even to give no prominence at all to the altar, instead emphasizing the pulpit; this was the case with Frank Lloyd Wright's influential design for the Unity Temple (now Unitarian Universalist Church) in Oak Park, Illinois, as long ago as 1904–1906.

Since 1970 the architectural scene has not remained static. There has been a recognition that a variety of buildings are needed for use as pastoral centers or to accommodate small groups, medium-sized congregations, and large assemblies. Indeed, what some would regard as bizarre designs have been realized; such was the drive-in church planned by Richard Neutra in 1959 for the Garden Grove community of Orange City in southern California, which was superseded by Philip Johnson's crystal cathedral opened in September 1980. The importance of mobility and flexibility has been acknowledged, with a consequent effect on furnishings and seating. The responsibility of the Christian community, not only to its own members but to the larger community within which it is set, has also led to the development of the idea of the multipurpose church, that is, one that accommodates not only worship but also other services for those in the neighborhood who are in need.

Reuse and reordering have also become important issues. The decline in attendance at worship in some areas and the movement of population in others (especially from the inner city) have made many churches virtually redundant. Some churches of little architectural or townscape interest have been demolished, while others have been adapted as libraries, museums, cultural centers, even dwelling places. Where a viable liturgical life is being maintained, there is often the need to redesign the interior of a building that was originally planned to accommodate hieratic forms of worship now regarded as belonging to the past. Beliefs, worship practices, and architecture continue to march in inextricable partnership, sometimes, but by no means always, producing less-than-major monuments, sometimes creating works of considerable beauty, in all cases and in all periods representing varying and valid traditions within the Christian denominations.

[*See also* Worship and Cultic Life, *article on* Christian Worship; Pilgrimage, *articles on* Roman Catholic Pilgrimage in Europe, Roman Catholic Pilgrimage in the New World, *and* Eastern Christian Pilgrimage; Relics; Shrines; *and* Tombs.]

BIBLIOGRAPHY

Blunt, Anthony, et al. *Baroque and Rococo: Architecture and Decoration.* London, 1978.

Conant, Kenneth J. *Carolingian and Romanesque Architecture, 800 to 1200.* 3d ed. Harmondsworth, 1973.

Davies, J. G. *The Secular Use of Church Buildings.* New York, 1968.

Davies, J. G. *Temples, Churches and Mosques. A Guide to the Appreciation of Religious Architecture.* New York, 1982.

Debuyst, Frédéric. *Modern Architecture and Christian Celebration.* London, 1968.

Frankl, Paul. *Gothic Architecture.* Harmondsworth, 1962.

Hammond, P. *Liturgy and Architecture.* London, 1960.

Kennedy, Roger G. *American Churches.* New York, 1982.

Krautheimer, Richard. *Early Christian and Byzantine Architecture.* Harmondsworth, 1965.

Murray, Peter. *The Architecture of the Italian Renaissance.* London, 1963.

J. G. DAVIES

BASIL OF CAESAREA (c. 329–379), called "the Great"; Christian theologian, bishop of Caesarea (modern Kayseri, Turkey), and one of three great Cappadocian fathers of the church (together with his friend, Gregory of Nazianzus, and his younger brother, Gregory of Nyssa).

Basil was born into a deeply Christian family of high social standing and extensive possessions. His grandmother Macrina, his parents Basil and Emmelia, his older sister Macrina, and his younger brothers Gregory of Nyssa and Peter of Sebaste are venerated as saints in both the Eastern Orthodox and Roman Catholic churches. Basil received a Christian education from childhood; his father, who was a rhetor, also gave him the beginnings of his secular training. After the early death of his father, Basil continued his secondary education in Caesarea (c. 345–347) and then pursued further studies in rhetoric and philosophy in Constantinople (c. 348–350), where he was probably a student of the famous pagan rhetor Libanius. Finally, he studied, together with Gregory of Nazianzus, in Athens (c. 350–355). Returning home, Basil seems to have taught rhetoric for a short time, but soon gave up a promising worldly career for the Christian ascetic ideal.

In accordance with the fourth-century custom of late baptism—even in fully Christian families—Basil was baptized and ordained a reader of scripture in Caesarea by Bishop Dianius, undertook a tour of monastic settlements in Syria, Mesopotamia, Palestine, and Egypt (c. 356–357), and then joined his mother and his sister Macrina in a semi-eremitical type of asceticism on a family estate at Annesi in Pontus. Dianius's successor, Eusebius, ordained Basil a priest (c. 364), and he soon became the actual leader of the diocese. After the death of Eusebius (c. 370), Basil was elected bishop of Caesarea and as such became metropolitan of Cappadocia. He fulfilled his office in an exemplary manner and extended his pastoral care to all aspects of the life of the church. He led the faithful, especially through his sermons, to a deeper understanding of their Christian faith. He supported the needy with social institutions, financed in great part from the selling of his possessions. He gave direction to the thriving, but often "sectarian" monastic movement and integrated it within the Christian community as a whole. He worked unceasingly against doctrinal and political divisions within the Eastern church and between Eastern and Western Christianity. Consumed by hard discipline and labors, he died on 1 January 379.

Because of the respect he enjoyed during his lifetime, Basil's works have been relatively well preserved. They reveal both his own quest for Christian perfection and his concerns as leader of the church. The *Philokalia*, apparently published posthumously, is an anthology of excerpts from Origen's writings, compiled by Basil and Gregory of Nazianzus during their retirement in Annesi. It reflects their critical assimilation of the theology of Origen and preserves many of his texts in the original Greek. In this same period he composed the *Moralia*, an anthology of more than 1,500 verses of the New Testament, distributed under eighty headings (rules), as guidelines for a perfect Christian life; it is directed, for the most part, to all believers, not only to monks and clergy. It was originally published with a preface, *On the Judgment of God*, to which Basil later added a second preface, *On the Faith*. During Basil's years as a priest he composed his "little" *Asceticon* (preserved in the Latin translation of Rufinus); the full version (the "great" *Asceticon*), completed during his later years as a bishop, consists of fifty-five "longer rules," or systematic regulations of the cenobitic life (i.e., monastic life in a community) and 313 "shorter rules," or practical answers to the questions emerging in such communities.

Basil's numerous letters (366 of which have been preserved) cover his life from the time of his return from Athens and contain precious information on the history of the church in the fourth century. His sermons are more difficult to date; some were preached during his priesthood, but the majority during his episcopate. Particularly famous are the nine *Homilies on the Hexaemeron* (i.e., on the story of creation in six days according to *Genesis*).

The most important of his dogmatic works are *Against Eunomius* (c. 364), a refutation of extreme Arianism (books 4 and 5 are not by Basil), and his substantial treatise *On the Holy Spirit* (c. 375), which is directed against those who denied that equal glory is to be given to the third person of the Trinity. The small treatise *On the Spirit*, a radical rewriting in the sense of the Christian Trinity of *Ennead* 5.1 of Plotinus ("founder" of Neoplatonism, c. 205–270), is probably not by Basil, although it seems to have influenced him. Particularly revered from the time of the European Renaissance is Basil's short treatise, *To the Young, on How They Might Derive Benefit from Greek Literature*, written probably in the last years of his life.

Basil's theology is both "theoretical" (i.e., contemplative) and "practical" (i.e., giving guidance for life). The strife-torn situation of the contemporary church, according to him, results primarily from the failure of Christians to live according to their faith (see *On the Judgment of God*). Only the grace of Christ and the guidance of the Holy Spirit can accomplish salvation, but in order to receive this, one should live according to God's precepts as manifested in the gospel, especially the two greatest commands, the love of God and of neighbor. Insisting on fidelity in practice, Basil was equally concerned with the purity of faith. He defended the divinity of the Son against the denial of the Arians (especially Eunomius), and the equal glory of the Holy Spirit against the so-called Pneumatomachians ("fighters against the spirit"), even though, to the disappointment of his friends, he did not demand an explicit confession of the divinity of the Holy Spirit. Clearly asserting, however, both the unity of the divine essence (*ousia*) and the distinction of the three persons (*hupostaseis:* that is, Father, Son, and Holy Spirit), Basil anticipated the definitive formulation of the trinitarian faith by the Council of Constantinople (381).

Basil had a profound and far-reaching influence on both Eastern and Western Christianity. His trinitarian faith, further clarified by the other two great Cappadocians, became normative for subsequent Christianity, and a basis for overcoming the divisions of the church that arose from the trinitarian controversies. Eastern monasticism, of crucial importance throughout the history of the church, still follows (with modifications) the rule of Basil, which was also one of the important resources of Western monasticism. The so-called "Liturgy of Saint Basil," still in use in the Eastern church, originated in his practice and writings. There can be no doubt that his life and teaching have been a source of inspiration for many Christians through the ages.

BIBLIOGRAPHY

Works by Basil of Caesarea. The only complete edition of the works of Basil in the original Greek with parallel Latin translation is that prepared by Julien Garnier and Prudentius Maran in 3 volumes (Paris, 1721–1730), reprinted in J.-P. Migne's *Patrologia Graeca,* vols. 29–32 (Paris, 1857, 1886). The photomechanical reprints of these volumes (Turnhout, 1959–1961) contain new introductions by Jean Gribomont, giving a survey of all editions and translations of Basil's works, with information on authenticity and chronology. A complete listing of Basil's works, indicating the best edition for each, with information as to authenticity, is given in Maurice Geerards's *Clavis Patrum Graecorum,* vol. 2 (Turnhout, 1974), pp. 140–178.

Basil's works can be found in English translation in *Letters and Selected Works,* translated by Blomfield Jackson, "Select Library of Nicene and Post-Nicene Fathers," 2d series, vol. 8 (1886; reprint, Grand Rapids, Mich., 1978–1979); *The Ascetic Works,* translated by W. K. L. Clarke (London, 1925); *Letters,* 4 vols., edited and translated by Roy J. Deferrari, "Loeb Classical Library" (Cambridge, Mass., 1926–1934), volume 4 of which also contains the *Address to Young Men on Reading Greek Literature* (pp. 363–435); *Ascetical Works,* translated by Monica Wagner, "Fathers of the Church," vol. 9 (Washington, D.C., 1950); *Letters,* translated by A. C. Way, "Fathers of the Church," vols. 13, 28 (Washington, D.C., 1951–1955); *Exegetic Homilies,* translated by A. C. Way, "Fathers of the Church," vol. 46 (Washington, D.C., 1963); and *Saint Basil on the Value of Greek Literature,* edited and translated by Nigel G. Wilson (London, 1975).

Works about Basil of Caesarea. *Basil of Caesarea: Christian, Humanist, Ascetic; A Sixteen-Hundredth Anniversary Symposium,* 2 vols., edited by Paul Jonathan Fedwick (Toronto, 1981), contains papers presented at an international symposium held in Toronto, 10–16 June 1979, on all major aspects of Basil's life, works, thought, and influence, by leading specialists, with extensive bibliography.

DAVID L. BALÁS, O.CIST.

BASQUE RELIGION. During the first millennium BCE, the religion of the Basque people of the western Pyrenees was influenced by various peoples with whom the Basques had contact, such as the Celts and, later, the Romans. Thus numerous myths, rites, and new beliefs from other traditions were incorporated into the Basque religion.

Mythology and Deities. Basque mythology is characterized by the existence of diverse deities in animal form: bulls, pigs, horses, goats, vultures, and serpents that generally lived in caves. Some Basque myths have parallels among other European peoples, such as the myth of the black hunter who, on stormy nights, accompanied by his pack of hounds, pursues a hare he never catches. One Basque myth, also found in similar form among other Indo-Europeans, tells of the *laminaks,* who are sometimes half woman and half fish and at other times half woman and half bird. Another myth, again with variants in Indo-European myths, is that of Basajaun, who resembles the Silvanus or Faunus of classical mythology and is likewise associated with grain; he is thought of as the first farmer, the first miller, and the first blacksmith. Tartarus (Span., Tartalo; Fr., Tartaro) is the Basque cyclops, an evil spirit who dwells in a cave, splits his prisoners in two, and eats them.

An important Basque deity is the Moon (Ilarqui). The moon is understood to be the recipient of reflected light or of the light of the dead. Consequently it is associated with death as well as with the month. On nights of the full moon the Basques held a religious festival associated with it. Vestiges of a moon cult have been found next to the remains of a cult to the god of the heavens (Ortzi), to the Sun (Ekhi), and to the Earth (Lur). Ekhi, who has the power to destroy evil spirits, is the daughter of Lur, who is depicted as a large receptacle.

Another important goddess in Basque religion is Mari, who dwells in a cave and assumes features of different animals, such as the cloven feet of a he-goat or the claws of a vulture. She is depicted as a wealthy woman, riding through the air in a chariot drawn by four horses. Every seven years she changes her place of residence. Her house is richly decorated with beds, chairs, combs, and the figure of a bull, all made of gold. At various times she appears as a burning tree, a white cloud, or the rainbow. She likes being remembered by her devotees with offerings, her preferred gift being a sheep. In the legends she appears as a chthonic deity, archaic and mysterious in character and sometimes malefic. Along with ruling the rains and the droughts, she punishes theft, lies, and pride. As can be seen, many diverse mythic themes come together in her. Her spouse, Maju, appears either as Mari or as a serpent. When the two meet rain and hail will follow.

The influence of Roman mythology shows in a number of Basque gods and spirits. Some of the major ones are as follows. Mari has two sons: Atarrabi is the good son, who has no shadow and mainly prevents his brother Mikelats from doing evil deeds. For his part, Mikelats brings on storms and destroys flocks and harvests. Another pair are Lamiñ, a female spirit with chicken feet, and Maide, a male spirit. Lamiñ dwells in caves, wells, and old castles but disappears when oxen are worked with. Maide comes to houses at night and takes the inhabitants' offerings. Another spirit who appears in houses at night is Inguma, a spirit of bad omen. He chokes people to frighten them. Prayers to keep him at bay are said to him before going to sleep.

Additionally, there are Lahe, a female deity, who is invoked during human illness, and Akerbeltz, who represents the goddess Mari and who cures animals. Azti, a magical character, cures maladies of the heart, protects harvests and animals, and brings on artificial rain through exorcism. Evil spirits include Beguizko, who has magical powers: he brings on the evil eye with a glance. Ashes, cinders, garlic, olives, and salt are charms used against him. Herensugue is a diabolical spirit in the form of a serpent. Sugaar, a male serpent who crosses the heavens as a ball of fire, is believed to presage strong winds. Gaueko, the spirit of night, punishes those who work at night or pretend not to be afraid.

Other spirits and deities include Aatxe, a young bull, who both punishes disobedient children and takes people to caves when they do not fulfill their religious duties; the Aiharra-haio, a group of familial spirits or goblins who help people when they perform certain ceremonies; Eate, the god of the storm and fire; Eluaso, the spirit of avalanches; Fagus, the spirit of the beech tree; and Galtxaggori, a very small, beneficent spirit in human shape. Alarabi, a mountain spirit, appears in human form but with only one eye and one leg, while Amilamia, a golden yellow female, is a very friendly deity who helps the poor.

Other Basque Beliefs and Rites. For the Basques, the house, represented by the spirit Itxe, was holy. Many houses were extensions of caves, which were a frequent motif in Basque religion. The kitchen hearth kept away ghosts who tried to visit. Certain plants, including ash and laurel, were used to sanctify the house. Before the spread of Christianity, which in the Basque country is recent, the house served as a grave, and sacrifices to the dead were made within it.

There was a highly developed cult of the dead among the Basques. The notion of the living corpse, nourished on light and on food laid out for the dead, was widespread. Masks, which appeared at festivals at the beginning of the year, very likely depicted the spirits of the dead. Animism, also, was highly developed. The Basques associated spirits with many different things; Mari, for example, was thought to take the form of a stalactite. Mari was also found in a burning tree, a white cloud, a rainbow, a ball of fire, a hearth, and so on.

Other beliefs held by the Basques included the idea that stalagmites were petrified beings and that touching them cured eczema. They also believed that the soul looked like light and could be influenced by a candle. The Basque people held religious dances, such as the masquerades from the region of Lanz (Navarre), in which a person disguised as a horse (Zamalzain) was pursued. A giant with a huge mask also took part in these events, which were intended to protect agriculture.

BIBLIOGRAPHY

Barandiarán, José Miguel de. *Die baskische Mythologie: Götter und Mythen im alten Europa.* Stuttgart, 1973.

Caro Baroja, Julio. *Sobre la religion antigua y el calendario del pueblo vasco.* San Sebastián, Spain, 1980.

José M. Blázquez

Translated from Spanish by Erica Meltzer

BAṢṬĀMĪ, AL-. *See* Biṣṭāmī, al-.

BATAK RELIGION.

The Batak societies, located around Lake Toba in North Sumatra, are among the more than three hundred ethnic minorities of Indonesia. Batak religion, like Batak culture as a whole, is ethnically diverse, syncretic, changing, and bound at once to both village social organizational patterns and the monotheistic national culture of Indonesia. Like many religious traditions of Indonesia, Malaysia, and the Philippines, Batak myths and rituals focus on the yearly cycle of rice cultivation activities and the local kinship system. Batak religions tie these two realms to a larger cosmological order, which is then represented in various religious art forms (traditional house architecture, village spatial layout, and wood sculpture) and ritual activities (dances, oratory, and gift-giving ceremonies). Batak kinship revolves around marriage alliances that link together lineages of patrilineal clans, called *marga.* This marriage system, which involves ritually superior and "holy" wife-providing lineages and their ritually subordinate, "mundane" wife-receiving lineages, is much celebrated in the indigenous Batak religions. Many village rites of passage, for instance, are largely occasions for eulogizing this asymmetrical marriage alliance system through hours of ritual oratory. Beyond these very localized ethnic patterns, however, Batak religious life extends outward into the world religions: the large majority of homeland Batak and virtually all migrants to cities in Sumatra and Java are Muslim or Christian. In fact, the Batak are stereotyped in Indonesia as uncommonly pious monotheists; both the southern Batak Muslim pilgrim to Mecca and the Toba Batak Protestant minister are stock characters in the national *dramatis personae* when members of other ethnic groups think of these Sumatran peoples. In this monotheistic environment, Batak village religion has undeniably lost some of its social and symbolic scope. However, through an inventive reinterpretation of symbols, other sectors of village belief and ritual continue to thrive in new forms.

There are six major Batak societies in the homeland region around Lake Toba. These societies are similar in village social structure and subsistence base (paddy rice farming with some dry field agriculture) but speak different dialects of Batak and have distinct ritual systems. These societies are commonly called the Toba Batak, Karo Batak, Pakpak and Dairi Batak, Simelungun Batak, Angkola and Sipirok Batak, and the Mandailing Batak (although some "Batak" rarely call themselves Batak). Their pre-monotheistic religions are impossible to reconstruct in detail from current evidence because Islam and Christianity have reshaped village ritual and folk memories of the past so thoroughly. It is common, for instance, for committed Muslim and Christian Batak to speak disparagingly of their "pagan" ancestors, who believed in populous spirit worlds before they "discovered that there was only one God." In other words, "traditional Batak religion" is in large part a figment of the contemporary Batak imagination. It is safe to say, however, that the Batak religions practiced before the 1820s (when Islam entered the southern Angkola and Mandailing homelands) and the 1850s and 1860s (when Protestant Christianity was introduced to Angkola and the Toba region by Dutch missionaries and the German Rheinische Mission Gesellschaft) shared many symbolic complexes with the related indigenous religions of Kalimantan's Dayaks, Sulawesi's highland societies, and the people of eastern Indonesia.

In all these regions, certain assumptions about the nature of the universe permeated village religion. Binary oppositions between life and death, humans and animals, the village and the forest, metal and cloth, masculinity and femininity, and warfare and farming were recurrent themes in ritual and myth. Both human and agricultural creativity and fertility were thought to come from the temporary, intensely powerful union of such complementary opposites as life and death, masculinity and femininity, and so on. Also important was the notion that the two opposing categories were aboriginally one. Ritual often endeavored to unite for a moment the binary opposites and then control the resulting release of power from the center. (For instance, at Batak weddings the bride-giving faction bestows ritual textiles on their bride-receivers while the latter bestow counter-gifts of metal and livestock. Such exchanges foster fertility in the marriage.) The Batak societies took these familiar pan-Indonesian concepts and fit them to their particular social structure. Toba origin myths, for instance, tell of a first human, Si Raja Batak, who fathered two sons (Guru Tateabulan and Raja Isumbaon), who in turn fathered the ancestors of the major Toba patrilineal clans. Related myths tell of the origin of farming and weaving and link clan clusters to certain valleys and upland regions. Other Toba myths warn of the consequences of clan incest and marriages that violate the asymmetrical alliance rules (men should not marry women from lineages that serve as their traditional wife-receivers).

All Batak religions had extensive soul concepts and generally posited a personal soul that could fragment when startled and escape from a person's head to wander haplessly in the countryside until recalled to his body in special soul-capture ceremonies. *Datu* or *guru* were diviner-sorcerers who performed such religious cures and also served the village chiefs as "village protection experts" in times of warfare, epidemic, or crop failure. Sacrificial rituals were central to the *datu*'s protective tasks; in a few areas there may have been occasional ritual cannibalism (a point that is hotly debated among Batak today). Common myth images include magic numbers, constellations of stars, the magic colors red, white, and black, the *baringin* tree (the banyan tree seen as the cosmic tree uniting the layers of the Batak cosmos), the *singa* (a powerful monster that is part human, part water buffalo, and part crocodile or lizard), the cosmic serpent Naga Padoha, the hornbill, and aboriginal boy-girl twins. In Toba and Karo such images animated an extensive range of art forms, including carved wooden sorcerers' staffs, textiles, funerary masks, and megalithic monuments. These art forms, and the larger religions surrounding them, also drew on Indian beliefs; like many Indonesian cultures the Batak came into contact with Hinduism and Buddhism via possible trading colonies near Barus, a temple community near Portibi, and through influence from the indianized ancient kingdoms of south Sumatra.

Contact with the monotheistic religions varies considerably from Batak society to society. Karo is an area of fairly recent conversions, with many animists. In this mixed Muslim and Protestant region, Christian proselytizing gained some converts in the 1930s, but the major switch to monotheism has come since 1965 as a result of the national government's identification of Indonesian patriotism with belief in a monotheistic religion. Toba is overwhelmingly Protestant; the original, German-sponsored missionary church, the HKBP (Huria Kristen Batak Protestan), has its headquarters in Tarutung. During the Padri Wars in the 1820s Minangkabau Muslims brought their religion to the southern Angkola and Mandailing homelands; today, Mandailing is entirely Muslim while Angkola is about 10 percent Protestant and 90 percent Muslim.

During the Suharto regime, the HKBP church has splintered into the parent church and a number of bickering class- and ethnicity-based new denominations. In religiously mixed areas, members of the churches tend to align themselves with Muslim families along class lines. In Angkola, for instance, where pre-national society was divided into an aristocracy, commoners, and slave descendants, Muslims from noble families often find political allies among highborn Christians. Early conversions in the 1850s and 1860s brought large numbers of slave descendants into the church, while later Dutch colonial policy led to favoritism for village chiefly lineages that became Christian. This policy has left southern Batak Christianity argumentative and faction-ridden.

In Angkola, members of the same social class often emphasize their common heritage "in the *adat*" (village custom) over their differences in monotheistic religion. Because *adat* encompasses much village ritual, this leads to much syncretism. In Muslim Mandailing and Christian Toba, by contrast, *adat* is often seen as conflicting with monotheistic religion. In all Batak societies, the area where *adat* meets monotheism promises to remain an important growing edge of culture in the coming decades.

[*See also* Southeast Asian Religions, *article on* Insular Cultures.]

BIBLIOGRAPHY

There is a large literature in Dutch, English, and Indonesian on the Batak societies. Toenggoel P. Siagian's "Bibliography on the Batak Peoples," *Indonesia* 2 (October 1966): 161–184, is a valuable guide to the main research before the mid-sixties, and the bibliographies in *Beyond Samosir: Recent Studies of the Batak Peoples of Sumatra*, edited by Rita Smith Kipp and Richard D. Kipp (Athens, Ohio, 1983), provide references for the last twenty years, a period of much American anthropological fieldwork in the area. Jacob Cornelis Vergouwen's *The Social Organization and Customary Law of the Toba-Batak of Northern Sumatra* (1933), translated by Jeune Scott-Kemball (The Hague, 1964), remains the premier descriptive ethnography of a Batak culture, with much information on non-monotheistic rituals and beliefs. Recent articles and monographs by anthropologists reflect a shift in research toward Batak symbol systems: Rita Smith Kipp's "The Thread of Three Colors: The Ideology of Kinship in Karo Batak Funerals," in *Art, Ritual, and Society in Indonesia*, edited by Judith Becker and Edward M. Bruner (Athens, Ohio, 1979), discusses Karo religion in its marriage alliance context; I discuss religious syncretism and change in *Adat, Islam, and Christianity in a Batak Homeland* (Athens, Ohio, 1981). Two major collections of anthropological essays on similar religious and social systems from other regions of Indonesia provide invaluable comparative material: *The Flow of Life: Essays on Eastern Indonesia*, edited by James Fox (Cambridge, Mass., 1980), and *The Imagination of Reality: Essays in Southeast Asian Coherence Systems*, edited by A. L. Becker and Aram A. Yengoyan (Norwood, N.J., 1979).

SUSAN RODGERS

BAUBO figures in the myth of the ancient Greek goddess Demeter as the perpetrator of an obscene spectacle that causes the goddess to laugh and that marks the end of her long period of mourning. The myth of Demeter tells of her inconsolable grief at the loss of her daughter Persephone (or Kore) and of her wanderings in search of her. [*See* Demeter and Persephone.] The aged Demeter finally comes out of mourning in the town of Eleusis, where she suddenly bursts into laughter. A double tradition relates how obscene words and gestures diverted and comforted this holy mother.

In the Homeric *Hymn to Demeter* (192–211), it is the maiden Iambe who cheers up the goddess with dirty jokes. The hymn says nothing about the specific content of these obscenities, but the effectiveness of Iambe's words is certain. Indeed, Demeter laughs, comes out of mourning, and ends her fast by accepting and drinking kukeon (a beverage made of wheat, water, and pennyroyal), which is offered to her by her hostess, Metanir, the wife of King Keleos.

In the writings of the church fathers, Baubo plays a role comparable to Iambe's. But whereas Iambe succeeds in comforting the goddess by telling jokes, Baubo does so not by words but by an obscene gesture: she suddenly lifts her gown to reveal her genitals. This indecent unveiling provokes laughter in the grieving mother, who then accepts and drinks the kukeon that Baubo offers her. Christian polemicists, who attribute the story of the obscene gesture to the Orphics, preserve two versions of the incongruous scene. Clement of Alexandria (*Protrepticus* 2.20.1–1.21.2) and Eusebius of Caesarea (*Praeparatio evangelica* 2.3.31–35) relate that the young Iacchos was found beneath Baubo's raised garment, laughing and waving his hand. Arnobius (*Adversus nationes* 5.25–26) presents a different, more detailed version in which Baubo's unveiled genitals, because of a cosmetic operation, look like the face of a baby.

This "spectacle" *(theama, spectaculum)* has given rise to numerous interpretations. In general, historians have understood it as an etiological myth justifying fertility rites, and certain specialists have recognized in Baubo the mythic memory of the manipulation of sexual articles at Eleusis. Baubo has also been associated, often confusedly, with anything obscene in the ancient world, particularly with obscene words and objects that evoke female sexuality.

Some earthenware figurines found at the beginning of this century in the temple of Demeter and Kore (fourth century BCE) at Priene, in Ionia, have been identified with Baubo. These "Baubos of Priene" merge the head, the belly, and the female sexual organ, with the genitals immediately below the mouth.

BIBLIOGRAPHY

Devereux, Georges. *Baubô: La vulve mythique.* Paris, 1983.

Graf, Fritz. *Eleusis und die orphische Dichtung Athens in vorhellenistischer Zeit.* Berlin, 1974.

Olender, Maurice. "Aspects de Baubô: Textes et contextes antiques." *Revue de l'histoire des religions* 202 (January–March 1985): 3–55.

Olender, Maurice. "Les manières de Baubô." In *Masculin et féminin en Grèce ancienne,* edited by Nicole Loraux. Paris, 1986.

Picard, Charles. "L'épisode de Baubô dans les mystères d'Éleusis." *Revue de l'histoire des religions* 95 (March–June 1927): 220–255.

MAURICE OLENDER
Translated from French by Kristine Anderson

BAUER, BRUNO (1809–1882), left-wing Hegelian critic of the Bible, Christianity, and Prussian society. Bauer began his career as a conservative (right-wing) Hegelian theologian. His earliest writings on the Old Testament (1838) argued that the Hebraic idea of a deity distinct from creation gradually developed toward the Christian doctrine of the immanence of God and humanity. As a Hegelian, he interpreted this to mean that the finite had become conscious of itself as infinite. In an essay of 1840 he also argued that the union of the Reformed and Lutheran churches in 1818 further confirmed the Hegelian view that the Prussian state had become the embodiment of true spiritual life.

Appointed to the faculty of Bonn University in 1839, he turned his attention to the New Testament and wrote what is now considered his most important work: *Kritik der evangelischen Geschichte der Synoptiker.* In it he tried to show that biblical criticism could advance the self-consciousness of humanity by extracting the kernel of truth in the Christian narratives—that is, that human self-consciousness is divine—from the contradictions resulting from the historical form of those narratives. He treated the New Testament Gospels as purely human documents and as literary products of the creative imagination of the authors, therefore concluding that they record little about the real Jesus but much about the mentality of the early church.

Dismissed from the faculty at Bonn, he returned in bitterness to Berlin and wrote attacks on Christianity, the Prussian state, and even Hegel. He came to believe that unremitting, rational criticism, unallied with any political party and without presuppositions of any kind, could bring about a transformation of society. Scornful of revolutionary action in 1848, he became disillusioned with Prussia until the advent of Bismarck. Although he returned to the problem of the origins of Christianity in later works, his views were largely ignorned. He spent his last years working in his family's tobacco shop.

BIBLIOGRAPHY

Unfortunately, not only is there no edition of Bauer's entire work, but there are no English translations of major individual works. His two best-known and most influential works, so far as New Testament criticism is concerned, are *Kritik der evangelischen Geschichte der Synoptiker,* 3 vols. (Leipzig, 1841–1842), and *Kritik der Evangelien und Geschichte ihres Ursprungs,* 4 vols. in 2 (Berlin, 1851–1855). His attack on Christianity is best represented by *Das entdeckte Christentum,* now reprinted in an edition by Ernst Banikol (Jena, 1927).

There are surprisingly few biographical studies of Bauer, the best being *Der Junghegelianer Bruno Bauer im Vormärz* by Dieter Hertz-Eichenrode (Berlin, 1959). In English there is only one book dealing solely with Bauer: Zvi Rosen's *Bruno Bauer and Karl Marx: The Influence of Bruno Bauer on Marx's Thought* (The Hague, 1977). There is a fine discussion of Bauer and his significance for Christian thought in Karl Löwith's *From Hegel to Nietzsche: The Revolution in Nineteenth-Century Thought* (Garden City, N.Y., 1967). Nor should one neglect Albert Schweitzer's discussion of Bauer's critical work in *The Quest of the Historical Jesus,* 2d ed. (1911; reprint, London, 1952). Other useful secondary sources are *The Young Hegelians* by William J. Brazill (New Haven, 1970), which contains very useful bibliographies, and *From Hegel to Marx: Studies in the Intellectual Development of Karl Marx* by Sidney Hook (New York, 1936).

VAN A. HARVEY

BAŪLS. *See* Bengali Religions.

BAUR, F. C. (1792–1860), German Protestant theologian, biblical scholar, and church historian. Ferdinand Christian Baur is best known as the leader of the "Tübingen school" and the practitioner of an allegedly Hegelian historial method. He was perhaps the most important German theologian between Friedrich Schleiermacher and Albrecht Ritschl. Over the years he has suffered from caricature and neglect, but reappraisal was made easier in the 1960s when selected works by him began to reappear in a new edition.

Baur was born in Schmiden, near Stuttgart, and educated mainly at Blaubeuren seminary and the University of Tübingen. In 1817 he returned to Blaubeuren as a teacher, and his thinking changed radically from the supernaturalism of the so-called Old Tübingen School to the conviction, learned from Schleiermacher, that Christianity cannot be studied in isolation from other religions, as though it alone had a divine origin. He moved in 1826 to a chair at his old university, Tübingen, where he remained until his death.

At Tübingen Baur led the secluded life of a dedicated

academic. But he became embroiled in two famous literary debates. The first was occasioned by the attempt of Johann Adam Moehler, of the Catholic theological faculty, to specify in his symbolics (1832) the doctrinal differences between Roman Catholics and Protestants. The second erupted when David Friedrich Strauss, one of Baur's former students from Blaubeuren, published his notorious *Life of Jesus* (1835) and was dismissed from his lectureship at Tübingen. Baur protested against the dismissal, but he endorsed neither Strauss's method nor his conclusions.

Unlike Strauss, Baur did not believe that criticism had proved the books of the New Testament to be virtually worthless as sources for reconstructing Christian origins. The documents themselves, according to Baur, give plain evidence of the historical situation through which they should be interpreted, namely, the clash between Jewish Christianity and gentile Christianity, which was later to be harmonized in the old Catholic church. The historical worth of the sources can be appraised by determining each author's "tendency," or theological proclivity, against this background of conflict. Baur concluded that John's gospel must be set aside in any serious attempt to write the history of the primitive church, that Matthew's is the earliest of the Gospels that have come down to us, and that Paul most likely wrote only four of the letters attributed to him *(Galatians, 1 Corinthians, 2 Corinthians,* and *Romans).* Further, while he rejected Schleiermacher's belief that in Christ the ideal became actual, he thought it possible, against Strauss, to trace the way in which the Christ of ecclesiastical dogma developed out of Jesus's own self-consciousness.

His critics read Baur's New Testament work as a doctrinaire application of the Hegelian dialectic of thesis, antithesis, and synthesis. Similarly, in his series of learned works in the history of dogma they discovered more speculation than history. Baur replied that objective history can be written only by one who first determines history's object—that is, what it is all about. The historian who is interested in something more than a senseless jumble of facts must take his point of departure from the thinking of his own day, and that meant, for Baur, the Hegelian vision of history as the progress of Mind through time in the medium of ideas. Church history, in particular, must start from the idea of the church, which is the idea of the reconciliation of God and man.

Whatever the merits of his Hegelianism, Baur was a scholar of massive erudition and a highly sophisticated methodologist. He held that history without philosophy is "eternally dumb," and that the only way to understand Christian doctrines is to trace their development in a process that has already begun within the New Testament itself. History, philosophy, constructive theology, and New Testament studies, Baur believed, belong together in a single grand enterprise.

BIBLIOGRAPHY

Baur's literary output was enormous. Of his greatest work, *Geschichte der christlichen Kirche,* 5 vols. (1853–1863; reprint, Leipzig, 1969), only the first volume was translated into English: *The Church History of the First Three Centuries,* 2 vols., translated from the third edition and edited by Allan Menzies (London, 1878–1879). The second edition of his major study of Paul (1866–1867) appeared in English as *Paul the Apostle of Jesus Christ, His Life and Work, His Epistles and His Doctrine: A Contribution to a Critical History of Primitive Christianity,* 2 vols., translated by Allan Menzies and Eduard Zeller (London, 1875–1876). Baur's survey of the epochs of church historiography (1852) and the introduction to his posthumously published lectures on the history of dogma (1865–1867) are translated in Peter C. Hodgson's *Ferdinand Christian Baur on the Writing of Church History* (New York, 1968). Hodgson's *The Formation of Historical Theology: A Study of Ferdinand Christian Baur* (New York, 1966) is a comprehensive guide to Baur's life and work. For the debate with Moehler, see Joseph Fitzer, *Moehler and Baur in Controversy, 1832–38: Romantic-Idealist Assessment of the Reformation and Counter-Reformation* (Tallahassee, 1974).

B. A. GERRISH

BAYḌĀWĪ, AL- (died sometime between AH 685 and 716, or 1286 and 1316 CE), fully Abū Saʿīd ʿAbd Allāh ibn ʿUmar ibn Muḥammad ibn ʿAlī Abū al-Khayr Naṣīr al-Dīn al-Bayḍāwī; Islamic religious scholar and judge. Born in Bayḍāʾ, near the city of Shiraz in Persia, al-Bayḍāwī was educated in the religious sciences in Baghdad and spent most of his life following in his father's footsteps in Shiraz as the chief justice of the province of Fārs. He belonged to the Shāfiʿī legal school *(madhhab)* and was a follower of the tradition of al-Ashʿarī in theology. He wrote some twenty works on various subjects, including jurisprudence, law, grammar, theology, and the Qur'anic sciences. While all of these works were written in Arabic, he also produced a world history in his native Persian.

Al-Bayḍāwī's fame and reputation rest mainly upon his commentary *(tafsīr)* on the Qur'ān, entitled *Anwār al-tanzīl wa-asrār al-ta'wīl* (The Lights of the Revelation and the Secrets of the Interpretation). This work examines the Qur'ān phrase by phrase in an attempt to present, concisely yet comprehensibly, the conclusions of earlier commentators in such a way as to express al-Bayḍāwī's own understanding of the orthodox Sunnī interpretation of the Qur'ān in his time. His main sources of interpretational information are the famous philosopher and Qur'anic commentator Fakhr al-Dīn al-Rāzī (d. 1209) and the Mu'tazilī theologian al-Zamakhsharī (d. 1144). The latter author was clearly more important for al-Bayḍāwī, whose commentary may be viewed to a great extent as a simplified summary of his predecessor's work, condensing what was found to be most essential in grammar, meaning, and textual variants. Omitted most of the time, although sometimes overlooked and allowed to remain, are statements which reflect al-Zamakhsharī's rationalist theological views. For example, in interpreting surah 3:8, "Our Lord, make not our hearts to swerve, after that thou hast guided us," al-Zamakhsharī takes "make not our hearts to swerve" to mean "do not withhold your grace from us after having already granted it to us," with the emphasis placed upon the notion of God's grace coming after man has acted to deserve it. Al-Bayḍāwī rejects this free-will, rationalist position, substituting the interpretation that since God does lead people astray, they must pray to God for the divine gift of guidance and grace.

Because of its concise nature, al-Bayḍāwī's commentary has proved valuable over the centuries for quick reference, although certainly not for full analysis. For this reason it has been widely read in the Muslim world and has attracted a large number of super-commentaries, and soon after Europeans made learned contacts with Islam it became the best-known Qur'ān commentary in the West. Representing what is best described as the consolidation of traditionalism in the field of Qur'anic interpretation, al-Bayḍāwī's *tafsīr* has been the basic textbook for all students of the subject in East and West alike.

BIBLIOGRAPHY

Anwār al-tanzīl wa-asrār al-ta'wīl has been edited and published numerous times both in the Islamic world and in Europe; the standard edition of the Arabic text is that edited by H. O. Fleischer (Leipzig, 1846–1848). Sections of the work are available in English translation, although they are often not completely understandable without at least some knowledge of Arabic. The commentary on surah 12, the story of Joseph, has appeared twice in translation, by Eric F. F. Bishop and Mohamed Kaddal in *"The Light of Inspiration and the Secrets of Interpretation," Chrestomathia Baidawiana: Translation of Surat Yusuf with Baidawi's Commentary* (Glasgow, 1957) and by A. F. L. Beeston in *Baiḍāwī's Commentary on Sūrah 12 of the Qur'ān* (Oxford, 1963). The commentary on surah 3 was translated by D. S. Margoliouth in *Chrestomathia Baidawiana: The Commentary of El-Baidāwī on Sura III* (London, 1894). The best place to start in order to experience al-Bayḍāwī's commentary in English is probably Kenneth Cragg's *The Mind of the Qur'ān: Chapters in Reflection* (London, 1973), which includes the commentary on surah 112. All of these works also provide some basic overview of al-Bayḍāwī and his significance. A number of articles by Lutpi Ibrahim have appeared on al-Bayḍāwī and his theological relationship to al-Zamakhsharī: "Al-Bayḍāwī's Life and Works," *Islamic Studies* (Karachi) 18 (1979): 311–321; "The Concept of Divine Justice According to al-Zamakhsharī and al-Bayḍāwī," *Hamdard Islamicus* 3 (1980): 3–17; "The Relation of Reason and Revelation in the Theology of al-Zamakhsharī and al-Baiḍāwī," *Islamic Culture* 54 (1980): 63–74; "The Concept of *Iḥbāṭ* and *Takfīr* According to az-Zamakhsharī and al-Bayḍāwī," *Die Welt des Orient* 11 (1980): 117–121; and "The Questions of the Superiority of Angels and Prophets between az-Zamakhsharī and al-Bayḍāwī," *Arabica* 28 (1981): 65–75.

ANDREW RIPPIN

BAY ÜLGEN. *See* Ülgen.

BEARS are an important part of the religious ritual life of several peoples, particularly the hunting peoples of northern Eurasia and North America. In these regions, where the harsh conditions of life make the killing of animals a necessity and where hunting rites consequently are an essential part of religious practice, the relationships between humans and animals are experienced in a particularly intimate way. Throughout the Arctic Circle one finds richly developed ceremonies, remarkably similar to one another, that focus on the bear. These bear ceremonies occupy a special place among the rites associated with big-game hunting all over the world.

Although the shamanism and hunting rituals of the northern peoples have often attracted the attention of students of religion, the bear ceremony itself has usually been studied in an incomplete, one-sided, or isolated fashion. Until the recent publication of new, not easily accessible primary data by field-workers, among them Russian and Japanese researchers, scholars were dependent upon sketchy reports often found in early travel literature. This older literature, together with the conclusions based on it, must now be critically reexamined. In addition, several general theoretical questions are also relevant to the study of the bear ceremony. These include the question of the relationship between religion and magic, the problem of the relationship between total structures and component elements, the question of how to account for similarities observed between separate regions (i.e., whether the similarities are of independent origin or are due to cultural contact), and questions regarding the migration of various population groups and the history of residential settlement.

Common Traits of the Bear Ceremony. Some traits characteristic of the ceremony are the guaranteeing of good fortune in the hunt through sacrifice, prayers, or divination, and by the use of language taboos; the exculpation or atonement rites performed immediately before or after killing the bear; the festive welcome of the dead animal, which receives homage and is served as an honored guest; taboos imposed upon women, who, for instance, are not allowed to eat certain parts of the bear meat; and finally the burial of the bear's skull and bones so that the mortal remains of the killed and eaten animal may secure a new life for it.

This treatment of the remains is particularly important and may be tinged with magic or addressed to a divinity. In the latter case, the divinity is perceived either as a special "owner" of the bear or as a "lord of the animals." At times the bear itself is regarded as a divinity that has assumed the guise of an animal in order to voluntarily offer itself as game. The bear is treated reverentially and given a ritual burial so that the resuscitated animal will once again offer itself as game to the hunter. Concern for the continued existence of the game (a scholar has compared it to modern legislation on game management) and the atonement for the killed animal (so that its soul does not take vengeance on the slayer) are two of the leading ideas in the ceremony.

Integral to the bear ceremonies is a myth that usually tells of a marriage between a woman and a bear. The bear subsequently allows himself to be killed by his wife's brother on the condition that his instructions on the ritual will be carefully observed in all future bear hunts.

The bear is regarded with both reverence and fear. He is considered to have superhuman qualities and can see and hear everything humans do, say, and even think about him. The special hunter's language thus constitutes a cautionary measure to protect the hunters from being understood by the bear.

At times the bear appears as an ancestor. When he decides to pay a visit to the human world in order to be shot, he conceals his human form with a bearskin. Sometimes he is regarded as a descendant of the sky god; sometimes he serves under the lord of the animals or the forest maiden, who send their subjects to be game for the hunter. [*See* Lord of the Animals.] When the bear happens to meet peaceable people, he good-naturedly moves out of the way; for instance, women picking berries need not fear him, if they show what sex they are. It is believed that in the winter lair the bear sustains itself by sucking his own paws, an idea attested early on by the Roman author Pliny the Elder.

Hunting rites, myths, practical experiences, and a rudimentary natural history are thus all elements included in the comprehensive complex constituted by the bear ceremony. This ceremony is found in its most elaborate form in northern Eurasia. A special bear festival is held among the peoples living along the lower course of the Amur River in eastern Russia, on the Russian island of Sakhalin, and on the Japanese island of Hokkaidō. In these places a bear brought up in captivity is killed and "sent away" with gifts to the Lord of the Mountains, who is regarded as the chief of the bears. By contrast, on either side of the Bering Strait and along the North American coast of the Arctic Ocean, the special position of the bear among game animals is not as pronounced. There, other game, such as the whale, the first salmon caught during the fishing season, the wolf, and the wolverine, all of which are associated with similar ceremonies, gain prominence. An earlier complex of bear ceremonies has all but disappeared among the North American Indians, although its original components can still be observed and classified without great difficulty in the Arctic Circle area. Such remnants appear most clearly among the northern, central, and eastern Algonquians (Montagnais-Naskapi, Cree, Ojibwa, Ottowa, the actual Algonquins, Menomini, Sauk, Fox, Micmac, Malecite, Penobscot, Abnaki, and the Delaware).

Scholars have tried different psychological, rational, and sociological explanations of ceremonies. These include an ambivalent attitude toward the animal, fostered by its being simultaneously dangerous and apparently good-natured; by its nearly humanlike walk and its almost uncanny similarity, after it has been skinned, to a human being; and by its long winter torpor. The collective hunt itself fosters fellowship. The hunters are united by the great practical value of their quarry. Some of these features are also characteristic, however, of hunts for other big game in completely different areas.

This leads to the question whether the bear rites are an expression of a general attitude to game that is characteristic of all hunting cultures—a kind of "elementary idea" *(Elementargedanke)* or archetype—or whether they constitute a unique complex with variations to be explained on the basis of the historical diffusion of culture. Even if the diffusion does exist, it is difficult to connect it with the head, skull, and bone offerings described by the so-called culture-circle school *(Kulturkreiselehre)*. According to this school, the sacrifice of skull and bones to a supreme being can be traced to the prehistoric caves of the European Alps and was later displaced by more magical hunting rites.

In fact, the relationship between sacrifice and the burial of the bear skull is unclear, as is the difference between religion and magic in the resuscitation rites, in which the lord of the animals is involved. In any event, the brain and the marrow do not constitute matter for sacrifice, as the representatives of the culture-circle school have maintained. On the other hand, a Saami (Lapp) missionary in the eighteenth century was justified to an extent in comparing the Old Testament ban on crushing the bone of the paschal lamb with the Saami's painstaking preservation of the bear's bones, even though this missionary went on to interpret the latter as a devilish mimicry of a holy act imposed by God. In both cases the bones are bearers of life (see *Ez.* 37). There is a similar story in Nordic mythology concerning the he-goats of the thunder god Thor, which are slaughtered in the evening only to rise again from their bones on the following morning. [*see* Bones.]

The precise manner of bear burial varies, even among neighboring groups of people. The Saami buried the remains; quite a number of such graves have been discovered in recent times. The Finns, by contrast, put bear skulls up in fir trees.

Examples from the Saami and Mansi. Two examples may be given in order to illustrate the above. The first, a description of the Saami's bear festival, was given by the Lutheran vicar Samuel Rheen in Jokkmokk (northern Swedish Lapland) in 1671. According to Rheen, the outcome of the hunt was first established with the aid of a magic drum, after which the hunters set off in carefully designated marching order. The bear was killed with spear and rifle shot while in hibernation and then dragged forward and beaten with slender switches, perhaps as a revivification ritual. Thereupon the hunters sang the bear song, giving thanks to the creator of game animals. Near their home with the quarry the Saami continued the bear song, in which they claimed to have come from Sweden, Germany, England, and other countries—a clear attempt to exculpate themselves by implying that foreigners, not the Saami, had been the killers. The wives of the hunters repeated these words in their song of welcome, after which the men crept in through the holy back door of the women's tent. At that moment they were sprinkled by bloodlike alder bark juice, prepared by the wives through chewing. The women spit it in their husbands' faces, probably as a protection against the vengeance of the bear. The husbands were not allowed to visit their wives for three days and nights. Instead, they ventured back to their huts where the bear was skinned, cooked, and eaten in the women's absence. The bones, which were not to be broken, were gathered and buried. The wives, blindfolded, then shot arrows at the bearskin in order to determine whose husband would get the bear next time. Finally, the husbands ran around the fire while their wives threw warm ashes mixed with coals at them. After that second protection rite they were allowed to visit their wives again.

A second example is provided by the Mansi (Voguls). The departure song that they sing to the bear in connection with the bear festival reflects their faith that the soul of the animal will remain on earth a few days while it occupies a series of successively larger new bodies. In the song, it is the bear himself that speaks, saying that, in the snow and fog, he has lost his place inside the people's cottage and now creeps around like a little mouse outside the cabin. He is struck with sorrow when, through the wall, he hears the children talking about him. The following night, as the people continue to sorrow over the bear's departure, he reaches the place where the women get snow for their cooking and has now grown to the size of an ermine. By the third night the bear reaches the end of the road that the husbands take on their squirrel hunts, and now he is as big as a wolverine. The next morning the bear resumes the guise of a sacred bear and makes a knapsack out of birch bark, in which he stows gifts from the people. At the site of the sacrifice, the bear is blasphemed by the village's protective gods, because he has become so lean; nevertheless he presents his own sacrificial gifts for the people and continues on his way. The bear finally goes to the golden abode where God the Father dwells. He sits on God's sable-clad knee and says, "Now I've returned!" Then he passes out the gifts from the people to God's children and relates that he was well treated on earth.

[*See also* Khanty and Mansi Religion *and* Ainu Religion.]

BIBLIOGRAPHY

Bakró-Nagy, Marianne Sz. *Die Sprache des Bärenkultes im Obugrischen.* Budapest, 1979. Language taboos and noa-words, or euphemisms, in connection with the bear.

Boratav, Pertev Nailî. *Les histoires d'ours en Anatolie.* Helsinki, 1955.

Diószegi, Vilmos, ed. *Popular Beliefs and Folklore Tradition in Siberia.* Budapest, 1968. A collection of important essays on Siberian religion, including bear rites, by one of the foremost experts on the circumpolar area.

Edsman, Carl-Martin."The Story of the Bear Wife in Nordic Tradition." *Ethnos* (Stockholm) 21 (1956): 36–56. Compares recent Scandinavian folklore and medieval Nordic sources with circumpolar myths and rituals.

Edsman, Carl-Martin. "The Hunter, the Games, and the Unseen Powers: Lappish and Finnish Bear Rites." In *Hunting and Fishing: Nordic Symposium on Life in a Traditional Hunting and Fishing Milieu in Prehistoric Times up to the Present Day,* edited by Harald Hvarfner, pp. 159–188. Stockholm, 1965. In part a more popular abstract, with references, of longer, scientific articles in Swedish.

Gill, Sam D. *Native American Traditions: Sources and Interpretations.* Belmont, Calif., 1983.

Hallowell, A. Irving. "Bear Ceremonialism in the Northern Hemisphere." *American Anthropologist* 28 (January–March 1926): 1–175. A classic work and still the only one that treats the whole circumpolar area. Needs to be rewritten now because of all the new material adduced by different specialists.

Hasselbrink, Gustav. "La chanson d'ours des Lapons: Essai d' interprétation d'un manuscrit du dix-huitième siècle concernant la chasse et le culte d'ours." *Orbis* 13 (1964): 420–480.

Holmberg, Uno. *Mythology of All Races, Finno-Ugric, Siberian.* vol. 4 (1927). New York, 1964. This description of the Saami bear rites contains an almost verbatim translation of the most exhaustive source in Swedish from 1755 combined with the document from about 1775 treated by Hasselbrink, above. Compare also works by the same author published in 1925 and 1938 (the last year under the name Harva).

Kannisto, Artturi. *Materialien zur Mythologie der Wogulen.* Helsinki, 1958.

Kitagawa, Joseph M. "Ainu Bear Festival (Iyomante)." *History of Religions* 1 (Summer 1961): 95–151. A useful introduction to Japanese research in particular.

Paproth, Hans-Joachim. *Studien über des Bärenzeremoniell,* vol. 1, *Bärenjagdriten und Bärenfeste bei den tungusischen Völkern.* Uppsala, 1976. The best critical study with a survey of the Northern Hemisphere as an introduction to the more limited research topic of bear hunt rites and festivals among the Tunguz. Reconsiders the large amount of comparative material and contains an exhaustive bibliography. The second volume, which is intended to treat the topic's mythological aspects, has not yet been published.

Speck, Frank G., and Jesse Moses. *The Celestial Bear Comes Down to Earth: The Bear Sacrifice Ceremony of the Munsee-Mahican in Canada as Related by Nekateit.* Reading, Pa., 1945.

Tschernjetzow, V. N. "Bärenfest bei den Ob-Ugriern." *Acta Ethnographica Academiae Scientiarum Hungaricae* 23 (1974): 285–319.

Zachrisson, Inger, and Elisabeth Iregren. *Lappish Bear Graves in Northern Sweden: An Archaeological and Osteological Study.* Stockholm, 1974.

CARL-MARTIN EDSMAN

Translated from Swedish by Verne Moberg

BEAUTY. *See* Aesthetics.

BEDE (c. 673–735), usually called "the Venerable"; Northumbrian monk and scholar. Bede's whole life was associated with the twin monasteries of Wearmouth and Jarrow, founded by Benedict Biscop in 673–681. It is difficult to improve on the summary of his life supplied by Bede himself in introducing the list of his works provided in the final chapter of his *Ecclesiastical History of the English People:*

> I was born on the lands belonging to this monastery and at the age of seven was given by my family to the most reverend Benedict [Biscop] and to Ceolfrid [his successor] to be educated. From that time onward I have lived my whole life in this same monastery, devoting all my time to the study of the scriptures. While observing the regular monastic discipline and singing the daily office in church, I have always taken delight in learning, teaching, and writing. In my nineteenth year I became a deacon, and in my thirtieth a priest. . . . And from the day of my priestly ordination to this, my fifty-ninth year [731], I have composed the following works on Holy Scripture, either for my own use or that of my brethren, drawing for this purpose on the works of the holy Fathers, and at times adding comments of my own to clarify their meaning and interpretation.

Bede then adds a list that, in addition to scriptural works, also contains lives of saints, histories, grammatical works, poetry, and treatises on computation.

Bede's *Ecclesiastical History of the English People*—basically a religious history written for Christian believers—is a remarkable work, able to win the admiration even of modern-day historians who may not share Bede's religious beliefs. It demonstrates Bede's scholarly gifts, his fine Latinity, his concern to find trustworthy sources, his dexterity in the use of these sources, and his sobriety of judgment even when handling miraculous elements. The *Ecclesiastical History* is also noteworthy for its introduction of *anno Domini* as a means of dating events in the Christian era, a practice that became customary throughout the Western world.

Although Bede is most famous in modern times for the *Ecclesiastical History,* it was his scriptural commentaries that were best known and most used in his own day and among medieval writers of later generations, not all of whom employed their typically allegorical method of interpretation with Bede's characteristic restraint. His works were so well respected and so often copied that most of them have survived. His numerous borrowings from the Fathers testify to the magnificent collection of books Benedict Biscop had accumulated in Rome and transported all the way to Northumbria.

Bede's writings display the working of a lively and inquiring mind, fascinated not only by problems of scripture but also by those of the natural world. Taken in their chronological order his works allow us to discern a constantly growing scholarly maturity, as well as an attractive and winning personality. Bede's work on the calendar deserves special mention. The controversy over the date of Easter was particularly acute in his time since it pitted Roman against Celtic usage. Bede tried to put order into the controversy through a work, *De temporum ratione,* whose modern editor remarks that it still remains "the best introduction to the ecclesiastical calendar."

We possess a moving eyewitness account of Bede's last days in a letter written by one of his disciples, Cuthbert, to another, Cuthwin. He continued working and teaching to the end. One of his last tasks—left incomplete—was a translation of John's gospel into Old English. He died on 26 May 735.

BIBLIOGRAPHY

The edition of Bede's works by J. A. Giles (1834–1844) was reprinted in *Patrologia Latina*, edited by J.-P. Migne, vols. 90–95 (Paris, 1850–1851). New editions of most of Bede's works have since appeared in *Corpus Christianorum, series latina*, vols. 118–122 (Turnhout, 1955–1969). For the Latin text of the *Ecclesiastical History*, Bertram Colgrave and R. A. B. Mynors's edition (Oxford, 1969) supersedes that of Charles Plummer (Oxford, 1896), although Plummer's historical notes retain much value.

The bibliography on Bede is large, especially in the form of articles in scholarly journals. Special mention should be made of Peter Hunter Blair's *The World of Bede* (London, 1970); *Bede, His Life, Times and Writings: Essays in Commemoration of the Twelfth Centenary of His Death*, edited by Alexander Hamilton Thompson (Oxford, 1935); and *Famulus Christi: Essays in Commemoration of the Thirteenth Centenary of the Birth of the Venerable Bede*, edited by Gerald Bonner (London, 1976). The best general introduction to Bede's *Ecclesiastical History* remains Jackson J. Campbell's "Bede," in *Latin Historians*, edited by T. A. Dorey (New York, 1966). Numerous aspects of Bede and his background have been examined in the "Jarrow Lectures" (1958–), a series too little known but published yearly by the rector of Jarrow (Saint Paul's Rectory, Jarrow, England).

PAUL MEYVAERT

BEGGING. *See* Almsgiving; Mendicancy; *and* Poverty.

BEING. *See* Ontology.

BEIT HILLEL AND BEIT SHAMMAI were two early Jewish schools of thought, or "houses" (*beit*, from Hebrew *bayit*, means "house of"), named after Hillel and Shammai, leading sages of Jerusalem in the latter half of the first century BCE and in the early first century CE. The schools actually represented two distinct approaches to the study of the oral law that were prevalent from the time of Hillel and Shammai until the beginning of the second century. While very few adherents of either school are known by name, it appears that the Shammaites managed to achieve dominance sometime before the destruction of the Temple in 70 CE. According to some scholars, the "Eighteen Matters" that Beit Shammai is said to have decreed despite the objections of Beit Hillel (J.T., *Shab.* 1.4, 3c, and parallels) refer to measures instituted during the first revolt against Rome (66–70 CE) in order to assure the separation of Jews and gentiles. In any event, Beit Hillel clearly emerges as the more influential school at Yavneh, where the sages of Israel convened after 70 CE. The Jerusalem (Palestinian) Talmud (*Ber.* 1.7, 3b) relates that a "heavenly echo" went forth at Yavneh and declared that the *halakhah* ("law") would henceforth be in accordance with Beit Hillel. Actually, the more than three hundred controversies between the two schools that have been preserved in Talmudic literature, many of which date to the Yavnean period, attest to what must have been a protracted struggle for ascendance before Beit Hillel prevailed in the early second century.

Though the Hillelites and Shammaites are said to have practiced love and friendship toward each other and even intermarried despite differences over marital law (B.T., *Yev.* 14b), it is clear that the rabbis regarded the schools as distinct factions. Thus the many controversies between Beit Hillel and Beit Shammai are attributed to the increase in the number of students of Hillel and Shammai "who did not wait upon [their masters]" sufficiently, which in turn led to the creation of two Torahs (Tosefta *Ḥag.* 2.9 [MS Vienna] and parallels), or, according to another version, two "parties," or *kittot* (J.T., *Ḥag.* 2.2, 77d). The tannaim generally considered Beit Shammai to be the school with the stricter viewpoint, calling attention to the few instances where this was not so (*'Eduy.* 4, 5).

Modern scholars have tried to clarify further the differences between the schools. The usual explanation is that the schools assumed the characteristics of Hillel and Shammai themselves, with Hillel representing the ideals of kindness, forbearance, and conciliation and Shammai, their opposites. Unfortunately, too few direct controversies between the two sages have been recorded to discern whether these characteristics played any major role in their differences.

Another theory is that there were socioeconomic differences between the schools; that is, that Beit Shammai expressed the attitudes of the upper classes and Beit Hillel, those of the lower. For example, when Beit Shammai maintained that on the eve of the Sabbath or a festival one should first recite the benediction over the day and then that over the wine and Beit Hillel contended that the wine should be blessed first (*Ber.* 8.8), each school's position may reflect its socioeconomic background. The wealthy commonly used wine at their meals, and so its use in no way indicated the festive nature of the Sabbath or festival. For the poor, however, the presence of wine at the table suggested the specialness of the day, so Beit Hillel decided that the benediction over it had to be recited first.

Some writers have maintained that the two schools had distinct hermeneutical approaches. For example, Beit Shammai tended to be more literal in its exegesis, explaining the verse "when thou liest down and when thou risest up" (*Dt.* 6:7) to mean that the Shema' should be recited in the evening while reclining and in the morning while standing. Beit Hillel understood the intention to be that the Shema' is said at the time when people are accustomed to lie down and when they arise (*Ber.* 1.3).

Still others have suggested that Beit Hillel insisted that a valid act had to be accompanied by intention, whereas Beit Shammai emphasized the deed itself. A common example pertains to the law that foods consumed on a festival must be prepared the day before. The question arose as to whether an egg laid on the festival day could be eaten (*Beits.* 1.1). Beit Shammai permitted its consumption because it viewed the egg as having been readied, albeit by the hen, the day before. Beit Hillel however, regarded this preparation as inadequate since no one could have anticipated that the egg would actually be laid on the festival day.

Finally, it has been suggested that Beit Hillel analyzed texts and concepts and broke them down into smaller components in order to understand them, while Beit Shammai emphasized the context and the whole. This understanding is actually an elaboration of the hermeneutical and intention-versus-deed explanations.

No one theory accounts for all or even most of the disputes between the two schools, so it must be concluded that aside from the generally strict perspective of Beit Shammai and the leniency of Beit Hillel, no general underlying principle can be discerned.

[*See also* Hillel.]

BIBLIOGRAPHY

The disputes between the houses are presented and evaluated in volume 2 of Jacob Neusner's *The Rabbinic Traditions about the Pharisees before 70*, 3 vols. (Leiden, 1971). See also the "Bibliographical Reflections" in volume 3 (pp. 320–368) of Neusner's work. Alexander Guttmann considers the relation of Hillel and Shammai to the schools and discusses the different approaches of Beit Hillel and Beit Shammai in his *Rabbinic Judaism in the Making: A Chapter in the History of the Halakhah from Ezra to Judah I* (Detroit, 1970), pp. 59–124. The socioeconomic understanding of the controversies is presented in Louis Ginzberg's "The Significance of the Halakhah for Jewish History," in his *On Jewish Law and Lore* (1955; reprint, New York, 1979), pp. 77–124. For the claim that the Hillelites had an "atomic-nominalistic" tendency, see Isaiah Sonne's "The Schools of Shammai and Hillel Seen from Within," in *Louis Ginzberg Jubilee Volume* (New York, 1945), pp. 275–291. The "Eighteen Matters" are discussed in Solomon Zeitlin's "Les 'dix-huit mesures,'" reprinted in his *Studies in the Early History of Judaism*, vol. 4 (New York, 1978), pp. 412–426.

STUART S. MILLER

BELIEF. *See* Doubt and Belief; Faith; *and* Knowledge and Ignorance.

BELLARMINO, ROBERTO (1542–1621), Jesuit theologian, controversialist, and cardinal; canonized saint of the Roman Catholic church. Roberto Francisco Romulo Bellarmino was born at Montepulciano in Tuscany on 4 October 1542. His father was an impoverished nobleman. His mother was a sister of Marcello Cervini, papal legate at the Council of Trent and later Pope Marcellus II (1555). Bellarmino entered the Society of Jesus in 1560. He studied philosophy at the Roman College and theology at Padua. He was frail as a youth and suffered from uncertain health all his life. As a student he was much devoted to literature and even wrote some poetry, most of which he later destroyed.

In 1569 Bellarmino was sent by his Jesuit superiors to Louvain in Flanders. The following year he was ordained priest by the bishop of Ghent and assumed his duties as lecturer in theology at the Jesuit house associated with the university. He was an immediate success in this capacity, so much so that by the end of his sojourn at Louvain, in 1576, he was offered prestigious positions at Paris and Milan. He was recalled instead to Rome, where a special chair of theological controversy was established for him at the Roman College. The lectures he delivered there, confuting all the leading Protestant spokesmen, were published in 1586 under the title *Disputationes de controversiis Christianae fidei adversus hujus temporis haereticos* (Lectures concerning the Controversies of the Christian Faith against the Heretics of This Time), a manual that soon became the standard of Roman positive, as distinguished from scholastic, theology. It had to pass first, however, through the displeasure of the imperious Pope Sixtus V, who threatened to put *Disputationes* on the Index of Forbidden Books because it argued that the pope's temporal jurisdiction is only indirect. Bellarmino was spared this embarrassment by the death of Sixtus in August 1590.

In 1591 Bellarmino was appointed spiritual director of the Roman College and a year later its rector. In 1595 he became Jesuit provincial in Naples, where he lived for three years until he was chosen by Clement VIII to be the papal theologian and grand penitentiary, a post that carried with it a red hat. Bellarmino was created cardinal under the title of Santa Maria in Via on 3 March 1599.

In the midst of his various administrative duties, Bellarmino continued to publish works in defense of Catholic doctrine and piety, as well as works on the Fathers, scriptural studies, and liturgy. All these books taken together amount to a considerable corpus, most conveniently consulted in the twelve large volumes edited by J. Fèvre in 1874.

Inevitably, Bellarmino was drawn into the sharp quarrel between the Jesuits and the Dominicans over the problem of the relation between grace and free will. It has been said that Bellarmino's position on this issue displeased the pope, who, for whatever reason, sent him off to be archbishop of Capua in 1602. When Clement died in March 1605, Bellarmino resigned his see, and Pope Paul V named him librarian of the Vatican. He remained active in the Curia Romana for the rest of his life and took an intellectual's part in many of the great events of the time, including the Venetian interdict (1606), the literary controversies with James I of England (1607–1609), and the debate on Gallicanism (1610–1612), which was the occasion for his celebrated treatise on the powers of the pope, *De potestate summi pontificis in rebus temporalibus* (Concerning the Powers of the Supreme Pontiff in Temporal Matters). In 1615 he was involved in the first curial interrogation of Galileo, a man for whom he had great regard and whom he treated with marked respect.

The process of Bellarmino's canonization began in 1627, six years after his death, but because of what was conceived to be his minimizing views about the papacy, it was not consummated until 1930. Roberto Bellarmino, personally austere, pious, and kindly, set the highest tone for the positive theology of the Counter-Reformation, not only because of his erudition and industry, but also because of the amiability and courtesy he brought to his controversial writings—characteristics rare indeed in his tumultuous era.

BIBLIOGRAPHY

The best short study of Bellarmino's life and work is Xavier-Marie Le Bachelet's entry, "Bellarmin, François-Robert-Romulus," in *Dictionnaire de théologie catholique* (Paris, 1932). Somewhat effusive but nevertheless useful is James Brodrick's *The Life and Work of Blessed Robert Francis Cardinal Bellarmine*, 2 vols. (London, 1928). E. A. Ryan's *The Historical Scholarship of Saint Bellarmine* (Louvain, 1936) examines the centerpiece of the subject's controversial writings. For a recent treatment of one of Bellarmino's controversies within his own communion, see Gustavo Galeota's *Bellarmino contra Baio a Lovanio* (Rome, 1966).

MARVIN R. O'CONNELL

BEMBA RELIGION. The Bemba, also known as Awemba, inhabit the northeastern part of present-day Zambia between lakes Tanganyika, Mweru, Malawi, and Bangweulu. According to oral traditions, three sons of the Luba king, Mukulumpe, who had fallen out with their father, led a migration of people from what is now the Shaba Province of southern Zaire to what became the Bemba territory. The royal clan of the Bemba traces its descent to these brothers and to their sister, Bwalya Chabala. By the mid-seventeenth century, the Bemba were established in their present territory. A paramount chief, or *citimukulu* (a title associated with Mukulumpe's sons), ruled the Bemba with the assistance of local chiefs, also of the royal clan, whom he appointed to govern the various districts under Bemba control.

The matrilineal clan structure of the Bemba can be traced to Bwalya Chabala's central role in the migrations from Shaba. According to tradition, the sons of Mukulumpe, after wandering in exile from their father's kingdom, realized that they needed the assistance of a royal woman to found their clan, so they went back to their father's compound and secretly carried Bwalya Chabala away with them. She is often mentioned as the person who brought the seeds and plants used in Bemba agriculture. In their tradition of a woman founding the royal clan as well as introducing agricultural knowledge, the Bemba assert the intimate connection between the principle of matrilineal descent and the fertility of the land. Bwalya Chabala's honored place in Bemba traditions can be seen in a sacred burial place, not far from the present-day Bemba capital, associated with her. Offerings of cloth and flour are brought to her burial shrine. A basket, which is said to be hers, hangs in the relic house of the *citimukulu*. Flour from this basket is used in several Bemba religious ceremonies.

Like other central African ethnic groups, the Bemba acknowledge a high god known as Lesa. Among the neighboring Lamba people, Lesa is thought to have been a man who lived on earth and helped his people. For the Bemba, however, Lesa was never a person. He is a creator god who controls the rains and the power of fertility manifested in humans, animals, and agriculture. He is the source of the creative power in the roots and shrubs that the Bemba use in healing and religious rituals. There is no organized cult associated with Lesa, and the Bemba do not ordinarily solicit his assistance. When serious problems of community-wide concern arise, however, they organize collective rituals to ask Lesa for help. These are particularly common in times of severe drought.

Spirits of the ancestors play a more central role in the day-to-day existence of the Bemba. Rituals are performed to seek assistance from the ancestors and to ensure that their considerable influence over the lives of the living becomes a force for good. Some of these ancestral spirits *(mipashi)* are considered benign; others, called *fiwa*, are more dangerous. The *fiwa* are the spirits of those who died with a sense of grievance or injury and who trouble their descendants until the wrong is corrected.

When a pregnant woman feels the child moving in her womb, she knows that the *mupashi* of an ancestor has entered her body. After the child is born, the identity of this ancestor is ascertained by divination. The child's *mupashi* is believed to guard him wherever he goes and remains as a guardian for his descendants after he dies.

For every man or woman who dies there is a special succession ceremony *(kupyamika)* in which a close relative assumes the dead man's bow or the dead woman's girdle. By doing so, the relative assumes some of the personal characteristics of the deceased as well as his or her position in the kinship system. Thus a young boy who is appointed in this way to succeed a dead man will thereafter address his fellow villagers using the same forms the deceased would have used; the villagers, in turn, will regard the boy as the husband of the dead man's widow and will speak of him as such.

The Bemba's paramount chief is said to succeed to the *mipashi* of his matrilineal ancestors, which dates back to the founding siblings. During the chief's succession ceremony, he is given a number of material objects associated with the *mipashi;* it is through these sacred relics that the *citimukulu* acquires power over his domains. This power can be weakened, however, by any failure of the chief to fulfill ritual obligations or to adhere to a series of sexual avoidances associated with his office. The ritual objects *(babenya)* inherited by the chief are kept in special spirit huts in the capital where they are looked after by hereditary "councillors" *(bakabilo)*, who also trace their ancestry to the foundation of the Bemba state. The shrines are also guarded by "wives of the dead," who are direct descendants of the wives of former chiefs. The approximately four hundred *bakabilo* are responsible for purifying the paramount chief before he approaches the spirit huts and for protecting him from harmful influences. They prevent the ritually impure from approaching the chief and guard his power by quickly removing from the capital anyone who is in imminent danger of dying.

Traditionally, when a paramount chief was at the point of death, the *bakabilo,* who traced their membership in the royal clan by paternal descent and were therefore ineligible to succeed him, gathered in the royal hut to ensure that the necessary rituals were carried out precisely as dictated by tradition. Their leader determined when the *bakabilo* should strangle the paramount chief. The *bakabilo* had to be careful to do this at the proper moment, for to strangle the king too soon would have been considered murder and to wait too long might have allowed the royal *mipashi* to escape, with devastating consequences for the entire kingdom. (The Bemba *citimukulu* may be seen as conforming to James G. Frazer's model of a "divine king.") After the death of the *citimukulu,* the *bakabilo* removed the ritual objects associated with the office and took them to a neighboring village for safekeeping until the succession ceremony took place.

The burial of the chief had to be done according to strict ritual procedures to ensure that the spiritual power of the office was not weakened. The corpse was washed by the three senior women—the chief's mother, his senior sister, and his head wife — then placed in the fetal position upon a platform made of branches. Hereditary royal buriers completed the rituals by pouring a special bean sauce over the body at dawn and at noon. The skin of a newly sacrificed bull was wrapped around the body, followed by a special cloth. At the end of a year-long mourning period and after the millet had been harvested, the chief's remains were moved to the sacred burial place *(mwalule).* Before the *bakabilo* set out for the burial place, the senior widow was slain in sacrifice. On their way to the burial site, the *bakabilo* sacrificed all the chickens and goats that they encountered. Commoners were supposed to hide from the burial procession. The chief's wives and servants were buried with his remains. Ivory tusks and other valuable goods were placed on top of his grave, which was guarded by the "wives of the dead."

The hereditary burier of the *citimukulu,* who was in charge of the royal burial ground, was known as *shinwalule* ("lord of the burial ground"). In addition to playing a prominent role in the succession ceremonies of the new chief, the *shinwalule* performed a variety of rituals associated with rain and the fertility of the land.

One of the most important Bemba rituals is the female initiation ceremony, Chisungu, held shortly after the onset of menstruation. Between one and three girls take part in the ceremony. During her first menstruation, a girl undergoes an individual purification rite designed to "bring her to the hearth" or "show her the fire," because it is believed that her condition has made her "cold." (Fire is often used in Bemba rituals to purify a person who has passed through a dangerous or impure condition.) Medicines treated with fire play an important part in the girl's purification ritual.

The actual Chisungu ritual is held at a convenient time relatively soon after the menstrual purification ritual. Chisungu is a nubility rite in the sense that it is less concerned with the physical transformations of puberty than with the social changes necessary for a woman to be ready for marriage. Normally the girl is already betrothed; the ritual is designed to protect the couple from the dangers associated with their first act of sexual intercourse and to establish the rights of the future husband to engage in sexual relations. It is also a time when women elders teach younger women the religious and social responsibilities of women in their community. The rite entails no physical operation but involves singing and dancing both within the village and in the bush. There is no comparable ritual for boys.

BIBLIOGRAPHY

For background history of the Bemba, see Andrew D. Roberts's *A History of the Bemba* (Madison, Wis., 1973). The following of my own works should also be consulted: "The Bemba of North-Eastern Rhodesia," in *Seven Tribes of British Central Africa,* edited by Elizabeth Colson and Max Gluckman (Oxford, 1951), pp. 164–193, gives a preliminary treatment of Bemba religion; *Land, Labour and Diet in Northern Rhodesia* (Oxford, 1939) contains accounts of religious ceremonies related to the economic life of the people; "Keeping the King Divine" in *Proceedings of the Royal Anthropological Institute of Great Britain and Ireland* (1968) draws on information provided by hereditary bearers of the *citimukulu;* and *Chisungu,* 2d ed. (London, 1982), examines this important female initiation ceremony. A. H. Muenya's "The Burial of Chitimukulu Mubanga," *African Affairs* 46 (1947): 101–104, offers an eyewitness account of the burial of a recent *citimukulu.*

AUDREY I. RICHARDS

BENARAS. *See* Banaras.

BENCHŌ (1162–1238), also known as Shōkōbō; posthumous name, Ben'a; founder of the Chinzei branch of the Japanese Jōdo (Pure Land) sect, the dominant branch of this sect. He is presently counted the second patriarch of the Jōdoshū.

Born in the province of Chikuzen in northern Kyushu, Benchō became a novice monk at the age of seven. At the age of twenty-two he left Kyushu and entered the head Tendai monastery of Enryakuji on the northeastern outskirts of Kyoto, then the capital of Japan. After six years of study there under the erudite scholar-monk Hōchibō Shōshin he returned to Chikuzen. Three years later, deeply shocked by the death of his stepbrother, he underwent a religious crisis in which he came to feel keenly the impermanence of things. On a trip to Kyoto in order to obtain a statue for a pagoda he had helped to reconstruct, Benchō met Hōnen and became his disciple. After delivering the statue to Chikuzen he returned to Kyoto in 1199 to study the Nembutsu (Chin., *nien-fo*) teachings under Hōnen.

Five years later he returned again to Kyushu, and from this time on was active in propagating the Pure Land Nembutsu teachings throughout the northern portion of Kyushu. Among his many disciples was Ryōchū (1198–1287), who was designated the heir of Benchō's transmission when the latter gave official sanction to Ryōchū's work, *Ryōge matsudai nembutsu jushuin shō.* Ryōchū was later instrumental in establishing Benchō's lineage as the dominant branch among the many offshoots of Hōnen's teaching.

Benchō held that practices other than the Nembutsu (the recitation of the words "Namu Amida Butsu") do not fundamentally accord with Amida's Original Vows *(hongan).* However, he did state that it was possible to attain birth in the Pure Land through non-Nembutsu practices insofar as they are performed in good faith. Thus he held that both Nembutsu and non-Nembutsu are qualitatively identical in that they can be the cause of birth in the Pure Land. He also emphasized the idea of "unperturbed mind at the deathbed" *(rinjū shōnen).* For Benchō, it is of utmost importance to recite the Nembutsu with an undisturbed mind at the time of one's death. Under these circumstances, the practitioner is said to be able to see the Buddha arriving to lead him to the Pure Land. This deathbed vision of the Buddha is considered crucial to one's birth in the Pure Land and eventual enlightenment there. Finally, Benchō placed strong emphasis on the actual recitation of the Nembutsu. This ultimately places him among the ranks of those who advocate "many-calling" *(tanen),* the constant repetition of the Nembutsu, and "self-power" *(jiriki),* the position that the Nembutsu is recited through one's own conscious effort.

[*See also* Jōdoshū; Nien-fo; *and the biography of* *Hōnen.*]

BIBLIOGRAPHY

Hōnen to sono monka no kyōgaku. Kyoto, 1972. Sponsored by Ryūkoku Daigaku Shinshū Gakkai.

Kodo Yasui. *Hōnen monka no kyōgaku.* Kyoto, 1968.

BANDO SHŌJUN

BENDIS. In Greek testimonies, this South Thracian goddess is known variously as Bendis, Béndis, or Mendis. Her name is uncontroversially explained as deriving from Indo-European **bhendh-,* "bind." She was probably a goddess of marriage whose function it was to watch over marital bindings.

As early as 429/8 BCE, Bendis was the object of a state cult in Athens. In the ceremonies called Bendideia, which took place on the nineteenth or twentieth of the month Thargetion, two processions took place, one composed of the rich and influential Thracians of Piraeus, the other of Athenians. The Bendideion, or temple of Bendis, was situated on the hill Munychia.

The Bendideia, as described in Plato's *Republic* (327a–c), was spectacular but did not contain any hint of the orgiastic character that is typical of rites performed in worship of a great goddess. Bendis was commonly identified with the Greek Artemis; it is therefore puzzling that Herodotus, who was very well acquainted with the Athenian Bendis, fails to mention her name in connection with the Thracian Artemis (*Histories* 4.33 and 5.7). Perhaps Herodotus had in mind another Thracian goddess, not Cotys, however, to whom the same objection would apply.

On reliefs and small statues, Bendis is represented as wearing Thracian garments and a pointed (Phrygian) cap. Her attributes are often a sacrificial cup in the right hand and a spear in the left hand. On Bythinian coins, however, she is represented as holding two spears in her right hand and a dagger in her left hand. On coins from Kabyle, she bears two torches, or one torch and a *patera*. Torches were also the attribute of the Greek goddess Hekate, with whom Bendis has also been often identified.

A temple consecrated to Bendis or Mendis existed in 188 BCE on the western shore of Hebros. Later testimonies mention another temple in Egypt, near Ptolemais. Her name is attested as an anthroponyme in both Thrace and Greece.

Notwithstanding her prominent role at Athens, Bendis is not to be considered an important divinity. The cult of Diana among the Roman soldiers in Dacia and south from the Danube does not necessarily have anything to do with Bendis.

BIBLIOGRAPHY

For further discussion, see Zlatozava Gočeva's essay "Der Bendiskult und die Beziehungen zwischen Thrakien und Kleinasien" in *Hommages à Maarten J. Vermaseren*, edited by Margaret B. de Boer and T. A. Edridge (Leiden, 1978), vol. 1, pp. 397–404.

IOAN PETRU CULIANU and CICERONE POGHIRC

BENEDICT, RUTH (1887–1948), American cultural anthropologist. Ruth Fulton grew up in a Baptist household in New York State. After four years at Vassar (1905–1909), schoolteaching, and marriage to Stanley Rossiter Benedict in 1914, she enrolled in the anthropology department at Columbia University. In 1923 she earned a doctorate under the aegis of Franz Boas.

On field trips to the Pueblo Indians between 1924 and 1926, Benedict elaborated on ideas about religion that she had formulated in prose sketches, poetry, and early anthropological writings. The significance of Zuni theocracy and ceremonialism is conveyed in her *Patterns of Culture* (1934). Through the 1930s, Benedict taught at Columbia, edited the *Journal of American Folk Lore*, and began to compare myths employed in primitive societies with the dreams of utopia current in complex societies. During World War II, at the Office of War Information, Benedict was assigned to work on Japan, a society whose beliefs and behaviors contrasted sharply with those of her own society. *The Chrysanthemum and the Sword* was published in 1946; Benedict died two years later.

According to Benedict, religion stems from human perception of a "wondrous power, a voltage with which the universe is believed to be charged" ("Religion," *General Anthropology*, p. 630). In an attempt to manipulate this power, people invent practices and accompanying beliefs; these constitute religion. People perceive "extraordinary power" either as a property of things *(mana)* or as analogous to human will and intention (animism). Each perception produces a distinct dogma and practice.

Benedict's interpretation centered on the individual, who needs reassurance and the security of knowing he can influence his own fate. Such psychological factors shape the universal elements of religion: vision, ceremonialism, ethical sanction, and dogma. All of these guide the individual through known and unknown forces. Because Benedict argued that religions exist to comfort human beings, she rejected the "cold," distant Christian God, the absolutist "good versus evil" of Western religions, and the abstract theologies of most stratified, literate societies. The Zuni religion was her model: gods resemble humans, humans dance as gods, religion is down-to-earth and sensual.

Religions also, in Benedict's view, express human imaginativeness. The capacity to envision a world beyond the ordinary provides the content of religion; in religion, humans symbolize their highest ideals. Whatever the precise form—quest, prayer, poem—dreaming represents an imaginative redoing of reality that can direct social change.

Benedict assumed that the human urge to control daily events precipitates fantasies, which are elaborate, imaginative transformations of culturally available means and ends. Her argument about religions echoes her theory of myth: just as myths give the plain details of everyday life an extraordinary character, so religion accords the mundane daydream a supernatural quality. The impulse to alter present conditions expands into a "desire to remodel the universe," although Benedict did not outline the process. An attempt to manipulate the "forces of the universe" is, by her definition, religious.

For Benedict, the dream had to be tied to reality. Cut loose from substantive, secular concerns, dream becomes delusion and the seed of mass deception. Benedict offered no way of ensuring the link to reality except her own faith that individual demands and the daily pressures of existence keep religions accountable. Reflecting human vulnerability and creativeness, religion is also a "technique for success" and a mode of survival. A religion that failed to perform these functions, Benedict hoped, would be rejected. This point illustrates a movement typical of Benedict's anthropology, from the psychological to the cultural: individual need leads to social phenomenon.

Benedict's view of religion fitted her humanistic and relativistic anthropology. Humanism provided the universal aspect: human response to perception of a "wondrous power" is an attempt to control and to comprehend this power. The one impulse issues in acts (prayer, ritual, liturgy), and the other issues in articulation (symbols, myths, theologies). Relativism emerged in her claim that religious content must be tied to the stuff of everyday life. The diversity of religions proves how thoroughly perceptions of the extraordinary are linked to the ordinary; the "supernatural" (or spiritual) has no meaning apart from the "natural" (for Benedict, the "cultural").

Although her writings do not offer a fully developed theory of religion, Benedict does provide insight into human religiosity. The humility, imaginativeness, pragmatism, and hope in humans gave birth to religions. In freeing religion from a specific kind of behavior and content, Benedict offered a concept with cross-cultural application. Her statements on religion reiterated her general anthropological theory: shared dilemmas of human existence produce a variety of cultural solutions.

BIBLIOGRAPHY

My book *Ruth Benedict: Patterns of a Life* (Philadelphia, 1983) contains a bibliography including all of Benedict's published writings, archival sources, and works of significance to her anthropology, as well as secondary sources relevant to her life and works. Here follows an annotated list of Benedict's more important works.

The Concept of the Guardian Spirit in North America. Menasha, Wis., 1923. Benedict's dissertation was a comparative discussion of the guardian spirit complex in North American Indian tribes. She explored notions of "vision," the links of vision to everyday life, and the importance of imagination. She also showed how borrowed traits are altered to fit an existing culture.

Tales of the Cochiti Indians. Washington, D.C., 1931. A collection of myths and tales from a Pueblo tribe, the volume anticipated Benedict's theory, articulated in later works, that myths and tales are two sides of one coin. The volume also contains an early version of the "compensation" theory she later outlined in *Zuni Mythology.*

Patterns of Culture. Boston, 1934. Benedict's best-known book presents portraits of Zuni, Dobu, and Kwakiutl cultures in order to urge changes in contemporary American culture. Saying that "culture is personality writ large," she argued that cultures acquire personality traits, that individuals are "molded" to their cultures, and that conformity can be variously suppressive of individual expression in different societies.

Zuni Mythology. 2 vols. New York, 1935. The introduction to and summary of these two volumes explicated a theory of myth. For Benedict, myths are "compensatory," a way of making up for the constraints and the failures of everyday life. Myths are also "wishes" for a better social order and for a "redesigned universe." The former she called "tales" and the latter, because of their religious content, "myths." The volumes contain a large number of Zuni stories.

"Religion." In *General Anthropology,* edited by Franz Boas. Boston, 1938. In this chapter of Boas's text, Benedict presented her theory of religion. The chapter is not entirely satisfactory; she focuses less on religious phenomena than on individual psychology and cultural diversity. The attempt to develop a cross-cultural definition of religion somewhat weakens the explanatory force of her theory.

The Chrysanthemum and the Sword. Boston, 1946. This book, the product of inquiries made during World War II, is an elegant portrait of Japanese society and individuals. Benedict's discussions of honor, debt, obligation, and childrearing are still classic, and her evocation of a unique Japanese "personality" has not been equaled even by anthropologists who have done the fieldwork Benedict could not do for her study.

JUDITH S. MODELL

BENEDICTINES. The Order of Saint Benedict (O.S.B.) is not a centralized religious order like the Franciscans, Dominicans, or Jesuits but rather a confederation of congregations of monks and nuns who follow the rule of Benedict of Nursia (c. 480–547). [*See the biography of Benedict.*] Each monastery is an autonomous community bound to other monasteries of the same congregation by loose juridic ties and associated with the rest of the confederation through common commitment to the rule. Benedict himself is known to have founded monasteries at Subiaco, Monte Cassino, and elsewhere in central Italy. Because of its wisdom and moderation his rule was also adopted in many of the other monasteries of Latin Christendom. Its widespread implementation was also fostered by the missionary zeal of the early Benedictine monks and by papal patronage.

Gregory the Great helped spread the influence of the rule in 596 when he sent Benedictine monks to evangelize the Anglo-Saxons. Augustine, their monastic leader, became the first archbishop of Canterbury, and their success also resulted in the development of schools and a flourishing scholarship, as seen especially in the work of the Venerable Bede (c. 673–735). Anglo-Saxon monks subsequently took up missionary work in Frisia and also in central Germany, where Boniface (680–754) firmly established monastic life according to the rule of Benedict. In the eighth and early ninth centuries, however, many monasteries fell into the hands of lay abbots, and consequently serious abuse and decadence crept into monastic life. Reform was initiated by Benedict of Aniane (c. 750–821), who insisted on a more literal observance of the rule; his approach to monasticism spread to other abbeys in Aquitaine. When Louis I, "the Pious," succeeded Charlemagne as emperor of the Holy Roman Empire in 814, Benedict was installed as superior of all monasteries in the empire. At Aachen in 817, the Frankish abbots agreed on a uniform discipline and encouraged a liturgy that was more elaborate and solemn than that provided for in the rule. As a result manual labor declined in importance. Such uniformity was not consonant with the spirit of the rule. Because more attention was given to external monastic structures than to the spirit of the rule, the Frankish attempt at reform was ultimately a failure. A new regularity of discipline was imposed in the Frankish houses during the first half of the ninth century and was accompanied by the development of scholarship, as indicated by the writings of Smaragdus, Paschasius Radbertus, Ratramnus, and Rabanus Maurus. However, the collapse of the empire in 843 resulted in a further decline in monastic life and discipline.

The tenth century saw a successful revival of Benedictinism, above all at Cluny, a monastery founded in 910 by William of Aquitaine and placed directly under papal patronage. Three distinguished and long-lived abbots, Majolus (abbot from 954 to 994), Odilo (994–1048), and Hugh (1049–1109), directed that house very effectively, establishing a high level of observance. They also established numerous other foundations so that in the twelfth century Cluny included a network of almost fifteen hundred monasteries, although many of them were very small houses. In reaction against the highly structured, economically wealthy, politically powerful, and liturgically elaborate form of monasticism that prevailed at Cluny and its larger daughter houses, other monastic families also developed during the eleventh century. These included the Camaldolese, the Vallumbrosans, the Carthusians, and the Cistercians, all of whom stressed a return to the basic elements of Benedict's rule, especially manual labor, corporate poverty, silence, prayer, and penitence. [*See* Cistercians.]

Monasticism was corrupted by the feudal system in the late Middle Ages; the observance of poverty and simplicity of life became particularly difficult to maintain. Popes Innocent III (d. 1216), Honorius III (d. 1227), and Gregory IX (d. 1241) sought reform, above all by having recourse to the Cistercian institution of the general chapter. In 1215 the Fourth Lateran Council mandated triennial provincial chapters that were to elect visitators to oversee the implementation of legislated reform measures, but this program was generally carried out only in England. In 1336 Benedict XII organized all Benedictine monasteries into thirty-two provinces and also prescribed a triennial chapter and visitation. Unfortunately, there was no way to implement this legislation effectively.

The institution that is known today as a Benedictine congregation was inaugurated in the fifteenth century by Luigi Barbo. In 1408 he became the abbot of Santa Giustina at Padua, where he established regular discipline. This attracted so many candidates that he went on to found new monasteries and reform existing ones, all of which were joined into a congregation in 1419. All of the Italian and Sicilian monasteries also eventually joined this congregation, which became known as the Cassinese Congregation when the abbey at Monte Cassino joined the congregation in 1504.

The Protestant Reformation destroyed about eight hundred of the approximately three thousand monasteries extant in Europe at the time. As a result of the Council of Trent (1545–1563), the congregational system was imposed on those monasteries that survived, and exemption from episcopal control was extended to all houses. By the eighteenth century Benedictine monasticism was generally in a healthy state, but it soon declined again as a result of the Enlightenment, the French Revolution, and widespread secularism. However, recovery and expansion followed during the nineteenth century. In 1833 Prosper Guéranger restored Benedictine life at Solesmes in France, prosperous houses developed in Germany at Metten in 1830 and at Beuron in 1863, and Boniface Wimmer, a monk of Metten, brought Benedictine monasticism to the United States in 1846. In 1888 Pope Leo XIII revived the Benedictine College of Sant' Anselmo in Rome, which had been founded by Innocent XI in 1687 as an international college for young Benedictine monks. The office of abbot primate was created in 1893. Elected by the Benedictine abbots of the world, the primate serves as head of the College of Sant' Anselmo and acts as an official representative of Benedictines to the Holy See; although he has no jurisdiction over individual abbeys throughout the world, he is a symbol of moral unity among Benedictines. On 21 March 1952 Pius XII approved the codification of the *Lex Proprio,* a particular code of law that governs the confederation of congregations. It is reviewed regularly at the congress of abbots held in Rome every four years.

The history of Benedictine women has not been well chronicled because of the scarcity of manuscript evidence. It seems that the Benedictine rule was first adopted in English convents in the seventh century, at the time the nuns Hilda and Etheldreda both ruled over double monasteries. When Boniface went as a missionary to Germany he was assisted by a distinguished group of nuns, including Lioba, Walburga, and Thekla. In the thirteenth century significant mystical writings were produced in Germany by Gertrude the Great, Mechthild of Hackeborn, and Mechthild of Magdeburg; it is not known, however, whether they were Benedictines or Cistercians. Post-Reformation nuns included Gertrude More (1606–1633); she achieved a high degree of holiness under the direction of Dom Augustine Baker while a member of the English community exiled at Cambrai in France. That community returned to Britain and finally settled at Stanbrook, near Worcester, in 1983. It is probably the most distinguished abbey of Benedictine nuns of the late twentieth century. Those nuns who came to the United States from Germany and Switzerland in the nineteenth century were forced to give up their solemn vows as nuns because of their apostolates outside the monastic enclosure; the majority of the women in the communities they founded are now Benedictine Sisters of pontifical jurisdiction.

In addition to the traditional life of work and prayer carried on within the enclosure of the monastery, Benedictine men and women in the 1980s are engaged in various ministries, including education, scholarship, health care, retreats, and parochial and missionary work. According to 1985 statistics, approximately 9453 monks live in 383 houses belonging to twenty-one congregations. There are approximately 7,911 nuns living in 351 monasteries, and approximately 11,273 sisters, many of whom work in diverse apostolates and live outside the monastery.

BIBLIOGRAPHY

A good introductory account of the Benedictines is to be found in Edward Cuthbert Butler's *Benedictine Monachism,* 2d ed. (1924; reprint, New York, 1961). *St. Benedict's Disciples,* edited by D. H. Farmer (Leominster, 1980), is a broad collection of essays on the past and present achievements of Benedict's followers, and through them of Benedict himself. *Saint Benedict: Father of Western Civilization,* prepared under the direction of Pieter Balsetier (New York, 1981), is a comprehensive and generously illustrated volume exploring many aspects of the Benedictine contribution to Christian humanism through art and architecture, as well as through scholarship. Statistical information can be found in *Catalogus monasteriorum O.S.B.,* 16th ed. (Rome, 1985), and J. P. Müller's *Atlas O.S.B.: Index monasteriorum* (Rome, 1975).

R. Kevin Seasoltz, o.s.b.

BENEDICT OF NURSIA (c. 480–547), Christian saint, monastic founder, and spiritual leader. Best known as the author of the monastic rule still followed by Benedictine and Cistercian monks and nuns, Benedict is looked upon as the father of Western monasticism because of the widespread influence of his rule. [*See* Benedictines *and* Cistercians.] Book 2 of the *Dialogues* of Gregory the Great, written about 593–594, is the only source of information on the details of Benedict's life. Although the primary purpose of the *Dialogues* is moral edification rather than biography in the modern sense, Gregory's work provides facts that conform to the general history of sixth-century central Italy; hence most scholars agree that the core of Gregory's information is basically reliable. His account of Benedict, however, concentrates mainly on miracles and encounters with demons.

Benedict was born in the Umbrian province of Nursia, northeast of Rome, into what the *Dialogues* describe as "a family of high station." The world of his time was in many ways chaotic. The Roman empire, already crumbling from within, was overrun by barbarians in the fifth century. In the sixth century Italy was devastated by war, famine, and plunder as Justinian I, the Byzantine emperor, attempted to reclaim control of the area. When Benedict was sent to Rome as a youth to study liberal arts, he was repelled by the immorality of the city; in about 500 he sought solitude, first at Enfide (modern-day Affide) and then at Subiaco, where he lived an eremitical life in a hillside cave. Sustained by the ministrations of a neighboring monk who brought him bread, he spent three years as a hermit but then reluctantly agreed to become the abbot of a nearby community of monks. Tensions between Benedict and the community, however, culminated in an attempt by members of the community to poison him. Benedict returned to Subiaco, where he was pursued by so many disciples that he established twelve small monasteries in the area. Because of the jealous opposition of a local priest, he migrated in about 525 to Casinum, approximately eighty miles south of Rome. Together with a small group of monks Benedict built his famous monastery, Monte Cassino, on the top of that imposing mountain in the central Apennines in place of a pagan shrine that he had destroyed.

The *Dialogues* portray Benedict in his relations with various personalities, including Totila, king of the Ostrogoths. Once a year he met with his sister Scholastica, who lived near Monte Cassino with a community of nuns. Benedict does not seem to have been ordained a priest. After founding the monastery he spent the rest of his life at Monte Cassino where he wrote the rule for monks, which has diffused his influence throughout the world for more than fourteen centuries. According to tradition, he died on 21 March 547. In about 590, Lombards ransacked the monastery at Monte Cassino and left it abandoned until it was reconstituted under Petronax of Brescia in about 720.

There are two traditions concerning Benedict's relics. One maintains that they were translated to the abbey of Saint-Benoît-sur-Loire in France some time during the seventh century; the feast of the translation of the relics has been celebrated on 11 July. According to the other tradition the relics were discovered at Monte Cassino in about 1069 by Abbot Desiderius, the future Pope Victor III. On 24 October 1964, Pope Paul VI declared Benedict the patron saint of Europe.

In Gregory's *Dialogues* Benedict's life is set out in four successive stages: confrontation with evil, or temptation; spiritual triumph, in which Benedict's virtue is demonstrated; a new situation in which his influence is shown more widely; and finally a fresh confrontation with the power of evil occasioned by this new position of influence. In this way Benedict's life unfolds as a search for God or a pilgrimage in which he finds God through temptations and trials. Benedict, as his name implies, is a man "blessed by God." His life illustrates the pattern set out in the rule itself, which invites the disciple to enter by the narrow gate in order to enjoy the freedom of living in the wide expanse of God. It also illustrates the paradox that fruitfulness emerges out of apparent sterility, that life comes forth from death.

It is the rule rather than the *Dialogues* that reveals Benedict's religious concerns. Impressive scholarship has been devoted to the question of the originality of the rule; the issue is in many ways of secondary importance. What is significant is that Benedict wisely took what he thought was good from existing rules and practices, evaluated that material in the light of his own experience, and blended the elements to form a balanced, positive, and flexible synthesis. The result is a clear code designed for a cenobitic rather than an eremitic form of monasticism: it combines sound spiritual teaching with pastoral details covering most aspects of community life. As Gregory noted, the rule is "outstanding for discretion." While setting out clear principles, it leaves much to the abbot's discernment.

The basic spiritual values affirmed by the rule are humility and unconditional obedience to God. Liturgical prayer, called the "work of God" in the rule, is to be carried out with a profound sense of God's presence, but that same awareness is also to permeate the whole of a monk's monastic life. A sense of the holiness of God generates a sense of compunction in the monk because of his sinfulness, but that awareness of weakness inspires confident trust in God's loving mercy rather than anxious fear.

Silence should prevail in the monastery so that the monk may be recollected and attentive to the word of God, especially during prayerful reading in which he is formed in accordance with the scriptures and the Christian monastic tradition. The monk's relationship of obedience with God is expressed especially through his relationship with his abbot, who is described in the rule as a sacrament of Christ. The abbot, however, is to reflect not only God's justice but his loving mercy as he "tempers all things so that the strong may have something to strive for and the weak may not recoil in dismay." The monk's relationship with God is also reflected in his relations with the other monks in the community as he shares all things in common, renounces self-will, forgives offences, and shows compassion for the weaknesses of others. Stability in the community provides the monk with his basic asceticism and supports and challenges him as he pursues his commitment to an ongoing conversion of life.

Work, whether manual or intellectual, is also an integral part of Benedict's vision of the monastic life. The rule proposes a set time for work not only because Benedict distrusted idleness but also because he wanted work to be kept in proportion with prayer and holy reading. Work is always situated in a communal context; it is not to degenerate into activism nor to promote self-sufficiency and arrogance. Pursued with an attitude of profound reverence for creation, work is meant to be a humanizing experience in which the monk serves both God and the community.

The rule of Benedict promotes a spirituality that is both broad and simple. Because of its flexibility and adaptability, it is capable of incorporating various local traditions. Whenever and wherever the rule is authentically incarnated in monastic men and women, both as individuals and communities, it results in a life that is biblical, contemplative, rooted in a community life of work and prayer, and productive of holiness and peace.

BIBLIOGRAPHY

The best critical edition of Gregory's *Dialogues* in Latin and French translation is edited by Adalbert De Vogüé, *Dialogues: Gregoire le Grand,* 3 vols. (Paris, 1978–1980). The rule of Benedict in Latin and French translation with extensive introduction, notes, and bibliography has also been edited by De Vogüé, *Le règle de Saint Benoît*, 7 vols. (Paris, 1971–1977). The final volume is available in English translation: *The Rule of Saint Benedict, a Doctrinal and Spiritual Commentary*, translated by John Hasbrouck (Kalamazoo, Mich., 1983). *RB 1980: The Rule of St. Benedict in Latin and English with Notes*, edited by Timothy Fry (Collegeville, Minn., 1981), is the best Latin edition of the rule accompanied by an English translation; it also contains excellent essays on specific topics in the rule. A balanced contemporary theology of Benedictine monasticism can be found in *Consider Your Call: A Theology of Monastic Life Today*, by Daniel Rees and others (Kalamazoo, Mich., 1980).

R. KEVIN SEASOLTZ, O.S.B.

BENGALI RELIGIONS. The religious profile of the Bengali-speaking region of eastern India (West Bengal) and Bangladesh (formerly East Pakistan) is pluralistic, complex and, like the active delta itself, ever-changing in contour. Two "great traditions," the Islamic and the Brahmanic Hindu, claim the allegiance of the vast majority of Bengalis. Yet in intimate relation to these there persist pockets of scarcely Hinduized tribal peoples, a hardy semi-tribal remnant of a once powerful Buddhist community, a cluster of Christian denominations, small urban settlements of non-Bengali Jains, Sikhs, Parsis, Chinese, and Jews, not to mention legions of Hindus and Muslims whose fundamental commitments or faith would seem to be in Marxist, radical humanist and other more or less "secular" forms.

This article treats each of the religious traditions separately but notes, where evident, their mutual impact and shared experience of common historical conditions. The fact of endemic exposure to religious (and social and cultural) plurality seems to have given a certain subtley or maleability to Bengali religious mentality, popular as well as learned. Bengal lies beyond the geographic-ethnic heartland of all of the religious "great traditions" (with the arguable exception of the Buddhist adherents dwelling in Bengal), a fact that seems to affect the way a tradition is perceived and applied in life. In the case of both the Brahmanic Hindu and the Islamic traditions there has been the development of distinctive "middle traditions," which use the Bengali vernacular and draw local cultural elements into a regional reformulation of the exogenous great tradition. The content and shape of such a Bengali "middle tradition"—as well as the readiness or reluctance with which a community undertakes its formulation—reveal distinctive Hindu and Muslim (and in principle other) conceptions of the meaning and value of Bengali cultural forms. It would seem from the evidence of Bengali religious history that sustained exposure to religious plurality and the experience of being outside the heartland of one's great tradition tend to accentuate regional particularities of religious life at the expense of alleged universalities of the exogenous great tradition. Also, in such a situation that is both plural and peripheral there seems to be a tendency to emphasize the more immediate humane aspects of piety and to relax somewhat the more transcendent, austere ones. These tendencies have been the occasion of both self-congratulation and scornful criticism from within the respective communities.

The Hindu Setting. The Hindu tradition has been, for perhaps two millennia, the most complex and culturally prolific religious tradition in Bengal (though self-consciously Hindu only after sustained contact with Muslims from the thirteenth century onward). It depends heavily upon the Brahmanic great tradition, with its Vedic and Sanskrit sacred texts, but it also draws much from myriad "little traditions" deriving symbolism and practices from indigenous non-Aryan (e.g., Kol-Munda, Dravidian, Tibeto-Mongolian) peoples. But what is most distinctive of the Hindu tradition in Bengal is the "middle (or regional) tradition," whose oral and written texts are in the vernacular Bengali language. The Hindu tradition provides the sociocultural matrix for Buddhists, Jains, and Sikhs as well as for Hindus in Bengal and constitutes the background from which have come most converts to the small Christian and the massive Muslim communities. It is for this reason that we treat Hinduism first.

Hindus represent about 75 percent of the population of West Bengal, and about 12 percent of that of Bangladesh. Fewer than 10 percent of Bengali Hindus are considered brahman (Skt., *brāhmaṇa*); most of the rest are *śūdra*, the latter divided among scores of endogamous groups known as *jāti*s, or subcastes. The two highest *jāti*s among the "clean" division of *śūdras*, the clerical *kāyastha*s and medical *baidyas*, share with brahmans the sociocultural status of *bhadralok* ("gentlemen"), a nonritualistic analogue to the ritualistic twice-born category of brahmans, *kṣatriyas*, and *vaiśyas* found elsewhere in Brahmanic Hindu society. Both brahmans and *kāyastha*s maintain the *kulin* ("possessing genuine lineage") system of hypergamous subdivisions, which in the past gave rise to excesses of polygamy no longer countenanced by law or custom. [*For further discussion of caste, see* Varṇa and Jāti.]

Bengali Hindus generally share the same sacred Sanskrit texts (Vedas, Dharmaśāstras, epics, and Purāṇas), the same pantheon, myths, rituals, and philosophical-theological heritage found throughout India, but with special emphases and exceptions. Vedic solemn *(śrauta)* rites are scarcely cultivated, though domestic *(gṛhya)* rites are maintained. Monumental religious architecture seems not to have flourished in Brahmanic (although it once did in Buddhist) circles, but smaller, gracefully curved temples of bamboo or brick, often embellished with terra-cotta relief, adorn the Bengali countryside. (Most impressive are those at Bisnupur in West Bengal, where a cluster of sixteenth- and seventeenth-century temples replicate Kṛṣṇa's sacred realm of Vṛndāvana.) Interestingly, the majority of Hindu temples in Bengal are dedicated to Śiva, the lord of the locality, while the favored objects of individual devotion *(bhakti)* and the preferred topics of Bengali religious texts are not Śiva, but overwhelmingly are either Kṛṣṇa or one of several goddesses.

Śāktism and Tantrism. Goddesses are especially prominent in Bengal. Most lavishly worshiped is the fair, ornately decorated Durgā, the multi-armed vanquisher of the buffalo demon. Her annual fall worship, Durgā Pūjā, extends over several days and supplants Dusserah in Bengal. [*See also* Durgā Hinduism.] *Pūjā* for the dark, naked goddess of blood, Kālī, supplants Dīvālī, the festival of lights. [*See* Dīvālī.] Other goddesses of eminence in Bengal include Caṇḍī/Umā/Pārvatī (spouse of Śiva), Sarasvatī (goddess of learning), Śītalā (goddess of smallpox and cholera), Ṣaṣṭhī (lit., "sixth," this goddess is the protector of children and is worshiped on the sixth day after childbirth), Manasā (goddess of snakebites, she is worshiped together with her devotee, the heroine Behulā), Annadā (goddess of grain and food in general), and Rādhā (idyllic lover of Kṛṣṇa). Childlike devotion to the Goddess as mother was late to appear in Bengal, but is manifest in Ramprasad Sen's (1718–1775) songs, *Śyāmāsaṅgīt*, and in Ramakrishna Paramahamsa's (d. 1886) ecstatic teasing devotion to Kālī. [*See the biography of Ramakrishna.*] The deltaic Bengal region itself is often imagined and apostrophied by Bengalis (non-Hindus as well as Hindus) as a quasi-divine mother, beautiful, bountiful, now caressing, now chastizing. [*See also* Goddess Worship, *article on* The Hindu Goddess.]

Loosely correlated with the preeminence of goddesses is the prominence of Tantrism in Bengal. The origins (Aryan and non-Aryan) of Tantrism are not yet clearly known, but from the mid-first millennium CE Bengal was a leading source of Sanskrit Tantric texts wherein brahman priests and Buddhist monks applied their respective learnings to Tantric principles of ritual and meditation. Hindu Tantra literature in Sanskrit flourished through the Pāla period (760–1142 CE), but declined under the Senas in the twelfth century. Not until the revival of sanskritic learning in Navadvīp in the sixteenth century is there evidence of renewed interest in Tantrism among Bengali brahmans.

However, a simplified variant of Tantrism, called Sahaja or Sahajiya ("natural, born together"), often of the "left" variety (i.e., using socially forbidden elements in ritualizing exercises), seems to have persisted in Bengal at least from the twelfth century (probably from much earlier), to the present. Sahaja Tantrism is an indigenous kind of yogic discipline specializing in symbolic interpretation and transformation of bodily substances. It selectively adapts from more sophisticated religious systems (Buddhist, Nāth, Śaiva-Śākta, Vaiṣṇava) elements of imagery, doctrine, and practice so as to forge hybrid systems of spiritual discipline *(sādhana)*. A hybrid Vaiṣṇava-Sahajiya flourished in the seventeenth and eighteenth centuries.

Many small circles of male and female adepts, often mendicant singers or musicians at the edge of Hindu society (i.e., Bauls, Śains, Kartābhajas), maintain their respective variants of simplified Tantra and gather periodically for festivals with fellow adepts of the same circle. The annual *mela* ("festival") of Jayadeva at Kenduli, West Bengal, attracts many Bauls. Several major sites of pilgrimage in West Bengal (for example, Bakresvar and Tarapith) have strong Tantric associations shared by Brahmanic and Sahajiya levels of Tantra. [*See also* Tantrism.]

Vaiṣṇavism. Vaiṣṇava piety in Bengal, like Śaivism and Śāktism, may go back to Mauryan times, certainly to Gupta and Pāla periods, from which iconographic and other detailed evidence survives. There are statues of Viṣṇu in many forms, of Śiva (*liṅga*s and anthropomorphic forms), of Śakti (as Durgā, Caṇḍī, Sarvāṇī, and other goddesses), and of Sūrya, Gaṇeśa, Indra, and Varuṇa. Images of Kṛṣṇa and Rāma are rare in pre-Islamic Bengal, but there is what appears to be a relief of Kṛṣṇa and Rādhā on the Buddhist stupa at Somapura near Pāhārpur. The most celebrated Sanskrit poem composed in Bengal, the *Gītagovinda* of Jayadeva (twelfth century), however, celebrates the love of Kṛṣṇa and his mistress, Rādhā. [*See the biography of Jayadeva.*] The theme was much favored in succeeding centuries by vernacular poets using Bengali and the closely related Maithili and Brajabuli languages. [*See also* Poetry, *article on* Indian Religious Poetry.]

Devotion *(bhakti)* to Kṛṣṇa (and to his divine lover Rādhā) has held a special place in Bengali religious life since the appearance of Kṛṣṇa-Caitanya (a brahman, born Viśvambhara Miśra; 1486–1533). [*See also* Bhakti.] An ecstatic revivalist, Caitanya was passionately dedicated to devout love *(prema)* to Kṛṣṇa through private meditation and public chanting *(saṃkīrtana)* of divine names. To Bengali Vaiṣṇavas he is the divine Kṛṣṇa or Rādhā and Kṛṣṇa combined. [*See also* Rādhā *and* Kṛṣṇa.] Most Vaiṣṇava temples in Bengal are now Kṛṣṇa temples, and many contain the image of Caitanya as well. Caitanya's birthplace, Navadvīp (Śrīmāyāpur) and other sites hallowed by his presence or that of his associates are the loci of periodic festivals, commemorating events of Caitanya's lifetime in addition to the annual round of Vaiṣṇava rituals, especially those specific to Kṛṣṇa. The Caitanya (or Gauḍīya, i.e., Bengali) Vaiṣṇava movement has bequeathed to Bengali culture a wealth of devotional literature in Sanskrit and Bengali: lyrics *(padāvalī)*, music *(kīrtan)*, drama, hagiography, and a systematic theology *(bhaktir-asaśāstra)* that combines Sanskrit poetics with Kṛṣṇaite philosophy of paradoxical difference and nondifference *(acintyabhedābheda)*. [*See also* Kṛṣṇaism.]

Caitanya's *bhakti* movement was but one of several surgings of religio-cultural creativity among Bengali Hindus early in the sixteenth century (under the protection of the independent Husain Shāhi sultans of Gaur). Raghunandan Śiromaṇi in the field of Dharmaśāstra, Raghunātha Tarkika Śiromaṇi in Navyanyāya (the new theistic logic), and Kṛṣṇānanda Āgamavāgīśa in Tantric scholarship all may have been contemporaries of Caitanya in Navadvīp. [*See also the biography of Caitanya.*]

Popular religious literature. From the sixteenth century we begin to get written versions of popular vernacular compositions that had been circulating orally long before. The foremost genre is the *maṅgal-kāvya* ("auspicious poem") in *pāyār* verse, intended for singing in ritual settings. A *maṅgal* recounts the glories of the god or goddess and the struggles and rewards of his or her worshipers, all set within a cosmological framework. There are *maṅgal*s dedicated to the deity Dharma (who protects certain local peoples); others feature *siddha*s ("adepts") of the Nāth tradition, and many inculcate worship of Manasā and other goddesses. An indigenous, composite deity, Dharma (neutral enough to stand for the supreme reality from varied Hindu, tribal, Buddhist, and even Muslim standpoints) stands out as a cosmogonic source in Dharma-, Nāth- and Manasā-*màngal*s. The *maṅgal* genre was utilized by biographers of Caitanya and by Muslim epic writers as well as by accomplished poets in the perennially vigorous Śākta tradition. A simpler genre of verse (to be recited rather than sung) is the *pāñcāli*, often utilized for extolling lesser local deities, spirits, and saints. [*See also* Music, *article on* Music and Religion in India.]

Classical religious literature. Drawing from the Brahmanic great tradition are numerous Bengali translations and paraphrases of Sanskrit epic, Puranic, and Tantric texts, the most influential being Kṛttivāsa's fifteenth-century *Rāmāyaṇa*, which in characteristic Bengali Vaiṣṇava fashion stresses compassionate human feelings more than heroism and duty. The most noted of many partial renderings of the *Mahābhārata* into Bengali is that by Kāśirāmdās and associates (seventeenth century), the *Pāṇḍavavijaya.* The earliest of many extant paraphrases of Purāṇas is the late fifteenth-century *Śrīkṛṣṇavijaya* of Mālādhara Vasu, who was honored by Barbak Shāh and by Caitanya. Much translation and adaptation of epic and Puranic texts was done under the patronage of Hindu *rājā*s on the periphery of Bengal (i.e., Kooch Bihar, Tipperah, Kachar, and Bisnupur), who secured their local privileges by acknowledging the sovereignty of the Sultan of Gaur or of the Mughals. But by and large the seventeenth and eighteenth centuries under imperial Mughal rule, in contrast to the sixteenth century, were a period of continuity and repetition rather than of creativity in the religious and literary life of Bengali Hindus.

Nineteenth-century renaissance. The nineteenth century, however, brought remarkable religious developments in the midst of profound political, economic, and cultural changes in Bengal. More than half a millennium of Muslim domination (initially destructive, occasioncally supportive, always, implicitly at least, intimidating) had ended. English soon replaced Persian in administration, courts, and higher education, thus opening up new cultural, professional, and business opportunities for those (initially, almost exclusively Hindu *bhadralok*) who would take part.

A floodtide of stimulation and challenge met those who exposed themselves to Western culture, secular and/or religious. Those Bengali *bhadralok* who came to the new colonial metropolis, Calcutta, became de facto the primary mediators between India and the West (until comparable elites emerged in secondary seats of British power). In this heady atmosphere they rapidly explored many avenues pertinent to their anomalous position between two cultures. Such avenues included radical criticism, even rejection, of the Hindu socioreligious tradition, as by those few of the new elite who became Christian or as by the iconoclastic Young India group inspired by Henry Derozio (1809–1831). Staunchly opposing (by argument, disapproval, or intimidation) these and less radical responses to Western religion and culture were diehard conservatives. Between these extremes were varied paths opened by Bengali *bhadralok* reformers who sought to remain within the Hindu tradition, but on terms consonant with their precarious position between two worlds.

Ram Mohan Roy (1774–1833), polyglot, intellectual,

and administrator, was the most effective of early nineteenth century *bhadralok* reformers. His appreciation for the oneness of a personal God (gained during youthful studies of Persian and Arabic) and admiration for the ethical teachings of Christ raised unfulfilled hope for his conversion among Christian and Unitarian missionaries, with whom he both cooperated and contended. He argued forcefully, if insensitively, against worship of images and amorous symbolism in myth, ritual, and song, and he campaigned successfully against the self-immolation of widows *(satī)* and other such socioreligious practices. [*See also the biography of Roy.*]

Roy was the first to translate selections from the Upaniṣads into Bengali and English. He founded the Brāhmo Samāj (Society of Theists), an elite congregation of Unitarian-style Hindus who professed faith in one personal God and who rejected image worship, animal sacrifice, and the harsher (to humanitarian, egalitarian sensibilities) aspects of the caste system. [*See also* Brāhmo Samāj.]

Succeeding Roy in leadership of the Brāhmo Samāj was the austere and meditative Debendranath Tagore (1817–1905), under whose guidance the Samāj gained a richer liturgy and stock of prayers. An enthusiastic younger Brāhmo, Keshab Chandra Sen (1838–1884), impatient with Debendranath's cautious socioritual stance, broke away to form the Brāhmo Samāj of India. This new group reflected the more radical social ideals of Sen as well as his preference for Vaiṣṇava-style *kīrtan* and his effusive devotion to Jesus Christ. A second schism, occasioned by Sen's failure to apply his radical socioritual principles in the marriage of his own daughter, resulted in yet a third Samāj, the Sādhāran Brāhmo Samāj. Although never attaining a large membership, the Brāhmo Samājes provided a crucial rallying place for Bengali *bhadralok* dissatisfied with the Hindu status quo but unwilling to foresake their tradition altogether. [*See also the biography of Sen.*]

Much of the rethinking of Hindu religious ideals and practices throughout the nineteenth century "Bengal Renaissance" was effected through novels, dramas, poems, and prose essays. An outstanding example is the novelist and social commentator Bankim Chandra Chatterji (1838–1894), whose novel *Ānanda Maṭh* (Abbey of Bliss) depicts militant struggle for independence as a mode of dedication to the Goddess and whose semischolarly *Kṛṣṇacarita* (Acts of Kṛṣṇa) extrapolates from the *Mahābhārata* an idealized humanistic Kṛṣṇa as model for modern Indians.

The most venerated nineteenth century Bengali religious figure was not of the English-trained elite: Ramakrishna (born Gadadhar Chatterji; 1836–1886) was engagingly simple in Bengali conversation and ecstatic in his devotion to the goddess Kālī. He sought to experience the divine through Śākta, Vaiṣṇava, Tantric, and Vedantic disciplines as well as through what he considered Christian and Muslim meditations. Ramakrishna and his wife, Śāradā Devī, are worshiped jointly by the devout: he as the divine descent *(avatāra)*, and she as the consort/power *(śakti)*. [*See also the biography of Ramakrishna.*]

The leading disciple of Ramakrishna, Vivekananda (born Narendranath Datta; 1863–1902), was a forceful speaker and writer (in Bengali and English) both in India—where he urged his countrymen to assert their Hindu Indian heritage—and overseas—where he projected a confident, irenic mode of Hindu faith and established in New York the first of several Vedanta Societies in the West. He organized the Ramakrishna Mission order of monks dedicated to religious uplift, education, medicine, and social services. [*See also the biography of Vivekananda.*]

Twentieth-century Hindu nationalism and internationalism. Incipient Hindu nationalism took on a more assertive and chauvinistic political character in the twentieth century, especially during the Bengali *bhadralok*'s swadeshi campaign to undo the 1905 partition of Bengal. The campaign succeeded but at the cost of further alienating Muslims. At the violent extreme of the campaign were youthful "Terrorists" who conceived of their acts of violence as sacrificial offerings to the Goddess/motherland. The profound and prolific England-educated Bengali Aurobindo Ghose (1872–1950) was himself briefly an "Extremist" before ecstatic experience while in prison in Calcutta helped redirect his energies into yogic meditations, religio-philosophic writing, and guidance—with the help of Mira Richard, "The Mother"—of a transnational community (based in Pondicherry, in southeastern India) seeking through Integral Yoga to advance the evolution of human consciousness. [*See the biography of Aurobindo Ghose.*]

Śākta imagery of the assertive, potentially violent sort seems to have inspired in a diffuse way nationalist politics in Bengal especially in the "Extremist" form embodied by Netaji Subhas Chandra Bose (1897–1945). Diffusion of the more accommodating and nonviolent Vaiṣṇava ethos into nationalist politics in Bengal was less pronounced, since Bose, rather than Gandhi, had captured the political imagination of Bengali Hindus. However, the mature work of Rabindranath Tagore (1861–1941), Nobel laureate in poetry (for *Gītāñjali*), novelist, dramatist, educator, musician, and artist—and very much a formative influence upon literate twentieth-century Bengalis—features certain Vaiṣṇava and Brāhmo ideals and attitudes prominently within its vision of global human solidarity. Tagore's "Religion of

Man" (as he entitled his Hibbert Lectures), stresses the creative, evolving, aesthetic, and interpersonal qualities of human experience as being at the heart of "religion" at its best. [*See also the biography of Tagore.*]

Traditional Hindu religious institutions flourished in the nineteenth and early twentieth centuries alongside the protean reform movements. Money and talent flowed into building and repairing temples and religious hostels and into evangelization via publishing, preaching, music, and drama. Scholarly editions of Bengali and Sanskrit religious texts were plentiful, and serious research on the Hindu (and also Buddhist) religious past proliferated in this period.

Vaiṣṇavas in the tradition of Caitanya were especially adept at utilizing the newer modes of evangelization, and within their specific tradition there were some vigorous movements of moderate innovation and reform. The most effective of these was begun by a layman, Bhakti Vinode Thakur (born Kedarnath Datta; 1838–1914), and was given institutional form by his son, Bhakti Siddhanta Sarasvati (born Bimala Prasad Datta; 1874–1937) as the Gauḍīya Maṭh (or Gauḍīya Mission), an order of preaching monks.

Independence and frustrations. The independence of India and Pakistan in 1947 meant the partition of Bengal, communal violence, and the migration of Hindu and Muslim refugees. West Bengal and Calcutta, suddenly cut off from the greater portion of the once proud Bengal Presidency, were stunted economically and politically and yet bound to assimilate millions of refugees. Starved for resources and with little prospect for relief, most institutions in West Bengal—including traditional and reformist religious ones—have languished since 1947, hanging on somehow, but rarely able to mobilize resources for creative or innovative endeavors.

One area in which there has been some innovation and vitality, though the key figures were mostly born long before independence, is that of individual *gurus* and their networks of disciples. It is too soon to assess the longterm import of this phenomenon. Among the more notable are Anandamayi Ma (born Nirmalasundari Bhattacarya; 1896–1982), a quiet, intuitive woman noted for the peace she radiates; Sri Chinmoy (born Chinmoy [Cinmay] Kumar Ghose, 1931–), a gifted musician with an international following seeking inner and outer peace, especially through music and vegetarian diet; A. C. Bhaktivedanta (born Abhay Caran De; 1896–1977), founder of the International Society for Krishna Consciousness (ISKCON), continuing in the tradition of Caitanyaite *bhakti.* [*See also* International Society for Krishna Consciousness.] The violence-plagued Ananda Marg and its political-economic affiliate, Progressive Utilization Theory (PROUT), have pockets of strength in rural West Bengal and in Calcutta.

The area of greatest creativity in post-independence Bengal is literature, with art, music, cinema, and political analysis also attracting creative minds. Most of what has been expressed in these areas, however, has taken secular humanist or even Marxist, rather than explicitly Hindu religious form. Yet one could argue that the passionately humanitarian films of a Ritwik Ghatak, the radical humanism of an M. N. Roy, and much of the poetry and fiction of post-independence Bengali writers—refugees and native West Bengalis alike—have a profoundly religious quality to them. They often embody a quest for human authenticity and/or social justice, and for transcendence of the status quo, thereby revealing continuities with themes found in earlier, explicitly religious, Bengali literature.

Meanwhile in East Pakistan and (from 1971) Bangladesh the conditions of the Hindu minority have been even less conducive to institutional and, with rare exceptions, individual creativity. Most wealthy and well-educated Hindus left at partition or during disturbances thereafter. Those who remained were preoccupied with day to day survival in an economically deprived and politically unsympathetic milieu. Sporadic harassment culminating in the atrocities and mass exodus in 1971 have been followed by the relative security of independent Bangladesh under the "secular" Awami League and the "Islamic," but not anti-Hindu, military regimes that have followed. Traditional Hindu institutions survive, but in severely depleted condition and, as in West Bengal, the more creative Hindu writers and artists generally speak an idiom that is humanistic rather than distinctively Hindu, but which may be profoundly religious for all that.

Religious Minorities. A significant number of Bengalis represent non-Hindu and non-Muslim religious traditions. To a certain extent these groups have accommodated to the dominant traditions, but they remain distinct communities nonetheless.

Buddhists. The largest concentration of Buddhists in Bengal is among the Barua/Maghas, Chakmas, and Marammas situated along the eastern periphery of Bangladesh. The Buddhist presence in Bengal goes back probably to Mauryan times and certainly to the early first millenium CE, when Buddhist monks (*bhikṣus*, lit., "mendicants") shared royal patronage with brahmans and Jains. Many rulers, especially among the Khaḍgas (late seventh century) and the Pālas, seem to have embraced the Buddhist faith. Under the Pālas several major monastic academies were constructed in Bengal and certain of these (e.g., Somapura near Pāhārpur and Śālban near Comilla) were endowed with massive sculptured stupas. Chinese travelers reported many *vihāras* (monasteries) with *bhikṣus* of several Buddhist persuasions: Mahāyāna, Sthavira, Sarvāstivāda, Tantrika, and Vajrayāna. Buddhist scholarship and art flourished for centuries in ancient Bengal, and during the long Pāla period Buddhist Tantra was assiduously cultivated. Subsequent discouragement by the Brahmanical Senas and destruction of remaining *vihāras* by the Turks in the thirteenth century brought about the dispersal of scholar-*bhikṣus* and their texts from Bengal, especially to Nepal and Tibet. [*See also* Buddhism, *article on* Buddhism in India.]

A hybrid Buddhist Sahaja Tantra, developed by the twelfth century at the latest, may well have survived in Bengal into the postconquest centuries only to have merged gradually with other hybrid forms of rustic piety. Traces of other Buddhist elements in later Bengali Hindu tradition are not implausible, but most are conjectural. Also conjectural is the extent of Buddhist influence among the lower rural strata before the Turkish conquest and the function, if any, of such prior Buddhist influence in facilitating Muslim conversion. In recent centuries there has been very little adherence to the Buddhist tradition by ethnic Bengalis. But several tribal peoples and the Barua/Maghas of southeast Bengal remained strongly committed to their respective forms of Buddhism; these were embedded in tribal and caste customs and were penetrated by Hindu Tantra and Śākta elements, but lacked properly initiated celibate *bhikṣus*.

In the middle of the nineteenth century a movement of reform was undertaken by a Theravāda monk from Arrakan (but a native of Chittagong), Sangaraj Saramedha. Aided by the Chakma queen, Kalindi, and the ongoing cooperation of the monks Punnacara Dhammodhara and Jnanalamkara Mahasthavir, Saramedha restored proper initiation, removed "offensive" Hindu practices, established educational facilities, and formed the Sangarāj Nikāya, an organization of reformed Buddhists characterized by a close interdependence of *bhikkus* and laymen. Not all Buddhists in what is now Bangladesh accepted the Sangarāj's reforms; the Mahāsthāvir Nikāya is an organization representing those who have held closer to the indigenous ways.

Many Buddhists in Bangladesh face an ominous threat to their way of life. The sparsely populated area that many of them inhabit has become coveted by others for hydroelectric projects, gas, minerals, timber, and land. Moreover, their tribal lands are now a sensitive border area, subjected to military and guerilla operations and liable to being declared off limits to outsiders.

The revival of Buddhism in West Bengal stems from the relocation in Calcutta of the Mahā Bodhi Society and the inauguration there of the Bauddha Dharmānkur Sabhā, both in 1892. Other associations, publications, and scholarship dealing with the Buddhist tradition soon sprang up and have continued into the present.

Jains. Most of the Jains in Bengal are Marwaris (i.e., Gujaratis and Rajasthanīs) and other non-Bengalis concentrated in the urban centers of West Bengal. They are noted for their splendid temple in Calcutta. Lay Jains have been prominent in Bengali finance and business at least since Mughal times. There were Jain ascetics (*nirgranthas*) in Bengal throughout the first millenium CE, but their ancient establishments have long since disappeared. The customs of certain lower-caste religious groups (e.g., Jugis, Jāti-Baiṣṇabs, etc.) may reflect distant Jain influence. [*See* Jainism.]

Sikhs. A substantial Sikh community is concentrated in Calcutta and other centers of business and transportation in West Bengal. Sikh and Vaiṣṇava hagiography both claim that Nānak visited eastern India early in the sixteenth century. Tegh Bahādur visited Sikhs residing in Dhaka in the late seventeenth century and most likely Sikh traders of the Punjabi *khatri* caste had settled in Bengal much earlier. Business opportunities under the British drew Punjabi Sikhs to Calcutta in the nineteenth century, and refugees from West Punjab (West Pakistan) augmented their numbers in 1947. Calcutta Sikhs maintain numerous *gurdwaras* (temples) and educational and welfare institutions. They bring out the noted *Sikh Review*. [*See* Sikhism.]

Parsis. Bengali Parsis are concentrated in Calcutta, where they came for banking and railways in the mid-nineteenth century. Prosperous and well-educated, they have had a fire temple since 1839 and have published a journal, *Navroz*, since 1917. [*See also* Parsis.]

Christians. The Christians in Bengal are socially, denominationally, and geographically diverse. The largest single denomination has been the Roman Catholic, the major portion of which derives from Portuguese traders of the sixteenth and later centuries and their mixed Portuguese-Bengali descendants. Protestant evangelization began in 1793 with the Baptist Mission, in the Dutch enclave, Serampore, where William Carey (1761–1843) and associates pioneered Bengali prose and printing and established Serampore College. Throughout the nineteenth century, Baptists, Lutherans, Anglicans, and Presbyterians were among the missionaries from several countries to establish congregations throughout Bengal.

Most converts were from lower Bengali social strata or from tribal peoples, but there were enough *bhadralok* conversions in the nineteenth century to spur Hindu reaction. Among *bhadralok* converts the Protestant Krishna Mohan Bannerji (1813–1885) and Brahmabandhab Upadhyay (1861–1907), Catholic theologian cum Hindu *saṃnyāsin* cum Indian nationalist, strove to forge indigenous Indian forms of the Christian church, but with meager results. Most denominations long remained dependent upon foreign leadership and models, but gradually indigenous clergies (and hierarchies), liturgies, and theologies have emerged, and some Protestant demoninations have amalgamated.

Christians in Bengal have long been associated with education, nursing, and social welfare. Indeed, the most esteemed saint in late twentieth-century West Bengal is probably the Albanian Catholic nun, Mother Theresa, whose nuns and brothers serve the dying destitutes, lepers, and foundlings with exemplary devotion. In Bangladesh Christians, both Bangladeshi and foreign, have been conspicuous in relief and development work. [*See also* Christianity, *article on* Christianity in Asia.]

Jews. There may be fewer than fifty resident Jews remaining in Calcutta, though their community was once much larger and more influential, as an impressive synagogue and large burial grounds in Calcutta bear witness. [*See also* Judaism, *article on* Judaism in Asia and Northeast Africa.]

The Islamic Majority. Muslims constitute the largest religious community among Bengalis (about 86 percent of Bangladeshis, and about 21 percent of West Bengalis); they are overwhelmingly Sunnī of Ḥanafi orientation, the few Shīʿah deriving mostly from Persian officials of the late Mughal period. The vast majority of Muslims in Bengal are ethnic Bengalis, thanks to massive conversion and natural increase since Muḥammad ibn Bakhtyār Khaljī's conquest of Bengal (c. 1203 CE). Ethnic and linguistic cleavage between immigrant (e.g., Arab, Turk, Afghan, Pathan, Mughal, and Persian) elite *(ashrāf)* and indigenous masses *(aṭrāf, ajlāf)* has affected deeply the character of Bengali Muslim life. The building of a vernacular-based middle tradition, which came so easily to Hindu Bengalis, has occasioned recurrent conflict, confusion, and anxiety for Muslims in Bengal. Indeed, the very use of the Bengali language and the acknowledgement of Bengali ethnicity have been problematic for them.

Conversion: pirs of the "little tradition." The process of conversion of the indigenous population of central and eastern Bengal remains a matter of conjecture due to lack of contemporary textual evidence. No doubt, rulers and governors established mosques, *madrasahs* (mosque colleges), and other Muslim institutions in those urban centers where immigrant Muslims congregated. But the greatest concentrations of Muslims are found not in such urban centers, but in the rural backcountry where the population would have been overwhelmingly indigenous, a mosaic of unevenly hinduized (with undetermined Buddhist influence) endogamous groups (*jātis*) and tribal peoples. Long after the event Bengali Muslim recollections attribute the massive evangelization to pirs (guides, typically Ṣūfī masters), but the Bengali category of pir is a protean one, embracing elements from legend, folklore, myth, and pre-Muslim rustic theology.

Some historical figures definitely are included among the pirs (e.g., Shāh Jalāl, who converted many in Sylhet, Ẓāfar Khān Ghāzi, the martyred warrior, and Khān Jahān ʿAlī, the clearer of forests). Many pirs who seem to have a historical foundation are remembered for alleged therapeutic, thaumaturgic, and pragmatic powers rather than for any Ṣūfī spirituality. Human pirs established free hostels *(āstānah, khānqāh)* in their lifetime and after death their tombs *(mazār, dargāh)* became foci of power of the "undying" *(zindah)* pir. Charismatic pioneering pirs were succeeded by sons and/or disciples. Other pirs seem to have no human referent, but to be transformations into the Muslim little tradition of minor deities, heroes, and spirits believed in the indigenous rural culture to have influence over a particular locality, illness, or occupation.

"Middle tradition": literary mediators. From the sixteenth century we begin to get written texts reflecting both the little tradition of Muslim pirs and the more sophisticated middle tradition of polished Bengali Islamic literature. Writers of these latter texts often expressed misgivings about their task, some simply noting and rebutting hostile elite criticism, others betraying their own ambivalence about expressing Islamic truth in a language and culture alleged to be unsuitable for it.

The resulting compositions are sometimes brilliant tours de force, transmutations of entire cosmic, mythic, and epic situations. The foremost authority on these "mediators" characterizes their work as "syncretistic," though this may unfairly characterize the effort as a whole. If one means by "syncretistic" that which is fundamentally hybrid, or which results in major alteration of basic patterns of thought and symbolism, then much of the mystical/meditational corpus is, indeed, syncretistic (i.e., more Tantric than Ṣūfī). Cosmological and mythic portions of epic texts have some syncretistic passages, but it is not clear that the overall message is syncretistic and not merely a restating of a basically unchanged pattern of meaning in an indigenous outer form. The texts on Muslim ritual and social practice are strictly within the realm of Islamic orthodoxy.

Islamic criticism and reform: Faraizis and jihād movements. The Bengali Muslim middle and little traditions, though scorned or ignored by the exogenous elite, had for centuries satisfied their respective literate and illiterate constituencies of Bengali-speaking Muslims. But by the early nineteenth century the traumatic loss of power by the Mughals to the British had set in motion processes that would destabilize the longstanding but problematic counterpoise of *ashrāf* versus *aṭrāf*, exogenous versus indigenous, and Persian/Urdu-speakers versus Bengali-speakers. There emerged vigorous movements of Muslim self-criticism and reform as responses to the loss of Muslim power, somewhat parallel to the Wahhābīyah in Arabia, but autonomous and firmly rooted in Bengali Muslim experience.

The Faraizi movement, led by Haji Shariatullah (1781–1840) and his son Dudu Miyan (1819–1862), sought to restore the fortunes of Islam by rejection of all sorts of indigenous practices, such as veneration of pirs, as un-Islamic, thus calling for—and to a remarkable extent achieving—a thoroughgoing alienation of indigenous rural Muslims from much of Bengali culture. They also called upon the exogenous elite to reject as un-Islamic such practices as acquiescing in British rule, adopting foreign customs, and withdrawing from fellowship with Muslims of lower social status. The Faraizis organized Muslim peasants to resist oppressive *zamīndārs* (landlords), who were mostly Hindu, and the government which supported them, thus giving a communal and revolutionary character to what was initially an internal Muslim reform.

The Tariqah-i-Muhammadiya, organized by Inayet Ali (1794–1858) and Wilayat Ali (1791–1853) of Patna, along with other *jihād* movements, stirred the enthusiasm of Muslims in Bengal and recruited men to fight in the northwest of India to restore sovereignty to Muslims. The *jihād* movements and the Faraizis helped shatter acceptance of the centuries-old religio-social status quo; they generated passionate concern for Islamic standards that would transcend Bengali particularity, and they motivated the Bengali Muslim masses to confront non-Muslim interests. Yet it was through the Bengali language, however much islamicized, and through the self-commitment of indigenous Bengali Muslims, that these movements had vitality. Forces were stirred that would outlast the movements that stirred them.

Muslim politics: urban elite and village mullahs. The Muslim elite in Bengal, by contrast with the masses, were at first somewhat benumbed by the trauma of loss of power to the British. At first they held back from learning English. But after the brutally decisive suppression of the "Mutiny" of 1857 they belatedly took to the English language and to lobbying the government through such elite organizations as Syed Ameer Ali's (1849–1929) National Muhammadan Association and Nawab Abdul Latif's (1828–1893) Mahomedan Literary Society. Neither of these organizations addressed the needs of the indigenous rural Muslims and both eschewed the Bengali language. [*See also the biography of Ameer Ali.*]

Of crucial importance in linking the urban Muslim sociopolitical elite with the millions of Bengali Muslim peasants were some of the urban *'ulamā'* and the rural *mullahs*, village level Muslim functionaries, ethnically Bengali but ideologically pan-Islamic. Though poorly trained, the latter were the only "authorities" on Islam at hand, and thus were of much influence among village Muslims. Though less radical than the Faraizis and advocates of *jihād*, the *'ulamā'* and *mullahs* shared pan-Islamic aspirations and together strove to "purify" Bengali Muslim life of "un-Islamic" elements, to encourage the use of Urdu, where feasible, and to islamicize Bengali, where necessary. When the urban elite at last, during the 1905–1911 partition controversy, stood forth as representing the rural masses, they found that the *'ulama'* and *mullahs* were already far advanced in convincing indigenous Bengali Muslims that their true solidarity of interests lay with fellow Muslims even beyond Bengal, rather than with Bengali Hindus of common locality or class. [*See also* Modernism, *article on* Islamic Modernism.]

Bengal Renaissance: Muslim phase. The "Bengal Renaissance" experienced a belated flowering, though less rich in content and of narrower appeal, among Bengali Muslim writers and intellectuals. They, like the authors of the sixteenth- to eighteenth-century Bengali "middle tradition," had to face severe criticism. Some, like Abdur Rahim (1859–1931) argued at length that Bengali can and must be developed as the Islamic language for those who have it as a mother tongue. Much of the renascent Bengali Muslim literature was steeped in Islamic piety, history, and legends (e.g., Musharaf Husain's [1847–1912] *Bisad Sindhu*, based on the Karbala tragedy). But there were more secular contributions such as those by Abdul Wadud (b. 1894) and others (Muslim and non-Muslim) in the Buddhir Mukti (freedom of intellect) movement and, later, the passionately humane poems of Qazi Nazrul Islam (1899–1976).

Independence: Islamic and secular states. The Muslim League's call for a separate state for Muslims met with overwhelming support in Bengal. Independence in East Pakistan—notwithstanding the agonies of partition and communal violence—began with exuberance, in contrast to the dismay among the Muslim minority left in West Bengal. But the perennial tension between indigenous and exogenous interests soon broke out anew. The attempt to impose Urdu as the sole national language met with resistance and martyrdom. Economic and political dissatisfaction reinforced resentment over language policy. The indigenous-exogenous tension took on the forms of incipient Bangladeshi nationalism *versus* Pakistani national integrity. The exogenous interests once again assumed the mantle of Islam, and the indigenous interests championed Bengali language and culture. The climax came in 1971 with Bangladeshi independence as the Bengali Muslim peasants, rejecting pleas that Islam was in danger, emphatically opted for the Bengali nationalist leadership of Mujibur Rahman (1920–1975).

The short-lived Awami League regime officially endorsed "secularism" (i.e., exclusion of religious parties from politics and religious neutrality by government) and successive military regimes have declared Bangladesh an "Islamic" state. But the former did not mean a rejection of Islam by Bengali Muslims, nor does the latter entail imposition of Islamic law in civil and criminal spheres or suppression of non-Islamic religion. Under both types of regime it has been common knowledge that Islamic religion and Bengali language and culture are fundamental components of Bangladeshi life, whatever the legal or symbolic niceties. However, there has been little constructive dialogue or debate between the *'ulamā'* and the more secular intelligentsia in Bangladesh over how the perennial tension between the imperatives of Islamic faith and the imperatives of Bengali language and culture may be resolved. Significant efforts were made in this direction, however, by the essayist and creative writer Abul Fazl (1903–1983). So long as a satisfactory resolution is not attained there remains the threat of renewed polarization and conflict among Muslims in Bengal. If a satisfactory resolution can be generated it will be an extremely creative and constructive achievement, releasing and directing into positive channels much energy that hitherto has been inhibited or expended in disruptive ways. The insights and conceptual breakthroughs that such a resolution would entail could have paradigmatic value beyond Bangladesh itself.

Tribal Peoples. There survive in the hilly periphery of Bengal a few hundred thousand persons of diverse tribal communities whose religious life entails little or no explicit involvement in any of the traditions treated above. As the economies and populations of India and Bangladesh expand, the number of tribal persons able to hold aloof from the larger social, cultural, and religious traditions generally diminishes and the tribal ways themselves tend to accommodate to the Brahmanic tradition. There is, however, some recent tribal self-assertiveness in the region that may for a while arrest the tide of assimilation or at least change the character of the accommodation that is involved. Most notable in this respect are the Santals of West Bengal and adjacent Indian states, who in recent years have embarked upon a major effort of self-conscious reassertion of their traditional Santali religious and sociocultural heritage.

[*All of the major religious traditions and many of the deities discussed in this article are the subject of independent entries. For similar overviews of other Indian regions, see* Hindi Religious Traditions; Tamil Religions; *and* Marathi Religions. *For further discussion of tribal religions in India, see* Indian Religions, *article on* Rural Traditions.]

BIBLIOGRAPHY

The two-volume *History of Bengal* by R. C. Majumdar (vol. 1, 1943; reprint, Dacca, 1963) and Jadunath Sarkar (vol. 2, Dacca, 1948) remains valuable, as does Majumdar's *History of Medieval Bengal* (Calcutta, 1973). Invaluable for background and religious data is Shashibhusan Dasgupta's *Obscure Religious Cults* (Calcutta, 1962). Especially useful for (not exclusively) Hindu authors is Sukumar Sen's *History of Bengali Literature* (1960; 2d rev. ed., New Delhi, 1971). For detailed treatment of Bengali religious literature, see Sukumar Sen's *Bāṅglā sāhityer itihās*, 4 vols. (vol. 1 in 2 parts; Calcutta, varied dates and editions for each volume from 1940) or Asit Kumar Bandyopadhyay's *Bāṅglā Sāhityer Itivṛtta*, 5 vols. (vol. 3 in 2 parts; Calcutta, dates and editions from 1959 to 1985).

There are two very useful, though not widely distributed, sources for papers and short translations relevant to Bengali religion: annual Bengal Studies Conference volumes, which appear among "Asian Studies Center Occasional Papers, South Asia Series," (Michigan State University, East Lansing), and *Learning Resources in Bengali Studies*, edited by Edward C. Dimock, Jr. (New York, 1974).

For Vaiṣṇava and Śākta piety in Bengal, see David Kinsley's *The Sword and the Flute: Kālī and Kṛṣṇa* (Berkeley, 1975); Alan E. Morinis's *Pilgrimage in the Hindu Tradition: A Case Study of West Bengal* (Delhi, 1984); Sushil Kumar De's *Early History of Vaiṣṇava Faith and Movement in Bengal* (Calcutta, 1961); Edward C. Dimock, Jr.'s *The Place of the Hidden Moon* (Chicago, 1966); and W. L. Smith's *The One-Eyed Goddess: A Study of the Manasā Maṅgal* (Stockholm, 1980).

Translations of texts important to religious life in Bengal include *Love Song of the Dark Lord: Jayadeva's Gītagovinda*, translated and edited by Barbara Stoler Miller (New York, 1977); *Love Songs of Vidyapati*, translated by Deben Bhattacharya; *Rama Prasada's Devotional Songs: The Cult of Shakti*, translated by Jadunath Sinha (Calcutta, 1966); and *The Gospel of Sri Ramakrishna*, translated by Swami Nikhilananda (New York, 1977).

For contrasting informed perspectives on nineteenth-century developments, see James N. Farquhar's *Modern Religious Movements in India* (New York, 1915) and David Kopf's *The Brahmo*

Samaj and the Shaping of the Modern Indian Mind (Princeton, 1979). For introductions to two creative modern Bengali figures, see *A Tagore Reader,* edited by Amiya Chakravarty (Boston, 1966), and *The Essential Aurobindo,* edited by Robert McDermott (New York, 1973).

For Buddhism in Bengal, see Gayatri Sen Majumdar's *Buddhism in Ancient Bengal* (Calcutta, 1983), Per Kvaerne's *An Anthology of Buddhist Tantric Songs: A Study of the Caryāgīti* (Oslo, 1977), and Sukomal Chaudhuri's *Contemporary Buddhism in Bangladesh* (Calcutta, 1982). Buddhists are among the tribal peoples treated in an excellent collection of papers edited by Mahmud Shah Qureshi, *Tribal Cultures in Bangladesh* (Rajshahi, 1984).

Accounts of Islam in the Bengal region include Asim Roy's *The Islamic Syncretistic Tradition in Bengal* (Princeton, 1983), Rafiuddin Ahmed's *The Bengal Muslims, 1871–1906: A Quest for Identity* (Delhi, 1981), and Mahmud Shah Qureshi's *Étude sur l'évolution intellectuelle chez les musulmans du Bengale, 1857–1947* (Paris, 1971).

JOSEPH T. O'CONNELL

BERBER RELIGION. It is difficult to refer with any sort of precision to "Berber religion" per se, even as it is difficult to speak about a "Berber people." The term *berber*—originally a derogatory name (cf. Gr. *barbaroi,* Eng. *barbarians*) applied by outsiders—designates the rather heterogeneous, indigenous population of North Africa extending from the Siwa Oasis in the western Egyptian desert to Morocco, Mauretania, and even as far as the great bend of the Niger River. These people, who have been in the region since prehistoric times, exhibit varying physical features, customs, and social organizations. They are united mainly by language. But even the language itself is highly variegated and is subdivided into a number of mutually unintelligible dialects and many localized vernaculars. In addition to language, another trait that has characterized the Berbers as a whole throughout history has been a strong spirit of local political, social, and cultural independence in the face of domination by civilizations that have imposed themselves upon the Maghreb (the Arabic name for western North Africa): Carthaginians, Romans, Vandals, Byzantines, Arabs, and, for a relatively short time, modern Europeans.

Ancient Berber Religion. Echoes of prehistoric Berber religiosity may be found in rock paintings and carvings from the Neolithic period. Many of these depictions are difficult to interpret, but some seem to indicate clearly the veneration of certain animals and perhaps even fetishism. The numerous animal sculptures in hard rock must certainly be idols. These include rams, bulls, and antelopes. By Punic and Roman times, however, zoolatry seems to have been a thing of the past. Augustine of Hippo singles out the Egyptians as animal worshipers, but he does not mention his fellow North Africans in this regard (*Sermons* 198.1).

Throughout the first half of the twentieth century, leading European scholars (e.g., Gsell, Basset, Bel, and Gautier) generally held that the Egyptian cult of Amun-Re was widespread across the Maghreb in antiquity. They based this supposition upon the iconography of a few rock drawings discovered in Algeria and upon the popularity in Carthage of the Punic deity Baal-Hammon, who was identified with Zeus-Amun of the Siwa Oasis. This interpretation, however, has been called into serious question by Gabriel Camps, who has argued that the depictions are of sacrificial animals with ornamental bonnets and not sun disks on their heads. The ram god of Siwa does not seem to have played any special role among the ancient Berbers beyond Libya.

If any deity enjoyed extensive popularity in classical times, it was Saturn. The omnipresence of depictions of this god and his associations with the Punic Baal-Hammon are evidence that he was the real master of the region. One of his iconographic representations, showing him seated on a lion (his animal attribute) and holding a serpent (the symbol of death and fertility), has continued in folk religion down to the present. Rabbi Ephraim Enqāwa of Tlemcen, a Jewish saint, who is venerated throughout the Berber regions of southern Morocco, is invariably depicted in the same fashion.

From Punic times onward, it seems that foreign gods were borrowed and syncretized with local North African deities. However, it is difficult to isolate the native Berber divinities from the overlay of official Punic and Roman religion. Because of its essentially popular character, Berber religious practice receives only occasional mention in classical sources or early Christian writings.

Most of the *dii Mauri* (i.e., Mauretanian gods), for whom some fifty-two names survive, were local spirits. Many of these have recognizably Berber names, such as Varsissima (Berb., *war ism,* "the nameless one") and Macurgum (Berb., *imqqor, amqran,* "the great one"), both members of the pantheon of seven deities worshiped at Vaga (modern Béja in Tunisia).

Natural phenomena were the main focuses of Berber veneration, and nature worship has continued to be the core of Berber religiosity into the modern era despite the official overlay of Islam. Writing nearly two thousand years apart, both Herodotus (*Histories* 4.188) and Ibn Khaldūn (*'Ibar* 6.94) relate that the Berbers worshiped the sun and the moon, although in what way we do not know. Inscriptions from the Roman period mention a god, Ieru, whose name corresponds to the Berber *ayyur* or *ior* ("moon"). Latin dedications to the sun have been found in Tunisia and Algeria, and Spanish writers report that the Guanches (the Berber natives of the Canaries) worshiped the sun, one of whose names was Amen, which in certain Tuareg dialects still means "lord" or "god."

Rocks, mountains, caves, and springs were frequently places of sanctity for the ancient Berbers, as they have continued to be for their modern descendants. Few of the spirits inhabiting these holy spots had names; they were impersonal forces, like so many of the *jnūn* of later Berber folk belief.

On the basis of archaeological evidence, it seems that the Berbers of antiquity had a well-developed funerary cult. Decorated rock-cut tombs, funeral altars, and tumuli—all with votive offerings—have been found throughout the region. Among the Numidians, charismatic rulers were venerated as gods after their death, a practice that had its parallel in the widespread saint and marabout cults of later Christian and Islamic times.

Berber Religion in Christian Times. During the early centuries of the common era, when Christianity began to spread throughout the Roman empire, many Berbers in the urbanized parts of North Africa adopted the Christian faith. However, Berber particularism frequently imparted to their Christianity an individualistic stamp. The cult of local martyrs was very strong and widely diffused. Many of the practices and votive offerings reflected earlier funerary cults. Certain customs from this period, such as the partaking by women of ritual meals at the grave site, continued after islamization.

Adherence to heretical schisms was another manifestation of Berber individualism. In addition to Donatism, which was an indigenous North African movement, there were active communities of Montanists, Pelagians, Arians, and Manichaeans. As in the pre-Christian era, there was a great deal of syncretizing of native religious traditions with the adopted religion of the dominant culture. [*See also* Christianity, *article on* Christianity in North Africa.]

Berber Religion in Islamic Times. According to Arab historians, the Berber tribes of North Africa submitted to Muslim rule and accepted Islam at the end of the seventh century, after more than fifty years of fierce resistance. This mass conversion was due more to political interest than to religious conviction. Since Arab settlement outside the few urban centers was very sparse indeed, the islamization of much of the interior and outlying regions must have been nominal at best. According to orthodox Muslim tradition, the Berbers seceded from Islam no fewer than twelve times. As late as the eleventh century, the Andalusian geographer al-Bakrī mentions Berber tribes who worshiped a stone idol named Kurzah (or Gurzah), which may be related to a Berber deity of Roman and Christian times known as Gurzil. Even in the major towns, Berber particularism made itself felt quite early by the widespread adherence to Khārijī sectarianism, whose egalitarian doctrines had great appeal in the wake of Arab domination and oppression.

New Berber religions appeared during the Middle Ages; influenced by Islam, they adopted aspects of its external form but remained native in language, rite, and usage. The earliest of these was the religion of the Barghawāṭah, who inhabited the Atlantic coastal region of eastern Morocco. During the eighth to twelfth centuries, they adhered to the faith of their prophet, Ṣāliḥ, as propagated and led by his descendants. The Barghawāṭah worshiped one god, Yākush, and had a Berber scripture consisting of eighty chapters. Their religion was highly ascetic and had a strict moral code. In contrast to Islam's five daily prayers, it had ten (five daily and five nightly). There were numerous food taboos: fish, animal heads, eggs, and cocks were all forbidden (some of these have modern parallels among particular families in Morocco for whom eating a taboo food is considered "inauspicious"—Berb., *tteaṯh;* Arab., *ṭīrah*). The charisma of the prophet Ṣāliḥ's family was a central element in Barghawāṭah communal life. As in the case of the late marabouts, their spittle was considered to have great spiritual and curative powers.

Another new Berber religion influenced by Islam was that of Ḥā-Mīm, who appeared among the Ghumārah tribe in the Rif province of northern Morocco during the tenth century. He too produced a Berber scripture, and had dietary taboos similar to those of the Barghawāṭah. However, Ḥā-Mīm's religion had only two daily prayers, at sunrise and sunset. An important place was accorded to Ḥā-Mīm's paternal aunt and sister, both of whom were sorceresses. According to al-Bakrī and Ibn Khaldūn, the Ghumārah sought their aid in times of war, drought, and calamity.

The Muslim reform movements of the Almoravids in the eleventh and twelfth centuries and of the Almohads in the twelfth and thirteenth centuries, although properly speaking a part of Islamic religious history, nevertheless show certain important affinities with the independent religious movements of the Barghawāṭah and Ghumārah. Tribal or regional Berber identity is very strong in all of them. In each instance the role of the charismatic leader is paramount (in the case of the Almoravids and Almohads this is truest at the early stages of their respective movements).

Although Islam had no rivals as the official religion

among the Berbers from the thirteenth century onward, many native Berber rites continued to be practiced within the Maghrebi Islamic context. These are particularly apparent in the highly developed cults of saints both living and dead, in the veneration of such natural phenomena as springs, caves, rocks, and trees, and in numerous rituals linked to agriculture and the seasons. Many Berber groups have retained a solar calendar alongside the Muslim one, which, because it is not only lunar but not intercalated, is of little use to farmers and pastoralists.

Certain dates of the solar year have traditionally been marked by widespread religious observances. For example, New Year's Day—called variously ʿĪḍ Ennayr (Feast of January); Asuggʷas Ujdid (New Year); Byannu, Bu-ini, Bubennāni, or Bumennāni (all apparently from the Latin *bonum annum*); and ʿĪd n-Ḥagūza (Feast of the Old Woman); is commonly celebrated with special meals, with household rites to ensure a good year, and, in some regions of Morocco and Algeria, with carnivals and bonfires.

Another important celebration in the solar cycle is the summer solstice, called variously *l-ʿanṣra, l-ʿanṣart,* and *tʿaynsāt* (Arab., *anṣārah*). It is celebrated all over Morocco and Algeria with bonfires, fumigation with braziers, and water rites that include ritual bathing, sprinkling, and water fights. The Jews of North Africa have incorporated playful water fights into the celebration of Shavuʿot, which takes place only a few weeks before the *ʿanṣrah.* (It should be noted that the very word *ʿanṣrah* has been linked by some scholars to the Hebrew *ʿatseret,* or "holy convocation," a term used to describe Shavuʿot.)

Although Islam has its own rogatory ceremony for rain in time of drought—the *istisqā'* ritual—the Berbers throughout North Africa have in addition their own practices for seeking divine intervention at such times of crisis. One ceremony involves the use of dolls called *tislātin* (sg., *taslit,* "bride"). These are frequently made from ladles or stirring sticks and are carried about by women and children who chant and pray. Even the North African Arabs who perform this ritual call the little effigies by their Berber name, which seems to underscore its autochthonous character.

In conclusion, it should be emphasized that, because of the many conquests of North Africa over the last three millennia and its domination by outside civilizations, it is extremely difficult to identify in many instances what is indigenous Berber religious practice. Even in those parts of the Maghreb where there has been a reassertion of Berber ethnic identity (e.g., in the Algerian Kabylia region), the primary emphasis has been ethnolinguistic and not religious. Islam—whether practiced normatively or not—still commands the Berbers' fundamental religious allegiance.

[*See also* Islam, *article on* Islam in North Africa.]

BIBLIOGRAPHY

There is no single work devoted to the history of Berber religion as a discrete entity, although there is an enormous literature on Maghrebi Islam and on popular beliefs and rituals. Berber religion receives extensive treatment within this broader context.

Though somewhat outdated in part, Alfred Bel's *La religion musulmane en Berbérie,* vol. 1 (the only volume to appear; Paris, 1938), remains the best survey of Berber religious history from antiquity through the later Islamic Middle Ages. An important bibliography precedes each chapter. The chapter on religion in Gabriel Camps's *Berbères: Aux marges de l'histoire* (Paris, 1980), pp. 193–271, goes a long way toward updating and correcting Bel and is especially good for the pre-Islamic periods. Edward A. Westermarck's *Ritual and Belief in Morocco,* 2 vols. (1926; reprint, New Hyde Park, N.Y., 1968), remains a classic source of information on popular religion in Morocco. In addition to a wealth of descriptive detail, the book offers much comparative data. Another valuable survey of popular religious practice is Edmond Doutté's *Magie et religion dans l'Afrique du Nord* (Algiers, 1909).

There are many studies on saint veneration in North Africa. The best dealing with holy men in a Berber society is Ernest Gellner's *Saints of the Atlas* (London, 1969). For a comparison of Muslim and Jewish saints, see my study "Ṣaddīq and Marabout in Morocco," in *The Sepharadi and Oriental Jewish Heritage,* edited by Issachar Ben-Ami (Jerusalem, 1982), pp. 489–500.

NORMAN A. STILLMAN

BERDIAEV, NIKOLAI (1874–1948), Russian philosopher and spiritual thinker. Nikolai Alexandrovich Berdiaev is one of the distinguished Christian existential philosophers of the twentieth century. His major themes were freedom, creativity, and eschatology. Born in Kiev, he died seventy-four years later in Clamart, a suburb of Paris, without realizing his desire to return to his homeland. Yet Berdiaev was first and foremost a Russian and a mystic, despite his indebtedness to the West.

Berdiaev's life can be divided almost evenly into three quarter-centuries: the years in Kiev, the years in Vologda, Saint Petersburg, and Moscow, and the years abroad in exile (primarily France). Berdiaev was the scion of a privileged family. His father held high military honors; his mother, born Princess Kadashev, had French royal blood. The family's means and status were quite comfortable; yet Berdiaev was restless. From his early youth he was disposed to regard the world about him as illusory, and to consider himself a part of another, "real" world. The child's consciousness of his spiritual aptitude—an eschatological and mystical yearning—was later to find expression in his principal works. He spoke of his early outlook in his autobiography, *Dream and Reality: An Essay in Autobiography* (1949): "I cannot remember my first cry on encountering the world, but I know for certain that from the very beginning I was aware of having fallen into an alien realm. I felt this as much on the first day of my conscious life as I do at the present time. I have always been a pilgrim" (p. 1).

Berdiaev's pilgrim personality is revealed in the following significant works (all available in English translation): *The Meaning of the Creative Act* (1916), *Dostoevsky* (1923), *Freedom and Spirit* (1927), *The Destiny of Man* (1931), *Solitude and Society* (1934), *The Origin of Russian Communism* (1937), *Slavery and Freedom* (1939), and *The Realm of Spirit and the Realm of Caesar* (1951). Throughout these works, he philosophized as an existentialist on the concrete human condition from a Christian perspective that was at times mystical and nonlogical.

Berdiaev's insights, reinforced by personal example, made him both a lonely and a prophetic figure among his contemporaries. He identified himself as belonging to the Russian intelligentsia of the turn of the century, who were permanently in search of truth. He inherited the traditions of both the Slavophiles and the westernizers, of Chaadaev, Khomiakov, Herzen and Belinskii, and also of Bakunin and Chernyshevskii. He saw himself in the line of Dostoevskii and Tolstoi, as well as of Vladimir Solov'ev and Nikolai Fedorov. In summarizing the traditions that influenced him he declared, "I am a Russian, and I regard my universalism, my very hostility to nationalism, as Russian" (*Dream and Reality*, p. xiv).

Appointed professor of philosophy at Moscow University in 1920, Berdiaev was expelled from the Soviet Union two years later for his unwillingness to embrace orthodox Marxism. His subsequent break with Marxism was inevitable. He questioned Marxist subordination of individuality and freedom in its worship of the collective. Furthermore, he found the Marxist view of reality too limited, denying any world other than a temporal-materialistic existence. For Berdiaev, life in one world was flat; he believed that the human spirit seeks transcendence—a striving toward the unlimited and the infinite. To live only in the realm of Caesar is to deny the realm of the spirit. Such restriction was contrary to his ideas of freedom, creativity, and hope. Only a Christian outlook, as embodied in his Russian Orthodox tradition, could satisfactorily embrace both heaven and earth and point to his understanding of the kingdom of God.

As a pilgrim philosopher, Berdiaev viewed the human task as stewardship toward God's End (eschatology); it was a view that called for a complete reevaluation of one's present values and style of life. For him the Christian outlook was far more revolutionary than Marxism.

The Christian gospel for Berdiaev pointed to an ethic of redemption culminating in the coming of the kingdom of God, a kingdom based on love rather than rights and rules. However, he felt strongly that the truth of the spiritual life cannot conform completely to earthly life. For him, there never had been, nor could there be, a Christian state, Christian economics, Christian family, Christian learning, or Christian social life. In the kingdom of God and in the perfect divine life there is no state, no economics, no family, no teaching, nor any other aspect of social life governed by law.

Berdiaev's vision of the Kingdom often led to misunderstandings throughout his lifetime. As a consequence, he was viewed as a maverick philosopher, with no desire for disciples to institutionalize his thoughts. The basic idealism in his thinking led Berdiaev to a serious devaluation of this world, a view that was more spiritualistic (gnostic-Manichaean) than biblical. Nevertheless, his lasting influence as a Christian philosopher and prophetic spirit lies in his ability to stimulate dialogue among divergent cultures and patterns of thought.

BIBLIOGRAPHY

Calian, Carnegie Samuel. *Berdyaev's Philosophy of Hope: A Contribution to Marxist-Christian Dialogue.* Minneapolis, 1968. Contains a complete list of Berdiaev's works.

Clarke, Oliver Fielding. *Introduction to Berdyaev.* London, 1950.

Lowrie, Donald A. *Rebellious Prophet: A Life of Nicholai Berdyaev.* New York, 1960.

Spinka, Matthew. *Nicolas Berdyaev, Captive of Freedom.* Philadelphia, 1950.

CARNEGIE SAMUEL CALIAN

BERENGAR OF TOURS (c. 1000–1088), rector of the schools of Saint-Martin in Tours and sometime archdeacon of Angers. Berengar was at the center of a eucharistic controversy in his own day and subsequently lent his name to a cluster of positions that more or less closely resembled his. He stands at one pole of a tension that has recurrently characterized Western thinking on the sacrament.

In 1059, under duress, Berengar took an oath formulated by Humbert, cardinal bishop of Silva Candida, to the effect that "the bread and wine which are laid on the altar are after consecration not only a sign [*sacra-*

mentum], but the true body and blood of our Lord Jesus Christ, and they are physically [*sensualiter*] touched and broken by the hands of the priests and crushed by the teeth of the faithful, not only in a sign [*sacramento*] but in truth." The oath of 1059 passed into canonical collections as orthodox doctrine, but its crudity embarrassed most later theologians.

Returning from Rome to Tours, Berengar repudiated and attacked the oath of Humbert and defended his own position that Christ's body and blood were received by the faithful figuratively rather than naturally. This time Lanfranc of Bec led the opposition with his *On the Lord's Body and Blood,* to which Berengar replied in *On the Holy Supper, against Lanfranc.* Berengar took a "spiritual" view of salvation, in which the mental memory of the Lord's life, passion, and resurrection apparently did not entail an earthly reception of Christ's physical body, which was in fact incorruptibly located in heaven. "Eternal salvation is given us if we receive with a pure heart the body of Christ, that is, the *reality* of the sign [*rem sacramenti*], while we are receiving the body of Christ in sign [*in sacramento*], that is, in the holy bread of the altar, which belongs to the temporal order" (Beekenkamp, 1941, vol. 2, p. 158).

At a Roman council in 1079, Gregory VII secured the reconciliation of Berengar by a considerably modified oath:

> The bread and wine which are placed on the altar . . . are converted substantially [*substantialiter*] into the true, proper, life-giving flesh and blood of Jesus Christ our Lord and after the consecration are, not merely in sacramental sign and power, but in the property of nature and truth of substance, the true body of Christ, which was born of the Virgin, and which as an offering for the salvation of the world hung upon the Cross, and sits at the right hand of the Father, and the true blood of Christ, which flowed from his side. (J.-P. Migne, ed., *Patrologia Latina* 150.411)

Berengar's account of the Roman council shows him still trying to interpret the late insertion of *substantialiter* in his own sense.

Berengar never ceased to quote Augustine: "That which you see on the altar is bread and wine, but faith insists that the bread is the body of Christ, and the wine is his blood." Berengar's interpretation of that principle, though rejected by the Roman Catholic church, finds clear echoes in the "receptionism" of parts of the Reformed tradition.

BIBLIOGRAPHY

Berengar's chief work was respectively introduced and edited by W. H. Beekenkamp in two volumes: *De avondmaalsleer van Berengarius van Tours* and *De Sacra Coena adversus Lanfrancum* (The Hague, 1941). Necessary corrections have been made by R. B. C. Huygens in "À propos de Bérengar et son traité de l'eucharistie," *Revue bénédictine* 76, no. 1–2 (1966): 133–139.

The background and sequel to the Berengarian controversy are described in Gary Macy's *The Theologies of the Eucharist in the Early Scholastic Period* (Oxford, 1984); see especially pages 1–72. An account of the affair is also given in Margaret T. Gibson's *Lanfranc of Bec* (Oxford, 1978). Roman Catholic scholars tend to stress the inadequacy of Berengar in terms of the later teaching of the Fourth Lateran Council, Thomas Aquinas, and the Council of Trent, as does Jean de Montclos in *Lanfranc et Bérenger: La controverse eucharistique du onzième siècle* (Louvain, 1971). On the other hand, a sympathetic appreciation of Berengar is offered by the Protestant A. J. Macdonald in *Berengar and the Reform of Sacramental Doctrine* (London, 1930).

GEOFFREY WAINWRIGHT

BERGSON, HENRI (1859–1941), French philosopher. Born in Paris and educated at Lycée Condorcet and École Normale Supérieure, Bergson taught at three lycées and the École Normale Supérieure before he was invited to the Collège de France in 1900, where he lectured until 1914, formally retiring in 1921. His popular lectures influenced listeners from a wide variety of disciplines. He served as the first president of the Commission for Intellectual Cooperation of the League of Nations. In 1927, already awarded France's highest honors, Bergson received the Nobel Prize for literature.

Although born Jewish, Bergson was increasingly attracted to Roman Catholicism. While declaring his "moral adherence" to Catholicism and requesting that a priest pray at his funeral, Bergson refused to abandon his fellow Jews in the face of Nazi anti-Semitism.

Bergson began his career as a disciple of Herbert Spencer, whose evolutionism exalted science and the individual. In the 1880s, however, Bergson decided that science provided an incomplete worldview, for its concept of time could not account for the experience of duration. From this disagreement came his first book, *Essai sur les données immédiates de la conscience* (1889; translated as *Time and Free Will,* 1910). He next examined the relationship of mind to body in *Matière et mémoire* (1896; *Matter and Memory,* 1911). *L'évolution créatrice,* his most famous work, appeared in 1907 (*Creative Evolution,* 1911). In it he expounded a nonmechanistic portrait of biological evolution, propelled toward higher levels of organization by an inner vital impulse *(élan vital). Les deux sources de la morale et de la religion* appeared in 1932 (*The Two Sources of Morality and Religion,* 1935). These four books constitute his major works.

In *Two Sources* Bergson distinguished between static

and dynamic morality. The first, a morality of obligation, sanctions behavior consistent with an ordered community. The second, a morality of attraction, issues from mystical experience. The vital impulse, communicated from God through the mystic to others, generates a dynamic morality guided by a vision of humanity as a whole. Whatever his earlier views, by 1932 Bergson was affirming a transcendent God of love who is creatively involved in human existence.

Because many found Bergson's thought liberating, his influence in the early twentieth century was important and widespread. Although he regarded science very seriously, there was still room in Bergson's universe for intuition as well as reason, for morality and religion as well as mechanics, for organic communities as well as isolated individuals. A gifted writer, he bridged the worlds of literature, philosophy, and science.

Bergson was a seminal thinker, prompting others to move beyond his own conclusions. There were few disciples and no one to transform his essays into a polished system. The American philosopher William James and the Jesuit philosopher of science and religion Pierre Teilhard de Chardin borrowed much and yet departed from him at significant points.

Bergson's influence continues among existentialists who borrow his distinction between conventional and "higher" morality and continues within various process theologies that abandon classical theism to find both divine and human creativity at work in an evolving world.

BIBLIOGRAPHY

The best introduction to Bergson's philosophy is the volume edited and introduced by Harold A. Larrabee, *Selections from Bergson* (New York, 1949). In addition to excerpts from Bergson's major works, it contains all but ten pages of his brief *Introduction to Metaphysics* (*Introduction à la métaphysique*, Paris, 1903). Translated by T. E. Hulme in 1913, this work, perhaps the best place to begin reading Bergson himself, has also been published separately with an introduction by Thomas Goudge (New York, 1955). Bergson's complete writings are available in one volume, *Œuvres* (Paris, 1959), introduced by Henri Gouhier and edited by André Robinet. P. A. Y. Gunter's *Henri Bergson: A Bibliography* (Bowling Green, Ohio, 1974) lists 4,377 entries: 470 refer to letters, articles, and books by Bergson himself, while 3,907 entries, some annotated, refer to essays on Bergson by various other authors. Two recent studies of his philosophy are Vladimir Jankélévitch's *Henri Bergson* (Paris, 1959; in French) and Daniel Herman's *The Philosophy of Henri Bergson* (Washington, D.C., 1980). Jankélévitch's book contains a chapter entitled "Bergson et le judaïsme." Herman's relatively brief interpretive essay surveys major topics in Bergson's thought while focusing on the role of finality in his philosophy.

DARRELL JODOCK

BERNARD OF CLAIRVAUX (1090–1153), monastic reformer, abbot of the Cistercian monastery of Clairvaux, France. Bernard is known principally through four biographical accounts written in his own century (which contain more legend than fact), through other writings of his contemporaries, and through his own works. Born to a noble family at the château of Fontaine, near Dijon, Bernard was educated by the canons of Saint-Vorles, Châtillon. At about the age of twenty he decided to commit himself to monastic life at the recently founded abbey of Cîteaux, which he entered in 1113. In 1115 he was sent to found the abbey of Clairvaux. So many recruits came that in 1118 he founded another abbey, and he continued to found one or more each year for a total of about seventy monasteries.

By 1125 Bernard had written three treatises: *The Steps of Humility, In Praise of the Virgin Mother,* and *Apologia to Abbot William.* His reputation spread. Around 1127 he wrote *On the Behavior and Duties of Bishops* and *On Grace and Free Choice; On Loving God* was composed between 1126 and 1141, and *In Praise of the New Knighthood* between 1128 and 1136. In 1133 he traveled to Italy to settle the schism in the papacy between Innocent II and Anacletus II. In about 1135 Bernard began the long series of sermons *On the Song of Songs,* leaving the last sermon, the eighty-sixth, unfinished at his death. In 1139 he began to participate in the controversy then raging over the writings of Abelard, as is particularly illustrated by his Letter 190, "Against the Errors of Abelard." At this time he wrote the treatise *On Conversion* for the students in Paris. Before 1144 he dedicated to some Benedictine monks *On Precept and Dispensation.* He also took an active part in church politics, first in the combat against the heresies of the Cathari in the south of France, and then in Flanders, the Rhineland, and Bavaria, to rally men for the Second Crusade, initiated in 1146 by Eugenius III, the first Cistercian pope, for whom Bernard wrote *Five Books on Consideration.* After 1148 he penned *The Life and Death of Saint Malachy,* a biography of the bishop of Armagh who died at Clairvaux. About five hundred of Bernard's many letters are extant, as are numerous sermons on various subjects. Bernard died at Clairvaux on 20 August 1153 and was canonized by Alexander III in 1174.

Bernard was essentially a monk and a reformer, and his way of being both was determined by his character. His extremely artistic literary style tended to conceal his natural spontaneity. One senses deep conflict in this man: a tendency to be aggressive and domineering versus a will to be humble, to serve only "the interests of Jesus Christ." By constant examination of his motivations Bernard acquired a certain self-control. Occasionally charity gave way to passion; however, his humanity toward all won him more friends than enemies.

Bernard reformed monasticism by introducing greater poverty and austerity among the monks of the older orders, such as those at Cluny and Saint-Denis. He encouraged the new orders, the Regular Canons and the Carthusians. He strove for similar reform in the papacy, in the Curia Romana, and among bishops, clergy, and laity. He continued the institutional reform of Gregory VII by a spiritual reform in favor of interiority.

In the controversies over Abelard, historians have detected a conflict between personal rather than doctrinal points of view. Bernard and Abelard were in basic agreement on most points of doctrine and especially on the necessity of the appeal to reason, but Bernard, ill informed about the details of Abelard's teachings, won the support of the clergy of his day more by the form of his presentation of Christian dogma than by his criticism of Abelard.

In the political field, and especially in connection with the continual warfare of his day, Bernard defended nonviolence and made every effort to bring about reconciliation. About the pagan Wendes he said, "We must persuade to faith, not impose it." Elsewhere, he pointed out that the faithful of the Eastern and the Western churches were united by faith. Further, he defended the persecuted Jews of the Rhineland.

Bernard's theology had its roots in his own spiritual experience and in scripture, which served as the norm of interpretation for experience. He affirmed that the Holy Spirit, who inspired the sacred authors, gives understanding to their readers. His style is a tapestry of biblical quotations and allusions, often worded as they are found in the liturgy or in the writings of the fathers of the church. He borrowed very little from profane authors.

His doctrine is founded on the idea that the image of God in man has been dimmed by sin but not effaced. This image is restored when grace gives true self-knowledge or humility. In Jesus Christ, God became imitable. The Holy Spirit enables us to share in the salvation brought by Christ by keeping alive in us his "memory"—through meditation, in the celebration of the "mysteries" (the sacraments), in the liturgy, and by following his example. Within the church—Christ's bride—ascesis and prayer lead to union with God, to peace and joy.

BIBLIOGRAPHY

The best critical edition of Bernard's writings is *Sancti Bernardi Opera*, 8 vols., edited by Jean Leclercq, C. H. Talbot, and H. M. Rochais (Rome, 1957–1977). English translations are available in the "Cistercian Fathers Series" (Kalamazoo, Mich.). For historical orientation, see N.-D. d'Aiguebelle's *Bernard de Clairvaux* (Paris, 1953), volume 3 in the series "Commission d'histoire de l'Ordre de Cîteaux." For discussions of Bernard's thought, see *Saint Bernard théologien*, edited by Jean Leclercq (Rome, 1953), volume 9, nos. 3–4, of the series "Analecta Sacri Ordinis Cisterciensis," and Gillian Evans's *The Mind of Saint Bernard of Clairvaux* (Oxford, 1983). Analyses of Bernard's work and influence are my own *Bernard of Clairvaux and the Cistercian Spirit*, translated by Claire Lavoie (Kalamazoo, Mich., 1976), and *Actualité de Saint Bernard: Dossier "H,"* edited by Christine Goémé (forthcoming).

Jean Leclercq

BERSERKERS. The Old Norse term *berserkr* was used to identify certain fierce warriors with animal characteristics. According to Old Norse literature, particularly the late romantic sagas from the thirteenth and fourteenth centuries, berserkers howled like animals in battle and bit their shields. They felt no blows and had unusual or supernatural strength, which gave way to languor after battle. Since warriors called *úlfheðnar* ("wolf skins") display similar characteristics, many scholars translate the term *berserkr* as "bearshirt," a reference to the warriors' shape-changing in the manner of werewolves and man-bears, or perhaps to animal cloaks they may have worn. [*See* Shape Shifting.] Others, however, believe the word means "bareshirted" and refers to the berserkers' lack of armor. Traditional explanations of the *berserksgangr* ("going berserk") include self-induced or group ecstasy, psychosis, or lycanthropy. [*See* Frenzy.]

In Norse mythology berserkers are associated primarily with the god Óðinn. In his *Ynglingasaga*—a euhemerized account of the origin of the royal line of the Ynglingar that constitutes the first saga in his famous *Heimskringla* (c. 1230)—the Icelandic mythographer Snorri Sturluson gives an explicit description of the *berserksgangr* and attributes it specifically to Óðinn's warriors (chap. 6). Óðinn also is master of the *einherjar*, dead warriors who inhabit Valhǫll, spending their days in battle, their evenings in feasting and drinking. [*See* Valhǫll.]

The religious complex suggested by these and other data is that of an ecstatic warrior cult of Óðinn, whose name, coming from the Proto-Germanic term **wōþanaz*, appears to mean "leader of the possessed." This cult probably involved strict rules of initiation, similar perhaps to those attributed by Tacitus to the Chatti (*Germania* 30). Óðinn's association with the *einherjar* may also imply worship of the dead within this cult. Its central moment, however, was presumably some form of religious esctasy.

Iconographic evidence for this cult includes cast-bronze dies from Torslunda, Sweden, which show dancing warriors with theriomorphic features.

BIBLIOGRAPHY

Fredrik Grøn's *Berserksgangens vesen og årsaksforhold* (Trondheim, 1929) treats the phenomenology of the *berserksgangr.* Hans Kuhn's "Kämpen und Berserkir," originally published in 1968 and reprinted in his *Kleine Schriften,* vol. 2 (Berlin, 1971), pp. 521–531, emphasizes possible Roman influence, especially gladiator traditions. In *Kultische Geheimbünde der Germanen,* vol. 1 (Frankfurt, 1934), Otto Höfler has offered the fullest treatment of the relationship between berserkers and Óðinn cult, *Männerbünde,* and worship of the dead, arguing the existence of a mystery cult that left traces in later folklore phenomena such as the Wild Hunt.

JOHN LINDOW

BERTHOLET, ALFRED (1868–1951), Swiss Protestant theologian, scholar in Old Testament and comparative religion. Bertholet was born in Basel, where he got his primary and secondary school education and enrolled at the university in order to study Protestant theology. He continued his studies at the universities of Strassburg and Berlin. His principal lecturers were Carl von Orelli, Bernhard Duhm, and Adolf von Harnack. After two years as minister to the German-Dutch parish in Leghorn he returned to Basel; there he obtained his doctorate in 1895 and became an assistant professor in 1896; from 1905 he occupied the chair of Old Testament, and extended his studies to the history of religions. After spending some years in Tübingen (1913) and Göttingen (1914–1928) he became professor at the University of Berlin, where he went into retirement in 1936, although he lectured until 1939. From 1945 until his death he was visiting professor of the history of religions at his home university in Basel. He died in the hospital of Münsterlingen, Switzerland.

Bertholet was appointed doctor *honoris causa* of the universities of Strassburg and Lausanne and of the Faculté Libre de Théologie Protestante de Paris. He was a fellow of the academy of Göttingen and an honorary member of the American Society of Biblical Literature and Exegesis. He organized and was secretary general of the international congress for the history of religions held in Basel in 1904. In 1938 he was the first historian of religions to be elected a fellow of the Prussian Learned Society (Preussische Akademie der Wissenschaften). With Gerardus van der Leeuw and C. Jouco Bleeker, he was one of the initiators of the Amsterdam congress for the history of religions in 1950.

The works of Bertholet, all written in German and not yet translated into other languages, include both Old Testament studies and investigations in the field of comparative religion. Among his contributions to the study of the Old Testament are commentaries and a history of the civilization of biblical Israel. His Old Testament thesis *Die Stellung der Israeliten und Juden zu den Fremden* (1896) was concerned with the relations of the Israelites and Jews to foreign peoples. His numerous writings on the subject of "foreign" religions, chiefly published in the series "Sammlung gemeinverstandlicher Vorträge und Schriften aus dem Gebiet der Theologie und Religionsgeschichte" (Tübingen), are concerned with themes of religious phenomenology and especially with the relationship of dynamism to personalism. These works prove Bertholet to be one of the founders of the phenomenology of religion. Bertholet was also active in stimulating the work of other scholars, and in editing many well-known works in the history of religions.

BIBLIOGRAPHY

Further details of Bertholet's life and work can be found in the *Festschrift Alfred Bertholet zum 80. Geburtstag gewidmet* (Tübingen, 1950), edited by Walter Baumgartner and others. This volume, which includes a useful bibliography compiled by Verena Tamann-Bertholet, should be supplemented by Leonhard Rost's "Alfred Bertholet, in Memorium," *Theologische Literaturzeitung* 77 (1952): 114–118.

GÜNTER LANCZKOWSKI

BERURYAH (second century CE), one of the few famous women in rabbinic Judaism of late antiquity. Rabbinic tradition states that she was the daughter of Ḥananyah ben Teradyon, and the wife of Me'ir.

In rabbinic sources Beruryah appears several times among the scholars who reestablished the Sanhedrin in the Galilean town of Usha after the Bar Kokhba Revolt. She is mentioned twice in the Tosefta (in Tosefta, *Kelim,* Bava' Metsi'a' 1.6 by name and in Tosefta, *Kelim,* Bava' Qamma' 4.17 as the daughter of Ḥananyah ben Teradyon) and seven times in the Babylonian Talmud.

Beruryah's contemporary importance lies in her prominence as one of the only female scholars accepted in the male-dominated rabbinic culture. David Goodblatt (1977) believes that Beruryah exemplifies the possibility, though quite uncommon, that a woman might receive formal education within rabbinic society. Goodblatt argues, however, that the traditions that ascribe rabbinic learning to Beruryah appear to be late accounts that do not reflect the situation in Roman Palestine, where Beruryah is said to have lived, but rather the situation in Sasanid Baylonia, where the traditions were formulated during the process of Talmudic compilation.

Whether historical or not, rabbinic tradition portrays Beruryah as a sensitive yet assertive figure. The Talmud recounts anecdotes illustrating her piety, compassion, and wit. In one source she admonishes her husband Me'ir not to be angry with his enemies and not to pray for their deaths. Instead, she suggests, he should pray that their sins cease and that they repent (B.T., *Ber.* 10a). When two of her sons died one Sabbath she delayed telling her husband until Saturday night when he had finished observing the Sabbath in peace (*Midrash Mishlei* on *Prv.* 31:10). The Talmud also recounts Beruryah's sharp tongue. When Yose the Galilean asked her for directions on the road she derided him for speaking too much with a woman (B.T., *'Eruv.* 53b).

The drama of her life climaxes in the so-called Beruryah Incident. A story preserved by the eleventh-century exegete Rashi (in his commentary to B.T., *'A.Z.* 18b) says that Beruryah mocked a misogynistic rabbinic tradition that labeled women as flighty. To test her own constancy, Me'ir sent one of his students to tempt her to commit adultery. According to the legend, she committed suicide after submitting to the student's advances.

BIBLIOGRAPHY

David M. Goodblatt, in "The Beruriah Traditions," in *Persons and Institutions in Early Rabbinic Judaism,* edited by William S. Green (Missoula, Mont., 1977), pp. 207–229, translates and analyzes all the materials relating to Beruryah in rabbinic literature.

TZVEE ZAHAVY

BESANT, ANNIE (1847–1933), theosophist and social reformer. Annie Besant, née Wood, was born in England into a devout Christian family. She married the Reverend Frank Besant, but growing doubts about the basic tenets of the Christian faith led her, in 1873, to leave her husband and to break with the church. She then joined the National Secular Movement, and in that organization she discovered her remarkable gift for oratory. In 1885 she joined the influential, socialist Fabian Society. Feminist, socialist, and political agitator, Besant is especially noted for her role during this period as a strike leader and union organizer. Throughout her life she remained devoted to social and educational reform.

In 1889, Besant was asked to review H. P. Blavatsky's *The Secret Doctrine,* and she subsequently met the author. Besant then joined the Theosophical Society, of which Blavatsky had been a founder, and resigned from the Fabian Society, to the great shock of her colleagues. In 1891 Blavatsky died in Besant's home in London while Besant was on a lecture tour of the United States. Besant succeeded her as head of the "inner school" of the society.

In 1893, Besant first traveled to India (she always described her arrival there as "coming home"), where she enjoyed great success. At this time, she met C. W. Leadbeater, an Anglican clergyman who purportedly had great psychic powers, and she began to develop her own latent psychic abilities.

Besant was elected president of the Theosophical Society in 1907. Shortly thereafter, she and Leadbeater met a small, frail boy in Adyar (near Madras). Believing this boy, Jiddu Krishnamurti, to have the potential to be a great spiritual teacher, she adopted him and had him educated in England. She lectured widely, proclaiming Krishnamurti a "world teacher."

Besant spent years promoting home rule for India, and in 1917 she was elected the first woman president of the Indian National Congress. Later, she lost her political influence because she differed with Mohandas Gandhi's ideas, believing that India should be free but remain part of the British Commonwealth. Her long interest in Indian education led her to found Central Hindu College (now Banaras University) and several other schools in India, and her contributions to India's education and political independence are still appreciated by the Indian people. Besant died in India in 1933.

Annie Besant was the most effective speaker in the Theosophical Society's history, and during the twenty-six years of her presidency the society grew and flourished. She was the author of numerous works on theosophy, writings that are characterized by the combination of Western occultism with Indian (chiefly Hindu) philosophies. Thus, her theory of human life in three worlds—the physical world, the world of desire, and the mental world—correlates elements of the Hindu conception of the *kośas,* or "sheaths," with theories of mediumship and astral projection. The themes of *karman* and reincarnation and of clairvoyance and spiritual evolution are central to her thought.

In her autobiography, Besant claims an experiential knowledge of the soul as the true self and of the soul's power to seek spiritual knowledge beyond the body. Rejecting the materialist beliefs that she had earlier held, she came to regard man as "Spiritual Intelligence, a fragment of Divinity clothed in matter" (*Man's Life in Three Worlds,* 1923, p. 3).

BIBLIOGRAPHY

Besant, Annie. *Annie Besant: An Autobiography* (1893). 2d ed. London, 1980.

Besant, Annie. *The Ancient Wisdom: An Outline of Theosophical Teachings* (1911). 2d ed. Adyar, India, 1939.
Nethercot, Arthur Hobart. *The First Five Lives of Annie Besant.* 4 vols. Chicago, 1960.
The Theosophist 69 (1947). A special issue commemorating the centenary of Besant's birth.

DORA KUNZ

BESHT, acronym of Ba'al Shem Ṭov ("master of the good name"), identifying Yisra'el ben Eli'ezer (1700–1760), founder of the Hasidic movement in eastern Europe. There are few historically authentic sources that describe the life of the Besht; most information must be gleaned from nineteenth-century hagiography, especially the collection of more than three hundred stories about him, known as *Shivḥei ha-Besht* (In Praise of the Besht; first printed in 1815), and the works of later Hasidic writers.

Born in the small town of Okopy in the southern Ukraine, Yisra'el ben Eli'ezer is said to have begun preaching around 1738, after a long period of seclusion in the Carpathian Mountains with his wife. According to other accounts, he served throughout his life as a popular healer, writer of amulets, and exorcist of demons from houses and bodies, which were the traditional roles of a *ba'al shem* ("master of the name") or *ba'al shem ṭov* ("master of the good name")—in other words, the master of the name that empowered him to perform what he wished.

In his wandering around many Jewish communities, the Besht came into contact with various circles of pietists. In some cases he was criticized by the rabbis, but his powers as a preacher and magician attracted disciples, including masters of Jewish law and Qabbalah such as Ya'aqov Yosef of Polonnoye (d. 1782) and Dov Ber of Mezhirich (d. 1772). As Gershom Scholem has suggested, the Besht should be regarded as the founder of the great eastern European Hasidic movement, even though our knowledge of his organizational work is scanty and even though the first Hasidic center was established only after his death by Dov Ber, who became the leader of the movement.

Although he was not a scholar in Jewish law, the Besht was well versed in Qabbalah and in popular Jewish ethical tradition, on which he relied when delivering his sermons and formulating his theories. He saw the supreme goal of religious life as *devequt* ("cleaving"), spiritual communion with God; this state can be achieved not only during prayers but also in the course of everyday activities. In his view, there is no barrier between the holy and the profane, and worship of God can be the inner content of any deed, even the most mundane one. Indeed, the Besht did not insist on following the complicated qabbalistic system of *kavvanot* ("intentions") in prayers and in the performance of the Jewish religious commandments but substituted instead the mystical devotion of *devequt* as the primary means of uplifting the soul to the divine world. His teachings also included the theory that evil can be transformed into goodness by a mystical process of returning it to its original source in the divine world and redirecting it into good spiritual power; this idea was further developed by his followers.

The Besht believed that he was in constant contact with the divine powers and saw his mission as that of correcting and leading his generation. In a letter preserved by Ya'aqov Yosef (whose voluminous works contain the most important material we have concerning the Besht's teachings), the Besht indicates that he practiced *'aliyyat neshamah,* or the uplifting of the soul. In this way, he explained, he communicated with celestial powers who revealed their secrets to him. According to the document, these included the Messiah, who told him that redemption would come when his teachings were spread all over the world (which the Besht interpreted as "in a long, long time").

The Besht was convinced that his prayer carried special weight in the celestial realm and that it could open heavenly gates for the prayers of the people as a whole. His insistence that there are righteous people in every generation who, like himself, carry special mystical responsibilities for their communities laid the foundations for the later Hasidic theory of the function of the *tsaddiq,* or leader, a theory that created a new type of charismatic leadership in the Jewish communities of eastern Europe.

[*See also* Hasidism, *overview article.*]

BIBLIOGRAPHY

Dan Ben-Amos and Jerome R. Mintz have translated and edited *Shivḥei ha-Besht* as *In Praise of the Ba'al Shem Tov: The Earliest Collection of Legends about the Founder of Hasidism* (Bloomington, Ind., 1970). Useful background information can also be found in Salo W. Baron's discussion of Hasidism in his *Social and Religious History of the Jews,* vol. 2 (New York, 1937), pp. 153–163. Gershom Scholem has discussed the Besht in *Major Trends in Jewish Mysticism,* 3d rev. ed. (New York, 1961), pp. 330–334, 348–349. Three papers concerning the Besht and Hasidism are included in his *The Messianic Idea in Judaism* (New York, 1972), pp. 176–250. Additional bibliographic references accompany the article "Israel ben Eliezer Ba'al Shem Tov" in *Encyclopaedia Judaica* (Jerusalem, 1971).

JOSEPH DAN

BETH, KARL (1872–1959), German historian of religions and Christian thinker. Karl Beth studied at the University of Berlin in the 1890s (under Adolf von Harnack, Otto Pfleiderer, and Wilhelm Dilthey), where he obtained his Ph.D. degree in 1898 with a dissertation entitled "Die Grundanschuungen Schleiermachers in seinem ersten Entwurf der philosophischen Sittenlehre"; he became an instructor of systematic theology at Berlin in 1901. Five years later he moved to Vienna and served at the university there, first as a lecturer and from 1908 onward as a full professor. The political developments that in 1938 brought an end to his academic career in Europe led him to emigrate to the United States in the following year. He served on the faculty of Meadville-Lombard Theological School in Chicago from 1941 to 1944, teaching the history of religions, a field that was a primary concern for him at several points in his life.

As early as 1901 in his inaugural address at Berlin, he argued that the study of the general history of religions—not merely the study of the religious environment of early Christianity—was necessary for understanding and defining the essence of Christianity. Shortly after he gave this address, he received a travel stipend that enabled him to visit areas around the Mediterranean under Greek and Turkish control, and the acquaintances he made with Christians living in these regions led to his publication of an account of Eastern Orthodox Christianity that opened the way for a new understanding of it among European Protestants (*Die orientalische Christenheit der Mittelmeerländer,* 1902; see also his article "Orthodox-anatolische Kirche" and several related entries in the second edition of *Religion in Geschichte und Gegenwart,* 1929-1932).

In the decade following 1902 much of Beth's work focused on the issue of Christianity and modern thought (e.g., *Das Wesen des Christentums und die moderne historische Denkweise,* 1904, and *Die Moderne und die Prinzipien der Theologie,* 1907). During this period he also dealt with specific issues such as the significance of the notion of evolution for Christian theology (comparing it, in *Der Entwicklungsgedanke und des Christentum,* 1909, with the significance of the idea of *logos* fifteen hundred years earlier) and with historical-critical questions regarding Jesus (in *Hat Jesus gelebt?,* 1910).

In the following years some of his major studies were again in the history of religions, particularly his book on religion and magic, *Religion und Magie bei den Naturvölkern: Ein religionsgeschichtlicher Beitrag zur Frage nach den Anfängen der Religion* (1914), in which he stresses *Ehrfurcht* ("reverence" or "awe") as a constituent element of religion, draws a sharp contrast between religion and magic, and assumes the existence of a historical stage preceding both. (He rejected James G. Frazer's hypothesis that magic was the forerunner of religion.) Also significant were his *Einführung in die vergleichende Religionsgeschichte* (1920) and his study on faith and mysticism (particularly within Christianity), *Frömmigkeit der Mystik und des Glaubens* (1927).

A third major field of involvement for Beth was the psychology of religion. He helped to establish the Research Institute for Psychology of Religion in Vienna in 1922, was editor of the *Zeitschrift für Religionspsychologie* from 1927 to 1938 (during which period he published more than twenty articles in that journal), and was instrumental in the organization of the First International Psychology of Religion Congress, held in Vienna in 1931 on the theme of the psychology of unbelief.

BIBLIOGRAPHY

Sources of biographical data include Beth's autobiographical essay in *Die Religionswissenschaft der Gegenwart in Selbstdarstellungen,* vol. 2, *Karl Beth,* edited by Eric Strange (Leipzig, 1926), and Erwin Schneider's article "Das Lebenwerk Karl Beths," in *Theologische Literaturzeitung* 78 (1958): 695–698, which is followed by an extensive bibliography of Beth's publications.

WILLEM A. BIJLEFELD

BEVERAGES. In addition to their nutritional role, all beverages are invested with a certain amount of symbolic and affectional content, and it seems likely that there is no beverage that has not taken on a profound religious significance somewhere or other in the world. Intoxicants and hallucinogens seem particularly well suited to this role, given the ways in which they open up startling new areas of experience to those who imbibe them, including ecstasy, enthusiasm, and vision. [*See also* Psychedelic Drugs.] Yet it is not just those drinks that are most extraordinary in their effects that come to be celebrated in myth, ritual, and sacred speculation, for often those drinks that are most ordinary—that is, most commonly used as a part of the normal diet and most unremarkable in their physiological and neurological effect—come to be invested with religious significance. Thus, for instance, among the Maasai and other cattle-herding peoples of East Africa, cow's milk is a staple part of the diet, but it is nevertheless regarded with the greatest of respect, for unlike virtually all other food items, milk can be obtained without causing the death of any living thing, animal or vegetable. For this reason, milk is set in marked contrast to beef, a food which has the same source as milk—cattle—but the procurement of which entails the violent death of the animal from which it is taken. The equation is explicitly drawn: milk is to meat as life is to death, and the two are not to be mixed within the same meal. The same prohibition is encountered in rabbinic law (itself an extension of the biblical prohibition, stated in *Exodus,* against cooking a kid in its mother's milk), perhaps arrived at by a similar line of reasoning.

To be sure, milk is understood as a perfect or paradisiacal fluid in many passages of the Hebrew scriptures, as for instance in those that refer to Israel as "the land of milk and honey" (*Ex.* 3:8 et al.), honey being—like milk—a nourishing and delicious food that may be obtained without doing violence to any living thing. Greek and Roman ritual also employed this symbolism, albeit in different fashion, for a libation offering of a fluid composed of milk and honey, called *melikraton,* had the power to reanimate the dead (*Odyssey* 10.519), while a potion known as *hermesias* was drunk by women before conception and while nursing in order to obtain children who were "excellent in soul and beautiful of body," that beverage being a symbolically charged mixture of milk, honey, pine nuts, myrrh, saffron, and palm wine (Pliny, *Natural History* 24.166).

In the *hermesias* concoction, we have come a long way from the simplicity and familiarity of milk, although the associations of milk—maternal nurturance and the gift of life—provide the symbolic starting point for a grander elaboration. Another simple beverage that came to be invested with a profound religious significance is tea, the preparation, distribution, and consumption of which are regarded as constituting nothing less than a master art and a way of knowledge and liberation in Japan, as is expressed in the common term *chadō* ("the way of tea"); the second element, *dō,* is the Japanese equivalent of the Chinese word *tao,* a term reserved for a select set of religio-aesthetic pursuits: painting, poetry, calligraphy, archery, flower arranging, and above all, tea. Originally used as a medicine in China, tea later came to be a more common beverage, the highly ritualistic preparation of which—with twenty-four carefully specified implements—was already systematized by Lu Yü (d. 804) in his *Ch'a ching* (Classic of Tea). Although there are indications that some tea may have come to Japan as early as the ninth century, its serious introduction came with Eisai (1141–1215), the founder of the Rinzai sect of Zen Buddhism in Japan, who also brought tea seeds and a knowledge of tea ceremonial with him after a period of study in China.

Although it is obvious from the title of Eisai's work on the art of tea—*Kissayōjōki* (The Account of Drinking Tea and Prolonging Life)—that he was interested in the medico-physiological effects of the drink, this never became a major part of the Japanese celebration of tea. Rather, as developed and explicated by such renowned tea masters as Daitō (1236–1308), Nōami (1397–1471), Ikkyū (1394–1481), Shukū (1422–1502), and above all Rikyū (1521–1591), it is the utter simplicity, serenity, and austere beauty of the tea ceremony *(cha no yu)* that were the foremost concerns. For within the small tearooms, meticulously cleansed of all impurities and equipped with perfectly chosen utensils and decorations, tea masters sought to create nothing less than a perfect microcosm, a thoroughly harmonious environment in which one might take refuge from the tribulations of the external world and encounter the Buddha nature that lies beyond the conflicts and fluctuations of life in the material world. Along these lines, the tea master Takuan observed:

> The principle of *cha-no-yu* is the spirit of harmonious blending of Heaven and Earth and provides the means for establishing universal peace. . . . The way of *cha-no-yu,* therefore, is to appreciate the spirit of a naturally harmonious blending of Heaven and Earth, to see the pervading presence of the five elements by one's fireside, where the mountains, rivers, rocks, and trees are found as they are in nature, to draw the refreshing water from the well of Nature, to taste with one's own mouth the flavor supplied by nature. How grand this enjoyment of the harmonious blending of Heaven and Earth! (Suzuki, 1959, p. 278)

Yet for all that the tea ceremony possesses a cosmic dimension and can be nothing less than a vehicle for full enlightenment, these lofty significances notwithstanding, it remains always also a celebration of the simple pleasures of the drink of tea. A celebrated poem of Rikyū, the greatest of all the recorded tea masters, stresses this point:

> The essence of the tea ceremony
> is simply to boil water,
> To make tea,
> And to drink it—nothing more!
> Be sure you know this.
> (Ludwig, 1974, p. 41)

In contrast, intoxicants are rarely regarded with such utter serenity and simplicity, given the drama, power, and even violence of their transformative effects. "Ale," observes one Icelandic text, "is another man" (*Jómsvikingasaga* 27). One may consider, for instance, the hallucinogenic decoction of vines called *yagé,* used throughout the upper Amazon; its use has been described at length by Gerardo Reichel-Dolmatoff (1975 and 1978). *Yagé* is ritually consumed; it produces nausea, vomiting, and diarrhea but also—aided by such other stimuli as torchlight and musical rhythms—induces brilliant visions that take regular and predictable forms to which interpretations based on mythic references are attached.

According to Reichel-Dolmatoff, the visions produced by *yagé* unfold in different stages, an initial phase of phosphenic patterns (i.e., colors and geometric shapes only) being followed by one or more coherent images of a hallucinatory nature. Indigenous interpretation of the first phase attaches specific iconographic meanings to given shapes—a diamond with a point in it represents an embryo in the womb, for example—and also makes use of color symbolism. Yellow and white are thus considered cold colors, and—more importantly—the embodiment of seminal and solar fertilizing energy. Red is considered hot, being associated primarily with the womb, fire, and menstrual blood. Finally, blue is an asexual color, being also morally ambiguous. A "good" vision in this first phase depends upon a proper balance of red and yellow, which is to say, of male and female, hot and cold principles.

Interpretation of the visions within the hallucinatory phase is somewhat more complex, and Reichel-Dolmatoff (1975) emphasizes the social nature of these visions and their imputed meanings: "The individual hallucinations do not constitute a private world, an intimate or almost secret experience; they are freely discussed, and anyone will ask questions and solicit answers." There is, then, a process of feedback, or reinterpretation and elaboration. This feedback process continually refers visions to the creation myths in order to make sense of them, myths which tell of the primordial incest of the Sun and his daughter. Through one's visions, one is felt to return to the time and place of creation, becoming a witness to and a participant in these events. Moreover, the ritual consumption of *yagé* is itself understood as a sexual experience of an incestuous and creative nature, for the *yagé* vessel is homologized to the mother's body, its opening to her vagina, and its interior to her womb. To drink *yagé* is thus to enter into sexual relations with one's mother and also to reenter her womb, becoming an embryo once more. Ultimately, as one emerges from the trance induced by the drug, one is felt to be reborn, re-created, renewed.

The myth of the creation of *yagé* is also of interest, for it exhibits a different kind of feedback process whereby details of the drug's physiological effects are appropriated to construct a mythic narrative. The story tells of the entrance of a primordial Yagé Woman into the first maloca, where the first ancestors of all the peoples of the Amazon were gathered. Yagé Woman gave birth to a child outside the maloca, and carried the infant inside. There, this child—who is *yagé* personified—shone radiant, white and yellow and red, those colors which are first seen during the phosphenic phase of *yagé* visions. Upon seeing this child, those gathered all experienced the various sensations brought on by *yagé*: nausea, bewilderment, and a sense of "drowning." According to Reichel-Dolmatoff's informants, the entrance of Yagé Woman and her child into the maloca is the high point of the myth, but there follows a curious episode. When Yagé Woman asked who was the father of the babe, all the assembled men claimed this honor, and fought over the rights to the child. Finally, all turned upon him and dismembered him, each taking a different part of his body. These bodily members then became the different vines used by the different peoples of the Amazon to prepare their own particular forms of *yagé*.

This same motif—the creation of an intoxicant from the body of a primordial divine being—is found in numerous other religious traditions, not least of which is the foundation of the Christian Eucharist. For at the end of the Last Supper, according to the synoptic Gospels, Jesus gave wine to his disciples, saying: "Drink of it, all of you; for this is my blood of the covenant, which is poured out for many for the forgiveness of sins. I tell you I shall not drink again of this fruit of the vine until that day when I drink it new with you in my Father's kingdom" (*Mt.* 26:27–29 and parallels). Throughout the history of the church, there has been disagreement as to how literally this passage ought to be interpreted, a disagreement which is at the heart of the theological debate over transubstantiation in the Mass.

Another account in which intoxicants derive from a quasi-sacrificial victim is the Iranian story of the origin of wine, which tells how the vine came into being from the blood of the primordial bovine when that animal was killed. Crushing grapes thus constitutes a reenactment of the bull's death, and the wine thereby produced is seen to be nothing less than the blood of the bull, which bestows the bull's strength, energy, and vital force upon one who drinks it (*Zādspram* 3.46), just as one who drinks sacramental wine takes Christ's essential nature and very blood within his or her own body, given a full-blown theory of transubstantiation.

Yet again one encounters a myth of intoxicants created from the blood of a murdered primordial being in the Norse account of the origin of mead, a story related by the god of poetry, Bragi, in response to the question "Whence came the art called poetry?" (*Skáldskaparmál* 2). The story begins at that moment when the two major groups of gods, the Æsir and Vanir, concluded their treaty of peace by spitting into a single vat and letting their saliva mingle. From the mixture, there grew a man by the name of Kvasir—who himself incarnates an intoxicant known in Russia as *kvas*, if his name is any indication—an individual gifted with exceptional wisdom, indeed, omniscience itself. Kvasir was subsequently murdered by two dwarfs, who mixed his blood with honey and made from it the first mead, a mead so powerful that it is said that "whoever drinks from it becomes a poet or a scholar."

Other stories pursue the fate of this "mead of poetry," telling how it fell first into the hands of the dwarves, then giants, from whom it was finally rescued by the wisest of gods, Odin himself, who assumed the form first of a serpent and then of an eagle in order to gain the precious mead. This myth of the mead's theft has important correspondences to myths elsewhere in the Indo-European world (see, for instance, the Indic text *Ṛgveda* 4.26) but it is that portion of the story that recounts the origin of the mead which provides a religious rationale and legitimation for its miraculous effect: that is, mead can bestow knowledge and inspiration because in origin and essence it is nothing less than the blood of the wisest of men and also the spittle of the gods.

The highly formalized, even solemn, consumption of mead, beer, ale, and/or wine has been a regular feature of banquets in Europe since antiquity, and may be seen to have a ritual origin and significance. As we have seen, such drinks as these are often felt to partake of divinity, and also demonstrably enable those who imbibe to transcend the limits of their ordinary human condition, bestowing upon them extraordinary powers of speech, intellect, physical strength, and well-being. Such potent fluids are also regularly offered as sacrificial libations, through which the same gifts are conferred upon gods, demigods, spirits of the dead, or the natural order itself.

Nowhere, however, have intoxicating drinks been elevated to a loftier position of religious significance than among the Indo-Iranian peoples, who knew both a profane intoxicant known as *surā* in India and *hurā* in Iran and a sacred drink (Indic *soma*, Iranian *haoma*), the latter of which was invested with both the status of a deity and a stunningly complex set of symbolic elaborations. [*See* Soma.] At the most concrete level, this beverage—prepared by pressing the sap from a specific plant to obtain a juice that is mixed with water, milk, or honey in different ritual contexts—had powerful hallucinogenic effects, but beyond this, it was understood to be an all purpose intensifier, which enhanced all human capabilities, giving health to the sick, children to the barren, eloquence to the poet, vision and insight to the priest, strength to the warrior, and long life to any who may drink it. Going still further, it was claimed that *soma* or *haoma* could grant freedom from death (Skt., *amṛta*, literally "nondeath"; often incorrectly translated as "immortality") both to gods and to humans, as for instance, in the exultant *Ṛgveda* 8.48.3:

> We have drunk soma; we have become free from death.
> We have gone to the light; we have found the gods!
> What now can joylessness do to us? What, truly, can
> the evil of mortality do, o you who are free from
> death?

Going further still, *soma* and *haoma* were considered nothing less than the universal life essence, the fluid that vivifies and invigorates all living beings. Moreover, the sacrificial offering of this elixir came to be regarded as the means to effect circulation of life energy throughout the entire cosmos. For in the last analysis, *soma* and *haoma* were not merely drinks, nor were they the plants from which drinks were made; rather, they were only temporary forms or incarnations of the life essence, of which there were many others. To pursue but one line of analysis found in the Indic manuals of esoteric speculation upon sacrificial ritual, we see that the juice extracted from some plants, when poured into the sacrificial fire, ascends to heaven in the form of smoke. This smoke coalesces to form clouds, from which the rains pour down to earth. Smoke, clouds, and rain—like *soma* juice—are all forms of the universal energizing fluid, and when rain falls upon the earth it brings forth plants (among them *soma*, the "king of plants," but all the others as well). These plants, in turn, are eaten by grazing animals. Having passed through rain and plants, in the bodies of male animals the elixir becomes semen, and in females, milk, both of which are but further transformations of *soma*. By eating plants, drinking water or milk, humans also absorb *soma* into their bodies, gaining life and energy thereby. But in all its various forms, *soma* is ultimately and inevitably destined for the sacrificial fire, for not only are plants, water, and milk offered along with the *soma* liquid proper, but the cremation fire is also a fire of sacrifice that returns the life fluids left in the corpse to the cosmic cycle.

This is but one system of symbolic speculation centering on *soma;* numerous others have also enjoyed currency, such as that which homologized the waxing moon to a vessel filled with the sacred fluid and the waning moon to a libation for the benefit of all the waters and plants (see, e.g., *Śatapatha Brāhmaṇa* 11.1.5.3). Ultimately, the symbolic importance of *soma* came to overshadow its use as an intoxicant, such that it mattered relatively little when either supplies of the original *soma* plant were cut off or the knowledge of its original identity was lost. For centuries the soma sacrifice has been performed with a substitute, the *Ephedra* plant, which has no hallucinogenic effect whatsoever, but which is treated with the same reverence as was its more potent predecessor. Although numerous attempts have been made to identify the original plant—the psychotropic mushroom *Amanita muscaria* being the most recent candiate—most Indologists consider it unlikely that it will ever be located.

In Iran, the *haoma* cultus developed somewhat differently, but Iranian data support the same general conclusion as do those from India: the symbolic possibilities of the drink were far more important than its physiological effects in the long run. [*See* Haoma.] The earliest mentions of *haoma* in any Iranian text are ringing condemnations of the intoxicating beverage. These are two verses within the most ancient and prestigious portions of the Avesta, attributed by the Zoroastrian tradition and most modern scholars to Zarathushtra himself (*Yasna* 32.4 and 48.10). In the latter of these, the speaker calls directly to Ahura Mazdā, the Wise Lord, pleading, "When will you strike down this piss of an intoxicant, with which the Karapan-priests and the wicked lords of the lands evilly cause pain?"

Expert opinion is divided on whether this implies a blanket condemnation of *haoma*, or only a rejection of certain abuses of the drink. What is clear is that by the Achaemenid period *haoma* once again stood at the center of Iranian cult, as is attested by hundreds of inscriptions at Persepolis. Later Zoroastrian texts also grant a privileged position to *haoma* as a sacred beverage, an elixir of life, and a deity who is celebrated with his own hymn, the famous *Hōm Yasht* (*Yasna* 9–11), a text that deserves much more careful and detailed study than it has received to date. This hymn appears to be a highly successful attempt to rehabilitate the *haoma* cultus, purifying it of the unseemly elements that led to Zarathushtra's denunciation while retaining many aspects of its symbolic significance, and reintegrating it into Zoroastrian worship. And to this day, the solemn preparation, consumption, and offering of *haoma*—now a drink devoid of intoxicating effect—is the central Zoroastrian ritual.

To these few examples, countless others might well be added, not least of which would be the clear magico-religious symbolism evident in advertisements for commercial soft drinks, as for instance "Come alive with Pepsi Cola," a slogan ineptly translated for the Taiwanese market as "Pepsi brings your ancestors back to life."

[*See also* Elixir.]

BIBLIOGRAPHY

To date, there is no satisfactory general summary of the variety of religious uses and significances of beverages. Rather, the literature exists in scattered form, most of it in languages other than English.

On the symbolic value of milk among the Maasai, see John G. Galaty's "Ceremony and Society: The Poetics of Maasai Ritual," *Man* 18 (June 1983): 361–382. On milk in antiquity, see Karl Wyss's *Die Milch im Kultus der Griechen und Römer* (Giessen, 1914), and specifically on milk and honey, note the still useful article of Hermann Usener, "Milch und Honig," *Rheinisches Museum für Philologie* 57 (1902): 177–195. On wine, see Karl Kirchner's *Die sakrale Bedeutung des Weines im Altertum* (Giessen, 1910).

Regarding the Japanese tea ceremony, several useful treatments are available. A. L. Sadler's *Cha-no-yu, the Japanese Tea Ceremony* (Rutland, Vt., 1962) provides a detailed description, but little in the way of analysis or interpretation. For these, see D. T. Suzuki's *Zen and Japanese Culture*, 2d ed., rev. & enl. (1959; reprint, Princeton, 1970), pp. 269–328; and Theodore M. Ludwig's "The Way of Tea: A Religio-Aesthetic Mode of Life," *History of Religions* 14 (1974): 28–50. For another excellent example of the religious valorization of a familiar beverage, see G. Mantovani's "Acqua magica e acqua di luce in due testi gnostici," in *Gnosticisme et monde hellénistique*, edited by Julien Ries (Louvain, 1982), pp. 429–439.

For use of intoxicants in the Amazon, the best sources to date are the writings of Gerardo Reichel-Dolmatoff, especially *The Shaman and the Jaguar* (Philadelphia, 1975) and *Beyond the Milky Way: Hallucinatory Imagery of the Tukano Indians* (Los Angeles, 1978). On the Germanic usage and mythology of mead, see the splendid work of Renate Doht, *Der Rauschtrank im germanischen Mythos* (Vienna, 1974).

On myths of the theft of an "immortality fluid," see the diverging interpretations in Adalbert Kuhn's *Die Herabkunft des Feuers und des Göttertranks* (Berlin, 1859); Georges Dumézil's *Le festin d'immortalité* (Paris, 1924); and David M. Knipe's "The Heroic Theft: Myths from Ṛgveda IV and the Ancient Near East," *History of Religions* 6 (May 1967): 328–360. On fluids of immortality in general, but with primary emphasis on the Greco-Roman world, the old work of W. H. Roscher, *Nektar und Ambrosia* (Leipzig, 1883), retains value.

There are numerous discussions on *soma* and *haoma*, the most valuable for its attention to the rich symbolism of these cult beverages being Herman Lommel's "König Soma," *Numen* 2 (1955): 196–205. The attempt to identify *soma* with the mushroom *Amanita muscaria* was made in R. Gordon Wasson's *Soma: Divine Mushroom of Immortality* (New York, 1968) but has been soundly refuted in John Brough's "Soma and Amanita Muscaria," *Bulletin of the School of Oriental and African Studies* 34 (1971): 331–362.

Bruce Lincoln

BEZA, THEODORE (1519–1605), Reformed theologian and successor to John Calvin as moderator of the Venerable Company of Pastors in Geneva, Switzerland. Born Théodore de Bèze and raised in Paris, he was trained as a lawyer (at Orléans) but preferred the company of humanists. His first publication, *Poemata*, evidenced considerable poetic talent. Upon his conversion from Catholicism to Protestantism in 1548, Beza fled France and, as a professor of Greek, joined Pierre Viret at the academy in Lausanne, Switzerland. Meanwhile, the French Parlement declared Beza an outlaw, confiscated his goods, and burned his effigy in Paris. It was at Lausanne that Beza wrote *A Tragedie of Abraham's Sacrifice* (1559; Eng. trans., 1575), the first biblical tragedy (a genre later utilized by Racine), as well as his theologically significant *Tabula praedestinationis* (1555), translated the following year as *A Briefe Declaraccion of the Chiefe Poyntes of the Christian Religion, Set Forth in a Table of Predestination.* The subject of predestination created such heated disputes that Viret and Beza left Lausanne in 1558. John Calvin then appointed Beza rector of the newly founded Academy of Geneva, a post that he held formally from 1559 to 1562, but Beza effectively directed the academy until he retired as professor of theology in 1599. Beza began three other significant works in Lausanne, which he continued in Geneva: the completion of the translation of the *Book of Psalms*, begun by the French poet Clément Marot; his New Testament commentaries; and his *Confession of the Christian Faith* (Fr., 1559; Lat., 1560). Beza's confession of faith was translated into every major European language and had a wide influence as a simple expression of Reformed belief.

In 1561, Beza was the primary spokesman for the French Reformed churches at the Colloquy of Poissy, summoned by Catherine de Médicis in the vain hope of preventing the bloody Wars of Religion, which broke out in 1563. In 1564, the dying Calvin designated Beza to succeed him as moderator of the Venerable Company of Pastors in Geneva, and Beza began his long career as the most influential pastor of the Genevan church and therefore of the Reformed French churches, for which Geneva trained pastors. From 1564 to 1599, Beza held the only regular chair in theology at the academy. His work included lectures, sermons, polemical and systematic publications, and numerous colloquies with Lutherans and Roman Catholics. Beyond his professorial and pastoral duties in Geneva, Beza advised the French Huguenot leaders, including Henry of Navarre (Henry IV), traveled to defend Reformed theology and church discipline, and, almost singlehandedly, kept the academy functioning during the sieges of Geneva by Savoy.

Out of his efforts to assist the Huguenots came his *On the Right of Magistrates* (1574), an important treatise for the history of political theory that supported the God-given right of the people through their magistrates to rebel against royal leaders if these latter were seriously misleading and mistreating the people. While with the Huguenot troops, Beza discovered what was at that time considered the oldest extant New Testament manuscript (the Codex Bezae), which Beza later sent to Cambridge University in an effort to gain Queen Elizabeth's support for the Huguenots and for plague-ridden and besieged Geneva.

As has been true of Calvin studies, Beza scholars dispute the degree to which the doctrine of predestination underlies all of Beza's theology. Scholars also disagree on the influence of Beza's work on the development of Reformed scholasticism in the seventeenth century. Beza's original contribution regarding the doctrine of the Lord's Supper, in which he taught the presence of Christ through the category of "relation" rather than of "substance," went unnoticed until the 1960s. Beyond dispute, however, is the contribution Beza made to the stability of the church and the Academy of Geneva for nearly forty years following Calvin's death.

BIBLIOGRAPHY

Beza's works are largely unavailable except as rare books. Most of his major treatises were rapidly translated into English and can be found in sixteenth-century editions. Beza collected his own most significant theological treatises in three volumes: collectively titled *Theodori Bezae Vezelii*, they are *Vol. tractationum theologicarum* (Geneva, 1570); *Vol. alterum tractationum theologicarum* (Geneva, 1573); and *Vol. tertium tractationum theologicarum*, 3 vols. in 1 (Geneva, 1582). Beza's correspondence is being meticulously edited in Geneva and published by Librairie Droz, 10 vols. to date (Geneva, 1960–).

A bibliography of Beza's works, which omits his biblical commentaries, has been gathered in Frédéric L. Gardy's *Bibliographie des œuvres théologiques, littéraires, historiques et juridiques de Théodore de Bèze* (Geneva, 1960). The standard biography is Paul F. Geisendorf's *Théodore de Bèze* (Geneva, 1967).

JILL RAITT

BHAGAVADGĪTĀ. The *Bhagavadgītā* is perhaps the most widely read and beloved scripture in all Indian religious literature. Its power to counsel and inspire its readers has remained undiminished in the almost two thousand years since its composition.

The *Bhagavadgītā* (Song of the Blessed Lord) is sacred literature, holy scripture—it is a text that has abundant power in its persistence and its presence. The pious Hindu, even if his piety is mild, will inevitably have access to the book or will be able to recite, or at least paraphrase, a few lines from it. The devout turn to it daily; they read it ritually, devotionally, with a sense of awe. The text is intoned during the initiation ceremony wherein one becomes a *saṃnyāsin* (renunciant); teachers and holy men expound upon it; professors translate it and write about it; the more humble listen to the words that, though heard countless times before, remain vibrant. The text is read by all Hindus, esteemed by Śaivas as well as by Vaiṣṇavas, venerated by the lower caste as well as by the high, savored by villagers as well as by the more urbane. Many times each day in India the consoling words of the *Gītā* are read or whispered into the ear of someone who, with eyes looking to the south in fear or hope or both, awaits death: "And whoever remembers Me alone when leaving the body at the time of death attains to My status of being" (8.5).

One may dispute whether the *Bhagavadgītā* teaches the dualistic Sāṃkhya philosophy or the nondualistic Vedānta, whether it is a call to action or renunciation; but what is beyond dispute is that it teaches devotion to god as a means to liberation, whether that liberation is understood as release from the world or freedom in the world: "Hear again My supreme word, the most secret of all: thou are greatly beloved by Me, hence I will speak for thy good. Center thy mind on Me, be devoted to Me, sacrifice to Me, revere Me, and thou shalt come to Me. I promise thee truly, for thou art dear to Me" (18.64–65).

The Text in Context. The *Bhagavadgītā* occupies a very small part of the *Mahābhārata*—it is but one of the Hundred Minor Books of that enormous epic, that elephantine tale of the great war between the Kauravas and the Pāṇḍavas, two descendant branches of the Kurus, the Lunar Race. Yudhiṣṭhira, the righteous leader of the Pāṇḍavas, having lost his family's portion of the kingdom to the Kauravas in a crooked game of dice, was forced, together with his four brothers, into forest exile for thirteen years. Afterward Yudhiṣṭhira asked for the just return of the kingdom, or at least five villages, one for each of the brothers. When this was refused, the great war became inevitable. [*See* Mahābhārata.]

Both armies sought allies. Kṛṣṇa, the princely leader of the Vṛṣṇis, another branch of the Lunar Race, in an attempt to remain neutral and loyal to both families, offered his troops to the Kauravas and his service as charioteer and counselor to his friend Arjuna, one of Yudhiṣṭhira's younger brothers. [*See* Arjuna.]

The battle was ready to begin: "Conches and kettledrums, cymbals and drums and horns suddenly were struck and the sound was tumultuous" (1.13). Suddenly, seeing his own kinsmen—teachers, fathers, uncles, cousins, and in-laws—arrayed for battle, Arjuna decided that he was unable to fight. Realizing that to kill them would destroy the eternal laws of the family and uncaring as to whether or not he himself would be slain, "Arjuna cast away his bow and arrow and sank down on the seat of his chariot, his spirit overcome by grief" (1.47).

In this dramatic setting the teachings of the *Bhagavadgītā* begin. Kṛṣṇa must show Arjuna why he must fight in this terrible war and, in so doing, he reveals the nature of reality and of himself. Military counsel becomes spiritual instruction; the heroic charioteer discloses his divinity. Kṛṣṇa-Vāsudeva is God, the highest reality and eternal self, beyond the world and yet of it as a preserver, creator, and destroyer. In the midst of the theophany Arjuna cries out: "Thou art the imperishable, the highest to be known; Thou art the final resting place of this universe; Thou are the immortal guardian of eternal law; Thou are the primal spirit" (9.18).

By the time the *Bhagavadgītā* was incorporated into the story of the great war (probably during the third century BCE), a conception of this world as a dreadful, burning round of death, a tedious prison in which we are trapped by transmigration, had taken hold and with it renunciatory ideals and impulses for liberation challenged more ancient, hieratic ideals of ritual action and aspirations for heavenly domains. The *Gītā* provided a synthesis of conflicting ideals and past and present norms. It harmonized Brahmanic values with a warrior's code, reconciled a traditional pantheism with a seemingly new theistic religiosity, and coalesced a variety of differing and potentially dissentient philosophical trends. This synthetic or syncretic quality of the text invested it with a pan-Indian appeal that it has retained.

Ancient Indian religious literature was formally classified as either a "revelation" (*śruti*—that which has been sacramentally "heard," the eternally existent Veda) or a "tradition" (*smṛti*—that which has been "remembered" from ancient times—the epics, Purāṇas, and various *sūtras* and *śāstras*). As a book within the *Mahābhārata*, the *Bhagavadgītā*, like Kṛṣṇa's later discourse, the *Anugītā*, and like the other didactic and philosophical portions of the epic, has the technical status of *smṛti*. But the *Bhagavadgītā* has attained the functional status of a gospel. Śaṅkara (eighth century), the major proponent of the Advaita Vedānta school of philosophy, quite typically begins his exegesis of the text with the comment that the *Gītā* contains the very quintessence of the Veda and that a knowledge of it leads to *mokṣa*, liberation from the bonds of worldly existence. Rāmānuja (eleventh century), who qualified the nondualistic position of Vedānta in order to expound his theology of a supreme and loving god, understood the *Gītā* as the actual revelation of the word of that god under the mere pretext of a discourse with Arjuna. And the Bengali saint Ramakrishna (1834–1886), like so many other modern commentators, declared the book to be "the essence of all scriptures" (*The Gospel of Sri Ramakrishna*, New York, 1949, p. 772). The *Bhagavadgītā*, particularly after the great flowering of the devotional strain within the Hindu tradition, became accepted as revelation within tradition. The text transcended its context.

The Philosophy of the Text. The individual human being, according to the *Bhagavadgītā,* is at once natural (a product of nature caught up in lawlike relations and filled with desires and longings) and spiritual (an embodiment of the divine). The individual is not, however, a walking dualism, for the spiritual aspect is one's higher nature and one must come to realize that one's natural existence, taken in itself, is only provisional and has meaning only from the standpoint of the spiritual.

The individual human being, Kṛṣṇa tells Arjuna early on in the text, is immortal. Possessed of an eternal, unchanging spirit, a person can only appear to be an autonomous actor in the natural world. This appearance derives from an ignorance of the true self. Normally identifying himself as an ego self-sufficiently working within the conditions of his psychophysical nature, a person must reidentify himself at a deeper level of integrated selfhood and thereby understand his true role as a social being.

Following the already traditional understanding of the ideal organization of society into classes (*varṇas*), the codified stages of life (*āśramas*) and aims in life (*puruṣārthas*), the *Bhagavadgītā* places much emphasis on one's need to follow or fulfill one's *dharma* ("social duty" or "role") as it is defined relative to one's place in the larger social order. The universe is sustained by *dharma.* Ideally each person works out his social career according to the dictates of his own nature *(svadharma)* as this is itself a product of past experience. *Dharma, karman* ("action" or "work"), and *saṃsāra* ("rebirth") belong together: action carried over innumerable lives must be informed by a sensitivity to the obligations one has in virtue of one's interdependence with others. Arjuna is a member of the warrior class and must fulfill the duties of this social position—he must fight.

But what is the nature of reality that makes this both possible and imperative? The *Gītā*'s answer to this is that reality, in its essence, is the presence of a personalized *brahman,* something higher than the impersonal *brahman,* the absolute reality described in the Upaniṣads. "There are two spirits in this world," Kṛṣṇa explains, "the perishable and the imperishable." The perishable is all beings and the imperishable is called *kūṭastha* ("the immovable"). But there is another, the Highest Spirit *(puruṣottama),* called the Supreme Self, who, as the imperishable Lord, enters into the three worlds and sustains them. "Since I transcend the perishable and am higher even than the imperishable, I am renowned in the world and in the Veda as the highest Spirit" (15.16–18).

This "Highest Spirit" then is not the nonpersonal, undifferentiated, unchanging *brahman* of Advaita Vedānta, but rather that being who while enjoying its status as a supreme reality, actively engages worlds of its creation. It has its higher and lower statuses as creative spirit and as the manifest natural world.

In its analysis of the lower status of the divine, the *Gītā* draws heavily upon the Sāṃkhya system of thought. Nature *(prakṛti)* is seen as an active organic field constituted by various strands (*guṇas*), which can best be understood as energy systems. Everything in nature, and particularly every individual human being, is constituted by a combination of these forces. *Sattva* represents a state of subtle harmony and equilibrium which is exhibited as clear intelligence, as light. At the other extreme is darkness, *tamas,* the state of lethargy, of heaviness. In between is *rajas,* agitation, restlessness, passion, the motivating force for actions. The *puruṣa* ("the individual spirit") caught up in *prakṛti,* is driven by the *guṇas* and is deluded into thinking that, as a given phenomenal fact, it is their master and not their victim. [*See* Sāṃkhya.]

The aim of human life in the *Bhagavadgītā* is to attain a self-realization that "I" am not a separate, autonomous actor but that "I" am at one with a divine reality, and that my ultimate freedom comes from bringing my actions into accord with that reality. "Everyone," the *Gītā* says, "is made to act helplessly by the *guṇas* born of *prakṛti*" (3.5). "I" can become a true actor only when my actions get grounded in a divine will. Freedom *(mokṣa)* is thus not a transcendence of all action but rather calls for my being a social persona fulfilling my *dharma* without ego-attachment, at one with the divine.

The realization of this aim of life is at the heart of the *Bhagavadgītā*'s teaching, and has been the most controversial among both modern and traditional interpreters of the text. Following Śaṅkara, whose commentary is one of the oldest to have survived, many have argued that the central yoga put forward by the *Bhagavadgītā* is the way of knowledge, *jñānayoga:* it alone provides the insight into reality that allows for genuine self-realization. [*See the biography of Śaṅkara.*] Taking the position of Rāmānuja, others have argued that *bhaktiyoga,* the discipline of devotion, remains the highest way for the *Gītā; bhakti,* in his understanding of the text, provides the basis for a salvific relationship between the individual person and a loving god with absolute power and supremacy over the world. [*See the biography of Rāmānuja.*] Still others have seen the *Gītā* as a gospel of works, teaching most centrally *karmayoga,* the way of action—of acting without attachment to the fruits of one's acts. This multiplicity of interpretations results from the fact that the *Bhagavadgītā* does extol each of these ways at various times. Each discipline or respective integration is said to have value. The text combines and assimilates the central features of the various paths. [*See* Yoga.]

The yoga of the *Bhagavadgītā* demands that actions be performed without attachment to their results, for otherwise, with attachment, comes bondage, not freedom. Actions, the *Gītā* says, must be performed as sacrifice *(yajña),* which means that actions must be performed in a spirit of reverence, with loving attention to the divine. But to do this one must understand how nature, as the lower status of the divine, acts according to its own necessity and that the individual actor is merely an expression of the *guṇas*. This understanding is the work of a preliminary *jñāna*—intellectual, philosophical analysis—which must then develop into a deeper insight into the nature of the self, one which allows for that discrimination between the higher and lower nature of both the human and the divine. It is only with this *jñāna* that actions can be carried out according to one's *dharma,* for that insight brings a fundamental axiological change. One sees the value of everything relative to the supreme value of reality itself. But according to the *Bhagavadgītā,* this knowledge is not sufficient for the realization of complete freedom, as it fails to provide a motivation or justification for any particular action. *Jñāna* must then recombine with *bhakti* at its highest level, which has as its object the divine in its own deepest personal nature. "Those who renounce all actions in Me and are intent on Me," Kṛṣṇa reveals, "who worship Me with complete discipline and meditate on Me, whose thoughts are fixed on Me—these I quickly lift up from the ocean of death and rebirth" (12.6–7). With the realization that one is entirely at one with an active, creative spiritual vitality, one can then imitate the divine—one can act according to *its* nature and realize thereby one's destiny. One rises above the ocean of death.

With such awareness Arjuna announced that his confusion and despair had passed. He picked up his bow and arrows: "I stand firm with my doubts dispelled; I shall act by Thy word" (18.73). The battle on the field of righteousness began.

The Persistence of the Text. By the eighth century the *Bhagavadgītā* had become a standard text for philosophical and religious exposition. The normative commentary of Śaṅkara generated subcommentaries and inspired responses, new interpretations, new commentaries and more subcommentaries. Rāmānuja's theistic exegesis set forth devotional paradigms for understanding the text which were to be elaborated by medieval Vaiṣṇava scholiasts. These latter commentators do not seem to have distinguished between the heroic Kṛṣṇa-Vāsudeva of the *Mahābhārata* and the originally distinct, erotic Kṛṣṇa-Gopāla of the Puranic and literary traditions. With the amalgamation of various Kṛṣṇas into one supreme God, the cool and detached *bhakti* of the *Bhagavadgītā* became subsumed into the emotional and passionate *bhakti* exemplified by the milkmaid lovers of Kṛṣṇa, the cowherd in the *Bhāgavata Purāṇa.* The meaning of the text changed—Madhva's commentary (thirteenth century) explains that Kṛṣṇa, the supreme lord, can only be approached or apprehended by the way of *bhakti* which is love *(sneha),* a love that is attachment. [*See the biography of Madhva.*]

Unabashedly classifying the overtly Vaiṣṇava *Bhagavadgītā* with their own ritual texts, the Āgamas, Śaiva exegetes produced their own corpus of commentarial literature. In the *Gītārthasaṅgraha* of the Kashmir Śaiva philosopher Abhinavagupta (eleventh century), which purports to reveal the "hidden meaning of the text," Kṛṣṇa is described as a protector of *dharma* and a guide to a *mokṣa* which is explicitly defined in the prefatory verses as "merger in Lord Śiva." [*See the biography of Abhinavagupta.*]

Beyond the exegetical tradition, the *Bhagavadgītā* became the prototype for a genre of devotional literature in which an Arjuna-like student is urged by a particular sectarian deity to absorb himself in the worship of that deity. So in the *Śivagītā* (eighth century), for example, Rāma is too disconsolate over his separation from Sītā to go into battle with Rāvaṇa; Śiva counsels and instructs him just as Kṛṣṇa did Arjuna. In the *Īśvaragītā* (ninth century) Śiva explains the paths to self-realization, the methods of liberation, to ascetics in a hermitage, in more or less the same words as were uttered in the prototype. The form and style of the original *Bhagavadgītā* seem to have imbued these later *gītās* with authority and legitimacy. Many of these texts are embedded within the Purāṇas (e.g., the *Śivagītā* in the *Padma Purāṇa,* the *Īśvaragītā* in the *Kūrma Purāṇa,* the *Devīgītā* in the *Devībhāgavata Purāṇa*). The later Purāṇas commonly give quotes from, resumés of, or eulogistic references to, the *Bhagavadgītā;* the *Padma Purāṇa* (eighth century) contains a glorification of the book, the *Gītāmāhātmya,* a paean to the text as the perfect distillation of supreme truth. The text about devotion became itself an object of devotion. It is carried like a talisman by many a wandering holy man.

Throughout Indian history the *Bhagavadgītā* has provided social theorists with axioms whereby political issues and problems could be understood in religious and traditional terms. Bal Gangadhar Tilak (1856–1920), one of the most important nationalist leaders of the modern Hindu renaissance, for example, while in prison in Mandalay for sedition, wrote the *Gītā rahasya,* an interpretation of the ancient text as a revolutionary manifesto, a call to the Indian people to take up arms against the British. Gandhi, on the other hand, who first became acquainted with the *Bhagavadgītā* through British Theosophists in London, asserted, without a trace of self-consciousness, that the *Bhagavadgītā* taught nonviolence. He urged his followers to read it assiduously and to live by it. He often referred to the book as *Mother Gita,* and would say, "When I am in difficulty or distress, I seek refuge in her bosom" (*Harijan,* August, 1934).

The *Bhagavadgītā* changes with each reader, fluctuates in meaning with each successive generation of interpreters, which is to say, it lives. This vitality constitutes its sacrality.

Caitanya (1486–1533), the ecstatic founder of Bengal Vaiṣṇavism, once came upon a man reading the *Bhagavadgītā* aloud in a temple, and as he read everyone laughed at him, for he mispronounced all of the words. The man himself was weeping and trembling, and Caitanya asked him which words made him cry so. "I don't know the meaning of any of the words," the man confessed, "but as I sound them out I see Kṛṣṇa in Arjuna's chariot. He is holding the reins in his hands and he is speaking to Arjuna and he looks very beautiful. The vision makes me weep with joy." Caitanya smiled: "You are an authority on the *Bhagavadgītā*. You know the real meaning of the text" (*Caitanyacaritāmṛta* of Kṛṣṇadāsa Kavirāja, *Madya-līlā* 9.93–103). [*See the biography of Caitanya.*]

It has not always been important for readers or hearers of the *Bhagavadgītā* to understand all the words; rather, what has been crucial for many Hindus has been to feel or experience the text, to participate in it, to allow the *Bhagavadgītā* to sanctify their lives and console them in death.

[*For a discussion of the moral and cosmological presuppositions that underlie the philosophy of the Gītā see* Dharma, *article on* Hindu Dharma. *The article on Kṛṣṇa discusses the mythology of the god;* Kṛṣṇaism *treats his cult in its various regional and historical contexts. For a discussion of Kṛṣṇa's role in the formation of Vaiṣṇava theology, see* Vaiṣṇavism. *The devotional practices and attitudes taught by Kṛṣṇa in the Gītā are discussed in* Bhakti *and are covered in more general form in* Devotion. *Many of the personalities and philosophical terms mentioned in this article are the subject of independent entries. See also* Vedānta.]

BIBLIOGRAPHY

The passages from the *Bhagavadgītā* cited in this article are from the translation of the text by Eliot Deutsch (New York, 1968). Since Charles Wilkins published his *The Bhăgvăt-gēētā, or, Dialogues of Krēēshnă and Ărjŏŏn in Eighteen Lectures, with Notes* in 1785 literally hundreds of translations of the text have been made into European languages. Gerald J. Larson has thoughtfully surveyed the stylistic and interpretive trends as exemplified by many of these translations in "The Song Celestial: Two Centuries of the *Bhagavad Gītā* in English," *Philosophy East and West* 31 (October 1981): 513–541. Of the readily available translations, Franklin Edgerton's (1925; reprint, Oxford, 1944) is the most literal, so literal in its attempt to preserve the Sanskrit syntax, in fact, that, for the sake of balance, it was originally published together with Sir Edwin Arnold's transformation of the text into Victorian poesy (Cambridge, Mass., 1944). Though Edgerton's always reliable translation is difficult to read, his lengthy commentary is masterful scholarship. The interpretive notes that accompany the translation by W. Douglas P. Hill (London, 1927) remain an important contribution to the literature. Étienne Lamotte's *Notes sur la Bhagavadgītā* (Paris, 1929) is a fine example of rigorous exegesis and reflection.

R. C. Zaehner's lucid translation (Oxford, 1969) is a pleasure to read and his analyses are as judicious as they are sensitivie; Zaehner introduces the insights of Śaṅkara and Rāmānuja where they are appropriate and he admits his penchant for the theistic interpretation of the latter. For a more detailed understanding of Rāmānuja's understanding of the text, see J.A.B. van Buitenen's *Rāmānuja on the Bhagavadgītā* (The Hague, 1953). Van Buitenen's own translation, *The Bhagavadgītā in the Mahābhārata* (Chicago, 1981), is heroic scholarship, translation at its best, and his introductory essay is no less insightful. The very important exegesis of Śaṅkara has been translated into English by Allādi Mahadeva Sastri: *The Bhagavad-Gita with the Commentary of Srî Sankarachâryâ,* 5th ed. (Madras, 1961). And the interesting commentary of Abhinavagupta, the *Gītārthasaṅgraha,* has been well translated into English and perceptively introduced by Arvind Sharma (Leiden, 1983).

For significant examples of modern Indian interpretations of the text, see *The Gospel of Selfless Action, or the Gita According to Gandhi,* edited and translated by Mahadev Desai (Ahmadabad, 1948); *Śrimad Bhagavadgītā Rahasya,* edited by B. G. Tilak (Poona, 1936); and Aurobindo Ghose's *Essays on the Gita* (Calcutta, 1926).

ELIOT DEUTSCH and LEE SIEGEL

BHAIṢAJYAGURU, the Buddha named Master of Healing, is an important member of the Mahāyāna Buddhist pantheon. He has been worshiped predominantly in East and Central Asian traditions of Buddhist practice.

Concepts of healing played a fundamental role in early Buddhism: Śākyamuni Buddha was sometimes given the epithet "supreme physician," and the Buddhist teachings were termed the "king of medicines" for their ability to lead beings out of suffering. In early Buddhist teachings, as in later times, the enlightenment process was equated with the healing process. Further, many monks were healers and physicians; such persons played a significant role in the spread of Buddhist teachings. Thus, when the Mahāyāna pantheon began to take form in the centuries directly before and after the beginning of the common era, several key figures were associated especially with healing abilities, both metaphorical and literal. Master of Healing ultimately was viewed as the most important figure of this group.

The principal scripture written about this Buddha, entitled *Scripture on the Merits and Original Vows of the Master of Healing, the Lapis Lazuli Radiance Tathāgata,* is a work that eventually became best known in the Chinese version translated by Hsüan-tsang in 650 CE (T.D. no. 450). As in other works of this type, most likely composed in the early centuries of the common era in the northwest borderlands of India, the historical Buddha Śākyamuni serves as a pivot between the human realms and celestial spheres, in this instance revealing to his listeners the existence of the enlightened celestial being Bhaiṣajyaguru. Following a pattern often seen in such texts, the Buddha and his pure land are described, his vows to aid all beings are detailed, and various methods are explicated for invoking his beneficent force. Here, Master of Healing is described as lord of a spirit realm located to the east, a land named Pure Lapis Lazuli, with level ground made of that radiantly blue stone, marked by roads of gold and various structures built of precious substances. Like the celestial fields of other Buddhas such as Amitābha, this realm is a refuge from suffering; it is an ideal site to listen without distraction to the pure principles taught by its lord, the Master of Healing, in association with the two leaders of his *bodhisattva* assembly, Sunlight (Sūryaprabha) and Moonglow (Candraprabha).

Master of Healing's twelve vows, first made when he set out to gain enlightenment, cover a wide range of benefits to sentient beings. The most widely known is the sixth vow, a pledge to alleviate the sickness and suffering of all beings. The fulfillment of this pledge forms the subject of much of the scripture. Yet, while Master of Healing has pledged to aid all beings who are sick and suffering, he must be called upon in order to invoke this potent aid. According to the scripture, methods of effective invocation range from the simple expedient of calling out his name to special rites involving prayer and worship before his image. In the case of life-threatening disease, a complex rite is outlined in the scripture (and described in great detail in special ritual texts) in which forty-nine cartwheel-shaped lamps are burned before seven images of the Buddha for forty-nine days, with many other ritual acts performed in units of seven or forty-nine. The number seven (and its square, forty-nine) is especially important in the Buddhist healing cults, most likely relating to the number of days in the intermediate state *(antarābhava)* between death and rebirth.

A fundamental feature of the healings bestowed by Bhaiṣajyaguru is the transformation of *karman,* that is, a concern for eradicating the patterned causes as well as the visible symptoms of suffering. This sense of transformation pervades the scriptural and ritual traditions associated with the cult. In this context, Master of Healing is especially important for his work in assisting beings to reach a momentous spiritual turning point known as the "aspiration to attain enlightenment," at which the drifting life is cast aside in order to seek spiritual fulfillment.

Standard images of Master of Healing depict him as a seated Buddha in monk's garb, either having skin the rich blue color of lapis lazuli or having a golden complexion with a halo and mandorla of lapis lazuli–colored rays. The Buddha holds a bowl or covered medicine jar on his lap with his left hand, while his right hand, resting on his right knee with palm outward, offers the medicinal myrobalan fruit; sometimes he is standing, holding the medicine jar in his left hand, with right hand upraised in the gesture of the banishment of fear. He is flanked by his *bodhisattva* assistants, Sunlight and Moonglow, who stand in princely garb. Encircling them are twelve *yakṣa* generals, each of whom is said to command seven thousand troops, all in aid of the Buddha's healing work. In some East Asian traditions, these twelve generals are clearly depicted as lords of the twelve hours of the day and the twelve years of the Jupiter-based cycle. The cosmic wholeness of this scene is striking: with lapis lazuli at the center that radiates like the depths of space, together with the two luminaries who are encircled by lords of time, it points to the profound nature of internal and external healing provided by this Buddha.

A somewhat later tradition, introduced to China in the early eighth century and eventually popular among Tibetans and Mongolians, focuses on seven brothers identified as healing Buddhas, the senior physician among them being Bhaiṣajyaguru. This group is often depicted with Śākyamuni Buddha, thus turning back to the roots of the Healing Buddha cult in the early tradition of Śākyamuni as spiritual healer.

[*See also* Celestial Buddhas and Bodhisattvas. *For a cross-cultural perspective, see* Healing.]

BIBLIOGRAPHY

The only extended study of Bhaiṣjyaguru is my *The Healing Buddha* (Boulder, 1979), which includes full translations from Chinese scriptures on this Buddha. This work provides a cross-cultural view of the cult, emphasizing its scriptural foundations and iconographic manifestations. Further information specific to the context of Chinese practice traditions can be found in my "Seeking Longevity in Chinese Buddhism: Long Life Deities and Their Symbolism," in *Myth and Symbol in Chinese Tradition,* edited by Norman Girardot and John S. Major, a special issue of the *Journal of Chinese Religions* 13 (1985). A comprehensive cross-cultural essay on Buddhist medical theory and healing traditions is admirably set forth in Paul Demiéville's *"Byō* (Disease)," in *Hōbōgirin,* fasc. 3 (Paris, 1937), pp. 224–270; Mark Tatz has translated this monographic study into English under the title *Buddhism and Healing: Demiéville's Article "Byō" from Hōbōgirin* (Lanham, Md., 1985).

RAOUL BIRNBAUM

BHAKTI. The Sanskrit term *bhakti* is most often translated in English as "devotion," and the *bhaktimārga,* the "path of devotion," is understood to be one major type of Hindu spiritual practice. The *bhaktimārga* is a path leading toward liberation *(mokṣa)* from material embodiment in our present imperfect world and the attainment of a state of abiding communion with a personally conceived ultimate reality. The word *devotion,* however, may not convey the sense of participation and even of mutual indwelling between the devotees and God so central in *bhakti.* The Sanskrit noun *bhakti* is derived from the verbal root *bhaj,* which means "to share in" or "to belong to," as well as "to worship." *Devotion,* moreover, may not suggest the range of intense emotional states so frequently connoted by *bhakti,* most of which are suggested by the inclusive English word *love.* God's love, however, whether answering or eliciting the devotee's love, is denoted with other words than *bhakti.* Thus *bhakti* is the divine-human relationship as experienced from the human side.

While *bhakti* is sometimes used in a broad sense to cover an attitude of reverence to any deity or to a human teacher, the *bhaktimārga* is understood to be a "path" of exclusive devotion to a divine or human figure representing or embodying ultimate reality, a path whose goal is not this-worldly benefits but supreme blessedness. Those who follow the path believe that ultimate reality is the personal Lord (Īśvara) who both transcends the universe and creates it. *Bhakti* is thus theistic and can be distinguished, not only (1) from those religious movements that deny the reality of Īśvara (including those of Buddhists and Jains), but also (2) from polytheistic beliefs in a number of deities within a divine cosmos, and (3) from philosophies that see Īśvara as an ultimately illusory appearance of the reality that transcends personal qualities, *nirguṇa brahman.* [*See also* Īśvara.]

In practice the boundaries of the *bhaktimārga* are indistinct and its forms are many and diverse, and it is differently defined by various sectarian communities. Nonetheless, there are some important common features found in different expressions of *bhakti,* and there is a discernible "history" of *bhakti* during the last fifteen hundred to two thousand years.

Modern historical approaches to Indian religion generally recognize some traces of *bhakti* in a few of the classical Upaniṣads and see it strikingly present in large sections of the epics (including notably the *Bhagavadgītā*). The earliest devotional poetry is considered that in praise of the Tamil god Murukaṉ, beginning about 200 CE, followed between the fifth and ninth centuries by the works of many poets in two distinct bodies of Tamil poetry, one in praise of Śiva, the other in praise of Viṣṇu. According to the traditional accounts, however, the Tamil poet-saints are scattered through the first five thousand years of the fourth and most degenerate age, the *kaliyuga.* This traditional dating fits a frequent theme, that *bhakti* is an easier path to salvation appropriate to an age of diminished spiritual capacities, but another theme sometimes crosses this: the assertion that the triumph of bands of singing and dancing devotees marks the breaking of the power of the demon Kali, and thus the end of Kali's evil age and the restoration of the age of spiritual perfection.

From a modern historical standpoint the flowering of *bhakti* is the coming together of considerably earlier theistic tendencies in three major religious traditions of ancient India: (1) the sacrificial cult of the invading Aryans and the recitation by *brāhmaṇa* priests that became the foundation of the Vedas; (2) the practice of bodily mortification and spiritual withdrawal by individuals and groups known as *śramaṇa*s, probably continuing traditions of earlier inhabitants of India but soon adopted and adapted by some of the Aryans; and (3) the pre-Aryan cults of spirits and village goddesses inhabiting trees and rocks and protecting special places or special groups.

All three traditions were subject to one type of reinterpretation that emphasized the great results of effective practice and a second type of reinterpretation that concentrated on the intuitive knowledge of the deities or ultimate powers of that tradition. There was also a third type of reinterpretation, however, that ascribed omnipotence to a particular deity, more or less personally conceived, and advocated single-minded devotion to this supreme deity. In the case of the Vedic tradition it was increasingly Viṣṇu who was regarded as both the essential core and the lord of the sacrifice. Some of the *śramaṇa*s sometimes regarded Śiva as the great yogin, paradoxically lord of fertility and sexual plenitude as well as of sexual abstinence. The more popular and polytheistic traditions have also had their *bhakti* forms, in which local goddesses are conceived as manifestations of the Mother, the great Power (Śakti) whose devotees sing her praises as the giver of both destruction and well-being.

Those who worship Viṣṇu (in any of his incarnations but particularly as Kṛṣṇa and Rāma) as the supreme deity are known as Vaiṣṇavas; likewise those who accord the supreme place to Śiva are called Śaivas, and those who are devotees of the Goddess, conceived not as the subordinate consort of Śiva but as the ultimate Power, are termed Śāktas. Each "sect" is in practice divided into a large number of groups marked by allegiance to particular forms of the supreme deity, to particular lineages of teachers and teachings in characteristic sectarian organizations, which usually include some form of initiation.

The major forms of *bhakti* are described by Hindus themselves, not only by their special relation to particular forms of deity, but also according to the various moods of the devotee. The classifications vary slightly; some are closely related to classical Indian aesthetic theory according to which a particular raw emotion *(bhāva)* is transformed in drama into a refined mood or essence *(rasa)*. Each combination of *bhāva* and *rasa* uses a particular human relationship: servant to master or child to parent (respectful subordination), friend to friend (joking familiarity), parent to child (maternal affection and concern), and beloved to lover (combining elements of the other three relationships in passionate love). Individual devotees as well as larger sectarian movements differ in their personal preference and doctrinal ranking among these relationships, but all are generally accepted as appropriate devotional stances.

When passionate attachment to the Lord is stressed, *bhakti* is a striking contrast to yoga and other ascetic paths to salvation that stress detachment and the overcoming of all passions, positive as well as negative. [*See* Yoga.] Yet many forms of *bhakti* also stress the detachment from all worldly beings that must accompany attachment to the Lord, or, like the *Bhagavadgītā*, which speaks of *bhaktiyoga*, they use the language of ascetic philosophy to extol the path of *bhakti*.

The *bhakti* movements generally stand religiously in between the more extreme ascetic paths and popular Hindu religiosity. (Less extreme forms of asceticism are often incorporated within the *bhakti* movements.) *Bhakti* generally shares the ascetic concern for *mokṣa:* release from finite existence and the realization of transcendent beatitude. What is primary, however, is communion with the Lord, and if *bhaktas* think of *mokṣa* as anything else than such communion, they will reject it as a goal that would deprive them of the very communion for which they fervently yearn. [*See also* Mokṣa.]

A few *bhaktas* make the total commitment of time and style of life characteristic of Hindu "renouncers," spending whole days in chanting and singing the praise of their Lord. Most, however, must find time for their devotion in the midst of their daily occupations, whether high or low, but may become "full time" devotees temporarily during a lengthy pilgrimage. Their being *bhaktas* is sometimes shown by the sectarian marks on their foreheads or by other signs that they have been initiated into a particular community.

Bhakti often shares with popular Hinduism the basic ritual of *pūjā:* worship of the deity in some image form with vegetables, fruits, and flowers, which are spiritually consumed—or worn—by the deity and then returned to the worshiper as *prasāda,* material substance filled with the Lord's grace. Such *pūjā* may take place in one's home shrine or local temple, or it may be done as the culmination of a lengthy and arduous journey to a center of pilgrimage. Most Hindus perform such *pūjā* in order to win the deity's favor for some request, or, in the case of a vow *(vrata),* to fulfill a promise made at the time of a request since favorably answered. [*See also* Pūjā, *article on* Hindu Pūjā.] True *bhaktas*, however, perform the very same ritual acts in a different spirit: in thanksgiving for divine gifts freely granted, in petition for the supreme gift of God's presence, sometimes expressed as the privilege of doing God some service, in obedient performance of duties to the deities God has ordained, which include sacrificial worship for the maintenance of the universe. *Bhaktas* recognize that the Lord they serve also grants worldly gifts to those who seek them, and moreover, even grants requests made to lower deities. This means that they often can practice common Hindu forms of worship and support temple establishments. On the other hand, some *bhakti* movements have at one time been or continue to be sharply critical of popular religion and/or the temple establishment. This was strikingly true of the Vīraśaiva poets in Karnataka from the twelfth to the fourteenth century CE. [*See* Śaivism, *article on* Vīraśaivas.] In North India Kabīr and Nānak (the first Sikh *gurū*) were sharply critical both of popular piety and of the religious establishments, Hindu as well as Muslim. [*See also the biographies of Kabīr and Nānak.*]

There are also distinctive *bhakti* rituals: the singing (sometimes communal) of hymns and chants, the performance of dramas, dances, and recitals of the heroic deeds or erotic sports of Viṣṇu's incarnations or of the mysterious appearances of Lord Śiva. Stories about the Lord may thus lead to stories about the great *bhaktas*. The recounting of their lives is almost as popular as the singing of their songs.

Here, too, there is a strong difference in emphasis between devotional and ascetic paths, for the distinctive rituals of *bhaktas* are generally not reserved for the few qualified initiates but open to all, whatever their motives or their qualifications in the socioreligious hierarchy. This egalitarian thrust of *bhakti*, although it has not always penetrated in practice to the untouchables, is usually praised in song and story. It is not the equality of modern Western individualism, but the openness to a divine seeking that transcends or even reverses the order of human society, sometimes precisely because humility is the necessary qualification for receiving the Lord's grace.

Bhakti means not only "sharing" with God but also some form of sharing or mutual participation among God's devotees. While there is a heroic loneliness in the lives of some of the great *bhaktas* corresponding to or even combined with the physical and spiritual isolation of more extreme asceticism, the dominant note in *bhakti* is community, between generations as well as among fellow devotees of the same generation. Within this devotional community there is usually both a hierarchical relationship between teacher and disciple and a more egalitarian relationship between fellow disciples.

The English word *movement* is particularly appropriate for most *bhakti* movements, for there is a spiritual movement between the divine and the human, an emotional movement affecting or even engulfing any particular community of devotees, and a movement through time celebrated in sacred story. The stories about the *bhakti* saints help to define particular devotional communities and sometimes to extend them. While the sacred history of many devotional movements is of interest only to their own members, there has also been, especially in North India since the fifteenth century, a combination of hagiographies known as the *Bhaktamāla* (The Garland of Devotees). The present evil age, the *kaliyuga*, is considered to be the one, in the vast recurring cycle of the four ages, in which the human capacity to live rightly is at its lowest. Yet this cycle of stories assumes that the present age is also the *bhaktikāla*, the time for devotion. The worst of times becomes the best of times for those who join together in fervent praise. Those who remember the Lord (as continuously as the flow of oil, in Rāmānuja's definition of *bhakti*) have already in this life a foretaste of the eternal communion that is their final goal and, in many Vaiṣṇava communities, the expected goal at the end of their present earthly life. *Bhaktas* thus share in a movement from eternity through time back to eternity.

Philosophically, Vaiṣṇava *bhakti* has expressed itself in a range of positions between the "pure nondualism" (*śuddhādvaita*) of Vallabha and the "dualism" (*dvaita*) of Madhva, and Śaiva *bhakti* ranges from the monistic philosophy of Kashmir Śaivism to the dualistic or pluralistic position of the Tamil Śaiva Siddhānta, yet almost all of these philosophical positions agree both on the infinitely superior quality of the divine reality and on some kind of subordinate reality for finite souls and material things.

The common goal of communion with the Lord can also be understood more or less monistically. One classification distinguishes between four degrees of communion: (1) *sālokya*, being in the same heaven with a continuous vision of the Lord; (2) *sāmīpya*, residing close to the Lord; (3) *sārūpya*, having the same form, understood to be the privilege of the Lord's intimate attendants, whose external appearance is similar to the Lord's; and (4) *sāyujya*, complete union through entering the body of the Lord.

In terms of religious practice and religious experience there is a somewhat comparable range of positions between the affirmation of the constant divine presence both within finite realities and surrounding them, on the one hand, and the lamenting of God's absence from the devotee's experience in this present life. The typical *bhakti* position is somehow to affirm both God's presence and God's absence, but there is considerable difference in emphasis, not only between different sects and different individuals, but also within the experience of the same *bhakta*. The moments of experienced union (*saṃśleṣa*) and anguished separation or desolation (*viśleṣa* or *viraha*) alternate, but the *bhakta*'s experience is still more complicated: the realization of the fleeting character of the experience of union may intrude into it, while, on the other hand, the grief at separation is sharpened by the memory of previous shared delight. That grief itself, if it passes the moment of despair, expresses itself as a passionate yearning for a new moment of divine presence or as a more serene confidence in the final goal of unending communion with God.

Those who express a devotion of passionate attachment to the Lord, especially when the Lord is conceived as Kṛṣṇa, are sometimes dissatisfied with merely spiritual union after this earthly life. They yearn for the Lord's physical embrace of their present embodied selves. *Bhaktas* differ as to whether such union of the human devotee's body with the Lord's body is possible. Within this life, however, ecstatic moments of perceived union are fleeting. Permanent union brings with it an end to the *bhakta*'s life in this world, as is dramatically portrayed in the stories of the merger of two of the Tamil Vaiṣṇava saints (Āṇṭāl and Tiruppān Āḻvār) into the Lord's image incarnation, Ranganātha. Similar stories are told of the Rājpūt woman saint Mīrā Bāī, absorbed with Kṛṣṇa's image at Dvarka, and of Caitanya, who, according to the local Oriya tradition in Puri, was absorbed into the image of Jagannātha. [*See also the biographies of Mīrā Bāī and Caitanya.*]

For the more monistic *bhakti* that regards permanent union as the end of the finite self's distinct personal existence, the state of separation may actually be preferred as ensuring the continued bittersweet experience of the Lord's absence. Certainly for *bhaktas* in many schools and sects, the moments of absence are conveyed in poetry of great intensity and beauty. There our common human experience of separation from the infinite source of being is transfigured by the special experience of that rare human being who has felt the divine presence or known the divine rapture and then experienced even more intensely the pain of separation from this incredibly beautiful and desirable Lord.

In the South Indian Vaiṣṇava *bhakti* of Rāmānuja, however, separation and union are coordinated in a hierarchical vision in which the Lord enters the heart of all finite beings as their inner controller, without obliterating the distinct existence and moral responsibility of the finite person. Here longing for God and belonging to God are not alternatives but mutually reinforcing coordinates in intensifying the *bhakta*'s experience. [*See also the biography of Rāmānuja.*]

From an outside vantage point the meaning of *bhakti* may be conveyed by two questions. One is a theological question: how can the infinite Lord be independent of all finite reality and yet be dependent on his devotees? Most *bhaktas* affirm both propositions. The second is the corresponding anthropological question: how can the *bhakta* be both the humble servant and the intimate companion of the Lord—not only the Lord's instrument but the Lord's bride? Since we recognize that these are no more than an outsider's "translation" of the *bhaktas'* own questions, we must add a third, what we might call a hermeneutical question: how can the outside student of Hindu *bhakti* (whether non-Hindu or non-*bhakta*) understand any particular form of Hindu *bhakti?* How can divine-human "sharing" be understood without sharing in it? While most of the Hindu tradition would find it difficult to imagine such external understanding as the question implies, and those in the Western Platonic tradition would reject the separation of loving and knowing, most Western study of religion in general and of Hindu *bhakti* in particular assumes that reasonable understanding is possible—enough to write this article, for example—*without* personally participating as a scholar in the *bhakta*'s experience. The very nature of *bhakti* as experienced participation, however, is a continuing challenge to the strong tendency of Western notions of understanding, especially the Western effort to "capture" all human experience in carefully crafted objective concepts.

To understand an alien experience we need to remember partially similar experiences familiar to us. *Bhakti* has both appealed to and puzzled Western students because they see in its central features Western monotheism combined with other elements that seem different or even totally alien. Many features of Hindu *bhakti* are also found in the more popular aspects of Jainism and Buddhism, and Pure Land Buddhism has incorporated much of *bhakti* at its very core. The Indian expressions of both Islam and Christianity, moreover, have developed their own *bhakti* poets and saints. In the case of Islam, *bhakti* has provided a bridge for a mutual interpenetration with Hindu piety that has given the piety of Muslims in South Asia a distinctive character; yet Islamic and Hindu *bhakti* did not merge. In the case of Christianity in the modern era, *bhakti* provided the basic vocabulary for Christian prayer and hymnody in most modern Indian languages, yet Christian *bhakti* has usually been so distinctive as to be unaware of its debt to the Hindu tradition. Perhaps *bhakti,* although distinctively Hindu, may be appropriated and developed, if not by the proud at least by the humble, in a great variety of religious and cultural communities.

[*Discussion of* bhakti *in varying contexts occurs in nearly all of the traditions of Hinduism. Most of the deities, sects, and religious leaders mentioned in this article are the subject of individual entries. For further specific discussion of* bhakti, *see* Bhagavadgītā; Devotion; *and* Poetry, *article on* Indian Religious Poetry.]

BIBLIOGRAPHY

Thus far, no complete textbook survey of *bhakti* is available. The short list of references that follows is thus necessarily incomplete.

Dhavamony, Mariasusai. *Love of God according to Śaiva Siddhānta.* Oxford, 1971.

Hardy, Friedhelm. *Viraha Bhakti: The Early Development of Kṛṣṇa Devotion in South India.* Oxford, 1981.

Hawley, John Stratton. *Sūr Dās: Poet, Singer, Saint.* Seattle, 1984.

Hawley, John Stratton, and Donna M. Wulff, eds. *The Divine Consort: Rādhā and the Goddesses of India.* Berkeley, 1982.

Hein, Norvin J. "Hinduism." In *A Reader's Guide to the Great Religions,* edited by Charles J. Adams, pp. 106–155. New York, 1977. See pages 126–140.

Ramanujan, A. K., trans. *Speaking of Śiva.* Harmondsworth, 1973.

Ramanujan, A. K., trans. *Hymns for the Drowning.* Princeton, 1981.

Schomer, Karine, and W. H. McLeod, eds. *The Sants: Studies in a Devotional Tradition of India.* Berkeley and Delhi, 1985.

Yocum, Glenn E. *Hymns to the Dancing Śiva.* New Delhi and Columbia, Mo., 1982.

Zelliot, Eleanor. "The Medieval Bhakti Movement in History: An Essay on the Literature in English." In *Hinduism: New Essays in the History of Religions,* edited by Bardwell L. Smith, pp. 143–168. Leiden, 1976.

JOHN B. CARMAN

BHĀVAVIVEKA (c. 490–570 CE), also known as Bhavya or (in Tibetan) Legs-ldan-'byed-pa; Indian Buddhist philosopher and historian, and founder of the Svātantrika-Mādhyamika school. Born to a royal family in Malyara, in South India (although some Chinese sources claim it was in Magadha, in North India), Bhāvaviveka studied both *sūtra* and *śāstra* literatures during his formative years. Having excelled in the art of debate, especially against Hindu apologists of the Sāṃkhya school, he is said to have been the abbot of some fifty monasteries in the region of Dhānyakaṭa, in South India. His chief influences were the writings of Nāgārjuna (second century CE), the founder of the Mādhyamika, and treatises on logic from the traditions of Buddhism (especially Dignāga's works) and Hinduism (especially the *Nyāyapraveśa*). His chief philosophical contribution was his attempt at formulating a synthesis of Mādhyamika dialectics and the logical conventions of his time.

As all of Bhāvaviveka's works are lost in the original Sanskrit and preserved only in Tibetan translations, the scholarly world came to know of him only through Candrakīrti (c. 580–650 CE), who refuted Bhāvaviveka's position in the first chapter of the *Prasannapadā.* It could therefore be argued that our understanding of the Mādhyamika in general has suffered from a one-sided perspective that relies solely on Candrakīrti's rival school, the Prāsaṅgika-Mādhyamika. However, contemporary scholarship no longer neglects Tibetan sources, and thus a more balanced approach has ensued, one that reads Nāgārjuna's seminal writings through the commentaries of both the Prāsaṅgikas and the Svātantrikas.

Nāgārjuna, especially as read through the commentaries of Buddhapālita (c. 470–550 CE), was characterized by many Indian philosophers as a *vaitaṇḍika,* a nihilist who refused to assume any thesis *(pratijñā)* in the course of the ongoing dialogue between Hindu thinkers of various schools and the Buddhists. While Mādhyamika thought had not asserted any claim about ultimate truth/reality *(paramārthasatya),* Bhāvaviveka's independent reasoning *(svatantra-anumāna)* was applied to conventional truth/reality *(samvṛtisatya)* as a means of rescuing logico-linguistic conventions *(vyavahāra)* from a systematic negation *(prasaṅga)* that opened the school to charges of nihilism. While Bhāvaviveka accepted the Mādhyamika view that ultimately *(paramārthataḥ)* no entities could be predicated with any form of existence, he was willing to employ such predication on a conventional level. In order to maintain the reality and utility of traditional Buddhist categories for talking about the path of spiritual growth while denying the ultimate reality of such categories, he employed a syllogistic thesis *(pratijñā),* a philosophic strategy that was nearly incomprehensible to scholars of the Mādhyamika, who knew this school only through Candrakīrti's Prāsaṅgika systematization.

In order to affirm a thesis on the conventional level while denying it ultimately, Bhāvaviveka creatively reinterpreted the key Mādhyamika doctrine of the two truths *(satyadvaya).* In his *Madhyamārthasaṃgraha,* he propounds two levels of ultimacy: a highest ultimate that is beyond all predication and specification *(aparyāya-paramārtha),* in conformity with all Mādhyamika teachings, and an ultimate that can be inferred logically and specified meaningfully *(paryāya-paramārtha);* this latter level was a bold innovation in the history of Mādhyamika thought. Of course, such a distinction was operative only within the realm of conventional thought. Again we must employ Bhāvaviveka's crucial adverbial codicil, *paramārthataḥ,* and follow him in claiming that such a distinction, like all distinctions, is ultimately unreal although conventionally useful.

Bhāvaviveka's two main philosophic contributions—his affirmation of a thesis on a conventional level and his reinterpretation of the two-truths doctrine—are evaluated diversely by contemporary scholars. Those unsympathetic to him see his work as an unhappy concession to the logical conventions of his day, a concession that dilutes the rigor of the Mādhyamika dialectic. Those with more sympathy see his contributions as a creative surge that rescued Buddhist religious philosophies from those dialectical negations that threatened the integrity of the Buddhist path itself.

Within the evolved Tibetan Buddhist tradition, Bhāvaviveka is especially known for two other contributions. His refutations of the rival Yogācāra school are considered to be among the clearest ever written. The fifth chapter of his *Tarkajvālā,* the "Yogācārattvaviniścaya," refutes both the existence of the absolute and the nonexistence of the conventional, both seminal Yogācāra positions.

He is also the forerunner of the literary style known as *siddhānta* (Tib., *grub-mtha'*), which became enormously popular within Tibetan scholarly circles. A *siddhānta* text devotes ordered chapters to analyzing the philosophic positions *(siddhāntas)* of rival schools, both Buddhist and Hindu. His *Tarkajvālā* contains systematic critiques of the positions held by the Hīnayāna and the Yogācāra, both Buddhist schools, and the Sāṃkhya, Vaiśeṣika, Vedānta, and Mīmāṃsā schools of Hindu philosophy.

Bhāvaviveka was also a keen historian. His *Nikāyabhedavibhaṅgavyākhyāna* remains one of our most important and reliable sources for the early history of the Buddhist order, and for information on the schisms within its ranks.

[*See also* Mādhyamika.]

BIBLIOGRAPHY

The most important philosophical works by Bhāvaviveka are his commentary on Nāgārjuna's *Mūlamadhyamakakārikā*, the *Prajñāpradīpa;* his verse work, the *Madhyamakahṛdayakārikā*, with the autocommentary the *Tarkajvālā;* his *Madhyamārthasaṅgraha;* and his *Karatalaratna*. All these works can be found in volumes 95 and 96 of *The Tibetan Tripiṭaka*, edited by D. T. Suzuki (Tokyo, 1962). Bhāvaviveka's work on the history of the Buddhist order, the *Nikāyabhedavibhaṅgavyākhyāna,* is included in volume 127.

Bhāvaviveka's biography can be found in Khetsun Sangpo's *Rgya gar paṇ chen rnams kyi rnam thar ngo mtshar padmo'i 'dzum zhal gsar pa* (Dharamsala, India, 1973). Perhaps the most definitive study of Bhāvaviveka is Malcolm David Eckel's "A Question of Nihilism: Bhāvaviveka's Response to the Fundamental Problems of Mādhyamika Philosophy" (Ph.D. diss., Harvard University, 1980). Shotaro Iida's *Reason and Emptiness: A Study in Logic and Mysticism* (Tokyo, 1980) studies Bhāvaviveka from the perspective of medieval Tibetan sources. Louis de La Vallée Poussin's essay "Bhāvaviveka," in volume 2 of *Mélanges chinois et bouddhiques* (Brussels, 1933), pp. 60–67, is the statement of classical Buddhology on the subject. Kajiyama Yuichi's "Bhāvaviveka and the Prāsaṅgika School," *Nava-Nalanda-Mahavihara Research Publication* 1 (n.d.): 289–331; my own "An Appraisal of the Svātantrika-Prāsaṃgika Debates," *Philosophy East and West* 26 (1976): 253–267; Peter Della Santina's "The Division of the Mādhyamika System into the Prāsaṅgika and Svātantrika Schools," *Journal of Religious Studies* 7 (1979): 40–49; and Ichimura Shohei's "A New Approach to the Intra-Mādhyamika Confrontation over the Svātantrika and Prāsaṅgika Methods of Refutation," *Journal of the International Association of Buddhist Studies* 5 (1982): 41–52, exemplify contemporary scholarship. One important source was unavailable to this author: Donald Lopez's "The Svātantrika-Mādhyamika School of Mahāyāna Buddhism" (Ph.D. diss., University of Virginia, 1982).

NATHAN KATZ

BHAVE, VINOBA (1895–1982), Indian social and religious reformer. Vinayak Narhari Bhave was closely associated with Mohandas Gandhi, who bestowed upon him the affectionate epithet Vinoba (Mar., "brother Vino"). He is generally acclaimed in India as the one who "stepped into Gandhi's shoes." As a young man Bhave studied Sanskrit and the Hindu religious tradition in Varanasi. It was here that he read accounts of Gandhi's patriotic speeches. Attracted by Gandhi's ideas, Bhave joined Gandhi as his disciple in 1916 and soon became one of his close associates. In 1921 Gandhi had Bhave move to a new ashram (retreat center) in Wardha in the state of Maharashtra. Here he began experimenting with many Gandhian ideas designed to implement self-rule for India. His main goal was to engage in village service for the benefit of the Indian masses. As a result, he became a skillful farmer, spinner, weaver, and scavenger. Many of these activities were later incorporated into several of his plans for the moral and spiritual uplift of all humanity. Impressed with his political and religious dedication, his spiritual way of life, and his belief in nonviolent methods of social action, Gandhi chose him in 1940 as the first *satyāgrahī* (one who uses nonviolent means to bring the opponent to the point of seeing the truth) in a protest against British rule.

After India's independence Bhave emerged from the shadow of his teacher as he began his *pad yātrā* ("journey on foot") to meet the people of India. The famous Bhoodān ("land gift") movement was born when on one such journey he sought a donation of land in order to distribute it among the landless poor. Later he designed a program to collect fifty million acres of land for the landless. For the rest of his life, he tirelessly worked for *grām swarāj* ("village self-rule") to free the people from the rich and the powerful. He retreated to his ashram in Paunar, near Wardha, in 1970 and died there in 1982.

Influences. Bhave's influence was greatest in his promotion of Gandhian principles. He became the chief exponent of the Sarvodaya ("welfare of all") movement and executed Gandhi's nonviolent philosophy through a series of activities known as "constructive works." These included such programs as promotion of *khādī* ("self-spun cloth"), *naī talīm* ("new education"), *strī śakti* ("woman power"), cow protection, and *śānti senā* ("peace brigade"). He created the Sarva Seva Sangha ("society for the service of all") in order to carry out the work of Sarvodaya, and served as its spiritual adviser. Bhave also launched a series of movements connected with the Land Gift movement in order to tackle the problem of exploitation of the farmers by their landlords. Although through these movements he sought to accomplish socioeconomic reform, for him they were part of a spiritual struggle to establish *rām rāj* ("kingdom of God") through *grām swarāj.* To this end, he adopted and promoted the Gandhian model of Sarvodaya. Bhave took the concept of "giving" *(dān)* further and asked that people donate their money, labor, intellect, and life for the work of Sarvodaya.

Bhave organized village councils (*grām sabhās*) to oversee the village development program. His aim was not only to bring self-sufficiency to the villages but also to establish a nonviolent society based on religious ideals. Through the constructive programs of Sarvodaya, Bhave sought to create a moral force in Indian society. The aim of his movement was not to promote the greatest good for the greatest number, but the greatest good for all people. The goal of Sarvodaya philosophy can be summarized as follows: in the social realm it advocates a casteless society, in politics it shares a democratic vision of the power of the people, in economics it promotes the belief that "small is beautiful," and in religion it asks for tolerance for all faiths. Its final goal is to promote peace for all mankind.

The failure of many of Bhave's plans to come to fruition ultimately led to dissension in the Sarvodaya. In the 1960s Jai Prakash Narayan, a Marxist-turned-Gandhian activist and an associate of Bhave, sought to steer the Sarvodaya movement in other directions. The controversy arose over the issue of whether Sarvodaya workers should participate in politics in order to initiate change in Indian society. Disenchanted with Bhave's nonpartisan religious approach and the slow moving program of *grām swarāj*, Narayan began taking an active part in contemporary politics. By the 1970s this led to a serious split within the organization of the Sarva Seva Sangha (the work agency of Sarvodaya) and the parting of ways of these two giants of the Gandhian movement. The conflict brought into focus various ideological differences that existed within the Sarvodaya movement. However, Bhave's supporters continued to maintain that his was a movement to "change the hearts of the people" through moral force and nonpartisan alliances. Since Bhave's death, many programs for social reform are still being carried out within the Sarvodaya movement by the *lok sevaks* ("servants of the people") whom he inspired.

[*See also the biography of Gandhi.*]

BIBLIOGRAPHY

Vinoba Bhave wrote relatively few books. However, many of his talks and speeches have been compiled into books and pamphlets. Most of these works are published by the Sarva Seva Sangha. The majority of his writings deal with the Bhoodān and Grāmdān movements, but he also wrote on a variety of topics related to Sarvodaya. His major English titles include *Bhoodan Yajna* (Ahmedabad, 1953), *Swaraj Sastra: The Principles of a Non-Violent Political Order*, translated by Bharatan Kumarappa (Wardha, 1955), *From Bhoodan to Gramdan* (Tanjore, 1957), *Thoughts on Education*, translated by Marjorie Sykes (Madras, 1959), *Talks on the Gita* (New York, 1960), *Democratic Values* (Kashi, 1962), and *Steadfast Wisdom*, translated by Lila Ray (Varanasi, 1966).

There are numerous secondary sources on Bhave. For a detailed biography, *Vinoba: His Life and Work* (Bombay, 1970) by Shriman Narayan is considered most authoritative. *Vinoba and His Mission* (Kashi, 1954) by Suresh Ramabhai is less biographical, but it gives a thorough description of the origin and progress of the movement started by Bhave. Vasant Nargolkar's *The Creed of Saint Vinoba* (Bombay, 1963) attempts to analyze Sarvodaya as interpreted by Vinoba. Among recent works, *Selections From Vinoba*, edited by Vishwanath Tandon (Varanasi, 1981), presents the "essential Vinoba." Finally, *Vinoba: The Spiritual Revolutionary*, edited by R. R. Diwakar and Mahendra Agrawal (New Delhi, 1984), presents Vinoba Bhave as others see him. It contains a series of articles by several scholars and close associates of Bhave covering a variety of topics dealing with Vinoba Bhave's thought.

ISHWAR C. HARRIS

BIBLICAL EXEGESIS. [*This entry consists of two articles, on Jewish and Christian traditions of biblical interpretation. Articles related to Jewish exegesis of the Bible are* Torah; Talmud; Midrash and Aggadah; *and* Qabbalah. *For philosophical discussion of critical approaches to texts, see* Hermeneutics. *See also the biographies of numerous biblical exegetes mentioned herein.*]

Jewish Views

The shift from rabbinic hermeneutics to medieval exegesis is marked by discrimination between different types of interpretation. It has been suggested, though not established, that this occurred, in the Arabic-speaking world, under the impetus of Karaism which, by rejecting the authority of rabbinic tradition, forced proponents and opponents alike to consider the literal meaning of the biblical text. The development of Arabic grammar and rhetoric may also have encouraged systematic study of the literal meaning.

The first major figure of medieval biblical exegesis is the Babylonian rabbinic leader Sa'adyah Gaon (d. 942), who, like his successors, engaged in translation into Arabic and commentary written in the same language. Sa'adyah insisted on literal interpretation, but discussed four circumstances in which deviation from the obvious literal meaning of the biblical text is justified: (1) when the literal meaning contradicts reason (e.g., "God is a consuming fire" [*Dt.* 4:24] must be interpreted metaphorically); (2) when the literal meaning contradicts sense-experience (e.g., Eve was not the "mother of all living beings" [*Gn.* 3:21] but rather the mother of human life; (3) when the literal meaning contradicts another biblical passage (e.g., "Thou shalt not test the

Lord" seemingly contradicts "Test me and see," thus necessitating reinterpretation); (4) when the literal meaning contradicts the oral tradition (e.g., "Thou shalt not seethe a kid in its mother's milk" [*Ex.* 23:19, 34:26; *Dt.* 14:21] is to be interpreted in conformity with the rabbinic view that this verse refers to all cooking of milk with meat).

The polemical thrust in Sa'adyah's exegesis manifests itself in various ways. For example, his insistence that *Psalms* is a prophetic rather than a devotional book is meant to controvert Karaite dismissal of rabbinic liturgy as a superfluous innovation.

Sa'adyah and the writers who succeeded him over the next century, under the sway of Islam, were to a great degree eclipsed, whether because they wrote in Arabic rather than Hebrew or as a result of their prolixity, by the popularity of Avraham ibn 'Ezra'. In fact, what influence they exerted was largely due to their citation by Ibn 'Ezra'. Included among these are commentators like Shemu'el ben Ḥofni (d. 1013), Yehudah ibn Bal'am, Mosheh ha-Kohen ibn Giqatilla; grammarians like Yehudah ibn Hayyuj and Yonah ibn Jannaḥ; and Karaite exegetes like Yefet ben 'Eli, who are generally treated neutrally by Ibn 'Ezra', except with regard to crucial polemical texts such as *Leviticus* 23:15, which divided the Karaites from the Rabbinites.

The peripatetic Ibn 'Ezra' wrote on almost all of the Bible, often writing multiple commentaries on the same book, not all of which have been published. Occasionally engaging in philosophical asides (e.g., *Ecclesiastes* 5 and 7), he is nonetheless committed to the straightforward interpretation of the text, governed by the principles of grammar. He is often skeptical of Midrashic elaboration upon the narrative, typically remarking, "If it is a tradition, we shall accept it." Regarding legal matters, he asserts his agreement with the oral law whenever its views are no less plausible than possible alternatives; otherwise, he accepts the oral law only as a normative legal tradition that has been attached to the verse.

The quest for exegetical simplicity led Ibn 'Ezra' to criticize some earlier approaches to the text. Thus he rejects Ibn Jannaḥ's view that the same Hebrew word can express contradictory meanings, as well as his willingness to transpose words or to substitute words for those in the text. By the same token, he sees no need to employ the rabbinic listing of *tiqqunei soferim* (euphemistic emendations of phrases referring to God). He is troubled neither by variations of phrase, so long as the meaning is conserved (for example, he considers the differences between *Exodus* 20 and *Deuteronomy* 4 insignificant), nor by orthographical inconsistencies.

Ibn 'Ezra' has been regarded as a precursor of the Higher Criticism which began with Barukh Spinoza (1632–1677). Several cryptic passages in his commentary (e.g., on *Gn.* 12:7, *Dt.* 1:2) allude to anachronisms in the Torah that have since been interpreted either as signs of a post-Mosaic hand (as first suggested by Yosef Bonfils in the fourteenth century) or as consequences of prophetic familiarity with the future. Attention has also been given his obscure remarks about the postexilic historical setting of *Isaiah* 40–66.

Franco-German Exegesis. The commentary of Rashi (Shelomoh ben Yitsḥaq, 1040–1105) to the Torah is the most influential work of Jewish exegesis. Combining philological sensitivity with generous quotations from rabbinic literature, it became, at the popular level, almost inseparable from the biblical text itself: until the nineteenth century no text of the Pentateuch was published with any commentary that did not include Rashi's as well. Rashi's popularity, as well as his laconic presentation, inspired hundreds of supercommentaries. The most important of these (e.g., Eliyyahu Mizraḥi and Yehudah Löw in the sixteenth century, David ha-Levi in the seventeenth, and the eclectic Shabbetai Bass) constitute a significant contribution to biblical exegesis in their own right. The contemporary leader of Lubavitch Hasidism, Menaḥem Mendel Schneersohn, has devoted the lion's share of his voluminous output to an investigation of Rashi's nuances.

Rashi several times distinguishes the literal meaning *(peshaṭ)* from the homiletical *(derash)*, identifying his own method, despite its heavy use of *aggadah*, with the former (e.g., on *Gn.* 3:8). His interpreters have generally inferred from this that all comments not explicitly labeled as Midrashic (and perhaps even these) are evoked by some peculiarity in the text that Rashi seeks to resolve. Reworking of and deviation from standard rabbinic exegesis occur both in narrative and in legal passages (for the latter, see, for example, *Exodus* 23:2). In his philology, Rashi is limited by his dependence on those grammarians who wrote in Hebrew (Menaḥem ben Saruq and Dunash ibn Labrat), employing, for example, the doctrine of the two-letter root, later superseded by the idea of a three-letter root. Among Rashi's predecessors, mention must also be made of Menaḥem ben Ḥelbo.

Among Rashi's contemporaries and successors, Yosef Qara' and Shemu'el ben Meir (Rashbam) are the most influential. The latter, who was Rashi's grandson, reflected on the innovation in the study of *peshaṭ* (see digression at *Genesis* 37:2): earlier generations, in their piety, had been concerned with the legal and moral lessons of scripture, leaving room for the "ever new facets of *peshaṭ* that are every day discovered." Rashbam is more reluctant than Rashi to erect his exegesis on rabbinic tradition, and he is more prone to seek exegetical alternatives in the legal passages (e.g., his preface to *Exodus* 21). Thus he asserts that day precedes night in *Genesis* 1:5, in contradiction to the halakhic exegetical tradition.

Other Franco-German scholars of note are Yosef Bekhor Shor, Eli'ezer of Beaugency, and Rashbam's brother Ya'aqov Tam (primarily for his grammatical remarks). Their works were overshadowed by Rashi's and did not enjoy wide circulation. More often republished are various collections of tosafistic exegetical works (e.g., *Da'at zeqenim*) that are homiletical in nature and often refer to Rashi. Also noteworthy are the many biblical exegetical comments found in *tosafot* to the Talmud. A significant manifestation of biblical study is found in Jewish-Christian polemical literature, such as the anonymous *Sefer nitstsaḥon yashan.*

Medieval Philosophical Exegesis. Philosophical concerns play a role in the work of Sa'adyah (who participates in Kalam philosophy) and the Neoplatonist Ibn 'Ezra'. Baḥye ibn Paquda's ethical treatise *Duties of the Heart* and Yehudah ha-Levi's *Kuzari* also contain remarks pertinent to biblical study. It is, however, with the *Guide of the Perplexed* of Moses Maimonides (Mosheh ben Maimon, 1135/8–1204) that the philosophical approach to scripture becomes central. Maimonides' doctrine of religious language leads him to reinterpret anthropomorphisms and anthropopathisms more rigorously than his predecessors. In addition to his interpretations of such sections as *Genesis* 1, *Ezekiel* 1, and *Job,* his concern for the symbolic functions of biblical imagery finds expression in an elaborate doctrine of prophecy and a tendency to allegorize many narratives. Lastly, his views on the "reasons for the commandments" occasionally emphasize the literal sense of the text at the expense of its normative application (e.g., the literalist rationale for the *lex talionis* in *Guide* 3.41), and more than occasionally justify the commandments in utilitarian terms relevant to the historical situation of Israel at the time of Moses (e.g., the purpose of the incense is fumigation of the Temple; many sacrificial and agricultural commandments are intended to counteract idolatrous practices).

The philosophical emphasis in Jewish biblical commentary flourished during the thirteenth to fifteenth centuries. Maimonides' views spread in commentaries on the Prophets and *Psalms* written by both David Kimḥi (known as Radaq, early thirteenth century) and Menaḥem Me'iri (late thirteenth century) of Provence. His terminology and concerns deeply affect the work of the antiphilosopher Yitsḥaq Arama (early fifteenth century) and the more ambivalent exegete and commentator on the *Guide,* Isaac Abravanel. Maimonides is also discussed by Moses Nahmanides (Mosheh ben Naḥman, thirteenth-century Spain) and the exegetical tradition stemming from him. Yosef Albo's *Sefer ha-'iqqarim* (Book of Principles), in which the greatest doctrinal affinity is to Albo's teacher Ḥasdai Crescas, a trenchant critic of Maimonides, should be cited for several homiletical sections.

The prolific Yosef ibn Kaspi (fourteenth-century Provence and Spain) displays a Maimonidean interest in the allegorization of prophetic stories (e.g., Jonah and the fish) along with strikingly original speculations (e.g., on the differences between *Samuel, Kings,* and *Chronicles*).

Levi ben Gershom (Gersonides, fourteenth-century Provence), a major Jewish philosopher, and more consistent an Aristotelian than Maimonides, is a major biblical commentator as well. Limiting divine providence, he offered rationalistic explanations of the stopping of the sun by Joshua and maintained that it was not Lot's wife but Sodom that became a pillar of salt. Like Maimonides before him, he interprets the *Song of Songs* as an allegory of God and the individual soul, not, as Rashi and Ibn 'Ezra' did, as an allegory of God's relationship with the Jewish people. Following Maimonides, he unraveled the speeches of Job and his friends as presentations of philosophical positions on providence. Gersonides affixed to his commentaries a list of *to'aliyyot* ("lessons") to be derived from scripture.

Eclectic Commentaries: Thirteenth–Fifteenth Centuries. David Kimḥi combines philological-grammatical perspicuity with liberal quotations from rabbinic literature, discussions of the Targum and its variants, fealty to Maimonides, and references to Rashi, Ibn 'Ezra', Yosef Kimḥi, who was his father, and his brother Mosheh (author of pseudo-Ibn 'Ezra' on *Proverbs* and *Ezra-Nehemiah).* Given the paucity of Rashi on Prophets, it is not surprising that Kimḥi is perhaps the most popular of medieval exegetes on the Prophets. A polemical contention with Christianity frequently comes to the fore, for example, contra the christological reading of the Immanuel prophecy (*Is.* 7). He evinces serious concern for variations in the received Masoretic text.

Nahmanides, like Rashi, is a major Talmudist who devoted himself to a commentary on the Torah; its impact over the centuries is second only to Rashi's. He attends to philology and law and comments on theological issues and psychological factors. Reaching the Land of Israel in his old age, he is occasionally able to draw upon an acquaintance with its geography and *realia.* A qabbalist, he is the first major commentator in whose work qabbalistic hints are common. Thus, by the fourteenth century, in the aftermath of Maimonides and Nahmanides, we encounter the fourfold division of biblical interpretation—PaRDeS—in which *remez* (hint) and *sod* (esoterica) join the familiar *peshaṭ* and *derash.* Nahmanides frequently quotes and discusses Rashi, particularly in legal sections, less frequently, Ibn ʿEzra', toward whom he adopts an attitude of "open rebuke and hidden love." He cites Maimonides, sometimes lauding his views, but on several crucial matters he disagrees sharply, for example, on the meaning of the sacrificial cult (*Lv.* 1:9) and the role of angels in prophecy (*Gn.* 18:1).

Nahmanides also employs typological interpretation to explain apparent superfluities in *Genesis.* While this method has its roots in Midrash ("the acts of the fathers are a sign for the sons"), it does not enjoy the popularity among Jewish medieval commentators that it attained in Christian exegesis. Of the Spanish commentators of import who flourished in the fourteenth and fifteenth centuries, several were strongly influenced by Nahmanides. Baḥye ben Asher includes a larger quota of homiletical and qabbalistic material. Yaʿaqov ben Asher's *Perush ha-ṭur ha-arokh* avoids such digressions. Nissim of Gerona, whose *12 Derashot* (Twelve Homilies) and commentary to *Genesis* 1–23 are occasionally critical of Nahmanides, nonetheless belongs to his sphere of influence.

Isaac Abravanel (Spain and Italy, d. 1508) represents the last stage of classic medieval commentary. Loquacious in style, he makes liberal use of the work of his predecessors, ranging over the philological, philosophical, and homiletical approaches. His psychological-political sense is keen; his philosophy, while tending toward fideism, is rooted in an extended and passionate involvement with Maimonides' *Guide;* philological originality, however, is not his strong suit. His prefaces to the biblical books are more elaborate than his predecessors', often devoting detailed attention to the authorship and provenance of the text; here he is willing to challenge rabbinic ascriptions, for example, attributing the *Book of Joshua* to Samuel instead of Joshua.

Abravanel makes use of such Christian scholars as Jerome and Nicholas of Lyra. His piety finds clear expression in his eschatological emphasis. Against Ibn Giqatilla, who interpreted most prophecies of redemption as references to the Second Temple period, and Ibn ʿEzra', who took a middle view, Abravanel is eager to read all such prophecies as messianic and is quick to respond to christological interpretations (e.g., *Is.* 7, 34).

The Sixteenth–Eighteenth Centuries. The centuries following the expulsion of the Jews from Spain have been erroneously characterized as a stagnant era for Jewish biblical study. Moshe Segal, in his survey of Jewish Bible study, includes only the *Metsuddat David* and *Metsuddat Tsion* (by the Altschuler family, late seventeenth-century Germany), a generally unoriginal selection from Rashi, Ibn ʿEzra', and Kimḥi that became a standard accompaniment to the study of the Prophets and Hagiographa. Jewish exegesis of this period, unlike that of Rashi, Ibn ʿEzra', Maimonides, and Kimḥi, does not exercise an impact on Christian scholarship. It innovates little of value as regards philology and grammar, beyond the achievements of the medievals (more specifically, the eleventh–thirteenth centuries). Moreover, the lack of willingness to develop alternatives to previous commentaries and rabbinic tradition brings innovation in reading the legal sections to a virtual standstill (despite the isolated examples culled by contemporary scholars). Typical of this change, which reflects the failure of the leading Talmudists of the period to make the Bible a major preoccupation, is Ibn Kaspi's preface to *Exodus* 21, in which he disclaims his own competence and defers to Rashi's exegesis of the legal matters.

Pace Segal, however, one cannot gainsay several contributions of the period. ʿOvadyah Sforno (sixteenth-century Italy), writing on the Torah and other biblical books, stresses both literal and philosophical interpretation. He follows Nahmanides in regarding the stories of *Genesis* as a typological "blueprint" of history. He is particularly concerned about the placement of legal sections among narrative units (e.g., the laws pertinent to the Land of Israel that follow the story of the spies, *Nm.* 15). Other major figures generally present their comments within a homiletical framework, with a not-infrequent mystical tendency. Efrayim of Luntshits's *Keli yaqar,* the work of a sixteenth-century Polish preacher, and the mystically oriented *Or ha-ḥayyim* of Ḥayyim ibn Attar (eighteenth-century Morocco) have become enshrined in many editions of *Miqra'ot gedolot,* the standard rabbinical Bible textbook, as have excerpts from the commentaries of the sixteenth-century Greek preacher Mosheh Alshekh. The aforementioned works find their continuation in nineteenth- and twentieth-century homiletical literature, of which the most outstanding examples are the classic works of the Hasidic movement, such as Yaʿaqov Yosef of Polonnoye's *Toledot Yaʿaqov Yosef* and Elimelekh of Lizhensk's *Noʿam Elimelekh* in the eighteenth century, and *Sefat emet* (by Alter of Gur) or *Shem mi-Shemu'el* (by Shemu'el of Sochatchov) in the late nineteenth to early twentieth century.

It should be noted that this period also marks the heyday of the major supercommentaries on Rashi, which apparently offered an outlet to rabbis interested in extending the medieval methods of study.

Traditional Developments in the Modern Period. Beginning in the late eighteenth century there is a renewal of interest, evident from several Torah commentaries, in the interaction between traditional rabbinic exegesis and extra-traditional exegesis. This renewal may derive from increased availabililty of the full panoply of rabbinic exegesis (i.e., *Sifra'*, *Mekhilta'*, *Sifrei*, the Jerusalem Talmud, and eventually *Mekhilta' de Rabbi Shim'on* and *Sifrei Zuṭa'*), which drew attention to hermeneutical results other than those preserved in the Babylonian Talmud. Whatever its sources, it is clearly motivated by a desire to defend the authenticity of the oral law against its skeptical ("enlightened" or Reform) detractors by showing the connection between the "text and tradition" (the title of Ya'aqov Mecklenburg's nineteenth-century commentary *Ketav ve-ha-qabbalah*).

One may distinguish between two types of works produced by these authors. The eastern Europeans, such as Eliyyahu ben Shelomoh Zalman, known as the gaon of Vilna (now Vilnius; d. 1796), Naftali Tsevi Berlin (d. 1892), and Me'ir Simḥah of Dvinsk (now Daugavpils; d. 1926) often present their own novel interpretations. Those who were most exposed to the aforementioned external challenges, in Germany (Mecklenberg and Samson Raphael Hirsch) or Romania (Malbim), are reluctant to propose legal interpretations contrary to tradition. Eliyyahu ben Shelomoh Zalman's treatment of the Bible is displayed in his commentary to *Proverbs*, to sections of other books, and in notes to others. He seeks an integration of all dimensions of Torah study, from the literal to the mystical. This involves the unification of oral and written laws but also precipitates an awareness of the differences between them. As an example of the latter one may point to his comment on *Leviticus* 16, where he recognizes two strata: 1–28 (referring to Aaron and oblivious to the Day of Atonement) and 29–34 (referring to the high priest and specifying the Day of Atonement). Both are, of course, Mosaic: the former pertaining to Aaron's priesthood; the latter, to the period after his death. Like his eastern European successors, he interprets many verses as allusions to the value of Torah study.

Berlin, in his *Ha'ameq davar* on Torah as well as his commentaries to halakhic *midrashim* and the *Shei'ltot* of Aḥa'i Gaon (eighth century), continues to cultivate both the unification and differentiation of *peshaṭ* and *derash*. His work on narrative sections is distinguished by psychological perspicuity that is enhanced rather than diminished by his reliance on the qabbalistic typology that identifies the patriarchs with particular *sefirot*. Me'ir Simḥah's *Meshekh ḥokhmah* is valued both for its insightful homiletical pieces and for his comments on, and alternatives to, classic rabbinic tradition.

Connected with these developments are such works as Barukh Epstein's *Torah temimah*, an anthology of rabbinic material with eclectic notes (1903) and Menaḥem Mendel Kasher's *Torah shelemah*, a heavily annotated encyclopedia work of the same nature. In addition one must note the aforementioned Hasidic exegesis and the homiletical literature produced by the Musar movement (e.g., Natan Finkel's *Or ha-tsafun)*, generally interpreting the text in the light of Midrash to derive a lesson illustrative of rigorous moral standards. There is also a quasi-exegetical literature seizing the text as an opportunity for halakhic analysis (e.g., *Beit ha-Levi* by the nineteenth-century Yosef Dov Soloveichik; *Tsafenat pa'aneaḥ* by the early-twentieth-century Yosef Rosin). Samson Raphael Hirsch, who as rabbi in Frankfort contended with Reform, maintained in his German commentaries to Torah and *Psalms* that the written law was dependent on the oral, as a set of notes is dependent on the lecture. Rabbinic hermeneutic, then, is less a matter of correct philology than of access to a code. In seeking to interpret the text, both narrative and legal, and justify tradition regarding the latter, Hirsch resorted to an idiosyncratic etymological method (occasionally used by Mecklenberg as well), whereby phonetically similar consonants are interchanged in order to locate the "essential" meaning of the word. Hirsch strongly criticized Maimonides' approach to "reasons for the commandments." Instead he offered a system of symbolic interpretation in which, for example, the upper half of the altar represents the higher nature of man, while the lower half symbolizes the lower aspects of human nature. Hirsch's rationales, unlike those dominant in the medieval literature, sought to explain not only the general purpose of the laws but their particular features as well, including those that are derived through rabbinic interpretation.

In contrast with Hirsch, Malbim proclaimed rabbinic hermeneutics to be the correct grammar of biblical Hebrew. From his premise about the perfection of biblical Hebrew he concludes that the Bible contains no redundancies of style or language: every seeming redundancy must be explained. Thus, Malbim (following Eliyyahu ben Shelomoh Zalmon and others) discovers many fine distinctions among the synonyms in biblical parallelism, rejecting the approach of Kimḥi and the *Metsuddot* that "the content is repeated in different words." Malbim's identification of rabbinic exegesis with philology is symbolized in his commentary to biblical law, where his independent commentary becomes, instead, a commentary to the corpus of halakhic *midrashim*, insofar as the latter provides the literal meaning of scripture.

Illustrative of the differences between Malbim and

some of his major medieval predecessors is his treatment of *qeri* (vocalization) and *ketiv* (Masoretic text). Ibn ʿEzraʾ had viewed the *qeri* as instructive of how the *ketiv* is to be read. Kimḥi had proposed that *qeri/ketiv* in the Prophets generally reflects alternative textual traditions, both of which were retained by the editors ("the men of the Great Assembly") out of uncertainty. Abravanel had gone so far as to suggest that the plethora of *qeri/ketiv* in *Jeremiah* derives from that prophet's orthographic deficiencies. For Malbim, however, both *qeri* and *ketiv* are divinely ordained and so must be interpreted.

Both Hirsch and Malbim had enough awareness of biblical criticism to address such problems as the doublets in biblical narrative through literary analysis. They are both oblivious, however, to the data provided by comparative Semitics or knowledge of the ancient Near East. David Tsevi Hoffmann (d. 1922), the last great traditional biblical exegete of western Europe, is fully aware of contemporary biblical scholarship and its ancillary disciplines. In his German commentaries to *Leviticus, Deuteronomy,* and *Genesis* and in *Die wichtigsten Instanzen gegen die Graf-Wellhausensche Hypothese* he marshaled his arguments against non-Mosaic dating of the Torah. A leading Talmudic authority, he concentrated on biblical law, attempting to establish that the laws ascribed to the P and D sources could best be understood within the context of Israel's desert experience, in the order narrated by the Torah, and that these laws were available in their present form during the First Temple period.

Enlightenment and Its Aftermath. The second half of the eighteenth century also marks the entry of Jewish exegesis into the world of general European culture. The founding father of the Jewish Enlightenment was Moses Mendelssohn (d. 1786), whose elegant German translation of the Torah was the first by Jewish hands; the translation was accompanied by a commentary (the *Bi'ur*) authored by Mendelssohn and his associates. This commentary follows in the footsteps of the classical medieval exegetes but is quite conservative in accepting rabbinic tradition regarding the legal sections; it is also concerned with aesthetic features of the text. That the *Bi'ur* was banned in many Orthodox circles had little to do with its content.

Nineteenth-century scholars like the Italian Samuel David Luzzatto (d. 1865) accepted the principles of contemporary biblical scholarship—up to a point—reluctant as they were to apply critical results to the text of the Torah. Luzzatto was willing to propose emendations outside the Torah. He stoutly resisted the thesis of postexilic authorship for *Isaiah* 40–66 on internal, not merely theological, grounds (though, by the turn of the century, Hoffmann's Orthodox colleague Jakob Barth recognized internal evidence for the later dating). Resistance to the Documentary Hypothesis continued, beyond Orthodox circles, into the twentieth century. The German Liberal rabbi Benno Jacob insisted on the literary integrity of the Torah and rejected textual emendation. The notes to British Chief Rabbi Joseph Hertz's popular English translation of the Pentateuch contain a lively attack on Higher Criticism. Umberto Cassuto and Moshe Segal, both professors at the Hebrew University in Jerusalem, rejected the Documentary Hypothesis without accepting the Orthodox position: Cassuto spoke of the post-Mosaic writing down of oral traditions, while Segal posited a significant number of interpolations. Their stances have been furthered by their more conservative student Y. M. Grintz. Such views maintain an attraction and influence among Jewish students of the Bible.

Contemporary Trends. Philosophical and literary contributions have also affected contemporary study. Yeḥezkel Kaufmann's insistence on the radical success of biblical monotheism is a theological as well as historical thesis. The literary sensitivity exhibited by Martin Buber and Franz Rosenzweig's German translation, particularly the notion of *Leitworten,* and Buber's own biblical studies have exerted an important influence, as has Me'ir Weiss's method of "total-interpretation." It is too early to assess the impact of Abraham Joshua Heschel's *The Prophets,* André Neher's theological studies, or Joseph B. Soloveitchik's (mostly unpublished) existential homilies.

The last generation has also seen a revival of interest, on the part of Jewish biblical scholars, in traditional exegesis. The teaching and writing of Nehama Leibowitz have made the traditional corpus attractive beyond the Orthodox camp. This development has further encouraged literary and theological concerns. It is not surprising to find scholars like Moshe Greenberg and Uriel Simon who, like Segal before them, combine research in the Bible with research in the history of exegesis. Thus the turn toward literature and, to a lesser extent, theology and the significant place accorded to Jewish exegesis have created a scholarly style that transcends, to some degree, the gap in belief between Orthodox and non-Orthodox.

Within the modern Orthodox community, two developments must be marked. The *Daʿat miqraʾ* series (which does not include the Torah) offers a semipopular commentary that incorporates the data of modern investigations into the framework of traditional scholarship. The somewhat idiosyncratic work of Mordecai

Breuer proclaims that the Torah, from a human point of view, speaks in multiple voices whose relation to one another must be clarified, along the lines of Hoffmann. Breuer also seeks to investigate textual variants with an eye to grasping the meaning of the canonized text.

BIBLIOGRAPHY

While several modern exegetical works have appeared in Western languages, such as those of Samson Raphael Hirsch and David Hoffmann, which were published in German, most of the primary literature has appeared in Hebrew. However, several primary sources are available in English translation. A mildly bowdlerized translation of Rashi's commentary on the Pentateuch was prepared and annotated by M. Rosenbaum and A. M. Silbermann under the title *Pentateuch with Targum Onkelos, Haphtaroth and Rashi's Commentary,* 5 vols. (New York,1934). C. B. Chavel's *Ramban (Nachmanides): Commentary on the Torah,* 5 vols. (New York, 1971–1976) is a complete and annotated translation of Nahmanides' commentary on the Pentateuch.

Other medieval biblical exegetes whose works have been translated into English include Avraham ibn 'Ezra' on *Isaiah (The Commentary of Ibn Ezra on Isaiah,* translated by Michael Friedländer, vol. 1, London, 1873); David Kimḥi's commentary on *Isaiah (The Commentary of David Kimhi on Isaiah* (1926), translated by Louis Finkelstein, reprinted, New York, 1966), as well as his work on *Hosea (The Commentary of Rabbi David Kimhi on Hosea* (1929), translated by Harry Cohen, reprinted, New York, 1965), and on *Psalms,* chaps. 120–150 (*The Commentary of Rabbi David Kimḥi on Psalms CXX–CL,* translated by Joshua Baker and E. W. Nicholson, Cambridge, 1973); Levi ben Gershom's commentary on *Job (Commentary of Levi ben Gerson on the Book of Job,* translated by A. L. Lassen, New York, 1946).

A complete listing of all editions of exegetical works written prior to 1540 is to be found in M. Kasher and Jacob B. Mandelbaum's *Sarei ha-elef,* 2d ed., 2 vols. (Jerusalem, 1978). Nehama Leibowitz's studies on each book of the Pentateuch have been translated into English and adapted by Aryeh Newman in six volumes (Jerusalem, 1972–1980) and provide an excellent guide to traditional Jewish commentary. Moshe Greenberg's *Understanding Exodus* (New York, 1969) integrates a generous amount of traditional exegesis.

Moshe Segal's *Parshanut ha-miqra',* 2d ed. (Jerusalem, 1971) is a fine survey of Jewish exegesis. Ezra Zion Melamed's *Mefarshei ha-miqra',* 2 vols. (Jerusalem, 1975), covers Rashi, Shemu'el ben Me'ir, Ibn 'Ezra', Kimḥi, Nahmanides, and the exegesis of rabbinic Targum in detail.

Some aspects of exegesis between Sa'adyah and Ibn 'Ezra' are dealt with by Uriel Simon in *Arba' gishot le-sefer Tehillim* (Ramat Gan, Israel, 1982). The exegesis of the medieval Franco-German Jewish scholars is described by Samuel Pozanański in his edition of Eli'ezer of Beaugency's *Perush Yeḥezqe'l ve-Terei 'Asar* (Warsaw, 1909).

An extensive bibliography of recent literature can be found in the *Entsiqeloppedyah miqra'it* (Jerusalem, 1982), in the lengthy entry on biblical exegesis that appears in volume 8 (pp. 649–737).

Shalom Carmy

Christian Views

As distinct from hermeneutical theory, which deals primarily with the phenomenon of understanding, biblical exegesis has to do with the methods and approaches used to explain a text. The value that interpreters attach to a document will determine the method of exegesis used. For example, a historical interest is attentive to such exegetical concerns as archaeological lore, grammatical and lexical data, exploration of sources, and the author's intention. Determination of the literal sense, or the "letter" of scripture, is traditionally associated with one or more facets of such approaches and in modern times is loosely linked with the terms *grammatical-historical* or *historical-critical.* On the other hand, interest in the biblical text as an instrument of contemporary instruction has led to emphasis on theological or life-related matters. In ancient times, this approach was understood as concern for the spiritual sense, and during most of the pre-Reformation era it found expression in allegorical method. In modern times, developments in linguistics and literary theory have focused attention on biblical texts as expressions of the human spirit that are capable of addressing all manners and circumstances of humanity.

Exegetical comment has taken a variety of forms. For understanding pre-Reformation modes of exposition, the following terms should be kept in mind. A terse comment on a word or phrase is ordinarily called a *gloss.* A continuous comment on a selected section of text is termed in Greek a *scholion.* When scholia are entered for an entire book of the Bible, the work qualifies as a *commentary;* a variation of this genre is the *postil,* a term introduced in the thirteenth century. A series of quotations extracted from the writings of the Fathers and used for explication of a text is termed a *catena* ("chain"). Many patristic interpreters used the homily, or sermon, as a medium for exposition.

Much of the sound and fury associated with the practice of biblical exegesis derives from the fact that the Bible, unlike most other classics, has been the object of incremental interpretation deposited by competing religious groups and individuals, often as the product of shifting worldviews and altered perspectives on moral responsibility. This article on biblical exegesis describes this sway within Christian circles.

Writers of the New Testament. The distinction between "letter" and "spirit," as applied to the canon of the Hebrew scriptures, is a dominant factor in the apostle Paul's exegetical approach and became an abiding paradigm. From Paul's perspective of faith, the "letter" incorporated what was superseded by God's action in Jesus Christ. Spirit has to do with understanding the very kernel, or heart, of divine intention and activity.

Similarly, the *Gospel of John* announces: "The Law was given through Moses; grace and truth came through Jesus Christ" (*Jn.* 1:17). As the Word of God (1:1), Jesus obviates the need for further prophecy. He is in his person the exposition of divine purpose.

For Mark, the words and work of Jesus clarify parts of the Old Testament, which in turn provides the outline for the story of Jesus.

Matthew explains the Old Testament principally in terms of the function of Jesus as executive of the communities of believers. His teaching, exemplified especially in the exegesis of Mosaic legislation (e.g., *Mt.* 5–7), is a model for instructing God's people (*Mt.* 28:19–20).

Luke's two-volume work (i.e., *Luke* and *Acts*) displays more extensive expository use of the Old Testament than do the gospels of Matthew and Mark. In it the basic decoding paradigm for assessing the significance of Jesus Christ is the reciprocity system, especially as reflected in the Greco-Roman understanding of the relation between civic benefactors and recipients of their bounty.

Demonstration of the superiority of Jesus Christ to all cultic media in Israel's previous history dominates *Hebrews*. Exegesis is embodied in a rhythmic succession of passages or data from the Old Testament, coupled with the author's exposition in terms of the controlling theme of superiority. Pastoral exhortation follows each stage of the theological exposition.

Typology plays a dominant role in *Revelation*. Much of the numerology and imagery in this book helps the writer's public to understand the current situation in the light of Israel's experience.

Apostolic Fathers. The writings of the apostolic fathers, a term used here in a broad sense, include a wide range of expository comment. *First Clement*, written by an unknown author near the turn of the first century at the behest of Christians in Rome and addressed to their fellow believers in Corinth, uses the Old Testament in an unimaginative manner as a source for moral instruction. Ignatius of Antioch discusses passages from *Matthew*, *Luke*, and *John* in language to which even gnostics could subscribe. The anonymous author of *Barnabas* takes pride in the possession of special knowledge, or gnosis, but denies any meaningful relevance of the Old Testament to non-Christian Jews. More restrained in allegorical approach is *2 Clement*, whose authorship, addressees, and date are uncertain.

Marcion and the Gnostics. Marcion, who in 144 broke with the dominant institutionalized Christianity, disavowed allegorical methodology in his exposition of the Old Testament. His lost commentary on *Luke* and the Pauline letters, excluding *1* and *2 Timothy* and *Titus*, bore the title *Antitheses*.

Gnostic Christians were apparently the first producers of biblical commentaries. Preeminent among gnostic teachers are Valentinus; two of his disciples, Heracleon and Ptolemy; and Basilides. Origen's numerous excerpts from Heracleon's commentary on *John*, apparently the first exposition of an entire gospel, reveal its thoroughgoing allegorical approach and denial of validity to the Old Testament. In a letter to an eminent woman named Flora, Ptolemy puts the Pentateuch under criticism in an attempt to show that Old Testament law is the work of an intermediate deity. Basilides, founder of a gnostic school in Alexandria, composed his own version of the Gospels and commented on it in a work entitled *Exegetica*. Of the Nag Hammadi texts, *A Valentinian Exposition* (11.2) discusses the origin of creation and the redemptive process. Another, *The Interpretation of Knowledge* (11.1), is of unknown authorship, with edifying comment based on selected passages from the New Testament.

Toward Consolidation. In the face of extreme elitist views on admittance to Christian privilege, representatives of the so-called orthodox apostolic tradition felt it was incumbent on them to develop exegetical theory that could challenge the expertise of those whom they considered heretics.

Justin of Rome to Didymus. Justin of Rome argued through allegorical interpretation that the entire Old Testament is a prophecy concerning Jesus, and Irenaeus lent support in a work titled *Against Heresies*. About the year 200, Clement of Alexandria became head of the catechetical school in that city. He defended allegorical method in the manner of Philo but with a Christocentric orientation, arguing that the Old Testament is enigmatic and requires such methodology to convey its meaning.

Origen, the first exponent of scientific biblical exegesis, extended allegorization to the interpretation of the New Testament. He explained his approach in the treatise *On First Principles*, with a practical demonstration in his *Commentary on John*. Origen ranged over the entire Bible, and his exegetical work is incorporated in scholia, homilies, and commentaries. Dionysius of Alexandria undergirded Origen's methodology by responding to its critics in a book titled *On the Promises*, in which he denied the Johannine authorship of *Revelation*.

More than a century later, Origen's methodology attracted Didymus, a nonclerical Alexandrian theologian who had been blind from the age of four or five. Admired by Jerome, Didymus is credited with commentaries on almost every biblical writing, including *Isaiah* 40–66, which he viewed as a complete book.

The Cappadocian fathers. The era of the Cappadocian fathers was a period of revitalization in the Eastern church. Under the influence of Origen and other Alexandrines, Basil of Caesarea, who said that "when he heard the word grass he understood that grass was meant," drew heavily in the fourth century on Greek science for his explanation of the creation account in nine homilies, collected in *On the Hexaemeron.* Gregory of Nyssa recognized the importance of the literal sense as he pursued Basil's interest in the creation account, but his numerous homilies and discussions of various other portions of the Bible convey his mystical absorption in allegorical exposition. Fondness for Greek rhetoric is evident in the writings of Gregory of Nazianzus, who like Cyril of Alexandria used the scriptures in the fight against Arianism in more than forty orations.

The Latins. Writing in Greek, Hippolytus of Rome produced what is now the oldest extant Christian exegetical treatise, a commentary on *Daniel.* His influence is apparent in the work of Victorinus of Pettau. Tertullian punctuated his own numerous writings with comments on scripture and introduced the West to theological Latin, but Victorinus was the first exegete, in the proper sense of the term, to write in Latin. His paraphrastic technique is displayed in an exposition of selected passages from *Revelation.*

As the Athanasius of the West, Hilary of Poitiers was the first Latin writer to introduce his part of the world to Eastern patristic theology. His discussions of *Matthew* and *Psalms* sound a homiletical tone, as do the works of Ambrose. Also among the enterprising was the Donatist Ticonius, of North Africa, whose *Book of Rules* is the first book relating to exegetical methodology to be written in Latin.

Jerome and Augustine. Origen's influence is evident in the earliest exegetical efforts of Jerome. Owing to Origen's loss of prestige in ecclesiastical circles, and to his own increasing interest in the Hebrew language, Jerome leaned markedly in the direction of the Antiochenes (see below), as attested especially in his exposition of *Jeremiah.*

In *De doctrina Christiana* (On Christian Doctrine), which pays homage to both allegory and to the letter of scripture, Augustine of Hippo summarized his views on the theologian's responsibility to scripture and the exegetical task and gave a masterful demonstration thereof in a commentary on *Psalms.* His emphasis on fidelity to tradition as a hermeneutical principle was later sharpened by Vincent of Lérins in the words "What is believed everywhere, always, and by all." The dictum also serves as an epitaph. Except for contributions of a homiletical nature by Gregory the Great on *Ezekiel* and *Job,* there is little indication of creative exegetical activity until the twelfth century.

From the fifth century to the twelfth, theologians proved themselves masters at piecing commentaries together out of patristic works. The term *catena,* that is, a chain of select citations, became standard after Thomas Aquinas published in 1484 a collection of excerpts, drawn from at least eighty sources, under the title *Catena aurea.* In the thirteenth century, Ibn al-ʿIbrī, better known as Bar Hebraeus, incorporated the work of Nestorian and Jacobite exegetes in a book titled *Storehouse of Mysteries.*

Champions of the Literal Sense. Allegorization, whether by representatives of mainstream tradition or by dissidents, threatened to make history an irrelevant concern of the church in the first five centuries. To offset the peril, a number of scholars, especially at Antioch, followed the lead of Jewish scholars and championed the literal sense. The Antiochenes would be followed by the Victorines in the twelfth century.

Antiochenes. For Antiochenes the literal sense covered a broad range of expression, including usage in a transferred sense. In addition to the literal sense there is a deeper meaning, called *theōria,* or "theory." A prophetic passage thus can express both a current historical phenomenon and a future development.

Outstanding among exegetes of the Antiochene school is Theodore of Mopsuestia, a disciple of Diodorus of Tarsus. Aspects of his methodology can be readily perceived in the substantial remains of his commentary on *Psalms,* in which he determines the historical situation of a psalm from its argumentative structure. The last of the great Antiochenes was Theodoret of Cyrrhus. Well grounded in the classics, he steered between the historical-literal approach of Theodore of Mopsuestia and a purely spiritual exposition. Besides commentaries on individual Old Testament books, he used a question-and-answer form for discussion of the Octateuch and *1* and *2 Kings.* His exposition of the Pauline letters rivals Chrysostom's homilies and the commentary by Ephraem of Syria on the same corpus.

Two Antiochene guides to interpretation have survived. The first, by a Syrian named Adrian from the first half of the fifth century, is titled *Introduction to the Divine Scriptures* and includes explanation of Hebrew idioms and phraseology and a discussion of the difference between prose and poetry. The second, by Junilius Africanus, from the time of Justinian I, is a free translation of a work by Paul the Persian and is titled *Regulative Institutes of the Divine Law.*

Victorines. With Hugh of Saint-Victor, who reworked Augustine's *On Christian Doctrine* in a treatise titled *Didascalion,* the role of scripture interpreted according to the letter became increasingly a subject of scientific discussion. Independence of judgment, emphasis on the literal sense, and reference to Jewish history and the Hebrew text of the Old Testament are characteristic of Hugh's exegesis. Of his two disciples, Richard and Andrew, it is Andrew who most sympathetically captured Hugh's method of inquiry and Jerome's respect for Hebrew lore.

A century later another Hugh, a Dominican from Saint-Cher, broke ground by organizing the production of a concordance of the Latin Vulgate. Also important are the *postillae* developed by the Dominicans as a supplement to the gloss. Whereas glosses presented detached comment on a page of text, *postillae* offered continuous and organized exposition of a book of scripture, as in Hugh's comments on *Wisdom of Solomon.* Since one of the goals was the rescue of the text from smothering or distorting glosses, the *postillae* in effect hastened the day when exegesis and speculative or systematic theology would take separate disciplinary paths.

Chiefly responsible for the continuation of the Victorine tradition at the end of the twelfth century are Peter Comestor, Peter the Chanter, and Stephen Langton. These three scholars glossed numerous portions of the scriptures, but Langton is also remembered for his development of a capitulation system, which in the main corresponds to the modern chapter division of the Bible.

Lending further support to the new but short-lived trend was the Dominican Roland of Cremona, a storehouse of lore on almost any subject. His scientific interest preserved him from Alexandrine speculation. Besides being enriched with references to Greco-Roman authors, his commentary on *Job* is the first exposition of that book in terms of its literal-historical sense. Fellow Dominican Albertus Magnus also could not resist flooding his numerous commentaries on Old and New Testament books with data from Greco-Roman, Arabic, and Jewish scientific sources.

Roger Bacon, a crotchety Franciscan celebrity, supported the fresh approaches taken by the Victorines and their successors. To remedy linguistic deficiencies, he wrote grammars for the study of Greek and Hebrew. Convinced that mathematics was the key to all sciences, he claimed that without it the literal sense of texts dealing, for example, with Noah's ark, the tabernacle, or Solomon's Temple could not be known. Dissatisfied with the textual condition of the Vulgate, he urged the pope to set up a commission for its revision by competent scholars.

The Victorines and their sympathizers were the advance people of the Renaissance, and one might have expected more from the fourteenth and fifteenth centuries, but the names of those who dared to challenge tradition are few, and that of the theologian and mystic Meister Eckhart, who died around 1327, leads the rest.

Other Medieval Exposition. In contrast to that of the Victorines, most of medieval exegetical production from 600 to 1500 had its roots in Alexandrine allegorization and the hermeneutical theory of Origen, who posited the somatic, the psychic, and the pneumatic as the three senses in scripture, corresponding to humanity's threefold nature: flesh, soul, and spirit. One text may manifest all three senses: literal, moral, and spiritual. Stimulated by the division of letter and spirit, as championed by Augustine and then by Gregory I, medieval theologians developed an intricate system of exposition that predicated a fourfold sense, summarized by Augustine of Dacia in this jingle:

> Through letter comes the history,
> And things of faith by allegory,
> For doing good we have the moral,
> To mount on high the anagogy.

The letter dealt with the visible and surface data of scripture; allegory conveyed the hidden or theological meaning and appealed especially to speculative and dialectical interests; practical guidance of Christians was derived from the moral or tropological sense; and the believer's final destiny was taught through the anagogical or eschatological sense, which appealed to the contemplative life.

Thomas Aquinas endorsed the traditional fourfold division, but his interest in dogmatic authority led him to celebrate, especially in commentaries on *Job* and the Prophets, the importance of the literal sense. The Franciscan Bonaventure augmented the fourfold sense, and Nicholas of Lyra tried to help his generation keep in touch with the original text. But following Nicholas, biblical exegesis displayed no creativity for almost two centuries.

The Renaissance and the Reformation. The work of Origen, the Victorines, and Nicholas of Lyra was prophetic of directions that would be taken when the right of systematic theology to control the meaning of sacred scripture came into question. But more efficient tools were needed to carry out the necessary functions of exegetical inquiry. The Renaissance, under the lead of popes Nicholas V, Sixtus IV, Alexander VI, and Clement VII, encouraged their shaping.

In six books on Latin rhetoric, Lorenzo Valla endeavored to upgrade the rhetorical taste of his time. His *On the False Donation of Constantine* was only incidentally a manifestation of critical inquiry, but it succeeded in demonstrating the vulnerability of institutionalized theology when confronted with careful research. Through his collation of manuscripts and critical comments on the New Testament, published by Desiderius Erasmus in 1505, Valla helped focus attention on basic data for exegetical study.

Commentators who were ignorant of Greek and Hebrew had long been able to project profundity through allegory, but more would be expected after Johannes Reuchlin, in the early sixteenth century, published two works on aspects of Hebrew grammar, thereby encouraging more intense cultivation of the literal sense. The Franciscan Konrad Pellikan, who officially adopted the Reformation cause in 1526, went beyond Reuchlin and became the first Christian to publish a Hebrew grammar. His *Commentaria Bibliorum* runs to seven volumes (1532–1539) and is a model of informed philological exposition.

Signs of things to come were evident in the work of James Cajetan, who used the Greek text of Erasmus, the last great representative of Renaissance humanism. Cajetan questioned the authenticity of *Mark* 16:9–20 and *John* 8:1–11 and cast doubt on the authorship of *Hebrews, James, 2 Peter, 2* and *3 John,* and *Jude.*

Martin Luther did not enter into a world of exegetical incompetence, for there were predecessors and contemporaries who outshined the reformer in exegetical precision. But Luther called attention to the basic dramatic issue in a way that the church had never seen. His presupposition that the word of God is not coextensive with the scriptures brought the relationship of the literal sense and the spiritual sense into sharper perspective. This view was synonymous with the reformer's hermeneutical principle of interpreting scripture in terms of its advancement of Christ. Luther's interpretation of *Galatians* (1519 and 1535), the only complete commentary by Luther on a book of the Bible, won admiration outside Germany from, among others, John Bunyan and John Wesley.

At the crest of his humanistic career, John Calvin produced a commentary on Seneca's *On Clemency,* an enduring achievement that exhibits Calvin's vigorous intellect and his ability to express himself in concise and lucid prose. In 1530 he joined Luther's sympathizers in the signing of the Augsburg Confession. Unlike Luther, who intertwined theology and exegesis in his biblical expositions, Calvin followed the lead of late Scholasticism and separated the domains of exegesis and theology, thus in effect heralding the type of philology that would later dominate Western exegesis. His commentaries consist of succinct comments on grammatical and historical matters, with careful attention to context and without homiletical excursion. The prophet Isaiah merited some of his best work.

Post-Reformation Period to the Twentieth Century. If the century after the Victorines was exegetically arid, the late sixteenth century and the seventeenth were somewhat cheerless in Protestant and Lutheran sectors.

Steps toward scientific exegesis. Luther had approached the scriptures as a totality whose center was Jesus Christ. Essentially there was but one dogma—God's outreaching love in Christ. And it was the task of the exegete to help protect the church against the threat of bondage under dogmatic theology. Apart from Luther's contributions, possibilities for original thought had trickled out of a work by Andreas Karlstadt, *On the Canonical Scriptures* (1520), in which Karlstadt expressed the view that Moses could not have written the Pentateuch as it was transmitted. But well-meaning followers of Luther needed only a few decades to remodel the dogmatic base and in the process lock exegesis within the confines of dogmatics. The principal sponsors of this latter-day scholasticism, enshrined in prodigious volumes, were Martin Chemnitz, Johann Gerhard, Abraham Calov, and Johann Quenstedt, who projected themselves as the official guardians of revelation. The most ponderous of their exegetical works in Calov's four-volume *Biblia illustrata* (1672–1676), which unwittingly hastened the era of the Enlightenment.

While adherents of the Augsburg Confession were retreating to scholastic enterprise, some of their erstwhile colleagues, championed by Roberto Bellarmino, leaned far out of scholasticism while remaining rooted in officially sanctioned doctrine. The Spanish exegete and Jesuit Johannes Maldonatus laid claim to the respect of posterity with a two-volume commentary of the four Gospels, published at the end of the sixteenth century. He stressed the literal sense and argued for a central point in parabolic interpretation. Sixtus of Siena, a convert from Judaism and a contemporary of Maldonatus, used the terms *protocanonical* and *deuterocanonical* in his *Bibliotheca sancta* (1566), which has been called the first modern introduction to the Bible.

In the vanguard of a fresh attempt at liberation of exegesis from thralldom to systematic theology are four scholars who span the years 1583–1754. Hugo Grotius found in the literal sense of the Old Testament guiding principles for the understanding of natural law. Many of his interpretations anticipate modern proposals for resolution of Old Testament problems, such as the dating of portions of *Zechariah*. His comments on the New Testament likewise exhibit philological-historical discernment. John Lightfoot's rabbinic exposition of the New Testament opened a new frontier. Johann J. Wetstein combined rabbinic and classical lore with textual-critical study in a two-volume work that ever since its publication in 1751–1752 has undergone pillaging, frequently without attribution. Johann Albrecht Bengel's one-volume commentary on the New Testament is far outweighed in kilograms by Calov's massive production, but it enjoys the kind of temporal durability that the centuries have accorded Euclid's geometry. One wonders what other advances might have been made during this period had scholars like Anna Maria van Schurman, the "Star of Utrecht," who composed an Ethiopian grammar and wrote occasional letters in Hebrew, been encouraged to enter the market where males determined the theological wares.

Although Roman Catholics failed to produce any significant expository work in the eighteenth century, two French scholars raised the curtain for glimpses into the future. Richard Simon made a valiant effort, but his work on the Old Testament was not recognized beyond the Oratory at Paris, where he published his *Histoire critique du texte Vieux Testament* (1678). Through this and numerous other books, Simon endeavored to bring scientific study of the Bible out of its incubation period, but he had no disciples to keep watch. Some cracking of the shell was heard in the work of Jean Astruc, private physician of Louis XV, who concluded that Moses probably used two major sources, one derived from an Elohist source and the other from a Yahvist source, besides ten smaller documents. Progress was indeed being made since the sixteenth century when Andreas Masius, the first European to compose a grammar and dictionary of Syriac, expressed some doubts about the traditional authorship of the *Book of Joshua* and certain parts of the Pentateuch.

The first commentary to incorporate observations concerning use of divine names in the Pentateuch was published by Henning Witter in 1711, but it received no scholarly attention for two centuries. Jean Astruc, on the other hand, had the good fortune to be noticed by Johann Eichhorn, who profited also from Johann Semler's and Johann Herder's contributions to the founding of historical-grammatical study of the Bible on a scientific basis. Eichhorn was the first scholar to apply such methodology to the study of the entire Bible, and together with Robert Lowth, professor of poetry at Oxford from 1741–1750, he is to be credited with the introduction of the concept of myth into biblical studies.

After Eichhorn, numerous variations of documentary analyses appeared, many of them vitiated by philosophical presuppositions. Hegelian philosophy permeated Wilhelm Vatke's study of the religion of the Old Testament, and evolutionary theory marked Julius Wellhausen's documentary hypothesis, for whose germination Eduard Reuss and Karl Graf could take credit. The complex cultic regulations described in the Pentateuch, concluded Wellhausen, belong not to the beginning of a development but to the end. Besides his contributions to the source criticism of the Old Testament, Wellhausen put New Testament students into his debt with comment on the four Gospels that echoes the pithiness of Bengel.

Reason versus dogma. The eighteenth and nineteenth centuries saw developments as revolutionary as those in the sixteenth. Ironically, the very intellectualism that transmuted Luther's central message into scholastic fine print became one of the primary catalysts for the deistic rationalism that pervaded much exegetical literature in the nineteenth century.

Soft words had been sounded in the latter half of the seventeenth century. Barukh Spinoza, a Jewish friend of Christians, combated religious intolerance. His exposition of the Old Testament is one of the earliest and important exhibits of biblical criticism that is not controlled by dogmatic considerations. And especially seminal near the end of the eighteenth century was G. E. Lessing's moderate view that a primitive oral gospel underlies the writings of the four evangelists. But the rationalistic type of methodology sponsored by post-Reformation orthodoxy unwittingly gave impetus to even more thoroughgoing criticism of the Bible by failing to prepare antidotes against the tendencies it helped engender. Consequently, when Lessing published the Wolfenbüttel fragments (1774–1778), selected abstracts of a work on reason and the Bible by a pious rector, Hermann S. Reimarus, the pulpits of orthodoxy trembled under indignant oratory. Institutionalized Christianity quaked at Reimarus's attack on the very integrity of the apostles. But Reimarus had helped initiate a new age for exegesis. The cultural lags that followed the Victorines and Luther were about to be overcome. The literal sense was to take on renewed meaning as Christians accepted the challenge to relieve history of the deadening weight of rationalism in both its orthodox and deistic forms. Defenders of the truth were to come from most unexpected quarters and find themselves under fire for what others would consider dubious assistance in time of disaster.

In the lead were Robert Lowth in England and Johann Semler in Germany. Semler's Pietist background provided personal acquaintance with the hazards of overintellectualization as posed by orthodoxy. Practiced in wariness, he moved against the threat of overextended deistic rationalism. Johann Ernesti had thought to withstand post-Reformation rationalism in its scholastic as well as its deistic forms through basic grammatical-historical research, with stress on philology. Semler went further, with an accent on history, and historical-critical methodology moved one step nearer to classification as a discipline. Semler did endeavor to make room for the Holy Spirit, but Herder's literary insight and empathy for the poetic dimension in the biblical writings promised more stable lodging for the spiritual sense of scripture. Through his emphasis on the human values of the Bible, Lowth helped liberate biblical research from bondage to dogmatic theology.

Immanuel Kant encouraged German scholars to shake the last traces of narrow dogma out of their theology and at the same time endeavored to undergird the moral sense of scripture. He sowed seeds that would bear fruit more than a century later with the emergence of linguistic science, but Friedrich Schleiermacher, a Moravian preacher, offered an interim solution that would atone for lack of justice to the affective dimension of human experience both in Kantian philosophy and in Semler's historical criticism. Self-anointed umpire of speculation and faith, Schleiermacher emphasized in a variety of publications the role of self-consciousness in calculating human capacity for knowledge of God. Again, it would take another century and more for Herder's and Schleiermacher's seed to sprout in full vigor after Edmund Husserl, Martin Heidegger, and Ferdinand de Saussure took up the problem of grammar at the depths of human identity. In the meantime, academia in the nineteenth century remained a battleground for the clients of history and of the spirit. Theologians endeavored to find a firm footing for truth, and G. W. F. Hegel thought that in dialectical law he had found the answer to the ultimate aspiration of the human spirit. Hegel's pupil David Friedrich Strauss skillfully exposed an array of inaccuracies and discrepancies in the Gospels, arguing in his two-volume life of Jesus (1835) that basic human ideas had come to expression in the myths of the New Testament. It was not necessary, he concluded, to renounce true Christianity.

Strauss's attack on the contents of the Gospels as data for historical reconstruction of events in the life of Jesus failed to account for the emergence of the evangelists' presentations, but he had succeeded in draping the coffin of rationalism after filling it with the remains of Heinrich Paulus's effort to reduce the miracle recitals of the New Testament to natural phenomena. What Strauss failed to accomplish, Ferdinand Christian Baur, professor at Tübingen, endeavored to effect with Hegelian tools. The New Testament is indeed the product of its times and cultural context, he argued, but *Acts* and the Pauline letters are specifically the expression of a debate between Petrine Jewish Christians and Pauline gentile Christians. His examination of the Gospels led him to view *John* as a basically unhistorical account and *Matthew* as the best historical source.

Gospel interrelationships: the synoptic problem. Baur's work induced new zeal, much of it directed toward solution of problems relating to the four Gospels. The spell of Augustine, that Mark's gospel epitomizes Matthew's, was broken in 1782 by Johann Koppe and in 1786 by Gottlob Storr. A study by Johann Griesbach titled *Inquiritur in fontes . . . .* (1783) echoed findings of Great Britain's Henry Owen (*Observations on the Four Gospels,* 1764) and exhibited the German scholar's preliminary solution to the question of synoptic interrelationships. Griesbach argued that *Mark* was written later than *Luke* and was dependent on *Matthew* and *Luke.* A thorough examination of Papias's second-century testimony concerning the Petrine influence on *Mark* led Schleiermacher to conclude in 1832 that the so-called sayings (logia) of *Matthew* did not constitute a gospel but were a collection of dominical sayings.

Contenders for the faith now thought they had a firm historical port in which to drop anchors. Also, it was but a short step to the two-document hypothesis—that *Matthew* and *Luke* are dependent on *Mark* and on a source consisting principally of sayings of Jesus that are common to *Matthew* and *Luke.* In 1826 Christian Wilke showed that *Mark* is basic to *Matthew* and *Luke,* and after Karl Lachmann demonstrated that the earliest source, or "Ur-gospel," was best preserved in *Mark,* Christian Weisse was able to water a seed sown by Herbert Marsh of England and argue that *Mark* incorporates more simply and fully an older document that was also used by *Matthew* and *Luke,* who in turn were dependent on a sayings source. Argument along these lines could have countered Strauss's alleged negative criticism of the Gospels as history, but this countervailing seed returned to dormancy until Heinrich Holtzmann, beginning in 1863, became its most persuasive nurturer. Soon the dependency of *Matthew* and *Luke* on both *Mark* and the sayings source, or what is now known as Q (the two-document, or two-source, hypothesis), became standard equipment in exegetical studies. The Griesbach hypothesis, in fulfillment of James Moffat's appraisal as an unluckly and prolific dandelion, blossomed midway in the later decades of the twentieth century under the husbandry of William Farmer and John Orchard, but the majority of scholars endeavored to eradicate it through application of the traditional two-source hypothesis. An important variation of the two-source hypothesis was Burnett Streeter's proposal in 1924 of a "proto-*Luke,*" compounded of *Mark* and Q, with two separate documents, M and L, underlying *Matthew* and *Luke*, respectively, for the material that they did not derive from *Mark* and Q. Karl Junack, under the direction of Kurt Aland, helped produce a synopsis of the four Gospels, which has seen general use since 1964. An ever-abiding port of call is John Hawkins's *Horae synopticae* (1909).

New Horizons. It had been thought that the establishment of a historical base through appeal to an early form of the Gospels would offer an impregnable fortress against the type of criticism used by Strauss, who found Griesbach's synoptic solution helpful in demolition of the extreme naturalistic views of Paulus. Confident of having found the historical Jesus, nondogmatists or "liberals" began to sketch psychological portraits of Jesus, with emphasis on his masterful moral instruction. Leading the parade was Ernest Renan (*Life of Jesus*, 1863). Adolf von Harnack, at the turn of the century, canonized the picture in *Das Wesen des Christentums* (What Is Christianity?). But Albert Schweitzer, taking the opening provided by Johannes Weiss, showed in his watershed book on the history of life-of-Jesus research, *Von Reimarus zu Wrede* (1906), translated as *The Quest for the Historical Jesus* (1910), that the liberal portrait lacked eschatological credentials. Reimarus had concluded that the Gospels' depiction of Jesus as Messiah was an *ex post facto* production by the followers of Jesus. And Wilhelm Wrede had called a halt to nineteenth-century psychologizing of Jesus, specifically his messianic self-consciousness, arguing in *Das Messiasgeheimnis* (The Messianic Secret, 1901) that the Christology evident in *Mark* transcends historical and biographical concerns.

Wrede's work helped awaken New Testament exegetes out of their dogmatic slumbers. A long drought in French scientific exegetical study ended with Alfred Loisy's two-volume work on the synoptic Gospels (1907–1908) and the publication of a commentary on *Mark* by Marie-Joseph Lagrange, who became the first director of Jerusalem's École Pratique d'Études Biblique (1890) and a leader in the revival of Roman Catholic biblical scholarship. Elsewhere, Old Testament scholars were nudged by Hermann Gunkel, who went beyond source criticism to the study of formal features in *Die Legenden der Genesis* (1901). American scholars might have made strides on their own in *Sachkritik*, or material criticism, of the Pentateuch had they listened to the challenge issued by Elizabeth Cady Stanton in *The Woman's Bible* (1895). About eight decades ahead of her time in literary-critical analysis, she asked a detractor why it was "more audacious to review Moses than Blackstone."

Post–World War I. History itself encouraged momentum for new constructions. World War I issued the quietus to human potential for ushering in the kingdom of God through intellectual and moral power. Marxism, offspring of a line of thought that found stimulation in Strauss and Hegel, offered an alternative and focused on the productive capacity of human beings in community as the point of realization of human identity. In 1913 Wilhelm Bousset had documented in *Kyrios Christos* the theological creativity of early Christian communities, and in 1919 Karl Schmidt and Martin Dibelius, followed in 1921 by Rudolf Bultmann, registered the tremor of the time and explored the Gospels as products of early Christian community enterprise. Schmidt observed that *Mark* provided a temporal and geographical framework for independent narratives. Bultmann first isolated the original formal units and then endeavored to trace their history. Dibelius began with the community's needs and interests and analyzed the forms of the tradition that served the church. *Sitz im Leben* ("life-situation") became a cliché. In answer to the question of genre, Clyde Votaw endeavored in 1915 (in the *American Journal of Theology*) to interpret the Gospels in terms of Greco-Roman biographies.

Research in history of religions and history of form was slow to take hold in England and the Americas. Aside from commentaries by Joseph B. Lightfoot on some of the Pauline letters and the publication of an edition of the Greek New Testament featuring the manuscript tradition of two Alexandrine manuscripts by Brooke Westcott and Fenton Hort, none of the English-speaking countries had produced anything of exceptional exegetical merit during most of the nineteenth century. Two biographers of Lightfoot remarked that his commentary on *Galatians*, published in 1865, contained the "novel" feature of examining the "historical setting of the original composition." Richard Trench resurrected the Fathers for support of his allegorized interpretation of the miracles and parables of Jesus.

Some originality was projected at the beginning of the twentieth century by Francis Burkitt, who in 1906 tackled the problem of the agreements of *Matthew* and *Luke* against *Mark*. A few years later Benjamin Bacon, in *Beginnings of the Gospel Story* (1909), found Loisy compatible. Streeter, on the other hand, took little account of fresh developments in France and Germany, relying on nineteenth-century scholarship. And forty years elapsed after the publication of Wrede's *Messianic Secret* before Vincent Taylor undertook a refutation through a modified form-critical approach in his glosses on *Mark* (1952).

The assault by Edwyn Hoskyns and Noel Davey in *The Riddle of the New Testament* (1931) on ideological views concerning Jesus prepared the way for acceptance of the work of Charles Dodd, who in various publications queried Schmidt's analysis of *Mark* and endeavored to demonstrate that *Mark* preserved contours of a genuine succession of events that were reflected in the apostolic preaching. Thomas Manson's *The Teaching of Jesus* (1931) and *The Sayings of Jesus* (1937 and 1949) contain a wealth of judicious exploration of the sayings source, or Q. In the United States, the so-called Chicago school, with Shirley Jackson Case in the lead, picked up on the form critics' environmental theme, and Burton Easton made allowance in 1928 for the validity of historical criticism in form-critical method. Henry J. Cadbury's contributions to the study of *Luke* and *Acts* rank in importance with the production of the five-volume *The Beginnings of Christianity* (1920–1933), edited by Foakes Jackson and Kirsopp Lake. Among Scandinavians, Harald Riesenfeld and Birger Gerhardson used Jewish pedagogical tradition to trace gospel units in part or in their entirety to Jesus.

In 1753 Lowth had written about parallelism in Hebrew poetry, and John Jebb later applied Lowth's principles to the New Testament in a book titled *Sacred Scripture* (1820), thus anticipating by a century Charles Burney, *The Poetry of Our Lord* (1925), in which appeal is made to Aramaic for explanation of the Gospels. Few have shared Charles Torrey's attempt to demonstrate that the Gospels were translations of Aramaic originals (1933), but publications by Matthew Black, Joachim Jeremias, Joseph Fitzmyer, and others have illumined a number of passages in the Gospels through reference to Aramaic. Numerous questions have been raised about the reliability of Paul Billerbeck's five-volume *Kommentar zum Neuen Testament aus Talmud und Midrasch* (1922–1928) for assessment of Jewish points of view. His work can be balanced by reading George Foot Moore's three-volume *Judaism in the First Centuries of the Christian Era* (1927–1930).

Near the end of the nineteenth century, Adolf Jülicher initiated a new era in research on the parables by rejuvenating Maldonatus's view of one controlling idea in each illustrative story told by Jesus. Paul Fiebig went on to compare the canonical parables with those of the rabbis in two publications (1904 and 1912). A. T. Cadoux, of Great Britain, opened another phase in parabolic interpretation, with emphasis in 1930 on the sociological situation of the early church. Following his lead, and in concert with Rudolf Otto's treatment in 1934 of the emergence of the kingdom of God in Jesus' parabolic teaching, Dodd proclaimed "realized eschatology" in *The Parables of the Kingdom* (1935), the importance of which was acknowledged by Joachim Jeremias in a work published in 1947 on the same subject.

Beginning in 1895, Adolf Deissmann had jostled philological complacency with various publications on the significance of papyrological finds for exegesis of the New Testament. A half-century later, discoveries of Hebrew manuscripts at Qumran and of Coptic texts at Nag Hammadi revitalized interest in the origins and development of Christian beliefs and practices.

Toward New Literary Criticism. With respect to dramatic developments in synchronic linguistics, biblical scholarship had displayed inexplicable indifference in the early decades of the twentieth century. Historical-philological glosses continued to dominate the commentaries. History of religion and cultures was featured in the annotations of the German series Handbuch zum Neuen Testament, begun by Hans Lietzmann in 1906. Little of the vitality manifested in related disciplines of literary-critical inquiry influenced the British-based International Critical Commentary series and the German series on the New Testament, Kritisch-exegetischer Kommentar über das Neue Testament, founded by Heinrich A. W. Meyer in 1829.

Karl Barth's publication in 1919 of a theologically impregnated commentary on *Romans* prophesied a new era. Moving beyond form criticism, Martin Dibelius in 1923 ascribed extraordinary creativity to the author of *Acts*. Twelve years later, Robert H. Lightfoot wrote the basic script *(History and Interpretation in the Gospels)* for editorial or redaction criticism, which recognizes the writers of the Gospels as authors in their own right.

With the advent of the 1940s, biblical writers appeared to receive even more recognition as masters of literary production. For the Gospels, paths cleared by Reimarus, Strauss, Wrede, and Robert H. Lightfoot converged in 1948 in an article in which Günther Bornkamm, a pupil of Rudolf Bultmann, showed that *Matthew* reinterprets *Mark*'s story of the stilling of the storm. In 1954 Hans Conzelmann produced a major study of *Luke's* theology. He was followed, in 1956, by Willi Marxsen, whose *Mark the Evangelist* used for the first time the term *redaction history*, that is, editorial or compositional criticism. Jack D. Kingsbury moved beyond a redaction-critical study of the parables of Jesus to a detailed analysis, in 1975, of *Matthew*'s Christology.

On 30 September 1943, seed sown by Jerome and the Roman Catholic scholars Simon, Astruc, and Lagrange brought a harvest of commendation for scientific study of the Bible in Catholic circles. The papal encyclical *Divino afflante spiritu* opened windows beyond medieval courtyards, and in the second half of the twentieth century apologetic and polemical glosses in major Roman Catholic exegetical works became so rare that the history of exegesis could be written without recourse to the ecclesiastical labeling that had been customary. A major contribution during this period was *The Jerome Biblical Commentary* (1968).

For students of the Old Testament, moves away from atomistic philology and across denominational lines were obvious in a number of commentaries published in the latter half of the twentieth century. Especially noteworthy is the work of Gerhard von Rad on *Genesis* (1952–1953), Brevard S. Childs on *Exodus* (1974), and Hans Hertzberg on *1* and *2 Samuel* (1965) in the Old Testament Library Series; George Wright on *Deuteronomy*, Samuel Terrien on *Job*, and Robert Scott on *Psalms* in the Interpreter's Bible; and Edward Campbell on *Ruth* and Delbert Hiller on *Lamentations* in the Anchor Bible, which was begun in 1964. Among the few voices raised in the world of biblical scholarship against Nazi anti-Semitism was Wilhelm Vischer's essay in 1937 on the *Book of Esther*. Lewis Paton, on the same book, can boast of one of the best works in the International Critical Commentary. Prolixity became endemic to commentaries of this period, and one of the champions, yet with much that is of abiding value, is Walther Zimmerli's three-volume work on *Ezekiel* in the series Hermeneia. The minor prophets also began to take the spotlight through the work of Hans Wolff.

The deuterocanonical, or apocryphal, books of the Old Testament have received a large share of comment in both ancient and modern times and across denominational lines. Beginning in 1974, with a commentary by Jacob Myers on *1* and *2 Esdras*, the publishers of the Anchor Bible encouraged even broader acquaintance with the contents and thought of these documents.

Besides becoming increasingly massive during the latter half of the twentieth century, many of the commentaries on the New Testament produced during that period reflected the older diachronic philology. Like their scholastic counterparts of other centuries, most of these commentaries added little that was new to an understanding of the ancient texts. The more durable among them took account of noetic and thematic structures. Vincent Taylor acquainted the English-speaking world with a modified version of form criticism in 700 pages of commentary on *Mark* (1952), but Rudolph Pesch took more conscientious account of *Mark's* literary and cognitive features in a two-volume work (1976–1977). Raymond E. Brown and Rudolf Schnackenburg became the principal exegetes of Johannine writings. Joseph Fitzmyer, in a determined attack on "thetical" positions, dedicated himself to *Luke* and *Acts*. Ernst Käsemann interviewed generations of theologians in an exposition of *Romans* (1973) for his *Handbuch zum Neuen Testament*, and the format signaled further disintegration of glossatorial philology. Well served was *1 Peter*, first by Edward G. Selwyn's commentary (1946) and twenty years later by John H. Elliott, whose *The Elect and the Holy*, which takes into account the entire letter in an exposition of *1 Peter* 2:4–10, deserves to be classed as one of the finest pieces of exegetical craftsmanship to come out of that period.

As the history of exegesis attests, biblical scholarship has ordinarily been a late bloomer. This is especially true with respect to awareness of the potential of modern linguistic theory for exegesis. Not until the publication of the first volume of the series Semeia in 1974 did biblical scholars in the United States begin earnestly to emulate work done in the study of other literatures and exhibit emphasis on synchronic rather than diachronic exegesis. Increased preoccupation with Heideggerian hermeneutics and post-Saussurian linguistic developments caused some in the exegetical craft to think that they were seeing a movement toward accent on the spirit as opposed to the letter, and idiosyncratic features of the new approach projected apparitions of arbitrary allegorizing methodology. The ghosts of Reitzenstein and Bousset encouraged a revival of interest in things Greco-Roman as an antidote, and exegetical studies at the end of the century once more became crammed with references to classical authors, papyri, and epigraphs. Hans Dieter Betz's commentary on *Galatians* in the Hermeneia series (1979) documents the trend. In *Home for the Homeless* (1981), Elliott, following the lead of John Gager, Gerd Theissen, and others, endeavored to determine the community profile of the recipients of *1 Peter* through application of modern sociological method.

For those who lacked sufficient competence in Greek or Latin, exegesis became predominantly a matter of compositional and comparative-literary analysis, displayed especially in studies designed for use in colleges. For those who could not read the signs of the times, the publication of *An Inclusive Language Lectionary: Readings for Year A* (1983) sent out a Reimarus-like shock wave. Nineteen centuries had passed without serious notice of women's contributions to biblical understanding. But after Rosemary Radford Ruether's various works and Elizabeth Schüssler Fiorenza's *In Memory of Her: A Feminist Theological Reconstruction of Christian Origins* (1983), the Anna Maria van Schurmans and Elizabeth Cady Stantons would no longer be denied access to indexes relating to the history of theological philology.

Biblical exegesis will continue in pursuit of status as a scientific discipline. The very multiplication of exegetical sects, as evidenced by the increasing number of task forces in the various learned societies, brings to mind a student cited in *The Epistles of Obscure Men* (1515–1517). The candidate solemnly attested that he had heard Ovid expounded "naturaliter, literaliter, historialiter, et spiritualiter." In search of an antidote to atomization, the first half of the twenty-first century should see heightened interest in interdisciplinary work, especially in the areas of anthropology, sociology, and psychology. Exegetes may be expected to take more account of the pseudoapostolic writings of the second century. Discoveries of hitherto unknown documents will probably enjoy more rapid publication than was the case with the gnostic texts of Nag Hammadi. Biblical studies will undoubtedly be done in even closer collegiality with students of other sacred literatures. The sayings of Jesus should certainly undergo ever more penetrating scrutiny. And in the spirit's quest for recognition over the dominance of the letter, it is quite probable that a revised genre of catena or florilegium will draw afresh, across ecclesiastical boundaries, from relatively untapped resources of patristic and other venerated writings.

BIBLIOGRAPHY

Helpful information on the personalities that figure in the history of exegesis can be found in the *New Catholic Encyclopedia*, 17 vols. (New York, 1967–1979), and in *Die Religion in Geschichte und Gegenwart*, 3d ed., 7 vols. (Tübingen, 1957–1965). *Semeia* (Philadelphia, 1975–) is an important journal published by the Society of Biblical Literature, which has also issued various informative volumes since the observance of its centennial in 1980. In addition to these basic sources, the following works can be consulted with profit.

Barth, Karl. *Protestant Theology in the Nineteenth Century: Its History and Background* (1947). Valley Forge, Pa., 1973. A discussion of theological and exegetical developments in political and cultural context.

Danker, Frederick W. *Multipurpose Tools for Bible Study*. 3d ed. Saint Louis, 1970. Descriptions and guides for the use of leading exegetical works. Much historical material.

Farrar, Frederic W. *History of Interpretation: Bampton Lectures, 1885* (1886). Reprint, Grand Rapids, Mich., 1961. Polemics intermingles with a wealth of reference to the principal personalities and interpretive approaches in the history of biblical exegesis.

Grant, Robert M. *A Short History of the Interpretation of the Bible*. Rev. ed. New York, 1963. Brief and nontechnical.

Kümmel, Werner Georg. *The New Testament: The History of the Investigation of Its Problems* (1958). Nashville, 1972. Concentrates on New Testament research from Johann S. Semler to Edwin Hoskyns, with summaries of each scholar's position illustrated by excerpts from the scholar's writings.

Neill, Stephen C. *The Interpretation of the New Testament, 1861–1961*. Oxford, 1964. Designed for the "nontheologian." Offers British antidote to overestimation of continental scholarship.

Rowley, Harold H., ed. *The Old Testament and Modern Study*. Oxford, 1951. A discussion of the main trends.

Schweitzer, Albert. *The Quest of the Historical Jesus: A Critical Study of Its Progress from Reimarus to Wrede* (1906). 2d ed. London, 1911. A probe of principal developments in life-of-Jesus research and so devastating that it practically terminated the production of the genre.

Smalley, Beryl. *The Study of the Bible in the Middle Ages*. 2d ed. Oxford, 1952. Principal resource for study of the organization, techniques, and objectives of biblical studies in northwestern Europe from the Carolingian renaissance to about 1300.

Spicq, Ceslaus. *Esquisse d'une histoire de l'exégèse latine au Moyen-Âge*. Paris, 1944. A fundamental resource for study of exegetical production in the Middle Ages.

FREDERICK W. DANKER

BIBLICAL LITERATURE.

[*This entry consists of three articles:*

Hebrew Scriptures
Apocrypha and Pseudepigrapha
New Testament

The first article discusses the books that make up the Hebrew Bible, known to Christians as the Old Testament and to Jews as the Tanakh. Related texts, which have been defined variously as canonical, extracanonical, deuterocanonical, and noncanonical, are treated in the second article. The third article concerns the New Testament. For discussion of the interpretation of biblical literature, see Biblical Exegesis.]

Hebrew Scriptures

The terms *Hebrew scriptures* and *Hebrew Bible* are synonyms here restricted to that received, definitive corpus of ancient literature, written in Hebrew except for some sections in Aramaic (*Genesis* 31:47, *Jeremiah* 10:11, and parts of *Daniel* and *Ezra*), that has been traditionally accepted by Jews and Christians alike as having been divinely inspired and, as such, authoritative in shaping their respective faiths and practices.

The word *Bible* is ultimately of Greek derivation and passed into many languages of the world through the medium of Latin. It meant simply "the Books" *par excellence*, the way in which the Jews of the Hellenistic world referred to their sacred scriptures, apparently in literal translation into Greek of the earliest known Hebrew designation current in Palestine. This latter is already reflected in *Daniel* 9:2.

Other names for the corpus that were current in ancient times are "Holy Books" and "Holy Writings."

More specific to Jews is the Hebrew term *miqra'*, widely used in the Middle Ages, but most likely going back to *Nehemiah* 8:8. Literally meaning "reading," this name underscores the fact that the public reading of the scriptures constituted the core of the Jewish liturgy. Another term commonly used among Jews is *tanakh*, the acronym (TaNaKh) composed of the initial consonants of the names of the three parts into which the Hebrew Bible is customarily divided: the Torah (Pentateuch), the Nevi'im (Prophets), and the Ketuvim (Writings, Hagiographa).

Among Christians, the Hebrew Bible has traditionally been referred to as the Old Testament (i.e., Covenant), in contradistinction to the New Testament—theological appellations based upon a christological interpretation of *Jeremiah* 31:30–34. In recognition of the partisan nature of this title, and under the impact of the ecumenical movement of recent times, many scholars have increasingly preferred instead to refer to the Hebrew Bible or Hebrew scriptures.

Canon. As generally used in scholarly parlance, the term *canon* relates particularly to the received and definitively closed nature of the sacred corpus. The noun derives from the Greek *kanōn*, itself borrowed from a Semitic word meaning "cane" or "measuring rod." The word was employed figuratively in Classical Greek, a usage adopted by the church fathers in the fourth century for a norm of faith or doctrine and applied by them to the collection of sacred scriptures.

The completed canon of the Hebrew Bible exerted a profound influence, first upon the Jewish people that produced it, and then upon a large section of the rest of humanity. It was the major factor in the preservation of the unity of the Jews at a time of desperate national crisis after the destruction of their state in the year 70 (or 68) CE and their subsequent wide dispersion. The wholly new and unique experience of Judaism as a book-centered religion became the direct inspiration for Christianity and its New Testament, while both religions served as the acknowledged analogue for the rise and development of Islam, based upon its own sacred book, the Qur'ān.

Contents. The tripartite division of the Hebrew Bible roughly describes its variegated contents, although, admittedly, some of the books of the third part would not be out of place in the second.

The Torah. More fully called the Torah of Moses, the Torah comprises the first five books of the biblical canon, usually known in English as the Pentateuch: *Genesis, Exodus, Leviticus, Numbers,* and *Deuteronomy.* These names, derived from the Greek, may translate Hebrew titles that were current among the Jews of Palestine. They more or less epitomize the subject matter of the books. Another system of designation, long in popular use among Jews, and probably earlier than the foregoing, is based upon the opening words of each book, a practice characteristic of ancient Mesopotamian literature: *Bere'shit, Shemot, Va-yiqra', Be-midbar,* and *Devarim.*

The Hebrew term *torah*, usually, but inaccurately, rendered "law," means "instruction, teaching." In the present context, the Pentateuch comprises a continuous narrative from the creation of the world to the death of Moses in which is embedded a considerable amount of legal and ritual prescription. *Genesis* constitutes a distinct work within the Torah corpus in that its first eleven chapters deal with universal history up to the birth of Abraham, and the rest of the book is devoted to the fortunes of a family, the ancestors of the people of Israel. *Deuteronomy,* too, forms a discrete entity, in that it is largely the summarizing discourses of Moses and is marked by its own characteristic style and theological tendency. The intervening three books deal with two generations of the people of Israel from the period of the Egyptian oppression and the Exodus through the wanderings in the wilderness. This section makes up the bulk of the Torah literature and comprises the record of the Egyptian oppression, the liberation, and the arrival at Mount Sinai (*Ex.* 1–18), God's self-revelation to Israel at this site with the divine legislation mediated there through Moses (*Ex.* 19–*Nm.* 10:10), and the events of the people's wanderings in the wilderness until they arrive at the plains of Moab ready to cross the Jordan River into the Promised Land (*Nm.* 10:11–chap. 36).

It is not certain how this corpus was materially preserved in early times. Two separate systems have survived. For convenience of study, the material was written on five separate scrolls, but for ideological reasons, in order both to delimit the Torah as a closed corpus and to emphasize its being a distinct unified composition, the Torah was also written on a single scroll. It is solely in this form that it has played a role in the Jewish synagogal liturgy.

The Nevi'im. The prophetic corpus naturally divides into two parts. What has come to be known as the Former Prophets continues the historical narrative of the Torah, beginning with Joshua's succession to leadership of Israel after the death of Moses and the conquest of Canaan, and closing with the destruction of the First Temple in Jerusalem, the end of the monarchy, and the Babylonian exile of the Judeans up to the year 560 BCE. This material is contained in the books of *Joshua, Judges, Samuel,* and *Kings.* They are incorporated into the prophetic corpus because they contain much information about the activities of prophets, and particularly because they constitute, in reality, a theological interpretation of the fortunes of the people of Israel presented from the perspective of prophetic teaching and judgment.

The second part of the Nevi'im, the Latter Prophets, comprises the works of the literary prophets in Israel and Judah from the eighth to the fifth centuries BCE. These are *Isaiah, Jeremiah,* and *Ezekiel,* and "the Book of the Twelve," known in English as the Minor Prophets: *Hosea, Joel, Amos, Obadiah, Jonah, Micah, Nahum, Habakkuk, Zephaniah, Haggai, Zechariah,* and *Malachi.* It should be noted that the adjective *minor* characterizes only the relative brevity of these works, and is by no means intended to be a judgment on their degree of importance.

The Ketuvim. The Writings, often also called Hagiographa in English, are actually a miscellany of sacred writings of several genres of literature, as the nonspecific nature of the name indicates. There is religious poetry *(Psalms* and *Lamentations);* love poetry (the *Song of Songs*); wisdom or reflective compositions *(Proverbs, Job,* and *Ecclesiastes);* historical works *(Ruth, Esther, Ezra-Nehemiah,* and *Chronicles);* and apocalypse *(Daniel).*

Tripartite canon. It is widely held that the tripartite nature of the canon represents three successive stages of canonization of the separate corpora. Repeated reference to this threefold division comes from the literature of the period of the Second Temple. *Ben Sira* 39:1, probably written around 180 BCE, mentions the "law of the Most High, the wisdom of all the ancients . . . , and . . . prophecies." About fifty years later, Ben Sira's grandson, who translated the work into Greek, writes in his prologue about "the law and the prophets and the others that came after them," which last are also called "the other books of our fathers" and "the rest of the books," while *2 Maccabees* (2:2–3, 2:13) has reference to "the law, the kings and prophets and the writings of David." In Alexandria, Egypt, the Jewish philosopher Philo Judaeus (d. 45–50 CE) mentions, besides "the law," also "the prophets and the psalms and other writings" (*De vita contemplativa* 3.25). The Jewish historian Josephus Flavius (37–c. 100 CE) tells of the Pentateuch of Moses, the "prophets" and "the remaining books" (*Against Apion* 1.39–41). Similarly, in the New Testament, the *Gospel of Luke* speaks of "the law of Moses and the prophets and the psalms" (24:4). This persistent allusion to the threefold division of the Hebrew scriptures, and the lack of any uniform title for the third collection of writings, in addition to the heterogeneous nature of that corpus, all argue in favor of two closed collections—the Torah and the Prophets—with a third being somewhat amorphous and having no uniform name, undoubtedly a sign of its late corporate canonicity.

Of course, the closing of a corpus tells nothing about the canonical history of the individual books within it. Some parts of the Ketuvim, such as the *Psalms,* for instance, would most likely have achieved canonical status before some of those included within the Nevi'im.

Samaritan canon. The religious community centered on Nablus (ancient Shechem) that calls itself Benei Yisra'el ("children of Israel") or Shomrim ("keepers," i.e., of the truth), and that is known by outsiders as Samaritans, claims to be directly descended from the Israelites of the Northern Kingdom who escaped deportation at the hands of the Assyrian kings who destroyed it in 722/1 BCE (*2 Kgs.* 17:5–6, 17:24–34, 17:41). Their canon consists solely of the Pentateuch, excluding the Prophets and the Writings. This fact has not been satisfactorily explained. The older view, that the final breach between the Samaritans and the Jews occurred in the time of Ezra and Nehemiah (fifth century BCE), before the canonization of the rest of the Hebrew Bible, is no longer tenable because both documentary and archaeological evidence leads to the conclusion that the schism was the culmination of a gradual process of increasing estrangement. A major step was the construction of a Samaritan shrine on Mount Gerizim early in the Hellenistic period; the destruction of the temple on that site by John Hyrcanus in 128 BCE completed the rupture. [*For further discussion of the Samaritan Bible, see* Samaritans.]

Canon at Qumran. The discovery of a hoard of more than five hundred manuscripts in the region of the sectarian settlement at Khirbat Qumran, northwest of the Dead Sea, has raised the question of the nature of the biblical canon recognized by that community, which came to an end about 70 CE. The question is legitimate both in light of the variant canon preserved by the Greek Septuagint, as discussed below, and because copies of extrabiblical books, apocryphal and pseudepigraphical works such as *Tobit, Ben Sira,* the *Letter of Jeremiah, 1 Enoch,* and *Jubilees,* not to mention the sect's own productions, were included among the finds.

A variety of factors combine to render a decisive conclusion all but impossible in the absence of a list that would determine contents and sequence. This lack is aggravated by the practice at that time of writing each biblical book on a separate scroll, and by the very fragmentary form of the overwhelming majority of extant scrolls. Furthermore, since the manuscripts had generally been hidden in the caves in great disorder, we cannot be sure whether we are dealing with a living library or a *genizah,* a storeroom of discarded works.

The following items of evidence are pertinent to the discussion. (1) With the exception of *Esther,* fragments of all the books of the Hebrew Bible have turned up; hence the Qumran canon would have included at least almost every book of the Hebrew Bible. (2) The category of Qumran literature known as the *pesharim,* or contemporizing interpretations of prophetic texts, is, so far, exclusively restricted to the books of the standard Hebrew canon. (3) The Manual of Discipline (*Serekh ha-yaḥad,* 1QS IX:11) expresses the hope for the renewal of prophecy, the same as is found in *1 Maccabees* 4:46. This suggests that the Qumran community recognized a closed corpus of prophetic literature. (4) The great psalms scroll (11QPs[a]), on the other hand, exhibits not only a deviant order of the standard psalms, but also contains other compositions, largely deriving from Hellenistic times. This scroll circulated in more than one copy, and several other Qumran manuscripts of psalms also vary in sequence and contents. At first glance it would seem that this phenomenon proves that the Qumran community could not have had a concept of a closed canon. However, it may be pointed out that the compiler of 11QPs[a] certainly was dependent on a Hebrew book of psalms much the same as that of the Hebrew Bible, and he may simply have been putting together a liturgical collection, not creating or copying a canonical work. Moreover, the caves of Qumran have yielded numerous psalters that contain only known canonical psalms, apparently without any deviation from the standard sequence. (5) As to the presence of noncanonical works, we have no means of knowing whether these had authority for the community equal with that of the standard Hebrew canonical books. (6) In sum, the evidence so far at hand does not justify the assumption that Qumran sectarians had a concept of canon different from that of their Palestinian Jewish brethren, although the opposite too cannot be proven.

Alexandrian canon (Septuagint). To meet the needs of worship and study, the populous hellenized Jewish community of Alexandria produced a Greek translation of the Hebrew Bible known as the Septuagint, begun in the third century BCE and completed before about 132 BCE. As it has come down to us, it differs from the traditional Hebrew Bible (the canonized books of the Masoretic text) both in content and form, and often textually (see "Greek Translations," below). It includes works that rabbinic Judaism rejected as noncanonical, and in it the books of the Prophets and Writings are not maintained as separate corpora but are distributed and arranged according to subject matter: historical books, poetry and wisdom, and prophetic literature. This situation has given rise to a widely held hypothesis of an Alexandrian or Hellenistic canon; that is to say, the Septuagint is said to represent a variant, independent concept of canon held by Diaspora Jewry. Alternatively, it is suggested that it derives from a rival canon that circulated in Jewish Palestine itself.

The evidence for either view is indecisive. First of all, it must be remembered that all extant complete manuscripts of the Septuagint—the Sinaiticus, the Alexandrinus, and the Vaticanus—are Christian in origin and are not earlier than the fourth century CE. There is a gap of at least four hundred years in our knowledge, which fact raises the possibility that the divergencies in content and arrangement from the traditional Hebrew Bible may have originated with the church. Moreover, there is no uniformity in the Greek manuscripts themselves in respect to the additional books included. Furthermore, the separate collections of the Torah and the Prophets were definitely known in Alexandria in the second century BCE, as is clear from the prologue to *Ben Sira* (which even speaks of their translation into Greek), as well as from *2 Maccabees* 2:13 and 15:9. At the same time, Ben Sira, his grandson who wrote the prologue, and Philo clearly distinguish between the books that make up the Hebrew Bible and other works of Jewish origin. In short, the problem of the origin of the contents and sequence in the Greek Bible cannot be solved in the present state of our knowledge.

Christian canon. The Christian canon of the Jewish scriptures differs in three ways from the Bible of the Jews. First, its text is not that of the received Hebrew, usually called the Masoretic text, but is based on the Greek and Latin versions. This fact is grounded in historical, not theological considerations. The early church functioned and missionized in a Greek-speaking environment, and thereafter took over the Jewish scriptures in their most readily available and convenient form, namely the (Greek) Septuagint version. Later, the Latin translation became authoritative. Second, although all the books officially recognized as canonical by the Jews were also accepted by the Christian church, many segments of the latter also included within its canon additional Jewish works that date from the days of the Second Temple. These, generally termed "deuterocanonical" by theologians of the Roman Catholic church, are books of historical and didactic content, composed in Hebrew or Aramaic. They were not sectarian in origin, and they circulated widely in both Palestine and the Greek-speaking Jewish Diaspora in their original language and in Greek translation long after the close of the Hebrew canon. Such books we often included in early manuscripts of the Septuagint, not as a separate group but appropriately interspersed among the undoubtedly canonical works. The books in question are *2 Ezra* (called *3 Esdras* in the Vulgate), *Tobit, Judith,* additions to *Esther*, the *Wisdom of Solomon, Ben Sira, 1 Baruch*, together with the *Letter of Jeremiah*, additions to *Daniel*, and *Maccabees*. It is to be noted that *Esther, Judith, Wisdom, 1* and *2 Maccabees, 1 Baruch*, chapters 1–5, and the Septuagint additions to *Daniel* and *Esther* have not yet turned up among the Dead Sea finds. [*For an extensive discussion of texts not included in the Hebrew canon, see the following article,* Apocrypha and Pseudepigrapha.]

The presence of the extra compositions in the manuscripts of the Septuagint long engendered controversy, and their status remained ambivalent. The authors of the New Testament books were certainly familiar with them and used them, but it remains a fact that New Testament citations from them are minimal. Further, the early lists of the Fathers emphasize a twenty-two-book canon identical with that of the Jews. In general, the Western church held the deuterocanonical books in high esteem, while the Eastern church downgraded them. The synods of the North African church held at Hippo (393 CE) and Carthage (397, 419 CE) confirmed the practice of the Western church. The powerful influence of the church theologian Augustine (354–430) weighed heavily in according the entire Septuagint equal and identical divine inspiration with the Hebrew Bible. The additional books remained in the Latin Vulgate, which became the official version of the Roman Catholic church at the Council of Trent (1545–1563).

On the other hand, the Latin father Jerome (347–420) did not recognize them as authoritative scripture, although he did concede them to be "ecclesiastical" or spiritually edifying, and he did translate them into Latin. The Syrian church utilized only the Jewish canon. It later succumbed to the influence of the Septuagint, a move resisted by the Nestorian (Chaldean or East Syrian) branch. In the Greek Orthodox church, the question remains unresolved to the present day, while it was not until the nineteenth century that the theologians of the Russian Orthodox church unanimously excluded the extra books from the canon.

The period of the Reformation and the Protestant appeal to the authority of the Hebrew Bible generated a renewed attack on their canonicity. John Wyclif (c. 1320–1384), forerunner of the Reformation, who initiated the first English translation of the Bible, omitted them entirely. Martin Luther, in his debates with Johann Maier of Eck (1519), denied their canonical status. His translation of the Bible (1534) included them as a group between the two Testaments, with the following rubric: "Apocrypha: these are books which are not held equal to the sacred Scriptures and yet are useful and good for reading." Luther's view became standard Protestant doctrine. The Thirty-Nine Articles of Religion of the Church of England (1563) asserted their worth for private study and edification but denied them any doctrinal value; and the Westminster Confession (1647), which established the confession of faith of English-speaking Presbyterians, definitively decreed that they were not divinely inspired, are to be excluded from the canon of scripture, and are devoid of authority. The King James Bible of 1611 had grouped the apocryphal books together before the New Testament, but in 1827 the British and Foreign Bible Society decided not to circulate the Apocrypha in whole or part. [*For the contemporary status of these works in different traditions, see* Apocrypha and Pseudepigrapha, *Table 1*.]

The third way in which the Christian canon diverges from the Jewish canon relates to the order of the books. The Hebrew tripartite division, clearly attested in *Luke* 28:44, was disregarded, and the contents were regrouped, as in the manuscripts of the Septuagint, according to literary categories—legal, historical, poetic-didactic, and prophetic. It is possible that the church selected one of the pre-Christian rival traditions already current in Palestine and the Diaspora. At any rate, the variant sequence was best suited to express the claim of the church that the New Testament is the fulfillment of the Hebrew scriptures of the Jews. The closing of the canon with Malachi's prophecy of the "day of the Lord" to be heralded by the return of Elijah provides a transition to the New Testament with John the Baptist as the new Elijah acclaiming his Messiah.

Number of books. Until the sixth century CE, it was customary among Jews for the scribes to copy each biblical work onto a separate scroll. The number of books in the biblical canon therefore relates to the number of scrolls onto which the completed Hebrew Bible was transcribed, and which were physically kept together as a unit. Josephus (*Against Apion* 1. 39–41, ed. Loeb, p. 179) is emphatic that there were no more than twenty-two such. What is not clear is whether this figure was arrived at by conjoining books, such as *Judges* and *Ruth*, and *Jeremiah* and *Lamentations*, or whether two books were not yet included in his canon, perhaps the *Song of Songs* and *Ecclesiastes*. The former suggestion seems more likely because this figure of twenty-two biblical books represents a widespread tradition in Palestine to which there are many Christian witnesses for several hundred years. It appears in a Hebrew-Aramaic list of titles that derives from the first half of the second century CE, and is repeated by several church fathers, such as Melito, bishop of Sardis in western Asia Minor (d. 190), Origen, theologian of Caesarea in southern Palestine (c. 185–c. 254), Eusebius, bishop of Caesarea (c.

260–339), who equates it with the number of letters of the Hebrew alphabet, Cyril, bishop of Jerusalem (d. 386), and the celebrated scholar Jerome. All of the aforementioned either visited Palestine or lived there for many years, and there can be no doubt that they reflect contemporary local Jewish practice. They all include the *Song of Songs* and *Ecclesiastes* in the canon.

A variant tradition counting twenty-four books eventually prevailed among Jews. This is first found in *2 Esdras* 14:45, written circa 100 BCE. The books are listed by name in a text that antedates 200 BCE cited in the Babylonian Talmud (*B.B.* 14b). Thereafter, this figure is explicitly given, and it becomes standard in rabbinic literature (cf. B.T., *Ta'an.* 5a). Whether the number has any significance is uncertain. In the case of Homer's *Odyssey* and *Iliad,* which are also each divided into twenty-four books, the division came about in the third century BCE because a scroll of more than a thousand verses was found to be too cumbersome to handle, and twenty-four is the number of letters in the Greek alphabet. It is of interest that the Old Babylonian bilingual lexical series known as Har-ra-Hubullu is inscribed on twenty-four tablets, the Mesopotamian *Epic of Gilgamesh* on twelve tablets, the Greek *Theogony* of Hesiod comes in twelve parts, and the old Roman law code was eventually codified as the Twelve Tablets (of wood). At any rate, in Jewish tradition, the biblical books become twenty-four by treating all the twelve Minor Prophets as one, since they were written on a single scroll, and by regarding *Ezra* and *Nehemiah* as a single work.

English Bibles (English version) have thirty-nine books because *Samuel, Kings,* and *Chronicles* are divided into two books each for reading convenience, and *Ezra* and *Nehemiah* are counted as separate works, as is each of the twelve Minor Prophets.

Canonizing Process. The available sources are silent about the nature and identity of the validating authorities, about the criteria of selectivity adopted in respect of the books included and excluded, and about the individual crucial stages in the history of the growth of the Hebrew biblical canon. This deficiency is aggravated by the fact that the literature that has survived represents at least six hundred years of literary creativity, in the course of which Israelite society underwent far-reaching, indeed metamorphic, change, much of it convulsive. Such a state of affairs militates against the likelihood of uniformity in the processes involved or of unbroken consistency in the considerations that swayed decision-making about individual works and collections of works. For these reasons, any reconstruction of the history of the phenomenon of the canonization of biblical literature must of necessity remain hypothetical.

Nonetheless, it should be noted that well before the year 1000 BCE, the libraries of the temples and palaces of Mesopotamia had organized the classical literature into a standardized corpus in some kind of uniform order and with a more or less official text. In similar manner, by order of Peisistratus, tyrant of Athens, the Homeric epics were codified in the sixth century and endowed with canonical authority. The idea of a canon was thus well based in the ancient world. There is every reason to assume that in Israel, too, temples served as the repositories of sacred texts from early times, and that the priests and scribes played an important role in the preservation and organization of literature. Hence, the formation of the biblical canon should not be viewed as a late development in Israel but as an ongoing process that is coextensive with the biblical period itself.

The definition of *canon* should, furthermore, be extended beyond the purely historical, external, formal aspects relating just to the end result of a process, to which it is usually restricted. In Israel, the conviction that the texts record the word of God or were divinely inspired, however these concepts were understood, would have been a decisive factor in their preservation. For the same reason, they would have been periodically read or recited, and the very force of repetition would inevitably and powerfully have informed the collective mind and self-consciousness of the community. This, in turn, would have subtly shaped and reshaped both the existing literature and new compositions in a continual process of interaction between the community and its traditions. A text that appears to be directed to a specific situation in time and space acquires a contemporizing validity and relevance that is independent of such restrictive dimensions and develops a life of its own. [*For further discussion of canonization, see* Canon.]

The earliest testimony to the canonizing process of the Torah literature comes from *Exodus* 24:1–11, which describes how Moses mediated the divine commands to the entire people assembled, how the people orally bound themselves to obedience, how Moses then put the stipulations into writing, and how a cultic ceremony was held at which the written record of the covenant just made was given a public reading. This was followed by a collective pledge of loyalty to its stipulations.

Another important text is *Deuteronomy,* chapter 31 (verses 9–13, 24–26). Here, too, Moses writes down the Teaching (Torah), this time entrusting the document to the ecclesiastical authorities for safekeeping, with provision for its septennial national public reading in the future. What is then called "this book of the Torah" is placed beside the Ark of the Covenant. In this case, the sanctity of the book is taken for granted, as is its permanent validity and authority, independent of the person of Moses.

The only other record of a preexilic public reading of Torah literature comes from near the end of the period of the monarchy. *2 Kings* 22–23 (cf. *2 Chr.* 34) recounts the chance discovery of "the book of the Torah" in 622 in the course of the renovations being carried out at the Temple in Jerusalem at the initiative of Josiah, then king. The scope of this work cannot be determined from the narrative, but the royal measures taken as a consequence of the find prove beyond cavil that it at least contained *Deuteronomy*. What is of particular significance is that it had long been stored in the Temple, that its antiquity, authenticity, and authority were recognized at once, and that its binding nature was confirmed at a national assembly. The ceremony centered upon a document that had already achieved normative status, but the impact of the event—the thoroughgoing religious reformation that it generated and sustained ideologically—left an indelible imprint on the subsequent literature and religion of Israel and constituted a powerful stimulus to the elevation of the Torah literature as the organizing principle in the life of the people. In this sense, the developments of 622 are an important milestone in the history of canonization. Between this year and 444 the process gathered apace. It is reasonable to assume that it was consummated in the Babylonian exile after 587/6, for it is impossible to explain the extraordinary survival of the small, defeated, fragmented community of Israelites, bereft of the organs of statecraft, deprived of its national territory, living on alien soil amid a victorious, prestigious civilization, other than through the vehicle of the book of the Torah, which preserved the national identity.

In the period of the return to Zion (the Land of Israel) and beyond, after 538 BCE, the convention of attributing the entire Torah to Moses is frequently attested—in *Malachi, Ezra-Nehemiah, Daniel,* and *Chronicles*. It also appears in *Joshua* (8:32, 23:6) and in *1 Kings* (2:3) and *2 Kings* (14:6, 23:25), but many scholars maintain that these references result from a later revision of these works. At any rate, by the year 444 the "Torah of Moses" had received popular acceptance. *Nehemiah* 8–10 records that in that year a public, national assembly took place in Jerusalem at which the people requested that "the scroll of the Torah of Moses with which the Lord had charged Israel" be read to them. This was done by Ezra, who is himself described as "a scribe, expert in the Torah of Moses," "a scholar in matters concerning the commandments of the Lord and his laws to Israel . . . a scholar in the law of the God of heaven" (*Ezr.* 7:6, 7:11–12, 7:21). It is quite evident that the stress is on the teaching, dissemination, interpretation, and reaffirmation of the Torah, long popularly recognized and accepted, not on its promulgation anew. Ezra had been commissioned by the Persian king Artaxerxes I "to regulate Judah and Jerusalem according to the law of God," which was in his care (*Ezr.* 7:14). True, the texts do not define the scope of this literature, but it can be safely assumed that it was little different from the Pentateuch that has come down to us, for the author of *Chronicles* who composed his history about 400 repeatedly refers to the "Torah of Moses," and it can be shown that this phrase in context applies comprehensively to the entire Pentateuch.

In the Pentateuch itself, however, there is no statement unambiguously asserting Mosaic authorship of the entire work, nor can the use of the term *torah* be shown to refer comprehensively to the complete Pentateuch. Rather, its applicability changes considerably, being variously restricted to an individual law, to a specific and limited collection of traditions, or to a large literary unit. The background to the tradition ascribing the authorship of the Pentateuch to Moses lies in the fact that, in biblical literature, Moses is the divinely chosen individual through whose instrumentality a social-religious revolution is effectuated. He is the leader *par excellence,* preeminent beyond compare; his is the only name associated with the term *torah;* he is the sole mediator of the word of God to the people; all laws are presented as divine communications to Moses; there are no collections of binding laws outside of the Torah. He is also the first person to whom the act of writing is ascribed. There can be no doubt that in a very real sense the Pentateuch would have been unthinkable were it not for his activity.

Compilation and Redaction. The composite nature of the biblical, especially the Pentateuchal, literature has long been recognized (see *Nm.* 21:14, *Jos.* 10:13). By the application of analytical criteria of consistent variations in style, phraseology, and theological viewpoint, of doublets and inconsistencies, of breaks in continuity with the obvious presence of connectives that conjoin separate homogeneous sections, critical research has concentrated on the disentanglement and isolation of the constituent literary strands.

The early founders of modern biblical criticism were Barukh Spinoza (1632–1677) and Jean Astruc (1684–1766). In the course of the nineteenth century, several important contributions were made by Wilhelm M. L. De Wette, Wilhelm Vatke, and Heinrich Ewald. It was Julius Wellhausen, however, who popularized what is known as the Documentary Hypothesis. He systematized and developed the work of his predecessors in several influential treatises: *Die Composition des Hexateuchs* (Berlin, 1876), *Geschichte Israels* (Berlin, 1878), and *Prolegomena zur Geschichte Israels* (Berlin, 1883).

The Documentary Hypothesis isolated four primary collections of traditions (sources) that it labeled J (because it employs the divine name *Jehovah,* in Hebrew, *YHVH*), E (because it uses *Elohim* for God), D (Deuteronomy), and P (Priestly). The isolation of the D and P sources, each with its distinctive content, style, and perspective, was less complicated than determining the literary parameters of J and E, on which there has been much difference of opinion. It became clear that the provenance, historical setting, and chronological sequence of these sources would yield the materials for reconstructing the history of the religion of Israel in biblical times. Accordingly, J, which was believed to have originally constituted the skeleton of the continuous narrative of *Genesis* through *1 Kings,* chapter 2, was assigned to the period of the united Israelite kingdom of David and Solomon in the tenth century and was thought to have derived from Judea. E was considered to be northern Israelite or Ephraimite from the ninth to eighth centuries. It was fused with J to become JE. D was regarded as the product of the reformation of Josiah in 622, and P as having been compiled in the Babylonian exile, between 587 and 560. The entire Pentateuch was taken to have reached its final form before Ezra's journey to Jerusalem in 458.

This hypothesis, with its evolutionary presuppositions, has been considerably modified since its systematic presentation in the nineteenth century. The major sources have themselves been dissected, and serious challenge has been posed to the dating and sequence of the reconstructed documents. Furthermore, it has been recognized that a distinction must be made between the age of the traditions, which may be of great antiquity, and the time of their assemblage and final editing. It has been noted that literary strands become interwoven, and sources tend to interact one with another, thus making the identification of the original documents far less secure. In addition, the creative work of the redactor(s) has come to be increasingly appreciated as an important factor in the development of biblical literature by scholars engaging in "redaction criticism."

Scholars of the school of "tradition criticism" have also paid attention to the process by which traditions were preserved and transmitted. It has been pointed out that much of the written material may well have had an oral prehistory. Traditions would have been recited in a cultic context at local and regional shrines, such as Bethel, Shiloh, Shechem, and Jerusalem (cf. *Dt.* 27:1–10). A series of major themes, like the divine promises to the patriarchs, the Exodus. the covenant of Sinai, and the wanderings in the wilderness would have been given public expression on sacral occasions to form the core of the Israelite religion. These units of tradition would become the focus of expansive tendencies, would be written down, assembled, and serve as the building blocks of extensive and complex narratives presented in a continuous form. The nature and characteristic properties of oral tradition, poetic or prose, its antiquity, reliability, and tenacity, its vicissitudes in the course of transmission, and the kinds of transformation it undergoes when reduced to writing have all been the subjects of intensive study, for they have direct bearing on the understanding of the development of biblical literature. [*See also the general discussion in* Oral Tradition.]

Finally, it has been acknowledged that any analysis that ignores the primary nature and function of the material must be incomplete. The formation of the scriptures was not motivated by literary, aesthetic considerations, or by the desire to write objective history. Rather, the literature is essentially religious, its purposes being theological interpretation and didactic function. This fact imposes considerable restraint on the simple application to it of the accepted literary-critical method.

The Bible and the Ancient Near East. The recovery of the languages and cultures of the lands of the ancient Near Eastern world demonstrate that the people of Israel arrived on the scene of history rather late, long after the great civilizations of Mesopotamia, Egypt, and the Hittite area had already passed their prime and produced a classical literature. Moreover, it is clear that this region, often referred to as the Fertile Crescent, constituted a cultural continuum, although, to be sure, each constituent, local entity possessed its own distinctive features. It is not surprising, therefore, that there exist numerous, close affinities in subject matter and form between the biblical writings and the literatures of the ancient Near East. This phenomenon is not necessarily to be explained in terms of dependency or borrowing, but more likely as a result of the sharing of a common cultural heritage. Furthermore, correspondences and parallels are not the same as identity. Contrast is as important a dimension as similarity, and it is the former that accords the Israelite productions their claim to singularity.

This point is illustrated by the fact that whereas all the diverse literary genres of the Bible are to be found in the neighboring cultures, the reverse is not the case, and the omissions are highly instructive. The huge literature belonging to the worlds of astrology and magic, omens, divination, and the like, and the considerable body of mythical texts, have no counterpart in the Hebrew scriptures (although the texts preserve evidence of these customs) because they are incompatible with Israel's fundamental monotheism. Moreover, it is apparent that what was drawn upon from the common Near Eastern stock was thoroughly refined and reshaped to bring it into conformity with the national religious ideology.

The primeval history in *Genesis,* chapters 1–11, well exemplifies this situation. The genealogies, for instance, belong to the same type of document as the Sumerian king-list, but they are used both as connectives to bridge the gap between narrative blocks and for theological purposes. Thus, ten generations are delineated to span the period between Adam and Noah, and another ten between Noah and Abraham, the symmetry being intended to convey the idea that history is the unfolding of God's predetermined plan for humankind. The Flood story has manifold and detailed points of contact with the corresponding episode in the Mesopotamian *Epic of Gilgamesh* and with its parent version, the Atrahasis epic. But the biblical version has a singularly didactic function and is uniquely placed within a spiritual and moral framework.

The law collection in the Pentateuch is another case in point. No less than six law codes have survived from the ancient Near East, the earliest probably deriving from about seven hundred years before Moses. All these, plus innumerable documents of law-court proceedings, leave no doubt of the existence of a common legal culture in the area that found expression in a similarity of content, legal phraseology, and literary form that Israel shared. Nevertheless, the scriptural exemplar features some fundamental and original departures from the general norm. The source and sanction of law are conceived in Israel to be entirely the revelation of divine will. The law is taken to be the expression of the covenant between God and Israel. There is no dichotomy, as elsewhere, between the secular and the religious. Social, moral, ethical, and cultic precepts are all equally and indiscriminately encompassed within the realm of the law. Also, there is an overwhelming preoccupation with the human person and with human life, and a lesser concern with matters of property, which is the reverse of the situation in the traditional codes. Finally, the biblical laws are encased within a narrative framework and are not isolated documents. [*For further discussion, see* Israelite Law.]

The genre that was truly an international phenomenon is that of biblical wisdom literature. It deals with observations on human behavior and the world order, drawn from experience. One such category has the individual as its focus of interest and is essentially pragmatic and utilitarian, containing precepts for success in living. Its artistic forms are mainly the maxim, the proverb, the pithy question, and the riddle. The other is reflective in nature and is more concerned with the human condition, and with the wider issues of divine-human relationships. Here the literary unit is much longer. Both Egypt and Mesopotamia produced an extensive body of literature of this type, and the analogues with *Proverbs, Job,* and *Ecclesiastes* are striking. Yet here, again, although these latter are mostly devoid of national or special Israelite content, they are distinctive in their uncompromising monotheism, in the absence of dream interpretation as an attribute of the sage, and in their insistence on the fear of the Lord as being the quintessence of wisdom. [*See* Wisdom Literature, *article on* Biblical Books.]

The *Book of Psalms* and the rich psalmody of Egypt and Babylon are closely related in both style and motifs. Both can be categorized under the more or less same limited number of literary genres. Although no Canaanite psalm has yet been recovered, the abundance of affinities with the poetry from ancient Ugarit (modern Ras Shamra) by way of poetic form, fixed pairs of words, the use of stereotyped phrases and of parallelism, is impressive. It is clear that biblical psalmody did not arise in cultural isolation from the neighboring civilizations. However, unlike the Mesopotamian psalms, the Hebrew scriptural compositions do not contain any cult-functional information, nor do they feature spells and incantations. Moreover, their conspicuous citation of history is unique, as are the spiritual experience and the soul-life of the Israelites that they mirror.

Historical Complexity of the Text. The model for printed editions of the Hebrew Bible was the second "Great Rabbinic Bible" published at Venice by Daniel Bomberg, 1524–1525, and edited by Ya'aqov ben Ḥayyim ibn Adoniyyah. All printed editions, as well as all extant medieval Hebrew manuscripts of the Bible—the earliest deriving from the ninth century CE—represent a single textual tradition, known as the Masoretic ("received") text (MT). This standard text comprises three distinct elements: the Hebrew consonants, vocalization signs, and accentuation marks. The last two components are relatively late additions. Their purpose is to preserve the proper traditional pronunciation and cantillation of the text for purposes of study and synagogue lectionary.[*See* Chanting.]

This normative uniformity notwithstanding, there is abundant evidence for a far more complex history of the Hebrew consonantal text than is suggested by the aforementioned manuscripts and the printed editions. Several different categories of testimony bear witness to an earlier era of textual transmission that was characterized by much diversity.

1. *Internal evidence* is represented by the duplication of several passages within the scriptures. These duplicates may display differences in content and arrangement, linguistic or grammatical variants, and orthographic diversity, testifying to the existence of divergent texts of one and the same composition as early as the period of the formation of biblical literature itself.

2. *Citations from the scriptures* are found in the Jewish literature of Second Temple times, such as the extracanonical books, the works of Philo Judaeus and the writings of Josephus, as well as in the New Testament. In all these sources, there can be no doubt that the citations, though in translation, often present genuine variant readings from an underlying Hebrew text that is independent of the Masoretic text and of the Septuagint.

3. *The Samaritan Pentateuch* exhibits many variants from the Masoretic text, the great majority of which relate to insignificant details, and even its manuscripts are not uniform. Although many of the disagreements are clearly the result of sectarian or dogmatic redactions and exegetical and editorial expansions, there remain several genuine variants, a goodly number of which coincide with Septuagint readings.

4. *Several ancient translations* were made directly from the original texts. None of these is identical in every respect with the Masoretic Hebrew. They are important because they were made prior to the emergence of one authoritative Hebrew text. (See "Aramaic Translations" and "Greek Translations" below.)

5. *Rabbinic sources* which supply rich and varied data make up the fifth type of testimony. Traditions, essentially anomalous ones, and hence of plausible credibility, have been preserved relating to the activities of the scribes in transmitting the sacred texts. These tell of "scribal corrections" and of divergent readings in different scrolls. In addition, there are reports of the existence of an official Temple model scroll from which other scrolls were corrected and of a class of "book-correctors" whose salaries were paid from Temple funds (e.g., B.T., *Ned.* 376, *Ket.* 106a; J.T., *Ta'an.* 4.2, 5.1; J.T., *Suk.* 3.2, *Sheq.* 4.3). A medieval source has retained a list of textual variants deriving from a Torah scroll deposited in the Severus Synagogue (or public building) in Rome and said to have been taken to Rome from Jerusalem after the destruction of the Second Temple, circa 70 CE (*Midrash Bere'shit Rabbati*, ed. C. Albeck, Jerusalem, 1940, p. 209, 45.8). Rabbinic literature also contains hundreds of citations from the Hebrew Bible that feature variants from the Masoretic text. While many of these may be discounted as having been caused by lapse of memory on behalf of the tradent or by the errors of medieval scribes, many also represent genuine variants. In addition, there are several examples of rabbinic exegesis based on consonantal texts not identical with the Masoretic text (see B.T., *San.* 4b).

6. *The Dead Sea Scrolls* are the last and most important, because the most direct, type of evidence. They consist of the Hebrew scrolls and fragments found in the Judean desert in modern-day Israel, which are now the earliest extant manuscripts of the period extending from the second half of the third century BCE to the fall of Jerusalem to the Romans in 70 (or 68) CE. The oldest of these antedate by about a thousand years the earliest Hebrew Bible manuscripts hitherto known. Some one hundred and eighty separate manuscripts of biblical books have come to light in various states of preservation, together with thousands of fragments. Every book of the Hebrew Bible, except *Esther*, is represented, several in multiple copies. Some Pentateuchal books, as well as *Job* fragments, are written in the Paleo-Hebrew script, a derivative of the ancient Hebrew script in use prior to the Babylonian exile of 587/6 BCE.

The great importance of these scrolls and fragments lies in the fact that they supply unimpeachable evidence for a degree of textual diversity that exceeds the limited three major witnesses previously known: the Masoretic text, the Septuagint, and the Samaritan Pentateuch. In fact, each biblical book displays a variety of individual texts that agree now with one of the above versions, now with another. It is to be emphasized, however, that none of the Hebrew scrolls from Qumran so far published can be seen to be actually identical in all respects with either the Septuagint or the Samaritan tradition. Particularly interesting and instructive are the direct citations from the Pentateuch found in the Qumran "Temple Scroll." These often agree with the Septuagint and occasionally with the Samaritan against the Masoretic text, but they differ from both more frequently than they agree with them. [*For further discussion, see* Dead Sea Scrolls.]

Development of the Masoretic Text. Examination of the evidence from the Judean desert yields the general conclusion that the profusion of variants increases in proportion to the antiquity of the manuscripts and decreases with the progression of time. Further, this diminution of variants works overwhelmingly in favor of the textual tradition close to that which eventually came to be known as Masoretic. This tradition is characterized, in the main, by a very conservative approach to the consonantal text that expresses itself in a minimum of expansiveness and harmonization. Difficult readings and archaic spellings and grammatical forms are carefully preserved. *Matres lectionis*, that is, the use of the weak letters (alef, he', vav, and yud) as vowel indicators, is sparsely employed. In the hoards of manuscripts from the Judean desert, the Masoretic-type exemplars are more numerous than the other text traditions. For instance, there are present no less than fourteen copies of *Isaiah* that are very close to our received Hebrew version.

These facts unmistakably point to the high prestige enjoyed by this particular tradition. Since there is no evidence for the biblical scrolls being a product of the Qumran community, this situation must reflect the text-type that eventuated in the Masoretic text, which was not only present very early at Qumran but was also already highly and widely esteemed in Palestine in Second Temple times. This implies its patronage by powerful and respected circles that could only have been located in the Temple at Jerusalem.

By the end of the first century CE this text tradition became authoritative and displaced all others. The process is clearly visible in the phenomenon of a revision at this time of the Septuagint to bring it into conformity with the proto-Masoretic text (see below, "Greek Translations"). The biblical manuscripts found at Masada are all but identical with our received texts from Wadi Murabbaat, deriving from the period of Bar Kokhba Revolt (132–135 CE).

The manuscript evidence for the development of a single authoritative text can be supplemented by secondary testimony. The recorded disputes between the Sadducees and the Pharisees never once center on or reflect differences in the text of scripture. Similarly, the Christians in the times of the New Testament do not claim a superior or different text from that used by the Jews. Also, early Christian-Jewish polemics frequently involved differences between Jewish and Christian citations of the Bible, but it was the Hebrew text of the Jews as against the Latin version of Jerome, not versus a different Hebrew existing text, that was the subject of dispute. This is in accord with another phenomenon of major importance. No differences of opinion regarding biblical readings appear in rabbinic literature, only varying interpretations of the same text. In fact, the above-cited rabbinic material that bears witness to the one time existence of divergent texts constitutes at the same time testimony to the tendency to reduce the plurality of readings; it communicates a desire to produce conformity to one text.

The above-mentioned existence of Temple-supported "book-correctors," of a model scroll kept in the Temple court, and of a hermeneutical derivation of a legal decision from the presence of a redundant conjunctive letter vav ("and") in the biblical text (*Soṭ.* 5.1) by a scholar who belonged to the generation of the destruction of the Temple—all presuppose a text fixed unalterably in spelling and content. The same conclusion is to be drawn even more emphatically from the reports of the literary activity of the *sofrim* (official scribes). This term is interpreted to mean "tellers" by the rabbis because the *sofrim* kept count of the number of letters in the Torah and marked its middle consonant, its middle words, and its middle verse to ensure the exact transmission of the Hebrew text. They did the same for the *Book of Psalms* (B.T., *Ḥag.* 15b, B.T., *Kid.* 30a).

Two other sources confirm that the concept of an official, fixed scriptural text was well rooted in Jewish learned circles. The Greek *Letter of Aristeas* (late second century BCE), which purports to tell of the origin of the Septuagint, knows of inaccurate copies of the Torah and reports an official Alexandrian request of the high priest in Jerusalem to supply an accurate Hebrew copy from which a Greek translation may be made. In the same vein, Josephus boasts that the Jews have always venerated their scriptures to the degree that none would dare to add, to remove, or to alter a syllable of the text (Josephus, *Against Apion* 1.6, 1.8).

The process by which the Masoretic text type achieved supremacy over all others and eventually supplanted them entirely is unclear. There is absolutely no evidence for an official promulgation on the subject by rabbinical authorities. The most plausible explanation for the phenomenon is that the very concept of a sacred canon of scripture on the basis of which Jewish communities established their identity, and the reading and studying of which formed the core of the organized public liturgy, would naturally tend toward the promotion of a stabilized, normative text. The specific text favored by scholarly and hierarchical circles in Second Temple times would acquire high prestige and serve as a model for less elitist groups. The trend toward uniformity would be hastened by the destruction of the Temple and the ever-widening Jewish Diaspora because a common text would act as a vital cohesive force. Laymen would cease to order and scribes would desist from copying any but the "official" text. All others would be discarded, and, being written on organic material, would perish—except for chance preservation in unusually favorable environmental conditions such as obtain in the Judean desert.

Aramaic Translations. The extensive imperial campaigns of the Assyrian kings during the eighth and ninth centuries BCE began the process that culminated in the aramaization of the Jewish people. Arameans and Chaldeans came to constitute a significant and powerful segment of the population under Assyrian domination. The diffusion of Aramaic was doubtless facilitated by the convenience and efficiency of the alphabet as opposed to the cumbersome cuneiform writing. The Aramaic language finally became the language of diplomacy and international trade throughout the Neo-Assyrian empire (see *2 Kings* 18:26). The fall of the northern kingdom of Israel in 722 to the Assyrian armies, and the subsequent large-scale population exchanges carried out by the conquerors, brought into Samaria and the Galilee various ethnic groups that seem to have had Aramaic as a common language. The importance of Aramaic was further enhanced during the days of the Neo-Babylonian empire (626–539). The destruction of the southern kingdom of Judah in 587, and the resultant Babylonian exile, soon caused a weakening of Hebrew and the adoption of Aramaic as the vernacular of the exiles. The return to Zion in the late sixth century BCE meant an influx into Judaea of Aramaic-speaking Jews who reinforced the existing bilingual situation. Throughout the Persian empire (539–333 BCE), Aramaic was the official language of the administration, and by the end of the period it was most likely the vernacular of a majority of Jews. While Hebrew still enjoyed pride of place as a literary language, this situation changed with the deteriorating fortunes of the organized Jewish rebellions against Roman rule in Palestine. The center of Jewish life shifted at the end of the first century from Judaea, where Hebrew had still managed to maintain its hold, to the Galilee, where Aramaic was the dominant language. The Jewish communities of Palestine and the widespread Diaspora of the East were now thoroughly aramaized. The emergence of Aramaic translations of the Hebrew scriptures was an inevitable development.

These Aramaic translations are known as *targumim* ("translations"; sg., *targum*). Their origins are ascribed in rabbinic sources to the time of Ezra and Nehemiah (fifth century BCE). *Nehemiah* 8:8 is adduced in support of this thesis (J.T., *Meg.* 4.1, 74d et al.). This tradition undoubtedly preserves a historical kernel, for the process certainly arose in connection with the public liturgical lectionary, most likely with the glossing in Aramaic of difficult Hebrew words and phrases. In the course of time, there arose the institution of the *meturgeman,* the official translator into Aramaic who stood beside the one who read the scriptural portion in Hebrew. According to rabbinic sources, the Aramaic had to be rendered extemporaneously, without the aid of a written text and without even a glance at the Torah scroll. The purpose was to ensure the exclusive authority of the original Hebrew text, and to prevent it from being superseded by a translation.

The existence of established Targums for private use is attested for the period of the Second Temple. The *Genesis Apocryphon* from Qumran is a typical aggadic Targum, that to *Job* from the same locale is a literal exemplar. The Greek translation of *Job,* probably made during the first century BCE, concludes with an addendum that seems to point to the existence of an earlier "Syriac" (probably Aramaic) Targum to that book. Another early written Targum to *Job* is mentioned in rabbinic sources (Tosefta, *Shab.* 13.2–3 *et al.*). Jesus' citation of *Psalms* 22:1 in Aramaic, rather than in Hebrew, at his crucifixion (*Mt.* 27:46, *Mk.* 15:34) testifies to a well-rooted tradition of Aramaic translation of *Psalms,* but whether it existed in oral or written form cannot be determined.

The almost total aramaization of the Jews of Palestine and the eastern Diaspora, and the unremitting retreat of Hebrew as a spoken language, made the Aramaic Targums to the scriptures a vital and effective tool of mass education. All resistance to their commitment to writing broke down. Some achieved official recognition to the extent that the private reading of the Targum together with the Hebrew text was actually prescribed (B.T., *Ber.* 8a–b).

Pentateuchal Targums. Targums to all books of the Hebrew Bible except *Daniel* and *Ezra-Nehemiah* have survived. Three that translate the Pentateuch are particularly important.

Targum Onkelos. Targum Onkelos was the official and single universally accepted Targum to the Torah. The ascription of its authorship is based on a passage in the Babylonian Talmud that refers to "Onkelos the proselyte" (B.T., *Meg.* 3a). From the corresponding passage in the Palestinian Talmud (J.T., *Meg.* 1.11, 71c) it is clear that the original reference was to the Greek translation of Aquila, a name pronounced "Onkelos" in the dialect of Babylonia. Because nothing was known about this Greek version in the East, that translation was there confused with the one to the Torah in Aramaic.

Identifying the dialect of Targum Onkelos presents a problem. It shares features characteristic of both Eastern and Western Aramaic, and is close to Middle Aramaic (200 BCE to 200 CE), whose place of origin seems to have been Palestine, which would point to a Palestinian provenance for Targum Onkelos. This conclusion is reinforced by linguistic evidence. In addition, its *aggadah* and *halakhah,* or homiletical and legal traditions, show unmistakable influence of the school of the Palestinian rabbi ʿAqiva' ben Yosef.

On the other hand, Targum Onkelos vanishes from Palestinian Jewish records for many hundreds of years after the end of the third century CE. It exhibits morphological features that are typical of Eastern Aramaic, and it was the official Targum of the academies of Babylon. It was transmitted with a Babylonian vocalization and a *masorah,* a text-critical apparatus that, written in the margins of the manuscript, reflects the Babylonian traditions regarding the form of the text, the spelling of words, directions for pronunciation, and other lexicographic details.

In light of the above data, it seems safe to assume that this Targum originated in Palestine and was brought to Babylon at the end of the second century CE. There it underwent a local, systematic redaction and was given official ecclesiastical recognition. It is a work composed of numerous and varied layers that represent a time span of hundreds of years.

Generally speaking, Targum Onkelos was executed with great care as a straightforward, literalistic rendering of the Hebrew source. It departs from this approach in the difficult poetic sections of the Pentateuch, as well as in those passages in which its pedagogic goals, namely, the Aramaic translation as an instrument for mass education, required change or expansion. Here it incorporated oral traditions, halakhic and aggadic, and it used circumlocutions and euphemisms to avoid misunderstanding on the part of the public as to the monotheistic concept of God, changing anthropomorphisms and anthropopathisms, and texts that might be misconstrued as suggesting direct physical contact between man and God.

Targum Onkelos was first printed at Bologna in 1482. The Sabbioneta text of 1557 served as the basis of Abraham Berliner's edition (Leipzig, 1877). A new edition, based on old Yemenite manuscripts and printed texts, was edited by Alexander Sperber in 1959. Alejandro Diez-Macho is publishing another edition for the Madrid Polyglot Bible.

Targum Jonathan. A second popular Targum to the Pentateuch was the Targum Jonathan (Heb., Yonatan). The name is a misnomer arising from a mistaken interpretation of an abbreviation, "T.Y.," which actually denotes Targum Yerushalmi (Jerusalem Targum). An earlier, widespread name for this translation was Targum of the Land of Israel. This Targum is also characterized by an aversion to anthropomorphisms, but it is free and expansive, replete with aggadic and halakhic material. Biblical toponyms are modernized. Its history is problematic. Internal evidence for its dating ranges from mention of the high priest John Hyrcanus (135–104 BCE) in the Targum to *Deuteronomy* 33:1, to mention of the "six orders of the Mishnah" (Targ. Jon., *Ex.* 26:9) that were edited only around 200 CE, to the presence of Khadījah, wife of Muḥammad (some texts read "Ayesha," another of his wives) and Faṭimah, his daughter (Targ. Jon., *Gn.* 21:21), to references to Ishmael and Esau as masters of the world (Targ. Jon., *Gn.* 49:26, *Dt.* 33:2), which can only refer to Islam and Byzantium of the seventh century CE at the earliest. A reference to Constantinople in the Targum on *Numbers* 24:19 seems to allude to the war of the caliph Sulaymān against the Byzantine capital in 716–718 CE.

A curious feature of this Targum is the number of passages in which the exegesis contradicts normative rabbinic *halakhah* (e.g., Targ. Jon., *Lev.* 18:21, cf. *Meg.* 4.9), and in several cases agrees with that of Philo and the sect of Karaites (eighth century CE on). As a result it is extremely hazardous to date this version. Its language is essentially Galilean Aramaic, and its origins certainly go back to Second Temple times. Innumerable accretions and the influence of Targum Onkelos on it have vastly complicated the task of reconstructing the history of its transmission.

Targum (Pseudo-) Jonathan was first printed at Venice, 1591. A British Museum manuscript was edited by Moses Ginsburger (Berlin, 1903) and published in a corrected edition by David Rieder (Jerusalem, 1974).

Neofiti 1. An early sixteenth-century manuscript known as Neofiti 1 represents a third Galilean Aramaic Targum to the Pentateuch. Discovered in the Vatican Library in 1956 by Diez-Macho, it has since been published in five volumes (1968–1978). The codex is complete and well preserved. It features a large number of marginal and interlinear variants and notes written in rabbinic script by different hands, the source of which may well be parallel readings in various Targums, since they often coincide with fragments preserved in the Cairo Genizah.

The dating of this Targum presents complex problems. Linguistic and other aspects point to the early centuries CE. It undoubtedly contains valuable textual variants paralleled in other ancient versions. It differs, however, in orthography, grammar, and the extent of paraphrastic material from the other Galilean Targums, and there is good reason to believe that the original underwent later revision. Another Palestinian Aramaic translation exists that is sometimes referred to as Targum Yerushalmi or Fragmentary Targum. It was first printed in the Bomberg Rabbinic Bible of 1517–1518, and subsequently, with additions, by Moses Ginsburger (Berlin, 1899). These fragments cover only about 850 of the 5,845 verses of the Pentateuch, and it is not clear whether it was ever complete.

The Samaritan Targum (or Targums). The Samaritan community produced for its own use a Targum based upon its recension of the Pentateuch. The dialect is that of the area of Shechem and the central highlands, very close to Galilean Aramaic. Linguistic criteria suggest an original date of composition sometime between the second and third centuries CE. Generally, the Samaritan Targum is characterized by extreme literalism even to the extent of reproducing anthropomorphisms.

A serious problem is the fact that the Samaritans never produced a definitive edition of their Targum, with the result that every manuscript exhibits its own peculiarities, the variants frequently reflecting changes and developments in their Aramaic dialect. Moreover, the later scribes, who did not know Aramaic, introduced numerous errors into their copies.

The first edition printed in the West was that of the Paris Polyglot (1645), but it is now clear that it was made from a decidedly inferior manuscript dating to 1514. Walton's London Polyglot of 1657 (vol. 6) reprinted this, but with numerous corrections. A version based on various manuscripts found in the Samaritan synagogue in Shechem was begun by Heinrich Petermann in 1872 and completed by Caroli Vollers in 1893, but the copies used were unreliable. A new edition for the projected Madrid Polyglot is being prepared by Jose Ramon Diaz.

Targum to the Prophets. Traditionally, the official Targum to the Prophets is ascribed to Jonathan son of Uzziel, based on a single Talmudic passage (B.T., *Meg.* 3a), which also makes him a contemporary of Haggai, Zechariah, and Malachi (sixth century BCE). However, another rabbinic text (B.T., *Suk.* 28a) has him a student of Hillel the Elder (end of first century BCE–beginning of first century CE). It has been noted that the name *Jonathan (Yonaton)* is a Hebrew rendering of the Greek name *Theodotion.* One of the second-century Greek versions of the Bible was executed by a certain Theodotion, and it is conjectured that in Babylonian Jewish circles he was confused with Jonathan ben Uzziel, who was then credited with translating the Prophets into Aramaic.

The Aramaic of the Targum to the Prophets is close to biblical Aramaic and to the Palestinian Jewish dialect. Its affinities with the *Pesher Habakkuk* (a commentary on *Habakkuk*) from Qumran and the exegetical traditions it shares in common with Josephus testify to the antiquity of some of its layers. At the same time, a definite dependence on Targum Onkelos to the Torah can be established. In assessing the date of Targum Jonathan's composition, account must also be taken of the fact that the Babylonian Talmud contains numerous citations of Aramaic renderings of passages from the Prophets, which are identical with those in Targum Jonathan, and which are given in the name of the Babylonian amora Yosef ben Ḥiyya' (d. 333 CE). These indicate that they were composed at least a generation earlier (B.T., *San.* 94b *et al.*).

It is possible that Yosef ben Ḥiyya' may have been connected with one of the revisions. At any rate, it is certain that the Targum is not the work of a single individual or of one period but has undergone much revision over a long period of time, until it reached its definitive form, by the seventh century CE.

The style of the Targum, especially to the Latter Prophets, is paraphrastic and expansive, probably because of the difficulties in translating the poetic oratory, which is replete with figurative language. It shares with Targum Onkelos to the Torah the general aversion to anthropomorphisms. Fragments of the Targum from Codex Reuchlinianus were edited by Paul de Lagarde as *Prophetae Chaldaice,* (1872). A critical edition of the Targum Jonathan to the Prophets was published by A. Sperber (1959, 1962).

Citations from another Palestinian Targum to the Prophets appear in the biblical commentaries of Rashi (Shelomoh ben Yitsḥaq, 1040–1105) and David Kimḥi (c. 1160–c. 1235) and in the rabbinic dictionary of Natan ben Yeḥiel of Rome (1035–c. 1110), known as the *Arukh,* as well as in the above-mentioned Codex Reuchlinianus. They have been collected by Lagarde and Sperber. While the Aramaic is Palestinian, the influence of the Babylonian Talmud upon this Targum is clear.

Targums to the Ketuvim. Ever since the Venice edition of 1518, rabbinic Bibles have carried Targums to all the books of the Ketuvim (Hagiographa) except *Daniel, Ezra,* and *Nehemiah.* Lagarde edited the series in *Hagiographa Chaldaice* (1873), and a critical edition was published by Sperber in 1964. These Targums are composed in the Palestinian Aramaic dialect, and presumably originate in Palestine. Each is distinctive, and there is no uniformity of style. None of them ever became authoritative or underwent formal redaction. Those to *Psalms* and *Job* share in common several distinctive features.

Rabbinic sources make clear that a Targum to *Job* already existed in Second Temple times (Tosefta, *Shab.* 13.2 et al.). The remains of such a one have been recovered from Qumran Cave 11, but whether it has any relationship to the former cannot be determined. The language of this Targum is close to biblical Aramaic and seems to go back to the late second century BCE.

The Targum to *Job* that appears in the printed editions has no relation to the preceding and appears to be a compilation from different periods. The Targum to *Proverbs* is unique in that it bears strong resemblance to the Peshitta, or Syriac version, leading to the most likely conclusion that both renderings go back to a common, older, Aramaic translation or to the influence of a Jewish transliteration of the Peshitta into Hebrew characters.

There are Targums to the Five Scrolls, but these are so expansive and paraphrastic that they are more collections of *midrashim* than true Targums. They were edited with an introduction by Bernard Grossfeld in 1973.

Greek Translations. The history of the Jewish community in Egypt can be traced back at least to the beginning of the sixth century BCE. There Jews spoke Aramaic and knew Hebrew, but the influx of Greek-speaking settlers had far-reaching effects on their cultural life. With the conquest of Egypt by Alexander the Great, the local Jewish population was swelled by a great wave of immigration attracted there by the opportunities afforded by the Ptolemies. The Jews concentrated mainly in Alexandria, where they formed an autonomous community with its own synagogues and sociocultural institutions, and where they came to form a significant segment of the population. They soon adopted Greek as their everyday language.

By the third century BCE, both liturgical and educational considerations dictated the need for a Greek translation of the scriptures, at least of the Pentateuch. The version known as the Septuagint was revolutionary in its conception, its execution, and its impact. No lengthy Eastern religious text had previously been translated into Greek, nor had a written translation of the Jewish scriptures been made hitherto. The Septuagint was one of the great literary enterprises of the ancient world, and it served to fashion and shape a distinctively Jewish-Hellenistic culture, which attempted to synthesize Hebraic and Greek thought and values. Eventually, it became a powerful literary medium for the spread of early Christianity throughout the far-flung Greek-speaking world, thereby transforming the culture and religion of a goodly segment of humanity.

The Septuagint ("seventy") received its Latin name from a legend current among the Jews of Alexandria that it was executed by seventy-two scholars in seventy-two days. Originally applicable only to the translation of the Pentateuch, this abbreviated title was gradually extended to the complete Greek rendering of the entire Jewish scriptures. In the course of time, the origins of the Septuagint came to be embroidered in legend and enveloped in an aura of the miraculous. The *Letter of Aristeas*, Philo's *Moses* (II, v-vii, 25–40) and rabbinic writings (e.g., B.T., *Meg.* 9a; *Avot de Rabbi Natan*, ms. b, 37) are the principal witnesses to this development, whereby the initiative for the translation was said to have come from Ptolemy II Philadelphus (r. 285–246 BCE).

The fullest and most popular version of the legend is that found in the first of the above-mentioned sources. That the *Letter* is a fiction is apparent from internal evidence, and it has been shown to have been composed by a hellenized Jew writing in the second half of the second century BCE, about a hundred years after the publication of the original Septuagint. It is certain that it was the needs of the Alexandrian Jewish community that called forth the translation in the course of the third century BCE. It is not impossible, however, that the project did receive royal approval, given the known interest and activities of the Ptolemies as patrons of culture. Furthermore, it is quite likely that the translators did come from Palestine and worked in Egypt.

The Greek of the Septuagint is essentially the Koine, that form of the language commonly spoken and written from the fourth century BCE until the middle of the sixth century CE by the Greek-speaking populations of the eastern Mediterranean. Hence, the Septuagint stands as a monument of Hellenistic Greek. However, it is distinctive in many ways. It abounds with lexical and syntactical Hebraisms and is often indifferent to Greek idiom. Neologisms are comparatively rare, but the translators frequently forced the meaning of common Greek words by using a standard rendering of a Hebrew term without regard to context. Further, Aramaic was still widely used, and the translators sometimes gave Aramaic rather than Hebrew meanings to certain words. On occasion, they rendered the original by Greek words that were similar in sound but quite dissimilar in meaning. Quite clearly they injected Palestinian exegetical traditions into their translations. All in all, the Septuagint was generally competently rendered. If its style is not consistent throughout, this is partly due to the multiplicity of translators and partly to the revolutionary nature of the undertaking in that the translators had neither experience nor real precedent to fall back on.

The rest of the Greek Bible displays a wide variety of styles and techniques ranging from the literal to the free and the paraphrastic. This is due to the piecemeal nature of the translations, to the long period of time it took to complete the entire scriptures—several hundred years—and to the fact that the books of the Prophets and Hagiographa were apparently privately executed. At least, no traditions about them have been preserved. The result was considerable fluctuations in the quality of the translations.

The Septuagint as it has come down to us often reflects readings at variance with the Masoretic Hebrew text. Two factors complicate the scholarly use of this version as a tool for biblical research. The first relates to its early external form, the second to its textual history.

With the spread of Christianity and the pursuit of missionary and polemical activity on the part of the church, the inconvenience of the traditional scroll format for the sacred books became more and more pronounced. The church, therefore, early adopted the codex or "leaf-book" format for its Bible, perhaps being additionally motivated by a conscious desire to differentiate its own from Jewish practice, which adhered to the scroll form for study purposes until at least the sixth century CE. Those who produced the early codices of the Greek Bible must have had great difficulty in assembling uniform copies of the individual scrolls that made up the scriptural canon. Accordingly, various scrolls of a heterogeneous nature were used by the copyists for their archetypes. A badly copied scroll might have been the only one available to the compiler.

The second factor concerns the tendency of later scholars to rework the original Greek translation. Scholars reworked translations because the manuscripts before them had been poorly made, or because the literary quality of the Greek rendering was deemed to be in need of improvement, or, what is most important, because the Greek reflected an underlying Hebrew text at variance with that current at the time, so that editors would attempt to bring the translation in line with the current Hebrew. As a result, multiple text traditions of the Septuagint arose, and the problem of recovering the pristine translation is a formidable one. Each book of the Septuagint must first be individually examined both in terms of its translation technique and style and of its own textual history and transmission. As a result, a rendering that appears to reflect a variant Hebrew text may turn out to be nothing of the sort and may be accounted for on quite different grounds. On the other hand, the Qumran scrolls often clearly display a Hebrew reading that the Septuagint translators must have had before them.

The problems relating to Septuagint studies are exacerbated by the large number of witnesses available, consisting of citations in the works of Philo Judaeus, Josephus, the writers of New Testament, and the church fathers; the manuscripts of the Septuagint itself; and the acknowledged revisions of it. Many of the variant quotations may, in fact, be independent personal renderings of the authors or not even be original to the works cited, having been tampered with by later copyists or editors. In the case of the New Testament, there is also the possibility of their having been rendered into Greek from an Aramaic version rather than the Hebrew. Nevertheless, there still remains a respectable residue of genuine Septuagint quotations that differ from the manuscripts. As to these last, the material is very extensive and stretches from the middle of the second century BCE (with the Dead Sea Scrolls material) to the age of printing.

The turning point in the production of Greek Bibles comes in the fourth century CE attendant upon the conversion to Christianity of Constantine (c. 280–337) and the conferring upon that religion of a privileged position in the Roman empire. An order from Constantine in 332 for fifty vellum Bibles for use in the new churches he was erecting in Constantinople afforded an immense stimulus to the creation of the great and handsome Greek Bibles known technically as majuscules or uncials ("inch high") because of the practice of the scribes to employ capital-size letters without ligatures. The three most important codices of this type that have come down to us in a reasonably complete state are the Codex Sinaiticus (usually designated for scholarly purposes by *S* or by the Hebrew letter alef), the Codex Alexandrinus (given the siglum *A*), and the Codex Vaticanus (indicated by the initial *B*). The Sinaiticus, executed in the fourth century CE, is not complete and in places has been seriously damaged by the action of the metallic ink eating through the parchment. Despite the often careless orthography, the manuscript is witness to a very early text tradition. The Vaticanus, also produced in the fourth century, is nearly perfect and constitutes the oldest and most excellent extant copy of the Greek Bible, even though it is not of uniform quality throughout. It was used as the basis of the Roman edition of 1587, the commonly printed Septuagint. The Alexandrinus, containing practically the entire Bible, was probably copied in the early fifth century. Its text is frequently at variance with that of the Codex Vaticanus. It too has suffered damage from corrosive ink.

Up to the eighth century, only uncials were produced, but thereafter appear the minuscules, written in small-size cursive writing. From the eleventh century, this type completely replaces the other. The minuscules were mainly intended for private reading, and hundreds are extant. Their value for Septuagint studies is small.

The adoption of the Septuagint instead of the Hebrew as the Bible of the church was itself a source of discomfort to Greek-speaking Jews. That the Greek rendering frequently departed from the by then universally recognized Hebrew text constituted additional and decisive cause for its rejection by the synagogue. Doubtless, the conviction on the part of the Jews that christological changes had been introduced into the original Septuagint also played a role. This reversal of attitude to the Septuagint on the part of the Jewish religious authorities is strikingly reflected in rabbinic literature. The Palestinian minor tractate *Soferim* (1.7) asserts, "The day that the Torah was rendered into Greek was as disastrous for Israel as the day in which the Golden Calf was made, for the Torah could not be adequately translated."

On the Christian side, the lack of uniformity and consistency within the Greek manuscripts themselves were to be an embarrassing disadvantage to Christian missionaries in their theological polemics with Jews. This situation would be exacerbated by the discrepancies between the translation used by Christian disputants and the Hebrew text, which was the only authoritative form of the scriptures recognized by Palestinian Jews. Exegetical debate could proceed only on the basis of a mutually acknowledged text, which in this case had to be the only Hebrew text tradition accepted by the Jews.

All the aforementioned factors led to conscious attempts by Jews and Christians to revise the Septuagint in order to bring it into closer harmony with the Hebrew. In the second century CE, three systematic revisions of the Greek translation took place, namely, those of Aquila, Theodotion, and Symmachus. Aquila, a Jewish proselyte from Pontus, Asia Minor, apparently worked under rabbinical supervision (J.T., *Meg.* 1.11, 70c). He adopted a mechanical, artificial technique of consistently using fixed Greek equivalents for Hebrew terms, and he coined words or forms to this end. This extreme literalness, to the extent of reproducing even minutiae of the original, yielded a recension that was often alien to one who knew no Hebrew. Aquila's motivation was to underline the authority of the standardized consonantal Hebrew text and to produce a Greek version that would be absolutely faithful to it. His work replaced the Septuagint in the synagogues of Greek-speaking Jews, and was used there for the lectionaries well into the sixth century CE. It has survived only in part.

It is not certain whether Theodotion was an Ebionite Christian or a Jewish proselyte. At any rate, he, too, displays excessive literalness. At times, he even transliterates Hebrew words into Greek letters, possibly for the benefit of Jews. His translation was not preserved in Jewish circles, but was highly regarded by the church. His Greek was readable, and his *Daniel* was incorporated into the Septuagint, displacing the inferior original Greek version of that book.

The third revision in the course of the second century CE was done by Symmachus. His origins are obscure. While he used the existing translations, his work has an independent quality about it. The style of the Greek is superior to that of the other two. He also exhibits a tendency to soften anthropomorphisms, as well as a marked influence of rabbinic exegesis. Very little of his work has survived.

The climax of a process of revision for the benefit of Christian missionaries and polemicists against the Jews was the work of the great church theologian of Caesarea, Origen (c. 185–257). He attempted both to provide a textbook for the study of Hebrew and to reduce the variety of Septuagint versions to order, taking as his base the standardized Hebrew text current among the Palestinian Jewish communities of his day. This was a bold step, for it made the Hebrew text superior to, and more authoritative than, the Septuagint, which the church had officially adopted and canonized. To achieve his goal, he arranged texts in six parallel columns. This bulky work, the product of prodigious industry, has come to be known as the Hexapla ("sixfold").

The first column of the Hexapla, the consonantal text in Hebrew characters, has wholly vanished, but the second, a Greek transliteration of the former, testifies to the fact that it was practically identical with the Masoretic Hebrew text. Origen's aim was apparently to indicate how to vocalize the consonants of the first column. Aquila's translation for the third column was the logical sequence since it was closest to the current Hebrew text, and that of Symmachus came next, apparently because it seems to have been based to a large extent upon Aquila, and it made that rendering more intelligible.

It is in the fifth column, a revised Septuagint, that Origen invested his main energies. In attempting to produce a "corrected" Greek translation, in the sense that it would faithfully represent the Hebrew of his first column, he devised a system for indicating to the reader the substantive differences between the latter and the Septuagint, and for remedying the "defects." The codex of Origen's Hexapla vanished completely sometime in the seventh century. However, his "restored" Septuagint text had been independently published and received wide circulation. In this way it considerably influenced subsequent copies of the Septuagint. Unfortunately, future scribes either neglected or carelessly reproduced the system of critical symbols, with the result that the text became chaotic and Origen's work was ruined.

One other edition of the Greek Bible is that of the Christian theologian Lucian of Antioch (c. 240–312). Lucian was heir to a still earlier Greek version that can now be shown, on the basis of Qumran readings, to have reflected an ancient Hebrew text. Where *Samuel* and *Kings* are concerned, at least, the "Proto-Lucian" was an early Jewish revision of the original Greek translation of which both Theodotion and Aquila seem to have known, if not the original itself, as some have claimed. At any rate, Lucian apparently revised this version on the basis of Origen's fifth column.

Translations Based on the Septuagint. The great prestige that the Septuagint acquired as the official, authoritative Bible of the church generated a number of secondary translations as Christianity spread to non-Greek-speaking lands and the churches had to accommodate themselves to the native language. Whereas the early translations had been the work of scholars who knew Hebrew, this was now no longer a requirement. The Greek itself served as the base for subsequent translations. Such was the case in respect to the Coptic, Ethiopic, Armenian, Georgian, Gothic, and Old Latin versions, all of which have little bearing on the history of the Hebrew text but are of lesser or greater importance for the study of the Septuagint itself.

The most important of all the secondary renderings of the Bible is the Latin. This language advanced with the expansion of Roman power, first throughout Italy, then into southern Gaul and throughout the Mediterranean coastal regions of Africa. In Rome itself, Greek remained the cultural language of the church until the third century, but in the African communities Latin was very popular, and it is most probable that the earliest translations thereinto emanated from these circles. The needs of the liturgy and the lectionary dictated renditions into the vernacular, which at first remained oral and by way of interlinear glosses. It is not impossible but cannot be proven that the earliest such efforts were made by Jews directly from the Hebrew. At any rate, by the middle of the second century CE, an Old Latin version, in the colloquial form of the language, based on the Septuagint, was current. Whether we are speaking here of a single text or a plurality of translations is a matter of dispute because of the great variety of readings to be found in extant manuscripts and citations. These divide roughly into African and European types, but it must be remembered that the two interacted with each other.

Despite the fact that the Old Latin is a translation of a translation, and for that reason must be used with extreme caution for text-critical studies, it is nevertheless important since it was made from a pre-Hexaplaric Greek text. For example, it has much in common with the Lucianic recension and with the Vatican and Sinaitic codices. In the case of *Job* and *Daniel*, it has renderings that presuppose a Greek reading that has not otherwise been preserved and that, in turn, indicates an original Hebrew text not identical with that received. The psalms, in particular, are significant for the numerous texts available as a consequence of their having been used in the liturgy, although they were frequently reworked.

Vulgate of Jerome. By the close of the fourth century, the confused state of the Old Latin texts had become acute, a source of embarrassment to the church in the lands of the West where Latin was the language of the intelligentsia and of literature. A stable and standardized Bible in that language was a desideratum. At the papal initiative of Damasus I (c. 382), Jerome undertook to revise the Old Latin version.

The Roman Psalter (384), a limited revision of the *Psalms* based on the Greek, seems to have been the first fruit of Jerome's labors in the Hebrew scriptures, although his authorship has been disputed by some scholars. This version was officially adopted into the church liturgy at Rome. It was soon generally superseded by the Gallican Psalter, so called because it was first accepted by the churches of Gaul. This was Jerome's revision of the Old Latin on the basis of the fifth column of the Hexapla, a rendering therefore very close to the Hebrew text of his day. This version, produced in Bethlehem, achieved preeminent status and is the one included in editions of the Vulgate to the present time, even though the fresh translation from the Hebrew more accurately reflects the original.

Jerome's involvement with Origen's Hexapla convinced him of the superiority of the Hebrew text over the Greek, and he set about creating a fresh Latin translation of the Hebrew scriptures, directly from the Hebrew text (the *Hebraica veritas*, the "Hebrew truth"). Doubtless, another motivation was the recognition that Christian theological polemic with Jews could not be conducted on the basis of a text, the Septuagint in this case, which had no authority for one of the parties.

Jerome completed his translation in 405, having enjoyed the assistance of both Jewish converts to Christianity and rabbinical scholars. Indeed, elements of rabbinic tradition and exegesis are embedded in his work, and it is evident that he was also influenced by Aquila's translation. Conscious of the implications of his audacious disregard of the Septuagint that the church had canonized, Jerome was careful to employ the terms and phrases of the Old Latin that had achieved wide currency, particularly those in the New Testament that had doctrinal coloration.

The new Latin translation, known since the sixteenth century as the Vulgate, or "common" edition, met with strenuous opposition, especially on the part of Augustine, but owing to its elegance and superior intelligibility it made headway, so that by the eighth century its preeminence was undisputed. However, because the Vulgate existed for several centuries side by side with the Old Latin, the two versions interacted with each other so that the manuscripts of the Vulgate became corrupted. Various attempts in the Middle Ages to produce a corrected and revised edition are recorded, but none gained lasting success.

The invention of printing finally made possible the long-sought goal of a standardized text, but this goal was not achieved at once. Jerome's Vulgate may have the distinction of being the first book printed from movable type to issue from Gutenberg's press at Mainz (1456), but it took almost another century of sporadic attempts at revision before a definitive, official edition was achieved. The achievement of a definitive edition was an outgrowth of the decision of the Council of Trent in 1546 to proclaim Jerome's Vulgate to be the authoritative Bible of the Catholic church. The hastily prepared three-volume edition of Sixtus V (1590), the "Sixtine Bible," proved to be unsatisfactory, and it was soon replaced by the "Clementine Bible" of 1592, promulgated by Clement VIII. This latter remained the one official text of the church until the twentieth century.

In 1907, a new critical edition of the Vulgate was commissioned by Pius X, and the task of preparation was entrusted to the Benedictine order. About eight thousand manuscripts were consulted, and it began to appear in 1926. By 1981, fourteen volumes had been published covering most of the books of the Hebrew Bible. A two-volume edition based on the foregoing was issued at Stuttgart in 1975, with a second edition in 1980.

The importance of the Vulgate as a major factor in the cultural and religious life of Western civilization cannot be overestimated. For a thousand years, it was the Bible of the churches of western Europe and served as the base at first for all translations into the respective developing vernaculars.

Syriac versions. Syriac is an Eastern Aramaic dialect within the Semitic group of languages that was current in southeastern Turkey and the Euphrates Valley. It was an important literary and liturgical language within the Christian church from the third century until the Arab Muslim invasion of the area. The Hebrew Bible was several times translated into Syriac, the many renderings necessitated by dialectic and theological considerations.

It is quite likely that there existed an early Syriac rendering that was the basis of the many later versions, most of which are extant only as fragments. The one complete translation to survive is the standard and most important recension, known since the ninth century as the Peshitta. This term means the "simple [version]," a designation it acquired either because of its popular style or, more likely, to contrast it with the more complicated renderings that were equipped with a text-critical apparatus. Ever since the third century, the Peshitta has been the official Bible of the Syrian church, common in one form or another to all its different branches.

The Peshitta is theoretically of the utmost significance for the textual criticism of the Hebrew Bible, since it was executed directly from the original long before the fixing of the Hebrew masoretic system, and because it is in a language closely related to Hebrew, in contrast to the Greek versions. This importance, however, is diminished by the facts that the version possesses a long complex history as yet imperfectly reconstructed, that the hundreds of manuscripts housed in the Western libraries display a large number of variants, and that all existing printed editions are unreliable.

No early trustworthy data about the provenance and date of the Peshitta or of the identity of the translators have been handed down. Weighty evidence has been adduced to prove both a Jewish and a Christian origin. If the former, the work would have originated in a Syriac-speaking community that maintained close relationships with Jerusalem. This immediately suggests the district of Adiabene in the upper region of the Tigris, situated between the rivers Great Zab and Little Zab, where a Jewish kingdom existed in the first century CE (Josephus, *Antiquities* 20.2.1–20.4.3, Loeb ed. XX.17–96). On the other hand, a Christian provenance can also be argued, since Christianity early took firm hold in the region of Adiabene, which already had Christian bishops by 123 CE. The ecclesiastical authorities, in preparing a version of scripture for the needs of the local Christian community, could have made use of earlier Jewish Aramaic translations and could have entrusted the task to Jewish Christians, whose presence in the area is attested. There is also the possibility that the Christian elements may be the result of the later redaction of an earlier Jewish work. It is impossible to generalize about the nature of the translation, which is the work of many hands and different periods and which lacks consistency.

Early in the fifth century, the Syriac church experienced a schism, dividing into Nestorians in the East and Jacobites in the West, with each group developing its own form of the Peshitta. Because of the relative isolation of the former, politically and geographically, in the area of Nisibin in southern Anatolia, the Eastern or Nestorian texts are regarded as having been less vulnerable to revisions on the basis of Hebrew or Greek sources.

The most important Peshitta manuscripts are those copied before the tenth century when the standardized Syriac biblical *masorah* was finally fixed. A critical *editio minor* of the Peshitta to the Hebrew Bible is currently in course of preparation by decision of the 1956 Strasbourg Congress of the International Organization for the Study of the Old Testament. When completed, the edition will offer the student an objective tool for the study of the Bible text and its history.

A Syriac version that is second in importance only to the Peshitta is the Syro-Hexapla. This is a rendering of the Septuagint version of the fifth column of Origen's Hexapla. It was commissioned to serve political and theological ends, and it was most likely executed in a Syrian monastery in Egypt by Paul, bishop of Tella, together with associates, and completed in 617. It never achieved its purpose of displacing the Peshitta, but it has its own inherent worth and is most valuable as a tool for reconstructing the lost column of the Hexapla on which it was based.

Another version of the Syriac Bible is the Syro-Palestinian. This version has only partially survived. Its script is distinctive, in that it used the Estrangela ("round script") type, as is also its dialect, which is a West Palestinian Aramaic spoken by a Christian community in certain areas of the Judean hills. This is a development of the dialect spoken by Jews who converted to Christianity around the year 400, and who intermingled with the Melchite church. The version bears close affinities with Jewish Aramaic Targums. Moshe H. Goshen-Gottstein together with H. Shirun assembled all printed remnants of this version as well as some unpublished material. The Pentateuch and the Prophets in Hebrew characters appeared in 1973.

Still another Syriac version, the Philoxenian, was commissioned by the leader of the Jacobite Monophysite church, Philoxenus, bishop of Mabbug-Hierapolis, near Aleppo, Syria, in 507–508. This version was not a revision of the Peshitta, but a new translation based on the Lucianic version of the Greek. Only fragments of *Isaiah* and *Psalms* have survived.

Finally, there is the attempt of Jacob (c. 640–708), bishop of Edessa, to modernize and popularize the style of the Syro-Hexapla while retaining the text-form of the former. For the first time, chapter divisions were introduced, and the Syrian Masoretic apparatus was utilized.

Arabic translations. Jewish and Christian communities existed in the Arabian Peninsula many centuries before the dawn of Islam, engaging in missionary activities among the pagan Arabs, often in competition with one another. In Yemen, in southwestern Arabia, the last of the Himyarite rulers, Dhu Nuwās, even converted to Judaism (517 CE). The buffer state of Al-Hīrah was a center of Arab Christianity between the third and sixth centuries. The Jews used their Hebrew Bible, the Christians either the Syriac or Greek translations. Since both religious communities were well integrated into Arabian life and culture, while retaining their distinctiveness, it seems plausible that at least parts of the Bible had been rendered into Arabic, if only in oral form, in pre-Islamic days, much the same way as Aramaic oral renderings long antedated the first written translations in that language. It was the Muslim invasions of western Asia and the concomitant arabization of the populace that prompted the systematic, written translation of the Bible into Arabic. The foremost Christian scholar and translator, Ḥunayn ibn Isḥāk (Johannitus, 808–873), is said to have produced such a version, basing himself on the Septuagint, but if there was such a version, it has not survived.

The first and most celebrated translation made directly from the Hebrew was that of Saʿadyah Gaon (882–942), leader of Babylonian Jewry. It has come down only in Hebrew script, and its appearance constituted a major turning point in the development of Judeo-Arabic culture. Saʿadyah tried to conform in his style to the genius of the Arabic language. He sought to eliminate anthropomorphisms and he rendered geographical names into contemporary usage.

The impact of Saʿadyah's translation was immense. It has continued to enjoy high prestige and to be read weekly by Yemenite Jews to the present day. It even influenced the Samaritan and Karaite communities, both of which produced their own Arabic versions of the Hebrew scriptures. The first Samaritan translator of the Pentateuch, Abū Saʿīd (thirteenth century), based himself on it; at the end of the tenth century, the foremost Karaite scholar, Yafet ben Eli, rendered the entire Bible anew into Arabic, which translation remained the standard text for all Karaite communities in the East. It, too, was indebted to Saʿadyah, even though its style and language were updated, more popular, and excessively literal.

Christian translations were generally not made from the Hebrew but were variously based on the Greek, Syriac, Latin, and Coptic versions, sometimes on more than one. In the sixteenth century, attempts were made to assemble a complete Bible in Arabic, but the different translators individually used different versions as their base. The resulting codex was a mixed text. The Paris Polyglot of 1629 first featured an almost complete Arabic text of the Bible, which was followed by the London Polyglot of 1657, but here again the result was a mixed text.

In the course of the nineteenth and twentieth centuries, as a result of renewed interest in the Arab world on the part of Western powers, Protestant and Catholic organizations set about producing translations into modern Arabic for missionary purposes. The most frequently used is that by the American Protestant mission in Beirut, completed in 1864, and made from the Hebrew. The most widely used Catholic translation is that in three volumes (1876–1880) made by the Jesuits in Beirut with the assistance of Ibrāhīm al-Yāzijt.

In sum, the Arabic translations, apart from that of Saʿadyah, are relatively late and are mostly secondary, so that they have no value for textual studies of the Hebrew original. They are, however, useful sources for the history of biblical exegesis, as well as witnesses to the earlier translations such as the Greek, the Aramaic, and the Syriac.

[*See also* Israelite Religion; Prophecy, *article on* Biblical Prophecy; Wisdom Literature, *article on* Biblical Books; Psalms; *and* Biblical Exegesis, *article on* Jewish Views.]

BIBLIOGRAPHY

The most reliable and comprehensive work on the Bible is *The Cambridge History of the Bible,* 3 vols., edited by Peter R. Ackroyd (Cambridge, 1963–1970). It summarizes the current state of scholarship in nontechnical language and each chapter is written by a specialist in the field. The excellent bibliographies are arranged by topic. For more concise introductions to the issues and approaches involved in the contemporary study of the Hebrew scriptures there are Herbert F. Hahn's *The Old Testament in Modern Research,* 2d exp. ed., with a survey of recent literature by Horace D. Hummel (Philadelphia, 1966), and John H. Hayes's *An Introduction to Old Testament Study* (Nashville, 1979). The latter work notes only items in English in the useful bibliographies that precede each chapter. Two most frequently used comprehensive traditional introductions to the Bible containing extensive bibliographies are Otto Eisfeldt's *The Old Testament: An Introduction,* translated from the third German edition by Peter R. Ackroyd (New York, 1965), and Georg Fohrer's *Introduction to the Old Testament* (Nashville, 1968).

Two classic works on the history of the canon are Frants Buhl's *Canon and Text of the Old Testament,* translated from the German by John Macpherson (Edinburgh, 1892), and H. E. Ryle's *The Canon of the Old Testament: An Essay on the Gradual Growth and Formation of the Hebrew Canon of Scripture,* 2d ed. (London, 1892). Both contain ample references to and quotations from rabbinic and patristic sources. *The Canon and Masorah of the Hebrew Bible,* edited by Sid Z. Leiman (New York, 1974), provides an indispensable collection of thirty-seven essays by as many scholars relating to various aspects of the biblical canon; all but four are in English. The work lacks an index. Leiman's original contribution to the subject is *The Canonization of Hebrew Scripture: The Talmudic and Midrashic Evidence* (Hamden, Conn., 1976). Extensive citations from rabbinic literature are given both in their original form and in translation. The work is enhanced by copious notes, bibliography, and indexes.

The new concept of canon as a process is explicated by James A. Sanders in his *Torah and Canon* (Philadelphia, 1972) and in his essay "Available for Life: The Nature and Function of Canon," in *Magnalia Dei', The Mighty Acts of God: Essays on the Bible and Archaeology in Memory of G. Ernest Wright,* edited by Frank Moore Cross et al. (Garden City, N.Y., 1976), pp. 531–560. *Introduction to the Old Testament as Scripture* by Brevard S. Childs (Philadelphia, 1979) seeks to describe the form and function of each book of the Hebrew Bible in its role as sacred scripture, and to understand the literature in that context. It contains detailed bibliographies. Contemporary concerns with canonical criticism are examined by James Barr in his *Holy Scripture, Canon, Authority, Criticism* (Philadelphia, 1983).

Ernst Würthwein's *The Text of the Old Testament,* translated from the German by Peter R. Ackroyd (Oxford, 1957), is a useful key to the critical apparatus of the Kittel edition of the Hebrew Bible. The text is illustrated by forty-four plates. The most detailed and readable work is that by Bleddyn J. Roberts, *Old Testament Text and Versions* (Cardiff, 1951). However, some of the data need to be updated in light of research into the Dead Sea Scrolls. The best all-around discussion of these last-mentioned is *The Ancient Library of Qumrân and Modern Biblical Studies,* rev. ed. (Garden City, N.Y., 1961), by Frank Moore Cross. This work is supplemented by a collection of scholarly essays assembled by the same author together with Shemaryahu Talmon in *Qumran and the History of the Biblical Text* (Cambridge, Mass., 1975). Paul E. Kahle's *The Cairo Genizah,* 2d ed. (New York, 1959), examines and evaluates the impact of the hoard of manuscripts found in the bibliocrypt of the synagogue in Old Cairo and in the caves of Qumran on the scholarship relating to the history of the biblical Hebrew text and the ancient translations, as well as on the ancient pronunciation of Hebrew. The history and critical evaluation of the methodology of textual criticism is given by M. H. Goshen-Gottstein in "The Textual Criticism of the Old Testament: Rise, Decline, Rebirth," *Journal of Biblical Literature* 102 (September 1983): 365–399.

A basic introduction to the Greek versions, their history, character, and the problems they present, is provided by the collection of thirty-five essays assembled by Sidney Jellicoe, *Studies into the Septuagint: Origins, Recensions, and Interpretations* (New York, 1974). Another important work for nonspecialists is Bruce M. Metzger's *Manuscripts of the Greek Bible: An Introduction to Greek Palaeography* (Oxford, 1981). Of a more technical and advanced nature is Imanuel Tov's *The Text-Critical Use of the Septuagint in Biblical Research* (Jerusalem, 1981). Henry Barclay Swete's *An Introduction to the Old Testament in Greek,* 2d ed. (Cambridge, 1902), still remains standard. Harry M. Orlinsky's essay "The Septuagint as Holy Writ and the Philosophy of the Translators," *Hebrew Union College Annual* 46 (1975): 89–114, contributes important insights into the nature of this version. *A Classified Bibliography of the Septuagint* by Sebastian P. Brock, Charles T. Fritsch, and Sidney Jellicoe (Leiden, 1973) is an indispensable scholarly tool.

For Targumic studies, there is Bernard Grossfeld's *A Bibliography of Targum Literature,* 2 vols. (Cincinnati, 1972–1977).

The Bible and the Ancient Near East: Essays in Honor of William Foxwell Albright, edited by G. Ernest Wright (Garden City, N.Y., 1961), contains fifteen studies by as many different scholars summarizing the course taken by scholarly research in various areas of Near Eastern studies bearing on the Bible. J. B. Pritchard has edited a superb collection, *Ancient Near Eastern Texts relating to the Old Testament,* 3d ed. (Princeton, 1969), which gives translations of pertinent texts drawn from all genres of literature, together with brief introductory notes and also indexes of names and biblical references. This collection is supplemented by *The Ancient Near East in Pictures relating to the Old Testament,* 2d ed. (Princeton, 1969), by the same author, which is arranged by topics, and is equipped with a descriptive catalogue giving in concise notation the significant details of each picture, and an index. *Near Eastern Religious Texts Relating to the Old Testament,* edited by Walter Beyerlin, translated from the German by John Bowden (London, 1978), is more restricted in scope, but includes several texts available only since 1969. The accompanying notes are fuller than in the preceding work. Another useful collection of this type, though far more limited in scope, and less up to date, is D. Winton Thomas's *Documents from Old Testament Times* (New York, 1961). Theodor H. Gaster's *Myth, Legend, and Custom in the Old Testament* (New York, 1969) is a comparative study based on James G. Frazer's *Folk-Lore in the Old Testament,* 3 vols. (London, 1919). The copious notes are especially valuable. A concise yet comprehensive introduction to the geographical and historical settings of the Hebrew Bible is provided by Martin Noth in his *The Old Testament World,* translated by Victor I. Gruhn (Philadelphia, 1966). Frederick G. Kenyon's *Our Bible and the Ancient Manuscripts,* revised by A. W. Adams, with an introduction by Godfrey R. Driver (New York, 1965), is particularly useful for a survey of the ancient versions.

NAHUM M. SARNA

Apocrypha and Pseudepigrapha

Well known are the documents canonized as the Hebrew scriptures (Old Testament) and dated from approximately 950 to 165/4 BCE. Less well known are the bodies of writings cognate to the Hebrew scriptures, called the Apocrypha and the Pseudepigrapha, and written by Jews during the Hellenistic and Roman periods. Closely related to the thirty-nine Old Testament books canonized by Jews and Christians and sometimes related to the twenty-seven New Testament books canonized by Christians, these documents were very influential and were frequently considered inspired by many Jewish and Christian communities. When the canons of scripture were closed, first by Jewish and then by Christian authorities, these writings were not included, and they quickly began to lose their influence and importance. Consequently, these documents are usually preserved only in late manuscripts that are translations of lost originals. Since the discovery of the Dead Sea Scrolls and the renewed appreciation of the diversities of thought at the time, scholars have agreed that the history of Early Judaism (250 BCE–200 CE) and Early Christianity (first–fourth centuries) cannot be written without consulting these bodies of so-called extracanonical writings, the Apocrypha and Pseudepigrapha.

The Apocrypha

The Apocrypha has been variously defined, for there is, of course, no set canon of either the Apocrypha or the Pseudepigrapha. The word *apokrypha* is a transliteration of a Greek neuter plural that means "hidden." By the fourth century CE the term *apocrypha* no longer denoted hidden esoteric secrets (cf. *Daniel* 12:9–10 and *4 Ezra* 14:44–48), but it was often used to name a category of discarded, heretical books. Jerome (c. 342–420), however, used the term to denote extracanonical, not heretical, documents. This position is the one adopted by Protestants today; Roman Catholics, since the Council of Trent (during session 4 on 8 April 1546), consider these works "deuterocanonical" and inspired, as do most Eastern Christians. These books are in the official Catholic canon because they are in the Vulgate (of the thirteen works in the Apocrypha, *2 Ezra,* which is *3 Esdras* in the Vulgate, is not included in the Catholic canon).

Since the first century CE, Jews and Christians have had widely divergent opinions regarding the Hellenistic literature collected into the Apocrypha and Pseudepigrapha of the Hebrew scriptures. It is essential now, while appreciating the varying status of each work in different religious denominations, to establish a set list of books in each collection, without delving into normative value judgments. It is best to limit the documents included in the Apocrypha to those contained in the fourth-century Greek codices of the Hebrew scriptures (these codices of the Septuagint contain more documents than the Hebrew scriptures) and to include documents occasionally found in some expanded collections of the Apocrypha under the larger collection called the Pseudepigrapha. The Apocrypha, then, contains thirteen writings (for the status of these writings in various religious traditions, see table 1), and the Pseudepigrapha contains fifty-two documents. In the following discussion, these writings will be arranged according to loosely defined genres and then presented according to the most probable chronological order.

The thirteen works in the Apocrypha have been dated by experts over a wide period, from the fourth century BCE to the late first century CE; most scholars today correctly date all of them from circa 300 BCE to 70 CE, when the Temple was burned by the Romans. Almost all were written in a Semitic language, except the *Wisdom of Solomon* and *2 Maccabees,* which were probably written in Greek. There probably is a consensus that none was written in Babylon, that all but two were written in Palestine, and that these two, the *Wisdom of Solomon* and *2 Maccabees,* were written in Egypt. In contrast to the Pseudepigrapha, the Apocrypha contains no examples of three literary genres—namely, apocalypses, testaments, and prayers, psalms, and odes. (The expanded Apocrypha, however, does include an apocalypse, *4 Ezra,* a prayer, the *Prayer of Manasseh,* and a psalm, Psalm 151.)

TABLE 1. *Inclusion of "Apocryphal" Writings in Various Canons.* Key: □ = not included or accorded religious value; ○ = not included but accorded some religious value; ● = included but not equal in status to the Old and New Testaments; ■ = considered part of the Old Testament canon.

	Religious Tradition								
		Western Christian		*Eastern Christian*					
				Eastern Orthodox		*Oriental Orthodox*			
Writing	Jewish[1]	Protestant[2]	Roman Catholic[3]	Greek[4]	Russian[4]	Armenian	Coptic	Ethiopian[5]	Syrian
Additions to *Esther*	□	○	■	■	●	■	□	■	○
Prayer of Azariah and the Song of the Three Young Men[6]	□	○	■	■	●	■	□	■	○
Susanna[6]	□	○	■	■	●	■	□	■	○
Bel and the Dragon[6]	□	○	■	■	●	■	□	■	○
1 Baruch	□	○	■	■	●	■	□	■	○
Letter of Jeremiah[7]	□	○	■	■	●	■	□	■	○
Tobit	□	○	■	■	●	■	□	■	○
Judith	□	○	■	■	●	■	□	■	○
2 Ezra[8]	□	○	○	■	●	■	□	□	○
Ben Sira	□	○	■	■	●	■	□	□	○
Wisdom of Solomon	□	○	■	■	●	■	□	■	○
1 Maccabees	□	○	■	■	●	■	□	■	○
2 Maccabees	□	○	■	■	●	■	□	■	○

[1]Ethiopian Jews accept the Old Testament canon of the Ethiopian Orthodox church as their canon.
[2]Protestant denominations vary in their regard for these writings, but all regard them as extracanonical.
[3]The Roman Catholic church accepts twelve writings as "deuterocanonical" (i.e., as a second collection of canonical writings), according to the ruling of the Council of Trent in 1546.
[4]Eastern Orthodox churches label these writings neither "canonical" nor "extracanonical." They prefer to regard them all as parts of scripture, but with varying degrees of inspiration. Individual authorities within these churches may differ on this question.
[5]The Ethiopian Orthodox church also includes in its canon *1 Enoch* and *Jubilees*, writings regarded as pseudepigraphal by other religious traditions.
[6]This writing is an addition to the *Book of Daniel.*
[7]Where included, the *Letter of Jeremiah* often appears as chapter 6 of *1 Baruch.*
[8]*2 Ezra* is titled *1 Esdras* in the Septuagint and *3 Esdras* in the Vulgate.

Legends, Romantic Stories, and Expansions of the Hebrew Scriptures. Nine documents of the Apocrypha can be regarded as forming a group of legends, romantic stories, and expansions of the Hebrew scriptures: the *Letter of Jeremiah, Tobit, Judith, 2 Ezra,* the additions to *Esther,* the *Prayer of Azariah and the Song of the Three Young Men, Susanna, Bel and the Dragon,* and *1 Baruch.*

Letter of Jeremiah. The *Letter of Jeremiah,* probably composed in Hebrew or Aramaic, is the oldest writing in the Apocrypha. A Greek fragment dating from around 100 BCE was found in Qumran Cave VII, and this discovery only disproves conjectures regarding a late date, such as Edgar J. Goodspeed's claim in *The Story of the Apocrypha* (Chicago, 1939, p. 105) that the *Letter of Jeremiah* was written late in the first century CE. Carey A. Moore (1977, pp. 327–329) concludes that the *Letter of Jeremiah* reflects the social setting of Palestine in the late fourth century BCE. A date between 323 and 100 BCE seems possible; perhaps around 300 is most likely (see Antonius H. J. Gunneweg, *Der Brief Jeremias* (Gütersloh, 1975, p. 186). A Palestinian provenience is relatively certain (not Alexandrian, as Goodspeed contends in *The Story of the Apocrypha,* p. 105).

The document is "a letter" *(epistolē)* pseudonymously

attributed to Jeremiah (verse 1); it contains seventy-two or seventy-three verses. The work is not a letter but a passionate sermon or plea to fellow Jews not to fear or worship idols; it is inspired by *Jeremiah* 10:1–16 (cf. *Isaiah* 44:9–21 and *Psalms* 115:3–8, 135:15–18), which is also a polemic against idolatry. The literary facade may have been stimulated by Jeremiah's letter to the exiles in Babylon (*Jer.* 29:1–23).

Tobit. Written in a Semitic language, probably Aramaic, around 180 BCE, and in Palestine—not in Egypt (*pace* D. C. Simpson, in Charles, 1913, p. 185)—*Tobit* is not a historical book, as some earlier critics claimed. It is a romantic story that attempts to edify the reader and to illustrate that God is efficacious and helps the righteous. The author fills the text with striking anachronisms: the tribe of Naphtali was exiled by Tiglath-pileser, not Shalmaneser (*Tb.* 1:2); Shalmaneser's successor was Sargon, not Sennacherib (*Tb.* 1:15); Nineveh was captured by Nabopolassar and Cyaxares, not Nebuchadrezzar and Ahasuerus (*Tb.* 14:15). These errors may have served to warn the attentive reader that the work is intended to be taken not as a history but as a folk tale, or fictional short story. Likewise, the angel Raphael's declaration that he appears before men not corporally but in a vision (*Tb.* 12:19) may indicate the author's refusal to play on the credulity of the simple, or it may perhaps reflect a theology that is against belief in angels. The author is learned, borrowing from the Hebrew scriptures (the Pentateuch and the Prophets especially), from the Pseudepigrapha (notably from Ahiqar, who is mentioned explicitly in *Tobit* 1:21–22, 2:10, 11:18, and 14:10), and perhaps from the fable of the Grateful Dead (Simpson, in Charles, 1913, p. 188; Pfeiffer, 1949, pp. 269–271).

Combining two ancient folk legends, those of the Grateful Dead and the Dangerous Bride, the author, in fourteen chapters, weaves a deeply religious story. Tobit, a righteous man in exile in Nineveh, risks the king's wrath and certain death by collecting the corpses of fellow Israelites and giving them an honorable burial. Forced to sleep outside, because of his impurity one night, he is blinded by sparrows' dung. After an altercation with Anna, his wife, he prays to God to die. Also praying to die on that same day is Sarah, whose seven bridegrooms had perished on their wedding night, slain by Asmodeus, a demon (his name means "destroyer").

Remembering ten talents of silver (a wealthy sum) he had left in Media with a certain Gabael, Tobit sends his son Tobias to Gabael. In words reminiscent of a "testament," Tobit instructs his son regarding his duties to his parents and to the Law and avows practical wisdom regarding daily life. Tobias sets off on his journey accompanied by Raphael (whose name means "God heals"), God's angel disguised as an Israelite. He captures a fish and removes its gall, heart, and liver. With these magical potents and Raphael's advice and help, Tobias successfully defeats Asmodeus. He then marries Sarah, at whose home they rested. Raphael collects Tobit's money. Tobias and Sarah return to Nineveh, with Tobit's talents and half of Sarah's father's wealth. Tobias heals his father's eyesight with the gall of the fish. Offered half the riches, Raphael respectfully declines, affirming that prayer and alms are superior to riches, and reports that God had sent him, one of the seven angels, to heal Tobit and Sarah (*Tb.* 3:17). Raphael ascends; Tobit and Anna live a full life and are honorably buried by their son, who moves from (wicked) Nineveh to Ecbatana, Sarah's hometown.

Judith. The dramatic and didactic story of Judith was written in Hebrew around 150 BCE in Palestine, not in the Diaspora (not Antioch, *pace* Solomon Zeitlin in *The Book of Judith*, Leiden, 1972, p. 32). The sixteen chapters can be divided into a description of the attack upon the Jews by Holofernes, the general of the Assyrian king Nebuchadrezzar (chaps. 1–7), and then the deliverance of the nation by God through Judith, who decapitates Holofernes (chaps. 8–16). Judith is reminiscent of numerous biblical heroines, notably Jael (*Jgs.* 4:17–22, 5:2–31), Deborah (*Jgs.* 4:4–5:31), and Esther (esp. *Est.* 2:15–8:17).

This literary masterpiece—a classic example of an ancient short story—was written in order to encourage fellow Jews to resist the evil enemy, and to exhort them to obey the Law strictly (see especially Achior's prophecy and celebration of the people "in the hill country," *Jdt.* 5:5–21). God's efficaciousness depends upon observance of the Law. Since the story circulated shortly after the beginning of the Maccabean revolution, which began in 167 BCE, it would have served to encourage the Jews who not only faced superior military forces but were weakened internally by the bewitching attractiveness of Greek culture. God is proclaimed in Judith's song as "the Lord who shatters wars" (*Jdt.* 16:2). During the early decades of the Maccabean revolution this thought characterized those zealous and faithful to the Law; they would have been encouraged also by Judith's victorious shout: "With us still is God, our God, to effect power in Israel and strength against our enemies" (*Jdt.* 13:11).

2 Ezra (1 Esdras in the Septuagint, 3 Esdras in the Vulgate). Probably written in Hebrew or Aramaic, this work is a reproduction and rewriting of parts of the Hebrew scriptures, especially *2 Chronicles* 35:1–36:23, all of *Ezra*, and *Nehemiah* 7:38–8:12. Although very difficult to date, the work may derive from the late second century, or around 150–100 BCE. It certainly must predate 100 CE; Josephus Flavius used it, and not the Septuagint parallels, as his source for the period 621–398 BCE in his *Jewish Antiquities* (esp. 11.1.1–11.5.5).

Although this document is, of all the apocryphal writings, the one most closely connected to the Hebrew scriptures, it contains one section that is without parallel therein. This passage, chapters 3:1–5:6, is not dependent on any biblical book, and it may be a rewriting and adaptation of an earlier Babylonian tale. It describes a great feast after which three young guardsmen attempt to ascertain which of three potents is strongest: wine, the king, or women. To these answers a fourth is appended at the end of the chapter (4:33–41; plus 4:13b); it shifts the answer from "women" to "truth" and has all the earmarks of being a Jewish editorial addition in order to bring the climax of the account to an acceptable Jewish affirmation: "Great is truth, and strongest of all" (cf. Vulgate: "Magna est veritas et praevalet").

While the purpose of the nine chapters in the document is unclear, some characteristics are notable. The author elevates Ezra and refers to him as "high priest" ("Esdras ho archiereus," 9:40; cf. 9:49). He puts considerable emphasis on the Temple and its cult, which is reflected in the numerous references to the Temple and in the magnification of Zerubabel, the winner of the contest, who is the only guardsman identified (4:13; 4:13b is an editorial addition). Zerubabel is linked closely with King Darius, who commends him as "the wisest" (*sophōteros*, 4:42) and rewards him by providing for the rebuilding of the Temple (see Myers, 1974, pp. 8–15).

Additions to Esther. The additions to Esther are not a separate book; they are six extensive expansions to the Greek version of the *Book of Esther:*

A. Mordecai's dream and his exposure of a conspiracy against King Artaxerxes (1:1a–1r or 11:2–12:6),
B. a letter by Artaxerxes, who orders the extermination of the Jews (3:13a–13g or 13:1–7),
C. prayers by Mordecai and Esther (4:17a–17z and 5:2a–2b or 13:8–15:16),
D. Esther's radiant and successful audience before the king (5:1a–1f., 5:2a–2b or 15:1–16),
E. a second letter by Artaxerxes, who rescinds his former edict and praises the Jews (8:12a–12x or 16:1–24), and
F. the interpretation of Mordecai's dream (10:3a–3l or 10:4–11:1).

These additions amount to 107 verses not found in the Hebrew scriptures.

Four of these additions reflect a Hebrew original, but additions B and E, the two letters, were probably composed in Greek (see Moore, 1977, p. 155). Modern scholars tend to accept the authenticity of the ending of the additions, which dates them before 114 BCE and situates them in Jerusalem ("In the fourth year of Ptolemy and Cleopatra's reign . . . the preceding Letter of Purim . . . had been translated by Lysimachus, son of Ptolemy, [who is among those Egyptians living] in Jerusalem," 31 or 11:1). Moore (1977, pp. 161, 165–167) argues (unconvincingly) that the letters, additions B and E, postdate 114 and may have originated in Alexandria. The date of the Hebrew sections (A, C, D, and F) is now an open issue: do they appreciably predate 114 BCE? Hans Bardtke in *Historische und legendarische Erzählungen: Zusätze zu Esther* (Gütersloh, 1973, p. 27), argues that the date of the additions to Esther is between 167 and 161 BCE, because *2 Maccabees* 15:36, which refers to "Mordecai's day," probably postdates these additions, and the celebration on this day was for the defeat and death of Nicanor in 161.

The purposes of these imaginative additions seem clear. First and foremost, they supply the religious dimension so singularly lacking in *Esther.* Second, they provide color and detail to the story. Third, they contain a strong apologetic for Judaism (see especially E and F): "We find the Jews are not evildoers, but they are governed by the most just laws. . . . Permit the Jews to live by their own laws."

Prayer of Azariah and the Song of the Three Young Men. Three additions to *Daniel* are collected into the Apocrypha. Two of these, the story of Susanna and the story of Bel and the dragon, are separate, self-contained works in the *Daniel* cycle; the third, the *Prayer of Azariah,* like the additions to Esther, should be read as an insertion of sixty-eight verses into the *Book of Daniel*; in the Septuagint these verses are numbered from 3:24 to 3:90 (hence, the addition begins after 3:23).

All three additions were probably written originally in Hebrew, or possibly in Aramaic, and not in Greek as many early scholars concluded. The date of the additions is difficult to discern; in their present form all, of course, must postdate 164/5, the date of the *Book of Daniel.* A date between 164/5 and 100 BCE is a reasonable guess for all three additions, provided we acknowledge the possibility that one or more, especially *Bel and the Dragon,* could have been added in the early decades of the first century BCE. The three additions are probably from different times. It is possible that all three, or portions of them, originally reflected a setting different from their present place in the Septuagint. In the second century BCE there probably existed two rival versions of *Daniel* in Hebrew, one that is represented in the present Hebrew Bible (Masoretic text), and the other a later Hebrew recension, which was translated into Greek (of which today there are two recensions, the Septuagint and the Theodotion).

Two caveats are necessary. First, these additions may originally have been composed without *Daniel* in mind; Moore (1977, pp. 26–29) argues that parts of the *Prayer of Azariah* come from the liturgy of the Temple or the synagogue, and that *Susanna* and *Bel and the Dragon* originally had "nothing at all to do with the prophet Daniel" (esp. pp. 26, 109). Second, while this possibility deserves careful examination, these three additions are now clearly related to *Daniel* and should be studied in light of the Danielic cycle, represented by previously unknown documents found among the Dead Sea Scrolls, especially the *Prayer of Nabonidus* (4QPsDan ar^{a-c}; cf. 4QPsDan A^{a}, 4QPrNab ar). A Palestinian provenience seems most likely for the additions.

The *Prayer of Azariah*, clearly composed in Hebrew (see Otto Plöger, *Züsatze zu Daniel*, Gütersloh, 1973, p. 68), emphasizes that there is only one God and that he is always just. This addition to *Daniel* shifts the focus from the evil king and his golden idol to three potential martyrs and their faithfulness in prayer.

Susanna. The colorful tale of Susanna, told in only sixty-four verses (in the Theodotion), may originally have been independent of the Danielic cycle and is perhaps considerably earlier than the *Book of Daniel.* It describes how a beautiful woman, Susanna, is brought to court, because she refuses to submit to two aroused influential men (elders, *presbuteroi,* and judges, *kritai*), who approached her while she was bathing. Her scream and the men's lies land her in court. There her fate is sealed; the people and judges condemn her without hearing her. As she is being led to be stoned, the Lord hears her cry (verse 44) and arouses a youth, Daniel, who asks the judge to cross-examine the accusors. The story illustrates how God hears and helps the faithful and virtuous woman, and it demonstrates the wisdom of God in Daniel. This story, however, does not permit us to claim unequivocally either that witnesses were privately cross-examined in court in the second century BCE or that the worth of the individual—even women—was accorded first priority in courts in Hellenistic Judaism.

Bel and the Dragon (Bel and the Snake). This story of forty-two verses contains two separate tales. The first, one of our earliest examples of a detective story, describes how Daniel, by pointing out footprints in the ashes he had strewn on the floor of a temple, reveals to the king that the priests, their wives, and children had been eating the food offered to Bel, the Babylonian idol. The king recognizes he has been duped, becomes enraged, sees the secret doors used by the priests, and orders their deaths. Daniel is told to destroy the idol and its temple. The second story tells how Daniel destroys an idol, which is shaped like a great dragon (*drakōn,* v. 23), and is subsequently thrown into a lions' den. He survives, and Habakkuk, with angelic aid, zooms to Babylon and feeds Daniel. The king releases Daniel and casts his enemies into the pit. The shout of the king is significant for the purpose of these two stories: "You are great, O Lord God of Daniel, and there is no other but you" (v. 41). These stories lack the polish and brilliance of *Tobit* and *Judith;* their purpose is to ridicule idolatry and affirm the importance of worshiping God alone.

1 Baruch. O. C. Whitehouse (in Charles, 1913, pp. 572–573) argued that *1 Baruch* had been written in Greek; but his editor, R. H. Charles, appended a significant footnote (pp. 573–574) in which he claimed it had been composed in Hebrew. Modern scholars have concluded that at least parts of this document were composed in Hebrew, others in Hebrew or perhaps Greek. Although the precise date of the document in its present form is unknown, there is wide agreement that it dates from the second or first centuries BCE. W. O. E. Oesterley (*An Introduction to the Books of the Apocrypha,* New York, 1935, p. 260) and Whitehouse (in Charles, 1913, p. 575) were certainly wrong to have dated *1 Baruch* after 70 CE. The provenience may be Palestinian.

The document is a composite: 1:1–3:8 is a prose composition and contains a confession of sins and a plea for God's compassion after the destruction of Jerusalem (cf. *Deuteronomy* 28–32 and *Daniel* 9:4–19); 3:9–4:4, by another writer, is in poetry and praises wisdom (cf. *Ben Sira* 24 and *Job* 28:12–28); 4:5–5:9, probably by the second writer, describes how Jerusalem's lament was heard. In *The Poetry of Baruch: A Reconstruction and Analysis of the Original Hebrew Text of Baruch 3:9–5:9* (Chico, Calif., 1982), David G. Burke argues that the second section, the poem on wisdom, is the earliest portion of the work and that the compilation dates somewhere from 180 to 100 BCE; he also attempts to reconstruct the original Hebrew of 3:9–4:4. This document is an example of Hellenistic Jewish theology, but noticeably absent are references to a messiah, eschatological or apocalyptic ideas, beliefs in a resurrection, and any signs of a dualism.

Wisdom and Philosophical Literature. Two books in the Apocrypha are from the wisdom school of Hellenistic Judaism, but while each is written by a single author, they are very different. *Ben Sira,* written in Hebrew, is by a conservative traditionalist from Palestine, perhaps even Jerusalem. The *Wisdom of Solomon,* written in Greek, is by a liberal thinker, thoroughly open to and influenced by non-Jewish ideas and philosophy—reminiscent to a certain extent of Philo Judaeus of Alexandria and *4 Maccabees;* it comes from Egypt, probably Alexandria.

Ben Sira (Sirach, Ecclesiasticus). The author addressed his work to fellow Jews and wrote it probably around 180 BCE. Fragments of the Hebrew original of 39:27–43:30 were discovered in 1964 in an eastern casemate wall at Masada. These twenty-six leather fragments must predate 74 CE, the date of the destruction of Masada, and paleographically they are from circa 125–25 BCE; they are middle or late Hasmonean (see the facsimiles in Yigael Yadin, *The Ben Sira Scroll from Masada,* Jerusalem, 1965, pls. 1–9 and pp. 2–11). The Qumran fragments of *Ben Sira* (2QSir) are also approximately of the same date; they are late Hasmonean or early Herodian (see M. Baillet in *Les "Petites Grottes" de Qumrân,* Oxford, 1962, p. 75 and pl. 15). Also, the Hebrew text of *Ben Sira* 51 (11QPs^{a}Sirach; see J. A. Sanders, ed., *The Psalms Scroll of Qumrân Cave 11,* Oxford, 1965, pp. 79–85, cols. 21 and 22) has been found in a Qumran manuscript dating from the first half of the first century CE. It is now certain that *Ben Sira* predates the first century BCE. Moreover, the Hebrew original must antedate the Greek translation (in the Septuagint) made by Ben Sira's grandson in Egypt not long after 132 BCE (see the prologue to *Ben Sira* in the Septuagint by the grandson, who refers to "the thirty-eighth year of the reign of Euergetes"). Finally, most scholars date the work to around 180, which seems reasonable, because in 50:1–24 the author refers to Shim'on (i.e., Simon II, 219–196 BCE) as if he had died recently (note the Hebrew of 50:24, *ye'amen 'im Shim'on ḥasdo;* see the text in Moses H. Segal, *Sefer ben Sira' ha-shalem,* Jerusalem, 1958, ad loc.).

A work of fifty-one chapters, *Ben Sira* is an apology for Judaism and is directed against the encroachments from Greek religion and culture. In particular, note the claim that Wisdom found a home in Israel and not in other nations (24:1–12). Some characteristic ideas in this long and major work are the following. The author believes in one God (explicit monotheism in 36:1–5) who is all-knowing (42:18), eternal (18:1), holy (23:9), just (35:12–13), and merciful (2:11, 48:20, 50:19). Ben Sira does not advocate an afterlife (17:27–28); immortality is through a son (30:4). Sin began with a woman (*me-ishshah teḥillat 'avon,* 25:24) and death then appeared; but the author is not affirming the concept of original sin or predestination. He rather affirms man's essential freedom to obey the Law because of the inclination (*be-yad yitsro,* 15:14) given to man by God (see the brilliant discussion "Sin and Death" by E. E. Urbach in *The Sages: Their Concepts and Beliefs,* 2 vols., Jerusalem, 1979, vol. 1, pp. 420–422). He reveres the Temple and the priests (45:6–25) and elevates the Law (viz. 9:15). Wisdom is both personified and divine (viz. 24:3–5). Noticeably absent are beliefs in angels and the coming of a messiah.

G. H. Box and W. O. E. Oesterley (in Charles, 1913, p. 283) argued that this document "in its original form, represented the Sadducean standpoint." Today, scholars are far more reluctant to assign the text, in any form, to the Sadducees. It is certain that many ideas in *Ben Sira* are similar to those attributed by Josephus to the Sadducees (*Antiquities* 18.1), but does that factor indicate that the document comes from the Sadducees? Would a Sadducean document have been accepted at Qumran, and at Masada?

Wisdom of Solomon. Addressed to non-Jews, to whom the author often accommodates his thought, and written probably in the first half of the first century CE (Winston, 1979, pp. 20–25) or conceivably as early as 100 BCE (Pfeiffer, 1949, p. 327; Metzger, 1957, p. 67), this document reflects the intriguing blend of ancient Israelite and Jewish wisdom traditions with earlier and contemporary Greek philosophy and Egyptian reflective thought. The influence of non-Jewish ideas often replaces earlier Jewish perspectives; for example, many scholars, notably Metzger (1957, p. 75) and Chrysostome Larcher (*Études sur le livre de la Sagesse,* Paris, 1969, pp. 43, 91, 104), correctly claim that the Platonic conception of the soul's immortality, and not the Jewish idea of the resurrection of the body (see esp. *2 Maccabees* 14:37–46) is presented in *Wisdom of Solomon* 3:1–19 (viz., verses 1 and 4: "But the souls of the righteous . . . their hope [is] full of immortality"; cf. also 1:15, 5:15, 8:13–20). As in *Ben Sira,* Wisdom has now become personified in Jewish thought; she even appears to be hypostatic (see 7:21–8:21). Winston (1979, p. 4) divides the document into three sections (1:1–6:21, Wisdom's Gift of Immortality; 6:22–10:21, Wisdom's Nature and Power and Solomon's Quest for Her; and 11:1–19:22, Wisdom in the Exodus) and distinguishes two "excursuses" (11:15–12:22, On Divine Mercy, and 13:1–15:19, On Idolatry).

Quasi-historical Books. It has been customary to refer to *1 Maccabees* and *2 Maccabees* as historical works; R. H. Charles (1913) arranged them, along with *2 Ezra* (*3 Esdras* in the Vulgate) and *3 Maccabees,* under the heading "Historical Books"; he put *Tobit* and *Judith* under the heading "Quasi-historical Books Written with a Moral Purpose." Today we recognize that *Tobit* and *Judith* are romantic and didactic stories, and that *1 Mac-*

cabees and especially *2 Maccabees* are far too tendentious and selective to be labeled anything more than "quasi-historical."

1 Maccabees. The sixteen chapters of *1 Maccabees* were written in Hebrew, in Palestine, perhaps Jerusalem, shortly before the end of the second century BCE. They recount the military exploits of the Maccabees and the history of Judaism from the incursions by Antiochus IV Epiphanes (175–164) and the zealous rejection of paganism by Mattathias to the rule of John Hyrcanus I (135/4–105/4). As Jonathan A. Goldstein (1976) has emphasized, the author of *1 Maccabees* held strong theological views: he is fervently pro-Hasmonean and is impressively silent about—and probably rejected—beliefs in immortality and resurrection. In contrast to the author of *2 Maccabees,* he apparently disavows the value of martyrdom in prompting God to action, and he clearly accepts the twelve-month Babylonian lunar calendar.

2 Maccabees. The fifteen chapters of *2 Maccabees,* compiled by an unknown author, are an epitome (or abridgment) of a lost five-volume work (which is our only example of the "pathetic history" genre) by Jason of Cyrene (*2 Mc.* 2:19–32), of whom we otherwise know nothing. The epitomist probably wrote in Greek in Alexandria—or possibly in Jerusalem—shortly after 124 BCE or early in the first century BCE; he wrote for a sophisticated, informed Jewish audience.

This abridged history of Jason's tomes, which emphasizes the holiness of the Jerusalem Temple (see Elias Bickerman, *The God of the Maccabees,* Leiden, 1979, p. 21), is often fundamentally different from *1 Maccabees.* It presents the clearest examples of the Jewish belief in the resurrection of the body (see esp. 7:1–42, 12:43–45, and 14:37–46). Martyrdom by faithful Jews is efficacious, moving God to act and ensuring military victories (7:37–38, 8:3–7). Miracles are employed to explain major events.

Perhaps the most significant difference between *1 Maccabees* and Jason's work, according to *2 Maccabees,* is that the former legitimizes the Hasmonean dynasty but the latter tends to disparage it (see 10:19–23, 12:39–43, and Goldstein, 1976, pp. 27–34). Robert Doran argues in *Temple Propaganda: The Purpose and Character of 2 Maccabees* (Washington, D.C., 1981) that the epitomist was anti-Hasmonean, because he rejected the late Hasmonean use of mercenary troops and attributed military success to God rather than to the Maccabees.

The larger part of *2 Maccabees,* 3:1–15:36, is commonly called the Epitome. The Epitome covers Jewish history from circa 180; it gives prominence to the high priest Onias III (d. 170 BCE) and to the defeat and death of Nicanor in 161. It thereby corresponds to *1 Maccabees* 1:10–7:50.

Appreciably different from the Epitome are the two letters that begin *2 Maccabees.* The first letter (1:1–10a) was probably written in Hebrew or Aramaic (the most likely language for official communications at that time), as both Charles Cutler Torrey (1945, pp. 78–79) and Jonathan A. Goldstein (1976, p. 35) have concluded. It appears to be an authentic letter from Jewish authorities in Jerusalem to Jews in Egypt (*2 Mc.* 1:1). While it dates from 124 BCE, it also quotes in verses 7–8 an earlier letter of 143/2 BCE. The purpose of the letter is to urge the proper celebration of Ḥanukkah (verse 9), and it may have been propaganda against Onias's temple at Leontopolis, as Goldstein (1976, p. 35) argues.

The character of the second letter (1:10b–2:18) continues to be debated among scholars. Probably no part of it is authentic (*pace* Arnaldo Momigliano, *Prime linee di storia della tradizione Maccabaica* [1931], Amsterdam, 1968, pp. 81–94), and probably it was not written in Aramaic (*pace* Torrey, 1945, pp. 78–79). It was most likely written in Greek and is inauthentic (Goldstein, 1976, p. 36; Martin Hengel, *Judaism and Hellenism,* Philadelphia, 1974, vol. 1, p. 100, vol. 2, p. 69; Christian Habicht, *Historische und legendarische Erzählungen: 2. Makkabäerbuch,* Gütersloh, 1976, pp. 170, 199–207). The date assigned to this forged letter and its possible provenience are uncertain; it may be as early as 103 BCE (Goldstein, 1976, p. 36) or as late as 60 BCE (Bickerman, *Studies in Jewish and Christian History,* Leiden, 1980, pp. 136–158), and it may derive from Jews in either Jerusalem or Alexandria.

Goldstein (1976, p. 36) suggests that both letters are anti-Oniad propaganda and that they were prefaced to the Epitome shortly after 78 or 77 BCE in order to create a liturgical text that would be proper for the celebration of Ḥanukkah and serve for that festival as *Esther* does for Purim.

It is difficult to identify or categorize the epitomist himself. Only 2:19–2:32 and 15:37–39, derived neither from letters nor from Jason of Cyrene, appear to have originated with him.

2 Maccabees is, therefore, a recital through prophetic perspectives of the highlights in Jewish history of the second century BCE. This deliberate alteration of history by theology tends to cast *1 Maccabees* as more reliable for a reconstruction of the paradigmatic and historic events by the Hasmoneans.

The Pseudepigrapha

The Pseudepigrapha has been inadvertently defined incorrectly by the *selections* from this corpus published in German under the editorship of Emil Kautzsch in *Die Apokryphen und Pseudepigraphen des Alten Testaments,* 2 vols. (Tübingen, 1900), and in English under the editorship of R. H. Charles in *The Apocrypha and Pseudepigrapha of the Old Testament,* 2 vols. (Oxford, 1913). Charles's edition of the Pseudepigrapha contains all the documents in Kautzsch's collection plus four additional writings: *2 Enoch, Ahiqar,* a Zadokite work, and *Pirkē Aboth (Pirqei avot).* The last two works belong, respectively, among the Dead Sea Scrolls and the rabbinic writings. All the others and many more, to a total of fifty-two writings plus a supplement that contains thirteen lost Jewish works quoted by the ancients, especially Alexander Polyhistor (c. 112–30s BCE), are included in *The Old Testament Pseudepigrapha,* 2 vols., edited by James H. Charlesworth (Garden City, N.Y., 1983–1984).

The fifty-two main documents in *The Old Testament Pseudepigrapha (OTP)*—which is not a canon of sacred writings but a modern collection of Jewish and Christian writings from circa 200 BCE to 200 CE—can be organized in five categories: (1) apocalyptic literature and related works; (2) testaments, which often include apocalyptic sections; (3) expansions of biblical stories and other legends; (4) wisdom and philosophical literature; and (5) prayers, psalms, and odes. (See figure 1.) To represent the corpus of the Pseudepigrapha within the confines of this relatively short article demands that comments on each category of writings be brief and sharply focused.

Apocalyptic Literature and Related Works. Nineteen pseudepigrapha can be grouped in the category of apocalyptic literature and related works (see figure 1). These nineteen works cover three overlapping chronological periods.

1. Antedating the burning of Jerusalem by the Romans in 70 CE, the great watershed in the history of Early Judaism (250 BCE–200 CE), are *1 Enoch,* some of the *Sibylline Oracles,* the *Apocrypha of Ezekiel,* and perhaps the *Treatise of Shem.*
2. After 70, the great varieties of religious thought in Judaism waned markedly as religious Jews, with great anxiety, lamented the loss of the Temple and pondered the cause of their defeat. *4 Ezra, 2 Baruch, 3 Baruch,* and the *Apocalypse of Abraham* are characterized by an intense interest in theodicy. *4 Ezra* is very pessimistic; its author finds it difficult to see

FIGURE 1. *The Pseudepigrapha, Arranged by Category*

Apocalyptic Literature and Related Works
1. Ethiopic *Apocalypse of Enoch (1 Enoch)*
2. Slavonic *Apocalypse of Enoch (2 Enoch)*
3. Hebrew *Apocalypse of Enoch (3 Enoch)*
4. *Sibylline Oracles*
5. *Treatise of Shem*
6. *Apocryphon of Ezekiel*
7. *Apocalypse of Zephaniah*
8. *Fourth Book of Ezra (4 Ezra)*
9. *Apocalypse of Ezra*
10. *Vision of Ezra*
11. *Questions of Ezra*
12. *Revelation of Ezra*
13. *Apocalypse of Sedrach*
14. Syriac *Apocalypse of Baruch (2 Baruch)*
15. Greek *Apocalypse of Baruch (3 Baruch)*
16. *Apocalypse of Abraham*
17. *Apocalypse of Adam*
18. *Apocalypse of Elijah*
19. *Apocalypse of Daniel*

Testaments
1. *Testaments of the Twelve Patriarchs*
2. *Testament of Abraham*
3. *Testament of Isaac*
4. *Testament of Jacob*
5. *Testament of Job*
6. *Testament of Moses*
7. *Testament of Solomon*
8. *Testament of Adam*

Expansions of Biblical Stories and Other Legends
1. *Letter of Aristeas*
2. *Jubilees*
3. *Martyrdom and Ascension of Isaiah*
4. *Joseph and Aseneth*
5. *Life of Adam and Eve*
6. *Pseudo-Philo*
7. *Lives of the Prophets*
8. *Ladder of Jacob*
9. *Fourth Book of Baruch (4 Baruch)*
10. *Jannes and Jambres*
11. *History of the Rechabites*
12. *Eldad and Modad*
13. *History of Joseph*

Wisdom and Philosophical Literature
1. *Ahiqar*
2. *Third Book of the Maccabees (3 Maccabees)*
3. *Fourth Book of the Maccabees (4 Maccabees)*
4. *Pseudo-Phocylides*
5. *Syriac Menander*

Prayers, Psalms, and Odes
1. Five More Psalms of David (Psalms 151–155)
2. *Prayer of Manasseh*
3. *Psalms of Solomon*
4. Hellenistic Synagogal Prayers
5. *Prayer of Joseph*
6. *Prayer of Jacob*
7. *Odes of Solomon*

any hope in his remorse. *2 Baruch* is much more optimistic than *4 Ezra;* the Temple was destroyed by God's angels because of Israel's unfaithfulness (7:1–8:5), not by a superior culture or the might of the enemy.

3. Later works are documents 3, some of 4, 9, 10, 11, 12, 13, 18, and 19, ranging in date from the lost purported Jewish base of (or traditions in) the *Apocalypse of Adam* in the first or second century CE to the *Apocalypse of Daniel* in the ninth. These works are important for an understanding of Early Judaism only because they apparently preserve some edited works and record some early Jewish traditions.

The most important pseudepigraphon in this group is the composite book known as *1 Enoch.* It is preserved in its entire, final form only in Ethiopic, although versions of early portions of it are preserved in other languages; of these the most important are the Greek and Aramaic. The Qumran Aramaic fragments, because of their paleographic age, prove that portions of *1 Enoch* date from the third, second, and first centuries BCE.

In *The Books of Enoch: Aramaic Fragments of Qumrân Cave 4* (Oxford, 1976), J. T. Milik not only published the *editio princeps* of the Aramaic fragments of *Enoch,* but he also claimed that chapters 37–71 must be Christian and postdate 260 CE. He obtained this surprising conclusion because of the absence of these chapters at Qumran, the striking similarity to the New Testament concepts of the Son of man and the Messiah, and the author's imagined reference to the "events of the years A.D. 260 to 270" (p. 96). These arguments are erroneous, and they have been rightly rejected by all specialists. The absence of fragments at Qumran is not so significant as Milik claims; the striking parallels to the New Testament are due either to a shared culture or to influences from *1 Enoch* 37–71 upon Jesus or the New Testament authors; the historical events of the third century CE are *not* reflected in *1 Enoch.* Moreover, all manuscripts of *1 Enoch* attest that chapters 37–71 move climactically to the elevation of Enoch as son of man (in 71:14, the angel says to Enoch, "You are the son of man."). Hence, all of *1 Enoch* is Jewish and predates 70.

1 Enoch consists of five works that were composed over three centuries. In chronological order they are *Enoch's Astronomical Book* (*1 Enoch* 72–82), from the third century BCE; *Enoch's Journeys* (*1 Enoch* 1–36), from pre-160 BCE; *Enoch's Dream Visions* (*1 Enoch* 83–90), from pre-160 BCE), *Enoch's Epistle* (*1 Enoch* 91–105), from the second or first century BCE; and *Enoch's Parables* (*1 Enoch* 37–71), from pre-70 CE. Addenda (*1 Enoch* 106–108) are of uncertain date.

Some of the chapters that begin and end the divisions in *1 Enoch* were added or edited as the separate works were brought together into one document; this composite work circulated in Palestine before 70. While the precise dates for these sections of *1 Enoch,* or *Books of Enoch,* are debated, it is clear that the ideas they contain, such as the advocation of a solar calendar, were characteristic of some Jews from the third century BCE to the first century CE. *1 Enoch* is one of our major sources for Hellenistic Jewish ideas on cosmology, angelology, astronomy, God, sin, and mankind.

Example: "Then an angel came to me [Enoch] and greeted me and said to me, 'You, son of man, who art born in righteousness and upon whom righteousness has dwelt, the righteousness of the Antecedent of Time will not forsake you'" (*1 En.* 71:14; trans. E. Isaac in *OTP*).

Testaments. Eight testaments, some of which include apocalyptic sections, make up a second group of pseudepigrapha (see figure 1). Of these, only the *Testament of Job* and the *Testament of Moses* clearly predate 70 CE. The *Testament of Adam,* in its present form, may be as late as the fifth century CE. The *Testament of Solomon* is earlier, perhaps from the third century CE. The *Testament of Isaac* and the *Testament of Jacob* were possibly added in the second or third century to the *Testament of Abraham,* which in its earliest form probably dates from the end of the first century or the beginning of the second century CE.

The most important—and most controversial—document in this group is the *Testaments of the Twelve Patriarchs.* Marinus de Jonge (for bibliographic data, see Charlesworth, 1981) has argued that this document is a Christian composition that inherits much Jewish tradition, both oral and written. Most scholars have concluded that, while the extant document is Christian, the Christian passages are clearly interpolations and redactions added to a Jewish document that dates from the second or first century BCE. This documents consists of twelve testaments, each attributed to a son of Jacob and containing ethical instruction often with apocalyptic visions.

Example: "A copy of the words of Levi: the things that he decreed to his sons concerning all they were to do, and the things that would happen to them until the day of judgment. . . . I, Levi, was born in Haran and came with my father to Shechem. . . . There I again saw the vision as formerly. . . . And now, my children, I know from the writings of Enoch that in the end time you will act impiously against the Lord . . . your brothers will be humiliated and among all the nations you shall become the occasion for scorn. For your father, Israel, is pure with respect to all the impieties of the chief priests [who laid their hands on the savior of the world *(sōtēra tou kosmou.)*], as heaven is pure above the earth; and you should be the lights of Israel as the sun and the moon" (*T. Levi* 1:1, 2:1, 8:1, 14:1–3; trans. H. C. Kee in *OTP;* brackets denote the Christian interpolation).

Expansions of Biblical Stories and Legends. The documents in the Hebrew Bible, because of their recognized divine authority and revered antiquity, profoundly affected the daily and religious life of Jews in the Hellenistic world. The three divisions of the Hebrew Bible—the Torah (Law), Prophets, and the Writings—moved toward canonicity during the years from 300 BCE to 200 CE. Almost all Jewish religious writings were categorically shaped on the literary norms, theological perspectives, and semiotic language already developed in the Hebrew Bible. Of the many ramifications caused by the normative force of the biblical books, one is singularly represented by the documents that expand upon the biblical stories, supplying details and providing answers—often through pictorially rich narratives—to questions aroused by careful and repeated readings of the sacred books. Thirteen documents fall into this category (see figure 1).

These thirteen documents represent Jewish expansions of stories in the Hebrew scriptures over many centuries. The *History of Joseph,* in a class by itself, is late, and perhaps reached its final form in the sixth century CE. Five writings, documents 8–12, date from the late first century to the late second century. The *History of the Rechabites,* however, was extensively expanded and reworked by early Christians; its present form in Syriac, and perhaps in Greek, was not complete until around the sixth century.

In this group the most important writings for Hellenistic Judaism are documents 1–7. Almost all these predate the destruction of Jerusalem in 70. The *Martyrdom and Ascension of Isaiah* is a significant exception; it continued to be expanded and was redacted by Christians up until about the fourth century. *Joseph and Aseneth* has been a controversial writing; while it has been dated by some scholars as early as the second century BCE, it probably dates from the early decades of the second century CE (see Charlesworth, 1981; Denis, 1970; and especially C. Burchard in *OTP*). *Jubilees* was probably composed in the years between 163 and 140 BCE.

Example: "And in the eleventh jubilee Jared took for himself a wife. . . . And she bore a son for him in the fifth week. . . . And he called him Enoch. This one was the first who learned writing and knowledge and wisdom. . . . And who wrote in a book the signs of the heaven according to the order of their months, so that the sons of man might know the (appointed) times of the years according to their order, with respect to each of their months" (*Jub.* 4:16–17; trans. Orval Wintermute in *OTP*).

Wisdom and Philosophical Literature. Mankind's search for understanding and wisdom crosses all boundaries, including the fictitious divides of centuries and the fluctuating contours of nations. Five pseudepigrapha constitute a Hellenistic Jewish record of mankind's insights into wisdom and present practical ethical rules and aphorisms for enlightened actions (see figure 1). *Syriac Menander,* as a collection, seems to date from the third century CE (see T. Baarda in *OTP*), but *Pseudo-Phocylides* and *4 Maccabees* date from the first century CE, and perhaps the former from even the first century BCE (see P. W. van der Horst in *OTP*). *3 Maccabees* was clearly composed in the first century BCE. *Ahiqar* is very early, dating from the fourth or even fifth century BCE, but it influenced the author of *Tobit* around 180 BCE.

Examples: "The love of money is the mother of all evil" *(Ps-Phoc.* 42; trans. van der Horst in *OTP).* "Long hair is not fit for boys, but for voluptuous women" *(Ps-Phoc.* 212; trans. van der Horst in *OTP).* "Do not laugh at old age, for that is where you shall arrive and remain" *(Syr. Men.* 11–12; trans. T. Baarda in *OTP).* "For reason [*logismos*] is the guide of the virtues and the supreme master of the passions" *(4 Mc.* 1:30; trans. H. Anderson in *OTP).*

Prayers, Psalms, and Odes. The Davidic Psalter, the hymnbook of the Second Temple, was gradually considered closed during the centuries that preceded the destruction of the Temple. Other poetic compositions were completed during the years from the conquests of Alexander the Great in 336–323 BCE until the final defeat of Shim'on Bar Kokhba in 135 CE. Many of these were incorporated into various pseudepigrapha to accentuate or illustrate a point or to raise the confessional level of the narrative. Others were collected into "hymnbooks" or "prayer books" that may be grouped as a fifth, and final, category of pseudepigrapha (see figure 1).

The *Odes of Solomon,* the earliest Christian "hymnbook," is modeled on the poetic style of the Davidic Psalter; it dates from the late first century or the beginning of the second century CE. The *Prayer of Joseph* and the *Prayer of Jacob* are Jewish compositions from perhaps as early as the first century CE. The "Hellenistic Synagogal Prayers," preserved in books 7 and 8 of the *Apostolic Constitutions,* are Christian in their present form, but they may well be remnants of Jewish prayers that date from the early centuries CE. The *Psalms of Solomon,* which seems to represent the piety of a circle of Jews living in Jerusalem, was certainly composed in the second half of the second century BCE. The *Prayer of Manasseh* is very difficult to date, but it probably comes from the turn of the eras. The Davidic Psalter itself was expanded with "Five More Psalms of David" (psalms

151–155), which date from various time periods, ranging from the third century (151) to the second or first century BCE (152–155). The original language of psalms 151, 154, and 155 is Hebrew; the others were composed in a Semitic language (Hebrew, Aramaic, or Syriac).

Example: "O Lord, do not condemn me according to my sins; / For no one living is righteous before you" (Psalm 155 [11QPs[a] 155]; trans. Charlesworth in *OTP*).

[*See also* Apocalypse, *overview article and article on* Jewish Apocalypticism to the Rabbinic Period.]

BIBLIOGRAPHY

The Apocrypha. The best bibliographical guide to the Apocrypha is Gerhard Elling's *Bibliographie zur jüdisch-hellenistischen und intertestamentarischen Literatur, 1900–1970,* "Texte und Untersuchungen," no. 106, 2d ed. (Berlin, 1975). An important introduction to parts of the Apocrypha and Pseudepigrapha, with insightful comments regarding their sources and historical setting, is George W. E. Nickelsburg's *Jewish Literature between the Bible and the Mishnah: A Historical and Literary Introduction* (Philadelphia, 1981). See also Robert H. Pfeiffer's *History of New Testament Times with an Introduction to the Apocrypha* (New York, 1984). A careful, well-written, and authoritative introduction (but a little dated now) is Bruce M. Metzger's *An Introduction to the Apocrypha* (New York, 1957). An earlier work is Charles C. Torrey's *The Apocryphal Literature: A Brief Introduction* (1945; reprint, London, 1963). Reliable introductions to the Apocrypha, from Roman Catholics who consider these books deuterocanonical, can be found in *The Jerome Bible Commentary,* edited by Raymond E. Brown, Joseph A. Fitzmyer, and Roland E. Murphy (Englewood Cliffs, N.J., 1968).

Critical Greek editions of the Apocrypha have been appearing in the Cambridge and Göttingen editions of the Septuagint. A handy Greek edition of the Apocrypha is Alfred Rahlfs's *Septuaginta,* 2 vols. (Stuttgart, 1935; reprint of 8th ed., 1965). A classic work on the Apocrypha is volume 1 of *The Apocrypha and Pseudepigrapha of the Old Testament in English: With Introductions and Critical and Explanatory Notes to the Several Books,* edited by R. H. Charles (Oxford, 1913). More recent and excellent translations are those in *The Jerusalem Bible* (Garden City, N.Y., 1966), which is translated by Roman Catholics, and in *The New Oxford Annotated Bible with the Apocrypha: Revised Standard Version,* exp. ed., edited by Herbert G. May and Bruce M. Metzger (New York, 1977).

The best current commentary series is the Anchor Bible. Volumes 41–44 (Garden City, N.Y., 1976–1983) include Jonathan A. Goldstein's *I Maccabees* (vol. 41, 1976) and *II Maccabees* (vol. 41A, 1983), Jacob M. Myers's *I and II Esdras* (vol. 42, 1974), David Winston's *The Wisdom of Solomon* (vol. 43, 1979; reprint, 1981), and Carey A. Moore's *Daniel, Esther, and Jeremiah: The Additions* (vol. 44, 1977). Also valuable, especially because the Greek text is printed opposite the English translation, is *Jewish Apocryphal Literature,* 7 vols., edited by Solomon Zeitlin (Leiden, 1950–1972). The fruit of the best German scholarship on the Apocrypha and Pseudepigrapha has been appearing in fascicles in the series titled "Jüdische Schriften aus hellenistisch-römischer Zeit" (JSHRZ), edited by Werner Georg Kümmel (Gütersloh, 1973–). Valuable tools for those who know Greek are Christian Abraham Wahl's *Clavis librorum veteris testamenti apocryphorum philologica* (1853; reprint, Graz, 1972) and Edwin Hatch and Henry A. Redpath's *A Concordance to the Septuagint and the Other Greek Versions of the Old Testament, including the Apocryphal Books,* 2 vols. (1897–1906; reprint, Graz, 1972). A model computer-produced reference work is now available for the Apocrypha (and part of the Pseudepigrapha): Bruce M. Metzger et al., *A Concordance to the Apocrypha-Deuterocanonical Books of the Revised Standard Version* (Grand Rapids, Mich., 1983).

The Pseudepigrapha

Charlesworth, James H. *The Pseudepigrapha and Modern Research with a Supplement.* Chico, Calif., 1981. This book succinctly introduces the documents in the Pseudepigrapha and provides a bibliography of publications from 1960 until 1979. All publications mentioned in this article are cited with complete bibliographic data.

Charlesworth, James H., ed. *The Old Testament Pseudepigrapha.* 2 vols. Garden City, N.Y., 1983–1985. This massive collection contains introductions to and English translations of fifty-two writings classified as pseudepigrapha and of thirteen other documents included in a supplement. The introductions by the editor clarify the problems in defining "apocalypses," "testaments," "expansions of the 'Old Testament,'" "wisdom and philosophical literature," and "prayers, psalms, and odes."

Denis, Albert-Marie. *Introduction aux pseudépigraphes grecs d'Ancien Testament.* Leiden, 1970.

Nickelsburg, George W. E. *Jewish Literature between the Bible and the Mishnah: A Historical and Literary Introduction.* Philadelphia, 1981.

Sparks, H. F. D., ed. *The Apocryphal Old Testament.* Oxford, 1984. A selection of some documents usually placed in the Pseudepigrapha.

JAMES H. CHARLESWORTH

New Testament

"New Testament" is the name commonly given to a collection of twenty-seven different writings that function as normative scripture within the Christian churches, namely, the gospel according to Matthew, the gospel according to Mark, the gospel according to Luke, the gospel according to John, the *Acts of the Apostles,* the letter of Paul to the Romans, the first and second letters of Paul to the Corinthians, the letter of Paul to the Galatians, the letter of Paul to the Ephesians, the letter of Paul to the Philippians, the letter of Paul to the Colossians, the first and second letters of Paul to the Thessalonians, the first and second letters of Paul to Timothy, the letter of Paul to Titus, the letter of Paul to Philemon, the *Letter to the Hebrews,* the *Letter of James,* the first and second letters of Peter, the first, second, and third letters of John, the *Letter of Jude*, and the *Revelation to John*. These writings were composed by various Christian authors over approximately one century (c. AD 50–150). They represent a significant portion of early Christian literature, but they do not in every instance represent the oldest extant Christian writings.

The collection and identification of this particular group of writings as a distinct and normative entity was the result of a complex development within the Christian churches. The process, known as canonization, took approximately four centuries. The oldest indisputable witness to the New Testament canon is Athanasius, a fourth-century bishop of Alexandria. Paraphrasing the prologue of the gospel according to Luke in an Easter letter addressed to his congregation in the year 367, Athanasius summarily cited the circumstances that led to the development of the canon. He wrote: "Forasmuch as some have taken in hand, to reduce into order for themselves the books termed apocryphal, and to mix them up with the divinely inspired Scriptures . . . it seemed good to me also . . . to set before you the books included in the Canon, and handed down, and accredited as Divine" (Philip Schaff and Henry Wace, eds., *The Nicene and Post-Nicene Fathers*, vol. 4, Grand Rapids, Mich., 1978, pp. 551–552). After listing the books belonging to the Old Testament, Athanasius continues:

> Again it is not tedious to speak of the books of the New Testament. These are the four Gospels, according to Matthew, Mark, Luke, and John. Afterwards, the Acts of the Apostles and Epistles (called Catholic), seven, viz., of James, one; of Peter, two; of John, three; after these, one of Jude. In addition, there are the fourteen epistles of Paul, written in this order. The first, to the Romans; then two to the Corinthians; after these, to the Galatians; next, to the Ephesians; then to the Philippians; then to the Colossians; after these, two to the Thessalonians, and that to the Hebrews; and again, two to Timothy; one to Titus; and lastly, that to Philemon. And besides, the Revelation to John. (ibid.)

Athanasius's remarks indicate that the process of canonization took place in the midst of some controversy, that it involved a distinction between writings identified as "canonical" and those deemed to be "apocryphal," and that the judgment as to the canonicity of writings was dependent upon tradition and the estimation that they were divinely inspired. Studies of the first four centuries of Christianity confirm the suggestions made by Athanasius. [*For further discussion of canonicity in broad religious perspective, see* Canon.]

The First Christian Generation

There is no evidence in the New Testament that the Christians of the first two or three generations were a literary group. The only indication that Jesus himself wrote anything is in *John* 8:6–8, a dubious reference in light of scholars' common estimation that *John* 7:53–8:11 did not originally belong to the text of John's gospel. According to the gospel evidence, Jesus' command to his disciples was that they should preach (e.g., *Mk.* 3:14, *Mt.* 28:20); nothing is said about a command or exhortation to write. The Lucan overview of early Christianity contained in the *Acts of Apostles* focuses on the preaching of the apostles. It specifically states that at least Peter and John were unlearned (*agrammatoi*, lit. "illiterate," in *Acts* 4:13). Moreover, even though the greater portion of *Acts* is devoted to Paul's activity, *Acts* presents Paul as a preacher and does not once mention his letter-writing. Paul did write letters, of course, and on occasion he referred to letters he has written (*1 Cor.* 5:9, *2 Cor.* 2:3–9; see also *2 Thes.* 2:3). The only New Testament indication of an authoritative command to write concerns the letters to the seven churches in the *Book of Revelation* (*Rv.* 1:11; see also *Rv.* 2:1, 2:8, 2:12, 2:18, 3:1, 3:7, 3:14). Thus there is no evidence in the New Testament itself that the earliest Christian communities experienced a need to have what later Christian generations would call a New Testament.

Apocalyptic Context. The Christian gospel was first preached in a variety of social and religious circumstances that generally militated against the production of a sacred literature. Not only were the first generations of Jesus' disciples largely unlearned, but the message that Jesus preached was couched in apocalyptic terms. He proclaimed, "The time is fulfilled, and the kingdom of God is at hand" (*Mk.* 1:15). This message, like that of John the Baptizer before Jesus, focused on the imminent coming of the reign of God. The apocalyptic proclamation of the coming of the kingdom of God was derived from the prophetic proclamation of the Day of the Lord. Not only did Jesus preach about the coming Kingdom, he was also an effective exorcist. The New Testament evidence suggests that Jesus himself, as well as his disciples, interpreted these early exorcisms as harbingers of the reign of God (see esp. *Mt.* 12:28, *Lk.* 11:20). Thus Jesus' activity is to be situated within the context of the Jewish apocalyptic movements of the first century AD. At the time there was widespread expectation that God would establish his reign by some definitive action. The coming of God's kingdom implied the end of the world order as it was then known.

Within a generation after the death of Jesus, the expectation of the coming of God's kingdom was associated with the expectation that Jesus himself would return as Son of man and Lord. This was the expectation of the Parousia ("presence" or "arrival," frequently identified in later Christian writings as the Second

Coming). Although Paul was a Hellenistic Jew, he too expected that Jesus would come as eschatological Lord during Paul's own lifetime (see *1 Thes.* 4:17). This expectation of an imminent Parousia was characteristic of the hope for the future that first-generation Christians held.

The New Testament is consistent in its affirmation that God raised Jesus from the dead. The Christians' belief in the resurrection of Jesus was the basis of their hope for the future. Jesus' resurrection was understood as an act of God and as the initial event in the eschatological drama. On more than one occasion, Paul attested that God first raised Jesus from the dead and that the resurrection of those who believed would subsequently follow. (See especially *1 Thessalonians* 4:13–17, *1 Corinthians* 15:12, and *1 Corinthians* 15:23–24 and such traditional kerygmatic texts as *Romans* 6:4, 8:11, *1 Corinthians* 6:14, and *2 Corinthians* 4:14. For a confirmation that this was a dominant point of view within the ambit of Pauline thought, see *Colossians* 1:15, 1:18.) More than a half-century after the death of Jesus, the gospel according to Matthew uses apocalyptic imagery (*Mt.* 27:51–54, 28:2–4) to attest that the death and resurrection of Jesus had been understood within Matthew's Jewish-Christian circles as an eschatological event.

The belief of the earliest Christians that God's kingdom was imminent not only gave a sense of urgency to the proclamation of Jesus' message by his disciples but also impeded production of a specifically Christian literature among the first generation of Jesus' disciples. For the most part they were incapable of literary activity; their expectation of an imminent Parousia rendered such activity redundant.

Belief in the Holy Spirit. Another factor tended to forestall the production of literature among the first generation of Christians: the role attributed to the Holy Spirit. Early Christian tradition affirms that the preaching and exorcisms of Jesus were the result of his having received the Holy Spirit. All four gospels—*Matthew* and *Mark* explicitly, *Luke* and *John* implicitly—describe Jesus' public activity as beginning with his baptism by John (*Mt.* 3:13–17, *Mk.* 1:9–11, *Lk.* 3:21–22, *Jn.* 1:31–34). The opening of the heavens (*Mt.* 3:16, *Mk.* 1:10, *Lk.* 3:21) served to characterize, in apocalyptic imagery, the beginning of Jesus' public ministry as an eschatological event. The spirit that descended upon Jesus at his baptism was the eschatological Holy Spirit, the manifestation of God's power associated with the reign of God. This was the Spirit of the end time, that is, the age to come. This eschatological Spirit empowered and impelled Jesus to proclaim the coming of the Kingdom and to effect exorcisms. As the fragment of a traditional creedal formula cited by Paul in *Romans* 1:4 explicitly attests, that same Holy Spirit continued to be operative in the resurrection of Jesus.

Because the spirit with which Jesus was endowed led him to proclaim the coming of the Kingdom, it was readily identified with the prophetic spirit of Jewish tradition. This point of view is developed in the gospel according to Luke, wherein Luke comments upon the tradition of Jesus' baptism and the descent of the Holy Spirit with an extended reflection to the effect that the gift of the Spirit should be understood as an anointing with the spirit of prophecy (*Lk.* 4:16–30). In the *Acts of the Apostles*, Luke highlights the continuity between the activity of Jesus' disciples and the activity of Jesus himself. He portrays the proclamation of the gospel by Jesus' disciples as also having been inaugurated by the gift of the Spirit (*Acts* 2:1–4). Subsequently *Acts* repeatedly ascribes the spread of the Christian message to the Spirit. *Acts* is effectively an extended affirmation that the prophetic spirit of God was at work in the spread of the gospel. By means of a citation of *Joel* 2:28–32 (see *Acts* 2:16–21), Luke avers that the Spirit, whose activity he is about to describe, is the Spirit of the end time. Having made a statement to that effect at the beginning of his work, Luke is subsequently content merely to affirm that he is describing the work of the prophetic Spirit of God.

The conviction that the proclamation of the Christian gospel was due to the power of the Spirit of God is also found in Paul's first letter to the Thessalonians, the earliest extant Christian writing. Paul explicitly attests that both the proclamation of the gospel and its reception are the work of the Spirit (*1 Thes.* 1:5–6). The apocalyptic tone of significant parts of that first letter suggests that it is indeed the Spirit of the final days to whom he attributes the power of the gospel.

The conviction that the echatological and prophetic Spirit of God was operative in their midst led the first generations of Christians to revere the voice of Spirit-inspired prophets, among whom Jesus was the paradigm. Even Paul, who avowed that he also had the Spirit of God (*1 Cor.* 7:40), boasted that he was a preacher (see *1 Cor.* 1:17, 2:1–5). He had recourse to writing only because the circumstances of his later preaching prevented him from being personally present to those whom he had previously evangelized and with whom he wished to be in additional communication (see, e.g., *1 Thes.* 2:17–3:10, *1 Cor.* 4:14–21). Paul appears to have valued personal presence and the spoken word over the written word.

Both Papias (AD 60–130) and Justin Martyr (c. 100–163/165) bear witness to the high regard in which oral tradition, as distinct from written documents, was held as late as the middle of the second century. In fact, Eusebius, the fourth-century church historian, writing at a time when there was considerable discussion among the Christian churches about which writings were traditional, and noting that some writings were commonly accepted by the churches and others were not, recalls that Papias had said: "I did not suppose that information from books would help me so much as the word of a living and surviving voice" (*Church History* 3.39.4). Thus, even when the process of canonization was reaching its climax, the foremost church historian of the time continued to recall that earlier generations of Christians had higher regard for the Spirit-inspired oral message than they did for written words.

The general illiteracy of the first Christians, the expectation of an imminent Parousia, and the high regard for Spirit-inspired prophetic utterance together ensured that the first generations of Christians would be itinerant, charismatic-type prophetic figures rather than scholarly authors of written works. Their social circumstances and their activity mutually served to prevent their producing written works.

Hebrew Scriptures. The early Christians were even less disposed to produce a specifically religious literature. Jesus and the twelve disciples already had their scriptures: the New Testament portrays Jesus and the disciples as being present in the Temple of Jerusalem and in synagogues, where the scriptures were expounded. The oldest literary attestation to one of Jesus' exorcisms is situated by Mark in the synagogue in Capernaum (*Mk.* 1:21–28), and Luke portrays Jesus in the synagogue in Nazareth, where he read from the scroll of the *Book of Isaiah* and commented upon its significance (*Lk.* 4:16–22). All four evangelists describe Jesus interpreting the scriptures, both in rabbinic-type disputation and by way of expository comment. While many of these descriptions owe as much to the creativity and theological purposes of the evangelists as they do to historical reminiscence and the conservative force of tradition, there is little doubt that Jesus accepted the scriptures of his people and his own religious tradition. For Jesus the Hebrew scriptures (*hai graphai* in Greek, the language in which the gospels were written) were a normative expression of the word of God.

Similarly, while the historical accuracy of Luke's account of Paul's formation at Jerusalem under Gamli'el (*Acts* 22:3) is doubtful, Paul's esteem for the Hebrew scriptures is certain. Although Paul was a Jew of the Diaspora, the scriptures were a preeminent authority in his religious vision. With the exception of the first letter to the Thessalonians and the letter to Philemon, Paul cites the Hebrew scriptures to illustrate and/or bolster his arguments. His manner of expounding the scriptures is remarkably similar to the expository techniques of the rabbis and the *pesharim* of Qumran. Even without Luke's idealized portrayal of Paul the synagogue preacher (see esp. *Acts* 13:14a–33), Paul's own letters offer abundant evidence that he held the Hebrew scriptures in the highest esteem.

Letters

Because the Hebrew scriptures were the scriptures *par excellence,* and because the first generation(s) of Christians were essentially Jews who acknowledged the risen Jesus as Christ or Lord, it was unlikely that these early Christians would have produced a sacred literature to compete with that of their Jewish tradition. Nonetheless, the high regard accorded the Hebrew scriptures within both Palestinian and Diaspora Judaism, and the apocalyptic perspective evidenced by the preaching of Jesus and the early writings of Paul, did not preclude the writing of letters. Letters are not literature in the proper sense of the term, as the Germans acknowledge by assigning letters to the category of *kleine Literatur* ("small written pieces"). Moreover, there is nothing about a letter that qualifies it as a particularly appropriate form for religious literature. Nonetheless the oldest extant Christian literature consists of the letters of Paul. These letters have always been found in the manuscript and printed editions of the New Testament following the four Gospels and the *Acts of the Apostles;* they are the oldest part of the New Testament.

Although an occasional voice within scholarly circles pleads that the letter of James, or the letter to the Galatians, or the second letter to the Thessalonians (each letter to the Thessalonians begins the same way) was the first New Testament letter to have been composed, it is almost unanimously recognized that the first letter to the Thessalonians represents the first piece of the documentation that was later collected together to form the New Testament. Written by Paul from Corinth to the church of the Thessalonians in AD 50 or 51, the letter was a further attempt by Paul to "supply what was lacking in the faith" of the Thessalonians (see *1 Thes.* 3:10) after receiving from Timothy, who had served as Paul's emissary to Thessalonica, a favorable report on the faith and love of the Thessalonian Christians. There is no suggestion in the letter that Paul is attempting to inaugurate a new mode of religious literature or that a letter is an especially suitable means of conveying the Christian message. As a letter, however, *1 Thessalonians* represents the propagation of the Christian message in a new form—the written composition. Thus, it merits Helmut Koester's description of it as an "experiment in

Christian writing." It was written in a particular set of circumstances, and it met the specific needs of those circumstances. Indeed, Paul had to request that the letter be read to all the brethren (*1 Thes.* 5:27). Therefore, *1 Thessalonians* is an "occasional writing" and must be interpreted within its historical situation. All writings are best understood within the historical circumstances of their composition, but this is especially true of letters, which by their very nature are situational.

The Hellenistic Model. Although A. J. Malherbe pleaded that *1 Thessalonians* be understood within the category of the paraenetic letter, it is more generally acknowledged that Paul employed the Hellenistic personal letter as a model for his own correspondence. Paul's first letter to the Thessalonians is substantially longer than the average personal letter of Hellenistic correspondents, but it has the essential form of such a letter.

Hellenistic letters typically followed a tripartite schema: the protocol (introduction), the body of the letter (the *homilia,* or basic message), and the eschatocol (conclusion). The protocol normally followed the format of "A to B, greetings and a health wish." Opening with "Paul, Silvanus, and Timothy, to the church of the Thessalonians in God the Father and the Lord Jesus Christ: Grace to you and peace," Paul's first letter to the Thessalonians followed the traditional format, with the exception of the health wish. The health wish is omitted from all the New Testament epistolary literature, with the exception of *3 John* (v. 2). As with all the Pauline letters deemed authentic by critical scholarship *(Romans, 1–2 Corinthians, Galatians, Philippians, 1 Thessalonians, Philemon),* other Christian evangelizers are associated with Paul in the sending of the greetings. The recipients of *1 Thessalonians* are an assembly (*ekklēsia,* "church") of believers, rather than a single individual. This too sets a precedent, since Paul's later letters were similarly addressed to churches. The greeting of *1 Thessalonians* clearly represents a modification of the typical Hellenistic greeting, a simple "greetings" (sg., *chaire;* pl., *chairete*). The greeting of *1 Thessalonians* is a literary neologism (*charis,* "grace"), somewhat homonymous with the Hellenistic greeting, expanded by the typical Semitic greeting (*eirenē,* "peace," the Greek equivalent of the Hebrew *shalom,* used as a greeting in personal encounters as well as in letters). Paul may well have taken the two-part greeting from the liturgical usage of the bicultural Christians at Antioch in Syria. Although the greeting of *1 Thessalonians* is the relatively simple "grace and peace," the formula was expanded in his later correspondence to become "grace to you and peace from God the Father and the Lord Jesus Christ." In short, Paul seems to have employed the typical Hellenistic introduction but adapted it to his own purposes.

The use of traditional form with marked personal adaptation is particularly remarkable with regard to the body of Paul's first letter. Typically the Hellenistic letter fulfilled three functions: it was an expression of friendship *(philophronensis),* it was a way of being present *(parousia),* and it conveyed a particular message. The body of the letter usually began with a thanksgiving, an expression of gratitude to one or another deity who had provided a specific benefit to the correspondents. (Some analysts of the Hellenistic letter prefer to distinguish the thanksgiving from the body of the letter and thus identify a four-part rather than a three-part schema in the letter.) The first letter to the Thessalonians actually contains two long thanksgiving periods (*1 Thes.* 1:2–2:12, 2:13–3:13), which together take up about half the letter. This phenomenon, among other factors, has led some scholars (particularly Walter Schmithals and Rudolf Pesch) to hold that *1 Thessalonians* is a composite text, that is, the result of an amalgamation of two shorter letters.

The First Letter to the Thessalonians. From the standpoint of Paul's appropriation of the personal-letter form, some specific features of *1 Thessalonians* are particularly noteworthy. Paul's use of the "recall motif," his constant allusions to being among the Thessalonians, shows that the letter is an occasional writing. Yet the body of the letter focuses upon God's activity among the Thessalonians. Paul gives thanks that the proclamation of the gospel has been effective among them. He represents his presence to the Thessalonians as that of an "apostle of Christ" (*1 Thes.* 2:7) so that there results a significant modification of the *parousia* function of the letter. Since Paul's presence is an apostolic presence, the section of the letter in which Paul specifically writes of his desire to be with the Thessalonians (*1 Thes.* 2:17–3:13) has been styled "the apostolic parousia" (Robert W. Funk). Paul's later letters have a similar feature.

But Paul's apostolic presence is overshadowed by a still greater presence, that of Jesus Christ the Lord. In *1 Thessalonians* Paul uses the technical term *parousia,* a term used elsewhere in the New Testament in this technical sense only in *2 Thessalonians* and *Matthew,* to express the object of Christian hope. Paul's second thanksgiving period concludes with a wish-prayer (*1 Thes.* 3:11–13) that focuses on the Parousia. Questions about the relationship between the Parousia of the Lord Jesus and the resurrection of the dead seem to have been singularly important among the specific concerns that prompted the writing of the first letter to the Thessalonians. However, Paul's concluding the second thanksgiving period (see also *1 Thes.* 2:12) with reference to the awaited and desired Parousia inaugurated a pattern of eschatological climax to the thanksgiving period that would characterize his later writings.

The eschatocol of the typical Hellenistic letter consisted of a series of greetings, prayers, and wishes. These elements are in the concluding verses of *1 Thessalonians* (5:23–27). Noteworthy is Paul's exhortation that the letter "be read to all the brethren" (v. 27), which shows that Paul intended that the letter be read to the entire assembly of the Thessalonian Christians. This is the first indication that Christian writings were to be read during the (liturgical) assemblies of Christians. The ensuing practice would be of major significance in the development of the New Testament canon in the following decades.

Paul's first letter to the Thessalonians proved to be a successful experiment. Within the course of a few years (AD 50–56), Paul wrote additional letters to the church of Corinth, to the churches of Galatia, to the church at Philippi, to Philemon, and to "God's beloved in Rome." The apostolic letter developed by Paul proved to be such a successful format for evangelization that a number of pseudepigraphal letters were composed by those of his disciples who wanted to capitalize on Paul's authority in confronting particular situations. During the latter part of the first century, an additional letter was written to the Thessalonians *(2 Thessalonians)*, and letters were written to the Ephesians, to the Colossians, to Timothy, and to Titus in Paul's name. Although later tradition attributed the letter to the Hebrews to Paul, that letter is not, strictly speaking, a pseudonymous writing because it does not make use of a patronymic "Paul" in the opening verses. Moreover, the letter to the Hebrews does not even have the format of a letter. The pseudonymous Pauline writings, on the other hand, do have the letter format. Prompted by specific circumstances, these writings enjoy the characteristic of occasional writings, but they are not authentic pieces of correspondence. They are documents upon which the epistolary format has been imposed to give them Pauline authority.

Post-Pauline Letters. The importance of Paul's experiment in Christian writing was also such that other apostolic letters included in the New Testament canon at the end of the fourth century were attributed to one or another apostle, for example, to James, Peter, John, and Jude. In patristic times these letters were described as "catholic" (*katholikae*, "universal" or "general") because they were not addressed to specific churches, as the Pauline letters were. Among these "catholic letters," *Jude, James,* and *2 Peter* were written to counteract libertine or gnostic tendencies resulting from Paul's teaching, and the Pauline influence is seen not only in the content of the writings but also in the choice of the apostolic letter format as a vehicle for conveying a message. In the case of the letter to James, it is especially clear that the document is not a real letter. The letter of James is a paraenetic treatise with an appended epistolary introduction consisting of but a single verse. The influence of Paul's experiment is also seen in the *Book of Revelation,* where the letters to the seven churches (*Rv.* 1:4, 2:1–3:22) evidence marked dependence upon Paul's compositional techniques. The last of the New Testament "letters" to have been composed is most likely *2 Peter,* written around AD 135.

Twenty-one apostolic letters have been included in the collection of New Testament writings, their composition spanning approximately eighty-five years. As a group they bear testimony to the importance of apostolic authority. They also demonstrate the significance of a traditional format as a mode of appeal for acceptance within the Christian churches. By writing a simple letter to the church of the Thessalonians, Paul had broken the implicit taboo on production of religious literature among Christians and had developed a literary form that brought forth a host of imitators, some of whose writings were later incorporated into the New Testament.

The Gospels

While reliance upon the voice of Christian prophets, the expectation of an imminent Parousia, and traditional respect for the scriptures impeded production of a specifically religious literature among early generations of Christians, these same factors imparted a sense of urgency to the oral proclamation of the gospel. The message that Jesus had preached was not only the simple, prophetic-like dictum "The time is fulfilled, and the kingdom of God is at hand; repent, and believe in the gospel" (*Mk.* 1:15). It also made use of proverbs, beatitudes, and especially parables. Proverbs and parables alike were types of *mashalim,* figures of comparative speech. Many of the sayings attributed to Jesus in the New Testament are similar to sayings attributed to rabbis and other sages in nonbiblical literature. These similarities allow these sayings to be typed and located in certain social settings.

Jesus himself was an apocalyptic preacher. His story was not written down until about forty years after his death, but in the intervening years his disciples believed that the reign of God Jesus had proclaimed had begun with his own death and resurrection. This conviction was a key element in the process whereby the gospel of Jesus came to be the gospel about Jesus. In the classic words of Rudolf Bultmann, the proclaimer became the proclaimed. What was written down in the form of gospel during the last third of the first century was not only what Jesus said but also what he did.

In the more than two generations that intervened between Jesus' death and the writing of the first gospel, the tradition about Jesus was handed down in oral fashion. The oral tradition was essentially the living memory of Jesus' immediate disciples and the first generations of Christians. Because it was memory, the oral tradition was essentially conservative, as a number of Scandinavian exegetes have pointed out; and because it was living, the oral tradition was essentially creative, as the early form-critics (especially Bultmann) have shown. An appreciation of the oral tradition about Jesus can only be had through an examination of the Gospels. The Gospels are the record of the church's proclamation of Jesus (Willi Marxsen). They are more than that, but they are the only available documentary evidence of that proclamation. [*See also* Gospel.]

The Synoptics. Since the late eighteenth century, it has been customary to identify *Matthew, Mark,* and *Luke* as the synoptic Gospels in distinction from the *Gospel of John.* Although John's gospel also provides an account of Jesus' activity from the time of his encounter with John the Baptist until the time of Jesus' death and resurrection, it differs in so many respects from the other three gospels that is should be treated apart from the others. The synoptic ("look-alike") Gospels are remarkably similar to one another, not only in structure but also in the choice of the events narrated and in details of the narration. This similarity of content, form, and structure gives rise to the so-called synoptic problem, namely, how to determine the literary relationship among these three remarkably similar documents.

The synoptic problem has been quite topical since the eighteenth century, not only from a literary viewpoint but also because of a significant historical question. If one wishes to know about the Jesus of history and one's source material is three interrelated documents, it is important to know how the texts are interrelated so that one can use them critically. By the end of the eighteenth century a scholarly consensus had been reached on the so-called two-source theory. Some demurrers to this approach continue to be formulated, notably among those who opt for Matthean priority (the Griesbach-Farmer hypothesis). According to the classic two-source theory, the gospel according to Mark has the greatest claim to literary priority among the synoptic Gospels. The extant gospels according to Matthew and Luke are dependent upon the Marcan work. In addition, Matthew and Luke made use of an additional written source, a sayings source, known as Q (from the German *Quelle,* "source"). Written in Greek, although giving evidence of a tradition of sayings originally uttered in Aramaic, the Q source contributed approximately 235 verses of discourse material to the later synoptic Gospels. In addition to their two major sources, each of these gospels also had its own proper source material.

Mark's gospel, written around AD 70, was thus the first written New Testament gospel. Just after World War I, Karl Ludwig Schmidt clearly demonstrated that the gospel genre was a Marcan literary creation. Mark was the originator of the genre insofar as he created a quasi-biographical framework into which he incorporated independent units of traditional material. Available to him were independent sayings and stories—some of which may have been previously joined together in small collections—handed down by means of the church's missionary, catechetical, and liturgical activity. These three types of activity were the typical settings in which the traditional material about Jesus was both handed down and shaped by the church. The church's activity thus served to stylize the tradition about Jesus, especially as it adapted the tradition to its own needs. In any event, the Gospels do not constitute a bland historical witness to Jesus of Nazareth. They are a witness in faith to the Jesus who has been acknowledged as Lord. The traditions about Jesus were transmitted by the church into its kerygmatic, didactic, and worship activity because of the belief that the Jesus who died on the cross was the Jesus who had been raised from the dead. Faith in Jesus as the Risen One colors the gospel narrative. This is true in all instances, but in some cases postresurrectional accounts have been retrojected into the gospel narrative. Mark's gospel has been described as a "passion narrative with an extended introduction" (Martin Kähler). The passion narrative concludes with a brief resurrection account that features the kerygmatic statement "He has risen; he is not here" (*Mk.* 16:1–8). As such the Marcan text demonstrates that the individual traditions about Jesus were to be understood in the light of Jesus' death and resurrection. The literary format suited to conveying that conviction was the product of Mark's religious and literary genius. Nonetheless, a few scholars (notably Charles H. Talbert) maintain that, as a literary form, the written gospel is dependent upon the Hellenistic form of the biographical sketch.

The specific circumstances of Mark's composition were not those of the Syrian Christian churches to which Matthew and Luke belonged in the eighties. Matthew's Hellenistic Jewish-Christian community had its own needs, as did Luke's largely gentile-Christian community. Accordingly both Matthew and Luke rewrote the Marcan narrative with the help of traditional material taken from other sources. Their compositions attest to the early church's need for a witness to Jesus that was pertinent to specific situations.

John. The gospel according to John was written in the last decade of the first century for the benefit of a Christian church that can be cryptically described as "the community of the Beloved Disciple" (Raymond E. Brown). That community had its origins in the circle of the disciples of John the Baptist. It had contacts with various forms of esoteric Judaism (many Johannine idioms and thought patterns are remarkably similar to both Qumranite and gnostic expressions and thoughts), and it had received an influx of Samaritan believers. Somehow this community had maintained a Christian existence in relative independence from other Christian communities, even to the point that some scholars believe it best to conceive of the Johannine community as a Christian sect. Only a relatively small number of scholars hold that the gospel produced within this community was literarily dependent upon one or another of the synoptic Gospels. Nonetheless, the literary form created by Mark had sufficient authority among the Christian churches of the late first century to ensure that the Johannine community's faith narrative about Jesus took the form of a gospel.

Foundations of the Canon

While the literary form of the apostolic letter had its origins in the middle of the first century, and the written gospel came into being about a quarter of a century later, forces at work within the Christian churches, forces that continued to be operative after a distinctively Christian literature had been produced, would eventually give rise to a discernible New Testament canon.

Authority. From the outset there was a concern about authentic expressions of the Spirit of God. Spirit-inspired authority was attributed to the scriptures. The Hebrew scriptures functioned as a hermeneutical tool in first-century Christianity. In a fashion similar to that of other first-century Jewish groups, the early Christians interpreted their experience in the light of the scriptures. The Second Isaian servant canticles, Psalms 2 and 100, were the key elements in the "scriptural apologetic" (Barnabas Lindars) of first-century Christianity. They served to place the Jesus experience in a meaningful context. It was especially the death and resurrection of Jesus that were interpreted "according to the scriptures" (see *1 Cor.* 15:3–4). In the exposition of this message, Paul argued from the Torah (e.g., *Gn.* 17:5 in *Rom.* 4:17), the prophets (*Hb.* 2:4 in *Rom.* 1:17), and the psalms (*Ps.* 51:4 in *Rom.* 3:4). Citations from and allusions to the Hebrew scriptures served to interpret Paul's own experience. There could be no doubt that the scriptures were authority for Jesus and the first generations of his disciples.

The word of the Lord. A real concern was with other Spirit-endowed authorities. Preeminent among these authorities was the word of the Lord Jesus. Barely a generation after Jesus' death, Paul appealed to the word of the Lord (*1 Thes.* 4:15) in an attempt to assuage the grief over the unexpected death of some Christians at Thessalonica. In *1 Corinthians* 7, Paul carefully distinguished the authority of the word of the Lord from his own. Contemporary with Paul's earliest letters was the collection of a number of Jesus' sayings in a florilegium, no longer extant, known to contemporary scholars as the Q source. Application of the criteria of multiple attestation (sayings contained in different texts and/or different literary forms) and dual exclusion (neither attested in contemporary Jewish sources nor serving specific ecclesiastical needs) allows scholars to judge that many of the gospel sayings derive from Jesus' own words. A history-of-tradition study of the *logia* (sayings of Jesus), as well as a comparative, redaction-critical study of a single saying contained in more than one of the Gospels, indicates that the sayings of Jesus were transmitted by the early Christians in such a way as to be applicable to later situations. Thus the sayings of Jesus enjoyed significant and relevant authority in the churches of the first generations. They were remembered from the past, but they were also applied to contemporary circumstances.

The apostles. In the *Acts of the Apostles*, Luke highlights the role of the twelve eyewitnesses to Jesus' life and ministry (see *Acts* 1:21–22; cf. *Acts* 1:8, *Lk.* 1:2). As witnesses, the apostles possessed considerable authority among the churches. [*See* Apostles.] *Acts* offers a stylized account of the authority enjoyed by Peter. Even more indicative is the biographical section of the letter to the Galatians, where Paul vehemently argues for his own authority on the basis that he had received a revelation of Jesus Christ (*Gal.* 1:12) but acknowledges the contacts he had with the Jerusalem apostles (1:18–19, 2:1). Despite the independence of his own apostolate, Paul felt constrained to visit with Cephas in Jerusalem.

Within the New Testament, the name "apostle" was not restricted to the twelve disciples, named apostles (*Lk.* 6:12–16, *Mk.* 3:13–19, *Mt.* 10:1–4). Paul himself was an apostle in his own right (*Gal.* 1:1), as even Luke acknowledges in *Acts* (14:4, 14:14). Not only did Paul preach in the power of the Holy Spirit, but he also used his Spirit-endowed authority to render authoritative decisions (see *1 Cor.* 7:10–11, 7:40). Those whom Paul had evangelized appealed to him to resolve disputes and uncertain matters (see *1 Cor.* 1:11, 7:1). He served as an authority for the churches he had founded, that is, those he had served as an apostle. The authority of the apostles is also attested to in the phenomenon of apostolic pseudepigraphy: works written by authors unknown to us were attributed to apostles so that they would have apostolic authority *(Ephesians, Colossians, 2 Thessalonians, 1–2 Timothy, Titus, James, 1–2 Peter, Jude)*.

Tradition. In the first century the tradition about Jesus became stylized and stereotyped in a variety of oral and literary forms. The New Testament evidence shows how important maintaining the tradition about Jesus was. One of the earliest indications of this was the emergence of creedal formulas that articulated the core content of the kerygma. In AD 50 three different creedal formulas were incorporated into the first letter to the Thessalonians (1:10, 4:14, 5:9–10). Paul used the technical language of the rabbinic schools, "receive" (Gr., *paralambanein;* Heb., *qibbel*) and "deliver" *(paradidomi, masar)*, to attest that he was handing along the tradition faithfully (*1 Cor.* 15:3–5). The creedal formulas principally articulated faith in the death and resurrection of Jesus, but the scope of tradition was broader. For example, it included the "liturgical" tradition of the Lord's Supper (see *1 Cor.* 11:23–32).

The later writings of the New Testament offer evidence of the importance placed on transmitting the tradition faithfully. Luke offers an exhortation on the faithful transmission of the gospel within the context of Paul's farewell discourse at Miletus (*Acts* 20:28–31). The Pastoral letters to Timothy and Titus portray the two as having been carefully taught by Paul (e.g., *1 Tm.* 1:2a) and charged with responsibility for conveying that teaching to others (e.g., *1 Tm.* 4:11). "The saying is sure" functions as a refrain, setting a seal of approval on authoritative pieces of tradition (e.g., *1 Tm.* 1:15).

Within early Christianity, Spirit-authority-tradition formed a constellation that can be perceived as constitutive of Christianity itself. The individual writings of the New Testament incorporated and bore witness to these elements in specific and concretized fashions. Each New Testament document was composed within a specific church situation and addressed to a specific situation.

Public Reading of Christian Texts. When Paul concluded his first letter by writing, "I adjure you by the Lord that this letter be read to all the brethren" (*1 Thes.* 5:27), he indicated that the letter would accomplish its purpose only if it were read aloud in a Christian assembly. Since all his letters were addressed to churches, they too were presumably intended to be read aloud to the assemblies to which they were addressed. Thus in the second generation of Christianity some Christian churches had already experienced the practice of a reading from Christian texts during the liturgical assembly. Some authors have suggested that, in the case of Paul's letters at least, such readings preceded the celebration of the Lord's Supper.

A few other New Testament texts suggest that the practice of reading Christian texts in the assembly was not limited to reading letters addressed to the churches. An aside (*Mk.* 13:14; cf. *Mt.* 24:15) in the Marcan apocalypse indicates that at least that much of the gospel text was read aloud. *Revelation* 1:3 shows that some portion of that book was to be read aloud, and some scholars use this passage as evidence that the office of reader existed in the late first century. The first letter to Timothy may well contain an allusion to Timothy's responsibility for the public reading of Christian texts (see *1 Tm.* 4:13).

Circulation and Collection of Texts. The author of the letter to the Colossians was undoubtedly inspired by the conclusion of Paul's first letter when he wrote, "And when this letter has been read among you, have it read also in the church of the Laodiceans, and see that you read also the letter from Laodicea" (*Col.* 4:16). The letter to the Laodiceans has been lost, unless the author's reference is to the letter to the Ephesians, cited more than once in early Christian literature as the "letter to the Laodiceans." The passage is also significant because it indicates that some Christian writings were already in circulation during the first century (as early as 60 if *Colossians* is authentic). It attests that (some) Christian writings were esteemed for reasons other than those implied by the concrete set of circumstances that occasioned their composition. In the case of the letter to the Colossians, "a letter to a church" was considered to be "a letter for the churches."

The author of *2 Peter,* writing approximately a full century after the death of Jesus and some seventy years after the death of Paul, apparently knew of a collection of Paul's writings. He wrote: "So also our beloved Paul wrote to you according to the wisdom given him, speaking of this as he does in all his letters. There are some things in them hard to understand, which the ignorant and unstable twist to their own destruction, as they do the other scriptures" (*2 Pt.* 3:15–16). The dispute over interpretation of Paul's teaching is otherwise attested in the New Testament; the letter of James, the second letter of Peter, and the letter of Jude were apparently composed in an effort to thwart exaggerated libertinistic interpretations of Paul's doctrine. In *2 Peter* the author's comparison between Paul's letters and "the other scriptures" *(tas loipas graphas)* is both novel and striking. It would seem to imply some similarity between Paul's writings and the Hebrew scriptures, whose function had been sacrosanct in first-century Christianity.

Second Century

In the judgment of most contemporary scholars, *2 Peter* is a pseudepigraphal writing composed in the second quarter of the second century AD. Polycarp of Smyrna (c. 69–155) is another second-century witness to the church's attitude toward the Pauline writings. Polycarp writes of Paul's "letters" as if he were aware of a collection of such letters. There is evidence that he considered at least one of these letters *(Ephesians)* as "scripture." Moreover, Polycarp sharply distinguishes the apostolic era from his own times. He includes Paul among the apostles and cites "the Lord," "the apostles, who brought us the gospel," and "the prophets, who foretold the coming of the Lord" as his authorities. Apparently he was even able to make use of a written copy of the gospel according to Matthew. In Rome, Polycarp's contemporary Justin Martyr wrote that the memoirs of the apostles or the writings of the prophets were read aloud during Sunday worship (*Apology* 67:3); by the memoirs of the apostles, Justin meant the three gospels that later became known as the synoptic Gospels.

By the middle of the second century, the origins of the New Testament canon were beginning to take shape. Christian texts were being read in liturgical assemblies. The Gospels (certainly the synoptic Gospels and probably also the Fourth Gospel) were read holistically, as a unity. A collection of Paul's letters had been made. The apostolic era was clearly identified (whether that identification was correct according to modern standards of historiography is a different issue). The witness of the apostles had become authoritative for the church.

Canonical Language. By the end of the second century, the technical language later used for the canon of the New Testament made its first appearance. In his monumental *Against Heresies* (c. 180), Irenaeus of Lyons presented the teachings of Jesus and the apostles as being so important that heretical teaching, such as that propounded by the Montanists and gnostics, would not be able to prevail. Within this context, Irenaeus wrote of the "canon of truth" *(kanōn tēs alētheias).* In Greek, *canon* originally signified a reed, then a rule or measuring instrument. Later it was used, almost metaphorically, to signify a norm or a list. As employed by Irenaeus, *canon* signified the basic content of the Christian faith. In 192, "New Testament" *(kainē diathēkē)* was used to characterize some Christian writings, but the usage may be somewhat older than that because Melito of Sardis had written of "the Old Testament" *(palaia diathēkē)* in 180. Among the gospels, the most widely used was the gospel according to Matthew. By the end of the century, four gospels were widely acknowledged as scripture on a par with the Hebrew scriptures. Irenaeus used the symbolic argument of the four winds and the four corners of the earth to affirm that the Lord "gave us the gospel in four forms but united by one spirit." In addition, the Pauline letters were acknowledged as having scriptural authority.

Other Christian Writings. The four gospels and the writings of Paul were not the only Christian texts that were widely circulated and held in high esteem during the second century. In Polycarp's judgment the letters of Ignatius of Antioch (c. 35–c.107) to the churches "contain faith, endurance, and all the edification which pertains to our Lord." The letter of Clement of Rome to the Corinthians (c. 96) and the pseudepigraphal epistle of Barnabas (late first century) were esteemed within various Christian churches. The *Didache* (Teaching of the Twelve Apostles), a Syrian text written in the late first or early second century, contained useful paraenetic and liturgical information. A pseudepigraphal second letter of Clement, in reality the earliest extant Christian homily (Egypt), and the *Shepherd of Hermas* (Rome) were composed during the first decades of the second century and were widely circulated and highly regarded by the various Christian churches. Later in the century there appeared the writings of such fathers of the church as Papias, Polycarp, Justin, and Irenaeus. These writings, though well regarded, did not merit comparison with the Hebrew scriptures and were not considered to be Christian "scriptures." The situation was, however, somewhat ambiguous for those earlier writings whose time of composition was more or less contemporaneous with many of the canonical New Testament texts. Among the so-called *Apostolic Fathers, 1 Clement, Barnabas,* and the *Shepherd* were read as scripture in the liturgical assemblies of some of the Christian churches.

The second century also saw production of a number of apocryphal works. The *Infancy Gospel of Thomas* and the *Protoevangelium of James* sought to fill in the gaps with regard to Jesus' childhood. The Nag Hammadi manuscripts discovered in 1946 at the site of Chenoboskon in Upper Egypt include a *Gospel of Thomas,* a *Gospel of Philip,* and a *Gospel of Truth.* The *Gospel of Peter,* the *Gospel of the Egyptians,* the *Gospel of the Ebionites,* and the *Gospel of the Hebrews,* all second-century compositions, were cited by various church fathers as having heretical tendencies. Along with this plethora of gospels there arose a number of letters attributed to Paul or other apostles. The *Acts of Paul* and the *Apocalypse of Peter* likewise appear on the scene of second-century Christianity.

Marcion. The process of forming the canon was a matter of discerning which Christian texts in this ever-growing body of literature represented the apostolic witness and authentic tradition. A key factor in the process was the work of Marcion, a second-century Roman who projected a radical incompatibility between Christianity and Judaism, between the loving Father and the God of wrath. His Bible consisted of the *Gospel of Luke*—which he tailored to his own theological insights—and the *Apostolicon*, a collection of ten Pauline writings: *Galatians, 1–2 Corinthians, Romans, 1–2 Thessalonians, Laodiceans (Ephesians), Colossians, Philippians,* and *Philemon.* Marcion's predilection for Paul, whose antinomianism he singularly valued, led him to include Luke's gospel in his Bible. Paul often writes of "the gospel," by which he means his oral proclamation of the good news of salvation. Marcion, however, believed that Paul meant some written work. Because tradition had it that Luke was Paul's companion, Marcion believed that the gospel to which Paul was referring was the written gospel of Luke.

Marcion intended that the collection of Christian writings for which he opted would stand in place of the Hebrew scriptures. As such his work (c. 150) represents a first attempt within Christianity to discern the contents of a closed collection of Christian writings that would function as ecclesiastical scriptures. He introduced each letter in his *Apostolicon* with a prologue. This provoked a series of anti-Marcionite prologues, some of which are still preserved among the writings of the fathers of the church. Basically the church fathers took issue with Marcion's whole project. In the words of Tertullian, "Marcion expressly and openly used the knife . . . since he made such an excision of the Scriptures as suited his own subject matter" (*On Prescription of Heretics* 38). [*See* Marcionism *and the biography of Marcion.*]

Thus the New Testament canon developed significantly during the second century, especially during the second half of the century. As the distance from the apostolic age grew, the several churches experienced a need to identify those writings considered to be authoritative witnesses of the Christian tradition. Criteria for discernment were in the air. A first attempt to construct a closed collection of authoritative works had been made. The reaction to Marcion precluded limiting a Christian canon to writings of Christian authors. As the four gospels were generally accepted and as a collection of Pauline letters was variously attested, a twofold canon was emerging. Appropriate terminology had been found to identify the process.

Third and Fourth Centuries

The process of determining the limits of the apostolic writing was, however, involved in further controversy that extended for almost two more centuries. The controversy had to do with the threat to orthodoxy represented by the Montanists and the gnostics. If Marcion had appropriated a bowdlerized version of *Luke* to his own advantage, there was hesitation on the part of some to accept that gospel. In the church of North Africa, Tertullian (160?–225?) wrote that Luke is "not even an apostle, but the disciple of an apostle, not a teacher but a pupil, and so decidedly a lesser figure than the teacher" (*Against Marcion* 4.2.4). Nevertheless, Tertullian accepted Luke because the work had been commisioned by the apostle Paul.

Because John's gospel had been appropriated by some Montanists and gnostics, its acceptability was even more tenuous than that of Luke's work. Montanus, a mid-second-century convert from paganism, had represented himself as the Spirit-Paraclete promised in the *Gospel of John* (see *Jn.* 14:15–26, 16:4–15). The second-century gnostic *Gospel of Philip* is clearly dependent on John's gospel. A Valentinian gnostic, Heracleon (c. 145–180), wrote the first commentary on *John.*

The response of some orthodox Christians was severe and reactionary. Epiphanius (315–403) pejoratively dubs a radical group of late-second-century anti-Montanists the Alogoi (*a-logoi,* "irrational") because they irrationally rejected the gospel that spoke of the Word (Logos). At the beginning of the third century, Gaius, a very orthodox Roman presbyter, rejected John's gospel and the *Book of Revelation* as the work of the gnostic Cerinthus (fl. about 100). Irenaeus's *Against Heresies* (3.11.9) took to task those who were so radical in their condemnation of Montanism that they rejected the gospel of John as well.

About that time (c. 180) there arose the early Christian tradition regarding the gospel according to John, namely, that the apostle John wrote the work in his old age. Irenaeus in Gaul, Tertullian in North Africa, and Clement in Alexandria—the three great church fathers of the late second century—accepted the gospel according to John, but their apologetic concern was evident in the way they wrote about the work. Clement presented *John* as a complement to the earlier gospels: after Matthew, Mark, and Luke had written about the outward facts (*ta sōmatika,* "the corporeal"), John composed "the spiritual gospel" *(euaggelion pneumatikon).* The apologetic concern received pointed expression in the fourth-century Muratorian fragment (a text that until recently had been thought to have come from the second century), which describes the origin of John's gospel this way: "The fourth of the Gospels was written by John, one of the disciples. When exhorted by his fellow disciples and bishops, he said, 'Fast with me this day for three days; and what may be revealed to any of us, let us relate it to one another.' The same night it was revealed to Andrew, one of the apostles, that John was to write all things in his own name, and they were all to certify." The fragment specifically affirms the apostolic origin of John's gospel.

In like fashion the Muratorian fragment affirmed the apostolic origin of Luke's gospel: "The third book of the Gospel, that according to Luke, was compiled in his own name on Paul's authority by Luke the physician." Behind the gospel according to Mark lay the apostolic authority of Peter. According to Eusebius, Papias, a second-century bishop of Hierapolis, had testified, "When Mark became Peter's interpreter, he wrote down accurately, although not in order, all that he remembers of what was said or done by the Lord ." In effect, although there may have been symbolic appropriateness for the fourfold witness to the one gospel of Jesus Christ, each of the four written gospels was accepted within the early church because it was thought to have enjoyed apostolic authority.

Irenaeus. Irenaeus was the first Christian author to theorize about the New Testament, but he did not use "New Testament" as specific nomenclature for his subject. According to him, *Acts* and the Pastoral letters *(1–2 Timothy, Titus)* are first clearly presented as having a useful ecclesiastical purpose. Irenaeus established the authority of *Acts* on the basis of its linkage to the gospel according to Luke. Among "the scriptures," Irenaeus cites the *Shepherd of Hermas,* but he explicitly excludes the first letter of Clement. While he does employ *1 Peter* and *1–2 John,* he does not include those works or *Revelation* in his scriptural argumentation. Tertullian accepted four gospels and the *Shepherd of Hermas* as scripture. Within the *Apostolos,* or corpus of apostolic writings, he placed thirteen Pauline letters, as well as *Acts, Revelation, 1 John, 1 Peter,* and *Jude,* but he cited *Hebrews* (his "Letter of Barnabas") as merely better received among the churches. *James, 2–3 John,* and *2 Peter* are not included among the "catholic letters." Clement of Alexandria included all these works, as well as the *Letter of Barnabas* and the *Apocalypse of Peter.*

From the time when the need for a canon began to emerge (mid-second century) until the fixation in the late fourth century, doubts about the acceptability of four of the "catholic letters" *(2–3 John, James, 2 Peter),* as well as the letter to the Hebrews, continued. Controversy about the origin of *John* and *Revelation* also remained. Toward the end of the fourth century the great Cappadocian fathers, Gregory of Nazianzus (c. 329–c. 389), Gregory of Nyssa (c. 330–c. 395), and Basil of Caesarea (c. 329–379), did not accept *Revelation* as scripture. Therefore, the *Book of Revelation* continued to be the most problematic for the Christian churches of the East, while *Hebrews* continued to be problematic in the West. The authority of Jerome (c. 342–420) and Hilary of Poitiers (c. 315–367), both formed in the East, eventually assured the acceptability of the letter to the Hebrews, but some manuscripts of the New Testament continued to be edited without *Hebrews* as late as the ninth century (especially the Augiensis [F] and Boernerianus [G] codices).

The state of the discussion during the fourth century is well represented by the church historian Eusebius. In his *Church History* (c. 303), Eusebius distinguishes three categories of Christian writings: (1) the *homologoumena,* the undisputed works; (2) the *antilegomena,* the disputed works; and (3) the *atopa pantē kai dusebē,* the altogether absurd and impious works. To the *homologoumena* Eusebius assigned four gospels, *Acts,* a fourteen-item Pauline corpus (including *Hebrews*), *1 Peter, 1 John,* and "if it seems correct," *Revelation.* A subunit of the *antilegomena* (i.e., *James, Jude, 2 Peter, 2–3 John*) is approved by many churches, while another subunit consists of works that are not generally accepted, namely the *Acts of Paul,* the *Apocalypse of Peter,* the *Shepherd of Hermas,* the *Letter of Barnabas,* the *Didache,* and "if it seems correct," *Revelation.* Eusebius attributes a similar type of categorization to the great Alexandrian theologian Origen (c. 185–c. 254), but there is reason to believe that this is a precedent-setting projection of his own views.

Canonization. Athanasius's Easter letter of 367 put an end to discussion of the internal limits of the New Testament canon within the Eastern church. From the works that he identifies as belonging to the canon *(kanōn),* Athanasius distinguished works that the church had rejected *(apokrupha),* and some that were suitable for reading aloud *(anaginōsomena)* and useful for baptismal instruction. The latter group contained such works as the *Didache* and the *Shepherd of Hermas* (contained, along with the *Letter of Barnabas,* in the Codex Sinaiticus after *Revelation*). The Eastern consensus on the internal limits of the canon was brought to the Western church through Jerome, who was the valued adviser of Pope Damasus I during the Roman synod of 382. The resultant Decree of Damasus states, "We must treat of the divine scriptures, what the universal catholic church accepts and what she ought to shun." It then lists the books of the Old Testament and cites "the order of the writings of the new and eternal testament which the holy and catholic church supports," the twenty-seven books specifically identified as "the canon of the New Testament."

Influenced by the Roman decree, a North African synod held at Hippo in 393 endorsed the twenty-seven-book canon of the New Testament. That resolution was repeated in a synod at Carthage in 397. In the meantime, under Jerome's influence, Augustine of Hippo had accepted the canon of Athanasius (see *On Christian Doctrine* 2.13; AD 396).

Some scholars hold that the earliest Western evidence of the canon of the New Testament is the fragment of Muratori, the so-called Muratorian canon, discovered in 1740. This mutilated seventh- or eighth-century manuscript cites four gospels, *Acts,* Paul's letters to seven churches, respectively located in Corinth, Ephesus, Philippi, Colossae, Galatia, Thessalonica, and Rome (with two letters each to Corinth and Thessalonica), *Philemon, 1–2 Timothy, Titus, 1–2 John,* the *Wisdom of Solomon, Revelation,* and the *Apocalypse of Peter.* However, it omits *Hebrews, James, 1–2 Peter,* and *3 John.* The fragmentary manuscript had been thought to represent a second-century Western text, but it is now thought to represent a fourth-century Eastern text. Thus the fixation of the New Testament canon is essentially an expression of the faith and practice of the fourth-century Greek church, which has been brought into the West through the influence of Jerome and Hilary.

By the beginning of the fifth century the Greek and Latin churches commonly accepted the twenty-seven-book canon. In the Syrian church there was still reluctance to accept *2 Peter, 2–3 John, Jude,* and *Revelation.* The fifth-century Peshitta, or common Bible of the Syrians, contained only twenty-two books. However, the sixth- and seventh-century revisions of the Syrian Bible, the Philoxenian and Harklian versions, contained the same twenty-seven books cited in the sister churches of the Greek East and Latin West.

Text of the New Testament

The New Testament was written entirely in Greek. Approximately five thousand ancient Greek New Testament manuscripts exist. These are categorized according to the material on which the texts are transcribed, the type of calligraphy, and the use made of the manuscripts. The oldest complete manuscript of the New Testament is the fourth-century Codex Sinaiticus, which originally contained both the Old and the New Testaments. Written on parchment, the New Testament portion of the codex is the only complete extant copy of the Greek New Testament written in uncial script. The codex was discovered by Konstantin von Tischendorf in the Monastery of Saint Catherine on Mount Sinai in 1844. To symbolize its antiquity, it has been designated in scholarship with the Hebrew letter alef.

Papyri. The oldest available manuscripts of the New Testament are papyrus fragments, none of which offers a complete text of any New Testament book. In the technical literature these fragments are indicated by a Gothic P with an Arabic numeral in exponent position indicating the specific papyrus. Eighty-eight New Testament papyri have been identified and cataloged thus far. The most ancient is P^{52}, a second-century fragment containing some letters from *John* 18:31–33 on the recto side and some letters from *John* 18:37–48 on the verso side. These letters are in an uncial script and written with no space between the words. The discovery of the fragment was particularly important because it led scholars almost unanimously to place the time of composition of the gospel according to John in the late first century, when the dominant tendency of critical scholarship was to identify that gospel as a second-century work.

The most important papyri that serve as witnesses to the text of the New Testament are those that belong to the Chester Beatty and Bodmer collections. Three third-century papyri were acquired by A. Chester Beatty in 1930–1931. P^{45} designates 30 leaves (of a 220-leaf codex) with parts of *Matthew, Mark, Luke, John,* and *Acts;* P^{46}, the oldest of the three papyri, consists of 86 leaves (of 104) with parts of *Romans, 1 Corinthians, 2 Corinthians, Ephesians, Galatians, Philippians, Colossians,* and *1 Thessalonians.* P^{47} has 10 leaves (of 32) with *Revelation* 9:10–17:2.

The five New Testament papyri acquired by Martin Bodmer in 1955–1956 are respectively designated P^{66}, P^{72}, P^{73}, P^{74}, and P^{75}. Of these, P^{66}, P^{72}, and P^{75} are considerably older than the other two papyri in the collection. Because P^{66}, dating from about AD 200, contains considerable portions of John's gospel; it is one of the longest fragments of the Greek New Testament among the ancient papyri. However, neither this papyrus nor any papyri of the *Gospel of John* contains *John* 5:3b–4 and 7:53–8:11. This omission is a major factor in the judgment of the majority of text critics, who deem that these two passages did not belong to the original text of the gospel. Bodmer's P^{72}, a third- or fourth-century papyrus, contains *1–2 Peter* and *Jude* in their entirety and represents the oldest extant text of these "catholic letters," the canonicity of two of which *(2 Peter, Jude)* was long a subject of dispute in the church. P^{75} is a third-century papyrus with 102 leaves, containing most of *Luke* (the oldest manuscript of that gospel) and considerable portions of *John.* Most of the papyri date from the third and fourth centuries, but some are as recent as the sixth century (perhaps even as late as the eighth century, as may be the case for the relatively unimportant P^{26} and P^{42}).

Parchment. Most New Testament manuscripts are written on parchment. For purposes of editing the text of the New Testament, the most important manuscripts are the parchment manuscripts written in uncial script, of which 274 are known to exist. These manuscripts are identified by a system of sigla devised by Johann Jacob Wettstein (1693–1754), who used the letters of the Latin and Greek alphabets to designate the ancient Greek manuscripts. The discovery of additional manuscripts and the recognition that some manuscripts that Wettstein had designated by a single letter were in fact parts of two manuscripts have rendered his system scientifically inadequate, but it is classic and remains in common use. A more exact system of classification was devised by Caspar René Gregory (1846–1917), who used Arabic numerals preceded by a zero (01, 02, 03, etc.) to designate the manuscripts. Thus the Codex Sinaiticus is designated by the Hebrew letter alef or 01. In addition to the Codex Sinaiticus, for purposes of editing the text of the New Testament, the more important uncial manuscripts are the Codex Alexandrinus, the Codex Vaticanus, the Codex Ephraemi Rescriptus, the Codex Bezae Cantabrigensis, the Codex Claromontanus, the Codex Regius, the Codex Washingtoniensis, and the Codex Koridethi.

The Codex Alexandrinus (A, 02) is a fifth-century manuscript. The leaves containing the greater portions of *Matthew* and *2 Corinthians* and some of *John* are missing. Along with the Codex Sinaiticus and the Codex Vaticanus, the manuscript is one of the oldest examples of the Alexandrian text type. The text of the four canonical gospels, however, has been identified as the oldest example of the Byzantine text type. The gospel text found in this manuscript is divided into chapters *(kephalaia)*, each of which is provided with a chapter heading *(titlos)*. There are 68 chapters in *Matthew*, 48 in *Mark*, 83 in *Luke*, and 18 in *John*. This division into chapters differs substantially from the modern division into chapters devised by Stephen Langton, a thirteenth-century archbishop of Canterbury. Langton divided *Matthew* into 28 chapters, *Mark* into 16, *Luke* into 24, and *John* into 21.

The Codex Vaticanus (B, 03), housed in the Vatican Library from before 1475, is one of the most valuable of all the manuscripts of the Bible in Greek. Some scholars claim that this manuscript, written in the middle of the fourth century, is even older than the Codex Sinaiticus. The manuscript originally contained the entire Bible, but its initial leaves (including *Gn.* 1–46) and final leaves are missing, as are others that contained a total of thirty psalms. Since the sequence of the New Testament books is that found in Athanasius's Easter letter, the missing section of this codex contained all of *Hebrews* after 9:14, *1–2 Timothy, Titus, Philemon,* and *Revelation.* Among textual critics, the Codex Vaticanus enjoys a position of undisputed prominence for the Gospels. *Matthew* is divided into 170 *kephalaia, Mark* into 62, *Luke* into 152, and *John* into 80. There is a single division of chapters for the entire Pauline corpus, beginning with the letter to the Romans.

The Codex Ephraemi Rescriptus (C, 04) is the oldest of the hitherto recovered fifty-two palimpsest New Testament uncial manuscripts. Palimpsests are parchment manuscripts whose original texts (in this case the New Testament text) have been erased. Modern technology allows the original text to be read despite the erasure. The Codex Ephraemi Rescriptus is the oldest of the extant New Testament palimpsests. A canon of the Trullan Council (AD 692) condemned the use of biblical manuscripts for other purposes, but many of the New Testament palimpsests date from after the council. The Codex Ephraemi Rescriptus is a fifth-century manuscript of the Greek Bible. It was erased in the twelfth century and used for a Greek translation of thirty-eight ascetical sermons of Ephraem of Syria, a fourth-century church father. The 145 leaves with the New Testament manuscript contain portions of every book of the New Testament with the exception of *2 Thessalonians* and *2 John*, but they do not contain any New Testament book in its entirety.

The Codex Bezae Cantabrigensis (D, 05) was presented to the University of Cambridge in 1581 by Theodore Beza, a Frenchman who succeeded John Calvin as a leader of the Calvinist church in Geneva. A biblical scholar, Beza published nine editions of the New Testament between 1565 and 1604. The codex that bears his name dates from the fifth century and contains the four canonical gospels and *Acts*. Its Greek text is on the left page, the Latin text is on the following page. The text of the Gospels is in the so-called Western order: the gospels attributed to the two apostles of Jesus appear first, with those attributed to the companions of apostles following (thus, *Matthew, John, Luke, Mark*). Among ancient manuscripts, the Codex Bezae diverges most from the commonly accepted text of the New Testament. When it does agree with other witness, it carries special weight as a witnesses to the Western text type of the Gospels.

The Codex Claromontanus (D, 06) is a sixth-century manuscript that contains the fourteen letters of the Pauline corpus. Although unrelated to the Codex Bezae (D, 05), it is like it in having a Greek text transcribed on the left page and the Latin text on the facing page.

The Codex Regius (L, 019) is an eighth-century manuscript of the Gospels from which a few leaves have been lost. The last few verses of *Matthew* (28:17–20) and *John* (21:15–25) are missing, but the manuscript contains two endings for the gospel of Mark. In the Codex Regius a "shorter ending," found in three other uncial manuscripts (044, 099, 0112) after *Mark* 16:8, is followed by the "canonical ending" (*Mark* 16:9–20). Most text critics judge both the shorter ending and the canonical ending to be later additions to *Mark*. On the whole, the text of the Codex Regius was written by a careless scribe, but in terms of its text type it serves as a valuable confirmation of the Alexandrian readings found in the Codex Vaticanus.

The Codex Washingtoniensis (Codex Freerianus), discovered at the beginning of the twentieth century, was acquired by Charles Freer of Detroit in 1906. Now housed in the Smithsonian Institution in Washington, D.C., the codex contains an early fifth-century manuscript of the Gospels in the Western order. The text type of the manuscript is a curious mixture; it gives the impression that the manuscript was transcribed from several different manuscripts belonging to different text types. In many places this codex offers an independent reading of the Gospels. A remarkable feature of the manuscript is the so-called Freer logion, an insertion after *Mark* 16:14. Part of the logion was known to Jerome, but its presence in the text of Mark's gospel is not otherwise attested in the ancient New Testament manuscripts.

The Codex Koridethi is a ninth-century manuscript containing the four canonical Gospels, with the exception of significant lacunae in the first five chapters of *Matthew*. Although the codex contains a number of independent readings, the text of *Matthew, Luke,* and *John* is similar to the Byzantine text type, but the text of *Mark* is similar to a type of text used by Origen and Eusebius in the third and fourth centuries. As such it represents the oldest sequential reading of a gospel text according to the Caesarean text type.

The Minuscules. The uncial style of transcribing New Testament manuscripts predominated for about five centuries. In the ninth century a minuscule or cursive style of writing was introduced. Most of the New Testament manuscripts written in the second millennium of Christianity are written in this minuscule style. Almost three thousand extant minuscule manuscripts of the New Testament exist, dating from the tenth century to the sixteenth century. As a group they are generally considered to bear witness to the Byzantine or ecclesiastical type of text, but a more recent trend identifies them simply as "the majority." In the technical literature they are simply identified by Arabic numerals. Some of the minuscules share such textual particularities with other manuscripts that they can be recognized as having some sort of dependence on one another. Among the groups so identified are the Lake (MSS 1, 18, 131, etc.) and Ferrar (MSS 13, 69, 124, 346, etc.) families, respectively named after Kirsopp Lake and William Hugh Ferrar, who first identified (Lake in 1902, Ferrar in 1868) the textual relationships among the manuscripts of the groups that today bear their names.

The Lectionaries. A final category of Greek manuscripts is the lectionaries. More than two thousand lectionaries have been classified thus far. The oldest fragmentary lectionary dates from the sixth century; the oldest complete lectionary dates from the eighth. The lectionaries contain New Testament texts arranged for liturgical reading. The text of the lectionaries is characterized by the insertion of appropriate introductory phrases and the additional use of proper nouns for clarity.

Editing the New Testament Text

While the lectionary readings represent a distinct text type, text critics generally characterize the readings found in the other New Testament manuscripts as Alexandrian (or Egyptian), Western, Caesarean, and Byzantine (or ecclesiastical). Because of the influence of such late-nineteenth-century scholars as Tischendorf in Germany and B. F. Westcott (1825–1901) and F. J. H. Hort (1828–1892) in England, the greatest value was commonly attributed to the Alexandrian type of reading. Westcott and Hort wrote about the "neutral text" of the New Testament, which was regarded as generally devoid of the tendentious readings of the ecclesiastical text type. Their "neutral text" was a text to which the Sinaiticus and Vaticanus codices gave witness.

While identification of text type is still important in New Testament textual criticism, recent criticism attaches considerable significance to the witness of the papyri, many of which were transcribed before the development of the text types. The relative importance of the papyri is reflected in the most recent popular editions of the Greek New Testament, especially the third edition of *The Greek New Testament* (1975) and the twenty-sixth edition of *Novum Testamentum Graece* (1979). The text of these popular editions was edited by an international committee composed of Kurt Aland, Matthew Black, Carlo Martini, Bruce M. Metzger, and Allen Wikgren in continuation of a work begun in 1898 by Eberhard Nestle and subsequently continued by his son Erwin.

These popular editions continue the work of printing the Greek text of the New Testament. The history of the printing of the Greek text dates back to 1514, when the first Greek New Testament came from the press. That was the fifth volume of a polyglot Bible, the Complutensian Polyglot, prepared under the patronage of Cardinal Francisco Jiménez de Cisneros (1437–1517), the primate of Spain. Although volume 5 of the work's six volumes was printed in 1514, the rest of the printing was not finished until 1517, and the work did not receive papal approbation until 1520. By that time Johann Froben of

Basel had succeeded in convincing the Dutch humanist Desiderius Erasmus (1469?–1536) to prepare an edition of the Greek New Testament. Erasmus completed his work in 1515, and the printing of it was finished on 1 March 1516, just six months after the task had been undertaken. Erasmus's edition was prepared on the basis of a few Greek manuscripts (principally the minuscule manuscripts 1 and 2), none of which was complete. Since not one of the available manuscripts contained *Revelation* 22:16–21, Erasmus completed his edition with a retroversion from the Latin Vulgate. Erasmus's work was done in haste, and as a result the large volume of about one thousand folio pages was full of errors. Nonetheless, it enjoyed considerable success, and a second edition was printed in 1519, followed by a third edition in 1522, a fourth in 1527 (with about ninety emendations of the text of *Revelation,* based on the Complutensian edition), and a fifth in 1535.

The success of Erasmus's work was assured not only because its second edition served as a basis for Luther's German translation of the New Testament but also because it gave rise to a number of unauthorized reprints and the work of subsequent editors who, to a large extent, based their work on Erasmus's pioneering efforts. Prominent among the subsequent editors was Robert Estienne (1503–1559), the Parisian printer who went by the Latin form of his name, Stephanus, and who published four editions of the Greek New Testament, respectively in 1546, 1549, 1550 (all in Paris), and 1551 (in Geneva). While the first two of Stephanus's editions were a composite of the Complutensian edition and Erasmus's work, the last two were akin to Erasmus's fourth and fifth editions. Stephanus's third edition (1550) was the first edition of the Greek New Testament to contain a critical apparatus, in this instance marginal citations of variant readings from fourteen Greek codices, including the Codex Bezae and the Complutensian Polyglot. Stephanus's fourth edition (1551) is best remembered as the first edition of the Greek New Testament with the text divided into verses.

Stephanus's fourth edition also served as the basis for the nine editions of the New Testament published between 1565 and 1604 by Theodore Beza. A posthumous tenth edition appeared in 1611. In Beza's edition the Greek text was accompanied by Jerome's Latin Vulgate, Beza's own translation into Latin, various annotations, and information collected from various Greek codices, including the Bezae and the Claromontanus. The significance of Beza's work lies principally in two subsequent developments. In 1611 a group of British scholars, acting on orders from James I, published a translation of the New Testament in English (the King James, or Authorized, Version of the New Testament), which was largely based on Beza's 1588–1589 and 1598 editions. In 1633 the Elzevir brothers published at Leiden the second edition of a Greek text of the New Testament which was principally based on Beza's work. The preface boasts, "Therefore you have the text now received by all *(textum . . . receptum),* in which we give nothing changed or corrupted." The strength of the boast was such that the text found in the Elzevir edition of 1633 is commonly called the Textus Receptus (Received Text) of the Greek New Testament.

For almost two hundred years the Textus Receptus was virtually the only text printed of the New Testament in Greek. Some editions were printed with an apparatus containing variant readings, but it was only in 1831 that a scholar was sufficiently free of bias in favor of the Textus Receptus to publish an edition of the Greek New Testament without reliance upon the earlier printed editions. This was Karl Lachmann (1793–1851), whose published edition of the Greek and Latin New Testaments marked a new era in the history of the New Testament text. Then between 1841 and 1872 Konstantin von Tischendorf (1815–1874), the prodigious editor of Greek New Testament manuscripts, published eight editions of the Greek New Testament. The eighth edition, completed in 1862 and published in two volumes (1869, 1872), was the first edition of the New Testament to make use of the Codex Sinaiticus. The critical apparatus that accompanies this *editio octava critica major* is so rich that it remains the largest single publication of textual data to the present time, even though additional textual material has since been discovered (especially the papyri and the Codex Washingtoniensis). In 1881 Westcott (1825–1901) and Hort (1828–1892) published *The New Testament in the Original Greek.* Its "neutral text" is based on the Codex Sinaiticus and the Codex Vaticanus and was published with virtually no critical apparatus apart from a few variant readings printed in the margins. The second volume of this two-volume work explains the author's editorial methodology and demonstrates the weakness of accepting the Greek text of the Textus Receptus principally because its readings are attested by a large number of manuscripts. Those manuscripts are for the most part relatively late. They represent the Byzantine text type and thus reflect a medieval ecclesiastical effort to standardize the Greek text.

The early editions (first to twenty-fifth) of Nestle's popular *Novum Testamentum Graece* were based on a comparison of the critical editions of Tischendorf and of Westcott and Hort and reflect these editors' predilection for the readings of the Sinaiticus and Vaticanus codices. The discovery of new manuscripts and the possibilities afforded by modern technology of making and collecting facsimile copies of virtually all New Testament manuscripts in a single place have created a new situation for the edition of the New Testament. Technological advances have also made it possible to read palimpsest more accurately, to identify manuscript corrections, to distinguish the work of one corrector from another, and to recover the reading of a manuscript prior to its correction. The Institute for New Testament Textual Research in Münster, Germany, is the principal center for New Testament textual study at the present time. In cooperation with the institute, the United Bible Societies has published *The Greek New Testament* (1966, 1968, 1975) to provide translators with a standard Greek text from which to work. The same Greek text, with some minor orthographical variants and some differences in punctuation, is printed in Nestle-Aland's twenty-sixth edition of the *Novum Testamentum Graece* (1979). Although individual text critics do not agree with every reading of the Greek text adopted by the editors, the Greek text of *The Greek New Testament—Novum Testamentum Graece* is the one in standard use today.

The Versions

The need for a translation of the Greek text of the New Testament into the vernacular is not limited to modern times. In the early fourth century, Augustine remarked, "Those who translated the scriptures from Hebrew into Greek can be counted, but the Latin translations are out of all numbers. For in the early days of the faith, every man who happened to gain possession of a Greek manuscript [of the New Testament] and who imagined he had any facility in both languages, however slight that might have been, dared to make a translation." The situation Augustine represented for Latin-language communities was not unlike that of churches in other localities where Greek was not or no longer the lingua franca. The missionary and catechetical needs of the young churches required that the New Testament be rendered into the vernacular.

Syriac. Syria was the locale of a Christian church within a generation after the death and resurrection of Jesus. In Antioch the disciples of Jesus were first called Christians (*Acts* 11:26). Throughout the remainder of the first century and well into the second century, Antiochene Christians continued to make use of the books of the New Testament in Greek. It is generally agreed that by the end of the second century the needs of the Syrian church were such that a Syriac version of the Gospels was required. Yet it is not known whether the first translation of the Gospels into Syriac consisted of a translation of each gospel or whether it took the form of a harmony of the Gospels.

A Syriac-language harmony of the four canonical gospels was produced by Tatian, a disciple of Justin Martyr, in about AD 170. Apart from a fourteen-line Greek fragment discovered at Dura-Europos in 1933, the text of the diatesseron is known only from secondary and tertiary sources. Scholars disagree about whether the work was originally composed in Greek and was then translated into Syriac, or whether it was originally written in Syriac. If the latter, was the diatesseron based on Greek texts or on Syriac versions of the Gospels? In any event, the work bears a Greek title, *Diatesseron* (Through the Four). The *Diatesseron* apparently begins with *John* 1:1. Thereafter Tatian produced his work by omitting parallel accounts and reconciling differences among the various gospel narratives. The text was widely used in the Syrian churches until the fifth century, when it was replaced by the four separate gospels.

Five different Syriac versions of all or parts of the New Testament are known. The Old Syriac version is found in two severely fragmented manuscripts, the Syrian Sinaiticus, a fourth-century palimpsest, and the Syrian Curetonian, a fifth-century manuscript whose text dates to AD 200. The fourth-century Syriac Sinaiticus contains the Gospels in the usual *Matthew-Mark-Luke-John* sequence, while the fifth-century manuscript has an unusual *Matthew-Mark-John-Luke* sequence. In the fifth century, before the split between the Nestorians and the Jacobites, the Syriac Peshitta, or common text, was prepared as a replacement for the Old Syriac texts then in circulation. A large percentage of the readings of the Peshitta are similar to those of the ecclesiastical text type, but approximately one-third of its readings are akin to the Western text type. Some scholars have held that the translation is the work of Rabbula, bishop of Edessa from 411 to 435, but this is doubtful. In any event, the oldest known manuscript of this twenty-two-book New Testament dates from 463 or 464.

The Syriac Philoxenian version is a revision of the Peshitta done for Philoxenus, bishop of Mabbug (Hierapolis), in 508 by a certain Polycarp. The bishop, who did not know Greek, desired a text in Syriac that would be more theologically accurate than the text in common circulation. A new Syriac version, slavishly adapted to the Greek text, was produced by Thomas of Harkel, bishop of Mabbug in 616. It is uncertain whether the Harklian version is a revision of the Philoxenian text or a new translation. Quite independent from the other Syriac versions is the Palestinian Syriac version. Its language is that of an Aramaic dialect, Christian Palestinian Syriac, used during the early Christian centuries. The oldest manuscripts representing this version date from the sixth century, but the date of the translation is uncertain. Many scholars situate the translation in the fifth century, but some believe it was done as early as the beginning of the fourth century.

Coptic. The Coptic language, the most recent form of the ancient Egyptian language, was spoken in at least a half-dozen different dialectical forms during the early centuries of the common era. During the second century Christianity was vibrant in Egypt, and by that time the Sahidic dialect had become the standard literary language of the country. Taken collectively, the extant Sahidic texts represent the entire New Testament, but the oldest dates to only about AD 300. The translation is relatively literal.

The only other Coptic dialect to become standardized is Bohairic, which became dominant after the eleventh century and is still used today in the Coptic liturgy. Although the Bohairic New Testament manuscripts are relatively late (the oldest complete gospel codex dates from 1174), scholars today believe that the translation of the New Testament into Bohairic took place in the fourth century. A fourth-century proto-Bohairic manuscript contains the gospel according to John. Relatively few Bohairic manuscripts contain the *Book of Revelation.*

The other Coptic dialects in use during the early Christian centuries—Akhmimic, Sub-Ackmimic, Middle Egyptian, and Fayyumic—were never standarized. Relatively few manuscripts attest to the translation of the New Testament in these dialects. Of these, the most important is a late-fourth-century Sub-Ackmimic manuscript containing almost half of John's gospel.

Latin. The origins of the Old Latin versions of the New Testament are obscure. The first theological writings in Latin in Rome date from about AD 190. The Old Latin version of the New Testament most likely originated in North Africa during the latter part of the second century through the practice of reading the scriptures first in Greek, then in the vernacular. Originally the vernacular rendition would have been oral, but it was eventually written down. The Old Latin version of the New Testament is not a single work. For two hundred years the New Testament was translated into Latin in various places, especially in North Africa, Spain, and Gaul. Each book was translated many times over, and so far as we know, no single person translated the entire New Testament. Even Jerome complained that there were almost as many Latin translations as there were manuscripts. Only ninety-two Old Latin New Testament manuscripts survive, none of which is complete. Many of these have a text that has been corrected according to the Vulgate or into which Vulgate-type passages have been inserted. The influence of Marcion's Bible upon the Old Latin texts is apparent. Among other peculiarities, the Old Latin texts are noted for words coined to denote spiritual realities (e.g., *sanctificatio*), for affinity to the Western text type of the Greek New Testament, and for the presence in the gospel according to John of the story of the woman taken in adultery (*Jn.* 7:53–8:11, likewise *Jn.* 5:3b–4).

The great differences among the Old Latin versions prompted Damasus I (r. 304–384) to ask Jerome (342–420), the most capable biblical scholar of the day, to prepare a revision of the Latin text. Summoned to Rome as Damasus's adviser in 382, Jerome was commissioned to revise the ancient texts. He was to decide which Latin texts agreed with the Greek original. In 384 Jerome presented the pope with a revision of the text of the four gospels. The text of the other books of the New Testament was revised in a much more cursory fashion, but it cannot be determined whether Jerome himself revised these remaining books. Augustine attests to the general reluctance to accept this new version. For some time Jerome's revision coexisted with the Old Latin versions, resulting in a considerable amount of textual mixture in the older manuscripts of the Vulgate (or common) version of the New Testament. As a result, several medieval scholars attempted to correct the Vulgate, most notably Alcuin (730/40–804) and Theodulf (750–821). These corrections only served to exacerbate the textual mixture.

The fourth session of the Council of Trent (8 April 1546) decreed that the Latin Vulgate version was to be the only authoritative text for Roman Catholics. Furthermore, it decided to have an authoritative edition published. In 1590 Sixtus V (r. 1585–1590) authorized the authoritative edition and decreed that variant readings not be printed in later editions. In 1592 Clement VIII (r. 1592–1605) recalled the copies in circulation and issued a new authoritative edition, the *Biblia Sacra Vulgatae Editionis Sixti Quonti Pont. Max. jussu recognita atque edita,* which contains almost five thousand readings that vary from the 1590 edition. An English translation of the Vulgate, known as the Douai-Reims version, was published in 1582. Revised by Richard Challoner in 1749–1750, it continued to be the English-language translation of the New Testament used by English-language Roman Catholics from 1750 until 1950. Among Roman Catholics, the Vulgate continued to represent the authoritatative version of the scriptures. The Second Vatican Council's Dogmatic Constitution on Divine Revelation (1963) spoke of the honor attributed to the ancient versions, "Eastern and Latin, especially the one known as the Vulgate," but no longer promulgated the exclusive authorities of the Vulgate.

Other Ancient Versions. During the third century, Christianity was introduced into Armenia, which then became the first kingdom to accept Christianity as its official religion. The beginning of Armenian literature, including biblical translations, dates to the start of the fifth century. The Armenian version was translated from the Greek, but it shows the influence of the Syriac to some extent. The text type is Syrian, but it has been revised according to a Byzantine standard. The oldest dated manuscript of the Gospels in Armenian is dated 887, but doubts have been raised about that dating. The oldest extant Armenian copy of the letters and *Revelation* comes from the twelfth century. A peculiarity of one Armenian manuscript (MS 2374) is that it ascribes the canonical ending of *Mark* to the presbyter Ariston.

Before the New Testament could be translated into Georgian, an alphabet had to be invented. The task was done, and the Gospels were translated perhaps as early as the late fourth century. The rest of the New Testament was translated into Georgian before the middle of the fifth century. Scholarly opinion remains divided on whether the Georgian version was made directly from the Greek. Some authorities hold that the translation was done on the basis of a Syriac or an Armenian text older than the extant Armenian version. A revision of the Georgian text was begun in the tenth century. It attempted to introduce greater conformity between the Georgian version and the Byzantine text. The first known translation of *Revelation* into Georgian, the work of Euthymius the Hagiorite (d. 1028), was part of this effort.

An alphabet was also developed for the translation of the New Testament into Gothic. This was the work of Ulfilas (d. around 382). Only a few fragmentary and to a large extent (six of eight) palimpsest Gothic manuscripts of the New Testament survive. They give evidence of a slavishly literal translation and of a Syrian text type. The Silver Codex (Codex Argentius), whose convoluted history is a saga in itself, contains the four canonical gospels in the Western order. A little more than half of its original leaves have survived.

Despite Luke's description of the conversion of the Ethiopian eunuch (*Acts* 8:26–40), the presence of Christianity in Ethiopia can be ascertained with certainty only from the end of the fourth century. Most of the Ethiopic manuscripts of the New Testament are very late, dating from the fourteenth and fifteenth centuries.

[*See the biographies of figures mentioned herein, especially those on John, Luke, Mark, Matthew, and Paul. For further discussion of the critical study of the New Testament, see* Biblical Exegesis, *article on* Christian Views.]

BIBLIOGRAPHY

Classic among the standard comprehensive works on the New Testament is Werner Georg Kümmel's *Introduction to the New Testament*, rev. ed. (London, 1975). This volume, which contains abundant bibliographic references, gives background material for each of the New Testament books, treats the collection of these books into the canon, and discusses transmission of the texts. Useful but less encyclopedic are Willi Marxsen's *Introduction to the New Testament: An Approach to Its Problems* (Philadelphia, 1968), Günther Bornkamm's *The New Testament: A Guide to Its Writings* (Philadelphia, 1973), and Norman Perrin and Dennis C. Duling's *The New Testament: An Introduction*, 2d ed. (New York, 1982).

An overview of the formation of the New Testament canon is given in chapter 1 of my *Introduction to the New Testament* (Garden City, N.Y., 1983). The classic study of the matter remains Hans von Campenhausen's *The Format of the Christian Bible* (London, 1972), although Charles F. Moule offers valuable insights in *The Birth of the New Testament*, rev. ed. (San Fransisco, 1981). Of particular interest is a study of the Muratorian fragment by Albert C. Sundberg, Jr., "Canon Muratori: A Fourth Century List," *Harvard Theological Review* 66 (1973): 1–41.

Helmut Koester's two-volume *Introduction to the New Testament* (Philadelphia, 1982) provides much information about the historical and religio-cultural conditions within which early Christian literature was written. Volume 1 is entitled *History, Culture, and Religion of the Hellenistic Age;* volume 2, *History and Literature of Early Christianity.* Various illustrative documents are presented by C. K. Barrett in *The New Testament Background: Selected Documents* (New York, 1961), by Howard Clark Kee in *The Origins of Christianity: Sources and Documents* (Englewood Cliffs, N.J., 1973), and by David R. Cartlidge and David L. Dungan in *Documents for the Study of the Gospels* (Cleveland, 1980). Useful historical studies are Floyd V. Filson's *A New Testament History: The Story of the Emerging Church* (Philadelphia, 1964) and Frederick F. Bruce's *New Testament History* (London, 1969). The religious, cultural, and social dimensions of the New Testament's environment are emphasized by Martin Hengel in *Judaism and Hellenism*, 2 vol. (Philadelphia, 1974), by Eduard Lohse in *The New Testament Environment* (London, 1976), by Gerd Theissen in *Sociology of Early Palestinian Christianity* (Philadelphia, 1978), and by Wayne A. Meeks in *The First Urban Christians: The Social World of the Apostle Paul* (New Haven, 1982).

A general study of the significance of letters in early Christianity is William G. Doty's *Letters in Primitive Christianity* (Philadelphia, 1973); more particular is Harry Gamble's "The Redaction of the Pauline Letters and the Formation of the Pauline Corpus," *Journal of Biblical Literature* 94 (1975): 403–418. Paul's use of the Hellenistic personal letter is analyzed in Helmut Koester's "I Thessalonians—Experiment in Christian Writing," in *Continuity and Discontinuity*, edited by F. Forrester Church and Timothy George (Leiden, 1979), pp. 33–44.

The three pioneering works in the form-critical approach to the New Testament, written in German just after the end of World War I, are still the classic studies of the formation of the synoptic Gospels. They are *The History of the Synoptic Tradition*, rev. ed. (New York, 1968), by Rudolf Bultmann; *From Tradition to Gospel* (New York, 1935) by Martin Dibelius; and

Der Rahmen der Geschichte Jesu (Berlin, 1919) by Karl Ludwig Schmidt.

The works of Bruce M. Metzger are among the most significant English-language publications on the transmission and editions of the text of the New Testament. Among them are *The Text of the New Testament: Its Transmission, Corruption, and Restoration*, 2d ed. (Oxford, 1968), *The Early Versions of the New Testament: Their Origin, Transmission and Limitations* (Oxford, 1977), and *Manuscripts of the Greek Bible* (Oxford, 1981). An overview of problematic aspects of textual transmission is given in chapter 3 of my *Introduction to the New Testament* (Garden City, N.Y., 1983). A useful introduction to the study of the New Testament manuscripts is Jack Finegan's *Encountering New Testament Manuscripts: A Working Introduction to Textual Criticism* (Grand Rapids, Mich., 1974).

The Cambridge History of the Bible, a three-volume work, remains the classic in this field. Volume 1 is *From the Beginnings to Jerome*, edited by P. R. Ackroyd and C. E. Evans (Cambridge, 1970); volume 2, *The West from the Fathers to the Reformation*, edited by G. W. Lampe (Cambridge, 1969); and volume 3, *The West from the Reformation to the Present Day*, edited by S. C. Greenslade (Cambridge, 1963). Two monographs offer useful surveys of the major translations of the New Testament into the English language: Frederick F. Bruce's *History of the Bible in English*, 3d ed. (New York, 1978), and W. Walden's *Guide to Bible Translations: A Handbook of Versions Ancient and Modern* (Duxbury, Mass., 1979).

RAYMOND F. COLLINS

BIBLICAL RELIGION.

See Israelite Religion.

BIBLICAL TEMPLE.

[*This entry is a discussion of the history, activities, and structure of the biblical Temple. For a full presentation of the religious functionaries in the Temple, see* Priesthood, *article on* Jewish Priesthood *and* Levites.]

The Hebrew Bible records various temples dedicated to God throughout ancient Israel. Recent archaeological discoveries generally have corroborated the record, while at the same time raising new questions about the character, functions, and locations of temples of the biblical period. Foremost among these temples were the First and Second Temples built in Jerusalem.

History and Design. The First Temple was built between 960 and 950 BCE during the reign of Solomon; it was destroyed in 587/6 with the Babylonian conquest of Judah. The Second Temple was built on the site of the First in 516, and was destroyed by the Romans in 70 CE. However, both Temples underwent periodic renovations, expansion, and even restructuring, so that in describing temples we are speaking of an ongoing process, rather than of single events. Furthermore, the term *Temple* is ambiguous since it may designate either the building specifically, the focus of cult activity, or the entire complex of buildings, gates, and walls that together constitute the institution. For the purposes of this article, *Temple* refers to the building, *Temple complex* to the institution.

Most of the physical changes that the two Temples underwent at various times came in response to corresponding changes in the urban environment that were brought about, in turn, by changing political circumstances. Increased population density and the fluctuating political status of Jerusalem stimulated a tendency to protect, even barricade, the Temples against the outside. To a degree, and according to conditions, such efforts may have been vital to defense. More consistently, however, they expressed specific religious attitudes: the Temple and cult were to be shut off from the sounds and movements of the world around.

Temples in antiquity generally were intended to be prominent, to stand out in relation to the environment. They were often located on the summits of hills, and if construction intensified in the area either the temple was elevated, or the courtyards and buildings in the vicinity were downgraded.

Solomon's Temple (The First Temple). The Temple of Solomon gained preeminence as a result of political and religious movements, most notably the conquest of the northern kingdom of Israel by the Assyrians, and the drive, for both religious and political causes, to eliminate local and regional temples. David, founder of the united Israelite kingdom, had made Jerusalem (more precisely, the City of David on Mount Zion) his capital after conquering it around 1000 BCE; he confirmed royal sponsorship of the cult of the Ark of the Covenant by bringing the Ark to the city, while at the same time sanctioning the city as his royal seat (*2 Sm.* 6–7).

The best functional definition of the Temple complex that eventually arose on Mount Zion is preserved in *Amos* 7:13, which originally applied to Bethel, not Jerusalem. Bethel was the most important cult center of the northern kingdom in the eighth century, and the priest of Bethel admonished Amos not to speak against the king at Bethel: "Don't ever prophesy again at Bethel; for it is a king's sanctuary and a royal domain." Indeed, the Temple was initially only one component of a royal acropolis built on the northern summit of Mount Zion.

As described in *1 Kings* 6–8, Solomon's Temple was an oblong, stone structure, reinforced by cedar beams. The interior was divided by a wooden partition into two sections: the *heikhal* (great hall), encountered upon entering the building through swinging wooden doors, followed by the *devir* ("shrine"), the holiest section of the Temple, sometimes called the Holy of Holies. The shrine was raised higher than the floor of the great hall, and was set upon a huge rock, known later in the Jewish tradition as *even ha-shetiyyah* ("the foundation stone") and in Arabic as *al-sakhrah* (the "rock"), over which the Dome of the Rock was later built.

There were no interior columns, for the roof rested on large beams, and rows of windows punctuated two walls of the Temple. The facade of the Temple included a portico *(ulam)* extending the width of the building, in front of which stood two massive, ornamental columns, *yakhin* and *bo'az,* that were probably insignia of the Davidic monarchy. The Temple lay on an east-west axis.

The design of Solomon's Temple points to Syrian and Phoenician models. The temple at Tell Tu'eimat (ancient Kunulua) on the Syrian coast is often mentioned by archaeologists, as are temples at Zinjirli in Northwest Syria, and at Carchemish and Byblos. The Kunulua temple was also an oblong structure, divided into three parts: portico, hall, and shrine. An earlier prototype may have been the late Bronze Age temple at Hazor in Galilee, dating from between the sixteenth and the thirteenth centuries.

What is unusual about Solomon's Temple is its east-west orientation. Some have suggested that this was to allow the sun's rays to penetrate the Temple; others have speculated that the alignment was to allow the sun, at certain times of the year, to shine through two successive doorways into the shrine itself.

The interior doors were paneled with cedar, as was the ceiling, and both were extensively decorated with floral motifs and cherubs, overlaid with gold. In the windowless shrine stood the Ark, and hovering over it were two cherubs, whose combined wingspan reached from one wall to the other. In the great hall, facing the entrance to the shrine, stood the incense altar, made of cedar wood and overlaid with gold, and two rows of five lampstands, ten in all, hammered of solid gold.

Abutting three of the outer walls of the Temple was a network of stone chambers three stories high, called the *yatsi'a,* through which one proceeded from chamber to chamber, climbing to the higher stories. Although the biblical text fails to specify the *yatsi'a*'s function, it undoubtedly was used for storing consecrated materials and for priestly preparations. The structure reached halfway up the Temple's walls, so that the great hall's windows on the north and south walls were not blocked.

The Temple was surrounded by an enclosed courtyard *(ḥatser),* in the center of which, facing the entrance to the Temple, stood the altar for burnt offerings. The Temple had three gates, on the east, north, and south. Upon entering to the right and again in front of the Temple was a huge bronze reservoir, the *yam* ("sea"), and ten mobile basins—all ornamented with beasts of burden, as if to indicate that these animals carried the sea and the basins.

As described in *1 Kings,* the Temple was more exposed initially than in later periods. A comparison of Solomon's Temple complex with the visionary descriptions of the Temple complex in *Ezekiel* 40–48 shows how the process of insulating the Temple from the outside world had proceeded from the tenth century to the early sixth century, prior to the Temple's destruction in 587/6. Serious doubt exists as to how realistic the descriptions of *Ezekiel* are, given their visionary, literary context, but they probably reveal somewhat how the Temple complex appeared in its last years.

Two periods of major renovation were the reign of Hezekiah in the late eighth and early seventh centuries, and the reign of Josiah in the late seventh century. Hezekiah's projects undoubtedly were motivated by the growth of the population of Jerusalem after the fall of the northern kingdom of Israel in 722, which left the Temple as the only national religious center.

2 Kings 22 tells of Josiah's Temple renovations. Both he and Hezekiah were, of course, devout Yahvists; Josiah, in particular, had a lasting impact on the historical importance of the Temple. However, not only pious, Yahvistic kings were motivated to undertake Temple renovation. Ahaz, Hezekiah's father and hardly a devout, Yahvistic monarch, installed an additional altar, modeled after one he had seen in Damascus, and he built a passageway leading from his palace to the Temple (*2 Kgs.* 16). Even Manasseh, characterized as wicked, who ruled during much of the seventh century, may not have neglected the Temple; indeed, Nahman Avigad's excavations in Jerusalem's upper city reveal the extent of Manasseh's construction efforts.

By the time of Ezekiel the Temple is described as enclosed in two courtyards; there were now three sets of gate houses, so that the Temple was approached by mounting three staircases; the burnt-offering altar was elevated, and numerous stores were near the walls and gates (*Ez.* 40–48).

The Second Temple. Returning Judahite exiles, under their Davidic king Zerubabel, rebuilt the Temple of Jerusalem on its original site pursuant to the edict of Cyrus II (the Great), issued in 538. Despite opposition from Samaritan leaders and other causes of delay, the Second Temple was dedicated in 516, its design resembling that of the First Temple. Measurements in *Ezra* 6:3, however, indicate that there may have been an upper story or attic above the ceiling of the Temple, as in later times, causing it to loom larger over the surrounding area than the First Temple.

As far as we know, no administrative buildings were located in the Temple complex, an absence that is understandable given the changed status of Jerusalem from capital of a sovereign kingdom to provincial temple city, one of many such entities throughout the Persian empire.

Since its inception, the Second Temple had been devoid of certain artifacts once considered essential to the sanctity of the First. For instance, the shrine held neither Ark nor cherubs. (These cultic objects are missing in Ezekiel's descriptions of the First Temple.) Also missing were the two ornamental columns in front of the portico, since they symbolized royal authority and the Jews no longer had their own king. Yet even though no attempt was ever made to fashion a new ark (or cherubs), the empty shrine nevertheless was believed to be the domicile of the God of Israel.

Nehemiah 7:2 describes a fortress, *birah,* built in the northwest corner of the acropolis. (It is also mentioned in the *Letter of Aristeas* in the third century BCE.) In Herod's time it was renamed the Antonia and heavily fortified.

Records from the Persian period (538 to around 330 BCE) are sparse, but once Hellenistic sources begin to appear, more information emerges. The writings of Josephus Flavius, a Jewish historian of the first century CE, early tractates of the Mishnah, and passages in the New Testament all afford considerable information. Josephus, in *Against Apion,* refers to a certain Hecateus of Abdera who visited the temple in Jerusalem in the late fourth century; from the third century come descriptions in the *Letter of Aristeas,* and Yehoshu'a son of Sirah *(Ben Sira)* mentions that Shim'on ha-Tsaddiq (Shim'on the Just) undertook Temple renovations around 200. The recently discovered Temple Scroll, a pre-Herodian, Hebrew document, preserves detailed plans for a Jewish temple, and archaeological excavations in the Temple complex area have yielded additional material of interest.

Two periods appear to be times of major renovations and structural changes in the Temple: one following the Maccabean liberation of the Temple in 164, and the other, beginning about 20 BCE when Herod undertook the rebuilding of the entire Temple complex, a project that continued virtually until the destruction in 70 CE. From 164 the Hasmonean (Maccabean) rulers maintained a degree of political autonomy, after ridding the Temple of the heterodox artifacts and cult practices introduced by the hellenizing priesthood of Jerusalem in the period leading up to the persecutions of Antiochus IV. During the Hasmonean period, construction began on a series of archways leading to the temple, connecting it to the city of Jerusalem. These are better known from the Herodian period.

Herod, descendant of the Idumeans who converted to Judaism, was a favorite of the Romans. His monumental Temple project was motivated by both his desire to rule over a majestic *polis* of the Roman empire, and at the same time be accepted by the religious leaders of the Jews. The accommodation struck by Herod produced a Temple complex conceived along Roman lines that nonetheless retained the traditional Temple building, by now probably heightened considerably.

Extensive archaeological excavations in the Temple mount area, initiated under the direction of Benjamin Mazar in 1968, have provided new information. It seems that Herod's Temple preserved earlier Temple design but the dimensions were considerably enlarged, including its height.

The inner area of Herod's Temple complex was prohibited to gentiles, and it was bounded by a balustrade called the *soreg.* Josephus mentions that inscriptions in Greek and Latin were posted at intervals warning gentiles not to pass beyond that point; two examples of these inscriptions have been discovered in modern times.

A visitor moving from east to west would perceive that the walled area of the temple was composed of two main sections. First, he would pass through the Beautiful Gate into the women's court and proceed up a staircase through the Nicanor Gate to the court of Israel, where male worshipers assembled. (Men and women did not worship together.) The court of Israel was set off in the eastern section of the inner court, and there was no wall separating it from the priests' court where the altar of burnt offerings stood. This entire walled section contained various chambers, including the Chamber of Hewn Stone, where the Sanhedrin, the high court of the Jews, convened prior to approximately 30 CE.

The altar for burnt offerings was situated in front of the Temple, slightly to the south of the staircase leading to the portico. In the Herodian period it was a raised altar reached by a ramp called the *kevesh.* Sacrificial animals were slaughtered in the northern front section of the court of priests, and a laver stood near the southern wall. The portico facade itself is described as exceedingly impressive and ornate; however, it included a golden eagle that aroused intense opposition because many Jews regarded the eagle as a pagan symbol.

The entire Temple mount, some of it resting on pillars, was enclosed by a high wall called the *ḥeil.* It undoubtedly served as a fortification, along with the Antonia fortress. The Temple mount had massive retaining walls, some of which have been exposed in recent archaeological excavations. (One is the so-called Western Wall.) On the periphery of the Temple mount were porticos, the best known of them being the royal portico, built along the southern side of the outer courtyards. This royal portico, which is profusely praised by Josephus, has been identified with the *ḥanuyyot* ("stores") mentioned in the Mishnah (*Ta'an.* 1.6). The Temple mount's outer dimensions prior to the destruction are estimated at 1,550 meters, an area twice the size of Trajan's forum in Rome.

The two Temples of Jerusalem, built on the same spot, had the cumulative effect of sanctifying that place for all subsequent generations of Jews.

The Cult of the Temples of Jerusalem. Information on the conduct of worship in the Temples of Jerusalem comes from several kinds of sources, all of which are problematic in one way or another. Most of the detailed descriptions of cultic praxis in biblical times come from the priestly codes of the Pentateuch, known as the P source. This source projects the sacrificial cult back to the time of the Sinai migrations, prior to Israelite settlement in Canaan. Historically these codes of practice, found primarily in *Exodus*, *Leviticus*, and *Numbers*, belong to a much later period and probably reflect the Jerusalem Temple cult. It is difficult, however, to ascertain whether the cult of the First or Second Temple is being described. While the P source, as we have it, is more logically the product of the early postexilic period, the time of Persian domination (538–c. 330), much of it, especially as pertains to types of sacrifices and their essential modes of presentation, was probably in effect in Judah in the latter part of the monarchic period, prior to the Babylonian exile. Today, the dating of the P source is a matter of considerable disagreement among scholars, with a substantial number favoring a preexilic provenance.

The *Letter of Aristeas* and the *Book of Ben Sira* contain a good deal of information from pre-Maccabean times about the Second Temple. For the Herodian period and thereafter (about the last one hundred years of the Temple), considerable information is preserved in the writings of Josephus. The Mishnah and Tannaitic literature may also be employed for the Herodian period even though they were not compiled until the early third century CE. *Megillat ta'anit* and the books of the New Testament also contain authentic information on Temple worship. It is warranted to assume a high degree of conservatism in the religious practice of ancient Jerusalem.

Structure of the cultic worship. The public cult of Jerusalem was, from earliest times, structured around a daily regimen, wherein the major sacrifice was offered in the morning, and a less elaborate one offered before sunset. This was the ancient Near Eastern pattern, according to which the day was defined as the daylight hours. This was the time frame for most worship, although certain types of ritual were conducted at night, magic and penitential worship for the most part. The daytime schedule expressed the basic aim of worship: the need to secure God's blessings and help in the practical pursuits of life, in the activities of each day.

Thus, the Bible tells us that Ahaz, king of Judah, instructed the priests of Jerusalem to offer "the burnt offering of the morning and the grain offering of the evening" (*2 Kgs.* 16:15). The late afternoon came to be referred to as the time "of the ascent of the grain offering" (*1 Kgs.* 18:29, 18:36). In *Ezekiel* 46:12–15, both a burnt offering and a grain offering were to be sacrificed each morning, but there is no mention of a second burnt offering later in the day, as is required by the laws of the Torah (*Ex.* 29:38–46; *Nm.* 28:1–8). It is likely, therefore, that the Torah codes which project two daily burnt offerings are postexilic, as suggested by Roland de Vaux.

On Sabbaths, New Moons, and festivals, additional or perhaps special sacrifices were offered. The Mishnah, especially in tractate *Tamid*, describes the daily regimen of the Second Temple, including the procedures for assignment of priests to various duties.

Basic kinds of sacrifice. *Leviticus* 1–3 and 5–7 outline the three basic types of sacrifice offered on the altar of burnt offerings:

1. *'Olah*, functionally translated as "burnt offering" or "holocaust," was a sacrifice burned to ash, no part of which was eaten by the priest or donors. Literally, *'olah* means "that which ascends [in smoke]." An *'olah* could consist of a bull, a sheep or goat, or certain birds. The donor of the sacrifice laid his hands on the animal's head and, following a set formula, assigned it as an *'olah;* the Mishnah (*'Arakh.* 5.5) preserves examples of such formulas used during the late Second Temple. The priest then slaughtered the animal, flayed it, washed certain internal organs, and decapitated and sectioned it. The blood of the sacrifice was then splashed on the altar. The *'olah* was also termed an *isheh* (offering by fire), a more general term for all burnt offerings, as well as a *qorban* ("offering").
2. *Minḥah* (grain offering) consisted of semolina wheat flour, finely ground, mixed with oil and frankincense into a dough. A scoop of the dough was burned on the altar, while the remainder was baked or cooked some other way. Any grain offering burned on the al-

tar had to be made of unleavened dough *(matsah)*. The reason for this restriction is not known. Portions of the *minḥah* were eaten by the priests.

3. *Zevaḥ shelamin* ("a sacred gift of greeting"; sometimes termed a "peace offering"). The term *zevaḥ* seems to mean "sacred meal," or "food." Such an offering could consist only of a bull, sheep, or goat. It too was assigned by the donor; its blood was splashed on the altar. But, in contrast to the first two kinds of sacrifice, this offering was shared with the donors. The altar received certain of the internal organs and the fat adhering to them, whereas the meat was divided between priests and donors and then boiled in pots (*1 Sm.* 2:13). In addition, libations of wine usually accompanied the major sacrifice (*Nm.* 15:1–16, 15:22–31).

Sacrifice as a mode of worship. The sacrificial regimen just outlined represents the outcome of a long process of development; left unanswered are questions about the history and meaning of sacrifice.

There were two basic sacrificial modes in biblical Israel: the presentation and the burnt offering. In the presentation offering, the deity is portrayed as looking upon the offering and accepting or rejecting it. Such offerings, once "set" or placed before God, were usually assigned to the priests who would partake of them. Examples include the offering of first fruits (*Dt.* 26:1–11); the "bread of display," placed on tables in the Temple for a week and then given to the priests (*Lv.* 24:5–9, *1 Sm.* 21:7); the leavened loaves of the thanksgiving offering (*Lv.* 6:11–13); and the offering of the sheaf from the new grain crop (*Lv.* 23:11, 23:17). Therefore, to a degree mode relates to substance, and presentations tended to consist of grain and fruits, very much in keeping with sacrifice in other ancient Near Eastern countries.

With the burnt offering, the deity is portrayed as inhaling the aromatic smoke of the sacrifice, typical of an incense offering—a kind of sacrifice in its own right (*Ex.* 30:7f, *Lv.* 6:12–15, *Is.* 1:13). Historically, the burnt offering may have originated in northern Syria, for it is known that it was adopted and widely used by the Hittites. It may not have been native to Canaan, although current research into this question is inadequate.

What is clear from biblical literature is the progressive ascendancy of the burnt offering in the public cult and in private donations. This can be traced in the adaptation of certain modes of sacrifice. The grain offering is a case in point. As prescribed in *Leviticus* 2 it can be analyzed as the accommodation of what was originally a presentation offering: only a scoop of dough was burned on the altar, the rest was given to the priests after having been offered first to the deity.

Yet another instance of accommodation is implicit in the term *tenufah* (raised offering). Before certain offerings were placed on the altar, they were held up and carried about for the deity to view (*Lv.* 10:4).

Procedures whereby offerings initially having nothing to do with the altar were adapted to the prevailing mode are also evident with respect to animal sacrifices. According to the old mode of sacrifice, the paschal lamb was roasted whole over an open fire without employing the altar (*Ex.* 12 and 13). But as prescribed in *Deuteronomy* 16:7 and like all other sacrifices of the *zevaḥ* variety, it was to be boiled in pots, with certain parts burned on the altar.

Generally, most sacrificial types and modes existed quite early in the biblical period, and some are mentioned independently by eighth-century prophets. What changes perceptibly is the elaborateness of composite, public rituals, such as those performed at festivals, or in purifying the Temple. The liturgical calendar in *Numbers*, chapters 28 through 29, shows the growth of a frequent and detailed sacrificial activity since an earlier period in *Leviticus* 23.

Certain very ancient sacrifices were revived after long periods; one was the water libation, mentioned in connection with David's early years (*1 Sm.* 23:16), and which figured in Elijah's confrontation with the Baal priests somewhere in the Carmel mountain range (*1 Kgs.* 18). It was revived in the early rabbinic period (*Sheq.* 6:3).

Interacting with mode and substance was motivation, the reason for the sacrifice. There were several types of sacrifices whose objective was expiation, through purification; two major ones were the *ḥaṭṭa't* ("sin offering") and the *asham* ("guilt offering"). The *asham* in particular had a votive aspect, and it could be donated in other than a sacrificial form (as silver, for instance), especially since the priesthood at different times preferred different kinds of revenue. The *asham,* as a sacrificial offering, had no role in the public cult, but the *ḥaṭṭa't* was used in Temple purification in rites such as those described for the Day of Atonement (*Lv.* 16). These sacrifices resembled others in substance, and usually consisted of large or small cattle, except that allowances were made for less expensive offerings from donors with limited means so as not to deny them expiation.

Private and public worship intersected in the Temple. Individuals donated public sacrifices; the Temple was a place to pronounce vows and fulfill pledges; new mothers, in accordance with *Leviticus* 12, brought pigeons and doves to the Temple following their specified periods of seclusion. Scattered among the legal discussions of the Talmudic sages are beautiful descriptions of celebrations in the late Second Temple period; for example, the description of the offering of first fruits in Jerusalem, as first commanded in *Deuteronomy* 20:1–11, and later recorded in the Mishnah, tractate *Bikkurim*, chapter 3.

Once consecrated, sacrificial materials became susceptible to defilement, and could not be left unused. Not only would certain foodstuffs spoil, which was a practical consideration, but there was always the fear that impurity would affect the entire Temple complex or, put another way, that demonic forces would contaminate sacrifices.

Sacrificial blood was utilized in the Temple cult in special ways. As such, blood from sacrifices was considered taboo, as was all blood from cattle, sheep, and goats used as food (*Gn.* 9:4; *Lv.* 3:17, 17:10f.; *Dt.* 12:16f.). In most sacrifices, the blood was splashed on the sides of the altar, and in some cases on the horns atop the altar. In certain expiatory rites, such as those performed in Temple purification, blood was also dabbed on the interior incense altar, on the curtains at the entrance to the great hall and the shrine, and even on the Ark and cherubs. Blood, as the vital fluid of living creatures, was to be returned to the earth, and the blood splashed on the sides of the altar would therefore be allowed to run down into the earth. What had once been a blood libation to chthonic powers became an offering to God. Other uses, such as dabbing blood on cult objects (and occasionally people), seem to have been intended to ward off demonic forces. Salt was applied to offerings to drain off residual blood after slaughter (*Lv.* 2:13), and the method of slaughter, later described in the Mishnah (*Ḥul.* 2.4), was to cut the jugular vein. An entire order of the Mishnah, *Qodashim* ("Sacred Things"), is devoted to procedures of sacrifice in late Second Temple times.

Apart from sacrifices, the Temple cult always included prayers and song, and probably dance as well (or at least orchestrated movement). The *Psalms* were first prayers, and one tradition has it that the Levites were the singers (*Ez.* 2:41, *Neh.* 7:44, *1 Chr.* 15:10), at least at the time of the Second Temple. This tradition is reflected in the captions of certain psalms that associate them with Levitical clans. But prayer and song were not regarded as the main events or even as sufficient modes of worship: only sacrifice and its rituals were ultimately efficacious. The *tamid* or daily sacrificial offering that in the Second Temple was burned twice each day was the mainstay of the cult, and when it was suppressed by decree great anxiety overtook Jewish people everywhere. [*For an extensive cross-cultural discussion, see* Sacrifice.]

Funding and Administration. Temple building and maintenance, the public cult, and the support of Temple personnel all required large outlays of funds. Who bore the costs? As with other matters pertaining to the Temples of Jerusalem, we are reliant primarily on the Hebrew Bible, since we lack contemporary documentation in the form of administrative records, such as those that have survived from the major ancient temples of Syria-Mesopotamia, or the inscribed ancient wall reliefs, for instance, that we find in Egypt. With the Hellenistic period, documentation begins to appear, and in the Roman period Jewish writings become available. Together these sources provide more specific information on the operation of the Second Temple.

In itself, the biblical record is complex and often confusing: the Torah tells one story, and the historical books of Hebrew scriptures—*Samuel, Kings, Ezra, Nehemiah, Chronicles*—another. The Torah gives little indication as to the role of the monarchy in biblical Israel, never venturing beyond stating the eventuality of a monarchy. Nor is there evidence of governmental taxation, only gifts to God—tithes, priestly emoluments, voluntary and obligatory sacrifices, and so forth. The various documentary sources of the Torah project legislation into the days of Moses, before the Israelite settlement of Canaan, when there was no king and no temple in Jerusalem. Historically misleading, all matters concerning the major temples of the land were controlled by the monarch, once established, in both Judaea and northern Israel. Although priestly groups probably originated independent of the monarchy, retaining traditional prerogatives, they nonetheless operated under royal jurisdiction for most of the preexilic period.

The contrast between the laws of the Torah, which provide so much detail on the performance of the cult, and the historical books of the Hebrew Bible, which contain little on these subjects but considerable information on governmental administration, can be demonstrated by the case of the tithe. The tithe amounted to one-tenth of the annual yield of grain and fruit, as well as an equal percentage of any increase in herds and flocks. In the Torah, such tithes are represented as cult dues or religious duties owed to the Levitical priests and the needy, without any governmental involvement in the process (*Dt.* 14:22–29, 15:19–23; *Lv.* 27:30). In contrast, the statement of royal jurisdiction preserved in *1 Samuel* 8 (especially verse 15) refers to the fact that kings are the ones who impose tithes on crop yield. Projecting back to Moses, so characteristic of the Torah, often masks the realities of royal administration that obtained during the preexilic period, as well as the realities of priestly administration under foreign rulers in the postexilic period. [*See* Tithes.]

Funding in the Second Temple. The preferred method of studying Temple funding would be to begin with the

Hellenistic period, for which we have contemporary evidence, and work backward. Elias Bickerman (1976) has clarified this subject for the Ptolemaic and Seleucid periods in Judaea and Jerusalem (c. 312–363 BCE) in a study of the mission of Heliodorus to the Temple of Jerusalem, as recounted in *2 Maccabees* 3 and as known well in later literature and art.

In later times, maintaining the Temple and cult in Jerusalem was a royal responsibility; tax revenues were allocated for this purpose, augmented by gifts from the nobility. Under the Romans (63 BCE–70 CE) the system was more complicated, as will become apparent.

The principle of royal sponsorship also applied during the earlier Achaemenid period (538–330); both Hebrew and Aramaic versions of the edict of Cyrus II of 538 have been preserved (*Ezr.* 1:2–3, 6:6–12). Of particular relevance are statements of the Aramaic version, in *Ezra* 6:8–9, relevant to the funds and materials required for the restoration of the public cult in Jerusalem:

> The expenses are to be paid to these men [the Judean elders] with dispatch out of the resources of the king, derived from the taxes of the province of Beyond the River, so that the work not be interrupted. They are to be provided daily, without fail, whatever they need of young bulls, rams and lambs as burnt offerings for the God of Heaven and wheat, salt, wine and oil, at the order of the priests in Jerusalem.

Further back in history, similar information about the funding of the First Temple under the national Judahite kings can be found.

Ezekiel 45 contains a statement on the prerogatives of the *nasi'* ("prince"; literally, "the one elevated, raised" above the people), Ezekiel's term for the future ruler of the restored Judahite community. It is not certain when this chapter was composed, but it is probably warranted, as in the matter of Temple design, to regard it as expressing the principle of royal funding in effect during the last days of the First Temple.

The chapter begins by designating a quarter inside Jerusalem to be set aside for the Temple complex (*Ez.* 45:1–8). Verses 9 through 17 establish standards of weights and measures, and specify a system of taxation based on percentage of annual yield. Verses 16 and 17 are particularly relevant:

> The entire population must pay this levy to the *nasi'*. It shall then be the responsibility of the *nasi'* to provide the holocausts, grain offerings and libations on the pilgrimage festivals, on New Moons and Sabbaths, on all the appointed celebrations of the House of Israel.

This passage has been variously interpreted by biblical historians, such as Jacob Jiver, who was undoubtedly correct in seeing it as reflecting royal sponsorship. In accounting terms royal sponsorship was a form of indirect funding. Taxes collected by government agents (sometimes priests served in this capacity) were partially or fully allocated to the Temple. Direct Temple funding came from the people, and was specifically earmarked for Temple use. The *nasi'*, a civil authority although he had sacral functions, was made responsible for the entire Temple restoration, and it was he who collected taxes for the Temple project and the public cult.

But Ezekiel's vision never materialized, because during the postexilic period Temple funding became a function of foreign kings, and indeed the Davidic king Zerubabel did not retain authority very long. Morton Smith has correctly understood the statement in *Zechariah* 6:12–13 as an official, prophetic endorsement of Zerubabel as sponsor of the rebuilt Temple of Jerusalem, with the authority of the high priest less precisely defined. He notes, however, that king and high priest are often addressed together, as coleaders of the people, (*Hg.* 1:1, 1:12, 1:14, 2:2; *Zec.* 3–4), and by placing two crowns in the Temple, their joint authority was memorialized. As time goes on, with priestly administration of the Temple under Persian jurisdiction as the everyday reality, much less is said in scripture about a Davidic restoration. So in effect Ezekiel's recast vision embodies the principle of royal sponsorship as it operated in the period of the First Temple. Further, *Samuel* and *Kings* clearly describe the First Temple as a royal agency, but say little about taxation other than that labor forces were conscripted for Temple projects and other royal enterprises.

Funding in the First Temple. One way to investigate Temple funding in the preexilic period is to discuss the royal and Temple treasuries, both mentioned in *1 Kings* 12:19, 14:26, and elsewhere, as separate agencies under royal control. We often read of "sanctuary weight" but hardly ever of royal standards of weights and measures. And yet, in a single, random passage (*2 Sm.* 14:26), we read of *'even ha-melekh* ("the royal weight"), which tells something about the degree to which even the historical chronicles mask administrative reality in a preoccupation with religious concerns.

Several biblical chronicles tell how Judahite kings, both "upright" in God's sight and those who "did what was evil," appropriated Temple treasures for other than cult purposes (*2 Kgs.* 18:15–16). In speaking of these acts, an assertion of royal authority over the Temple, *Kings* usually refers to Temple treasures as "sacred gifts" *(qodashim)* donated by the various Judean kings and their ancestors, as if to imply that they, in turn, had the right to expropriate them.

Chapters 12 and 22 in *2 Kings* are particularly informative on the subject of Temple funding during the period of the Judahite monarchy. Chapter 12 tells of Joash, a king who ruled in the late ninth century, who used Temple treasures for tribute. The chapter's present arrangement has the confrontation with the Aramean king, Hazael, after Temple renovations undertaken by Joash, as seen in verses 18 and 19, yet it is quite logical to regard the renovations mentioned in verses 1 through 17 as actually taking place subsequent to Joash's payment to Hazael.

Payments to Hazael left Temple coffers empty. The chapter opens with an edict issued by Joash to the priests: all silver brought into the Temple as votaries was to be collected by the priests and used for Temple renovation. This was apparently an exceptional measure, and the priests were lax to resort to votaries for this purpose, expecting instead royal allocations to cover their cost. After a time the king, seeing that repairs had not been made, summoned the chief priest of the Temple and, prevailing over the priest's objections, insisted that his edict be carried out. The priest installed a collection box near the altar where all donors were to deposit their votaries. At appropriate intervals the priest would tally donations, in the presence of the royal scribe, and the silver would be melted down into ingots; these, in turn, were paid out to craftsmen working on the Temple who apparently were so trustworthy that no accounting system was required for them. A freeze was placed on the manufacture of cultic vessels of silver and gold in order that all available funds could be used for needed repairs. The only exemption, for penalties brought to the Temple by worshipers in need of expiation, was granted so that atonement would not be delayed.

2 Kings 22 describes a similar situation under Josiah, king of Judah, in the late seventh century; both chapter 12 and this chapter are drawn from the same kind of royal chronicles. Again, all silver, this time collected by the Temple gatekeepers, was to be melted down into ingots to pay Temple workers. Josiah's coffers were also empty after the long period of Manasseh's reign.

Both chapters report that the king had jurisdiction over the Temple, royal scribes supervised Temple accounting procedures, and craftsmen were paid by royal order. In part records were preserved to credit Judean kings for proper maintenance of the First Temple of Jerusalem and for attending to necessary repairs. And yet they also point to another fairly constant source of Temple revenue and serve to link the historical books of the Hebrew Bible to the laws of the Torah.

Sacred vessels and sacrificial offerings were regularly donated (or "devoted") to the Temple by individual Israelites and their families. Votaries mentioned in *2 Kings* 12, in fact, are the subject of Torah legislation in *Leviticus* 27, where specific payments are determined separately for men and women by age group. Such devotions often assumed large proportions. The writings of Josephus and rabbinic sources describe large-scale devotions from prominent Diaspora Jews, such as Helene, the queen of Adiabene. These donations were usually prompted by the motive of sponsorship.

The priesthood, for its part, relied on popular support, which, however, was not always adequate to sustain the priests and their families. People were exhorted to pay tithes and vows on time and to devote sacrifices; indeed, the Torah sets down the dues payable to the Levitical priesthood and includes a whole schedule of offerings (*Nm.* 18).

Fiscal responsibilities. The main problem here is to determine who bore responsibility for the Temples of Jerusalem—the government (so to speak), or the private sector. No persistent policy of support by the private sector is evident until late Hasmonean or early Roman times. Basing his work on Bickerman's, Jiver meticulously surveyed the background of this development, showing that the first reference to popular funding of the Temple is found in the writings of Josephus (*Jewish Antiquities* 18:312), who tells of the annual head tax of one-half shekel (at times, equal to two Roman drachmas); *Matthew* 17:24 through 17:27 speaks about the collection of this tax in Capernaum, in the early first century CE. In the Mishnah (*Sheq.* 1:3–6) the tax is called *terumat ha-lishkah* ("the levy of the bureau," for the bureau in the Temple complex where it was collected); it was used mainly to fund the *tamid* or daily sacrifice that was the mainstay of the public Temple cult. It was not accepted from gentiles, thereby excluding them from any role in supporting the cult. But more specifically, at some prior time Jewish religious leaders decided that the cult should be supported "by all Israel," and not by foreign rulers—Herodian or Roman. This decision is first recorded in the *scholia*, or comments, affixed to *Megillat ta'anit* concerning a dispute involving the early Pharisees. The text states that Boethusians (perhaps the Sadducees, or some other anti-Pharisaic sect) claimed:

> The *tamid* sacrifices may be brought from private contributions: one person may offer it for one week, another may offer it for two weeks, and still another for thirty days.
>
> The Sages [Pharisees] retorted: "You are not permitted to act in this way, because this sacrifice may only be contributed by all Israel . . . and all of them [the sacrifices] are to come from the 'levy of the bureau.' " When they [the Phari-

sees] prevailed over them and defeated them, they instituted that all should weigh out their shekels and deposit them in the bureau, and *tamid* sacrifices were henceforth offered from popular funds.

(quoted in Lichtenstein, 1931–1932, p. 325)

We cannot date the enactment of which this passage speaks, but historically it may have been the result of Pharisaic displeasure with the later Hasmoneans; some scholars trace it to the reign of Salome Alexandra (76–67 BCE). Whatever the case, Jewish communities from all over the Diaspora contributed their shekels.

The policy of refusing royal support was based on several Torah traditions that speak of all Israelites as contributing to the building of the Tabernacle in the Sinai wilderness. These traditions have baffled biblical historians, who have searched for a historical situation that could account for them. Since no such principle is known for either the First Temple or the Second, both of which relied on royal funding, the question remains as to when popular funding came to function as a system.

The Torah traditions are preserved primarily in the priestly sources of *Exodus* and *Numbers*. Beginning with *Exodus* 30:11 through 16, a law required every adult Israelite male to contribute one-half shekel "to Yahveh" to support the Tabernacle; it was to be collected in the course of a census.

In its context, this law was formulated as a one-time obligation. *Exodus* 25 and the following chapters appealed to all Israelites to contribute voluntarily to the construction ofgold and silver objects for the Tabernacle, valuable fabrics, and the like. This fund-raising effort was very successful, and sufficient materials were donated. The half-shekel was for the "service" of the Tabernacle, to support its sacrifical cult. Of course it is possible that in *Exodus* 25 and 30 parallel traditions on funding exist: one recording a fixed tax, the other a voluntary contribution.

Either way, these traditions, reinforced by *Numbers* 7, which tells that the chieftains of the twelve tribes contributed identical vessels and sacrificial materials for the dedication of the Tabernacle, quite clearly idealize popular support for the Temple and its public cult. Nonetheless, all Israelites participated in its support, making it an institution of and for the people, even though it was conducted by the priesthood.

Since it is virtually out of the question to date these Torah traditions to the late first century BCE, it is difficult to identify their historical situation. Most likely Julius Wellhausen and others were right in attributing the head tax of *Exodus* 30 with the period of Nehemiah, the late fifth century; he was a Jew who served for two terms under the Persians as governor of Judah. In *Nehemiah* 10 is a record of a popular assembly, or "constitutional convention," that some historians date to around 438, although *Nehemiah* may have been written considerably later.

Under Nehemiah the people, along with priestly leaders and civil officials, assembled in Jerusalem and pledged to fulfill the Torah of Moses. In fact, however, they also instituted some new marriage restrictions, reinforced the observance of the Sabbath, and assumed certain financial obligations in support of the Temple cult. They pledged one-third shekel a year in support of the cult and cast lots to determine who would provide wood for the altar fire. In addition, they promised to pay tithes, redeem firstlings and firstborns by remitting their set value to the Temple, and offer first fruits of the harvest—all of which brought profit to the Temple.

It is reasonable to see the priestly traditions as the institutionalization of a temporary policy change that occurred in the late Persian period when the economic fortunes of the empire declined, threatening the continuity of the cult. According to the *Book of Nehemiah*, especially chapter 5, taxes were heavy and Jewish leaders had to help matters along. With the conquest of Alexander the Great, and the initiation of Ptolemaic and Seleucid rule in Jerusalem and Judaea, the economic situation improved substantially, and royal sponsorship functioned well once again.

The Torah traditions also correlate with other references to popular responsibility for the public cult in *Ezra* and *Chronicles*, although these references reach into the fourth century BCE. (See *Ezra* 1:4, an addendum to the Cyrus Edict, also *Ezra* 3:5, 8:28; *2 Chronicles* 31:14, 35:8.)

2 Chronicles 24:4 through 14 is a late recasting of *2 Kings* 12, discussed earlier. In this version, Joash orders the priests and Levites to travel to every town in Judaea to collect silver for Temple repairs, from "all Israel." When the Levites fail to do their part, he rebukes them (*2 Chr.* 24:6). Thus, this preexilic chronicle's version of Temple votary expropriation was recast as the record of a tax collected throughout the land from all the people.

The Torah traditions, whenever composed, became epitomes ultimately of a democratic ideal—the liberation of the Temple cult from royal domination. The Jews took charge of the Temple and limited the authority of foreign kings over the conduct of religious life. Perhaps for the first time, these kings, who had spent a fortune on the Temples from taxes collected from the people, were no longer permitted to claim exclusive sponsorship of the worship of God.

The Torah speaks of "consecrations" to the Temple (*Lv.* 27), with an assured profit of 20 percent on "redemptions" of land or real estate so designated. Land was also permanently bequeathed to the Temple, making itthe beneficiary of private estates. More than likely, the Temple served as a channel for tax exemptions.

The Mishnah describes how the Temple operated on a day-to-day basis in Herodian times and prior to its destruction. Like the prophet Jeremiah before him, Jesus certainly had reason to object to the atmosphere of the marketplace that characterized the Temple complex, but such was the nature of holy cities everywhere. Great numbers of sacrificial animals, as well as large quantities of incense, flour, wine, and oil, were stocked in the Temple stores; priests and their agents attended to the business of the Temple, selling to worshipers the goods that they required and collecting various payments. Priests were assigned to Temple duty, usually of a week's duration. Ancient records of these tours (*mishmarot*) have been discovered in recent archaeological investigations, such as those at Beit She'an. The Temple proper was inspected every morning; a daily duty roster was used, with one priest placed in charge of work assignments each day; treasurers kept Temple accounts. Indeed, the Temple complex was the very hub of Jerusalem.

Temple Function and Phenomenology. Throughout biblical literature, the temple of Jerusalem is called *beit YHVH* ("the House of Yahveh"). This role emerges clearly from *1 Kings* 8, a mixed text that presents both an early statement on the functions of this house and a later postexilic reinterpretation. Its primary function is best conveyed in verses 12 and 13: "Then Solomon spoke: Yahveh has chosen to abide in dense cloud. I have accordingly built for You a royal house, a dais for Your eternal enthronement."

The Temple served as an earthly residence for God and was designed to replicate his celestial estate. In the heavens, God is enveloped by dense cloud (*2 Sm.* 22; *Ps.* 18, 97:2; *Jb.* 38:9); his heavenly throne-room was, in graphic terms, an arrested version of his chariot, fashioned as a winged sphinx and cherub (*Ez.* 28:14, *Ps.* 18:11). God rode his chariot across heaven, as "rider amid the clouds" (*Ps.* 68:5) and as "Yahveh of the [heavenly] hosts, seated astride the cherubim" (*1 Sm.* 4:4, *2 Sm.* 6:2)—a projection now recognized as a very ancient Near Eastern image known in Ugaritic mythology.

Also basic to celestial depictions is the obscurity that afforded protection from view and access. Moses climbed Mount Sinai, "into the dense cloud where God is" (*Ex.* 20:21); God had descended there to communicate with Moses, a dramatic move in keeping with other visible manifestations of the deity (*2 Sm.* 20:10, *Ps.* 18:10).

The Temple was a divine palace. In the ancient Near Eastern tradition of inverting reality, earth was perceived as a replica of heaven, yet poets and writers depicted heaven according to what they knew on earth—an inversion seemingly endemic to the human imagination. The earthly residence of God in Jerusalem contained a shrine without windows, a dark room; in it the Ark served as God's footstool, and his throne was formed by the arched, winged cherubs. He was present, but invisible and immaterial. On those rare occasions that the high priest entered the shrine, he bore incense, partly to protect himself, but also to cloud the immediate area of the shrine where the deity was thought to be seated (*Lv.* 16:13).

The term for great hall, *heikhal*, goes back to Sumerian *egal* ("big house"); Akkadian *hekallu*, and Ugaritic *hkl*. The Egyptian title *pharaoh (pr)* literally means "big house," the ruler who lives in a palace. The great hall was a veritable audience room or parlor, where priests (perhaps originally worshipers as well) offered gifts to the resident divine monarch. There was a table for presentations and an incense altar, so that the air would be sweetened for God's pleasure. The cedar-paneled walls and ceiling were decorated with motifs suitable for a divine residence—cherubs and floral motifs. Here was an effort to simulate a heavenly "garden," such as described in *Ezekiel* 27–28. Such decorations were not thought to contradict the ban on iconography so basic to Israelite monotheism (*Ex.* 20:4, *Dt.* 5:8). [*See* Iconography, *article on* Jewish Iconography.] And, like a palace, the Temple had a portico, so that one would not enter into the presence of the deity abruptly.

Offerings. In the open-air courtyard stood the altar of burnt offerings, facing the entrance of the Temple. Every day sacrifices were burned on this altar, and other installations and artifacts were also present to serve the priests' needs.

The classic plan of Solomon's Temple and of all its successors represented the integration of two originally separate concepts: that of a house, closed and covered by a roof, and that of an open-air encampment. Within the "house" gifts were presented to the deity, and his "looking upon" them with favor constituted his acceptance of them. Normally, such gifts were assigned to the priests, who partook of them in a sacred meal.

The offerings of incense inside the great hall point to another kind of divine response—inhalation. In this respect, incense and the burnt offerings of animals, birds, and grain belonged together on the outdoor altar. Therefore, two modes of sacrifice took place in the great hall: presentation, which was intended to evoke a visual response from God, and aromatic smoke, intended for inhalation by the deity. A description of the open-air ceremony will help us to understand the phenomenology of incense offerings. On the altar of burnt offerings were placed parts of animals and fowl and scoops of dough that were reduced to ash by the fire. The smoke ascended heavenward, there inhaled by God and in this manner accepted by him. When God disapproved of the worshipers or the manner of their worship, he angrily refused to inhale the aromatic smoke of their burnt offerings (*Am.* 5:21, *Lv.* 26:31).

The open-air altar was oriented vertically and the effects of the rite directed heavenward, which helps explain the preference for mountaintops and high places. As the sacrificial rite began, God was thought to be in heaven, not yet present; once the smoke rose to heaven, it was hoped that he would be attracted by the sweet aroma, and come to his worshipers (*Ex.* 20:24). Once God drew near he could be entreated and petitioned for the blessings of life. This was the basic phenomenology of the open-air burnt offering. In liturgical terms it was a form of invocation, and this seems to be the original function of the burnt offering referred to as *ʿolah* (literally, "that which *ascends*," in aromatic smoke, to heaven).

The presentation clearly had a horizontal orientation. The deity was perceived as already present in his "house." This is the basic difference between a "house" and the open-air setting. The Temple "house" was God's permanent residence, affording him shelter and the necessities of life (so to speak), whereas an altar or *bamah* ("high place") was a site visited by him on occasion. [*For a cross-cultural discussion of this subject, see* Altar.] Consequently, it is likely that the incense offering was originally an open-air ritual. Archaeological evidence seems to suggest this; many incense stands have been found in front of temples, or outside their entrances. But it is also reasonable to assume that the venue of the incense offering was, in certain instances, shifted to the Temple's interior.

Structure. As a projection of differing patterns of human habitation, the typical temple plan—including both an open-air court and a closed, covered "house"—combines the encampment and the town, the pastoral and the more settled, agricultural bases of economic life into one expression.

Wood was preferred for temple architecture, particularly the fine, aromatic cedar from Lebanon. The Sumerian king Gudea used cedar wood in his temple, built more than a thousand years before Solomon's Temple. In many areas of the ancient Near East there seems to be an almost symbolic preference for wood, persisting long after stone and mud brick became the functional materials for construction. In the earliest temple tombs of Egypt, wooden motifs were retained long after stone was used. It was conventional to romanticize more ancient modes of construction, while for practical purposes utilizing stronger, more lasting materials.

The huge reservoir, *yam* ("sea"), located in the courtyard also had its particular meaning; in Mesopotamian temples similar reservoirs were called *apsu* ("the deep"). Aside from their practical purposes, their names reflect a common cosmic or mythological concept. *Zechariah* 14:8 states that the Temple rested on the fountainhead of the earth and was connected to the deep wellsprings. As in heaven, where gods lived at the junctures of cosmic streams, so too on earth the divine palace was associated with water. The man-made reservoir was called "sea" to symbolize the purifying and fructifying properties of "living water."

Gods normally desired an earthly house or palace built by worshipers (usually their king) more fervently than they desired altars and high places. This desire is beautifully expressed (and with considerable pathos) in ancient Near Eastern literature from Sumer to Ugarit. Biblical historiography reports this suprisingly sophisticated attitude as attributed to the God of Israel when he, in effect, initially refuses David's offer to build a temple in his honor. He states that only when the Davidic dynasty is established and the conquest of the promised land accomplished will he insist on a "house." In *2 Samuel* 7 "house" *(bayit)* undergoes an ingenious semantic transaction: both David's dynasty and the Temple are houses, and only when David's dynasty is established, in the days of his son, will the time be right to build God his house.

The Temple is thus a royal project *par excellence*, a fact further demonstrated by the other components of Solomon's acropolis. The two pillars in front of the portico *(yakhin* and *boʿaz)* were apparently royal insignia, although the precise meaning of their names remains elusive. The hall of justice demonstrates the judicial role of the king, as the one responsible for establishing justice in the land, and as a court of last resort for the redress of grievances. The king, chosen by God to rule in his name, exercised judicial authority over the Temple complex; documents were stored for safekeeping near the Temple, as was the practice in other temples. Oaths were pronounced in God's name, often in his presence, that is in the Temple (*Ex.* 21:7). Priests served as judges as well as cultic officiants, determining innocence or culpability according to a code of instruction (a *torah*), and the king was commanded to consult God's law in arriving at his judgments (*Dt.* 17:18–20). This set of functions is articulated in *Deuteronomy* 17:8f.:

> If a case is too baffling for you to decide . . . you shall

> promptly repair to the place which the Lord your God will have chosen, and appear before the Levitical priests, or the magistrate in charge at the time and present your problem.

Reference to the "the place which the Lord your God will have chosen" is *Deuteronomy*'s way of referring to the central temple of the land, ultimately identified as the Temple of Jerusalem.

Until soon before the Roman destruction of the Second Temple in 70, the Sanhedrin convened in a chamber of the inner Temple complex; around 30 CE it moved out to the portico, in the outer Temple area.

Sanctity. The Temple area itself was considered sacred space; this very ancient notion that certain spaces are sacred goes back to animism, the belief that power (or "life") is immanent in mountains, rivers, trees, and the like. Biblical statements on the subject of sanctity rarely (if ever) define it as immanent, but rather as property attributed to a certain place, object, person, act, or time. It was therefore important to know how and when a particular site had become sacred in the first place. A story or poem that relates how a place became sacred is known as *hieros logos,* and the Bible presents quite a few examples. A classic example is found in *Genesis* 28, which tells how Bethel, the major cult center of the northern kingdom of Israel, first achieved its sanctity: the partriarch Jacob once spent the night there and experienced a theophany.

The sanctity of Jerusalem is recounted in several biblical sources. In addition to the historiographies and oracles of *2 Samuel* 6 and 7 and the chronicle of *1 Kings* 8, a *hieros logos* in *2 Samuel* 24 relates that David, after fighting many battles, angered God by conducting a census and imposing new conscriptions and taxes on the already weary people of Israel. God's anger was unleashed in a plague that at the critical moment was stopped when David confessed his sinfulness. This confession took place in front of a threshing floor owned by Aravnah, the Jebusite, most probably the Canaanite ruler of Jerusalem. Realizing that the spot was propitious, David obeyed a prophetic order to worship the God of Israel there. He purchased the facility from Aravnah, as well as sacrifical animals, insisting on making full payment. He then offered sacrifices to God. In addition, the episode of Abraham and the king of Salem, Melchizedek (*Gn.* 14:18–20), has been interpreted as a veiled allusion to Jerusalem, in that Salem is traditionally equated with [Jeru]salem. This is further suggested by Psalm 110, wherein Melchizedek is praised and promised the priesthood of Zion.

In other words, biblical literature preserves stories about the sanctity of Jerusalem (and Zion) as the divinely chosen site for the Temple, just as it does for other similar sites, such as Bethel, Shiloh, and elsewhere. While these accounts seem to sanction changing political realities, in terms of religious phenomenology they explain the basis for the sanctity of certain "spaces." In the case of Jerusalem, we have an entire genre of psalms in which the divine selection of Jerusalem (Zion) is recounted (for example, Psalms 48, 78, and 122).

Historically, however, sites like Bethel were sacred to the Canaanites before sanctification by the Israelites, as is evident from the intensive archaeological excavations that have been carried out at Bethel, Shechem, and other sites. Information about pre-Israelite Jerusalem is less precise, but there are indications of cultic history there as well. The Israelites, notwithstanding their distinctive religion, were not averse to appropriating sacred space and worshiping the God of Israel where others had worshiped pagan gods. Sanctity of space seems to have cut across religious and national boundaries, and once attributed to a space, no matter by whom, such sanctity was permanent.

The Jerusalem Temple complex was a sacred space in which the farther one penetrated, the greater the sanctity, and, accordingly, the greater the restrictions on those who may enter and the greater the degree of purity required. Precise information is lacking on the "graduated" sanctity of the First Temple of the kind available on the Second Temple in its later period. The priestly writings of the Torah, projecting an elaborate system of purity and describing a Tabernacle with demarcated zones of graduated sanctity, may not have reflected the First Temple in detail, but rather the postexilic Temple. Nevertheless, it is quite certain that in principle there were, from the outset, limitations on who could enter the Temple, and there were rites of purification for all who desired entry. It is reasonable to conclude that only priests who were consecrated could enter the Temple, or stand in the courtyard near the Temple, although Judean kings may not have always respected this rule. Sacrificial animals and other materials used in worship had to conform to certain specifications; cult artifacts were also subject to specific standards, and in this connection the introduction of pagan or otherwise improper cult objects into the Temple or its courtyards defiled the sanctity of the Temple. Certain kings were guilty of such acts of defilement, and others—the more upright in God's sight—piously removed the improper cult objects from the Temple and its courts, thus restoring its condition of purity.

Whereas the preexilic prophets concentrated their denunciations on paganism and on social evils for which no ritual remedy existed (*Isaiah* 1 is a good example), early postexilic prophets, taking their cue from Jeremiah, Ezekiel, and "Second Isaiah," begin to attack the problem of defilement more pointedly. Thus, the *Book of Malachi* insists on ritual purity and quite explicitly condemns improper sacrifice. It is reasonable to place the elaborate priestly regimen of *Exodus, Leviticus,* and *Numbers* in the early postexilic period, when the Temple became the center of the restored Judean community, and certainly by the end of the fourth century the degree of ritual stringency with respect to sacred spaces had increased considerably, as can be gathered from *1* and *2 Chronicles,* and from passages of *Ezra* and *Nehemiah*—all literary products of that century.

This priestly tradition was the basis for the later rabbinic codification of law relating to the Temple and cult, preserved primarily in the Mishnah and other tannaitic sources. In other words, early rabbis utilized the complete Torah, drawing on it selectively to produce a regimen of purification. [*For further discussion, see* Rabbinic Judaism in Late Antiquity.]

With the changing designs of both the First and Second Temples of Jerusalem, progressively, the Temple and its inner courts were further protected or barricaded against the outside world by the addition of more walls, gates, and courtyards. Since a great deal is known about the Herodian temple, it is possible to be specific on the subject of "graduated" sanctity. The design of the structure prohibited entry to gentiles beyond a balustrade that encircled the inner Temple complex: this then was the first graduation. Such a restriction is actually presaged in principle in the priestly writings of the Torah; *Ezekiel* 44:63 is the first to mention explicit oppostion to the presence of gentiles within the Temple, in a passage that is exilic at the very earliest.

Within the compound open to all Jews, the next graduation pertained to the exclusion of women. There is no explicit evidence from preexilic sources that women were excluded from those areas of the Temple complex that were open to men. Even if the laws of *Leviticus* 12 are preexilic (which is less likely than some suppose), the exclusion would have affected menstruating women and new mothers, and only for a limited length of time. But little information exists on the status of women and sacred space until late in the postexilic period; it is known, however, that women were never considered legitimately acceptable as priests, although they undoubtedly served in that capacity under heterodox sponsorship.

The next graduation pertained to the priesthood itself. In the Herodian Temple complex, the court of Israel was not separated by a wall from the court of the priests, but probably by a marker. Opposed to the increasingly greater emphasis on purity was the ancient notion that the donor of the sacrifice, the Israelite who offered the gift to God, should "appear" before him and stand in his presence (*Ex.* 23:17). According to priestly law, the donor was to lay his hands upon the sacrifice (*Lv.* 1:4), so no wall or absolute barrier could stand between donor and altar.

Beyond the court of Israel was the court of the priests and the Temple itself. The shrine, the Holy of Holies, was out of bounds to priests, even to the high priest for the most part. Only when ritual purification of the Temple was obligatory could the high priest penetrate its space. We do not know how early in the biblical period the laws of *Leviticus* 16 detailing the purification of the Temple were in force, but prior to the end of the Persian period at the very latest there was an annual day of purification, Yom Kippur.

Following any defilement, purification of the Temple complex and its ground was both possible and necessary (*2 Kgs.* 18, 23; *1 Mc.* 1). Depending on the material of construction, many cultic vessels had to be destroyed, and sacrificial materials—meat and other foodstuffs—usually were not susceptible to purification and had to be likewise eliminated. Generally people could be purified, certainly as long as the Temple cult was in operation. Ultimately, the Temple complex and grounds withstood all the defilements recorded in literature and retained their sanctity through the ages.

Sanctification of space could also be affected by a ritual process, usually based on "mythic" models. At the first level, Israelites visited sites thought to be holy; in all cases, however, formal consecration was required. Jacob anointed the foundation stone of the temple at Bethel and offered sacrifices on an altar (*Gn.* 28). Usually there were specific recitations and celebrations, proclaiming the sanctity of the site; the process was then inverted and a myth created: it was declared that God had chosen the site and manifested himself there. But the myth was never quite sufficient, however, and communal sanctification was required.

Pilgrimage. There is no clearer demonstration of how the notion of sacred space worked than the religious pilgrimage. Important, often obligatory, the pilgrimage supported the belief that worshiping God at a sacred site is more efficacious than worship elsewhere.

In biblical Israel the three annual festivals—*matsot* in the early spring, the spring grain harvest, and the autumn fruit harvest—were all referred to as *ḥag,* which means "pilgrimage." On these occasions an Israelite was required to appear before God, bearing gifts, at a proper pilgrimage center (*Ex.* 23, 34). *1 Samuel* 1 tells the story of a family undertaking an annual pilgrimage to Shiloh, in the Ephraimite mountains. The occasion was not a scheduled religious festival but instead an annual clan gathering.

Throughout most of the preexilic period, there were temples and altars throughout the Land of Israel. An open-air cult site was called *bamah* ("high place") in Judaea and *maqom* ("cult site") in northern Israel. Political and demographic realities determined their relative prominence as pilgrimage centers. [*For discussion of pilgrimage by Jews to biblical sites, see* Pilgrimage, *article on* Contemporary Jewish Pilgrimage.]

Heterodoxy and Centralization of the Cult. Experience with local and regional temples, high places, and altars, both in Judah and in northern Israel, was usually troublesome from the point of view of piety because of the almost inevitable tendency to introduce pagan elements into the ritual. There were even temples dedicated to pagan gods. These trends were regularly denounced by the prophets, such as the northern Israelite Hosea. *1* and *2 Kings,* since they reveal a strong pro-Judahite bias, tell less about heterodoxy in Judah and Jerusalem, although there must have been similar problems there as well.

1 Kings 18:4 tells that Hezekiah, king of Judah after the fall of the northern kingdom of Israel, removed the *bamot.* However, no record of a follow-up exists, and historians assume that the efforts of this "upright" king were not effective, especially since, following Hezekiah, his son Manasseh, who reigned for many years, pursued a decidedly heterodox policy. The next attempt to remove the *bamot,* an issue that pervades *1* and *2 Kings,* was during the reign of Josiah (*2 Kgs.* 22, 23). In response to the horrendous execrations found in an old document that had been deposited in the Temple, Josiah closed down the local and regional cult sites in the towns of Judah, ordering all the priests to report to Jerusalem. He destroyed what remained of the temple and necropolis of Bethel, the major cult site of the erstwhile northern kingdom. Josiah further proclaimed a celebration of the paschal sacrifice in the Temple of Jerusalem for the first time, thereby altering in a basic way the relevance of what had been a domestic, clan-centered sacrifice.

To understand just how the site of the temples of Jerusalem eventually became the unique sacred space in Jewish religion, the background and consequences of Josiah's (and Hezekiah's) edicts need to be discussed. One of the major preoccupations of modern Bible scholarship has been to define the historical relationship between the events recorded in *2 Kings* 22 and 23 and the doctrine in *Deuteronomy* 12 and 16. The narrative setting of *Deuteronomy* is projected back into the presettlement period of Israelite history, a projection consistent with Torah traditon. Chapters 12 and 16 state that once the Israelites have securely settled in their land, they must discontinue their customary practice of offering sacrifice at cult sites throughout the land and paying tithes locally, and they must do all of these things only at a central temple, to be built in a town selected by God.

At first, modern scholars tended to regard this doctrine of cult centralization as a seventh-century Judahite movement, a reaction to the heterodox policies of Manasseh. H. L. Ginsberg (1982) has made a good case for regarding the core of *Deuteronomy,* wherein this doctrine is expounded, as the product of the mid- to late eighth century, in northern Israel. He compares the language of *Hosea* and *Deuteronomy,* showing the unique correspondences, and argues that the doctrine of cult centralization grew out of the extreme dissatisfaction of northern Israelite prophets and leaders with the cults of the many local altars operating there, and eventually with the major temples of Dan and Bethel as well. They sought a solution in the form of a new, central temple, perhaps in Shechem on Mount Gerizim, which was still sacred to the Samaritans. *Deuteronomy* never refers to Jerusalem, even by allusion, but after the fall of the northern kingdom, it was logical to identify the proper site of the central temple as Jerusalem and to evoke the myth of Jerusalem's selection by God. So, some forty years before the Babylonian destruction (c. 622), Josiah taught this doctrine by devout priests who had educated him, acted in fulfillment of *Deuteronomy's* doctrine. In the short run he probably failed to remove all local cult sites, but in the long run he succeeded.

The real motivations behind cult centralization as a means of control over religious worship can only be guessed at. From the beginning of the monarchy, there were at least two factions or "parties" in Judah and the northern kingdom: what Morton Smith (1971) called "the Yahveh-alone" party, and a party that accepted Yahveh as the national god of Israel but saw no reason not to allow (or even sponsor) worship of other gods as well.

In 587/6 the Babylonians conquered all of Judah and destroyed the Temple of Jerusalem. At that point religious life, both in the devastated land and among the exiles in Babylonia, Egypt, and elsewhere, could have gone one of two ways. Sacrificial worship might have been undertaken at substitute sites, which would have been the normal course. As it happened, Jewish leadership opposed substitute sites and insisted on a restoration theology—sacrifice would be resumed only at the site of a rebuilt Jerusalem Temple, as God had promised.

There were several Jewish temples in the Diaspora—the best known were one near Heliopolis, a suburb of

Cairo, and one at Aswan (Elephantine) in Upper Egypt. There is also evidence of temples in Transjordan and possibly elsewhere in the Land of Israel. But in the main the Jewish religious leadership during the exilic period opposed such worship, and a clue to this policy may be preserved in *Ezekiel* where the elders of Israel approached Ezekiel in Babylonia and apparently inquired of him as to whether it would be proper to erect an altar to the God of Israel while in exile. The unequivocal response of the prophet: only when God restores his people to his holy mountain and to the Land of Israel will he once again be worshiped by sacrifice. Meanwhile, God would be present among the exiles, and there was no need for a temple in exile (*Ez.* 20:40–44).

During the period of the Second Temple, the religious pilgrimage and support of the priesthood and cult of Jerusalem became mainstays of Jewish religious life throughout the expanding Diaspora. The statements in *Deuteronomy* about being distant from the central temple (*Dt.* 12:21) took on a new, somewhat pathetic interpretation: dispersed Jews must attend upon the cult of Jerusalem's Temple. *Tobit,* a pseudepigraphical work probably writen well before the Maccabean period, relates that Tobit made regular pilgrimages to Jerusalem and contributed hisdues to the Temple (*Tb.* 1). The Jewish military colony of Elephantine, active in the fifth century BCE, which had its own temple, nevertheless maintained a steady relationship to the Temple of Jerusalem, as is known from the archives of that community.

During the period of the Second Temple, the Jewish synagogue came into being as a local institution devoid of any cultic status, strictly speaking. Jews in Israel and Diaspora communities assembled at synagogues for prayer and the reading of sacred writ, to attend to communal matters, and to celebrate in their own way Sabbaths and festivals, while the cult of the Temple of Jerusalem was in full operation. [*See* Synagogue, *article on* History and Tradition.] The true and sufficient worship of the God of Israel took place in the Temple, and delegations of pilgrims were dispatched to Jerusalem to attend the offering of sacrifices as representatives of the far-flung communities (*Ta'an.*, chap. 4).

In *1 Kings* 8 great emphasis is placed on prayer and song as forms of religious devotion. Prayers are heard by God in heaven when recited at the Temple. Prayer assumed an importance it did not have in the preexilic Temple, although the psalms, many of them preexilic in origin, show evidence that prayer and sacrifice coexisted even in earlier periods. [*See* Psalms *and, for a cross-cultural discussion,* Music, *article on* Music and Religion in the Middle East.]

From praying "at" the Temple to praying elsewhere "toward" or "facing" it is a fascinating step in religious phenomenology, having relevance not only to postbiblical Judaism but to Christianity and Islam as well. Islam substituted Mecca for Jerusalem but insisted that in every mosque in the world the *qiblah* ("niche") be oriented toward a central spot, the focus of pilgrimage. Daniel, the wise seer of the exile, turned toward Jerusalem thrice daily when praying to God while in exile (*Dn.* 6:11).

Throughout the centuries, Jewish pilgrims attempted and often succeeded in visiting the site of the Temple in Jerusalem, but in fact Judaism accommodated itself to the loss of the Temple—to living without sacred space. It is still too soon to speculate on the effects upon the Jewish religion of the modern resettlement of Israel, except to take note of the renewed importance of sacred space, as identified with Jerusalem.

[*For a discussion of the centralization of the cult within the context of contemporary belief see* Israelite Religion.]

BIBLIOGRAPHY

Th. A. Busink's *Der Tempel von Jerusalem: Von Salomo bis Herodes,* 2 vols. (Leiden, 1970–1980), is the most exhaustive study, encyclopedic in nature, on the two temples of Jerusalem, providing discussion of everything from design and architecture to function, with numerous references to recent scholarly investigations. These volumes are replete with comparative evidence and are amply illustrated. The results of recent excavations in the area of the Temple mount are summarized, along with a survey of the physical history of Jerusalem by the leader of the excavations, Benjamin Mazar, in *The Mountain of the Lord* (Garden City, N.Y., 1975). This volume is well illustrated and synthesizes the archaeological and the textual evidence. It is popular in presentation but authentic. As a companion to Mazar's volume, the reader is referred to Nahman Avigad's *Discovering Jerusalem* (Nashville, 1983), a fascinating and well-illustrated report of the archaeologist's recent discovery of the upper city of Jerusalem, whose buildings, public and private, help to define the relation of the city to the Temples of Jerusalem, both in the preexilic and postexilic periods.

Henri Frankfort's *The Art and Architecture of the Ancient Orient* (New York, 1969) remains the most penetrating treatment of temple architecture and its relation to meaning and function in the ancient Near East. Using examples drawn from Syria—Mesopotamia and Egypt—Frankfort analyzes the physical development of major temples, and his insights shed light on the temples of Jerusalem as well.

On the subject of cult and ritual and the phenomenology of worship in biblical Israel, two works, based on differing methods, may be consulted: Menahem Haran's *Temples and Temple-Service in Ancient Israel* (Oxford, 1978) and my own *In the Presence of the Lord* (Leiden, 1974). A collection of studies on various forms of sacrifice and their religious significance is provided in Jacob Milgrom's *Cult and Conscience: The Asham and the Priestly Doctrine of Repentence* (Leiden, 1976). An earlier work, highly influential in its impact on present-day cultic studies, is G. B. Gray's *Sacrifice in the Old Testament* (1925), which I have reissued with a prolegomena (New York, 1971).

Recent encyclopedias offer informative "state of the field" investigations. The *Encyclopedia of Archaeological Excavations in the Holy Land,* 4 vols., edited by Michael Avi-Yonah (Englewood Cliffs, N.J., 1975–1978), is a heavily illustrated reference work that will lead the reader to information on the modern exploration of ancient sites in biblical lands.

The *Encyclopaedia Judaica,* 16 vols. (Jerusalem, 1971), contains many easily located and informative articles on Jerusalem, the Temple, cult and ritual, with extensive bibliography. For those who read Hebrew, volume 5 of the *Encyclopedia Biblica,* edited by Haim Beinart and Menahem Haran (Jerusalem, 1968), contains a series of articles by Menahem Haran and Samuel Yeivin under "Miqdash" that are unexcelled for sound scholarly judgment, breadth of view, and attention to detail.

Several specialized studies contribute to our understanding of the foundations of the two Temples of Jerusalem. The administration and funding of the Second Temple under the Seleucids is incisively clarified in Elias J. Bickerman's "Heliodore au Temple de Jerusalem," in his *Studies in Jewish and Christian History* (Leiden, 1976), pp. 151–191. The movement toward cult centralization, as reflected in *Deuteronomy,* is explored with new insights by H. L. Ginsberg in his *The Israelian Heritage of Judaism* (New York, 1982). Ginsberg traces this religious movement to northern Israel of the eighth century, and shows how it eventually overtook Judaea, as well. The political implications of the Temples and their priesthoods are investigated by Morton Smith in *Palestinian Parties and Politics That Shaped the Old Testament* (New York, 1971).

The phenomenology of the Temple as a house built for God is explored in my "On the Presence of the Lord in Biblical Religion," *Religions in Antiquity: Essays in Memory of Erwin Ramsdell Goodenough,* edited by Jacob Neusner (Leiden, 1970), pp. 71–87.

The reader will also want to consult ancient sources outside the Bible, referred to in this article. The best available English translation of the Mishnah is Herbert Danby's *Mishnah* (Oxford, 1933). The writings of the ancient historian Josephus Flavius, translated by Henry St. J. Thackeray and Ralph Marcus, are available in volumes 1–5 and 7 of the "Loeb Classical Library" (Cambridge, Mass., 1950–1961). *Apocrypha and Pseudepigrapha of the Old Testament,* 2 vols., edited by R. H. Charles (Oxford, 1913), includes such works as *Ben Sira. Aristeas to Philocrates,* or the *Letter of Aristeas,* has been edited and translated by Moses Hadas (New York, 1951). The *Ta'anit Scroll (Die Fastenrolle)* has been edited by Hans Lichtenstein in "Die Fastenrolle: Eine Untersuchung zur Judisch-Hellenistischen Geschichte," *Hebrew Union College Annual* 8–9 (1931–1932): 257–351. A newly discovered Hebrew document, named the Temple Scroll, dating from the pre-Herodian period, and containing plans for a Jewish temple and laws for its cult, has been published in a three-volume English edition, translated and edited by Yigael Yadin (Jerusalem, 1977).

BARUCH A. LEVINE

BINDING. The motif of binding is widespread in the history of religions, in both the so-called primitive religions and in the religions of both ancient and modern higher civilizations. Its many, complex transpositions, often quite original, vary according to the cultural milieu and the historical moment of which they are the expressions.

Drawing on extraordinarily rich examples taken from the most diverse civilizations, phenomenologists of religion have called attention to the enormous sacred potential that is polarized around acts of physical and symbolic binding, to the concretization of this potential in the form of knots, and to the importance of the opposing act of loosening a bond. In many traditional cultures, important mythical events are believed to be the result of the fastening or loosening of bonds. Actions of binding and loosing frequently occur at the center of rituals, both cultic rituals that involve superhuman beings, and autonomous rituals that are efficacious in themselves, such as the so-called rites of passage, rites of purification, and, above all, magic.

The agents of these actions of binding and loosing vary according to circumstances. They may be superhuman beings of the most diverse kinds, whether located at the time of origins (as, for example, the creator, the first man, the *dema,* the trickster, the culture hero, the totemic ancestor, and so on), or believed to be still acting in the present (as, for example, the supreme being, the earth mother, fetishes, spirits, ancestors, polytheistic gods, or the god of monotheistic religions). Or it may be ordinary mortals who bind and loose, especially those who belong to a specialized sacred group (priests, shamans, wizards, magicians, etc.). The materials with which the bond is made are extremely diverse but generally may be distinguished as either concrete or abstract. Equally numerous are the ends that the binding or loosing action is intended to serve, whether positive or negative. This variety has been well illustrated in the works of Arnold van Gennep, Gerardus van der Leeuw, and Mircea Eliade.

Scholarly interest in binding began in the first half of the nineteenth century, when scholars such as Jacob B. Listing (1847) and Peter Guthrie Tait (1879) became interested in the question of knots. It was James G. Frazer, however, who finally brought the problem to the attention of historians of religion in the first decade of the present century. In the wake of his studies of the concept of taboo and the binding action it exercised, Frazer (1911) saw the need to broaden the scope of his research to include the special type of restraint constituted by the bond as such, its varieties and its functions. Given Frazer's predominant interest in magic, it is not surprising that he interpreted bonds as magical impediments. Despite the problems involved with such an emphasis on the magical—itself inadequately conceived as prior to or even opposed to religion—Frazer's work had the merit of interpreting sacred bonds in terms of the specific historical circumstances in which they are found, showing that the significance of a bond is relative to the positive or negative nature of what it restrains. This latter aspect of Frazer's work unfortunately left little trace in the works of his successors, such as Isidor Scheftelowitz (1912) and Walter J. Dilling (1914). Today this historical dimension to the study of bonds and binding, initially opened up by the great English scholar, remains to be developed.

The less positive side of Frazer's theory, namely the emphasis on magic, has by contrast provided the direction for more recent studies. This can be seen in the case of Georges Dumézil. Dumézil's researches, carried out in the 1930s, were based upon studies of deities of the Vedic religion of ancient India, Varuṇa most especially, but also Mitra, Vṛtra, Indra, Yama, and Nirṛti. These deities were believed to possess snares or at least to be endowed with the ability to bind their enemies and ensnare evil human beings. Accepting the thesis of the magical value of binding *in toto* and uncritically, Dumézil identified a structure of magical binding within the royal function of ancient Indo-European culture, a function that was itself associated with magic.

Dumézil's findings were based largely on Indo-European cultures. A decade later, however, Eliade, in an elegant effort to reinterpret Dumézil's conclusions, demonstrated the presence of what he called the "binding complex" in other civilizations as well, both higher civilizations (for example, in the Semitic world) and in primitive ones, and on several different planes: cosmological, magical, religious, initiatory, metaphysical, and soteriological. Although he initially followed the Frazer-Dumézil line, Eliade soon departed from it, distancing himself from the conflicts over the presumed necessity of interpreting every binding action exclusively in terms of magic or in strict accordance with French trifunctionalism. Beyond the diverse historical forms assumed by the binding motif in the most diverse cultural surroundings, Eliade attempted to identify an archetypal form of binding that would find different realizations on an infinite variety of levels. In the process, he demonstrated that it was possible to interpret the various forms of binding in nonmagical terms. At the same time, however, his work was indicative of the problematic status that the question of binding continues to have in historical comparative studies. Although there are particular studies concerning this or that type of sacred bond that are founded on a rigorously historical basis, in general the scholarly world continues to address the issue merely on the phenomenological level, thereby leaving the question of the historical foundations of the binding motif unresolved.

On the properly historical level, however, it seems possible, and indeed necessary, to establish the precise relation between the sacred value of the bond and the type of reality that lies at the origin of this value; to explain why such a phenomenon arises, and under what circumstances.

The fact that sacred bonds are known in even the most archaic cultures suggests that we should seek an answer to these questions in primitive societies before confronting them on the level of higher civilizations, with their more abstract symbolism. To take only one example, an observation made by Raffaele Pettazzoni in his comparative study of the confession of sins contributes more to our understanding of the "snares" used by the Vedic god Varuṇa than does the sophisticated trifunctional theory of Dumézil. Pettazzoni noted how often primitive peoples try to concretize their sins in the form of knots, tied in various kinds of material (ropes, lianas, vegetable fibers, etc.). He went on to interpret the Vedic motif of binding as "the primitive idea of evil-sin as a fluid wrapping the sinner like the meshes of a net" (*La confessione dei peccati,* vol. 1, Bologna, 1929, p. 230).

It is characteristic of the religions of primitive peoples that sacred bonds, of whatever type they may be and whatever their function, are viewed in a way that is not at all dissimilar to the normal, concrete bonds used in the most varied circumstances of everyday life: the means by which a shaman attempts to "capture" the soul of a sick person to bring it back to the body is an ordinary lasso, of the type ordinarily used to stop a running animal or to prevent it from straying off. Similarly, among the Aranda, an ordinary rope represents the means by which the Tjimbarkna demons tie up at night men whom they want to harm. Akaanga, the lord of the dead for the Aranda inhabitants of Harvey Island, Australia, is believed to capture the deceased by means of a real net, of the kind used by fishermen. There are many such examples.

The same parallel between sacred and ordinary bonds is found in the mythologies of primitive peoples. Here the lassos, traps, nets, and so forth, with which the sun, moon, or clouds are captured, or with which one snares the spirits, are the same as those with which on other occasions poles are tied together in the construction of a hut, wild animals are captured, and fish caught. There is nothing extraordinary in these bonds, except for the increase in power that their use normally confers on the person who employs them.

These facts should lead us to reflect on the enormous

importance that fibers used for weaving and spinning, ropes, lassos, nets, and other means of binding have for peoples with a technology that is still at a rudimentary level. Such simple materials and implements are needed for the capture and domestication of animals, and for making weapons, garments, utensils, containers, pottery, and so on. These are the tools and instruments by which the labor potential of *homo faber* can be significantly increased beyond its natural limits, so as to enable the social group to establish greater control over reality, especially over those sectors that most closely concern economic interests and that would otherwise be too difficult to master. There is nothing strange, therefore, in the constant tendency of primitive cultures to transpose the techniques and the tools used to perform a binding action onto a superhuman level. The main goal of this transposition is to strengthen their supposedly extraordinary nature and to place their beneficial effects under the care of the supernatural beings who are often believed to be the source of these marvels. In this way their use can also be protected from possible risks by means of appropriate ritual practices.

Spinning and weaving provide numerous examples of such transposition. These techniques in particular involve the activity of binding and tying (one thinks of the countless loops, weaves, and knots to be found in even a tiny piece of fabric). For example, among the Bambara of Mali, the spindle and the batten, originally the possessions of Faro, the lord of the waters, were granted by him to human beings, whom he also instructed in their use. Thus the first work of a weaver cannot be used, but must be thrown into the river in honor of the superhuman being. The Dogon, on the other hand, link the invention of spinning and weaving directly with the myth of the origin of the world. Among the Ashanti various sacred precautions are taken to protect weaving. It is usually exclusively reserved for men, or else for women who have passed menopause; the work cannot be begun or finished on Friday, the day on which, according to tradition, the use of weaving had been introduced into the land; menstruating wives of weavers must not touch the loom or speak to their husband for the entire duration of the period of impurity; and in the case of adultery with another weaver, a goat must be sacrificed on the loom. In the so-called weaving schools found among the Maori of New Zealand, the technical procedures and the sacred practices are taught at the same time. The sacred practices must be scrupulously observed throughout the work in order to increase the weaver's skill. Weavers must be initiated into the profession by a priest, and are required to follow various alimentary taboos and protect their work from the harmful gaze of strangers, in order to prevent the loss of their own inventiveness and mastery. [*See* Webs and Nets.]

In addition to spinning and weaving, other specific binding actions, such as the working of fibers and wicker to produce ropes, baskets, nets, traps, and so forth, are projected onto the sacred plane. In the beginning they are the exclusive property of superhuman beings of various kinds, who decide at a certain point to transmit the practice to human beings. The Athapascan-speaking Wailaki of northwestern California relate that the culture hero Kettanagai taught people to weave ropes, baskets, and fishing nets after the flood. Among the Diegueño of southern California the art of working wicker through weaving was included in the comprehensive knowledge that exploded from the head of the primordial serpent and spread throughout the world. The Hopi, for their part, maintain that Spider Woman, a superhuman being connected for several reasons with spiders, and who had directly collaborated in creation, taught the Indians to spin and weave cotton. Among the eastern Pomo (north central California), Marunda first created men by weaving his own hair and, immediately thereafter, wicker; he then taught the art of working wicker to humanity.

The ever closer relationship that is being established by the comparative history of religions between the sphere of work and the sphere of the sacred in the explanation of the activity of binding may furnish us with the possibility of going back to quite precise and concrete historical roots, and to the corresponding economic substrata of all types of bonds, temporarily bypassing the complex and sophisticated symbolism with which they are often associated in higher civilizations. This more complex symbolism, once condemned to obscurity through the now outmoded label of "magical," may itself finally find a more fitting, definite, and substantial clarification.

Thus we may expect to find that behind the "snares" so skillfully manipulated by this or that god in the Indo-European, Indo-Iranian, or Semitic areas (zones with a pastoral economy in antiquity) in order to prevent deviations from the just order of things stand the actual snares (or lassos) with which the society of primitive stockbreeders, during their continual migrations in search of new pastures, maintained control over their herds, the almost unique source of their subsistence. Snares stood, therefore, as a precious guarantee of the proper course of reality.

[*See also* Knots.]

BIBLIOGRAPHY

For research on the extent to which binding is associated with religious activity, three works dating from the 1910s are still indispensable: James G. Frazer's *The Golden Bough*, 3d ed., rev. & enl., vol. 3, *Taboo and the Perils of the Soul* (London, 1911); Isidor Scheftelowitz's *Das Schlingen- und Netzmotiv im Glauben und Brauch der Völker* (Giessen, 1912); and Walter J. Dilling's "Knots," in the *Encyclopaedia of Religion and Ethics*, edited by James Hastings, vol. 7 (Edinburgh, 1914). Rich in examples of the use of sacred bonds are Arnold van Gennep's *Les rites de passage* (Paris, 1909), translated as *The Rites of Passage* (Chicago, 1960); Gerardus van der Leeuw's *Phänomenologie der Religion* (Tübingen, 1933), translated as *Religion in Essence and Manifestation*, rev. ed. (New York, 1963); and Mircea Eliade's *Patterns in Comparative Religion* (New York, 1958). More detailed studies are two now-classic works of Georges Dumézil, *Ouranós-Váruṇa* (Paris, 1934) and *Mitra-Varuṇa*, 4th ed. (Paris, 1948), and Mircea Eliade's "The 'God Who Binds' and Symbolism of Knots," in his *Images and Symbols: Studies in Religious Symbolism* (New York, 1961), chap. 3.

Reinterpretations of the concept of magic in rigorously historical terms can be found in *Il mondo magico*, by Ernesto de Martino (Turin, 1948), and in *Magia: Studi di storia delle religioni in memoria di Raffaela Garosi*, edited by Paolo Xella et al. (Rome, 1976). Enrico Cerulli discusses the sublimation at the sacred level of the arts of spinning and weaving in "Industrie e tecniche," in *Ethnologica*, vol. 2, *Le opere dell'uomo*, edited by Vinigi Grottanelli (Milan, 1965). On the theme of binding action and bonds, see both Raffaele Pettazzoni's *Miti e leggende*, 4 vols. (Turin, 1948–1963), and G. M. Mullett's *Spider Woman Stories* (Tucson, 1979).

GIULIA PICCALUGA
Translated from Italian by Roger DeGaris

BIOGRAPHY. The subject here is best termed *sacred biography*, which most precisely designates the written accounts of lives of persons deemed to be holy, although its usage is extended also to oral traditions concerning such figures. The reason for allowing this wider usage is clear: in most contexts it was oral traditions that not only preceded but also largely shaped the later, written versions. The category of sacred biography is bounded on one side by mythology—that is, narratives concerning gods and other beings thought to be supernatural—and on the other side by biography, efforts to reconstruct credible accounts of the lives of ordinary human beings. It might also be defined as a genre that mixes myth and biography: unlike the former, its subjects are held even today to have actually lived but, unlike the latter, the received versions of their lives are often heavily mythologized. [*See also* Oral Tradition; Myth; *and* Hero, The.]

Whereas mythology will usually tell only of random deeds of deities in a largely episodic and nonconsecutive manner, the subjects of a sacred biography will tend to be treated as persons whose life stories need to be told as discrete and continuous lives. The subject of a sacred biography will tend to be treated as someone whose life story can be told from birth to death and, to that degree at least, as it would be treated in a secular biography. The difference from the latter, however, lies in the degree to which such a subject will be represented as carrying out a divinely planned mission, being the possessor of a "call" or visions authenticating such a mission, and having either infallible knowledge or supernatural powers. Individual instances of this genre differ in the degree to which they exemplify either the empirical or the mythological sides of the spectrum, but some degree of combination is present in all. Most sacred biographies are written either about the founders of the major religions or about saints—in which case this rubric overlaps with hagiography. In order to illustrate the genre our consideration here will focus upon sacred biographies of the founders. [*For discussion of saints, see* Sainthood.]

History of the Designation "Sacred Biography." The detection or designation of sacred biography as a genre of oral and written literature with its own structure and rules was initially a concomitant of that nineteenth-century scholarship which, under the aegis of positivist expectations and the use of an objective historical method, had sought to disentangle the incontrovertible "facts" of the life of Jesus of Nazareth from the overlay both of pious fabrications and christological dogma. The intention of this process of winnowing and reconstruction was captured best in Albert Schweitzer's phrase "the quest of the historical Jesus." [*See* Jesus *and the biography of Schweitzer.*] To some extent Schweitzer's work, while not terminating the search for verifiable facts, did signal the end of the nineteenth-century scholars' confidence that they could simply circumvent or dispense with the piety and Christology of the early Christian community and thereby disclose the "facts" of Jesus' life. When twentieth-century scholarship abandoned that part of the earlier "quest," it became possible to see that the Gospels are not merely flawed or failed biographies but a form of devotional literature of the early church, and, to that extent, examples of a genre with its own intentions and norms. As a result scholars came to see the rubric of sacred biography as discrete and legitimate for the first time. They recognized that the documents in question ought not merely to be sifted through for the purpose of separating fact from fiction, but that they had to be subjected to the more sophisticated type of analysis known as "form criticism."

With this perspective such studies could also become comparative and cross-cultural for the first time. Important in this development was Martin Dibelius's *Die Formgeschichte des Evangeliums* (Tübingen, 1919), translated as *From Tradition to Gospel* (New York, 1935). Dibelius referred to a "law" at work in such biographies and noted that there existed "many points of agreement between Buddha-legends and Jesus-legends" as well as between the saints of otherwise very different traditions. He claimed that this was a "law of biographical analogy leading to formulations constantly renewed" rather than a pattern that arose from cultural borrowing or diffusion. As examples he noted that various traditions separately articulate "a fixed idea of the life of the holy man: such a man may neither be born nor die without the significance of the event being proclaimed from heaven." Likewise his calling is announced in his youth and he has divine powers at his disposal throughout his life.

Although Dibelius arrived at this formulation through his analysis of the literary form of the Christian Gospels, his attribution of intrinsic value to sacred biography implicitly recognized that the early Christian community had quite properly had the decisive role in shaping the account of the life of Jesus according to its own ideals and expectations; modern scholars neither could nor should simply circumvent the contributions of the church in an attempt to reconstruct an "objective" biography of its founder.

This shift in attitude coincided with the embryonic development of the sociology of religion. [*See* Sociology.] Joachim Wach interpreted and applied Max Weber's concept of charisma and its routinization in his *Sociology of Religion* (Chicago, 1944). He discussed in some detail the founders of the great religions and took note that the term *founder* "does not denote any intrinsic quality or activity of the personality but refers to the historical and sociological effect of his charisma." He went on to state that "virtually all the founders became objects of religious veneration themselves." Although Wach tended to give causal priority to the founder and his teaching, he went further than others before him in recognizing an element of *reciprocal* generation in this phenomenon: at least in a sociological sense, the religious community creates its founder almost as much as the founder creates the community. Therefore, the message of the founder will often tend to be "implemented by miraculous acts, such as healing, feeding, transforming matter, etc." In this "hagiographical development" will be illustrated "the specific personal charisma which designates the man of God in an unmistakable and uninterchangeable way."

Wach, who brought a detailed knowledge of many religious traditions to his comparative efforts, tried as much as possible to retain the particularity of the separate traditions. His focus on the social matrix of religious traditions also led him to emphasize the relationship that each founder of a major religion had to his own circle of disciples. His 1924 essay on this topic shows how central it was in his thinking (Eng. trans., "Master and Disciple: Two Religio-Sociological Studies," *Journal of Religion* 42, 1962, pp. 1–21). The importance of this essay is that it reconstructs the psychological and social interaction between a master and his disciples—precisely the element that would seem to have frequently been the prelude to a later mythic embellishment of the deceased master's life in the form of sacred biography.

Although Mircea Eliade did not specifically elaborate a new theory of sacred biography, his discussions of the paradigmatic and exemplary nature of sacred time had a deep impact upon many scholars working on biographical materials of the past. This influence is clearly evident in the most comprehensive study of this topic to date, namely, *The Biographical Process: Studies in the History and Psychology of Religion*, edited by Frank E. Reynolds and Donald Capps (The Hague, 1976).

Sacred Biography and the Great Founders. The crucial importance of the concept of sacred biography in modern scholarship is that it has forced attention to certain kinds of materials that had tended to be slighted, dismissed, or regarded as uninteresting to intellectual historians and positivist text critics. It acknowledges that the formation of the major religions and religiously based philosophies was not merely the result of individual geniuses and their ideas but equally the product of social groupings and the projection of their shared ideals onto that person who, precisely through this reciprocity, was coming to be regarded as the "founder" of the new community. In the section above we looked at the process through which the Christian Gospels came to be gradually recognized as such a form of sacred biography. But a similar process was present in the formation of the received "lives" of the founders of the other major religions as well, and we focus here upon the Buddha, Muḥammad, and Confucius by way of illustration.

Although the scholarly study of Buddhism in nineteenth-century Europe made great strides in linguistic and textual matters, the recognition of the received biographies of the Buddha as a form of sacred biography was comparatively late. [*See* Buddha.] The reason for this was that scholarship on the life of the Buddha tended to oscillate between the two positions just beyond the boundaries of the sacred biography spectrum: pure mythology on one side and "factual" biography on the other. Advocates of the former, scholars working mostly with Sanskrit texts, saw the Buddha's life story as a variety of myth—solar myth in this case. The two principal proponents of this view were Émile Senart in his *Essai sur la légende du Bouddha, son caractère et ses origines* (Paris, 1882) and Hendrik Kern in his *Der Buddhismus und seine Geschichte in Indien* (Leipzig, 1882–1884). Their position was strenuously opposed by T. W. Rhys Davids and others in England who, working with and usually trusting the antiquity and reliability of the newly discovered Pali texts, were convinced that, with the carrying out of requisite analyses, the authentic life of the Buddha could be extracted from these sources. Although their materials were many and various, the scholars of the London school of Pali studies saw their task as different from that of their counterparts working on the life of Jesus, inasmuch as the Pali texts tended to present the Buddha—especially in his adult years—as an unparalleled but fully human teacher, not as an incarnate deity performing miracles. In that sense their texts themselves resembled ordinary biography much more than mythology.

Posed in this way between the alternatives of myth on one side and ordinary biography on the other, scholars working on the life of the Buddha had difficulty recognizing the presence and integrity of sacred biography in their texts. Only with the collapse of the solar-myth hypothesis and the gradual recognition that the Pali sources were more complex and mythicized than had been previously assumed did it finally become possible to see the life of the Buddha as a variety of sacred biography. Edward J. Thomas's *The Life of Buddha as Legend and History* (London, 1927) makes some tentative steps in that direction. By the middle of the twentieth century scholars had generally accepted the fact that, even though the Buddha had existed and had lived within a detectable time frame, it was impossible to ignore the role that the ideals of the early *saṃgha* (the Buddhist order) had played in shaping and elaborating the received narratives of their founder's life. To that extent the impassable presence of sacred biography has been recognized even though individual scholars differ considerably in their analyses of the process of its composition and its movement from oral tradition to scripture. [*See also* Buddhist Literature.]

Once the sacred biographies of the Buddha could be seen not merely as excrescences to be scaled off but as research topics with their own intellectual importance, the relationship of these to the specific cultural matrix of India could be studied as well. In particular, the Indian presupposition that life involves multiple lives could be positively assessed: the Jātakas, tales of the earlier lives of the Buddha, could be studied as part of the later sacred biographical tradition.

Quite soon after the death of Muḥammad in 632—at least by the eighth century—biographies appeared that demonstrated the growing tendency to idealize the Prophet as sinless and capable of performing miracles. [*See* Muḥammad.] Throughout most subsequent history the received accounts of the life of Muḥammad were clearly in the genre of sacred biography. Beginning with William Muir's *The Life of Mahomet and History of Islam, to the Era of Hegira* (London, 1861), this view was challenged, especially by Ignácz Goldziher's *Muhammedanische Studien* (Halle, 1888–1890). The Qur'ān itself was subjected to analyses in order to locate reliable data for the reconstruction of what European scholars regarded as a verified account of the life of Muḥammad. This was much to the consternation of Muslims, for whom the Qur'ān is special and divinely derived revelation, not a source among other sources for a critical study of the Prophet's life. The first reaction to this approach on the part of Muslim scholars themselves came in the last quarter of the nineteenth century in the form of many new biographies of Muḥammad, works clearly intended to state the facts of his life correctly from within the faith-framework of Islam. Although these biographies did tend to stress the prophetic in Muḥammad's life and to play down the miraculous, to many Western scholars they nevertheless seem continuous in some sense with the classical sacred biographies' tendency to idealization.

Within this context the study of sacred biographies of Muḥammad has been relatively difficult. Tor Andrae, best known for his *Mohammed: The Man and His Faith* (London, 1936), contributed earlier and substantially to this topic in his *Die person Muhammeds in lehre und glauben seiner gemeinde* (Stockholm, 1918). Distinguished by its skillful use of comparative materials, Andrae's book amply demonstrated the growth of legends that formed over time around the person of the Prophet—so much so that as a superhuman exemplary figure he eventually came to have status almost equal to that of the Qur'ān for some Muslims. More recent studies include *Divine Word and Prophetic Word in Early Islam* by William A. Graham (Paris, 1977), a work that uses and adapts Mircea Eliade's conception of "sacred time" to insist that later Muslims looked back on the whole period of Muḥammad's life as such a paradigmatic age even though it was historical time as well. Graham notes that, although passages in the Qur'ān distinguish mortal Muḥammad from immortal God, the tradition also includes materials showing that "the divine authority of [Muḥammad's] role as God's Apostle was a major factor in the tendency to divinize his person" and that as such he became "the paradigm for Muslim life" (p. 23). In an important essay Earle H. Waugh focuses upon later (Ṣūfī) materials but also uses Eliade's studies of shamanism to analyze the legends concerning Muḥammad's Miʿrāj as a form of shamanic ascension. He also explores the exemplary role of these legends in the spiritual life of individual Ṣūfīs ("Following the Beloved: Muhammed as Model in the Ṣūfī Tradition," in Reynolds and Capps, 1976, pp. 63–85). Perhaps what makes the study of sacred biography in the Islamic tradition both difficult and fascinating is the fact that its very existence—suggesting as it does the apotheosis of the founder—could only exist and develop in some state of tension with Islamic orthodoxy's insistence upon the uncompromisable transcendence of God.

The study of sacred biography as it exists in the Chinese cultural context has presented scholars with very different kinds of problems. Because there remain serious questions about any historical fact underlying the accounts of the life of Lao-tzu, the reputed founder of Taoism, it is best here to restrict our consideration to Confucius (511–479 BCE). [*See* Confucius.] If sacred biography is characterized by the forging together of myth and history, accounts of the life of Confucius certainly tend to remain closer to the history side of this combination. In addition, since the *Analects (Lun-yü)* clearly shows that Confucius himself turned attention away from the gods and spirits and toward man and society, modern scholars, sensing this way of thought to be remarkably consonant with the temper of the modern West, have tended to find the subsequent sacralization of Confucius within China to be intellectually uninteresting at best and reprehensible at worst. It is not incidental, therefore, that the latter of these views informs the approach taken in what remains to date the most important and influential biographical study, H. G. Creel's *Confucius: The Man and the Myth* (New York, 1949), republished as *Confucius and the Chinese Way* (New York, 1960).

There was indeed a tradition of sacred biography that grew up around the figure of Confucius, but his apotheosis was shaped by distinctly Chinese cultural norms. This is shown in the fact that the Master's apotheosis was expressed through the extension of his sagacity rather than his power; in a work such as the *K'ung-tzu chia yü* (Discourses of the Confucian School) of the third century BCE, Confucius is presented as infallible, not as a miracle worker. In a similar fashion the *Tso chuan,* which was composed around 300 BCE, attributes to him not supernatural deeds but knowledge of arcane and supernatural matters—things that seem rather far removed from the Confucius of the *Analects.* Also in the *Tso chuan* his lineage is presented as derived from that of the Sage-Kings of archaic times; some scholars such as D. C. Lau (in his translation *The Analects,* London, 1979) do not find this exceptionable, but Creel judged it to be so. If it was, in fact, part of the developing sacred biography of Confucius, it also shows the imprint of the pattern of the culture. In subsequent centuries, especially in the writings of what was called the New Text school, Confucius was viewed as having received a mandate from Heaven and was often also treated as a supernatural being (See Donald J. Munro's *The Concept of Man in Early China,* Stanford, 1969, p. 40).

The cult of Confucius increased over the centuries, often to the neglect of his writings. As late as the early twentieth century K'ang Yü-wei (1858–1927) advocated Confucianism as a state religion for China. Although much less work has been done on Confucius than on the other founders considered above, the tradition of reverence for him as a founder presents difficult but important problems for any theory of the nature of sacred biography. It demonstrates that, whatever tendency may exist for sacred biography to develop around a figure who comes to be recognized as a religious founder, that development occurs in distinctive *cultural* patterns. Confucius's life is certainly presented as a paradigmatic one, but he is the exemplar of the teacher and sage. There seem to be specific cultural restraints—perhaps even derived from the doctrinal content of the *Analects* itself to the exfoliation of the mythic dimension in this case. Wach's explication of the master-disciple relationship may well be the most useful methodological tool to apply in connecting the sacred biographies of Confucius with those of the other founders of the great religions.

Recent Directions in Scholarship. Current scholarship shows a marked tendency to focus upon the varieties of sacred biographical composition found within a specific cultural context. The research tradition that began it all—namely, the one initially concerned with the Gospels and the quest for the historical Jesus—remains in the forefront in terms of detailed and innovative studies. The scope has been widened to include a variety of types of hagiography and sacred biography found throughout the Hellenistic period extending to late antiquity. Although Eliade's point about sacred biographies being paradigmatic and exemplary is widely accepted and employed, there is increasing attention to both intertextuality in these matters and to the particularity of special kinds of idealized figures within a given cultural context. One example is the hypothesis that there exists a connection between the Gospels and the aretalogies of the Greco-Roman period—proposed especially by Morton Smith in his "Prolegomena to a Discussion of Aretalogies, Divine Men, the Gospels, and Jesus" (*Journal of Biblical Literature* 90, 1971, pp. 174–199) and Jonathan Z. Smith in his "Good News Is No News: Aretalogy and Gospel" (in *Christianity, Judaism, and Other Greco-Roman Cults,* edited by Jacob Neusner, Leiden, 1975, vol. 1, pp. 21–38).

Also important is the growing attention to the combination of religious with sociopolitical aspirations in every specific community that projected its ideals onto its founder or its saints. Not only the specific social matrix of the community that shaped its sacred biographies but also the history of such popular piety deserves attention. In his critique of the "two-tiered model" that has long relegated popular piety to the inferior status of something that is always and everywhere the same, Peter Brown (*The Cult of the Saints: Its Rise and Function in Latin Christianity,* Chicago, 1981) charts a direction that could be profitably followed by students of sacred biography generally. Another important new study—again focused on the Greco-Roman world—is Patricia Cox's *Biography in Late Antiquity: A Quest for the Holy Man* (Berkeley, 1983). Especially valuable is her discussion of paradigms of the divine sage in that period.

Aside from Frank E. Reynolds and Donald Capps's *The Biographical Process* and Michael A. William's *Charisma and Sacred Biography* (1982), real comparative work on this genre seems nonexistent in recent literature. (This is in keeping with the concentration of recent studies upon intertextuality and the continuities within a specific cultural area.) Perhaps after this phase of scholarship has attained its objectives, new energies and techniques can again be directed toward comparative work on sacred biography.

[*See also* Autobiography.]

BIBLIOGRAPHY

Brown, Peter. *The Making of Late Antiquity.* Cambridge, Mass., 1978.

Dungan, David L., and David R. Cartlidge, eds. and trans. *Sourcebook of Texts for the Comparative Study of the Gospels.* 4th ed. Missoula, Mont., 1974. See part 1, "Selections of Popular Religious Biographies."

Hadas, Moses, and Morton Smith. *Heroes and Gods: Spiritual Biographies in Antiquity.* Freeport, N.Y., 1970.

Jaspers, Karl. *Socrates, Buddha, Confucius, Jesus: The Paradigmatic Individuals.* New York, 1962.

Reynolds, Frank E., and Donald Capps, eds. *The Biographical Process: Studies in the History and Psychology of Religion.* The Hague, 1976. Includes an extensive bibliography on this and related topics. See especially Joseph M. Kitagawa's "Kūkai as Master and Savior" (pp. 319–341) and my "The Death and 'Lives' of the Poet-Monk Saigyō: The Genesis of a Buddhist Sacred Biography" (pp. 343–361).

Scholem, Gershom. *Sabbatai Sevi: The Mystical Messiah, 1626–1676.* Princeton, 1973.

Waugh, Earle H. "Images of Muḥammad in the Work of Iqbal: Tradition and Alterations." *History of Religions* 23 (1983): 156–168.

Williams, Michael A., ed. *Charisma and Sacred Biography.* Chico, Calif., 1982.

Wright, Arthur F. "Biography and Hagiography: Huei-chiao's Lives of Eminent Monks." In *Silver Jubilee Volume of the Zinbun-Kagaku-Kenkyūsho,* pp. 383–432. Kyoto, 1954.

Wright, Arthur F. "Sui Yang-Ti: Personality and Stereotype." In his *Confucianism and Chinese Civilization,* pp. 158–187. New York, 1964.

William R. LaFleur

BIRDS are primarily the epiphanies of the gods and spirits, but they also appear as messengers of the heavenly divine beings. They announce new situations in advance and serve as guides. Moreover, birds symbolize man's soul or spirit as it is released from the body in ecstasy or in death; the bird is a symbol of absolute freedom and transcendence of the soul from the body, of the spiritual from the earthly. Hence, a bird is often associated with divinity, immortality, power, victory, and royalty.

Birds and bird-masked figures are clearly attested as early as the Paleolithic period. In the cave painting at Lascaux in the Dordogne, dating from approximately 15,000 BCE, a bird-masked person is depicted as falling backward before a bison confronting him. At his feet lies his spear-thrower, and the spear that he has discharged has pierced the bison's body. Quite close to them is a bird perched on a pole. Most scholars interpret this scene as depicting a hunting tragedy: wearing a bird mask, the hunter has been killed by the bison. The mask may have been used as a device to enable the hunter to approach his prey without being noticed. The bird on a pole may represent the soul of the dead man or the totem and mythical ancestor of the tribe to which he belongs. For other scholars, the scene presents the shamanic trance. The man wearing a bird mask is a shaman; he lies unconscious while his soul has departed for the ecstatic journey to the world beyond. A companion on this spiritual journey is his helping spirit, here symbolized by the bird on a pole. The bison is possibly a sacrificial animal.

Although it is still uncertain whether shamanism originated in the Paleolithic period, birds undoubtedly occupy a very important place in the spiritual world of hunters generally and of northern Eurasia in particular, where shamanism has been a dominant magico-religious force. In fact, the shaman of Inner Asia and Siberia receives help from the spirits of wild animals and birds when undertaking an ecstatic journey. Bird spirits (especially those of geese, eagles, owls, and crows) descend from heaven and enter the shaman's body to inspire him as he beats his drum, wearing the shamanic costume of the bird type. Otherwise, they move into his drum or sit on his shamanic costume. This is precisely when shamanic ecstasy occurs; the shaman is transformed into a spiritual being, a bird in his inner experience. He moves, sings, and flies like a bird; his soul leaves the body and rises toward the heavens, accompanied by bird spirits. This motif of the ascending bird spirit has been revalorized by Taoism on a new spiritual plane: in the *Chuang-tzu*, dating from the third century BCE, for example, a huge bird named P'eng appears as the symbol of the soaring spirit that enjoys absolute freedom and is emancipated from mundane values and concerns. When a shaman dies among the Yakuts, the Tunguz, and the Dolgans, it is customary to erect on his tomb poles or sticks with a wooden bird at each tip. The bird symbolizes the soul of the departed shaman.

Birds appear in the myths of creation that center on the theme of the cosmogonic dive or the earth diver. In the beginning, when only the waters exist, aquatic birds (ducks, swans, geese, or swallows) dive to the bottom of the primeval ocean to fetch a particle of soil. Birds dive sometimes by God's order and sometimes by their own initiative, but in some variants God transforms himself into a bird and dives. This motif of the diving bird, common among such Altaic peoples as the Buriats and the Yakuts, is also found among the Russians and such Uralic peoples as the Samoyeds, the Mansi, the Yenisei, and the Mari. Earth divers also appear in a certain number of Indian cosmogonic myths of North America. The result of the courageous dive is always the same: a small particle of soil that has been brought up grows miraculously until it becomes the world as it is today. In Finnish and Estonian cosmogonic myths, God flies down as a bird onto the primeval ocean and lays on it the cosmic eggs from which the world emerges. This motif is also found in Indonesia and Polynesia.

Myths of kingship in northern Eurasia are often imbued with the symbolism of birds. According to the Mongolians, a golden-winged eagle gave them the *yasa*, or basic rules of life on the steppes, and helped them to establish the foundation of the Mongol empire by installing Chinggis Khan on the royal throne. Japanese myths tell how a crow (or raven) and a golden kite flew down as messengers of the heavenly gods and served Jimmu, the first mythical emperor of Japan, as guides in his march through the mountains to Yamato, where he established his imperial dynasty. The Hungarians have the tradition that the Magyars were guided by a giant *turul* (falcon, eagle, or hawk) into the land where Árpád founded the Hungarian nation. The *turul* is known as the mythical ancestor of the Árpáds.

These myths of creation and kingship reveal the prominent role played by birds in the formation of the cosmic order. As an epiphany of a god, demiurge, or mythical ancestor, a bird appears in the beginning of the world, and its appearance serves as an announcement of the creation of the universe, of the alteration of the cosmic structure, or of the founding of a people, a dynasty, or a nation. The eagle in Siberia, as well as the raven and thunderbird in North America, is especially invested with the features of the culture hero. Often described as the creator of the world, the bird is the divine being who familiarizes the people with knowledge and techniques, endows them with important cultural inventions, and presents them with the rules of life and social institutions.

In the ancient Near East and the Greco-Mediterranean world, birds are charged with a complex of symbolic meanings. Here, as elsewhere, the bird is essentially an epiphany of deity. In the Near East the dove usually symbolizes the goddess of fertility by whatever name she is known, and in Greece it is especially an epiphany of Aphrodite, the goddess of love. The eagle is a manifestation of the solar deity, as is clearly illustrated by the winged sun disks of Mesopotamia and later of Persia. The eagle is often represented as engaged in fighting with the snake or dragon. This archaic motif, attested in the Near East, India, and the southern Pacific, shows the tension that exists between the celestial solar principle and that of the maternal chthonic forces, but it also reveals man's inextinguishable aspiration for universal oneness or wholeness, which can be achieved by the cooperation and synthesis of conflicting powers.

The bird, and particularly the dove, often symbolizes love as an attribute of the goddess of fertility. In the cults of Dumuzi and Adonis, the goddess appears as a mother who laments over her son's captivity in the underworld and descends there to rescue him, to raise him from the dead. It is possible that the dove's moaning contributed to making it the special symbol of the goddess of love in the ancient Near East. In Greece the dove is an epiphany of divinity, but divinity in its amorous aspect, as can be seen from the dove's association with Aphrodite. In the Greco-Mediterranean world the dove has never lost this erotic connotation.

The eagle, the king of birds, is inseparably associated with royalty as well as with the solar deity. Indeed, royalty has never severed its symbolic ties with the sun and the eagle. In the Near East certain coins depict Hellenistic kings wearing a tiara with a pair of eagles on it facing the sun between them. In utilizing these symbols, the kings declare that they are divine by nature or deified. The divinity of the Roman emperor is expressed through the symbolism of Sol Invictus ("the invincible sun") and the eagle.

More generally, birds in the ancient Near East also signify the immortal souls of the dead. This celebrated image seems to have survived in Islam, where it is believed that the souls of the dead will remain as birds until the Day of Judgment. In Greece, images of the dove on graves may symbolize the soul of the departed, the divinity coming to help the departed, or the soul now in divine form. In Syria, the eagle depicted on tombs is the psychopomp, who leads the soul of the deceased to heaven. On Egyptian tombs the soul of the dead is represented as an androcephalic bird. However, soul birds (hawks, ducks, or geese) in Egypt have more than one function, usually in connection with the mummy. Certainly they are immortal souls, but they also symbolize divine presence and protection; birds bring all sorts of nourishment to the corpse to revive it. Thus in Egypt as elsewhere, the bird is both the soul of the departed and the divinity, regardless of what bird is depicted. The peacock, which in the Greco-Roman world may have symbolized man's hope for immortality, is of Indian origin. In Buddhism not only the peacock but also the owl and many other birds appear as epiphanies of the Buddhas and *bodhisattvas*, preaching the message of enlightenment and compassion. The *bodhisattva* Mayūrāsana, for example, is usually portrayed riding on a peacock.

In Judaism the dove and the eagle, the two most important birds, seem to have kept much the same symbolic values intact although they have been given specific Jewish colorings. The dove depicted on Jewish tombstones, in the wall paintings of Jewish catacombs, and on the ceilings of synagogues signifies Israel the beloved of God, the individual Israelite, or the salvation and immortality given to the faithful by God. In rabbinic tradition, too, the dove symbolizes not only the soul departing at death, but especially Israel the beloved. Moreover, the dove serves as the psychopomp. The eagle is equally multivalent; it is an epiphany of God or the power of God, but it is symbolic also of man's hope for eternal life and immortality.

The Christian symbolism of the dove and the eagle has also undergone a process of revalorization. The dove signifies the Holy Spirit in the baptism of Jesus, but it also becomes the erotic and impregnating force in the Annunciation. The motif of soul birds is well attested in early Christian literature and iconography. The soul becomes a dove at baptism; it identifies thereby with the Holy Spirit, the dove of Jesus' baptism. As a dove, the soul of the departed becomes immortal, soaring up to heaven at death, especially at martyrdom. The eagle as a Christian symbol is bound up with a complex of ideas and images. For early Christians the eagle was symbolic of John the Evangelist because at the beginning of his gospel it is implied that John has risen to the heights of the genealogy of the Logos. But the eagle also symbolizes Jesus Christ himself, and it is believed that as an eagle Christ has accompanied John on his flight in quest of visions. Moreover, the eagle represents the Logos itself, just as in Judaism it signifies God or his power. Finally, the eagle depicted on Christian sarcophagi is inseparably associated with the hope for eternal life, light, and resurrection; it serves as the escort of the souls of departed Christians into immortal life with God.

In Islamic literature and folklore, the symbolism of birds abounds. Farīd al-Dīn ʿAṭṭar's famous epic *Manṭiq al-ṭayr* (Conversation of the Birds) uses the imagery of birds as human souls that journey through the seven valleys and, at the end of the road, discover their identity with the Simurgh, the divine bird that "has a name but no body," a perfectly spiritual being. The Turkish saying "Can kuşu uçtu" ("His soul bird has flown away"), uttered when someone dies, expresses the same concept. And throughout Persian and Persianate poetry and literature, one finds repeatedly the image of the nightingale *(bulbul)* in love with the radiant rose *(gul)*, representing the soul longing for divine beauty.

Birds are not yet deprived of symbolic meanings. Dreams of flying birds still haunt us. In his masterpiece *Demian*, Hermann Hesse has given new life to bird symbolism when he speaks of the "bird struggling out of the egg." Modern man's aspiration for freedom and transcendence has also been admirably expressed by the sculptor Constantin Brancuşi through images of birds.

[*For more detailed discussions of specific birds, see* Cocks; Eagles and Hawks; Owls; *and* Swans.]

BIBLIOGRAPHY

The supreme importance of ornithomorphic symbolism and shamanism in the religious life of Paleolithic hunters has been stressed by Horst Kirchner in his article "Ein archäologischer Beitrag zur Urgeschichte des Schamanismus," *Anthropos* 47 (1952): 244–286. On the shaman's ecstasy and his transformation into a bird, there is much useful material in Mircea Eliade's *Shamanism: Archaic Techniques of Ecstasy* (New York, 1964). The bird type of the shamanic costume is illustrated in two works by Uno Harva (formerly Holmberg): *The Mythology of All Races*, vol. 4, *Finno-Ugric, Siberian* (Boston, 1927), and *Die religiösen Vorstellungen der altaischen Völker* (Helsinki, 1938). On the cosmogonic myths of the earth-diver type in which birds play a prominent role, see Mircea Eliade's "The Devil and God," in his *Zalmoxis, the Vanishing God: Comparative Studies in the Religions and Folklore of Dacia and Eastern Europe* (Chicago, 1972), pp. 76–130. On birds and kingship in Inner Asia and North Asia, see my article "Birds in the Mythology of Sacred Kingship," *East and West*, n.s. 28 (1978): 283–289. The symbolism of birds in Judaism has been admirably studied by Erwin R. Goodenough in *Pagan Symbols in*

Judaism (New York, 1958), volume 8 of his *Jewish Symbols in the Greco-Roman Period.* The best single book by a folklorist on folk beliefs and customs concerning birds is Edward A. Armstrong's *The Folklore of Birds: An Enquiry into the Origin and Distribution of Some Magico-Religious Traditions,* 2d ed., rev. & enl. (New York, 1970).

MANABU WAIDA

BIRTH. The mystery associated with birth forms a central motif in every religion. The motif may be appreciated in its irreducible physical form or may become a highly abstract symbol or ritual. Religiously, birth is not regarded as merely a physiological process, or even a ritualized physiological event, but is associated with the evolution and transcendence of spiritual powers or the soul. Transmuted through myth, ritual, and symbol, the concept of birth becomes a major cipher for understanding existence and expressing wonder at creation.

Most religions explore the motif of birth through these three areas of myth, ritual, and symbol. Mythic narratives about important births or mythic figures who give birth are found in most religious traditions, and these myths shed light on the theological and ethical importance of rituals surrounding birth and rebirth. The ritual concerning physical childbirth itself makes this physiological event a religious experience. A third important motif is symbolic rebirth. Many religions speak of the central transformations in the religious life as rebirth. Whether as a collective initiation or as a solitary conversion, members of most religions are expected to undergo a second birth, which sometimes closely duplicates the first, physiological birth. At other times it is intended to undo the inadequacies of the first birth, so that there is an opposition between physiological birth and spiritual or social rebirth. This kind of second birth can often involve great tension or even hostility between women and men. This second birth can be so abstract that the way in which it duplicates one's first birth is unclear.

Primal Religions. Statues of pregnant women dating from the Paleolithic period are important as indicators of the earliest attachment of religious significance to birth. Found in archaeological sites from Spain to Russia, these statues date from about 25,000 BCE on. Since they are found in the remains of old settlements and dwellings, they are thus assumed to be part of domestic religion. Although the exact use and significance of these figures cannot be determined, it seems undeniable that they reflect and express concern with birth specifically and with feminine energy in general as central existential and religious symbols.

For the Neolithic period, the evidence for a religion centered on goddesses and for a matrifocal society in Old Europe between 6500 and 3500 BCE is convincingly presented by Marija Gimbutas (1982). According to Gimbutas, the appropriate collective title for the goddesses is "the Goddess-Creatrix in her many aspects." Among the most important of these aspects is "the life-giving goddess, her legs widely parted" (p. 176). Reliefs of this goddess found in the temples of the Anatolian village of Çatal Hüyük (excavated and reported by James Mellaart) have become especially well known. Contemporary interpreters of this culture have suggested that one may contemplate the impact of entering a religious sanctuary and finding the large, central, elevated image of the Great Birth-Giver with widely parted legs. Such sanctuaries were common in Çatal Hüyük for at least a millennium. In addition, according to Gimbutas, the schematic diagram for this birth-giving goddess was widespread in Old Europe. [*See* Prehistoric Religions, *article on* Old Europe.]

The religious significance of birth in primal religions can also be studied in the context of the present ethnographic data. Rituals surrounding first and second birth have been minutely described and analyzed for many societies. Small-scale societies provide reference points for many classic analyses of birth and rebirth ritual. The links between these rituals of birth and mythologies about birth have not been thoroughly studied, but many small-scale societies also possess a significant mythology concerning births.

Physiological birth is the occasion for rituals in almost all small-scale societies. The well-known pattern for transition rituals—withdrawal, seclusion, and return—is evident in the activities surrounding physiological childbirth. In this case there is an especially close connection between physiological requirements and ritual elaboration. Other transition rituals do not carry the same physiological necessity for withdrawal and seclusion, which strengthens the hypothesis that the experience of giving birth is the model upon which other transition rituals are based. This observation also intensifies the impression that the religious meaning of birth extends far beyond physiological childbirth, which is nevertheless one of the most powerful and pervasive root metaphors of religion.

The pattern of withdrawal, seclusion, and return can take many forms and can include other ritual details. The withdrawal may begin some time before the actual delivery, or it may begin only with the onset of labor, as among the !Kung of southern Africa. The seclusion may be short and solitary, an unusual pattern found among the !Kung and, among them, only for uncomplicated deliveries. Usually the woman giving birth is secluded with appropriate relatives and helpers. Though there are exceptions, as among the inhabitants of Tikopia and the Marquesas, one of the most reliable generalizations that can be made about childbirth seclusion in primal religions is the absence of men. Usually their absence is not merely an accident or a practical arrangement but rather a deeply felt religious requirement. However, the woman's husband may participate vicariously in childbirth through practicing couvade, a series of work and food taboos, physical symptoms, and seclusion. These practices are especially associated with South American Indians. While male absence from childbirth is a general requirement, exceptions are sometimes made in special circumstances such as a difficult delivery; then the shaman or the father may attempt to help the delivery.

After childbirth, the seclusion for the woman continues usually for at least a few days and frequently for a month or more. During this seclusion period, both mother and child receive special treatment and are subject to special restrictions. In most cases, during the entire period of the withdrawal, seclusion, and return, normal routines of eating, working, and human association are disrupted. Normal activities or associations may be restricted to protect either the mother and child or those with whom the mother comes in contact or both. On the other hand, the mother may also be indulged with special foods, a lighter workload, and the solicitous companionship of her friends and relatives. Generally, some ritual elaboration of physiological childbirth seems to be universal among the women of primal cultures.

Almost all of the observances of childbirth outlined above are found among the Aboriginal Australians. The ethnographic literature on these groups concentrates heavily on the second birth, or initiation, as the important birth. In fact, many analyses of Australian Aboriginal religion suggest that physiological birth is the low point in the life cycle relative to membership in the sacred or religious community, and that this situation begins to change only with a second or so-called real birth during initiation. For the birth-giver, however, childbirth is definitely a religious experience that also serves to advance her ritual status. She experiences and practices all the rituals associated with participation in a sacred ceremony and thus emulates models from the mythic Dreaming that sanction her experience and behavior.

For members of many primal religions, birth is believed to be something that must be reexperienced at least once, especially by men. [*See* Initiation.] Frequently, for this purpose, boys are forcibly removed from their familiar surroundings, isolated from women, subjected to painful ordeals and physical operations, and taught secret lore that only men may know (although, in fact, women often surreptitiously find out these secrets). When the boys are reintegrated into the society, they have become "men" through the agency of their male initiators.

Though there are exceptions, as among the Mende of West Africa, this process of a prolonged and tedious rebirth is more typically expected of males than of females. Some scholars analyze this male rebirth ritual as a symbolic gesture whereby boys enter the masculine realm and are freed of the feminine world in which they had previously lived. The second-birth ceremonies of Australian Aborigines may also be seen as experiences that serve as a transition from profane to sacred status. This analysis suggests that the second symbolic birth is the *real* birth, and that male initiation is needed to accomplish what women cannot do when they give birth. This analysis stresses the differences and tensions between the two modes of birth—that given by women and that given by men—and focuses often on male-female tension and hostility in the culture. However, other analyses emphasize the continuity between first and second births and see the second birth as a duplication rather than an undoing of the first birth. More significantly, the male initiators finally experience vicarious childbirth in a kind of delayed couvade as they duplicate the pattern of childbirth. This kind of analysis stresses the extent to which the ceremonies of male second birth are based on awe of, not scorn for, the women's accomplishment in giving birth.

Aboriginal Australian male ceremonies of second birth give clear evidence for the dual meaning of second birth as both a transformation of boys into men and as a birth-giving experience for men. During the ceremonies, boys are carried about by men in the same way that women carry babies. After the initiation operation, the boys are taught a new language, and the men engage in the same purificatory and healing practices as do women after childbirth like the mythic sisters of the Dreaming. The operation itself is symbolic of severing the umbilical cord. In other ceremonies, a trench, symbolizing a uterus, is dug on sacred ritual ground and boys are made to lie in it until the proper time for their emergence, which is indicated by the correct sequence in the dance dramas conducted by the men. In some ceremonies, men ritually wound themselves and correlate their blood with the blood that flows in childbirth.

Many primal religions focus on mythic births and birth-givers. No mythological system among primal religions is devoid of female personalities and activities that focus on birth and rebirth. Among the Aborigines of Australia, there are several well-known mythologies of birth-givers, who are also models for current ritual practices that both women and men engage in. Ronald M. Berndt has reported on two major myth cycles in *Kunapipi* (Melbourne, 1951) and *Djanggawul* (Melbourne, 1952). The Djanggawul epic concerns a brother and two sisters who travel together; the sisters are perpetually pregnant and constantly give birth, assisted by their brother. The other epic concerns two sisters, the Wawalag, one of whom is pregnant and gives birth. The sisters reveal their experiences to men through dreams that become the basis for the men's ritual drama that accompanies second birth. In some Aboriginal mythologies, the ritual process of second birth is itself identified with the great All-Mother or Birth-Giver.

Indian Religions. In the Indian religious context, especially in Indian folk religions, childbirth remains an occasion for religious observances. These rituals follow familiar patterns of withdrawal, seclusion, return, and disruption of normal daily routines. Usually both women and men take part in some birth observances, though the rituals are much more extensive for women. Indian childbirth practices are characterized by uniquely Hindu notions and practices of ritual purity and pollution and are colored by the highly patriarchal character of the Indian family.

The childbirth rituals of an Indian village have been described in a study by Doranne Jacobsen (1980). Though restrictions on food and activity during pregnancy are minimal, with the onset of labor the woman giving birth is separated from others. It is believed that during labor and for a short period immediately following childbirth, the woman and her baby are in a highly polluted and polluting state, similar to the state of people in the lowest untouchable classes. Anyone who contacts the mother and child contracts this pollution, so the two are carefully isolated. Only the midwife, who belongs to a very low class because of the polluting nature of her work, and one married female relative stay with the woman. This childbirth pollution extends to a lesser extent to all members of the husband's family. They also observe some of the restrictions incumbent upon one in a state of pollution and undergo purificatory practices.

The delivery is followed by a series of ceremonies gradually reintegrating the woman and child into the ongoing life of the village. On the evening of the birth girls and women gather in the courtyard of the house to sing. After three days, the level of pollution is lessened when the woman is given purifying baths; she then begins to have limited contact with her household. After ten days, in an important women's ceremony, the woman and her baby leave the house momentarily for the first time, and the mother blesses the family water pots and water supply. For the next month, the woman is still in a transitional state, participating in some of the family's activities, but not cooking or participating in worship services for the deities. Usually the pollution period ends about forty days after the birth, when the mother performs a ceremony at the village well at night, symbolically extending her fertility to the village water supply and completing her reintegration into the community.

This transition period in the woman's life is significant not only for her but for her entire family and community. Both male and female members of her husband's family, who often make the young wife's life very difficult, recognize the new mother's ritual status and must change their behavior appropriately. For the new mother herself, the forty-day seclusion is not so much a period of liability and deprivation as a period of healthful rest and indulgence. She receives special foods, attention, and a new, respected status in her husband's family, especially if she has just given birth to her first son. These rituals surrounding childbirth support and validate women's vital role in a society that often expresses ambivalence toward women and projects strong male dominance.

Second symbolic birth is important in some Indian castes and some religious groups. During the Vedic period (c. 1500–900 BCE) and in those castes that are still heavily involved in rituals and privileges having Vedic antecedents, second birth is an important affair. During Vedic times it was important in its own right; in contemporary Hinduism it is more important because of the privileges associated with being eligible to undergo a second birth.

The upper levels of Hindu society call themselves "twice-born"; their second birth gives them privileges, status, and responsibilities unavailable to the rest of the population. The privileges include the right to study the Vedic sacred texts and to practice religious ceremonies derived from Vedic models. The visible symbol of this status is a cotton cord worn by men across the left shoulder and resting on the right hip. A boy's second birth occurs when he is invested with this sacred thread, receives a sacred verse from his mentor, and undertakes, for at least a few moments, the ascetic discipline of a religious student.

The ancient texts regarding this initiation ceremony regard it as a second birth conferred by the male preceptor. The preceptor transforms the boy into an embryo, conceiving him at the moment when he puts his hand on the boy's shoulder. The preceptor becomes the boy's mother and father and symbolically carries him in his belly for three nights; on the third day the boy is reborn as a member of the privileged twice-born group. After his initiation the twice-born man can perform further sacrifices, which also begin with an initiation involving return to embryonic status and rebirth. Some Indian cultic traditions that still rely heavily on initiation continue to employ these motifs. For example, some Buddhist initiations begin with a series of rites in which the neophyte, deliberately compared to an infant, is washed, dressed, decorated, taught to speak, given a name, and so on.

However, though the theme of second birth occurs in the Indian contexts, many of the great soteriological themes of the Indian tradition do not rely on metaphors of birth and rebirth. Neither Hindu yoga nor the Buddhist Eightfold Path are a process of second birth; neither Hindu *brahman* nor Buddhist *nirvāṇa* results from second birth. They destroy delusion and result in insight and understanding. Images of maturation and death, rather than images of birth and rebirth, more accurately describe this attainment of an otherworldly attitude.

In the Indian context both stories of mythic birth and images of great birth-givers are ambiguous. The two most familiar birth stories, that of the Buddha and that of Kṛṣṇa, are highly unusual. Rather than serving as paradigms of birth-giving, they tell of the extraordinary futures awaiting the infants Buddha and Kṛṣṇa. Goddesses are numerous and important, but they are never simple mother goddesses. Though the creative power of the goddesses is stressed, none of the great goddesses of Hindu mythology experiences a pregnancy and delivery with which a human female could identify, not even Pārvatī, the wife of Śiva and the mother of two of his children. But the veneration of symbols of male and female sexuality is widespread. Temple reliefs of goddesses, naked, hands on hips, knees turned outward to display their sex, recall the Creatrix of Çatal Hüyük. As Śakti, vital energy, she is the energy that fuels the entire phenomenal world. Moreover, without the touch of her energizing dancing feet even the greatest god, Śiva, is a mere *sava* or corpse.

Monotheistic Religions. In the ancient Near East, the concept of monotheism involved the suppression of the goddess as the legitimate symbol of divine creativity and resulted in her replacement by a solitary sovereign, an abstract and nonsexual, though male, creator. Many mythologies from the third millennium onward display an increasing attempt to present males as primordially creative, even as the first birth-givers. They become pregnant and give birth, despite their anatomical limitations. Even if they are not directly involved in birth-giving, they are depicted as performing creative acts. Perhaps the most dramatic account of this reversal occurs in the creation epic of ancient Mesopotamia (mid-second millennium BCE). The older generation of gods are the primordial parents Apsu and Tiamat. After Apsu is killed by younger gods, Tiamat engages in battle against the younger gods. The battle is a confrontation between Marduk, a young male hero, and Tiamat, the Original Mother. He kills her and creates the cosmos out of her lifeless body. The gender identification of the two protagonists, though often ignored, is extremely significant. It is also found in one of the most important myths of Western culture, the creation of the female (Eve) out of the male (Adam).

Against this mythological background, physiological childbearing is not an especially important or religiously valued activity in monotheistic religions. The pains of childbirth are explained as punishment for Eve's curiosity and disobedience; the most noteworthy birth, Jesus' virgin birth, can no more be a model for ordinary women than can the births of the Buddha or Kṛṣṇa. Throughout the centuries, though women have been exhorted to bear children and even have been declared saved by their childbearing (*1 Tm.* 2:15), their childbearing has neither been given value by significant religious rituals nor been utilized as a significant symbol in the mythological system. In the Christian, Jewish, and Muslim traditions, childbirth has nevertheless been surrounded by folk rituals, taboos, and superstitions. Even in modern secular societies, the activities surrounding childbirth are highly ritualized, as has been pointed out by several anthropological analyses of modern Western cultures. These rituals are changing at present, as indicated by the growing popularity of home births, birthing centers, and so on, and by much more direct participation of fathers in the childbirth process than is found in most other societies.

In the context of these Western religious traditions, mothering as an activity has been a more significant religious symbol than birth itself, as is evidenced by the madonna-and-child imagery that is popular in Christian piety. Scholars are beginning to notice aspects of motherly energy in the symbolism of the divine. Yahveh of the Hebrew scriptures is also depicted as a mother eagle. The word for his mercy *(raḥamim)* derives from the word meaning "womb" *(reḥem);* some suggest that the phrase "merciful father" could be translated as "motherly father." The words for his spirit may be masculine or feminine, while the word for his wisdom is definitely feminine, as is *shekhinah,* the term for his presence on earth. In medieval times Christ was depicted as being motherly and feminine. Anselm, in his ontological proof of the existence of God, pictured Christ as a mother hen, an image that appears in the Bible (*Mt.* 23–37, *Lk.* 13–34).

Second birth has remained a central motif in monotheistic religions, especially in Christianity. Physiological birth by itself is insufficient to initiate a person into complete membership in the religious community, which is accomplished by the second and *real* birth. In Judaism and Islam the circumcision ritual does not stress, or even recognize, circumcision as rebirth. In Judaism it is simply "entry into the covenant," and is the first religiously significant event, but is not modeled on an earlier birth.

In Christianity, the necessity of second birth has been especially strong. The contrast between the "Old Adam" and the "New Man" is deeply built into the Christian symbol system. Transition from one birth to the other is a necessary individual experience, verified in baptism, or more recently, in the psychological experience of being "born again." Inasmuch as baptism is performed by a traditionally all-male clergy, the ritual resembles the second births performed by men in other religions. However, rebirth is not a duplication of physiological childbearing but instead emphasizes the need to die to the "old life." In Christianity, everyone, whether female or male, needs to be individually reborn. In this way the Christian understanding of true rebirth departs significantly from other traditions. However, this rebirth occurs through the ritual agency of a male clergy and is almost always understood as a rebirth into the graces of a male monotheistic deity. Perhaps in no other context is the need to be reborn so strongly felt yet so strongly removed from the arenas of feminine symbolism and replication of female activity.

[*See also* Couvade.]

BIBLIOGRAPHY

Literature about rituals of birth and rebirth as well as the mythology and symbolism of the Great Birth-Giver is scattered in many sources. Only rarely, or not at all, are such materials easily found in a few sources. Two classic discussions of transition rituals are Mircea Eliade's *Rites and Symbols of Initiation: The Mysteries of Birth and Rebirth* (New York, 1958) and Arnold van Gennep's *The Rites of Passage* (Chicago, 1960). More recent books that include significant comparative discussions of birth rituals include Martha Nemes Fried and Morton H. Fried's *Transitions: Four Rituals in Eight Cultures* (New York, 1980) and Sheila Kitzinger's *Women as Mothers: How They See Themselves in Different Cultures* (New York, 1978).

The Old European religion is discussed in Marija Gimbutas's *The Goddesses and Gods of Old Europe, 6500–3500 B.C.* (Berkeley, 1982) and in Anne Barstow's "The Prehistoric Goddess," in *The Book of the Goddess: Past and Present*, edited by Carl Olson (New York, 1983). The ceremonies of birth and rebirth among Aboriginal Australians are summarized in my essay "Menstruation and Childbirth as Ritual and Religious Experience among Native Australians," in *Unspoken Worlds*, edited by Nancy Auer Falk and me (San Francisco, 1980), where Doranne Jacobson's "Golden Handprints and Red-Painted Feet: Hindu Childbirth Rituals in Central India" can also be found. Rebirth ceremonies are described in David G. Mandelbaum's *Society in India*, 2 vols. (Berkeley, 1970), and Abbé Jean Antoine Dubois's *Hindu Manners, Customs and Ceremonies*, 3d ed. (1906; reprint, Oxford, 1968). The many qualities of Hindu goddesses and mythic birth-givers can be seen in N. N. Bhattacharyya's *The Indian Mother Goddess*, 2d ed. (Columbia, Mo., 1977), and in *The Divine Consort*, edited by John Stratton Hawley and Donna Marie Wulff (Berkeley, 1982).

Shifts in the core symbolism of the ancient Near East become apparent when the older worldview is first studied. Diane Wolkstein and Samuel Noah Kramer present a moving portrait in *Inanna: Queen of Heaven and Earth* (New York, 1983). The prebiblical shifts in symbolism are presented by Thorkild Jacobsen's *The Treasures of Darkness* (New Haven, 1976), and the struggle to enforce the biblical shift in symbolism is discussed by Raphael Patai's *The Hebrew Goddess* (New York, 1967). For symbolism of second birth in Christianity, see Marion J. Hatchett's *Sanctifying Life, Time and Space* (New York, 1976) and Joseph Martos's *Doors to the Sacred* (New York, 1982). Finally an older source containing much valuable information, including chapters on Palestine and the church, is E. O. James's *The Cult of the Mother Goddess* (New York, 1959).

RITA M. GROSS

BĪRŪNĪ, AL- (AH 362–442/973–1051 CE), more fully known as Abū Rayḥān Muḥammad ibn Aḥmad al-Bīrūnī; Muslim scientist and polymath. Among the most brilliant, eclectic, and fertile minds produced by Islamic civilization in its peak middle period, al-Bīrūnī is a genius to be compared to but two contemporary Muslim literati, Ibn Sīnā (Avicenna; d. 1037), the medical philosopher, with whom he maintained an intermittent correspondence, and Firdawsī (d. 1020), author of the heralded and often illustrated Persian epic, the *Shāhnāmah*. Firdawsī shared with al-Bīrūnī the unhappy fate of being a scholar-prisoner in the court of the Turkic warrior Maḥmūd of Ghaznah (r. c. 1000–1030).

Life. Al-Bīrūnī's life illustrates the keen interest that Persian-Turkic dynasts of the tenth and eleventh centuries had in promoting scientific learning and literary productivity. It also reveals the extent to which all scholars, like all branches of scholarship, were dependent on the taste—and sometimes the whim—of powerful political patrons. While official support allowed al-Bīrūnī to travel widely, to gather disparate data, and to develop a broad network of contacts in Central and South Asia, certain of his patrons, especially Maḥmūd, may have impeded as much as they aided his intellectual undertakings. Only kings and princes, in his view, "could free the minds of scholars from the daily anxieties for the necessities of life and stimulate their energies to earn more fame and favor," but, he adds, "the present times are not of this kind. They are the very opposite, and therefore it is quite impossible that a new science or any new kind of research should arise in our days. What we have of sciences is nothing but the scanty remains of bygone better times" (E. C. Sachau, trans., *Alberuni's India*, vol. 1, p. 152).

Despite that harsh judgment, al-Bīrūnī's biography serves to highlight the manner in which a genius, though subject like other mortals to political strictures and the vagaries of fate, nonetheless maximizes the narrow opportunities provided him. Born near Khorezm, just south of the Aral Sea in modern Soviet Central Asia, he studied under eminent local scientists. Though he favored mathematics and astronomy, he gained competence and even renown in several fields. Political disturbances constantly uprooted him; from 995 until 1004 he found employment under patrons of the Samanid and Ziyarid dynasties. After his return to Khorezm in 1004, he was caught up in diplomatic as well as academic pursuits until 1017, the date of the Ghaznavid conquest of his native region. Pressing al-Bīrūnī into his royal entourage, Maḥmūd sent him first to Ghaznah (Afghanistan) and then to parts of India during prolonged military compaigns there. Maḥmūd died in 1030, but al-Bīrūnī remained in Ghaznah , where he served first under Maḥmūd's son and successor, Mas'ūd, and then under weaker dynasts, until his own death in 1051.

Works. Al-Bīrūnī's scholarship transcends the limiting circumstances of his life and reveals a mind of broad interests and encyclopedic learning. He was first and foremost an empiricist, fascinated by discoveries of the physical world derived through precise observation and careful calculation. Benefiting from the comprehensive curricular resources available to the intellectual elite of the eastern Muslim world by the eleventh century, he studied and wrote about astronomy, mathematics, geology, pharmacology, languages, and geography. He also concerned himself with history, philosophy, and religion. During his lifetime al-Bīrūnī wrote approximately thirteen thousand pages of publishable text, most of it highly technical in nature. This may be sorted out into 138 titles, although some have said he wrote 146 or even 180 independent volumes. Only 22, however, are known to have survived: most were written in Arabic, his preferred scholarly language, although some also exist in Persian versions. Among the most notable are the following:

1. *Al-āthār al-bāqiyah 'an al-qurūn al-khāliyah* (Vestiges of Bygone Days), his first major work, completed around 1000 but subsequently revised. In it al-Bīrūnī sets forth a comparative chronology of the eras and festivals of various ethnic and religious groups.
2. *Qānūn al-Mas'ūdī* (The Canon Mas'udicus), compiled over several years but dedicated in 1031 to Maḥmūd's son and successor, Mas'ūd. It is the most systematic and comprehensive of his numerous works on astronomy and includes an appendix on astrology that leaves little doubt about his personal distaste for it as a pseudoscience, despite its popularity among his coreligionists.
3. *Kitāb taḥqīq mā lil-Hind min maqbūlah lil-'aql aw mardhūlah* (The Book Confirming What Pertains to India, Whether Rational or Despicable), often simply known as the *India*, composed in 1030. This work is based on al-Bīrūnī's study of Sanskrit scientific texts and his conversations with Indian pandits whom he met while forced to accompany Maḥmūd on military campaigns against their patrons. Neither the *Āthār* nor the *Qānūn* nor any of his extant works can surpass the *India's* sheer breadth of learning and novel sense of cosmopolitan objectivity.

Al-Bīrūnī's work as a comparative religionist is rated high on the scale of his total scholarly output primarily because of the *India*. In it he not only distances himself from his warlike patron, Maḥmūd, for whose brutality he expresses barely veiled contempt, but he also attempts to understand what it was that made Indians think as they did; he prejudges neither the truth nor the falsehood of their religious beliefs and ritual practices. If the *India* reveals any weakness, it is al-Bīrūnī's constant preference for literary evidence over ethnographic observation and his predilection to posit the underlying metaphysical unity of Hindu, Greek, and Muslim elites, with disregard bordering on disdain for the views of nonelites. But the shortcomings of the *India* pale in comparison with its achievement, a vast, unprecedented, and unrepeated compendium that details the cultural traits of a conquered people from the point of view of one of their conquerors.

Al-Bīrūnī's vast erudition and innovative scholarship should have commended his works to Muslims of his own and later generations. Unfortunately, he stands out as an exception to his time rather than a model for others to respect or emulate. His scientific work did gain him a reputation as the outstanding authority in fields as diverse as astronomy, geology, and pharmacy, yet his contribution as a comparativist inspired no Muslim successors. It remained for nineteenth-century European scholars to rediscover al-Bīrūnī's legacy as a cultural historian and to spark an interest in the further study of him, both among educated Muslims and Western scholars of Islam. One mark of al-Bīrūnī's continued success is the large number of his extant writings that have been edited, published, and translated during the past fifty years, some of them by Soviet scholars laying claim to a native son.

BIBLIOGRAPHY

While there is no dearth of secondary literature on al-Bīrūnī, there is a dearth of essays providing a competent overview of the range and significance of his writings for the study of religion. The best introductory article to all aspects of his life and work is E. S. Kennedy's "al-Biruni," *Dictionary of Scientific Biography* (New York, 1970), vol. 2, pp. 147–158. Less critical, especially on his attitude toward astrology, but otherwise valuable is Seyyed Hossein Nasr's *An Introduction to Islamic Cosmological Doctrines: Conceptions of Nature and Methods Used for Its Study by the Ikhwān al-Safa', al-Bīrūnī, and Ibn Sīnā* (Cambridge, 1964), pp. 107–174. For an assessment of his religious data in the *Āthār* and *India*, see Arthur Jeffery's "Al-Biruni's Contribution to Comparative Religion," in *Al-Biruni Commemoration Volume* (Calcutta, 1951), pp. 125–160, now to be supplemented by more recent articles in *The Scholar and the Saint: Studies in Commemoration of Abu'l-Rayhan al-Bīrūni and Jalal al-Din Rūmī*, edited by Peter J. Chelkowski (New York, 1975), pp. 1–168; *Biruni Symposium: Iran Center, Columbia University*, edited by Ehsan Yarshater and Dale Bishop (New York, 1983); and select papers from *Al-Bīrūnī Commemorative Volume* (Karachi, 1979), edited by Hakim Mohammed Said. An attractive abridgement of Edward C. Sachau's translation of the *India* has been done, with introduction and notes, by Ainslie T. T. Embree (New York, 1971). Soviet scholarship can be traced by reference to M. S. Khan's "A Select Bibliography of Soviet Publications on Al-Biruni," *Janus* 62 (1975): 279–288.

A fuller appreciation of his contribution to the Muslim study of non-Muslim religions must be derived from unpublished or incomplete studies, such as Michael H. Browder's "Al-Biruni as a Source for Mani and Manichaeism" (Ph.D. diss., Duke University, 1982) and Shlomo Pines and Turia Gelblum's "Al-Bīrūnī's Arabic Version of Patañjali's Yogasūtra," a text that preceded and informed his evaluation of Brahmanic beliefs in the *India*, published seriatim in the *Bulletin of the School of Oriental and African Studies* 29, no. 2 (1966): 302–325 (chap. 1), 40, no. 3 (1977): 522–549 (chap. 2), and 46, no. 2 (1983): 258–304 (chap. 3). The fourth and final chapter is forthcoming.

BRUCE B. LAWRENCE

BISṬĀMĪ, AL- (AH 161-234/777-848 CE), more fully Abū Yazīd Ṭayfūr ibn ʿIsā ibn Sharūshān al-Bisṭāmī; early Muslim mystic. A native of Bisṭām in northeastern Iran, al-Bisṭāmī was the grandson of a Magian convert to Islam. Adopting the Ṣūfī way of life when he was about ten, he left Bisṭām and wandered from place to place for thirty years while serving a large number of Ṣūfī masters and disciplining himself to ascetic practices. At about forty years of age, al-Bisṭāmī returned to his native town and devoted himself to mystical practices and to the teaching of disciples. There he had contacts with a number of important Ṣūfīs of his time, including Abū Mūsā al-Daybūlī and Aḥmad (ibn) Khaḍrūyah, who visited him, and Yaḥyā al-Rāzī and Dhū al-Nūn Miṣrī, who corresponded with him a number of times. He died in Bisṭām, where his tomb is still a place of pilgrimage for many. The death date of 848 is established by his disciple al-Sahlāgī and should be considered more reliable than those offered by later writers.

No writings are attributed to al-Bisṭāmī. Al-Junayd (d. 910?) quoted and wrote commentaries on some of his sayings, and fragments of these have been preserved in the *Kitāb al-lumaʿ* of al-Sarrāj (d. 988). A more complete source of information on al-Bisṭāmī is the *Kitāb al-nūr* (Book of Light) of al-Sahlāgī (d. 1093?), a Ṣūfī of Bisṭām who belonged to the Bisṭāmī tradition.

Al-Bisṭāmī's life and thought were characterized by extremism. He had an unusually sharp sense of what is and what is not permissible, an acute sense of devotion to his mother, and an extraordinary sense of humility before God and his creatures. It is said that his fear of God's majesty was so great that at the time of prayer people near him could hear the crackling of his shoulder blades from the convulsing of his shoulders. In practicing a rigorous form of asceticism, he completely denied *nafs* ("self") as the source of passions and desires. He is said to have put *nafs* in the furnace of discipline, burned it in the fire of self-mortification, and finally invoked the Muslim formula of divorce with the intention of never returning to it again. In states of mystical trance he made many unusual utterances such as "Praise be to me; how great is my majesty," "To see me once is better for you than to see God a thousand times," and "My banner is greater than Muḥammad's." Because of these extravagant claims he was persecuted by the *ʿulamāʾ* (religious scholars) and on seven different occasions was exiled from Bisṭām for short periods. These claims, however, made him well known in the history of Sufism. He was also the first to reenact the Prophet's *miʿrāj* (night journey), step by step, in his own mystical experience.

The question of Indian influence on al-Bisṭāmī remains controversial. There is little evidence to prove any direct link between his thought and Indian systems, and as I have shown elsewhere, his thought can be explained with reference to Islamic contexts.

Al-Bisṭāmī gave Sufism new concepts, images, and metaphors that proved meaningful in the expression of mystical experience, and he also elaborated some of the existing Ṣūfī ideas. In terms of influence on the later development of the Ṣūfī tradition, he was perhaps the greatest Ṣūfī up to his time.

BIBLIOGRAPHY

Arberry, A. J. "Bisṭamiana." *Bulletin of the School of Oriental and African Studies* 25 (1962): 28–37.

Rabb, Muhammad Abdur. *Persian Mysticism: Abū Yazīd Al-Bis-*

lūmī. Dhaka, 1971. Revised version of my doctoral dissertation, Institute of Islamic Studies, McGill University.

MUHAMMAD ABDUR RABB

BLACK ELK (1863–1950), Lakota spiritual leader, known in Lakota as Hehaka Sapa. Few American Indian spiritual leaders have gained greater national and indeed international recognition than this Oglala Lakota of the western American plains. Although Nickolas Black Elk was well known by his own people as a holy person *(wicaša wakan),* it was the poetic interpretation given to his life and sacred experiences in *Black Elk Speaks* (1932) by John G. Neihardt that first caught the attention and imagination of a much wider public. A second book, on the seven rites of the Lakota, was dictated at Black Elk's request to Joseph Epes Brown. This work, *The Sacred Pipe* (1963), further stimulated interest in the man and his message, both of which became, especially during the 1960s, meaningful symbols for a generation seeking alternate values. In his introduction to the 1979 edition of *Black Elk Speaks,* the Dakota writer Vine Deloria, Jr., referred to these books as the "Black Elk theological tradition" and predicted that they will become "the central core of a North American Indian theological canon which will someday challenge the Eastern and Western traditions as a way of looking at the world."

Of the Big Road band of Lakota, Black Elk was born in December 1863 on the Little Powder River within the borders of present-day Wyoming. In those early nomadic days following their adoption of the horse, his people hunted west of the Black Hills (Lakota, Pa Sapa) until 1877, when they were forced to move east to the area of their present reservation at Pine Ridge in South Dakota. At the age of thirteen Black Elk was present at General Custer's defeat at the Battle of the Little Bighorn. He remembered the murder at Fort Robinson of his relative the great warrior and spiritual leader Crazy Horse, and recalled the years during which his people sought refuge with Sitting Bull's band in Canada. He was also present at the tragic massacre at Wounded Knee (1890), which ended the revitalistic Ghost Dance movement. Against that background of traumatic historical events, Black Elk at the age of nine involuntarily received the first of a long series of sacred visionary experiences that set him upon a lifelong quest to find the means by which his people could mend "the broken hoop" of their lives, could find their sacred center where "the flowering tree" of their traditions could bloom again. This first of many vision experiences was of terrifying thunder beings, the powers of the West; whoever received their power was obliged to become a *heyoka,* or sacred clown. Shaken by his experience, Black Elk could not bring himself to reveal the vision until the age of seventeen. Then he confided it to the holy man Black Road, who instructed Black Elk in the spring of 1881 to enact part of his visionary experience, the Great Horse Dance, so that the people might share in the power of his vision.

It was in part his mission to find a means for helping his people that led Black Elk to join Buffalo Bill's Wild West Show in 1886. He appeared in New York and then in England in 1887–1888 for the Golden Jubilee of Queen Victoria, whom he apparently met. He subsequently joined another "western" show and toured France, Germany, and Italy, finally returning to South Dakota in 1889. There, under the influence of Roman Catholic missionaries, and still seeking a way for his people, Black Elk turned to Christianity and even became a catechist for the church. A devout Christian, he nevertheless was able to accommodate both religious traditions without inner conflict. Like many American Indians through history who have had to adapt and borrow selectively in order to survive, Black Elk could be neither traditional Indian nor complete convert, for he had realized the truth of both religions. When he died on 19 August 1950, in his log cabin at Manderson, South Dakota, there was for him no contradiction in the fact that he was holding a Christian rosary as well as a Lakota sacred pipe, which he had never given up smoking in the ceremonial manner.

Although Black Elk may have died feeling he had failed to revive his people's culture, the question of his success remains for history to answer. Black Elk knew something of the power of the printed word. He was thus willing to give through two books details of his visions with their force of mission, as well as accounts of the rites and metaphysics of his people. The widespread popularity of these two books, among both Indians and non-Indians, and the subsequent revitalization of traditional ceremonies across the reservations by younger tribespeople attest that Black Elk still speaks.

BIBLIOGRAPHY

Brown, Joseph Epes, ed. *The Sacred Pipe: Black Elk's Account of the Seven Rites of the Oglala Sioux.* Norman, Okla., 1953.

DeMallie, Raymond J., ed. *The Sixth Grandfather: Black Elk's Teachings Given to John G. Neihardt.* Lincoln, Nebr., 1984.

Neihardt, John G. *Black Elk Speaks: Being the Life Story of a Holy Man of the Oglala Sioux.* Rev. ed. Lincoln, Nebr., 1979.

JOSEPH EPES BROWN

BLACKFEET RELIGION. The Blackfeet Indians are a people of Algonquian linguistic stock. Their historic territory was bounded on the north by the Saskatchewan River in the present province of Alberta, Canada; on the south by the Missouri River in the present state of Montana; on the west by the Rocky Mountains; and on the east by a line running through Saskatchewan and eastern Montana at approximately 105° west longitude.

The Blackfeet are a confederacy of closely related peoples: the Siksika, or Blackfeet proper; the Kainah, or Blood; and the Piegan. Before conquest, the Blackfeet proper occupied the northern part of their traditional homeland, while the Blood were located in the middle and the Piegan in the south. Today, these divisions live in roughly the same geographical configuration on three reserves in Alberta and one in northwestern Montana.

Population figures for the three divisions of the Blackfeet may be viewed in historical perspective. In 1780, for example, the total population was estimated at 15,000. By 1909, as a consequence of wars and disease, that population had dropped to 4,635, of whom 2,440 were in Canada and 2,195 were in the United States. By 1978, the population had risen to a total of 21,466, of whom 9,879 were in Canada and 11,587 were in the United States. As of June 1982, official population figures for Blackfeet in the United States were 12,298; figures for the Canadian reserves were not available.

Before their migration onto the Great Plains, the Blackfeet probably lived in the woodlands to the east. But by the time they were met by Europeans, the Blackfeet had become typical Plains dwellers, living in conical tipis and depending upon buffalo for their livelihood. Blackfeet culture, like that of other Plains tribes, was marked by periods of rapid social change associated with new economic conditions, such as the acquisition of the horse and the gun in the mid-eighteenth century.

The Blackfeet believed in a sacred power pervading all things. This power was symbolically represented by the nourishing radiance of the sun. Sun power manifested itself to humans in a variety of ways, being especially visible through the activities of important sky, earth, and water beings. Sun, Moon, and Morning Star were powerful sky beings, as were Thunder and Eagle. Potent earth beings included Buffalo and Bear; water beings included Otter and Beaver.

Vision Experiences. A central theme in traditional Blackfeet religious life was the experience of vision. Such experiences might overtake individuals in the midst of their waking lives, but more commonly they irrupted in dreams. So important were these experiences that they were actively sought, especially by young men, although their occurrence was not limited by age or sex. Young men sought visions by retiring to lonely places, there to fast and pray until the vision world opened up to them.

Typically, vision experiences involved the transfer of sacred power to a person. Beings that appeared in dreams or waking visions might include significant animals or powerful natural forces, such as thunder. The form of these dream beings was not always fixed: animals might change into persons, becoming animals again at the conclusion of the dream or vision. The moment when these beings spoke was especially powerful, and through such communication sacred power was transferred to the dreamer or visionary.

Medicine Bundles. In the vision, the dream being instructed the visionary to acquire certain special objects, such as skins of animals, which would be gathered together in a personal medicine bundle. Instructions concerning appropriate songs, dances, body paints, and other ritual acts might also be communicated in the dream. The bundle was the symbolic representation of sacred power, but it was the ritual that was of central importance. The material objects contained in the bundle might be lost or destroyed, but as long as the person preserved the ritual, the bundle could be reconstructed.

A person who experienced an important communication of power might transfer this power to another person. The transfer ceremony required a gift of property, as well as instruction by the owner in the ritual associated with the bundle. Once the bundle was transferred, the former owner could no longer call upon its sacred power for assistance.

In addition to such personal bundles, there were among the Blackfeet other more important bundles. These bundles derived from a special relationship that had been established with the people by powerful sky and water beings. A variety of oral traditions preserved the origin myths of such bundles, and, although they were individually owned, they had significance for the welfare of the entire tribe. Like personal bundles, the power of these larger bundles could also be transferred.

Perhaps the most ancient of these bundles was believed to have been given to the Blackfeet by Beaver, a powerful water being. The ritual of the Beaver bundle was complex, and the songs associated with its opening ran into the hundreds. Years were required to learn the details of the ritual. Among the important powers of this bundle, which its owner was called upon to exercise in times of scarcity, was the ritual for calling the buffalo. Beaver bundle owners also kept track of tribal time by means of special counting sticks, and in their bundles were kept the seeds used for planting sacred tobacco. It is probable that the Sun Dance bundle was originally a part of the Beaver bundle. Another important bundle was transferred to the Blackfeet by Thunder, who gave the people a sacred pipe. The medicine pipe bundle was traditionally opened at the sound of the first thunder in the spring. Among other things, it was believed to be efficacious in the healing of illnesses.

Persons who owned such a complex bundle as the medicine pipe or the Beaver bundle were required to become knowledgeable in all aspects of its care and in the details of its rituals. In some cases, the owner might obtain the services of a more experienced person to assist in opening the bundle. Owners of bundles were highly respected among the people, and there were several of these sacred objects distributed among the Blackfeet confederacy. At the turn of the century, for example, there were at least seventeen medicine pipe bundles.

Major Ceremonies. Most important ceremonies, such as the opening or transfer of bundles, were accompanied by ritual purification of the individuals principally involved. Purification ceremonies took place in a sweat lodge, normally constructed of willow branches and covered with skins or blankets. Heated stones were passed into the lodge. Water was sprinkled upon the stones, producing steam and intense heat. Individuals participating in this ritual engaged in a variety of symbolic acts and sang a number of songs. Typically, songs were addressed to Sun, Moon, Morning Star, or important constellations. Through such ritual acts, individuals were removed from the profane world and prepared to enter into relations with sacred powers.

The great tribal ceremony among the Blackfeet was the Sun Dance. Widely distributed among the Plains tribes, this complex religious ceremony was essentially a ritual of individual, social, and world renewal. Each year the Sun Dance was sponsored by a woman of impeccable character. In times of illness or other social crisis, such a virtuous woman would come forward, vowing to sponsor the dance. The vow constituted a public pledge to acquire by transfer a Sun Dance bundle and to bear, along with relatives, the significant expenses and personal sacrifices required by the performance of the ceremony.

The entire tribe participated in the construction of the Sun's lodge, which was built in the form of a circle, perhaps symbolizing the world or the universe itself. Especially sacred was the center pole that symbolically linked the earth with the sacred powers of the sky, principal among which was the Sun. Through the medium of the center pole, sacred power that nurtured all of life flowed into the world. Through the complex ritual of the Sun Dance, individuals, the social world, and nature were renewed.

The Sun Dance ritual formed a rich symbolic universe. There were transfers of important bundles, shamanistic activities, and the performance of dances before the Sun's pole. Upon occasion, sacrifices of flesh were offered by both men and women. In one important male sacrifice, skewers were inserted under the flesh of both sides of a man's chest; ropes were attached to the skewers and then tied to the center pole. The man would dance, leaning against the ropes until the flesh was torn. Persons who performed flesh sacrifices were considered especially sacred and possessed of more than ordinary powers. [*For further discussion, see* Sun Dance.]

Blackfeet religious life was suffused with a rich symbolism that permeated all major phases of ritual activity—sweat lodge ceremonies, bundle openings, and the Sun Dance. Symbolic dances, such as those that traced the cardinal directions, were prominent, as were dances that imitated powerful animals, such as the beaver and the bear. Color symbolism was pervasive, both in the form of body painting and in the decoration of tipis and other objects. The colors red and black were much used, often symbolizing the sun and the moon, respectively. Shapes that symbolized sacred powers were also numerous, such as the circle and representations of the sun, the moon, and the morning star. Sacred objects, both large and small, were commonly depicted. Among these was the buffalo skull, symbolizing the great animal upon which the people were dependent for life and for sacred power.

Despite well over a century of Christian missionary activity, survivals of traditional religious forms can still be observed among some modern Blackfeet. Sacred objects such as the medicine pipe bundle are still owned and opened, and the Sun Dance is still performed, although not always every year. This evidence suggests that a core of traditional religious meaning still persists in the experience of some Blackfeet.

BIBLIOGRAPHY

The best general work on the Blackfeet is John C. Ewers's *The Blackfeet: Raiders on the Northwestern Plains* (Norman, Okla., 1958). For works on Blackfeet mythology, consult Clark Wissler and D. C. Duvall's "Mythology of the Blackfoot Indians," *Anthropological Papers of the American Museum of Natural History* 2 (1908): 1–63, and George Bird Grinnell's *Blackfoot Lodge Tales* (Lincoln, Nebr., 1962). Detailed descriptions of Blackfeet bundles and of the Sun Dance can be found in Wissler's "Ceremonial Bundles of the Blackfoot Indians," *Anthropological Papers of the American Museum of Natural History* 7 (1912): 65–269, and "The Sun Dance of the Blackfoot Indians," *Anthropological Papers of the American Museum of Natural History* 16 (1918): 223–270. For a discussion of the impact of Christian missions upon Blackfeet religion and culture, see my *Mission among the Blackfeet* (Norman, Okla., 1971).

HOWARD L. HARROD

BLACK MUSLIMS. *See* Afro-American Religions; *see also the biographies of Elijah Muhammad and Malcolm X.*

BLADES, such as those of swords, knives, axes, scythes, scissors, and saws, are instruments for cutting things apart. As hierophanies of divine power, blades manifest the instrumental function of intentional or purposeful cutting, dividing, separating, splitting, cleaving, or articulating.

The divine cutting power epiphanized by blades acts creatively or constructively when it differentiates a primordial entity; multiplies one into many by cutting something into parts; releases or receives some fructifying substance by cutting something open; orders a confused state by dividing it into parts; or purifies or brings something to its perfected form by cutting away a nonessential admixture. The same cutting power acts in a negating, limiting, or destructive way when it brings about a premature end by cutting off further development, by establishing an impassable boundary, or by destroying the necessary integrity or organic unity required for the continuance of something.

Blades are man-made instruments designed for implementing conscious intentions; they require craft for their manufacture and both training and discipline for their use. This quality of consciousness enables them to symbolize the divine intellect, purpose, will, judgment, craft, cunning, or wisdom that wields or guides the cutting power.

Blades manifest their divine power in all domains of existence—agriculture, warfare, civil administration, service to the gods, and meditative disciplines. For instance, cutting power in the form of the sickle is an attribute of divinities connected with agriculture as a sacred institution. The ancient Italian god of seedtime and harvest, Saturnus, carries a sickle. The Greek earth goddess, Gaia, invented the sickle and urged her son Kronos to castrate his father with it because he was preventing her children from coming into the light.

Cutting power in the form of a sword is an attribute of divinities connected with meditative disciplines. In Hinduism, for example, the sword Nandaka ("source of joy"), which is held by the god Viṣṇu, represents pure knowledge *(jñāna),* whose substance is wisdom *(vidyā).* The flaming sword of knowledge is the powerful weapon that destroys ignorance. Generally, in whatever domain of existence the divine cutting power manifests itself it does so as the sacred blade of a numinous agent who wields the blade and whose essential nature is represented by it.

Blades as attributes of the ruling gods of the sky in various religious traditions manifest cutting power in both its constructive and its negative connotations. The blades of the sky gods have their natural analogue in the phenomenon of lightning. For example, the Vedic ruler of heaven, the cloud-dwelling god Indra, is deity of space, dispenser of rain, thrower of the thunderbolt *(vajra),* and principle of lightning—the energy of cosmic and animal life, which is stored as the semen *(vīrya)* of all beings. When the priest of Indra brandishes the ritual wooden sword *(sphyha),* he is regarded as raising the thunderbolt used by Indra to behead Vṛtra, the dragon (or demon) that caused drought. In the epic *Mahābhārata,* Indra's thunderbolt is equated with the penis, and in the Tantras it is equated with sexual power as the fundamental energy.

According to Ananda Coomaraswamy, "the Japanese sword, Shinto, royal, or samurai, is in fact the descendant or hypostasis of the sword of lightning found by Susa-no-Wo-no-Mikoto in the tail of the Dragon of the Clouds, whom he slays and dissevers, receiving in return the last of the daughters of the Earth, whose seven predecessors have been consumed by the Dragon" (*Selected Papers,* Princeton, 1977, vol. 1, p. 434).

Lightning is also a metaphor expressive of the flashing sword of judgment wielded by Yahveh. "I have posted a sword at every gate to flash like lightning, polished for havoc" (*Ez.* 21:20). After Adam and Eve are expelled from the Garden of Eden, Yahveh posts "the cherubs, and the flame of a flashing sword, to guard the way to the tree of life" (*Gn.* 3:24).

The ax is also an attribute of sky gods. Indra is incarnated as the god Rāma-with-the-Ax, Parasic-Rāma. Rāma's ax is the cutting power in the service of reestablishing the proper social order by means of war. Rāma was given the ax and trained in its use by Śiva, the god or principle of disintegration, dispersion, and annihilation. Zeus is another example of a sky god whose warrior power is represented by the ax. At the time of his birth on Mount Ida in Crete the mountain brought forth the Kouretes, youths armed with battle-axes and shields, who danced around the divine child to conceal his cries from Kronos, his murderous father. The birthplace of Zeus on Crete is also a major site of the cult of the double ax. Apparently the double ax itself was worshiped, and in later representations Zeus is shown shouldering the ax.

Blades are attributes of sun gods and solar heroes. These blades have their natural analogue in the form and activity of sunbeams and rays of sunlight. The Babylonian sun god, Shamash, who was a judge, lawgiver, and fertility deity, is depicted holding a saw with which to cut decisions. His heroic and kingly agent, Gilgamesh, carries a battle-ax and a sword with which he kills both the monster Huwawa, who rules the wilderness, and the Bull of Heaven, sent against him by the goddess Ishtar, whose seduction he rejects. In general, the blades associated with sun gods and solar heroes manifest the divine cutting power serving the interest of establishing the human order, civilization, and kingship.

Swords are almost universally found as a part of royal regalia, for the sovereign is the temporal counterpart of the divine principle that rules through cutting power. For example, there are five swords in the regalia of the British monarch: the sword of state, a smaller sword substituted for it that is used during the coronation ceremony, the sword of spiritual justice, the sword of temporal justice, and the sword of mercy, which has a blunted tip.

Scissors are particularly connected with the power of terminating or cutting something off. For example, the Moirai or goddesses of fate in the pre-Olympian Greek religion spun and determined the length of the threads of human lives. One of them, Atropos, snipped off the threads with scissors. In Hindu iconography the goddess Kālī is sometimes depicted with scissors, which she uses to snip the thread of life.

Kālī or Mahā-Kālī, the transcendent power of time that dissociates all things, is often shown holding a sword, which represents the destructive power of time to cut off life. The sword is also an instrument of sacrifice in the rites of Kālī.

Blades are also attributes of gods of the underworld. For instance, Yama, the Hindu sovereign of the infernal regions and judge of the dead, carries a sword, an ax, and a dagger. The name *Yama* means "binder, restrainer." When Yama is identified with the principle of time (Kālā) he is shown as an old man carrying a sword and shield, as this concept has to do with endings.

In the biblical *Book of Revelation* (15:14–16) the end of time is represented by the image of the Son of man appearing on a cloud with a sickle in his hand. "Then another angel . . . shouted aloud to the one sitting on the cloud, 'Put your sickle in and reap: harvest time has come and the harvest of the earth is ripe.' Then the one on the cloud set his sickle to work on the earth. . . ." The judging Word of the Lord is also represented in the image of the Son of man with the double-edged sword coming from his mouth (*Rv.* 1:16).

Thus the divine cutting power manifested in blades works toward a multiplicity of ends in all domains of existence. Depending upon the context in which it appears, the blade traditionally symbolizes the instrument of creativity, liberation, justice, power, authority, fertility, purification, enlightenment, punishment, death, execution, destruction, martyrdom, and limitation.

BIBLIOGRAPHY

Further discussion can be found in Alain Daniélou's *Hindu Polytheism* (New York, 1964).

RICHARD W. THURN

BLASPHEMY. [*This entry consists of two articles on the concept of blasphemy in monotheistic religions:* Judeo-Christian Concept *and* Islamic Concept. *For discussion of comparable phenomena in broader religious perspective, see* Sacrilege.]

Judeo-Christian Concept

The word *blasphemy* derives from a Greek term meaning "speaking evil," but in the Judeo-Christian religious tradition the word refers to verbal offenses against sacred values or beliefs. A seventeenth-century Scottish jurist epitomized blasphemy by calling it "treason against God." The concept of blasphemy has never remained fixed. It has ranged from the ancient Hebrew crime of cursing the ineffable name of God to irreverent statements that outrage the religious sensibilities of others. What is deemed blasphemous varies from society to society and may differ with time and place, but whatever is condemned as blasphemy is always regarded as an abuse of liberty and reveals what a society cannot and will not tolerate. Blasphemy constitutes a litmus test of the standards a society feels it must enforce to preserve its religious peace, order, morality, and above all, salvation. Wherever organized religion exists, blasphemy is taboo.

Yet the Judeo-Christian religious tradition holds no monopoly on the concept of blasphemy. Every society will punish the rejection or mockery of its gods. Because blasphemy is an intolerable verbal violation of the sacred, it affronts the priestly class, the deep-seated beliefs of worshipers, and the basic religious values that a community shares. Punishing the blasphemer may serve any one of several social purposes in addition to setting an example to warn others. Punishment is also supposed to propitiate the offended deities by avenging their honor, thereby averting their wrath in the shape of earthquakes, infertility, lost battles, floods, plagues, or crop failures. Public retribution for blasphemy also vindicates the witness of believers, reaffirms communal values, and avoids the snares of toleration. Toleration sanctions the offense, inviting others to commit it, and sheds doubt on orthodox truths.

Periclean Greece cherished liberty yet prosecuted its blasphemers. Anaxagoras the philosopher, by imagining a superior intellect that had imposed a purposeful order on the physical world, insulted the Greek gods; Phidias the sculptor, by carving a figure of himself on the shield of his colossal statue of Athena, profaned her; Euripides the tragic poet seemed to doubt the sanctity of oaths witnessed by the gods; Alcibiades the general supposedly mocked the sacred rites honoring Demeter, the grain goddess; Protagoras the mathematician and Diagoras the poet confessed to agnosticism. Finally, Socrates, whose trial for blasphemy is the best known in history next to that of Jesus, was charged with corrupting the youth by disbelieving in the gods of the state and advocating deities of his own.

Christendom's concept of blasphemy derived from the Mosaic injunction of *Exodus* 22:28, which declares, "You shall not revile God." The precedent for punishing blasphemy as a crime is in *Leviticus* 24:16, where one who cursed the name of the Lord was put to death by stoning. None of the Old Testament references to the commission of blasphemy quotes the actual crime for fear of repeating it. The Hebrew scriptures distinguished blasphemy from other offenses against religion, in contrast to the Septuagint. Where, for example, Greek usage showed a preference for *blasphemy* and used that term somewhat loosely, the Hebrew scriptures referred more precisely to "idolatry" or "sacrilege," as in *Isaiah* 66:3 and *1 Maccabees* 2:6, or sometimes to "speaking anything against God," as in *Daniel* 3:29. On the other hand, the term for "blasphemy" in the Hebrew scriptures is *linqov*, which means "to specify, enunciate, or pronounce distinctly"; but *Leviticus* 24:10–23 uses it in conjunction with *qillel*, which means "curse." The word cannotes also "to pierce [the name of God], rail, repudiate, derogate, speak disrespectfully, denounce, insult, and abuse." The blasphemy of Rab-Shakeh in *2 Kings* 18–19 shows the offense to mean speaking disrespectfully of God, doubting his powers, and comparing him to idols. However, only cursing the personal name of the Lord merited the death penalty; for a lesser blasphemy, the punishment was probably excommunication. To curse was a far more serious offense than in our time. "God damn," a familiar curse, is today mere profanity; in the biblical sense, to curse meant uttering an imprecation in the name of God for the purpose of calling upon his power to perform an evil deed. [*See* Cursing.] Although the Septuagint tends to use *blasphemy* as a broad term for any offenses against religion, with the exception of *Ben Sira* 3:16 no Greek-Jewish text uses the word or any form of it that is not God-centered. Only God can be blasphemed in Jewish thought. And nowhere in Old Testament or Greek-Jewish sacred books is *blasphemy* a synonym for *heresy*. Indeed, no equivalent for the concept of heresy exists in the pre-Christian era. Christianity, though greatly influenced by Greek-Jewish texts, would use the two terms *blasphemy* and *heresy* as equivalents and as more than a God-centered offense. Not until Christianity began did the meaning of *blasphemy* change.

As the term *blasphemy* broadened in Christian usage, it narrowed in Jewish usage. Jewish law avenges God's honor but not that of the Jewish religion. Reviling sacred customs, beliefs, and institutions, whether of Judaism itself, the Temple, the sacerdotal hierarchy, particular rituals, or holy dogmas, did not constitute blasphemy. The Talmud focused on *Exodus* 22:28 and narrowed the capital crime. In rabbinic thought, not even cursing God deserved death unless the blasphemer used the name of God to curse God. The Talmud requires cursing the name of God by the name of God, as in "May Yahveh curse Yahveh." Cursing God, the tetragrammaton *(YHVH)*, or one of the names of God (*Adonai* or *Elohim*) did not suffice to constitute the crime. And no degree of blasphemy could be committed unless the name of God were accompanied by disrespect or contempt (see B.T., *San.* 56a, 60a). The Talmud's discussion of blasphemy, so tightly defined, represents a road not taken by Christianity.

The New Testament retained the God-centeredness of the Mosaic code but expanded the concept of the offense to include the rejection of Jesus and the attribution of his miracles to satanic forces. Although only Mark and Matthew depict a formal trial and condemnation of Jesus by the Sanhedrin, all four evangelists employ the motif that the Jewish rejection of Jesus was blasphemy. Readers understand that whenever the Gospels depicted the Jews as describing Jesus as blasphemous for performing some miracle, or healing on the Sabbath, or forgiving sins, none of which constituted the crime of blasphemy in Jewish law, the Jews by their rejection, and not Jesus, were blasphemous. Thus in the climax of the trial scenes before the Sanhedrin, those who found Jesus guilty were blasphemers because they did not recognize him as the Son of God and the Messiah. Jesus' answer to Caiaphas in *Mark* 14:62 ("I am") should be understood as post-Easter theology, but it became the basis for a new, expanded concept of blasphemy in Christian thought.

For four centuries after the crucifixion, many different interpretations of Christianity competed with each other as the true faith, producing accusations of blasphemy. Jesus, having joined God as a divine majesty in

Christian thought, though not in Arianism, became a target of blasphemers or, rather, the basis for leveling the charge of blasphemy against variant professors of Christianity. Cursing, reproaching, challenging, mocking, rejecting, or denying Jesus Christ became blasphemy. Posing as Jesus, claiming to be equal to him, or asserting powers or attributes that belonged to him, became blasphemy. Ascribing evil or immoral inspiration to any work of God or of the Holy Spirit that moved Jesus also became blasphemy, as did any denial or renunciation of the faith, and any discord, false beliefs, or dissent from Jesus' teachings. Denying the incarnation or calling the Son of God a human being only resulted in the same charge. Blasphemy was a concept of primary concern to Christians, as well as a vile epithet with which to blacken religious enemies. During the four centuries it took for Christianity to define itself and develop its faith, every faction accused its opponents as blasphemers. In time, heresy, which originally meant a factionalism arising from the willful choice of an untrue faith, became not just a form of blasphemy that exposed the true faith to contention; it became a term that eclipsed blasphemy. A point implicit in the deutero-Pauline epistles became explicit in *2 Clement,* which stated that blasphemy means "you do not do what I desire" and therefore consists of anything that contravened ecclesiastical authority. This viewpoint became a fixed position in Christian thought.

Any religious view contrary to church policy was blasphemy, a form of heresy, but the doctrine of the Trinity became the focal point in the controversy over blasphemy. The conflict between Arians and Athanasians involved more than a dispute over the right faith; it concerned the right road to salvation for all Christians. The authority of the church, when backed by the coercion of the state, settled the controversy by fixing on the Nicene Creed, which ultimately became the test of orthodoxy. Constantine's decrees against Arians and Arian books eventually led to the Theodosian Code of 438, enthroning Catholic Christianity as the exclusive religion of the empire, and Christians began persecuting each other. Heresy then superseded blasphemy as the great crime against Christianity. Unfreighted with Old Testament origins, heresy was more flexible and spacious a concept than blasphemy and had as many meanings. Both Athanasius and Augustine freely intermixed accusations of blasphemy and heresy, as if the two terms were interchangeable. But heresy became the encompassing term, because the church faced abusive criticism and competing doctrines about the faith, not abusive speech about God. Augustine developed a theory of persecution that lasted more than a millennium. Blasphemers, he wrote, "slay souls," causing "everlasting deaths." Rape, torture, and death were nothing compared to rejection or corruption of the pure faith. The church persecuted "out of love," he declared, "to save souls." Toleration intensified the heretic's damnation and passed his guilt to church and state for allowing him to contaminate others, multiplying his eternal fate among the faithful. Those who knew the revealed truth yet permitted disloyalty to it committed a greater crime than those who rejected it. Indulging willful error in a matter of salvation betrayed the faith and risked the worst calamity in the hereafter. Blasphemy, Augustine wrote, was the most "diabolical heresy."

Theologians who discussed blasphemy in the times of Bede, Gratian, Aquinas, Bernard Gui, and Bellarmine said nothing significantly different from Augustine. Aquinas regarded blasphemy as saying or thinking something false against God; he therefore understood it as a species of unbelief meriting death. But he also condemned all heresies as blasphemy: heretics, he thought, ought to be punished for crimes worse than treason or murder because they victimized God, not merely other human beings. According to Aquinas, "heretics . . . blaspheme against God by following a false faith."

Protestants during the Reformation had to reinvent the crime of blasphemy on the fiction that it was distinguishable from heresy. Because "heresy" was the Catholic description for Protestantism, Protestant leaders tended to choke on the word *heretic* and preferred to describe as "blasphemy" anything they disliked or disagreed with, just as the church had used "heresy." Luther, for example, impartially if promiscuously condemned as blasphemies Anabaptism, Arianism, Catholicism, Judaism, and Islam. Any denial of an article of Christian faith as he understood it was blasphemy. So too, sin was blasphemy, opposing Luther was blasphemy, questioning God's judgments was blasphemy, persecution of Protestants by Catholics was blasphemy, Zwinglian dissent from Lutheranism was blasphemy, missing church was blasphemy, and the peasantry's political opinions were blasphemy. Luther abused and cheapened the word, but he certainly revived and popularized it. It became part of the Protestant currency. In 1553 Calvin's Geneva executed Michael Servetus, the first systematic antitrinitarian theorist, for his "execrable blasphemies" that scandalized the Trinity and entailed the murder of many souls. Of all the blasphemy cases of the sixteenth century the strangest was that of Ferenc Dávid, the head of the Unitarian church in Transylvania. His allies, the Socinians, denounced and prosecuted him as a blasphemer because of his belief that Christians should not worship Christ. In 1579 the Hungarian Diet convicted him of blasphemy and sentenced him to life imprisonment.

During the seventeenth century blasphemy increasingly became a secular crime. The state began to supplant the church as the agency mainly responsible for instigating and conducting prosecutions. The connection between religious dissent and political subversion and the belief that a nation's religious unity augmented its peace and strength accounted in part for the rising dominance of the state in policing serious crimes against religion. Governments intervened more frequently to suppress nonconforming sectarians and intellectuals. Although Rome had charged Giordano Bruno with blasphemy and burned him for heresy in 1600, Protestant precedents were not without some influence. The church condemned for heresy, the state increasingly for blasphemy, even in Catholic states. On the continent, blasphemy prosecutions continued into the present century, although the death penalty for the crime was abandoned during the eighteenth century.

In England the prosecution of heresy as a capital crime had begun to die out in the reign of Elizabeth. The earliest Protestant codification of ecclesiastical law in England (1553) had the first separate section on blasphemy. Elizabeth burned five or six Arians and Anabaptists whose crimes included the beliefs that Christ was not God and that infant baptism was unnecessary. The last English executions for religion occurred in 1612; both victims were antitrinitarians, the principal targets of suppression throughout the century. John Biddle, the Socinian father of English Unitarianism, was persecuted for seventeen years and finally died in prison in 1662.

In 1648 Parliament had enacted a statute against blasphemy that reached the doctrines of Socinianism but not those of Ranterism, a phenomenon of the disillusioned and defeated political left that turned to religion for expression. Ranters believed that, as God's grace is unbounded, nothing is sinful. Antinomian sentiment run amok into religious anarchy, the Ranters were seditious, obscene, and blasphemous in ways as flagrantly offensive as possible. A 1650 act against blasphemy cataloged Ranter beliefs but punished them lightly compared to Scotland, which carried out the death penalty. The Ranters, believing that life should be enjoyed, recanted easily and disappeared. Unlike the Socinians or the Quakers, they did not have the stuff of martyrs.

George Fox, the founding Quaker, who was prosecuted for blasphemy four times, and his followers endured violent persecution. Their belief in the Christ within seemed blasphemous. In 1656 James Nayler, then the greatest Quaker, was convicted by Parliament for blasphemy because he reenacted Jesus' entry into Jerusalem on Palm Sunday as a sign of the imminent Second Coming. Nayler was savagely beaten and imprisoned. The first person imprisoned for blasphemy after the Restoration was William Penn, accused of antitrinitarianism.

In 1676 John Taylor, a farmer who really blasphemed ("Religion is a cheat" and "Christ is a bastard"), was convicted by the King's Bench. Chief Justice Matthew Hale delivered an opinion that made Taylor's case the most important ever decided in England; he ruled that the secular courts had jurisdiction of blasphemy and could punish blasphemers, because Christianity is part of the law of the land and the state has to prevent dissolution of government and religion. After the crime of nonconformity died in consequence of the Toleration Act of 1689, blasphemy remained an offense punishable by the state. A blasphemy act of 1698 targeted antitrinitarians, showing that England still regarded them as execrable atheists.

English precepts about blasphemy made the Atlantic crossing. Virginia's first code of laws (1611) specified death for anyone blaspheming the Trinity or Christianity, and most other colonies followed suit. But the actual punishments consisted of fines, branding, whipping, banishment, and prison. Massachusetts regarded Quakers as blasphemous but inflicted the death penalty, technically, for defiance of banishment decrees. In the eighteenth century, the Age of Enlightenment, blasphemy prosecutions on both sides of the Atlantic diminished. All the American colonies produced only half a dozen convictions, and the worst sentence was boring through the tongue and a year in prison. In Great Britain, where there were a dozen convictions, the cases involved important defendants, serious legal issues, and heavier sentences. In one case the first minister to call himself a Unitarian was convicted for writing a book that temperately argued the subordination of Christ to God. A biblical scholar who mocked literal interpretations of miracles lost his appeal when the high court of Britain relied on the judgment in Taylor's case. As the century closed, a series of blasphemy prosecutions began against the publishers and sellers of Thomas Paine's *Age of Reason.*

The number of blasphemy cases peaked in England and the United States in the first half of the nineteenth century. Between 1821 and 1834 English trials produced seventy-three convictions. The defendants, who in the past had professed to be believing Christians, increasingly became agnostics, deists, and secularists who relied on freedom of the press more than freedom of religion, with as little success. In the American cases the courts maintained the legal fiction that the law punished only malice, never mere difference of opinion. The law aimed, that is, not at what was said but the way it was said; the judicial cliché on both sides of the Atlantic rested on the doctrine that manner, not matter, determined criminality. That seemed so in an important New York case of 1811 *(People* v. *Ruggles),* in which the court ruled that only Christianity could be blasphemed and judged guilty the defendant, who had declared that Jesus was a bastard, his mother a whore. Such malicious blasphemy found no protection in constitutional guarantees of freedom of expression or separation of church and state. But in the leading American case *(Commonwealth* v. *Kneeland),* decided in 1838 in Massachusetts, arguments based on liberty of conscience and press failed even though the defendant was a pantheist who declared in language devoid of scurrility that he did not believe in God, Christ, or miracles. The view that received no judicial endorsement in the nineteenth century was that espoused in 1825 by two old men, John Adams and Thomas Jefferson, who agreed that blasphemy prosecutions conflicted with the principle of free inquiry; Jefferson also sought to prove that Christianity was not part of the law of the land and that religion or irreligion did not belong to the cognizance of government. In 1883 the Lord Chief Justice of England supposedly liberalized the law by holding that decency of expression would exempt from prosecution even an attack on the fundamentals of Christianity—a fairly subjective test. Moreover, the decencies of controversy were also subjective in character. Indeed, the authors of most of the books of the Old and New Testaments as well as many leading saints and the originators of most Protestant denominations and sects gave such offense that they would not have passed the legal tests that prevailed in England and America.

In the twentieth century, blasphemy prosecutions have dwindled in number. In 1977 Massachusetts refused to repeal its three-hundred-year-old act against blasphemy, even though the last prosecutions in that state were conducted in the 1920s and had failed. But in the same year a prosecution succeeded in London, the first in over half a century. In the United States no prosecution has occurred since 1968, despite laws against blasphemy, and no prosecution ending in a conviction could survive judicial scrutiny on appeal, given the contemporary interpretations of First Amendment freedoms by the Supreme Court. Blasphemy prosecutions, relics of the Anglo-American world, are becoming obsolete even elsewhere in Christendom. People seem to have learned that Christianity is capable of surviving without penal sanctions and that God can avenge his own honor.

BIBLIOGRAPHY

Theodore Albert Schroeder's *Constitutional Free Speech Defined and Defended in an Unfinished Argument in a Case of Blasphemy* (1919; New York, 1970) is, despite its misleading title, a comprehensive history by a passionate, freethinking radical lawyer who opposed any restraints on expression. Not factually accurate, it is nevertheless a still useful pioneering work. Gerald D. Nokes's *A History of the Crime of Blasphemy* (London, 1928) also has a misleading title. It is a brief and narrowly legalistic study of English cases only, but is well executed. Leonard W. Levy's *Treason against God: A History of the Offense of Blasphemy* (New York, 1981) is easily the fullest treatment of the concept from Moses to 1700; covering religious thought as well as legal history, it is oversympathetic to victims of prosecution, according to reviewers. A promised sequel will bring the subject up to date. Levy's *Blasphemy in Massachusetts: Freedom of Conscience and the Abner Kneeland Case* (New York, 1973) reprints the major primary sources on the most important American case. Roland Bainton's *Hunted Heretic: The Life and Death of Michael Servetus* (Boston, 1953) is the best introduction to the most important blasphemy case of the Reformation. Donald Thomas's *A Long Time Burning: The History of Literary Censorship in England* (New York, 1969) is a vivid account that views the subject of blasphemy against a broad canvas. William H. Wickwar's *The Struggle for the Freedom of the Press, 1819–1832* (London, 1928) is a splendid, scholarly book that recounts prosecutions for blasphemy in England at a time when they peaked in number. George Holyoake's *The History of the Last Trial by Jury for Atheism in England* (1851; London, 1972) is a short autobiographical account by a freethinking victim of a prosecution. Hypatia Bradlaugh Bonner's *Penalties upon Opinion: Or Some Records of the Laws of Heresy and Blasphemy* (London, 1912) is a short account by an opponent of all blasphemy prosecutions and the daughter of the victim of one. William Wolkovich's *Bay State "Blue" Laws and Bimba* (Brockton, Mass., n.d.) is a well-documented study of a 1926 prosecution. Alan King-Hamilton's *And Nothing But the Truth* (London, 1982) is a judge's autobiography containing a chapter on a noted blasphemy case in England.

LEONARD W. LEVY

Islamic Concept

Offering insult *(sabb)* to God, to the prophet Muḥammad, or to any part of the divine revelation is a crime in Islamic religious law, fully comparable to blasphemy. In the Christian tradition, blasphemy properly denotes mockery or *lèse majesté* of God. There is no exact equivalent to *blasphemy* in the Islamic tradition, although the Qur'anic phrase "word of infidelity" *(kalimat al-kufr)* comes fairly close. From the viewpoint of Islamic law, blasphemy may be defined as any verbal expression that gives grounds for suspicion of apostasy *(riddah)*. In theological terms, blasphemy often overlaps with infidelity *(kufr)*, which is the deliberate rejection of God and revelation; in this sense, expressing religious opinions at variance with standard Islamic views could easily be looked upon as blasphemous. Blasphemy can also be seen as the equivalent of heresy *(zandaqah)*, a pre-Islamic Persian term used in reference to the revolutionary teachings of Mani and Mazdak; in this sense, it can mean any public expression of teachings deemed dangerous to the state. Thus, in describing the Islamic concept of blasphemy, it is necessary to include not only insulting language directed at God, the Prophet, and the revelation, but also theological positions and even mystical aphorisms that have come under suspicion.

Blasphemy in Early Islam. During his own lifetime, the prophet Muḥammad (d. AH 10/632 CE) encountered strong opposition from the leaders of the Arab clans of Mecca when he preached the worship of the one God and attacked the traditional polytheism of the Arabs. Most frequently, this opposition took the form of verbal disputes and abuse, by which the pagan leaders rejected and ridiculed the Qur'anic teachings on the unity of God and the resurrection. Muḥammad's opponents, moreover, mocked his claim to be an inspired prophet and accused him variously of being possessed, a soothsayer, a magician, a poet, or an unscrupulous power-seeker. From the beginning, as the Qur'ān attests, the blasphemous language of the Prophet's opponents thus consisted of calling divine revelation a lie *(takdhīb)*. Insult to the Prophet was particularly blasphemous, since Muḥammad was the chief medium of that revelation. Among Muḥammad's opponents the Qur'ān (surah 111) singles out Abū Lahab above all as destined to punishment in hellfire; according to traditional accounts, the Qur'ān turns back on Abū Lahab the very words that he had used to curse Muḥammad. The followers of Muḥammad who killed two poets who had written satires on the Prophet evidently considered this kind of mockery to be blasphemy. The Qur'ān stresses the opposition that previous prophets experienced, as in the notable case of the pharaoh who called the revelation to Moses a lie, saying, "I am your highest Lord" (79:24). As a rejection of divine lordship, this saying is usually considered to be the height of blasphemy. Within the early Islamic community itself, the "hypocrites" *(munāfiqūn)* uttered blasphemous jests about God and the Prophet (9:65–66). Such mockery constituted infidelity *(kufr)* after professing faith *(īmān)* and invalidated whatever good deeds they might have previously performed (5:5).

Blasphemy in Islamic Law. Building upon the descriptions of and pronouncements on blasphemy found in the Qur'ān and the example *(sunnah)* of the Prophet, the various legal schools have elaborated upon the nature, conditions, and punishments for blasphemy. Jurists describe it as the expression of denigration *(istikhfāf)*, contempt *(iḥānah)*, or scorn *(ḥaqārah)* for God, the Prophets, the Qur'ān, the angels, or the traditional religious sciences based on revelation. The legal handbooks of the Ḥanafī school, in particular, offer numerous examples of blasphemous sayings, usually classified under the heading of "words of infidelity" (*kalimāt al-kufr;* see surah 9:74). Since most of the classical collections of case-judgments *(fatāwā)* of this school derive from Iranian and Central Asian jurists of the eleventh and twelfth centuries, the blasphemous sayings are usually given not in Arabic but in Persian, which was the spoken language of those regions. The sayings, many of which were doubtless uttered in levity or in the heat of emotion, are generally wisecracking remarks, oaths, and imprecations of an intemperate or irreligious nature. Some examples are borderline cases, which are judged ambiguous or declared innocent. Later works, which include several separate monographs on "words of infidelity," give even larger collections of examples, with special prominence for those remarks that give offense to religious scholars as a class. An insult to religious scholarship is equivalent to rejection of religious knowledge and, hence, gives the lie to divine revelation. Under the same heading, the handbooks also include acts of sacrilege, such as donning the clothing of Jews or Zoroastrians, or participating in non-Islamic religious festivals. To claim that forbidden acts are permitted, or to invoke the name of God while committing sins, is blasphemy. A very small proportion of blasphemous statements (primarily in Ḥanafī texts) concern doctrinal matters, such as the formula used to declare oneself as a faithful worshiper.

Legal authorities agree that the conditions for blasphemy include adulthood, lack of duress, and being of sound mind, and it is immaterial whether the offender is a Muslim or not. Accidental blasphemy is, in general, not excused, although Ḥanafī jurists allow suspicious statements to be construed innocently if a legitimate case can be made for the interpretation. The Mālikī school permits an excuse to be made for one who has converted to Islam from another religion, but otherwise views blasphemy as entailing apostasy *(riddah)*.

The punishment for blasphemy differs somewhat from one school to another. The Ḥanafīyah define blasphemous statements as acts of infidelity *(kufr)* and strip the blasphemer of all legal rights: his marriage is declared invalid, all religious acts worthless, and all claims to property or inheritance void. The death penalty is a last resort that most authorities try to avoid, especially if some element of accident or doubt is present. Repentance, however, restores all previous rights, although it is necessary to renew marriage. A few cases are mentioned in which a woman uttered blasphemies as a stratagem to annul her marriage, with the intention of repenting later to regain her other rights. The Mālikīyah, treating blasphemy as apostasy, call for immediate execution of the offender; as in cases of apostasy, they do not offer the chance to repent. An exception is made for female blasphemers, who are not to be executed but punished and encouraged to repent. In cases of minor blasphemies, or cases supported by only a single witness, the Mālikīyah prescribe a discretionary punishment in place of the death penalty.

Blasphemy in Islamic Theology and Philosophy. As indicated above, certain doctrinal propositions found their way into the lists of blasphemous statements. One of the earliest credal documents in Islam, the *Fiqh Akbar I* attributed to the jurist Abū Ḥanīfah (d. 767), includes two blasphemous statements about the prophets and God and calls them infidelity. But with the development of theological dogma, there was a tendency for scholars to label opposing doctrinal positions as forms of infidelity, even though only highly abstract arguments were involved. The legal consequences of such accusations were quite serious, as noted above, so it was natural that cooler heads insisted on moderating the use of such anathemas in theological debate. The great religious thinker Abū Ḥāmid al-Ghazālī (d. 1111) clarified this problem by removing infidelity (and hence blasphemy) from the realm of doctrine altogether. Insisting that infidelity is strictly a legal matter, al-Ghazālī defined it as calling the Prophet a liar in any respect; this is to equate infidelity with blasphemy. He further stipulated that no one who prays toward Mecca and repeats the Muslim confession of faith should be accused of infidelity, unless there is clear proof regarding a matter essential to the faith. In doctrinal terms, there are only three teachings that al-Ghazālī regards as infidelity in this sense. These teachings, all drawn from the works of philosophers such as Ibn Sīnā (Avicenna, d. 1037), are the doctrines that (1) the world is eternal and not God's creation; (2) God does not know particulars; and (3) the resurrection is not bodily but spiritual. Although al-Ghazālī enumerates many other doctrines that he considers objectionable, these alone appear to contradict the Prophet and divine revelation on essential matters (creation, divine omniscience, and eschatology). Thus teaching these doctrines is a blasphemous act punishable by death. It is worth noting that the Andalusian philosopher Ibn Rushd (Averroës, d. 1198) disputed al-Ghazālī's findings on both doctrinal and legal grounds, and later Iranian philosophers, such as Mullā Ṣadrā (d. 1637), certainly upheld similar theses. Although the doctrines of Greek philosophy seem far removed from the scurrilous insults that generally constitute blasphemy, certain of these teachings were potentially in serious conflict with the traditional Islamic understanding of revelation. Insofar as philosophy could be seen as calling the Prophet a liar, it constituted blasphemy.

Blasphemy in Ṣūfī Mysticism. The concept of blasphemy is applied rather differently in the case of mysticism. The growing Ṣūfī movement, which was centered on meditative practices that interiorized the Qur'ān and the ritual prayer, distinguished itself also by creating a technical vocabulary to express the states of mystical experience. Legalists challenged this innovation as a departure from the usage of the Qur'ān. More suspicious still were the ecstatic sayings *(shaṭḥīyāt)* that uncontrollably burst forth from the mystics. Ṣūfīs such as Abū Yazīd (Bāyazīd) al-Bisṭāmī (d. 874) and al-Ḥallāj (executed in 922) were notorious for such sayings as the former's "Glory be to Me! How great is My Majesty!" and the latter's "I am the Truth." Such proclamations appeared to be pretensions to divinity or prophecy, and readily fell into the category of blasphemy. Other sayings of this type criticized mechanical performance of ritual, made light of the punishments of hell, and, in general, made claims of great audacity.

Since Islamic law did not take formal cognizance of the existence of mystical states, the legal reaction to ecstatic sayings was not systematic. Certain Ṣūfīs, such as Nūrī (d. 907), ʿAyn al-Quḍāt (d. 1131), and the abovementioned al-Ḥallāj, were put on trial and even executed, but such trials were heavily politicized and did not reflect correct juridical procedure. Contrary to popular opinion, however, Ṣūfīs such as al-Ḥallāj were not executed on account of their utterances; historical accounts reveal a mixture of charges, including radical Shiism, philosophical atheism, pretension to divinity and prophecy, and libertinism. Al-Ḥallāj was formally accused of maintaining the legitimacy of private ritual that could substitute for pilgrimage to Mecca. The Ḥanafī legal textbooks give a few examples of blasphemous statements that savor of mysticism. These generally consist of claims to know the unseen *(ghayb)*, the assertion that only God exists, and the recognition of the omnipresence of God. Authentic ecstatic sayings were far more audacious than these examples cited by the jurists. One of the few jurists to review ecstatic sayings in detail was Ibn al-Jawzī (d. 1200), who severely criticized these utterances in his polemical treatise, *The*

Devil's Delusion. Later jurists frequently criticized the theosophical writings of the Andalusian Ṣūfī Ibn al-ʿArabī (d. 1240) as blasphemous; he drew fire, in particular, for upholding the validity of Pharaoh's confession of faith, though it was made even as the waters of the Red Sea fell upon him (10:90). This was not so much a contradiction of the Qur'ān as it was a rejection of the dominant learned opinion.

Some authorities attempted a compromise on the subject of ecstatic sayings by considering them the products of intoxication *(sukr).* As such, they were like the ravings of a madman and hence were not punishable as blasphemy. From this point of view, ecstatic sayings were neither accepted nor condemned. Ṣūfīs, on the other hand, maintained that they were symbolic of inner experiences and could only be understood by those who had attained to esoteric knowledge. Legalists were thus incapable of the spiritual exegesis *(ta'wīl)* that alone could provide the correct interpretation of ecstatic sayings. A significant minority of legal scholars accepted this distinction and so excused ecstatic sayings from the charge of blasphemy, on the grounds that they were symbolic.

BIBLIOGRAPHY

The Qur'anic references to the Meccans' verbal criticism of Muḥammad are conveniently listed and discussed in W. Montgomery Watt's *Muhammad at Mecca* (London, 1953), pp. 123–131. For the legal status of blasphemy insofar as it relates to apostasy, see Rudolph Peters and Gert J. J. de Vries's "Apostasy in Islam," *Die Welt des Islams,* n.s. 17 (1976–1977): 1–25, especially pages 2–4. Most of the legal treatises dealing with blasphemy remain unedited in manuscript form, but a French translation from the *Mukhtaṣar* by the Mālikī jurist Sīdī Khalīl (d. 1374) has been made by Léon Bercher, "L'apostasie, le blasphème et la rébellion in droit Musulman malékite," *Revue tunisienne* 30 (1923): 115–130 (occasioned by the controversy over the "naturalized" Tunisian Muslims who became subject to French instead of Islamic law). Other important legal discussions of blasphemy and apostasy can be found in David Santillana's *Istituzioni di diritto musulmano malichita con riguardo anche al sistema sciafiita,* vol. 1 (Rome, 1925), pp. 167–170 (Mālikī and Shāfi'ī); Eduard Sachau's *Muhammedanisches Recht nach Schafiitischer Lehre* (Stuttgart, 1897), pp. 843–846; and Neil B. E. Baillie's *A Digest of Moohummdan Laws,* 2 vols. (Lahore, 1965) (see the index for *apostacy* and *apostate*). A. J. Wensinck discusses the *Fiqh Akbar I* in *The Muslim Creed: Its Genesis and Historical Development,* 2d ed. (New Delhi, 1979), pp. 102–124. Al-Ghazālī's treatise on heresy and blasphemy has been translated by Richard Joseph McCarthy in *Freedom and Fulfillment* (Boston, 1980), pp. 145–174. Ibn al-Jawzī's censure of blasphemy of Sufism has been translated by David S. Margoliouth in " 'The Devil's Delusion' of Ibn al-Jauzi," *Islamic Culture* 10 (1936): 363–368 and 21 (1947): 394–402. An analysis of the legal criticisms of Ṣūfī sayings is available in my book *Words of Ecstasy in Sufism* (Albany, N.Y., 1985), in which see especially part 3.

CARL W. ERNST

BLAVATSKY, H. P. (1831–1891), principal founder of the modern theosophical movement. Helena Petrovna Blavatsky, née Hahn-Hahn, was born in Ekaterinoslav (present-day Dnepropetrovsk), Russia, of noble parentage. From earliest childhood she displayed remarkable paranormal powers, and these, coupled with her tempestuous personality and unconventional behavior, made her the controversial figure she remains to this day—attacked and vilified by some, honored and respected by others.

Married at seventeen, Blavatsky soon left home and husband. The very figure of an emancipated woman, she spent years traveling alone in Europe, the Americas, Egypt, and India, fighting with Giuseppe Garibaldi in Italy and even reaching Tibet, where she at last met the personage she claimed was the "master" who had long appeared to her in dreams.

Although she had little formal education, Blavatsky wrote encyclopedically, ranging over ancient as well as living religious traditions, drawing upon the sciences of her day, and quoting extensively from scholarly sources. This last aspect of her works led to charges of plagiarism, but she defended herself by saying that she was merely the transmitter, not the originator, of theosophical doctrines, which she traced to ancient Greek as well as Asian origins. She maintained that the real authors of her works were those she called her "masters," enlightened guardians of an ancient mystery tradition that lies at the heart of all religions and unifies them.

Restlessly seeking the work she felt appointed to do, Blavatsky reached New York in 1873 and quickly became involved in the spiritualist movement, which she saw as a force for penetrating the defenses of both scientific materialism and religious orthodoxy. She openly criticized spiritualist practices, however, thereby attracting the attention of inquirers interested in the philosophical aspects of the subject. Most notable among these inquirers was Colonel Henry S. Olcott, who joined with Blavatsky and others in forming the Theosophical Society in New York City on 17 November 1875. Two years later Blavatsky published *Isis Unveiled,* in which she introduced the Eastern and Western esoteric teachings that she later developed more fully. *The Secret Doctrine* (1888), her major work, expatiates upon three fundamental propositions: (1) that there is an omnipresent, eternal, boundless, and immutable Reality, of which spirit and matter are complementary aspects; (2) that there is a universal law of periodicity, or evolution through cyclic change; and (3) that all souls are identical with the universal Oversoul, which is itself an aspect of the unknown Reality.

In 1878, Blavatsky and Olcott left for India, where they founded *The Theosophist,* a journal dedicated to uniting Eastern spirituality with Western advances in thought. Blavatsky's increasing renown brought her into contact with many prominent people, and the Theosophical Society grew rapidly. But her outspoken criticism of Anglo-Indian attitudes toward Hindus and Hinduism, as well as the striking phenomena her followers claimed she produced, aroused the hostility of missionaries and other establishment figures, who tried to discredit her and her teachings. Often accused of being an impostor and even a Russian spy, she was, in the "Hodgson Report" (1885) that was issued by the London Society for Psychical Research, denounced as a fraud who had forged the letters she claimed to have received from her Tibetan mahatmas—a charge that was finally retracted in 1963. These allegations were vigorously protested by her many supporters as being false to Blavatsky's character and purpose, but the atmosphere of suspicion aggravated her already poor health, and she decided to leave India in 1885.

The remaining years of Blavatsky's life were spent in England and Europe. In spite of her increasing illness, she founded a new journal, *Lucifer,* wrote two works (*The Voice of the Silence* and *The Key to Theosophy,* both 1889), and completed *The Secret Doctrine,* which was published two and a half years before her death on 8 May 1891, a date still commemorated by members of the Theosophical Society as White Lotus Day.

[*See also* Theosophical Society *and the biography of Annie Besant.*]

BIBLIOGRAPHY

Thirteen volumes of Blavatsky's published work have so far been republished under the title *Collected Writings,* edited by Boris de Zirkoff (Los Angeles, 1950–). Two useful biographies are A. P. Sinnett's *Incidents in the Life of Madame Blavatsky* (London, 1913) and Howard Murphet's *When Daylight Comes* (Wheaton, Ill., 1975).

The so-called Hodgson Report, which denounced Blavatsky but which was retracted eighty years after its publication, is actually entitled "Account of Personal Investigations in India and Discussions of the Authorship of the 'Koot Hoomi' Letters by Richard Hodgson" and appears in the *Proceedings of the Society for Psychical Research* 3 (London, 1885), pp. 207–317.

EMILY SELLON

BLEEKER, C. JOUCO (1898–1983), Dutch historian of Egyptian religion and leading figure in the field of phenomenology of religion. Claas Jouco Bleeker was born in Beneden Knijpe, the Netherlands, and attended school in Leeuwarden. He went on to study theology at the University of Leiden. There he specialized in Egyptology and the history of religions, chiefly under the tutelage of W. Brede Kristensen, whose work influenced him greatly. He continued his studies at the University of Berlin, and in 1929 he received his Th.D. from the University of Leiden for his thesis *De beteekenis van de Egyptische godin Ma-a-t* (The Significance of the Egyptian Goddess Maat). In 1925 Bleeker began a career as a minister in the Dutch Reformed church, serving first in the town of Apeldoorn. He held pulpits in various Dutch cities until 1946 when he was appointed professor of the history of religions and the phenomenology of religion at the University of Amsterdam. He remained in that post until his retirement in 1949.

Bleeker's interest both in the religion of ancient Egypt and in religious phenomenology continued throughout his life. His writings on Egyptian religion consist for the most part of studies of individual deities, such as *Die Geburt eines Gottes: Eine Studie über den ägyptischen Gott Min und sein Fest* (The Birth of a God: A Study on the Egyptian God Min and His Festival; 1956), and research on particular aspects of Egyptian religious life, such as *Egyptian Festivals: Enactments of Religious Renewal* (1967).

His work in the field of phenomenology was strongly influenced by Kristensen and Gerardus van der Leeuw. Bleeker was concerned with establishing phenomenology of religion as a distinct scholarly discipline that would examine the meaning of religious phenomena in the light of their realized "essence." He understood religion to be structured in terms of "(a) a holy vision of the Supreme Being or of the being and the will of the Deity, (b) a holy path that a man must pursue in order to be freed from his sin and suffering, and (c) a holy action that the believer must carry out in the cult and in his personal religious life" (*The Rainbow,* 1975, p. 8). He proposed three main objectives for phenomenology of religion. First, it must seek to understand individual phenomena that appear in all or many religious systems, such as prayer (this type of inquiry he called "theōria"). Second, it must try to discover the inner laws that determine the structure of a particular religion ("logos"). Finally, it should attempt to elucidate the way in which religions develop and evolve ("entelecheia").

Bleeker viewed the study of religion as an examination of humanity's varied relationships with God, and he attempted to understand mankind in light of its various attitudes toward divinity. Furthermore, he believed that the science of religion could engender greater mutual respect and understanding among religious groups holding widely differing opinions.

An able and energetic administrator, Bleeker served as secretary-general of the International Association for the History of Religions from 1950 to 1970. From 1960 to 1977 he edited the I.A.H.R.'s review *Numen* and supervised that journal's supplementary monograph series "Studies in the History of Religions." With Geo Widengren he coedited the important, two-volume handbook *Historia Religionum* (1969–1971). He also oversaw the publication of the proceedings of several important international conferences.

Upon his retirement Bleeker was honored with a festschrift, *Liber Amicorum* (1969). Thereafter, until the time of his death, he remained active as a scholar, organizer, and editor.

BIBLIOGRAPHY

The fullest account of Bleeker's life is J. H. Kamstra's "In Memoriam Prof. Dr. C. J. Bleeker," *Nederlands theologisch tijdschrift* 38 (January 1984): 67–69 (in Dutch). See also the obituary by R. J. Zwi Werblowsky in *Numen* 30 (December 1983): 129–130. For assessments of Bleeker's contribution to scholarship, see Geo Widengren's "Professor C. J. Bleeker, A Personal Appreciation" in the festschrift *Liber Amicorum: Studies in Honour of Professor Dr. C. J. Bleeker* (Leiden, 1969), pp. 5–7, and J. G. Platvoet's "The Study of Rites in the Netherlands," in *Nederlands theologisch tijdschrift* 37 (July 1983): 177–188.

A complete bibliography of Bleeker's works up to 1969 may be found in the *Liber Amicorum*. To this list may be added *Hathor and Thoth: Two Key Figures in Ancient Egyptian Religion* (Leiden, 1973). Many of Bleeker's articles are collected in two volumes: *The Sacred Bridge: Researches into the Nature and Structure of Religion* (Leiden, 1963) and *The Rainbow: A Collection of Studies in the Science of Religion* (Leiden, 1975).

M. Heerma van Voss

BLESSING.

BLESSING. The term *blessing* has two fundamental meanings. In its first meaning, it is a form of prayer; it is man's adoration and praise of God. In its second meaning, the meaning that will be dealt with here, blessing is a divine gift that descends upon man, nature, or things; it is a material or spiritual benefit that results from divine favor. In this second meaning, blessing is the transfer of a sacred and beneficent power, a power that emanates from the supernatural world and confers a new quality on the object of the blessing.

Blessing is part of the life of *homo religiosus,* who both seeks and expects gifts and favors from divinity. Hence, this study will first examine the phenomenology of blessing as it appears in the behavior of *homo religiosus*—behavior determined by the belief in the sacred as a reality that transcends this world but which is nevertheless manifested in it. Second, it will elaborate a typology of blessing in different religions throughout the world.

Phenomenology of Blessing. Man as *homo religiosus* "believes that there is an absolute reality, the *sacred,* that transcends this world but manifests itself in this world, thereby sanctifying it and making it real" (Mircea Eliade, *The Sacred and the Profane,* New York, 1959, p. 202). He employs blessings as a means of remaining in contact with this reality in order to receive its beneficent influence. Through the blessing the sacred becomes manifest. A blessing is thus a type of hierophany. It is one of those mysterious acts through which a transcendent power becomes immanent in this world. In every blessing, therefore, a power intervenes to bestow benefits of divine origin upon a being or object.

Considered as an action, every blessing includes three elements: first, the establishment of a relationship with the realm of the Wholly Other, which is the source of the desired beneficial effect; second, the transfer, to a being or object, of an efficacious quality emanating from that realm, through some form of mediation; finally, the enhancement of the existence of the being or object that receives this quality. A blessing is not limited, therefore, simply to the expression of a vow or wish in favor of a particular person or object; it also involves the thought, will, and action that are involved in bringing about the transfer of a quality from the transcendent realm.

Power. At different times and places, man has given names to the transcendent power or reality that is the source of all blessings. [*See* Power.] One of the best known of these is *mana.* Of Melanesian origin, *mana* denotes a supernatural reality attached to beings or things—a reality full of the power, authority, and strength inherent in life and truth, all experienced as both real and effective. Indeed, the idea of a real and effective power is found again and again in nonliterate traditions throughout the world, receiving such names as *orenda* (Iroquois), *manitou* (Algonquian), *wakan* (Lakota), and *uxbe* (Pueblo). In the high civilizations of antiquity, it appears as *brahman* (India), *tao* (China), *kami* (Japan), *khvarenah* (ancient Iran), *me* (Sumer), and *melammu* (Mesopotamia). This power was often more precisely expressed in terms of a celestial theophany and was frequently personified, as can be seen most clearly in the cases of Judaism, Christianity, and Islam.

Transfer. However conceived, this transcendent power is transferred to the human realm through the blessing. The divine will can carry out this transfer *motu pro-*

prio, without the aid of an intermediary. Nevertheless, a blessing commonly makes use of some form of mediation. The intermediary, who uses both ritual and symbols, may be a king or a priest, a saint, a prophet, or the head of a family. By ritual means he animates the mysterious forces that make communication with the transcendent power possible and thereby creates a special relationship with the divinity. This ritual mediation requires special gestures since the body is the instrument with which the intermediary expresses intelligence, will, or emotion. Such gestures and postures are filled with meaning since they are understood within the context of a group of recognized symbols. Of particular significance is the position of the right hand. Indeed, the hand is capable of creating a language of its own, and it is ceaselessly active throughout the ritual. [*See* Hands.]

The spoken word occupies a special place in the symbolism of mediation—so special, in fact, that F. Max Müller could claim that *nomina sunt numina.* The mystical power of words is particularly prominent among archaic peoples. In Australia, the voices of the bull-roarers, symbols of the Great Spirit's presence, are heard throughout every initiation ceremony. In Vedism, *vāc* is the celestial word, an aspect of the *brahman;* and the syllable *oṃ* is believed to encompass the universe, the *brahman,* the sound that gives fullness to the sacrifice. The word is also the instrument of divine power, which may be invoked by the civilizing word, the prophetic word, or in the evocation of holy names. The presence of theophoric names and all manner of incantations in all ancient civilizations demonstrates man's belief in the power of the word. Indeed, the Akkadian *amatu* and the Hebrew *davar* refer to the word understood as coincidental with reality itself.

Just as it is the sign of the divine presence and the instrument of divine power, so the word is creative. In Egypt and Mesopotamia, creation takes place through the pronunciation of the holy name. The belief in creation through God's word pervades both the Bible and the Qur'ān. In initiation ceremonies, neophytes are given words filled with power, words that must be used wisely, in accord with the ritual formula. That formula, combined with the rhythm and tonality of the words, provides the secret of the rite's effectiveness. Ultimately, the word is creative as an aspect of the sacred's self-manifestation, or hierophany. [*See* Language, *article on* Sacred Language.]

Gifts and favors. The third element of a blessing is the actual benefit that a being or object receives through contact with the transcendent power. This power is dynamic. The Sanskrit *ojas,* the Avestan *aojō,* and the Latin *augustus* all have the sense of an enabling power, one that literally empowers its possessor to fulfill the religious function allotted to him. In this sense, the ritual of blessing brings about a participation in the sacred itself, that is, in the real that is powerful, effective, and lasting. Thus, in Vedic India, a new territory is settled by the erection of an altar to Agni, god of fire and messenger of the gods. By this act, the territory is set apart from the profane and is established in a new and sacred dimension. In *Genesis* 9:1, God blesses Noah and his sons directly, saying to them, "Be fruitful and multiply." In *Numbers* 6:22–27, the sacerdotal blessing is intended to assure divine protection, benevolence, and peace to the faithful. Blessings may also produce less spiritual results: fertility, health, and long life in men or animals, bountiful harvests, material prosperity. Whatever the nature of the gifts or favors he receives, man is always conscious of their divine origin, acknowledging the transcendent power that lies behind the effectiveness of blessing.

Typology of Blessing. This section presents a selective survey of the great variety of forms of blessing practiced by *homo religiosus* at different times and places. The typology developed here does not consider the different conceptions of the divine power itself and the different types of benefits that it confers (the first and third elements discussed above). Instead it will classify types of blessing according to the methods of transfer that they employ, the methods that actually set the blessing in motion. In particular, it will focus on three essential aspects of such methods: language, gesture, and ritual.

Religions of peoples with oral traditions. Among peoples without writing, blessing is intimately linked to myth. Indeed, in the life of these peoples, myth constitutes a sacred history that puts man in contact with the supernatural world, joining present and primordial time and linking present action to the initial acts of creation. This sacred history furnishes archaic man with models for his life. In addition, he grasps the meaning of the celestial archetype through the symbolic language of myth; blessing constitutes one of the archaic ritual forms that he uses in his various efforts to orient himself in reference to that archetype. Within the vast magico-religious context of archaic ritual, word and gesture are inseparably linked.

In a great many religious traditions, the sacred word, the word spoken by God, appears at the first moment of creation. Among the Dogon, for example, the Nommo spoke three times, pronouncing words of light, of dampness, and of music. In archaic belief, man's spoken word, addressed to the Wholly Other, allows him to participate in divine power or, at least, to benefit from it. Such a belief, admirably documented in the stone prayer carvings of Valcamonica, underlies the beginnings of prayer and is expressed in the incantations that are part of every people's patrimony—incantations that seek to constrain divine power through the repetition of spoken words. In sub-Saharan Africa, the word approaches its fullest power to the extent that it is joined with rhythm and image, its most effective mediators. The hand also carries meaning, and among the Dogon, the Bambara, and the Fali, the thumb is the symbol of power. Word, rhythm, and gesture are fully integrated in the rituals associated with myths of fertility and initiation; indeed, when used in celebrations of myth, they reestablish, through the reactualization of the archetypal event, the complete harmony believed to have existed at the beginning. Africans have created from myth, word, and ritual an effective symbolic unity used to reestablish the original harmony. Ancestors are also important in these rituals, for they exist in primordial time and have a major role in the transfer of favors to the living. Likewise, the human intermediary has an important role in the ritual of blessing.

In Australia, the Aboriginal doctor gains access to the primordial sacred universe once he is initiated; as the intermediary between the tribal group and its mythic ancestors, he effects a transfer of divine power that supports him in his role as healer and rainmaker. Moreover, working with the Aboriginal doctor is a group of initiates who also have made effective contact with the sacred. In fact, archaic man benefits from divine power as a result of initiation, which establishes a link with primordial history.

Among the ethnically related groups in Burundi and Rwanda in central Africa, all religious life revolves around belief in Imana, the supreme being, omnipotent creator, good and omniscient protector of man and nature. A child is placed under Imana's blessing at birth, and on the eighth day his father gives him a name associated with the god. Imana's importance in the life of the Rundi people of the Nyarwanda ethnic group is clear in the impressive list of theophoric names transmitted by the oral tradition: Haremimana ("God creates"), Hategekimana ("God commands"), Hakizimana ("God makes happy"), Hagenimana ("God predestines"), Ndagijimana ("God is my guardian"). In fact, theophoric names signify Imana's permanent blessing and guidance of those who bear them. Human intermediaries, especially heads of families, play an important role in obtaining the effects of blessing. During Kurya Umwaka, the New Year festival celebrated in Burundi in May, the father presides over a meal that consists of "eating the old year"; acting as both intermediary of the god and head of the family, he distributes food from Imana and pronounces wishes for happiness in the new year. Another intermediary in Burundi is the *mupmufu*, the prophet, magician, and healer who has the responsibility of transmitting the word of Imana. In a ceremony after the building of a hut, he blesses it with lustral water. When sickness appears in the hut, he is called upon, as Imana's emissary, to bless the inhabitants.

Symbols of the right hand. Biblical texts are filled with references to the hand of God, which touches man and causes him to share in divine power, but these are by no means the only religious writings that give an important, beneficent role to the hand. A number of Mediterranean and Eastern religions have particularly emphasized the symbolic role of the right hand. [*See also* Left and Right.] In the Syrian cults of Jupiter Dolichenus, Atargatis, and Hadad, as in the Phrygian cult of the god Satazius, votive hands indicate the divine presence and symbolize God's power. In Africa, the raised hand, a substitute for divinity, appears in the tympanium on the front of Punic stelae (Leglay, 1978). Statuaries from both the East and—especially—the West furnish many examples of gods extending their hand in a gesture of blessing and protection; indeed, Zeus is sometimes called Hyperdexios, the protector with the extended hand. This gesture is also represented on effigies of Asklepios, the god of healing. In all these artifacts invoking the vast symbolic system surrounding blessing, the right hand is both a sign of power and the expression of a benevolent divine will, of the gods' transfer of part of their strength and power.

The symbolism of the hand appears in another form in the *dexiōsis*, the handshake—always of right hands—that creates mysterious bonds of union. A number of documents concerning the *dexiōsis* come from the Roman world, where the gesture was associated with the *fides*, an agreement of alliance and voluntary, reciprocal obligation. Representations of the *dexiōsis* sometimes show clasped hands together with ears of wheat, symbols of the prosperity that comes from concord, itself the result of the divine blessing of the goddess Fides; here, the *dexiōsis* shifts notions of concord and obligation into the religious domain of the blessing. The *dexiōsis* is found in the liturgy of the cults of Dionysos, Sabazios, and Isis; in all these cults, the ritual signifies both the celestial apotheosis of the god and the entrance of the devout into the elite group of initiates who have received divine gifts. The *dextrarum iunctio* is a gesture binding the initiate to his god's power; as ancient Latin authors wrote, "Felix dextra, salutis humanae pignus."

Dexiōsis and blessing in Mithraism and Manichaeism. The *dexiōsis* played a major role in the myth and ritual that are intertwined in Mithraic liturgy. A number of illustrated documents from Rome, Dura-Europos (present-day Salahiyeh, Syria), and the Danubian area represent the *dexiōsis* of Mithra and Helios, seated together in the celestial chariot; the scene evokes the apotheosis of the young Mithra, conqueror of evil and darkness, and at the same time presents the mythical archetype to which the ritual *dexiōsis* alludes in the Mithraic initiation. At the conclusion of the initiation ceremony, the *pater,* the *magister sacrorum* ("chief priest") of the Mithraic community, welcomes the initiate by extending his right hand to him; by this gesture, the initiate becomes one of the participants in the rite, who then join in the same gesture and are thereby introduced to the cult's salvation mysteries. This *dexiōsis* seals the agreement between Mithra and the initiate and creates a bond that insures the initiate's salvation. By joining their right hands, the initiates take part in the mystic *dexiōsis* of Mithra and Helios and at the same time ensure, through this authentic ritual of blessing, the transfer of the benefits of salvation promised by Mithra to those inducted into his mysteries.

The ritual of the *dexiōsis* in Mithraic mysteries of the Roman empire has been clarified by evidence recently discovered at Nimrud-Dagh and at Arsameia Nymphaios in the ancient province of Commagene, between Cilicia and the Euphrates River, where Mithraism was a royal cult during the centuries immediately preceding the Christian era. Several representations show the gods Mithra, Herakles, Zeus, and Apollo extending their right hands to King Antiochus I, son of the cult's founder, Mithradates I Kallinikos. The king, an inscription states, believes that he is the instrument of "religious piety" *(eusebeia)* and that he fulfills the will of the gods; he places the sanctuary he has just built under divine protection and entrusts the maintenance of the cult to a sacerdotal college. Such evidence reflects the syncretism of Hellenistic cults, resulting from the encounter of Greek and Eastern religious ideas; in the example from Arsameia, the *dexiōsis* has become a rite through which divine power was transferred to the person of the king.

The pattern uniting myth, ritual, and *dexiōsis* is found again in Manichaeism in Mani's great myth of the struggle between Light and Darkness. The Living Spirit, second messenger of the Father of Greatness, walks toward the boundary of the Realm of Darkness to save Primordial Man, prisoner of Darkness; he lets out a great cry, "Tōchme," heard by Primordial Man, who replies, "Sōtme." The Living Spirit then extends his right hand; grasping it, Primordial Man, the savior saved, regains the Paradise of Light. Used similarly in the Manichaean community, the saving gesture of the *dexiōsis* became the gnostic gesture *par excellence* since it both symbolized and realized the communication of the dualistic mysteries, the sources of salvation.

Power of the word. The energy of the word is central to Indian religious thought; indeed, the word is considered a power in itself. [*See* Logos.] Sanskrit includes a number of words that are close in meaning to "blessing" or "to bless" or that suggest the result of a blessing: *āśis* ("wish, blessing"), *āśirvāda* ("benediction"), *kuśala* ("prosperous"), *dhanya* ("that which brings good fortune"), *kalyāṇa* ("excellent"). The word *kuśalavāda* confers "benefits," and *kuśalam* is "the benefit received, the desirable thing, the blessing." *Maṅgala* signifies "the spoken blessing, the word of good augur"; *maṅgalācāra* is "the rite that assures happiness" and *maṅgalāyana* "the route of felicity." The word *brahman* means "sacred word"; originally, it signified "the word that causes growth."

Brahmanaspati, or Bṛhaspati, is chaplain of the gods, charged with reciting the sacred formulas. "O Bṛhaspati," begins the Vedic hymn "The Word" (Ṛgveda 10.71.1), "then it was, the first beginning of the word, when they were set in motion, giving a name to things." As *purohita,* or chief priest of the gods, he is charged with reciting the sacred formulas; they become beneficent in his mouth. Indeed, to be effective, the formulas must be pronounced, but once pronounced they are real, beneficent, and effective by themselves, not through the chaplain's mediation. The Vedic priest, the *brāhmaṇa,* sometimes asks for the help of Brahmanaspati, who can suggest effective words to him. "I put a splendid word in your mouth," the *purohita* says to the *brāhmaṇa* (*Ṛgveda* 10.98.2). Words of blessing are also spoken by the father at the birth of a son: "Be imperishable gold. Truly you are the One called son. Live a hundred autumns."

Blessing in the Hebrew scriptures. The Semitic root *brk,* "bless," was the common property of all peoples of the ancient Near East. Likewise, the Assyrian word *karabu* was used frequently to denote the formulas of blessing pronounced by the gods. But the most abundant evidence of the importance of blessing comes from ancient Israel. The root *brk* and the noun *berakhah* ("blessing") appear 398 times in the Old Testament (Hebrew scriptures). *Barukh,* the qualifying past participle, denotes the condition of possessing the *berakhah;* hence, God is *barukh* since he possesses, and dispenses, the truths of salvation. In its plural form, *brk* is used to indicate the act of blessing, which may be carried out by God, angels, or men. In addition to designating the transfer of benefits from God to men, *brk* means "praise raised up to God by man," but this meaning, which describes a form of prayer, is not discussed in this article.

In the typology of blessing found in the Hebrew scriptures a first major tendency is exemplified by God's dispensation of benefits among people or among created things generally. After the creation, he blesses the beings he has just made (*Gn.* 1:22–28); after the Flood, he blesses Noah and his children (*Gn.* 9:1). Likewise, he blesses the patriarchs Abraham, Isaac, and Jacob, and finally, all the children of Israel (*Gn.* 12:2–3, 27:16, 35:9; *Dt.* 1:11), all of whom become *barukh,* beneficiaries of divine blessing. This blessing can also apply to nonliving things that assist in the execution of the divine plan: the Sabbath (*Gn.* 2:3), bread and water (*Ex.* 23:25), the home of the righteous (*Prv.* 3:33). Faith in the value of God's blessing underlies the many wishes for good fortune found in the Hebrew scriptures: "Blessed be Abram by God Most High" (*Gn.* 14:19). This faith, together with the value accorded divine benefits and favors, is also involved in the salutation given to visitors, the wishes exchanged between host and guest, and the greeting of peace—for peace is considered a gift of God (see *2 Kgs.* 4:29). Although some of these concerns are part of the common patrimony of ancient Semitic peoples, only the Old Testament is categorical: God alone is the source and the absolute master of every blessing.

In addition to the forms discussed, blessing appears in the Old Testament in a truly original way, one that goes well beyond the conventional Semitic meaning of *brk.* To the ancient Hebrews, blessing was also the expression of the divine favor stemming from God's choice of a particular people whom he surrounds with his solicitude. This favor was first manifested in the vocation of Abraham (*Gn.* 12:2–3); the superabundant blessing that God gave to Abraham will be poured over the chosen people and, ultimately, over all peoples. This spiritual and universal idea of divine blessing finds its fullest development in the Covenant and the teachings of the prophets, where the blessing conferred on Abraham becomes a program of salvation upon which God insists (*Gn.* 18:18–19, 22:16–18, 26:4–5, 28:13–15). Israel's mission, which is the Covenant, and the prophetic movement are rooted in God's blessing of Abraham; hence, this blessing is part of the history of salvation.

The second important tendency in the Old Testament typology of blessing involves the blessing conferred by God through an intermediary—family head, king, or priest—charged with a mission. At first, this tendency merely reflected a number of Semitic cultural and religious influences. Among the Phoenicians and the Arameans, the father of the family was the intermediary, addressing the gods on behalf of his wife and children; among the nomadic clans of Syria and Canaan, the ancestral cult and the chiefs' hereditary authority strongly influenced life in the clan and were, in fact, as important in malediction as in blessing. Nevertheless, while this Semitic heritage is present in certain customs of the chosen people, the Hebrew scriptures are marked chiefly by the presence of God in the midst of the people whom he has chosen for himself and whom he leads through selected intermediaries. The effects of the patriarchs' blessings continue to be felt (*Gn.* 27:27–29, 48:15); the nuptial blessing becomes part of the chosen people's life (*Ru.* 4:11, *Tb.* 10:11). Words of blessing pronounced by the king, or in his favor, are rooted in God's choice of David and of his dynasty (*2 Sm.* 7:29, *1 Chr.* 17:27). The father of the family gives his blessing by both the spoken word and the laying on of hands, a practice that seems to be a specific mark of the chosen people. An archetypal rite that goes back to the patriarchal period, the laying on of hands is described at length in *Genesis* 48:1–20 and appears throughout both the Old and the New Testaments.

As the religious institutions of the chosen people who had become the holy nation of God were fixed, and their liturgical organization refined, the priests, successors of Aaron, gradually assumed the responsibility of blessing the children of Israel, of offering official blessings in God's name. The sacerdotal blessing, the archetype of which is found in *Numbers* 6:22–27, involves three supplications, each invoking God's name. The precious benefits to be assured to the faithful are God's protection, his benevolence, and his peace, a peace that epitomizes all that is good on the earth. This view of blessing is far removed from the simple good wishes or salutations found in the pagan cults of the archaic Semitic world. In the covenant with his people, God gives assurance that he will bless those who receive the sacerdotal blessing; the priests, in their mission as God's intermediaries, transform the sacerdotal power of blessing into an institution of the Hebrew scriptures. The laying on of hands, considered since earliest times a private ritual of blessing, now becomes part of official liturgy. Likewise, the ritual elevation of the hands becomes part of Jewish priestly custom; at the end of the worship ceremony, a priest blesses the congregation, which replies, "Amen."

Barakah among the Arabs and in Islam. In the Arab world, the Semitic root *brk* seems originally to have meant both "blessing" and "crouching." The verb *baraka* was used to designate the appearance of a camel in a crouching position; *bark* signified a herd of kneeling camels. According to Joseph Chelhod (1955), a shift in meaning toward the idea of mating gave the sense of procreation or strength to *baraka.* Thus, in the pre-Islamic Arab world, *baraka* came to mean "having many descendants"; it also suggested the transfer of strength and fertility from father to children. Additionally, *baraka* meant "to prosper, to enjoy large herds, abundant grasses, and rich harvests"; it denoted a quality in beings and things that brought them prosperity and success. In the Arab mind, the idea seems to have developed of transferring this quality; *barakah* (noun; pl., *barakāt*) could be transferred to such acts as kissing a hand or touching a holy object. [*See* Touching.] In popular Islam, traces of this nomadic notion of *barakah* remain in attitudes toward localities, historical personalities, and sacred objects.

In the uncompromising monotheism of Islam, the omnipotence and omnipresence of God stand at the center of the life of the faithful and the community. God is the source of all that is sacred; the sacred refers only to the will of Allāh, the holy God, Al-Quddūs, a term that implies the power, strength, and mastery that God alone can possess. In the Qur'ān, *barakāt* are sent to people by God; *barakah* is God's blessing, the gift that he makes to mortals of the power to dispense his benefits, all of which proceed from him. Linked to the holiness of God, *barakah* is an influence that proceeds from all that touches God closely: the Qur'ān, the Prophet, the Five Pillars of Islam, the mosques, and the saints. Yet because Islam has neither clergy nor ministry, *barakah* finds no human intermediary: all blessing comes from God.

Christian blessing. The Septuagint translates *berekh* with the word *eulogein,* which in the Vulgate is *benedicere. Berakhah* is rendered by *eulogia,* a word that can denote either the praise creatures lift up to God or the gifts God makes to his creatures—the sense in which it is discussed here. *Eulogia* results from an act of blessing; it is the blessing itself, the gift given to a being. *Eulogēsis* denotes the act through which the blessing is conferred, the action of the church's minister, who gives the blessing. In the Vulgate, *benedictio* carries the meaning of both *eulogia* and *eulogēsis;* in the Septuagint, *eulogētos* corresponds to the Hebrew *barukh.*

The Gospels report a number of Jesus' blessings of persons and things. He blesses little children (*Mk.* 10:16) and the bread that he will multiply (*Mt.* 14:19); immediately before his ascension, he blesses his disciples (*Lk.* 24:50). The editors of *Luke* and *Mark* also recorded Jesus' gestures. He blessed the children by laying his hands on them, while to the disciples he raised his hands in blessing. Such gestures of blessing were already familiar to the Jews. According to the Talmud, the priests gave the blessing in the temple daily, during the morning sacrifice; they remained standing, their arms upraised, during the ceremony. Rabbis also followed the custom of blessing little children, which explains the behavior of the mothers who presented their children to Jesus. But Christ's gestures were not limited to the customs of his time. The description of the ceremony of blessing in *Matthew* 14:19 emphasizes the fact that Jesus "looked up to heaven," a gesture characteristic of his blessings, intended to indicate God's transcendence.

The expression "Pax vobis," used by Jesus when speaking with his disciples, is an authentic formula of blessing (*Lk.* 24:36, *Jn.* 20:19, 20:21). Christ charges those whom he sends forth to pronounce this blessing in their apostolic work (*Mt.* 10:12, *Lk.* 10:5, *Jn.* 20:21); Paul uses it repeatedly in his letters (*Rom.* 1:7, *Phil.* 4:7, *Col.* 3:15); John of Patmos places it at the beginning of the *Revelation* (*Rv.* 1:4). As the epistles of Ignatius of Antioch attest, the church quickly took up this formula, thus establishing what will become a long ecclesiastical tradition. The "Pax vobis" is by no means intended merely as a polite greeting. It is, rather, a blessing that brings to its recipients the messianic peace, with all that that implies. The apostles' use of the words *charis* ("grace") and *eirēnē* ("peace") should be understood in the context of this blessing (*Rom.* 1:7, *1 Cor.* 1:7, *1 Pt.* 1:2).

Jesus' words and gestures of blessing passed into the various Christian communities. Referring in the *Paedagogus* to Jesus' blessing of the children, Clement of Alexandria uses a concise formulation—*cheirothesia eulogias,* blessing by the laying on of hands—that is evidence of the ceremonial during his time (*Paedagogus* 2.5). Elsewhere, he writes that this ritual was also used in the gnostic circle of Basilides to help sustain the brotherhood (*Stromateis* 3.1.2–5). From the *Clementine Homilies* and the *Acts of Thomas,* it is clear that the ritual of blessing was customary in Christian circles. At a very early date, blessing appears in liturgical regulations such as the *Apostolic Tradition.* In the *Apostolic Constitutions,* the right of blessing is reserved to priests and bishops, since, in the thinking of the church fathers, the power of blessing went hand in hand with the church's mandate to sanctify the world and things. In the eyes of the church, the sacerdotal blessing is effective because it comes from God through his priests, who are also his ministers. Hence, the Council of Laodicea (c. 363) prohibited receiving blessings from the hands of heretics, and theologians later defined blessing as a sacred ritual through which the church brings divine favors—primarily spiritual favors—upon people and things.

Ancient documents dealing with rites of blessing are plentiful. Catacomb paintings and references in literature show that in the second century the usual gesture of Christian blessing was the laying on of hands; during the third century, this gesture was gradually replaced by the *sphragis tou Christou* ("the sign of the cross"). Indeed, it is evident from the *Sibylline Oracles,* from writings of Tertullian and Cyril of Jerusalem, and from mural paintings and the first Christian sarcophagi that the sign of the cross pervaded Christian customs from the third century onward. The shift from the laying on of hands to the sign of the cross as the characteristic gesture of blessing, combined with the increased use of prayer formulas, shows that Christians were aware of the transcendence of the ritual of blessing and hence were indifferent about actual physical contact with the hand or hands, and about the hands' position, in the ritual itself. Hence they could easily adopt a number of finger gestures borrowed from orators of the Greco-Roman world after the disappearance of paganism. Moreover, documents of the Eastern, Western, and African churches, through their explicit discussion of the gestures and prayers associated with blessing, make clear the importance of the rite and the effect that was attributed to it; the invocation of the names of Jesus and of the other persons of the divinity assured the effectiveness of the episcopal or sacerdotal ritual. Over the centuries, blessings multiplied and took different forms in different countries; until the Middle Ages, they were grouped with other rites of the church under the general name of sacraments. In the twelfth century, however, from the influence of Hugh of Saint-Victor (d. 1142), Abelard (d. 1142), and Alger of Liège (d. 1131), the denomination of sacred rite was given to blessing, and emphasis in the rite was placed more upon its formula than upon gestures. This emphasis was accentuated by Luther's Reformation. To the reformers, God's presence and action are known and carried out through the word; in the word, therefore, is found the whole effectiveness of blessing.

Conclusion. This brief study has shown the importance and role of blessing in the life of *homo religiosus*. Conscious of the existence of an absolute reality transcending this world, religious man tries to draw the favors of that reality toward himself in order to give a dimension of perfection to his life. Blessing is one of the efforts set in motion to bring about the transfer of divine power to man or things; to *homo religiosus*, this effort achieves its greatest effectiveness through the proper combination of word and gesture. In Christianity, through the archetype of Jesus Christ, the typology of blessing reaches its fullest development. Christ, the divine Logos that manifests itself in the human condition, himself performs the gestures of blessing that the church will continue through the ministry of its bishops, priests, and pastors.

BIBLIOGRAPHY

Bianchi, Ugo, ed. *Mysteria Mithrae: Proceedings of the International Seminar on the Religio-Historical Character of Roman Mithraism, with Particular Reference to Roman and Ostian Sources, Rome and Ostia, 28–31 March 1978*. Leiden, 1979. Includes numerous documents; a veritable compendium on Mithraism.

Chelhod, Joseph. "La baraka chez les Arabes." *Revue de l'histoire des religions* 148 (July–September 1955): 68–88.

Coppens, Joseph. *L'imposition des mains et les rites connexes dans le Nouveau Testament et dans l'église ancienne*. Paris, 1925.

Eliade, Mircea. *Patterns in Comparative Religion*. New York, 1958.

Junker, Hubert. "Segen als heilsgeschichtliches Motivwort im Alten Testament." In *Sacra Pagina*, edited by Joseph Coppens et al., vol. 1, pp. 548–558. Paris, 1959.

Keller, C. A., and G. Wehmeier. "*Brk*, segnen." In *Theologisches Handwörterbuch zum Alten Testament*, vol. 1, pp. 359–376. Munich, 1971.

Leeuw, Gerardus van der. *Religion in Essence and Manifestation*. 2d ed. 2 vols. New York, 1963.

Leglay, Marcel. "La dexiôsis dans les mystères de Mithra." In *Études mithriaques*, edited by Jacques Duchesne-Guillemin, pp. 279–303. Tehran, 1978. A thorough study of the *dexiōsis* in Hellenistic and Roman religions.

Scharbert, Josef. *Solidarität in Segen und Fluch im Alten Testament und in seiner Umwelt*. Bonn, 1958.

Thomas, Louis-Vincent, and René Luneau. *La terre africaine et ses religions*. Paris, 1974.

Walmann, Helmut. *Die kommagenischen Kultreformen unter König Mithradates I: Kallinikos und seinem Sohne Antiochos I*. Leiden, 1973. A precise study of archaeological evidence and Mithraic inscriptions from Commagene.

Westermann, Claus. *Blessing: In the Bible and the Life of the Church*. Philadelphia, 1978.

JULIEN RIES

Translated from French by Jeffrey C. Haight
and Annie S. Mahler

BLONDEL, MAURICE (1861–1949), French Roman Catholic philosopher. Blondel was born at Dijon and educated at the École Normale Supérieure, where he was a pupil of Léon Ollé Laprune, to whom he dedicated his thesis, published as *L'action*, which he presented at the Sorbonne in 1893. He was professor of philosophy at Aix-en-Provence from 1897 to 1927. *L'action* aroused much interest and controversy because of its originality. Blondel claimed that from purely philosophical premises he had reached theological conclusions. Unlike the positivists, who were dominant in the university, and the scholastics, who controlled the theological schools, Blondel worked from a subtle analysis of what was involved in human experience, and maintained that it pointed to, and in the end required, the supernatural. Thus by what was known as "the method of immanence" he arrived at the transcendent. By "action" he did not mean only activity but all that is involved in the human response to reality, including affection, willing, and knowing.

Blondel was not a lucid writer, and his teaching was regarded as complicated and obscure. He spent the rest of his life in trying to clarify his meaning and seeking to distinguish his ideas from those of others with which they were liable to be confused. He waited for many years before publishing a revised edition of *L'action,* which, with other works, won for his thought a widespread influence in France. Most important among these other works were *Le problème de la philosophie catholique* (The Problem of Catholic Philosophy; 1932), *La pensée* (Thought; 1934), *L'être et les êtres* (Being and Beings; 1935), and *La philosophie et l'esprit chrétien* (Philosophy and the Spirit of Christianity; 1944–1949). One of his closest collaborators was Lucien Laberthonnière, but eventually Blondel fell out with him, as he did with most of his contemporaries. He was involved in the modernist movement and obviously desired a renewal of the church's teaching, but he insisted that he did not share the views of modernists such as Alfred Loisy, Édouard Le Roy, and Friedrich von Hügel. Though sometimes threatened with ecclesiastical censure, he avoided it, and indeed received a certificate of orthodoxy from Pope Pius X.

BIBLIOGRAPHY

In addition to *L'action* (1893; reprinted in 2 vols., Paris, 1936), *The Letter on Apologetics, and History and Dogma* (New York, 1964), and the other works mentioned above, several volumes of Blondel's correspondence have been published. In English there is the *Correspondence of Pierre Teilhard de Chardin and Maurice Blondel,* translated by William Whitman (New York, 1967), and *Maurice Blondel and Auguste Valensin, 1899–1912,* 2 vols. (Paris, 1957). None of Blondel's major works has been translated into English.

A comprehensive 240-page Blondel bibliography was produced by René Virgoulay and Claude Troisfontaines, *Maurice Blondel: Bibliographie analytique et critique* (Louvain, 1975). The following works about Blondel can be recommended: Frédéric Lefèvre's *L'itinéraire philosophique de Maurice Blondel* (Paris, 1928); Paul Archambault's *Vers un réalism intégral: L'œuvre philosophique de Maurice Blondel* (Paris, 1928); Henri Bouillard's *Blondel and Christianity* (Washington, D.C., 1970); and René Virgoulay's *Blondel et le modernisme: La philosophie de l'action et les sciences religieuses* (Paris, 1980). Blondel's work is also discussed in Bernard M. G. Reardon's *Roman Catholic Modernism* (Stanford, Calif., 1970) and in Gabriel Daly's *Transcendence and Immanence: A Study in Catholic Modernism and Integralism* (Oxford, 1980).

ALEC VIDLER

BLOOD. Among the religions of the world one finds many ambivalent or contradictory attitudes toward blood. Blood is perceived as being simultaneously pure and impure, attractive and repulsive, sacred and profane; it is at once a life-giving substance and a symbol of death. Handling blood is sometimes forbidden, sometimes mandatory, but usually dangerous. Rites involving blood require the intervention of individual specialists (warriors, sacrificers, circumcisers, butchers, or executioners) and always the participation of the group or community.

In many primitive societies, blood is identified as a soul substance: of men, of animals, and even of plants. The Romans said that in it is the *sedes animae* ("seat of life"). In pre-Islamic times, Arabs considered it the vegetative, liquid soul that remains in the body after death, feeding on libations. For the Hebrews, "the life of the flesh is in the blood" (*Lv.* 17:4).

The spilling of blood is often forbidden. This ban applies to certain categories of humans and animals: sacrificial victims, royalty, game, and so on. The Iroquois, the Scythians (Herodotus, 4.60–61), and the old Turco-Mongols, as well as the rulers of the Ottoman empire, forbade shedding the blood of persons of royal lineage. There is reason to believe that the Indian Hindu religions that have abolished sacrifices, and the feasting that goes with sacrifice, have done so more to avoid the shedding of blood than to comply with the dogmas of nonviolence and reincarnation. According to *Genesis* 9:4, the eating of raw meat is forbidden: "But you must not eat the flesh with the life, which is the blood, still in it." [*See* Omophagia.] The Islamic tradition has similar restrictions.

Attitudes toward blood can be divided into two general categories: toward the blood of strangers, foreigners, or enemies and toward the blood of members of one's own community.

The blood of enemies usually is not protected by any taboo. It has been suggested that one justification for war is the perceived necessity of shedding blood in order to water the earth. One frequently encounters the idea that the earth is thirsty for blood—but only for licit blood. It can refuse blood that is not licit or cry out for vengeance against such illicit bloodshed, as the biblical passages *Isaiah* 26:21 and *Job* 16:18 illustrate. In pre-Columbian America blood was essential to the survival of the Sun, and in other countries it was demanded by the gods. [*See* Human Sacrifice.]

The killing of enemies is sometimes mandatory. Among the Turkic peoples in ancient times and again during the Islamic period in the sixteenth century, an adolescent did not acquire his adulthood, his name, and thus his soul until he committed his first murder. Killing—and being killed—has been the *raison d'être* for the Ojibwa and Dakota Indian tribes, as well as, to a certain extent, the Muslim "martyrs" of holy war and the Japanese samurai. At one time, a bloody death at the hand of an enemy seemed more to be envied than a natural death. However, concerning the caste of Hindu warriors in India, it was believed that one whose vocation was killing awaited his own immolation.

The blood of the enemy is rarely dangerous, even though the qualities and strengths of the soul remain in it. In antiquity people attempted to appropriate these qualities of blood by drinking it or washing themselves in it. Herodotus (17.64) notes that the Scythians drank the blood of the first victims they killed.

Within the community, however, attitudes toward blood and killing are different. Members of the community are connected by consanguinity, and they share collective responsibility for one another; the blood of each is the blood of all. The group's totemic animals may be included in this community, which is connected to the animals by adoption or alliance. A stranger can enter the group through marriage or "blood brotherhood," a custom practiced among the Fon of West Africa and among Central Asian peoples. Relations between blood brothers can be established in various ways, often through the juxtaposition of cuts made in their wrists or by pouring a few drops of blood into a cup, mixing it with wine (called "the blood of the vine" in antiquity), and drinking it. The Turkic peoples, Scythians, and Tibetans used the tops of skulls for drinking cups.

Murder within the community is forbidden. To kill one's relative is tantamount to shedding one's own blood; it is a crime that draws a curse that lasts for generations. When Cain murdered Abel, Abel's "blood cried out for vengeance," and Cain's descendants suffered as a result. When Oedipus unknowingly killed his father, he gouged out his own eyes to confess his blindness, but his punishment fell upon his children. After Orestes executed his mother, Clytemnestra, he was followed by the Furies, spiritlike incarnations of blood. The death of the just and innocent brings vengeance. King David protested: "I and my kingdom are guiltless before the Lord forever from the blood of Abner. . . . Let it rest on the head of Joab, and on all his father's house" (*2 Sm.* 3:28–29). According to Matthew, after the sentencing of Jesus to be crucified the Jews cried: "Let his blood be upon us and upon our children" (27:25).

A murder between families or between clans is a grave wrong that must be avenged by killing the guilty party. The latter, who in turn becomes the victim, will have his own avenger from among his relatives. Thus develops the cycle of vendetta killing, which can be broken only by "paying the blood price." [*See* Revenge and Retribution.] Vendetta killing is found in ancient Greece, pre-Islamic Arabia, modern Corsica, and among the Nuer of the Sudan. The Jewish and Muslim demands of "an eye for an eye" may be similar to this phenomenon.

Under certain circumstances killing is perceived as a creative act, especially in the realm of the gods, where suicide or parricide sometimes leads to birth or new life. Mesopotamian and Babylonian cosmogonies feature gods who were slain in order to give life. The Greek Kronos severed the testicles of his father Ouranos (Sky) with a billhook while the latter lay in a tight embrace with Gaia (Earth). The blood of Ouranos's genital organs gave birth to new beings and, according to some traditions, to Aphrodite herself. This kind of suicide—relinquishing a part to preserve the whole—was sometimes magnified into a supreme act of love or redemption: Odin gave up one eye for the sake of supernatural "vision"; Attis emasculated himself; Abraham was prepared to slit the throat of his only son; Jesus accepted death voluntarily.

Some kinds of sacrifice are centered around blood. [*See* Sacrifice.] Blood is the drink of the gods or the drink shared by mortals with the gods. Blood sacrifices are varied in form and function. In Jewish sacrifice (abolished since the destruction of the Temple), the victim is not human but animal; its death has reconciliatory and expiatory value. In Muslim sacrifices, the gift of meat is the price paid by the genuinely guilty; there is no blessing or grace expected, and reconciliation and expiation are not involved.

In the Christian concept of sacrifice, the slitting of an animal's throat is abolished, and the animal is replaced by the "Lamb of God," Jesus on the cross. Crucifixion and asphyxiation, although not bloody in themselves, are perceived as fundamentally bloody. The sacrifice (at least, as it is understood outside Protestantism) is renewed daily; it is both expiatory and redemptory. The sacrifice is accompanied by a communal meal (Eucharist) where the believer is invited to eat bread, symbolizing the body of Christ, and to drink wine, symbolizing his blood. Charles Guignebert has noted that the bread has been of less interest than the wine; the wine "is the symbolism of blood that dominates in the Eucharist . . . and affirms its doctrinal richness" (Guignebert, 1935, p. 546). Christ, who offers the cup to his disciples, says, "This is the blood of the new testament that is shed for many for the remission of sins."

Judaism had already established that the covenant between God and his people was one of blood, of circumcision and sacrifice. Moses sprinkled the people with the blood of sacrificed bulls, saying, "Behold the blood of the covenant which the Lord hath made with you" (*Ex.* 24:8).

The idea of establishing a covenant through blood is found in many cultures. People create covenants among themselves as well as between their gods and themselves. Some peoples in Central Asia, in Siberia, and on the steppes of eastern Europe cut a dog or other animal in two to seal a treaty or to take a solemn oath, thus guaranteeing their loyalty. The protective force of blood is illustrated in the covenant between God and Israel in *Exodus* 13:7–13; the Israelites, remaining in their homes, which were marked with blood, were spared from the death that struck the Egyptians. A similar idea is expressed in Indonesia when the doors and pillars of houses are smeared with blood during sacrifices of domestic dedication.

Blood can eliminate flaws and weaknesses. In Australia, a young man would spread his blood on an old man in order to rejuvenate him. Some Romans, in honor of Attis, emasculated themselves and celebrated the *dendrophoria* by beating their backs, hoping thus to escape the disease of death and to wash themselves of its stain. Similarly, Shīʿī flagellants relive the martyrdom of Ḥusayn ibn ʿAlī, grandson of the prophet Muḥammad. [*See* Mortification.]

The most common type of self-inflicted wound is circumcision. [*See* Circumcision.] In the female the incision of the clitoris sometimes corresponds with this rite. [*See* Clitoridectomy.] Male circumcision is required in Hebrew tradition, where it is the sign of a covenant with God. It is common also in Islam. Many explanations have been given for this almost universal rite. It is seen primarily as a manifestation of the desire to eliminate any traces of femininity in the male. It is doubtful that circumcision is an attempt to imitate the menses. If the sexual act is considered a defilement, the removal of the foreskin could, in effect, rid the sexual organ of impurity transmitted from the mother. Yet there are some societies where the circumcised male is considered to be as impure as the menstruating female and where he is treated as if he were one.

The menses are universally considered the worst impurity, due to the involuntary and uncontrollable flowing of blood. Menstruating women are believed to pose great dangers to men, and for this reason many peoples of New Guinea, Australia, Polynesia, Africa, Central Asia, and the Arctic have feared them and imposed innumerable bans on them. One finds similar fears in the Hebrew (*Lv.* 20:18), Islamic, and Hindu traditions. Researchers have not yet properly emphasized the implications of the interruption of menstruation during pregnancy; one can surmise that the fetus, believed to be fed with the impure blood, acquires this impurity, which has to be removed at birth. The impurity only indirectly appears to be a function of the sexual act or of the vaginal bleeding at delivery.

BIBLIOGRAPHY

Nearly all works on the history of religions mention blood, but there are no valuable monographs on the subject other than G. J. M. Desse's *Le sang dans le rite* (Bordeaux, 1933). The reader is referred also to Lucien Lévy-Bruhl's *The "Soul" of the Primitive* (New York, 1928) and to Mircea Eliade's *Rites and Symbols of Initiation* (New York, 1958). Numerous facts on the topic are found in Bronislaw Malinowski's *Sex and Repression in Savage Society* (London, 1927) and *Crime and Custom in Savage Society* (New York, 1926). W. Robertson Smith's *Lectures on the Religion of the Semites*, 3d ed. (London, 1927), is still fundamental in the study of sacrifice. Charles Guignebert discusses the symbolism of blood as found in the Christian Eucharist in *Jesus* (London, 1935). On circumcision, see B. J. F. Laubscher's *Sex, Custom and Psychopathology* (London, 1937). On blood brotherhood, see Georges Davy's *La foi jurée* (Paris, 1922). Bruno Bettelheim's *Symbolic Wounds: Puberty Rites and the Envious Male* (Glencoe, Ill., 1954) and Paul Hazoumé's *Le pacte de sang au Dahomey* (Paris, 1937) are also worth consulting.

JEAN-PAUL ROUX
Translated from French by Sherri L. Granka

BOAS, FRANZ (1858–1942), German-American anthropologist. Boas was born at Minden, Prussian Westphalia, on 9 July 1858, the son of Jewish parents of comfortable means, both of whom were assimilated into German culture. His education was largely at the local state school and gymnasium. He seems not to have had significant Jewish religious instruction. His mother, Sophie Meyer Boas, who had been part of a circle of liberal and Marxist intellectuals dedicated to the revolutionary principles of 1848, was a major influence in his youth. He studied the sciences at the universities of Heidelberg (1877), Bonn (1877–1879), and Kiel (1879–1881), but he decided upon geography as a career. Shortly after receiving his doctorate, he left for a twelve-month expedition to Baffin Island, studying local geography and anthropology. He qualified as a university instructor at Berlin in 1886 but never taught, instead going to the United States, where he undertook a research trip to the Northwest Coast, whose Indians became the subjects of his most intensive ethnological scrutiny. He worked for a number of scholarly institutions in the United States and Canada from 1887 until 1896, when he found secure employment in New York City at the American Museum of Natural History and Columbia University. He left the museum in 1906 but continued at Columbia until his retirement in 1936. In his later years he became increasingly involved in public affairs, speaking out especially against racialist ideas. He died in New York on 22 December 1942.

Boas published in a wide range of anthropological

fields, exercising a dominating influence on American anthropology both in his own right and through a network of associates and former students, including A. L. Kroeber, Paul Radin, Alexander Goldenweiser, Robert H. Lowie, Ruth Benedict, Leslie Spier, J. R. Swanton, and Margaret Mead. Many of these, Radin and Lowie in particular, were more systematically concerned with religion than he.

Boas was himself a rationalist without conscious religious views. One of the mainsprings of his intellectual life was the search for an explanation of the "psychological origin of the implicit belief in the authority of tradition," a belief foreign to his own mind, and thus for an explication of how "the shackles that tradition has laid upon us" might be recognized and then broken. Alongside this, however, went a relativist's tolerance of the beliefs and values of others.

Boas's anthropological methodology was so strongly particularistic that his religious descriptions usually have little generalizing value in themselves; his approach was so concerned with the integrated totality of a culture that religion often seems to occur only as a by-product in his work. However, the enormous amount of material, especially texts, that he published on mythology, ceremonialism, and secret societies contains rich material for the study of beliefs, and his shorter treatments, including the religion entry in the *Handbook of American Indians* and his discussion of esoteric doctrines and the idea of future life among primitive tribes, are valuable.

The fundamental concept bearing on the religious life of the North American Indians, Boas wrote, was a belief in the existence of a "magic power," the "wonderful qualities" of which are believed to exist in objects, animals, men, spirits, or deities and that are superior to the natural qualities of man. The actions of the Indians were regulated by the desire to retain the good will of powers friendly to them and to control those that were hostile. Taboos, guardian spirits, charms, offerings and sacrifices, and incantations were all means to these ends. Boas also clearly associated religion with social structure in totemic kinship groups, in ceremonialism, and in explanatory mythology.

BIBLIOGRAPHY

Boas's publications are numerous and scattered. He collected some essays into *Race, Language and Culture* (New York, 1940), including "The Idea of the Future Life among Primitive Tribes" and "The Ethnological Significance of Esoteric Doctrines." George W. Stocking, Jr., edited another collection, including the essay "The Religion of American Indians," in *The Shaping of American Anthropology, 1883–1911: A Franz Boas Reader* (New York, 1974), with a fine introduction. Some of Stocking's other studies of Boas are in his *Race, Culture, and Evolution*, 2d ed. (Chicago, 1982). Boas's *Kwakiutl Ethnography* (Chicago, 1966) is, with *The Social Organization and the Secret Societies of the Kwakiutl Indians* (1897; reprint, New York, 1970), his most important discussion of the Kwakiutl. Åke Hultkrantz's *The Study of American Indian Religion* (New York, 1983), contains a discussion of Boas and his students on the subject. See also Boas's "An Anthropologist's Credo," in *The Nation* 147 (27 August 1938): 202.

DOUGLAS COLE

BOATS.

It is not surprising that those who live by the sea or on a river often visualize man's last journey as being undertaken in a boat. We encounter the use of boats in the burial rites of such peoples as well as in their mythology. Although boats figure in strikingly similar ways in the rituals and mythologies of peoples from all over the globe, their exact significance in a given culture or religion and the precise relationship between their cultic use and their appearance in myth are often far from clear. In some cases a specifically religious significance may be lacking, or the actual use of boats in the cult may bear no discernible relation to their role in mythology. These thoughts should be kept in mind as one considers individual cases of the use of boats or boat symbolism in the history of religions.

The Mythic Ferry across the Waters of Death. The use of a boat to cross the waters of death is fairly common in the ancient Near East and in classical antiquity. The Assyrian version of the well-known Babylonian *Epic of Gilgamesh* (c. 1200 BCE) provides us with a particularly striking example. The tenth episode of the epic describes the hero's long and arduous attempt to reach Utanapishtim, the Akkadian Noah, and obtain the secret of immortality. In order to do so Gilgamesh must cross the sea and the Waters of Death, something no mortal has ever done. Only Shamash, the sun god, is able to cross the sea. However, with the help of Urshanabi, Utanapishtim's boatman, Gilgamesh manages to cross the waters in a boat equipped with 120 stout, ferruled punting poles, each 60 cubits in length. Since the Waters of Death must not be touched by human hands, each pole can be used for only a single thrust. As the final pole is used, Gilgamesh and Urshanabi arrive at the dwelling of Utanapishtim, the keeper of the plant of immortality.

Most of the elements contained in later accounts of the journey to the otherworld can be found in the Gilgamesh epic. Thus one can understand the enthusiasm of the German Assyriologist Peter Jensen (1861–1936), who thought he could detect traces of it in all subsequent epic writings.

In classical antiquity we find a boat being used by Charon, the ferryman of the underworld. According to ancient Greek belief, first documented in the fragmentary epic *Minyas* and in paintings found at Delphi, Charon used a boat to ferry the dead across the rivers of the underworld to the gates of Hades, which were guarded by Kerberos. Vergil, in the sixth canto of the *Aeneid,* describes Charon's repulsive appearance and adds that his services are reserved for the dead alone. It was customary to bury the dead with an obol (a small coin) for Charon left in the mouth to make sure that he would perform the necessary service. Charon has survived in neo-Grecian Christian belief as the figure Charos.

We owe a description of Charon's boat to the Greek satirist Lucian. In *The Downward Journey,* Lucian has Charon describe his vessel to Hermes, who has just delivered to him over three hundred souls ready for the crossing: "Our ship is ready and very well prepared for putting to sea. It is bailed out, the mast is raised, the sail is ready hoisted and each of the oars is furnished with its thong. Nothing prevents us, as far as I am concerned, from weighing anchor and taking off."

Egyptian Grave Boats. Boats and ships were part of Egyptian burial gifts since earliest times. The simple clay representations of boats found in prehistoric times were replaced, during the Old Kingdom period (c. 3000–2200 BCE), by reliefs or by references to boats in the sacrificial lists. Near the end of the sixth dynasty (c. 2350–2260 BCE), representations of boats in wall decorations gave way to simple sculptures, including model ships complete with crews and cabins where the dead rested. Sailboats were to be used for the journey up the Nile toward the south, rowboats for the journey downstream toward the north. During the New Kingdom period (c. 1569–1085 BCE), the use of such models was discontinued for all but the royal tombs.

The primary function of these boats was to facilitate the continued journeys of the dead to specific places in the otherworld, just as they had facilitated journeys in life. The presence of war ships and hunting boats suggests a continuity between this life and the next. There was also a belief in a journey to the west. A model boat or the ceremonial "formulas for bringing a ferry" were believed to guarantee that the deceased would successfully reach his goal. Some of the boats found in or around the tombs lack equipment and in all probability were intended not as burial gifts but for use during the funeral ceremonies.

As worship of Osiris, god of the dead, gained ground, boats acquired yet another function: to take the dead to Busiris and Abydos, the shrines of Osiris, so that they could partake of the life-giving blessings of the god. During the journey, the mummy rested on a bier under a canopy while a priest made offerings of incense and read from the sacred texts. Still later, the deceased acquired a superhuman quality, assuming an Osiris-like form during the course of the journey.

Toward the end of the Old Kingdom, models of the two sun boats—the ships in which the eye of the day traveled across the evening and morning sky—made their appearance. These are known from Tutankhamen's tomb dating from the New Kingdom period. From the *Book of Going Forth by Day* (often called the *Book of the Dead*) we know that these particular burial gifts expressed the desire to be united with Re, the sun god, and to accompany him in his sun boat. According to texts found in the pyramids, the dead king would thus be able to share in the governance of the world. Later this privilege was extended to commoners, and the sun boats were laden with food offerings to be shared among the fellow travelers.

Ship Burials. Boats and ships constitute the most frequently encountered images in the Bronze Age rock carvings of central and southern Sweden (c. 1600–500 BCE). Interpretation is difficult because no written sources exist from this period or the one immediately following. The images consist of two parallel lines that curve upward at the ends and are joined by cross strokes, one of which sometimes terminates in an animal head. The fact that several contain men obviously handling paddles argues against the theory that these images actually represent sleds. Occasionally, depictions of a steering oar or helmsman are found. The ships may be outrigged canoes or, in the case of the carvings found in northern Scandinavia, skin boats similar to the Inuit (Eskimo) kayaks. It is unclear, however, whether these images represent real boats, cultic objects associated with solar worship, or even scenes from mythology.

Ships and other objects represented in these rock carvings are also found in Bronze Age graves. The end of this period marks the appearance of both ship graves and ship settings (stones erected spaced so that they form the outline of a ship's deck). The island of Gotland in the Baltic contains around three hundred such ship settings from the late Bronze Age. After an interval of about a thousand years, ships were once more used as funeral symbols on memorial stones found on the same island. They remained in use until the end of the pagan era. These memorials stem mainly from the late Iron Age (c. 400–1050 CE). The dead were sometimes buried in boats, or a ship setting was erected either on top of the actual grave or as a memorial over an empty grave. All kinds of equipment were buried with the dead for use in the otherworld.

At about the same time, boat burials came into use in Sweden, Norway, and, through Norse invaders, in East Anglia. Seventh-century grave fields containing unburned boats have been uncovered in the Swedish province of Uppland (Vendel, Valsgärde, Ultuna, and Tuna in Alsike). The dead that the boats contain—in all probability they were wealthy yeomen and heads of families—have been equipped with costly weapons and ample provisions. Ordinary family members, by contrast, were cremated and their remains buried in mounds in a routine fashion. Numerous boat graves have also been found along the Norwegian coast—at the ancient trading center by the Oslo Fjord, for instance. However, the best-known Norwegian ship graves are in Oseberg and Gokstad in the southern part of the country. The ships found here are lavishly equipped seagoing vessels, leading one to suspect that the dead men were kings. The same applies to the famous Sutton Hoo find made in Suffolk in 1939, which also dates from the seventh century.

By 1970, Michael Müller-Wille had found a total of 190 Norse graves that contained boats. Graves containing burned boats or ships, however, are most numerous in Scandinavia (where a total of 230 have been found) and in the territories colonized by Norsemen, for example, in Knoc y Doonee, Parish of Andreas, and Balladoolee, Parish of Arbory, on the Isle of Man, and on Colonsay in the Hebrides. Evidence from the Hebrides makes it clear that women followed their men in death. A ship grave also has been discovered on the Île de Groix off the Brittany coast. Only a few cases of ship burial are known from Denmark (e.g., Ladby, c. 900 CE). Five boat graves from the tenth century have been found so far in Iceland.

Thus there is a wealth of Norse archaeological material attesting to the custom of real boat burial, a custom unique to Europe and limited both chronologically and geographically to a single ethnic group. Similar customs in the Near East and among North American Indians do not include burial of the actual boat. Nevertheless the significance of the Norse practice remains unclear. What can be the explanation for this way of burying the dead (or at least the most prominent among the dead)? Icelandic literary sources mention the practice of placing the dead in a ship that was then covered with a burial mound, but they offer no explanation of why this was done.

One could reasonably assume that boat graves are in some way tied to the notion of a voyage on the water. Norse mythology in fact knows several worlds of death, all of which are reached by a long journey. The Icelandic epic poet Snorri Sturluson (c. 1179–1241) tells us that the wicked go to Hel and thence to Misty Hel (Niflhel, Niflheimr). The journey passes north through deep and dark valleys, and the traveler must be well equipped. Nastrand ("the shore of corpses") and the Land of Death, surrounded by rushing rivers, lie to the north. Still, neither the journey to the underworld nor the way to Valhǫll calls for sailing ships. The ships of the dead that are sometimes set ablaze and launched, such as those mentioned in *Beowulf,* the *Ynglingasaga,* the *Skjoldungasaga,* and the *Gylfaginning,* all trace their origins to Celtic legends and are thus not thought to be associated with Norse burial customs. Nor may we draw any sure conclusions from the early medieval German usage of the words *naufus* or *naucus* ("ship") alongside *truncus* ("trunk"), used to denote a coffin. These may well be terminological relics of the ancient custom of boat burial but only the terms survive.

We must conclude, therefore, that the Norse sources ultimately fail to explain the purpose behind boat burials. While the introduction of the boat into burial customs is certainly an interesting innovation, it may well have been intended merely as an addition to such other burial paraphernalia as weapons and food. Such boats do not necessarily have to be understood as burial ships designed to carry the dead to a distant and unknown land.

There is some evidence, however, that at least in some instances the funeral boat was understood as such. A famous and detailed eyewitness account of the funeral of a Norse chieftain on the banks of the Volga in 922 CE was given by an Arabian diplomat, Ibn Faḍlān, a member of a delegation sent by a caliph in Baghdad to the Bulgars along the Volga. According to Ibn Faḍlān's description, all the grave offerings were first placed in a ship, then, as a final offering, a servant woman was brought forward to follow her master into death. Before being killed, she looked three times over a kind of door frame to see what was awaiting her and told the men who lifted her that she could see her father, her mother, and her dead relatives. The last time she was lifted she added: "I can see my master, seated in Paradise, and Paradise is green and fair. . . . He is calling me; send me to him." She was then killed by an old woman known as "the angel of death," and everything was subsequently consumed by a fire lit by the nearest kinsman. A mound was built up over the site and crowned by a wooden monument. Ibn Faḍlān also reported that the Norsemen deride the Arabs for giving their dead to the earth and the worms: "We burn him in a moment, so that he enters paradise at once. . . . His master, out of love for him, sent him the wind to carry him off in an hour."

Although this description has been colored by Ibn Faḍlān's Islamic preconceptions and by his manner of presentation, the purpose of the funeral rites is clear, even though the role played by the ship remains uncertain. Does the wind refer to the breeze fanning the flames or to a sailing wind? If the latter is the case, we may conclude that, at least in this case, the burial ship was indeed intended to carry the dead man to the otherworld, although this may not have been its only purpose. In addition to the report by Ibn Faḍlān, other studies confirm a link between eschatological myth and burial rites among the Norse.

Among certain North American Indians, burial customs involving boats and a journey to the land of the dead have been documented. For instance, the typical grave of the Twana and other Coast Salish Indians consists of a canoe suspended on poles or on an elevated platform. A grieving husband traditionally spends four days and four nights near the canoe, waiting for his wife to depart for the otherworld. According to a Twana tale, the inhabitants of the realm of the dead come in a canoe to claim the newly deceased. Late at night it is said that one can hear their paddles in the water as they come to carry away their new companion.

The same vivid imagination characterizes a song from an entirely different part of the world, the Trobriand Islands, north of the eastern point of New Guinea. The tale is told of a warrior's sweetheart who, fearing that her lover has fallen in battle, waits by the shore to greet him in his spirit boat as he travels to the otherworld.

In Late Megalithic cultures near the beginning of our era, we find a belief among certain island people that their ancestors had arrived at their present location by canoe, having come across the sea from the west. On the Tanimbar Islands in Indonesia, for instance, this belief is reflected in the roofs of the ceremonial huts, which are shaped like canoes and have gables that are referred to as "stems" and "sterns." Canoes and stone or wooden representations of canoes also figure prominently in burial rites. The underlying thought is that the spirits of the dead journey across the sea in a spirit boat to the land of their ancestors in the west. The organization of the community itself is modeled on that of a ship's crew, exactly as it is in ancient Scandinavia.

Throughout central Polynesia the dead are placed in canoes or canoe-shaped coffins or receptacles. Robert W. Williamson (1977) speculates that the spiritual essence of the visible canoe was intended to carry the soul on its journey to the spirit land called Hawaiki. The voyage could be undertaken symbolically as well in miniature boats containing bones and images of the dead person. In the case of inhumation and cremation, the grave on land could be shaped like a ship, or pictures of ships could be carved on top of the memorials. The canoe was also used as an instrument for the removal of a dead person's sins.

Celtic Tales of Sea Journeys to Mythical Lands. The Celtic imagination is especially fertile when it comes to depicting the adventures of the deceased on the way to their final resting place. This place is represented as an earthly Elysium—the abode of the gods—a notion that is clearly derived from Classical Greek sources. This paradise on earth has many names, such as Magh Mór ("great plain"), Magh Mell ("plain of delights"), Tír na nÓg ("land of the young"), Annwn ("abyss"), and Tír nam Béo ("land of the living"). Tales are told of a sea voyage *(imram)* to various scattered islands, often involving a magic ship or vessel. In what is possibly the earliest of these tales, the *Voyage of Bran* (eighth century), the hero sails from one marvelous island to another: the Land beneath the Waves, the Island of Laughter, and the Island of Women. Other islands are mentioned in the *Voyage of Maeldúin* (ninth to eleventh century), in which the voyager builds the boat himself. The same elements, combined with other motifs, are also found in the widespread account of the *Navigation of Saint Brendan* (c. tenth century), where the journey ends in the Land of Promise, or Paradise. In this case, the story is obviously colored by Christian legends. The role of the seagoing vessel appears to have faded in the medieval visionary literature and in the extracanonical apocrypha and apocalypses, possibly because of its pagan connotations.

Medieval allegories, ballads, and romances, as well as historical legends, contain stories about magic ships, often rudderless and unpiloted. Marie de France, the earliest known French female writer (twelfth century), describes such a ship in her lay *Guigemar.* Its sails are made of silk, the timbers of ebony, and it contains a sumptuous bed in a pavilion. It carries a wounded hero to a castle in an ancient town where he encounters a fairy endowed with healing powers. This same motif of a rudderless boat is found in *Beowulf* where Scyld (Skjold), the founder of the Danish dynasty of the Skjoldunger, is said to arrive as a child in an unpiloted ship. He also departs for an unknown destination in a burial ship. The story appears to be patterned on the theme of the journey to the otherworld but may also reflect notions connected with ship burials.

Ship Symbolism. Ship symbolism was very highly developed in the Hellenistic world, a fact that helps explain its importance in Christian sources. But the Greeks did not go to sea with undiluted joy. "The sea is an evil thing, seafaring is a hazardous and dangerous undertaking," declares the Greek rhetorician Alciphron; "the sailor is the neighbor of death." But the danger, though mortal, was nevertheless considered wonderful and tempting, worthy of men who are like gods. Courage, hope, and joy characterize the names of the Athenian ships—names that might as easily refer to the ship of the church—and they are always feminine: *Salvation, Grace, Bringer of Light, Blessed, Victorious, Virgin, Dove, Savior, Providence, Help,* and *Peace.*

Allusions to ships are frequent in classical literature. The ancient ship of Theseus, in which the planks of the hull are successively exchanged, is compared by Plutarch to the human body that is also in a process of constant renewal. Meleager, the Greek epigrammatist (first century BCE), turns this image the other way around and refers to his beloved in her old age as an old frigate: the various members of her withered body are compared with nautical precision to the different parts of a ship. Love is like a hazardous voyage; the cunning Greek or Roman "turns his sheet windward"; death overtakes us "with swelling sails." To act to one's own detriment was expressed by the ancient Greek or Roman as "drilling holes through the hull." To give up a fight was "to take down the sail"; from beginning to end was "from fore to aft." An expression we still use, "to be in the same boat," is borrowed from Cicero. A good ship is necessary for the voyage through life.

Three classical images are of special importance and exerted a strong influence on the development of Christian symbolism: the ship of state, the ship of the soul, and the ship of the world. In the shared fate of the crew and in their dependence on their captain—reflected in such expressions as "our governor" and "to be at the helm"—the Greek sailors saw a clear allegorical reference to their own city-state. We find it in the Greek lyrical poet Alcaeus who wrote around 600 BCE of "the storm-tossed ship of state." He is echoed by many, Horace among them. The Greek writers of tragedy, Aeschylus and Sophocles, used the same symbols, which entered the field of political philosophy through Plato: all is well on a ship where all obey the captain *(nauklēros),* while nothing but misfortune awaits a ship where the captain is ignorant and each sailor wants to be in command. The human body too is likened to a ship where the soul and reason are the helmsman, and the eyes and ears constitute the lookout. Cooperation is vital, just as governors and governed must cooperate in a good state. Aristotle maintains that the common goal of all good citizens, regardless of their tasks and rights, must be a good voyage (that is, the welfare of the state). Nautical symbols are found in Demosthenes, Plutarch, and Cicero, as well as in the writings of emperors and church fathers.

The idea of the body as the ship of the soul is based on the image of a hull under construction: the spine is likened to the keel, the frame timbers represent the ribs, and the place of the helmsman is the head (see Ovid, *Metamorphoses* 14.549–554). This comparison between the human body and a ship later becomes important in the characterization of the ship as a symbol of the church. The church fathers perceived Noah's ark as a symbol of the church and interpreted it in terms of the human body. In this way, the images of the mystical body of Christ and the ship of the church were able to merge. What applies to the church as the collectivity of the redeemed applies as well to the individual soul, itself conceived of as a vessel, a *navicula animae.*

The relationship between body and soul, which in Platonism and Neoplatonism is likened to the dependence of a ship on its captain, is a recurring image in the Christian sermon. Death is spoken of as a shipwreck. The emperor Constantine talks of the flotsam of the body on the underworld river Acheron. In the image of Charon and his ferry, death becomes a voyage to the other side. The fluidity of such symbolism allows the images to merge independently of any restraints imposed by logic. This in turn leads to the Christian reference to "the blessed haven."

The Stoic philosopher Chrysippus claims that reason *(logos)* governs man like a ship. Plutarch further develops this metaphor: the governing part of the soul is itself governed by God like a rudder, or it listens like an experienced helmsman to the divine captain. Jerome, in commenting on Psalm 103, is therefore able to preach to his attentive monks: "Who among us is such a sturdily built ship that he is able to escape this world without going down or running aground on a rock—if he wants to reach salvation, the right sense *(sensus)* must be his pilot." The philosophical *logos* has thereby been replaced by reason enlightened by faith, and Christ as the true Logos becomes the real pilot of the soul. The ascetic tradition refers to "the ship of the soul," "the ship of the heart," and "the ship of life." Augustine gives further impetus to the notion of Christ dwelling in the heart as in a ship.

The divinely governed world is also likened to a ship. Although worshiping the thing created is as reprehensible as mistaking the ship for its captain, it is nevertheless possible to deduce the builder from the ship. Platonic, Neoplatonic, and Stoic thought lends itself especially well to adoption and christianization. The large eye, which is still painted on the bows of Mediterranean boats, is interpreted by ancient philosophers and Christians alike as a symbol of Providence. Furthermore, the ship of the world must perish one day; only the ship of the church will survive.

The image of the ship of the church or of salvation can be further extended so that the cross becomes the mast and the yard, a spiritual wind fills the sails, and Christ himself is at the helm. The account of Odysseus, fettered to the mast in order not to succumb to the sirens' song, is also easily christianized. The ship of salvation sails across the sea of time, past all temptations, toward the heavenly haven.

BIBLIOGRAPHY

Arbman, Holger. "Begravning." In *Kulturhistorisk Leksikon för Nordisk Middelalder,* vol. 1. Copenhagen, 1956.

Baldwin, B. "Usituma! Song of Heaven." *Oceania* 15 (March 1945): 201–238. Includes a canoe and a war song from the Trobriand Islands, where the author served as missionary.

Bar, Francis. *Les routes de l'autre monde: Descentes aux enfers et voyages dans l'au-delà.* Paris, 1946. A good short survey treating European folklore, Asian, American, Near Eastern, and classical material, Jewish and Christian apocrypha, Norse and Celtic stories, medieval literature on visions, and parodies from antiquity.

Bonnet, Hans. *Reallexikon der ägyptischen Religionsgeschichte.* Berlin, 1952.

Davidson, Hilda R. Ellis, ed. *The Journey to the Other World.* Totowa, N.J., 1975. See pages 73–89. The South Sea and Egypt are touched on as an introduction to the Norse material. Caution is needed.

Foote, Peter, and David M. Wilson. *The Viking Achievement: The Society and Culture of Early Medieval Scandinavia.* New York, 1970. A chapter on religion treats the ship burials.

Fredsjö, Åke, Sverker Janson, and C.-A. Moberg. *Hällristningar i sverige.* Stockholm, 1956. A short critical survey of Swedish rock carvings written by trained archaeologists.

Hultkrantz, Åke. *The North American Indian Orpheus Tradition: A Contribution to Comparative Religion.* Stockholm, 1957. Tales of the recovery of a beloved person from the land of the dead.

Meuli, Karl. *Gesammelte Schriften,* 2 vols. Basel, 1975.

Müller-Wille, Michael. *Bestattung im Boot: Studien zu einer nordeuropäischen Grabsitte.* Neumünster, West Germany, 1970. Outstanding scientific monograph.

Müller-Wille, Michael, David M. Wilson, Hayo Vierck, and Heinrich Beck. "Bootgrab." In *Reallexikon der Germanischen Altertumskunde,* edited by Johannes Hoops, vol. 3. Berlin and New York, 1978. A concentrated, well-documented survey with an extensive bibliography.

Patch, Howard R. *The Other World according to Descriptions in Medieval Literature.* Cambridge, Mass., 1950. A reliable study starting with Oriental and classical material, as well as Celtic and German mythology.

Pritchard, J. B., ed. *Ancient Near Eastern Texts relating to the Old Testament.* 3d ed. Princeton, 1969. Contains Egyptian, Sumerian, and Akkadian myths of death and the otherworld.

Rahner, Hugo. *Symbole der Kirche: Die Ekklesiologie der Väter.* Salzburg, 1964. Half of this learned, voluminous work of a patristic scholar contains the Christian symbolism of the ship and its classical background.

Strömberg Krantz, Eva. *Des Schiffes Weg mitten im Meer: Beiträge zur Erforschung der nautischen Terminologie des Alten Testaments.* Lund, 1982. Study of the nautical terminology of the Israelites and of the small traces in it of their contact with seafaring people ever since their entrance into Palestine.

Turville-Petre, E. O. G. *Myth and Religion of the North: The Religion of Ancient Scandinavia.* New York, 1964.

Vendel Period Studies. Stockholm, 1983. A multi-author work of twenty specialists that was connected with an exposition in Stockholm of the boat graves from Vendel, Valsgärde (Sweden), and Sutton Hoo (England). A good, popular summary of the actual state of research. Contains a rich bibliography.

Vroklage, Bernardus A. G. "Das Schiff in den Megalithkulturen Südostasiens und der Südsee." *Anthropos* 31 (1936): 712–757. The author belongs to the Kulturgeschichtliche Schule.

Wachsmuth, Dietrich. *Pompimos ho daimon: Untersuchung zu den antiken Sakralhandlungen bei Seereisen.* Exp. ed. Berlin, 1967. A very substantial study of all religious rites in connection with classical seafare.

Williamson, Robert W. *Religious and Cosmic Beliefs of Central Polynesia* (1933). 2 vols. New York, 1977. A careful, systematic survey based on an extensive literature.

CARL-MARTIN EDSMAN
Translated from Swedish by Kjersti Board

BOCHICA was a major deity of the Muisca (Chibcha) Indians of the highlands around Bogotá, Colombia, at the time of the Spanish conquest, in the sixteenth century. Early Spanish chroniclers report varying mythical dates for Bochica's appearance in Muisca territory. He was called by several names or titles, one of which means "sun," another "disappearing one." Said to be a foreigner from the east (i.e., present-day Venezuela), he appeared as an old man with a waist-length beard, long hair, and a mantle. He preached and taught virtuous behavior, religious ritual, and crafts, particularly spinning, weaving, and cloth painting. Traveling to the west through the Muisca region, then eastward again, he arrived at Sogamoso, on the eastern Muisca border. There, according to different accounts, he died, disappeared, or became the Sun. At the time of the Conquest, there was an important Temple of the Sun at Sogamoso. One Muisca myth tells that the world was created there, and one of Bochica's titles was "messenger of the creator."

Bochica combines the culture hero, sun, and transformation aspects characteristic of many New World gods. He was the patron of chieftains and goldsmiths, the latter perhaps because of his association both with the sun and with craft. Worked gold was offered to him. When an angry local god once caused a destructive flood, so a tale relates, the Muisca people appealed to Bochica, who appeared on a rainbow to strike and shatter a rock with his golden staff, releasing the floodwaters from the Bogotá plateau and creating the great Tequendama waterfall, one of the wonders of the South American landscape.

According to one set of mythical stories, a beautiful goddess taught the people promiscuity, pleasure, and dancing—the opposite of Bochica's instructions. In some accounts, she was the Moon, or was changed by Bochica into the Moon; because she was evil, she was permitted to shine only at night. She was sometimes called the wife of the Sun (presumably Bochica). In one tale, the goddess was turned by Bochica into an owl.

BIBLIOGRAPHY

The best summary in English of early source material on Bochica is A. L. Kroeber's "The Chibcha," in the *Handbook of South American Indians*, edited by Julian H. Steward, vol. 2 (Washington, D.C., 1946). In Spanish, José Pérez de Barradas's *Los Muiscas antes de la Conquista*, vol. 2 (Madrid, 1951), quotes the chroniclers, with references. Harold Osborne's *South American Mythology* (London, 1968) publishes material taken largely from Kroeber, without citation of early sources; it is the most comprehensive recent discussion.

ELIZABETH P. BENSON

BODHIDHARMA (fl. c. 480–520), known in China as Ta-mo and in Japan as Daruma; traditionally considered the twenty-eighth patriarch of Indian Buddhism and the founder of the Ch'an (Jpn., Zen) school of Chinese Buddhism.

The "Historical" Bodhidharma. Accounts of Bodhidharma's life have been based until recently on largely hagiographical materials such as the *Ching-te ch'uan-teng lu* (1004). However, the discovery of new documents among the Tun-huang manuscripts found in Central Asia at the turn of this century has led Chinese and Japanese scholars to question the authenticity of these accounts. The oldest text in which Bodhidharma's name is mentioned is the *Lo-yang ch'ieh-lan chi*, a description of Buddhist monasteries in Lo-yang written in 547 by Yang Hsüan-chih. In this work, a monk called Bodhidharma from "Po-ssu in the western regions" (possibly Persia) is said to have visited and admired the Yung-ning Monastery. This monastery was built in 516 and became a military camp after 528. Consequently, Bodhidharma's visit must have taken place around 520. But no other biographical details can be inferred from this, and the aged western monk (he was purportedly one hundred and fifty years old at the time) bears no resemblance to the legendary founder of Chinese Ch'an.

The most important source for Bodhidharma's life is the *Hsü kao-seng chuan*, a work written by Tao-hsüan in 645 and revised before his death in 667. It states that Bodhidharma was a brahman from southern India. After studying the Buddhist tradition of the Greater Vehicle (Mahāyāna), Bodhidharma decided to travel to China in order to spread Mahāyāna doctrine. He arrived by sea at Nan-yüeh, in the domain of the Liu Sung dynasty (420–479), and later traveled to Lo-yang, the capital of the Northern Wei (386–534). In Lo-yang, he attempted to win converts, apparently without great success. Nonetheless, he eventually acquired two worthy disciples, Hui-k'o (487–593) and Tao-yü (dates unknown), who studied with him for several years. He is said to have transmitted the *Laṅkāvatāra Sūtra*, the scripture he deemed best fitted for Chinese practitioners, to Hui-k'o. Bodhidharma seems also to have met with some hostility and slander. Tao-hsüan stresses that Bodhidharma's teaching, known as "wall-gazing" *(pi-kuan)*, or as the "two entrances" (via "principle," *li-ju*, and via "practice," *hsing-ju*), was difficult to understand compared to the more traditional and popular teachings of Seng-ch'ou (480–560). Tao-hsüan concludes by saying that he does not know where Bodhidharma died. In another section of the text, however, Tao-hsüan states that Bodhidharma died on the banks of the Lo River. That Bodhidharma's teachings evoked hostility in China is evident from the fact that after his death, his disciple Hui-k'o felt it necessary to hide for a period. Since the locale mentioned is known to have been an execution ground, it is possible that Bodhidharma was executed during the late Wei rebellions.

Although Tao-hsüan's account is straightforward, succinct, and apparently fairly authentic, it presents some problems. Most important, it presents two different, almost contradictory, images of Bodhidharma—as a practicer of "wall-gazing," intent on not relying on the written word, and as a partisan of the *Laṅkāvatāra Sūtra*. Tao-hsüan clearly has some difficulty in reconciling his divergent sources. Primarily, he draws on the preface to the so-called *Erh-ju ssu-hsing lun* (Treatise on the Two Entrances and Four Practices), written around 600 by Bodhidharma's (or Hui-k'o's) disciple T'an-lin (dates unknown) and on information concerning the reputed transmission of the *Laṅkāvatāra Sūtra*. This latter had probably been given to Tao-hsüan by Fa-ch'ung (587?–665), an heir of the tradition. In any case, at the time of Tao-hsüan's writing, Bodhidharma was not yet considered the twenty-eighth patriarch of Indian Buddhism.

In Tao-hsüan's time, a new school was developing on the Eastern Mountain (Tung-shan, in modern Hunan) around the *dhyāna* masters Tao-hsin (580–651) and Hung-jen (601–674). The latter's disciples, Fa-ju (638–689), Shen-hsiu (606–706), and Hui-an (attested dates 582–709), spread this new teaching, known as the "Tung-shan doctrine," in the region of the T'ang capitals (Ch'ang-an and Lo-yang). Fa-ju's epitaph and two historiographical works of this metropolitan Ch'an written in the first decades of the eighth century, the *Ch'uan fa-pao chi* and the *Leng-ch'ieh shih-tzu chi,* succeeded in linking the Tung-shan tradition to the *Laṅkāvatāra* tradition. Bodhidharma and Hui-k'o were defined in these texts as the first two Chinese patriarchs of the Ch'an school and Tao-hsin and Hung-jen were designated the fourth and fifth patriarchs. The missing link was conveniently provided by an obscure disciple of Hui-k'o, Seng-ts'an (d. 606)—baptized "third patriarch." Having established its orthodoxy and spiritual filiation, the new Ch'an school, popularly known as the Ta-mo-tsung (Bodhidharma school) or the Leng-ch'ieh-tsung (*Laṅkāvatāra* school), quickly developed as the main trend of Chinese Buddhism and its "founder" Bodhidharma accordingly acquired legendary status.

The Legend of Bodhidharma within the Ch'an Sect. About one hundred fifty years after Bodhidharma's death, his legend had already grown considerably. His Indian origin plus the very scarcity of information available from the *Hsü kao-seng chuan* seem to have been the essential factors in Bodhidharma's posthumous assumption of the status of "first patriarch" of the new Ch'an school. In 686, Fa-ju settled at Sung-shan, near Lo-yang (in modern Honan). Sung-shan was already a Buddhist stronghold; Seng-ch'ou, Bodhidharma's lucky rival, had once studied under another Indian monk named Fo-t'o (dates unknown) at Sung-shan. Fo-t'o was revered by the Northern Wei emperor, Hsiao-wen-ti (r. 471–499), who, after moving the capital to Lo-yang in 496, had the Shao-lin Monastery built for him at Sung-shan. It seems that later, in Fa-ju's circle, an amalgam was made of the legends of Fo-t'o, Seng-ch'ou, and Bodhidharma. This may be the reason why Bodhidharma became associated with the Shao-lin Monastery. According to the *Ch'uan fa-pao chi,* Bodhidharma practiced wall-gazing at Sung-shan for several years. He thus became known as the "wall-gazing brahman," the monk who remained without moving for nine years in meditation in a cave on Sung-shan (eventually losing his legs, as the popular iconography depicts him). There he also met Hui-k'o, who, to show his earnestness in searching for the Way, cut off his own arm. (The *Ch'uan fa-pao chi* severely criticizes Tao-hsüan for claiming that Hui-k'o had his arm cut off by bandits.) This tradition, fusing with the martial tradition that developed at Sung-shan, resulted in Bodhidharma becoming the "founder" of the martial art known as Shao-lin boxing (Jpn., Shōrinji *kempō*).

Bodhidharma's legend continued to develop with the *Li-tai fa-pao chi* (c. 774), the *Pao-lin chuan* (801), and the *Tsu-t'ang chi* (Kor., *Chodangjip,* 952), and reached its classical stage in 1004 with the *Ching-te chuan-teng lu.* In the process, it borrowed features from other popular Buddhist or Taoist figures such as Pao-chih or Fu Hsi (alias Fu Ta-shih, "Fu the Mahāsattva," 497–569, considered an incarnation of Maitreya). But its main aspects were already fixed at the beginning of the eighth century. For example, the *Ch'uan fa-pao chi* contains the following account concerning Bodhidharma's "deliverance from the corpse" (a typical Taoist practice): On the day of his death, he was met in the Pamir Mountains by Sung Yün, a Northern Wei emissary on his way back from India. After his arrival in China, Sung Yün told Bodhidharma's disciples of his encounter. The disciples, opening their master's grave, found it empty except for a single straw sandal. Bodhidharma returning to his home in the western regions on one sandal has become a standard motif in Ch'an iconography.

Another important—if somewhat later—motif is Bodhidharma's encounter with Liang Wu-ti (r. 502–549) on his arrival in China. This story, which became a favorite theme of Ch'an "riddles" or *kung-an* (Jpn., *kōan*), has its prototype in Fu Hsi's encounter with Liang Wu-ti. In both cases, the emperor failed to understand the eminence of the person he had in front of him. [*See the biography of Liang Wu-ti.*]

It is also noteworthy that many early Ch'an works formerly attributed to Bodhidharma have recently been proved to have been written by later Ch'an masters such as Niu-t'ou Fa-jung (594–657) or Shen-hsiu (606–706). That so many works were erroneously attributed to Bodhidharma may be due simply to the fact that the Ch'an school was at the time known as the Bodhidharma school, and that all works of the school could thus be considered expressive of Bodhidharma's thought. Whatever the case, these works have greatly contributed to the development of Bodhidharma's image, especially in the Japanese Zen tradition. Further confusing the issue is the "discovery," throughout the eighth century, of epitaphs supposedly written shortly after his death. In fact, these epitaphs were products of the struggle for hegemony among various factions of Ch'an.

Bodhidharma in Popular Religion. The *Genkōshakusho,* a well-known account of Japanese Buddhism written by a Zen monk named Kokan Shiren (1278–1346), opens with the story of Bodhidharma crossing over to

Japan to spread his teachings (a development of the iconographic tradition representing him crossing the Yangtze River). In Japan, Bodhidharma's legend seems to have developed first within the Tendai (Chin., T'ien-t'ai) tradition brought from China at the beginning of the Heian period (794–1191) by the Japanese monk Saichō (767–822) and his disciples. One of them in particular, Kōjō (779–858), was instrumental in linking the Bodhidharma legend to the Tendai tradition and to the legend of the regent Shōtoku (Shōtoku Taishi, 574–622), who was considered a reincarnation of Nan-yüeh Hui-ssu (515–577), one of the founders of the T'ien-t'ai school (notwithstanding the fact that Shōtoku was born before Hui-ssu died). In his *Denjutsu isshin kaimon*, a work presented to the emperor, Kōjō mentions the encounter that took place near Kataoka Hill (Nara Prefecture) between Shōtoku and a strange, starving beggar—considered a Taoist immortal in the version of the story given by the *Kojiki*. Kōjō, arguing from a former legendary encounter between Hui-ssu and Bodhidharma on Mount T'ien-t'ai in China, and from Bodhidharma's prediction that both would be reborn in Japan, has no difficulty establishing that the beggar was none other than Bodhidharma himself. [*See the biography of Shōtoku Taishi.*]

This amalgam proved very successful and reached far beyond the Tendai school. Toward the end of the Heian period a Zen school emerged from the Tendai tradition, and its leader, Dainichi Nōnin (dates unknown), labeled it the "Japanese school of Bodhidharma" (Nihon Darumashū). This movement was a forerunner of the Japanese Zen sect, whose two main branches were founded by Eisai (1141–1215) and Dōgen (1200–1253) at the beginning of the Kamakura period (1192–1337). This eventually led to the publication of a *Daruma sanchōden* (Biography of Bodhidharma in the Three Kingdoms [India, China, and Japan]) during the Edo period.

But it is in popular religion that Bodhidharma's figure developed most flamboyantly. Early in China, Bodhidharma not only borrowed features from Taoist immortals but became completely assimilated by the Taoist tradition; there are several Taoist works extant concerning Bodhidharma. In Japan, Bodhidharma's legend developed in tandem with that of Shōtoku Taishi; a temple dedicated to Daruma is still to be found on the top of Kataoka Hill. The Japanese image of Daruma, a legless doll known as *fuku-Daruma* ("Daruma of happiness"), presides over many aspects of everyday life (household safety, prosperity in business, political campaigns, etc.). This figure, impressed on every child's mind, has come to play an important role in Japanese art and culture.

[*See also* Ch'an.]

BIBLIOGRAPHY

Demiéville, Paul. "Appendice sur 'Damoduolo' (Dharmatrā[ta])." In *Peintures monochromes de Dunhuang (Dunhuang baihua)*, edited by Jao Tsong-yi, Pierre Ryckmans, and Paul Demiéville. Paris, 1978. A valuable study of the Sino-Tibetan tradition that merged Bodhidharma and the Indian translator Dharmatrāta into a single figure, which was subsequently incorporated into the list of the eighteen legendary disciples of the Buddha.

Dumoulin, Heinrich. "Bodhidharma und die Anfänge des Ch'an-Buddhismus." *Monumenta Nipponica* (Tokyo) 7, no. 1 (1951): 67–83. A good summary of the first Sino-Japanese reexaminations of the early Ch'an tradition.

Sekiguchi Shindai. *Daruma no kenkyū.* Tokyo, 1967. An important work, with an abstract in English, on the Chinese hagiographical tradition concerning Bodhidharma.

Yanagida Seizan. *Daruma.* Tokyo, 1981. The most recent and authoritative work on Bodhidharma. It examines the historical evidence and the development of the legend in Ch'an (Zen) and in Japanese popular religion and also provides a convenient translation in modern Japanese of Bodhidharma's thought as recorded in the *Erh-ju ssu-hsing lun.*

BERNARD FAURE

BODHISATTVA PATH. The English term *bodhisattva path* translates the Sanskrit *bodhisattvayāna*, "vehicle of the *bodhisattvas*," or, more frequently, *bodhisattvācāryā*, "the practice of the *bodhisattva*," terms widely employed in Mahāyāna Buddhist texts. In Pali literature the word *bodhisattva* appears quite often, but the Pali equivalents of the aforementioned Sanskrit words do not, reflecting the quite different conception of the *bodhisattva* enjoyed by Hīnayāna and Mahāyāna Buddhism.

Etymologically, *bodhisattva* is a term compounded out of *bodhi*, meaning here "enlightenment [of the Buddha]," and *sattva*, denoting "living being." Thus, *bodhisattva* refers either to a person who is seeking *bodhi* or a "*bodhi* being," that is, a being destined to attain Buddhahood. Another interpretation, "one whose mind *(sattva)* is fixed on *bodhi*," is also recognized by the tradition.

In early Buddhism and in conservative schools such as the Theravāda, the term *bodhisattva* designates a Buddha-to-be. It refers in this context merely to one of a very limited number of beings in various states of existence prior to their having attained enlightenment. Its principal use was thus confined to the previous lives of the Buddha Śākyamuni; however, the existence of other *bodhisattvas* in aeons past was acknowledged, as was the bodhisattvahood of the future Buddha, Maitreya. Śākyamuni's previous existences as a *bodhisattva* are the subject of the Jātaka literature, which illustrates the religious career of the future Buddha as he perfects himself in his quest for enlightenment.

History and Development of the Term. In early and Pali Buddhism the idea of the *bodhisattva* was especially popular among the laity. A large number of the Jātakas, accounts of the prior births of the Buddha, were based on popular stories, including animal tales, current in the traditions of the time. These were transformed to more didactic ends as the *bodhisattva* idea was later woven into the Jātaka narrative structure as a whole. Beyond this, however, the notion of the *bodhisattva* underwent little further elaboration until the rise of Mahāyāna Buddhism around the beginning of the common era. It was the Mahāyāna, with its vastly altered understanding of Buddhahood and the path of spiritual sanctification, that transformed the notion from its very limited initial application to a vehicle of universal salvation.

Early Buddhism maintained that there was only one Buddha in any one epoch within our world system. The career of the being destined to become the Buddha Gautama was held to have begun with a vow *(praṇidhāna)* to attain enlightenment taken before another Buddha (Dīpaṃkara) ages ago. This vow was confirmed by a prophecy *(vyākaraṇa)* by Dīpaṃkara that at such-and-such a time and such-and-such a place the being who had taken this vow would become the Buddha for our particular world age. During countless subsequent births the future Buddha labored to perfect himself in a variety of virtues (*pāramitās*, "perfections"), principal among which were wisdom *(prajñā)* and selfless giving *(dāna)*. This mythic structure was also held to obtain for Buddhas in other epochs, all of whom had uttered a vow, undertaken religious practices *(bhāvanā)*, and perfected themselves in various ways prior to their enlightenment. This religious path, then, was conceived as the exclusive domain of a very small number of beings (eight or twenty-five by the most common reckonings), whose appearance in the world as Buddhas was deemed metaphorically "as rare as the appearance of the *udumbara* blossom." In early Buddhism, the liberation of beings other than Buddhas seems to have entailed insight into the same truths as those discovered by the Buddhas, that is, the tradition initially appears to have discerned little difference in the content or depth of their awakening. However, profound differences remained in the religious *paths* taken by the respective practitioners. The path of those who merely heard the Buddha preach, the so-called *śrāvakas*, or "listeners," was held to culminate not in Buddhahood but in the attainment of arhatship. Unlike a Buddha, an *arhat* (Pali, *arahant*) comes to the Dharma through hearing it preached by others; he does not participate in the cosmic drama that results in the appearance of a Buddha in the world.

Mahāyāna Buddhism, on the other hand, developed a radically different view of the path of religious practice, a view that embodied a critique of the *arhat* ideal. Our sources suggest that within a century or so of the death of the Buddha the *arhat* was viewed by some Buddhists, notably the Mahāsāṃghikas, as embodying a distinctly less exalted spiritual state than that of a Buddha. Accounts of the first schism in the *saṃgha* credit the Mahāsāṃghikas with maintaining that the *arhat* is subject to doubt, is plagued by remnants of desire, specifically sexual desire, and retains vestiges of ignorance on nonreligious topics. Although there is no direct evidence linking the Mahāsāṃghikas to the origins of the Mahāyāna community, it is clear that the critique of the *arhat* was a contributing factor in the development of alternate religious paths in the Buddhist community. [*See* Mahāsāṃghikas.]

The Mahāyāna probably had its origins in groups of clergy and laity outside of the formal *nikāyas* who took as their base the stupas (Skt., *stūpa*), or reliquary mounds of the Buddha. Members of these "orders" appear to have centered their practice on devotion to the Buddha and to have referred to themselves as *bodhisattvas*. [*See* Stupa Worship.] Although we know little of these early groups, the movement they spawned emerged by the second century of the common era with a literature that championed a much different view of the *bodhisattva*. For the Mahāyāna, the path of the *arhat* is one characterized by a self-centered concern for personal salvation and a distinctly less than complete insight into the nature of things. Here, in other words, the enlightenment of the *arhat* is held inferior to that of Buddhas.

Mahāyāna texts propose that the end of religious practice properly conceived is nothing less than the universal insight achieved by the Buddha, that is, that the goal of religious practice ought to be Buddhahood itself. They further insist that it is ultimately meaningless to speak of the liberation of an individual alone, for enlightenment inevitably entails a wholly selfless compassion for others *(karuṇā)* that mandates concern for their spiritual welfare. [*See* Karuṇā.] For the Mahāyāna, all those who, like the Buddha Śākyamuni, commence their religious career with a vow to become a Buddha and to work tirelessly for the enlightenment of others are by definition *bodhisattvas*, and the career of the *bodhisattva* is conceived here as open to any and all beings who undertake with right resolve to become Buddhas. What is more, some Mahāyāna texts proclaim, the career leading to Buddhahood is in fact the only real path preached by the Buddha. All other soteriologies, these texts aver, are merely strategies employed by the Buddha against those whose understanding was not sufficiently developed for the Mahāyāna teachings. It is this new and more universal soteriology that lent to the movement its self-designation *Mahāyāna*, the "Greater Path" to salvation.

Ultimately then, by the early centuries of the common era the tradition recognized the existence of at least two distinct paths of religious practice: the *śrāvakayāna* (as the Mahāyānists termed it) and the *bodhisattvayāna*. The former expounded a practice that emphasized self-liberation; the latter embraced a more socially-oriented ideal that stressed the salvation of others. Believing that the salvation of one entails the salvation of all beings, Mahāyāna *bodhisattvas* vow to postpone their own liberation and to remain in the world as Śākyamuni did following his enlightenment, exercising compassionate concern for others until all beings have been saved.

As Mahāyāna Buddhism developed doctrinally it came to propose an elaborate Buddhology (notions concerning the nature of the Buddha) to explain how Buddhas and *bodhisattvas* function in the world to save sentient beings. In brief, these doctrines held that Buddhas and *bodhisattvas*, through their long aeons of spiritual practice, had accumulated vast funds of religious merit that they could freely transfer to others in order to help them to salvation. The mechanism of this transfer of merit *(pariṇāmanā)* varied over the tradition, but in general it was believed that at a certain point in the stages *(bhūmi)* of the path a *bodhisattva* could assume a form at will in any of the realms of being, there to exert a beneficent effect on the course of the beings inhabiting them. [*See* Merit, *article on* Buddhist Concepts.] A *bodhisattva* could, if he chose, be born in one of the various hells to be a boon to its denizens. On their part, sentient being were encouraged in many texts to pay homage to various Buddhas and *bodhisattvas* by meditating on them, making offerings to them, and reciting their names. Consonant with this was the cult rendered certain great or "celestial" *bodhisattvas*, figures with distinct personalities in the Buddhist pantheon who were believed to be *bodhisattvas* of the very highest attainment. Chief among these frankly mythological figures were Avalokiteśvara, Mañjuśrī, Maitreya, and Kṣitigarbha, all of whom enjoy significant cultic followings throughout Buddhist Asia. These *mahāsattvas*, or "great beings," became the subjects of an elaborate iconography that emphasizes their majesty, insight, and concern to save others. [*See* Iconography, *article on* Buddhist Iconography.]

Often, the *bodhisattva* path is held to be one of three vehicles to liberation: the path of the *bodhisattva*, the path of the *arhat*, and a path that culminates in a Buddhahood attained by one who has never heard the Dharma preached, but who by his own efforts naturally comes to an understanding of *pratītya-samutpāda* (the doctrine of causality). Because of the special circumstances under which these *pratyekabuddhas*, as they are called, achieve enlightenment, they are held incapable of transmitting the Dharma to others. This threefold formulation is very early; both the Sarvāstivādins and the Theravādins recognized the existence of three distinct soteriologies. The Pali *Upāsakajanālaṅkāra*, for instance, speaks of three types of liberation: *sāvaka (śrāvaka) bodhi*, *pacceka (pratyeka) bodhi*, and *samyaksaṃbodhi* (that of a fully enlightened Buddha), although their understanding of the three terms is naturally incommensurate with the Mahāyāna view. Various Mahāyāna texts treat the relationship between the vehicles, but the most radical view is that of the *Saddharmapuṇḍarīka Sūtra* (Lotus Sutra), which holds that the Buddha preached the *śrāvakayāna* and the *pratyekabuddhayāna* as mere expedients *(upāya)* designed to draw beings of varying spiritual capacities to the Dharma. [*See* Upāya.] For the *Lotus*, the three vehicles are in reality one vehicle *(ekayāna)*, which is Buddhahood itself. The *Lotus* is famous for its insistence that all beings who hear the Dharma and conceive of faith and confidence in its message will eventually become Buddhas.

Bodhisattva Practice. The career of the *bodhisattva* is traditionally held to begin when the devotee first conceives the aspiration for enlightenment *(bodhicitta)* and formulates a vow to become a Buddha and work for the weal of all beings. The uttering of this vow has profound axiological consequences for the *bodhisattva:* henceforth, it will be the vow that will be the ultimate controlling factor in onc's karmic destiny, inaugurating one on a path of spiritual perfection that will take aeons to complete. The specific contents of this vow vary from case to case: all *bodhisattvas* take certain vows in common, among which, of course, are the resolve to postpone one's own enlightenment indefinitely while endeavoring to save others, to freely transfer merit to others, and so forth; but the *sūtras* also record vows specific to the great figures of the Buddhist pantheon. Amitābha, for instance, while the *bodhisattva* Dharmākara, is said to have formulated a series of vows in which he resolves to create a "Pure Land" where beings can be reborn to hear the Dharma preached by a Buddha. [*See* Amitābha.] The *Daśabhūmika Sūtra* enumerates ten "great aspirations" *(mahāpraṇidhāna)* of the *bodhisattva*, among which are the resolve to provide for the worship of all Buddhas, to maintain the Buddha's Dharma, to bring all beings to spiritual maturity, and to practice the *pāramitās*. Similarly, Queen Śrīmālā and the *bodhisattva* Samantabhadra are each said to have given issue to ten vows.

Ultimately, the *bodhisattva* path calls for the practitioner to perfect a series of six or ten virtues called *pāramitās*, "perfections." The (probably earlier) enumeration of six virtues, found in such texts as the Prajñāpāramitā Sūtras or the *Lotus*, consists of *dāna* ("giving"), *śīla* ("morality, the precepts"), *kṣānti* ("patience, forbearance"), *vīrya* ("effort"), *dhyāna* ("contemplation"), and *prajñā* ("transcendental insight"). Later texts such as the *Daśabhūmika Sūtra* add *upāya* ("skill in means"), *praṇidhāna* ("resolution," i.e., the *bodhisattva* vow), *bala* ("strength"), and *jñāna* ("knowledge"). [*See especially* Prajñā *and* Jñāna.]

The *pāramitās* were meant as an explicitly Mahāyāna counterpart to the older scheme of spiritual development—*śīla, dhyāna,* and *prajñā*—that prevailed among the Hīnayāna practitioners, but lists of *pāramitās* are not unknown to the Hīnayāna scriptures. For instance, enumerations of *pāramitās* were used in all traditions as a scheme for interpreting the Jātaka tales, now regarded as instances of the Buddha's accomplishment of the Perfections. The *pāramitās* as a systematic outline of *bodhisattva* practice are treated *inter alia* in Śāntideva's *Bodhicaryāvatāra*. [*See* Pāramitās.]

Another enumeration of *bodhisattva* practices is afforded by the thirty-seven so-called *bodhipakṣya dharmas*, or "principles conducive to enlightenment." These comprehend four *smṛtyupasthānāni*, or "states of mind fulness"; four *prahāṇāni*, or "abandonments"; four *ṛddhipādāḥ*, or "elements of supernatural power"; the five *indriyāṇi*, or "moral faculties"; five *balāni*, or "moral powers"; seven *bodhyaṅgāni*, or "components of perception"; and the Noble Eightfold Path. This list the Mahāyāna holds in common with the Hīnayāna, save for the fact that the Mahāyāna adds to it the practice of the *pāramitās* and the enumeration of ten *bodhisattva* stages, known as the *bodhisattva bhūmis*.

The classic enumeration of the *bhūmis* occurs in the *Daśabhūmika Sūtra*, although a variety of alternate schema also exist. Here, the *bodhisattva* path is conceived of as an ascent through levels of spiritual accomplishment that, in this text at least, are symmetrically linked with the practice of the ten *pāramitās*. The list clearly betrays an older enumeration of but seven *bhūmis*, as is evidenced by the fact that at the seventh *bhūmi* the practitioner is held to have undertaken those disciplines sufficient to win *nirvāṇa*, although his vow constrains him to remain in *saṃsāra*. Traditionally, the seventh *bhūmi* is also regarded as the stage at which no spiritual retrogression is possible: from this level the enlightenment of the *bodhisattva* is inevitable.

The *bodhisattva bhūmis* of the *Daśabhūmika* are as follows:

1. *Pramuditā* ("joyful"). Rejoicing in *bodhi* and in the fact that he shall succor all beings, the *bodhisattva* perfects himself in *dāna*.
2. *Vimalā* ("pure"). Perfecting himself in morality *(śīla)*, the *bodhisattva* is free from all impurities.
3. *Prabhākarī* ("light giving"). The *bodhisattva* brings the light (of his insight) to the world and perfects himself in *kṣānti*.
4. *Arciṣmatī* ("radiant"). Perfecting himself in *vīrya* and in the thirty-seven *bodhipakṣya dharmas*, the *bodhisattva*'s practice burns away ignorance.
5. *Sudurjayā* ("difficult to conquer"). Endeavoring to perfect himself in *dhyāna* and in the practice of the Four Noble Truths, the *bodhisattva* is not easily conquered by the forces of Māra, the tempter of the Buddhas.
6. *Abhimukhī* ("face to face"). Perfecting himself in *prajña* and insight into *pratītya-samutpāda*, the *bodhisattva* stands "face to face" with *nirvāṇa*.
7. *Dūraṃgamā* ("far-going"). With this stage, the practical aspects of the *bodhisattva*'s career are brought to fruition. Able now to comprehend reality just as it is, the *bodhisattva* stands at the "basis of existence" *(bhūta-koṭivihāra)* and is said to perfect himself in *upāya*, the "skillful means" necessary to help beings to salvation (although the text also calls for the *bodhisattva* to cultivate all ten *pāramitās* at this stage).
8. *Acalā* ("immovable"). The *bodhisattva*, unmoved by thoughts either of emptiness or phenomena, cause or non-cause, cultivates *praṇidhāna* and manifests himself at will throughout the various levels of existence.
9. *Sādhumatī* ("stage of good beings"). The *bodhisattva* acquires the four *pratisaṃvids* (analytical knowledges) and perfects himself in *bala*.
10. *Dharmameghā* ("cloud of the Dharma"). Just as space is dotted with clouds, so is this stage dominated by various trances and concentrations. The *bodhisattva* acquires a radiant body befitted with gems, and works miracles for the aid of beings. Perfecting himself in *jñāna*, he obtains the ten "deliverances" of the *bodhisattva*.

The *Daśabhūmika* maintains that the *bodhisattva* enters the first *bhūmi* immediately upon giving rise to *bodhicitta*. Other schemes, however, call for variety of intervening stages. One popular outline consists of fifty-two *bodhisattva* stages: ten degrees of faith, ten "abodes," ten degress of action, ten degrees of "diversion" (alt., the transfer of merit), the ten *bhūmis*, and two subsequent stages of highest enlightenment. Then again, some schools, particularly in East Asia, decried the tendency to divide the path into ever finer increments and insisted on the suddenness of the enlightenment experience. The Ch'an and Zen sects, for instance, virtually ignore the formal outline of the *bhūmis* in their insistence that enlightenment is a sudden, radical break in consciousness. The Esoteric traditions as well, while still prescribing a rigorous and detailed path of spiritual training, insist that Buddhahood can be attained "in this very body"; they thus minimize the importance of the traditional *bodhisattva* path, with its inconceivably long period of spiritual preparation necessary to attain Buddhahood.

Bodhisattva Disciplines. The formation of Mahāyāna did not entail a total rupture of the Buddhist community. Monks who professed the Mahāyāna soteriology did not necessarily leave the monastic compounds of the Hīnayāna *nikāyas* and, indeed, continued to be ordained according to their Vinayas. [*See* Vinaya.] Because of the nature of their practice and aspirations, however, practitioners of Mahāyāna did come to formulate guidelines for their life as a community, particularly for clerical life. These guidelines did not reject the Vinaya precepts so much as they did provide for supplemental practices and attitudes consistent with the altruistic spirit underlying Mahāyāna thought. The greater flexibility and liberality of Mahāyāna practice and doctrine also tended to create a role of enhanced importance for the laity, for the Mahāyāna typically rejected the assertion, prominent in Hīnayāna texts, that only as a cleric was one able to fulfill the religious life and win liberation. Thus, Mahāyāna ethics continued to endorse the legitimacy of lay life as a field of religious action and to provide religious sanction for the duties and obligations incumbent upon householders.

The disciplines of the *bodhisattva* are set forth in the *Bodhisattvabhūmi*, traditionally ascribed to Maitreyanātha. Here are described the so-called Threefold Pure Precepts of the *bodhisattva: saṃvaraśīla*, or adherence to the Prātimokṣa, aims at suppressing all evil acts on the part of the practitioner; *kuśaladharma samgrāhakam śīlam*, "practicing all virtuous deeds," aims at cultivating the roots of virtuous acts *(karman)* of body, speech, and mind; *sattvārtha-kriyā śīlam*, "granting mercy to all beings," aims at inculcating in others the practice of compassion and mercy toward all beings. The latter two practices comprise the specifically Mahāyāna component of the *bodhisattva* discipline, emphasizing as they do not merely the suppression of unwholesome acts but the positive injunction to do good on behalf of others. Another text, the *Brahmajāla Sūtra* (Sutra of Brahma's Net), was widely esteemed in East Asia as a source of precepts for *bodhisattvas*. Although in China monks continue to be ordained according to the Vinaya of the Dharmaguptaka school, in Japan, the *Brahmajāla Sūtra* provided a set of Mahāyāna precepts (Jpn., *bonmōkai*) observed by Tendai ordinands in lieu of the Vinaya altogether. Other Mahāyāna precepts appear in the *Bodhisattvaprātimokṣa Sūtra* (identical with the *Vinayaviniścaya-upālipariprcchā*) and the *Śrīmālādevī Sūtra*. The vows of Queen Śrīmālā in this latter work constitute a discipline all their own, prohibiting transgressions against morality, thoughts of anger, covetousness, jealousy, and disrespect toward others, and enjoining liberality, sympathy, help to those in need, and faith and confidence in the Dharma.

[*See also* Buddhism, Schools of, *article on* Mahāyāna Buddhism; Celestial Buddhas and Bodhisattvas; Soteriology, *article on* Buddhist Soteriology; *and* Buddha.]

BIBLIOGRAPHY

Dayal, Har. *The Bodhisattva Doctrine in Buddhist Sanskrit Literature* (1932). Reprint, Delhi, 1970.

Kajiyama Yūichi. "On the Meaning of the Words Bodhisattva and Mahāsattva." In *Indological and Buddhist Studies: Articles in Honor of Professor J. W. de Jong*, edited by L. A. Hercus et al., pp. 253–270. Canberra, 1982.

Nakamura Hajime. *Indian Buddhism: A Survey with Bibliographical Notes*. Osaka, 1980.

NAKAMURA HAJIME

BODILY MARKS. The human body is constantly being altered by natural and cultural processes. These alterations leave visible traces, which, in many societies, are associated with religious ideas, beliefs, and forces. Biological growth itself leaves marks on the body. Adolescence brings changes in physical structure to members of both sexes. Ageing alters the coloring and density of body hair. Firm flesh wrinkles; teeth drop out. Furthermore, accidents at work and play mar, scar, mutilate, and deform the body. Such biological and accidental changes may in many cultures be evidence of the operation of invisible beings or powers, such as deities, ancestors, or witchcraft. Or compensatory, supernormal powers may be attributed to the lame, to the malformed, to the blind, and to albinos. Just as certain kinds of diviners may read hidden meanings in such natural phenomena as the flight of birds or the spoor of foxes in sand, so, too, may the will of invisible entities be read into the natural marks left on the body by growth, illness, and violent mishap.

But nature lags far behind culture in the use of the body as a "canvas," as manipulable material for the expression of meaning. Clothing, headgear, ornaments, and regalia are, of course, salient agencies for the situational communication of personal and social identity, religious and secular values, and social status. Masks, too, have similar functions. Such external coverings indicate cultural transformations, particularly those of a transitory and repeatable character. It must be stressed, however, that in ritual settings in many cultures the same concepts and beliefs may be expressed by the marking of the body and by its clothing and masking. Ritual enlists many sensory codes, nonverbal and verbal, and orchestrates them to convey many-layered messages about the meaning of the human condition.

Bodily marking proper may be divided into two main types. The first, permanent marking, involves surgical or quasi-surgical operations on the surface of the body by means of cutting or piercing instruments, such as knives, needles, or razors. The general purpose here is to leave indelible marks on the body, mute messages of irreversible status-change, permanent cultural identity, or corporate affiliation. The second category, temporary marking, includes the application to the body of decorations through such media as chalk, charcoal, paint, or other substances that can readily be washed or dusted off. In a sense, such bodily marks are less durable than clothing, but when they are used in ritual contexts, they may convey more tellingly important aspects of the cosmological order.

Radical alteration of the genitalia is common to many cultures. [*See* Circumcision *and* Clitoridectomy.] It should, however, be noted that such operations, both in preindustrial societies and among adherents of some of the major historical religions, take place in a religious context, often to mark an important stage of the patient's life cycle. Symbolic action reinforces the surgical message that the patient, also an initiand, is undergoing an irreversible change in status and mode of being as culturally defined. Religious as well as cultural definitions and evaluations—gender, age, social segmentation, and cultic, tribal, and national affiliation—are given permanent expression precisely in the surgical refashioning of those bodily parts through which the very existence of the patient's group is genetically transmitted.

Many authorities hold that, generally speaking, tattooing has flourished most among relatively light-skinned peoples, while scarification and cicatrization are mostly found among dark-skinned peoples, since raised scars and keloids are more easily seen as pattern elements than the darker pigments. In contrast to body painting, however, all forms of piercing, cutting, or cauterizing the body involve contact with nerve endings resulting in pain, hence their not infrequent association with initiatory ordeals, in which respect they find common ground with such practices as genital excision, scourging, and the knocking out of teeth. Neuroscience may someday discover the precise effects on the central nervous system and on such concomitant psychological functions as memory and sexuality that are produced by these often prolonged operations on the subcutaneous neuronic network.

With the spread of Western culture, many societies that formerly practiced surgical bodily marking in religious contexts have abandoned these customs. Certainly, the three major religions "of the book"—Judaism, Christianity, and Islam—have interdicted tattooing since early times. Body marking was forbidden to Jews by God in the Torah (*Lv.* 19:28, *Dt.* 14:1). In AD 787 a Roman Catholic council forbade tattooing. Tattooing was also forbidden by Muḥammad. Nevertheless, tattooing has been frequently practiced, for therapeutic or decorative reasons, by nominal adherents of these three religions: for example, by Bosnian Catholics, where it may be a survival of an ancient puberty rite (reported by Durham, 1928, pp. 104–106), by Muslims in the Middle East (exhaustively discussed in Field, 1958), and (very rarely) among Middle Eastern and North African Jews.

Tattooing. European explorers during the fifteenth to eighteenth centuries were struck by the marks that they found on the bodies of the peoples they encountered in hitherto unknown lands. Captain John Smith in Virginia and Captain James Cook in Polynesia (to whom we owe the term *tattoo,* from the Tahitian word *tattau,* meaning "to mark") were struck by this form of body marking "by inlaying the Colour Black under their skins in such a manner as to be indelible" (W. J. L. Wharton, *Captain Cook's Journal during his First Voyage Round the World in H. M. Bark "Endeavour," 1768–1771,* London, 1893, p. 93). European explorers found tattooing in general practice among the Maori of New Zealand and most other Polynesian islands. The custom was also common throughout New Guinea, Melanesia, Micronesia, the Malay Archipelago, and the Malay Peninsula. On mainland Asia certain peoples of India, Burma, and the fringes of Tibet employed tattooing. Some African groups, including the Nama Khoi, also practiced the art. Tattooing was relatively frequent among North and South American Indians.

Tattooing resembles painting, with the face and body as canvas, while scarification resembles sculpture or woodcarving. Both processes can be painful, but tattooing seems to be less so than scarification, though a full design may take longer to apply. Perhaps the relative quickness of scarification and cicatrization is one of the reasons why they figure so prominently in rites of passage and other religious and therapeutic rituals, since they literally mark a sharp contrast between the initiand's previous and subsequent state and status. Nevertheless, if such rites include a lengthy period of seclusion from the mundane domain, the slower, more cumulative operation of tattooing may proceed at a more leisurely pace.

Full-body tattooing may take years to complete, and may be accomplished in several ritually significant stages. Wilfred D. Hambly (1925) reports, for example, that among the Motu Koita of New Guinea tattooing played a prominent role in rituals celebrating the physical development of the female body. At about five years old, the hands and forearms were tattooed. Between five and ten years of age, the chin, nose, lower abdomen, and inner thighs were tattooed as they lost their infantile appearance and grew firmer. At puberty, the breast, back, and buttocks were tattooed as they took on adult contours. During marital rites, and then at motherhood, the final designs were placed. Each phase of maturation had its own design: indeed, the Motu believed that tattooing not only signified growing up but even helped to cause it (Hambly, 1925, p. 32).

In a religious context, as distinct from a purely decorative context, tattoo marks are clearly symbolic. Hambly, for example, shows how the tattooing of initiands in girls' puberty rituals among the Omaha of North America was originally associated with rites devoted to the sun, the dominant power in their universe. The Omaha deified day and night as the male and female cosmic powers, akin to the Chinese opposition of *yang* and *yin*. At the apogee of solar ritual, a nubile girl is the focus of ritual dances, painting, and tattooing. She is tattooed with a disk representing the sun and a star standing for night. Four points on the star signify the four life-giving winds. The two marks together express the message that night gives way to the sun, a presage of the girl's marriage. The tattoos are believed to confer life energy and potential fecundity on the developing woman during this liminal phase. If her tattoo sores do not heal quickly, this is thought to indicate the displeasure of spirits because she has been unchaste (ibid., pp. 83–84). This example illustrates how ritual tattooing inscribes—or, one might even say, incarnates—cosmological ideas and forces, leaving a permanent impress, both subjectively and objectively.

There is archaeological evidence for puncture tattooing in the Middle East at least as early as the second millennium BCE. Puncture marks on mummy skins with duplicate signs painted on figurines have been found in Nubian burials from this period. Just as in preliterate societies, the polytheistic cultures of the eastern Mediterranean world saw tattooing as an efficacious means of communication between the invisible and visible domains, here regarded as divine and human. For example, the pharaoh Akhenaton (Amunhotep IV) is represented in reliefs as bearing the name *Aton* on his body. Although Akhenaton was reared in a polytheistic tradition, he tried to develop a solar monotheism and encouraged naturalistic art at the expense of symbolism. Hence his tattoo was a name, not a symbol. The great monotheistic religions went even further in forbidding the marking of symbols of deities on the body. Henry Field (1958, p. 4) supplies further evidence of rapport between humans and deities effected by tattooing. The symbol of the goddess Neit, for example, was tattooed on the arms and legs of Libyan captives figured on the tomb walls of Sety I (1318–1304 BCE). Even today in North Africa a tattoo pattern called "Triangle of Tanit" has been identified as the symbol of the Carthaginian goddess Tanit, who was herself perhaps the Libyan goddess Ta-Neit taken over by the Carthaginians. Field also mentions that the devotees of Dionysos were stamped with that god's symbol, the ivy leaf. In Syria-Palestine, the worshipers of the moon goddess Mylitta were tattooed with her figure or symbol on their hands or the backs of their necks.

Subsequently, despite religious interdictions, both Christians and Muslims bore tattoos as evidences of having made pilgrimages to the sacred places. This practice apparently derived from the time of the Crusades. Coptic pilgrims are tattooed with the word *Jerusalem*, with the date of the visit beneath it, or a standardized religious emblem. Moses Maimonides, commenting on the prohibition against tattooing in *Leviticus*, reiterated the central Judaic argument against idolatry as its motive force, while other scholars in his tradition stress the integrity of the human body made in the express image and likeness of God as justification for the ban.

In the cultural history of tattooing, certain main trends are discernible. In antiquity and in many of the reports of travelers in the early modern period, tattooing in preindustrial societies dominantly relates the tattooed person to a social group or category (totemic clan, age or sex category, secret society or warrior association, unmarried or married categories, the widowed, and the like). Sometimes the tattooing process is embedded in an encompassing ritual process. In other instances, as we have seen, cumulative tattooing may operate independently from rites of passage, stressing individual development rather than collective affiliation. As societies increase in scale, grow more complex, and the division of economic and social labor becomes more refined, tattooing becomes more a matter of individual choice and serves the purpose of self-expression, stressing the decorative rather than the religious and corporate functions. Instead of classing individuals together, homogenizing them symbolically, it now differentiates them. An antinomian character invests tattooing. As the technology of the art develops (for example, the invention of the electric tattooing needle), so do the designs and colors multiply, allowing considerable scope for self-expression and for making statements about the self, not only to others but also to oneself, indelibly imprinting a complex image of one's identity upon one's body.

In societies where tattooing is strongly interdicted or frowned upon for religious or political reasons, tattooing comes to mark and identify not only recalcitrant individuals but also marginal groups that otherwise have few means to display identity in mainstream society. A considerable literature exists on tattooing among such diverse categories as enlisted men in World Wars I and II, criminals, prostitutes, homosexuals, juvenile delinquents, and motorcycle gangs such as the Hell's Angels.

In Japan, where the art of tattooing *(irezumi)* has been long established and may have had, as in Polynesia, ritual connections, the practice fell under interdict in the late Tokugawa period, but it was strongly revived after 1881 when it ceased to be a penal offense. According to Robert Brain (1979), the Japanese—who embroider the whole body with artistic designs, the equivalent of a suit of clothes to a culture that has never hallowed the nude—"use tattooing to give personality to the naked body. . . . Even the bare skin, incorporated into the overall design, acquires an appearance of artificiality" (p. 64). The designs are traditional and include the dragon, "giver of strength and sagacity," the horse and the carp (mutations of the dragon), epic heroes such as Yoshitsune, Chinese sages, and the gods whose deeds are recorded in the *Kojiki* and *Nihonshoki.* In Japan it has often been difficult to distinguish, in Western style, the religious from the aesthetic and social. Contemporary tattooed men and women wear on their bodies subtle and beautiful expressions of a continuous tradition that links deity, nature, and humankind.

As tattooing became detached from its earlier religious contexts, it seems to have become increasingly associated with the magical protection of individuals and with curative rites performed in cases of individual affliction. Field (1958) provides innumerable examples of tattooing in Syria, Iraq, Iran, Kuwait, Saudi Arabia, Palestine, Baluchistan, and West Pakistan used as prophylaxis, cure, and subsequent prevention of a variety of diseases and ailments, mostly thought to be due to supernatural causes such as the evil eye, witchcraft, or demons. Therapeutic tattooing is found in many cultures. For example, the Sarawak Kaya of Borneo believe that sickness is caused by the soul leaving the body. A ritual therapist, the *dayong,* is called in to perform a ritual, including dancing and incantations, to recall the patient's soul to its body. After he is sure that the soul is back, the *dayong* tattoos an emblem on the patient to keep it from straying again. Similar uses may be found cross-culturally in abundance.

Mention should be made of the recent growth of tattooing in the United States, particularly in California during the late 1970s. After World War II, the practice had subsided, but because of the influence of the "counterculture" of the late sixties, the role of electronic media in bringing the practices of other cultures into the American home, extensive tourism, a general emphasis on individuality (in dress, sexual mores, art, and religion), and improvements in the techniques of professional tattooing, there has been a marked revival in the art. The ancient connection with religion has not been forgotten. For example, at the Fifth World Convention of Tattoo Artists and Fans, held in Sacramento in 1980, the prize tattoo was "a large back mural, which included the Virgin of Guadalupe, set on a bed of bright roses, framed in the lower corners by a skull face and a human face, and in the upper, by flowing angels" (A. B. Gobenar, "Culture in Transition: The Recent Growth of Tattooing in America," *Anthropos* 76, 1981, p. 216).

Scarification and Cicatrization. Whereas tattooing is the insertion of pigment under the skin, involving pricking instruments ranging from thorns, fish spines, cactus spikes, shells, and bones to steel and electric needles, scarification and cicatrization are more drastic ways of marking the body. Many anthropologists equate these terms, but, strictly speaking, scarification is the operation of marking with scars, while cicatrization is the subsequent formation of a scar at the site of a healing wound, that is, the healing process. It might be useful to distinguish *scarification,* meaning "the production of long cuts," from *cicatrization,* meaning "the deliberate formation of keloids, sharply elevated, often round or oval scars due to the rich production of collagen in the dermal layer." David Livingstone, in his *Last Journals in Central Africa* (London, 1874), gives us the classic definition of keloid formation, when writing of the Makwa, who have double lines of keloids on the face: "After the incisions are made, charcoal is rubbed in, and the flesh pressed out, so that all the cuts are raised above the level of the surface" (vol. 1, p. 33). In many parts of sub-

Saharan Africa, cicatrization follows the work of two instruments: a hooked thorn to raise the skin and a small blade to slice it. The more the skin is raised, the more prominent the resulting keloid.

In many preindustrial societies, the cicatrization process is embedded in a complex ritual sequence. In *The Drums of Affliction* (Oxford, 1968), I reported upon such a ritual sequence among the Ndembu of Zambia. During the seclusion phase of a girl's puberty ritual, the initiand is cicatrized by a woman skilled in the work. The girl is said to feel much pain while the incisions are being made, but after the operation, she is allowed to revile the operator, in compensation, just as boys are permitted to swear at the circumciser during the corresponding male initiation rites. Groups of horizontal incisions converge on the navel from either side, like several sentences of braille. Other keloids are made beneath the navel toward the pubes and on the small of the back. Black wood ash, mixed with castor oil, is rubbed into the cuts. The raised cicatrices beside the navel constitute a kind of erotic braille and are "to catch a man" by giving him enhanced sexual pleasure when he plays his hand over them. Initiands who can stand the pain are also cicatrized on the mid-chest above the breast line. Two parallel cuts are made, known by a term signifying "to deny the lover." The first keloid, to the left, represents the initiand's premarital lover; the second, to the right, her husband-to-be. The girl is told never to mention her lover's name to her husband, for the two men should "remain friends" and not fight each other.

Although tattooing, cicatrization, and scarification have much in common, may be combined in various ways, or may each be applied in different contexts in the same society, it may be broadly concluded that tattooing, like body painting, lends itself well to decorative use and personal art. The body becomes a canvas on or under the skin of which may be depicted naturalistic scenes and portraits, abstract designs, and symbolic patterns. Cutting and scarring flesh, although this, too, may result in aesthetic effects of a quite sophisticated character, also constitutes a visible record of incarnate religious forces and a sacred chronicle of a culture's life-crisis ceremonies. Here the incised body itself proclaims carnally the disciplines involved in the cultural definition of its age, gender, and communal and structural identifications and alliances. In certain societies, these marks are believed to be inscribed on the ghost or spirit after death, enabling the gods or spirits to recognize the membership and status of the deceased and to send him or her to an appropriate place of posthumous residence. It is interesting that the Roman Catholic and Orthodox branches of Christianity have sublimated similar beliefs, while condemning body marking itself, in the notion that sacraments of baptism, confirmation, and ordination confer indelible marks upon the soul.

Body Painting. Of the many languages of bodily adornment, several may coexist in a single culture. Terence S. Turner (1977) points out, for example, that the Chikrí, a Ge-speaking group in central Brazil, possess elaborate body painting, adorn themselves with earplugs, lip plugs, and penis sheaths, and put on cotton leg and arm bands in ritual contexts. Turner argues that such body adornments are a kind of symbolic language. Body painting is a code that expresses a wide range of information about social status, sex, and age. More than this, writes Turner, it "establishes a channel of communication *within* the individual, between the social and biological aspects of his personality" (p. 98).

Color symbolism is most important here, especially the colors red, black, and white, all of which are used in determinate ways. Red is always applied on bodily extremities, forearms and hands, lower legs and feet, and the face. Black is used on the trunk and the upper parts of the limbs, as well as for square cheek patches and borders along the shaved areas of the forehead. Black face paintings, executed with great care, are often covered immediately by a heavy coat of red that renders them almost invisible. This practice may be explained by the symbolic values of the colors. Red, according to Turner, represents energy, health, and "quickness," both in the sense of swiftness and of heightened sensitivity. Black, *per contra*, is associated with transitions between clearly defined states or categories, with liminal conditions, or regions where normal, precisely defined structures of ideas and behavioral rules are "blacked out." Black also means "dead" and is adjectivally applied to a zone of land outside the village, separating it from the wild forest, that is used for graveyards and seclusion camps for groups undergoing rites of passage. The Chikrí see death itself as a liminal phase between life and complete oblivion. Ghosts survive for one generation in the village of the dead before they "die" once more, this time forever. White represents the pure, terminal state of complete transcendence of the normal social world, for white is the color of ghosts, and white clay is the food of ghosts. The Chikrí paint over the black designs with red to make a symbolic statement, clearly uninfluenced by aesthetic considerations. According to Turner, the black designs represent the socialization of the intelligent part of the person, which is then energized by the biological and psychic life force represented by the thick red overpainting.

Turner's conclusion that body painting at this general level of meaning "really amounts to the imposition of a second, social 'skin' on the naked biological skin of the individual" (p. 100) has a very wide cross-cultural range of applications. The etymological link between *cosmos* and *cosmetics* has often been noted; both derive from the Greek term meaning "order, ornament, universe." When the face and body are painted with designs and colors, the cosmeticized ones are living links between the individual and the sociocultural order with which he is temporarily identified. But, as with tattooing, in complex industrial societies body painting may assume an antinomian function; bizarre and extravagant designs may betoken rebellion against a society's most cherished values. Or it may become merely an expression of personal vanity and love of adornment.

Marks of Supernatural Election. A considerable literature exists on bodily marks that are believed to be signs of election to high religious status. These must be distinguished from blemishes or birthmarks taken to be indications of reincarnation. In many sub-Saharan societies, for example, recently born infants are carefully inspected for marks corresponding to conspicuous scars and moles found on some deceased relative. Among the Ndembu of Zambia, a child was called Lupinda because marks resembling scratches on his thigh were similar to the scar marks of a leopard-inflicted wound on the thigh of his mother's brother, the great hunter Lupinda. It was expected that the boy, Lupinda reborn, would likewise excel at the chase. Similar beliefs have been reported among the Haida and Tlingit of northwestern North America.

In the great historical religions, founders, prophets, saints, and notable teachers of the faith are sometimes associated with supernaturally generated bodily characteristics. For example, it is reported that when Siddhartha Gautama, who became the Buddha, was born, his body bore the thirty-two auspicious marks *(mahāpuruṣa lakṣaṇāni)* that indicated his future greatness, besides secondary marks *(anuvyañjanāni)*. The Indian poet Aśvaghoṣa, who wrote his *Buddhacarita* (Life of the Buddha) in the second century CE, mentions some of these marks: the sign of a wheel on one foot, webbing between his fingers and toes, and a circle of hair between his eyebrows. In Islam, too, there is a tradition of a person bearing bodily marks signifying divine election. Muḥammad's son-in-law ʿAlī predicted that the Mahdi, the "divinely guided one," would come to restore justice and righteousness to the world and that he would be recognized by certain bodily traits, among them a balding forehead and a high, hooked nose. A birthmark on his right cheek, a gap between his front teeth, and a deep black beard were also predicted. Muḥammad Aḥmad, who was believed to be the Mahdi by many living in the Sudan during the nineteenth century, was said to have all the looked-for attributes.

Christianity also has its tradition of bodily marks divinely imposed. For Christians, the term *stigmata* refers to wounds some people bear on hands and feet, and occasionally on the side, shoulder, or back, that are believed to be visible signs of participation in Christ's passion. Francis of Assisi (d. 1226) is said to have been the first stigmatic. Since his time, the number has multiplied. Historically, the stigmata have taken many different forms and have appeared in different positions on the body, hands, and feet of stigmatics. For example, Francis's side wound was on the right, while that of the celebrated modern stigmatic Padre Pio was on the left. For the Catholic church, stigmata do not by themselves indicate sanctity. Of the several hundred stigmatics listed since the thirteenth century, only sixty-one have been canonized or beatified. Father Herbert Thurston, S.J., an authority on this phenomenon, was extremely reluctant to attribute stigmatization to a miracle ("The Problem of Stigmatization," *Studies* 22, 1933, p. 223). Other theologians are ready to await the verdict of neuroscientific research to settle the problem. Moreover, it has been pointed out by C. Bernard Ruffin, a Lutheran minister, that "for every genuine stigmatic, whether holy or hysterical, saintly or satanic, there are at least two whose wounds are self-inflicted" (Ruffin, 1982, p. 145).

Summary. In many societies, birthmarks, blemishes, deformities, and other natural signs have been regarded as visible indicators of the permanent or transient presence of invisible, preternatural forces and influences, whether of a magical or religious character. They may be linked with notions of reincarnation, illness caused by spirits or witches, election to a priestly or shamanic role, or the marking of basic group identity. However, the deliberate shaping of the body as an artifact by cultural means is the most widely practiced marker of group identity, an identity that in the simpler societies is also religious identity. Here the body becomes a deliberately created badge of identity. Both permanent and temporary changes are made for this purpose. In addition to the means described above, one might cite tooth-filing, piercing or otherwise changing the shape of ears, nose, tongue, and lips, and changes made in the body's extremities, such as hair, feet, fingers, and nails. Although discussion of clothing, the identifying medium for all kinds of religions in all cultures, is beyond the scope of this article, as is detailed discussion of the relationship between aesthetic and ritual bodily marking, it is clear that the body, whether clad or unclad, painted or unpainted, smooth or scarred, is never religiously neutral: it is always and everywhere a complex signifier of spirit, society, self, and cosmos.

[*For discussion of other modes of religious differentiation, see* Clothing; Masks; *and* Nudity. *See also* Human Body.]

BIBLIOGRAPHY

Brain, Robert. *The Decorated Body.* London, 1979. A readable cross-cultural description of the decoration of the human body by an anthropologist, somewhat polemical in tone against the Western phenomenon of fashion.

Durham, Mary E. *Some Tribal Origins and Customs of the Balkans.* London, 1928. Includes a brief but interesting account of the survival of tattooing among Bosnian Catholics.

Field, Henry. *Body-Marking in Southwestern Asia.* Papers of the Peabody Museum of Archaeology and Ethnology, Harvard University, vol. 45, no. 1. Cambridge, Mass., 1958. Results obtained from fieldwork in Southwest Asia by several investigators attached to expeditions undertaken by the Peabody Museum, the Field Museum, and Oxford University, between 1925 and 1955. A rich store of ethnographic information, but with little in the way of theory.

Hambly, Wilfrid D. *The History of Tattooing and Its Significance, with Some Account of Other Forms of Corporal Marking* (1925). Reprint, Detroit, 1975. Still the classic study on tattooing.

Polhemus, Ted, ed. *The Body Reader: Social Aspects of the Human Body.* New York, 1978. A set of significant contemporary articles on body image, alteration, and adornment, dealing with a wide range of theories about bodily marks.

Ruffin, C. Bernard. *Padre Pio: The True Story.* Huntingdon, Ind., 1982. A critical, sober, essentially nonhagiographical account of the life of this century's best-known stigmatic. The medical evidence about his stigmata is thoroughly discussed.

Strathern, Andrew, and Marilyn Strathern. *Self-Decoration in Mount Hagen.* Toronto, 1971. The most comprehensive account of body decoration and its meaning in a single society, that of Mount Hagen, New Guinea.

Turner, Terence S. "Cosmetics: The Language of Bodily Adornment." In *Conformity and Conflict,* 3d ed., edited by James P. Spradley and David W. McCurdy, pp. 91–108. Boston, 1977. A seminal article on bodily adornment among the Chikrí of Brazil. The author deciphers the complex code underlying various modes of decoration to reveal their meaning and suggests that body decorations have similar functions in all societies.

VICTOR TURNER

BODY. *See* Human Body.

BODY PAINTING. *See* Bodily Marks.

BOEHME, JAKOB (1575–1624), Protestant visionary and theologian. Born into a Lutheran farming family in the village of Alt Seidenberg near Görlitz, Saxony, Boehme was apprenticed to a shoemaker following his elementary education. In 1599 he became a citizen of Görlitz, where he opened a shoemaking business and married. Boehme was early associated with various religious groups in the city, and through them he encountered the work of the alchemist Paracelsus (1493–1551) and the nature mystic Valentine Weigel (1533–1588). He also shared with his religious associates an interest in Qabbalah.

In 1600 Martin Moller (d. 1606) came to the city as Lutheran pastor and formed the Conventicle of God's Real Servants, which Boehme joined following a religious conversion. Deeply concerned with the problem of theodicy, Boehme in 1612 completed *Aurora,* but when a copy of the manuscript fell into the hands of the local Lutheran pastor, the book was confiscated and the author banned from further writing. Seven years later, as the result of an illumination, Boehme broke his silence with the publication of *On the Three Principles of Divine Being,* a work abounding in alchemic imagery, which was to shape the form of his arguments for the next several years. [*For broad examination of the relation of religion and alchemy, see* Alchemy.] In 1620 there appeared *On the Three-fold Life of Man, On the Incarnation, Six Theosophical Points,* and *Six Mystical Points.* Other major works followed quickly, including, *Concerning the Birth and Designation of All Being, On Election to Grace,* the large commentary on *Genesis* entitled *Mysterium magnum,* and the various tracts that make up *The Way to Christ.* As a result of these publications, Boehme was involved in bitter controversy, and suffered exile for a short time. He died in Görlitz on 17 November 1624.

In an attempt to solve the problem of theodicy, Boehme began with the nothing (unknown even to itself), which, as a single unified will, wills a something. In this act of willing, the Son is begotten. In this begetting the nothing discovers the something within itself, which is itself the ground of the abyss. Simultaneously the will proceeds from the Son as Holy Spirit to an eternal contemplation of itself as wisdom (Sophia).

In this contemplation are conceived the various possibilities of being present in the Word (the Son) and created by it. The will of the nothing looks out to the something as light (love) and returns into itself as a desiring fire (wrath). In the knowledge that results, eternal nature has its being. The two fused principles of fire and light reflect in themselves a third, the being of the universe, which is progressively manifested through seven properties: harshness; attraction; dread; the ignition of fire, which is the basis of sensitive and intellectual life; love, which overcomes the individualism of the first four; the power of speech; and speech itself. All properties are present in all being. Further, the seven properties can be categorized according to three principles. The first three properties represent the fire (wrath) principle. The fifth and sixth properties represent the light (love) principle. The seventh property represents the third principle (being of the universe). The fourth property is the center on which all turn. All beings of the third principle are free and can turn to either of the first two principles, thereby upsetting the balance. Searching for the controlling fire of light, Lucifer refused to accept the light principle within himself and as a result fell.

At the moment of Lucifer's fall, temporal creation came into existence. At its height stood Adam, a perfect balance of the four elements fire and light, male and female. But Adam, too, chose to know the principles separately and fell. In the loss of the balance, these four elements were awakened and male and female divided. Thereafter human beings have chosen the fiery origin that, untempered by light, love, or the spiritual water of the new life, would destroy each individual human being. In his mercy, however, God fully revealed the light element in the New Man, Christ, in whose perfect balance each human being can once more live in harmony with the divine contemplation, the virgin Sophia. [*See* Sophia.]

Following Boehme's death, his disciples, chief among whom was Abraham von Franckenberg (1593–1649), spread his ideas throughout Europe. The Silesian poet Angelus Silesius (Johann Scheffler, 1624–1677) used Boehme's images extensively in his poetry before and after his conversion from Lutheranism to Roman Catholicism. By 1661 Boehme's works appeared in English translation, and under the direction of Jane Leade (1623–1704) the Philadelphian Society was founded in London on Boehmist principles. In England alone Boehme's influence can be traced in the seventeenth century to persons of such stature as the Cambridge Platonist Benjamin Whichcote, the poet John Milton, and the physicist Isaac Newton, and in the eighteenth century to the spiritual writer William Law and the visionary poet William Blake. In the Low Countries, Boehme's thought was popularized by the most important of his editors and students, Johann Georg Gichtel (1638–1710), and by radical Quietists such as Antoinette Bourignon (1616–1680) and Pierre Poiret (1646–1719).

BIBLIOGRAPHY

Boehme, Jakob. *Sämmtliche Schriften.* 10 vols. Edited by Will-Erich Peuckert. Stuttgart, 1955–1960.

Koyré, Alexandre. *La philosophie de Jacob Boehme* (1929). Reprint, New York, 1968. The fullest introduction to Boehme's thought.

Peuckert, Will-Erich. *Das Leben Jakob Böhmes* (1924). Reprint, Stuttgart, 1961. A detailed biography of Boehme.

Stoudt, John Joseph. *Sunrise to Eternity.* Philadelphia, 1957. The best introduction to Boehme's life and thought in English.

Thune, Nils. *The Behmenists and the Philadelphians.* Uppsala, 1948. A limited but useful outline of the Boehmist heritage.

PETER C. ERB

BOETHIUS (c. 475–c. 525), more fully Anicius Manlius (Torquatus) Severinus Boethius, late Roman philosopher, theologian, and statesman. Because of the paucity of sources concerning Boethius's life, no more than the most shadowy biographical sketch is possible. A member of one of the great Roman families, Boethius was almost certainly born at Rome. The Rome in which he lived had lost much of its importance—imperial control had given way to the reign of the barbarian king Odoacer about the time of his birth—but the prestige of the Anician family remained intact, as shown by the consulship of Boethius's father in 487. Upon completing his schooling, which he presumably received at Rome, Boethius continued his education by studying philosophy, probably at Alexandria, but possibly in his native city. Of his public life, it is known only that he served as consul in 510 and that, about 523, he became master of offices, one of the highest civil officials in the court of the Ostrogothic king of Italy, Theodoric. While master of offices, Boethius was implicated in a treasonable conspiracy with the Eastern emperor, which apparently centered upon a plot to overthrow Theodoric. Although Boethius resolutely maintained his innocence, he was imprisoned. During his imprisonment he wrote *On the Consolation of Philosophy,* his most famous work, which he completed only shortly before his execution.

Much more important than his public career, which was not unusual for a person of his standing, was his literary career. In one of his early works, he described his projected program of philosophical writings: in a world in which the Latin West was rapidly losing its knowledge of Greek, Boethius wished to translate into Latin all the works of Plato and Aristotle and to show, through a series of commentaries on these works, that there was no essential conflict between the Platonic and Aristotelian traditions. He did not realize this plan in its entirety, but he did translate a number of the logical works of Aristotle (the so-called *Organon*) and wrote (or possibly only translated from the Greek) several commentaries on these writings. In doing so, he rendered a very important service to the early medieval West by providing the only Latin translations of Aristotle available until the gradual introduction of the "new learning" in the late Middle Ages.

Despite his failure to translate any of the works of Plato, Boethius did provide the medieval world with one of its most important source books of Neoplatonic thought, *On the Consolation of Philosophy,* one of the most widely read books of the Middle Ages. Cast in the form of a cosmological revelation by Lady Philosophy to the imprisoned and perplexed Boethius, the *Consolation* presents a highly sophisticated and systematic Neoplatonic worldview. The curious fact that Boethius, who was certainly a Christian, looked to Neoplatonism rather than to Christianity to console him is inexplicable.

Boethius's chief creative contribution to the intellectual tradition of the West comes in his five brief Christian theological works. Although these works are highly Augustinian in their content, Boethius established his independence from Augustine in matters of terminology and method. In *On the Trinity,* he employed the term *theology* for the first time as a technical Christian term denoting the philosophical inquiry into the nature of God. Methodologically, his contribution lies in the use of formal Aristotelian demonstrative logic for the first time in the service of Christian theology. In doing so, he anticipated the fundamental character of the Thomistic method of "scientific" theology by some five and one-half centuries.

BIBLIOGRAPHY

Most of Boethius's works have not been translated into English, but *The Theological Tractates* and *The Consolation of Philosophy,* translated by H. F. Stewart and E. K. Rand, are widely available in a Loeb Classical Library edition (Cambridge, Mass., 1926). The best work in English on Boethius's writings in general is Pierre Courcelle's *Late Latin Writers and Their Greek Sources,* translated by Harry E. Wedeck (Cambridge, Mass., 1969). For specific discussion of the Christian theological works, see my study entitled "Boethius' Conception of Theology and His Method in the Tractates" (Ph.D. diss., University of Chicago, 1974).

A. Rand Sutherland

BON. There are two organized religious traditions in Tibet: Buddhism and a faith that is referred to by its Tibetan name, Bon. Since its introduction into Tibet in the eighth century, Buddhism has been the dominant religion; in the person of the Dalai Lama, present-day Tibetan Buddhism has an articulate and internationally respected spokesman.

The Bon religion is much less well known, although the number of its adherents in Tibet is by all accounts considerable. In the West, the traditional view of Bon has been less than accurate. It has been characterized as "shamanism" or "animism," and as such, regarded as a continuation of what supposedly were the religious practices prevalent in Tibet before the coming of Buddhism. It has also been described in rather unfavorable terms as a perversion of Buddhism, a kind of marginal countercurrent in which elements of Buddhist doctrine and practice have either been shamelessly copied or inverted and distorted in a manner that has been somewhat imaginatively compared with satanic cults. It is only since the mid-1960s that a more accurate understanding of this religion has emerged (first and foremost thanks to the efforts of David L. Snellgrove), so that Bon is now recognized as closely related to the various Buddhist schools in Tibet (in particular the Rñiṅ-ma-pa order) and yet possessed of an identity of its own that justifies its status as a distinct religion.

Problems of Definition. An adherent of the Bon religion is called a Bon-po, again using the Tibetan term. A Bon-po is "a believer in *bon,*" and for such a believer the word *bon* signifies "truth," "reality," or the eternal, unchanging doctrine in which truth and reality are expressed. Thus *bon* has the same range of connotations for its believers as the Tibetan word *chos* (corresponding to the Indian word *dharma*) has for Buddhists.

A problem, however, arises when one is confronted with the fact that an important group of ritual experts in pre-Buddhist Tibet were likewise known as *bon-pos*. It is possible that their religious practices were styled Bon (although scholars are divided on this point); certainly they were so designated in the later, predominantly Buddhist historiographical tradition. Be that as it may, their religious system was essentially different not only from Buddhism, but also, in certain important respects, from the Bon religious tradition as practiced in later centuries. For example, the pre-Buddhist religion of Tibet gives the impression of being preoccupied with the continuation of life beyond death. It included elaborate rituals for ensuring that the soul of a dead person was conducted safely to a postmortem land of bliss by an appropriate animal—usually a yak, a horse, or a sheep—which was sacrificed in the course of the funerary rites. Offerings of food, drink, and precious objects likewise accompanied the dead. These rites reached their highest level of elaboration and magnificence in connection with the death of a king or a high nobleman; as was the case in China, enormous funerary mounds were erected, and a large number of priests and court officials were involved in rites that lasted for several years. The purpose of these rites was twofold: on the one hand, to ensure the happiness of the deceased in the land of the dead, and on the other, to obtain their beneficial influence for the welfare and fertility of the living.

The term *Bon* refers not only to these and other religious practices of pre-Buddhist Tibet, but also to the religion that apparently developed in close interaction with Buddhism from the eighth century onward and that still claims the adherence of many Tibetans. It is with the latter religion that this article is concerned. The Bon-pos claim that there is an unbroken continuity between the earlier and the later religion—a claim that, whatever its historical validity, is significant in itself.

The matter is further complicated by the fact that there has always existed a vast and somewhat amorphous body of popular beliefs in Tibet, including beliefs in various techniques of divination, the cult of local deities (connected, above all, with certain mountains), and conceptions of the soul. In Western literature, such beliefs are frequently styled "Bon," and reference is made to "Bon animism" and other supposedly typical Bon attributes. This has, however, no basis in Tibetan usage, and since this popular, unsystematized religion does not form an essential part of Buddhism or Bon (although it is, to a large extent, sanctioned by and integrated into both religions), an appropriate term for it is the one coined by Rolf A. Stein, "the nameless religion."

The Bon-po Identity. Although limited to Tibet, Bon regards itself as a universal religion in the sense that its doctrines are true and valid for all humanity. For this reason it styles itself G'yuṅ-druṅ Bon, "Eternal Bon." According to its own historical perspective, it was introduced into Tibet many centuries before Buddhism and enjoyed royal patronage until it was supplanted and expelled by the "false religion" (Buddhism) coming from India.

Before reaching Tibet, however, it is claimed that Bon prospered in a land known as Źaṅ-źuṅ and that this country remained the center of the religion until it was absorbed by the expanding Tibetan empire in the seventh century. There is no doubt as to the historical reality of Źaṅ-źuṅ, although its exact extent and ethnic and cultural identity are far from clear. It does, however, seem to have been situated in what today is, roughly speaking, western Tibet, with Mount Kailāśa as its center.

The ultimate homeland of Bon, is, however, to be sought farther to the west, beyond the borders of Źaṅ-źuṅ. The Bon-pos believe that their religion was first proclaimed in a land called Rtag-gzigs (Tazik) or 'Ol-mo Luṅ-riṅ. Although the former name suggests the land of the Tajiks (in present-day Soviet Central Asia), it has so far not been possible to identify this holy land of Bon in a convincing manner.

In Rtag-gzigs, so the Bon-pos claim, lived Ston-pa Gśen-rab (Tönpa Shenrap), a fully enlightened being who was, in fact, nothing less than the true Buddha of our world age. The Bon-pos possess a voluminous biographical literature in which his exploits are extolled. Without entering into details, or discussing the many problems connected with the historical genesis of this extraordinary figure, one may at least note that his biography is not closely related to the biographical traditions connected with Śākyamuni, the Buddha on whose authority the Buddhists base their doctrines. Ston-pa Gśen-rab was a layman, and it was as a prince that he incessantly journeyed from his capital in all directions to propagate Bon. It is remarkable that this propagation also included the institution of innumerable rituals, the supervision of the erection of temples and stupas, and the conversion of notorious sinners. His numerous wives, sons, daughters, and disciples also played a significant role (in a way for which there is no Buddhist parallel) in this soteriological activity. It was only late in his life that he was ordained as a monk, and at that point in his career he retired to a forest hermitage. On the other hand, Ston-pa Gśen-rab is considered to have been a fully enlightened being from his very birth, endowed with numerous supernatural powers. His importance in the Bon religion is crucial; it is he who—directly or indirectly—lends authority to the religious literature of the Bon-pos, and he is the object of their intense devotion.

Religious Beliefs and Practices. In the same way as the Buddhists of Tibet divide their sacred scriptures into two vast collections, the Bon-pos also—probably since the middle of the fourteenth century CE—possess their own Bka'-'gyur (Kanjur, texts considered to have been actually expounded by Ston-pa Gśen-rab) and Brten-'gyur (Tenjur, later commentaries and treatises), comprising in all approximately three hundred volumes. Since the middle of the nineteenth century wooden blocks for printing the entire collection have been available in the principality of Khro-bcu in the extreme east of Tibet, and printed copies of the canon were produced until the 1950s. (The blocks were destroyed during the Cultural Revolution). Large portions of the Bka'-'gyur and Brten-'gyur may be reconstituted on the basis of texts published by Bon-po exiles living in India, and it seems that a complete set of the printed edition has survived the ravages of war and of the Cultural Revolution in Tibet itself.

A common division of the Bon-po Bka'-'gyur is the fourfold one into Sūtras *(mdo),* Prajñāpāramitā texts *('bum),* Tantras *(rgyud),* and texts dealing with the higher forms of meditation (*mdzod,* lit. "treasure-house"). The Brten-'gyur is divided into three basic textual categories: "External," including commentaries on the Vinaya, the Abhidharma, and the Sūtras; "Internal," comprising the commentaries on the Tantras and the rituals focusing on the major Tantric deities, as well as the cult of *ḍākinīs*, *dharmapālas*, and worldly rituals of magic and divination; and finally, "Secret," a section that treats meditation practices. A section containing treatises on grammar, architecture, and medicine is appended.

For the sake of convenience, the Indian (Buddhist) terms corresponding to the Tibetan have been used here, but it must be kept in mind that although the Bon-pos employ the same Tibetan terms as the Buddhists, they do not accept their Indian origin, since they trace, as explained above, their entire religious terminology to Źaṅ-źuṅ and, ultimately, to Rtag-gzigs.

As this review of Bon-po religious literature indicates, the doctrines they contain are basically the same as those of Buddhism. The concepts of the world as suffering, of moral causality and rebirth in the six states of existence, and of enlightenment and Buddhahood are basic doctrinal elements of Bon. Bon-pos follow the same path of virtue and have recourse to the same meditational practices as do Buddhist Tibetans.

In the early fifteenth century—and indeed even earlier—the Bon-pos began to establish monasteries that were organized along the same lines as those of the Buddhists, and several of these monasteries developed into large institutions with hundreds of monks and novices. The most prestigious Bon-po monastery, founded in 1405, is Sman-ri in central Tibet (in the province of Gtsaṅ, north of the Brahmaputra River). Fully ordained monks, corresponding to the Buddhist *dge-sloṇ* (Skt., *bhikṣu*), are styled *draṅ-sroṅ* (a term that in Tibetan otherwise translates *ṛṣi,* the semidivine "seers" of the Vedas). They are bound by all the rules of monastic discipline, including strict celibacy.

Over the centuries the monastic life of Bon has come increasingly under the influence of the tradition of academic learning and scholastic debate that characterize the dominant Dge-lugs-pa school, but the older tradition of Tantric yogins and hermits, constituting an important link between the Bon-pos and the Rñiṅ-ma-pas, has never been quite abandoned. [*See* Dge-lugs-pa.]

An important class of religious experts, which likewise finds its counterpart in the Rñiṅ-ma-pa tradition, consists of the visionaries—both monks and laymen—who reveal "hidden texts." During the Buddhist persecution of Bon in the eighth and nineth centuries, the Bon-pos claim, their sacred texts were hidden in caves, buried underground, or walled up in certain temples. Later (apparently from the tenth century onward) the texts were rediscovered—at first, it would seem, by chance, and subsequently through the intervention of supernatural beings who would direct the chosen *gter-ston* ("treasure finder") to the site. Later still, texts would be revealed in visions or through purely mental transference from divine beings. The greater part of the Bon-po Bka'-'gyur and Brten-'gyur consists of such "rediscovered" or supernaturally inspired texts. "Treasure finders" have been active until the present, and indeed may be said to play an important role in the revival of religious activities in Tibet today, as texts that were hidden for safekeeping during the systematic destruction of the 1960s and 1970s are once more being removed from their hiding places.

As is the case in Tibetan religion generally, these texts are particularly important in that they serve, in an almost literal sense, as liturgical scores for the innumerable and extremely complex rituals, the performance of which occupies much of the time and attention of the monks. Many of these rituals do not differ significantly from those performed by the Buddhists, except that the deities invoked—although falling into the same general categories as those that apply to the deities of Mahāyāna Buddhism—are different from the Buddhist ones. They have different names, iconographical characteristics, evocatory formulas (*mantras*), and myths. A systematic study of this pantheon remains, however, to be undertaken, and likewise, our knowledge of the rituals of the Bon-pos is still extremely incomplete.

The laypeople are confronted by many of these deities, impersonated by monks, in the course of mask dances. The lay Bon-pos have the same range of religious activities as Tibetan Buddhist laypeople: the practice of liberality toward monks and monasteries (in exchange for the performance of rituals); the mechanical multiplication of prayers by means of prayer flags and prayer wheels; and journeys of pilgrimage to the holy places of Bon, such as Mount Kailāśa in the western Himalayas, or Bon-ri ("mountain of Bon"), in the southeastern province of Rkoṅ-po.

The Diffusion of Bon. Both Buddhists and Bon-pos agree that when Buddhism succeeded in gaining royal patronage in Tibet in the eighth and ninth centuries, Bon suffered a serious setback. By the eleventh century, however, an organized religious tradition, styling itself Bon and claiming continuity with the earlier, pre-Buddhist religion, appeared in central Tibet. It is this religion of Bon that has persisted to our own times, absorbing doctrines and practices from the dominant

Buddhist religion but always adapting what it learned to its own needs and its own perspectives. This is, of course, not just plagiarism, but a dynamic and flexible strategy that has ensured the survival, indeed the vitality, of a religious minority.

Until recent years, much has been made in Western literature of the fact that the Bon-pos perform certain basic ritual acts in a manner opposite to that practiced by the Buddhists. Thus, when circumambulating sacred places and objects or when spinning their prayerwheels, the Bon-pos proceed counterclockwise rather than following the (Indian and Buddhist) tradition of *pradakṣiṇā,* or circumambulation "toward the right." For this reason, it has been said of Bon that "its essence lay largely in contradiction and negation," and Bon's "willful perversions and distortions" have been pointed out. The error of such views cannot be too strongly emphasized. The Bon-pos are conscious of no element of "contradiction and negation" in their beliefs and practices but regard their religion as the pure path to liberation from suffering and rebirth. It is true that down through the centuries Bon-po historiographers have generally regarded the introduction of Buddhism into Tibet as a catastrophe, which they have ascribed to the accumulated collective "evil karma" of the Tibetans. On the other hand, conciliatory efforts have not been lacking; thus one source suggests that Ston-pa Gśen-rab and Śākyamuni were really twin brothers.

It is difficult to assess just how large the Bon-po community of Tibet is. Certainly the Bon-pos are a not insignificant minority. Particularly in eastern Tibet, whole districts are populated by Bon-pos. Scattered communities are also to be found in central and western Tibet, particularly in the Chumbi Valley (bordering Sikkim) and among nomads. In the north of Nepal, too, there are Bon-po villages, especially in the district of Dol-po. At a point in history that remains to be determined precisely, Bon exerted a strong influence on the religion of the Na-khi people in Yunnan Province in southwestern China; with this exception, the Bon-pos do not seem to have engaged in missionary enterprises. In India, Bon-pos belonging to the Tibetan refugee community have established (since 1968) a large and well-organized monastery in which traditional scholarship, rituals, and sacred dances are carried on with great vigor. Since 1980, when religious life was revived in Tibet itself, the Bon-pos there have rebuilt several monasteries (albeit on a reduced scale), installed monks, and resumed—to the extent that prevailing conditions permit—many aspects of traditional religious life. It would thus seem that there is good reason to believe that Bon will continue to exist, and even, with certain limits, to flourish.

[*For further discussion of the religious traditions of Tibet and their relationship to Bon, see* Tibetan Religions, *overview article, and* Buddhism, Schools of, *article on* Tibetan Buddhism.]

BIBLIOGRAPHY

When it was published in 1950 and for many years thereafter, Helmut Hoffman's *Quellen zur Geschichte der tibetischen Bon-Religion* (Wiesbaden, 1950) was the most reliable and comprehensive study of Bon, based as it was on all sources available at the time. Since 1960, Tibetan Bon-po monks in exile have collaborated with Western scholars. The first major work to result from this entirely new situation was *The Nine Ways of Bon: Excerpts from the gZi-brjid,* edited and translated by David L. Snellgrove (1967; reprint, Boulder, 1980), in which doctrinal material from the important fourteenth-century Bon-po text *Gzi-brjid* was presented for the first time. In the following year, David L. Snellgrove and Hugh E. Richardson presented a historical framework for the development of Bon in *A Cultural History of Tibet* (1968; reprint, Boulder, 1980) that has since been generally accepted. An excellent and up-to-date presentation of Bon is also given by Anne-Marie Blondeau in her article "Les religions du Tibet," in *Histoire des religions,* edited by Henri-Charles Puech, vol. 3 (Paris, 1976), pp. 233–329.

An important survey of the Bon religion is Samten G. Karmay's "A General Introduction to the History and Doctrines of Bon," *Memoirs of the Research Department of the Tōyō Bunko,* no. 33 (1975): 171–218 (also printed as a separate booklet, *The M.T.B. Off-prints Series,* no. 3; Tokyo, 1975). The same scholar has also translated a history of Bon written by the Bon-po scholar Śar-rdza Bkra-śis Rgyal-mtshan (1859–1935) in 1922 under the title *The Treasury of Good Sayings: A Tibetan History of Bon* (London, 1972).

On Bon literature, see Per Kvaerne's "The Canon of the Bonpos," *Indo-Iranian Journal* 16 (1975): 18–56, 96–144, and Samten G. Karmay's *A Catalogue of Bonpo Publications* (Tokyo, 1977). The monastic life of Bon (based on information from Sman-ri monastery) is outlined in Kvaerne's "Continuity and Change in Tibetan Monasticism," in *Korean and Asian Religious Tradition,* edited by Chai-shin Yu (Toronto, 1977), pp. 83–98. On meditational practices, see Kvaerne's "'The Great Perfection' in the Tradition of the Bonpos," in *Early Ch'an in China and Tibet,* edited by Whalen Lai and Lewis R. Lancaster (Berkeley, 1983), pp. 367–392.

A detailed description of a Bon-po ritual has been provided in Per Kvaerne's *Tibet, Bon Religion: A Death Ritual of the Tibetan Bonpos* (Leiden, 1984). The same book analyzes the extensive iconography connected with that particular ritual. General studies of Bon-po iconography are still lacking. Detailed descriptions of a few painted scrolls are, however, provided in Kvaerne's "Art Bon-po: Art du bouddhisme lamaïque," in *Dieux et démons de l'Himâlaya* (Paris, 1977), pp. 185–189; and in his "A Bonpo Version of the Wheel of Existence," in *Tantric and Taoist Studies in Honour of R. A. Stein,* edited by Michel Strickman (Brussels, 1981), vol. 1, pp. 274–289. The biography of Ston-pa Gśen-rab has been studied intensively on the basis of the *Gzi-rjid* and a series of paintings in Per

Kvaerne's "Peintures tibétaines de la vie de *sTon-pa-gçen-rab,*" *Arts asiatiques* 41 (1986).

PER KVAERNE

BONAVENTURE, religious name of Giovanni di Fidanza (c. 1217–1274), Italian scholastic theologian, minister general of the Friars Minor, cardinal bishop of Albano, doctor of the church, and Christian saint.

Life and Works. Information concerning the early life of Bonaventure is scant. His parents were Giovanni di Fidanza, who was a doctor in Bagnoregio in Tuscany, and Maria di Ritello. Bonaventure himself tells that he was cured of a serious childhood illness through his mother's prayer to Francis of Assisi. After early schooling at the Franciscan friary in Bagnoregio, Bonaventure began his studies at the University of Paris in 1235. After earning a master of arts degree, he entered the Franciscan order (Friars Minor), probably in 1243, pursuing the study of theology first under the Franciscan masters Alexander of Hales and John of La Rochelle and later under Odo Rigaldi and William of Meliton.

After he received a bachelor of scripture degree in Paris in 1248, Bonaventure began lecturing on the Bible. Although not all his commentaries survived, those on *Luke* and *John* remain important sources for his early theological viewpoints. After giving his courses on the *Sentences* of Peter Lombard between 1250 and 1252, he was ready to receive the licentiate and the doctorate in theology. Although there is some debate concerning the exact date of his formal acceptance into the masters' guild, there is strong evidence indicating that he functioned as regent master at the school of the Friars Minor at Paris from 1253 to 1257. During this period, he composed at least three well-known sets of disputed questions: *On Evangelical Perfection, On Christ's Knowledge,* and *On the Mystery of the Trinity.* Because of his election as minister general, Bonaventure had to resign his university post to take up the pressing tasks of administration. Even though he no longer lectured at the university, he made Paris his headquarters and preached frequently to the students and masters gathered there.

During his first years as minister general of the Friars Minor, Bonaventure produced three works that are important sources for his system of thought: a concise handbook of theology called the *Breviloquium* (1257), a brief tract entitled *Retracing the Arts to Theology* (date unknown), and a synthesis of his speculative and mystical theology known as *The Journey of the Mind to God* (1259). Most of the writings coming from his years as minister general are directly religious or ascetical in nature, including many sermons, letters, and regulations for the friars, two lives of Francis of Assisi, and the *Defense of the Mendicants* (c. 1269). Of particular importance for insight into the development of Aristotelianism are three sets of conferences held for the friars of Paris: *On the Ten Commandments* (1267), *On the Seven Gifts of the Holy Spirit* (1268), and *On the Six Days of Creation or the Illuminations of the Church* (1273). The final set of conferences was left unfinished when Bonaventure was named cardinal bishop of Albano by Pope Gregory X in 1273.

Bonaventure left Paris to help with preparations for the Council of Lyons, which convened on 7 May 1274, and he took an active part in the council until his unexpected death on 15 July 1274. Canonized by Sixtus IV in 1482, he was declared a doctor of the church by Sixtus V in 1588 with the title "Seraphic Doctor."

Theological Teaching. Although not a stranger to philosophy, Bonaventure is known primarily as a theologian. He acknowledged philosophy as a legitimate and important level of reflection, but he believed that it must be transcended by speculative theology and finally by mystical union with God. Bonaventure's theology was influenced not only by the spirituality of Francis of Assisi and the thought of Augustine but also by Dionysius the Areopagite, Boethius, Joachim of Fiore, Richard of Saint Victor, Aristotle, and Ibn Gabirol (Avicebron).

Bonaventure's theological system is strongly Christocentric. While his early *Commentary on John* describes a view emphatically centered around the Word, his final work, *Collations on the Six Days of Creation,* reveals a system for which the Word as incarnate is the point of departure for theological reflection. While Christ is the historical foundation of Christian theology, reflection on Christ reveals the ontological foundation of theology, which is the triune God.

Doctrine on God. Bonaventure is deeply Augustinian in his conviction that the existence of God cannot be denied (*Opera,* vol. 1, p. 155; vol. 5, pp. 45–51). Human reason can be called on either to affirm or to deny the existence of God. Bonaventure develops three approaches that he sees not as philosophical demonstrations but as spiritual exercises that make one aware of the closeness of God to the human spirit. Any doubt concerning the existence of God can arise only from some deficiency in the human subject. Ultimately, knowledge of God is not an affair of the intellect alone. Love pushes beyond reason. The knowledge of God through love is the goal to which the intellectual analysis is directed and to which it is subordinate (*Opera,* vol. 3, pp. 689, 775).

Bonaventure's theology of the Trinity begins with the New Testament perception of God as a mystery of goodness and love. This theme is developed into metaphysical reflection on the nature of goodness and love by drawing on the insights of Dionysius the Areopagite, Richard of Saint Victor, Aristotle, and the *Liber de causis*, an influential Neoplatonic work of uncertain authorship. This perception of God as supreme love that is necessarily triune is the highest level of metaphysical insight available to the human mind in this world. Open to us only through revelation, it leads us beyond philosophical metaphysics, which is constrained to reflect on the supreme reality under the name of being (*Opera*, vol. 5, p. 308). As supreme, self-communicative goodness and love, God is conceived as *plenitudo fontalis*, an overflowing fount of being and life that first flows into the two internal emanations through which the Son is generated and the Spirit is breathed forth, then flowing outward into creation. Peculiar in Western trinitarian theology is the emphasis given to the primacy of the Father within the Trinity. As the Trinity is first with respect to the created world, the Father is first with respect to the divine persons (*Opera*, vol. 5, p. 115).

Christology. From the centrality of Christ in the spirituality of Francis of Assisi, Bonaventure moves to systematic reflection on Christ as the center. The core of the christological mystery is that in Christ the center of reality has become incarnate and has been made historically visible. The theme of the center becomes ever more important in Bonaventure's thought, finding its most extensive development in his *Collations on the Six Days of Creation*. The Son who from eternity is the center of the Trinity mediates all the divine works of creation, illumination, and consummation. When the Son became incarnate in Jesus, he assumed his place as the center of the created universe and its history.

The concept of Christ as center is grounded in Bonaventure's understanding of exemplarity. As a metaphysical concern, exemplarity is the question of the original reality in whose likeness all the copies in creation are formed. The Platonic influence in Bonaventure's thought is apparent in his conviction that exemplarity is the most basic metaphysical question. The Word is the most compact expression of the original divine reality, copies of which are scattered throughout the created cosmos. When the Word becomes incarnate in a particular human being, that human being provides the crucial key to unlock the mystery of reality. As the incarnate Word, Jesus is both the temporal and the eternal exemplar (*Opera*, vol. 8, pp. 242–243). Therefore, his moral teaching and example have normative significance in the search for authentic human existence. For Bonaventure, spirituality is above all the journey of the human soul to God. This journey is made through the person of Christ, who mediates grace to the soul and draws the human person to respond to God by shaping human life in terms of the normative values that have been lived and taught by Christ.

Creation and salvation. Creation and salvation are symbolized by the two sides of a circle whereby Bonaventure expresses the spiritual journey that is the mainspring of world history. Emanation and return (*egressus* and *reditus*) speak of the origin and finality of creation. These paired concepts indicate that in Bonaventure's system creation and salvation are inseparably related. Creation is the movement of finite being from nothing toward that fullness of life that constitutes salvation. Salvation is the actualization of the deepest potential latent in finite reality by reason of the creative love of God.

Bonaventure's understanding of creation coheres with his understanding of God as *plenitudo fontalis*. Since God is the fullest abundance of being, creation is like an immense river that flows from the fecund love of God. Emanating from the depths of the Father through the mediation of the Son and the Spirit, creation circles back to its point of origin. Emanation is always a movement toward return.

The world of created reality takes shape in a hierarchical order based on degrees of God-likeness. The faintest reflection of God is found in the shadow *(umbra)* or vestige *(vestigium)* at the level of inorganic substances and lower forms of life. By nature, man is an image *(imago)* principally because of his soul. As the image is reformed by grace, it becomes a likeness *(similitudo)* of God. An angel, by reason of its purely spiritual nature, is also a similitude. Bonaventure employs the doctrine of Dionysius the Areopagite on the angelic and ecclesiastical hierarchies as a means of elaborating the structure of the angelic world and the mediatorial nature of the church.

To the enlightened eye, the entire created world may become a road that leads the human person to God and thus to the fulfillment of creation's destiny. The return of creation to God (technically, *reductio*), which takes place in and through the spiritual journey of humanity, is above all the work of the illumination and grace mediated through Christ. The redemptive process, begun decisively in Christ, includes the overcoming of sin (satisfaction) and the completion of the creative work of God (cosmic fulfillment). The theology of redemption is the elaboration of the return of an incomplete and fallen creation to God.

Spiritual life. Bonaventure has long been regarded as one of the masters of the spiritual life. Reflecting the spirituality of Francis of Assisi, the spiritual doctrine of Bonaventure is centered around Christ as mediator of grace and interior teacher of the soul. Christ's historical life and teaching manifest the basic values by which human life is transformed in its response to God's grace. As risen Lord, Christ functions as a hierarch, exercising the three hierarchical acts of purgation, illumination, and perfection, which Bonaventure draws from Dionysius the Areopagite (*Opera*, vol. 8, pp. 3–27). Through its response to Christ's action, the soul becomes hierarchized as the disorder of sin is replaced by order. The goal of the spiritual journey is contemplative union in love with God. All philosophical and theological reflection is subordinate to this end. Bonaventure follows Dionysius in describing a level of ecstatic, loving contact with God that transcends all purely intellectual knowledge of God. At this point, apophatic theology and silence are appropriate (*Opera*, vol. 5, pp. 312–313).

The doctrine of the soul's journey integrates the spirituality of Francis into the broader context of Augustinian and Dionysian mysticism. Finally, the journey of the individual soul is integrated into the journey of the church, and Francis of Assisi becomes the model of the destiny of the church as *ecclesia contemplativa.*

Theory of knowledge. While Bonaventure agrees with Aristotle that knowledge of the external world is dependent on sensation, he attempts to integrate elements of Aristotle's empiricism with Augustine's doctrine of illumination. Convinced that the experience of certitude can be accounted for neither in terms of mutable objects nor in terms of the mutable human mind, Bonaventure suggests a mode of divine cooperation whereby the human mind is elevated by the light of the divine ideas and thus is able to arrive at certitude even though all the objects of experience are mutable (*Opera,* vol. 5, p. 23). The divine ideas function as a regulatory and motivating influence that illumines the mind so that it can judge in accord with the eternal truth. Illumination is involved especially in the full analysis of finite being, which leads ultimately to absolute being. Such analysis, or reduction, is possible only if the human mind is aided by that being that is "most pure, most actual, most complete and absolute" (*Opera,* vol. 5, p. 304).

Though the soul is dependent on the senses for knowledge of the external world, it enjoys a relative independence of the senses in its knowledge of itself and its own activity. Thus Bonaventure departs from the Aristotelian view that there is nothing in the intellect that is not first in the senses, and he incorporates into his theory of knowledge the way of interiority inherited from Augustine and found in a variety of mystical systems.

Theology of history. Among the great theologians of history, Bonaventure is one of the most consistently apocalyptic. Influenced by Joachim of Fiore's theory of exegesis, Bonaventure interpreted Francis of Assisi as a positive sign of the dawning of a new contemplative age. The adulteration of the wine of revelation by the water of philosophy was seen as a negative sign of apocalyptic import. To Bonaventure it seemed that his own time was experiencing the crisis of the "sixth age" of history. This would be followed by an age of full revelation and peace prior to the end of the world, an age in which the Holy Spirit would lead the church into the full realization of the revelation of Christ, making all rational philosophy and theology superfluous.

Influence. Bonaventure's theological views were instrumental in consolidating late-thirteenth-century opposition to radical Aristotelianism. In the context of the controversy concerning Thomas Aquinas's philosophy, Franciscans, including John Pecham, Roger Marston, William de la Mare, Walter of Bruges, Matthew of Aquasparta, and others, developed a form of neo-Augustinianism that drew much inspiration from the work of Bonaventure. It is hardly possible, however, to speak of a Bonaventurian school in the fourteenth century. The founding of the College of Saint Bonaventure at Rome by Sixtus V in 1587 was intended to foster Bonaventurian studies. The most significant contribution of the college was the first complete edition of the works of Bonaventure (1588–1599). An attempted Bonaventurian revival in the seventeenth century met with little success. The College of Saint Bonaventure at Quaracchi, near Florence, founded in the late nineteenth century, produced the critical edition of Bonaventure's works, which provides the basis for the many studies that appeared in the twentieth century.

The influence of Bonaventure as a master of the spiritual life has been extensive, especially in Germany and the Netherlands during the late Middle Ages. The *Soliloquy* and the *Threefold Way* were widely disseminated in vernacular translations and influenced Germanic education, piety, and theology for centuries. In *Bonaventura deutsch* (Bern, 1956), Kurt Ruh calls Bonaventure "an essential factor in the history of the German mind" (p. 295).

BIBLIOGRAPHY

The most complete and reliable edition of Bonaventure's works is the critical edition published as *Opera omnia,* 10 vols. (Quaracchi, 1882–1902).

Of the English translations available, those being published in the series "Works of Saint Bonaventure," edited by Philotheus Boehner and M. Frances Laughlin (Saint Bonaventure, N.Y., 1955–), are most useful because of their scholarly introductions and commentaries. This series has published *Retracing the Arts to Theology,* translated by Emma Thérèse Healy (1955); *The Journey of the Mind into God,* translated by Philotheus Boehner (1956); and *Saint Bonaventure's Disputed Questions on the Mystery of the Trinity,* translated by me (1979). A five-volume series of translations by José de Vinck entitled *The Works of St. Bonaventure* (Paterson, N.J., 1960–1970) provides no commentary. Three sermons on Christ with commentary offering an orientation to the Christology of Bonaventure are found in my edited volume *What Manner of Man?* (Chicago, 1974). Ewert H. Cousins's *Bonaventure* (New York, 1978) provides fresh translations of *The Soul's Journey*, the *Tree of Life*, and the *Life of Saint Francis* with an introduction relating the spiritual doctrine to Bonaventure's theology.

Jacques Guy Bougerol's *Introduction to the Works of Bonaventure* (Paterson, N.J., 1964) is a useful resource for information on the sources, chronology, and stylistic characteristics of Bonaventure's writings.

John Francis Quinn's *The Historical Constitution of Saint Bonaventure's Philosophy* (Toronto, 1973) gives a full historical account of the modern controversy concerning Bonaventure's philosophy together with an excellent bibliography. On the philosophical aspects of Bonaventure's thought, Étienne Gilson's *The Philosophy of Saint Bonaventure* (Paterson, N.J., 1965) is still the classic exposition. Examining the inner structure of Bonaventure's thought from the perspective of archetypal thought-patterns, Ewert H. Cousins's *Bonaventure and the Coincidence of Opposites* (Chicago, 1978) offers a challenging and controversial analysis.

An excellent resource for Bonaventure's trinitarian theology is Konrad Fischer's *De Deo trino et uno* (Göttingen, 1978). A full, systematic exposition of Christology emphasizing the synthesis of spirituality and speculative thought is presented in my book *The Hidden Center* (New York, 1981). Joseph Ratzinger's *The Theology of History in Saint Bonaventure* (Chicago, 1971) is an important study of the mature work of Bonaventure and its relation to Joachim of Fiore. The first four volumes of *S. Bonaventura, 1274–1974*, edited by Jacques Guy Bougerol (Grottaferrata, 1973–1974), include discussion of iconography and articles on philosophy, theology, and spirituality. Volume 5 contains the most extensive and up-to-date bibliography.

ZACHARY HAYES, O.F.M.

BONES resist decay longer than any other parts of the body. Thus the bones of humans and animals are regarded in many parts of the world as the real seat of life, whether "life" be understood as a rather vague life force or more specifically as the soul (the "bone soul"). For this reason, skulls and skeletons are often given special burial after the soft parts of the body have decomposed, or they are preserved in some manner, treated with special veneration, and, in many instances, used for purposes of magic. This underlying conception explains why, among some Siberian peoples, a man who is in training as a shaman will, as a result of autosuggestion, experience in imagination his own dismemberment and restoration to life beginning at the skeletal stage.

The idea of reanimation beginning with the bones occurs with particular frequency among the peoples of northern Eurasia, some of them hunters, others nomadic herders, and others practicing both ways of life side by side, as for instance the Saami, Mansi, Khanty, Buriats, Giliaks, Yukagirs, and Chukchi. This northern Asiatic conception regarding bones as the seat of life has also been linked to the ritual importance that human bones have in Tibetan Lamaism. The motif—originating probably in a hunting culture—of reanimation beginning with the bones is also found among agrarian peoples and in economically more complex cultures (especially in those in which hunting is still practiced, even if only incidentally). Thus it crops up in myths, legends, and fairy tales among the ancient Germans and the peoples of the Caucasus, and in Africa, South America, Oceania, and Australia. Among the ancient civilizations the following in particular should be mentioned: Iran, Egypt, Mesopotamia, and Ugarit.

Traces of this conception are also to be found in Arab-Islamic traditions and legends as well as among the Israelites, both in the Old Testament and in postbiblical Jewish literature. Especially in poetic texts of the Old Testament, bones often appear as subjects of existence and personality; a certain consciousness, feelings, and activities are attributed to them (e.g., *Jb.* 4:14; *Ps.* 6:3, 31:11, 32:3, 34:21, 35:10, 38:4, 51:10, 53:6, 102:4, 109:18; *Prv.* 12:4; *Is.* 38:13; *Jer.* 23:9; *Lam.* 3:4). For this reason, great importance is attached to the preservation and safekeeping of bones (*Gn.* 50:25, *Ex.* 13:19, *Jos.* 24:32, *1 Sm.* 31:13, *2 Sm.* 21:12–14). A trace of these ideas is also seen in Ezekiel's vision of the reanimation of the dead bones (*Ez.* 37:1–14).

Proscriptions for the treatment of bones occur even more frequently than explicit statements about bones as the seat of life. Thus there are many proscriptions against breaking or in any way harming the bones of animals (especially bears, reindeer, and other animals who are hunted); instead, such bones are to be carefully collected and disposed of. They are buried, or exposed in trees or on platforms, or wrapped in the bark of trees, or covered with stones, brush, and so on. Such practices are attested especially for northern Eurasia and North America, where they are found not only among the people mentioned earlier but also among the Cheremis, Samoyeds, Kazakh-Kirgiz, Tunguz, Yakuts, Ainu, Inuit, and others. When the animals in question are marine mammals, the bones are thrown into the sea; the skeletons of fish are also often thrown back into the water. Furthermore, the ancient Greek sacrificial custom, according to which the Olympian gods received only the bones of the sacrificial animal, wrapped in its fat, while the flesh was eaten at a sacrificial meal, has been plausibly explained as a survival (its significance later forgotten) from the ancient customs of hunters.

The best-known example of the prohibition against the breaking of bones is the proscription that the Israelites were not to break a single bone of the Passover lamb (*Ex.* 12:46, *Nm.* 9:12); this proscription receives a typological interpretation in the New Testament (*Jn.* 19:36).

In many instances we know only of these prohibitions or rituals as such, without any explicit explanation of them being given. And when explanations are in fact given, it must be assumed that sometimes they are secondary explanations for practices whose original meaning is no longer understood. For this reason numerous, more or less speculative, interpretations of the original meaning have been attempted. Of these, many can claim validity only for a limited area and time, as for example the explanation of the practices as being apotropaic rites: the bones of hunted or sacrificed animals are not to be broken, lest broken bones occur in human beings and domestic animals. Other explanations must be regarded as unfounded or as possessing limited probability; only two of the proposed explanations deserve further attention.

1. According to Alexander Gahs (1928), behind these customs lay an original sacrifice of firstlings offered to the supreme being in gratitude for a successful hunt; the actual object sacrificed was the brain and marrow (which were regarded as delicacies and, therefore, as especially valuable parts of the animal), for which the skull and long bones served simply as vessels. The use of bones in magical rituals for ensuring reproduction appeared later on. Wilhelm Schmidt accepted this interpretation, applied it extensively (even outside the northern Eurasian area) to rites involving skulls and long bones, and defended it in various publications (1929–1948). Gahs and Schmidt, in agreement with prehistorians Oswald Menghin, Emil Bächler, and Heinz Bächler, also applied the theory to data from prehistory, namely, to prehistoric deposits of the skulls and long bones of cave bears. This, however, elicited opposition from prehistorians Hugo Obermaier, Hans-Georg Bandi, and Johannes Maringer. A discussion in which many ethnologists and historians of religion also took part yielded some scholarly agreement: there are many clear cases of sacrificial offerings of skulls and long bones (not only among herders but among hunters as well); these, however, are meant rather as symbolic sacrifices of the entire animal and rarely as explicit sacrifices of the brain and marrow as such; in any event, not all rites and proscriptions involving bones can be traced back to an original offering of firstlings.

2. However, the most reasonable explanation of the widespread proscription against breaking the bones of animals continues to be the original belief of hunters in a reanimation beginning with undamaged bones. This belief was often no longer a conscious one, although the pertinent rites, now in a "fossil" stage, continued to be practiced.

BIBLIOGRAPHY

Closs, Alois. "Zerstückelung in autosuggestiver Imagination, im Mythos und im Kult." *Temonos* (Helsinki) 15 (1979): 5–40.

Eliade, Mircea. "Les sacrifices grecs et les rites des peuples primitifs." *Revue de l'histoire des religions* 133 (1947–1948): 225–230. A review of Meuli (1946).

Friedrich, Adolf. "Knochen und Skelett in der Vorstellungswelt Nordasiens." *Wiener Beiträge zur Kulturgeschichte und Linguistik* 5 (1943): 189–247. A fundamental study.

Gahs, Alexander. "Kopf-, Schädel- und Langknochenopfer bei Rentiervölkern." In *Festschrift, publication d'hommage offerte au P. W. Schmidt*, edited by Wilhelm Koppers, pp. 231–268. Vienna, 1928.

Henninger, Joseph. "Zum Verbot des Knochenzerbrechens bei den Semiten." In *Studi orientalistici in onore di Giorgio Levi Della Vida*, vol. 1, pp. 448–458. Rome, 1956.

Henninger, Joseph. "Neuere Forschungen zum Verbot des Knochenzerbrechens." In *Studia Ethnographica et Folkloristica in honorem Béla Gunda*, pp. 673–702. Debrecen, 1971.

Henninger, Joseph. "La défense de briser les os d'un animal." In *Les fêtes de printemps chez les Sémites et la Pâque israélite.* Paris, 1975.

Meuli, Karl. "Griechische Opferbräuche." In *Phyllobolia: Für Peter Von der Mühll zum 60. Geburtstage*, pp. 185–288. Basel, 1946.

Paproth, Hans-Joachim. *Studien über das Bärenzeremoniell*, vol. 1, *Bärenjagdriten und Bärenfeste bei den tungusischen Völkern.* Uppsala, 1976. See especially pages 11–47.

Robinson, H. Wheeler. "Bones." In *Encyclopaedia of Religion and Ethics*, edited by James Hastings, vol. 2. Edinburgh, 1909.

JOSEPH HENNINGER
Translated from German by Matthew J. O'Connell

BONHOEFFER, DIETRICH (1906–1945), Lutheran pastor, theologian, and martyr. The sixth of eight children, Bonhoeffer was raised in Berlin in the upper-middle-class family of a leading neurologist. He received his doctorate in theology from the University of Berlin. A student of Adolf von Harnack, Bonhoeffer was deeply influenced by the writings of the young Karl Barth. From 1930 to 1931, he studied at Union Theological Seminary in New York with Reinhold Niebuhr. He then returned to Berlin, teaching theology and becoming student chaplain and youth secretary in the ecumenical movement.

As early as 1933 Bonhoeffer was struggling against the nazification of the churches and against the persecution of the Jews. Disappointed by the churches' non-action against Nazism, he accepted a pastorate for Germans in London. However, when the Confessing church (i.e., Christians who resisted Nazi domination) founded its own seminaries, he returned to Germany to prepare candidates for ordination, a task he considered the most fulfilling of his life. As a result of this work, he was forbidden to teach at the University of Berlin. In 1939, after conflicts with the Gestapo, he accepted an invitation to the United States, again to Union Theological Seminary. After four weeks, however, he returned to Germany, convinced he would be ineffectual in the eventual renewal of his nation were he to live elsewhere during its most fateful crisis. He then became an active member of the conspiracy against Hitler. On 5 April 1943 he was imprisoned on suspicion. After the plot to assassinate Hitler failed, Bonhoeffer was hanged (on 9 April 1945), along with five thousand others (including three other members of his family) accused of participating in the resistance.

Bonhoeffer's writings have been widely translated. His early work reflects his search for a concrete theology of revelation. His first dissertation, "Sanctorum Communio," published in Germany in 1930 (also under that title in London, 1963; and as *The Communion of Saints,* New York, 1963), relates the revelational character of the church to its sociological features. An original statement at the time, it remains evocative. His second dissertation, "Act and Being," was written in 1931 against a background of such opposing philosophies as Kantian transcendentalism and Heideggerian ontology. This work tries to reconcile an existential theological approach with an ontological one. According to Bonhoeffer, these approaches work themselves out in the church, in which revelational contingency and institutional continuity merge.

Turning to the actual life of the church and to criticism of it, Bonhoeffer, in 1937, published his controversial *The Cost of Discipleship* (New York, 1963). Asserting that "cheap grace is the deadly enemy of our Church," this work, which is based on the Sermon on the Mount, critiques a Reformation heritage that breaks faith and obedience asunder. In *Life Together* (New York, 1976), Bonhoeffer's most widely read book, the author considers experiments to renew a kind of monastic life for serving the world. In 1939 Bonhoeffer began to write a theological ethics, the work he intended to be his lifework, but he only completed fragments of it (*Ethics,* New York, 1965). These fragments reveal Bonhoeffer as moving beyond a situational ethic to a Christ-centered one.

The most influential of Bonhoeffer's posthumous publications has become *Letters and Papers from Prison* (New York, 1972). Among his daily observations was a vision of a future Christianity ready for "messianic suffering" with Christ in a "nonreligious world." To Bonhoeffer "religion" was a province separated from the whole of life—providing cheap escapism for the individual—and a tool in the hands of the powers that be for continuing domination of dependent subjects. Bonhoeffer was critical of Western Christianity because of its complicity with the Holocaust; his letters reveal his conviction that a life with Christ means "to exist for others." It was his belief in a "religionless Christianity"—that is, a praying church that responds to Christ out of the modern (not sinless) strength of human beings and their decisions—that enabled Bonhoeffer to begin to write a revised theology of "Jesus, the man for others," and to participate in the conspiratorial counteraction against the deadly forces of Hitler.

Bonhoeffer's thought emerged from his cultural heritage of German liberalism. He suffered when he experienced its weakness in the face of Nazism. He rethought this heritage within a Christocentric theology, thus becoming a radical critic of his contemporary church and of contemporary theology because they seemed to him to touch only the insignificant corners of life.

The originality of Bonhoeffer's thought may be summarized in three ways. First, by employing biblical and modern criticism of religion, he gave to theology and piety epochal stress on the idea that the God who is not of this world posits a requisite "this-worldliness" of faith, which is not, however, absorbed by immanentism. Second, Bonhoeffer's words and deeds teach that each generation must discern its own particular means to express its contribution to faith and action. Third, in areas where developments press toward a "confessing church," Bonhoeffer challenges Christians to analyze and to resist ideological syncretism with any zeitgeist, whether the result is a Greek, a Teutonic, or an American Christ.

His influence is worldwide for two reasons. First, his life as theologian and thinker was sealed by martyrdom. Second, Bonhoeffer's legacy has stimulated ecumenism beyond his own national, spiritual, and institutional borders, including influence among Roman Catholics and Jews who see in him a Christian theologian who never cheaply evaded controversial issues.

BIBLIOGRAPHY

For a comprehensive listing of primary and secondary literature, see Clifford J. Green's "Bonhoeffer Bibliography: English Language Sources," *Union Seminary Quarterly Review* (New York) 31 (Summer 1976): 227–260. This admirable work is continually revised and amended in *The News Letter* of the English Language Section of the International Bonhoeffer Society for Archival Research.

In addition to the works by Bonhoeffer mentioned in the article, see three collections of letters, lectures, and notes titled *No Rusty Swords* (New York, 1965), *The Way to Freedom* (New York, 1966), and *True Patriotism* (New York, 1973). For works about Bonhoeffer, see my *Dietrich Bonhoeffer: Theologian, Christian, Contemporary*, 3d abr. ed. (New York, 1970); André Dumas's *Dietrich Bonhoeffer: Theologian of Reality* (New York, 1971); Clifford J. Green's *The Sociality of Christ and Humanity: Dietrich Bonhoeffer's Early Theology, 1927–1933* (Missoula, Mont., 1972); and Keith W. Clements's *A Patriotism for Today: Dialogue with Dietrich Bonhoeffer* (Bristol, 1984).

EBERHARD BETHGE

BONIFACE (673–754), the most distinguished in the group of English missionaries who, in the eighth and succeeding centuries, felt impelled to cross the seas and to preach the gospel to the peoples of the continent of Europe who were still non-Christians. Winfrith, to whom the pope, as tradition has it, gave the name Boniface in 722, was a missionary, founder of monasteries, diffuser of culture, and church organizer. Born in Devonshire, he was introduced to monastic life at an early age. Here he grew up in an atmosphere of strict observance of the Benedictine rule and acceptance of the vivid culture which was spreading abroad from Northumbria. His many gifts would have assured him of a distinguished career in the growing English church but he felt within himself an intense inner call to carry the gospel to the as yet non-Christian world.

Two attempts at missionary work with Willibrord in Friesland led to nothing, perhaps because of temperamental differences between the two. In 719, Winfrith made the journey to Rome and received a commission from the pope as missionary to the Frankish lands. This commission was later strengthened by his consecration as bishop. Before long the missionary convictions of Boniface became firmly settled on three points: that the missions of the Western church must be controlled and directed by the central authority in Rome, that religious houses both for men and women must be founded to supply the necessary continuity of Christian life in a period of almost ceaseless military disturbance, that regular dioceses must be founded and supplied with loyal and well-trained bishops.

The first period of Boniface's work was marked by notable successes in Hesse and Thuringia. At Geismar he dared to fell the sacred oak of Thor. This episode was understood by the people of the time as a conflict between two gods. When Boniface felled the oak and suffered no vengeance from the resident Germanic god, it was clear that the God whom he preached was the true God who alone is to be worshipped and adored.

Boniface was successful in securing the confidence and support, first of the all-powerful Frankish ruler, Charles Martel, who in 732 defeated the Muslims at the battle of Tours, and, after Charles's death in 741, of Martel's sons Carloman and Pepin. This helped Boniface greatly in his work of restoring or creating order in the churches in the dominions of the Franks, the goal of his second period of the work. He was successful in creating four bishoprics in Bavaria, where churches existed but without settled order. He also called into being four dioceses in the territories to the east of the Rhine. During this period he brought in many colleagues, both men and women, and founded a number of religious houses. His favorite was Fulda (744), where he was buried, and which for more than a thousand years was a great center of church life in Germany.

Until 747 Boniface had been a primate and archbishop without a diocese. In 747 he was appointed archbishop of Mainz. In the meantime his influence had extended westward, until it was felt in many parts of what is now France. In 742 he was able to hold a synod of the French churches, commonly known as the German Council, and in 744 an even more important meeting at Soissons. It is to be noted that the decrees of the earlier council were issued in the name of Carloman and became the law of the church as well as of the state.

Two special features of the work of Boniface are to be noted. Boniface was too busy to become an accomplished scholar but was deeply concerned for the spread of culture and used his monasteries as centers for the diffusion of knowledge. He himself wrote Latin clearly and elegantly, coming between the over-elaborate style of Aldhelm (d. 709) and the rather flat scholastic Latin of the Middle Ages. Frank Stenton has called him the one great writer produced by the early schools of southern England and a man of individual genius.

The part played by women in the development of the church in this period is astonishing. At a time at which the vast majority of women were illiterate, the religious houses of England produced a number of aristocratic and highly cultivated nuns, a number of whom Boniface brought over to Europe to be the abbesses of his newly founded monasteries. To Leobgytha (Leoba), abbess of Tauferbischofsheim, he was bound, as the letters exchanged between them show, in a relationship of specially affectionate friendship. She survived him by more than a quarter of a century, and when she died in 780, she was buried near her venerable friend at Fulda, in accordance with her earnest desire.

In 752, Boniface, feeling that his work was done, and perhaps wearied by the increasing opposition of the Frankish churchmen to the English dominance, resigned all his offices and returned as a simple missionary to Friesland, where he had begun his missionary career. Great success marked the first year of this enterprise. But on 4 June 754 Boniface and his companions found themselves surrounded by a band of pagans, determined to put a stop to the progress of the gospel. Boniface forbade armed resistance, and he and fifty-three of his followers met their death with the quiet fortitude of Christian martyrs.

The English are accustomed to speak of these years as "the dark ages," but, as the eminent German church historian K. D. Schmidt once remarked, "to us this was the period of light, when the light of the Gospel and of Christian civilization came to us." Boniface, the apostle of Germany, was one of those burning and shining lights.

BIBLIOGRAPHY

The primary authority is the large collection of the letters of Boniface, to be found in Latin, *Bonifacius: Die Briefe des heiligen Bonifacius and Lullus*, vol. 1 (Berlin, 1916), admirably edited by Michael Tangl. A good many of these letters are available in English in *The Anglo-Saxon Missionaries in Germany*, edited and translated by Charles H. Talbot (New York, 1954). For those who read German the outstanding modern work is Theodor Schieffer's *Winfrid Bonifatius und die christliche Grundlegung Europas* (Darmstadt, 1972). In English the pioneer work is William Levison's *England and the Continent in the Eighth Century* (Oxford, 1946). Among more popular works, Eleanor S. Duckett's *Anglo-Saxon Saints and Scholars* (New York, 1947), pages 339–455, can be specially recommended as both scholarly and readable.

STEPHEN C. NEILL

BONIFACE VIII (Benedetto Gaetani, c. 1235–1303), pope of the Roman Catholic church (1294–1303). Connected by family relationship not only with the earlier popes Alexander IV and Nicholas III but also with the Orsini and Colonna families, Gaetani studied law at Bologna, worked as a notary at the Curia Romana, served on embassies to France and England, discharged the office of papal legate in France, and by 1291 had become cardinal priest of San Martino. A capable, experienced, and energetic administrator, he was by temperament bold, hardheaded, formidably stubborn, and, at least in his latter years, prone to damaging outbursts of irascibility that some have attributed in part to painful bouts with "the stone." Unfortunately, the juxtaposition of his energetic pontificate with the brief (and chaotic) reign of his predecessor, the devout hermit-pope Celestine V, proved to be a case of the wrong men in a crucial role at the wrong time and in the wrong sequence. The troubles besetting the two pontificates are usually taken to mark the great turning point in the fortunes of the late medieval papacy.

Certainly, the difficulties and disputes that marked the reign of Boniface VIII have served to obscure for posterity the pope's more positive achievements. These were real enough. His reordering of the curial fiscal and administrative system, his publication in 1298 of the *Liber sextus*, a legal compilation supplementary to the decretals of Gregory IX, his sponsorship in 1300 of the Jubilee Year at Rome, his decisive ruling of that same year on the relationship between the diocesan clergy and the clergy of the mendicant orders, his foundation in 1303 of a *studium generale* at Rome—all had important, and some of them enduringly positive, consequences. Nonetheless, even such unquestionably positive achievements sometimes generated problems for Boniface. Thus, the increase in financial support and papal prestige stemming from the enormous flow of pilgrims to Rome during the Jubilee may well have bolstered Boniface's self-assurance and encouraged him to be too unyielding in his subsequent dealings with the French king. Similarly, while they were impartially and carefully framed, the measures he introduced to remedy the dissension and disorder in diocesan government spawned by the extensive exemptions and privileges previously granted to the mendicant orders nevertheless succeeded in alienating many of the friars. Yet again, his tightening of the papal fiscal system after the chaos of the previous pontificate, and, within the papal territories, his success in suppressing disorder, enforcing papal control, and extending the property holdings of his Gaetani kin led him into a fatal conflict with the landed interests of the powerful Colonna family.

Problems with Philip IV, king of France, had begun already in 1296 and centered on the right of monarchs to tax the clergy of their kingdoms. Hostilities between Philip and Edward I of England had broken out in 1294, and even in the absence of papal consent the two kings had taken it upon themselves to tax their national churches. Responding to a protest launched by the French Cistercians, Boniface moved in the bull *Clericis laicos* (24 February 1296) to proscribe (in the absence of explicit papal permission) all lay taxation of the clergy. In the prevailing climate of opinion, with lay sentiment in the two kingdoms favoring the monarchs and some of the clergy inclining to support them too, threats of excommunication proved to be of no avail. The prestige of the papacy had fallen too low to permit the successful deployment of such spiritual weaponry—so low, indeed, that in 1297, confronted also by the combined opposition in Italy of the Colonna family and the Spiritual

Franciscans, Boniface was forced to compromise on the question of taxation and in effect to concede the principle he had attempted to establish.

That concession, however, did not prevent his reacting with great firmness when in 1301 Philip IV arrested Bernard of Saisset, bishop of Pamiers, tried him, threw him into prison, and demanded that the pope endorse those actions. Boniface responded by issuing the bulls *Salvator mundi* and *Ausculta fili*, demanding the bishop's release, revoking the taxing privileges earlier granted to the French king, and commanding attendance of the French bishops at a council to be held at Rome in November 1302 in order to consider the condition of religion in France.

Defeated by a Flemish army at Courtral in the summer of 1302, Philip adroitly used the excuse of a national emergency to prohibit attendance of the French bishops at the Roman council. The abortive nature of that assembly, however, did not prevent Boniface from issuing in November 1302 the bull *Unam sanctam*, a rather derivative document but one culminating with the famous declaration "It is altogether necessary to salvation for every human creature to be subject to the Roman pontiff." Philip's response was even more forceful. Rallying national opinion during the spring of 1303 at a series of assemblies in Paris, and echoing the old Colonna call for convocation of a general council to judge the pope, Philip also authorized his adviser Guillaume de Nogaret to lead an expedition to Italy to seize the person of the pope and bring him back for judgment.

Hence evolved the extraordinary chain of events leading up to the "outrage of Anagni" on 7 September 1303: the attack on the papal palace by Nogaret and Sciarra Colonna, the humiliation of the aged pope, his subsequent rescue by the citizens of Anagni, and his demise soon after at Rome. French pressure by no means ended with his death, and Boniface VIII has since been portrayed as the pope who, while advancing some of the most ambitious claims ever made for the power of the medieval papacy, contrived also to precipitate its decline.

BIBLIOGRAPHY

Boase, T. S. R. *Boniface VIII.* London, 1933.

Digard, G. A. L. *Philippe le Bel et le Saint-siège de 1285 à 1304.* 2 vols. Paris, 1936.

Digard, G. A. L., et al. *Les registres de Boniface VIII.* 4 vols. Paris, 1904–1939.

Dupuy, Pierre, ed. and trans. *Histoire du différend d'entre le Pape Boniface VIII et Philippe le Bel.* Paris, 1655.

Rivière, Jean. *Le problème de l'église et de l'état au temps de Philippe le Bel.* Paris, 1926.

Scholz, Richard. *Die Publizistik zur Zeit Philipps des Schönen und Bonifaz VIII* (1903). Reprint, Amsterdam, 1962.

FRANCIS OAKLEY

BOOK. *See* Scripture; *see also* Canon *and* Qur'ān, *article on* The Text and Its History.

BOOTH, WILLIAM (1829–1912), English evangelist, founder of the Salvation Army. William Booth was born on 10 April 1829 in Nottingham, England, the only son of the four surviving children of Samuel and Mary Moss Booth. The elder Booth, an unsuccessful building contractor, and his wife were no more than conventionally religious, but William, intelligent, ambitious, zealous, and introspective, was earnest about Christianity from an early age. He was converted at the age of fifteen and two years later gave himself entirely to the service of God as the result of the preaching of James Caughey, a visiting American Methodist revivalist. From the age of thirteen until he was twenty-two Booth worked as a pawnbroker's assistant, first in Nottingham and, after 1849, in London. His zeal and compassion for the poor among whom he passed his youth drove him to preach in the streets and, in 1852, to become a licensed Methodist minister. Although Booth had been forced by his father's financial ruin to withdraw from a good grammar school at age thirteen, he read avidly, sought instruction from older ministers, and developed an effective style in speech and writing. In 1855 he married Catherine Mumford, a woman of original and independent intelligence and great moral courage, who had a strong influence on him. They had eight children.

In 1861 Booth began to travel as an independent and successful evangelist, sometimes appearing with Catherine, who publicly advocated an equal role for women in the pulpit. In 1865 the couple established a permanent preaching mission among the poor in the East End of London, in a place where Booth had conducted an especially effective series of meetings. This new endeavor, which soon included small-scale charitable activities for the poor, was known for several years as the Christian Mission. In 1878 the mission was renamed the Salvation Army.

The military structure suggested by the new name appealed to the Booths and to the co-workers they had attracted to their work. Booth remained an orthodox Methodist in doctrine, preaching the necessity of repentance and the promise of holiness—a voluntary submission to God that opened to the believer a life of love for God and for humankind. A premillennialist as well, he was convinced that the fastest way to complete the work of soul winning that would herald the return of Christ was to establish flying squads of enthusiasts who would spread out over the country at his command. The General, as Booth was called, saw evangelism as warfare against Satan over the souls of men; the militant tone of scripture and hymn were not figurative to Booth and his officers, but literal reality. The autocracy of military command was well suited to Booth's decisive and uncompromising personality; and it appealed both to his close associates, who were devoted to him and who sought his counsel on every matter, and to his more distant followers, the "soldiers" recently saved from sin, most of them uneducated, new to religion, and eager to fit themselves into the great scheme.

William and Catherine were convinced from the beginning of their work in London that it was their destiny to carry the gospel to those untouched by existing religious efforts; to them this meant the urban poor. Their sympathy for these people led them to supplement their evangelism by immediate and practical relief. They launched campaigns to awaken the public to the worst aspects of the life of the poor, such as child prostitution and dangerous and ill-paid piecework in neighborhood match factories. Soup kitchens, men's hostels, and "rescue homes" for converted prostitutes and unwed mothers became essential parts of the Army's program.

In 1890 William Booth published *In Darkest England and the Way Out,* which contained a full-fledged program to uplift and regenerate the "submerged tenth" of urban society. The heart of the scheme was a sequence of "city colonies" (urban missions for the unemployed), "land colonies" (where rest would be combined with retraining in agricultural skills), and "overseas colonies" (assisted emigration to America or one of Britain's colonies). The book also explained existing programs like the rescue homes and promised many new schemes in addition to the colonies: the "poor man's lawyer," the "poor man's bank," clinics, industrial schools for poor children, missing-persons inquiries, a "matrimonial bureau," and a poor-man's seaside resort, "Whitechapel-by-the-Sea." The *Darkest England* scheme, which was widely endorsed, represents an important turning point in public support for the Army.

Booth would not have claimed to be a saint in any conventional sense, and there are certainly controversial aspects to his life and work. Always overworked and chronically unwell, he often had strained relationships with his close associates, especially after the death of Catherine in 1890. Many of his statements about the Army overlooked the fact that much of its program was not original. He offered no criticism of the basic social and political structure that surrounded him, and his confidence in the desirability of transferring the urban unemployed to the more healthful and "natural" environment of the country was romantic and impractical. Yet the fact remains that Booth combined old and new techniques of evangelism and social relief in an immensely effective and appealing program. He displayed great flexibility in adapting measures to the needs of the moment, altering or eliminating any program, however dear to him, if it had ceased to function. He abandoned anything in the way of theology (like sacraments) or social theory (like the then still popular distinction between the "worthy" and "unworthy" poor) that might confuse his followers or dampen their zeal for soul winning and good works.

Guileless and unsentimental, Booth showed a rare and genuine single-mindedness in the cause of evangelism. His last public message, delivered three months before his death on 20 August 1912, is still cherished by the Army that is his most fitting memorial. The concluding words of the message were these: "While there yet remains one dark soul without the light of God, I'll fight—I'll fight to the very end!"

[*See also* Salvation Army.]

BIBLIOGRAPHY

William Booth has received surprisingly little attention from serious scholarship. Incomparably the best published biography remains St. John Ervine's *God's Soldier: General William Booth,* 2 vols. (New York, 1935). Harold Begbie's *The Life of General William Booth, the Founder of the Salvation Army,* 2 vols. (New York, 1920) is still valuable. William Booth's *In Darkest England and the Way Out* (1890; reprint, London, 1970) is indispensable to an understanding of Booth and his work. The best biography of Catherine Booth remains that of her son-in-law, Commissioner Frederick de Latour Booth-Tucker, *The Life of Catherine Booth, the Mother of the Salvation Army,* 2 vols. (London, 1892).

EDWARD H. MCKINLEY

BORNEAN RELIGIONS. From earliest times, the coasts of Borneo have been visited by travelers going between ancient centers of civilization in Asia. Since the sixteenth century Islam has slowly spread from coastal trading centers, such as Brunei in the north and Banjarmasin in the south. Immigrant Chinese have brought the practices of their homeland, and in the last century Christian missionaries have been increasingly successful in the interior, prompting syncretic revivalist cults. This article, however, is concerned with the indigenous religions of the great island. Many of these have passed out of existence or are imminently about to do so without being studied in depth. The existing data indicate wide variation in belief and practice. Nevertheless, there are features widely characteristic of Bornean religions, and it is these that are summarized here.

Ethnic Diversity. All the indigenous peoples of Borneo speak Austronesian languages, but they exhibit bewildering ethnic diversity. There is still no generally agreed upon taxonomy, and many of the most familiar ethnic terms are vague. In the south and west there are large, politically fragmented populations that nevertheless manifest considerable cultural uniformity. Examples of these are the Ngaju and Iban, both numbering some hundreds of thousands. To the north the terrain is mountainous and the rivers difficult to navigate. Here are found many small groups, each at most only a few thousand strong. The ethnic diversity is of immediate consequence for religions, because the religions are rooted in the local community and contribute to much of its identity.

The General Concept of Religion. Many of the cultures of interior Borneo lack the concept of a separate domain of religion. Instead, ritual observance is incorporated into a spectrum of prescribed behaviors that includes legal forms, marriage practices, etiquette, and much else. All of these are matters of collective representations shared by autonomous communities. Such communities often consist of a longhouse with a few hundred inhabitants and are separated from neighboring villages by tracts of jungle. There is no notion of conversion to another religion; if an individual moves to another community—for instance, as the result of a marriage—he or she simply adheres to the ritual forms of that place. Significantly, members of a community often exaggerate their ritual peculiarity. An outside observer readily identifies items shared with neighboring groups, but the patterns of distribution are complex, reflecting migration and borrowing over many centuries.

The religions of interior Borneo are rich in both ritual and cosmology. In perhaps the best known account, Schärer (1963) describes the subtle notions of the godhead found among the Ngaju, replete with dualistic aspects of upper world and underworld, multilayered heavens, and complex animal and color symbolism. Other peoples have comparably extensive spirit worlds. Because of the archaeologically attested antiquity of contact with India, some authors have discerned elements of Hindu belief. Schärer (1963, p. 13) attributes one of the names of the Ngaju supreme deity to an epoch of Indian influence. In the north there are features of the religion—for instance, in number symbolism—that may indicate influence from China, but there is no overall similarity to Indian or Chinese religions.

The Prominence of Mortuary Ritual. One element of ancient Southeast Asian provenance is a central feature of many Bornean religions: that is, a focus on death and, in particular, on secondary treatment of the dead. This mortuary complex has been associated with Borneo at least since the publication of Robert Hertz's classic essay (1907). By no means did all interior peoples practice secondary disposal in recent times. The custom is found across much of the southern third of the island but has only a scattered distribution further north. Stöhr (1959) surveys the variety of death rites across the island. Where secondary treatment occurs, it is part of an extended ritual sequence, often the most elaborate of that religion (Metcalf, 1982). The occurrence of secondary treatment also draws attention to the importance of the dead in indigenous cosmologies. Other life-crisis rituals are generally celebrated on a smaller scale, one that does not involve the participation of entire communities.

Agricultural Rites. Major calendrical rituals are usually coordinated with the agricultural cycle. This is especially true among the Iban, who speak of the soul of the rice in anthropomorphic terms, and focus rites upon it at every stage of cultivation (Jensen, 1974, pp. 151–195). In some areas, however, notably the northwestern subcoastal belt, reliance on hill rice is relatively recent. In these areas, where sago is produced, rice ritual is less prominent.

Head-hunting Rites. Head-hunting is another practice commonly associated with Borneo. Formerly prevalent, it usually occurred in the context of warfare or as an adjunct to mortuary rites. Frequently heads were required in order to terminate the mourning period for community leaders. In contrast to other parts of Southeast Asia, heads were the focus of much ritual. Hose and McDougall describe the techniques of warfare and head-hunting found among the Kayan and Kenyah of central northern Borneo, and also the large festivals periodically held to honor the heads (Hose and McDougall, 1912, vol. 1, p. 159; vol. 2, pp. 20–22, 41, 47).

Ritual Specialists. Even in societies with little technological and political specialization, ritual specialists are important. But there is great variation in the particular combinations of roles played by priest, shaman, and augur. Women often play a major part. Among the Dusun of northern Borneo, for example, priestesses officiate at all major rituals (Evans, 1953, p. 42). Often in association with death rites there are psychopomps to conduct the deceased to the land of the dead. In all of this, ritual languages are prominent. Often the major function of priests and priestesses is to recite long chants that deal with mythical events. These chants are complexly structured in terms of parallel phraseology; even prayers uttered by laymen in small family rituals display formal structure (Evans, 1953, pp. 42–56). Ritual is often accompanied by the sacrifice of chickens, pigs, or buffalo.

Shamanism is found everywhere and typically involves the recovery of errant souls through séances. Concomitantly, theories of illness usually focus on soul loss, in which all manner of nonhuman, malign agencies are implicated. Yet there is often a complementary theory of illness that results from the infraction of primordial taboo. Although not entirely absent, there is remarkably little concern with witchcraft.

Ritual and Social Differentiation. Some societies of interior Borneo are hierarchically stratified, while others are egalitarian. But even in the latter, major public rituals are closely bound up with the forms of leadership and social control. There is a dearth of rites of prestation, in which wealth passes between similar collectivities. This may in part be a result of social organization that is predominantly cognatic, that is, lacking groups defined by fixed rules of descent. In large-scale festivals, however, leaders coordinate the efforts of entire communities in order to feed guests and erect monuments.

BIBLIOGRAPHY

Evans, Ivor H. N. *The Religion of the Tempasuk Dusuns of North Borneo.* Cambridge, 1953. Describes in list format the beliefs and ceremonies of a subgroup of the extensive but culturally varied Dusun people of Sabah. The major emphasis is on folklore and mythology.

Hertz, Robert. "A Contribution to the Study of the Collective Representation of Death" (1907). In *Death and the Right Hand,* two of Hertz's essays translated from the French by Rodney Needham and Claudia Needham. New York, 1960. A brilliant essay by a prominent student of Émile Durkheim concerning the significance of mortuary rites, particularly secondary treatment of the dead. Hertz utilized published sources, and much of his data came from the Ngaju of southern Borneo.

Hose, Charles, and William McDougall. *The Pagan Tribes of Borneo.* 2 vols. London, 1912. Despite the title, these volumes mostly concern the people of central northern Borneo, particularly the Kayan. Based on Hose's years of experience as a government officer. Contains much useful information; most of that on religion is in volume 2.

Jensen, Erik. *The Iban and Their Religion.* Oxford, 1974. A readable ethnographic account based on Jensen's seven years among the Iban as an Anglican missionary and community development officer. Emphasizes world view, cosmology, and longhouse festivals.

Metcalf, Peter. *A Borneo Journey into Death: Berawan Eschatology from Its Rituals.* Philadelphia, 1982. Describes in detail the elaborate mortuary ritual sequence, involving secondary treatment of the dead, in a small ethnic group of central northern Borneo. Shows how these rites reflect Berawan concepts of the soul in life and death.

Schärer, Hans. *Ngaju Religion: The Conception of God among a South Borneo People* (1946). Translated from the German by Rodney Needham. The Hague, 1963. Schärer was a missionary with the Baseler Mission in southern Borneo for seven years and later studied under J. P. B. de Josselin de Jong at Leiden. His account of Ngaju cosmology is impressive, but he unfortunately gives little idea of the social or ritual context.

Stöhr, Waldemar. *Das Totenritual der Dajak.* Ethnologica, n.s. vol. 1. Cologne, 1959. A compendium of sources on death practices from the entire island. Contains no analysis but is useful as a guide to bibliography.

PETER METCALF

BORROMEO, CARLO (1538–1584), reforming archbishop of Milan, cardinal, and canonized saint of the Roman Catholic church. Carlo Borromeo, second son of Count Gilberto Borromeo and Margherita de' Medici, was born at Arona, northwest of Milan, on 2 October 1538. From 1552 he attended the University of Pavia, where he received a doctorate in civil and canon law in 1559. At the end of that year his maternal uncle, Gian Angelo de' Medici, was elected Pope Pius IV and immediately bestowed upon his twenty-one-year-old nephew the archbishopric of Milan, a collection of other wealthy benefices, and a cardinal's hat. Borromeo, however, proved by his seriousness and personal austerity to be an atypical beneficiary of nepotism; thus when his elder brother died heirless and his family attempted to persuade him to revert to lay status, marry, and assume the noble title, he refused and instead had himself secretly ordained a priest 17 July 1563.

Borromeo's most significant role in the pontifical government of his uncle was his work as liaison between the Curia Romana and the third session of the Council of Trent (1560–1563). Afterward he served on various postconciliar commissions and oversaw the preparation of the *Catechism of the Council of Trent*—not so much a catechism in the ordinary sense as a doctrinal manual for the use of parish priests. This book was completed in 1564 and published in 1566.

Among the most important reforms of the Council of Trent was the requirement that bishops reside in their dioceses, but Pius IV would not allow his nephew to fulfill this obligation. Borromeo did however visit Milan in September and October of 1565, during which time he summoned and presided over his first provincial council. Recalled to Rome to assist at his uncle's deathbed, he participated in the conclave that followed and was instrumental in the election of his fellow-reformer, Pius V, on 8 January 1566.

Borromeo returned to Milan in April 1566 and labored there for the rest of his life. He became during those years the ideal of the Counter-Reformation bishop, not only because his own spiritual life was rich and deep and in accord with the ascetic principles of his time, but also because he reconstructed his great diocese and province along the lines mandated by the Council of Trent. He was present everywhere to oversee the moral reform of clergy, laity, and religious, either through tireless journeys of episcopal visitation or through the six provincial and eleven diocesan synods he held during his tenure. He founded six seminaries and a special missionary college to train priests to work in nearby Switzerland. He established hundreds of catechetical centers, which by the time he died were serving regularly more than twenty thousand children. He founded orphanages, hospitals, and homes for abandoned women. In his educational projects he worked closely with the new Society of Jesus. He was punctilious in carrying out his pastoral duties and careless of his personal safety, notably during the plague years of 1570 and 1576.

Borromeo's severity earned him enemies as well as adherents. In 1569 a friar attempted to assassinate him. He was constantly at odds with the Spanish authorities who governed the duchy of Milan, and particularly with the redoubtable viceroy, Requesens, whom he excommunicated. But Borromeo never heeded opposition, and during his relatively short span of years he established the model of the Tridentine bishop, a model destined to perdure for nearly four centuries. He was canonized on 1 November 1610.

BIBLIOGRAPHY

Borromeo's own works, especially letters and devotional literature, are in *Opere complete di S. Carlo Borromeo*, 5 vols., edited by J. A. Sassi (Milan, 1747–1748). His reform legislation is found in *Acta ecclesiae mediolanensis*, 2 vols. (Lyon, 1683). The standard life is Andreé Deroo's *Saint Charles Borromée, cardinal, réformateur, docteur de la pastorale* (Paris, 1963); a popular treatment is Margaret Yeo's *A Prince of Pastors: St. Charles Borromeo* (New York, 1938). A particularly incisive treatment of Borromeo's work is Roger Mols's "Saint Charles Borromée, pionnier de la pastorale moderne," *Nouvelle revue théologique*, 79 (1957): 600–622.

MARVIN R. O'CONNELL

BRAHMĀ is the creator in Hindu mythology; sometimes he is said to form a trinity with Viṣṇu as preserver and Śiva as destroyer. Yet Brahmā does not have the importance that creator gods usually have in mythology, nor is his status equal to that of Śiva or Viṣṇu. Though Brahmā appears in more myths than almost any other Hindu god, as the central figure in quite a few, and as a bit player in many more, he was seldom worshiped in India; at least one important version of the myth in which Śiva appears before Brahmā and Viṣṇu in the form of a flaming phallus explicitly states that Brahmā will never again be worshiped in India (to punish him for having wrongly sworn that he saw the tip of the infinite pillar). Brahmā's ability to create is little more than an expertise or a technical skill that he employs at the behest of the greater gods; he is called upon whenever anyone is needed to create something, or even to create a pregnant situation—to give power to a potential villain so that the action of the conflict can unfold. But if one were to create a functional trinity of gods who wield actual power in Hindu mythology, one would have to replace Brahmā with the Goddess.

Brahmā's mythology is derived largely from that of the god Prajāpati in the Brāhmaṇas. Unlike Brahmā, Prajāpati is regarded as the supreme deity, and he creates in a variety of ways: he casts his seed into the fire in place of the usual liquid oblation; he separates a female from his androgynous form and creates with her through incestuous intercourse; or he practices asceticism in order to generate heat, from which his children are born. In this way he creates first fire, wind, sun, moon; then all the gods and demons (the *deva*s and *asura*s, who are his younger and older sons); then men and animals; and then all the rest of creation. In the epics and Purāṇas, when Brahmā takes over the task of creation he still uses these methods from time to time, but his usual method is to create mentally: he thinks of something and it comes into existence. While he is under the influence of the element of darkness *(tamas)* he creates the demons; under the influence of goodness *(sattva)* he creates the gods. Or he may dismember himself, like the Ṛgvedic cosmic man (Puruṣa), and create sheep from his breast, cows from his stomach, horses from his feet, and grasses from his hairs. Paradoxically (or perversely), he usually employs less abstract methods (such as copulation) to produce the more abstract elements of creation (such as the hours and minutes, or the principles of logic and music).

Brahmā's name is clearly related both to *brahman*, the neuter term for the godhead (or, in earlier texts, for the principle of religious reality), and to the word for the priest, the *brāhmaṇa*. In later Hinduism Brahmā is committed to the strand of Hinduism associated with *pravṛtti* ("active creation, worldly involvement") and indifferent, or even opposed, to *nivṛtti* ("withdrawal from the world, renunciation"). He therefore comes into frequent conflict with Śiva when Śiva is in his ascetic phase, and competes with Śiva when Śiva is in his phallic phase. Brahmā's unilateral attachment to *pravṛtti* may also explain why he alone among the gods is able to grant the boon of immortality, often to demon ascetics: he deals only in life, never in death. This habit unfortunately causes the gods serious problems in dealing with demons, who are usually overcome somehow by Śiva or Viṣṇu. Immortality (or release from death) is what Brahmā bestows in place of the *mokṣa* (release from rebirth and redeath) that Śiva and Viṣṇu may grant, for these two gods, unlike Brahmā, are involved in both *pravṛtti* and *nivṛtti*. This one-sidedness of Brahmā may, finally, explain why he failed to capture the imagination of the Hindu worshiper: the god who is to take responsibility for one's whole life must, in the Hindu view, acknowledge not only the desire to create but the desire to renounce creation.

[*See also* Śiva; Prajāpati; *and* Indian Religions, *article on* Mythic Themes.]

BIBLIOGRAPHY

The best study of Brahmā is Greg Bailey's *The Mythology of Brahmā* (Oxford, 1983), which also contains an extensive bibliography of the secondary literature. Many of the relevant texts are translated in my *Hindu Myths* (Baltimore, 1975), pp. 25–55, and interpreted in my *Śiva: The Erotic Ascetic* (Oxford, 1981), pp. 68–77 and 111–140.

WENDY DONIGER O'FLAHERTY

BRAHMAN. In the Vedic hymns the neuter noun *bráhman* denotes the cosmic principle or power contained in the priestly or inspired utterance. As such, it came to be viewed as embodied in the Veda when the latter was fixed in a body of texts. The masculine form of the word, *brahmán*, denotes the priest who knows and speaks such utterances; in the later standardized Vedic ritual he is one of the four main priests who, mostly silently, oversees and rectifies errors in the sacrificial proceedings. The derivative term *brāhmaṇa* has two denotations. One indicates the Vedic prose texts that expound the *śrauta* ("solemn") ritual; these texts are also known in English as the Brāhmaṇas. The other indicates a person of the first of the four *varṇas*, or "castes"; in English this becomes *brahman* or *brahmin*. Finally, Brahman or Brahmā is a name for the creator god in Hinduism.

Etymology. Notwithstanding many and various attempts to establish the linguistic derivation of *brahman*, the question remains unsettled. The old equation with Latin *flamen* has been vigorously and repeatedly championed by Georges Dumézil. Louis Renou suggests derivation from the root *barh* (or *brah*), which would mean to speak in riddles. Jan Gonda wants to derive *brahman* from the root *bṛh* ("to be strong"), a view that he finds supported by the ancient Indian exegetes and that has the advantage of bringing together the two largely interchangeable Vedic divinities Bṛhaspati and Brahmaṇaspati. Paul Thieme, rejecting Gonda's reliance on traditional Indian exegesis, starts from a basic meaning of "form(ing), formulation" and pleads for connecting it with Greek *morphē*. These, as well as other proposed etymologies, run into formal or semantic difficulties. Much depends on the view one takes of the basic meaning. Consensus tends to look for the basic meaning in the sphere of (sacred) word or formulation, as is in accordance with abundant textual evidence. The main problem, however, is the multi-interpretability of the element *brah*, which keeps frustrating attempts to arrive at a satisfactory solution.

Mythology. In the Brāhmaṇas and especially in the Upaniṣads, *brahman* comes to designate the impersonal eternal principle and first cause of the universe. It plays, however, no distinct role in Vedic cosmogony. Its connection—under the form of the god Brahmā—with the cosmogonic myth of the golden germ or egg *(hiraṇyagarbha)* is post-Vedic. In the *Laws of Manu* (1.5ff.) the golden egg is said to have arisen from Brahmā's seed, which he deposited in the primordial waters. After remaining in this embryonic state, Brahmā is born from the golden egg as the cosmic man, Puruṣa-Nārāyaṇa. The essential point of this and similar passages is that Brahmā as the single principle and cause of the universe is "self-existent" *(svayaṃbhū)* and therefore can only put the cosmogonic process into motion by reproducing himself. In the same line of self-reproduction we find the motif of Brahmā's incest with his daughter, Vāc ("speech")—a motif transferred from the Vedic creator god Prajāpati, lord of creatures. Though fused with the cosmic man, Puruṣa, and with Prajāpati, he has not given rise to a cosmogonic myth specific to him. In Hindu cosmology he is either a presiding but inactive deity—not unlike the brahman priest in the sacrificial ritual—or a demiurge who comes into his own only in the second stage of the cosmogony, when the phenomenal world starts its deployment. He is then seated on the lotus that grows out of Viṣṇu's navel, or, again, he is born from the cosmic egg *(brahmāṇḍa)*.

In the Hindu pantheon, Brahmā is united, as the static center, with the dynamic supreme deities Viṣṇu and Śiva in the *trimūrti*, the triple form of the divine. Iconographically, he is represented with four bearded heads and four arms. His attributes are the four Vedas, the water vessel, the offering ladle, the rosary (emblems of the brahman), the lotus, and the scepter (or bow), while his mount is the *haṃsa* or goose. The otherwise abundant Hindu mythology does not, however, give much attention to Brahmā, nor is there clear evidence of a cult. In essence, *brahman* remained an abstract concept that was elaborated in the Upaniṣads and the monistic Vedānta philosophy.

Semantic Development. Hermann Oldenberg summarized the general meaning of *brahman* (neuter) as the sacred formula and the magic power inherent in it ("die heilige Formel und das sie erfüllende Fluidum der Zauberkraft"; 1917, vol. 2, p. 65). Although this is consistent overall with Vedic usage, it still leaves a large distance between sacred formula and the later meaning of *principium omnium.* Moreover, the Vedic *brahman,* far from being eternal and immutable, is said to be made or "carpented." Gonda's view of *brahman* as "power," derived from the verbal root *bṛh* ("to be strong"), is useful but too general to answer the problem in more precise terms. Thieme's analysis leading to "form(ing), formulation" *(Formung, Gestaltung, Formulierung)* as the original meaning, especially in the sense of (improvised) poetic formulation and later (stereotyped) truth formulation, goes a long way toward filling the gap. Renou, apart from the doubtful etymology proposed by him, draws attention to a particular dimension of the formulation. In his view, *brahman* is distinguished by its enigmatic or paradoxical nature. The *brahman,* then, is the formulation of the cosmic riddle, a riddle that cannot be solved by a direct answer but only formulated in paradoxical terms that leave the answer—the (hidden) connection *(bandhu, nidāna)* between the terms of the paradox—unexpressed. In Renou's felicitous phrase, the *brahman* is the "énergie connective comprimée en énigmes" (1949, p. 43).

Yet another element must be taken into account in fixing the semantic range of *brahman,* namely, the verbal contest. This element is preserved, albeit in fixed and ritualized form, in the Brahmodya of the Vedic ritual, especially in the horse sacrifice, or Aśvamedha. It consists of a series of rounds of verbal challenges and responses. In each round two contestants put riddle questions to each other. The point of the riddle contest is to show that one has "seen" or understood the hidden "connection" by responding with a similar, if possible even more artfully contrived, riddle. The one who holds out longest and finally reduces his opponent to silence is the winner, the true *brahman,* holder of the hidden connection. Hence the importance of silence stressed by Renou. In the elaborate Brahmodya of the horse sacrifice the last round is concluded by the brahman priest who asserts himself, apparently as the winner, with the words: "This *brahman* is the highest heaven of speech" *(brahmāyaṃ vācaḥ paramaṃ vyoma).* In the last resort, then, man as a contestant must place himself in the open gap of the unresolved cosmic riddle and vindicate himself as the live "connection" that holds together the cosmos.

The original Brahmodya, therefore, is not an innocuous riddle game but a matter of life and death. This still transpires in the Brahmodya-like debates of the Upaniṣads, where the losing contestant who fails to submit to his superior opponent and goes on challenging him has to pay for his boldness with his life or, more precisely, with his head. As a contest, the Brahmodya takes its place among other contests, such as chariot races, surviving in fixed, ritualized form. In fact, the Vedic sacrifice itself appears originally to have been a perilous and violent contest for the goods of life. However, the Vedic sacrificial ritual, as the prose texts describe it, is a perfectly peaceful and all but obsessively ordered procedure that has no place for adversaries and real contests. It is the exclusive affair of an individual sacrificer.

This fundamental change is expressed in interesting fashion in a ritualistic myth relating the decisive sacrificial contest between Prajāpati and Mṛtyu, or Death (*Jaiminīya Brāhmaṇa* 2.69–2.70). Prajāpati wins his final victory by his "vision" of equivalence that enables him to assimilate his adversary's sacrificial panoply and thereby to eliminate him once and for all. "Since then," the text concludes, "there is no sacrificial contest anymore." But this also meant that the formulation of the cosmic life-death riddle with its hidden connection was replaced with flat and artless statements of equivalence, establishing the identification of the elements of macro- and microcosmos with those of the standardized ritual. Thus the so-called "four *hotṛ*" *(caturhotṛ)* formulas are still said to be "the highest hidden *brahman* of the gods" and their original context appears indeed to have been the verbal contest. However, in the way these formulas are given in the texts, they are no more than a string of simple identifications—"Thinking is the ladle, thought is the ghee, speech is the altar . . ."—without mystery or enigma, to be learned and recited by rote. The dynamic tension of the hidden connection has collapsed into flat and static identification. The uncertain outcome of the contest has been replaced by the ritualistic knowledge of him "who knows thus" *(ya evam veda),* namely the identifications that concentrated the whole of the universe in the ritual proceedings and, ultimately, in the single sacrifice.

In the context of the ritual's development and fixation the *brahman* evolves from the visionary formulation of the cosmic riddle to comprise the immutably fixed corpus of Vedic texts. From the subjective truth of the visionary poet it has become the objective truth of the suprahuman, transcendent law of the universe, realized in the ritual and underpinned by identification. This also meant that the function of the *brahman* (masc.), that is, the speaker or knower of *brahman* (neuter), was narrowed down to that of the mostly silent *brahman* priest in the ritual, while the *brāhmaṇa* became (ideally) the human carrier of the Veda (hence the scriptural stress on its oral preservation and transmission by the brahman).

At the same time, the *brahman* kept up its intimate connection with speech, which gave rise to the later speculations on the primordial utterance as the cosmic principle *(śabda-brahman)* and to philosophy of language, as well as to grammatical description.

On the other hand, identification made it possible to concentrate the whole of the spoken and acted proceedings of the ritual in the person of the single sacrificer, who in this way internalizes the whole of the ritual, that is, the transcendent cosmic order, and so becomes identical with *brahman*. This was already prefigured in the *brahman* who, as we saw, identifies himself with "the highest heaven of speech." Here the development leads over to the Upaniṣadic doctrine of the unity of *ātman*, the principle of individuation or the individual "soul," and *brahman*, which gave rise to the monistic philosophy of the Vedānta.

[*For further discussion of the concept of (the neuter term)* brahman, *see* Upaniṣads *and* Vedānta; *for the priestly caste, see* Varṇa and Jāti *and* Priesthood, *article on* Hindu Priesthood; *for the Hindu creator deity, see* Brahmā.]

BIBLIOGRAPHY

The most original view of *brahman* is presented by Louis Renou (with the collaboration of Liliane Silburn) in "Sur la notion de brahman," *Journal asiatique* 237 (1949): 7–46, reprinted in his *L'Inde fondamentale* (Paris, 1978). Jan Gonda's *Notes on Brahman* (Utrecht, 1950) brings in anthropological materials concerning power concepts. He is criticized by Paul Thieme, who presents a balanced view of the semantic development, in "Brahman," *Zeitschrift der Deutschen Morgenländischen Gesellschaft* 102 (1952): 91–129, reprinted in Thieme's *Kleine Schriften*, vol. 1 (Wiesbaden, 1971). For a discussion of Gonda's and Thieme's views, see also Hanns-Peter Schmidt's *Bṛhaspati und Indra* (Wiesbaden, 1968), pp. 16–22, 239ff. The element of verbal contest is stressed in my essay "On the Origin of the Nāstika," *Wiener Zeitschrift für die Kunde Sud- und Ostasiens* 12–13 (1968–1969): 171–185, which has been revised and reprinted in my *The Inner Conflict of Tradition* (Chicago, 1985). For the equation of *flamen* and *brahman*, see Georges Dumézil's *Flamen-Brahman* (Paris, 1935); see also the *Revue de l'histoire des religions* 38 and 39 for Dumézil's responses to criticism. For Oldenberg's views, see his *Die Religion des Veda* (Stuttgart, 1917) and his *Kleine Schriften* (Wiesbaden, 1967), pp. 1127–1156. A critical survey of the various etymologies is to be found in Manfred Mayrhofer's *Kurzgefasstes etymologisches Wörterbuch des Altindischen*, vol. 2 (Heidelberg, 1963), pp. 453–456.

The philosophical developments and the concept of *śabda-brahman* are discussed in Madeleine Biardeau's *Théorie de la connaissance et philosophie de la parole dans le brahmanisme classique* (Paris, 1964).

JAN C. HEESTERMAN

BRĀHMAṆAS AND ĀRAṆYAKAS. The Brāhmaṇas are the oldest Indian Sanskrit prose texts, usually dated from the first half or the middle of the last millennium BCE. Their chronology, like that of most classical Indian texts, is uncertain and hinges on equally uncertain external factors such as the dates for the *Ṛgveda*, for the grammarian Pāṇini, and for the Buddha; moreover, the time span between their first formulation and their final redaction may have been considerable. The word *brāhmaṇa* means a statement on *brahman*, that is, on the cosmic importance or meaning of the Vedic sacrificial ritual, whether of each individual act *(karman)* and formula *(mantra)*, or of the combination of such acts and formulas that constitute a particular sacrifice. *Brāhmaṇa* then becomes the generic term applied to such collections of statements or commentaries. As a class of texts, they deal in a step-by-step, rite-by-rite manner with the whole of the *śrauta* ("solemn") ritual. Together with the usually metrical *mantras*, the prose Brāhmaṇas constitute the *śruti* (whence the adjective *śrauta*), the corpus of the "revealed" Veda.

The Brāhmaṇas follow the division of the four Vedas and the corresponding parts of the ritual—*Ṛgveda*, recitation; *Yajurveda*, performance; *Sāmaveda*, chanting; and *Atharvaveda*, officiating. The central and oldest group of Brāhmaṇas are those of the *Yajurveda*, which is concerned with the overall scheme of the ritual process. In the older versions or *śākhās* ("branches") of the *Yajurveda*, the *mantra* and Brāhmaṇa parts are intermingled in the Saṃhitās of the relevant "branch" (*Kāṭhaka, Maitrāyaṇī*, and *Taittirīya Saṃhitās* together forming the *Kṛṣṇa* or "Black" *Yajurveda*). In the younger *Śukla* or "White" *Yajurveda*, the Saṃhitā with the *mantras* pertaining to the ritual acts is separated from the Brāhmaṇa (the *Śatapatha Brāhmaṇa*), as is also the case with the *Ṛgveda* and the *Sāmaveda*, while the *Atharvaveda* has appended to its Saṃhitā (which stands apart from the basic threefold Veda) a Brāhmaṇa that is only loosely connected and derivative. In this way the Brāhmaṇas developed into a separate class or genre characterized by a standardized expository prose style. As a genre they remained, however, tied up with the *śrauta* ritual and came to a halt with the ultimate institutionalization of the associated ceremonies. On the other hand they spawned the productive genre of the Upaniṣads, which originally were part of the Brāhmaṇa literature but eventually turned away from the ritual to treat meta-ritualistic and esoteric speculation.

The ritualistic thought of the Brāhmaṇas owes its origins to a fundamental change in worldview that gave rise to a new conception of sacrifice. Though direct and coherent information on the ritual of sacrifice preceding the Brāhmaṇa texts is lacking, they do contain in their explanations many scattered and archaic but telling references that allow us to reconstruct a rough outline of previous ritual practices. In fact, the Brāhmaṇa authors show themselves to be aware of restructuring the sacrifice within the context of a new, rationalized system of ritual. The old pattern of sacrifice was intimately bound up with conflict, contest, and battle, corresponding with the mythological motif of the enmity and combat between the conquering gods (*deva*s) and their adversaries, the lordly *asura*s. The agonistic sacrificial festival was the central institution in an essentially tragic-heroic worldview. Its destructive violence is preserved in hypertrophic form in the all-embracing epic war of the *Mahābhārata*. The constant threat of sacrally sanctioned violence, death, and destruction provided the impetus for the intensive reflection on sacrifice and the construction of the *śrauta* ritual expounded in the Brāhmaṇas.

The main thrust of this new exposition of ritual practice served to remove the agonistic festival with its unsettling dangers and uncertain outcome from its central position and to replace it with the absolutely failsafe order of a mechanistic, rational rite. To this end, sacrifice was taken out of its agonistic context. This meant the exclusion of the adversary from the place of sacrifice. With that, sacrifice became a strictly personal affair of the individual sacrificer (acting in perfect unison with the priestly technicians of the ritual engaged by him for the purpose). Hence the striking absence of *sacra publica* from the *śrauta* ritual. Even in the royal rituals the king is just a single sacrificer and as such no different from a commoner. In other words, sacrifice was desocialized and set apart in a separate sphere of its own, transcending the social world. Outside society the sacrificer creates his own conflict-free, perfectly ordered universe, subject only to the absolute rules of the ritual.

Mythologically, this ritualized *agon* is expressed in the identification of the sacrificer with the creator god Prajāpati, the Lord of Creatures, who personifies the monistic conception of sacrifice, being himself both victim and sacrificer. Through sacrifice Prajāpati makes the beings go forth from his dismembered body, recalling the relatively late *Ṛgveda* hymn (10.90) that celebrates the cosmogonic sacrifice by the gods of Puruṣa, the Primordial Being. In this respect Prajāpati supersedes the warrior-god Indra and his cosmogonic martial exploits. The outcome no longer depends on prowess in the sacrificial contest involving martial arts such as charioteering and verbal skills, but on unerring knowledge of the complicated but systematic (and therefore readily learnable) body of ritual rules. [*See also* Prajāpati.]

In contrast to the poetic or visionary metaphor, which was based on numerical equivalence *(saṃpad, saṃkhyāna)*, the mainstay of Brahmaṇic thought in elaborating the ritual system was identification in uncomplicated "this-is-that" terms. Elements of the ritual (*mantra*s, recitations, chants, acts, ritual implements, the place of sacrifice and its various parts) are identified with those of the universe and of the self. In this way the course of the universe, of man, and of his life are reduced to the denominator of the ritual. In the last resort it is the sacrificer who, through his identification with Prajāpati, the God-Sacrifice, integrates the ritually ordered universe in himself. We are here on the threshold of the Upaniṣadic doctrine of the identity of the *ātman*, the self, with the *brahman (principium omnium)*—a doctrine that announces itself already in a passage of the *Śatapatha Brāhmaṇa* (10.6.3.1–2). [*See also* Brahman.]

It is possible to view the Brāhmaṇas' conception of sacrifice as "a piece of magic pure and simple," enabling the sacrificer to obtain fulfillment of his wishes—cattle, progeny, prestige, power, health, long life—and indeed the texts are effusive in promising such rewards to the sacrificer. It is, however, a subtly different matter when, as is frequently the case, heaven and immortality are brought in. The problem of death appears as the central motif of the Brahmanic cosmico-ritual system, which is aimed at escaping from the cyclic life-death alternation (the dreaded "re-death," *punarmṛtyu*) by making for oneself an immortal body in the hereafter in accordance with the transcendent order of the ritual. Although the ritual system of the Brāhmaṇas remains open to magic interpretation, this should not obscure their rigorously systemic reflection on the sacrifice resulting in the maximization of the structuring capacity of ritual and the construction of an absolute, comprehensive, and exhaustive system of rules. In this sense we can speak of a "science of ritual" (cf. Hermann Oldenberg's view of the Brāhmaṇas as "vorwissenschaftliche Wissenschaft"). Although the term *brāhmaṇa* refers primarily to the ritual's cosmic importance, expressed in the form of identifications, the *śrauta* tradition gives pride of place to the system of rules as such. Thus the Brāhmaṇas are already characterized early on as ritual injunctions *(codanā)*, while the explanatory discussions *(arthavāda)*—including the statements of the cosmic importance of the rites, illustrated by mythological tales and relations of past events—are qualified as secondary, a mere "remainder." Only the pure systematics of the ritual count. In the final analysis, the potential for magic is rejected. The ritual system stands by itself, divorced from mundane reality and unaffected by its uses or abuses.

At this point the development of the ritual bifurcates. On the one hand, the doctrine of the Brāhmaṇas gave rise to the prescriptive handbooks, the Śrautasūtras, and ultimately, via the meta-rules contained in them, to the classical Mīmāṃsā school of jurisprudence. On the other hand, the statements on *brahman*, that is, the cosmic importance of the rites contained in the *arthavāda* parts, prefigure the musings of the Upaniṣads, which go on to form the final series of Sanskrit prose commentaries and speculation classified as Vedānta, the "conclusion of the Veda."

Āraṇyaka, literally pertaining to the wilderness *(araṇya)*, is the name of a loosely defined class of texts that form part of or are attached to the Brāhmaṇas. Their distinctive trait is that the material contained in them—both *mantra* and Brāhmaṇa—is traditionally qualified as secret or dangerous and therefore has to be studied outside the settled community *(grāma)* in the wilderness while submitting to restrictive rules of behavior *(vrata)*. Why these texts should be so classified is not explained. Although the Āraṇyakas vary in their contents, they are mainly concerned with the Mahāvrata, originally a New Year festival with agonistic and orgiastic features, and with parts of the ritual concerning the fire, especially the Pravargya (milk offering), featuring an earthen pot brought to glowing temperature in the fire, while funerary rites also occur. The latter item might explain the putatively secret or dangerous nature of the Āraṇyakas, but funerary rites as such do not form a commonly shared or preeminent part of these texts. Perhaps their common denominator could be found in that their contents were still recognized as being specifically bound up with life outside the settled community, that is, not, as has been erroneously thought, the life of the ascetic *(vānaprastha)*, but of the nomadic warriors of old setting out with their fires and cattle into the wilds. An indication to this effect may be contained in the formulas giving the names of the divine warriors, the Maruts, and in those celebrating the dread forms or bodies *(ghorā tanvaḥ)* of the fire. Since systematization of the ritual was aimed at the exclusion of the warrior and his deeds, the relevant traditions were relegated to the margin of the ritualistic Brāhmaṇas. On the other hand, the wilderness was of old the typical locus of revelatory vision, which therefore became associated with the warrior. The links between wilderness, warrior, and vision may have been the original basis for the reputation of danger and secrecy attached to the Āraṇyakas, while their marginalization may explain the mixed and disjointed nature of their contents (to which later materials may have been added) as hallowed remnants of the otherwise discredited world of the warrior that could not be easily fitted into the ritual system. For the same reasons, however, it would seem that the Āraṇyakas offered the proper slot for attaching the Upaniṣads to the ritualistic Brāhmaṇas. In this respect it is interesting that in their form the Upaniṣads recall an important aspect of the warrior-and-seer phenomenon, namely the verbal contest *(brahmodya)* on the hidden cosmic connection.

[*See also* Vedism and Brahmanism; Vedas; *and* Upaniṣads.]

BIBLIOGRAPHY

A general survey of the Brāhmaṇa and Āraṇyaka literature is to be found in Jan Gonda's *Vedic Literature* (Wiesbaden, 1975), pp. 339–432.

The classic studies of the Brāhmaṇa texts are Sylvain Lévi's *La doctrine du sacrifice dans les Brâhmaṇas* (1898; 2d ed., Paris, 1966) and Hermann Oldenberg's *Die Weltanschauung der Brāhmaṇa-Texte* (Göttingen, 1919). The proto-scientific nature of these texts has recently been emphasized again in Frits Staal's P. D. Gune Memorial Lectures, *The Science of Ritual* (Poona, 1982); see also his "The Meaninglessness of Ritual," *Numen* 26 (1979): 2–22, which, however, passes over the Brāhmaṇa explanations based on cosmic identifications; see my own comment in *Festschrift R. N. Dandekar* (Poona, 1984).

For the Āraṇyakas see Hermann Oldenberg's still valuable "Āraṇyaka," *Nachrichten von der Kgl. Gesellschaft der Wissenschaften zu Göttingen* (1915), pp. 382–401, reprinted in *Kleine Schriften*, edited by Klaus Janert (Wiesbaden, 1967), pp. 419–438. Louis Renou's "Le passage des brāhmaṇa aux upaniṣad," *Journal of the American Oriental Society* 73 (1953): 138–144, traces the linkage between Brāhmaṇa, Āraṇyaka, and Upaniṣad.

Translations include Julius Eggeling's *The Śatapatha-Brāhmaṇa*, 5 vols. (1882–1900; reprint, Delhi, 1963); Arthur Berriedale Keith's *The Veda of the Black Yajus School Entitled Taittirīya-Sanhitā*, 2 vols. (1914; reprint, Delhi, 1967), and *Rigveda Brahmaṇas* (1920; reprint, Delhi, 1971); and Willem Caland's *Pañcaviṃśa Brāhmaṇa* (Calcutta, 1931) and *Das Jaiminīya-Brāhmaṇa in Auswahl* (Amsterdam, 1919). Of the Āraṇyakas Keith has translated the Śānkhyāna (London, 1908) and the Aitareya (Oxford, 1909).

JAN C. HEESTERMAN

BRĀHMO SAMĀJ. The Brāhmo Samāj, also known as Brāhma Samāj and Brāhmo (or Brāhma) Sabhā, was the first modern Hindu reform movement. It was founded in Calcutta in 1828 by Ram Mohan Roy (1772–1833). As an expression of the social and religious views of a small but influential group of westernized Indians, the Brāhmo Samāj ("congregation of *brahman*") sought to create a purified form of Hinduism, a Hindu *dharma* free of all Puranic elements such as temple rituals and image worship. Led by a series of prominent Bengali intellectuals, the movement was a major factor in shaping Hindu responses to both secular and Christian influence from the West and thus helped pave the way for the so-called Hindu Renaissance in the late 1800s. The Brāhmo Samāj, along with the Ārya Samāj, was one of the most important religio-political influences in the Independence movement, the Brāhmo Samāj being a reform movement and the Ārya Samāj tending toward a revitalistic concern for the religious heritage of the Vedas mediated through new social and theological forms.

The Hindus involved in the Brāhmo Samāj were not broadly representative of the Bengal Hindu population, but instead belonged to a group of castes and families that had prospered in the late eighteenth and early nineteenth centuries after Mughal domination had given way to rule by the British East India Company. The Bengalis who gained money and land during this difficult economic period were mainly those who served as suppliers, agents, or bankers for the British. In the early period of company rule, those who were prepared to take this westernizing route to new wealth were mostly Hindus from a few select castes, and it was they and their descendants who provided the leadership and most of the membership of the Brāhmo Samāj.

The initial Indian response to British rule in Bengal was strongly influenced by caste and religious factors. Muslims deprived of political power and related social privileges largely withdrew from involvement with their conquerors, while Hindu response was divided between what were known in Bengal as *kulīna* and non-*kulīna* castes. In the unique Bengal hierarchy, the highest status was given to five *kulīna* ("superior") brahman castes and three *kulīna* castes of *kāyastha*s (traditional writer/clerical castes of *śūdra* origin). Faced with British rule these *kulīna* castes remained aloof, as they previously had from Muslim rulers, in order to preserve their ritual purity. The upper echelons of non-*kulīna*s, however, were less concerned about purity and were in many cases accustomed to relations with non-Hindu rulers. Members of these castes, whose ranks included the non-*kulīna* brahman families of Roy and Tagore as well as non-*kulīna kāyastha*s and *vaidya*s, recognized the benefits of working with the British, and using this involvement to their advantage, they had emerged by the early 1800s as wealthy entrepreneurs and landowners more receptive than other Bengalis to Western social and religious influences.

The newly affluent non-*kulīna* Hindus formed a natural constituency for Hindu reform. They were wealthy, but within the traditional Hindu system they had to accept religious leadership from *kulīna*s. Although attracted to Western culture, most were unwilling to reject Hinduism in favor of Christianity—a choice increasingly urged on them after the British East India Company opened Bengal to Christian missionaries in 1813. If they were to acquire Western culture, retain their Hindu identity, and also improve their religious status, a new form of Hinduism in which they could set the terms and take the leading role was necessary. Thanks to the genius of Ram Mohan Roy, this need was met by the creation of the Brāhmo Samāj in 1828.

The son of a non-*kulīna* brahman and himself a successful entrepreneur, Roy had a passion for reason and universality that led him by 1815 to reject Hindu polytheism and image worship in favor of the monotheism of the early Vedānta texts, the Upaniṣads and the *Brahma Sūtra,* which he interpreted as teaching the worship of *brahman* as the sole creator and supporter of the universe. Applying his standards to Christianity, he concluded that Jesus' ethical teachings had universal validity, though he rejected trinitarian theology. For a brief period in the early 1820s he aligned himself with the Unitarian movements in England and America, but when he saw that Hindus could not satisfy their spiritual and religious needs by becoming Unitarians, he founded the Brāhmo Samāj as a Hindu counterpart.

As Roy conceived it, the Brāhmo Samāj was a rational and ethical expression of Vedantic monotheism, reformist rather than radical in its ideas and goals. One radical element, however, was the assumption of religious leadership by Roy himself, a worldly self-taught non-*kulīna* who rejected traditional priestly authority. Once this example was accepted, the way was open for a new type of religious leader. In Bengal, this meant the recognition of upper non-*kulīna*s such as the Tagores, the Sens, and the Dutts as valid religious guides, and it was they in fact who provided leadership for most of the new religious movements throughout the nineteenth century.

Roy's successors in Brāhmo leadership, Debendranath Tagore (1817–1905) and Keshab Chandra Sen (1838–1884), converted the fledgling enterprise into a vital movement for religious and social reform. Between 1843 and 1858, Tagore recruited hundreds of new members, codified Brāhmo teachings, and campaigned actively against Christian proselytizing. Sen, the son of a Vaiṣṇava *vaidya* banker, expanded the efforts for social reform and brought the movement national attention with his charismatic missionary activities. Most significantly, as non-*kulīnas*, both men reinforced Roy's principle that religious authority rests on reason and ability and not on priestly caste.

By the time Sen died, the Brāhmo Samāj had largely completed its mission, having met the initial impact of Christianity and Western culture and having shown how they could be used to strengthen Hinduism instead of destroying it. In the process, the movement created a new and lasting religious model that could release the creative energies of a class of people who formerly had been patrons rather than leaders in the Hindu system. Although the Brāhmo Samāj survived as an independent organization, the energies of that class after 1884 were largely expressed in other movements of religious, social, and political reform. Such nonpriestly religious leaders as Vivekananda and Gandhi, however, were certainly both beneficiaries and worthy successors to Roy's initial vision.

[*See also* Ārya Samāj *and the biographies of Roy, Sen, Tagore, Vivekananda, and Gandhi.*]

BIBLIOGRAPHY

The Brāhmo Samāj has inspired a massive literature from Ram Mohan Roy to the present. The best work on the movement as a whole is David Kopf's *The Brahmo Samaj and the Shaping of the Modern Indian Mind* (Princeton, 1979). J. N. Farquhar's *Modern Religious Movements in India* (New York, 1915) gives an interesting early description of the Brāhmo Samāj in the context of other nineteenth-century Indian religious developments. Two recent and more analytic studies of the religious views of the movement and its founder are provided in Spencer Lavan's, "The Brahmo Samaj: India's First Modern Movement for Religious Reform" and in James N. Pankratz's "Rammohun Roy," in *Religion in Modern India,* edited by Robert D. Baird (New Delhi, 1981), pp. 1–25, and pp. 163–177. The standard source for more detailed information on Roy is Sophia Dobson Collet's *The Life and Letters of Raja Rammohun Roy,* 3d ed. rev., edited by Dilip Kumar Biswas and Prabhat Chandra Ganguli (Calcutta, 1962), and many of his important writings have been collected in the single-volume edition of *The English Works of Raja Rammohun Roy,* edited by Kalidas Nag and Debajyoti Burman (Calcutta, 1958). Narayan Chaudhuri's *Maharshi Devendranath Tagore* (New Delhi, 1973) provides a good description and evaluation of Tagore's contributions to the Brāhmo movement, and Meredith Borthwick's *Keshub Chunder Sen: A Search for Cultural Synthesis* (Calcutta, 1977) gives an excellent scholarly assessment of his successor. The unique and complex caste system of Bengal is explained in detail in Ronald B. Inden's *Marriage and Rank in Bengali Culture* (Berkeley, 1976).

THOMAS J. HOPKINS

BRANDON, S. G. F. (1907–1971), English historian of religions and of the early Christian church. Born in Devonshire, Samuel George Frederick Brandon was trained for the priesthood of the Church of England at the College of the Resurrection, Mirfield, during which time he also studied history at the University of Leeds. He was graduated in 1930 and was ordained two years later. After seven years as a parish priest in the west of England, he became in 1939 a chaplain in the British army, serving in the European and North African campaigns and taking part in the Dunkirk evacuation. He remained in the regular army until 1951, when he was appointed professor of comparative religion at the University of Manchester despite a lack of previous academic teaching experience; he held the post until his death.

Brandon's work centered on two areas. The first and more controversial was the early history of the Christian church. Here he took with the utmost seriousness the older theory of a conflict in the early church between a Petrine, Jewish group and a Pauline, gentile community, the latter gaining the upper hand only after AD 70. This was the theme of his first book, *The Fall of Jerusalem and the Christian Church* (1951). Over a decade later he returned to the subject of Christian origins in *Jesus and the Zealots* (1967) and *The Trial of Jesus of Nazareth* (1968), in which he emphasized that Jesus had been executed by the Romans for sedition, and drew parallels between Jesus' followers and the violent anti-Roman movements of the time. Coming as they did at a highly volatile period in Western religious history, these books gained him a considerable (and to Brandon, unwelcome) radical following, and much international attention, owing to reports in *Time, Newsweek,* and other newsmagazines.

Brandon's other major interest was centered on the belief that religion is a human response to the inexorable passage of time. His thesis was stated in *Time and Mankind* (1951), and was repeated in various ways in such books as *Man and His Destiny in the Great Religions* (1962), *History, Time, and Deity* (1965), and *The Judgment of the Dead* (1967). Wider interests were revealed in *A Dictionary of Comparative Religion* (1970), planned, edited, and to a great extent written by him, and in his last work, published after his death, *Man and God in Art and Ritual* (1975). Here the focus shifted to iconography, but the underlying theme remained that of history and time.

In 1970 Brandon was elected general secretary of the International Association for the History of Religions, but his unexpected death a little more than a year later prevented him from exercising any permanent influence on that organization.

Despite his years as a parish priest and chaplain, after 1951 Brandon virtually lost touch with the church, and as a professor he had no interest in Christian apologetics. He was a historian pure and simple, who saw Western religion as having been in irreversible decline since the high Middle Ages, and who believed that understanding of religious traditions could be gained only from a study of their origins. His view of the interrelations of religion and the sense of time was undoubtedly valid; however, being uninterested in psychology, philosophy, or phenomenology—or in methodological questions generally—he seldom carried his investigations far enough. Although he was a disciplined scholar and a fastidious writer, his mind lacked flexibility, and his short academic career can now be seen as having marked the end of the era of traditional comparative religion in Britain. In the area of Christian origins, his views were too controversial to win ready acceptance, but it was important that he drew attention to the political setting of early Christianity, a field in which much work remains to be done.

BIBLIOGRAPHY

Sharpe, Eric J. "S. G. F. Brandon, 1907–1971." *History of Religions* 12 (August 1972): 71–74.

Sharpe, Eric J. "Comparative Religion at the University of Manchester, 1904–1979." *Bulletin of the John Rylands Library* (Manchester) 63 (Autumn 1980): 144–170.

Sharpe, Eric J., and J. R. Hinnells, eds. *Man and His Salvation: Studies in Memory of S. G. F. Brandon.* Manchester, 1973. Includes a personal appreciation of Brandon by H. C. Snape, a summary of Brandon's contribution to scholarship by E. O. James, and a bibliography of Brandon's works.

Simon, Marcel. "S. G. F. Brandon, 1907–1971." *Numen* 19 (August–December 1972): 84–90.

ERIC J. SHARPE

BREAD. We learn from the *Epic of Gilgamesh* that bread was offered to the gods over five thousand years ago. Since that time, wherever grain has been cultivated, bread has held a place of honor in rituals. Bread is the staff of life and often, as in the Lord's Prayer, stands for food in general.

Raised bread was invented by the Egyptians, who made it the basis of their administrative system. Although the Israelites used bread in many of their religious rites and the Greeks honored a bread goddess, it was Jesus who exalted bread to the highest religious value when he said, "This is my body."

In early agricultural societies, the first fruits of the harvest were offered to the gods (cf. *Lv.* 23:15–22). For the harvest feast, Shavu'ot, the Feast of Weeks, the Israelites were instructed to bring two loaves of bread made of wheaten flour as an oblation to Yahveh. Because the festival occurred fifty days (seven weeks) after Passover, it came to be known by the Greek name *Pentecost* and commemorated the giving of the Law at Sinai.

Ḥag ha-Matsot, the Feast of Unleavened Bread, was one of the three great agricultural festivals celebrated by the Israelites after they settled in Canaan. Originally a rite of thanksgiving at the beginning of the grain harvest, it was later linked to the nomadic pastoral feast of Passover as a historical commemoration of Israel's deliverance from Egypt. For seven days, only unleavened bread was eaten, as a sign of a new beginning (cf. *1 Cor.* 5:6–8).

Somewhat similar to first fruits was the "bread of the presence" (shewbread), which the Israelites laid out before the Holy of Holies in the Temple (*Lv.* 24:5–9). Twelve cakes of pure wheaten flour, representing the twelve tribes of Israel and their unending covenant with Yahveh, were placed on a table in two lines. Each Sabbath they were replaced and then eaten by the priests. Because incense was burned while the loaves were being replaced, scholars have viewed the bread as either a sacrificial or a thanks offering.

From the seventh century BCE, the Greeks celebrated the mysteries of Demeter, the bread goddess of Eleusis, whose cult was the established religion of Athens. Demeter was also the intercessor in the realm of the dead. Her two roles were complementary, for grain must die in the earth before it regenerates. Little else is known about the Eleusinian mysteries because adherents took a vow of secrecy.

Bread was among the food offerings that the ancient Egyptians provided for their deceased. An incantation in the *Book of Going Forth by Day* was to be recited if an enemy challenged the deceased's right to bread. In the *Book of Tobit* (4:18), Tobias is told to "be generous with bread and wine on the graves of virtuous men."

The ritual use of bread may have originated as an offering of nourishment to the deity. But since the God of the Israelites refused all nourishment (*Jgs.* 13:16), the loaves became a symbol of communion between Yahveh and his people. In cultures where bread was the staple of life, it was natural that communion be symbolized by the sharing of bread, since eating together has always been a sign of fellowship.

Bread was elevated to a symbol of supreme importance when Jesus spoke of himself as the "bread of life" that would give eternal life to those who believed in him, quite unlike the manna that the followers of Moses fed upon in the desert (*Jn.* 6). In New Testament accounts of sharing bread at a meal, a recurrent series of words (*took, gave thanks* or *blessed, broke,* and *gave*) describes the actions of Jesus at the Last Supper when he instituted the Eucharist. By the ritual act of breaking bread (*Acts* 2:42, 20:7) and eating it, Christians would become one with Christ and his Father in heaven.

The bread that becomes the body of Christ has an interesting parallel among the Aztec, who made a dough-like paste from the crushed seeds of the prickly poppy and molded it into a figure of the god Huitzilopochtli. The ritual involved "god-eating": the bread body was broken into pieces and eaten.

Bread presented by the faithful for the Eucharist but not used for that purpose was called the *eulogia.* The bishop blessed it and had it distributed to catechumens and to absent members of the community. By the fourth century, Christians were sending the *eulogia* to one another as a symbol of their union. Hippolytus of Rome (170–235) pointed to another sign of the special unity that bound early Christians together when he spoke of the bread of exorcism that should be given to catechumens in place of eucharistic bread.

Bread as a symbol has also had negative aspects. The good wife does not eat the "bread of idleness" (*Prv.* 31:27). The ungodly "eat the bread of wickedness" (*Prv.* 4:17). The "bread of deceit" has a sweet taste but leaves the mouth full of gravel (*Prv.* 20:17). Yahveh, when angry with his people, sends the "bread of adversity" (*Is.* 30:20) or the "bread of tears" (*Ps.* 80:5). These expressions evolved from a recollection of God's curse on Adam, who was to earn his bread by the sweat of his brow (*Gn.* 3:19).

[*See also* Leaven.]

BIBLIOGRAPHY

Borgen, Peder. *Bread from Heaven: An Exegetical Study of the Concept of Manna in the Gospel of John and the Writings of Philo.* Leiden, 1965. A careful study of John's sixth chapter in relation to Jewish concepts about the "bread from heaven."

Jacob, Heinrich E. *Six Thousand Years of Bread: Its Holy and Unholy History.* Garden City, N.Y., 1944. A popular history that should be used with caution.

JAMES E. LATHAM

BREATH AND BREATHING. The concept of breath figures prominently in the development of thought in many religions. Egyptian *ka,* Hebrew *nefesh* and *ruaḥ,* Greek *psuchē* and *pneuma,* Latin *anima* and *spiritus,* Sanskrit *prāṇa,* Chinese *ch'i,* Polynesian *mana,* and Iroquoian *orenda* all demonstrate that the theme of breath has had a major place in man's quest for religious understanding. Moreover, theological conceptions of breath have led many of the world's traditions to feature respiratory exercises in their religious disciplines, especially in Asia and among groups influenced directly or indirectly by practices from the Indian subcontinent.

Breath and the Religious Understanding of Man. The centrality of breath in defining man has focused on understanding what it is that gives man life and under what circumstances man defines his own death. Moreover, the theme of breath, along with related notions of vitality and energy, has been associated with views of the soul and with questions regarding the mortal and immortal aspects of human life.

Greek views. Although the theme of breath is seldom mentioned by Plato and Aristotle, some of their predecessors, for whom the universe was a quasi-living organism, saw air, wind, or breath as central to the definition of the soul. Pre-Socratic philosophers identified two qualities of the soul, movement and knowledge. Empedocles, for example, believed that because the soul knows all natural things, and because natural things can be analyzed into four constituent parts—fire, air, water, and earth—the soul must be made up of a combination of these four elements, together with the principles of love and strife.

Diogenes, taking up the position of the Ionians (one of whom, Anaximenes, described the soul as having an air-like nature that guides and controls the living being), credited air itself with sentience and intelligence. For Diogenes, air was the element most capable of originating movement, because it was the finest element in grain; in this characteristic, he thought, lay the grounds of the soul's own powers of knowing and of originating movement. Moreover, he stated, the internal air in the body had an important role in the functioning of each of the sense organs. Similarly, some of the Pythagoreans believed that the particles in the air, or the force that moved them, were soul, and Heraclitus declared that the soul as first principle was a "warm exhalation" of which everything else was composed.

Of the words Plato used for "soul," including *nous, sōma, psuchē,* and *genesis, psuchē* was the closest to a concept that incorporated breath. In Homer, *psuchē* refers to the life that is lost at death, as well as to the shade or wraith that lives on. Like the ancient Egyptian *ka* ("breath"), the "double" of man that was born with him but survived death and remained close to the tomb, the Homeric soul was an airy, ethereal entity identified with the breath of life. In Plato, however, *psuchē* designates a comprehensive personal soul, the divine aspect of man that is the seat of rational intelligence and moral choice, entirely separate from the body. Although, from the beginning of Greek philosophy, *psuchē* referred to the "life force" in all its psychosomatic connotations, it was not always related to breath *per se*. Because Greek philosophy placed such a premium on the intellectual life of the soul, the "breath of life" came to be relegated to a place of little stature.

Biblical views. In the Bible, the role of breath rests on several concepts: *ruaḥ, neshamah, nefesh, psuchē,* and *pneuma*. Of these, *nefesh* and *psuchē* refer specifically to the individual as the subject of life, while *ruaḥ* and *pneuma* refer to a more generic understanding of breath as a symbol of life and even as life itself.

The Hebrew term *ruaḥ* means "breath, wind," or "spirit." As a concept of nature, it refers to the winds of the four directions, as well as to the wind of heaven. For humans as a species, *ruaḥ* is a general principle, covering such things as the physical breath that issues from the mouth and nostrils, words carried forth on this breath, animated emotions (such as agitation, anger, vigor, courage, impatience, bitterness, troubled disposition, discontent, uncontrollable impulse, and jealousy), and, occasionally, mental activity and moral character. *Ruaḥ* is also the spirit in man that gives him life; because this spirit is created and preserved by God, it is thus understood to be God's spirit (the *ruaḥ elohim* of *Genesis* 1:2), which is breathed into man at the time of creation. Biblical literature sees evidence of God's spirit in such phenomena as prophecy (whereby human beings utter instructions or warnings), ecstatic states of frenzy and possession, and situations of authority through which divine wisdom is revealed.

The term *neshamah,* although used considerably less often than *ruaḥ,* nevertheless carries many of the same meanings: the breath of God as wind (hot, cold, life creating, or life destroying), the breath of man as breathed into him by God, and breath as found in every living thing.

The individual soul of man is usually designated by the term *nefesh*. From a root probably meaning "to breathe" (cf. Akkadian *napashu,* "expand"), *nefesh* occasionally designates the neck or throat (which opens for breathing), but is more often the concrete sign of life, the breathing substance, and then the soul or inner being, in man. Moreover, since the living are distinguished from the dead by breath, *nefesh* indicates the individual, the person or "I," which after death goes to She'ol. As the life force in individual beings, *nefesh* is mentioned in referring to both animals and humans, and is that which makes flesh alive. The relation between *neshama,* as "breath," and *nefesh,* denoting "person," is seen in *Genesis* 2:7: "Then the Lord God formed man of dust from the ground, and breathed into his nostrils the breath [*neshamah*] of life; and man became a living being [*nefesh*]." This belief in the unity of body and soul is continued from the biblical period into later Jewish philosophy.

Like *ruaḥ, pneuma* in the New Testament denotes "spirit," and it refers both to the Holy Spirit and the spirit of an individual person, as well as to the evil spirits or demons that are responsible for mental illness. Although it has the same psychosomatic implications as *ruaḥ,* its ties to the notion of breath are less obvious.

The New Testament term *psuchē,* on the other hand, although it continues to carry the old Greek sense of life force, corresponds more to the Hebrew notion of breath of life than it does to its use in Plato or the pre-Socratics. Like *nefesh, psuchē* is the individual soul, the "I" that feels, loves, and desires, and that lives only because it has been infused with breath. Nevertheless, under Greek influence, the *nefesh*-become-*psuchē* concept was gradually opposed to the mortal body and used to designate the immortal principle in man.

Breath is of little importance in later Christian investigations of the soul. Tertullian, however, relying on the Stoic tradition, emphasized the union of soul and body, and said that the soul is "born of the breath of God, immortal, corporeal, and representable"—though it was only Adam's soul that was created by God, as all others have come into being by an act of generation.

Islamic views. Arabic terms related to breath parallel the Hebrew. In pre-Qur'anic poetry, for example, *nafs* is the "self" or "person" and *rūḥ* is breath and wind. Beginning with the Qur'ān, *nafs* takes on the additional meaning of "soul," while *rūḥ* comes to refer to an angel, or heavenly messenger, or to a special divine quality. The two words are eventually synonymous in post-Qur'anic literature, where they refer equally to the human spirit, to angels, and to *jinn* (supernatural beings). The term *nafas,* "breath" and "wind," is cognate to *nafs* through its root and to *rūḥ* in some meanings. It first appears in Islamic literary history in the early poetry.

Classical Islamic philosophy gives a central role to breath in the perfection of man within the cosmos. According to Ibn Sīnā, God created the left side of the heart, the main organ of breathing, to be a source and storehouse for breath, which is the rallying point for the faculties of the soul and the conveyor of these faculties to various parts of the body. Breath begins as a divine emanation moving from potentiality to actuality, proceeding without interruption until each form is complete and perfect. There is one breath that acts as the origin of the others; this principal breath arises in the heart and moves throughout the body, giving its parts their proper temperament. It is identified with the force of life itself and is thus the link between the bodily and spiritual aspects of man's being. The principal breath of man, then, makes possible the perfect equilibrium and balance of the elements—a condition necessary for the manifestation of the divine.

Hindu views. The Sanskrit term *prāṇa* is a word of broad import that can refer to breath, respiration, life, vitality, wind, energy, and strength. In general, it is used in the plural to indicate the vital breaths in the body, but is also related to speculation about the individual soul. Early Indian literature proposed a variety of notions about the relation between man's breath *(prāṇa),* its natural correlate the atmospheric wind, and the cosmic order. The most important of these equated the atmospheric wind with the breath of Puruṣa, the cosmic man (*Ṛgveda* 10.90.13), who was, like the Egyptian god Amun, a deity manifest in the wind and, as breath, the mysterious source of life in men and animals.

Indian medical theory, the basis for *haṭhayoga,* identifies five *prāṇas* operative within the body: *prāṇa,* the "breath of the front," or thoracic breath, which ensures respiration and swallowing; *udāna,* the "breath that goes upward," which produces speech; *samāna,* "concentrated breath," which provides air to the internal "cooking" fire for digesting food; *apāna,* the "breath that goes downward," or abdominal breath, which controls the elimination of urine and feces; and *vyāna,* the "diffused breath," which circulates throughout the entire body and distributes the energy derived from food and breath. The general process of inhalation and exhalation is referred to by the compound *prāṇāpānau.*

In addition, there are five subsidiary "winds" or *vāyūs*: *nāga,* which relieves abdominal pressure through belching; *kūrma,* which controls the movements of the eyelids, thereby preventing foreign matter and bright light from entering the eyes; *kṛkara,* which controls sneezing and coughing, thereby preventing substances from passing up the nasal passages and down the throat; *devadatta,* which provides for the intake of extra oxygen into the tired body by causing a yawn; and *dhanaṃjaya,* which remains in the body after death, often bloating up the corpse.

There is some debate about the relation of yogic *prāṇa* to the cosmic forces in the universe. In modern literature on yoga, *prāṇa,* even in the compound *prāṇāyāma,* "the restraint of breath," is often interpreted as a subtle psychic force or cosmic element. This is not borne out by the early texts, however, and Patañjali, from whom we receive our first real exposure to yoga, uses the term *prāṇāyāma* to refer only to respiratory movements. Later *haṭhayoga* texts do use the word *prāṇa* to indicate a subtle psychic force, but this is the force awakened by the process of *prāṇāyāma* and not *prāṇāyāma* itself. [*See* Prāṇa.]

The Brāhmaṇas and Upaniṣads equate breath, as "vital breath," with the *ātman* or soul (cf. German *Atem,* "breath") and with *brahman,* the cosmic essence. The vital air in the upper part of the body is here thought to be immortal and to be the inspirer of thoughts. Moreover, it is by the breath of his mouth that Prajāpati created the gods and by the *prāṇa* of his lower body that he created the demons. Finally, in the Vedic sacrifice, bricks for the altar are sniffed by the sacrificial horse, who thereby bestows "breath" upon them—explained as a "sniff-kiss" in which the horse transfers beneficent power to ritual objects.

Chinese views. In ancient China, each person was thought to have two souls, both composed of very subtle matter: the *hun* ("air soul") came from the upper air and was received back into it at death, while the *p'o* ("earth soul") was generated by the earth below and sank back at the end to mingle with it. Of the two, it was the *hun* that was the object of ancestor worship. This two-part system corresponded to the *yin-yang* equilibrium, the *hun* soul being the *yang* aspect, in which the spiritual dominates, and the *p'o* being the *yin* aspect, in which the demonic dominates. In later tradition, the *hun* soul was thought to give rise to the seminal and mental essences, while the *p'o* was responsible for the existence of the flesh and bones of the body.

Breath and Religious Disciplines. Many of the major religious traditions are familiar with some type of respiratory practice. The oldest known and most comprehensive of these breathing disciplines is that of Hindu yoga, from which the disciplines of Jainism and Buddhism are derived. Some scholars have suggested that other traditions as well (particularly Taoism and Islam) have been influenced, at least in part, by Indian practices.

Hindu yoga. The Indian science of respiratory discipline, *prāṇāyāma,* fits within the larger complex of Hindu yoga, the most important type of which, for understanding breath control, is *haṭhayoga.* In general, yoga has as its goal the steady control of the senses and mind, leading to the abolition of normal consciousness and to freedom from delusion. *Prāṇāyāma,* the rhythmic control of the breath, is the fourth in the traditional eight states of yoga, coming after *āsana,* posture, and before *pratyāhāra,* withdrawal of the senses. Its main purpose is to change the ordinarily irregular flow of breath—which can be upset by indigestion, fever, cough, and cold, or by emotions like fear, anger, and lust—by bringing the breath under conscious control so that its rhythm becomes slow and even and respiratory effort is eliminated. By means of *prāṇāyāma* not only are the lungs cleansed and aerated, the blood oxygenated, and the nerves purified, but longevity as well as subtle states of consciousness leading to spiritual release are promoted. Although *prāṇāyāma* came to be a yogic exercise of great importance, Patañjali allots only three *sūtras* to it (1.34, 2.29, 2.49). The technical details for *prāṇāyāma* were then elaborated in the commentaries of Vyāsa, Bhoja, and Vācaspati Miśra, and especially in the classical works on *haṭhayoga*.

Although extraordinary feats resulting from respiratory discipline have been documented in numerous sources, including submersion in water or burial alive for unbelievable lengths of time, more frequent mention is made of the dangerous results of improper breathing. Practitioners are cautioned to undertake *prāṇāyāma* only under the instruction of a knowledgeable teacher, and to proceed with the exercises very slowly at first and according to their own capacity; otherwise they will incur disease or even death. By improper practice of *prāṇāyāma*, for example, a pupil can introduce disorders into his system, such as hiccups, wind, asthma, cough, catarrh, pains in the head, eyes, and ears, and severe nervous irritation; by proper practice, however, one is freed from these and most other diseases. The classic example of improper respiratory discipline is that of the nineteenth-century Hindu saint Ramakrishna. When he was young, Ramakrishna's practice of yoga almost always ended in blackout. He later developed bloodshot eyes, then bleeding of the gums, and finally the cancer of the throat from which he died. In this regard, the classical tradition holds that when *prāṇāyāma* is too intensive, that is, when the body becomes overloaded with *prāṇa*, colored flames dance before the eyes and blackout inevitably occurs.

The respiratory rhythm of *prāṇāyāma* is measured in units of time called *mātrāprāmāṇa*, one *mātrā* being the time necessary for one respiration. This rhythm is achieved by harmonizing the three basic activities of inhalation *(pūraka)*, retention of breath *(kumbhaka)*, and exhalation *(recaka)*. The most favored proportion of *pūraka* to *kumbhaka* to *recaka* is 1:4:2, although other traditions recommend 1:2:2 (for beginners) or an equal measure for all three parts. Still another tradition recommends that beginners not practice *kumbhaka* at all. Although this particular terminology is not used by either Patañjali or Vyāsa, it is traditional in *haṭhayoga* texts, where *kumbhaka* alone can sometimes refer to all three respiratory processes. A more detailed analysis describes two different states of "breath retention," *antara kumbhaka*, when breathing is suspended after full inspiration (the lungs being full), and *bāhya kumbhaka*, when breathing is suspended after full exhalation (the lungs being empty).

The technique of *prāṇāyāma* is thought to transform the natural processes already at work in the body. It is believed that every living creature breathes the prayer "So'ham" ("The immortal spirit, he am I") with each inward breath, and " 'Haṃsaḥ" ("I am he, the immortal Spirit") with each outgoing breath. This unconscious repetitive prayer goes on throughout life, and is to be brought into full consciousness through the discipline that begins with breathing.

Prāṇāyāma should be undertaken only when the third stage of yoga has been mastered, for it is only when correct posture has been achieved and complete relaxation has set in that breath can be made to flow freely. The student of *prāṇāyāma* should be sure that the bowels and bladder are empty, and especially that the stomach has little or no food in it when he or she begins the practice: for the physical culturist, *prāṇāyāma* should take place at least one half hour before the next meal and four and a half hours after the last; for the spiritual culturist, one meal a day is best, but at least six hours should have elapsed since the last meal was eaten. For serious students, *prāṇāyāma* should be practiced four times a day (early morning, noon, evening, and midnight), with a count of eighty cycles per sitting. The best seasons to begin are spring and fall, when the climate is equable, and the best place to practice is one that is well ventilated but without a strong draft. Traditionally *prāṇāyāma* was performed on a carpet of *kuśa* grass covered with a deer hide and then with a clean thick cloth, but current rules prescribe a folded blanket on the floor. The eyes should be fixed in a special gaze (usually directed ahead or at the tip of the nose), while the mind is passive but alert. The breathing itself is directed through the nostrils only, not through the mouth. Specific rules for *prāṇāyāma* differ according to the authority in question, but in most treatises, special respiratory rules are given for pregnant women and those just completing childbirth.

Breath is made to flow through the yogin's body by an elaborate system of controls designed to prevent internal damage: the *bandha*s are postures in which certain organs or parts of the body are contracted and controlled; the *nāḍī*s are tubular channels in the body through which the breath energy flows; and the *cakra*s are the flywheels controlling the body's machinery. The three most important *bandha*s are the *jālandhara bandha* ("chin lock"), whereby the chin is pressed against the chest and the abdomen is withdrawn; the *uḍḍīyāna bandha* ("raising of the diaphragm"), whereby the diaphragm is pulled up and the abdominal organs are brought against the back and held toward the spine; and the *mūla bandha* ("anal contraction"), whereby the sphincter muscle is tightened. These postures affect what most authorities believe are the seventy-two thousand *nāḍī*s, along which the breath or life current flows to all parts of the body. Some *nāḍī*s are more important than others, the single most important being the *suṣumnā*, identified with the spinal cord. The breath energy flowing through the *nāḍīs* is then regulated by the *cakras*, control points placed at crucial locations in the body.

Respiratory discipline is central in bringing about the unification of consciousness, the goal of yoga. From an early period, mind and breath were held to be intimately connected, and the arousal or cessation of one was known to affect the other. Patañjali, for example, recommended *prāṇāyāma* for achieving equanimity and inner peace, and Bhoja noted that through the suspension of sense activity, breath control could bring about single-pointed concentration (the fifth stage of yoga, *pratyāhāra*). The classical image used here is that of the chariot, according to which the mind is a chariot yoked to a pair of powerful horses, one of which is breath *(prāṇa)*, the other, desire. The chariot moves in the direction of the more powerful animal; if breath prevails, desires are controlled, but if desires prevail, breath becomes irregular. Through *prāṇāyāma*, which ensures the controlled progress of the chariot, the advanced yogin can penetrate the four basic structures of consciousness—waking, sleeping with dreams, sleeping without dreams, and the *turīya* state—thereby unifying all four within himself. [*See* Yoga.]

With the development of Tantrism, the yogic disciplines of posture and breath control were combined with sexual practices that served to unite the practitioner with cosmic energy or *śakti*, as symbolized by the great goddess. According to Tantric texts, the object of *prāṇāyāma* is to arouse *kuṇḍalinī*, the divine cosmic force in the body, symbolized by a coiled and sleeping serpent that lies dormant in the lowest nerve center *(cakra)* at the base of the spinal column. Once aroused by *prāṇāyāma*, this energy rises up through the spinal column, piercing each *cakra* on its way until it reaches the head and there unites with the supreme soul. [*See* Tantrism.]

Buddhist meditation. For Theravāda Buddhists, respiratory discipline is counted as part of the contemplation of the body—*ānapānasati* ("mindfulness of breathing"). The Pali canon describes the meditation as "mindfully he breathes in, mindfully he breathes out," and then enumerates sixteen ways in which mindful breathing can be practiced. The work begins with developing an awareness of "breathing in a long breath, breathing out a long breath, breathing in a short breath, breathing out a short breath," and continues through the practices until discursive thinking has been cut off and full concentration attained. Unlike yogic breathing techniques, however, Buddhist mindfulness of breath does not hold or control the breath but lets it come and go naturally, with the goal only to become fully aware of all states of the breathing process.

In Tibetan Buddhism, breathing is a part of the complex process of visualization by which a deity is mentally created in front of the practitioner out of his internal psychic elements. Tibetan Buddhists believe that breath or vitality in the body enters not only through the nose but also through the eyes, ears, mouth, navel, male or female organ, anus, and head and body hair pores. Since these "winds" act as a mount or basis for consciousness, the mind's scattering is stopped when they are restrained. Visualization, therefore, can proceed only when vitality (or breath) and exertion (or distraction) have been controlled. To achieve the mental stability needed for visualization, the meditator is advised to practice "wind yoga," that is, to hold his breath—"hold the wind"—while simultaneously holding his mind on the divine body that is the object of meditation. When he can no longer retain the breath, he should let it out gently, see himself clarified as the deity, and then hold his breathing again, keeping in mind, as before, one aspect of the deity. It is only when the mind is thus stabilized that the divine body will appear.

Taoist yoga. In China, breathing exercises go back to an early period. Lao-tzu and Chuang-tzu were familiar with a "methodical breathing," and a Chou dynasty inscription, dating from as early as the sixth century BCE, prescribes a precise collection and circulation of the breath inside the body that is designed to achieve long life. Also known were archaic shamanic techniques that imitated the movements and breathing of animals—a practice reflected later in the Taoist notion that the deep and silent breathing of ecstasy is like the breathing of animals in hibernation.

Unlike the many alchemical practices of Chinese tradition, which use aphrodisiacs to restore sexual activity, Taoist yoga aims primarily at restraining and rechanneling the sexual urges of the body. Through the regulation of breathing and other yogic techniques, the practitioner learns to sublimate the generative force that produces sexual fluid, and to prevent this fluid from following its normal course of satisfying desires and producing offspring. The correct method of breathing is essential in Taoist yoga, for it serves to circulate an inner fire through a microcosmic orbit and so immobilize the generative force, causing the genital organ to retract and stopping the drain of vitality caused by the emission of semen.

The ultimate purpose of stemming the generative force is to obtain *ch'ang sheng* ("long life"), a state understood as a material immortality of the body. The practitioner begins by holding the breath through a period of 3, 5, 7, 9, and 12 normal respirations, then up to

120 or even more. To attain immortality, however, one must hold the breath through 1,000 respirations. The practitioner will, in the end, enter a state of serenity characterized by the qualities of *nien chu* ("thoughtlessness"), *hsi chu* ("breathlessness"), *mo chu* ("pulselessness"), and *mieh chin* ("unmindfulness of worldly existence").

Taoist respiratory disciplines are not, like *prāṇāyāma,* preliminary or auxiliary exercises in meditation to prepare the yogin for spiritual concentration but, rather, techniques that actually accomplish the purpose of the yoga itself: the indefinite prolongation of bodily life. The question whether there may be a historical relation between Taoist and Indian practices has not been resolved. Some scholars believe that Neo-Taoism borrowed from Tantric yoga practices. Others have noted that Taoism must have taken the notion of a physiological role of breath from India, for ancient Chinese medicine—Taoism's most likely source—had no such notion. Whatever the case, the results of both yogas are, in some instances, very similar, for the Taoist's ability to enter the water without drowning or walk on fire without being burned resemble Indian yogic powers or *siddhis*.

The aim of the breathing exercises is to try to return to the type of breathing experienced by the embryo in the womb; when the umbilical cord was cut at birth, this initial type of breathing was replaced by breathing through the nostrils. During the practice, inspiration and expiration are kept as quiet as possible, and breath is held closed up in the body—"swallowed," some texts say—until it is intolerable, and then let out through the mouth. "Embryonic breathing" or "immortal breathing" is thus a restoration of profound fetal breathing; it wipes out all postnatal conditions so that prenatal vitality can be transmuted and the seed of immortality nurtured. As a stage in the quest for immortal breath, the embryonic breathing of Taoism is not merely a checking of respiration, but an internal circulation of vital principles whereby the individual can remain completely airtight. If, however, breathing through the nostrils and mouth is used (and used randomly) in advanced stages of this yoga, then the psychic center in the heart will burst and the practitioner will become deranged.

Central to the yogic endeavor of Taoism is the theory of the five vital breaths located in the heart, spleen, lungs, liver, and kidneys that keep these organs functioning, and without which the body perishes. These vitalities have their source in the brain, and when they converge again in the head into one vitality, a golden light is made manifest. This system of vital breaths is held to correspond to the interaction in the body of the five basic elements: heart (fire), spleen or stomach (earth), lungs (metal), liver (wood), and kidneys (water).

The vital breaths are linked to one another by a network of eight main psychic channels that, when clear, have two distinct roles: the unimpeded flow of the generative force and the unrestricted circulation of the vital breaths. This network contains a microcosmic orbit with four cardinal points: at the root of the penis, where the generative force is gathered; at the top of the head; and at the two points between them in the spine and in the front of the body, where the generative force is cleansed and purified during the microcosmic orbiting.

Dysfunctional breathing in Taoism is designated by the "nine unsettled breaths." They are caused by anger, which lifts the breath, and fear, which lowers it; joy, which slows it down; grief, which disperses it; terror, which throws it out of gear; thinking, which ties it up; toil, which wastes it; cold, which collects it; and heat, which scatters it.

Islamic prayer. The Muslims belonging to the school of Ibn al-ʿArabī practiced a technique comparable to the *prāṇāyāma* of Hinduism. In breathing out, the words *lā ilāha* ("There is no god") are formed, while the inward breath coincides with the words *illā Allāh* ("but God"), resulting in a profession of faith. Breath control is practiced by Islamic mystics in *dhikr* ("remembrance"), a practice dedicated to the glorification of God that repeats certain fixed phrases in a ritual order, either out loud or in the mind, and is accompanied by certain breathing and physical movements. Although it is not known exactly when methods of breath control (*ḥabs-i dam,* "keeping one's breath in recollection") were adopted into Sufism, there is a twelfth-century text prescribing the following: the breath is "emitted above the left breast (to empty the heart); then the word *lā* is exhaled from the navel (against the sexual demon); then *ilāha* is uttered on the right shoulder, and *illā* at the navel; finally *Allāh* is strongly articulated in the empty heart."

For the Ṣūfī, every breath that goes out without remembering God is "dead," while every breath that goes out in recollection of the Lord is "alive" and connected with him. In *dhikr* one is enjoined not to speak much but rather, in a variant form of the above text, to say, three times in one breath, "Lā ilāha illā Allāh" from the right side and then, having brought the breath down to the heart, to bring forth "Muḥammad rasūl Allāh" from the left side. The importance of breath regulation in *dhikr* to the advanced Ṣūfī is seen in the following example from Pashto poetry: "Thy every breath is a pearl and a coral of inestimable price / Be careful, therefore, and guard every respiration well!" Directions are given in various texts for the exact count and duration of the respiratory cycle in *dhikr,* and some sources state that the experienced mystic is often able to hold his breath for almost three hours. *Dhikr* is also used for healing purposes. Even today the recitation of the *Fātiḥah* or some other prayer, together with a "breathing upon" the sick, is common in the Muslim world.

The extent to which the breath control used by Ṣūfīs in their *dhikr* developed under the influence of Indian practices is not certain. We know that regulated breathing existed among the Ṣūfīs of eastern Iran before Sufism spread to India, but in the later period when there was contact with India, yogic practices undoubtedly further colored numerous aspects of Ṣūfī life.

Christian prayer. Respiratory techniques similar to those used in Hindu yoga can be found in the Christian tradition of hesychasm. Hesychasm is a type of prayer in Eastern Christianity based on a control of physical faculties and a concentration on the Jesus Prayer to achieve peace of soul and union with God. Although the earliest descriptions of the hesychastic method of contemplation go back at least to the fifth century, to John of Jerusalem, the earliest datable combination of the Jesus Prayer with respiratory techniques is in the writings of Nikephoros the Solitary (fl. 1260). Nikephoros writes: "Sit down, compose your mind, introduce it—your mind, I say—into your nostrils; this is the road that the breath takes to reach the heart. Push it, force it to descend into your heart at the same time as the inhaled air. When it is there, you will see what joy will follow."

The traditional breath control that begins hesychastic contemplation is used, like *prāṇāyāma,* to prepare for mental prayer, that is, to bring about a "return of the mind." In a quiet cell, with the door closed, one sits in the corner and presses the (bearded) chin against the upper part of the chest, much as in the *jālandhara bandha* of Hindu yoga. One then directs the eye—and with it all the mind—to the navel, and compresses the inspiration of air in the nose so that normal breathing does not come easily, all the while ceaselessly repeating the Jesus Prayer: "Lord Jesus Christ, Son of God, have mercy on me!" This exercise prepares one for the attainment of absolute quietude of the soul and for the experience of divine light.

[*See also* Life *and* Inspiration.]

BIBLIOGRAPHY

Good summaries of the role of breath in biblical theology can be found in *The Interpreter's Dictionary of the Bible,* 4 vols., edited by George A. Buttrick (New York, 1962), under such headings as "man," "soul," and "spirit." Likewise, important discussions of breath and the soul in Christian and Jewish theology appear in the *New Catholic Encyclopedia,* 17 vols. (New York, 1967), and in the *Encyclopaedia Judaica,* 16 vols. (Jerusalem, 1971). David B. Claus's *Toward the Soul: An Inquiry into the Meaning of* ψυχή *before Plato* (New Haven, 1981) is an important, but often very technical, survey of the development of the concept "psyche" in pre-Socratic thought. Jean Gouillard's *Petite Philocalie de la prière du cœur* (Paris, 1953), on the tradition of hesychasm, has a good bibliography and an excellent sampling of textual translations. On the respiratory technique in Islamic *dhikr,* see Louis Gardet's "La mention du nom divin, *dhikr,* dans la mystique musulmane," *Revue Thomiste* (Paris) 52 (1952): 642–679 and 53 (1953): 197–216.

The best book on *haṭhayoga* is B. K. S. Iyengar's *Light on Yoga (Yoga Dīpikā)* (New York, 1966). It has an excellent introduction and detailed yet accessible sections on *prāṇāyāma.* Svāmī Kuvalayānanda's *Prāṇāyāma,* 4th ed. (Bombay, 1966), is a comprehensive handbook on the breathing process and respiratory technique in Hinduism. Kuvalayānanda's work also appears in the quarterly journal *Yoga-Mīmāṁsā* (Lonavla, Poona District, India, 1924–), which contains vast scientific information on actual laboratory and clinical experiments done on yogic breathing. Hans-Ulrich Rieker's excellent translation of the *Haṭhayogapradīpikā* called *The Yoga of Light,* translated from the German by Elsy Becherer (New York, 1971), describes the combination of the two yogic paths *haṭha* and *rāja,* and makes special reference to the arousal and control of the *kuṇḍalinī.* Mircea Eliade's *Patañjali and Yoga* (New York, 1969) and *Yoga: Immortality and Freedom,* 2d ed. (Princeton, 1969), contain excellent summaries of respiratory techniques in various traditions, as well as abundant bibliographic references. Finally, for those who may wish to go directly to the source, Georg Feuerstein's recent translation of *The Yoga-Sūtras of Patañjali* (Folkestone, England, 1979) has an exceedingly helpful commentary.

A good introduction to breathing and mindfulness meditation in Buddhism is Bhikkhu Khantipālo's *Calm and Insight: A Buddhist Manual for Meditators* (London, 1981). For a basic sourcebook on breathing in Taoist yoga, see *Taoist Yoga, Alchemy, and Immortality,* translated by Charles Luk (K'uan Yü Lu) (London, 1970); the classic article on the topic is, of course, Henri Maspero's "Les procédés de 'nourrir le principe vital' dans la religion taoïste ancienne," *Journal asiatique* 229 (1937): 177–252, 353–430.

Ellison Banks Findly

BRELICH, ANGELO (1913–1977), Italian historian of religions. After completing his academic studies in Hungary under Károly Kerényi and Andreas Alföldi, Brelich became the assistant to the chair of history of religions at the University of Rome, a chair then held by Raffaele Pettazzoni, whom he succeeded as professor ordinarius in 1958. His first publication, *Aspetti della morte nelle iscrizioni sepolcrali nell'Impero romano* (Aspects of Death in the Sepulchral Inscriptions of the Roman Empire; 1937), was based upon a thorough exploration of the *Corpus inscriptionum Latinarum* and anticipated Brelich's future interest in methodological reflection. There followed in 1949 *Die geheime Schutzgottheit von Rom* (The Secret Protecting Deity of Rome) and *Vesta,* which show the strong influence of his teacher Kerényi and bear witness to Brelich's own search for scientific originality. In these two books, which were conceived as a unit, Brelich distinguishes between "analytical research," aimed at delineating the fundamental elements of themes present in a divine figure, and "historical research," which is concerned with the figure's specific content and further developments.

A new period in Brelich's studies began in the 1950s. *Tre variazioni romane sul tema delle origini* (Three Roman Variations on the Theme of Origins; 1955) emphasizes the theme of historical creativity. Unlike the evolutionist notion of survival (i.e., the notion of vestigial cultural elements surviving merely as erratic blocks in the living stream of more recent cultural formations), Brelich's notion of historical creativity implies the validation of elements already found within different mythological and religious horizons on the part of new, emerging cultural-historical settings. Brelich also makes use of a basic opposition between primordial chaos or "non-order" and the order that results from the organization of the cosmos. These methodological principles recur in the volume *Gli eroi greci* (The Greek Heroes; 1958), where Brelich advocates the inclusion of the study of the religions of the classical world within the problematic of the history of religions. In the same book, Brelich also reflects on the type of the hero, especially as the object of a funerary cult and in its connection with cosmogonic themes. He was later to alter those views expressed here, however, because of the radicalization of his analytic hermeneutics.

During this period Brelich became deeply interested in polytheism, which had been a rather neglected topic in the field of comparative, cultural-historical studies. He saw in polytheism a religious phenomenon typical of the archaic "high cultures" such as were found in Japan, India, Mesopotamia, Egypt, and Greece, as well as in Central America and Peru. He believed that the polytheistic conception of "god" or deity was to be distinguished from both the ghosts of animism and the *dei otiosi* ("idle gods") of some nonliterate cultures. Polytheism for Brelich is a *sui generis* phenomenon and the proper object of historical research aimed at discovering its structure and *raison d'être* in the religious history of mankind.

Guerre, agoni, e culti nella Grecia arcaica (Wars, Ritual Competitions, and Cults in Archaic Greece; 1961) marked Brelich's growing interest in initiatory institutions. These institutions are central to his *Paides e Parthenoi* (1969), which is a study of the way in which tribal initiation rites were adapted to use in the Greek polis once their original purpose had been lost. Here again we see Brelich's interest in historical creativity. He showed less interest in soteriological and eschatological aspects of these institutions.

Brelich left unfinished a complex history of the cult of Jupiter, a history that was to trace Jupiter's development from the status of an Indo-European prepolytheistic heavenly being to that of the head of an entire pantheon, noting especially the political implications of this development. As for his view of religion as a general phenomenon, Brelich's introduction to Henri-Charles Puech's *Histoire des religions* (1970) seems to indicate that he accepted functionalist explanations.

BIBLIOGRAPHY

A notable work by Brelich not mentioned in the text is his posthumously published *Storia delle religioni: Perche?* (Naples, 1979). Two memorial volumes for Brelich have appeared. They are *Perennitas: Studi in onore di Angelo Brelich,* edited by Giulia Piccaluga (Rome, 1980), and *Religioni e civiltà: Scritti in memoria di Angelo Brelich* (Bari, 1982).

UGO BIANCHI

BRETHREN OF PURITY. *See* Ikhwān al-Ṣafā'.

BREUIL, HENRI (1877–1961), French scholar of prehistoric man. Henri-Édouard-Prosper Breuil was born in Mortain, Manche. As a youth, he developed an interest in natural history and the history of early man, which he pursued during his years at the seminary of Issy. Ordained a priest in 1900, he devoted the rest of his scholarly life to human paleontology. Breuil was introduced to Paleolithic studies by Émile Cartailhac, with whom in October 1902 he opened the Altamira cave in Spain, and his studies of Paleolithic art and artifacts were furthered by Édouard Iette and Joseph-Louis Capitan. In these early stages, Breuil's work was actively supported by Prince Albert of Monaco.

After having taught from 1905 to 1910 at the University of Fribourg, Breuil became professor of prehistoric ethnography at the Institut de Paléontologie Humaine in Paris. From 1929 to 1947 he served as professor of prehistory at the Collège de France. During his career, Breuil taught also in Lisbon (1941–1942) and Johannesburg (1942–1945). He traveled extensively in Europe and southern Africa, and even journeyed to China, searching for survivals of Paleolithic man.

Through his global studies of Paleolithic cave art and the tools and techniques of Paleolithic craftsmen, Breuil greatly increased our knowledge of the conditions of life and the creative work of Paleolithic man. He drew attention, for example, to the religious aspects (i.e., the symbolic and possible ritual functions) of paintings such as that of "the Sorcerer" in the cave of Les Trois Frères, discovered in 1916 in southern France. He was also interested in the religious meaning of funerary practices and their hieratic manifestations, to which he ascribed a common origin. Breuil gave the first scholarly description of the famous caves of Lascaux (1940). In his thinking about human evolution (and the evidences for such evolution that he found in humanity's early religious history), Breuil envisaged a developing cosmic order moved by energy. Pierre Teilhard de Chardin, who for some time was associated with Breuil, developed these ideas more systematically.

BIBLIOGRAPHY

Most of Breuil's publications are descriptions of the more than eighty painted caves he studied in France and Spain and the hundreds of rock paintings he investigated in Spain, Ethiopia, and southern Africa. An excellent example of these descriptions is his *Les peintures rupestres schématiques de la Péninsule ibérique,* 4 vols. (Lagny-sur-Marne, 1932–1935). Breuil's more extensive works, done in collaboration with other scholars, include *Afrique* (Paris, 1931), which Breuil edited with Leo Frobenius and which contains Breuil's essay "L'Afrique préhistorique" (pp. 60–119), and *Les hommes de la pierre ancienne* (Paris, 1951). A significant example of Breuil's works on the religion of early man is his piece "Pratique religeuses chez les humanités quaternaires, " in *Scienza e civiltà* (Rome, 1951), pp. 47–73. Among Breuil's books that have been translated into English, the following should be mentioned: *Rock Paintings of Southern Andalusia,* written with M. C. Burkitt and Montagu Pollock (Oxford, 1929); *The Cave of Altamira at Santillana de Mar,* written with Hugo Obermaier (Madrid, 1935); *Beyond the Bounds of History: Scenes of the Old Stone Age* (London, 1949); and *Four Hundred Centuries of Cave Art* (Montignac, 1952). A bibliography of Breuil's writings is contained in *Hommage à l'abbé Henri Breuil pour son quatre-vingtième anniversaire,* compiled by G. Henri-Martin (Paris, 1957).

Publications on Breuil's life and work include "Recollections of the Abbé Breuil" by Mary Boyle and others, *Antiquity* 37 (1963): 12–19; Alan H. Brodrick's *The Abbé Breuil: Prehistorian* (London, 1963); and Nicolas Skrotzky's *L'abbé Breuil* (Paris, 1964).

JACQUES WAARDENBURG

BRIDGES. All over the world, in different religions and cultures, there are vivid descriptions of a perilous way that the dreamer, the ecstatic visionary, or the deceased has to follow on his journey to the otherworld. One of the perils may be a bridge leading across a chasm, a rapacious stream, or the void. Success in crossing the bridge may depend on the traveler's own behavior during life or on the sacrifices he or his surviving relatives have performed. Ethical qualifications are not always needed.

Parallel with these eschatological ideas, actual bridge-building on earth has been connected with sacrifices and with religious, folkloric, and magical conceptions. At times, the construction of a tangible bridge—whether for day-to-day use or for ritual use only—is related to the soul's passage to the afterlife. Finally, the bridge in itself has often been a very useful symbol to signify the transcendence of the border between two realms or the ascension from a lower to a higher dominion.

History. One of the striking characteristics of the bridge as symbol is its universality among traditions from all over the world.

Indo-Iranian religions. In the Hindu religion, from the *Ṛgveda* (9.41.2) onward, the bridge occurs as a link between earth and heaven, the world of illusion *(māyā)* and reality. The sacrifice terminology and the lofty speculations of the Upaniṣads use it in a figurative rather than a literal sense, though the popular imagination might suppose the latter to be the case. Just as the gods enter the heavenly world by means of the "southern fires" (*dakṣiṇās*) in the Agnicayana ritual, using them as steps and ladders, so the sacrificer "crosses a bridge and enters into the world of heaven" (*Yajurveda, Kāṭhakam* 28.4). It is necessary to make a ladder or a bridge with sacrificial gifts in order to ascend into that heavenly realm.

On the other hand, this luminous *brahman* world is attained by recognition of *ātman,* the spiritual reality. To the extent that this universal self is conceived of as a person, God himself is called "the highest bridge to immortality" (*Svetāśvatara Upaniṣad* 6.19). That bridge, God, in itself is not ethical, but all evil is excluded from the *brahman* world: "Therefore, if a blind man goes over the bridge he receives his sight, if a wounded man, he is cured; therefore, if the night crosses the bridge, it is turned to day" (*Chāndogya Upaniṣad* 8.4.1).

According to Herman Lommel (1930, pp. 264ff.), the greatest significance of the ancient Indian bridge is that it holds two worlds, heaven and earth, apart. But, speaking of the Nāciketas fire—"the bridge of the sacrificers to that eternal highest *brahman*"—Lommel does not mention some later lines where the road is described as the "sharp edge of a razor, difficult to pass over" (*Kāṭhaka Upaniṣad* 3.14). The bridge, however, is not explicitly mentioned in this connection.

If we compare the Indian and Iranian sources, we find common as well as differing conceptions of the bridge and of the whole structure of ideas to which it belongs. The paradisiacal delights of the virtuous are pictured in a very concrete way in *Kauśītaki Upaniṣad* 1.4: "Five hundred nymphs [*Apsaras*] go to meet him, one hundred with fruit in their hands, one hundred with ointment in their hands, one hundred with wreaths, one hundred with raiment, one hundred with fragrant powder in their hands" (Lommel, p. 270).

Space does not allow a thorough account here of the Iranian sources with their various chronologies, varying content, and difficulties of philological interpretation (cf. Lommel, pp. 263ff., with Nyberg, 1966, pp. 180ff.). Some general ideas may be summarized, however, with the help of a present-day specialist.

In ancient Iran, the ceremonies of the first three days after death were regarded as very important for the soul of the dead person. It had to be protected against evil powers and had to be strengthened before the dangerous journey to the otherworld. Originally, at least, princes, warriors, and priests might hope to come to a luminous paradise with all its delights. The "crossing of the Separator" (Av., Chinvatō Peretu) was imagined as passing over a bridge that began on top of Mount Harā and ended on the road to Heaven. Only worthy souls, perhaps those who had given rich offerings, could reach the heavenly way; the others fell down into the subterranean Hell (Boyce, 1979, pp. 13ff.).

Zarathushtra taught that everyone had the possibility of gaining Paradise and that the successful passing of the bridge depended on the moral qualities of the departed, not on social rank or costly sacrifices. Three godly judges weigh the soul's good and bad thoughts, words, and deeds. If the good are heavier, the bridge is made broader, and the soul can pass, accompanied by a beautiful maiden, Daēnā, its own heavenly double or good conscience. Otherwise, the bridge gets as narrow as a blade edge, and the soul is propelled into the place of torment by an ugly hag (Boyce, 1979, p. 27). The classical sources of this short abstract are the ritual law contained in the Younger Avesta, *Vendidad* 19.28–32, combined with the fragment of the *Hadhōkht Nask* belonging to the same canon, composed in pre-Christian times and supplemented with later Pahlavi literature, from the ninth century CE (*Mēnōg ī Khrad* 2; *Bundahishn* 30), as quoted in detail by Nyberg (pp. 180ff.; cf. Duchesne-Guillemin, 1973, pp. 333f.).

Judaism and Islam. Probably through Iranian influence, a similar conception appears in Judaism. It has been mistakenly cited as existing in the Jewish apocalypse of Ezra (*2 Esdras* 7:8ff., end of first century CE). There, according to Silverstein (1952, pp. 95f.), the bridge, whose width accommodates only a single person's feet, becomes broader when the righteous cross it and narrower for the sinners. But this passage actually refers to two different ways (not bridges), one belonging to this earthly world, the other to the heavenly one. The ordeal of crossing the bridge over the Valley of Jehoshaphat, which according to Jewish eschatology occurs in the Last Judgment, is of a later date.

The corresponding eschatological ideas in Islam also seem to be dependent on Iranian tradition, perhaps with a Jewish intermediary. The Islamic name of this bridge is Ṣirāṭ, which simply means "way." Thus it has been possible to discover the bridge in Qur'anic passages concerning the afterlife that refer only to a way (36:66, 37:23f.). But the later tradition *(ḥadīth)* describes a real bridge, "thinner than a hair and sharper than the edge of a sword," which leads the dead over Hell's uppermost part, Jahannam. Out of compassion or in recognition of the good deeds of the person concerned, God makes it possible for believers to pass over the bridge. The just and those who have received forgiveness come over without mishap, while sinful Muslims plunge down into Hell and remain there for a limited time in a sort of purgatory. Unbelievers, however, remain in those portions that function as places of punishment. Gabriel stands before the bridge and Michael upon it; they question those who pass over about the lives they have led (Gardet, 1968, p. 87).

According to a tradition that goes back to Ibn Mas'ūd, everyone must cross the bridge. In accordance with their works, they do it more swiftly or more slowly: as the wind, as a bird, as a fine horse or a camel, as a running man, or as a man walking only on the big toes of his feet, who is immediately shaken off into the fire by the sharp, slippery bridge bristling with barbs. In his passage, the walker is also attacked by angels with fiery pitchforks (Jeffery, 1962, p. 247). The bridge may be arched, ascending for a thousand years, running level for a thousand, and descending for a thousand years. In this tradition, the gate of Paradise is opened only if the deceased gives the right answers. Then he is accompanied over the now soft and level bridge by an angel (Coomaraswamy, 1944/1945, p. 203, with references).

Christianity. In the literature of classical antiquity and in the Bible, no soul-bridge is known. But the classical writer of the Syrian church, Ephraem (fourth century), speaks of the cross of Christ as a bridge leading over the terrible abyss with its menacing fire. This river or sea of fire as an obstacle on the journey of the soul can be transcended in other ways, too; the righteous may even pass through it without being damaged. Because of their vividly striking descriptions, it is sometimes difficult to say whether these passages are to be taken literally or figuratively (Edsman, 1940, pp. 121ff.; cf. pp. 52ff.).

In medieval Russian spiritual songs, which represent popular religion, the language is very realistic (Edsman, 1959, pp. 106ff.). In medieval times, the world of folk imagery knew well the perilous bridge. It also has a place in the literature of Christian visionaries, with its roots in the ancient church's rich outpouring of apocalyptic descriptions of the hereafter. To a great extent, these descriptions are found in the extracanonical apocrypha; these, in turn, are descended from Judaism and Iran.

However, the classic Christian image of a bridge, which has been very influential throughout history, is contained in the *Dialogues* of Gregory I (c. 540–604). The framework is the same as in the famous vision of Er in the last book of Plato's *Republic:* one who seems to be dead revives and tells those around him what he has experienced. In Gregory's story, it is a certain soldier who tells of a bridge under which a dark and stinking river runs, but that leads to the heavenly green meadows and shining mansions inhabited by men in white clothes. Any wicked person who tries to go over the bridge tumbles down into the river, whereas the righteous pass safely across. The soldier also saw a fight between angels and demons over a person who had slipped on the bridge so that half his body was hanging over the edge (*Dialogues* 4.36). As Howard Rollin Patch (1950, pp. 95f.) points out, Gregory quotes *Matthew* 7:14 as part of his interpretation: "For very narrow is the path which leads to life." This quotation, in turn, demonstrates the technique of combining biblical and extrabiblical source material.

The bridge motif occurs in many different categories of medieval literature and belongs to Celtic and Germanic mythology also (Patch, 1950; Dinzelbacher, 1973). It can have greater or lesser importance in the Christian representations of the general topography of the otherworld, where the account of the soul's union with the Savior on the other shore may outweigh the description of the horrors on the way (Dinzelbacher, 1978). Moreover, the eschatological ideas were combined with the practical construction of a bridge; this was considered a pious work that was also helpful for the future fate of the builder. Frequently, a bridge had its own chapel for prayers and often its own hospital. Papal and episcopal indulgences encouraged such construction. Consequently, legacies became common, and bridge-building brotherhoods were founded beginning at the end of the twelfth century (Knight, 1911, p. 856; Boyer, 1967, p. 798).

Buddhism. That the soul-bridge also turns up in Buddhism is hardly surprising, since Buddhism is a daughter religion of Hinduism. As conceptions of an afterlife influenced by Islam can be found in the great stretches of Central Asia into which the Muslim religion has penetrated (Paulson, 1964, 152f.; cf. Eliade, 1964, pp. 482ff.), so a corresponding eschatology has followed Buddhism into East Asia. But here a new feature is observed. Even though people have tried in various ways in the different religions to affect the fate of deceased persons (for example, during the Christian Middle Ages, by accomplishing the actual construction of a bridge as a spirit-gift for the deceased), it is only in "northern" Buddhism that there is found a comprehensive symbolic bridge-building ceremony combined with the funeral. One of the classical Sinologists, J. J. M. de Groot, has written in careful detail about the Buddhist rites for the dead in Amoy, which lies in Fukien opposite Taiwan (1885, pp. 97ff.). According to de Groot, the bridge ceremony that takes place in connection with these rites is based on a quotation from a relatively late description of Hell. According to the latter, no less than six bridges of different materials lead from the underworld to the world of rebirth. There, the souls are sorted out, and their impending fates in the six different forms of existence are decided in detail.

The rites for the dead are intended to help the souls over some of these bridges. If a deceased person has not completely atoned for his crimes by enduring the torments of Hell or has not, through the actions of clergy, been freed from his remaining punishment, he has to plunge down into the pit, which is filled with snakes and writhing monsters. Therefore, in the room where the rites for the dead are being carried out, the priests build a temporary bridge out of boards that are laid upon chairs or out of a long bench without a back. The soul-bridge is also provided with railings of bamboo and cloth or paper, sometimes even with an overhead canopy. As soon as the ceremony, which is called "the beating of Hell," is completed, they undertake "the crossing of the bridge." The happy completion of this is reported to the powers of the underworld, so that they will not be able to hinder the soul in its progress.

Just as the variations in such rituals are numerous, the afterlife concepts that lie behind them also change. Thus, Nai-ho Bridge ("the bridge without return") is also found in the popular color illustrations that the Jesuit father Henri Doré reproduced in his instructive and comprehensive work on what he calls "superstitions" in China (1914, pp. 194f., fig. 52). The text quoted by Doré describes the picture exactly: souls receive the wine of forgetfulness from the ten underworld judges before they continue to what is also called the Bridge of Pain, which goes over a red foaming stream in a hilly region. When the souls have read a text on the conditions of existence, they are seized by two devils, Short Life and Quick Death, who hurl them into the stream. They are swept out through the stream into new existences to live as men, four-footed animals, birds, fish, insects, or worms. As late as after World War II such ceremonies were carried out both in mainland China (Hsu, 1948, p. 165) and on Taiwan.

Ritual Sacrifices. The Latin word *pontifex* is composed of the noun *pons* and the verb *facere,* and it signifies "he who makes or builds bridges." One cannot prove historically that the incumbents of this ancient Roman office literally had such a function. [*See* Pontifex.] However, the etymology, which existed as early as the Roman librarian and scholar Varro (116–27 BCE), is disputed both in antiquity and among modern researchers. Evidently an old Indo-European meaning is hidden in *pons,* giving it the sense of a "path" or "way," not necessarily over a river (Szemler, 1978, cols. 334ff.).

Discussing the various interpretations of the term *pontifices* and rejecting that of "bridge builders," the Greek writer Plutarch (b. 46?–d. around 119 CE) gives us the arguments of those who defend that theory: the name refers to the sacrifices performed at the very ancient and sacred bridge Pons Sublicius over the Tiber, which were necessary to prevent a sacrilegious demolition of the entirely wooden construction (*Numa* 9.2). The Roman poet Ovid (43 BCE–17 CE) makes reference to this ceremony, at which the Roman high priest, *pontifex maximus,* officiated together with the first Vestal: "Then, too, the Virgin is wont to throw the rush-made effigies of ancient men from the oaken bridge" (*Fasti* 5. 621f.). This ancient festival in the middle of May is also mentioned by another historian, Dionysius of Halicarnassus (fl. 20 BCE). Dionysius already understands that the puppets are a substitute offering for men (1.38.3).

The purpose of this and corresponding sacrifices is interpreted in different ways by both ancient and modern authors. According to James G. Frazer, the river god must be propitiated when man intrudes into his domain and transcends a border. Or, as Eliade (1957) explains, any building, to withstand its hardships, ought to have a life and soul that are transferred to it by a bloody sacrifice. [*See* Foundation Rites.]

A Greek folk song, "The Bridge at Arta," which speaks of this matter, has become famous. The song describes how people keep on building the bridge for three years, but the last span is never finished because what is built by day collapses by night. When the builders begin to complain, the demon or *genius loci,* perhaps originally the river god, lets his voice be heard: he tells the people that unless they sacrifice a human life, no wall is securely founded. They are not, however, to give an orphan child, a traveler, or a foreigner but instead the construction foreman's beautiful wife. From one of the Ionian islands, Zante (Gr., Zákinthos), there is the tale that, as late as the second half of the nineteenth century, the people had wanted to sacrifice a Muslim or a Jew at the building of the more important bridges. There is also a legend that a black person was walled up in an aqueduct near Lebadea in Boeotia (Lawson, 1910, pp. 265f., 276f.; Armistead and Silverman, 1963). In 1890, China's department of public works paid the price of ten pounds for a human bridge sacrifice, if one is to believe a highly respected English reference work (Knight, 1911, p. 850). In Western countries sacrificial ceremonies at the building of bridges have survived as only partly understood reminiscences; they take the form of children's games (Knight, 1911, p. 852; Edsman, 1959).

Symbolism. In Christian metaphorical language, life is likened to a pilgrimage. One is not to become so captivated with the joy of traveling, whether by wagon or ship, that one forgets the destination. It is a matter of using the world, not of enjoying it. Augustine conveys this theme in *On Christian Doctrine* (1.4), while in his discourses on the *Gospel of John* (40.10) he speaks of the world as a lodging where one has temporarily stopped over during one's journey.

This metaphor can easily be reformulated using the bridge symbol. We can then consider a saying of Jesus that is lacking from the New Testament, a so-called agraphon, that has survived in Islamic tradition. It is best known through the inscription that, in 1601, Emperor Akbar caused to be affixed at the chief entrance to the great mosque in Fathepur Sikri in North India: "Jesus, peace be upon him, has said: 'The world is a bridge, walk over it, but do not sit down on it.'" The saying can be traced through Islam as far back as the seventh century (Jeremias, 1955).

Among the extremes of modern psychoanalytical interpretations of the bridge is the Freudian-inspired theory that the bridge constitutes a phallic symbol, with all that suggests about sexual fantasies, castration complexes, and incest (Friedman, 1968). A different interpretation is found in the writings of Hedwig von Beit, who was inspired by C. G. Jung to apply his categories to research into fairy tales. The bridge, which divides two land areas, would thus reflect a psychic situation in which a gap in consciousness occurs or where a transition is occurring to another area. It is at just such a point that the "demons" of the unconscious are free to make an appearance (Reimbold, 1972, pp. 66f., pp. 71f.).

Mircea Eliade, who has also been influenced by Jung, gives a phenomenological interpretation of the bridge symbol in the initiation of shamans among the Mongolian Buriats of southern Siberia. A climbing ceremony is involved in which the candidate climbs nine birches that are tied together with a rope and called a "bridge." Eliade interprets the red and blue ribbons, which further bind this arrangement with the yurt, as a symbol of the rainbow. This would lend support to the interpretation that Eliade gives to the whole ceremony: it is a visualization of the shaman's heavenly journey, his rite of ascension. Therefore, the initiation of the Mongolian shaman can be connected with the crossing of the Chinvat Bridge in ancient Iranian eschatology, which also constitutes a test or an initiation. [*See* Chinvat Bridge.] But both pertain to an even larger framework: the reinstitution of the paradisiacal antiquity when men and gods could converse with each other without difficulty, thanks to the bridge that then connected them (Eliade, 1964, pp. 116ff.; cf. Berner, 1982). Eliade has treated this theme in his fiction, in a tale entitled "Bridge" (1963) included in his collection *Phantastische Geschichten* (1978), as Berner has pointed out. Eliade's critics, in turn, consider a hermeneutic of this kind fantastic; other specialists (e.g., Blacker, 1975) have found his interpretation confirmed by their own material.

BIBLIOGRAPHY

Armistead, Samuel G., and Joseph H. Silverman. "A Judeo-Spanish Derivate of the Ballad of the Bridge of Arta." *Journal of American Folklore* 76 (January–March 1963): 16–20. Contains a rich bibliography.

Berner, Ulrich. "Erforschung und Anwendung religiöser Symbole in Doppelwerk Mircea Eliades." *Symbolon* 6 (1982): 27–35.

Blacker, Carmen. "Other World Journeys in Japan." In *The Journey to the Other World,* edited by Hilda R. Ellis Davidson, pp. 42–72. Totowa, N.J., 1975.

Boyce, Mary. *Zoroastrians: Their Religious Beliefs and Practices.* Boston, 1979.

Boyer, Marjorie Nice. "Bridgebuilding." In *New Catholic Encyclopedia,* vol. 2, p. 798. Washington, D.C., 1967.

Coomaraswamy, Luisa. "The Perilous Bridge of Welfare." *Harvard Journal of Asiatic Studies* 8 (1944/1945): 196–213.

Dienzelbacher, Peter. *Die Jenseitsbrücke im Mittelalter.* Vienna, 1973.

Dinzelbacher, Peter. "Ida von Nijvels Brückenvision." *Ons Geestelijk Erf* 52 (June 1978): 179–194.

Doré, Henri. *Recherches sur les superstitions en Chine,* vol. 2. Shanghai, 1914.

Duchesne-Guillemin, Jacques. *La religion de l'Iran ancien.* Paris, 1962. Translated as *Religion of Ancient Iran* (Bombay, 1973).

Edsman, Carl-Martin. *Le baptême de feu.* Uppsala, 1940.

Edsman, Carl-Martin. "Själarnas bro och dödens älv." *Annales Academiae Regiae Scientiarum Upsaliensis* 3 (1959): 91–109.

Eliade, Mircea. "Bauopfer." *Die Religion in Geschichte und Gegenwart,* 3d ed., vol. 1, p. 935. Tübingen, 1957.

Eliade, Mircea. *Shamanism: Archaic Techniques of Ecstasy* (1951). Rev. & enl. ed. New York, 1964.

Friedman, Paul. "On the Universality of Symbols." In *Religions in Antiquity: Essays in Memory of Erwin Ramsdell Goodenough,* edited by Jacob Neusner, pp. 609–618. Leiden, 1968.

Gardet, Louis. *Islam* (1967). Cologne, 1968.

Groot, J. J. M. de. "Buddhist Masses for the Dead." In *Actes du Sixième Congrès International des Orientalistes tenu en 1883 à Leide,* vol. 4, pp. 1–120. Leiden, 1885.

Hsu, Francis L. K. *Under the Ancestors' Shadow: Chinese Culture and Personality* (1948). Enl. ed. Stanford, 1971.

Jeffery, Arthur, ed. *A Reader on Islam: Passages from Standard Arabic Writings Illustrative of the Beliefs and Practices of Muslims.* The Hague, 1962.

Jeremias, Joachim. "Zur Überlieferungsgeschichte des Agraphon: Die Welt ist eine Brücke; Zugleich ein Beitrag zu den Anfängen des Christentums in Indien." *Nachrichten der Akademie der Wissenschaften in Göttingen* 4 (1955): 95–103.

Knight, G. A. Frank. "Bridge." In *Encyclopaedia of Religion and Ethics,* edited by James Hastings, vol. 2. Edinburgh, 1911.

Lawson, John Cuthbert. *Modern Greek Folklore and Ancient Greek Religion: A Study in Survivals* (1910). Reprint, New York, 1964.

Lommel, Herman. "Some Corresponding Conceptions in Old India and Iran." In *Dr. Modi Memorial Volume,* pp. 260–272. Bombay, 1930.

Nyberg, H. S. *Die Religionen des alten Iran.* 2d ed. Osnabrück, 1966.

Patch, Howard Rollin. *The Other World According to Descriptions in Medieval Literature.* New York, 1950. See the index, s.v. *Bridge.*

Paulson, Ivar. "Jenseitsglaube der finnischen Völker: In der wolgafinnischen und permischen Volksreligion." *Arv* 20 (1964): 125–164.

Reimbold, Ernst T. "Die Brücke als Symbol." *Symbolon* 1 (1972): 55–78.

Silverstein, Theodore. "Dante and the Legend of the Miʿrāj: The Problem of Islamic Influence on the Christian Literature of the Otherworld." *Journal of Near Eastern Studies* 11 (1952): 89–110, 187–197.

Szemler, G. J. "Pontifex." In *Real-encyclopädie der klassischen Altertumswissenschaft,* supp. vol. 15, cols. 331–396. Munich, 1978.

CARL-MARTIN EDSMAN
Translated from Swedish by David Mel Paul and Margareta Paul

BRINDAVAN. *See* Vr̥ndāvana.

BROADCASTING, RELIGIOUS. *See* Religious Broadcasting.

BROWNE, ROBERT (c. 1550–1633), leading Protestant Separatist from the Church of England in the reign of Elizabeth I. Although he finally conformed, his teaching anticipated much in later Independency, or Congregationalism. He was born at Tolesthorpe in Rutlandshire. For about twenty years after leaving Cambridge, he was an active Separatist. On receiving the bishop's license to preach in 1579, he threw it in the fire, asserting that he preached "not as caring for or leaning on the Bishop's authority, but only to satisfy his duty and conscience." He helped gather a dissenting congregation in Norwich in 1518 and was frequently imprisoned. In 1582 he was in exile in Holland.

During exile, he wrote the tracts that later became influential among more radical Protestants in which he insisted on the voluntary nature of church membership. The best-known is *A treatise of Reformation without Tarying for Anie* (1582). *A Booke which Sheweth the life and Manner of All true Christians* (1582) is the first outline of an Independent church polity.

Browne was a contentious individualist who frequently had to be rescued from trouble by his kinsman Lord Burghley. He fell out with his fellow Separatists Henry Barrow and John Greenwood over the eldership. In 1586, he became master of Saint Olave's School in Southwark but continued to minister to dissenting congregations. In 1591, however, Burghley presented him with the living of a church in Northamptonshire, where he remained for the rest of his life. He appears to have continued to be contentious even in conformity, because he died in Northampton jail after assaulting a constable.

Browne is best thought of as a precursor rather than a founding father of the later Congregational churches. The word *Brownists* became a general term of abuse for English Protestants who favored a democratic church polity.

BIBLIOGRAPHY

Little book-length literature is available other than an edition of Browne's writings in Albert Peel and Leland H. Carlson's *The Writings of Robert Harrison and Robert Browne* (London, 1953). See also Champlin Burrage's *The True Story of Robert Browne, 1550?–1633, Father of Congregationalism* (Oxford, 1906).

DANIEL JENKINS

BRUNNER, EMIL (1889–1966), Swiss Protestant theologian. Brunner was a critic of liberalism and secularism. His writing on knowledge and faith was influenced by Kant; his stress on religious experience by Kierkegaard and Husserl; and his stress on God's transcendence and the need for vigorous social and political action by Luther and Calvin.

Brunner anticipated Martin Buber's notion of the I–Thou relationship, elucidating throughout his *Dogmatics* the encounter between humanity and God as humanity's most significant existential experience. In *The Divine Imperative,* Brunner argues that the source of Christian ethics lies in God's imperative. He deemed personhood to be the center of human-divine interaction, deploring the reductionism of positivism and behaviorism. Although sympathetic to philosophy, he opposed its attempts to stand in judgment of theology, as well as attempts by Paul Tillich and others to use such philosophical terms as *being* and *ground of being* in reference to God. In contrast to Barth, Brunner asserted that even sinful man can attain some knowledge of God but that, apart from the Christian revelation, this knowledge has no salvific value.

Brunner's theology is rich in the areas of ethics and sociopolitical thought. We are told in his *The Divine Imperative, Christianity and Civilization,* and *Justice and the Social Order* that God's command is to love and that the person who has faith in Jesus Christ responds to God's love by living a life of hope and love in "orders of creation"—the family, the economy, the state, the culture, and the church. Though the New Testament contains no blueprint for a socio-economic-political order, Brunner believed that human institutions could be informed by love and by justice in the service of God.

BIBLIOGRAPHY

Brunner's three-volume *Dogmatics* (Zurich, 1946–1960) is the definitive statement of his theology. The first two volumes have been translated into English by Olive Wyon, and the third by David Cairns and T. H. L. Parker (Philadelphia, 1950–1962). Crucial to an understanding of Brunner's ethics and his Reformed stance is *Das Gebot und die Ordnungen* (Tübingen, 1932), translated by Olive Wyon as *The Divine Imperative* (Philadelphia, 1947). The existentialist and personal aspects of Brunner's thought are best exhibited in *Wahrheit als Begegnung* (Berlin, 1938), translated by Amandus W. Loos as *The Divine-Human Encounter* (Philadelphia, 1943), and *Der Mittler* (Tübingen, 1927), translated by Olive Wyon as *The Mediator: A Study of the Central Doctrine of the Christian Faith* (Philadelphia, 1947). For a critical evaluation of all Brunner's works, see my *The Theology of Emil Brunner* (New York, 1962). This volume contains works by Brunner, interpretative essays, replies to these essays by Brunner, and a complete bibliography.

CHARLES W. KEGLEY

BRUNO, GIORDANO (1548–1600), Italian philosopher. Bruno was a brilliant and encyclopedic though erratic thinker of the Italian Renaissance, a man who synthesized and transformed thought in terms of the situation of his own times. Born in Nola, Bruno joined the Dominican order in Naples at the age of fifteen. He was expelled for his views on transubstantiation and the immaculate conception and fled Rome about 1576. After wandering over half of Europe, he finally returned to Italy, only to be imprisoned by the Roman Inquisition for his cosmological theories and burned as a heretic, the "martyr of the Renaissance."

Bruno was strongly influenced by the German philosopher Nicholas of Cusa and the latter's theory of the "coincidence of opposites," namely, that the infinitely great coincides with the infinitely small, and that God relates to the world as does one side of a piece of paper to the other side (panentheism). Drawing on Neoplatonic philosophy in developing his theories about the universe, Bruno rejected Aristotle's conception of the structure of the universe, held to a theory of animate monads, taught the relativity of space, time, and motion, and maintained that the universe is infinite in extension and eternal in its origin and duration.

Bruno was a prolific author and, especially in his Italian works, a beautiful writer, though some of his Latin works were prolix and confused. He had obsessions, such as his preoccupation with mnemonic theories, and he was easily distracted by thinkers, such as Ramón Lull (c. 1235–1315). Among Bruno's better-known works are *On Heroic Rages*, expounding a Neoplatonic theodicy cast in mythical form, describing the soul's ascent to God as its return to the original and highest unity; *An Ash Wednesday Conversation*, discussing the Copernican heliocentric theory; *On the Infinite Universe and Worlds*, an ecstatic vision of a single infinite universe; *The Expulsion of the Triumphant Beast*, an allegory dealing mostly with moral philosophy; and *On the Beginnings, Elements and Causes of Things*, his cosmic philosophy. Bruno's writings influenced Jakob Boehme, Spinoza, Leibniz, Descartes, Schelling, and Hegel.

BIBLIOGRAPHY

Virgilio Salvestrini's *Bibliografia delle opere di Giordano Bruno* (Pisa, 1926) is an excellent comprehensive bibliography of Bruno's works, including references to him by other writers. The best book in English on Bruno is Dorothea Waley Singer's *Giordano Bruno: His Life and Thought with Annotated Translation of His Work "On the Infinite Universe and Worlds"* (New York, 1968). An authoritative treatment of his thought is Giovanni Gentile's *Giordano Bruno e il pensiero del rinascimento*, 2d ed. (Florence, 1925). Irving Louis Horowitz's *The Renaissance Philosophy of Giordano Bruno* (New York, 1952) offers a general introduction to his natural philosophy or ontology and an analysis of the interactions of his philosophical system and method. Frances A. Yates's *Giordano Bruno and the Hermetic Tradition* (London, 1964) relates his thought to the mystical and Platonic tradition.

LEWIS W. SPITZ

BUBER, MARTIN (1878–1965), Jewish philosopher and educator. Born in Vienna, where he was raised by his paternal grandparents, Buber studied at universities in Vienna, Leipzig, Zurich, and Berlin, and received his Ph.D. from Vienna in 1904 after completing a dissertation on Nicholas of Cusa and Jakob Boehme. Buber was married to Paula Winkler, a well-known German writer, and they had two children, Raphael and Eva (Strauss). Alienated from traditional Judaism, Buber returned to the Jewish community through the newly formed Zionist movement, whose official journal *(Die Welt)* he edited from 1901 to 1904.

Buber advocated a renewal of Jewish spiritual nationalism and wrote extensively on Judaism and Jewish nationalism. A five-year intensive study of Hasidism produced two volumes in German: *Tales of Rabbi Nachman* (1906) and *The Legends of the Baal Shem* (1908), followed by volumes of essays and translations including *For the Sake of Heaven* (1945), *Tales of the Hasidim* (1947), and *The Origin and Meaning of Hasidism* (1960), which first appeared in Hebrew, and *Hasidism and Modern Man* (1954). Other early writings include studies in mysticism: *Ekstatische Konfessionen* (1909) and *Reden und Gleichnisse des Tschuang-Tse* (1910), as well as two collections of essays on Jewish national and religious renewal: *Die Judische Bewegung* (2 vols., 1916–1920) and *Reden über das Judentum* (On Judaism; 1923). He edited a monographic series, *Die Gesellschaft* (1904–1912) and a journal, *Die Jude* (1916–1924).

Widely regarded by Jewish youth as a spiritual leader, Buber taught at the University of Frankfurt from 1923 to 1933. He was also active in Jewish cultural life and lectured at the Frankfurt Judische Lehrhaus directed by Franz Rosenzweig. His lectures and writings were a source of spiritual inspiration for the besieged Jewish community in Nazi Germany. After emigrating to Palestine in 1938, he became professor of social philosophy at the Hebrew University in Jerusalem and was active in adult education. Buber was a founder and active participant in Berit Shalom and Iḥud, movements for Arab-Jewish rapprochement. In this function he endorsed, until 1948, a binational state.

Philosophy of Judaism. Inspired by the emphasis placed in Hasidism on the hallowing of mundane, physical acts, Buber detached the teachings of that eighteenth-century pietist movement from their traditional rabbinic framework and revised them to create a unique, existential interpretation of Judaism. Rejecting orthodoxy, he espoused creative, spontaneous, individual "religiosity" over static, institutionalized "religion." In his emphasis on myth and mysticism, he diverged sharply from conventional Jewish historical scholarship and rationalist theology.

In such works of biblical interpretation as *Kingship of God* (1932), *Moses* (1946), *Prophetic Faith* (1949), and *On The Bible* (1968), Buber combined existential insight and scholarly method as he attempted to recover the living situations from which the biblical text emerged. Based upon his view of biblical texts as derived from oral tradition, his German translation of the Hebrew Bible emphasizes the sensuous, poetic force of the Hebrew language and reflects Buber's view of the Bible as a record of Israel's ongoing dialogue with God. Initially undertaken with the collaboration of Franz Rosenzweig, the project was completed in 1962.

Philosophy of Relation and Dialogue. Under the influence of mystics (Boehme, Eckhart), existentialists (Kierkegaard, Nietzsche), and German social theorists (Tönnies, Simmel, Weber), Buber held that modern life and thought estrange the individual from his authentic self, other persons, nature, and God. Following World War I, however, he shifted from an individualistic philosophy to one rooted in social experience, and he coined the word *interhuman (das Zwischenmenschliche)* to describe the unique sphere of relation between persons. He set forth the basic concepts of his philosophy of relation and dialogue in *Ich und Du* (1923; translated as *I and Thou*).

Buber eschewed systematic philosophy. Like Kierkegaard and Nietzsche, he endeavored to change the way in which people understand their relation to other human beings, the world, and God. His philosophy centered around two basic modes of relation, "I–You" and "I–It." In the "I–It" mode, which is characterized by a goal-oriented, instrumentalist attitude, we relate to others in terms of their use and value. Assuming a detached, analytic stance, we categorize others according to measurement and type. However, whereas such an approach is appropriate to technology and practical activities, the intrusion of the I–It mode into the realm of interhuman relationships leads to widespread alienation. Rather than relate to others as unique beings, we reduce them to the status of objects or tools, utilizing them for our own needs and purposes.

An alternative to the conventional form of human relationship is the I–You mode. Through direct, nonpurposive relations one relates to another as an end (You), rather than a means (It), confirming and nurturing that person's uniqueness. The moments of I–You relating provide us with a basic sense of meaning and purpose; the absence of such experiences has a dehumanizing effect. Whereas structured, ordered I–It relations perdure, I–You relations are fleeting, unplannable, and fluid, eventually reverting back to I–It relationships. "Every you in the world is doomed by its nature to become a thing, or at least to enter into thinghood again and again" (*I and Thou,* trans. Walter Kaufmann, New York, 1970, p. 69).

Through I–You relations, we actualize our humanity. Continually shaped by interactions with others, each person has a twofold wish: "to be confirmed as what he is, even as what he can become, by men; and the innate capacity to confirm his fellow men in this way" (*Knowledge of Man,* New York, 1965 p. 68). In genuine dialogue, we accept, affirm, and confirm the other as the person that he is and can become. Buber's philosophy of relation, elaborated in such volumes as *Between Man and Man* (1961) and *Knowledge of Man* (1965), provided the foundation for his philosophical anthropology and social theory.

Religious Faith and the Eternal You. Buber developed a relational conception of religion, elaborated in *Two Types of Faith* (1951), *Eclipse of God* (1952), and *Good and Evil* (1953). Although he admitted the possibility of direct divine-human encounters, he emphasized the "interhuman" as the locus of genuine religious life. I–You relations between persons, when extended, "intersect in the Eternal You" (*I and Thou,* p. 123). We live religiously by hallowing those human and other living beings whom we encounter. By confirming their unique qualities and potential, we nurture the divine spark in each of them, thereby actualizing God in the world.

Speaking of the divine as the "Eternal You," Buber asserted the impossibility of relating to it through the I–It mode. In revelation, we directly encounter a "presence," receiving a ground of meaning that we must translate into action. Moments of divine-human encounter, like all significant moments of relation, elude conceptual speech and are best conveyed through myth and poetry.

Genuine relation both presupposes and fosters genuine community, rooted in authentic relations between members and between members and leader. To Buber, Israel's unique vocation is to actualize true community in its daily life. Like his mentor, the romantic socialist and anarchist Gustav Landauer (1870–1919), Buber advocated a community based on "utopian socialism," that is, mutual ownership and mutual aid.

Judaism and Genuine Community. Buber's conception of Jewish existence is characterized by a simultaneous commitment to humanity and the Jewish people. The Jews are a people united by common kinship, fate and memory, who, from its beginnings, accepted responsibility for actualizing genuine dialogue and genuine community in its daily life. Israel fulfills its responsibility as a nation by actualizing in its social life genuine, non-exploitative, confirming relations between people. In the Israeli *kibbuts,* Buber saw one of history's most successful examples of genuine community based upon mutual responsibility.

To live as a Jew means to dedicate oneself to actualizing genuine relation in all spheres of life. Rejecting all prepackaged recipes, norms, and principles, Buber emphasized Israel's continuing responsibility to draw anew the "line of demarcation" separating just from unjust action. For Buber, the Arab-Jewish conflict is the greatest test of the Jewish people's ability to actualize its vocation.

Buber was a major spokesman for a small group of Jews espousing Arab-Jewish rapprochement. Advocating a binational state in which Jews and Arabs would live as two culturally autonomous people with absolute political equality, he reluctantly accepted the state of Israel as necessitated by historical circumstances. Nevertheless, he continually criticized Israel's political leadership for shifting the context of the Arab-Jewish debate from the realm of human relationships to the realm of power politics.

For Buber, Israel was a microcosm of general humanity. The religious responsibility to actualize true community and dialogue in daily life is incumbent upon all nations and is a prerequisite for world peace. Criticizing the existential mistrust that permeates modern society and the centralized power of the nation state, he envisioned a network of decentralized communities based upon mutual production and direct relations.

Influence. Buber's influence among European Jewish youth was great. In Israel, however, his stand on Arab-Jewish rapprochement and his unique synthesis of religious existentialism and cultural nationalism made him unacceptable to the majority of secular and religious Israelis alike. Consequently, his influence was limited to a small circle of *kibbuts* members. In the United States, many rabbis rejected his strongly anti-institutional orientation to religion. However, his influence was strongly felt by a limited number of rabbis and Jewish theologians such as Will Herberg, Arthur A. Cohen, and Eugene B. Borowitz, as well as by Christian theologians such as Paul Tillich and H. Richard Neihbuhr. His philosophy of relation influenced the psychiatrists R. D. Laing, Irvin Yalom, and Leslie Farber; the philosophers Gabriel Marcel, Phillip Wheelwright, and Ernst Becker; and the anthropologist Victor Turner. As secretary general of the United Nations (1953–1961) Dag Hammarskjöld was deeply influenced by the political implications of Buber's philosophy of relation, and at the time of his death was in the process of translating Buber's writings into Swedish.

[*See also* Jewish Thought and Philosophy, *article on* Modern Thought.]

BIBLIOGRAPHY

A comprehensive bibliography of Buber's writings is *Martin Buber: A Bibliography of His Writings, 1897–1978* by Margot Cohn and Rafhael Buber (Jerusalem and New York, 1980). Available works by Buber not mentioned in the body of the article include *Israel and The World: Essays in a Time of Crisis,* 2d ed. (New York, 1963), which includes important essays on Judaism, the Bible, and Zionism; *A Believing Humanism: My Testament, 1902–1965,* translated and with an introduction and explanatory comment by Maurice S. Friedman (New York, 1967); and *Pointing the Way,* translated, edited, and with an introduction by Maurice S. Friedman (New York, 1957). A valuable collection of writings on the Arab question is *A Land of Two Peoples: Martin Buber on Jews and Arabs,* edited with an incisive introductory essay and notes by Paul R. Mendes-Flohr (Oxford, 1983). *The Writings of Martin Buber,* selected, edited, and introduced by Will Herberg (New York, 1956), is a useful collection, but includes none of Buber's writings on Hasidism.

The specifics of Buber's life, previously available only to the reader of German in Hans Kohn's fine study *Martin Buber: Sein Werk und seine Zeit* (Cologne, 1961), can now be found in Maurice S. Friedman's three-volume biography, *Martin Buber's Life and Work* (New York, 1981–1984). Friedman's *Martin Buber: The Life of Dialogue,* 3d ed. (Chicago, 1976), still remains the most comprehensive introduction to his thought in English. Grete Shaeder's *The Hebrew Humanism of Martin Buber,* translated by Noah J. Jacobs (Detroit, 1973), emphasizes the aesthetic and humanistic dimension of Buber's writings, traced biographically. Important criticisms with Buber's response are found in *The Philosophy of Martin Buber,* edited by Paul A. Schilpp and Maurice S. Friedman (Lasalle, Ill., 1967), and *Philosophical Interrogations,* edited by Sydney Rome and Beatrice Rome (New York, 1964), pp. 15–117.

For recent discussions of Buber's philosophy, see the proceedings (translated into English) of the Buber Centenary Conference held in 1978 at Ben Gurion University in Israel in *Martin Buber: A Centenary Volume,* edited by Haim Gordon and Jochanan Bloch (New York, 1984). Valuable critical insights into Buber's life and thought in the context of modern Jewish culture are provided in several articles by Ernst Simon: "Martin Buber and German Jewry," *Yearbook of The Leo Baeck Institute* 3 (1958): 3–39; "The Builder of Bridges," *Judaism* 27 (Spring, 1978): 148–160; and "From Dialogue to Peace," *Conservative Judaism* 19 (Summer, 1965): 28–31. These and other articles by Simon on Buber appear in his *Ye'adim, zematim, netivim: Haguto shel Mordekhai Martin Buber* (Tel Aviv, 1985). A brief discussion of Buber's early writings up to *I and Thou* is found in my article "Martin Buber: The Social Paradigm in Modern Jewish Thought," *Journal of the American Academy of Religion* 49 (June, 1981): 211–229.

LAURENCE J. SILBERSTEIN

BUCER, MARTIN (1491–1551), Christian humanist and reformer. Best known as the chief reformer of the Free Imperial City of Strasbourg, Bucer illustrates the combining of Martin Luther's evangelical theology with aspirations and traditions that predated the Reformation. A Dominican, Bucer was thus trained in the *via* *antiqua* of Thomas Aquinas but early fell under the spell of Erasmian humanism. Meeting and hearing Luther for the first time at the Heidelberg Disputation (1518) led him to become increasingly dissatisfied with his vocation and finally to secure release from his vows. He thus arrived in Strasbourg (1523) as a dispossessed and married cleric who could only appeal to that city's authorities for protection from the episcopal court. Friends arranged a position for him; he led in the efforts to abolish the Mass (1529), to erect a new church (1533–1534), and to construct the city's policy of mediation in the Sacramentarian Controversy. Eventually he became president of the Company of Pastors, but he was forced because of his opposition to the Interim (a temporary religious settlement arranged by Charles V) to flee to England, where he participated in the revision of *The Book of Common Prayer* shortly before his death. Ostensibly he appeared to have broken decisively with the intellectual and religious traditions that predated his encounter with Luther.

Bucer was thoroughly evangelical—and a follower of Luther—in the basic outline of his theology, but prior allegiances were apparent in his actions. At colloquies with representatives of Rome in the 1540s, he agreed to a theory of "double justification," according to which a Christian cooperates with God after the gift of salvation, a claim that may hark back to Thomas. In the Sacramentarian Controversy, although he was an early adherent to Zwingli's spiritualist view of the elements and later agreed with Luther in the Wittenberg Concord (1536), he consistently argued that the true meaning of the Lord's Supper was communion among the believers and with Christ. His mediatory efforts both flowed directly from this view and reflected the earlier influence of Erasmus and northern humanism.

These prior traditions and aspirations showed through most clearly in the sort of reformation Bucer promoted and the manner in which he did so. Like many others who translated Luther's theology into practice, Bucer sought a thorough reform of all of Christian society, as is well summarized in his posthumously published *De regno Christi*, dedicated to Edward VI. Outlined there is the program he followed throughout his entire career. Not only did he advocate that the Mass be abolished and proper Christian worship and doctrine be put in its place. He also helped found schools that had the humanist educational program at the heart of the curriculum. He laid the groundwork for creating in Strasbourg and elsewhere an educated clergy, who in turn made religion even at the popular level a matter of the mind as well as of the heart. And he helped to establish civil authority over relief for the poor and over marriage and morals. Finally, throughout his career he sought to tame the turbulent reform movement by working with the Christian magistrates, as he called the princes and city councils, so that peace might prevail and Christian society flourish.

BIBLIOGRAPHY

Martin Bucer's works are collected in *Martin Bucers deutsche Schriften*, 6 vols. to date, edited by Robert Stupperich (Gütersloh, 1960–), and in *Martini Buceri opera Latina*, 2 vols. to date, edited by François Wendel (Paris, 1954–). See also *Correspondance de Martin Bucer*, edited by Jean Rott (Leiden, 1979–). A good English biography is Hastings Eells's *Martin Bucer* (1931; New York, 1971). For bibliography, see *Bibliographia Bucerana*, by Robert Stupperich (Gütersloh, 1952), and *Bucer und seine Zeit*, edited by Marijn de Kroon and Friedhelm Krüger (Wiesbaden, 1976).

JAMES M. KITTELSON

BUDDHA. Etymologically, the Sanskrit/Pali word *buddha* means "one who has awakened"; in the context of Indian religions it is used as an honorific title for an individual who is enlightened. This metaphor indicates the change in consciousness that, according to Buddhism, is always characteristic of enlightenment. It suggests the otherness and splendor associated with those named by this epithet in various Buddhist traditions. *Buddha* is also related etymologically to the Sanskrit/Pali term *buddhi*, which signifies "intelligence" and "understanding." A person who has awakened can thus be said to be "one who knows."

Within the traditional Buddhist context *buddha* is an appellative term or title—that is, a term or title that is inclusive in character. As with all titles of office (e.g., king), the term *buddha* denotes not merely the individual incumbent but also a larger conceptual framework. As an appellative, *buddha* describes a person by placing him or her within a class, instead of isolating and analyzing individual attributes. It emphasizes the paradigm that is exhibited, rather than distinctive qualities or characteristics.

The designation *buddha* has had wide circulation among various religious traditions of India. It has been applied, for example, by Jains to their founder, Mahāvīra. [*See* Mahāvīra.] The definition of the inclusive category has varied, however, and *buddha* has been used to describe a broad spectrum of persons, from those who are simply learned to those rare individuals who have had transforming and liberating insight into the nature of reality. Buddhists have, in general, employed the term in this second, stronger sense.

Buddhists adopted the term *buddha* from the religious discourse of ancient India and gave it a special imprint, just as they have done with much of their vocabulary. It seems, however, that the early Buddhists may not have immediately applied the term to the person—the historical Gautama—whom they recognized as the founder of their community. In the accounts of the first two Buddhist councils (one held just after Gautama's death, the other several decades later) Gautama is spoken of as *bhagavan* ("lord," a common title of respect) and *śāstṛ* ("teacher"), not as *buddha*. However, once the term *buddha* was adopted, it not only became the primary designation for Gautama but also assumed a central role within the basic structure of Buddhist thought and practice.

We will begin our discussion by focusing on the question of the historical Buddha and what—if anything—we know about him and his ministry. This issue has not been of particular importance for traditional Buddhists—at least not in the way that it is formulated here. But it has been of major significance for modern scholars of Buddhism, and it has become of great interest to many contemporary Buddhists and others who have been influenced by modern Western notions of history.

We will then turn to the term *buddha* as it has been employed within the various traditions that constitute classical Buddhism. As an appellative term utilized in classical Buddhist contexts, *buddha* has had three distinct, yet interwoven, levels of meaning. It has referred, first of all, to what we will call "the Buddha"—otherwise known as the Gautama Buddha or the Buddha Śākyamuni ("sage of the Śākyas"). Most Buddhists recognize Gautama as the buddha of our own cosmic era and/or cosmic space, and they honor him as the founder of the existing Buddhist community. As a perfectly enlightened being, Gautama is understood to have perfected various virtues (*pāramitā*s) over the course of numerous lives. [*See* Pāramitās.] These prodigious efforts prepared Gautama to awake fully to the true nature of reality just as other Buddhas had awakened before him. The preparation also gave him—as it did other Buddhas—the inclination and ability to share with others what he had discovered for himself. Following his Enlightenment, Gautama became a teacher who "set in motion the wheel of Dharma" and oversaw the founding of the Buddhist comunity of monks, nuns, laymen, and laywomen.

The second level of meaning associated with *buddha* as an appellative term has to do with "other Buddhas." Many Buddhas of different times and places are named in Buddhist literature. Moreover, anyone who attains release *(mokṣa, nirvāṇa)* from this world of recurring rebirths *(saṃsāra)* can be called—in some contexts at least—a Buddha. Buddhas, then, are potentially as "innumerable as the sands of the river Ganges." But all Buddhas are not equal: they possess different capabilities according to their aspirations and accomplishments. The enlightened insight of some is greater than that of others. Some attain enlightenment only for themselves (e.g., *pratyekabuddha*), others for the benefit and welfare of many (e.g., *samyaksaṃbuddha*). Some accomplish their mission through their earthly careers, others through the creation of celestial Buddha fields into which their devotees seek rebirth.

Finally, the term *buddha* as an appellative has a third level of meaning that we will designate as Buddhahood—a level that provides its widest conceptual context. This level is constituted by the recognition that the Buddha and other Buddhas are, in a very profound sense, identical with ultimate reality itself. Consequently, Buddhists have given the more personal and active connotations associated with the Buddha and other Buddhas to their characterizations of absolute reality as *dharma* (salvific truth), *śūnyatā* ("emptiness"), *tathatā* ("suchness"), and the like. At the same time, the term *Buddhahood* has on occasion given a somewhat depersonalized cast to the notions of the Buddha and other Buddhas. For example, early Buddhists, who were closest to the historical Buddha, were reluctant to depict Gautama in anthropomorphic forms and seem to have intentionally avoided biographical structures and iconic imagery. They used impersonal and symbolic representation to express their perception that the Buddha whose teachings they had preserved was fully homologous with reality itself. In some later traditions the pervading significance of this third level of meaning was expressed through the affirmation that the Buddha's impersonal and ineffable *dharmakāya* ("*dharma* body") was the source and truth of the other, more personalized manifestations of Buddhahood.

The Historical Buddha

The scholars who inaugurated the critical study of Buddhism in the late nineteenth and early twentieth centuries were deeply concerned with the question of the "historical Buddha." But their views on the subject differed radically. The field was largely divided between a group of myth-oriented scholars, such as Émile Senart, Heinrich Kern, and Ananda Coomaraswamy, and a group of more historically oriented philologists, such as Hermann Oldenberg and T. W. and C. A. F. Rhys Davids. The myth-oriented interpreters placed emphasis on the study of Sanskrit sources and on the importance of those elements in the sacred biography that pointed in the direction of solar mythology; for these scholars, the historical Buddha was, at most, a reformer who provided an occasion for historicizing a classic solar myth.

In contrast, the historically oriented philologists emphasized the texts written in Pali, as well as those elements in these texts that they could use to create (or reconstruct, in their view) an acceptable "historical" life of the Buddha. From the perspective of these scholars, the mythic elements—and other supposedly irrational elements as well—were later additions to a true historical memory, additions that brought about the demise of the original Buddhism of the Buddha. Such pious frauds were to be identified and discounted by critical scholarship.

More recently, scholars have recognized the inadequacy of the older mythic and historical approaches. Most scholars working in the field at present are convinced of the existence of the historical Gautama. The general consensus was well expressed by the great Belgian Buddhologist Étienne Lamotte, who noted that "Buddhism would remain inexplicable if one did not place at its beginning a strong personality who was its founder" (Lamotte, 1958, p. 707). But at the same time scholars are aware that the available tests provide little information about the details of Gautama's life.

The difficulties involved in saying anything significant about the historical Buddha are illustrated by the lack of certainty concerning the dates of his birth and death. Since different Buddhist traditions recognize different dates, and since external evidence is slight and inconclusive, scholars have ventured diverging opinions.

Two chronologies found in Buddhist texts are important for any attempt to calculate the date of the historical Buddha. A "long chronology," presented in the Sri Lankan chronicles, the *Dīpavaṃsa* and the *Mahāvaṃsa,* places the birth of the historical Buddha 298 years before the coronation of King Aśoka, his death 218 years before that event. If we accept the date given in the chronicles for the coronation of Aśoka (326 BCE), that would locate the Buddha's birth date in 624 BCE and his death in 544. These dates have been traditionally accepted in Sri Lanka and Southeast Asia and were the basis for the celebration of the 2500th anniversary of the Buddha's death, or *parinirvāṇa,* in 1956. However, most modern scholars who accept the long chronology believe, on the basis of Greek evidence, that Aśoka's coronation took place around 268 or 267 BCE and that the Buddha's birth and death should therefore be dated circa 566 and circa 486, respectively. These later dates are favored by the majority of Buddhologists in Europe, America, and India.

A "short chronology" is attested to by Indian sources and their Chinese and Tibetan translations. These sources place the birth of the Buddha 180 years before the coronation of Aśoka and his death 100 years before that event. If the presumably reliable Greek testimony concerning Aśoka's coronation is applied, the birth date of the Buddha is 448 and the date of his death, or *parinirvāṇa,* is 368. This short chronology is accepted by many Japanese Buddhologists and was spiritedly defended by the German scholar Heinz Bechert in 1982.

Although there seems to be little chance of resolving the long chronology/short chronology question in any kind of definitive manner, we can say with some certainty that the historical Buddha lived sometime during the period from the sixth through the fourth centuries BCE. This was a time of radical thought and speculation, as manifested in the pre-Socratic philosophical tradition and the mystery cults in Greece, the prophets and prophetic schools of the Near East, Confucius and Lao-tzu in China, the Upaniṣadic sages and the communities of ascetic wanderers (*śramaṇas*) in India, and the emergence of "founded" religions such as Jainism and Buddhism. These intellectual and religious movements were fostered by the formation of cosmopolitan empires, such as those associated with Alexander in the Hellenistic world, with the Ch'in and Han dynasties in China, with Darius and Cyrus in Persia, and with the Maurya dynasty in India. Urban centers were established and soon became the focal points around which a new kind of life was organized. A significant number of people, cut off from the old sources of order and meaning, were open to different ways of expressing their religious concerns and were quite ready to support those engaged in new forms of religious and intellectual endeavor.

The historical Buddha responded to this kind of situation in northeastern India. He was a renouncer and an ascetic, although the style of renunciation and asceticism he practiced and recommended was, it seems, mild by Indian standards. He shared with other renunciants an ultimately somber view of the world and its pleasures, and he practiced and recommended a mode of religious life in which individual participation in a specifically religious community was of primary importance. He experimented with the practices of renunciants—begging, wandering, celibacy, techniques of self-restraint (yoga), and the like—and he organized a community in which discipline played a central role. Judging from the movement he inspired, he was not only an innovator but also a charismatic personality. Through the course of his ministry he gathered around him a group of wandering mendicants and nuns, as well as men and women who continued to live the life of householders.

Can we go beyond this very generalized portrait of the historical Buddha toward a fuller biography? Lamotte has advised caution, observing in his *Histoire* that writing the life of the historical Gautama is "a hopeless enterprise" (p. 16). There are, however, a few details that, though they do not add up to a biography, do suggest that there is a historical core to the later biographical traditions. These details are presented in almost identical form in the literature of diverse Buddhist schools, a reasonable indication that they date from before the fourth to third centuries BCE, when independent and separate traditions first began to develop.

Some of these details are so specific and arbitrary or unexpected that it seems unlikely that they were fabricated. These include the details that Gautama was of the *kṣatriya* caste, that he was born in the Śākya clan (a more distinguished pedigree could have been created), that he was marrried and had a child, that he entered the ascetic life without the permission of his father, that his first attempts to share the insights that he had gained through his Enlightenment met with failure, that his leadership of the community he had established was seriously challenged by his more ascetically inclined cousin, and that he died in a remote place after eating a tainted meal. But these details are so few and disconnected that our knowlege of the historical Buddha remains shadowy and unsatisfying. In order to identify a more meaningful image of Gautama and his career we must turn to the Buddha who is explicitly affirmed in the memory and practice of the Buddhist community.

The Buddha

The general history of religions strongly suggests that the death of a founder results in the loss of a charismatic focus. This loss must be dealt with if the founded group is to survive. In his classic article "Master and Disciple: Two Religio-Sociological Studies," Joachim Wach suggests that "the image" of the beloved founder could produce a unity sufficient for the group to continue (*Journal of Religion* 42, 1962, p. 5).

Each founded religion has developed original ways of preserving the image of their master: Christians with the Gospels and later artistic expressions, Muslims with *ḥadīth* and Miʿrāj stories of Muḥammad's journeys to heaven, and so on. Buddhists, it seems, have addressed this crisis with the assumption—explicitly stated in the words of a fifth-century CE Mahāyāna text known as the *Saptaśatikā-prajñāpāramitā*—that "a Buddha is not easily made known by words" (Rome, 1923, p. 126). This recognition has not proved to be a restraint but has instead inspired Buddhists to preserve the image of Gautama through the creation and explication of epithets, through a variety of "biographical" accounts, and through a tradition of visual representation in monumental architecture and art. The image of the founder became, in Joachim Wach's phrase, "an objective center of crystalization" for a variety of opinions concerning the nature and significance of his person.

The creative preservation of the image of the Buddha was closely related to evolving patterns of worship—including pilgrimage, contemplation, and ritual—in the Buddhist community. This reminds us that the various ways of portraying the Buddha are the result of innumerable personal efforts to discern him with immediacy, as well as the product of the desire to preserve and share that image.

Epithets. Certainly one of the earliest and most ubiquitous forms in which Buddhists have expressed and generated their image of Gautama Buddha was through the medium of epithets. For example, in the *Majjhima Nikāya* (London, 1948, vol. 1, p. 386), a householder named Upāli, after becoming the Buddha's follower, acclaims him with one hundred epithets. The Sanskrit version of this text adds that Upāli spoke these epithets spontaneously, as an expression of his faith and respect. Over the centuries the enumerations of these and other epithets focused on the extraordinary aspects of the Buddha's person, on his marvelous nature. In so doing they became a foundation for Buddhist devotional literature, their enunciation a support of devotional and contemplative practice.

Countless epithets have been applied to the Buddha over the centuries, but *buddha* itself has been a particular favorite for explanation. Even hearing the word *buddha* can cause people to rejoice because, as the Theravāda commentary on the *Saṃyutta Nikāya* says, "It is very rare indeed to hear the word *buddha* in this world" (London, 1929, vol. 1, p. 312). The *Paṭisambhidā*, a late addition to the Theravāda canon, explored the significance of the word *buddha* by saying that "it is a name derived from the final liberation of the Enlightened Ones, the Blessed Ones, together with the omniscient knowledge at the root of the Enlightenment Tree; this name "buddha" is a designation based on realization" (*The Path of Purification*, translated by Ñyāṇamoli, Colombo, 1964, p. 213). Sun Ch'o, a fourth-century Chinese writer, explicated the *buddha* epithet in a rather different mode, reminiscent of a Taoist sage: "'Buddha' means 'one who embodies the Way'. . . . It is the one who reacts to the stimuli (of the world) in all pervading accordance (with the needs of all beings); the one who abstains from activity and who is yet universally active" (quoted in Erik Zürcher's *The Buddhist Conquest of China*, Leiden, 1959, p. 133).

Particular epithets accentuate specific qualities of the Buddha that might otherwise remain unemphasized or ambiguous. Thus the epithet "teacher of gods and men" *(satthar devamanussānāṃ)* is used in the *Mahāniddesa*, another late canonical text in the Theravāda tradition, to display the Buddha as one who helps others escape from suffering. The techniques used—exploiting ordinary polysemy and puns and deriving elaborate etymologies—are favorites of Buddhist commentators for exposing the significance of an epithet.

> He teaches by means of the here and now, of the life to come, and of the ultimate goal, according as befits the case, thus he is Teacher *(satthar).*
>
> "Teacher *(satthar)*": the Blessed One is a caravan leader *(satthar)* since he brings home caravans. Just as one who brings a caravan home gets caravans across a wilderness. . . gets them to reach a land of safety, so too the Blessed One is a caravan leader, one who brings home the caravans; he gets them across . . . the wilderness of birth.
>
> (Ñyāṇamoli, p. 223)

Some of the epithets of the Buddha refer to his lineage and name: for example, Śākyamuni, "sage of the Śākya tribe," and his personal name, Siddhārtha, "he whose aims are fulfilled." Some refer to religio-mythic paradigms with which he was identified: *mahāpuruṣa* means "great cosmic person"; *cakravartin* refers to the "universal monarch." the possessor of the seven jewels of sovereignty who sets in motion the wheel of righteous rule. Some—such as *bhagavan*—convey a sense of beneficent lordship. Others—such as *tathāgata* ("thus come," or "thus gone")—retain, at least in retrospect, an aura of august ambiguity and mystery.

Various epithets define the Buddha as having attained perfection in all domains. His wisdom is perfect, as are his physical form and manner. In some cases the epithets indicate that the Buddha is without equal, that he has attained "the summit of the world." André Bareau concluded his study "The Superhuman Personality of the Buddha and its Symbolism in the *Mahāparinirvāṇa-sūtra,*" which is largely an examination of the epithets in this important text, by stating that through these epithets the authors "began to conceive the transcendence of the Buddha. . . . Perfect in all points, superior through distance from all beings, unique, the Beatific had evidently taken, in the thought of his followers, the place which the devotees of the great religions attributed to the great God whom they adored" (*Myths and Symbols*, ed. Charles H. Long and Joseph M. Kitagawa, Chicago, 1969, pp. 19–20).

The epithets of the Buddha, in addition to having a central place in Buddhist devotion, are featured in the *buddhānusmṛti* meditation—the "recollection of the Buddha." This form of meditation, like all Buddhist meditational practices, had as its aim the discipline and purification of the mind; but, in addition, it was a technique of visualization, a way of recovering the image of the founder. [*See* Nien-fo.] This practice of visualization by contemplation on the epithets is important in the Theravāda tradition, both monastic and lay, and it was also very popular in the Sarvāstivāda communities in northwestern India and influential in various Mahāyāna traditions in China. It was instrumental in the development of the Mahāyāna notion of the "three bodies" *(trikāya)* of the Buddha, particularly the second, or visualized, body that was known as his *saṃbhogakāya* ("body of enjoyment").

Biographies. Like the tradition of uttering and interpreting epithets that extolled the exalted nature and virtues of the Buddha, the tradition of recounting biographical episodes is an integral part of early Buddhism. Episodic fragments, preserved in the Pali and Chinese versions of the early Buddhist literature, are embedded in sermons attributed to the Buddha himself and illustrate points of practice or doctrine. Such episodes are also used as narrative frames to provide a context indicating when and where a particular discourse was taught. It appears certain that other episodic fragments were recounted and generated at the four great pilgrimage centers of early Buddhism—the sites that were identified as the locations of the Buddha's birth, of his Enlightenment, of the preaching of his first sermon, and of his death, or *parinirvāṇa.* Some of the scattered narratives do seem to presuppose a developed biographical tradition, but others suggest a fluidity in the biographical structure. Thus, a crucial problem that is posed for our understanding of the biographical process in the Buddhist tradition is when and how a more or less fixed biography of the Buddha actually took shape.

The most convincing argument for the very early development of a comprehensive biography of the Buddha has been made by Erich Frauwallner (1956). Frauwallner argues, on the basis of a brilliant text-critical analysis, that a no longer extant biography of the Buddha, complete up to the conversion of the two great disciples, Śāriputra and Maudgalyāyana, was written approximately one hundred years after the Buddha's death and well prior to the reign of King Aśoka. This biography, he maintains, was composed as an introduction to the *Skandhaka*, a text of monastic discipline (Vinaya) that was reportedly confirmed at the Second Buddhist Council held at Vaiśālī. Appended to the *Skandhaka*, according to Frauwallner, was an account of the Buddha's death, or *parinirvāṇa*, and of the first years of the fledgling monastic community. Frauwallner contends that all subsequent Buddha biographies have been derived from this basic ur-text. The fragmentary biographies found in the extant Vinaya literature of the various Buddhist schools indicate a crumbling away of this original biography; later autonomous biographies are versions cut from the original Vinaya context and subsequently elaborated.

A different argument has been made, also on the basis of close text-critical study, by scholars such as Alfred Foucher, Étienne Lamotte, and André Bareau. They have argued that there was a gradual development of biographical cycles, with only a later synthesis of this material into a series of more complete biographies. According to this thesis, the earliest stages of the development of the Buddha biography are the fragments in the Sūtra and Vinaya texts, which show no concern for chronology or continuity. The Sūtra literature emphasizes stories of the Buddha's previous births *(jātaka)*, episodes leading up to the Enlightenment, the Enlightenment itself, and an account of his last journey, death, and funeral. André Bareau states that the biographical material in the Sūtras was "composed for the most part of episodes taken from separate traditions, from which the authors chose with complete freedom, guided only by their desire to illustrate a particular point of doctrine" (Bareau, 1963, p. 364). The Vinaya texts, on the other hand, focus on the Buddha as teacher and incorporate—in addition to accounts of the events associated with his Enlightenment—narratives that describe the early days of his ministry, including an account of the conversion of his first disciples. The air of these Vinaya fragments seems to be to confer authenticity on the monastic rules and practices set forth in the rest of the text.

The oldest of the surviving autonomous biographies is the *Mahāvastu*, an unwieldly anthology written in Buddhist Hybrid Sanskrit about the beginning of the common era. Other more tightly constructed biographies were produced soon after the *Mahāvastu*—notably, the *Lalitavistara*, which played an important role in various Mahāyāna traditions; the *Abhiniṣkramaṇa Sūtra*, which was especially popular in China, where at least five Chinese works were, nominally at least, translations of it; and the very famous and popular *Buddhacarita*, attributed to Aśvaghoṣa. Much later, between the fourth and fifth centuries, still another autonomous biography, known as the Vinaya of the Mūlasarvāstivādins, was given its final form. This voluminous compendium of biographical traditions provided later Mahāyāna schools with a major source for stories about the Buddha and his career.

These new autonomous biographies continued to incorporate stories that had developed at the pilgrimage sites associated with the Buddha's birth and great renunciation, his Enlightenment, and his first sermon. For example, in the *Lalitavistara* an episode is recounted that is clearly related to a specific shrine at the Buddhist pilgrimage site at Kapilavastu—namely, the story in which the Buddha's charioteer leaves him and returns to the palace in Kapilavastu. What is more, these new autonomous biographies also continued to exhibit structural elements that had been characteristic of the biographical segments of the older Vinaya literature. For example, all of the early autonomous biographies (with the exception of the "completed" Chinese and Tibetan versions of the *Buddhacarita*) follow the Vinaya tradition, which ends the story at a point soon after the Buddha had begun his ministry.

These new autonomous biographies testify to three important changes that affected the traditions of Buddha biography during the centuries immediately following the death of King Aśoka. The first is the inclusion of new biographical elements drawn from non-Buddhist and even non-Indian sources. The autonomous biographies were the products of the cosmopolitan civilizations associated with the Śātavāhana and Kushan (Kuṣāṇa) empires, and therefore it is not surprising that new episodes were adapted from Greek and West Asian sources. Somewhat later, as the autonomous Buddha biographies were introduced into other areas, changes were introduced to accentuate the Buddha's exemplification of new cultural values. Thus, in a fourth-century Chinese "translation" of the *Abhiniṣkramaṇa*, great emphasis was placed on the Buddha's exemplification of filial piety through the conversion of his father, King Śuddhodana.

The second important change exhibited by these new autonomous biographies was the ubiquitous inclusion of stories about the Buddha's previous lives *(jātaka)* as a device for explicating details of his final life as Gautama. This is particularly evident in the *Mahāvastu* and in certain versions of the *Abhiniṣkramaṇa Sūtra*, in which, according to Lamotte, "the Jātakas become the prime mover of the narration: each episode in the life of the Buddha is given as the result and reproduction of an event from previous lives" (Lamotte, 1958, p. 725).

The third discernible change is the increasing placement of emphasis on the superhuman and transcendent dimensions of the Buddha's nature. Earlier narratives refer to the Buddha's fatigue and to his susceptibility to illness, but in the autonomous biographies he is said to be above human frailties. There is a tendency to emphasize the Buddha's superhuman qualities, not only of mind, but also of body: "It is true that the Buddhas bathe, but no dirt is found on them; their bodies are radiant like golden amaranth. Their bathing is mere conformity with the world" (*Mahāvastu*, trans. J. J. Jones, London, 1949, vol. 1, p. 133). As a function of this same emphasis on transcendence, the Buddha's activities are increasingly portrayed in the modes of miracle and magic. With the emergence and development of Mahāyāna, new narratives began to appear that portrayed the Buddha preaching a more exalted doctrine, sometimes on a mountain peak, sometimes in a celestial realm, sometimes to his most receptive disciples, sometimes to a great assembly of *bodhisattvas* (future Buddhas) and gods.

Whereas the Mahāyāna accepted the early autonomous biographies and supplemented them with additional episodes of their own, the Theravāda community displayed a continuing resistance to developments in the biographical tradition. For almost nine centuries after the death of Gautama, the various elements of the Buddha biography were kept separate in Theravāda literature. But in the fifth century CE, about half a millennium after the composition of the first autonomous biographies, the Theravādins began to create their own biographical genres. These brought together and synthesized, in their own, more restrained style, many of the previously fragmented narratives.

Two types of Buddha biographies have had an important impact and role in the later history of the Theravāda tradition. The model for the classical type is the *Nidānakathā,* a text that serves as an introduction to the fifth-century *Jātaka Commentary* and thus continues the pattern of using biography to provide a narrative context that authenticates the teaching. It traces the Buddha's career from the time of his previous birth as Sumedha (when he made his original vow to become a Buddha) to the year following Gautama's Enlightenment, when he took up residence in the Jetavana Monastery. Subsequent Theravāda biographies, based on the *Nidānakathā,* continued the narration through the rest of Gautama's ministry and beyond.

The second type of Theravāda biography—the chronicle *(vaṃsa)* biography—illustrates a distinctive Theravāda understanding of the Buddha. From very early in their history the Theravādins had distinguished between two bodies of the Buddha, his physical body *(rūpakāya)* and his body of truth *(dharmakāya).* After the Buddha's death, or *parinirvāṇa,* the *rūpakāya* continued to be present to the community in his relics, and his *dharmakāya* continued to be present in his teachings. In the fourth to fifth centuries CE the Theravādins began to compose biographical chronicles that focused on these continuing legacies. These begin with previous lives of the Buddha, then provide an abbreviated account of his "final" life as Gautama. They go on to narrate the history of the tradition by interweaving accounts of kings who maintain the physical legacy (in the form of relics, stupas, and the like) with accounts of the monastic order, which maintains his *dharma* legacy (in the form of proper teaching and discipline). Examples of this type of biographical chronicle are numerous, beginning with the *Dīpavaṃsa* and *Mahāvaṃsa* and continuing through many other *vaṃsa* texts written in Sri Lanka and Southeast Asia.

Throughout the premodern history of Buddhism, all of the major Buddhist schools preserved biographies of the Buddha. And in each situation, they were continually reinterpreted in relation to contemporary attitudes and experiences. But in the modern period, a new genre of Buddha biographies has been introduced. This new type of biography has been influenced by Western scholarship on Buddhism and by Western attempts to recover the historical Buddha, who had—from the modernist perspective—been hidden from view by the accretions of tradition. New, largely urbanized elites throughout the Buddhist world have sought to "demythologize" the Buddha biography, deleting miraculous elements of the Buddha's life and replacing them with an image of the founder as a teacher of a rationalistic ethical system or a "scientific" system of meditation or as a social reformer committed to the cause of democracy, socialism, or egalitarianism. This new genre of Buddha biography has appeared in many Buddhist contexts and has made an impact that has cut across all the traditional lines of geographical and sectarian division.

Visual Representations. The images of the founder that Buddhists have generated and expressed visually are more enigmatic than the images presented in epithets and biographies. The history of Buddhist monumental architecture, art, and sculpture does not neatly fit such accustomed categories as "mythologization" or "divinization." Furthermore, the association of various kinds of visual representation with veneration and worship challenges many stereotypes about the secondary place of cult activity in the Buddhist tradition. The situation is further complicated by the fact that the function and significance of visual representations of the Buddha are only explained in relatively late Buddhist literature, after both doctrine and practice had become extremely complex.

The most important of the very early visual representations of the Buddha was the burial mound, or stupa (Skt., *stūpa*). The interment of the remains of kings and heroes in burial mounds was a well-established practice in pre-Buddhist India. Buddhists and Jains adopted these mounds as models for their first religious monuments and honored them with traditional practices. In the Pali *Mahāparinibbāna Suttanta* and its parallels in Sanskrit, Tibetan, and Chinese, the Buddha gives instructions that his funeral rites should be performed in the manner customary for a "universal monarch" *(cakravartin),* an epithet that was applied to the Buddha.

[*See* Cakravartin.] After his cremation his bones were to be deposited in a golden urn and placed in a mound built at the crossing of four main roads. Offerings of flowers and garlands, banners, incense, and music characterized both the funeral rites themselves and the continuing worship at a stupa.

As Buddhism developed, the stupa continued to serve as a central visual representation of the founder. Seeing a stupa called to memory the greatness of the Buddha and—for some at least—became equivalent to actually seeing the Buddha when he was alive. Since the Buddha's physical remains could be divided, replicated, and distributed, new stupas containing relics could be constructed. They became a focal point for worship wherever Buddhism spread, first within India and then beyond. What is more, the stupa had symbolic connotations that exerted a significant influence on the way in which the Buddha was perceived. For example, stupas had a locative significance through which the Buddha was associated with specific territorial units. They also came increasingly to represent a cosmology and cosmography ordered by Buddhist principles, thus symbolically embodying the notion of the Buddha as a cosmic person.

The later literature explains that a stupa is worthy of worship and reverence not only because it contains a relic or relics but also because its form symbolizes the enlightened state of a Buddha, or Buddhahood itself. In some texts the stupa is described as the *dharmakāya*, or transcendent body, of the Buddha, and each of its layers and components is correlated with a set of spiritual qualities cultivated to perfection by a Buddha. Such symbolic correlations made evident what, in some circles at least, had been long accepted, namely, the notion that the stupa represents the Buddha's spiritual, as well as his physical, legacy.

The beginnings of Buddhist art are found on post-Aśokan stupas, such as those found at Bhārhut, Sāñcī, and Amarāvatī. These great stupas and their gates are decorated with narrative reliefs of events from the Buddha's life and with scenes of gods and men "rendering homage to the Lord." The Buddha is always depicted symbolically in these reliefs, with emblems appropriate to the story. For example, in friezes depicting scenes associated with his birth he is often represented by a footprint with the characteristic marks of the *mahāpuruṣa* (the cosmic man destined to be either a *cakravartin* or a Buddha). In scenes associated with his Enlightenment he is often represented by the Bodhi Tree under which he attained Enlightenment, or the throne on which he was seated when that event occurred. When the subject is the preaching of his first sermon he is often represented by an eight-spoked wheel that is identified with the wheel of *dharma*. When the subject is his death, or *parinirvāṇa*, the preferred symbol is, of course, the stupa. [*See also* Stupa Worship.]

The motivation for this aniconic imagery is not clear, especially since the friezes abound with other human figures. However, it is probable that abstract art was more adaptable to contemplative uses that we have already seen emphasized in connection with the epithets of the Buddha and with the symbolic interpretation of the stupa. It may also be that these aniconic images imply a conception of the Buddha as a supramundane being similar to that of the docetic portrayals found in the autonomous biographies that appear somewhat later. This suggests that at this time Buddhism may have been richer in its concrete reality, in its practice, than in its doctrine, as it took centuries for a doctrinal understanding of the significance of these first representations to be formulated in the literature.

The stupa and other aniconic symbols emblematic of the Buddha have remained an integral component of Buddhist life in all Buddhist areas and eras. Toward the end of the first century BCE, however, another form of visual representation began to appear, namely, the anthropomorphic image that subsequently assumed paramount importance in all Buddhist countries and sects. The first of these images are contemporary with the autonomous biographies of the Buddha, and, like these texts, they appropriate previously non-Buddhist and non-Indian motifs to express Buddhist conceptions and experiences. At Mathurā, in north-central India, where the first statues seem to have originated, sculptors employed a style and iconography associated with *yakṣas*, the popular life-cult deities of ancient India, to create bulky and powerful figures of the Buddha. At Gandhāra in northwestern India, another major center of early Buddhist image-making, the artists sculpted the Buddha images quite differently, appropriating Hellenistic conventions introduced into Asia by the Greeks, who ruled the area in the centuries following the invasions of Alexander the Great.

A great many styles have developed for the Buddha image; and just as at Mathurā and Gandhāra, local conventions have been fully exploited. There has been a continuity, however, to all these creations: the Buddha image has consistently served a dual function as both an object of worship and a support for contemplation. It seems clear that the basic form of the image was shaped by conceptions of the Buddha as *lokottara* (supramundane), *mahāpuruṣa*, *cakravartin*, omniscient, and so on, and standardized iconography was used to convey these various dimensions. The sculpted (and later painted) image was both an expression of, and an aid for, the visualization of the master and the realization of his presence.

If aniconic symbols lend themselves especially well to contemplative uses, anthropomorphic images seem more appropriate to emotion and prayer, as well as to worship as such. In fact, the patterns of veneration and worship that developed in connection with Buddha images show a strong continuity with the ancient devotional and petitionary practices associated with the *yakṣas* and other folk deities. Throughout Buddhist history the veneration and worship of Buddha images have involved sensuous offerings of flowers, incense, music, food, and drink, and have often been closely tied to very immediate worldly concerns.

Later Buddhist literature explains that the Buddha image is worthy of honor and worship because it is a likeness of the Buddha. Popular practice often ascribes a living presence to the statue, whether by placing a relic within it or by a ritual of consecration that infuses it with "life." Thus the image of the Buddha, like the stupa, is both a reminder that can inspire and guide and a locus of power. [*See also* Iconography, *article on* Buddhist Iconography.]

Other Buddhas

The representations of the Buddha in epithet, biography, and image have been shared in their main outlines by the great majority of Buddhist schools. However, the recognition of other Buddhas, the roles other Buddhas have played, and the evaluation of their significance (and hence the role and significance of Gautama himself) have varied greatly from one tradition to another.

Buddhas of the Past and Future. Quite early, Gautama is perceived as one of several Buddhas in a series that began in the distant past. In the early canonical literature, the series of previous Buddhas sometimes appears as a practically anonymous group, deriving probably from the recognition that Gautama could not have been alone in achieving enlightenment. It is thus not surprising that in texts such as the *Saṃyutta Nikāya* the interest in these previous Buddhas focuses on their thoughts at the time of enlightenment, thoughts that are identical with those attributed to Gautama when he achieved the same experience.

The most important early text on previous Buddhas is the *Mahāvadāna Sutta,* which refers to six Buddhas who had appeared prior to Gautama. This text implicitly contains the earliest coordinated biography of the Buddha, for it describes the pattern to which the lives of all Buddhas conform. Thus, describing the life of a Buddha named Vipaśyin, Gautama narrates that he was born into a royal family, that he was raised in luxury, that he was later confronted with the realities of sickness, aging, and death while visiting a park, and that he subsequently took up the life of a wandering mendicant. After Vipaśyin realized the truth for himself, he established a monastic order and taught what he had discovered to others. In the narratives of the other Buddhas, some details vary; but in every instance they are said to have discovered and taught the same eternal truth.

There is clear evidence that Buddhas who were thought to have lived prior to Gautama were worshiped in India at least from the time of Aśoka through the period of Buddhist decline. In the inscription, Aśoka states that he had doubled the size of the stupa associated with the Buddha Konākamana, who had lived earlier than Gautama and was his immediate predecessor. During the first millennium of the common era, successive Chinese pilgrims recorded visits to Indian monuments dedicated to former Buddhas, many of them attributed to the pious construction activities of Aśoka.

The *Buddhavaṃsa* (Lineage of the Buddhas), which is a late text within the Pali canon, narrates the lives of twenty-four previous Buddhas in almost identical terms. It may be that the number twenty-four was borrowed from Jainism, which has a lineage of twenty-four *tīrthaṃkaras* that culminates in the figure of the founder, Mahāvīra. The *Buddhavaṃsa* also embellished the idea of a connection between Gautama Buddha and the lineage of previous Buddhas. It contains the story that later came to provide the starting point for the classic Theravāda biography of Gautama—the story in which the future Gautama Buddha, in his earlier birth as Sumedha, meets the previous Buddha Dīpaṃkara and vows to undertake the great exertions necessary to attain Buddhahood for himself.

According to conceptions that are closely interwoven with notions concerning previous Buddhas, the appearance of a Buddha in this world is determined not only by his own spiritual efforts but also by other circumstances. There can only be one Buddha in a particular world at a given time, and no Buddha can arise until the teachings of the previous Buddha have completely disappeared. There are also cosmological considerations. A Buddha is not born in the beginning of a cosmic aeon *(kalpa)* when human beings are so well off and live so long that they do not fear sickness, aging, and death; such people, like the gods and other superhuman beings, would be incapable of insight into the pervasiveness of suffering and the impermanence of all things and therefore would not be prepared to receive a Buddha's message. Furthermore, Buddhas are born only in the continent of Jambudvīpa (roughly equivalent to India) and only to priestly *(brāhmaṇa)* or noble *(kṣatriya)* families.

The idea of a chronological series of previous Buddhas, which was prominent primarily in the Hīnayāna traditions, accentuates the significance of Gautama by designating him as the teacher for our age and by providing him with a spiritual lineage that authenticates his message. This idea also provides a basis for hope because it suggests that even if the force of Gautama's person and message has begun to fade, there remains the possibility that other Buddhas are yet to come.

The belief in a future Buddha also originated in the Hīnayāna tradition and has played an important role in various Hīnayāna schools, including the Theravāda. The name of this next Buddha is Maitreya ("the friendly one"), and he seems to have come into prominence in the period after the reign of King Aśoka. (Technically, of course, Maitreya is a *bodhisattva*—one who is on the path to Buddhahood—rather than a Buddha in the full sense. However, the degree to which the attention of Buddhists has been focused on the role that he will play when he becomes a Buddha justifies consideration of him in the present context.) [*See* Maitreya.]

According to the Maitreyan mythology that has been diffused throughout the entire Buddhist world, the future Buddha, who was one of Gautama Buddha's disciples, now dwells in Tuṣita Heaven, awaiting the appropriate moment to be reborn on earth, where he will inaugurate an era of peace, prosperity, and salvation. As the Buddha of the future, Maitreya assumed many diverse roles. Among other things he became an object of worship, a focus of aspiration, and a center of religiopolitical interest both as a legitimator of royalty and as a rallying point for rebellion. [*See especially* Millenarianism, *article on* Chinese Millenarian Movements.]

The wish to be reborn in the presence of Maitreya, whether in Tuṣita Heaven or when he is reborn among humans, has been a sustaining hope of many Buddhists in the past, and it persists among Theravādins even today. The contemplation and recitation of the name of Maitreya inspired devotional cults in northwestern India, Central Asia, and China, especially between the fourth and seventh centuries CE. But in East Asia his devotional cult was superseded by that dedicated to Amitābha, a Buddha now existing in another cosmic world.

Celestial and Cosmic Buddhas. The recognition that there could be other Buddhas in other world systems described in Buddhist cosmology builds on implications already present in the idea of past and future Buddhas. Like the first Buddhas of the past, the first Buddhas associated with other worlds are largely anonymous, appearing in groups to celebrate the teaching of the Buddha Gautama. The many epithets of the Buddha were sometimes pressed into service as personal names for individual Buddhas who needed to be identified.

The idea of Buddhas existing in other worlds comes to the fore in the early Mahāyāna literature. It was first employed, as in the *Saddharmapuṇḍarīka Sūtra* (Lotus of the True Law), to authenticate new teachings, just as the tradition of former Buddhas had done for the teachings of the early community. In the course of time, some of these Buddhas came to be recognized individually as very powerful, their worlds as indescribably splendid and blissful. They were Buddhas in superhuman form, and their careers, which were dedicated to the saving of others, lasted for aeons. Their influence was effective beyond their own worlds, and they could provide assistance—through the infinite merit they had accumulated—to the inhabitants of other world systems, including our own. The traditions that have focused attention on these Buddhas have inevitably deemphasized the importance of Gautama Buddha by removing his singularity in human experience and by contrasting him with more powerful Buddhas who could make their assistance and influence immediately and directly available. [*See also* Pure and Impure Lands; Merit, *article on* Buddhist Concepts; *and* Cosmology, *article on* Buddhist Cosmology.]

While the number of such coexisting celestial Buddhas is, in principle, infinite, and a great number are named in Buddhist literature, distinct mythological, iconic, and devotional traditions have only developed in a few cases. Amitābha ("boundless light") is one of the most important of the Buddhas who did become the focus of a distinctive tradition. Originating in Northwest India or Central Asia, his appeal subsequently spread to China, Tibet, and Japan. Amitābha rules over a paradise that contains all the excellences of other Buddha lands. He offers universal accessibility to this Pure Land (called Sukhāvatī), granting rebirth to those who practice the Buddha's determination to be reborn in it, and even to those who merely recite his name or think of him briefly but with faith. In the Amitābha/Pure Land traditions, which have had continuing success in China and Japan, we see a concentration on patterns of contemplation, visualization, and recitation first developed in connection with the epithets of the Buddha. [*See* Amitābha.]

Another celestial Buddha who came to hold a position of importance in the Buddhist tradition is Bhaiṣajyaguru, the Master of Medicine. Bhaiṣajyaguru rules over his own paradisiacal realm, which, in contrast to Amitābha's western paradise, is traditionally located in the east. Unlike Amitābha, he does not assist human beings in reaching final liberation, nor does he even offer rebirth in his land. Rather, the repetition or rememberance of his name relieves various kinds of suffering, such as sickness, hunger, and fear. The ritual worship of his statue brings all things that are desired. In the cult dedicated to Bhaiṣajyaguru—popular in China and Japan, where it was often influenced by Amitābha traditions—we see a magnification of the patterns of worship that had originally coalesced around the stupa and the Buddha image. [*See* Bhaiṣajyaguru.]

In other contexts, conceptions of integrated pantheons of Buddhas were developed and exerted widespread influence. For example, in the traditions of Esoteric Buddhism a strong emphasis was placed on a primordial, central Buddha. He was taken to be the essence or source of a set of Buddhas who were positioned in the form of a cosmic *maṇḍala* ("circle") that was vividly depicted in iconography and ritual, for example, in the *tanka* paintings of Tibet. In certain Indo-Tibetan traditions the central Buddha was Vajradhara ("diamond holder") or sometimes, when the emphasis was more theistic, the Ādi ("primordial") Buddha. In other Indo-Tibetan traditions the central Buddha was Vairocana ("resplendent"), who also served as the preeminent Buddha in the Esoteric (Shingon) tradition of Japan, where he was identified with the all-important solar deity in the indigenous pantheon of *kami.* [*See* Mahāvairocana.] In both cases—the one associated with Vajradhara and the Ādi Buddha and the one associated with Vairocana—the pantheon encompassed other Buddhas (and sometimes their "families"), who were identified with subsidiary cosmic positions. These included the east, a position often occupied by Akṣobhya ("imperturbable"); the south, often occupied by Ratnasaṃbhava ("jewel-born"); the west, often occupied by Amitābha; and the north, often occupied by Amoghasiddhi ("infallible success"). In both cases the pantheon had a macrocosmic reference to the universe as a whole and a microcosmic reference in which the Buddhas of the pantheon were homoligized with the mystic physiology of the human body. [*See also* Buddhism, Schools of, *article on* Esoteric Buddhism.]

Living Buddhas. In addition to the Buddha, *pratyekabuddhas*, previous Buddhas, the future Buddha, celestial Buddhas, and cosmic Buddhas, still another kind of Buddha was recognized by some Buddhists—what we shall call a "living Buddha." Living Buddhas are persons in this world who have, in one way or another, achieved the status of a fully enlightened and compassionate being. In some cases these living Buddhas have attained Buddhahood through various, usually Esoteric, forms of practice; in others they are incarnations of a Buddha, ordinarily a celestial Buddha, already included in the established pantheon. The presence of living Buddhas tends, of course, to diminish to a new degree the significance of Gautama Buddha (except in rare cases where it is he who reappears). However, their presence also reiterates with new force two characteristic Mahāyāna-Vajrayāna emphases: that the message of the Buddhas continues to be efficaciously available in the world and that the community still has direct access to the kind of assistance that only a Buddha can provide.

Like the notions of previous Buddhas and the Buddhas of other worlds, the concept of living Buddhas began to be elaborated in a context in which a new kind of teaching and practice was being introduced. In this case the new teaching and practice was Esoteric in character and was focused on ritual activities that promised to provide a "fast path" to Buddhahood. Thus the new kind of Buddha—the living Buddha—was both a product of the new movement and a mode of authenticating it. The analogy between the earlier development of the notion of celestial Buddhas and the later development of the notion of living Buddhas can be carried further. Just as only a few celestial Buddhas received their own individual mythology, iconography, and devotional attention, so too a limited number of living Buddhas were similarly singled out. It is not surprising that many of these especially recognized and venerated living Buddhas were figures who initiated new strands of tradition by introducing practices, revealing hidden texts, converting new peoples, and the like. A classic example of a living Buddha in the Tibetan tradition is Padmasambhava, the famous missionary from India who is credited with subduing the demons in Tibet, converting the people to the Buddhist cause, and founding the Rñiṅ-ma-pa order. [*See the biography of Padmasambhava.*] An example of the same type of figure in Japan is Kūkai, the founder of the Esoteric Shingon tradition, who has traditionally been venerated both as master and as savior. [*See the biography of Kūkai.*]

The notion of living Buddhas as incarnations of celestial Buddhas also came to the fore with the rise of Esoteric Buddhism. In this case there seems to have been an especially close connection with Buddhist conceptions of kingship and rule. In both the Hīnayāna and Mahāyāna contexts, the notion of the king as a *bodhisattva*, or future Buddha, was ancient; in the case of the rather common royal identifications with Maitreya, the distinction between the king as an incarnation of the celestial *bodhisattva* and the king as a living Buddha had been very fluid. With the rise of the Esoteric Buddhist traditions a further step was taken. Thus, after the Esoteric tradition had been firmly established in the Khmer (Cambodian) capital of Angkor, the king came to be explicitly recognized and venerated as Bhaiṣajyaguru, Master of Medicine. Somewhat later in Tibet, the Panchen Lamas, who have traditionally had both royal and monastic functions, were identified as successive incarnations of the Buddha Amitābha.

Buddhahood

The epithets, biographies, and images of Śākyamuni and other Buddhas weigh the distinctiveness of each Buddha against his inclusion within a series or assembly of similar beings. However, as the appellative character of the term *buddha* suggests, at the level of Buddhahood each tradition has affirmed the ultimate identity of all those they have recognized as Buddhas. Even the Theravādins, who have consistently given pride of place to Gautama, have acknowledged this final level at which differentiations are not relevant. The same is true for those movements that focus primary attention on Amitābha or Mahāvairocana. The consensus of Buddhists in this respect is voiced by the *Milindapañha* (The Questions of King Milinda), a Hīnayāna text dating from the beginning of the common era: "There is no distinction in form, morality, concentration, wisdom, freedom...among all the Buddhas because all Buddhas are the same in respect to their nature" (London, 1880, p. 285).

This initial consensus concerning the ultimate identity of all Buddhas notwithstanding, the actual delineation of Buddhahood has varied significantly from one Buddhist tradition to another. This third level of meaning of the term *buddha* has always been discussed in connection with questions concerning the nature and analysis of reality. Early Buddhists believed that a Buddha awoke to and displayed the causal process (*pratītya-samutpāda*, co-dependent origination) that perpetuates this world, allowing himself and others to use those processes to end further rebirth. [*See* Pratītya-samutpāda.] The early Mahāyāna, especially in the Prajñāpāramitā literature, saw Buddhahood as awakening to the absence of self-nature in all things *(śūnyatā)* and proclaimed this absence as the ultimate reality *(tathatā)*. [*See* Śūnyam and Śūnyatā *and* Tathatā.] Later Mahāyāna schools, such as the Yogācārins, held a more idealistic worldview; for them Buddhahood was the recovery of an originally pure and undefiled mind. The Hua-yen (Jpn., Kegon) school, an East Asian tradition based on the *Avataṃsaka Sūtra*, posited the infinite mutual interaction of all things and developed a striking conception of a universal, cosmic Buddha who is all-pervasive. In such contexts Buddhahood itself became an alternative way of describing reality. [*See* Yogācāra *and* Hua-yen.]

Between the consensus about the identity of all Buddhas and the diversity of interpretations, there are at least two different languages in which Buddhahood has traditionally been conceived and described. The first is the identification of Buddhahood in terms of the special characteristics associated with a Buddha. The second is the discussion of the Buddha bodies that make up Buddhahood. These two clusters of concepts allow us to see patterns of continuity in the midst of the very different ways in which Buddhahood has been understood.

Buddhist scholasticism developed subtle catalogs of the unique powers and qualities of a Buddha, culminating in lists of *āveṇika dharmas* (special characteristics). These special characteristics vary in number from 6 to 140, depending on the text and context. What interests us here is not the multitude of qualities and powers that are mentioned but, rather, the fact that these qualities and powers are often grouped under four major headings. These four headings are conduct and realization, which apply to the attainment of Buddhahood, and wisdom and activity, which apply to the expression of Buddhahood.

Throughout Buddhist history these four dimensions of Buddhahood have been interpreted in different ways. For example, Hīnayānists have tended to emphasize motivated conduct as a means to the realization of Buddhahood, whereas Mahāyānists and Vajrayānists have tended to stress that Buddhahood (often in the form of Buddha nature) is in important respects a necessary prerequisite for such conduct. [*See* Buddhist Ethics.] Similarly, Hīnayānists have often recognized a certain distance between the attainment of wisdom and a commitment to compassionate activity, whereas in the Mahāyāna and Vajrayāna traditions the stress has been placed on the inseparable fusion of wisdom on the one hand and the expression of compassion on the other. [*See* Prajñā, Karuṇā, *and* Upāya.] These differences notwithstanding, the four basic dimensions are present in virtually all Buddhist conceptions of Buddhahood.

When we turn to the way Buddhahood has been expressed through the language of Buddha bodies, we discern the same sort of continuity in the midst of difference. In the early Buddhist literature (e.g., *Dīgha Nikāya*, vol. 3, p. 84) the Buddha is described as having a body "born of *dharma*," that is, a *dharmakāya*. In this early period, and in the subsequent Theravāda development, the notion that Gautama possessed a *dharmakāya* seems to have served primarily as a metaphor that affirmed a continuity between the personal realizations that he had achieved and truth or reality itself. In some later Hīnayāna traditions such as the Sarvāstivāda, and in the Mahāyāna, the notion of *dharmakāya* took on a stronger meaning. It served as a primary means through which an increasingly transcendent vision of Buddhahood could subsume the inescapable fact of

Gautama's death. According to such texts as the *Saddharmapuṇḍarīka*, the *dharmakāya* is the true meaning of Buddhahood; Buddhas such as Gautama who appear, teach, and die among human beings are mere manifestations. In this early Mahāyāna context, however, the correlated notions of Buddhahood and *dharmakāya* are still conditioned by their close association with philosophical conceptions such as *śūnyatā* ("emptiness") and *tathatā* ("suchness").

The *dharmakāya* is given a more ontological cast in other Mahāyāna and Vajrayāna traditions. In these cases, *dharmakāya* denotes a "ground" or "source" that is the reality that gives rise to all other realities; this provides the basis for a new understanding of the whole range of Buddha bodies. Buddhahood comes to be explicated in terms of a theory of three bodies. The *trikāya* ("three bodies") are the *dharmakāya*, the primal body that is the source of the other two; the emanated *saṃbhogakāya* ("enjoyment body"), a glorious body seen in visions in which Buddhas of other worlds become manifest to devotees in this world; and the "magical" and ephemeral *nirmāṇakāya*, the physical body in which Gautama, for example, appeared among his disciples.

In some Mahāyāna and Vajrayāna contexts, this more ontological conception of the Buddhahood and *dharmakāya* was also connected with the important soteriological notion of a Buddha nature, or *tathāgata-garbha* (tathāgata is an epithet for a Buddha, *garbha* means "womb"), which is the source and cause of enlightenment as well as its fruit. In these traditions, Buddha nature, or *tathāgata-garbha*, is taken to be the *dharmakāya* covered with defilements. Enlightenment, and therefore Buddhahood, is the recovery of this pure, original state of being that is identical with ultimate reality itself. In other Mahāyāna and Vajrayāna contexts, even the dichotomy between purity and defilement is transcended at the level of Buddhahood. [*See* Tathāgata-garbha.]

Conclusion

In the course of our discussion of *buddha* as an appellative term we have distinguished three basic levels of meaning—those associated with Gautama Buddha, with other Buddhas, and with Buddhahood as such. However, it is important to note that Buddhist usage has always held the three levels of meaning closely together, with the result that each level has had a continuing influence on the others. Thus, even though a distinction between the different denotations of *buddha* is helpful for purposes of interpretation and understanding, it cannot be drawn too sharply.

In fact, these three meanings represent three different modes of reference that, according to some Indian theories of denotation, are common to all names. The word *cow*, for example, refers to individual cows ("a cow"), the aggregation of cows, and the quality of "cowness" common to all cows. There are obvious parallels to the uses of *buddha*. It might be helpful for those unfamiliar with such theories to think of *buddha* in terms of set theory: individual Buddhas are members of subsets of the set of Buddhahood. Just as mathematical sets exist without members, so Buddhahood exists, according to the affirmation of Buddhists, even when it is not embodied by individual Buddhas.

[*For further discussion of the nature of Buddhas and Buddhahood see* Celestial Buddhas and Bodhisattvas *and* Tathāgata. *The religious career culminating in Buddhahood is treated in* Bodhisattva Path. *"Enlightenment" is discussed in* Buddhist Philosophy *and* Nirvāṇa.]

BIBLIOGRAPHY

Scholarship that is available in European languages generally treats the different levels of meaning of the appellative *buddha* in isolation. The interrelations among the different levels of meaning still remain largely unexplored.

Two books by Edward J. Thomas, if read in conjunction, can serve as a suitable introduction to the subject. *The Life of Buddha as Legend and History* (1927; 3d rev. ed., London, 1949) remains the standard work on the biography of the Buddha in English. *The History of Buddhist Thought* (1933; 2d ed., New York, 1951) surveys the development of ideas of other Buddhas and Buddhahood against the backdrop of the Indian Buddhist tradition. Thomas, however, does not include any of the developments in Tibet or East Asia, and his work has a definite bias in favor of the Pali tradition. A useful supplement for Tibet is David L. Snellgrove's *Buddhist Himālaya* (Oxford, 1957), which provides an introduction to the Vajrayāna interpretations. East Asian innovations were largely in connection with the meaning of Buddhahood. They may be approached through Junjirō Takakusu's *The Essentials of Buddhist Philosophy*, edited by Wing-Tsit Chan and Charles A. Moore (Honolulu, 1947), although, as the title suggests, Takakusu is not primarily concerned with Buddhological patterns as such.

Heinz Bechert's important article "The Date of the Buddha Reconsidered," *Indologica Taurinensia* 10 (1982): 29–36, provides helpful summaries of the arguments favoring the long and short chronologies for calculating the date of the Buddha, although his conclusion in favor of the short chronology is by no means definitive. The cultural context of the historical Buddha is outlined by Padmanabh S. Jaini in his "*Śramaṇas:* Their Conflict with Brāhmaṇical Society," in *Chapters in Indian Civilization*, rev. ed., edited by Joseph W. Elder (Dubuque, 1970) vol. 1, pp. 39–81. This article should be read together with J. A. B. van Buitenen's "Vedic and Upaniṣadic Bases of Indian Civilization," which immediately preceeds it in the same volume (pp. 1–38).

A helpful starting point for the study of the Buddha biography is Frank E. Reynolds's "The Many Lives of Buddha: A Study of Sacred Biography and Theravada Tradition" in *The Biographical Process*, edited by Reynolds and Donald Capps

("Religion and Reason Series," vol. 11, The Hague, 1976). It provides a survey of the patterns of interpretation that have developed in connection with the Buddha biography in Western scholarship, as well as an overview of the relevant Hīnayāna and later Theravāda texts.

The most important recent research on the biographies of the Buddha is written in French. An argument for successive stages in the development of the Buddha biography is found in Étienne Lamotte's *Histoire du bouddhisme indien* (Louvain, 1958), pp. 707–759, in which Lamotte responds to Erich Frauwallner's thesis that there was a very early, complete biography. Frauwallner presented this thesis in *The Earliest Vinaya and the Beginnings of Buddhist Literature* (Rome, 1956). An indispensable aid to serious work on the Buddha biography is André Bareau's *Recherches sur la biographie du Buddha dans les Sūtrapitaka et les Vinayapiṭaka anciens*, 2 vols. (Paris; 1963–1971). In these volumes Bareau documents and improves upon Lamotte's arguments in favor of a gradual development of the biographical cycles.

Alfred Foucher presents a composite biography of the Buddha from the beginning of the common era in *The Life of the Buddha according to the Ancient Texts and Monuments of India*, abridged translation by Simone B. Boas (Middletown, Conn., 1963). Foucher also includes an introduction that is of particular importance because it highlights the significance of early Buddhist pilgrimages in the development of the biographical tradition.

Several of the autonomous biographies, as well as some later biographies from Tibet, China, and Southeast Asia, have been translated into European languages. The most readable is Aśvaghoṣa's *Buddhacarita, or, Acts of the Buddha*, 2 vols. in 1, edited and translated by Edward H. Johnston (Calcutta, 1935–1936; 2d ed., New Delhi, 1972). This translation should be supplemented by Samuel Beal's translation of the Chinese version of the same text, *The Fo-Sho-hing-tsan-king: A Life of Buddha by Asvaghosha Bodhisattva* (Oxford, 1883; reprint, Delhi, 1966).

The role of the stupa as a preeminent Buddha symbol in Buddhist thought and practice is introduced in the collection *The Stūpa: Its Religious, Historical and Architectural Significance*, edited by Anna Libera Dallapiccola in collaboration with Stephanie Zingel-Ave Lallemant (Wiesbaden, 1980). Gustav Roth's article in this collection, "Symbolism of the Buddhist Stupa," is especially significant for its investigation of the symbolic interpretation of the stupa in Buddhist literature. A convenient and beautiful survey and appraisal of the visual representations of the Buddha throughout the Buddhist world is *The Image of the Buddha*, edited by David L. Snellgrove (London, 1978).

Modern research on "other Buddhas" is much less extensive than the research focused on the biographies and symbols associated with Gautama. Those interested in short, well-done introductions to Akṣobhya, Amitābha (Amita), and Bhaiṣajyaguru should consult the *Encyclopaedia of Buddhism*, edited by G. P. Malalasekera (Colombo, 1968). Vairocana is discussed by Ryūjun Tajima in his *Étude sur le Mahāvairocana sūtra (Dainichikyō)*, (Paris, 1936). Material on "living Buddhas" can be gleaned from various sections of Giuseppe Tucci's *The Religions of Tibet*, translated from the Italian and German by Geoffrey Samuel (Berkeley, 1980).

A work of monumental importance for the study of the concept of the Buddha and of Buddhism in general, is Paul Mus's *Barabuḍur*, 2 vols. (1935; reprint, New York, 1978). It is perhaps the only academic work that exploits the full potential of the appellative character of the term *buddha*. It contains seminal discussions of Buddhology in early, Hīnayāna, and Mahāyāna traditions; of the symbolism of the stupa and the relics; of celestial and cosmic Buddhas; and of the origin of Pure Land symbolism and thought. Unfortunately, this ponderously long work has not been translated, and the French is extremely difficult.

Readers seeking more specialized references (e.g., available translations of biographical texts or studies of particular developments) should consult the annotated entries in Frank E. Reynolds's *Guide to Buddhist Religion* (Boston, 1981), especially section 8, "Ideal Beings, Hagiography and Biography," and section 9, "Mythology (including Sacred History), Cosmology and Basic Symbols."

FRANK E. REYNOLDS and CHARLES HALLISEY

BUDDHAGHOSA (fl. fifth century CE), one of the greatest Buddhist commentators. Participating in the Buddhist heritage as it neared completion of its first millennium, Buddhaghosa is most acclaimed for providing a commentarial and interpretive structure for the Theravāda tradition. He took the many strands of contemporary Buddhist teachings and traditions, both oral and written, and through patience and methodical scholarship wove them together to produce the standard Theravāda orientation for interpreting the teachings of the Buddha. He accomplished this by coordinating, collating, translating, and editing the vast, imposing body of the Theravāda canon.

Very little about the life of Buddhaghosa can be established definitely. That he was held in great esteem in the Theravāda tradition is seen in the *Buddhaghosuppatti*, a late Pali text of uncertain origin, date, and authorship, which presents a legendary account of his life and work. The *Mahāvaṃsa*, the chronicle of Sri Lanka written and preserved by the monastic community there, provides some information about this figure, but in a section (chap. 37, vv. 215ff.) considered to have been written seven to eight centuries after his life. From the silence regarding biographical information about such a prolific commentator, one may infer that his enormous industry and productivity were the consequence of a consistently self-effacing purpose. His foremost aim was to provide a commentarial framework in the language of the canonical texts that would contribute to a clearer understanding of the canonical teachings and ensure the continuity of these teachings and interpretations for posterity.

Although an old Burmese tradition has claimed that Buddhaghosa was a native of Thaton, in lower Burma (a position generally discredited, but argued anew on occasion), it appears that Buddhaghosa was from India, but opinions vary as to whether he came from the region of Bodh Gayā or from Andhra, or from an area farther to the south, around Kāñcīpuram.

Buddhaghosa received his ordination into the monastic order, came to Sri Lanka, and resided either at the Mahāvihāra in Anurādhapura or in nearby monastic dwellings. His purpose there was to study the Theravāda exegetical tradition. When he arrived in the early fifth century, he found approximately twenty-five sources forming a multifaceted collection of commentarial literature written in Sinhala, the predominant language of Sri Lanka. At least one additional commentarial source seems to have been preserved in a Dravidian language. These sources had developed over several centuries and by the end of the first century CE had reached the state in which Buddhaghosa found them.

It was against this historical background that Buddhaghosa wrote in Pali the *Visuddhimagga* (The Path of Purity), his first literary effort in Sri Lanka. This encyclopedic work, structured upon a cardinal tripartite theme in the Buddhist heritage—virtue (Pali, *sīla*), concentration *(samādhi)*, and wisdom *(paññā)*—demonstrates Buddhaghosa's talent in arranging the complex details of the Buddhist teachings at his disposal. He brought together details drawn from practically all of the canonical Pali texts, a few postcanonical works, and several Sinhala commentarial sources. His classic work remains the scholar's gateway to a Theravāda perspective on the canonical teachings and through which those canonical teachings subsequently passed into the continuing tradition.

Buddhaghosa continued his labor to assure a wider dissemination of the received commentarial interpretations of Sri Lanka by translating into Pali the Sinhala exegetical literature on many of the canonical texts. The chronological order of his works remains uncertain, however. He drew from his sources to provide a commentary on the Vinaya Piṭaka, the voluminous *Samantapāsādika*. He also provided a particular commentary, the *Kaṅkhāvitaraṇī*, on a portion of the Vinaya known as the *Pātimokkha*. He further provided commentaries on the four sections of the Sutta Piṭaka: the *Sumaṅgalavilāsinī* on the *Dīgha Nikāya;* the *Papañcasūdanī* on the *Majjhima Nikāya;* the *Saratthappakāsinī* on the *Saṃyutta Nikāya;* and the *Manorathapūraṇī* on the *Aṅguttara Nikāya*. Each work testifies, in its prologue, that it represents a translation of the Sinhala commentaries established by Mahinda, who is said to have brought the *buddhadhamma* to Sri Lanka in the middle of the third century BCE; these commentaries were preserved in the Mahāvihāra.

Although the point remains open to debate, it appears that Buddhaghosa also wrote commentaries on the seven texts comprising the third major division of the Pali canon, the Abhidhamma Piṭaka: on the *Dhammasaṅganī* he provided a commentary called *Atthasālinī;* on the *Vibhaṅga*, the *Sammohavinodanī;* and on the remaining five texts, one work called *Pañcappakaraṇaṭṭhakathā*. The commentaries note that they are based on the older Sinhala commentaries and follow the tradition of interpretation endorsed at the Mahāvihāra.

A few years after completing these commentaries, political turmoil disrupted the calm of the Mahāvihāra when Anurādhapura was overrun by invaders. This probably was the cause of Buddhaghosa's departure from Sri Lanka and the reason he did not complete commentaries on all the canonical texts. The weight of tradition says that he returned to India, although some accounts claim that he left Sri Lanka for lower Burma. Additional commentaries have been ascribed to Buddhaghosa, but they were probably the work of others. Buddhaghosa was followed by other notable commentators, namely Buddhadatta, Dhammapāla, Upasena, and Mahānāma.

[*See also* Theravāda.]

BIBLIOGRAPHY

Adikaram, E. W. *Early History of Buddhism in Ceylon* (1946). Reprint, Colombo, 1953.

Law, Bimala Churn. "Buddhaghosa." In *Encyclopaedia of Buddhism*, edited by G. P. Malalasekera, vol. 3, fasc. 3. Colombo, 1973. A condensation of his *The Life and Work of Buddhaghosa* (1923; reprint, Delhi, 1976).

Malalasekera, G. P. *The Pali Literature of Ceylon* (1928). Reprint, Colombo, 1958.

Ñyāṇamoli, trans. *The Path of Purification (Visuddhimagga) by Bhadantācariya Buddhaghosa.* 2d ed. Colombo, 1964.

JOHN ROSS CARTER

BUDDHAPĀLITA (c. 470–540), Indian Buddhist dialectician belonging to the Madhyamaka (Mādhyamika) school. According to the Tibetan historian Tāranātha, Buddhapālita (Tib., Saṅs-rgyas-skyaṅs; Chin., Fo-hu; Jpn., Butsugo) was born at Haṃsakrīḍa (Ṅaṅ-pas-rtse-ba) in the South Indian district of Tambala. Having taken religious ordination there, he learned much about the scriptures of Nāgārjuna from Saṃgharakṣita (Dge-

'dun-bsruṅ-ba), a disciple of Nāgamitra (Klu'i-bśes-gñen). He attained the highest knowledge through intense meditation and had a vision of Mañjuśrī. Residing in the Dantapurī monastery, he delivered many sermons on the Dharma and composed commentaries on treatises by such authors as Nāgārjuna and Āryadeva. Finally, he attained the miraculous powers *(siddhi)*. More or less the same account of his life is given in Bu-ston's *Chos 'byuṅ* (History of Buddhism) and Sum-pa-mkhan-po's *Dpag bsam ljon bzaṅ*, although these works exist only in fragments.

Buddhapālita is one of the traditionally reported "eight commentators" on Nāgārjuna's *Mūlamadhyamakakārikā*, the seven others being Nāgārjuna himself, Bhāvaviveka, Candrakīrti, Devaśarman, Guṇaśrī, Guṇamati, and Sthiramati (the last four commentators are Yogācāras). According to tradition, he composed commentaries on many Madhyamaka treatises, but only one has survived: the *(Buddhapālita) Mūlamadhyamakavṛtti*. The original Sanskrit text is actually lost; the work is only preserved in the Tibetan translation made by Jñānagarbha and Klu'i-rgyal-mtshan in the beginning of the ninth century. This commentary is one of the six extant commentaries on the *Mūlamadhyamakakārikā*, the five others being (1) the *Akutobhayā* (Derge edition of the Tibetan Tripiṭaka 3829, hereafter cited as D.; Peking edition of the Tibetan Tripiṭaka 5229, hereafter cited as P.); (2) Ch'ing-mu's (Piṅgala?) *Chung-lun* (T.D. no. 1824); (3) Bhāvaviveka's *Prajñāpradīpa* (D. 3853, P. 5253); (4) Sthiramati's *Ta-sheng chung-kuan shih-lun* (T.D. no. 1567); (5) Candrakīrti's *Prasannapadā* (Sanskrit ed. by L. de La Vallée Poussin in Bibliotheca Buddhica 4; D. 3860, P. 5260).

Buddhapālita's commentary consists of twenty-seven chapters in accordance with its basic text the *Mūlamadhyamakakārikā*. Chronologically, it was composed between the *Akutobhayā* and the *Prajñāpradīpa*. It incorporates most of the *Akutobhayā*'s passages; the last five chapters are almost identical. Chapter titles in Buddhapālita's commentary are the same as those of the *Akutobhayā* and the *Prajñāpradīpa* (perhaps because the translators of these three commentaries are the same: Jñānagarbha and Klu'i-rgyal-mtshan), but they differ slightly from the titles of Candrakīrti's *Prasannapadā* (particularly chapters 2, 3, 7, 11, 13, 15, 18, and 20). Buddhapālita's titles thus represent an older text of the *Mūlamadhyamakakārikā*, which was known to these translators before the revision by Pa-tshab Ñi-ma-grags (b. 1055) and his collaborators when they translated the *Prasannapadā*. The main authorities cited by Buddhapālita in his commentary are Nāgārjuna *(Mūlamadhyamakakārikā)*, Āryadeva *(Catuḥśataka)*, Rāhulabhadra *(Prajñāpāramitāstotra)*, and 'Phags-pa-'jigs-med (Aryābhaya?).

Buddhapālita's main philosophical methodological approach consisted of his explaining the philosophy of Nāgārjuna by the method of *prasaṅgavākya (reductio ad absurdum)*. That is, without himself maintaining any thesis or proposition to be established, he tried to point out the necessary but undesired consequences resulting from a non-Madhyamaka opponent's thesis. This method was strongly criticized by Bhāvaviveka, who wanted to make use of independent inferences *(svatantrānumāna)* to prove the Madhaymaka standpoint, but it was later defended by Candrakīrti. The Tibetan doxographers accordingly classified Buddhapālita with Candrakīrti as members of the Prāsaṅgika (Thal-'gyur-ba) school, while Bhāvaviveka was classed in the Svātantrika (Raṅ-rgyud-pa) school.

[*See also* Mādhaymika.]

BIBLIOGRAPHY

Lindtner, Christian. "Buddhapālita on Emptiness." *Indo-Iranian Journal* 23 (1981): 187–217.

Ruegg, David S. *The Literature of the Madhyamaka School of Philosophy in India*. Wiesbaden, 1981.

Saito, A. "A Study of the Buddhapālita-Mūlamadhyamaka-vṛtti." Ph.D. diss., Australian National University, 1984.

MIMAKI KATSUMI

BUDDHISM. [*This entry consists of an overview and nine surveys of the regional dispersion of Buddhism:*

These articles survey, principally, the historical development of Buddhism in the various areas in which it has flourished. Buddhist thought and practice are introduced with greater specificity in Buddhism, Schools of.]

An Overview

[*This article attempts to identify certain of the elements and structures that have constituted the Buddhist tradition as it has evolved over the past twenty-five hundred years. It traces a complex of social and ideological for-*

mations that have allowed it to develop from a small religious community to a "universal" religion associated with empire, to an important component in the several cultures of Buddhist Asia, to a tradition faced with the problems raised by modernity and contact with the West.]

The concept of Buddhism was created about three centuries ago to identify what we now know to be a pan-Asian religious tradition that dates back some twenty-five hundred years. Although the concept, rather recent and European in origin, has gradually, if sometimes begrudgingly, received global acceptance, there is still no consensus about its definition. We can, however, identify two complementary meanings that have consistently informed its use. First, it groups together the thoughts, practices, institutions, and values that over the centuries have—to use a phrase coined by the French Buddhologist Louis de La Vallée Poussin—"condensed around the name of the Buddha." The implicit conclusion of this usage is that Buddhism is, in short, whatever Buddhist men and women have said, done, and held dear. Second, the concept suggests some unifying character or order in the overwhelming diversity encompassed by the first usage. The beginning of this ordering process has often been to consider Buddhism as an example of larger categories, and thus Buddhism has been variously labeled a religion, a philosophy, a civilization, or a culture. It must be admitted, however, that no single ordering principle has been found that takes full account of the data included within the first meaning. This admission stands as a rebuke of the limitations of our current understanding, and as a continuing challenge to go further in our descriptions and explanations.

When the first meaning of Buddhism, which emphasizes its encompassment of accumulated traditions, is placed in the foreground, the resulting conception is indeed comprehensive. The further scholarship proceeds, the more comprehensive this conception becomes, because Buddhists have done in the name of the Buddha almost everything that other humans have done. Buddhists have, of course, been concerned with living religiously, some with the aim of salvation, and they have created traditions of belief and practice that help to realize these aspirations. But they have been concerned with much more as well. Buddhists have built cities sanctified by monuments dedicated to the Buddha and they have cultivated their crops using blessings that invoke his name. They have written self-consciously Buddhist poems and plays as well as highly technical works of grammar and logic that begin with invocations to the Buddha. They have commended nonviolence, but they have also gone to war with the name of Buddha on their lips. They have valued celibacy, but have also written erotic manuals and rejoiced in family life, all in the name of Buddha. Buddhists have created subtle philosophical concepts, such as the absence of self *(anātman)*, which are contravened by other ideas and values they have held. Like other human beings, Buddhists have been inconsistent and even contradictory, and they have been both noble and base in what they have said and done.

Although most scholars have at some level accepted this first conception of Buddhism as a diverse cumulative tradition, few have been content to allow this encompassing notion to prevail. They have sought to discover what ideals and values have inspired Buddhists, or to formulate generalizations that will help us to see the behavior of individuals as distinctively Buddhist. Some scholars have singled out a pattern, an idea, or a cluster of ideas that they felt was important enough to provide continuity through Buddhist history, or at least sufficient to suggest a coherence to the variety. Important candidates for this "key" to Buddhism are the purported teaching of the founder of Buddhism, Gautama, which provides an essence that has unfolded over the centuries; the monastic organization *(saṃgha)*, whose historical continuity provides a center of Buddhist practice and a social basis for the persistence of Buddhist thought and values; the closely related ideas of nonself and emptiness *(anātman, śūnyatā)*, realized through insight, which are said to mold Buddhist behavior; and the goal of *nirvāṇa* as the purpose of life. While such patterns and notions are very important for Buddhist sociology and soteriology, they also omit a great deal. Moreover, we can see that the element that is singled out as important is often distictive to Buddhism only in comparison with other religions or philosophies and cannot serve as a core that informs the entire corpus of Buddhist beliefs, rituals, and values.

Scholars have also sought to identify the characteristic order of Buddhism by dividing the cumulative tradition into more manageable parts, whether by chronology, by school, or by country. Some scholars, following the Buddhist historians Bu-ston (1290–1364) and Tāranātha (1574–1608), have divided Buddhism into three periods, mainly along philosophical lines. A first phase, represented by the early Theravāda (Way of the Elders) and Sarvāstivāda (All Things Are Real) schools, emphasized the no-soul idea and the reality of the constituents (*dharmas*) of the world. A middle phase, represented by the Mādhyamika (Middle Way) school, introduced the idea of the ultimate emptiness *(śūnyatā)* of all phenomena. A third period, represented by the Vijñānavāda (Consciousness Only) school, was philosophically idealistic in character. The limitations of this philosophical division are severe in that it only touches certain aspects of Buddhism and acknowledges no significant development after the fifth century CE.

Other scholars have elaborated a schema based on polemical divisions within the Buddhist community. They have focused attention on three great Buddhist "vehicles" *(yāna)* that are characterized by different understandings of the process and goal of salvation. The Hīnayāna, or Lesser Vehicle, elaborated a gradual process of individual salvation, and in that context distinguished among the attainment of an *arhat*, the attainment of a *pratyekabuddha* (one who achieves enlightenment on his own but does not become a teacher), and the attainment of a fully enlightened Buddha who teaches others the way to salvation. The Theravāda and Sarvāstivāda schools mentioned above are two of the major schools that are included under the Hīnayāna rubric. The term *Hīnayāna* was in its origins a pejorative name coined by the adherents of a new movement, self-designated as the Mahāyāna, or Great Vehicle, which generated new texts and teachings that were rejected by the Hīnayānists.

Like the adherents of the Hīnayāna, the Mahāyānists elaborated a gradual path of salvation lasting over many lifetimes, but their emphasis was different in two very important and related respects. They held that an individual's soteriological process could be aided and abetted by what some Mahāyāna schools came to designate as "other-power," and they recognized, ultimately, only one soteriological goal—the attainment of fully realized Buddhahood. The Vajrayāna (Diamond Vehicle), which is also known as Mantrayāna (Sacred Sounds Vehicle), Esoteric Buddhism, or Tantric Buddhism, accepted the basic approach and goal of the Mahāyāna, but felt that individual realization could be accomplished more quickly, in some cases even in this present life. The Vajrayānists described the practices that lead to this attainment in texts called *tantras* that were not accepted by either the Hīnayāna or the Mahāyāna schools. Although this Hīnayāna/Mahāyāna/Vajrayāna schema is probably the most common one used by scholars to divide Buddhism into more manageable segments, it too has serious drawbacks. It underestimates the significance of developments after the first millennium of the common era and it tends to overemphasize certain traits therein as extreme differences, beyond what is warranted by history.

Finally, scholars have recognized that Buddhism has always been deeply shaped by its surrounding culture. The Buddhist tradition has been more accretive in its doctrine and practice than the other great missionary religions, Christianity and Islam. It has shown an enduring tendency to adapt to local forms; as a result we can speak of a transformation of Buddhism in various cultures. The extent of this transformation can be seen in the difficulty that the first Western observers had in recognizing that the religion they observed in Japan was historically related to the religion found in Sri Lanka. This cultural division of Buddhism into Tibetan Buddhism, Chinese Buddhism, and so forth has been most successfully applied to the more recent phases of Buddhist history, especially to contemporary developments. Its dangers are, of course, quite obvious: above all, it conceals the Buddhist tradition's capacity to transcend the boundaries of culture, politics, and nationality.

The general trends of scholarship on Buddhism in this century have been within such accepted divisions of the cumulative tradition, with the result that our sense of Buddhism's historical continuity has been greatly obscured. Theodore Stcherbatsky, a Soviet Buddhologist, is in this regard a representative example. He adopted Bu-ston's tripartite "philosophical" division of Buddhist history and, in his *Conception of Buddhist Nirvāṇa* (Leningrad, 1927), commented on the transition between the first phase and the second phase as follows: "the history of religions has scarcely witnessed such a break between new and old within the pale of what nevertheless continued to claim common descent from the same religious founder" (p. 36). Similar statements pointing to radical discontinuity have been made from the perspective of the soteriological and cultural forms of Buddhism as well.

The investigation of each segment of the Buddhist cumulative tradition is now generally done in isolation from other segments. This strategy has had remarkable success in our discovery of the imprint of Buddhist thought and practice in areas far beyond the monasteries, beyond the level of elite groups. In small domains scholars have begun to see patterns in the full extent of phenomena grouped under the name of Buddhism. At the same time, contemporary scholarship often risks missing the forest for the trees. Our advances in particular areas of research may be at the price of the scholar's unique vision of Buddhism as a pan-Asian tradition.

As is often the case in the study of religion, however, the scale of investigation is decisive. This article will discuss Buddhism on a general level and will highlight continuities rather than disjunctions within the tradition. These continuities cannot be found in any static essence or core threading its way through all of Buddhist history. They will be traced here by following certain elements that have been preserved in a changing series of structures, expanded to meet new needs, and brought into relation with new elements that are continuously being introduced. We will, in other words, identify various elements and successive structures that have constituted Buddhism as it developed from a small community of mendicants and householders in northeastern India into a great "universal" religion associated with empire, civilization, and culture in various parts of Asia, and ultimately with "modernity" and the West as well.

Buddhism as Sectarian Religion

Buddhism began around the fifth or fourth century BCE as a small community that developed at a certain distance, both self-perceived and real, from other contemporary religious communities, as well as from the society, civilization, and culture with which it coexisted. Thus, we have chosen to characterize the Buddhism of this period as "sectarian."

It is quite probable that Buddhism remained basically a sectarian religion until the time of King Aśoka (third century BCE). Whether this was a period of approximately two hundred years, as some scholars, dating the death of the Buddha around 486 BCE, maintain, or of approximately one hundred years (accepting a death date around a century later) as others contend, it was by all accounts a crucial period in which many elements and patterns were established that have remained fundamental to subsequent phases of Buddhist thought and life. Despite the importance of this early phase of Buddhist history our knowledge about it remains sketchy and uncertain. Three topics can suggest what we do know: the source of authority that the new Buddhist community recognized, the pattern of development in its teaching and ecclesiastical structures, and the attitude it took toward matters of political and social order. In discussing these three topics we shall identify some of the main scholarly opinions concerning them.

One primary factor that both accounts for and expresses Buddhism's emergence as a new sectarian religion rather than simply a new Hindu movement is the community's recognition of the ascetic Gautama as the Buddha ("enlightened one") and of the words that he had reportedly uttered as a new and ultimate source of sacred authority. The recognition of the Buddha's authority was based on an acceptance of the actuality and relative uniqueness of his person and career, and of his enlightenment experience in particular. [*See* Buddha *and* Tathāgata.] It was based on the conviction that through his enlightenment he had gained insight into the Dharma (the Truth). [*See* Dharma, *article on* Buddhist Dharma and Dharmas.] This included the aspect of truth that he had formulated more "philosophically" as, for example, in the teaching concerning the dependent co-origination *(pratītya-samutpāda)* of the various elements that constitute reality, and also the aspect of truth he had formulated more soteriologically, as summarized, for example, in the classic delineation of the Four Noble Truths (that reality is permeated with suffering, that desire is the cause of suffering, that the cessation of suffering is a possibility, and that there is a path that leads to a cessation of suffering). [*See* Soul, *article on* Buddhist Concepts; Pratītya-samutpāda; Four Noble Truths; Eightfold Path; *and* Arhat.] Finally, the Buddha's authority was based on the confidence that the teachings and actions that had flowed from his enlightenment had been accurately transmitted by those who had heard and seen them. [*See* Saṃgha, *overview article, and* Vinaya.]

From certain stories preserved in the tradition it seems that there were some challenges to the Buddha's authority. For example, there are numerous reports that even during his own lifetime a more ascetically inclined cousin named Devadatta tried to take over leadership of the new movement. Such challenges were successfully met by the Buddha and by those who carried on the tradition. As a result, later controversies concerned not so much the authority of his teachings and actions as their content and correct interpretation.

There is less scholarly agreement concerning the more specific content of the early Buddhist teaching and about the closely related question of the structure of the early Buddhist community. Three conflicting interpretations have been set forth, each defended on the basis of detailed text-critical research. Some scholars have maintained that early Buddhism was a movement of philosophically oriented renouncers practicing a discipline of salvation that subsequently degenerated into a popular religion. A second group has contended that Buddhism was originally a popular religious movement that took form around the Buddha and his religiously inspiring message, a movement that was subsequently co-opted by a monastic elite that transformed it into a rather lifeless clerical scholasticism. A third group has argued that as far back as there is evidence, early Buddhist teaching combined philosophical and popular elements, and that during the earliest period that we can penetrate, the Buddhist community included both a significant monastic and a significant lay component. This argument, which is most convincing, has included the suggestion that the philosophical/popular and monastic/lay dichotomies should actually be seen as complements rather than oppositions, even though the understandings of the relative importance of these elements and their interrelationships have varied from the beginning of the Buddhist movement.

By the time of the Second Buddhist Council, held in the city of Vaiśālī probably in the fourth century BCE, the Buddhist community already encompassed two competing assemblies whose members espoused positions that correspond to the modern scholarly group of those who associate the "original" or "true" Buddhism with an elite monastic tradition, and those who associate it with a more democratic and populist tradition. [*See* Councils, *article on* Buddhist Councils.] A split occurred at or shortly after the Second Council: those who adhered to the former position came to be known in Sanskrit as Sthaviravādins (Pali, Theravādins; the proponents of the Way of the Elders), while those who adhered to the latter position came to be known as the Mahāsāṃghikas (Members of the Great Assembly).

The third area of discussion about early Buddhism has focused on its sectarian character. While it is not disputed that during the pre-Aśokan period the Buddhist community was a specifically religious community only tangentially involved with issues of political order and social organization, it is less clear whether this distance was a matter of principle or simply an accident of history. Some scholars have argued that early Buddhists were so preoccupied with individual salvation, and the early monastic order so oriented toward "otherworldly" attainments, that early Buddhism's sectarian character was intrinsic, rather than simply circumstantial. While individualistic and otherworldly strands played an important role in some segments of the early Buddhist community, there are balancing factors that must also be taken into account. Early Buddhists were concerned to gain royal patronage and were often successful in their efforts; they appropriated royal symbolism in their depiction of the Buddha and his career; they maintained their own explicitly anti-Brahmanic conception of kingship and social order, in the *Aggañña Sutta,* for example; and they encouraged a respect for authority and moral decorum conducive to civil order and tranquillity. Thus, within the sectarian Buddhism of the early period, there were a number of elements that prepared the way for the "civilizational Buddhism" that began to emerge during the reign of King Aśoka.

Buddhism as Civilizational Religion

Buddhism has never lost the imprint of the sectarian pattern that characterized its earliest history, largely because the sectarian pattern has been reasserted at various points in Buddhist history. But Buddhism did not remain a purely sectarian religion. With the reign of King Aśoka, Buddhism entered a new phase of its history in which it became what we have chosen to call a "civilizational religion," that is, a religion that was associated with a sophisticated high culture and that transcended the boundaries of local regions and politics. By the beginning of the common era Buddhism's civilizational character was well established in various areas of India and beyond. By the middle centuries of the first millennium CE, Buddhism as a civilizational religion had reached a high level of development across Asia. However, the signs of the transition to a new stage had already begun to appear by the sixth and seventh centuries CE.

History and Legend of the Aśokan Impact. Aśoka (r. circa 270–232 BCE) was the third ruler in a line of Mauryan emperors who established the first pan-Indian empire through military conquest. In one of the many inscriptions that provide the best evidence regarding his attitudes and actual policies, Aśoka renounced further violent conquest and made a commitment to the practice and propagation of Dharma. In other inscriptions Aśoka informs his subjects concerning the basic moral principles that form his vision of the Dharma; he mentions related meditational practices that he commends to his subjects as well as festivals of Dharma that he sponsored. He also tells of sending special representatives to ensure that the Dharma was appropriately practiced and taught by the various religious communities within his realm.

It would seem from Aśoka's inscriptions that the Dharma that he officially affirmed and propagated was not identical to the Buddhist Dharma, although it was associated with it, especially insofar as Buddhist teaching impinged on the behavior of the laity. However, the inscriptions give clear evidence that if Aśoka was not personally a Buddhist when he made his first commitment to the Dharma, he became so soon thereafter. His edicts indicate that he sponsored Buddhist missions to various areas not only within his own empire, but in the Greek-ruled areas of the northwest and in Sri Lanka to the south. They indicate that he maintained a special interest in the well-being and unity of the Buddhist *saṃgha,* that he was concerned to emphasize the importance of Buddhist texts that dealt with lay morality, and that he undertook a royal pilgrimage to the sites associated with the great events in the Buddha's life.

Aśoka's actual policies and actions represent only one aspect of his impact in facilitating the transition of Buddhism from a sectarian religion to a civilizational religion. The other aspect is evidenced in the legends of Aśoka that appeared within the Buddhist community in the period following his death. These legends vary in character from one Buddhist tradition to another. For example, the Theravādins present an idealized portrait of Aśoka and depict him as a strong supporter of their own traditions. Another widely disseminated Aśokan text, the *Aśokāvadāna*, composed in Northwest India probably in a Sarvāstivāda context, depicts an equally imposing but more ambivalent figure, sometimes cruel in behavior and ugly in appearance. But all of the various Aśokan legends present in dramatic form an ideal of Buddhist kingship correlated with an imperial Buddhism that is truly civilizational in character. [*See* Cakravartin; Saṃgha, *article on* Saṃgha and Society; Kingship, *article on* Kingship in Southeast Asia; *and the biography of Aśoka.*]

During the Aśokan and immediately post-Aśokan era there are at least three specific developments that sustained the transformation of Buddhism into a civilizational religion. The first, a realignment in the structure of the religious community, involved an innovation in the relationship and balance between the monastic order and its lay supporters. [*See* Monasticism, *article on* Buddhist Monasticism.] Prior to the time of Aśoka the monastic order was, from an organizational point of view, the focus of Buddhist community life; the laity, however important its role may have been, lacked any kind of independent institutional structure. As a result of the Aśokan experience, including both historical events and the idealized example he set as lay participant *par excellence* in the affairs of the *saṃgha*, the Buddhist state came to provide (sometimes as a hoped-for possibility, at other times as a socioreligious reality) an independent institution that could serve as a lay counterpoint and counterbalance to the order of monks. In addition, this realignment in the structure of the Buddhist community fostered the emergence of an important crosscutting distinction between monks and laypersons who were participants in the imperial-civilizational elite on the one hand, and ordinary monks and laypersons on the other.

The transformation of Buddhism into a civilizational religion also involved doctrinal and scholastic factors. During the Aśokan and post-Aśokan periods, factions within the monastic community began to formulate aspects of the teachings more precisely, and to develop those teachings into philosophies that attempted to explain all of reality in a coherent and logically defensible manner. As a result, the literature in which the community preserved its memory of the sermons of the Buddha (the Sūtras) and of his instructions to the monastic order (Vinaya) came to be supplemented by new scholastic texts known as Abhidharma ("higher Dharma"). [*The formation of the canon, the range of Buddhist texts, and the problems raised in their interpretation are treated in* Buddhist Literature.] Given the philosophical ambiguities of the received traditions, it was inevitable that contradictory doctrines would be put forward and that different religio-philosophical systems would be generated. This led to controversies within the community, and these controversies led to the proliferation of Buddhist schools and subschools, probably in conjunction with other more mundane disputes that we do not have sufficient data to reconstruct. Some sources list a total of eighteen schools without any consistency in names. The institutional and ideological boundaries between groups and subgroups were probably very fluid. [*See* Buddhism, Schools of, *article on* Hīnayāna Buddhism; Mahāsāṃghika; Sarvāstivāda; Sautrāntika; *and* Theravāda.]

Developments in the areas of symbolism, architecture, and ritual were also significant components in the transformation of Buddhism into a civilizational religion. Some changes were related to the support Buddhism received from its royal and elite supporters. For example, royal and elite patronage seems to have been crucial to the emergence of large monastic establishments throughout India. Such support was also a central factor in the proliferation of stūpas (Skt., *stūpas*), memorial monuments replete with cosmological and associated royal symbolism that represented the Buddha and were, in most cases, believed to contain a portion of his relics. These stupas were an appropriate setting for the development of Buddhist art in which the Buddha was represented in aniconic forms such as a footprint, a Bodhi ("enlightenment") Tree, a royal throne, the wheel of the Dharma, and the like. Merit making and related rituals proliferated and assumed new forms around these stupas. Pilgrimages to the sacred sites associated with the great events of the Buddha's life became more popular. The veneration and contemplation of stupas and other symbolic representations of the Buddha became increasingly widespread. Moreover, the notion of merit making itself was expanded so that it came to include not only merit making for oneself but the transfer of merit to deceased relatives and others was well. [*See also* Iconography, *article on* Buddhist Iconography; Pilgrimage, *article on* Buddhist Pilgrimage in South and Southeast Asia; Temple, *article on* Buddhist Temple Compounds; Stupa Worship; *and* Merit, *article on* Buddhist Concepts.]

Imperial Buddhism Reasserted and Transcended. Despite the importance of Aśoka to the history of Buddhism, the imperial order that he established persisted only a short time after his death. Within fifty years of his death (i.e., by the year 186 BCE), the Buddhist-oriented Mauryan dynasty collapsed and was replaced by the Śuṅga dynasty, more supportive of Brahmanic Hindu traditions. The Buddhist texts claim that the Śuṅgas undertook a persecution of Buddhism, although the force of any such persecution is rendered dubious by the fact that Buddhism and Buddhist institutions continued to flourish and develop within the territory ruled by the Śuṅgas. Moreover, Buddhism emerged as a dominant religion in areas outside northeastern India where the Śuṅgas were unable to maintain the authority and prestige that their Mauryan predecessors had enjoyed.

During the three centuries from the second century BCE through the first century CE Buddhism became a powerful religious force in virtually all of India, from the southern tip of the peninsula to the Indo-Greek areas in the northwest, and in Sri Lanka and Central Asia as well. [*See* Missions, *article on* Buddhist Missions.] New polities seeking to secure their control over culturally plural areas emulated Aśoka's example and adopted Buddhism as an imperial religion. This happened in Sri Lanka, probably when Duṭṭhagāmaṇī brought about the unification of the island kingdom in the mid-second century BCE. [*See the biography of Duṭṭhagāmaṇī.*] It happened in central India when the rising Śātavāhana dynasty became a supporter of the Buddhist cause. It happened to some extent in northwestern India when certain Greek and invading Central Asian kings converted to Buddhism. And it happened more fully in northwestern India during and after the reign of King Kaniṣka (first to second century CE), who ruled over a vast Kushan empire that extended from northern India deep into Central Asia. By this time Buddhism had also begun to penetrate into trading centers in northern China and to spread along land and sea routes across Southeast Asia to South China as well.

A major aspect of the transformation of Buddhism into a fully civilizational religion was the differentiation that occurred between Buddhism as a civilizational religion and Buddhism as an imperial religion. During late Mauryan times the civilizational and imperial dimensions had not been clearly differentiated. However, by the beginning of the common era Buddhism had become a civilizational religion that transcended the various expressions of imperial Buddhism in particular geographical areas. As a direct correlate of this development, an important distinction was generated within the elite of the Buddhist community. By this period this elite had come to include both a truly civilizational component that maintained close international contacts and traveled freely from one Buddhist empire to another and beyond, as well as overlapping but distinguishable imperial components that operated within the framework of each particular empire.

At this time Buddhist texts and teachings were being extended in a variety of ways. In some schools, such as the Theravāda and the Sarvāstivāda, canons of authoritative texts were established, but even after this had occurred new elements continued to be incorporated into the tradition through commentaries. In the case of the Sarvāstivādins, a huge collection of commentaries known as the *Mahāvibhāṣā* was compiled at a Buddhist council held by King Kaniṣka. In other schools the Piṭakas themselves were still being enriched by the incorporation of a variety of new additions and embellishments. There also began to appear, on the fringes of the established schools, a new kind of *sūtra* that signaled the rise of a new Buddhist orientation that came to be known as the Mahāyāna. [*See* Buddhism, Schools of, *article on* Mahāyāna Buddhism.] The earliest of these were the Prajñāpāramitā Sūtras, which put forward the doctrine of *śūnyatā* (the ultimate "emptiness" of all phenomena) and proclaimed the path of the *bodhisattva* (future Buddha) as the path that all Buddhists should follow. [*See* Bodhisattva Path.] Before the end of the second century CE the great Buddhist philosopher Nāgārjuna had given the perspective of these *sūtras* a systematic expression and thereby established a basis for the first of the major Mahāyāna schools, known as Mādhyamika. [*See* Mādhyamika; Śūnyam and Śūnyatā; *and the biography of Nāgārjuna.*]

This extension of Buddhist traditions of texts and teachings was accompanied by two other developments that also contributed to their civilizational efficacy. During this period the older Buddhist schools (hereafter collectively called the Hīnayāna) that had previously limited themselves to the oral transmission of tradition, and the newly emerging Mahāyāna fraternities as well, began to commit their versions of the Buddha's teaching to writing. Some Buddhist groups began to translate and write their most authoritative texts in Sanskrit, which had become the preeminent civilizational language in India.

The rapid development of Buddhism led to major changes in Buddhist ways of representing the Buddha and relating to him ritually. Some Hīnayāna schools produced autonomous biographies of the Buddha. The most famous of the biographies is the *Buddhacarita* (Acts of the Buddha), by Aśvaghoṣa, written in refined Sanskrit in a classic literary form *(kavya)*. The Hīnayāna schools provided the context for the production of anthropomorphic images of the Buddha, which became a major focal point for sophisticated artistic expression on the one hand, and for veneration and devotion on the other. These schools also made a place within the Buddhist system for a new and very important figure who became a focus for new forms of devotional practice and, in later phases of Buddhist history, new forms of religio-political symbolism and activity as well. This new figure was the future Buddha Maitreya ("the friendly one"), who was believed to be residing in the Tuṣita Heaven awaiting the appropriate time to descend to earth. [*See* Maitreya.] By the beginning of the common era other buddhological trends were beginning to surface that were exclusively Mahāyāna in character. For example, *sūtra*s were beginning to appear that focused attention on a celestial Buddha named Amitābha ("infinite light") and portrayed practices of visualization that could lead to rebirth in the western paradise over which he presided. [*See* Amitābha *and* Pure and Impure Lands.]

Closely associated developments were taking place at the level of cosmology and its application to religious practice. In the Hīnayāna context the most important development was probably the rich portrayal of a set of six cosmological *gati*s, or "destinies" (of gods, humans, animals, *asura*s or titans, hungry ghosts, and beings who are consigned to hell), which depicted, in vivid fashion, the workings of *karman* (moral action and its effects). [*See* Karman, *article on* Buddhist Concepts.] These texts, which were probably used as the basis for sermons, strongly encouraged Buddhist morality and Buddhist merit-making activities. Other Hīnayāna works of the period suggested the presence of a vast expanse of worlds that coexist with our own. In the new Mahāyāna context this notion of a plurality of worlds was moved into the foreground, the existence of Buddhas in at least some of these other worlds was recognized, and the significance of these Buddhas for life in our own world was both affirmed and described. [*See* Cosmology, *article on* Buddhist Cosmology.] Finally, there are indications that during this period both Hīnayāna and Mahāyāna Buddhists increasingly employed exorcistic rituals that depended on the magical power of various kinds of chants and spells (*paritta* in Pali, *dhāraṇī* in Sanskrit).

Buddhism as Pan-Asian Civilization. From the second to the ninth century, Buddhism enjoyed a period of immense creativity and influence. Prior to the beginning of the sixth century, Buddhist fortunes were generally on the rise. Buddhism flourished in Sri Lanka, India, and Central Asia. Through already familiar processes involving its introduction along trade routes, its assimilation to indigenous beliefs and practices, and its adoption as an imperial religion, Buddhism became firmly entrenched in both northern and southern China and in many parts of Southeast Asia. After about 500 CE, these well-established dynamics of expansion continued to operate. Buddhism became the preeminent religion in a newly unified Chinese empire, it continued its spread in parts of Southeast Asia, and it was established in important new areas, first in Japan and then in Tibet. However, during this latter period its successes were coupled with setbacks, and by the middle of the ninth century the era of Buddhism as a pan-Asian civilization was rapidly drawing to a close.

The geographical expansion of Buddhism was both a cause and an effect of its civilizational character. But Buddhism's role as a pan-Asian civilization involved much more than a pan-Asian presence. Buddhist monasteries, often state supported and located near capitals of the various Buddhist kingdoms, functioned in ways analogous to modern universities. There was a constant circulation of Buddhist monks, texts, and artistic forms across increasingly vast geographical areas. Indian and Central Asian missionaries traveled to China and with the help of Chinese Buddhists translated whole libraries of books into Chinese, which became a third major Buddhist sacred language alongside Pali and Sanskrit. In the fifth century Buddhist nuns carried their ordination lineage from Sri Lanka to China. Between 400 and 700 a stream of Chinese pilgrims traveled to India via Central Asia and Southeast Asia in order to visit sacred sites and monasteries and to collect additional scriptures and commentaries. Some of these, such as Fa-hsien, Hsüan-tsang, and I-ching, wrote travel accounts that provide information concerning Buddhist civilization in its fullest development. In the sixth century Buddhism was formally introduced into Japan; in the following century Buddhists from Central Asia, India, and China made their way into Tibet. Beginning in the eighth and ninth centuries monks from Japan visited China in order to receive Buddhist training and acquire Buddhist texts. These are only a few illustrations of the kind of travel and interaction that characterized this period. [*See the biographies of Fa-hsien; Hsüan-tsang; and I-ching.*]

While Buddhism was reaching its apogee as a civilizational religion, the teachings of the Hīnayāna tradition were further extended and refined. New commentaries were produced in both Sanskrit and in Pali. During the fifth century these commentaries were supplemented by the appearance of two very important manuals, Vasubandhu's *Abhidharmakośa*, composed in the Sarvāstivāda-Sautrāntika context in Northwest India, and Buddhaghosa's *Visuddhimagga* (Path of Purification), written in the Theravādin context in Sri Lanka. [*See the biographies of Vasubandhu and Buddhaghosa.*] Moreover, many Hīnayāna themes remained basic to the other Buddhist traditions with which it coexisted. Most Buddhists continued to recognize the Buddha Gautama as an important figure, and to focus attention on the single-world cosmology that posited the existence of three realms—the realm beyond form associated with the most exalted gods and the highest meditational states, the realm of form associated with slightly less exalted gods and meditational states, and the realm of desire constituted by the six *gatis* previously mentioned. This latter realm was especially prominent as the context presumed by pan-Buddhist teachings concerning karmic retribution and the value of giving, particularly to the members of the monastic community.

Within the Mahāyāna tradition this period of Buddhist efflorescence as a civilizational religion was characterized by a high level of creativity and by a variety of efforts toward systematization. In the earlier centuries the Mahāyānists produced a rich and extensive collection of new *sūtras*, including the *Saddharmapuṇḍarīka Sūtra* (Lotus of the True Law), the *Mahāparinirvāṇa Sūtra*, the *Laṅkāvatāra Sūtra*, and the *Avataṃsaka Sūtra*. With the passage of time, voluminous commentaries were written on many of these *sūtras* in India, Central Asia, and China. These *sūtras* and commentaries developed new teachings concerning the emptiness of the phenomenal world, the storehouse consciousness *(ālaya-vijñāna)*, and the "embryo of the Tathāgata" *(tathāgata-garbha)*. [*See* Ālaya-vijñāna *and* Tathāgata-garbha.] These teachings were given scholastic forms in various Mahāyāna groups such as the Mādhyamika and Yogācāra schools, which originated in India, and the T'ien-t'ai and Hua-yen schools, which originated in China. [*See* Yogācāra; T'ien-t'ai; *and* Hua-yen.] In addition, these *sūtras* and commentaries recognized a vast pantheon of Buddhas and *bodhisattvas* (future Buddhas) and acknowledged the existence of a plurality, even an infinity, of worlds. Some went on to affirm the reality of an eternal, cosmic Buddha whom they took to be the ultimate source of these innumerable Buddhas, *bodhisattvas*, and worlds (and of all else as well). Some of these texts highlighted various kinds of soteriological help that particular Buddhas and *bodhisattvas* could provide to those who sought their aid. In addition to Maitreya and Amitābha, mentioned above, other Buddhas and *bodhisattvas* who became particularly important include Bhaiṣajyaguru (the Buddha of healing), Avalokiteśvara (the *bodhisattva* exemplar of compassion), Mañjuśrī (the *bodhisattva* patron of the wise), and Kṣitigarbha (the *bodhisattva* who specialized in assisting those who suffer in hell). [*See* Bhaiṣajyaguru; Avalokiteśvara; Mañjuśrī; Kṣitigarbha; *and* Celestial Buddhas and Bodhisattvas.]

By the second half of the first millennium CE a new strand of Buddhist tradition, the Vajrayāna, or Esoteric Vehicle, began to come into the foreground in India. This new vehicle accepted the basic orientation of the Mahāyāna, but supplemented Mahāyāna insights with new and dramatic forms of practice, many of them esoteric in character. The appearance of this new Buddhist vehicle was closely associated with the composition of new texts, including new *sūtras* (e.g., the *Mahāvairocana Sūtra*), and the new ritual manuals known as *tantras*. By the eighth and ninth centuries this new vehicle had spread through virtually the entire Buddhist world and was preserved especially in Japan and in Tibet. But before the process of systematization of the Vajrayāna could proceed very far the infrastructure that constituted Buddhist civilization began to break down, thus at least partially accounting for the very different form that this tradition took in Tibet and in Japan, where it became known as Shingon. [*See* Buddhism, Schools of, *article on* Esoteric Buddhism *and* Mahāsiddhas.]

During the period of its hegenomy as a pan-Asian civilization, Buddhism retained a considerable degree of unity across both the regional and text-oriented boundaries that delimited particular Buddhist traditions. In each cultural area and in each of the three *yānas* there were ascetics and contemplatives who practiced Buddhist meditation; there were ecclesiastics and moralists whose primary concern was Buddhist discipline; there were monks and laypersons who were involved in Buddhist devotion; and there were those who took a special interest in Buddhist magic and exorcism. These diverse groups and individuals shared—and many realized that they shared—beliefs, attitudes, and practices with like-minded Buddhists in distant areas and other *yānas*.

Moreover, during the period of its ascendancy as a civilizational religion, Buddhism provided a successful standard of cultural unification such that other religious traditions, including the Hindu in India, the Manichaean in Central Asia, the Taoist in China, the Shintō in Japan, and the Bon in Tibet, responded to it with their own innovations shaped by Buddhist ideas and values. [*See the articles on these traditions.*] During this period, in other words, Buddhism set the standards, religious, philosophical, artistic, and so on, to which a whole range of other Asian traditions were forced to respond. Buddhism also served as a civilizational religion by encompassing other elements—logic, medicine, grammar, and technology, to name but a few—that made it attractive to individuals and groups, including many rulers and members of various Asian aristocracies who had little or no interest in the spiritual aspect of religion.

Buddhism as Cultural Religion

For more than a thousand years, from the time of King Aśoka to about the ninth century, Buddhism exhibited a civilizational form that began as pan-Indian and ultimately became pan-Asian in character. Like the sectarian pattern that preceded it, this civilizational pattern left an indelible mark on all subsequent Buddhist developments. Buddhism never completely lost either its concern for inclusiveness or its distinctively international flavor. But beginning in about the fifth century the civilizational structure suffered increasingly severe disruptions, and a new pattern began to emerge. All across Asia, Buddhism was gradually transformed, through a variety of historical processes, into what we have chosen to call "cultural religion."

The Period of Transition. Buddhist civilization, which characteristically strove for both comprehensiveness and systematic order, was dependent on the security and material prosperity of a relatively small number of great monasteries and monastic universities that maintained contact with one another and shared common interests and values. This institutional base was, in fact, quite fragile, as was demonstrated when historical events threatened the well-being of these monasteries and their residents. New developments arose within the Buddhist community as a result of these vicissitudes, developments that eventually transformed Buddhism into a series of discrete cultural traditions.

Some indication of these developments can be seen quite early, even as Buddhist civilization was at the peak of its brilliance. Events in Central Asia during the fifth and sixth centuries were not favorable to the Buddhist kingdoms along the Silk Route that connected Northwest India and northern China. These kingdoms were invaded and in some cases conquered by different nomadic peoples such as the Huns, who also invaded India and the Roman empire. The Chinese pilgrim Hsüan-tsang, who visited Sogdiana in 630, saw only ruins of Buddhist temples and former Buddhist monasteries that had been given over to the Zoroastrians.

The instability in the crucial linking area between India and China during the fifth and sixth centuries seems to have been sufficient to weaken Buddhism's civilizational structure. For the first time we see the emergence of new Buddhist schools in China that are distinctively Chinese. The appearance of synthetic Chinese schools like T'ien-t'ai and Hua-yen suggests a continuation of the civilizational orientation. These schools sought to reconcile the divergent views found in Buddhist literature through an extended elaboration of different levels of teaching. This is, of course, characteristic of Buddhism as a civilizational religion, but the manner of reconciliation reflects a style of harmonization that is distinctively Chinese.

The increasing importance of Tantra in late Indian Buddhism and the success of the Pure Land (Ching-t'u) and Ch'an (Zen) schools in China during the Sui and T'ang period (598–907) are further indications that the Buddhist tradition was becoming more local in self-definition. [*See* Ching-t'u *and* Ch'an.] Chinese Buddhism had a new independent spirit in contrast to the earlier India-centered Buddhism. Moreover, the new movements that emerged at that time seem to be the result of a long development that took place apart from the major cosmopolitan centers. Far more than in the past, expressions of Buddhism were being made at all levels of particular societies, and there was a new concern for the interrelation of those levels within each society.

During the last centuries of the first millennium CE, Buddhist civilization developed a new, somewhat independent center in China that reached its peak during the Sui and T'ang dynasties. Thus, when Buddhist texts and images were introduced into Japan during the sixth century they were presented and appropriated as part and parcel of Chinese culture. The new religion gained support from the prince regent, Shōtoku Taishi, who wanted to model his rule after that of the Buddhist-oriented Sui dynasty. Chinese Buddhist schools such as Hua-yen (Jpn., Kegon) also prospered in the Nara period in Japan (710–784) as Chinese cultural influence continued to flourish. [*See the biography of Shōtoku Taishi.*]

The two centers of Buddhist civilization, China and India, also competed with each other, as can be seen in a situation that developed in Tibet. Buddhism had been brought to Tibet by King Sroṅ-bstan-sgam-po (d. 650), who established the first stable state in the area. Buddhist texts were translated into Tibetan from both Sanskrit and Chinese. A later king, Khri-sroṅ-lde-bstan (755–797), officially adopted Buddhism as the state religion and determined to resolve the tension between Indian and Chinese influence. He sponsored the famous Council of Lhasa, in which a Chinese party representing a Ch'an "sudden enlightenment" point of view debated an Indian group that advocated a more gradualist understanding of the Buddhist path. Both sides claimed victory, but the Indian tradition gained predominance and eventually translations were permitted only from Sanskrit. [*See the biography of Kamalaśīla.*]

During the ninth and tenth centuries the two Buddhist civilizational centers in India and China were themselves subject to attack, both internally and externally. The combination of Hindu resurgence and Muslim invasions led to the effective disappearance of the Buddhist community in India by the thirteenth century. [*See* Islam, *article on* Islam in South Asia.] Repeated invasions by Uighurs and Turkic peoples, as well as official persecutions and the revival of the Confucian tradition, resulted in a decisive weaking of institutional

Buddhism in China. [*See* Turkic Religions *and* Confucianism, *article on* Neo-Confucianism.]

The processes of acculturation that had first become evident in the sixth century in India and China repeated themselves beginning in the tenth century in Japan, Korea, Tibet, Sri Lanka, and Southeast Asia. In each of these areas distinct cultural forms of Buddhism evolved. There was a reorganization of the Buddhist community with an increased emphasis on the bonds between elite and ordinary Buddhists in each particular area. There was a renewed interest in efficacious forms of Buddhist practice and the Buddhist schools that preserved and encouraged such practice. Within each area there was a development of Buddhist symbols and rituals that became representative of distinct Buddhist cultures, particularly at the popular level.

In Central Asia the Buddhist community had no success in surviving the Muslim expansion. [*See* Islam, *article on* Islam in Central Asia.] Buddhism had some limited success in India during the last centuries of the first millennium. It benefited from extensive royal and popular support in northeastern India under the Pāla dynasty from the eighth to the twelfth century, but Hindu philosophy and theistic *(bhakti)* movements were aggressive critics of Buddhism. Hardly any distinct Buddhist presence continued in India after the last of the great monasteries were destroyed by the Muslims. In China there was more success, although the Confucian and Taoist traditions were powerful rivals. As a result of persecutions in the ninth century, Buddhism lost its distinctively civilizational role, but it continued as a major component of Chinese religion, becoming increasingly synthesized with other native traditions. In Sri Lanka, Southeast Asia (except for Indonesia and the Malay Peninsula, where Buddhism suffered the same fate that it suffered in India), Japan, Korea, and Tibet (from whence it eventually spread to Mongolia), areas where Buddhism did not have to compete with strongly organized indigenous traditions, it was successful in establishing itself as the dominant religious tradition. The religious creativity of these areas, once the periphery of the Buddhist world, resulted in a Buddhist "axial age" that dramatically transformed the tradition as a whole.

Monastic Order, Royal Order, and Popular Buddhism. The transformation of Buddhism from a civilizational religion to a cultural religion depended on a fundamental realignment in the structure of the Buddhist community. As a civilizational religion, Buddhist community life had come to include a largely monastic elite that traveled extensively, was multilingual, and operated at the civilizational level; an imperial elite made up of monks and laypersons associated more closely with royal courts and related aristocracies; and a less exalted company of ordinary monks and laypersons living not only in urban areas but in the countryside as well. In Buddhism's zenith as a civilizational religion the central organizing relationship was that between the largely monastic civilizational elite and the imperial elites, consisting of kings, queens, and other high-placed members of the laity on the one hand, and the monks whom they supported on the other. The ordinary members of the laity and the less exalted monks played a role, of course, but in most areas at most periods of time they seem to have been somewhat distanced from the mainstream of Buddhist community life. With the transformation of Buddhism into a cultural religion, however, this situation was drastically altered.

One aspect of this transformation was major changes that took place at three different levels: monastic, imperial, and popular. The demise of the monastic network through which the civilizational aspect of Buddhism had been supported and maintained was decisive. To be sure, there were elements of the monastic community that never lost their international vision, and travel and exchanges between specific cultural areas was never totally absent, particularly between China and Japan, China and Tibet, and Sri Lanka and mainland Southeast Asia. Nevertheless, it would be difficult to speak of a pan-Asian Buddhist elite after the ninth or tenth century.

The pattern at the imperial level was altered by the loss of monastic power and influence coupled with increased state control in monastic affairs. During the period that Buddhism was an effective civilizational religion its great monasteries functioned practically as "states within the state." Monasteries commanded extensive resources of land and labor and were often actively involved in commercial enterprises. This public splendor made the monasteries inviting targets, especially after their usefulness as civilizational centers had declined. If the monasteries were not simply destroyed, as they were in India and Central Asia, they were often deprived of their resources, as occurred at one time or another in virtually every Buddhist area. With the decline of monastic influence at the imperial level, the control of the state over monastic affairs inevitably increased. In China and Japan, and to a lesser extent in Korea and Vietnam, state control became thoroughly bureaucratized. In Sri Lanka and the Theravāda areas of Southeast Asia, state control was implemented more indirectly and with considerably less efficiency by royal "purifications" of the *sangha.* Specific local conditions in Tibet led to a unique situation in which monastic and royal functions became so tightly interlocked that they were often completely fused.

The demise of the international Buddhist elite and the weakening of the large and powerful establishments were counterbalanced by a strengthening of Buddhist life at the grass-roots level. Smaller, local institutions that for a long time had coexisted with the great monasteries took on new importance as focal points in Buddhist community life. For example, smaller so-called merit cloisters *(kung-te yüan)* supported by wealthy laymen were significant components in the development and life of Chinese Buddhism. In Sri Lanka and Southeast Asia the emergence of cultural Buddhism was closely associated with monks who were called *gāmavāsins* (village dwellers) and who strengthened Buddhist influence among the people in the major cities and in the more distant provinces as well. In contrast to civilizational Buddhism, in which the crucial structural alignment was that between the civilizational elite and the monks and laity at the imperial level, the crucial structural alignment in cultural Buddhism was between the monks and laity of the imperial or state elites, who were located primarily in the capital cities, and the ordinary people who inhabited local monasteries and villages.

The Preeminence of Practice. The era of comprehensive Buddhist philosophizing and the formulation of original systems of thought came to an end, for the most part, with the demise of Buddhism as a civilizational religion. There continued to be philosophical innovations, and some of the great systems that were already formulated were adjusted to meet new circumstances. However, the real creativity of Buddhism as a cultural religion came to the fore in schools and movements that emphasized efficacious modes of Buddhist practice.

A major component in the development of various Buddhist cultures is the ascendancy of schools or movements that combined a strong emphasis on the importance of discipline (particularly although not exclusively the monastic discipline) with an accompanying emphasis on meditation. [*See* Meditation, *article on* Buddhist Meditation.] In China and Japan, Ch'an and Zen, with their emphasis on firm discipline and meditative practices such as "just sitting" and the contemplation of *kung-an* (Jpn., *kōan;* enigmatic verses), are representative of this kind of Buddhist tradition. [*See* Zen.] These were the schools that became more prominent as Mahāyāna Buddhism emerged as a cultural religion in East Asia, and they continued to exert influence on the various East Asian political and aesthetic elites from that time forward. The Āraññikas, or "forest-dwelling monks," represented an analogous orientation and played a similar role in Sri Lanka and subsequently in Southeast Asia. The Āraññikas appeared on the Sri Lankan scene in the ninth and tenth centuries as a group of monks who had chosen to withdraw from the wealthy monasteries of the capital, to adopt a strictly disciplined mode of life, and to devote themselves to study and/or meditation. In the twelfth century the Āraññikas led a major reform in Sri Lanka and in subsequent centuries they extended their reform movement throughout the Theravāda world, which included not only Sri Lanka but also Burma, Thailand, Cambodia, and Laos. The Āraññikas in the Theravāda world, like the Ch'an and Zen practitioners in East Asia, were closely affiliated with the elite segments of the various societies in which they were active. A similar kind of emphasis was placed on discipline, study, and meditation in Tibet, where the Vajrayāna tradition was established by Atīśa, the monk who in the eleventh century inaugurated the "second introduction" of Buddhism into the country. In the fifteenth century another infusion of discipline-oriented reform was provided by reformers who established the Dge-lugs-pa, the so-called Yellow Hats, which became the preeminent Tibetan (and Mongolian) school subsequently headed by the well-known line of Dalai Lamas. [*See* Dge-lugs-pa; Dalai Lama; *and the biography of Atīśa.*]

Each expression of Buddhism as a cultural religion generated, as a kind of counterpoint to its more elitist, discipline-oriented schools and movements, other schools and movements that focused on more populist forms of devotional or Esoteric (Tantric) practice. In the East Asian Mahāyāna areas the most important development was the increasing prominence of the Pure Land schools in the early centuries of the second millennium CE. The Chinese Pure Land schools remained in close symbiosis with the practitioners of Ch'an and retained a relatively traditional mode of monastic practice. Their Japanese counterparts, however, became more differentiated and considerably morc innovative. During the Kamakura period (1185–1333) a number of new, distinctively Japanese Pure Land and related schools were founded by charismatic leaders such as Hōnen, Shinran, and Nichiren; these schools took on a distinctively Japanese cast. For Nichiren, the Pure Land was Japan itself. [*See* Jōdoshū; Jōdo Shinshū; Nichirenshū; *and the biographies of Hōnen, Shinran, and Nichiren.*]

Although less important than Pure Land and related kinds of devotion, Esoteric or Tantric modes of religion also were a significant part of cultural Buddhism in East Asia. In China the Esoteric elements were closely related to influences from the Vajrayāna tradition in Tibet as well as interactions with forms of indigenous Taoism. [*See* Chen-yen.] In Japan more sophisticated Esoteric elements persisted in the Tendai (Chin., T'ien-t'ai) and Shingon schools, while more rustic and indigenous elements were prominent in groups that were integrated into these schools, for example, the Shugendō community that was made up of mountain ascetics known as *yamabushi*. [*See* Shūgendō; Tendaishū; *and* Shingonshū.]

In Sri Lanka in the twelfth and thirteenth centuries (the period of Hōnen, Shinran, and Nichiren in Japan) devotional religion also seems to have been influential in the Buddhist community, generating new genres of Buddhist literature that were written primarily in Sinhala rather than Pali. Although no specifically devotional "schools" were formed, a whole new devotional component was incorporated into the Theravāda tradition and subsequently diffused to the Theravāda cultures in Southeast Asia. Similarly, there were, as far as we know, no "schools" that were specifically Esoteric or Tantric in character. However, there is some evidence that indicates that Esoteric elements played a very significant role in each of the premodern Theravāda cultures. This kind of influence seems to have been particularly strong in northern Burma, northern Thailand, Laos, and Cambodia.

In Tibet and Mongolia, as one would expect given their Vajrayāna ethos, the primary counterpoints to the more discipline-oriented traditions were the schools, such as the Rñiṅ-ma-pa and Bka'-brgyud-pa, that emphasized the performance of Esoteric and Tantric rituals in order to achieve worldly benefits and to proceed along a "fast path" to salvation. However, just as in the other Buddhist cultures devotion was supplemented by recourse to Esoteric and Tantric techniques, so in Tibet and Mongolia Esoteric and Tantric techniques were supplemented by the practice of devotion.

Another important component of Buddhism as a cultural religion was the mitigation, in some circles at least, of traditional distinctions between monks and laity. This trend was least evident in the more discipline-oriented contexts, but even here there was some movement in this direction. For example, in the Ch'an and Zen monasteries, monks, rather than being prohibited from engaging in productive work as the Vinaya had stipulated, were actually required to work. In the Pure Land schools in Japan, and in some of the Esoteric schools in Japan and Tibet, it became permissible and common for clergy to marry and have families. Also, certain kinds of monastic/lay and purely lay associations played important roles in China and Japan. These included both straightforward religious associations devoted to the various Buddhist causes, and, particularly in China, a number of secret societies and messianically oriented groups. [*See* Millenarianism, *article on* Chinese Millenarian Movements.] Even in Sri Lanka and Southeast Asia tendencies toward the laicization of the monastic order can from time to time be observed, but in these strongly Theravāda areas the process was always thwarted by royal intervention before the innovations could take root.

The Pervasiveness of Ritual. Alongside the particular schools and movements that characterized Buddhism as a cultural religion there were also modes of Buddhist practice that, although influenced by those schools and movements, were more pervasively involved in Buddhist cultures as such. Pilgrimage was in the forefront of these practices.

Virtually every instance of Buddhism as a cultural religion had its own particular patterns of Buddhist pilgrimage. [*See* Pilgrimage, *articles on Buddhist pilgrimage*.] In many cases these pilgrimage patterns were a major factor in maintaining the specificity of particular, often overlapping, religious and cultural complexes. In some contexts these pilgrimage patterns delimited Buddhist cultural complexes that supported and were supported by particular political kingdoms. An example of this situation was the Sinhala pattern, in which there were sixteen major sites systematically distributed throughout all of Sri Lanka. In other situations, for example in Southeastern Asia, these patterns often delimited Buddhist cultural complexes that cut across political divisions.

Many of the sites that were the goals of major Buddhist pilgrimages were mountain peaks or other places that had been sacred from before the introduction of Buddhism and continued to have sacred associations in other traditions that coexisted with Buddhism. [*See also* Mountains.] Through pilgrimage practices at these sites Buddhism assimilated various deities and practices associated with local religious traditions. At the same time, of course, the Buddhist presence imbued those deities and practices with Buddhist connotations. In Japan, Buddhas and *bodhisattvas* became virtually identified in many situations with indigenous *kami* (divine spirits). In China great *bodhisattvas* such as Kṣitigarbha, Mañjuśrī, and Avalokiteśvara became denizens of sacred mountains that were popular pilgrimage sites, and in those pilgrimage contexts underwent a thoroughgoing process of sinicization. Stupas, footprints, and other Buddhist objects of pilgrimage in Southeast Asia became, for many who venerated them, representations in which the Buddha was closely associated with indigenous spirits (e.g., *nats* in Burma, *phī* in Thailand, etc.) who served as the local guardians or protectors of Buddhist institutions. [*See* Nats.]

Wherever Buddhism developed as a cultural religion it penetrated not only the sacred topography of the area but also the cycle of calendric rites. In China, for example, the annual cycle of Buddhist ritual activities included festivals honoring various Buddhas and *bodhisattvas*, festivals dedicated to significant figures from Chinese Buddhist history, a great vegetarian feast, and a very important "All Soul's" festival in which the Chinese virtue of filial piety was expressed through offerings intended to aid one's ancestors. While these rituals themselves involved much that was distinctively Chinese, they were interspersed with other festivals, both Confucian and Taoist, and were supplemented by other, lesser rituals associated with daily life that involved an even greater integration with non-Buddhist elements. In Sri Lanka the Buddhist ritual calendar included festivals honoring events of the Buddha's life; a festival that celebrated the coming of Mahinda, Aśoka's missionary son, to establish Buddhism in Sri Lanka; a festival in the capital honoring the Buddha relic that served as the palladium of the kingdom; and the monastic-centered *kathin* (Pali, *kaṭhina;* giving of robes) ceremony that marked the end of the rainy season. These Buddhist rituals were interspersed with non-Buddhist celebrations that were, in this case, largely Hindu. These large-scale rituals were supplemented by more episodic and specialized rites that involved an even wider variety of indigenous elements such as offerings to local spirits. In the Tibetan cultural area the Buddhist calendar encompassed great festivals sponsored by monasteries in which the introduction of Buddhism to Tibet was celebrated as the Buddhist defeat of indigenous demons, as well as festivals honoring Buddhist deities (e.g., Tārā) and Tibetan Buddhist heroes (e.g., Padmasambhava). [*See* Tārā *and the biography of Padmasambhava.*] The Tibetan Buddhist calendar also included other large- and small-scale rituals in which Buddhist and indigenous shamanistic elements were combined. [*See* Buddhist Religious Year.]

Buddhism in its various cultural expressions also became associated with life cycle rites, especially those of the male initiation into adulthood and those associated with death. The Buddhist involvement in male initiation rites was limited primarily to Southeast Asia. In many Buddhist countries children and young men were educated in the monasteries, but only in Southeast Asia did temporary initiation into the order, either as a novice (as in Burma) or at a later age as a full-fledged monk (as in central Thailand), become a culturally accepted necessity for the attainment of male adulthood. Buddhist involvement in funerary rituals was, on the other hand, a phenomenon that appeared again and again all across Asia. For example, in the Theravāda countries where Buddhism has been the dominant cultural religion elaborate cremations patterned after the ceremony reportedly performed for the Buddha himself have become the rule for members of the royal and monastic elites. Simpler ceremonies, based on the same basic model, were the norm for those of lesser accomplishment or status. Even in cultures where Buddhism coexisted with other major religions on a more or less equal basis, Buddhists have been the preferred officiants in the funerary context. [*See* Priesthood, *article on* Buddhist Priesthood.] The prime example is China, where Buddhists developed elaborate masses for the dead that were widely used throughout the whole of society. Originally introduced into China by the now defunct Chen-yen (Vajrayāna) school, these masses for the dead were adapted to their new Chinese environment and became an integral component of Chinese Buddhist culture.

All across Asia Buddhism expressed itself as a cultural religion through different kinds of ritual at different levels of society. It was through these ritual forms, more than in any other way, that it became an integral component in the life of different Asian peoples, molding cultures in accordance with its values and being itself molded in the process. Once Buddhism became established as a cultural religion, it was these rituals that enabled it to maintain its position and influence, and to do so century after century on into the modern era. [*See* Pūjā, *article on* Buddhist Pūjā, *and* Worship and Cultic Life, *articles on Buddhist cultic life.*]

Buddhism in the Modern World

The beginnings of European mercantilism and imperialism in the sixteenth century initiated a chain of events that continue to stimulate and to threaten the Buddhist community in its parts and as a whole. Traditional social and economic patterns on which the various Buddhist cultures depended were disrupted and eventually displaced by new patterns. These new patterns inextricably linked individual Buddhist societies to a global community and especially to the West. As a result, all of the profound transformations that have occurred in European civilization in the last three centuries, the advent of rationalism, scientific materialism, nationalism, relativism, technology, democracy, and communism, have challenged Buddhists in Asia just as they have challenged religious men and women in Europe and the Americas.

The modern encounter of cultures and civilizations has not been monolithic. Three stages can be identified in Buddhist Asia. The first was the arrival of missionaries with traders in various parts of Asia. These missionaries came to convert and instruct, and they brought printing presses and schools as well as Bibles and catechisms. There was a missionary onslaught on Asian religious traditions, including Buddhism, in Sri

Lanka, Southeast Asia, China, and Japan. This onslaught was sometimes physically violent, as in the Portuguese destruction of Buddhist temples and relics in Sri Lanka, but for the most part it was an ideological assault. A second stage was more strictly colonial, as some European powers gained control over many different areas of the Buddhist world. Some Buddhist countries, such as Sri Lanka, Burma, and the Indochinese states, were fully colonized while others, such as Thailand, China, and Japan, were subjected to strong colonial influences. In virtually every situation (Tibet was a notable exception), the symbiotic relationship between the political order and the monastic order was disrupted, with adverse effects for Buddhist institutions.

The twentieth-century acceptance of Western political and economic ideologies, whether democratic capitalism or communism, represents a third stage. Buddhists in China, Mongolia, Tibet, and parts of Korea and Southeast Asia now live in communist societies, and the future of Buddhist communities in these areas looks bleak. Capitalism has been dominant in Japan, South Korea, Sri Lanka, and parts of Southeast Asia (Thailand being the prime example), and greater possibilities for the Buddhist tradition are presumed to exist in these areas. But capitalism, as well as communism, has undercut the claim that Buddhist thought and values are of central significance for contemporary life. Buddhist monuments and institutions are in many cases treated as museum pieces, while Buddhist beliefs are often banished to the sphere of individual opinion. In many situations Buddhism is deplored as backward and superstitious, and is for that reason criticized or ignored. As Edward Conze noted in his *A Short History of Buddhism* (London, 1980), "One may well doubt whether capitalism has been any more kind to Buddhism than communism" (p. 129).

Despite the difficulties that Buddhists have faced, they have responded creatively to the turmoil of recent history. They have engaged in many efforts to adapt to their changing environment, just as they have done repeatedly in the past. Thus far, however, they have drawn on their traditional heritage for suitable models, and their varied responses can thus be grouped as cultural, civilizational, and sectarian.

Cultural Responses. The initial responses to European civilization were cultural in character, and often reactionary. Some Buddhist kingdoms, after an initial exposure to elements of European civilization, attempted to isolate themselves as a way of preserving their cultural identity. This was done in Japan, Korea, and Tibet, and was attempted in China. In other cases, Buddhist revivals were inspired by the missionary challenges. In Sri Lanka and China, Buddhist intellectuals responded to the efforts of Christian missionaries to criticize Buddhism with their own spirited apologetics. These intellectuals readily adopted the methods and instruments of the Christian missionary, the printing press and the school, as well as his militancy, to promote the Buddhist cause. Some processes that began in the period of Buddhist culture, especially the mitigation of distinctions between monks and laity, were also stimulated by these innovations. Modern technology, such as improved modes of transportation, also made it easier for more people to engage in traditional practices like pilgrimage.

The Buddhist revivals often were inspired by cultural loyalism. To choose Buddhism as one's religious identity in the face of the Christian challenge also meant that one was choosing to be Sinhala, Thai, or Chinese. It was an emphatic denial that things Chinese, for example, were inferior, even if this was suggested by the power and prestige of Christianity and European civilization.

The association between Buddhism and cultural loyalism has been strongest in Sri Lanka and Southeast Asia. Buddhists, both laity and monks, were actively involved in the local independence movements. In these contexts Buddhism has been given a sharply defined nationalistic character by drawing on both the heritage of indigenous Buddhist culture and the example of Aśoka's imperial religion. Buddhism has been used as an instrument for national integration in postcolonial politics and elements of Buddhism have been appropriated by emerging civic religions in Sri Lanka, Burma, and Thailand.

The colonial disestablishment of Buddhism in Sri Lanka and Southeast Asia, and its analogues in Ch'ing-dynasty China and Meiji Japan, altered again the lay-monk relationship and encouraged the emergence of an active lay leadership. Monasteries, deprived of government maintenance and generally without sufficient resources of their own, found it necessary to cultivate the support of local patrons. A larger number of people from various economic and social levels thus became actively involved in religious affairs focusing on the monasteries. This, of course, often led to controversy, with further segmentation of the monastic communities resulting. It also created an environment in which laity and monks could come together in new kinds of associations, much as had happened in the development of Buddhist cultures. Some of the strikingly successful "new religions" of Japan and Korea, such as Reiyūkai (Association of the Friends of the Spirit) and Won Buddhism, are products of this environment. [*See*

New Religions, *article on* New Religions in Japan, *and* Reiyūkai Kyōdan.]

The disestablishment of Buddhism also encouraged the development of an active lay leadership among the new urban elites who were most influenced by European civilization. These elites introduced "reformed" interpretations of elements of the Buddhist tradition in order to bring those elements into harmony with the expectations of European civilization. Modern reformers' interpretations of the Buddha's biography have emphasized his humanity and his rational approach to the problem of human suffering. Some modernists have sought to relate Buddhist thought to Western philosophical perspectives and also to scientific patterns. Many Buddhist reformers have stressed the relevance of Buddhist teachings to social and ethical issues.

Civilizational Responses. The encounter between European civilization and Buddhist cultures encouraged a new awareness among Buddhists of their common heritage. New contacts among Buddhists began on a significant scale, and, as a result, there was also a renewed sense of Buddhism as a civilizational religion.

This sense that Buddhism could again be a civilizational standard that could encompass the conflicting ideologies present in modern Asia and the world had great appeal to the new urban elites. In many countries Buddhist apologists maintained that Buddhism could be the basis for a truly democratic or socialist society and, as a nontheistic religion, could be the basis for world peace and unity. Sōka Gakkai (Value Creation Society), a Japanese "new religion" stemming from the Nichiren tradition, for example, presents an understanding of Buddhism as the "Third Civilization," which can overcome the opposition of idealism and materialism in thought and, when applied to the economy, can bring about a synthesis of capitalism and socialism. [*See* Sōka Gakkai.]

New missionary efforts to Asian countries such as India, Indonesia, and Nepal, where Buddhist influence had waned, and to the West have been encouraged by this view of Buddhism as "the supreme civilization" and the antidote to the spiritual malaise generated by European civilization.

Sectarian Developments. New sectarian developments in the modern period have resulted from the expansion of Buddhism, through missionary work, and from Buddhist losses that have occurred through the encounter with European civilization. These developments are evidence that the idea of a new Buddhist civilization remains, as yet, more an aspiration than a reality.

Sectarian developments resulting from expansion can be seen in the establishment of Buddhism in the West, which has been accomplished at a certain distance from the mainstream communities, whether among immigrant groups or among intellectuals and spiritual seekers disaffected by Western cultures and religious traditions. Another sectarian development resulting from expansion is the neo-Buddhist movement among *harijans*, or scheduled castes, in India, led by B. R. Ambedkar. [*See the biography of Ambedkar.*]

A resurgence of sectarian patterns, resulting from Buddhist losses, can be seen in totalitarian communist areas. These developments tend to be pragmatic and defensive in character. Buddhists have attempted to isolate their community from the mainstream of communist society and thus avoid criticism and attack, but these efforts have rarely been successful. Sectarian isolation, however, has often been enforced by new communist governments as a way of weakening and discrediting Buddhist influence. Through a combination of criticism of Buddhist teaching by communist ideology and the radical disestablishment of Buddhist monasteries, communist governments have been able to divest Buddhist leaders and institutions of their cultural power and influence very quickly. This has occurred in the Soviet Union, Mongolia, North Korea, Vietnam, and with special ferocity in Cambodia (Kampuchea) and Tibet.

The Tibetan experience provides a tragic example of a new sectarian development in Buddhism. Buddhist institutions and leaders have been subject to a brutal attack as part of the effort to incorporate Tibet into the People's Republic of China. This has often taken the form of sinicization, with Buddhism being attacked because of its central place in traditional Tibetan culture. Following the Chinese invasion of 1959, thousands of Tibetans, including the Dalai Lama, fled the country. They have established refugee communities in North America, Europe, and India, where they are trying to preserve the heritage of Tibetan Buddhist culture.

Finally, the growth of millenarian movements among Buddhists in the modern period, especially in Burma, Thailand, and Vietnam, may be described as sectarian developments resulting from Buddhist losses. Like so much else of Buddhism in the modern period, Buddhist millenarian movements were transitory responses to crises of power and interpretation within the Buddhist community.

Conclusion

Buddhism as a whole has not yet developed a distinctive character in the modern period. On the contrary, there is a great deal of continuity between the historical development of Buddhism and the current responses and innovations. Thus the sectarian, civilizational, and cultural patterns continue to exert a predominant influence in the evolution of Buddhist tradition.

At the same time, we can see that Buddhism, like other world religions, participates in a modern religious situation that is, in many respects, radically new. Buddhism has thus come to share certain modern elements with other contemporary religions. We can see such elements in the search for new modes of religious symbolism, as is found in the writings of the Thai monk Buddhadasa and the Japanese Kyoto school of Buddhist philosophy. We can also see these common elements in the preoccupation with the human world and this-worldly soteriology that is emerging in many Buddhist contexts. A modern Sinhala Buddhist, D. Wijewardena, expressed this attitude in a polemical tract, *The Revolt in the Temple* (Colombo, 1953), by saying that Buddhists must pursue "not a will-o'-the-wisp Nirvana secluded in the cells of their monasteries, but a Nirvana attained here and now by a life of self-forgetful activity . . . [so that] they would live in closer touch with humanity, would better understand and sympathize with human difficulties" (p. 586).

This diversity, representing both tradition and present situation, reminds those of us who would study and understand Buddhism and Buddhists that, in the end, the decisive meaning of our concept of Buddhism must be that of cumulative tradition. Our concept must remain open-ended to allow for future transformations of the Buddhist tradition for as long as men and women associate their lives with the name of Buddha.

[*For further discussion of the doctrinal and practical stance(s) of the tradition, see* Buddhist Philosophy; Soteriology, *article on* Buddhist Soteriology; Language, *article on* Buddhist Views of Language; Nirvāṇa; *and* Buddhist Ethics. *For an overview of some of the means by which Buddhism and local cultures become syncretized, see* Folk Religion, *article on* Folk Buddhism. *Various regional surveys treat Buddhism as a component of local and regional cultures. See in particular* Indian Religions, *overview article;* Southeast Asian Religions, *article on* Mainland Cultures; Tibetan Religions, *overview article;* Chinese Religion, *overview article;* Mongol Religions; Korean Religions; *and* Japanese Religion, *overview article. Each of these articles provides further cross-references to Buddhist-inspired elements in local art, architecture, literature, dance, and drama.*]

BIBLIOGRAPHY

"A Brief History of Buddhist Studies in Europe and America" is provided by J. W. de Jong in two successive issues of *Eastern Buddhist*, n.s. 7 (May and October 1974): 55–106 and 49–82, which he has brought up to date in his "Recent Buddhist Studies in Europe and America 1973–1983," which appeared in the same journal, vol. 17 (Spring 1984): 79–107. One of the few books that treats a significant theme within this fascinating scholarly tradition is G. R. Welbon's *The Buddhist Nirvāṇa and its Western Interpreters* (Chicago, 1968).

Among the book-length introductory surveys of Buddhism, the second edition of Richard H. Robinson and Willard L. Johnson's *The Buddhist Religion* (Encino, Calif., 1977) is, overall, the most satisfactory. The only modern attempt to present a full-scale historical survey by a single author is to be found in the Buddhism sections of Charles Eliot's three-volume work *Hinduism and Buddhism*, 3d ed. (London, 1957), taken together with his *Japanese Buddhism* (1935; reprint, New York, 1959). Although these books are seriously dated (they were first published in 1921 and 1935, respectively), they still provide a valuable resource. Five other important works that attempt cross-cultural presentations of a particular aspect of Buddhism are Junjirō Takakusu's *The Essentials of Buddhist Philosophy*, 3d ed., edited by Wing-tsit Chan and Charles A. Moore (Honolulu, 1956); Paul Mus's wide-ranging *Barabuḍur: Esquisse d'une histoire du bouddhisme fondée sur la critique archéologique des textes*, 2 vols. (Hanoi, 1935); Robert Bleichsteiner's *Die gelbe Kirche* (Vienna, 1937), which was translated into French and published as *L'église jaune* (Paris, 1937); W. Randolph Kloetzli's *Buddhist Cosmology* (Delhi, 1983); and David L. Snellgrove's edited collection *The Image of the Buddha* (London, 1978).

Many of the most important studies of the early, sectarian phase of Buddhism in India extend their discussions to the later phases of Indian Buddhism as well. This is true, for example, of Sukumar Dutt's *Buddhist Monks and Monasteries of India* (London, 1962) and of Edward Conze's *Buddhist Thought in India* (Ann Arbor, 1967). For those interested in Buddhist doctrines, Conze's book may be supplemented by David J. Kalupahana's *Causality: The Central Philosophy of Buddhism* (Honolulu, 1975), which focuses on sectarian Buddhism, and Fredrick J. Streng's *Emptiness: A Study in Religious Meaning* (New York, 1967), which examines the work of the famous early Mahāyāna philosopher Nāgārjuna.

A historical account that is focused more exclusively on the sectarian period and the transition to civilizational Buddhism is provided by Étienne Lamotte in his authoritative *Histoire du bouddhisme indien: Des origines á l'ère Śaka* (Louvain, 1958). A somewhat different perspective on the same process of development is accessible in three closely related works that can profitably be read in series: Frank E. Reynolds's title essay in *The Two Wheels of Dhamma*, edited by Frank E. Reynolds and Bardwell L. Smith, "AAR Studies in Religion," no. 3 (Chambersburg, Pa., 1972); John C. Holt's *Discipline: The Canonical Buddhism of the Vinayapiṭaka* (Delhi, 1981); and John Strong's *The Legend of King Aśoka: A Study and Translation of the Aśokāvadāna* (Princeton, 1983).

Good books that treat Buddhism as an international civilization are hard to come by. Three that provide some assistance to those interested in the topic are Trevor O. Ling's *The Bud-*

dha: Buddhist Civilization in India and Ceylon (London, 1973); Erik Zürcher's *The Buddhist Conquest of China: The Spread and Adaptation of Buddhism in Early Medieval China*, 2 vols. (Leiden; 1959); and René Grousset's *In the Footsteps of the Buddha*, translated by J. A. Underwood (New York, 1971). Works that focus on the process of acculturation of Buddhism in various contexts include Hajime Nakamura's *Ways of Thinking of Eastern Peoples*, the revised English translation of which was edited by Philip P. Wiener (Honolulu, 1964); Alicia Matsunaga's *The Buddhist Philosophy of Assimilation* (Tokyo and Rutland, Vt., 1969); and Kenneth Ch'en's *The Chinese Transformation of Buddhism* (Princeton, 1973).

Studies of particular Buddhist cultures are legion. Some valuable studies focus on Buddhism in the context of the whole range of religions that were present in a particular area. Good examples are Giuseppe Tucci's *The Religions of Tibet*, translated by Geoffrey Samuel (Berkeley, 1980), and Joseph M. Kitagawa's *Religion in Japanese History* (New York, 1966). Other treatments of particular Buddhist cultures trace the Buddhist tradition in question from its introduction into the area through the period of acculturation and, in some cases, on into modern times. Two examples are *Religion and Legitimation of Power in Sri Lanka*, edited by Bardwell L. Smith (Chambersburg, Pa., 1978), and Kenneth Ch'en's comprehensive *Buddhism in China* (Princeton, 1964). Finally, some interpretations of particular Buddhist cultures focus more narrowly on a specific period or theme. See, for example, Lal Mani Joshi's *Studies in the Buddhistic Culture of India* (Delhi, 1967), which deals primarily with Buddhist culture in Northeast India during the seventh and eighth centuries; Daniel Overmyer's *Folk Buddhist Religion: Dissenting Sects in Late Traditional China* (Cambridge, Mass., 1976); and William R. La Fleur's *The Karma of Words: Buddhism and the Literary Arts in Medieval Japan* (Berkeley, 1983).

There is also a myriad of books and articles that consider the development of Buddhism in the modern period. The most adequate overview of developments through the early 1970s is provided in *Buddhism in the Modern World*, edited by Heinrich Dumoulin and John Maraldo (New York, 1976). In addition, there are two excellent trilogies on particular traditions. The first, by Holmes Welch, includes *The Practice of Chinese Buddhism, 1900–1950* (1967), *The Buddhist Revival in China* (1968), and *Buddhism under Mao* (1972), all published by the Harvard University Press. The second, by Stanley J. Tambiah, includes *Buddhism and the Spirit Cults in North-East Thailand* (1970), *World Conqueror and World Renouncer: A Study of Buddhism and Polity in Thailand against a Historical Background* (1976), and *The Buddhist Saints of the Forest and the Cult of Amulets* (1984), all published by the Cambridge University Press.

For those interested in pursuing the study of Buddhism in a cross-cultural, thematic manner, Frank E. Reynolds's *Guide to the Buddhist Religion* (Boston, 1981), done with the assistance of John Holt and John Strong, is a useful resource. It provides 350 pages of annotated bibliography of English, French, and German materials (plus a preface and 65 pages of index) organized in terms of eleven themes, including "Historical Development," "Religious Thought," "Authoritative Texts," "Popular Beliefs and Literature," "Social, Political and Economic Aspects," "The Arts," "Religious Practices and Rituals," and "Soteriological Experience and Processes: Path and Goal."

FRANK E. REYNOLDS and CHARLES HALLISEY

Buddhism in India

A contemporary visitor to the South Asian subcontinent would find Buddhism flourishing only outside the mainland, on the island of Sri Lanka. This visitor would meet small pockets of Buddhists in Bengal and in the Himalayan regions, especially in Ladakh and Nepal, and as the dominant group in Bhutan and Sikkim. Most of the latter Buddhists belong to the Mahāyāna and Vajrayāna forms of Buddhism and represent denominations and orders of Tibetan and Nepalese origin. Buddhists may also be found in the subcontinent among Tibetan refugees (mostly in Himachal Pradesh and Bangalore), among the Ambedkar Buddhists of Maharashtra, and among pilgrims and missionaries flocking to the sacred sites of India. The diversity of manifestations is not new, but the specific forms are not representative of what Indian Buddhism was in the past.

Origins

Approximately twenty-five hundred years ago the founder of the Buddhist religion was born into the Śākya tribe in a small aristocratic republic in the Himalayan foothills, in what is today the kingdom of Nepal. In his youth he descended to the Ganges River valley in search of spiritual realization. After several years of study at the feet of spiritual masters he underwent a profound religious experience that changed his life; he became a teacher himself, and lived for the rest of his adult life as a mendicant peripatetic. His worldview and personal preoccupations were shaped in the cultural milieu of India of the sixth century BCE; the religious communities that trace their origin to him developed their most distinctive doctrines and practices in Indian soil.

Sources and Setting. Unfortunately, we do not possess reliable sources for most of the history of Buddhism in its homeland; in particular, we have precious little to rely on for its early history. Textual sources are late, dating at the very least five hundred years after the death of the Buddha. The archaeological evidence, abundant as it is, is limited in the information it can give us. A few facts are nevertheless well established. The roots of Indian Buddhism are to be found in the "shramanic" movement of the sixth century BCE, which owes the name to its model of religious perfection, the *śramaṇa*, or wandering ascetic. The *śramaṇas* set religious goals that stood outside, and in direct opposition to, the religious and social order of the *brāhmaṇas* (brahmans), who represented the Indo-Aryan establishment. Most of the values that would become characteristic of Indian, and therefore Hindu, religion in general were shaped by the interaction of these two groups, especially by a process of assimilation that transformed the Brahmanic order into Hindu culture. [*See* Vedism and Brahmanism.]

The appearance of two major shramanic religions, Buddhism and Jainism, marked the end of the Vedic-Brahmanic period and the beginning of an era of cross-fertilization between diverse strata of Indian culture. This new age, sometimes called the Indic period, was characterized by the dominant role of "heterodox" or non-Hindu religious systems, the flourishing of their ascetic and monastic orders, and the use of the vernaculars in preference to Sanskrit.

We can surmise that this new age was a time of social upheaval and political instability. The use of iron had changed radically the character of warfare and the nature of farming. The jungle was cleared, farmland could support a court bureaucracy, and palaces and city walls could be built. A surplus economy was created that made possible large state societies, with concentrated populations and resources, and consequently with heightened political ambition.

The Buddha must have been touched directly by these changes: shortly before his death the republic of the Śākyas was sacked by the powerful kingdom of Kośala, which in turn would shortly thereafter fall under the power of Magadha. At the time of the Buddha sixteen independent states existed in north-central India, a century later only one empire would rule in the region, and in another hundred years this empire, Magadha, would control all of northern India and most of the South. The unity of the empire was won at a price: political and social systems based on family or tribal order crumbled; the old gods lost their power.

As the old order crumbled, the brahmans claimed special privileges that other groups were not always willing to concede. Those who would not accept their leadership sought spiritual and moral guidance among the *śramaṇas*. Although recent research has shown that the interaction between these two groups was more complex than we had previously imagined, it is still accepted that the shramanic movement represented some of the groups displaced by the economic and political changes of the day, and by the expansion of Brahmanic power. The *śramaṇas,* therefore, were rebels of sorts. They challenged the values of lay life in general, but especially the caste system as it existed at the time. Thus, what appeared as a life-style designed to lead to religious realization may have been at the same time the expression of social protest, or at least of social malaise.

The shramanic movement was fragmented: among the shramanic groups, Buddhism's main rival was Jainism, representing an ancient teaching whose origin dated to at least one or two generations before the Buddha. A community of mendicants reformed by Vardhamāṇa Mahāvīra (d. around 468 BCE) shortly before the beginning of Buddha's career, Jainism represented the extremes of world denial and asceticism that Buddhism sought to moderate with its doctrine of the Middle Way. Buddhists also criticized in Jainism what they saw as a mechanistic conception of moral responsibility and liberation. Another school criticized by early Buddhists was that of Makkhali Gosāla, founder of the Ājīvikas, who also taught an extreme form of asceticism that was based, strangely, on a fatalistic doctrine. [*See* Jainism; Mahāvīra; Ājīvikas; *and the biography of Gośāla.*]

We have to understand the shramanic movements as independent systems and not as simple derivations or reforms of Brahmanic doctrine and practice. One can find, nevertheless, certain elements common to all the movements of the age: the *śramaṇas*, called "wanderers" (*parivrājakas*), like the forest dwellers of Brahmanism, retired from society. Some sought an enstatic experience; some believed that particular forms of conduct led to purity and liberation from suffering; others sought power through knowledge (ritual or magical) or insight (contemplative or gnostic); but most systems contained elements of all of these tendencies.

Among the religious values formed during the earlier part of the Indic age, that is, during the shramanic period, we must include, above all, the concept of the cycle and bondage of rebirth *(saṃsāra)* and the belief in the possibility of liberation *(mokṣa)* from the cycle through ascetic discipline, world renunciation, and a moral or ritual code that gave a prominent place to abstaining from doing harm to living beings *(ahiṃsā).* This ideal, like the quest for altered states of consciousness, was not always separable from ancient notions of ritual purity and spiritual power. But among the shramanic movements it sometimes took the form of a moral virtue. Then it appeared as opposition to organized violence—political, as embodied in war, and religious, as expressed in animal sacrifice.

The primary evil force was no longer envisioned as a spiritual personality, but as an impersonal moral law of cause and effect *(karman)* whereby human actions created a state of bondage and suffering. In their quest for a state of rest from the activities of *karman,* whether the goal was defined as enstasy or knowledge, the new religious specialists practiced a variety of techniques of

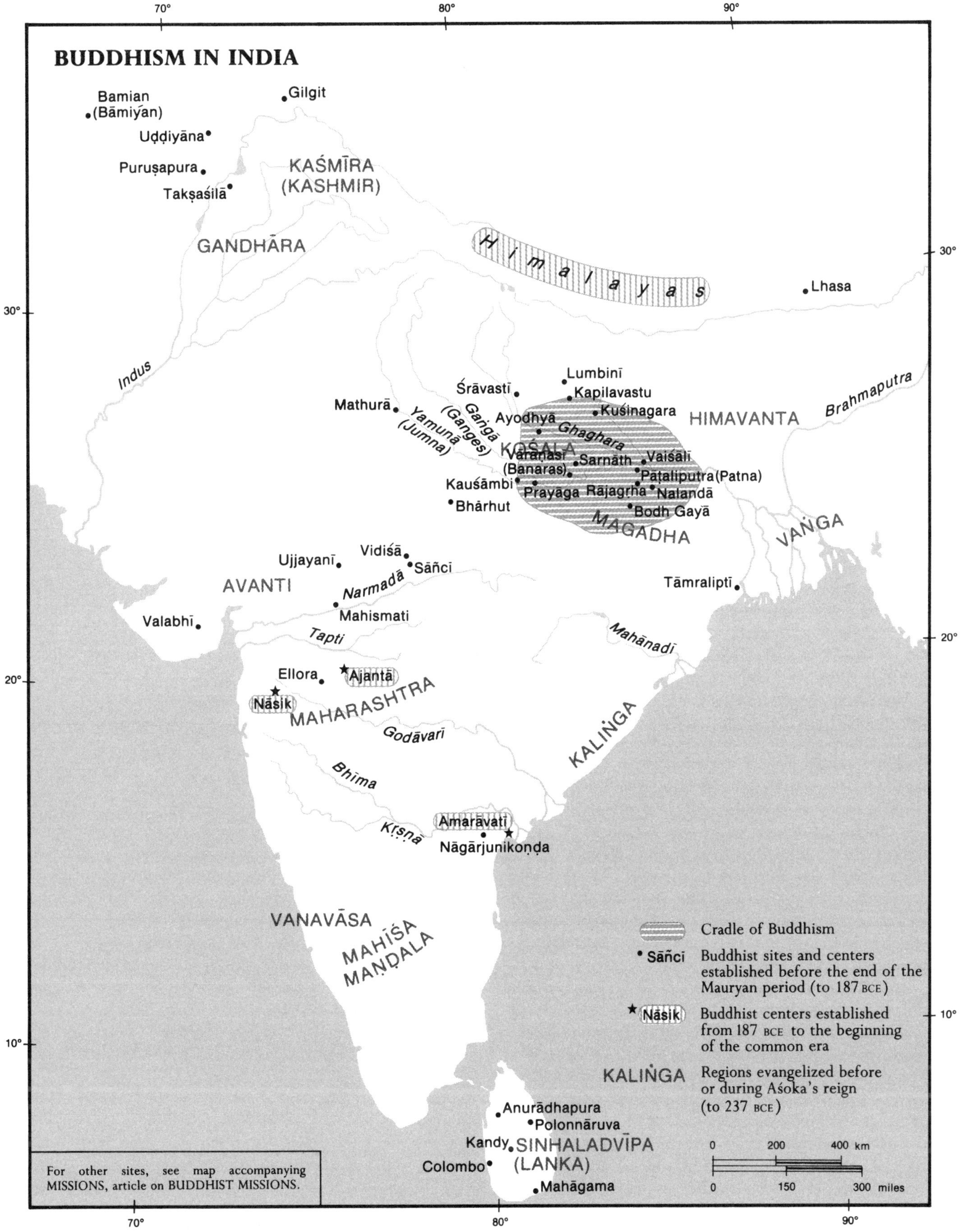
BUDDHISM IN INDIA
Bamian
(Bāmiyan)
Gilgit
Uḍḍiyāna
Puruṣapura
Takṣaśilā
KAŚMĪRA
(KASHMIR)
GANDHĀRA
Himalayas
Lhasa
Indus
Lumbinī
Kapilavastu
Śrāvastī
Mathurā
Gaṅgā
(Ganges)
Yamunā
(Jumna)
Ayodhyā
Kuśinagara
HIMAVANTA
Brahmaputra
Ghaghara
KOŚALA
Vārāṇasī
(Banaras)
Sarnāth
Vaiśālī
Pāṭaliputra(Patna)
Kauśāmbi
Prayāga
Rājagṛha
Nālandā
Bhārhut
Bodh Gayā
MAGADHA
VAṄGA
Vidiśā
Ujjayanī
Sāñcī
AVANTI
Narmadā
Tāmraliptī
Valabhī
Mahismati
Tapti
Mahānadī
Ellora
Ajantā
Nāsik
MAHARASHTRA
Godāvarī
KALIṄGA
Bhīma
Amarāvatī
Kṛṣṇā
Nāgārjunikoṇḍa
VANAVĀSA
MAHIŚA
MAṆḌALA
Cradle of Buddhism
Sāñcī Buddhist sites and centers established before the end of the Mauryan period (to 187 BCE)
Nāsik Buddhist centers established from 187 BCE to the beginning of the common era
KALIṄGA Regions evangelized before or during Aśoka's reign (to 237 BCE)
Anurādhapura
Polonnāruva
Kandy
SINHALADVĪPA
(LANKA)
Colombo
Mahāgama
0 200 400 km
0 150 300 miles
For other sites, see map accompanying MISSIONS, article on BUDDHIST MISSIONS.
70°
80°
90°
30°
20°
10°

self-cultivation usually known as *yogas*. The sustained practice of this discipline was known as a "path" *(mārga)*, and the goal was a state of peace and freedom from passion and suffering called *nirvāṇa*. [*See* Karman, *article on* Hindu and Jain Concepts; Mokṣa; Yoga; Saṃsāra; Ahiṃsā; *and* Saṃnyāsa.]

As a shramanic religion, Buddhism displayed similar traits but gave to each of these its unique imprint. The conception of rebirth and its evils were not questioned, but suffering was universalized: all human conditions lead to suffering, suffering has a cause, and that cause is craving, or "thirst" *(tṛṣṇā)*. To achieve liberation from the cycle of rebirth one must follow the spiritual discipline prescribed by the Buddha, summarized in the Eightfold Path. The follower of Buddhism was expected to renounce the lay life and become a wandering ascetic, an ideal epitomized by the spiritual career of the founder.

Most shramanic groups made provisions for their lay supporters, essentially members of the community who by circumstance or choice could not follow the wanderer's path. Buddhist laymen could begin moving in the right direction—with the hope of being able to renounce the world in a future birth—by "taking refuge" *(śaraṇagamana)*, that is, by making a confession of faith in the Buddha, his teachings, and his monastic order, and by adopting five fundamental moral precepts *(pañcaśīla)*: not to deprive a living thing of life, not to take what is not given to you, not to engage in illicit sexual conduct, not to lie, and not to take intoxicating drinks.

The Three Jewels. Perhaps all we can say with certainty about the roots of Buddhist doctrine and doctrinal continuity in Buddhism is that the figure of the Buddha and his experience dominate most of Buddhist teachings. If we wish to understand Buddhism as a doctrinal system, we can look at its oral and written ideology—including its scriptures—as the effort of diverse Buddhist communities to explore and define the general issues raised by the Buddha's career. These include questions such as the following: Does the Buddha "exist" after liberation? Is the experience of awakening ineffable? Which of the two experiences, awakening or liberation, is the fundamental one?

On the other hand, if we wish to understand Buddhism as a religion rather than as a system of doctrines, its focus or fulcrum must be found in the religious communities and their objects of veneration. The early community was represented primarily by the gathering of mendicants or monks called the *saṃgha*, held together by ascetic or monastic codes *(prātimokṣa)* attributed to the Buddha himself, and by the objects of worship represented by (1) the founder himself as the "Awakened One" *(buddha)*; (2) his exemplary and holy life, his teachings and his experience *(dharma)*; and (3) the community *(saṃgha)* itself, sustained by the memory of his personality and teaching. These objects of veneration are known as the "Three Treasures" *(triratna)*, and the believer's trust in these ideals is expressed, doctrinally and ritually, in the "Three Refuges" (to rely on the Buddha, the Dharma, and the Sangha). To this day, this formula serves at once as an indication of the meaning of monastic ordination and a lay confession of faith.

Buddha. No Western scholar today would claim to know the exact details of the founder's biography, or for that matter the exact content of his teachings. The above is merely an educated guess based on formulations from a time removed by several centuries from their origins. Scholars agree, nevertheless, on the historicity of the founder. That is to say, though they may doubt the accuracy of the information transmitted in traditional "biographies" (beginning with his personal name, Siddhārtha Gautama) or in legends about the Buddha's sermons, Western scholars accept the existence of an influential religious figure, called Śākyamuni ("the sage of the Śākya tribe") by his disciples, who at some point in the sixth century BCE founded in the Ganges River valley the community of wandering mendicants that would eventually grow into the world religion we now call Buddhism.

Scholars generally tend to accept the years 563 to 483 BCE as the least problematic, if not the most plausible, dating for the life of Gautama Buddha. (Other dating systems exist, however, that place his life as much as a century later.) Assuming, moreover, that the legend is reliable in some of its details, we can say that the history of the religion begins when Śākyamuni was thirty-five (therefore, in about 528), with his first sermon at Sārnāth (northeast of the city of Vārāṇasī).

Before and after his enlightenment, Śākyamuni followed the typical career of a wanderer. At twenty-nine he abandoned the household and sought a spiritual guide. An early legend claims that Śākyamuni actually studied under two teachers of the age, Āḷāra Kālāma and Udraka Rāmaputra. From such teachers the young ascetic learned techniques of meditation that he later rejected, but the imprints of which remain in Buddhist theories of meditation. Dissatisfied with what he had learned, he tried the life of the hermit. Finally, after six years of struggle, he "awakened" under a pipal tree *(Ficus religiosa)* near the border town of Uruvilvā (Bodh Gayā).

His first sermon was followed by forty-five years of wandering through the Ganges River valley, spreading his teachings. Although tradition preserves many narratives of isolated episodes of this half century of teaching, no one has been able to piece together a convincing account of this period. For the tradition this was also a time for the performance of great miracles, and historical accuracy was never an important consideration.

At the age of eighty (c. 483), Siddhārtha Gautama, the Buddha Śākyamuni, died near the city of Kuśināgara. To his immediate disciples perhaps this fading away of the Master confirmed his teachings on impermanence, but the Buddha's death would soon come to be regarded as a symbol of his perfect peace and renunciation: with death he had reached his *parinirvāṇa,* that point in his career after which he would be reborn no more. His ashes, encased in a reliquary buried in a cairn, came to stand for the highest achievement of an awakened being, confirming his status as the one who had attained to truth, the Tathāgata—an epithet that would come to denote ultimate truth itself. [*See* Buddha *and* Tathāgata.]

Dharma. The first preaching, known as the "First Turning of the Wheel of Dharma" (or, in the West, the "Sermon at Banaras" or the "Deer Park Sermon"), symbolizes the appearance in history of the Buddhist teaching, whereas Śākyamuni's enlightenment experience, or "Great Awakening" *(mahābodhi),* which occurred in the same year, represents the human experience around which the religion would develop its practices and ideals. This was the experience whereby Śākyamuni became an "Awakened One" *(buddha).* His disciples came to believe that all aspects of Buddhist doctrine and practice flow from this experience of awakening *(bodhi)* and from the resultant state of freedom from passion, suffering, and rebirth called *nirvāṇa.* The teachings found in the Buddha's sermons can be interpreted as definitions of these two experiences, the spiritual practices that lead to or flow from them, and the institutions that arose inspired by the experience and the human beings who laid claim to it. [*See* Nirvāṇa.]

However, it is difficult, if not impossible, to surmise which, if any, among the many doctrines attributed by tradition to the founder are veritably his. Different Buddhists, even when they can agree on the words, will interpret the message differently. Although most would find the nucleus of Śākyamuni's teachings in the "First Sermon," especially in the doctrine of the Four Noble Truths allegedly preached therein, a host of other doctrinal statements compete for the central position throughout the history of Buddhism in India and beyond. Moreover, a number of texts that can claim great antiquity are not only silent about the Four Noble Truths but actually do not seem to presuppose them in any way. The same can be said about other doctrines that would become central to the development of Buddhist doctrinal speculation, for instance, the principle of conditioned arising *(pratītya-samutpāda)* and the analysis of the human personality into its constitutent parts (*skandha*s, etc.).

It is difficult to determine to what extent early Buddhism had an accompanying metaphysics. Some of the earliest strata of Buddhist literature suggest that the early community may have emphasized the joys of renunciation and the peace of abstention from conflict—political, social, and religious—more than a philosophical doctrine of liberation. Such are the ascetic ideals of one of the earliest texts of the tradition, the *Aṭṭhakavagga (Suttanipāta).* The mendicant abstains from participating in the religious and metaphysical debates of brahmans, *śramaṇa*s, and sages. He is detached from all views, for

> Purity is not [attained] by views, or learning,
> by knowledge, or by moral rules, and rites.
> Nor is it [attained] by the absence of views,
> learning, knowledge, rules, or rites.
> Abandoning all these, not grasping at them,
> he is at peace; not relying, he would not
> hanker for becoming. (*Suttanipāta* 839)

There is in this text a rejection of doctrine, rule, and rite that is a critique of the exaggerated claims of those who believed they could become pure and free through ritual, knowledge, or religious status. The lonely ascetic seeks not to become one thing or the other and avoids doctrinal disputes.

If such statements represent some of the earliest moments in the development of the doctrine, then the next stage must have brought a growing awareness of the need for ritual and creed if the community was to survive. This awareness would have been followed in a short time by the formation of a metaphysic, a theory of liberation, and a conscious system of meditation. In the next strata of early Buddhist literature these themes are only surpassed in importance by discussions of ascetic morality. The ascetic ideals of the early community were then expanded and defined by doctrine—as confession of faith, as ideology, and as a plan for religious and moral practice. The earliest formulations of this type are perhaps those of the Eightfold Path, with its triple division into wisdom, moral practice, and mental concentration. The theoretical or metaphysical underpinnings are contained in the Four Noble Truths and in the Three Marks (impermanence, sorrow, and no-self), both traditionally regarded as the subject matter of the Buddha's first sermons. [*See* Four Noble Truths; Eightfold Path; Karman, *article on* Buddhist Concepts; Soul, *article on* Buddhist Concepts; *and* Dharma, *article on* Buddhist Dharma and Dharmas.]

Saṃgha. With the first sermon the Buddha began a ministry that would last forty-five years. During this period he established a religious order—perhaps only a mendicant order in its beginnings—and trained a number of distinguished disciples who would carry on the teaching after the founder's death. Tradition preserves the names of many of his disciples and immediate heirs to his teaching: Kauṇḍinya, the first convert to be admitted into the Buddha's religious order *(saṃgha);* Yasa, the first householder to receive full lay initiation with the Three Refuges; Śāriputra, the master of wisdom; Maudgalyāyana, the great thaumaturge; Upāli, the expert in the monastic code; Ānanda, the Buddha's cousin and beloved disciple; Mahāprajāpati, the first woman admitted into the monastic order; and Mahākāśyapa, who undertook to preserve the Buddha's teaching and organized the First Council. The Buddha's disciples represented a wide spectrum of social classes. Yasa was the son of a wealthy gild master; Upāli, a humble barber; Śāriputra, a brahman; Ānanda, a member of the nobility *(kṣatriya).* Among the early followers we find not only world renouncers but believers from a variety of walks of life; King Bimbisāra, the wealthy banker Anāthapiṇḍika, the respectable housewife Viśākhā, and the courtesan Amrapālī, for instance.

Although the Buddhist monastic community was an integral part of Indian society, serving as an instrument of legitimation and cohesion, it also served on occasions as a critic of society. Especially in its early development, and in particular during the period of the wandering mendicants, the *saṃgha* was a nonconformist subgroup. The variety of social classes represented by the roster of early disciples in part reflects the fluid state of Indian society at the time; but it also reflects the Buddha's open opposition to the caste system as it existed then. Although the challenge was religious and political as well as social, the Buddha's critique of Brahmanism made his order of mendicants an alternative community, where those who did not fit in the new social order could find a sense of belonging, acceptance, and achievement. Buddhist reforms and institutions would waver in their function as rebels and supporters of social order until Buddhism ultimately became absorbed into Hinduism during the centuries following the first millennium of the common era.

We can surmise that the earliest community did not have a fixed abode. During the dry season the Buddhist *śramaṇas* would sleep in the open and wander from village to village "begging" for their sustenance—hence their title *bhikṣu,* "mendicant" (fem., *bhikṣuṇī).* They were persons who had set forth *(pravrajyā)* from the household to lead the life of the wanderer *(parivrājaka).* Only during the rainy season would they gather in certain spots in the forest or in special groves provided by lay supporters. There they would build temporary huts that would be dismantled at the end of the rainy season, when they would set out again in their constant wandering to spread the Buddha's Dharma.

The main ideals of the mendicant life of the "wanderers" is expressed in a passage that is presented as the creed or code (the Prātimokṣa) recited by the followers of the "former Buddha" Vipaśyin when they interrupted the wandering to meet and renew their common ideals:

> Enduring patience is the highest austerity,
> *nirvāṇa* is the highest condition—say the Buddhas.
> For he who injures another is not a true renouncer,
> He who causes harm to others is not a true ascetic.
> Not to do any evil, to practice the good,
> to purify one's own mind:
> This is the teaching of the Buddhas.
>
> Not to speak against others, not to harm others,
> and restraint according to the rule *(prātimokṣa),*
> Moderation in eating, secluded dwelling,
> and the practice of mental cultivation *(adhicitta):*
> This is the teaching of the Buddhas.
>
> *(Mahāpadāna Suttanta)*

These verses outline important aspects of the early teaching: the centrality of *ahiṃsā,* the two aspects of morality—abstention and cultivation—and the practice of meditation, all in the context of a community of ascetics for whom a life of solitude, poverty, and moderation was more important than the development of subtle metaphysics. [*For a discussion of ascetic practices, see* Soteriology, *article on* Buddhist Soteriology.]

Probably—and the earliest scriptures suggest this—the first aspect of Buddhist teachings to be systematized was the rule, first as a confession of faith for dispersed communities of mendicants, soon as a monastic rule for sedentary ascetics. Also at an early stage, the community sought to systematize its traditions of meditation, some of which must have been pre-Buddhistic (the Buddha himself having learned some of these from his teachers). Thus, Buddhist techniques of meditation represent a continuation of earlier processes of yoga, though we cannot be certain as to the exact connection, or the exact content of the early practices.

The first of these developments brought the community closer together by establishing a common ritual, the recitation of the rule *(prātimokṣa)* at a meeting held on the full and new moon and the quarter moons *(uposatha).* The second development confirmed an important but divisive trait of the early community: the primary source of authority remained with the individual monk and his experience in solitude. Thus, competing systems of meditation and doctrine probably developed more rapidly than differences in the code. [*See* Saṃgha, *especially the overview article.*]

The Cenobium

As India moved into an age of imperial unity under the Maurya (322–185) and Śuṅga dynasties (185–73), the Buddhist community reached its point of greatest unity. Although the *saṃgha* split into schools or sects perhaps as early as the fourth century BCE, differences among Buddhists were relatively minor. Transformed into a monastic brotherhood, Buddhism served a society that shared common values and customs. Unity, however, was shortlived, and Buddhism, like India, would have to adapt rapidly to new circumstances as the first invasions from Central Asia would put an end to the Śuṅga dynasty in 175. Until then, however, during the approximately three hundred years from the death of the founder to the beginning of the age of foreign invasions, Buddhist monks and laymen began the process of systematization that defined the common ground of Indian Buddhism in practice, scripture, and doctrine.

The primary element of continuity became the Prātimokṣa, the rules for the maintenance of the community and the liturgical recitation thereof; differences in this regard would be more serious than differences of doctrine. Thus the Second Council, which is supposed to have caused the most serious split in the history of the community, is said to have been called to resolve differences in the interpretation and formulation of minor details in the monastic regulations. In order to justify and clarify the rules that held the community together a detailed commentary of the Prātimokṣa rules had to be developed. The commentary, attributed to the Buddha himself, eventually grew into the Vinaya, an extensive section of the canon.

But the full development of the monastic code presupposes a sedentary *saṃgha.* We can surmise that not long after the Buddha's death the retreat for the rainy season began to extend into the dry season, perhaps at the invitation of the lay community, perhaps owing to dwindling popular support for the mendicant wanderers. Soon the temporary huts were replaced by more or less permanent structures build of wood, and the community of wanderers became a cenobium. The stone and gravel foundation of one of the earliest monasteries remains in the vicinity of Rājagṛha (Bihar). These are the ruins of the famous "Jivaka's Mango Grove" (Jivakāmravaṇa) Monastery, built on a plot of land donated to the order at the time of the Buddha. In its early history it may have been used only during the rainy season, but it already shows the basic structure of the earliest monasteries: living quarters for the monks and a large assembly hall (perhaps for the celebration of the Uposatha).

As the community settled down, rules and rituals for regulating monastic life became a necessity. At least some of the items in the *Prātimokṣa* section of the Vinaya and some of the procedural rules discussed in the *Karmavācanā* may go back to the time of the Buddha. The rule and the procedures for governing the *Saṃgha* are clearly based on republican models, like the constitution of the Licchavis of Vaiśālī, which is praised in the canonical texts. If this admiration goes back to the founder, then we can say that the Buddha ordered his community of wandering mendicants on the political model provided by the disappearing republics of North India. Such a rule would encourage order and harmony on the one hand, and peaceful disagreement and individual effort on the other. It provided for mutual care and concern in matters of morals, but lacked a provision for a central authority in political or doctrinal matters. [*See* Vinaya *and* Monasticism, *article on* Buddhist Monasticism.]

The Common Doctrinal Ground. The Buddha realized the true nature of things, their "suchness" *(tathatā),* and therefore is one of those rare beings called Tathāgatas. Yet, whether there is a Tathāgata to preach it or not, the Dharma is always present, because it is the nature of all things *(dharmatā).* Four terms summarize this truth known by the Tathāgatas: impermanence, sorrow, no-self, *nirvāṇa.* The first implies the second, for attachment to what must change brings sorrow. Our incapacity to control change, however, reveals the reality of no-self—nothing is "I" or "mine." The experience of no-self, on the other hand, is liberating; it releases one from craving and the causes of sorrow; it leads to peace, *nirvāṇa.*

These principles are summarized also in a doctrine recognized by all schools, that of the Four Noble Truths: sorrow, its cause, its cessation, and the path leading to cessation. Buddhist tradition, therefore, will spend much of its energy in understanding the causes of suffering and the means to put an end to it, or, in doctrinal shorthand, "arising" and "cessation." Since cessation is in fact the obverse of arising, a proper understanding of arising, or causation, becomes central to Buddhist speculation in India. The most important doctrine for this aspect of the religion is the principle of dependent arising *(pratītya-samutpāda):* everything we regard as "the self" is conditioned or compounded; everything conditioned depends on causes and conditions; by understanding the causes of our idea of the self and of the sorrow that this idea brings to us we can become free of suffering. [*See* Pratītya-samutpāda.] This doctrine is summarized in a stanza that has become one of the best known Buddhist creeds throughout Asia:

> The Tathāgata has proclaimed the cause,
> as well as the cessation,
> of all things *(dharma)* arising from a cause.
> This is the Great *Śramaṇa's* teaching.
> (*Mahāvastu* 2.62; Pali *Vinaya* 1.40)

Abstract theories of causation were perceived as having an ultimately soteriological meaning or function, for they clarified both the process of bondage (rebirth forced upon us as a consequence of our actions) and the process of liberation (freedom from rebirth by overcoming our ignorance and gaining control over the causes of bondage). Liberation was possible because the analysis of causation revealed that there was no reincarnating or suffering self to begin with.

Impermanence and causation were explained by primitive theories of the composition of material reality (the four elements) and mental reality (the six senses, the six types of sense objects, etc.) and, what is more important, by the theory of the constituents (*skandhas*) of human personality. These notions would become the main focus of Buddhist philosophy, and by the beginning of the common era they were being integrated into systematic treatments of the nature of ultimately real entities *(dharma)*. [*See* Dharma, *article on* Buddhist Dharma and Dharmas.]

Although the themes of impermanence and causation will remain at the heart of Buddhist philosophical speculation for several centuries, from the religious point of view the question of no-self plays a more important role. At first seen as an insightful formulation of the meaning of awakening and liberation, the doctrine of no-self raised several difficulties for Buddhist dogma. First, it was not at all obvious how moral (or karmic) responsibility could be possible if there was no continuous self. Second, some Buddhists wondered what was the meaning of liberation in the absence of a self.

Closely related to these issues was the question of the nature and status of the liberated being. In other words, what sort of living being is a Tathāgata? Some Buddhists considered the Tathāgata as a transcendent or eternal being, while others saw him as someone who by becoming extinct was nonexistent; still others began to redefine the concept of liberation and no-self in an attempt to solve these questions and in response to changes in the mythological or hagiographic sphere. These issues are an essential part of the changes in doctrine and practice that would take place during the age of invasions, culminating in the emergence of Mahāyāna Buddhism.

Worship and Ritual. The most important ritual of the monastic community continued to be Upavasatha or Uposatha, a gathering of the *saṃgha* of a given locality or "parish" *(sīmā)* to recite the rules of the Prātimokṣa. These meetings were held at every change in the moon's phase. A similar ceremony, but with greater emphasis on the public confession of individual faults, was held at the end of the rainy season. At this time too was held the *kaṭhina* ceremony, in which the monks received new robes from the lay community. Other rituals, such as the ordination ceremony, had a more limited impact on the community at large but were nevertheless important symbols of the status of the religious specialist in society at large.

Above all other rituals, one of shramanic origin offered continued reinforcement of the ties that bound the religious order with the laity. The *bhikṣu,* as his title indicates, was expected to receive his sustenance from the charity *(dāna)* of pious laymen and laywomen. Accordingly, the monks would walk the villages every morning to collect alms. By giving the unsolicited gift the layperson was assured of the merit *(puṇya)* necessary to be reborn in a state of being more favorable for spiritual or material progress. According to some traditions, the monk received the benefits of helping others gain merit; but some believed the monk could not gain merit except by his own virtue.

In the early stages lay followers were identified by their adherence to the fivefold moral precept *(pañcaśīla)* and the formal adoption of the Three Refuges. These practices continued throughout the history of Indian Buddhism. It is also likely that participation of lay members in Upavasatha meetings with the *saṃgha* was also an early and persistent practice.

At first the cenobitic life of the monks probably had no room for explicit acts of devotion, and the monk's religion was limited to a life of solitude and meditation. The early monastic ruins do not show evidence of any shrine room. It was essential to have the cells open onto a closed courtyard, to keep out the noise of the world; it was essential to have an assembly hall for teaching and the recitation of the Prātimokṣa; a promenade *(caṅkrama)* for walking meditation was also necessary. But there were no shrine rooms.

With the institutionalization of Buddhism, however, came new forms of lay and monastic practice. The monastic brotherhood gradually began to play a priestly role; in tandem with the lay community, they participated in nonmonastic rituals, many of which must have been of pre-Buddhist origin. [*See* Priesthood, *article on* Buddhist Priesthood.] One practice that clearly was an important, nonascetic ritual, yet characteristic of Buddhism, was the worship of the relics of the Buddha and his immediate disciples. The relics were placed in a casket, which was then deposited in a cairn or tumulus *(stūpa, caitya),* to which the faithful would come to present their offerings. Already by the time of Aśoka (mid-third century BCE) we find evidence of a flourishing cult of the relics, often accompanied by the practice of pilgrimage to the sacred sites consecrated by their role in the life of Śākyamuni—especially the birth place, the site of the Great Awakening, the site of the First Sermon, and the spot where the Buddha was believed to have died. [*See also* Pilgrimage, *article on* Buddhist Pilgrimage in South and Southeast Asia.] Following an ancient custom, tumuli were built on these spots—perhaps at first as reliquaries, later as commemorative monuments. Monasteries near such sites assumed the role of shrine caretakers. Eventually, most monasteries became associated with stupas.

Aśoka erected columns and stupas (as many as eighty thousand, according to one tradition) marking the localities associated with the life of the Buddha as well as other ancient sacred sites, some associated with "former Buddhas," that is, mythical beings believed to have achieved Buddhahood thousands or millions of lives before the Buddha Śākyamuni. The latter practice and belief indicates the development of a new form of Buddhism, firmly based on the mythology of each locality, that expanded the concept of the Three Treasures to include a host of mythical beings who would share in the sanctity of Śākyamuni's experience and virtue and who were therefore deserving of the same veneration as he had received in the past.

The cairn or tumulus eventually became sacred in itself, whether there was a relic in it or not. Chapels were built to contain the *caitya.* The earliest surviving examples of these structures are built in stone and date from the first or second century BCE, but we can surmise that they existed in wood from an earlier date. These "*caitya* halls" became the standard shrine room of the monastery: a stylized memorial tumulus built in stone or brick, housed in an apsidal hall with a processional for the ritual circumambulation of the tumulus. [*See* Temple, *article on* Buddhist Temple Compounds.]

Reliefs at the *caitya* hall at Bhājā in western India (late Śuṅga, c. end of the second century BCE) suggest various aspects of the cult: the main form of worship was the ritual of circumambulation *(pradakṣiṇa),* which could be carried out individually or in groups. The stupa represented the sacred or cosmic mountain, at whose center was found the *axis mundi* (now represented by the Buddha's royal parasol); thus the rite of circumambulation expressed veneration for the Buddha and his teaching, while at the same time it served as a symbolic walking of the sun's path around the cosmic mountain.

Stupas were often erected at ancient sacred sites, hills, trees, the confluence of streams, which in many cases were sacred by virtue of non-Buddhist belief. Thus, pre-Buddhist practice, if not belief, survived side by side, and even within, Buddhist liturgy and belief. There is ample evidence of a coexisting cult of the tree (identified with the "Tree of Awakening"), of forest spirits *(yakṣas)* and goddesses *(devatā),* and the persistence of Vedic deities, albeit in a subordinate role, beside a more austere, and presumably monastically inspired, cult of aniconic symbolizations of Buddhahood: the tree and the throne of enlightenment standing for the Great Awakening, the stupa representing the *nirvāṇa,* the wheel representing the doctrine of the Buddha. But one must not assume that the implied categories of "high tradition" and popular cult were mutually exclusive. [*See* Stupa Worship *and* Nāgas and Yakṣas. *For a discussion of Buddhist/local syncretism, see* Folk Religion, *article on* Folk Buddhism. *See also* Worship and Cultic Life, *article on* Buddhist Cultic Life in Southeast Asia.]

The Councils and the Beginning of Scriptural Tradition. The First Council, or Council of Rājagṛha, if a historical fact, must have served to establish the Buddhist *saṃgha* and its doctrine for the community of the Magadhan capital. In all probability the decisions of the Council were not accepted by all Buddhists. Further evidence of disagreement, and geographical fragmentation is found in the legend of the Second Council, one hundred years after the Buddha's death.

Since the early community of wanderers, there had been ample room for disagreement and dissension. But certain forces contributed to maintaining unity: the secular powers, for instance, had much at stake in preserving harmony within the *saṃgha,* especially if they could maintain some kind of control over it. Thus, as the legends have it, each of the three major councils were sponsored by a king: Ajātaśatru, Kālāśoka, and Aśoka, respectively. Within the *saṃgha,* there must have been interests groups, mainly conservative, seeking to preserve the religion by avoiding change—two goals that are not always conciliable. There must have been, therefore, a strong pressure to recover the ideal unity of the early community (as we have seen, probably a fantasy), by legislation. These efforts took two forms: in the first place, there was the drive to establish a common monastic code, in the second place, there was the drive to fix a canon of scriptures. Both tendencies probably became stronger toward the beginning of the common era, when a number of political factors recreated a sense of urgency and a yearning for harmony and peace similar to the one that had given rise to the religion. [*See* Councils, *article on* Buddhist Councils.]

The most important result of the new quest for harmony was the compilation and redaction of scriptures. Transmitted and edited through the oral tradition, the words of the Buddha and his immediate disciples had suffered many transformations before they came to be compiled, to say nothing of their state when they were eventually written down. We have no way of determining which, if any, of the words contained in the Buddhist scriptures are the words of the founder: in fact we have no hard evidence for the language used by the Buddha in his ministry. Scholars have suggested an early form of Māgadhī, since this was probably the lingua franca of the kingdom of Magadha, but this is at best an educated guess. If it is correct, then none of the words of the Buddha have come to us in the original language.

Although the Theravādin tradition claims that the language of its canon, Pali, is the language spoken by the Buddha, Western scholars disagree. Evidently, the Pali canon, like other Buddhist scriptures, is the creation, or at least the compilation and composition, of another age and a different linguistic milieu. As they are preserved today, the Buddhist scriptures must be a collective creation, the fruit of the effort of several generations of memorizers, redactors, and compilers. Some of the earliest Buddhist scriptures may have been translations from logia or sayings of the Buddha that were transmitted for some time in his own language. But even if this is the case, the extant versions represent at the very least redactions and reworkings, if not creations, of a later age.

Since the *saṃgha* was from the beginning a decentralized church, one can presume that the word of the Buddha took many forms. Adding to this the problem of geographical isolation and linguistic diversity, one would expect that the oral transmission would have produced a variegated textual tradition. Perhaps it is this expectation of total chaos that makes it all the more surprising that there is agreement on so many points in the scriptures preserved to this day. This is especially true of the scriptures of the Theravāda school (preserved in Pali), and fragments of the canon of the Sarvāstivāda school (in the original Sanskrit or in Chinese translation). Some scholars have been led to believe, therefore, that these two traditions represent the earliest stratum of the transmission, preserving a complex of pericopes and logia that must go back to a stage when the community was not divided: that is, before the split of the Second Council. Most scholars tend to accept this view; a significant minority, however, sees the uniformity of the texts as reflecting a late, not an early stage, in the redaction of the canon.

The early canon, transmitted orally, must have had only two major sections, Dharma and Vinaya. The first of these contained the discourses of the Buddha and his immediate disciples. The Vinaya contained the monastic rules. Most Western scholars agree that a third section, Abhidharma, found in all of the surviving canons, could not have been included in early definitions of canonicity, though eventually most schools would incorporate it in their canon with varying degrees of authority.

Each early school possessed its own set of scriptural "collections" (called metaphorically "baskets," *piṭaka*). Although eventually the preferred organization seems to have been a tripartite collection of "Three Baskets," the Tripiṭaka, divided into monastic rules, sermons, and scholastic treatises (Vinaya, Sūtra, Abhidharma), some schools adopted different orderings. Among the collections that are now lost there were fourfold and fivefold subdivisions of the scriptures. Of the main surviving scriptural collections, only one is strictly speaking a Tripiṭaka, the Pali corpus of the Theravādins. (The much later Chinese and Tibetan collections have much more complex subdivisions and can be called Tripiṭakas only metaphorically.) [*See* Buddhist Literature, *article on* Canonization.]

The Age of Foreign Invasions

The decline and fall of the Maurya dynasty (324–187) brought an end to an age of assured support for Buddhist monastic institutions. Political circumstances unfavorable to Buddhism began with persecution under Puṣyamitra Śuṅga (r. about 187–151). The Śuṅga dynasty would see the construction of some of the most important Buddhist sites of India: Bhārhut, Sāñcī, and Amarāvatī. But it also foreshadowed the beginning of Hindu dominance. The rising cult of Viṣṇu seemed better equipped to assimilate the religion of the people and win the support of the ruling classes. Although Buddhism served better as a universal religion that could unite Indians and foreign invaders, the latter did not always choose to become Buddhists. A series of non-Indian rulers—Greek, Parthian, Scythian (Saka), Kushan—would hesitate in their religious allegiances.

Among the Greek kings, the Buddhist tradition claims Menandros (Milinda, c. 150 BCE) as one of its converts. The Scythian tribe of the Sakas, who invaded Bactriana around 130 BCE, roughly contemporaneous with the Yüeh-chih conquest of the Tokharians, would become stable supporters of Buddhism in the subcontinent. [*See*

Inner Asian Religions.] Their rivals in South India, the Tamil dynasty of the Śātavāhana (220 BCE–236 CE), sponsored in Andhra the construction of major centers of worship at Amarāvatī and Nāgārjunīkoṇḍa. The Yüeh-chih (Kushans) also supported Buddhism, though perhaps less consistently. The most famous of their rulers, Kaṇiṣka, is represented by the literature as a pious patron of Buddhism (his dates are uncertain; proposed accession in 78 or 125 CE). During the Kushan period (c. 50–320 CE) the great schools of Gandhāra and Mathurā revolutionized Indian, especially Buddhist, art. Both the northern styles of Gandhāra and Mathurā and the southern school of Andhra combined iconic and aniconic symbolization of the Buddha: the first Buddha images appeared around the third century of the common era, apparently independently and simultaneously in all three schools.

The Appearance of Schools and Denominations. Any understanding of the history of composition of the canons, or of their significance in the history of the religion, is dependent on our knowledge of the geographic distribution, history, and doctrine of the various sects. Unfortunately, our knowledge in this regard is also very limited. [*See* Buddhism, Schools of, *overview article.*]

Developments in doctrine and in scholastic speculation. As the original community of wandering mendicants settled in monasteries, a new type of religion arose, concerned with the preservation of a tradition and the justification of its institutions. Although the "forest dweller" continued as an ideal and a practice—some were still dedicated primarily to a life of solitude and meditation—the dominant figure became that of the monk-scholar. This new type of religious specialist pursued the study of the early tradition and moved its doctrinal systems in new directions. On the one hand, the old doctrines were classified, defined, and expanded. On the other hand, there was a growing awareness of the gap that separated the new developments from the transmitted creeds and codes. A set of basic or "original" teachings had to be defined, and the practice of exegesis had to be formalized. In fact, the fluidity and uncertainty of the earlier scriptural tradition may be one of the causes for the development of Buddhist scholasticism. By the time the canons were closed the degree of diversity and conflict among the schools was such, and the tradition was overall so fluid, that it was difficult to establish orthodoxy even when there was agreement on the basic content of the canons. In response to these problems Buddhists soon developed complicated scholastic studies.

At least some of the techniques and problems of this early scholasticism must go back to the early redactions of the Sūtra section of the canon, if not to a precanonical stage. The genre of the *mātṛkā*, or doctrinal "matrices," is not an uncommon form of Sūtra literature. It is suggested in the redaction of certain sections of the Pali and Sarvāstivādin canons, is found in early Chinese translations (e.g., the *Dharmaśarīraka Sūtra* and the *Daśottara Sūtra*), and continues in Mahāyāna Sūtra literature. It is a literary form that probably represents not only an exegetic device but an early technique of doctrinal redaction—a hermeneutic that also served as the basis for the redaction of earlier strata of the oral transmission.

The early sects. Given the geographical and linguistic diversity of India and the lack of a central authority in the Buddhist community one can safely speculate that Buddhist sects arose early in the history of the religion. Tradition speaks of a first, but major, schism occurring at (or shortly after) the Second Council in Vaiśālī, one hundred years after the death of the founder. Whether the details are true or not, it is suggestive that this first split was between the Sthaviras and the Mahāsāṃghikas, the prototypes of the two major divisions of Buddhism: "Hīnayāna" and Mahāyāna.

After this schism new subdivisions arose, reaching by the beginning of the common era a total of approximately thirty different denominations or schools and subschools. Tradition refers to this state of sectarian division as the period of the "Eighteen Schools," since some of the early sources count eighteen groups. It is not clear when these arose. *Faut de mieux*, most Western scholars go along with classical Indian sources, albeit with a mild skepticism, and try to sort out a consistent narrative from contradictory sources. Thus, we can only say that if we are to believe the Pali tradition, the Eighteen Schools must have been in existence already in the third century BCE, when a legendary Moggaliputtatissa compiled the *Kathāvatthu*. But such an early dating raises many problems. [*See the biography of Moggaliputtatissa.*]

In the same vein, we tend to accept the account of the Second Council that sees it as the beginning of a major split. In this version the main points of contention were monastic issues—the exact content and interpretation of the code. But doctrinal, ritual, and scholastic issues must have played a major role in the formation of separate schools. Many of the main points of controversy, for instance, centered on the question of the nature of the state of liberation and the status of the liberated person. Is the liberated human *(arhat)* free from all moral and karmic taint? Is the state of liberation *(nirvāṇa)* a condition of being or nonbeing? Can there be at the same time more than one fully awakened person *(samyaksaṃbuddha)* in one world system? Are persons already on their way to full awakening, the *bodhisattvas* or future Buddhas, deserving of worship? Do they have the ability to descend to the hells to help other sentient beings?

Among these doctrinal disputes one emerges as emblematic of the most important fissure in the Buddhist community. This was the polemic surrounding the exalted state of the *arhat* (Pali, *arahant*). Most of the Buddhist schools believed that only a few human beings could aspire to become fully awakened beings *(samyaksaṃbuddha)*, others had to content themselves with the hope of becoming free from the burden of past *karman* and attaining liberation in *nirvāṇa*, without the extraordinary wisdom and virtue of Buddhahood. But the attainment of liberation was in itself a great achievement, and a person who was assured of an end to rebirth at the end of the present life was considered the most saintly, deserving of the highest respect, a "worthy" *(arhat)*. Some of the schools even attributed to the *arhat* omniscience and total freedom from moral taint. Objections were raised against those who believed in the faultless wisdom of the *arhat*, including obvious limitations in their knowledge of everyday, worldly affairs. Some of these objections were formalized in the "Five Points" of Mahādeva, after its purported proponent. These criticisms can be interpreted either as a challenge to the belief in the superhuman perfection of the *arhat* or as a plea for the acceptance of their humanity. Traditionally, Western scholars have opted for the first of these interpretations. [*See* Arhat.]

The controversies among the Eighteen Schools identified each group doctrinally, but it seems unlikely that in the early stages these differences lead to major rifts in the community, with the exception of the schism between the two trunk schools of the Sthavira and the Mahāsāṃghika; and even then, there is evidence that monks of both schools often lived together in a single monastic community. Among the doctrinal differences, however, we can find the seeds of future dissension, especially in the controversies relating to ritual. The Mahīśāsakas, for instance, claimed that there is more merit in worshiping and making offerings to the *saṃgha* than in worshiping a stupa, as the latter merely contains the remains of a member of the *saṃgha* who is no more. The Dharmaguptakas replied that there is more merit in worshiping a stupa, because the Buddha's path and his present state (in *nirvāṇa*) are far superior to that of any living monk. Here we have a fundamental difference with both social and religious consequences, for the choice is between two types of communal hierarchies as well as between two types of spiritual orders. [*For further discussion of sectarian splits in early Buddhism, see* Buddhism, Schools of, *article on* Hīnayāna Buddhism. *For specific* nikāyas, *see* Sarvāstivāda; Sautrāntika; Mahāsāṃghika; *and* Theravāda.]

Developments in the Scriptural Tradition. Apart from the Theravāda recension of the Pali canon and some fragments of the Sarvāstivādin Sanskrit canon nothing survives of what must have been a vast and diverse body of literature. For most of the collections we only have the memory preserved in inscriptions referring to *piṭakas* and *nikāyas* and an occasional reference in the extant literature.

According to the Pali tradition of Sri Lanka, the three parts of the Tripiṭaka were compiled in the language of the Buddha at the First Council. The Second Council introduced minor revisions in the Vinaya, and the Third Council added Moggaliputtatissa's *Kathāvatthu*. A few years later the canon resulting from this council, and a number of extracanonical commentaries, were transmitted to Sri Lanka by Mahinda. The texts were transmitted orally *(mukhapāṭhena)* for the next two centuries, but after difficult years of civil war and famine, King Vaṭṭagāmaṇī of Sri Lanka ordered the texts written down. This task was carried out between 35 and 32 BCE. In this way, it is said, the canon was preserved in the original language. Although the commentaries were by that time extant only in Sinhala, they continued to be transmitted in written form until they were retranslated into Pali in the fifth century CE.

Modern scholarship, however, questions the accuracy of several points in this account. Pali appears to be a literary language originating in Avantī, western India; it seems unlikely that it could be the vernacular of a man who had lived in eastern India all his life or, for that matter, the lingua franca of the early Magadhan kingdom. The Pali texts as they are preserved today show clear signs of the work of editors and redactors. Although much in them still has the ring of oral transmission, it is a formalized or ritualized oral tradition, far from the spontaneous preaching of a living teacher. Different strata of language, history, and doctrine can be recognized easily in these texts. There is abundant evidence that already at the stage of oral transmission the tradition was fragmented, different schools of "reciters" *(bhāṇaka)* preserving not only different corpuses (the eventual main categories of the canons) but also different recensions of the same corpus of literature. Finally, we have no way of knowing if the canon written down at the time of Vaṭṭagāmaṇī was the Tripiṭaka as we know it today. There is evidence to the contrary, for we are told that the great South Indian scholar Buddhaghosa revised the canon in the fifth century when he also edited the commentaries preserved in Sinhala and translated them into Pali, which suggests that Pali literature in general had gone through a period of deterioration before his time.

Most scholars, however, accept the tradition that would have the Pali canon belong to a date earlier than the fifth century; even the commentaries must represent an earlier stratum. However late may be its final recension, the Pali canon preserves much from earlier stages in the development of the religion.

Of the Sanskrit canon of the Sarvāstivāda school we only possess a few isolated texts and fragments in the original, mostly from Central Asia. However, extensive sections survive in Chinese translation. This canon is supposed to have been written down at a "Fourth Council" held in Jālandhara, Kashmir, about 100 CE, close to the time when the same school systematized its Abhidharma in a voluminous commentary called the *Mahāvibhāṣa*. If this legend is true, two details are of historical interest. We must note first the proximity in time of this compilation to the date of the writing down of the Pali canon. This would set the parameters for the closing of the "Hīnayāna" canons between the first century BCE and the first century CE. Second, the close connection between the closing of a canon and the final formulation of a scholastic system confirms the similar socio-religious function of both activities: the establishing of orthodoxy.

Developments in Practice. The cult at this stage was still dominated by the practice of pilgrimage and by the cult of the *caitya*, as described above. However, we can imagine an intensification of the devotional aspect of ritual and a greater degree of systematization as folk belief and "high tradition" continued to interact. Sectarian differences probably began to affect the nature of the liturgies, as a body of liturgical texts became part of the common or the specific property of different groups of Buddhists. Among the earliest liturgical texts were the hymns in praise of the Buddha, especially the ones singing the many epithets of the Awakened One. Their use probably goes back to the earliest stages in the history of monastic ritual and may be closely connected with the practice of *buddhānusmṛti*, or meditation on the attributes of the Buddha. [*See also* Nien-fo.]

Pilgrimage sites and stupas. Many Buddhist practices and institutions remain apparently stable in the subcontinent until the beginnings of the common era. The monuments of Bhārhut and Sāñcī, for example, where we find the earliest examples of aniconic symbolism, represent a conservative Buddhism. Other signs of conservatism, however, confirm a continuous nonliterary cult. The oldest section at Sāñcī, the east gateway, dating from perhaps 90 to 80 BCE, preserves, next to the illustrated Jātakas, the woman and tree motifs, *yakṣas* and *yakṣīs* (with the implied popular cult of male and female fertility deities), and the aniconic representations of the wheel, the footprint, the throne, and the tree.

The most advanced or innovative trait is the increasing iconographic importance of the previous lives of the Buddha, represented in the reliefs of Jātakas. These indicate a developed legend of the Buddha's past lives, a feature of the period that suggests the importance of past lives in the cult and in the future development of Mahāyāna. The most important cultic development of the pre-Mahāyāna period, however, was the shift from the commemorative ritual associated with the stupa and the aniconic symbol to the ritual of worship and devotion associated with the Buddha image.

After the beginning of the Christian era major developments in practice reflect outside influence as well as new internal developments. This is the time when the sects were beginning to commit to writing their sacred literature, but it is also the time of foreign invasions. These may have played a major role in the development of the Buddha image. Modern scholarship has debated the place of origin of this important cultic element and the causal factors that brought it about. Some, following Foucher, proposed a northwestern origin, and saw the Buddhas and *bodhisattvas* created under the influence of Greco-Roman art in Gandhāra (Kushan period) as the first images. Others, following Coomaraswamy, believed the first images were created in Andhra, as part of the natural development of a South Indian cult of the *yakṣas*, and in the north central region of Mathurā. Be that as it may, the Buddha image dominates Buddhist iconography after the second century CE; stupas and Jātaka representations remain but play a secondary role.

There seems to be, especially in Mathurā art, an association between the Buddha image and solar symbolism, which suggests Central Asian or Iranian influences on Buddhism and may be closely related to the development of the new doctrinal conceptions, such as those that regarded the Buddha as "universal monarch" *(cakravartin)* and lord of the universe, and Buddhas and *bodhisattvas* as radiant beings. [*See* Cakravartin.] The abundance of *bodhisattva* images in Gandhāra, moreover, suggests the beginning of a gradual shift towards a conception of the ideal being as layman, or at least a shift in the way the *bodhisattva* was conceived (from merely an instance of a Buddha's past to the central paradigm of Buddhahood). [*See* Iconography, *article on* Buddhist Iconography.]

As a balance to the growing importance of the past lives of the Buddha, the process of redacting the scriptures also brought about the necessity of formulating a biography of the Buddha. The first "biographies" appear at the beginning of the common era, perhaps as late as the second century CE. Partial biographies appear in the literature of the Sarvāstivādins *(Lalitavistara)* and Lokottaravādins *(Mahāvastu)*. The first complete biography is a cultured poem in the *kāvya* style, the *Buddhacarita* of Aśvaghoṣa.

This is also a time when noncanonical literature flourished. Poets wrote Buddhist dramas and poetical recastings of canonical parables and legends. Aśvaghoṣa, for instance, wrote a drama on the life of Śāriputra, and a poem narrating the conversion of Nanda *(Saundarānanda)*. Developments in the literary tradition perhaps should be seen as reflecting other strata of the living tradition. Thus, the vitality of the Jātaka tradition is seen in its appearance as a literary genre in the *Jātakamālā* of Āryaśūra (fl. c. 150 CE). This classical poet is sometimes identified with Mātṛceṭa, who in his works (e.g., *Śatapañcaśatka*) gives us a highly cultured reflection of the hymns of praise (*stotras*) that must have been a regular part of the Buddhist cult of the day. In these hymns we already see the apotheosis of the Buddha figure, side by side with the newly redefined *bodhisattva* ideal.

Mystics and intellectuals. The development of devotional Buddhism did not obscure the ascetic and contemplative dimensions of the religion. The system of meditation contained in the Nikāyas probably achieved its final form during this period. Diverse techniques for the development of enstasy and insight were conflated first in the canonical Sūtra literature, then in the Abhidharmic texts.

Side by side with the development of popular and monastic cults a new elite of religious specialists appeared, seeking to follow the Buddha's path through systematic study into the scriptures. They belonged to the tradition of the *mātṛkās* and composed treatises purporting to treat the "higher" Dharma *(abhidharma)*—or, what is perhaps the more correct etymology, treatises "on the Dharma." Although the analysis of meditational categories was an important aspect of these traditions, the scholar-monks were not always dedicated meditators. In fact, many of them must have made scholarship the prime objective of their religious life, leaving the practice of meditation to the forest monks. For the scholars, the goal was to account for the whole of Buddhism, in particular, the plethora of ancient doctrines and practices found in the canon. Above all, they sought to define and explain the ultimately real components of reality, the *dharmas*, into which one could analyze or explode the false conception of the self.

This critique was not without soteriological implications. The goal was conceived at times as ineffable, beyond the ken of human conception. Thus canonical literature describes the liberated person, the *arhat*, as follows:

> When bright sparks fly
> as the smith beats red-hot iron,
> and fade away,
> one cannot tell where they have gone.
>
> In the same way, there is no way of knowing
> the final destination of those who are truly free,
> who have crossed beyond the flood, bondage, and desire,
> obtaining unshakable bliss. (*Udāna*, p. 93)

But side by side with the tradition of ineffability, there was a need to define at the very least the process of liberation. For the gradual realization of selflessness was understood as personal growth. Accordingly, a set of standard definitions of liberation was accompanied by accepted descriptions of the stages on the path to liberation, or of degrees of spiritual achievement. The canonical collections already list, for instance, four types of saints *(āryapudgala):* the one who will be reborn no more *(arhat);* the one who will not come back to this world, the "non-returner" *(anāgamin);* the one who will return only once more *(sakṛdāgamin);* and the one who has entered the path to sainthood, the "stream-enterer" *(srotāpanna)*. [*See also* Soteriology, *article on* Buddhist Soteriology.]

Canonical notions of levels or hierarchies in the path to liberation became the focus of much scholastic speculation—in fact, the presence of these categories in the canons may be a sign of scholastic influence on the redaction of the scriptures. The construction of complex systems of soteriology, conceived as maps or detailed descriptions of the path, that integrated the description and analysis of ethical and contemplative practices with philosophical argumentation, characterized the Abhidharmic schools. This activity contributed to the definition of the doctrinal parameters of the sects; but it also set the tone for much of future Buddhist dogmatics. The concerns of the Abhidharmists, ranging from the analysis of enstasy and the contemplative stages to the rational critique of philosophical views of reality, had a number of significant doctrinal consequences: (1) scholars began devising "maps of the path," or theoretical blueprints of the stages from the condition of a common human being *(pṛthag-jana)* to the exalted state of a fully awakened being *(samyaksaṃbuddha);* (2) Buddhist scholars engaged other Indian intellectuals in the discussion of broad philosophical issues; (3) various orthodox apologetics were developed, with the consequent freezing of a technical terminology common to most Buddhists; (4) the rigidity of their systems set the stage for a reaction that would lead to the creation of new forms of Buddhism.

The Sects and the Appearance of Mahāyāna

Most of the developments mentioned above overlap with the growth of a new spirit that changed the religion and eventually created a distinct form of Buddhist belief and practice. The new movement referred to itself as the "Great Vehicle" (Mahāyāna) to distinguish itself from other styles of Buddhism that the followers of the movement considered forms of a "Lesser Vehicle" (Hīnayāna). [*See* Buddhism, Schools of, *article on* Mahāyāna Buddhism.]

The Early Schools Outside India. If we accept the general custom of using the reign of Aśoka as the landmark for the beginning of the missionary spread of Buddhism, we may say that Buddhism reached the frontiers of India by the middle of the second century BCE. By the beginning of the common era it had spread beyond. In the early centuries of the era Mahāyāna and Hīnayāna spread in every direction; eventually certain areas would become predominantly Mahāyāna, others, predominantly Hīnayāna. [*See* Missions, *article on* Buddhist Missions, *and the biography of Aśoka.*]

Mahāyāna came to dominate in East and Central Asia—with the exception of Turkistan, where Sarvāstivādin monasteries flourished until the Muslim invasion and conversion of the region. Hīnayāna was slower to spread, and in some foreign lands had to displace Mahāyāna. It lives on in a school that refers to itself as the Theravāda, a Sinhala derivative of the Sthavira school. It spread throughout Southeast Asia where it continues to this day.

The Great Vehicle. The encounter of Buddhism with extra-Indian ethnic groups and the increasing influence of the laity gradually transformed the monastic child of shramanic Buddhism into a universal religion. This occurred in two ways. On the one hand, monasticism adapted to the changing circumstances, strengthened its ties to the laity and secular authorities, established a satisfactory mode of coexistence with nonliterary, regional forms of worship. Both Mahāyāna and Hīnayāna schools participated in this aspect of the process of adaptation. But Buddhism also redefined its goals and renovated its symbols to create a new synthesis that in some ways may be considered a new religion. The new style, the Mahāyāna, claimed to be a path for the many, the vehicle for the salvation of all sentient beings (hence its name, "The Great Vehicle"). Its distinctive features are: a tilt toward world affirmation, a laicized conception of the human ideal, a new ritual of devotion, and new definitions of the metaphysical and contemplative ideals.

The origins of Mahāyāna. The followers of Mahāyāna claim the highest antiquity for its teachings. Their own myths of origin, however, belie this claim. Mahāyāna recognizes the fact that its teachings were not known in the early days of Buddhism by asserting that Śākyamuni revealed the Mahāyāna only to select *bodhisattvas* or heavenly beings who kept the texts hidden for centuries. One legend recounts that the philosopher Nāgārjuna had to descend to the underworld to obtain the Mahāyāna texts known as the "Perfection of Wisdom" (Prajñāpāramitā).

Western scholars are divided on the question of the dates and location of the origins of Mahāyāna. Some favor an early (beginning of the common era) origin among Mahāsāṃghika communities in the southeastern region of Andhra. Others propose a northwestern origin, among the Sarvāstivādins, close to the second and third centuries CE. It may be, however, that Mahāyāna arose by a gradual and complex process involving more than one region of India. It is clear that Mahāyāna was partly a reform movement, partly the natural development of pre-Mahāyāna Buddhism; still in another sense, it was the result of new social forces shaping the Indian subcontinent.

The theory of a southern origin assumes that the Mahāsāṃghika monastic centers of Andhra continued to develop some of the more radical ideals of the school, until some of these communities saw themselves as a movement completely distinct from other, so-called Hīnayāna schools. This theory also recognizes external influences: the Iranian invaders as well as the non-Aryan substratum of southern India, the first affecting the mythology of the celestial *bodhisattvas*, the second incorporating non-Aryan concepts of the role of women into the mainstream of Buddhist religious ideals.

For the sake of clarity one could distinguish two types of causes in the development of Mahāyāna: social or external, and doctrinal or internal. Among the first one must include the Central Asian and Iranian influences mentioned above, the growing importance of the role of women and the laity, especially as this affected the development of the cultus, and the impact of the pilgrimage cycles. The foreign element is supposed to have introduced elements of light symbolism and solar cults, as well as a less ascetic bent.

Doctrinal factors were primarily the development of the myth of the former lives of Śākyamuni and the cult of former Buddhas, both of which contributed to a critique of the *arhat* ideal. The mythology of the Buddha's former lives as a *bodhisattva* led to the exaltation of the *bodhisattva* ideal over that of the *arhat*. The vows of the *bodhisattva* began to take the central role, especially as they were seen as an integral part of a developing liturgy at the center of which the dedication of merit was transformed as part of the exalted *bodhisattva* ideal.

It seems likely, furthermore, that visionaries and inspired believers had continued to compose *sūtras*. Some of these, through a gradual process we can no longer retrace, began to move away from the general direction of the older scholastic traditions and canonical redactors. Thus it happened that approximately at the time when the older schools were closing their canons, the Mahāyāna was composing a set of texts that would place it in a position of disagreement with, if not frank opposition to, the older schools. At the same time, the High Tradition began to accept Mahāyāna and therefore argue for its superiority; thus, a Mahāyāna *śāstra* tradition began to develop almost at the same time as the great Sarvāstivādin synthesis was completed.

In the West, the gap between Mahāyāna and Hīnayāna is sometimes exaggerated. It is customary to envision Mahāyāna as a revolutionary movement through which the aspirations of a restless laity managed to overcome an oppressive, conservative monastic establishment. Recent research suggests that the opposition between the laity and the religious specialists was not as sharp as had hitherto been proposed. Furthermore, it has become apparent that the monastic establishment continued to be a powerful force in Indian Mahāyāna. It seems more likely that Mahāyāna arose gradually and in different forms in various points of the subcontinent. A single name and a more or less unified ideology may have arisen after certain common aspirations were recognized. Be that as it may, it seems evident that the immediate causes for the arising of this new form of Buddhism were the appearance of new cultic forms and widespread dissatisfaction with the scholastic tradition.

Merit, bodhisattvas, and the Pure Land. Inscriptional evidence shows that the doctrine of merit transference had an important role in the cultus even before the appearance of Mahāyāna. Although all Buddhists believe that virtuous thoughts and actions generate merit, which leads to a good rebirth, it appears that early Buddhists believed that individuals could generate merit only for themselves, and that merit could only lead to a better rebirth, not to liberation from the cycle of rebirth. By the beginning of the common era, however, some Buddhists had adopted a different conception of merit. They believed that merit could be shared or transferred, and that it was a factor in the attainment of liberation—so much so that they were offering their own merit for the salvation of their dead relatives.

Dedication of merit appears as one of the pivotal doctrines of the new Buddhism. Evidently, it served a social function: it made participation in Buddhist ritual a social encounter rather than a private experience. It also contributed to the development of a Buddhist high liturgy, an important factor in the survival of Buddhism and its assimilation of foreign elements, both in and outside India. [*See* Merit, *article on* Buddhist Concepts.]

This practice and belief interacted with the cult of former Buddhas and the mythology of the former lives to create a Buddhist system of beliefs in which the primary goal was to imitate the virtue of Śākyamuni's former lives, when he was a *bodhisattva* dedicated to the liberation of others rather than himself. To achieve this goal the believer sought to imitate Śākyamuni not as he appeared in his last life or after his enlightenment, when he sought and attained *nirvāṇa*, but by adopting a vow similar to Śākyamuni's former vow to seek awakening *(bodhi)* for the sake of all sentient beings. On the one hand, this shift put the emphasis on insight into the world, rather than escape from it. On the other hand, it also created a new form of ideal being and object of worship, the *bodhisattva*. [*See* Bodhisattva Path.]

Contemporary developments in Hindu devotionalism *(bhakti)* probably played an important role in the development of Buddhist liturgies of worship *(pūjā)*, but it would be a mistake to assume that the beginnings of Mahāyāna faith and ritual can be explained adequately by attributing them merely to external theistic influences. [*See* Bhakti.] For instance, the growth of a faith in rebirth in "purified Buddha fields," realms of the cosmos in which the merit and power of Buddhas and *bodhisattvas* create an environment where birth without suffering is possible, can be seen as primarily a Buddhist development. The new faith, generalized in India through the concept of the "Land of Bliss" (the "Pure Land" of East Asian Buddhism), hinged on faith in the vows of former *bodhisattvas* who chose to transfer or dedicate their merit to the purification of a special "field" or "realm." The influence of Iranian religious conceptions seems likely, however, and one may have to seek some of the roots of this belief among Central Asian converts. [*See* Pure and Impure Lands *and* Amitābha.]

Formation of a new scriptural tradition. With the new cult and the new ideology came a new body of scriptures. Mahāyāna *sūtras* began to be composed probably around the beginning of the Christian era, and continued to be composed and redacted until at least the fifth or sixth century CE. Unlike the canons of the earlier schools, the Mahāyāna scriptures do not seem to have been collected into formal, closed canons in the land of their origin—even the collections edited in China and Tibet were never closed canons.

In its inception Mahāyāna literature is indistinguishable from the literature of some of the earlier schools.

The *Prajñāpāramitā* text attributed to the Pūrvaśailas is probably an earlier version of one of the Mahāyāna texts of the same title; the *Ratnakūṭa* probably began as part of a Mahāsāṃghika canon; and the now lost *Dhāraṇī Piṭaka* of the Dharmaguptaka school probably contained prototypes of the *dhāraṇī-sūtras* of the Mahāyāna tradition. The Mahāyānist monks never gave up the pre-Mahāyāna Vinaya. Many followed the Dharmaguptaka version, some the Mahāsāṃghika. Even the Vinaya of a school that fell squarely into the Hīnayāna camp, the Sarvāstivāda, was used as the basis for Mahāyāna monastic rule.

Still, the focus of much Mahāyāna rhetoric, especially in the earlier strata of the literature, is the critique of non-Mahāyāna forms of Buddhism, especially the ideal of the *arhat*. This is one of the leading themes of a work now believed to represent an early stage in the development of Mahāyāna, the *Raṣṭrapālaparipṛcchā*, a text of the *Ratnakūṭa* class. In this text, the monastic life is still exalted above all other forms of spiritual life, but the *bodhisattva* vows are presented for the first time as superior to the mere monastic vows.

It is difficult, if not impossible, to establish with any degree of certainty the early history of Mahāyāna literature. It seems, however, that the earliest extant Mahāyāna *sūtra* is the *Aṣṭasāhasrikāprajñāpāramitā*, or its verse rendering, the *Ratnaguṇasaṃcayagāthā*. Both reflect a polemic within Buddhism, centering on a critique of the "low aspirations" of those Buddhists who chose not to take the vows of the *bodhisattvas*. The *Ratnaguṇa* defines the virtues of the *bodhisattva*, emphasizing the transcendental insight or "perfect wisdom" *(prajñāpāramitā)* that frees him from all forms of attachment and preconceived notions—including notions of purity and world renunciation. An important aspect or complement of this wisdom is skill in means *(upāyakauśalya)*—defined here as the capacity to adapt thought, speech, and action to circumstances and to the ultimate purpose of Buddhist practice, freedom from attachment. This virtue allows the *bodhisattva* to remain in the world while being perfectly free from the world.

The *Aṣṭasāhasrikā* treats these same concepts, but also expands the concept of merit in at least two directions: (1) dedication of merit to awakening means here seeing through the illusion of merit as well as applying merit to the path of liberation, and (2) dedication of merit is an act of devotion to insight (wisdom, *prajñā*). As the goal and ground of all perfections *(pāramitā)*, Perfection of Wisdom is personified as the Mother of All Buddhas. She gives birth to the mind of awakening, but she is present in concrete form in the Sacred Book itself. Thus, the *Aṣṭasāhasrikāprajñāpāramitā Sūtra* is at the same time the medium expressing a sophisticated doctrine of salvation by insight and skill in means, the rationalization of a ritual system, and the object of worship. [*See* Pāramitās; Prajñā; *and* Upāya.]

Another early Mahāyāna text, the *Saddharmapuṇḍarīka* (Lotus Sutra), also attacks the *arhat* ideal. This *sūtra* is considered the paradigmatic text on the developed Buddhology of the Mahāyāna: the Buddha is presented as a supernatural being, eternal, unchanging; at the same time he is Buddha by virtue of the fact that he has become free from all conceptions of being and nonbeing. The Buddha never *attained* awakening or *nirvāṇa*—because he *is* Buddhahood, and has been in awakening and *nirvāṇa* since eternity, but also because there is no Buddhahood or *nirvāṇa* to be attained.

The widespread, but clearly not exclusively popular, belief in the Land of Bliss (Sukhāvatī) finds expression in two texts of the latter part of the early period (c. first to second century CE). The two *Sukhāvatī sūtras* express a faith in the saving grace of the *bodhisattva* Dharmākara, who under a former Buddha made the vow to purify his own Buddha field. The vows of this *bodhisattva* guarantee rebirth in his Land of Bliss to all those who think on him with faith. Rebirth in his land, furthermore, guarantees eventual enlightenment and liberation. The Indian history of these two texts, however, remains for the most part obscure.

The attitude of early Mahāyāna *sūtras* to laity and to women is relatively inconsistent. Thus, the *Ugradattaparipṛcchā* and the *Upāsakaśīla*, while pretending to preach a lay morality, use monastic models for the householder's life. But compared to the earlier tradition, the Mahāyāna represents a significant move in the direction of a religion that is less ascetic and monastic in tone and intent. Some Mahāyāna *sūtras* of the early period place laypersons in a central role. The main character in the *Gaṇḍavyūha*, for instance, is a young lay pilgrim who visits a number of *bodhisattvas* in search of the teaching. Among his teachers we find laymen and laywomen, as well as female night spirits and celestial *bodhisattvas*. The *Vimalakīrtinirdeśa* is more down-to-earth in its exaltation of the lay ideal. Although not without its miraculous events, it represents the demythologizing tendencies of Mahāyāna, which are often carried out to the extreme of affirming that the metaphoric meaning of one doctrine is exactly its opposite.

The Development of Mahāyāna

Although Buddhism flourished during the classical age of the Guptas, the cultural splendor in which it grew was also the harbinger of Hindu dominance. Sanskrit returned as the lingua franca of the subcontinent, and Hindu devotionalism began to displace the ideals of the Indic period. Mahāyāna must have been a divided movement even in its inception. Some of the divisions found in the Hīnayāna or pre-Mahāyāna schools from which Mahāyāna originated must have carried through into Mahāyāna itself. Unfortunately, we know much less of the early sectarian divisions in the movement than we know of the Eighteen Schools. It is clear, for instance, that the conception of the *bodhisattva* found among the Mahāsāṃghikas is different from that of the Sarvāstivādins. It appears also that the Prajñaptivādins conceived of the unconditioned *dharmas* in a manner different from other early schools. However, though we may speculate that some of these differences influenced the development of Mahāyāna, we have no solid evidence.

As pre-Mahāyāna Buddhism had developed a scholastic system to bolster its ideological position, Mahāyāna developed special forms of scholarly investigation. A new synthesis, in many ways far removed from the visionary faith underlying the religious aspects of Mahāyāna, grew in the established monasteries partly as a critique of earlier scholastic formulations, partly due to the need to explain and justify the new faith. Through this intellectual function the monastery reasserted its institutional position. Both monk and layman participated in giving birth to Mahāyāna and maintaining its social and liturgical life, but the intellectual leadership remained monastic and conservative. Therefore, Mahāyāna reform brought with it an element of continuity—monastic institutions and codes—that could be at the same time a cause for fossilization and stagnation. The monasteries would eventually grow to the point where they became a burden on society, at the same time that, as institutions of conservatism, they failed to adapt to a changing society.

Still, from the beginning of the Gupta dynasty to the earlier part of the Pāla dynasty the monasteries were centers of intellectual creativity. They continued to be supported under the Guptas, especially Kumāra Gupta I (414–455), who endowed a major monastery in a site in Bihar originally consecrated to Śāriputra. This monastic establishment, called Nālandā after the name of a local genie, probably had been active as a center of learning for several decades before Kumāra Gupta decided to give it special recognition. It would become the leading institution of higher learning in the Buddhist world for almost a thousand years. Together with the university of Valabhī in western India, Nālandā represents the scholastic side of Mahāyāna, which coexisted with a nonintellectual (not necessarily "popular") dimension, the outlines of which appear through archaeological remains, certain aspects of the Sūtra literature, and the accounts of Chinese pilgrims.

Some texts suggest a conflict between forest and city dwellers that may in fact reflect the expected tension between the ascetic and the intellectual, or the meditator and the religious politician. But, lest this simple schema obliterate important aspects of Buddhist religious life, one must note that there is plentiful evidence of intense and constant interaction between the philosopher, the meditator, and the devotee—often all three functions coinciding in one person. Furthermore, the writings of great philosophical minds like Asaṅga, Śāntideva, and Āryadeva suggest an active involvement of the monk-*bodhisattva* in the social life of the community. The nonintellectual dimensions of the religion, therefore, must be seen as one aspect of a dialectic that resolved itself in synthesis as much as rivalry, tension, or dissonance.

Mahāyāna faith and devotion, moreover, was in itself a complex phenomenon, incorporating a liturgy of the High Tradition (e.g., the *Hymn to the Three Bodies of the Buddha,* attributed to Aśvaghoṣa) with elements of the nonliterary and non-Buddhist religion (e.g., pilgrimage cycles and the cult of local spirits, respectively), as well as generalized beliefs such as the dedication of merit and the hope of rebirth in a purified Buddha Land.

Developments in Doctrine. In explaining the appearance of Mahāyāna, two extremes should be avoided carefully. On the one hand, one can exaggerate the points of continuity that link Mahāyāna with pre-Mahāyāna Buddhism; on the other, one can make a distinction so sharp that Mahāyāna appears as a radical break with the past, rather than a gradual process of growth. The truth lies somewhere between these two extremes: although Mahāyāna can be understood as a logical expansion of earlier Buddhist doctrine and practice, it is difficult to see how the phenomenon could be explained without assuming major changes in the social fabric of the Indian communities that provided the base for the religion. These changes, furthermore, are suggested by historical evidence.

The key innovations in doctrine can be divided into those that are primarily critiques of early scholastic constructs and those that reflect new developments in practice. In both types, of course, one should not ignore the influence of visionary or contemplative experience; but this aspect of the religion, unfortunately, cannot always be documented adequately. The most important doctrine of practical consequence was the *bodhisattva* doctrine; the most important theoretical development was the doctrine of emptiness *(śūnyatā)*. The first can be understood also as the result of a certain vision of the concrete manifestation of the sacred; the second, as the expression of a new type of mystical or contemplative experience.

The bodhisattva. In pre-Mahāyāna Buddhism the term *bodhisattva* referred primarily to the figure of a Buddha from the time of his adoption of the vow to attain enlightenment to the point at which he attained Buddhahood. Even when used as an abstract designation of an ideal of perfection, the value of the ideal was determined by the goal: liberation from suffering. In the teachings of some of the Hīnayāna schools, however, the *bodhisattva* became an ideal with intrinsic value: to be a *bodhisattva* meant to adopt the vow *(praṇidhāna)* of seeking perfect awakening *for the sake of living beings;* that is, to follow the example set by the altruistic dedication of the Buddha in his former lives, when he was a *bodhisattva,* and not to aspire merely to individual liberation, as the *arhat*s were supposed to have done. The Mahāyāna made this critique its own, and the *bodhisattva* ideal its central religious goal.

This doctrinal stance accompanied a shift in mythology that has been outlined above: the belief in multiple *bodhisattva*s and the development of a complex legend of the former lives of the Buddha. There was likewise a change in ritual centered around the cult of the *bodhisattva,* especially of mythical *bodhisattva*s who were believed to be engaged in the pursuit of awakening primarily, if not exclusively, for the sake of assisting beings in need or distress. Closely allied with this was the increasing popularity of the recitation of *bodhisattva* vows.

Whereas the *bodhisattva* of early Buddhism stood for a human being on his way to become a liberated being, the *bodhisattva* that appears in the Mahāyāna reflects the culmination of a process of change that began when some of the Hīnayāna schools extended the apotheosis of the Buddha Śākyamuni to the *bodhisattva*—that is, when they idealized both the Buddha and the spiritual career outlined by the myth of his previous lives. Mahāyāna then extended the same religious revaluation to numerous mythical beings believed to be far advanced in the path of awakening. Accordingly, in its mythology Mahāyāna has more than one object of veneration. Especially in contrast to the more conservative Hīnayāna schools (the Sarvāstivāda and the Theravāda, for instance), Mahāyāna is the Buddhism of multiple Buddhas and *bodhisattva*s, residing in multiple realms, where they assist numberless beings on their way to awakening. [*See* Celestial Buddhas and Bodhisattvas.]

Accordingly, the early ideal of the *bodhisattva* as future Buddha is not discarded; rather it is redefined and expanded. As a theory of liberation, the characteristic position of Mahāyāna can be summarized by saying that it emphasizes *bodhi* and relegates *nirvāṇa* to a secondary position. Strictly speaking, this may represent an early split within the community rather than a shift in doctrine. One could speculate that it goes back to conflicting notions of means to liberation found among the shramanic religions: the conflict between enstasy and insight as means of liberation. But this analysis must be qualified by noting that the revaluation of *bodhi* must be seen in the context of the *bodhisattva* vow. The unique aspiration of the *bodhisattva* defines awakening as "awakening for the sake of all sentient beings." This is a concept that cannot be understood properly in the context of disputes regarding the relative importance of insight.

Furthermore, one should note that the displacement of *nirvāṇa* is usually effected through its redefinition, not by means of a rejection of the basic concept of "freedom from all attachment." Although the formalized texts of the vows often speak of the *bodhisattva* "postponing" his entrance into *nirvāṇa* until all living beings are saved, and the Buddha is asked in prayer to remain in the world without entering *nirvāṇa,* the central doctrine implies that a *bodhisattva* would not even consider a *nirvāṇa* of the type sought by the *arhat.* The *bodhisattva* is defined more by his aspiration for a different type of *nirvāṇa* than by a rejection or postponement of *nirvāṇa* as such. The gist of this new doctrine of *nirvāṇa* can be summarized in a definition of liberation as a state of peace in which the liberated person is neither attached to peace not attached to the turmoil of the cycle of rebirth. It is variously named and defined: either by an identity of *saṃsāra* and *nirvāṇa* or by proposing a *nirvāṇa* in which one can find no support *(apratiṣṭhita-nirvāṇa).* [*See* Soteriology, *article on* Buddhist Soteriology.]

As noted above, in the early conception a *bodhisattva* is a real human being. This aspect of the doctrine is not lost in Mahāyāna, but preserved in the belief that the aspiration to perfect awakening (the *bodhicita*) and the *bodhisattva* vow should be adopted by all believers. By taking up the vow—by conversion or by ritual repetition—the Mahāyāna Buddhist, monk or layperson, actualizes the *bodhicitta* and progresses toward the goal of becoming a *bodhisattva.* Also uniquely Mahāyāna is the belief that these human aspirants to awakening are not alone—they are accompanied and protected by "celestial *bodhisattvas,*" powerful beings far advanced in the path, so perfect that they are free from both rebirth and liberation, and can now choose freely if, when, and where they are to be reborn. They engage freely in the process of rebirth only to save living beings.

What transforms the human and ethical ideal into a religious ideal, and into the object of religious awe, is the scale in which the *bodhisattva* path is conceived. From the first aspiration to awakening *(bodhicitta)* and the affirmation of the vow to the attainment of final enlightenment and liberation, countless lives intervene. The *bodhisattva* has to traverse ten stages *(bhūmi)*, beginning with the intense practice of the virtue of generosity (primarily a lay virtue), passing through morality in the second stage, patience in the third, then fortitude, meditation, insight, skill in means, vows, powers, and the highest knowledge of a Buddha. The stages, therefore, correspond with the ten perfections *(pāramitā)*. Although all perfections are practiced in every stage, they are mastered in the order in which they are listed in the scheme of the stages, suggesting at one end of the spectrum a simple and accessible practice for the majority of believers, the human *bodhisattva*, and at the other end a stage clearly unattainable in the realm of normal human circumstances, reserved for semidivine Buddhas and *bodhisattvas*, the object of worship. Although some exceptional human beings may qualify for the status of advanced *bodhisattvas*, most of these ideal beings are the mythic objects of religious fervor and imagination.

Among the mythic or celestial *bodhisattvas* the figure of Maitreya—destined to be the next Buddha of this world system after Śākyamuni—clearly represents the earliest stage of the myth. His cult is especially important in East Asian Buddhism. Other celestial *bodhisattvas* include Mañjuśrī, the *bodhisattva* of wisdom, the patron of scripture, obviously less important in the general cultus but an important *bodhisattva* in monastic devotion. The most important liturgical role is reserved for Avalokiteśvara, the *bodhisattva* of compassion, whose central role in worship is attested by archaeology. [*See also* Maitreya; Mañjuśrī; *and* Avalokiteśvara.]

Emptiness. The doctrine of emptiness *(śūnyatā)* represents a refinement of the ancient doctrine of no-self. In some ways it is merely an extension of the earlier doctrine: the denial of the substantial reality of the self and what belongs to the self, as a means to effect a breaking of the bonds of attachment. The notion of emptiness, however, expresses a critique of our common notions of reality that is much more radical than the critique implicit in the doctrine of no-self. The Mahāyāna critique is in fact unacceptable to other Buddhists, for it is in a manner of speaking a critique of Buddhism. Emptiness of all things implies the groundlessness of all ideas and conceptions, including, ultimately, Buddhist doctrines themselves.

The doctrine of emptiness was developed by the philosophical schools, but clearly inspired by the tradition of the Mahāyāna *sūtras*. Thus we read: "Even *nirvāṇa* is like a magical creation, like a dream, how much more any other object or idea *(dharma)*. . . ? Even a Perfect Buddha is like a magical creation, like a dream. . ." (*Aṣṭasāhasrikā*, p. 40). The practical correlate of the doctrine of emptiness is the concept of "skill in means" *(upāya):* Buddhist teachings are not absolute statements about reality, they are means to a higher goal beyond all views. In their cultural context these two doctrines probably served as a way of making Buddhist doctrine malleable to diverse populations. By placing the truth of Buddhism beyond the specific content of its religious practices, these two doctrines justified adaptation to changing circumstances and the adoption of new religious customs.

But emptiness, like the *bodhisattva* vows, also reflects the Mahāyāna understanding of the ultimate experience of Buddhism—understood both as a dialectic and a meditational process. This experience can be described as an awareness that nothing is self-existent. Dialectically, this means that there is no way that the mind can consistently think of any thing as having an existence of its own. All concepts of substance and existence vanish when they are examined closely and rationally. As a religious experience the term *emptiness* refers to a direct perception of this absence of self-existence, a perception that is only possible through mental cultivation, and which is a liberating experience. Liberation, in fact, has been redefined in a way reminiscent of early texts such as the *Suttanipāta*. Liberation is now the freedom resulting from the negation of all assumptions about reality, even Buddhist assumptions.

> The cessation of grasping and reifying,
> calming the plural mind—this is bliss.
> The Buddha never taught any thing/doctrine [*dharma*]
> to anyone anywhere. (*Madhyamakakārikā* 25.24)

Finally, emptiness is also an affirmation of the immanence of the sacred. Applied to the turmoil of the sphere of rebirth *(saṃsāra)*, it points to the relative value and reality of the world and at the same time transforms it into the sacred, the experience of awakening. Applied to the sphere of liberation *(nirvāṇa)*, emptiness is a critique of the conception of liberation as a religious goal outside the world of impermanence and suffering. [*See* Śūnyam and Śūnyatā.]

Other views of the Absolute. Mahāyāna developed early notions of the supernatural and the sacred that guaranteed an exalted status to the symbols of its mystical and ethical ideals. Its notion of extraordinary beings populating supernal Buddha fields and coming to the aid of suffering sentient beings necessitated a metaphysic and cosmology that could offer concrete images of a transcendent sacred. Accordingly, the abstract, apophatic concept of emptiness was often qualified by, or even rejected in favor of, positive statements and concrete images.

Pre-Mahāyāna traditions had emphasized impermanence and no-self: to imagine that there is permanence in the impermanent is the most noxious error. Mahāyāna introduced the notion of emptiness, urging us to give up the notion of permanence, but to give up the notion of impermanence as well. Within the Mahāyāna camp others proposed that there was something permanent within the impermanent. Texts like the [*Mahāyāna*] *Mahāparinirvāṇa Sūtra* asserted that the Buddha himself had taught a doctrine of permanence: the seed of Buddhahood, innate enlightenment, is permanent, blissful, pure—indeed, it is the true self, present in the impermanent mind and body of sentient beings.

The Tathāgata as object of worship was associated with "suchness" *(tathatā)*, his saving actions were seen as taking effect in a world formed in the image of the Dharma and its ultimate truth *(dharmadhātu)*, and his form as repository of all goodness and virtue represented his highest form. [*See* Tathatā.]

A doctrine common to all Mahāyānists sought to establish a link between the absolute and common human beings. The Tathāgata was conceived of as having several aspects to his person: the human Buddha or "Body of Magical Apparition" *(nirmāṇakāya)*, that is, the historical persons of Buddhas; the transcendent sacred, the Buddha of the paradises and Buddha fields, who is also the form that is the object of worship *(saṃbhogakāya)*; and the Buddha as Suchness, as nonduality, the Tathāgata as embodiment of the *dharmadhātu*, called the "Dharma Body" *(dharmakāya)*.

Developments in Practice. The practice of meditation was for the Mahāyānist part of a ritual process beginning with the first feelings of compassion for other sentient beings, formulating the vow, including the expression of a strong desire to save all sentient beings and share one's merit with them, followed by the cultivation of the analysis of all existents, reaching a pinnacle in the experience of emptiness but culminating in the dedication of these efforts to the salvation of others.

Worship and ritual. The uniquely Mahāyāna aspect of the ritual is the threefold service *(triskandhaka)*. Variously defined, this bare outline of the essential Mahāyāna ritual is explained by the seventh-century poet Śāntideva as consisting of a confession of sins, formal rejoicing at the merit of others, and a request to all Buddhas that they remain in the world for the sake of suffering sentient beings. A pious Buddhist was expected to perform this threefold ritual three times in the day and three times in the night.

A text known as the *Triskandhaka*, forming part of the *Upālipariprcchā*, proves the central role of confession and dedication of merit. The act of confession is clearly a continuation of the ancient Prātimokṣa ritual. Other elements of continuity include a link with early nonliterary tradition (now integrated into scripture) in the role of the dedication of merit, and a link with the general Buddhist tradition of the Three Refuges.

More complicated liturgies were in use. Several versions remain in the extant literature. Although many of them are said to be "the sevenfold service" *(saptavidhānuttarapūjā)*, the number seven is to be taken as an abstract number. The most important elements of the longer liturgies are the salutation to the Buddhas and *bodhisattva*s, the act of worship, the act of contrition, delight in the merit of others, and the dedication of merit. Hsüan-tsang, the seventh-century Chinese pilgrim to India, describes, albeit cursorily, some of the liturgies in use in the Indian monasteries of his time.

Most common forms of ritual, however, must have been less formalized and less monkish. The common rite is best represented by the litany of Avalokiteśvara, preserved in the literature and the monuments. In its literary form it is a solemn statement of the *bodhisattva*'s capacity to save from peril those who call on his name. But in actual practice, one can surmise, the cult of Avalokiteśvara included then, as it does today in East Asia, prayers of petition and apotropaic invocations.

The basic liturgical order of the literary tradition was embellished with elements from general Indian religious custom, especially from the styles of worship called *pūjā*. These included practices such as bathing the sacred image, carrying it in procession, offering cloth, perfume, and music to the icon, and so forth. [*See* Pūjā, *especially the article on* Buddhist Pūjā.]

Ritual practices were also expanded in the monastic tradition. For instance, another text also going by the title *Triskandhaka* (but preserved only in Tibetan translation) shows an intimate connection between ritual and meditation, as it integrates—like many monastic manuals of meditation—the typical daily ritual cycle with a meditation session.

Meditation. The practice of meditation was as important in the Mahāyāna tradition as it had been before. The maps of the path and the meditation manuals of Mahāyāna Buddhists give us accounts, if somewhat idealized ones, of the process of meditation. Although no systematic history of Mahāyāna meditation has been attempted yet, it is obvious that there are important synchronic and diachronic differences among Mahāyāna Buddhists in India. Considering, nevertheless, only those elements that are common to the various systems, one must note first an element of continuity with the past in the use of a terminology very similar to that of the Mahīśāsakas and the Sarvāstivāda, and in the acceptance, with little change, of traditional lists of objects and states of contemplation. [*See* Meditation, *article on* Buddhist Meditation.]

The interpretation of the process, however, and the definition of the higher stages of contemplation differed radically from that of the Hīnayāna schools. The principal shift is in the definition of the goal as a state in which the object of contemplation *(ālambana)* is no longer present to the mind *(nirālambana)*. All the mental images (or "marks," *nimitta, saṃjñā*) that form the basis for conceptual thought and attachment must be abandoned through a process of mental calm and analysis, until the contemplative reaches a state of peaceful concentration free of mental marks *(ānimitta)*, free of conceptualizations *(nirvikalpa-samādhi)*.

These changes in contemplative theory are closely connected to the abandonment of the *dharma* theory and the doctrine of no-self as the theoretical focus of speculative mysticism. One may say that the leading theme of Mahāyāna contemplative life is the meditation on emptiness. But one must add that the scholastic traditions are very careful to define the goal as constituted by both emptiness and compassion *(karuṇā)*. The higher state of freedom from conceptions (the "supramundane knowledge") must be followed by return to the world to fulfill the vows of the *bodhisattva*—the highest contemplative stage is, at least in theory, a preparation for the practice of compassion. [*See* Karuṇā.]

The new ethics. The *bodhisattva* ideal also implied new ethical notions. Two themes prevail in Mahāyāna ethical speculation: the altruistic vow and life in the world. Both themes reflect changes in the social context of Buddhism: a greater concern, if not a stronger role for, lay life and its needs and aspirations and a cultural context requiring universal social values. The altruistic ideal is embodied in the *bodhisattva* vows and in the creation of a new set of ethical rules, commonly known as the "Bodhisattva Vinaya." A number of Mahāyāna texts are said to represent this new "Vinaya." Among these, the *Bodhisattvaprātimokṣa* was especially important in India. It prescribes a liturgy for the ritual adoption of the *bodhisattva* vows, which is clearly based on the earlier rites of ordination *(upasaṃpadā)*. Although the Mahāyāna Vinaya Sūtras never replaced in India the earlier monastic codes, they preserved and transmitted important, and at times obligatory, rites of monastic and lay initiation, and were considered essential supplements to traditional monastic Vinaya. [*See also* Buddhist Ethics.]

The High Tradition and the Universities

The most important element in the institutionalization of Mahāyāna was perhaps the establishment of Buddhist universities. In these centers of learning the elaboration of Buddhist doctrine became the most important goal of Buddhist monastic life. First at Nālandā and Valabhī, then, as the Pāla dynasty took control of East Central India (c. 650), at the universities of Vikramaśīla and Odantapurī, Mahāyāna scholars trained disciples from different parts of the Buddhist world and elaborated subtle systems of textual interpretation and philosophical speculation.

The Mahāyāna Synthesis. Although eventually they would not be able to compete with more resilient forms of Buddhism and Hinduism, the Mahāyāna scholars played a leading role in the creation of a Mahāyāna synthesis that would satisfy both the intelligentsia and the common believers for at least five hundred years. Devotion, ritual, ethics, metaphysics, and logic formed part of this monument to Indian philosophical acumen. Even as the ruthless Mihirakula, the Ephthalite ("White") Hun, was invading India from the northwest (c. 500–528) and the Chalukya dynasty was contributing to a Hindu renaissance in the southwest (c. 550–753), India allowed for the development of great minds—such distinguished philosophical figures as Dignāga and Sthiramati, who investigated subtle philosophical issues. Persecution by Mihirakula (c. 550) was followed by the reign of one of the great patrons of Buddhism, Harṣa Vardhana (c. 605–647). Once more Buddhism was managing to survive on the seesaw of Indian politics.

Schools. The scholastic tradition of Mahāyāna can be divided into three schools: Mādhyamika (Madhyamaka), Yogācāra, and the school of Sāramati. The first two dominated the intellectual life of Mahāyāna in India. The third had a short-lived but important influence on Tibet, and indirectly may be considered an important element in the development of East Asian Buddhism.

Mādhyamika. The founder of this school can also be regarded as the father of Mahāyāna scholasticism and philosophy. Nāgārjuna (fl. c. 150 CE) came from South India, possibly from the Amarāvatī region. Said to have been the advisor to one of the Śātavāhana monarchs, he became the first major philosopher of Mahāyāna and a figure whose ideas influenced all its schools. The central theme of his philosophy is emptiness *(śūnyatā)* understood as a corollary of the pre-Mahāyāna theory of dependent origination. Emptiness is the Middle Way between affirmations of being and nonbeing. The extremes of existence and nonexistence are avoided by recognizing certain causal relations (e.g., the path and liberation) without predicating a self-existence or immutable essence *(svabhāva)* to either cause or effect. To defend his views without establishing a metaphysical thesis, Nāgārjuna argues by reducing to the absurd all the alternative philosophical doctrines recognized in his day. For his own "system," Nāgārjuna claims to have no thesis to affirm beyond his rejection of the affirmations and negations of all metaphysical systems. Therefore, Nāgārjuna's system is "the school of the Middle" *(madhyamaka)* both as an ontology (neither being nor nonbeing) and as a logic (neither affirmation nor negation). In religious terms, Nāgārjuna's Middle Way is summarized in his famous statement that *saṃsāra* and *nirvāṇa* are the same. [*See the biography of Nāgārjuna.*]

Three to four centuries after Nāgārjuna the Mādhyamika school split into two main branches, called Prāsaṅgika and Svātantrika. The first of these, represented by Buddhapālita (c. 500) and Candrakīrti (c. 550–600), claimed that in order to be faithful to the teachings of Nāgārjuna, philosophers had to confine themselves to the critique of opposing views by *reductio ad absurdum*. The Svātantrikas, on the other hand, claimed that the Mādhyamika philosopher had to formulate his own thesis; in particular, he needed his own epistemology. The main exponent of this view was Buddhapālita's great critic Bhāvaviveka (c. 500–550). The debate continued for some time but was eclipsed by other philosophical issues; for the Mādhyamika school eventually assimilated elements of other Mahāyāna traditions, especially those of the logicians and the Yogācārins. [*See the biographies of Buddhapālita, Bhāvaviveka, and Candrakīrti.*]

Mādhyamika scholars also contributed to the development of religious literature. Several hymns *(stava)* are attributed to Nāgārjuna. His disciple Āryadeva discusses the *bodhisattva*'s career in his *Bodhisattva-yogācāra-catuḥśataka*, although the work deals mostly with philosophical issues. Two anthological works, one attributed to Nāgārjuna, the *Sūtrasamuccaya*, and the other to the seventh-century Śāntideva, the *Śikṣāsamuccaya*, became guides to the ritual and ethical practices of Mahāyāna. Śāntideva also wrote a "guide" to the *bodhisattva*'s career, the *Bodhicaryāvatāra*, a work that gives us a sampling of the ritual and contemplative practices of Mādhyamika monks, as well as a classical survey of the philosophical issues that engaged their attention. [*See also* Mādhyamika *and the biographies of Āryadeva and Śāntideva.*]

Yogācāra. Approximately two centuries after Nāgārjuna, during the transition period from Kushan to Gupta power, a new school of Mahāyāna philosophy arose in the northwest. The founders of this school, the brothers Asaṅga (c. 310–390) and Vasubandhu (c. 320–400), had begun as scholars in the Hīnayāna schools. Asaṅga, the elder brother, was trained in the Mahīśāsaka school. Many important features of the Abhidharma theories of this school remained in Asaṅga's Mahāyāna system. Vasubandhu, who converted to Mahāyāna after his brother had become an established scholar of the school, began as a Sautrāntika with an extraordinary command of Sarvāstivādin theories. Therefore, when he did become a Mahāyānist he too brought with him a Hīnayāna scholastic grid on which to organize and rationalize Mahāyāna teachings.

The school founded by the two brothers is known as the Yogācāra, perhaps following the title of Asaṅga's major work, the *Yogācārabhūmi* (sometimes attributed to Maitreya), but clearly expressing the centrality of the practice of self-cultivation, especially through meditation. In explaining the experiences arising during the practice of yoga, the school proposes the two doctrines that characterize it: (1) the experience of enstasy leads to the conviction that there is nothing but mind *(cittamātratā)*, or the world is nothing but a perceptual construct *(vijñaptimātratā)*; (2) the analysis of mind carried out during meditation reveals different levels of perception or awareness, and, in the depths of consciousness, the basis for rebirth and karmic determination, a storehouse consciousness *(ālaya-vijñāna)* containing the seeds of former actions. Varying emphasis on these two principles characterize different modes of the doctrine. The doctrine of mind-only dominates Vasubandhu's *Viṃśatikā* and *Triṃśikā*; the analysis of the *ālaya-vijñāna* is more central to Asaṅga's doctrine. Since both aspects of the doctrine can be understood as theories of consciousness *(vijñāna)*, the school is sometimes called Vijñānavāda.

One of the first important divisions within the Yogācāra camp reflected geographical as well as doctrinal differences. The school of Valabhī, following Sthiramati (c. 500–560), opposed the Yogācārins of Nālandā, led by Dharmapāla (c. 530–561). The point at issue, whether the pure mind is the same as the storehouse consciousness, illustrates the subtleties of Indian philosophical polemics but also reflects the influence of another school, the school of Sāramati, as well as the soteriological concerns underlying the psychological theories of Yogācāra. The debate on this point would continue in the Mādhyamika school, involving issues of the theory of perception as well as problems in the theory of the liberated mind. [*See also* Yogācāra; Vijñāna; Ālaya-vijñāna; *and the biographies of Asaṅga, Vasubandhu, Sthiramati, Dharmapāla, and Śīlabhadra.*]

***Tathāgata-garbha* theory.** Another influential school followed the tendency—already expressed in some Mahāyāna *sūtras*—toward a positive definition or description of ultimate reality. The emphasis in this school was on the ontological basis for the experience and virtues of Buddhahood. This basis was found in the underlying or innate Buddhahood of all beings. The school is known under two names; one describes its fundamental doctrine, the theory of *tathāgata-garbha* (the presence of the Tathāgata in all beings), the other refers to its purported systematizer, Sāramati (c. 350–450). The school's emphasis on a positive foundation of being associates it closely with the thought of Maitreyanātha, the teacher of Asaṅga, to whom is often attributed one of the fundamental texts of the school, the *Ratnagotravibhāga*. It may be that Maitreya's thought gave rise to two lines of interpretation—*tathāgata-garbha* and *cittamātratā*.

Sāramati wrote a commentary on the *Ratnagotravibhāga* in which he explains the process whereby innate Buddhahood becomes manifest Buddhahood. The work is critical of the theory of emptiness and describes the positive attributes of Buddhahood. The *bodhisattva*'s involvement in the world is seen not so much as the abandonment of the bliss of liberation as it is the manifestation of the Absolute *(dharmadhātu)* in the sphere of sentient beings, a concept that can be traced to Mahāsāṃghika doctrines. The *dharmadhātu* is a positive, metaphysical absolute, not only eternal, but pure, the locus of ethical, soteric, and epistemological value. This absolute is also the basis for the *gotra*, or spiritual lineage, which is a metaphor for the relative potential for enlightenment in living beings. [*See also* Tathāgatagarbha.]

The logicians. An important development in Buddhist scholarship came about as a result of the concern of scholastics with the rules of debate and their engagement in philosophical controversies with Hindu logicians of the Nyāya school. Nāgārjuna and Vasubandhu wrote short treatises on logic, but a creative and uniquely Buddhist logic and epistemology did not arise until the time of Dignāga (c. 480–540), a scholar who claimed allegiance to Yogācāra but adopted a number of Sautrāntika doctrines. The crowning achievement of Buddhist logic was the work of Dharmakīrti (c. 600–650), whose *Pramāṇavārttika* and its *Vṛtti* revised critically the whole field. Although his work seems on the surface not relevant for the history of religion, it is emblematic of the direction of much of the intellectual effort of Mahāyāna scholars after the fifth century. [*See the biographies of Dignāga and Dharmakīrti.*]

Yogācāra-Mādhyamika philosophers. As India moved away from the security of the Gupta period, Mahāyāna Buddhist philosophy gradually moved in the direction of eclecticism. By the time the university at Vikramaśīla was founded in the eighth century the dominant philosophy at Nālandā was a combination of Mādhyamika and Yogācāra, with the latter as the qualifying term and Mādhyamika as the core of the philosophy. This movement had roots in the earlier Svātantrika Mādhyamika and like its predecessor favored the formulation of ontological and epistemological theses in defense of Nāgārjuna's fundamental doctrine of emptiness. The most distinguished exponent of this school was Śāntirakṣita (c. 680–740); but some of his theories were challenged from within the movement by his contemporary Jñānagarbha (c. 700–760). The greatest contribution to religious thought, however, came from their successors. Kamalaśīla (c. 740–790), a disciple of Śāntirakṣita who continued the latter's mission in Tibet, wrote a number of brilliant works on diverse aspects of philosophy. He traveled to Tibet, where he wrote three treatises on meditation and the *bodhisattva* path, each called *Bhāvanākrama*, which must be counted among the jewels of Indian religious thought. [*See the biographies of Śāntirakṣita and Kamalaśīla.*]

New Scriptures. The philosophers found their main source of inspiration in the Mahāyāna *sūtras*, most of which did not advocate clearly defined philosophical theories. Some *sūtras*, however, do express positions that can be associated with the doctrines of particular schools. Although scholars agree that these compositions are later than texts without a clear doctrinal affiliation, the connection between the *sūtras* and the schools they represent is not always clear.

For instance, some of the characteristic elements of the school of Sāramati are clearly pre-Mahāyānic, and can also be found in a number of *sūtras* from the *Avataṃsaka* and *Ratnakūṭa* collections. However, Sāramati appealed to a select number of Mahāyāna *sūtras* that clustered around the basic themes of the school. Perhaps the most famous is the *Srīmālādevīsiṃhanāda*, but equally important are the *[Mahāyāna] Mahāparinirvāṇa Sūtra*, the *Anūnatvāpūrṇatvanirdeśa*, and the *Dhāraṇīrāja*.

A number of Mahāyāna *sūtras* of late composition were closely associated with the Yogācāra school. Although they were known already at the time of Asaṅga and Vasubandhu, in their present form they reflect a polemic that presupposes some form of proto-Yogācāra theory. Among these the *Laṅkāvatāra* and the *Saṃdhinirmocana* are the most important from a philosophical point of view. The first contains an early form of the theory of levels of *vijñāna*.

Decline of Mahāyāna. It is difficult to assess the nature and causes of the decay of Mahāyāna in India. Although it is possible to argue that the early success of Mahāyāna led to a tendency to look inward, that philosophers spent their time debating subtle metaphysical, logical, or even grammatical points, the truth is that even during the period of technical scholasticism, constructive religious thought was not dormant. But it may be that as Mahāyāna became more established and conventional, the natural need for religious revival found expression in other vehicles. Most likely Mahāyāna thinkers participated in the search for new forms of expression, appealing once more to visionary, revolutionary, and charismatic leaders. But the new life gradually would adopt an identity of its own, first as Tantric Buddhism, eventually as Hinduism. For, in adopting Tantric practices and symbols, Mahāyāna Buddhists appealed to a symbolic and ritual world that fit naturally with a religious substratum that was about to become the province of Hinduism. [*For Hindu Tantrism, see* Tantrism *and* Hindu Tantric Literature.]

The gradual shift from Mahāyāna to Tantra seems to have gained momentum precisely at the time when Mahāyāna philosophy was beginning to lose its creative energy. We know of Tantric practices at Nālandā in the seventh century. These practices were criticized by the Nālandā scholar Dharmakīrti but apparently were accepted by most distinguished scholars of the same institution during the following century. As Tantra gained respectability, the Pāla monarchs established new centers of learning, rivaling Nālandā. We may say that the death of its great patron, King Harṣa, in 657 signals the decline of Mahāyāna, whereas the construction of the University of Vikramaśīla under Dharmapāla about the year 800 marks the beginning of the Tantric period. [*For Buddhist Tantrism, see* Buddhism, Schools of, *article on* Esoteric Buddhism.]

Tantric Innovations

As with Mahāyāna, we must assume that Tantra reflects social as well as religious changes. Because of the uncertainties of the date of its origin, however, few scholars have ventured any explanation for the arising of Tantra. Some advocate an early origin for Tantra, suggesting that the literature existed as an esoteric practice for many centuries before it ever came to the surface. If this were the case, then Tantra must have existed as some kind of underground movement long before the sixth century. But this theory must still explain the sudden appearance of Tantrism as a mainstream religion.

In its beginnings, Buddhist Tantra may have been a minority religion, essentially a private cult incorporating elements from the substratum frowned upon by the Buddhist establishment. It echoed ancient practices such as the critical rites of the *Atharvaveda* tradition, and the initiatory ceremonies, Aryan and non-Aryan, known to us from other Brahmanic sources. Starting as a marginal phenomenon, it eventually gained momentum, assuming the same role Mahāyāna had assumed earlier; a force of innovation and a vehicle for the expression of dissatisfaction with organized religion. The followers of Tantra became the new critics of the establishment. Some asserted the superiority of techniques of ritual and meditation that would lead to a direct, spontaneous realization of Buddhahood in this life. As wandering saints called *siddhas* ("possessed of *siddhi,*" i.e., realization or magical power), they assumed the demeanor of madmen, and abandoned the rules of the monastic code. [*See* Mahāsiddhas.] Others saw Tantra as the culmination of Mahāyāna and chose to integrate it with earlier teachings, following established monastic practices even as they adopted beliefs that challenged the traditional assumptions of Buddhist monasticism.

The documented history of Tantra, naturally, reveals more about the second group. It is now impossible to establish with all certainty how the substratum affected Buddhist Tantra—whether, for instance, the metaphoric use of sexual practices preceded their explicit use, or vice versa. But it seems clear that the new wandering ascetics and their ideology submitted to the religious establishment even as they changed it. Tantra followed the pattern of cooperation with established religious institutions set by Mahāyāna in its relationship to the early scholastic establishment. Tantric monks would take the *bodhisattva* vows and receive monastic ordination under the pre-Mahāyāna code. Practitioners of Tantra would live in the same monastery with non-Tantric Mahāyāna monks. Thus Tantric Buddhism became integrated into the Buddhist high tradition even as the *siddhas* continued to challenge the values of Buddhist monasticism.

Although it seems likely that Tantric Buddhism existed as a minority, esoteric practice among Mahāyāna Buddhists before it made its appearance on the center stage of Indian religion, it is now impossible to know for how long and in what form it existed before the seventh century. The latter date alone is certain because the transmission of Tantra to China is marked by the arrival in the Chinese capitals of Tantric masters like Śubhākarasiṃha (arrives in Ch'ang-an 716) and Vajrabodhi (arrives in Lo-yang 720), and we can safely assume that the exportation of Tantra beyond the Indian border could not have been possible without a flourishing activity in India. [*See the biographies of Vajrabodhi, Śubhākarasiṃha, and Amoghavajra.*] Evidence for an earlier origin is found in the occasional reference, critical or laudatory, to *mantras* and *dhāraṇīs* in the literature of the seventh century (Dharmakīrti, Śāntideva) and the presence of proto-Tantric elements in Mahāyāna *sūtras* that must date from at least the fourth century *(Gaṇḍavyūha, Vimalakīrtinirdeśa, Saddharmapuṇḍarīka)*.

Tantra in general makes use of ritual, symbolic, and doctrinal elements of earlier form of Buddhism. Especially the apotropaic and mystical formulas called *mantras* and *dhāraṇis* gain a central role in Tantrayāna. [*See* Mantra.] The *Mahāmāyūrī*, a proto-Tantric text of the third or fourth century, collects apotropaic formulas associated with local deities in different parts of India. Some of these formulas seem to go back to *parittas* similar to those in the Pali canonical text *Āṭāṇātiya Suttanta* (*Dīgha Nikāya* no. 32). Although one should not identify the relatively early, and pan-Buddhist, genre of the *dhāraṇī* and *paritta* with the Tantrayāna, the increased use of these formulas in most existing forms of Buddhism, and the appearance of *dhāraṇī-sūtras* in late Mahāyāna literature perhaps marks a shift towards greater emphasis on the magical dimension of Buddhist faith. The Mahāyāna *sūtras* also foreshadow Tantra with their doctrine of the identity of the awakened and the afflicted minds *(Dharmasaṅgīti, Vimalakīrtinirdeśa)*, and innate Buddhahood (Tathāgata-garbha *sūtras*).

Varieties of Tantra. Whatever may have been its prehistory, as esoteric or exoteric practice, the new movement—sometimes called the third *yāna*, Tantrayāna—was as complex and fragmented as earlier forms of Buddhism. A somewhat artificial, but useful classification distinguishes three main types of Tantra: Vajrayāna, Sahajayāna, and Kālacakra Tantra. The first established the symbolic terminology and the liturgy that would characterize all forms of the tradition. Many of these iconographic and ritual forms are described in the *Mañjuśrīmūlakalpa* (finished in its extant form c. 750), the *Mahāvairocana Sūtra*, and the *Vajraśekhara* (or *Tattvasaṃgraha*) *Sūtra*, which some would, following East Asian traditions, classify under a different, more primitive branch of Tantra called "Mantrayāna." The Sahajayāna was dominated by long-haired, wandering *siddhas*, who openly challenged and ridiculed the Buddhist establishment. They referred to the object of their religious experience as "the whore," both as a reference to the sexual symbolism of ritual Tantra and as a challenge to monastic conceptions of spiritual purity, but also as a metaphor for the universal accessibility of enlightenment. The Kālacakra tradition is the farthest removed from earlier Buddhist traditions, and shows a stronger influence from the substratum. It incorporates concepts of messianism and astrology not attested elsewhere in Buddhist literature.

Unfortunately, the history of all three of these movements is clouded in legend. Tibetan tradition considers the Mantrayāna a third "turning of the wheel [of the Dharma]" (with Mahāyāna as the second), taking place in Dhānyakaṭaka (Andhra) sixteen years after the enlightenment. But this is patently absurd. As a working hypothesis, we can propose that there was an early stage of Mantrayāna beginning in the fourth century. The term *Vajrayāna* could be used then to describe the early documented manifestations of Tantric practice, especially in the high tradition of the Ganges River valley after the seventh century.

Sahajayāna is supposed to have originated with the Kashmirian yogin Lūi-pa (c. 750–800). The earliest documented Sahajayānists are from Bengal, but probably from the beginning of the ninth century. Regarding the Kālacakra, Western scholarship would not accept traditional views of its ancient origins in the mythic land of Shambhala. It must be dated not earlier than the tenth century, probably to the beginning of the reign of King Mahīpāla (c. 974–1026). Its roots have been sought in the North as well as in the South.

The Vajrayāna. The Vajrayāna derives its name from the centrality of the concept of *vajra* in its symbolism. The word *vajra* means both "diamond" and "cudgel." It is therefore a metaphor for hardness and destructiveness. Spiritually, it represents the eternal, innate state of Buddhahood possessed by all beings, as well as the cutting edge of wisdom. The personification of this condition and power is Vajrasattva, a deity and an abstract principle, which is defined as follows:

> By *vajra* is meant emptiness;
> *sattva* means pure cognition.
> The identity of these two is known
> as the essence of Vajrasattva.
> (*Advayavajra Saṃgraha*, p. 24)

Behind this definition is clearly the metaphysics of Yogācāra-Mādhyamika thought. Vajrasattva stands for the nondual experience that transcends both emptiness and pure mind. In religious terms this principle represents a homology between the human person and the essence of *vajra*: in the human body, in this life, relative and absolute meet.

The innate quality of the nondual is also represented by the concept of the "thought of awakening" *(bodhicitta)*. But innate awakening in Vajrayāna becomes the goal: enlightenment is present in its totality and perfection in this human body; the thought of awakening *is* awakening:

> The Thought of Awakening is known to be
> Without beginning or end, quiescent,

Free from being and nonbeing, powerful,
Undivided in emptiness and compassion.
(*Guhyasamāja* 18.37)

This identity is established symbolically and ritually by a series of homologies. For instance, the six elements of the human body are identified with different aspects of the body of Mahāvairocana, the five constituents of the human personality (*skandhas*) are identified with the five forms of Buddha knowledge.

But the most characteristic aspect of Tantric Buddhism generally is the extension of these homologies to sexual symbolism. The "thought of awakening" is identified with semen, dormant wisdom with a woman waiting to be inseminated. Therefore, wisdom *(prajñā)* is conceived as a female deity. She is a mother *(jananī)*, as in the Prajñāpāramitā literature; she is the female yogi *(yoginī)*; but she is also a low-caste whore *(ḍombī caṇḍālī)*. Skillful means *(upāya)* are visualized as her male consort. The perfect union of these two *(prajñopāya-yuganaddha)* is the union of the nondual. Behind the Buddhist interpretation, of course, one discovers the non-Aryan substratum, with its emphasis on fertility and the symbolism of the mother goddess. [*See* Goddess Worship, *article on* The Hindu Goddess.] But one may also see this radical departure from Buddhist monkish prudery as an attempt to shock the establishment out of self-righteous complacency.

Because the sexual symbolism can be understood metaphorically, most forms of Buddhist Tantra were antinomian only in principle. Thus, Vajrayāna was not without its vows and rules. As *upāya*, the symbols of ritual had as their goal the integration of the Absolute and the relative, not the abrogation of the latter. Tantric vows included traditional monastic rules, the *bodhisattva* vows, and special Tantric rules—some of which are contained in texts such as the *Vinayasūtra* and the *Bodhicittaśīlādānakalpa*.

The practice of the higher mysteries was reserved for those who had mastered the more elementary Mahāyāna and Tantra practices. The hierarchy of practice was established in systems such as the "five steps" of the *Pañcakrama* (by the Tantric Nāgārjuna). Generally, the order of study protected the higher mysteries, establishing the dividing line between esoteric and exoteric. Another common classification of the types of Tantra distinguished external daily rituals (Kriyā Tantra), special rituals serving as preparation for meditation, (Caryā Tantra), basic meditation practices (Yoga Tantra), and the highest, or advanced meditation Tantras (Anuttarayoga Tantra). This hermeneutic of sorts served both as an apologetic and a doctrinal classification of Tantric practice by distinguishing the audience for which each type of Tantra was best suited: respectively *śrāvakas*, *pratyekabuddhas*, Yogācārins, and Mādhyamikas.

Elements of Tathāgata-garbha theory seem to have been combined with early totemic beliefs to establish a system of Tathāgata families or clans that also served to define the proper audience for a variety of teachings. Persons afflicted by delusion, for instance, belonged to Mahāvairocana's clan, and should cultivate the homologies and visualizations associated with this Buddha—who, not coincidentally, represents the highest awakening. This system extends the homologies of *skandhas*, levels of knowledge, and so forth, to personality types. This can be understood as a practical psychology that forms part of the Tantric quest for the immanence of the sacred.

The Sahaja (or Sahajiyā) movement. Although traditional Sahaja master-to-disciple lineages present it as a movement of great antiquity, the languages used in extant Sahaja literature belong to an advanced stage in the development of New Indic. These works were written mostly in Apabhrāṃśa (the *Dohākośa*) and early Bengali (the *Caryāgīti*). Thus, although their dates are uncertain, they cannot go as far back as suggested by tradition. Scholars generally agree on a conjectural dating of perhaps eighth to tenth century.

Works attributed to Sahaja masters are preserved not only in New Indian languages (Saraha, c. 750–800, Kaṇha, c. 800–850, Ti-lo-pa, c. 950–1000); a few commentaries exist in Sanskrit. The latter attest to the influence of the early wandering *siddhas* on the Buddhist establishment.

The basic doctrinal stance of the Sahaja movement is no different from that of Vajrayāna: *sahaja* is the innate principle of enlightenment, the *bodhicitta,* to be realized in the union of wisdom and skillful means. The main difference between the two types of Tantra is in the life-style of the adept. The Sahajiyā was a movement that represented a clear challenge to the Buddhist establishment: the ideal person was a homeless madman wandering about with his female consort, or a householder-sorcerer—either of which would claim to practice union with his consort as the actualization of what the high tradition practiced only in symbolic or mystical form. The Vajrayāna soon became integrated into the curriculum of the universities, controlled by the Vinaya and philosophical analysis. It was incorporated into the ordered program of spiritual cultivation accepted in the monasteries, which corresponded to the desired social and political stability of the academic institutions and their sponsors. The iconoclastic saints of the Sahaja, on the other hand, sought spontaneity, and saw monastic life as an obstacle to true realization. The force of their challenge is seen in quasi-mythic form in the legend that tells of the bizarre tests to which the *siddha* Ti-lo-pa submitted the great scholar Nā-ro-pa when the latter left his post at Vikramaśīla to follow the half-naked madman Ti-lo-pa.

This particular Tantric tradition, therefore, best embodied the iconoclastic tendencies found in all of Tantra. It challenged the establishment in the social as well as the religious sphere, for it incorporated freely practices from the substratum and placed women and sexuality on the level of the sacred. In opposition to the bland and ascetic paradises of Mahāyāna—where there were no women or sexual intercourse—Tantrism identifies the bliss of enlightment with the great bliss *(mahāsukha)* of sexual union.

The Kālacakra Tantra. This text has several features that separate it from other works of the Buddhist tradition: an obvious political message, suggesting an alliance to stop the Muslim advance in India, and astrological symbolism and teachings, among others. In this work also we meet the concept of "Ādibuddha," the primordial Buddha, whence arises everything in the universe.

The high tradition, however, sees the text as remaining within the main line of Buddhist Tantrism. Its main argument is that all phenomena, including the rituals of Tantra, are contained within the initiate's body, and all aspects of time are also contained in this body. The concept of time *(kāla)* is introduced and discussed and its symbolism explained as a means to give the devotee control over time and therefore over the impermanent world. The *Sekoddeśaṭīkā*, a commentary on part of the *Kālacakra* attributed to Nā-ro-pa (Nāḍapāda, tenth century), explains that the time *(kāla)* of the *Kālacakra* is the same as the unchanging *dharmadhātu,* whereas the wheel *(cakra)* means the manifestations of time. In *Kālacakra* the two, absolute and relative, *prajñā* and *upāya*, are united. In this sense, therefore, in spite of its concessions to the substratum and to the rising tide of Hinduism, the *Kālacakra* was also integrated with mainline Buddhism.

Tantric Literature. The word *tantra* means "thread" or "weft" and, by extension, "text." The sacred texts produced as the new dispensation, esoteric or exoteric, were called Tantras, and formed indeed a literary thread interwoven with the secret transmission from master to disciple. Some of the most difficult and profound Tantras were produced in the early period (before the eighth century); the *Mahāvairocana, Guhyasamāja,* the earlier parts of the *Mañjuśrīmūlakalpa,* and the *Hevajra*. By the time Tantra became the dominant system and, therefore, part of the establishment, a series of commentaries and authored works had appeared. Nāgārjuna's *Pañcakrama* is among the earliest. The Tantric Candrakīrti (ninth century) wrote a commentary on the *Guhyasamāja,* and Buddhaguhya (eighth century) discussed the *Mahāvairocana*. Sanskrit commentaries eventually were written to fossilize even the spontaneous poems of the Sahaja saints.

Tantra and the High Tradition. Thus, Tantra too, like its predecessors, eventually became institutionalized. What arose as an esoteric, intensely private, visionary and iconoclastic movement, became a literary tradition, ritualized, often exoteric and speculative.

We have abundant evidence of a flourishing Tantric circle at Nālandā, for instance, at least since the late seventh century. Tantric masters were by that time established members of the faculty. Especially during the Pāla dynasty, Tantric practices and speculation played a central role in Buddhist universities. This was clearly the period of institutionalization, a period when Tantra became part of the mainstream of Buddhism.

With this transformation the magical origins of Tantra were partly disguised by a high Tantric liturgy and a theory of Tantric meditation paralleling earlier, Mahāyāna theories of the path. Still, Tantric ritual and meditation retained an identity of their own. Magic formulas, gestures, and circles appeared transformed, respectively, into the mystical words of the Buddhas, the secret gestures of the Buddhas, and charts (*maṇḍalas*) of the human psyche and the path.

The mystical diagram *(maṇḍala)* illustrates the complexity of this symbolism. It is at the same time a chart of the human person as it is now, a plan for liberation, and a representation of the transfigured body, the structure of Buddhahood itself. As a magic circle it is the sphere in which spiritual forces are evoked and controlled, as religious symbol it is the sphere of religious progress, experience, and action. The primitive functions remain: the *maṇḍala* is still a circle of power, with apotropaic functions. For each divinity there is an assigned meaning, a sacred syllable, a color, and a position within the *maṇḍala*. Spiritual forces can thus be evoked without danger. The sacred syllable is still a charm. The visualization of Buddhas is often inseparable from the evocation of demons and spirits. New beings populate the Buddhist pantheon. The Buddhas and *bodhisattvas* are accompanied by female consorts—these spiritual sexual partners can be found in explicit carnal iconographic representations. [*See* Maṇḍala, *article on* Buddhist Maṇḍalas.]

Worship and ritual. Whereas the esoteric ritual incorporated elements of the substratum into a Buddhist doctrinal base, the exoteric liturgies of the Tantric high tradition followed ritual models from the Mahāyāna tradition as well as elements that evince Brahmanic ritual and Hindu worship. The daily ritual of the Tantric Buddhist presents a number of analogies to Brahmanic *pūjā* that cannot be accidental. But the complete liturgical cycle is still Buddhist. Many examples are preserved, for instance, in the Sanskrit text *Ādikarmapradīpa*. The ritual incorporates Tantric rites (offering to a *maṇḍala,* recitation of *mantras*) into a structure composed of elements from pre-Mahāyāna Buddhism (e.g., the Refuges), and Mahāyāna ritual (e.g., confession, vows, dedication of merit).

More complex liturgies included rites of initiation or consecration *(abhiṣeka)* and empowerment *(adhiṣṭhāna),* rites that may have roots going as far back as the *Atharvaveda*. The burnt-offering rites *(homa)* also have Vedic and Brahmanic counterparts. Elements of the substratum are also evident in the frequent invocation of *yakṣas* and *devatās*, the propitiation of spirits, and the underlying sexual and alchemical symbolism.

Meditation. The practice of Tantric visualization *(sādhana)* was even more a part of ritual than the Mahāyāna meditation session. It was always set in a purely ritual frame similar to the structure of the daily ritual summarized above. A complete *sādhana* would integrate pre-Mahāyāna and Mahāyāna liturgical and contemplative processes with Tantric visualization. The meditator would first go through a gradual process of purification (sometimes including ablutions) usually constructed on the model of the Mahāyāna "sevenfold service." He would then visualize the mystical syllable corresponding to his chosen deity. The syllable would be transformed into a series of images that would lead finally to clear visualization of the deity. Once the deity was visualized clearly, the adept would become one with it. But this oneness was interpreted as the realization of the nondual; therefore, the deity became the adept as much as the adept was turned into a deity. Thus, the transcendent could be actualized in the adept's life beyond meditation in the fulfillment of the *bodhisattva* vows.

Tantric doctrine. Tantric symbolism was interpreted in the context of Mahāyāna orthodoxy. It is therefore possible to explain Tantric theoretical conceptions as a natural development from Mahāyāna. The immanence of Buddhahood is explicitly connected with the Mahāyāna doctrine of the identity of *saṃsāra* and *nirvāṇa* and the teachings of those Yogācārins who believed that consciousness is inherently pure. The magical symbolism of Tantra can be traced—again through explicit references—to the doctrine of the *bodhisattva* as magician: since the world is like a dream, like a magical apparition, one can be free of it by knowing the dream as dream—knowing and controlling the magical illusion as a magician would control it. The *bodhisattva* (and therefore the *siddha*) is able to play the magical trick of the world without deceiving himself into believing it real.

One should not forget, however, that what is distinctively Tantric is not limited to the externals of ritual and symbolism. The special symbolism transforms its Mahāyāna context because of the specifically Tantric understanding of immanence. The Buddha is present in the human body innately, but the Buddha nature is manifested only when one realizes the "three mysteries," or "three secrets." It is not enough to be free from the illusion of the world; one becomes free by living *in* illusion in such a way that illusion becomes the manifestation of Buddhahood. Tantra seeks to construct an alternative reality, such that a mentally constructed world reveals the fundamental illusion of the world and manifests the mysterious power of the Buddha through illusion. The human body, the realm of the senses, is to be transformed into the body of a Buddha, the senses of a Buddha.

The body, mind, and speech of the Buddha (the Three Mysteries) have specific characteristics that must be recognized and reproduced. In ritual terms this means that the adept actualizes Buddhahood when he performs prostrations and ritual gestures (*mudrās*); he speaks with the voice of the Buddha when he utters *mantras*; his mind is the mind of the Buddha when he visualizes the deity. The magical dimension is evident: the power of the Buddha lives in the formalized "demeanor of a Buddha." But the doctrine also implies transforming the body by a mystical alchemy (rooted in substratum sexual alchemy) from which is derived the soteriological meaning of the doctrine: the ritual changes the human person into a Buddha, all his human functions become sacred. Then this person's mind is the mind of an awakened being, it knows all things; the body assumes the appearance appropriate to save any living being; the voice is able to speak in the language of any living being needing to be saved. [*See also* Soteriology, *article on* Buddhist Soteriology.]

The Decline of Buddhism in India

With Harṣa's death Indian Buddhism could depend only on the royal patronage of the Pāla dynasty of Bihar and Bengal (c. 650–950), who soon favored the institutions they had founded—Vikramaśīla (c. 800), Odantapurī (c. 760). The last shining lights of Nālandā were the Mādhyamika masters Śāntirakṣita and Kamalaśīla, both of whom participated actively in the conversion of Tibet. Then the ancient university was eclipsed by its rival Vikramaśīla, which saw its final glory in the eleventh century.

Traditionally, the end of Indian Buddhism has been

identified with the sack of the two great universities by the troops of the Turk Muḥammad Ghūrī: Nālandā in 1197 and Vikramaśīla in 1203. But, although the destruction of Nālandā put an end to its former glory, Nālandā lingered on. When the Tibetan pilgrim Dharmasvāmin (1197–1264) visited the site of the ancient university in 1235 he found a few monks teaching in two monasteries remaining among the ruins of eighty-two others. In this way Buddhism would stay on in India for a brief time, but under circumstances well illustrated by the decay witnessed by Dharmasvāmin—even as he was there, the Turks mounted another raid to further ransack what was left of Nālandā.

For a long time scholars have debated the causes for the decline of Buddhism in India. Although there is little chance of agreement on a problem so complex—and on which we have precious little evidence—some of the reasons adduced early are no longer widely accepted. For instance, the notion that Tantric Buddhism was a "degenerate form" of Buddhism that contributed to or brought about the disappearance of Buddhism is no longer entertained by the scholarly community. The image of a defenseless, pacifist Buddhist community annihilated by invading hordes of Muslim warriors is perhaps also a simplification. Though the Turkish conquerors of India were far from benevolent, the Arabs who occupied Sindh in 711 seem to have accepted a state of peaceful coexistence with the local population. Furthermore, one must still understand why Jainism and Hinduism survived the Muslim invasion while Buddhism did not.

Buddhist relations with Hindu and Jain monarchs were not always peaceful—witness the conquest of Bihar by the Bengali Śaiva king Śaśīṅka (c. 618). Even without the intervention of intolerance, the growth of Hinduism, with its firm roots in Indian society and freedom from the costly institution of the monastery, offered a colossal challenge to Buddhism. The eventual triumph of Hinduism can be followed by a number of landmarks often associated with opposition to Buddhism: the spread of Vaiṣṇavism (in which the Buddha appears as a deceptive *avatāra* of Viṣṇu); the great Vaiṣṇava and Śaiva saints of the South, the Āḷvārs and Nāyaṉārs, respectively, whose Hindu patrons were openly hostile to Buddhism and Jainism; the ministry of Śaṅkara in Mysore (788–850), a critic of Buddhism who was himself accused of being a "crypto-Buddhist"; and the triumph of Śaivism in Kashmir (c. 800). [*See* Vaiṣṇavism, *overview article;* Ālvars; Śaivism, *overview article and article on* Nāyaṉārs; Kṛṣṇaism; Avatāra; *and the biography of Śaṅkara.*]

But the causes for the disappearance of Buddhism were subtle: the assimilation of Buddhist ideas and practices into Hinduism and the inverse process of the Hinduization of Buddhism, with the advantage of Hinduism as a religion of the land and the locality. More important than these were perhaps the internal causes for the decline: dependence on monastic institutions that did not have broad popular support but relied exclusively on royal patronage; and isolation of monasteries from the life of the village community, owing to the tendency of the monasteries to look inward and to lose interest in proselytizing and serving the surrounding communities.

The disappearance of Buddhism in India may have been precipitated by the Muslim invasion, but it was caused primarily by internal factors, the most important of which seems to have been the gradual assimilation of Buddhism into Hinduism. The Muslim invasion, especially the Turkish conquest of the Ganges Valley, was the *coup de grace;* we may consider it the dividing line between two eras, but it was not the primary cause for the disappearance of Buddhism from India. [*See* Islam, *articles on* Islam in Central Asia *and* Islam in South Asia.]

Buddhist Remnants and Revivals in the Subcontinent

After the last days of the great monastic institutions (twelfth and thirteenth centuries) Indian Buddhism lingered on in isolated pockets in the subcontinent. During the period of Muslim and British conquest (thirteenth to nineteenth century) it was almost completely absorbed by Hinduism and Islam, and gave no sign of creative life until modern attempts at restoration (nineteenth and twentieth centuries). Therefore, a hiatus of roughly six hundred years separates the creative period of Indian Buddhism from its modern manifestations.

Buddhism of the Frontier. As the Turk occupation of India advanced, the last great scholars of India escaped from Kashmir and Bihar to Tibet and Nepal. But the flight of Buddhist talent also responded to the attraction of royal patronage and popular support in other lands. The career of Atīśa (Dīpaṃkara Śrījñāna, 982–1054), who emigrated to Tibet in 1042, is emblematic of the great loss incurred by Indian Buddhism in losing its monk-scholars. He combined extensive studies in Mahāyāna philosophy and Tantra in India with a sojourn in Sumatra under the tutorship of Dharmakīrti. He had studied with Bodhibhadra (the successor of Nā-ro-pa when the latter left Vikramaśīla to become a wandering ascetic), and was head master *(upādhyāya)* of Vikramaśīla and Odantapurī at the time of King Bheyapāla. He left for Tibet at the invitation of Byaṅ-chub-'od, apparently attracted by a large monetary offer. [*See the biography of Atiśa.*]

The migration of the Indian scholars, and a steady stream of Tibetan students, made possible the exportation of Buddhist academic institutions and traditions to Tibet, where they were preserved until the Chinese suppression of 1959. The most learned monks were pushed out to the Himalayan and Bengali frontiers in part because the Indian communities were no longer willing to support the monasteries. Certain forms of Tantra, dependent only on householder priests, could survive, mostly in Bengal and in the Himalayan foothills. But some Theravādin Buddhists also survived in East Bengal—most of them taking refuge in India after the partition, some remaining in Bangladesh and Assam. [*See* Bengali Religions.]

Himalayan Buddhism of direct Indian ancestry remains only in Nepal, where it can be observed even today in suspended animation, partly fused with local Hinduism, as it must have been in the Gangetic plain during the twelfth century. Nepalese Buddhists produced what may very well be considered the last major Buddhist scripture composed in the subcontinent, the *Svayaṃbhū Purāṇa* (c. fifteenth century). This text is an open window into the last days of Indian Buddhism. It reveals the close connection between Buddhist piety and non-Buddhist sacred localities, the formation of a Buddhist cosmogonic ontology (the Ādibuddha), and the role of Tantric ritual in the incorporation of religious elements from the substratum. Nepalese Buddhism survives under the tutelage of married Tantric priests, called *vajrācāryas*. It is therefore sometimes referred to as "Vajrācārya Buddhism."

Buddhism of Tibetan origin survives in the subcontinent mostly in Ladakh, Sikkim, and Bhutan, but also in Nepal. [*See* Himalayan Religions.] Perhaps the most significant presence in modern India, however, is that of the Tibetan refugee communities. The Tibetan diaspora includes about eighty thousand persons, among which are several thousand monks. Some have retained their monastic robes and have reconstructed in India their ancient Buddhist academic curricula, returning to the land of origin the disciplines of the classical universities. So far their impact on Indian society at large has been insignificant and their hope of returning to Tibet dwindles with the passing of time. But the preservation, on Indian soil, of the classical traditions of Nālandā and Vikramaśīla is hardly a trivial accomplishment.

Attempted Revival: The Mahābodhi Society. Attempts to revive Buddhism in the land of its origin began with the Theosophical Society, founded in Colombo, Sri Lanka in 1875 by the American Henry S. Olcott. Although the society eventually became the vehicle for broader and less defined speculative goals, it inspired new pride in Buddhists after years of colonial oppression. [*See* Theosophical Society.] The Sinhala monk Anagārika Dharmapāla (1864–1933; born David Hewavitarane) set out to modernize Buddhist education. He also worked untiringly to restore the main pilgrimage sites of India, especially the temple of Bodh Gayā, which had fallen in disrepair and had been under Hindu administration for several centuries. To this end he founded in 1891 the Mahābodhi Society, still a major presence in Indian Buddhism.

Ambedkar and "Neo-Buddhism." The most significant Buddhist mass revival of the new age was led by Dr. Bhimrao Ramji Ambedkar (1891–1956). He saw Buddhism as the gospel for India's oppressed and read in the Buddhist scriptures ideals of equality and justice. After many years of spiritual search, he became convinced that Buddhism was the only ideology that could effect the eventual liberation of Indian outcastes. On 14 October 1956 he performed a mass "consecration" of Buddhists in Nagpur, Maharashtra. The new converts were mostly from the "scheduled caste" of the *mahārs*. Although his gospel is in some way on the fringes of Buddhist orthodoxy, Buddhist monks from other parts of Asia have ministered to the spiritual needs of his converts, and inspired Indian Buddhists refer to him as "Bodhisattva Ambedkar." [*See* Marathi Religions *and the biography of Ambedkar*.]

Other Aspects of Modern Buddhism. The most fruitful and persistent effort in the rediscovery of Indian Buddhism has been in the West, primarily among Western scholars. The achievements of European scholars include a modern critical edition of the complete Pali canon, published by the Pāli Text Society (founded in London in 1881), and the recovery of original texts of parts of the canon of the Sarvāstivāda. The combined effort of Indian, North American and European historians, archaeologists, and art historians has placed Indian Buddhism in a historical and social context, which, though still only understood in its rough outlines, allows us to see Buddhism in its historical evolution.

Japanese scholarship has also made great strides since the beginning of the twentieth century. The publication in Japan of three different editions of the Chinese canon between 1880 and 1929 may be seen as the symbolic beginning of a century of productive critical scholarship that has placed Japan at the head of modern research into Indian Buddhism. [*See* Buddhist Studies.]

Another interesting phenomenon of the contemporary world is the appearance of "neo-Buddhists" in Europe and North America. Although most of these groups have adopted extra-Indian forms of Buddhism, their interest in the scriptural traditions of India has created an audience and a demand for research into India's Buddhist past. The Buddhist Society, founded in London in 1926, and the Amis du Bouddhisme, founded in Paris in 1928, both supported scholarship and encouraged the Buddhist revival in India.

In spite of the revived interest in India of the last century, the prospects of an effective Buddhist revival in the land of Śākyamuni seem remote. It is difficult to imagine a successful living Buddhism in India today or in the near future. The possibility of the religion coming back to life may depend on the reimportation of the Dharma into India from another land. It remains to be seen if Ambedkar and Anagārika Dharmapāla had good reasons for hope in a Buddhist revival, or if in fact the necessary social conditions for the existence of Indian Buddhism disappeared with the last monarchs of the Pāla dynasty.

[*See also* Indian Religions.]

BIBLIOGRAPHY

Bareau, André. "Le bouddhisme indien." In *Les religions de l'Inde*, vol. 3, pp. 1–246. Paris, 1966. In addition to this useful survey, see Bareau's "Le bouddhisme indien," in *Histoire des religions*, edited by Henri-Charles Puech vol. 1, (Paris, 1970), pp. 1146–1215. Bareau has written the classical work on the question of the dating of the Buddha's life, "La date du Nirvāṇa," *Journal asiatique* 241 (1953): 27–62. He surveys and interprets classical documents on the Hīnayāna schools in "Les sectes bouddhiques du Petit Véhicule et leurs Abhidharmapiṭaka." *Bulletin de l'École Française d'Extrême-Orient* 50 (1952): 1–11; "Trois traités sur les sectes bouddhiques dus à Vasumitra, Bhavya et Vinitadeva," *Journal asiatique* 242–244 (1954–1956); *Les premiers conciles bouddhiques* (Paris, 1955); *Les sectes bouddhiques de Petit Véhicule* (Saigon, 1955); "Les controverses rélatives à la nature de l'arhant dans le bouddhisme ancien," *Indo-Iranian Journal* 1 (1957): 241–250. Bareau has also worked extensively on the "biography" of the Buddha: *Recherches sur la biographie du Bouddha*, 3 vols. (Paris, 1970–1983); "Le parinirvāṇa du Bouddha et la naissance de la religion bouddhique," *Bulletin de l'École Française d'Extrême-Orient* 61 (1974): 275–300; and, on a more popular but still scholarly bent, *Le Bouddha* (Paris, 1962).

Basham, A. L. *The Wonder That Was India*. London, 1954. This is the most accessible and readable cultural history of pre-Muslim India. A more technical study on the religious movements at the time of the Buddha is Basham's *History and Doctrine of the Ājīvikas* (London, 1951).

Beal, Samuel. *Travels of Fa-hian and Sung-Yun, Buddhist Pilgrims from China to India (400 A.D. and 518 A.D.)*. London, 1869. The travel records of two early pilgrims. See also Beal's *Si-yu-ki: Buddhist Records of the Western World*, 2 vols. (London, 1884). Translation of Hsüan-tsang's accounts of his travels to India.

Bechert, Heinz. "Zur Frühgeschichte des Mahāyāna-Buddhismus." *Zeitschrift der Deutschen Morgenländischen Gesellschaft* 113 (1963): 530–535. Summary discussion of the Hīnayāna roots of Mahāyāna. On the same topic, see also "Notes on the Formation of Buddhist Sects and the Origins of Mahāyāna," in *German Scholars on India*, vol. 1 (Varanasi, 1973), pp. 6–18; "The Date of the Buddha Reconsidered," *Indologica Taurinensia* 10 (1982): 29–36; "The Importance of Aśoka's So-called Schism Edict," in *Indological and Buddhist Studies in Honour of Prof. J. W. de Jong* (Canberra, 1982), pp. 61–68; and "The Beginnings of Buddhist Historiography," in *Religion and Legitimation of Power in Sri Lanka*, edited by Bardwell L. Smith (Chambersburg, Pa., 1978), pp. 1–12. Bechert is also the editor of the most recent contribution to the question of the language of Buddha and early Buddhism, *Die Sprache der ältesten buddhistischen Überlieferung / The Language of the Earliest Buddhist Tradition* (Göttingen, 1980).

Bechert, Heinz, and Georg von Simson, eds. *Einführung in die Indologie: Stand, Methoden, Aufgaben*. Darmstadt, 1979. A general introduction to Indology, containing abundant materials on Indian history and religion, including Buddhism.

Bechert, Heinz, and Richard Gombrich, eds. *The World of Buddhism*. London, 1984. This is by far the most scholarly and comprehensive survey of Buddhism for the general reader. Indian Buddhism is treated on pages 15–132 and 277–278.

Demiéville, Paul. "L'origine des sectes bouddhiques d'après Paramārtha." In *Mélanges chinois et bouddhiques*, vol. 1, pp. 14–64. Brussels, 1931 1932.

Demiéville, Paul. "A propos du Concile de Vaiśālī." *T'oung pao* 40 (1951): 239–296.

Dutt, Nalinaksha. *Aspects of Mahāyāna Buddhism and Its Relation to Hīnayāna*. London, 1930. Although Dutt's work on the development of the Buddhist sects is now largely superseded, there are no comprehensive expositions to replace his surveys. His *Mahāyāna Buddhism* (Calcutta, 1973) is sometimes presented as a revision of *Aspects*, but the earlier work is quite different and far superior. Most of Dutt's earlier work on the sects, found hidden in various journals, was compiled in *Buddhist Sects in India* (Calcutta, 1970). See also his *Early Monastic Buddhism*, rev. ed. (Calcutta, 1960).

Dutt, Sukumar. *The Buddha and Five After-Centuries*. London, 1957. Other useful, although dated, surveys include *Early Buddhist Monachism* (1924; new ed., Delhi, 1960) and *Buddhist Monks and Monasteries in India* (London, 1962).

Fick, R. *The Social Organization in Northeast India in the Buddha's Time*. Calcutta, 1920.

Frauwallner, Erich. "Die buddhistische Konzile." *Zeitschrift der Deutschen Morgenländischen Gesellschaft* 102 (1952): 240–261.

Frauwallner, Erich. *The Earliest Vinaya and the Beginnings of Buddhist Literature*. Rome, 1956.

Frauwallner, Erich. "The Historical Data We Possess on the Person and Doctrine of the Buddha." *East and West* 7 (1956): 309–312.

Fujita Kotatsu. *Genshi jōdoshisō no kenkyū*. Tokyo, 1970. The standard book on early Sukhāvatī beliefs.

Glasenapp, Helmuth von. "Zur Geschichte der buddhistischen

Dharma Theorie." *Zeitschrift der Deutschen Morgenländischen Gesellschaft* 92 (1938): 383–420.

Glasenapp, Helmuth von. "Der Ursprung der buddhistischen Dharma-Theorie." *Wiener Zeitschrift für die Kunde des Morgenlandes* 46 (1939): 242–266.

Glasenapp, Helmuth von. *Buddhistische Mysterien*. Stuttgart, 1940. Discusses most of the theories on early Brahmanic influence on Buddhist doctrine.

Glasenapp, Helmuth von. *Buddhismus und Gottesidee*. Mainz, 1954.

Gokhale, Balkrishna Govind. *Buddhism and Aśoka*. Baroda, 1948. Other of this author's extensive writings on the social and political contexts of early Buddhism include "The Early Buddhist Elite," *Journal of Indian History* 43 (1965): 391–402; "Early Buddhist View of the State," *Journal of the American Oriental Society* 89 (1969): 731–738; "Theravāda Buddhism in Western India," *Journal of the American Oriental Society* 92 (1972): 230–236; and "Early Buddhism and the Brāhmaṇas," in *Studies in History of Buddhism*, edited by A. K. Narain (Delhi, 1980).

Gómez, Luis O. "Proto-Mādhyamika in the Pāli Canon." *Philosophy East and West* 26 (1976): 137–165. This paper argues that the older portions of *Suttanipāta* preserve a stratum of the tradition that differs radically from the dominant themes expressed in the rest of the Pali canon, especially in its Theravāda interpretation. The question of dedication of merit in the Mahāyāna is discussed in "Paradigm Shift and Paradigm Translation: The Case of Merit and Grace in Buddhism," in *Buddhist-Christian Dialogue* (Honolulu, forthcoming). On Mahāyāna doctrine and myth, see also my "Buddhism as a Religion of Hope: Polarities in the Myth of Dharmākara," *Journal of the Institute for Integral Shin Studies* (Kyoto, in press).

Grousset, René. *The Civilizations of the East*, vol. 2, *India*. London, 1931. One of the best surveys of Indian history. See also his *Sur les traces du Bouddha* (Paris, 1957) for a modern expansion and retelling of Hsüan-tsang's travels.

Hirakawa Akira. *Indo bukkyōshi*. 2 vols. Tokyo, 1974–1979. A valuable survey of Indian Buddhism from the perspective of Japanese scholarship (English translation forthcoming from the University Press of Hawaii). The development of the earliest Vinaya is discussed in *Ritsuzō no kenkyū* (Tokyo, 1960) and in *Shoki daijō bukkyō no kenkyū* (Tokyo, 1969). The author's "The Rise of Mahāyāna Buddhism and Its Relationship to the Worship of Stupas," *Memoirs of the Research Department of the Tōyō Bunko* 22 (1963): 57–106, is better known in the West and summarizes some of the conclusions of his Japanese writings.

Horner, I. B. *Early Buddhist Theory of Man Perfected*. London, 1936. A study of the *arhat* ideal in the Pali canon. See also Horner's translation of the dialogues between King Menander and Nāgasena, *Milinda's Questions* (London, 1964), and *Women under Primitive Buddhism* (1930; reprint, Delhi, 1975).

Horsch, P. "Der Hinduismus und die Religionen der primitivstämme Indiens." *Asiatische Studien / Études asiatiques* 22 (1968): 115–136.

Horsch, P. "Vorstufen der Indischen Seelenwanderungslehre." *Asiatische Studien / Études asiatiques* 25 (1971): 98–157.

Jayatilleke, K. N. *Early Buddhist Theory of Knowledge*. London, 1963. Discusses the relationship between early Buddhist ideas and śramaṇic and Upaniṣadic doctrines.

Jong, J. W. de. "A Brief History of Buddhist Studies in Europe and America." *Eastern Buddhist* 7 (May 1974): 55–106, (October 1974): 49–82. For the most part these bibliographic surveys, along with the author's "Recent Buddhist Studies in Europe and America: 1973–1983," *Eastern Buddhist* 17 (1984): 79–107, treat only the philological study of Indian Buddhism. The author also tends to omit certain major figures who are not in his own school of Buddhology. These articles are nonetheless the most scholarly surveys available on the field, and put forth truly excellent models of scholarly rigor.

Joshi, Lal Mani. *Studies in the Buddhistic Culture of India*. Delhi, 1967. Indian Buddhism during the middle and late Mahāyāna periods.

Kajiyama Yūichi. "Women in Buddhism." *Eastern Buddhist* 15 (1982): 53–70.

Kajiyama Yūichi. "Stūpas, the Mother of Buddhas, and Dharma-body." In *New Paths in Buddhist Research*, edited by A. K. Warder, pp. 9–16. Delhi, 1985.

Kimura Taiken. *Abidammaron no kenkyū*. Tokyo, 1937. A survey of Sarvāstivāda Abhidharma, especially valuable for its analysis of the *Mahāvibhāṣā*.

Lamotte, Étienne. "Buddhist Controversy over the Five Propositions." *Indian Historical Quarterly* 32 (1956). The material collected in this article is also found, slightly augmented, in Lamotte's *magnum opus*, *Histoire du bouddhisme indien des origines à l'ère Śaka* (Louvain, 1958), pp. 300–319, 542–543, 575–606, 690–695. This erudite work is still the standard reference tool on the history of early Indian Buddhism (to circa 200 CE). Unfortunately, Lamotte did not attempt a history of Indian Buddhism for the middle and late periods. He did, however, write an article on the origins of Mahāyāna titled "Sur la formation du Mahāyāna," in *Asiatica: Festschrift Friedrich Weller* (Leipzig, 1954), pp. 381–386; this is the definitive statement on the northern origin of Mahāyāna. See also *Der Verfasser des Upadeśa und seine Quellen* (Göttingen, 1973). On early Buddhism, see "La légende du Buddha," *Revue de l'histoire des religions* 134 (1947–1948): 37–71; *Le bouddhisme de Śākyamuni* (Göttingen, 1983); and *The Spirit of Ancient Buddhism* (Venice, 1961). Lamotte also translated a vast amount of Mahāyāna literature, including *Le traité de la grande vertu de sagesse*, 5 vols. (Louvain, 1944–1980); *La somme du Grand Véhicule d'Asaṅga*, 2 vols. (Louvain, 1938); and *L'enseignement de Vimalakīrti* (Louvain, 1962), containing a long note on the concept of Buddha field (pp. 395–404).

La Vallée Poussin, Louis de. *Bouddhisme: Études et matériaux*. London, 1898. One of the most productive and seminal Western scholars of Buddhism, La Vallée Poussin contributed to historical studies in this and other works, as *Bouddhisme: Opinions sur l'histoire de la dogmatique* (Paris, 1909), *L'Inde aux temps des Mauryas* (Paris, 1930), and *Dynasties et histoire de l'Inde depuis Kanishka jusqu'aux invasions musul-*

manes (Paris, 1935). Contributions on doctrine include *The Way to Nirvāṇa* (London, 1917); *Nirvāṇa* (Paris, 1925); "La controverse du temps et du pudgala dans la *Vijñānakāya*," in *Études asiatiques, publiées à l'occasion du vingt-cinquième anniversaire de l'École Française d'Extrême-Orient*, vol. 1 (Paris, 1925), pp. 358–376; *La morale bouddhique* (Paris, 1927); and *Le dogme et la philosophie du bouddhism* (Paris, 1930). On Abhidharma, see "Documents d'Abhidharma," in *Mélanges chinois et bouddhiques*, vol. 1 (Brussels, 1931–1932), pp. 65–109. The Belgian scholar also translated the most influential work of Abhidharma, *L'Abhidharmakośa de Vasubandhu*, 6 vols. (1923–1931; reprint, Brussels, 1971). His articles in the *Encyclopaedia of Religion and Ethics*, edited by James Hastings, are still of value. Especially useful are "Bodhisattva (In Sanskrit Literature)," vol. 2 (Edinburgh, 1909), pp. 739–753; "Mahāyāna," vol. 8 (1915), pp. 330–336; and "Councils and Synods (Buddhist)," vol. 7 (1914), pp. 179–185.

Law, B. C. *Historical Gleanings*. Calcutta, 1922. Other of his numerous contributions to the early history of Buddhism include *Some Kṣatriya Tribes of Ancient India* (Calcutta, 1924), *Tribes in Ancient India* (Poona, 1943), and *The Magadhas in Ancient India* (London, 1946).

Law, B. C., ed. *Buddhistic Studies*. Calcutta, 1931. A collection of seminal essays on the history and doctrines of Indian Buddhism.

Legge, James. *A Record of Buddhist Kingdoms*. Oxford, 1886. English translation of Fa-hsien's accounts.

Majumdar, R. C., ed. *History and Culture of the Indian People*, vols. 2–5. London, 1951. A major survey of the periods of Indian history when Buddhism flourished.

Masson, Joseph. *La religion populaire dans le canon bouddhique Pāli*. Louvain, 1942. The standard study on the interactions of high tradition Buddhism with the substratum, not superseded yet.

Masuda Jiryō. "Origins and Doctrines of Early Indian Buddhist Schools." *Asia Major* 2 (1925): 1–78. English translation of Vasumitra's classical account of the Eighteen Schools.

May, Jacques. "La philosophie bouddhique de la vacuité." *Studia Philosophica* 18 (1958): 123–137. Discusses philosophical issues; for historical survey, see "Chūgan," in *Hōbōgirin*, vol. 5 (Paris and Tokyo, 1979), pp. 470–493, and the article coauthored with Mimaki (below). May's treatment of the Yogācāra schools (including the school of Sāramati), on the other hand, is both historical and doctrinal; see "La philosophie bouddhique idéaliste," *Asiatische Studien / Études asiatiques* 25 (1971): 265–323.

Mimaki Katsumi and Jacques May. "Chūdō." In *Hōbōgirin*, vol. 5, pp. 456–470. Paris and Tokyo, 1979.

Mitra, Debala. *Buddhist Monuments*. Calcutta, 1971. A handy survey of the Buddhist archaeological sites of India.

Mitra, R. C. *The Decline of Buddhism in India*. Calcutta, 1954.

Nagao Gadjin. "The Architectural Tradition in Buddhist Monasticism." In *Studies in History of Buddhism*, edited by A. K. Narain, pp. 189–208. Delhi, 1980.

Nakamura Hajime. *Indian Buddhism: A Survey with Bibliographical Notes*. Tokyo, 1980. Disorganized and poorly edited, but contains useful information on Japanese scholarship on the development of Indian Buddhism.

Nilakanta Sastri, K. A. *Age of the Nandas and Mauryas*. Varanasi, 1952. See also his *A History of South India from Prehistoric Times to the Fall of Vijayanagar* (Madras, 1955) and *Development of Religion in South India* (Bombay, 1963).

Oldenberg, Hermann. *Buddha, sein Leben, seine Lehre, seine Gemeinde* (1881). Revised and edited by Helmuth von Glasenapp. Stuttgart, 1959. The first German edition was translated by W. Hoey as *Buddha, His Life, His Doctrine, His Order* (London, 1882).

Paul, Diana. *The Buddhist Feminine Ideal: Queen Śrīmālā and the Tathāgatagarbha*. Missoula, Mont., 1980. See also her *Women in Buddhism* (Berkeley, 1980).

Prebish, Charles S. "A Review of Scholarship on the Buddhist Councils." *Journal of Asian Studies* 33 (February 1974): 239–254. Treats the problem of the early schools and the history and significance of their Vinaya. Other works on this topic include Prebish's "The Prātimokṣa Puzzle: Facts Versus Fantasy," *Journal of the American Oriental Society* 94 (April–June 1974): 168–176; and *Buddhist Monastic Discipline: The Sanskrit Prātimokṣa Sūtras of the Mahāsāṅghikas and the Mūlasarvāstivādins* (University Park, Pa., 1975).

Prebish, Charles S., and Janice J. Nattier. "Mahāsāṅghika Origins: The Beginning of Buddhist Sectarianism." *History of Religions* 16 (1977): 237–272. An original and convincing argument against the conception of the Mahāsāṃghika as "liberals."

Rhys Davids, T. W. *Buddhist India*. London, 1903. A classic, although its methodology is questionable. Also of some use, in spite of its date, is his "Sects (Buddhist)," in the *Encyclopaedia of Religion and Ethics*, edited by James Hastings, vol. 11 (Edinburgh, 1920), pp. 307–309.

Robinson, Richard H. "Classical Indian Philosophy." In *Chapters in Indian Civilization*, edited by Joseph Elder, vol. 1, pp. 127–227. Dubuque, 1970. A bit idiosyncratic, but valuable in its attempt to understand Buddhist philosophy as part of general Indian currents and patterns of speculative thought. Robinson's "The Religion of the Householder Bodhisattva," *Bharati* (1966): 31–55, challenges the notion of Mahāyāna as a lay movement.

Robinson, Richard H., and Willard L. Johnson. *The Buddhist Religion: A Historical Introduction*. 3d rev. ed. Belmont, Calif., 1982. A great improvement over earlier editions, this book is now a useful manual, with a good bibliography for the English reader.

Ruegg, David S. *The Study of Indian and Tibetan Thought*. Leiden, 1967. The most valuable survey of the main issues of modern scholarship on Indian Buddhism, especially on the early period. The author has also written the definitive study of the Tathāgata-garbha doctrines in *La théorie du tathāgatagarbha et du gotra* (Paris, 1969). See also on the Mādhyamika school his "Towards a Chronology of the Madhyamaka School," in *Indological and Buddhist Studies in Honour of J. W. de Jong* (Canberra, 1982), pp. 505–530, and *The Literature of the Madhyamaka School of Philosophy in India* (Wiesbaden, 1981).

Schayer, Stanislaus. "Precanonical Buddhism." *Acta Orientalia* 7 (1935): 121–132. Posits an early Buddhism not found explicitly in the canon; attempts to reconstruct the doctrines of Buddhism antedating the canon.

Schopen, Gregory. "The Phrase *'sa pṛthivīpradeśaś caityabhūto bhavet'* in the *Vajracchedikā*: Notes on the Cult of the Book in Mahāyāna." *Indo-Iranian Journal* 17 (1975): 147–181. Schopen's work has opened new perspectives on the early history of Mahāyāna, emphasizing its religious rather than philosophical character and revealing generalized beliefs and practices rather than the speculations of the elite. See also "Sukhāvatī as a Generalized Religious Goal in Sanskrit Mahāyāna Sūtra Literature," *Indo-Iranian Journal* 19 (1977): 177–210; "Mahāyāna in Indian Inscriptions," *Indo-Iranian Journal* 21 (1979): 1–19; and "Two Problems in the History of Indian Buddhism: The Layman/Monk Distinction and the Doctrines of the Transference of Merit," *Studien zur Indologie und Iranistik* 10 (1985): 9–47.

Schlingloff, Dieter. *Die Religion des Buddhismus*. 2 vols. Berlin, 1963. An insightful exposition of Buddhism, mostly from the perspective of canonical Indian documents.

Snellgrove, David L., ed. *Buddhist Himālaya*. Oxford, 1957. Although the context of this study is modern Himalayan Buddhism, it contains useful information on Buddhist Tantra in general. Snellgrove's two-volume *The Hevajra Tantra: A Critical Study* (London, 1959) includes an English translation and study of this major Tantric work. In *The Image of the Buddha* (Tokyo and London, 1978) Snellgrove, in collaboration with other scholars, surveys the history of the iconography of the Buddha image.

Stcherbatsky, Theodore. *The Central Conception of Buddhism and the Meaning of the Word "Dharma"* (1923). Reprint, Delhi, 1970. A classic introduction to Sarvāstivādin doctrine. On the Mādhyamika, Stcherbatsky wrote *The Conception of Buddhist Nirvana* (Leningrad, 1927). On early Buddhism, see his "The Doctrine of the Buddha," *Bulletin of the School of Oriental Studies* 6 (1932): 867–896, and "The 'Dharmas' of the Buddhists and the 'Guṇas' of the Sāṃkhyas," *Indian Historical Quarterly* 10 (1934): 737–760. Stcherbatsky categorized the history of Buddhist thought in "Die drei Richtungen in der Philosophie des Buddhismus," *Rocznik Orjentalistyczny* 10 (1934): 1–37.

Takasaki Jikidō. *Nyoraizō shisō no keisei—Indo daijō bukkyō shisō kenkyū*. Tokyo, 1974. A major study of Tathāgata-garbha thought in India.

Thapar, Romila. *Asoka and the Decline of the Mauryas*. London, 1961. Controversial study of Aśoka's reign. Her conclusions are summarized in her *History of India*, vol. 1 (Baltimore, 1965). Also relevant for the study of Indian Buddhism are her *Ancient Indian Social History: Some Interpretations* (New Delhi, 1978), *Dissent in the Early Indian Tradition* (Dehradun, 1979), and *From Lineage to State* (Bombay, 1984).

Thomas, Edward J. *The Life of the Buddha as Legend and History* (1927). New York, 1960. Still the only book-length, critical study of the life of Buddha. Less current, but still useful, is the author's 1933 work *The History of Buddhist Thought* (New York, 1975).

Varma, V. P. *Early Buddhism and Its Origins*. New Delhi, 1973.

Vetter, Tilmann. "The Most Ancient Form of Buddhism." In his *Buddhism and Its Relation to Other Religions*. Kyoto, 1985.

Warder, A. K. *Indian Buddhism*. 2d rev. ed. Delhi, 1980. One of the few modern surveys of the field, this work includes a bibliography of classical sources (pp. 523–574). Unfortunately, the author does not make use of materials available in Chinese and Tibetan translation.

Watanabe Fumimaro. *Philosophy and Its Development in the Nikāyas and Abhidhamma*. Delhi, 1983. The beginnings of Buddhist scholasticism, especially as seen in the transition from Sūtra to Abhidharma literature.

Watters, Thomas. *On Yuan Chwang's Travels in India*. 2 vols. London, 1904–1905. Extensive study of Hsüan-tsang's travels.

Wayman, Alex. *The Buddhist Tantras: Light on Indo-Tibetan Esotericism*. New York, 1973. Not a survey or introduction to the study of Indian Tantra, but a collection of essays on specific issues and problems. Chapter 1.2 deals with the problem of the early history of Tantra. See also Wayman's *Yoga of the Guhyasamājatantra: The Arcane Lore of Forty Verses; A Buddhist Tantra Commentary* (Delhi, 1977). In his "The Mahāsāṅghika and the Tathāgatagarbha (Buddhist Doctrinal History, Study 1)," *Journal of the International Association of Buddhist Studies* 1 (1978): 35–50, Wayman discusses possible connections between the Mahāsāṃghika subsects of Andhra and the development of Mahāyāna. His "Meditation in Theravāda and Mahīśāsaka," *Studia Missionalia* 25 (1976): 1–28, is a study of the doctrine of meditation in two of the leading schools of Hīnayāna.

Winternitz, Moriz. *Geschichte der indischen Literature*, vol. 2. Leipzig, 1920. Translated as *A History of Indian Literature* (Delhi, 1983). Largely dated but not superseded.

Zelliot, Eleanor. *Dr. Ambedkar and the Mahar Movement*. Philadelphia, 1969.

LUIS O. GÓMEZ

Buddhism in Southeast Asia

Conventional wisdom labels the Buddhism of Southeast Asia as Theravāda. Indeed, customarily a general distinction pertains between the "southern," Theravāda, Buddhism of Southeast Asia, whose scriptures are written in Pali, and the "northern," Sanskrit Mahāyāna (including Tantrayāna), Buddhism of Central and East Asia. A Thai or a Burmese most likely thinks of the Buddhism of his country as a continuation of the Theravāda tradition, which was allegedly brought to the Golden Peninsula (Suvaṇṇabhūmi) by Aśoka's missionaries Soṇa and Uttara in the third century BCE. But modern scholarship has demonstrated that prior to the development of the classical Southeast Asian states, which occurred from the tenth or eleventh century to the fifteenth century CE, Buddhism in Southeast Asia—the area covered by present-day Burma, Thailand, Vietnam,

Cambodia (Kampuchea), and Laos—defies rigid classification. Both archaeological and chronicle evidence suggest that the religious situation in the area was fluid and informal, with Buddhism characterized more by miraculous relics and charismatic, magical monks than by organized sectarian traditions. In short, the early period of Buddhism in Southeast Asia was diverse and eclectic, infused with elements of Hindu Dharmśāstra and Brahmanic deities, Mahāyāna Buddhas such as Lokeśvara, Tantric practices, Sanskrit Sarvāstivādin texts, as well as Pali Theravāda traditions.

The classical period of Southeast Asian Buddhism, which lasted from the eleventh to the fifteenth century, began with the development of the monarchical states of Śrīvijaya in Java, Angkor in Cambodia, Pagan in Burma, Sukhōthai in Thailand, and Luang Prabang in Laos, and culminated in the establishment of a normative Pali Theravāda tradition of the Sinhala Mahāvihāra monastic line. Hence, by the fourteenth and fifteenth centuries the primary, although by no means exclusive, form of Buddhism in Burma, Thailand, Laos, and Cambodia was a Sinhala orthodoxy that was dominated doctrinally by "the commentator" (Buddhaghosa) but enriched by various local traditions of thought and practice. By this time, what is now Malaysia and Indonesia, with the exception of Bali, had been overrun by Islam, and the popular religion there was an amalgamation of animism, Brahmanic deities, and the religion of the Prophet. The colonial interregnum, which infused Western and Christian elements into the religious and cultural milieu of Southeast Asia, gradually challenged the dominance of the Indian Buddhist worldview and its symbiotically related institutional realms of kingship *(dhammacakka)* and monastic order *(sāsanacakka)*. From the nineteenth century onward Buddhism in Southeast Asia has faced the challenges of Western science; provided cultural and ideological support for modern nationalist movements; offered idiosyncratic, sometimes messianically flavored, solutions to the stresses and strains of political, economic, and social change; and formulated doctrinal innovations challenging the Abhidammic orthodoxy of Buddhaghosa that characterizes the Sinhala Theravāda.

The following essay will examine Buddhism in Southeast Asia in terms of its early development, the establishment of a normative Theravāda orthodoxy, and the diverse responses of this tradition to the challenges of the modern period. The future of Buddhism in Southeast Asia may not hang in the balance; nevertheless, it does appear to be problematic. Political events in Cambodia (Kampuchea) and Laos have threatened the very foundations of institutional Buddhism in those countries. Thailand's rapid and widespread modernization and secularization have undermined many traditional aspects of the religion *(sāsana)*, and internal political strife in Burma has had severe, detrimental effects on the *sangha* (Skt., *saṃgha*). Our attention to Southeast Asian Buddhism should not ignore its fragility or its potential contribution to the continuing self-definition and self-determination of these civilizations.

Early Development. From its earliest beginnings to the establishment of the major monarchical states, Buddhism in Southeast Asia can only be characterized as diverse and eclectic. Its presence was felt as part of the Indian cultural influence that flourished throughout the area. During these early centuries Buddhism competed successfully with indigenous forms of magical animism and Brahmanism, undoubtably becoming transformed in the process. Its propagation probably followed the same pattern that was seen in Central and East Asia, with which we are more familiar: Padmasambhava-type monks subjugating territorial guardian spirits; monks accompanying traders and bringing in objects of power and protection, such as relics and images, as well as a literary tradition in the forms of magical chants in sacred languages and also written texts. We glean something of this pattern from Buddhist chronicles in Pali and in Southeast Asian vernacular languages of a later time. When the *Sāsanavaṃsa* of Burma or the *Mūlasāsana* of Thailand relates the story of the Buddha's visit to these countries to establish the religion, we interpret myth in historical terms, reading "the Buddha" to mean "unnamed Buddhist monks" who were bearers of a more advanced cultural tradition. While the chronicles, more so than the early inscriptions, paint a picture of dubious historical accuracy, they correctly associate Buddhism with a high continental way of life in contrast to the less sophisticated life of tribal peoples. Buddhism, then, abets the development of a town or urban culture, provides symbols of translocal value, and articulates a worldview in which diverse communities can participate and find a new identity, a language in which they can communicate, and institutions in which an organized religious life can be pursued and systematically taught.

Such a general description of the early centuries of Buddhism in Southeast Asia does not preclude the establishment of identifiable Buddhist traditions in the area. These include not only strong Pali Theravāda tradition but also other Buddhist sects and schools representing Mahāyāna and Tantric traditions. Pali inscriptions found in Hmawza, the ancient Pyu capital of Śrīkṣetra in lower Burma, indicate the existence of Theravāda Buddhism by the fifth or sixth century CE. Their Andhra-Kadamba script points to connections with Kāñcīpuram, Negapatam, and Kāverīpaṭṭanam in

South India. The Chinese traveler I-ching, who visited Shih-li-cha-to-lo (Śrīkṣetra, or Prome) in the seventh century, mentions the presence of not only Theravādins (Āryasthaviras) but also the Āryamahāsāṃghika, Āryamūlasarvāstivāda, and Āryasammatīya schools. We know of the Mahāsāṃghikas as among the forerunners of the Mahāyāna tradition. While their original home was in Magadha, their tradition established itself in parts of northern, western, eastern, and southern India. The Amarāvatī and Nāgārjunikoṇḍa inscriptions, for instance, mention the Mahāsāṃghikas and state that their canon was written in Prakrit. The three other sects are Hīnayāna schools. The Mūlasarvāstivāda, according to one tradition, was one of the seven branches of the Sarvāstivādin tradition and was widespread in India, although it was especially strong in the north, whence it was propagated under the aegis of King Kaniṣka during the late first century CE. Its canon was written in a Buddhist Hybrid Sanskrit. The Sammatīya sect, also known as the Vātsīputrīya or Vajjipattaka, came from Avanti, but inscriptions point to its presence in Sārnāth during the fourth century and in Mathurā during the fifth century. The great early seventh-century ruler Harṣavardhana is thought to have supported the Sammatīyas in the early part of his reign. Hence, the four sects whose presence in the Prome area was attested to by I-ching are all associated with important Indian Buddhist centers and with the reigns of powerful monarchs reputed to have been supporters of various Buddhist sectarian traditions.

Evidence of the diverse nature of sectarian Buddhism during the formative period of Southeast Asian history comes from Burmese and other sources in both mainland and insular Southeast Asia. The T'ang dynastic chronicles (seventh to tenth century CE) state that Buddhism flourished in the P'iao (Pyu) capital of Shih-li-cha-to-lo (Śrīkṣetra) in the eighth and ninth centuries. Archaeological and sculptural evidence of the same period from Prome and Hmawza portray the Buddha in scenes from the Jātakas and from popular commentarial stories. Terra-cotta votive tablets depicting scenes from the life of the Buddha and of the Mahāyāna *bodhisattvas* have also been found, as well as inscriptions written in Sanskrit, Pali, mixed Pali and Sanskrit, and Pyu written in South Indian alphabets. Evidence from ruined stupas in Hmawza, which date from the fifth to the eighth century, reinforce the claim to a strong but diverse Buddhist presence.

The Mon, or Talaing, lived south of the Pyu, occupying the coastal area of lower Burma, with flourishing centers at Pegu (Haṃsavatī) and Thaton (Sudhammavatī). This region, known as Rāmaññadesa in Burmese and Thai chronicles, extended over much of present-day Thailand; one major Mon center was as far north as Haripuñjaya (present-day Lamphun). In Nakorn Prathom, thirty miles southwest of Bangkok, archaeological evidence points to a flourishing Mon Buddhist culture in the region known as Dvāravatī, in which forms of both Hīnayāna and Mahāyāna Buddhism were present. Amarāvatī-style Buddha images in the vicinity of Nakorn Prathom and Pong Tuk date from the fourth to fifth century CE, and images of both early and late Gupta are also found there. While Mon-Dvāravatī Buddhism in Thailand and lower Burma lacked the homogeneity attributed to it by later chroniclers, both archaeological and textual evidence suggest a strong Pali Theravāda presence, especially in comparison to that found in Pagan.

Pagan, near the sacred Mount Popa on the Irrawaddy Plains of upper Burma, had become the locus of power of the Mrammas, a Tibeto-Dravidian tribe who eventually dominated and consequently named the entire region. During the tenth and eleventh centuries, the Buddhism present among people of the Pagan-Irrawaddy River basin seems to have been dominated by an eclectic form of Mahāyāna Tantrism similar to that found in esoteric Śaivism or in animistic *nāga* cults. According to the Burmese chronicles, the monks of this sect, who are referred to as Ari, rejected the teachings of the Lord Buddha. They believed in the efficacy of magical *mantras* over the power of *karman* and propagated the custom of sending virgins to priests before marriage. In addition to numerous figures of Mahāyāna *bodhisattvas*, such as Avalokiteśvara and Mañjuśrī, findings include remnants of murals that depict deities embracing their consorts.

According to the *Hmannān mạha yazạwintawkyī* (Glass Palace Chronicle, begun 1829) of Burma, the country's political and religious history was changed by the effect of Shin Arahan, a charismatic Mon Theravāda monk from Thaton, on the Burmese ruler Aniruddha (Anawratha), who ascended to power in Pagan in 1044 CE. According to this account, Shin Arahan converted Aniruddha to a Theravāda persuasion, advising him to secure relics, *bhikkhus* (monks), and Pali texts from Manuha (Manohari), the king of Thaton. Manuha's refusal became the excuse for Aniruddha's invasion of Thaton, the eventual subjugation of the Mons in lower Burma, and the establishment of Theravāda under Kyanzittha (fl. 1084–1113) as the dominant, although by no means exclusive, Buddhist sect.

As part of the Indian cultural expansion into "greater India," Mahāyāna, Tantric, and Hīnayāna forms of Buddhism were established in other parts of mainland and insular Southeast Asia from the fifth century onward. Guṇavarman is reputed to have taken the Dharmaguptaka tradition from northern India to Java in the fifth century, and by the seventh century Buddhism was apparently flourishing in the Sumatra of Śrīvijaya. An inscription from 684 CE, for instance, refers to a Buddhist monarch named Jayanāsā. I-ching, who spent several months in Java on his return to China in order to copy and translate Buddhist texts, indicates that both Hīnayāna and Mahāyāna forms of Buddhism were present at that time. Indonesia was also visited by Dharmapāla of Nālandā University and by two prominent South Indian monks, Vajrabodhi and Amoghavajra, both adherents of a Tantric form of Buddhism. Two inscriptions from the late eighth century refer to the construction, under the aegis of Śailendra rulers, of a Tārā temple at Kalasan and an image of Mañjuśrī at Kelunak. The Śailendras were great patrons of the North Indian Pāla form of Mahāyāna Buddhism. [*See the biographies of Dharmapāla, Vajrabodhi, and Amoghavajra. Evidence for the flourishing of Tantric forms of Buddhism in Southeast Asia is treated in* Buddhism, Schools of, *article on* Esoteric Buddhism.]

The rulers of Champa, in southern Annam (Vietnam), also patronized Buddhism. According to I-ching, the dominant tradition in Champa was that of the Āryasammatīya *nikāya,* but the Sarvāstivādins were also present. Amarāvatī-style Buddha images and monastery foundations from the ninth century have been discovered in Quang Nam Province, and an inscription of the same period from An-Thai records the erection of a statue of Lokanātha and refers to such Mahāyāna deities as Amitābha and Vairocana.

Although Hinduism was initially the dominant religion in Cambodia, there is some evidence of Buddhism from the fifth century CE. Jayavarman of Fu-nan sent representatives to China in 503 CE who took as gifts a Buddha image; and an inscription by Jayavarman's son, Rudravarman, invokes the Buddha. In the eleventh century Sūryavarman was given the posthumous Buddhist title of Nirvāṇapada, and Jayavarman VII, the Khmer empire's greatest monarch and builder of Angkor Thom, patronized Buddhism of the Mahāyāna variety. A Pali inscription from 1308, during the reign of Śrīndravarmadeva, refers to a Hīnayāna form of Buddhism, and a Chinese source from about the same time refers to Hīnayāna Buddhism as flourishing in Cambodia at that time.

The evidence cited supports the contention that throughout much of Southeast Asia Buddhism was present as part of the larger Indian cultural influence. Various sources, ranging from testimony of Chinese and indigenous chronicles, diaries of Chinese monk-travelers, as well as a large amount of archaeological and inscriptional evidence, support the contention that both Mahāyāna and Hīnayāna forms of Buddhism existed side by side, dependent on such factors as the particular regional Indian source and the predilection of a given ruler. Clearly, before the emergence of the major classical Southeast Asian states, no standard form of Buddhism existed.

It is also true that various types of Buddhism in this period competed with autochthonous forms of animism as well as Brahmanic cults. Were the early states in Burma, Cambodia, Thailand, and Indonesia—such as Fu-nan, Champa, Śrīkṣetra, Dvāravatī, and so on—Buddhist or Hindu? Or were these great traditions themselves so accommodated and transformed by the Southeast Asian cultures that they qualified the labels "Buddhist" and "Hindu" almost beyond recognition? Although rulers in these preclassical states may be characterized as Hindu or Buddhist and their brand of Buddhism defined by a given sect or school, in all probability they supported a variety of priests, monks, and religious institutions and worshiped various gods and spirits ranging from territorial guardians to Viṣṇu, Śiva, and Vairocana. In some cases we are prone to assign labels when, in reality, the diversity of the situation makes labeling a problematic enterprise at best. Such a qualification does not mean that we are unable to make certain claims about the nature of Buddhism in Southeast Asia in the formative period; however, evidence supporting the presence of particular Buddhist schools and sects should be understood within the general framework of the varied and eclectic nature of Buddhism in this era.

Classical Period. While diversity and eclecticism continue to mark the character of Buddhism during the period of the foundation of the classical Southeast Asian monarchical states, homogeneity of form and institutional orthodoxy began to emerge during this period. On the one hand, Buddhism and Hinduism contributed to the development of the nature and form of Southeast Asian kingship. On the other hand, the symbiotic relationship that developed between the monarchy and the Buddhist *sangha* tended to support a loose religious orthodoxy. Historically, this orthodoxy follows the Sinhala Theravāda tradition and accompanies the ascendancy of the Burmese and the Tai in mainland Southeast Asia. Vietnam, Malaysia, and Indonesia, however, depart from this pattern: Vietnamese culture was strongly influenced by China, and Malaysia and Indonesia were affected by the advent and spread of Islam during the thirteenth century. We shall first examine Buddhism at the level of the nature and form of classical Southeast Asian kingship and then trace the emergence of Sinhala Theravāda Buddhism as the normative tradition in Burma, Thailand, Cambodia, and Laos after the thirteenth century.

Buddhism and monarchy. The relationship between Buddhism and the rise of the monarchical states in the classical period of Southeast Asian history is customarily referred to as symbiotic, that is, one of mutual benefit. Rulers supported Buddhism because it provided a cosmology in which the king was accorded the central place and a view of society in which the human community was dependent on the role of the king. Ideologically, Buddhism legitimated kingship, providing a metaphysical rationale and moral basis for its existence. The Buddhist *sangha,* in turn, supported Southeast Asian monarchs because the material well-being, success, and popularity of institutional Buddhism depended to a significant degree on the approval, support, and largess of the ruling classes.

The Theravāda picture of the cosmos, set forth classically in the *Aggañña Suttanta* of the *Dīgha Nikāya,* depicts the world as devolving from a more perfect, luminous, undifferentiated state to a condition of greater opacity and differentiation. Imperfection results because differences in sex, comeliness, size of rice fields, and so on engender desire, greed, lust, and hatred, which, in turn, lead to actions that destroy the harmony and well-being of the inhabitants of the world. Recognizing the need to correct the situation, the people select a person whose comeliness, wisdom, virtue, and power enable him to bring order to this disharmonious, chaotic situation. That person, the ruler or king, is referred to in the text as *mahāsammata* because he is chosen by the people. He is *rāja* (king) because he rules by the Dhamma, and he is also *khattiya,* or lord of the fields, responsible for maintaining the economic and political order. Social order is dependent upon the righteous ruler, who creates and maintains the fourfold social structure (the traditional Indian *varṇa* hierarchy). Such a peaceful and harmonious situation also allows for the sustenance of *bhikkhu*s, who seek a higher, nonmundane end, that is, *nibbāna* (Skt., *nirvāṇa*). The ruler, then, is responsible for the peace, harmony, and total well-being of the people, which includes the opportunity to pursue a religious or spiritual life.

Buddhism's contribution to the classical conception of Southeast Asian kingship is particularly noteworthy in its emphasis on Dhamma and on the role of the ruler as a moral exemplar. The king is a *cakkavattin,* one whose rule depends upon the universal Dhamma of cosmic, natural, and moral law. His authority stems from the place he assumes in the total cosmic scheme of things. But his power and, hence, his effectiveness rest on his virtue. While the king rules by strength of arms, wealth, intellect, able ministers, and the prestige of his own status, his embodiment of the Dhamma and, hence, his ability to rule depend on his maintenance of the ten *rājadhamma*s: liberality, good conduct, nonattachment, straightforwardness, mildness, austerity, suppression of anger, noninjury, patience, and forbearance. The ideal king should cleanse his mind of all traces of avarice, ill will, and intellectual confusion and eschew the use of force and weapons of destruction. These moral virtues represent the highest ideals of Theravāda Buddhism, an overlapping of two "wheels" *(cakka),* or realms: the mundane *(ānācakka, lokiya)* and the transmundane *(sāsanacakka, lokuttara),* or the ideals of the political leader *(cakkavattin)* and the religious exemplar (Buddha).

This symbiotic relationship between political and religious leadership roles takes a particular mythic pattern in many of the classical Southeast Asian chronicles, such as the *Jinakālamālipakaraṇaṃ* (The Sheaf of Garlands of the Epochs of the Conqueror), a pattern also present in the Pali chronicles of Sri Lanka (e.g., the *Mahāvaṃsa*). Essentially, the chroniclers hold that the Budda sacralizes a region by visiting it. He frequently converts the indigenous populations and teaches them the Dhamma. To be sure, the monastic authors had a vested interest in establishing the precedence of Buddhism in the land, but the Buddha's visits to such places as the Tagaung kingdom of Burma and Haripuñjaya in northern Thailand serve the additional purpose of grounding a later interrelationship between Buddhism and kingship. In the northern Thai chronicles, for example, when the Buddha visits the Mon-Lava state of Haripuñjaya in the Chiangmai Valley, he predicts that his bone relic will be discovered by King Ādicca (Āditarāja), one of the principal twelfth-century monarchs of this state. This tale not only points to royal support of the *sāsana,* it makes the king the symbolic actualizer of the tradition, which he celebrates by building a *cetiya* for the relic. Furthermore, the Buddha in effect engenders the monarch with the power necessary to rule, a magical potency inherent in the relic. The *cetiya* reliquary mound thus functions as a magical center, or *axis mundi,* for the kingdom. In Haripuñjaya, alliances between the northern Tai kingdom of Lānnā and other states were sealed in front of the magical center. The Emerald Buddha image has played a similar role in Lao and Tai religious history, with various princes of the kingdom swearing fealty to the reigning monarch who possessed it.

The nature of the interrelationship between Buddhism and classical monarchical rule in Southeast Asia manifests itself architecturally in the great *cetiya* or stupa (Skt., *stūpa*) monuments of Borobudur, Angkor, Pagan, and other ancient capitals. The earliest of these, Borobudur, was constructed on the Kedu Plain outside of present-day Jogjakarta on the island of Java in the mid-eighth century CE under a dynasty known as the Śailendras, or "kings of the mountain." The monument's strong Mahāyāna influence is reflected in bas-reliefs that depict stories from the *Lalitavistara*, *Divyāvadāna*, *Jātakamālā*, and *Gaṇḍavyūha*. The seventy-two perforated, hollow stupas on the top of three circular platforms cover seated images of the Buddha Vairocana. Scholars have argued that the monument, as a cosmic mountain, connects royal power with the Dharma, the basis of all reality; it may also synthesize an autochthonous cult of "kings of the mountain" with the Ādibuddha, or universal Buddha nature. In support of this connection it is speculated that Śailendra inscriptions use the Sanskrit term *gotra* to signify both "line of the ancestors" as well as "family of the Buddha," thereby identifying the Śailendra ancestral line with that of the Tathāgata.

Angkor, in Cambodia, has been even more widely studied as a source for understanding the interrelationships between Southeast Asian kingship and religion, especially regarding the *devarāja* (god-king) concept. It may be that this concept originated in Fu-nan, a Chinese term derived from the Mon-Khmer *bnam*, meaning "mountain" and possibly referring to a cult of a national guardian spirit established by the founder of the state. In the early ninth century the Khmer ruler Jayavarman II built on this background, adopting Śaivism as the state religion and thus requiring that the king be worshiped as a manifestation of Śiva. This identification was symbolized by a *liṅga* that was set upon the central altar of a pyramidal temple as an imitation of Mount Meru and the center of the realm. The *devarāja* cult took on Mahāyāna Buddhist forms under Sūryavarman I in the early eleventh century and under Jayavarman VII (1181–1218), who constructed the great Bayon Temple, in which Jayavarman and Lokeśvara appear to be identified, at Angkor Thom at the end of the twelfth century. It can be inferred that in the tradition of the *devarāja*, Sūryavarman and Jayavarman became *buddharājas*, or incarnate Buddhas.

Other classical Southeast Asian capitals and major royal and religious monuments exhibit the influence of both Hindu and Buddhist worldviews. The remains of over five thousand stupas can be seen at the site of ancient Pagan, an area covering sixteen square miles. It was unified by Aniruddha (1040–1077) and the commander of his forces and successor, Kyanzittha (fl. 1084–1113). The Schwezigon Pagoda, possibly begun by Aniruddha but certainly completed by Kyanzittha, enshrines three sacred Buddha relics, symbolizing the power of the *cakkavattin* as the defender of the sacred order of things *(dhamma)*. Other stupas, such as the Mingalazedi, which was completed in the late thirteenth century, reflect the basic macro-micro cosmological symbolism of Borobudur; it has truncated pyramidal and terraced bases and a central stairway on each side. The Ānanda Temple, the stupa that dominated Pagan, was constructed by Kyanzittha in the late eleventh century and combines both cosmic mountain and cave symbolism: an ascetic's cave in which the Buddha meditates and a magical *axis mundi* that empowers the entire cosmos. A small kneeling image facing the large Buddha image in the temple is thought to represent Kyanzittha, corroborating inscriptional claims that he saw himself as a *bodhitsatta* and *ṣakkavattin*.

The mythic ideal of the *cakkavattin* is embodied in the moral example of Aśoka Maurya. Similarly, the *cakkavattin* of the Suttas provides the legendary charter for the idealized kingly exemplar of the Southeast Asian Theravāda chronicles. Aśoka was the moral exemplar *par excellence*, in whose footsteps, so say the chronicles and inscriptions, the monarchs of Burma, Thailand, and Laos follow. Aśoka's conversion divides his biography into two halves—the first tells of warring, wicked Aśoka (Pali, Caṇḍāsoka) and the second of the just, righteous Aśoka (Pali, Dhammāsoka). Similarly Aniruddha kills his brother to become the ruler of Pagan but then becomes a patron of Buddhism, and Tilokarāja (1441–1487) of Chiangmai revolts against his father but then devotes much of his attention to the prosperity of the Buddhist *sangha*. Southeast Asian rulers are also reputed to have called councils, as did Aśoka, in order to purify the *sangha* and regularize the Tipiṭaka. These activities, which supported Buddhism, represented ways the monarch could uphold his reputation for righteousness in ruling the state and in his dealings with the people. In his famous 1292 inscription, Rāma Khamhaeng (Ramkhamhaeng) of Sukhōthai says that the king adjudicates cases of inheritance with complete impartiality, does not kill or beat captured enemy soldiers, and listens to the grievances of his subjects. This paternalistic model of the dhammically righteous king is obviously indebted to the Aśoka model. [*See* Kingship, *article on* Kingship in Southeast Asia; Cakravartin; *and the biography of Aśoka*.]

Dominance of Sinhala Theravāda Buddhism. The shift to a Sinhala Theravāda orthodoxy in what became, in the true sense, Buddhist Southeast Asia (Burma, Thailand, Laos, and Cambodia) took place gradually from the late eleventh to the early thirteenth century and onward. This development reflected several factors: the decline of Buddhism in parts of Asia that had influenced the Southeast Asian mainland; the rising influence of Sri Lanka under Vijayabāhu I (1055–1110) and Parākramabāhu I; the consolidation of power by the Burmese and Tai; an increasing interrelationship among Sri Lanka, Burma, and Thailand; and the spread of popular Theravāda practice among the general population of mainland Southeast Asia. The general outline of the story of the establishment of Sinhala Theravāda Buddhism in Southeast Asia is reasonably clear, although disparities between epigraphic and chronicle sources make historical precision difficult. Consequently, scholars disagree on dates, and historical reconstructions keep on changing.

Pali Theravāda and Sanskrit Hīnayāna forms of Buddhism were present at a relatively early time. Pali inscriptions found in central Thailand and lower Burma and associated with Mon culture support this claim, as does chronicle testimony, such as the story of Aniruddha's excursion into Rāmaññadesa to secure Pali scriptures. Inscriptional evidence makes it reasonable to assume that the roots of Mon Theravāda lay in the Kāñcīpuram area along the east coast of India. Even the popular Burmese tradition that holds that Buddhaghosa, who has been associated with Kāñcī, either came from Thaton or went there after visiting Sri Lanka may contain a kernel of historical truth, namely, the spread of Kāñcī Theravāda Buddhism into the Mon area. The presence of Pali Theravāda Buddhism among the Mon, who strongly influenced both the Burmese and Tai, provides the religio-cultural backdrop to the eventual consolidation of Sri Lankan forms of Theravāda Buddhism. As we shall see, both the Burmese and the Tai assimilated elements of Mon culture: its religion, legal traditions, artistic forms, and written script. Mon Theravāda, in effect, mediated Sinhala Theravāda. On the one hand, Theravāda Buddhism from Sri Lanka provided continuity with Mon religio-cultural traditions; on the other, it enabled the Burmese and Tai to break away from a Mon religio-cultural dominance. We must now explore some of the details of this story of cultural transformation and religious consolidation.

Burma. Contact between Burma and Sri Lanka dates from the establishment of the Pagan era by Aniruddha. Because of the disruption of Sri Lanka caused by wars with the Cōḷas in the mid-eleventh century, Vijayabāhu I, knowing of the strength of the Mon Theravāda traditions, sought help from Aniruddha to restore valid ordination. Aniruddha responded by sending a group of monks and Pali scriptures to Sri Lanka. In turn, Aniruddha requested, and was sent, a replica of the Buddha's tooth relic and a copy of the Tipiṭaka with which to check the copies of the Pali scriptures acquired at Thaton. The tooth relic was enshrined in Pagan's Schwezigon Pagoda, which became Burma's national palladium. Although archaeological evidence calls into question the chronicler's claim regarding the acquisition of the entire Pali Tipiṭaka, the tale might well be interpreted to indicate the growing importance of Sinhala Buddhism, not simply because the texts were more authoritative, but because the alliance between the king and the new sectarian tradition legitimated his authority over the Mon religio-cultural tradition.

Sinhala Buddhism flourished during the reign of Narapatisithu (1173–1210), and the Mahāvihāra tradition became normative at this time. Sinhala Buddhism, in particular the Mahāvihāra tradition, gained position partly through visits of distinguished Burmese monks to Sri Lanka. Panthagu, successor to Shin Arahan as the nominal head of the Pagan Buddhist *sangha*, visited the island in 1167. The Mon monk Uttarajīva Mahāthera followed in his predecessor's footsteps by journeying to Sri Lanka in 1180 with a group of monks that included a Mon novice named Chapaṭa, who was to figure most prominently in establishing the precedent authority of the Mahāvihāra. Chapaṭa and four others remained in Sri Lanka for ten years and were reordained as Mahātheras in the Mahāvihāra lineage. Their return to Burma marked the permanent establishment of Sinhala Buddhism in mainland Southeast Asia and brought about a schism in the Burmese Buddhist *sangha* between the Theravāda school of Thaton and Kāñcī, characterized by Shin Arahan's orthodoxy; and the Sinhala Theravāda tradition. When Chapaṭa returned to Pagan, Narapatisithu requested that he and the other four Mahātheras reordain Burmese monks of the Shin Arahan tradition, thereby establishing the superior legitimacy of the Sinhala orthodoxy over the Mon form of Theravāda. The chronicles refer to the Shin Arahan tradition as the "early school" *(purimagaṇa)* and to Chapaṭa's Sīhaḷa Sangha simply as the "late school" *(pacchāgaṇa).* Owing to disciplinary and personal reasons, the *pacchāgaṇa* was to divide into several branches each loyal to one or another of the Mahātheras who had returned from Sri Lanka. One point of dispute among the branches was whether gifts could be given to particular monks or to the *sangha* at large.

The Sīhaḷa order was introduced to lower Burma at Dala, near Rangoon, by Sariputta, who bore the title Dhammavīlasa, meaning a scholar of great repute. This tradition is referred to as the Sīhaḷapakkhabhikkhu Sangha, in contrast with the Ariyārahantapakkhabhikkhu Sangha, which represents the Mon Theravāda tradition. The chronicles also call this school the Kambojasanghapakka on the grounds that it was headquartered near a settlement of Kambojans (Cambodians). This title may reflect historical fact or refer to the earlier Theravāda of the Mon-Khmer areas to the east (i.e., Dvāravatī), which found its way into lower Burma. The Sīhaḷa Sangha was also introduced to Martaban by two Mon monks, Buddhavaṃsa Mahāthera and Mahāsāmi Mahāthera, who had been reordained in Sri Lanka. According to the Kalyāṇī inscriptions of Pegu, by the thirteenth century six Buddhist schools—the Mon Ariyārahanta and five Sīhaḷa sects—existed in Martaban. Sectarianism in Burmese Theravāda has continued into the modern period and contrasts with the relative homogeneity of Theravāda Buddhism in Thailand.

Buddhism prospered during the reign of Narapatisithu (1173–1210). Many beautiful temples were built under his sponsorship (e.g., Sulamani, Gawdawpalin), and Pali scholarship flourished. For example, Chapaṭa (also known as Saddhammajotipāla) wrote a series of famous works dealing with Pali grammar, discipline (Vinaya), and higher philosophy (e.g., *Suttaniddesa, Sankhepavaṇṇanā, Abhidhammatthasangha)*, and Sariputta wrote the first collection of laws composed in Rāmaññadesa, known as the *Dhammavīlasa* or *Dhammathāt.* The shift away from a dominant Mon influence that occurred during Narapatisithu's reign is also reflected in the architectural style and the use of Burmese in inscriptions.

Thailand. The development of Buddhism among the Tai followed roughly the same pattern as in Burma. As the Tai migrated from southwestern China into the hills east of the Irrawaddy (home of the Shans), the upper Menam Plain (the Siamese), and farther east to the Nam U (the Lao), and as they gradually moved into the lowland area dominated by the Mons and the Khmers, they came into contact with Theravāda and Mahāyāna forms of Buddhism as well as with Brahmanism. After Khubilai Khan's conquest of Nan-chao in 1254 caused ever greater numbers of Tai to push south, they began to establish domination over the Mon and Khmer and to absorb elements of these more advanced cultures. As was the case in Burma, Mon Buddhism in particular became a major influence on the Tai as they extended their sway over much of what we now know as modern Thailand. This influence is seen in the establishment of two major Tai states in the late thirteenth and fourteenth centuries, Sukhōthai and Chiangmai.

Both Sukhōthai and Chiangmai became powerful centers of Tai settlement under the leadership of the able rulers Rāma Khamhaeng (r. c. 1279–1299) and Mengrai respectively. Sukhōthai, which had been a Khmer outpost from at least the time of Jayavarman VII, became an independent Tai state in the middle of the thirteenth century. Two Tai chieftains, Phe Mu'ang and Bang Klang Hao, seized Śrī Sajanalāya and drove the Khmer governor from Sukhōthai. Bang Klang Hao was installed as ruler of Sukhōthai with the title Indrāditya. Indrāditya's third son, Rāma Khamhaeng, was to become Sukhōthai's greatest monarch and one of the exemplary Buddhist kings of Tai history. During his reign, which extended over the last two decades of the century, Rāma Khamhaeng asserted his sway over a large area extending from Haṃsavatī (Pegu) to the west, Phrae to the north, Luang Prabang to the east, and Nakorn Sri Dhammaraja (Nagara Śrī Dharmarāja; Ligor or Tambraliṅga) to the south. Nakorn Sri Dhammaraja, although dominated by Śrīvijaya from the eighth to the twelfth century and later by the Khmer, was an important center of Theravāda Buddhism by the eleventh century. Prior to Rāma Khamhaeng's ascendance to power in Sukhōthai, Chandrabhānu of Nagara Śrī Dharmarāja had sent a mission to Sri Lanka, and the *Cūlavaṃsa* reports that Parākramabāhu II invited Dhammakitti Mahāthera, a monk from Nagara Śrī Dharmarāja, to visit Sri Lanka. Rāma Khamhaeng, who was well aware of the strength of Theravāda Buddhism at Nagara Śrī Dharmarāja, invited a Mahāthera from the forest-dwelling tradition *(araññaka)* there to reside in Sukhōthai. Rāma Khamhaeng's famous 1292 stela inscription refers to various religious sanctuaries in Sukhōthai, including the *araññaka* monastery (Wat Taphan Hin), a Khmer temple (Wat Phra Phai Luang), and a shrine to the guardian spirit of the city, Phra Khaphung. In short, while we have definitive evidence that Rāma Khamhaeng supported Theravāda Buddhism, religion in thirteenth-century Sukhōthai was varied and eclectic.

During the reigns of Rāma Khamhaeng's successors—his son Lö Tai (1298–1347), and his grandson Lü Thai (1347–1368/74?)—Sinhala Buddhism became normative. According to the *Jīnakālamāli,* a Sukhōthai monk named Sumana studied under, and received ordination from, a Sinhala Mahāthera, Udumbara Mahāsāmi, who was resident in Martaban. Sumana returned to Sukhōthai to establish the Sīhaḷa Sangha there, and, along with his colleague Anōmadassī, he proceeded to spread the Sīhaḷa order throughout much of Thailand (Ayuthayā, Pitsanulōk, Nān, Chiangmai, and Luang Prabang). King Lü Thai, in particular, was noted for his piety and his support of Buddhism. He brought Buddha relics and images and established Buddha "footprints" *(buddhapada)* in an effort to popularize Buddhist practice throughout his realm. A Buddhist scholar of note, he was particularly known as the author of the *Traibhūmikathā* (Verses on the Three Worlds), thought to be the first systematic Theravāda cosmological treatise.

About the same time that Sinhala Buddhism was coming into its own in Sukhōthai, it was also being spread to Tai states to the north and northeast, namely,

Chiangmai and Luang Prabang. Chiangmai was established as the major Tai state in northern Thailand by Mengrai, who expanded his authority from Chiangsaen to encompass Chiangrai, Chiangkhong, and Fāng. He subjugated the Mon-Lava center of Haripuñjaya in 1291 before founding Chiangmai in 1296. According to both inscriptional and chronicle evidence, Sumana Mahāthera brought the Sinhala Buddhism he had learned from his preceptor in Martaban to Chiangmai in 1369 at the invitation of King Küna (1355–1385). Küna built Wat Suan Dọk to house the Buddha relic brought by Sumana, and Sinhala Buddhism gained favored status over the Mon Theravāda traditions of Haripuñjaya. As in the case of Sukhōthai and Pagan, Sinhala Buddhism functioned not only as a means to build continuity with the Mon Theravāda tradition over which the Tai and the Burmese established their authority but also as a means to assert their unique religio-cultural traditions.

The apogee of the development of the Sīhaḷa order in Chiangmai was reached during the reigns of Tilokarāja, one of the greatest of the Tai monarchs, and Phra Mu'ang Kaew (1495–1526). Tilokarāja legitimated the overthrow of his father, Sam Fang Kaen, through the support of the Mahāvihāra order, which had been brought to Chiangmai in 1430. According to the Mūlasāsana of Wat Pa Daeng in Chiangmai, the center of this sect, this tradition was brought to Thailand by a group of thirty-nine monks from Chiangmai, Lopburi, and lower Burma who had visited Sri Lanka in 1423 during the reign of Parākramabāhu VI of Kotte. They returned to Ayutthayā, a Tai state that subjugated Sukhōthai under the Indrarāja in 1412, and dominated central Thailand until they were conquered by the Burmese at the end of the eighteenth century. According to the northern Tai chronicles, members of this mission spread throughout central and northern Thailand, reordaining monks into the new Sīhaḷa order. Tilokarāja made this Wat Pa Daeng-Mahāvihāra group the normative monastic tradition in Chiangmai at a general council in 1477. The Pa Daeng chronicles depict Tilokarāja as a great supporter of the *sangha* and as a righteous and exemplary monarch in the Aśokan mode. During the reign of Tilokarāja's successor, Phra Mu'ang Kaew, Pali Buddhist scholarship in Chiangmai flourished. The *Māṅgaladīpaṇi*, a Pali commentary on the *Māṅgala Sutta*, was written at this time and is still used as the basis of higher-level Pali studies, and the most important northern Tai chronicle, the *Jīnakālamālipakaraṇa*, also dates from this period.

Contemporaneous with the apogee of Buddhism in Chiangmai was the reign of Dhammaceti (1472–1492), who ruled Burma from Pegu, in the lower part of the country. According to the northern Tai and Burmese chronicles as well as the Kālyaṇī inscriptions, during Dhammaceti's reign there were several religious missions to Sri Lanka from Pegu and Ava, and Sīhaḷa monks, in turn, visited Burma. Burmese monks were reordained and visited sacred shrines on the island. Like Tilokarāja, Dhammaceti wanted to unify the *sangha* and used the new ordination to unite Buddhists in the Pegu kingdom. Monks from all over lower Burma, Ava, Tougoo, from the Shan kingdoms, Thailand, and Cambodia came to Pegu to be ordained during what the chronicles portray as the "golden age" of lower Burma.

Cambodia and Laos. Theravāda Buddhism was introduced to Cambodia by the Mon of the lower Menam Chaophraya River valley. In the eleventh and twelfth centuries, Theravāda also existed alongside Mahāyāna forms of Buddhism as well as Brahmanism. Mahāyāna Buddhism certainly received royal patronages in the eleventh century, and Jayavarman VII, the builder of the Bayon Temple at Angkor Thom, was identified with the Buddha Lokeśvara in the divine-royal symbiosis of the Khmer *devarāja/buddharāja* cult. Yet, typical of the classical Southeast Asian monarchs, Jayavarman's patronage of Mahāyāna Buddhism was not exclusive. According to the Kālyaṇī inscriptions and *The Glass Palace Chronicle*, a Cambodian monk, possibly Jayavarman's son, was part of the Burmese mission to Sri Lanka in the twelfth century. There was certainly an influx of Mon Buddhists from the Lopburi region in the face of Tai pressure in the thirteenth and early fourteenth centuries. Testimony of Chau Ta Kuan, a member of a late thirteenth century mission to Angkor, indicates that Theravāda monks were present in the Khmer capital during that period. The *Jīnakālamāli* account of the Chiangmai mission to Sri Lanka in 1423 CE includes reference to eight Khmer monks who brought the Sīhaḷa order of the Mahāvihāra to Cambodia.

The development of Buddhism in Laos was influenced by both Cambodia and Thailand. According to the Lao chronicles, Jayavarman Parmesvara (1327–1353) helped Phi Fa and Fa Ngum establish the independent kingdom of Lān Chāng, which earlier had been under the political hegemony of Sukhōthai. An inscription at Wat Keo in Luang Prabang refers to three Sinhala Mahātheras—including Mahāpasaman, Fa Ngum's teacher at Angkor—who went from Cambodia to Lān Chāng as part of a religious mission. Certainly, from the late fourteenth century onward, Buddhism in Laos and Cambodia was primarily influenced by the Tai as a consequence of their political dominance in the area. Even in the modern period, Theravāda sectarian developments in Thailand were reflected in Cambodia and Laos, and prior to the Communist revolution, monks from Cambodia and Laos studied in the Buddhist universities in Bangkok.

Summary. During the period that marks the rise of the classical Southeast Asian states, Buddhism existed in many guises. Pali Theravāda was introduced principally through the Mon of Dvāravatī and lower Burma and was considered a "higher" culture appropriated by the Burmese and the Tai. A strong Mahāyāna Buddhist presence is apparent not only in Śrīvijaya and Angkor but also in Pagan and the early Tai states. Furthermore, these forms of Buddhism competed with, and were complemented by, autochthonous animistic cults and Brahmanism. Buddhism made a decisive contribution to the conception of Southeast Asian kingship and monarchical rule through its ideal of the *dhammarāja,* who was not only represented by King Aśoka in India but by such Southeast Asian monarchs as Kyanzittha, Rāma Khamhaeng, and Tilokarāja.

Sri Lanka played the decisive role in the increasing dominance of Theravāda Buddhism in mainland Southeast Asia. Several factors contributed to this development, but I have singled out two: the rise to power of the Burmese and the Tai, who appropriated the Theravāda Buddhism of the Mon; and their subsequent adoption of Sinhala Buddhism as a way of establishing their own distinctive cultural and religious identity. While Sinhala influence can be traced to the eleventh century, the Sīhaḷa order only became dominant with the rise and development of the classical states from the mid-twelfth to the end of the fifteenth century. Sinhala Buddhism contributed to the legitimation of the ruling monarchies through its worldview, interpretation of history, monastic institution, education, and language; however, just as important, it became the religion of the masses through the worship of relics and sacred images and through the development of popular syncretic cults.

Vietnam has been largely excluded from the story of the development of the classical Buddhist Southeast Asian states because of the predominance of Hinduism among the Chams during early Vietnamese history and the overwhelming cultural influence of China on the country. Until the eleventh century the Vietnamese were effectively a group within the Chinese empire, and they looked to China for cultural inspiration even after they achieved independence under the Ly dynasty (1009–1224). Mahāyāna Buddhism was certainly part of the Chinese cultural influence, and the Ch'an (Viet., Thien) school, allegedly first established in 580 CE by Ti-ni-da-lu'u-chi, was the major Buddhist tradition in Vietnam. The elite eventually came to prefer Confucianism, but Buddhism continued to be important among the masses.

Southeast Asian Buddhism in the Modern Period. The classical Southeast Asian religio-cultural synthesis, of which Theravāda Buddhism has been a major component, has given the cultures of Burma, Thailand, Cambodia, Laos, and Vietnam a unique sense of identity and has sustained them to the present. Faced with Western imperialistic expansion from the seventeenth century onward and the challenge of modernity, the classical religious worldview, institutional structures, and cultural ethos have been changed, modified, and reasserted in a variety of ways. We shall examine how Buddhism has adapted to this challenge, its role in the development of the modern nation-state, and what the most recent trends suggest for the future of Buddhism in the region.

The condition of Southeast Asian Buddhism in the modern period reflects, to a large degree, the forces unleashed during the colonial period, especially during the nineteenth and twentieth centuries. Although modern religious histories of Burma, Thailand, and Indochina differ because of internal factors as well as the uniqueness of their colonial experiences—just as the Enlightenment fundamentally challenged the medieval synthesis of Christian Europe—the last century and a half has called into question the traditional Buddhist-Brahmanic-animistic synthesis of Southeast Asia and, consequently, the institutions and values associated with that worldview. The challenge to the classical worldview, and to the traditional moral community that was based on it, occurred on many fronts. Throughout the region the educational role of the *sangha* has been undermined by Western education. The status of the monk as one who was educated and as an educator and the significance of what was traditionally taught have also suffered. In Burma, the destruction of the institution of Buddhist kingship in 1885, as well as the relatively open posture of the British toward Buddhism, left the *sangha* in disarray, without the authority and direction the king traditionally provided. Thailand's rapid urbanization over the past fifty years has dramatically changed the village or town milieu that has historically informed and supported Buddhist religious practice. The communist revolutions in Laos, Cambodia, and Vietnam have displaced Buddhism as the fundamental mediator of cultural values. These are but a few of the challenges that Southeast Asian Buddhism has faced in the modern and contemporary periods.

Modernization and reform. The eve of the assertion of colonial power in the Buddhist countries of Southeast Asia found them in differing states and conditions. The Burmese destruction of Ayutthayā in 1767 provided the Thai (the designation applied to Tai living in the modern nation-state) the opportunity to establish a new capital on the lower Chaophraya River at present-day Bangkok. Because of its accessibility to international commerce the new site was much better situated for the new era about to dawn; the new dynastic line was better able to cope with the increasing impact of Western influence and was also committed to building a new sense of national unity. The Burmese, on the other hand, tired of wars under Alaungpaya and his son, were beset by religious and ethnic fractionalism. They were disadvantaged by the more isolated location of their capital (Ava, Amarapura, and then Mandalay), and governed by politically less astute rulers such as King Bagyidaw, who lost the Arakan and lower Burma to the British in the Anglo-Burmese Wars. Cambodia, in the eighteenth and early nineteenth centuries, basically fell victim to either the Thai or the Vietnamese until the French protectorate was established over the country in the 1860s. The Lao kingdoms of Luang Prabang and Vientiane were subject to Thai dominance in the nineteenth century until King Norodom was forced to accept French protection in 1863. Only in the 1890s were the French able to pacify Cochin China, Annam, and Tongkin, which, together with Cambodia, were formed into the Union Indochinoise in 1887. With the rest of Buddhist Southeast Asia disrupted by the colonial policies of France and Great Britain, Thailand's independence and able leadership under Mongkut (Rama IV, 1851–1868) and Chulalongkorn (1868–1910) abetted religious modernization and reform, making Thailand the appropriate focus for this topic.

The classical Thai Buddhist worldview had been set forth in the *Traibhūmikathā* of King Lü Thai of Sukhōthai. In one sense this text must be seen as part of Lü Thai's program to reconstruct an administrative and political framework and to salvage the alliance structure that had collapsed under the policies of his predecessor. In laying out the traditional Buddhist stages of the deterioration of history, Lü Thai meant to affirm the meaningfulness of a karmically calculated human life within a given multitiered universe. As a Buddhist sermon it urges its listeners to lead a moral life and by so doing to reap the appropriate heavenly rewards. Within its great chain of being framework of various human, heavenly, and demonic realms, the text focuses on a central figure, the universal monarch, or *cakkavattin*, exemplified by the legendary king Dharmaśokarāja. Lü Thai's traditional picture of the world, the role of the king, the nature of karmic action, and the hope of a heavenly reward provide a rationale for Sukhōthai political, social, and religious order. That King Rāma I (1782–1809), who reestablished the fortunes of the Thai monarchy, commissioned a new recension of the *Traibhūmi* testifies to its longevity and also to its utility as a charter for order and stability during yet another time of political and social disruption.

The worldview of the *Traibhūmi* was soon to be challenged by the West, however. European and American missionaries, merchants, and travelers came to Bangkok in the 1830s and 1840s, and by 1850 Thailand, or Siam, had signed commercial treaties with several Western nations. Led by Mongkut, who was crowned king in 1851, and by Chao Phraya Thiphakorawong, his able minister of foreign affairs, the Siamese noble elite proved to be interested in and open to Western technology and culture. A pragmatic type of scientific empiricism began to develop among them, leading even the devout Mongkut to articulate a demythologized Buddhism somewhat at odds with the traditional *Traibhūmi* worldview. This critique was formally set forth in 1867 in Chao Phraya Thiphakorawong's *Kitchanukit* (A Book Explaining Various Things), which explains events not in terms of traditional cosmological and mythological sources but using astronomy, geology, and medicine. For example, he argues that rain falls not because the rainmaking deities venture forth or because a great serpent thrashes its tail but because the winds suck water out of clouds; illness, he says, is caused not by a god punishing evil deeds but by air currents. Although the explanations were inaccurate, they were naturalistic rather than mythological or religious. The *Kitchanukit* presents Buddhism as primarily a system of social ethics; heaven and hell are not places but have a moral or pedagogical utility; *kamma* (Skt., *karman*) is not an actual causal force but a genetic principle that accounts for human diversity. Mongkut's successor, his son Chulalongkorn, moved even further from the mythic cosmology of the traditional Southeast Asian Buddhist worldview, declaring the *Traibhūmi* simply an act of imagination.

Modernization of the Thai Buddhist worldview was accompanied by a reform of the Buddhist *sangha*, led initially by Mongkut and continued during the reign of Chulalongkorn. Before his coronation in 1851 Mongkut had been a monk for twenty-five years. During that time his study of the Pali scriptures and his association with Mon monks of a stricter discipline convinced him that Thai Buddhism had departed from the authentic Buddhist tradition. He advocated a more serious study of Pali and Buddhist scripture as well as the attainment of proficiency in meditation. His efforts at religious reform resulted in an upgrading of monastic discipline in an effort to make it more orthodox. The group of monks who gathered around Mongkut at Wat Bovornives called themselves the Thammayut ("those adhering to the doctrine") and formed the nucleus of a new, stricter sect of Thai Buddhism. With its royal origins and connections, the Thammayut, or Dhammayuttika, sect has played a very influential role in the development of modern Thai Buddhism. In 1864 the Khmer royal family imported it to Cambodia, where it played a similar role. Its impact in Laos, however, was less significant. [*See the biography of Mongkut.*]

The development of a reformist Buddhist tradition that embodied Mongkut's ideals brought about further changes in the monastic order, especially as the *sangha* became part of the policies and programs of Mongkut's son Chulalongkorn. At the same time that he implemented reforms designed to politically integrate outlying areas into the emergent nation-state of Thailand, Chulalongkorn also initiated policies aimed at the incorporation of all Buddhists within the kingdom into a single national organization. As a consequence, monastic discipline, as well as the quality of monastic education, improved throughout the country. A standard monastic curriculum, which included three levels of study in Buddhist history, doctrine, and liturgy, and nine levels of Pali study, was established throughout the country. In addition, two Buddhist academies for higher studies were established in Bangkok.

The modernization and reform of Buddhism in Thailand in the late nineteenth and early twentieth centuries stand out, but the Thai case must be seen as part of a general trend in all the Southeast Asian Buddhist countries. In the area of text and doctrine a new scripturalism, epitomized by the new redaction of the Tipiṭaka in conjunction with the general Buddhist council held in Burma in 1956 and 1957, has emerged. Doctrinal reinterpretation has followed three major lines: an emphasis on the ethical dimensions of the tradition at the expense of the supernatural and mythical; a rejection of magical elements of popular thought and practice as incompatible with the authentic tradition; and a rationalization of Buddhist thought in terms of Western categories, along with an apologetic interest in depicting Buddhism as scientific. Some apologists, such as U Chan Htoon of Burma, have claimed that all modern scientific concepts preexisted in Buddhism. Others make less sweeping claims but cite specific correlations between such Buddhist doctrines as interdependent co-arising (*paṭicca samuppāda;* Skt., *pratītya-samutpāda)* and Einstein's relativity theory. Generally speaking, Buddhist apologists have attempted to prove that Buddhism is more scientific than other religions, particularly Christianity; that the empirical approach or methodology of Buddhism is consistent with modern science; and that science proves or validates particular Buddhist teachings.

Institutional modernization and reform have also taken place along the lines that we have examined in some detail in regard to Thailand. Cambodia, for example, not only adopted the Dhammayuttika sect from Thailand but also reorganized the *sangha* along national lines. In Laos and Burma various Buddhist organizations and associations with reformist intent emerged, often under lay leadership.

Buddhism and the modern nation-state. Buddhism proved to be a crucial factor during the end of the colonial and the postcolonial periods, as Burma, Thailand, Cambodia, Laos, and Vietnam became modern nation-states. On the one hand, Buddhism contributed decisively to the development of the new nationhood; on the other, it resisted in various ways to changes forced upon traditional Buddhist thought and practice. We shall first examine the Buddhist contributions to the national independence movements and to the maintenance of national identity and unity; second, we shall explore Buddhist resistance to pressures put on the tradition by the organization of the modern nation-state.

Historically, Buddhism played an important role in the definition of the classical Southeast Asian states. It was inevitable, therefore, that it would be a crucial factor in the redefinition of these states. In those cases, for example, in which a country was dominated by a colonial power, nationalist movements grew out of, or were identified with, a religious base or context. Take Burma as a case in point. Buddhism provided the impetus for the independence movement that arose there during the first decades of the twentieth century. The YMBAs (Young Men's Buddhist Association) of Rangoon and elsewhere in Burma quickly assumed a political role. The first issue of major consequence was the "no footwear" controversy of 1918. The YMBAs argued that Europeans, in keeping with Burmese custom, should be prohibited from wearing shoes in all pagodas; accordingly, the British government allowed the head monk of each pagoda to decide the regulations applying to footwear. During the next decade the nationalist cause was led primarily by the General Council of Burmese Associations and by such politically active monks as U Ottama, who was imprisoned for urging a boycott of government-sponsored elections, and U Wisara, who became a martyr to the independence movement when he died during a hunger strike in a British jail.

When U Nu became prime minister in January 1948, following Aung San's assassination, he put Buddhism at the heart of his political program. Although he rejected Marxism, he espoused a Buddhist socialism. In essence, he believed that a national community could be constructed only if individuals are able to overcome their own self-acquisitive interests. Sufficient material needs should be provided for everyone, class and property distinctions should be minimized, and all should strive for moral and mental perfection. The state was to meet the material needs of the people and Buddhism their spiritual needs. To this end he created a Buddhist Sasana

Council in 1950 to propagate Buddhism and to supervise monks, appointed a minister of religious affairs, and ordered government departments to dismiss civil servants thirty minutes early if they wished to meditate. In 1960 U Nu committed himself and his party to making Buddhism the state religion of Burma, an unpopular move with such minorities as the Christian Karens. This attempt was one of the reasons given for General Ne Win's coup in March 1962, which deposed U Nu as prime minister. While in many ways naive and politically unrealistic, U Nu's vision of Buddhist socialism harked back to an earlier vision of the political leader as one who ruled by *dhamma* and who would engender peace and prosperity by the power of his own virtue. But such a vision proved incompatible with the political realities of the 1960s.

Buddhism figured prominently in other Southeast Asian countries, both as a basis of protest against ruling regimes and as an important symbolic component of political leadership. In the 1960s politically active Vietnamese monks contributed to the downfall of the Diem regime, and afterward the United Buddhist Association, under the leadership of Thich Tri Quang and Thich Thien Minh, remained politically active. In Cambodia, Prince Sihanouk espoused a political philosophy based on Buddhist socialism and was the last Cambodian ruler to represent, although in an attenuated way, the tradition of classical Southeast Asian Buddhist rule.

In addition to providing the inspiration for political independence movements, contributing to a political ideology with uniquely Buddhist features, and being the motivating force challenging political power structures, Southeast Asian Buddhism has been used to promote political unity within the boundaries of the nation-state. U Nu's hope that making Buddhism the state religion would promote national unity was naive; it did not take into account the contending factions within the Buddhist *sangha* and the presence of sizable non-Buddhist minorities who feared they might be threatened by covert, if not overt, pressure from the Buddhist majority.

In Thailand the centralization of the Thai *sangha* under King Chulalongkorn and his able *sangharāja*, Vajirañāṇa, not only improved monastic discipline and education but also integrated the monastic order more fully into the nation-state. Chulalongkorn's successor, Vajiravudh (1910–1925), made loyalty to the nation synonymous with loyalty to Buddhism; in effect, he utilized Buddhism as an instrument to promote a spirit of nationalism. In particular, he glorified military virtues and identified nationalism with the support of Thai Buddhism. He founded the Wild Tigers Corps, resembling the British Territorial Army; the Tiger Cubs, a branch of the corps, was later assimilated into the Boy Scout movement. Both encouraged loyalty to nation, religion (i.e., Buddhism), and the king.

Buddhism has continued to be an important tool in the government's policy to promote national unity. In 1962 the Buddhist Sangha Act further centralized the organization of the monastic order under the power of the secular state. In the same year the government organized the Dhammadhuta program, and in 1965 the Dhammacarika program. The former supported Buddhist monks abroad and those working in sensitive border areas, especially the northeastern region of the country, while the latter has focused on Buddhist missions among northern hill tribes.

Buddhism, however, has not only functioned as a kind of "civil religion," contributing to the definition and support of the new Southeast Asian nation-states in the postcolonial period. It has also resisted the kind of accommodation and change brought on by the new nationalism. In some cases this resistance has been generated by the desire to maintain traditional religious practices and more local autonomy; in others, it has come in the form of armed rebellion and messianic, millenarian movements. As an example of the former we cite Khrūbā Sīwichai, a northern Thai monk of the early twentieth century, and of the latter we cite the Saya San rebellion (1930–1931) in Burma.

While the vast majority of the Buddhist *sangha* in Thailand cooperated with the central government's attempts in the early twentieth century to standardize monastic organization, discipline, and education, there were a few notable exceptions. Khrūbā Sīwichai of the Chiangmai region of northern Thailand was one of them. He ran into problems with the *sangha* hierarchy because he ordained monks and novices according to northern Thai custom although he had not been recognized as a preceptor by the national order. He also singlehandedly raised vast sums of money to rebuild monasteries that had fallen into disrepair and to construct a road, using manual labor, to the famous Mahādhātu Temple on Doi Sutēp Mountain, overlooking Chiangmai. Because of his success in these enterprises, miraculous powers were attributed to him. In 1919, however, he was ordered to report to Bangkok to answer charges of clerical disobedience and sedition, but high Thai officials, fearing the repercussions that punishment of Khrūbā Sīwichai might have, intervened on his behalf. Although eventually Sīwichai submitted to the laws of the Thai national monastic order, *sangha* officials tacitly agreed to permit the northern clergy to follow some of its traditional customs.

Other, more radical Buddhist responses to the emerging nation-state developed in various parts of Southeast

Asia and usually centered on a charismatic leader who was sometimes identified as an incarnation of the *bodhisattva* Maitreya. In Burma several rebellions in the early twentieth century aimed to overthrow British rule and to restore the fortunes of both Burmese kingship and Burmese Buddhism. One of these was led by Saya San, who had been a monk in the Tharrawaddy district in lower Burma but disrobed to work in a more directly political way to overthrow the British. Saya San's movement had a strongly traditional religious and royal aura, and much of his support came from political monks associated with nationalistic associations *(wunthanu athins)* that had formed in the 1920s. Saya San was "crowned" as "king" in a thoroughly traditional Burmese manner in a jungle capital on 28 October 1930. An armed group was trained and the rebellion launched toward the end of December. As the conflict spread throughout lower Burma and into the Shan States, the British army was called in to help the police forces repress the rebellion. Only after eight months of fighting did the warfare end.

Recent trends. The chapter on Southeast Asian Buddhism's future within the context of the modern nation-state has yet to be closed. The disestablishment of the *sangha* in Cambodia and Laos has shaken, but by no means rooted out, the tradition, even though Pol Pot's genocidal regime attempted such wholesale destruction in the aftermath of American withdrawal from the war in Indochina. Laos and Cambodia, however, have experienced a breakdown of the traditional religio-cultural synthesis. This is taking place more slowly in Thailand and even in Burma, which has been much more isolated from Western influences since the early 1960s. The political and economic contexts of Southeast Asian Buddhism, in short, have obviously affected the state of Buddhism in Southeast Asia. The trends that have emerged seem paradoxical, if not contradictory. We shall examine three sets or pairs: increasingly active lay leadership and the veneration of monks to whom supernatural powers are ascribed; a revival of meditation practice and an emphasis on active political and social involvement; rampant magical, syncretic ritual practice and insistence on the purity of the authentic teaching.

The modern period has seen increased lay leadership at various levels of religious life. The YMBAs of Burma and the Buddhist "Sunday schools" that have arisen in Thailand have obviously been influenced by Western Christian models. Lay associations have developed for various purposes. For example, prior to the revolution Cambodia had the Buddhist Association of the Republic of Cambodia (1952), the Association of Friends of the Buddhist Lycée (1949), the Association of Friends of Religious Welfare Aid Centers, the Association of Religious Students of the Republic of Cambodia (1970), the Association of the Buddhist Youth of Cambodia (1971), and so on. Buddhist laity have also been actively involved in the worldwide Buddhist movement. Most notable of the laity groups are the World Fellowship of Buddhists, which has headquarters in Bangkok, and the World Council of Churches, which holds interreligious dialogue consultations.

The increasingly significant role of the laity in a religious tradition noted for the centrality of the monk reflects many developments in modern Southeast Asian countries, not the least of which is the spread of secular, Western education among the elites. Coupled with this phenomenon, however, we find a polar opposition—a persistent cult of the holy man to whom supernatural powers are attributed. In some instances the holy monk becomes a charismatic leader of a messianic cult (e.g., the Mahagandare Weikzado Apwegyoke in Burma), while in others the form of veneration is more informal and generalized (e.g., Phra Acharn Mun in Thailand). In many cases the holy monk makes few, if any, miraculous or supernatural claims, but these will be ascribed to him by his followers. Hagiographic literature, describing cosmic portents of the monk's birth, extraordinary events during his childhood, and other characteristics of this genre, will often emerge. While the monk as miracle worker is not a new phenomenon in Theravāda Buddhism, it has persisted to the present time and, some observers claim, has been on the upswing in the contemporary period.

Meditation has always been the *sine qua non* of Buddhist practice, but traditionally it was the preserve of the forest-dwelling *(araññavāsī)* or meditating *(vipassana dhura)* monk. In the modern period, meditation has been more widely practiced as part of the routines of ordinary Buddhist temples and, more particularly, in meditation centers that either include or are specifically for lay practice. The lay meditation movement was especially strong in Burma under the leadership of such meditation masters as U Ba Khin and Ledi Sayadaw (1856–1923). Westerners have been particularly attracted to some of Southeast Asia's renowned meditation teachers, such as Acharn Cha of Wat Pa Pong in Ubon Ratchathani. Some meditating monks have also gained reputations not only for their method of meditation or for holiness but for the attainment of extraordinary powers as well.

While meditation has become a lay as well as monastic practice in contemporary Southeast Asian Buddhism, this development has not precluded a movement to formulate a strong, activist social ethic. The Vietnamese Zen monk Thich Nhat Hahn attempted to work out a Buddhist solution to the military conflict in his country during the 1960s, and there has been a widespread interest in formulating a Buddhist theory of economic development that is critical of Western capitalism but not necessarily indebted to Marxism. Buddhists have also acted to solve particular social problems, such as drug addiction, and have spoken out strongly against the proliferation of nuclear arms. Southeast Asian Buddhists have also joined with members of other religious groups, both within their own countries as well as in international organizations, to work for such causes as world peace and basic civil rights for all peoples. Buddhist interpreters, such as the Thai monk Bhikkhu Buddhadāsa, have referred to Buddhism as a practical system of personal and social morality.

Buddhadāsa has also been strongly critical of conventional Thai Buddhist religious practice, which has stressed merit-making rituals. These are aimed at obtaining personal benefit and propitiating various supernatural powers for protection or good luck. In his writings and at his center in Chaiya, southern Thailand, he emphasizes the importance of overcoming greed and attachment. *Nibbāna*, for Buddhadāsa, is the state that is achieved when egoism is overcome. This is the goal of all Buddhists, not just monks. Indeed, he argues, this is the purpose of all religions. Buddhadāsa's critique reflects the magical nature of popular Buddhist ritual practice not only in Thailand but, more generally, in Southeast Asian Buddhism, the goal of which is to improve one's life materially through the mechanism of gaining merit or improving one's karmic status. Buddhadāsa's proposal that such teachings as *nibbāna* and *anatta* (not-self), which represent the essence of the Buddha's teachings, must be part of every Buddhist's religious practice exemplifies an interest on the part of many contemporary Buddhist thinkers to restore the kernel of the authentic tradition, which has often been hidden beneath layers of cultural accretions. Thus, while the popular religious ethos is syncretic and emphasizes the attainment of worldly goals, various apologists in Burma and Thailand are attempting to make the core of the tradition a part of the understanding and practice of the Buddhist populace at large. Some critical observers have referred to this trend as a "protestantizing" of Southeast Asian Buddhism.

The contemporary ethos of Buddhism in Southeast Asia reflects an ancient heritage but also points in new directions. It is difficult to predict how the *sangha* will fare under the Marxist regimes in Laos and Cambodia or, for that matter, in the urban and increasingly materialistic environment of Bangkok and Chiangmai. Can the Theravāda monk maintain his place in society when his education cannot compare with that of the elite? Can Buddhism effectively address problems of overpopulation, prostitution, malnourishment, and economic exploitation? To what extent can the tradition change with the times and retain its identity? These and other questions face a religion that has not only been fundamental in the identity of the Burmese, Thai, Laotians, Cambodians, and Vietnamese but has also contributed much to world culture.

[*For a discussion of the institutional history of the Buddhist order in Southeast Asia, see* Theravāda. *An examination of the relationship between the* saṃgha *and the larger societies of which it is a part can be found in* Saṃgha, *article on* Saṃgha and Society. Southeast Asian Religions, *article on* Mainland Cultures *treats local Buddhist traditions in Southeast Asia. See also* Buddhism, *article on* Folk Buddhism; Pilgrimage, *article on* Buddhist Pilgrimage in South and Southeast Asia; Worship and Cultic Life, *article on* Buddhist Cultic Life in Southeast Asia; Burmese Religion; Khmer Religion; Lao Religion; Thai Religion; *and* Vietnamese Religion.]

BIBLIOGRAPHY

Works on Buddhism in Southeast Asia include text translations and doctrinal studies, histories of the development of Buddhism in various Southeast Asian countries, anthropological treatments of popular, village Buddhism, and studies of Buddhism and political change. Georges Coedès's studies, *The Indianized States of Southeast Asia*, edited by Walter F. Vella and translated by Susan Brown Cowing (Canberra, 1968), and *The Making of South-East Asia*, translated by H. M. Wright (Berkeley, 1966), are standard treatments of the region, as is Reginald Le May's *The Culture of South-East Asia* (London, 1954). The classic study of Southeast Asian religion and kingship is Robert Heine-Geldern's *Conceptions of State and Kingship in Southeast Asia* (Ithaca, N.Y., 1956). A readable, general study of the history of Theravāda Buddhism in Southeast Asia and its present teachings and practices is Robert C. Lester's *Theravada Buddhism in Southeast Asia* (Ann Arbor, 1973). My *Buddhism and Society in Southeast Asia* (Chambersburg, Pa., 1981) is an analysis of Theravāda Buddhism in terms of the themes of syncretism, political legitimation, and modernization. The theme of Buddhism and political legitimation is discussed in several seminal articles in *Buddhism and Legitimation of Power in Thailand, Laos, and Burma*, edited by Bardwell L. Smith (Chambersburg, Pa., 1978).

The monumental work on the early Pagan period is Gordon H. Luce's *Old Burma—Early Pagán*, 3 vols. (Locust Valley, N.Y., 1969–1970). Two of the important Burmese chronicles have been translated: *Hmannān mạha yazạwintawkyī: The Glass Palace Chronicle of the Kings of Burma*, translated by Pe Maung Tin and G. H. Luce (London, 1923); and Pannasami's *The History of the Buddha's Religion (Sāsanavaṁsa)*, translated by B. C. Law (London, 1952). Standard treatments of both Pali and Sanskritic Buddhism in Burma are Nihar-Ranjan Ray's *An Introduction to the Study of Theravāda Buddhism in Burma* (Calcutta, 1946), and his *Sanskrit Buddhism in Burma* (Calcutta, 1936). A more recent study is Winston L. King's *A Thousand*

Lives Away (Cambridge, Mass., 1964). Two standard anthropological studies are Melford E. Spiro's *Buddhism and Society: A Great Tradition and its Burmese Vicissitudes*, 2d. ed. (Berkeley, 1982), and Manning Nash's *The Golden Road to Modernity* (New York, 1965). Nash was also the general editor of *Anthropological Studies in Theravada Buddhism* (New Haven, 1966), which contains valuable articles on Burmese and Thai Buddhism by Nash, David E. Pfanner, and Jasper Ingersoll. E. Michael Mendelson's *Sangha and State in Burma*, edited by John P. Ferguson (Ithaca, N.Y., 1965), although difficult going is a mine of information. Buddhism and the early nationalist period are studied in Emanuel Sarkisyanz's *Buddhist Backgrounds of the Burmese Revolution* (The Hague, 1965), and Donald E. Smith's *Religion and Politics in Burma* (Princeton, 1965).

The standard Thai history with much information about Thai Buddhism is David K. Wyatt's *Thailand: A Short History* (New Haven, 1984); Kenneth E. Wells's *Thai Buddhism: Its Rites and Activities* (Bangkok, 1939), while somewhat dated and rather dry is still very useful. One of the major northern Thai chronicles, Ratanapanya's *Jinakālamālīpakaranam*, has been translated by N. A. Jayawickrama as *The Sheaf of Garlands of the Epochs of the Conqueror* (London, 1968). Frank E. Reynolds and Mani B. Reynolds have translated the major Thai cosmological treatise, *Trai Phūmi Phra Rūang*, as *Three Worlds according to King Ruang* (Berkeley, 1982). Prince Dhani-Nivat's *A History of Buddhism in Siam*, 2d ed. (Bangkok, 1965), provides a brief historical overview of the development of Buddhism in Thailand. Much recent, significant work on Thai Buddhism has been done by anthropologists; see especially Stanley J. Tambiah's *World Conqueror and World Renouncer* (Cambridge, 1976) and several articles by Charles F. Keyes, for example, "Buddhism and National Integration in Thailand," *Journal of Asian Studies* 30 (May 1971): 551–567. Historians of religion have also contributed to our knowledge of Thai Buddhism. Frank E. Reynolds has written several articles including, "The Holy Emerald Jewel: Some Aspects of Buddhist Symbolism and Political Legitimation in Thailand and Laos," in *Religion and Legitimation of Power in Thailand, Laos, and Burma*, edited by Bardwell L. Smith (Chambersburg, Pa., 1978), pp. 175–193. I have analyzed a major northern Thai monastery in *Wat Haripuñjaya: A Study of the Royal Temple of the Buddha's Relic, Lamphun, Thailand* (Missoula, Mont., 1976).

French scholars have made the major contribution to the study of Buddhism in Laos, Cambodia, and Vietnam. Louis Finot's "Research sur la littérature laotienne," *Bulletin de l'École Française d'Extrême-Orient* 17 (1917) is an indispensable tool in the study of Lao Buddhist literature. Marcel Zago's *Rites et cérémonies en milieu bouddhiste'lao* (Rome, 1972) provides a comprehensive treatment of Lao religion, although Charles Archaimbault's "Religious Structures in Laos," *Journal of the Siam Society* 52 (1964): 57–74, while more limited in scope is very useful. Lawrence Palmer Brigg's "The Syncretism of Religions in Southeast Asia, especially in the Khmer Empire," *Journal of the American Oriental Society* 71 (October–December 1951): 230–249, provides a survey of the development of religion in Cambodia. Adhémard Leclère's classic study, *Le bouddhisme au Cambodge* (Paris, 1899) remains the standard work. The classic study of Vietnamese religion is Leopold Michel Cadière's *Croyances et pratiques religieuses des Viêtnamiens*, 3 vols. (Saigon, 1955–1958), but more accessible is the brief sketch in the trilingual volume by Chanh-tri Mai-tho-Truyen, *Le bouddhisme au Vietnam, Buddhism in Vietnam, Phatgiao Viet-nam* (Saigon, 1962). Thich Thien-An's *Buddhism and Zen in Vietnam in Relation to the Development of Buddhism in Asia*, edited by Carol Smith (Los Angeles, 1975), studies the development of Buddhist schools from the sixth to the seventeenth century. Thich Nhat-Hanh's *Vietnam: Lotus in a Sea of Fire* (New York, 1967) puts the Buddhist situation in the 1960s into historical perspective.

Interested readers may also wish to consult the following works: Heinz Bechert's three-volume study, *Buddhismus, Staat und Gesellschaft in den Ländern Theravāda-Buddhismus* (Frankfurt, 1966–1973); *Religion in South Asia*, edited by Edward B. Harper (Seattle, 1964), especially the articles by Michael Ames and Nur Yalman; and *Religion and Progress in Modern Asia*, edited by Robert N. Bellah (New York, 1965).

DONALD K. SWEARER

Buddhism in Central Asia

It is not known exactly how or when Buddhism first spread northward into Bactria, but there is strong evidence that it was actively promoted in the Indo-Iranian border region as a result of the missionary activity encouraged by the Indian emperor Aśoka in the third century BCE. Aśoka set up inscriptions in widely distant parts of his kingdom. The most famous are the so-called Rock Edicts and Pillar Edicts, which are of varied content but consistently promulgate the ethical standards of Buddhist teaching that he wished to inculcate. Two Aśokan inscriptions have been found as far north as Qandahar in Afghanistan. Aśoka was renowned also for his building activity and he is credited by popular legend with the erection of eighty-four thousand stupas. The stupas of the time of Aśoka and his immediate successors were markedly distinct in style from those built later under the Kushans. This difference had already been noticed by the famous seventh-century Chinese pilgrim Hsüan-tsang, who observed a large number of stupas in the Aśokan style in the northwest, for example, three at Taxila, two in Uḍḍiyāna, five in Gandhāra, three near Nagarahāra (Jelalabad), dozens in Jāguḍa (near Qandahar), and even one at Kāpiśī (Begram). [*See the biography of Aśoka.*]

The first centuries of the common era saw the consolidation and expansion of the Kushan empire founded by Kujula Kadphises. The Kushans were a people of uncertain extraction who in Gandhāra adopted as their official language an East Iranian language nowadays called Bactrian. They controlled the famous caravan route that proceeded from Taxila via Bamian to Balkh and thence to Termez on the Afghan border. Archaeological remains of Kushan Buddhist occupation have been found along the entire route and to the east of it.

A new era in Indian history is associated with the most renowned Kushan ruler, Kaniṣka I (first to second century CE). Kaniṣka is celebrated in Buddhist sources as a second Aśoka and similar legends arose concerning him, but it is likely that his patronage of Buddhism proceeded from his tolerance rather than from his conversion. Although the figure of a Buddha is depicted on one of his coins, they portray a varied pantheon. Archaeological evidence indicates that the Kushans mainly worshiped Śiva and the Iranian goddess Ardoxšo, but that Buddhism was gaining ground. Kaniṣka is traditionally associated with the famous Buddhist authors Aśvaghoṣa, Mātṛceṭa, and Vasubandhu, as well as with the well-known physician Caraka. Such traditions have little value beyond confirming what we know otherwise, namely, that under Kaniṣka Buddhism flourished and spread as never before.

The Kushan empire embraced various peoples living side by side. In particular, several Iranian tribes were represented as well as Greeks and Indians. Greeks had been living in Bactria and Gandhāra since the time of Alexander in the fourth century BCE; Saka tribes penetrated the area in the second century BCE. It is generally agreed that it was due to Greek influence in communities where religious tolerance was observed that the style of Buddhist art known as Gandharan developed. The most noticeable feature of this style was the depiction in human form of the Buddha, whose person had previously been considered beyond the reach of artists and who had accordingly been represented in art only symbolically, for example by a wheel. Also noteworthy is the common portrayal of the Buddhist laity in this art. One episode often depicted is the giving of food to the Buddha by the two merchant brothers Trapusa and Bhallika, who were shown in a second-century relief at Shotorak as bearded and dressed in an Indo-Scythian manner. Bhallika has traditionally been associated with Balkh.

It is also significant that the cult of the *bodhisattva* is reflected early in Gandharan art. Best known are the representations of the *bodhisattva* Maitreya, the future Buddha. As recently as 1977 there came to light in Mathurā a fragmentary sculpture of the Buddha Amitābha. It is identified by an accompanying inscription that dates the sculpture to 106 CE.

Much controversy surrounds the question of the date and place of origin of Mahāyāna Buddhism. There are, however, many indications that it arose during the first century CE in a cosmopolitan environment such as Gandhāra. The depiction of the Buddha in human form certainly betrays Greek influence, but at the same time it conforms with Mahāyāna Buddhist teaching that the historical Buddha Śākyamuni should be regarded merely as one of many Buddhas.

Kushan influence is known to have spread northwards into Khorezm and Sogdiana, but it seems clear that those regions were never actually under Kushan rule, and there is not much evidence of Buddhism there in the time of the Kushans. The sites excavated at Varakhsha near Bukhara, and at Afrāsiyāb and Panjikent near Samarkand, are conspicuously non-Buddhist, while the Buddhist sites further east at Ajina Tepe near Kurgan-Tyube, at Kuva in Ferghana, and at Ak-Beshim near Frunze all belong to the seventh or eighth century. Even at this date Buddhism cannot have been well established around the capital, as the sites near Bukhara and Samarkand show clearly enough. Hsüan-tsang found little Buddhist adherence in Samarkand in the seventh century, and despite Hsüan-tsang's claim to conversions there, the Korean pilgrim known by his Chinese name Hui-ch'ao found only a solitary Buddhist monastery with a single monk when he visited Samarkand in the eighth century. [*See the biography of Hsüan-tsang.*]

Although the Kushans adopted Bactrian as the official language for their coins and for the inscription at the dynastic temple at Surkh Kotal, the language of their administration was Indian, the so-called Gāndhārī Prakrit written in Kharoṣṭhī script. Kushan influence extended well into China during the first centuries CE and administrative documents dating from the period between 200 and 320 written in Gāndhārī have been found in the kingdom of Shan-shan (Kroraina), which stretched from the Niya River a short distance east of Khotan as far as Lob Nor. A Kharoṣṭhī well inscription probably dating from the second half of the second century was found at Lo-yang in China. Gāndhārī was the language used by a Hīnayāna Buddhist sect, the Dharmaguptakas, whose *Dīrghāgama* and Vinaya were translated into Chinese by Buddhayaśas between 410 and 413. One of the Niya documents contains the final verses of the Dharmaguptaka recension of the *Prātimokṣa Sūtra,* and we know from the Chinese traveler Fa-hsien that in 400 there were more than four thousand Hīnayāna monks in Shan-shan.

One of the oldest manuscripts of any Indian text is the Gāndhārī recension of the *Dharmapada,* which also is the only extant literary text written in the Kharoṣṭhī script. It came to light in the vicinity of Khotan, but although it is said to have come from Kohmari Mazar it has not been possible to establish any connection with an archaeological site. It is written in essentially the same dialect as that used for the Niya documents from the nearby kingdom of Shan-shan and it may in fact have been written in one of the monasteries there. The Gāndhārī *Dharmapada* may date to the second century, and its discovery in the vicinity of Khotan lends support to the thesis that the first Buddhist mission to eastern Central Asia was led by the Dharmaguptakas. Whether the Dharmaguptakas came to Khotan or not, speakers of Gāndhārī certainly did, as the Khotanese language is in its oldest strata already permeated by loanwords from Gāndhārī.

By the Kushan period monks of another Buddhist Hīnayāna sect, the Sarvāstivāda, were spreading throughout Central Asia, taking with them palm-leaf manuscripts written in Buddhist Sanskrit. The earliest manuscripts have been found mainly in the cave monasteries of the Kuchā oasis and near Qarashahr. During the Kushan period works on Abhidharma and poetic literature predominated. Recent paleographic research has established a close connection between the monasteries in Bamian and Gilgit on the one hand and those in Eastern Turkistan on the other. There is thus good reason for assuming that missionary activity on the part of the Sarvāstivādins had its point of departure in Afghanistan and Kashmir.

The precise date of Buddhism's initial establishment in Khotan is unknown. A late tradition would indicate about 84 BCE, which is not unlikely. According to Chinese sources, there was a Buddhist community in Khotan by the second century CE, and, as mentioned above, the Gāndhārī *Dharmapada* found near Khotan probably dates to the second century. Chu Shih-hsing, who studied Prajñāpāramitā literature at Lo-yang in the third century, went west in search of the *Pañcaviṃśatisāhasrikā-prajñāpāramitā Sūtra*, which he found in Khotan. Mokṣala, who translated this work into Chinese in 291, was a Khotanese, and another Khotanese, Gītamitra, took a copy of the same text with him to Ch'ang-an (modern Sian) in 296. Thus, Khotan was already a well-established center of Mahāyāna studies in the third century.

Many fragments of Sanskrit manuscripts of Prajñāpāramitā literature have been found in Khotan but most of them await publication. Already published is an incomplete text of the *Vajracchedikā*, of which fourteen out of nineteen folios are extant. A complete manuscript of a Khotanese translation of this popular Mahāyana work is also extant. It dates from a much later period and incorporates some interesting commentatorial additions. The fact that so many fragments of Mahāyāna manuscripts have been found in Khotan testifies to the reliability of Chinese reports concerning the dominance of the Mahāyāna in Khotan. Much of this material still awaits publication. One large manuscript of the *Saddharmapuṇḍarīka Sūtra*, which must originally have come from Khotan, has been the object of much study in recent years. It contains several colophons written in Late Khotanese.

The Central Asian recensions of Buddhist Sanskrit texts are of particular interest because they shed light on the way in which these texts were transmitted to Tibet and China. It was only at a relatively late date that the Sanskrit texts were translated into Central Asian languages. The Buddhist scriptures were first translated into Chinese from Gāndhārī and thereafter from Sanskrit. Many of the early translators of Indian works into Chinese spoke Central Asian languages themselves. Typical is the complaint of a Khotanese poet: "The Khotanese do not value the [Buddhist] Law at all in Khotanese. They understand it badly in Indian. In Khotanese it does not seem to them to be the Law. For the Chinese the Law is in Chinese." It must have been particularly frustrating for the poet to find so little appreciation in view of the efforts of Khotanese missionaries such as Devaprajña, Śikṣānanda, and Śīladharma in translating Buddhist texts into Chinese at Lo-yang and Ch'ang-an.

The king of Khotan is said to have converted Kashgar to Buddhism in about 100 CE. At this date the Mahāyāna had probably not yet fully emerged and Khotan would have followed Hīnayāna teaching. Hīnayāna was mainly followed in Kashgar and its subsequent links were rather with the cities of the northern route across the Takla Makan. The same is true of Tumshuq, whose Buddhist monastery is thought to date from the fourth or fifth century. Nothing is known of its history but the style of its artistic remains shows connections with Qizil in the Kuchā region. That it was inhabited by Saka monks is shown by the discovery of a manuscript fragment containing the ceremonial formulas for the ordination of Buddhist laywomen. It is written in a Middle Iranian dialect closely related to Khotanese but in the same kind of Brāhmī script used for writing Tocharian. The many archaic features of Tumshuqese reveal that it separated very early from Khotanese, which developed along different lines. Archaeological evidence indicates that the monastery complex was destroyed by fire about the tenth century, which would be the time when the Karakhanids imposed Islam on the area.

Although there is not much evidence of Buddhism in the heart of Sogdiana, the Sogdians were one of the main peoples responsible for the diffusion of Buddhism throughout Central Asia and China. They were merchants who established trading colonies all along the northern Silk Route as far as the Chinese capital at Lo-yang. The Sogdians took with them not only Buddhism but also Manichaeism and Christianity, and we have translations into the Middle Iranian Sogdian language of the scriptures of all three religions. The Sogdians acquired a knowledge of Chinese for trading purposes, but they put it to use by translating Chinese Buddhist literature into Sogdian. Moreover, some of the early translators of Buddhist Sanskrit literature into Chinese were of Sogdian extraction such as K'ang (i.e., Samarkand) Meng-hsiang, who worked at Lo-yang from 194 to 199.

Still extant are four letters written in Tun-huang in the Sogdian language. They can be dated with considerable certainty to the year 313. Thus, there was a Sogdian colony in Tun-huang before building began in 366 at the famous site of Ch'ien-fo-tung ("caves of the thousand Buddhas"), nine miles southwest of the city. It was among the hundreds of cave-temples there that a famous medieval library of Central Asian manuscripts was discovered at the beginning of the present century. Among other things, this library included the largest proportion of extant Khotanese literature and most of the surviving Buddhist Sogdian manuscripts.

Buddhism must have come to Tun-huang by the beginning of the common era, but it is first attested in literature in the third century. The greatest translator of Buddhist texts before Kumārajīva was the Indo-Scythian Dharmarakṣa (Chin., Fa-hu), who was born in Tun-huang around 230 CE. He is known to have traveled extensively throughout Central Asia in search of Buddhist scriptures and to have acquired knowledge of many Central Asian languages. He collaborated with Indians and Kucheans, with a Yüeh-chih, a Khotanese, and probably also a Sogdian. It was one of his Chinese disciples, Fa-ch'eng, who in about 280 founded a large monastery in Tun-huang.

The earliest inscription in a Turkic language is a funeral stela discovered near Bugut about 170 kilometers from the site of the eighth-century royal Turkic inscriptions at Orkhon in Mongolia. It is the epitaph of a prince of the Eastern Turks who became kaghan in 571. The inscription, which dates to approximately 581, is written in Sogdian and in the kind of Sogdian writing found in the later Buddhist Sogdian manuscripts. From this kind of Sogdian writing the Uighur script used by the Eastern Turks for their translations of Buddhist works later developed. The inscription mentions the establishment of a Buddhist community, and there is evidence that two of the rulers of the Eastern Turks mentioned in it were Buddhists. It is known that a Buddhist monk from Kāpiśī (Begram) called Jinagupta (528–605), who had spent some time in Khotan, taught Buddhism at the court of the Eastern Turks.

Kocho, modern Karakocho, a few miles east of Turfan, was the principal city of the Turfan region until the end of the fourteenth century. The name of the city in Chinese sources is usually Kao-ch'ang or Ho-chou. It began as a Chinese military colony in the first century BCE. In about 790 it was conquered by the Tibetans and after the fall of the Uighur empire in the Orkhon Basin in 840–843 the Uighurs made Kocho their southern capital. The Uighurs who came from the Orkhon region were Manichaeans, not Buddhists, but Kocho had long been inhabited by Sogdians and Chinese professing Buddhism. Most of the Buddhist texts in the Uighur language were found in the Turfan region and derive from the Sarvāstivāda and Mahāyāna canons. The language of these texts has been profoundly influenced by Sogdian, and it may be assumed accordingly that the Sogdians played an important role in instructing the Uighurs in Buddhism. However, most of the texts seem to have been translated from Chinese, perhaps with the help of Sogdian translators. The Sogdians themselves usually translated Buddhist literature from Chinese into Sogdian. The Buddhist communities in the Turfan area and elsewhere remained in contact with Tibetan Buddhists; from the eleventh to the fourteenth century a number of Tantric texts were translated from Tibetan into Uighur.

The most famous Buddhist text in Uighur is the *Maitrisimit* (Skt., *Maitreya-samiti*). It was evidently quite popular, as indicated by the number of copies found in different places. It bears a colophon according to which a Sarvāstivādin called Prajñārakṣita translated it from Tocharian. A substantial amount of the Tocharian version is extant but most of it awaits publication. The Tocharians were a non-Turkic people speaking an Indo-European language, of which two dialects are attested. East Tocharian, or Tocharian A, is the dialect spoken mainly in Qarashahr; West Tocharian, or Tocharian B, is the dialect spoken mainly in Kuchā. East Tocharian is the better known dialect and it is in this that the *Maitrisimit* and the well-known *Puṇyavanta Jātaka* were written. However, much material written in West Tocharian remains unpublished. Most of the Tocharian Buddhist texts were translated from Sanskrit works of the Sarvāstivādins and date from the sixth to eighth century.

There are indications that Buddhism probably was present in Kuchā before the beginning of the common era. It was certainly well established by the time of the famous translator Kumārajīva (344–413). Kumārajīva was the son of an Indian father and a Kuchean mother. His mother, a younger sister of the king of Kuchā, became a Buddhist nun. Before the age of twenty, Kumārajīva turned from Hīnayāna to Mahāyāna. During his lifetime he translated numerous works, both Hīnayāna and Mahāyāna, into Chinese, but he is chiefly remembered in China for having introduced the Chinese to Mādhyamika philosophy. Owing to his influence, the

Mahāyāna was held in high esteem in Kuchā for some time. [*See the biography of Kumārajīva.*] However, an Indian monk called Dharmakṣema reported that at the beginning of the fifth century most of the population of Kuchā followed the Hīnayāna. Around 583 the king of Kuchā was an adherent of Mahāyāna, but in 630 Hsüan-tsang reported that most Kucheans followed the Hīnayāna teaching. According to the eighth-century Korean pilgrim Hui-ch'ao, the local population followed the Hīnayāna whereas the Chinese inhabitants were devotees of Mahāyāna. At the beginning of the fourth century a prince of Kuchā called Po Śrīmitra introduced to southern China the Kuchean art of melodic recitation of Buddhist texts.

From the brief review above it is clear that throughout the first millennium CE the whole of Central Asia was under strong Buddhist influence. Several centers of Buddhist learning emerged in Eastern Turkistan: Khotan, Turfan, Kocho, Tun-huang. Various peoples were converted to Buddhism: Iranian peoples, especially the Tumshuqese, Khotanese, and Sogdians; the Tocharians; Turkic peoples such as the Eastern Turks and the Uighurs; and the Chinese. Expatriate Indians took their religion with them, but it was the Sogdians and the Chinese who were especially active as missionaries. It is difficult to assess the contribution made by Central Asian Buddhists to the development of Buddhism. The Sogdians and the Tocharians appear to have confined themselves to translation of the scriptures and propagation of the religion. There is some evidence that the Khotanese and the Uighurs, like the Chinese, brought original ideas to bear upon the traditions they had adopted. Khotan may have played a role in the development of the Mahāyāna and of the later kinds of Tantric Buddhism, for the Tibetans came in contact with Khotanese Buddhism during their occupation of Khotan and Tun-huang.

[*See the maps accompanying* Missions, *article on* Buddhist Missions, *and* Chinese Religion, *overview article. See also* Inner Asian Religions.]

BIBLIOGRAPHY

The most detailed survey of Buddhism in Central Asia is provided by Lore Sander's article "Buddhist Literature in Central Asia," in the *Encyclopaedia of Buddhism,* edited by G. P. Malalasekera, vol. 4, fasc. 1 (Colombo, 1979). This article, however, contains many inaccuracies of detail and must be used with caution. The article by B. A. Litvinskii in the same volume, although entitled "Central Asia," deals with Buddhism in Soviet Central Asia and Afghanistan only. The same applies to his book *Outline History of Buddhism in Central Asia,* edited by G. M. Bongard-Levin (Moscow, 1968). *Buddhism in Afghanistan and Central Asia,* 2 vols., by Simone Gaulier, Robert Jera-Bezard, and Monique Maillard (Leiden, 1976), is a brief commentary on the artistic treasures as exemplified by 124 illustrations. Annemarie von Gabain's well-known article "Buddhistische Türkenmission," in *Asiatica: Festschrift Friedrich Weller* (Leipzig, 1954), pp. 160–173, is confined to the part played by the Turks. Her undocumented article "Der Buddhismus in Zentralasien," in *Religionsgeschichte des Orients in der Zeit der Weltreligionen* (Leiden, 1961), pp. 496–514, neglects the role played by the Iranian peoples. For this, see my chapter "Buddhism among Iranian Peoples," in *The Cambridge History of Iran,* edited by Ehsan Yarshater (Cambridge, 1983), pp. 949–964. Useful surveys of Buddhist literature in Central Asia are my *A Guide to the Literature of Khotan* (Tokyo, 1979); David A. Utz's *A Survey of Buddhist Sogdian Studies* (Tokyo, 1978); Wolfgang Scharlipp's "Kurzer Überblick über die buddhistische Literatur der Türken," *Materialia turcica* 6 (1980): 37–53; and Werner Thomas's "Die tocharische Literatur," in *Die Literaturen der Welt in ihrer mündlichen und schriftlichen Überlieferung,* edited by Wolfgang von Einsiedel (Zurich, 1964), pp. 967–973.

RONALD ERIC EMMERICK

Buddhism in Mongolia

Early Mongolian contacts with Buddhism are dated to the fourth century CE, when the activities of Chinese monks among the population of this border area are reported in contemporary Chinese sources. Buddhist influences spread as far as the Yenisei region by the seventh century, as evidenced by Buddhist temple bells with Chinese inscriptions found there. Another factor in the spread of Buddhism into Mongolia was the flourishing of Buddhist communities in the predominantly Uighur oasis-states along the Silk Route. Furthermore, the palace that was built by Ögedei Khan (r. 1229–1241) in Karakorum, the Mongol capital, was constructed on the foundations of a former Buddhist temple; some of the murals from this temple have been preserved. Sources for this early Buddhist activity are rather scarce.

Reports in Mongolian sources on the early spread of Buddhism shroud these missionary activities in a cloak of mysterious events that testify to the superiority of Tantric Buddhism over other religions during the reign of Khubilai Khan (r. 1260–1294). Contacts with the Saskya *paṇḍita* Kun-dga'-rgyal-mtshan (1182–1251) were established during Ögedei's reign, but Buddhism only gained influence with the Mongols after their expeditions into Tibet, which resulted in the sojourn of Tibetan monks as hostages at the Mongol court. The activities there of the lama (Tib., *bla ma*) 'Phags-pa (1235–1280) resulted in an increase in conversions to Buddhism; his invention, in 1269, of a block script led to the translation into Mongolian of great numbers of Buddhist religious literature, the translations often based on already existing Uighur translations. The legend that Chinggis Khan had previously invited the Sa-skya abbot Kun-dga'-sñiṅ-po (1092–1158) lacks proof.

In spite of the extensive translation and printing of Buddhist tracts, conversion seems to have been limited to the nobility and the ruling families. Judging from the Mongols' history of religious tolerance, it is rather doubtful that Buddhism spread among the general population on a large scale. Syncretic influences resulted in the transformation of popular gods into Buddhist deities and the acceptance of notions from other religions during this period.

After Mongol rule over China ended in 1368 the practice of Buddhism diminished among the Mongols, deteriorating into mere superstition or giving way once again to the indigenous religious conceptions of the Mongols and to shamanism. It was not until the sixteenth century that a second wave of Buddhist conversion began, brought about by the military expeditions of Altan Khan of the Tümet (1507–1583) into the eastern border districts of Tibet, which resulted in contacts with lamaist clerics. Within the short period of fifty years, beginning with the visit of the third Dalai Lama to Altan Khan's newly built residence, Köke Khota, in 1578, practically all of the Mongolian nobility was converted to Buddhism by the missionary work of many devoted lamaist priests. The most famous of these were Neyiči Toyin (1557–1653), who converted the eastern Mongols, and Zaya Paṇḍita, who converted the western and northern Mongols. Sustained by princes and overlords who acted according to the maxim "huius regio, eius religio," inducing the adoption of the new faith by donations of horses, dairy animals, and money, the population willingly or forcedly took to Lamaism. Shamanism was outlawed, its idols sought out and burned. The establishment of many new monasteries opened to a greater part of the population the opportunity to become monks, resulting in a drain on Mongolian manpower. The monasteries, however, became similar to those of early medieval Europe; they were the cradles of literature and science, particularly of Buddhist philosophy. By 1629 many other lamaist works were translated into Mongolian, including the 1,161 volumes of the lamaist canon, the Bka'-'gyur (Kanjur). Tibetan became the lingua franca of the clerics, as Latin was in medieval Europe, with hundreds of religious works written in this language.

During the Ch'ing dynasty in China, particularly during the K'ang-hsi, Yung-cheng, and Ch'ien-lung reign periods, the printing of Buddhist works in Mongolian was furthered by the Manchu emperors as well as by the Mongolian nobility. Donating money for copying scripture, cutting printing blocks, and printing Buddhist works were thought of as meritorious deeds. Works on medicine, philosophy, and history were also published and distributed. The spiritual life of Mongolia became strongly influenced by religious and semireligious thoughts and ethics. Sponsored by the K'ang-hsi emperor, a revised edition of the Mongolian Bka'-'gyur was printed from 1718 to 1720; translation of the Bstan-'gyur (Tanjur) was begun under the Ch'ien-lung emperor in 1741 and was completed in 1749. Copies of the completed edition (in 108 and 223 volumes, respectively, for the Bka'-'gyur and Bstan-'gyur) were given as imperial gifts to many monasteries throughout Mongolia.

In the eighteenth century elements of indigenous Mongolian mythology were incorporated into a national liturgy composed entirely in Mongolian. A century later there were about twelve hundred lamaist temples and monasteries in Inner Mongolia and more than seven hundred in the territory of the present-day Mongolian People's Republic. More than a third of the entire male population of Mongolia belonged to the clergy. The monasteries, possessing their own economic system and property, formed a separate administrative and political organization. In the twentieth century the decline of monasteries and Lamaism was brought about by inner strife and a changing moral climate as well as by political movements and new ideologies. Only recently have some monasteries been reopened in the Mongolian parts of China, in the Mongolian People's Republic, and in Buriat-Mongolia in the U.S.S.R., but the question of whether the younger members of the population will embrace the faith again remains open.

[*See also* Mongol Religions.]

BIBLIOGRAPHY

Heissig, Walther. *Die Pekinger lamaistischen Blockdrucke in mongolischer Sprache.* Wiesbaden, 1954.

Heissig, Walther. "Zur geistigen Leistung der neubekehrten Mongolen des späten 16. und frühen 17. Jahrhunderts." *Ural-Altaische Jahrbücher* 26 (1954): 101–116.

Heissig, Walther. *The Religions of Mongolia.* Translated by Geoffrey Samuel. Berkeley, 1980.

Ligeti, Lajos. *Catalogue du Kanjur mongol imprimé.* Budapest, 1942–1944.

Tucci, Giuseppe. *Tibetan Painted Scrolls.* 2 vols. Translated by Virginia Vacca. Rome, 1949.

Tucci, Giuseppe. *The Religions of Tibet.* Translated by Geoffrey Samuel. Berkeley, 1980.

WALTHER HEISSIG

Buddhism in Tibet

Buddhism in Tibet constitutes an immensely complex phenomenon. Its rich and subtle philosophy is combined with a highly developed depth psychology that involves advanced techniques such as visualization coupled with other transformative operations. It has developed a cosmology that in a certain sense is a joint enterprise of philosophy, psychology, and the arts and sciences, as well as religion. "Religion" in this context may be defined as a blend of a deeply moving inner experience and an evocative theory that attempts to communicate rationally and discursively what is experienced and felt holistically. As such, religion enters into an intimate relationship with society by catering to the aspirations and anxieties of individuals, and by regulating their relationships to each other. Indeed, Buddhism never lost sight of living man, who is held to construct within his mind, from all the information he receives, the various "worlds" with their welter of gods and other, primarily human, beings.

Tibetan Buddhism developed in the wake of Mahāyāna Buddhism, which was marked by a growing social awareness expressed by the guiding image of the *bodhisattva,* who stands in the service of mankind, as contrasted with the Hīnayāna guiding image of the *arhat,* who allegedly stands aloof from the rest of society. Since a *bodhisattva* is not necessarily a monk, but may come from any walk of life, the emphasis on his social character introduced a tension between this newer guiding image and that of the *arhat,* who could come only from the ranks of the monks, who had a privileged status in the early phase of Buddhism, and who tried to maintain that status even when social and economic conditions had changed. In Tibet this tension led to a proliferation of monastic establishments that struggled for political power. [*See also* Bodhisattva Path.]

From an intellectual and spiritual point of view, Mahāyāna Buddhism is represented by an epistemology-oriented approach to the human situation, codified in the Sūtras, and an experiential approach, codified in the Tantras. The Indian word *tantra* means, literally, "loom." In its expanded sense, the term may also refer to "living one's possibilities." These possibilities constitute the individual's indestructible core and value: the individual presents a value by virtue of his being, not because of some hypothetical *ātman* or "self." The indigenous Indian term for this indestructible core and value is *vajra.* This term, rich in connotations, is better left untranslated in order to avoid perpetuating the many past misconceptions about its meaning.

Initial Transmission. In addition to being its own "way," Buddhism has had a tendency to gather within it, if not take credit for, disparate folk customs and religious rituals by reinterpreting whatever it has absorbed. At the time that Buddhism arrived in Tibet (beginning in the eighth century CE) it found itself in a highly developed intellectual climate, one that later followers, once Buddhism had become firmly established, tended to belittle. Our picture of this early climate is obscured by two major factors. One is the fact that before Buddhism was officially recognized the dominant intellectual force was Bon, itself still a subject of considerable uncertainty due to lack of early sources. Besides adherents of Bon, called Bon-pos, there were storytellers *(sgruṅ)* and riddlemasters *(lde'u),* who represented the "religion of men" *(mi chos).* Buddhism claimed to have superseded both *mi chos* and Bon, the "religion of gods" *(lha'i chos).* That it could make this claim was due to the fact that the ground for its reception had already been prepared by Buddhist ideas that had come from Central Asia and China. The other factor that contributed to confusion was the notion that whatever had preceded the predominantly Indian version of Buddhism that reached Tibet was something uncivilized, primitive, and barbarous. In fact, the religious situation in Tibet at the time of the arrival of Buddhism was already far from primitive.

It is important to note that Buddhism was well received by the highly sophisticated world of governmental and educated people, but in order to become firmly established, it needed official patronage as well. Thus, almost from its very beginning in Tibet, Buddhism was involved in activities that today would be termed "political," including rivalries of families and clans as well as feuding between pro-China and pro-India factions. It was this involvement in politics that eventually led to Tibet's status as an ecclesiastical state operating on two levels, that of the central government and that of the more or less independent local states. Every lay official had his monastic counterpart. Underlying this division is the age-old problem of the One and the Many, which in the Tibetan context has been solved through the concept of incarnate beings. Through the symbol of Avalokiteśvara, mankind is seen as One (i.e., mankind's spiritual unity); through the symbol of incarnate beings, mankind is seen as the Many (i.e., mankind's physical plurality). Each Dalai Lama is considered to be the reincarnation of his historical, physical predecessor; similarly, the hierarchs of the various schools of Tibetan Buddhism are held to be reincarnations of their predecessors.

The whole history of Buddhism in Tibet reflects the complementarity of two structural movements, one of which takes precedence over, but does not exclude, the other. These two movements are a prereflective-nonthematic, nonobjectifying (and hence also nonsubjectifying), "mystical" thinking and a reflective-thematic, objectifying (and hence also subjectifying), representational, "rational" thinking. Mystical thinking attempts to keep the immediacy of experience alive and perhaps to recapture it by reaching out and merging with the universe (a movement that—if it happens—happens all at once); rational thinking stands outside of experience, as it were, analyzes it, makes distinctions, catalogs what has taken place, and argues about it endlessly.

Historical events related to the official recognition of Buddhism bear out this underlying complementarity. Mes-ag-tshom, the father of King Khri-sroṅ-lde-btsan (756–797?), showed an interest in Buddhism even at this early date and sent emissaries to India to invite some monks who were engaged in mystical contemplation inthe Źaṅ-źuṅ area. They, however, merely sent him some texts in reply. Because of the anti-Buddhist feeling in court circles the king surreptitiously sent a certain Saṅ-śi of the Sba (alt., Rba) clan to China to procure additional Buddhist texts. On his return Saṅ-śi had to go into hiding, because the old king had died while his son and heir was still a minor, and the various calamities that subsequently befell the court were ascribed to the interest in Buddhism. When on attaining majority, Khri-sroṅ-lde-btsan took charge, he renewed, with due caution, his father's interest in Buddhism. The young king sent Gsal-snaṅ of Sba, who later was ordained as a monk under the name Ye-śes-dbaṅ-po, to India and Nepal with an invitation for the Indian *paṇḍita* Śāntirakṣita. However, the *paṇḍita* had to leave Tibet almost as soon as he arrived because of internal turmoil. It was only after the anti-Buddhist party was ousted by exiling its followers and assassinating its leader, Ma-źaṅ Khrom-pa-skyes, that Śāntirakṣita was able to return to Tibet.

Śāntarakṣita had no success in Tibet. As a follower of the Yogācāra-Svātantrika-Mādhyamika school of Indian Buddhism, he emphasized rational thought and its accompanying tendency to argue for argumentation's sake. [*See the biography of Śāntirakṣita.*] Realizing his limitations, the *paṇḍita* advised the king to invite the monk Padmasambhava, about whose life no available sources agree (except about the fact that he had to leave Tibet under threat) and whose birthplace, Uḍḍiyāna, has not yet been satisfactorily located. Padmasambhava seems to have been capable of thinking both mystically and rationally by starting from a common experiential source and thereby avoiding the "nothing-but" fallacy that dictates a choice between mysticism and rationality. Relating his teaching to praxis-oriented experience, Padmasambhava was not content with mere abstractions or purely perceptual analysis. To label this figure an exorcist, as some scholars have done, is to misunderstand what mysticism means and to confuse it with occultism. In fact, it was through Padmasambhava that a link could be forged with those "mystical"—but non-Buddhist—elements in Tibetan civilization that have given Tibetan Buddhism its distinct flavor. [*See also the biography of Padmasambhava.*] This holds true especially for the Rdzogs-chen teaching to which both Bon and Buddhism lay claim. This school regards as one of its patrons Myaṅ Tiṅ-ne-'dzin, who led the revolt against Ye-śes-dbaṅ-po and replaced him by Dpal-dyaṅs, a prominent member of the mystical tradition with links to Ch'an Buddhism (Hwa-śaṅ Mahāyāna). Myaṅ Tiṅ-ne-'dzin was also chosen by the then ruling king as the guardian of the throne's heir, Khri-lde-sroṅ-btsan. Nevertheless, Ye-śes-dbaṅ-po fought back by inviting Kamalaśīla, another representative of the "rationalist" (Yogācāra-Svātantrika) trend in Buddism. [*See the biography of Kamalaśīla.*] The outcome of the alleged debate of Bsam-yas, according to late and hence not very trustworthy Tibetan sources, marked the ascendence of the purely Indian rationalist and monastic trend. In the political bickering between rationalism-only and/or mysticism-only, their complementarity was overlooked, and the rift grew ever wider. Furthermore, while mysticism emphasized the immediacy of experience as being copresent with and pervading all particular experiences, rationalism insisted on a gradual passage from one spiritual state to another, which requires for its success that the person or community involved in this process be supported by donations.

Persecution and Revival. The ensuing establishment of monastic centers soon gave rise to self-governing economic units active in business transactions and even in trade. The monasteries, having gradually acquired large estates that had been bequeathed to them by wealthy families, became powerful landowners themselves, and smaller landowners, unable to hold out against them, eventually became their tenants. Since the monasteries were tax-exempt, the state was deprived of considerable resources in both manpower and revenue. As the monastic centers grew in economic power, they became increasingly arrogant and demanded more and more privileges. These were the main reasons for the persecution of Buddhism by Glaṅ-dar-ma (838–842).

The persecution deprived Buddhism not only of its court patronage, but also of all its property. However, on the political front, the assassination in 842 or 846 of Glaṅ-dar-ma by a monk, Dpal-gyi-rdo-rje of Lha-luṅ, did not save Tibet from political fragmentation. (After this deed Dpal-gyi-rdo-rje fled to the area of Hsünhwa, in Amdo, where he is said to have been indirectly instrumental in reviving monastic ordination.) Chinese frontier towns such as Tun-huang and Sha-chou, which had been occupied for some time by the Tibetans, were lost; the minister in command was beheaded (866) and his army scattered into splinter groups along the borderlands, where they formed the nucleus of evolving communities. Shortly thereafter the Tibetans were expelled from Turkistan by the Uighurs and Karluk Türk. On the spiritual-intellectual side the sobering influence of the monasteries and religious communities was no longer felt.

After Glaṅ-dar-ma's assassination his two sons, Yum-brtan (by his first wife, or at least brought up by her, as he is said to have been kidnapped from another woman) and 'Od-sruṅ (by his second wife), ruled separately over parts of Tibet. 'Od-sruṅ's son, Dpal-'khor-btsan, is said to have been a pious Buddhist who was slain by his subjects. Dpal-'khor-btsan's two sons took western Gtsaṅ, which once had been part of the central kingdom, and the three lands of Mṅa'-ris: Mar-yul (which lasted as a Buddhist kingdom until about 1100), Spu-hraṅ(s), and Źaṅ-źuṅ or Gu-ge, respectively. The son and grandson of Dpal-'khor-btsan's first son founded local principalities at Guṅ-thaṅ, as well as in Ñaṅ/Myaṅ, at Tsoṅ-kha in Amdo, and in Yar-kluṅ. Thus, in these areas Buddhism continued and was eventually revitalized, at first in the eastern part of what had been Tibet. (Accounts found in Tibetan chronicles are open to doubt, since their authors had a vested interest in validating their claims to the continuity of the lineage to which they belonged.)

What is of interest in the process of this revival of Buddhism in the east is the fact that the connection with Chinese or non-Indian Buddhism was retained. The story goes that during the period of persecution three Buddhist monks, Rab-gsal of Gtsaṅ, G.yo-dge-'byuṅ of Bo-doṅ, and Dmar Śākyamuni of Stod-luṅ, set out via Ladakh and the region held by the Karluk Türk to the west, passed through the region held by the Uighurs, and ended up in Amdo. An ex-Bon-po who lived there, Dge-rab-gsal of the Mu-zi (Mu-zu) clan (822–915? or 892–975?) from Tsoṅ-kha, had been converted to Buddhism, which in its Rdzogs-chen form seems to have flourished in this area due to the presence of Vairocana, a follower of Padmasambhava, who had been banished during the reign of Khri-sroṅ-lde-btsan. Impressed by the conduct of the three monks, Dge-rab-gsal wanted to be ordained as a monk also. Since ordination requires the presence of five ordained monks, two Hwa-shaṅ monks were added to make up the quorum. In this connection it should be noted that the pro-India Tibetan Buddhists, in their hostility against anything non-Indian, have consistently failed to distinguish between Hwa-śaṅ, probably a Chinese Taoist, and Hwa-śaṅ Mahāyāna, a Chinese Buddhist.

The account of the arrival of Buddhism in the central part of Tibet is modeled after the events that had taken place in the eastern part and, for this reason alone, is highly suspicious. During the ninth and tenth centuries, events of tremendous importance for the subsequent history of Buddhism in Tibet took place in the western part of the land through the efforts of the kings of Mṅa'-ris. King 'Khor-re abdicated in favor of his younger brother Sroṅ-ṅe, and took the robe under the name (Lha Bla-ma) Ye-śes-'od. He sent several young men to study the monastic tradition in Kashmir. Kashmir at that time retained the last splendors of Buddhism (which had practically disappeared from India). Here both the mystical and the rational approaches to the Buddhist teaching were still flourishing. "Rational" here refers to the Sarvāstivāda, Sautrāntika, Mādhyamika, and Yogācāra schools of Buddhism, all of which were classified by the Tibetans as *rgyu-mtshan,* that is, epistemology-oriented, or what may be typified as "causality." "Mystical," on the other hand, refers to the *rgyud* (Skt., *tantra*) or experience-oriented "existential" approach.

When the young men returned to their homeland at the end of their studies, they brought with them a number of teachers and artists. This rekindled interest in Buddhism quickly spread to the central parts of Tibet, and soon a continual stream of pilgrims passed between Tibet and India.

Two figures dominated the western Tibetan scene during this time, the Tibetan Rin-chen-bzaṅ-po (958-1055), one of the young men sent to India by Ye-śes-'od, and Atīśa Dīpaṃkara Śrījñāna (982–1054), described as the son of the king of Zahor and said to be well versed in all aspects of Buddhism. Atīśa Dīpaṃkara Śrījñāna was invited to Gu-ge by Byaṅ-chub-'od, nephew or grandnephew of Ye-śes-'od, and he arrived there in 1042. [*See also the biography of Atīśa.*]

Rin-chen-bzaṅ-po was active in the erection of numerous chapels. (Tradition puts the number at 108, but it must be noted that 108 recurs frequently as one of the sacred numbers in Indian religious thought.) The largest temple founded by him in western Tibet is Mtho-liṅ, famous for its frescoes. It is likely that he founded Tabo and Nako in Spiti. He also was active in the translation of Buddhist texts from India. (These translations included original texts as well as revisions of already translated texts.) A total of 158 of these texts were included in the large collections of the Bka'-'gyur (Kanjur; the texts claimed to have been "spoken" by the Buddha) and the Bstan-'gyur (Tanjur; treatises by Indian scholars analyzing and commenting on the "Buddha word"). Rin-chen bzaṅ-po marks the dividing line between the "new " tradition and the "old" tradition, a division relating to the texts of a mystical nature. This division, applicable only to Tibet, has distinctly political (i.e., pro-Indian) overtones, and seems to have been made arbitrarily on the basis of whether or not "older" texts were available in an Indian (either Sanskrit or Prakrit) version. Texts that were said to have been translated from an extinct Indian source were simply excluded and branded as "spurious" or "incorrect."

Atīśa found Buddhism in the process of renewal as he traveled to the heartland of Tibet. At Sñe-thaṅ, a few kilometers from Lhasa, he came into contact with a group of monks from Khams who became his disciples. One of its leading members was 'Brom-ston Rgyal-ba'i-'byuṅ-gnas (1008–1064), a native of Dbus, who had brought back the monastic discipline from Khams; there the spiritual lineage of Padmasambhava had been kept alive through Vairocana, among whose disciples was the daughter of the king of that region. Vairocana's specific Rdzogs-chen teaching was transmitted to a former Bon-po Ya-zi Bon-ston, who also had been taught by an ascetic (A-ro Ye-śes-'byuṅ-gnas), who continued both the Indian and Chinese traditions. This ascetic was established at Ldan Gloṅ (Kloṅ-thaṅ), where a monk from Nepal, Smṛti by name, had founded a school for the study of the *Abhidharmakośa*. Smṛti had been a teacher of 'Brom-ston before he moved to Liangchow. A-ro Ye-śes-'byuṅ-gnas taught Roṅ-zom Chos-kyi-bzaṅ-po the Rdzogs-chen teaching according to the Khams tradition. One of Roṅ-zom Chos-kyi-bzaṅ-po's works is *Theg pa chen po'i tshul la 'jug pa'i sgo* (The Gate to enter the Practice of Mahāyāna), a profound Rdzogs-chen treatise that was highly praised by Atīśa, who had met Roṅ-zom during his travels.

The Bka'-gdams-pa Order. Atīśa himself wrote a small work, *Bodhipathapradīpa* (The Lamp on the Road to Enlightenment), which became very influential. It is related that when 'Brom-ston asked Atīśa whether the texts (*bka'*, "Buddha word," and *bstan bcos*, exegetic works by Indian scholars) or one's teacher's instruction were of greater importance, Atīśa replied that the teacher's instructions were more important, since such directness would guarantee a correct understanding of the concealed intention to which the disciple was committed or had an obiligation *(gdams)*. In fact, the importance of the teacher or lama (Tib., *bla ma*) in his direct contact with the disciple gave Tibetan Buddhism its often used epithet Lamaism. In this personal relationship the function of the teacher was to become increasingly indispensable and unquestionable; in a certain sense, the teacher was considered to be the living presence of Buddhahood. The mediator of Buddhahood was known as a "spiritual friend," and many of Atīśa's followers, who formed the first indigenous school of Buddhism in Tibet, the Bka'-gdams-pa, were considered to belong to this category. Addressing the laity, they aimed at cleansing their listeners' minds of preconceived notions by the use of illustrative stories. The whole approach, however, remained predominantly rational; even the mystical aspect, although not totally rejected, was given an intellectualist twist. This may be the reason why Atīśa's teaching had no wide appeal. His favorite disciple, 'Brom-ston, avoided every kind of publicity, even refusing to give instruction, and after founding the monastery of Rwa-sgreṅ in 1059 lived in his cell in utter seclusion until his death.

While the teacher-disciple relationship was strictly personal, on the communal level there was a close reciprocal connection between the lay world and the religious community within it. The religious community provided the laity with spiritual sustenance and was, in turn, materially supported by the laity; this led not only to rivalries among orders but also to their political and economic expansion. Furthermore, the resultant reestablishment of monasteries began to serve a double function. First, they became centers of learning, and thus contributed to the general high standard of cultural life; second, they also became receiving centers for surplus population, and thus contributed to a fairly high level of economic existence by avoiding parcellation of arable land into unproductive lots. Nevertheless, the monks' rational approach to the problems of human existence, together with such injunctions as those imposed upon members of the Bka'-gdams-pa order—abstention from marriage, intoxicants, travel, and the possession of money—had little impact, above all because this approach left out a vital component of man's complex nature: the mystical, emotionally moving, and spiritually satisfying side. Most prominent among those who sought to fill the vacuum were 'Brog-mi (992–1072) and Mar-pa (Marpa, 1012–1096).

The Sa-skya-pa Order. 'Brog-mi, with financial assistance from the local rulers of western Tibet, had set out for India and Nepal. Having studied Sanskrit extensively in Nepal, he then pursued his studies at Vikramaśīla under the guidance of the *mahāsiddha* ("accomplished master") Śānti-pa, who had written a commentary on the *Hevajra Tantra*. This text explains the experiential character of spiritual growth, expressed in the symbols and images of femininity. However, 'Brog-mi received most of his teaching in Tibet from an Indian master after paying him a considerable sum of money. 'Brog-mi later translated the *Hevajra Tantra* into Tibetan, and it became one of the basic texts of the Sa-skya-pa order. This order is named after the place where one of 'Brog-mi's disciples, Dkon-mchog Rgyal-po of the 'Khon family, founded a monastery in 1073. The monastery lies on the trade route linking the Nepal valley with the rich agricultural area around Shigatse, with further extensions into the nomad lands that supply the order with butter and wool. Thus trade and natural resources contributed to the growing wealth of the areas dominated by the Sa-skya-pa. Dkon-mchog Rgyal-po's son and successor, the great Sa-skya Kun-dga'-sñiṅ-po (1092–1158), formulated the tenets of this school, which became known as Lam-'bras ("the path and its fruition"), and ultimately can be traced back to another Indian *mahāsiddha*, Virūpa.

Supported by wealthy landowners and using his own organizational capacity Kun-dga'-sñiṅ-po laid the foundation for the greatness of the Sa-skya-pas. Eventually they were granted sovereignty over Tibet by Khubilai Khan of the Yüan dynasty (the Mongol rulers of China), through the good office of 'Phags-pa (1235–1280?). Apart from their involvement in political struggles, the scholars of the Sa-skya-pa order were most active in the fields of philosophy and linguistics. Thus Bsod-nams-rtse-mo (1142–1182) worked on the systematization of Tantric literature; Grags-pa-rgyal-mtshan (1147–1216) was the author of the first history of the early development of Buddhism in Tibet, but also wrote on medicine. Sa-skya *paṇḍita* Kun-dga'-rgyal-mtshan (1182–1251) wrote on grammar, poetics, and logic. His monumental work, the famous *Tshad ma rigs pa'i gter,* is a distinct development of Buddhist logic beyond Dharmakīrti's *Pramāṇavārttika,* from which it starts. Finally, 'Phags-pa, a prolific writer on every conceivable topic in Buddhism, not only wrote stylistically elegant letters to the Mongol princes, but also devised for the Mongolian language a script that goes by his name. A truly independent thinker in this order was Roṅ-ston Smra-ba'i-seṅ-ge (1367–1449), author of sixty-four exegetic and instructional works. He came from a Bon-po family.

The scholar and artist Bu-ston (1290–1364) was not strictly a Sa-skya-pa but a follower of the Źwa-lu-pas (so named after the monastery of Źwa-lu in Gtsaṅ which had been founded in 1040 by Lce). Bu-ston (1290–1364), who hardly differed in outlook from the Sa-skya-pas, undertook the immense task of revising and arranging the vast literature contained in the Bka'-'gyur and Bstan-'gyur. His prejudice against the works of the "older" order (Rñiṅ-ma-pa)—only out of deference to one of his teachers did he include a few such works—is at the root of the growing hostility in later times against the Rñiṅ-ma-pas, particularly on the part of the Dge-lugs-pas. [*See also the biography of Bu-ston.*]

The Bka'-brgyud and Karma-pa Orders. Mar-pa, whose real name was Chos-kyi-blo-gros of Mar, was born in the fertile district of Lha-brag in southern Tibet of very wealthy parents. Since he had a violent temper, his parents sent him to 'Brog-mi. For twelve years he studied under the guidance of Nā-ro-pa (Naḍapāda) whose "Six Principles" he brought back to Tibet. Mar-pa's most important student was Mi-la-ras-pa (Milarepa, 1040–1123), who continued the ascetic tradition of India, which by that time had succumbed to physically oriented techniques. He is mostly known for his beautiful and moving songs (*mgur*) modeled after the *dohās* in which Indian *mahāsiddhas* expressed their peak experiences. The order thus initiated became known as the *Bka'-brgyud* ("continuity of the Buddha word"); its teaching centers on the *mahāmudrā* ("great seal") experience. It highlights the principle of complementarity, whose realization is aimed at by the synthesis of the multiple "phenomenal" *(snaṅ-ba)* and the unitary "nothing" *(stoṅ pa).* As contrasted with the pure, mystical teaching of the Rdzogs-chen tradition, the *mahāmudrā* teaching has slightly rational overtones. [*See the biographies of Mar-pa, Nā-ro-pa, and Mi-la-ras-pa.*]

Mi-la-ras-pa's most important disciple was Sgam-po-pa (1079–1153), whose influence was far-reaching. He was born of a noble family and first studied medicine, but was drawn more and more to the contemplative arts. At Dwags-po he founded a monastery, where he actively guided the most learned men of his time. He is the first to have written a guide to the "stages on the path" *(lam rim),* which found countless imitations. One of his three greatest immediate disciples and successors, Phag-mo-gru (1110–1170), spent his life in a simple grass hut that was enshrined in the great and wealthy monastery of Gdan-sa-mthil that developed after his death due to the support of the noble family of Klaṅs, which then provided the religious head of the monastery and the chief lay administrative officer. The monastery remained a family affair, however, and despite its influence failed to establish a definite line of thought. A disciple of Phag-mo-gru, Mi-ñag Sgom-rin (fl. c. twelfth century), set up 'Bri-guṅ monastery, but its real foundation was the work of 'Jig-rten-mgon-po, also known as 'Bri-guṅ Rin-po-che (1143–1212), a monk from 'Dan, in 1179. It soon rose to fame and power and came into conflict with the Sa-skya-pas. Dus-gsum-mkhyen-pa (1110–1193), a native of Khams and second of Sgam-po-pa's three most important disciples, founded in 1147 the Karma Gdan-sa Monastery and (among other monasteries) in 1185 the monastery of Mtshur-phu, the modern seat of the Karma-pas. These lamas spent most of their time traveling from one monastery to another; having no wealthy patrons, they were supported by landed and nomad families. They derive their name from a black hat symbolizing the totality of all Buddha activities *(phrin-las;* Skt., *karman).* The representatives of this order reign to this day as the "Black Hat" lineage.

A related line, known as the "Red Hats," originated with Grags-pa-seṅ-ge (1283–1345). Sgom-pa (1116–1169), the third eminent disciple of Sgam-po-pa, established another school through his disciple Lama Źaṅ (1123–1193) at Guṅ-thaṅ, near Lhasa, in the district of Mtshal. The name *Mtshal* was applied to the school as well as to the family supporting the school. The family became active in politics, and one of its members negotiated the Tibetan submission to Chinggis Khan. Among the many other "sub-orders" the 'Brug-pa and the Śaṅs-pa must be mentioned. The former order, founded by Gliṅ-ras-pa Padma-rdo-rje (1128–1188), derived its name from the monastery at 'Brug in Dbus. This order became most active in Bhutan and the western Himalayas. Padma-dkar-po (1526–1592) was one of its outstanding scholars; his *Phyag chen gan mdzod* is a mine of information. The Śaṅs-pa order traces its origin to Khyuṅ-po-rnal-'byor, a Bon-po who converted to Buddhism; he received his teaching from many Indian scholars, but particularly from Ni-gu-ma, the wife (sister?) of Nā-ro-pa. Its main instructions passed through the Jo-naṅ-pa order, which was made famous by Śes-rab-rgyal-mtshan (1296–1361) and counted among its followers and sympathizers such illustrious figures as 'Ba-ra-ba Rgyal-mtshan-dpal-bzaṅ (1310–1391); Thaṅ-stoṅ-rgyal-po (1385–1464), noted for his construction of iron chain bridges and who became the patron saint of the theater under the nickname "the Madman of the Empty Valley"; and the historian Tāranātha (b. 1575). Its distinctive philosophical position, partly based on the syncretistic *Kālacakra Tantra,* became the target of Dge-lugs-pa intolerance. The Dge-lugs-pa ruthlessly destroyed or converted the Jo-naṅ-pa monasteries into Dge-lugs-pa monasteries and even burned the books of the Jo-naṅ-pa school.

Two other ascetic orders that originated in the philosophical and religious ferment of the eleventh and twelfth centuries were the Źi-byed ("pacifiers of suffering"), founded by a South Indian ascetic, and the Gcod ("cutting through the affective processes"), founded by Ma-gcig Lab-kyi-sgron-ma (1055–1145), a remarkable woman disciple of Pha-dam-pa. The order, which later divided into two lines, the "male" Gcod and "female" Gcod, still has followers in the western Himalayas.

The Dge-lugs-pa Order. This intellectual activity, which emphasized its Indian source of inspiration, lost its spiritual force and died away in the face of political power struggles between monasteries, feuds between noble houses, and growing Mongol and Chinese expansionism. Thus, the Karma-pas were eclipsed by the Sa-skya-pas, and these, in turn, by the Dge-lugs-pas who, through the intervention of Gu-śri Khan were given, in the person of the Fifth Dalai Lama, Ṅag-dbaṅ-blo-bzaṅ-rgya-mtsho (1617–1682), the authority to reign over all Tibet, although he had to accept a "governor" imposed upon him by his Mongol patron.

The Dge-lugs-pas consider Tsoṅ-kha-pa Blo-bzaṅ-grags-pa (1357–1419) to be the founder of their movement, which gained prominence through the determination of his ambitious and power-hungry disciples. Tsoṅ-kha-pa was the son of an official in the Kokonor region and in his youth studied under the most famous lamas of his time, but a lasting influence was exerted on him by the Sa-skya lama Red-mda'-pa, who had been a disciple of Roṅ-ston Smra-ba'i-seṅ-ge, and the Bka'-gdams-pa lama Dbu-ma-pa, who made him familiar with the teaching of Atīśa. At the age of forty he joined the Bka'-gdams-pa monastery of Rwa-sgreṅ, where he is said to have had a vision of Atīśa.

Tsoṅ-kha-pa earned his fame because of personal integrity. He was not an independent thinker; his noted *Lam rim chen mo* (The Great Exposition of the Stages on the Path), expatiating on Atīśa's *Bodhipathapradīpa,* is basically a voluminous collection of quotations from Indian texts that are either still extant in their original Sanskrit or long lost. Similarly, his *Sṅags rim chen mo,* purporting to deal with the mystical aspect of Buddhism, emphasizes a meticulous enumeration and description of ritualistic implements. Passed on to his followers, his doctrine was transformed into dogmatism with strong political overtones. A remarkable exception is the fifth Dalai Lam, whose wide-ranging interest included a personal concern for Rñiṅ-ma-pa forms of meditation; for this reason the Rñiṅ-ma-pas escaped persecution during his time. In 1408 Tsoṅ-kha-pa instituted the Smon-lam Chen-mo (the annual New Year ceremony of the Great Prayer), at teh Jo-khaṅ temple in Lhasa, thought to have been built by Sroṅ-btsan-sgam-po. One year later he founded his own monastery of Ri-bo Dga'-ldan where he taught and wrote and supervised the fledgling community according to strict monastic rules. His two chief disciples founded two other monasteries that were to become famous, 'Bras-spuṅs in 1416 and Se-ra in 1419. However, it was Tsoṅ-kha-pa's own circumscribed interests that set the tone and the political direction of the Dge-lugs-pa movement, which from the outset came into conflict with the orders already established, in many cases themselves torn by inner strife. The political preoccupation of the Dge-lugs-pas climaxed in the succession of the various Dalai Lamas by means of reincarnation, an idea first developed by the 'Bri-guṅ-pas and Sa-skya-pas. Despite the mystique that surrounds this notion, as a device for preventing the wealth and power of a family or monastery from passing into the hands of others it was essentially too lucrative to be passed up by any one order—even by the Rñiṅ-ma-pas, who had no political pretensions. Another aspect of this notion was that the declaration that the most gifted were "reincarnations" naturally enhanced the intellectual standard of the establishment to which they were attached. On the whole, this ingenious device worked very well. [*See also the biography of Tsoṅ-kha-pa.*]

The Rñiṅ-ma-pa Order. As already noted, the most remarkable figure in the Rñiṅ-ma tradition is Padmasambhava, who is credited with having written the first *lam rim* text, the *Gsaṅ sṅags lam gyi rim pa rin po che gsal ba'i sgron me,* an explanation of the experiential character of Buddhism. This little work belongs to the group of works that Padmasambhava is said to have hidden in order that they might be rediscovered at propitious times. This kind of literature is known as *gter ma* ("hidden treasures"). Many of these works are certainly apocryphal, but many others are adaptations of genuine documents; examples of this latter category are the *Bka' thaṅ lde lṅa* and the *Padma thaṅ-yig,* which, though it was constantly rewritten, contains the testament of Khri-sroṅ-lde-btsan. It should be noted that the term *gter ma* does not merely refer to texts concealed in caves or under rocks, but also to what a person might bring out of the hidden recesses of his mind and thus to what can be described as contributing to the development of thought and innovative ideas. Such "discoveries" began at a very early stage, with Saṅs-rgyas-bla-ma (c. 1000–1080), the first 'discoverer' *(gter ston).* Other notable "discoverers" were Ñaṅ-ral Ñi-ma-'od-zer (1124–1192), ruler of Ñaṅ; Guru Chos-kyi-dbaṅ-phyug (1212–1270 or 1273) and his wife Jo-mo Sman-mo (1248–1283); O-rgyan Gliṅ-pa (1323–c. 1360), and Ratna Gliṅ-pa (1403–1479), collector and compiler of the *Rñiṅ ma rgyud 'bum,* which Bu-ston had excluded from his codification of the Bka'-'gyur and Bstan-'gyur. In this connection, Dṅos-grub-rgyal-mtshan, also known as Rig-'dzin Rgod-kyi-ldem-'phru-can (1337–1408), a representative of the northern *gter ma* tradition, must be mentioned; the southern tradition is linked with Lo-chen Dharma-śrī (1654–1717), younger brother of Gter-bdag Gliṅ-pa (1646–1714) of the monastery of Smin-grol-gliṅ, which was supported by the fifth Dalai Lama. This monastery and the monastery of Rdo-rje-brag, the seat of the northern tradition, were both destroyed during the Dzungar revolt of 1717–1718 in which Lo-chen Dharma-śrī was murdered.

As I have mentioned above, Roṅ-zom Chos-kyi-bzaṅ-po represents the Rdzogs-chen line of thought. But the most outstanding representative is Kloṅ-chen Rab-'byams-pa (1308–1363/64). To this day Kloṅ-chen has remained a lone figure, unmatched in the lucidity of his presentation, a poet in his own right, who for all his erudition is never pedantic but always thought-provoking. His *Mdzod bdun* (Seven Treasures) and *Skor gsum gsum* (Three Sets with Three Members Each) are indispensable for the understanding of Rdzogs-chen thought and practice, and his *Sñiṅ thig ya bzhi,* a summary of Vimalamitra's teaching, is the very quintessence of Rdzogs-chen experience. It is not too much to say that Kloṅ-chen Rab-'byams-pa *is* Rñiṅ-ma and Rdzogs-chen philosophy. Since Rñiṅ-ma thought is essentially a process philosophy and religion in which experience is of utmost importance, it frequently came under attack by the various structure-oriented schools with their reductionist tendencies of accepting as authentic only that which came from India. Among those who countered these attacks, at least three authors stand out prominently. The first, 'Gos-lo-tsā-ba Gźon-nu-dpal (1392–1481), wrote the *Deb ther sṅoṅ po* (Blue Annals), a masterpiece of historical writing and a critique of Bu-ston (who, as I have noted, was responsible for the exclusion of the Rñiṅ-ma *tantras* from the canonical collection of Buddhist writings). Also important is Mṅa'-ris Paṇ-chen Padma-dbaṅ-rgyal (1487–1542), whose *Sdom gsum rnam ṅes* (The Definitive Gradation of the Three Statuses) is in its psychological insight far superior to Sa-skya Paṇḍita's *Sdom gsum rab dbye,* an attack on the *Dgoṅs gcig* theory propounded by Dbon-po Śes-rab-'byuṅ-gnas (1187–1241), a nephew of the 'Bri-guṅ-pa master 'Jig-rten-mgon-po. The third major defendant of Rñiṅ-ma thought is Sog-zlog-pa Blo-gros-rgyal-mtshan ("repeller of the Mongols"; 1552–1624), who is supposed to have defended his area at one time against a Mongol invasion force (hence the epithet Sog-zlog-pa). He was most famous as a physician and for having written a history of Buddhism. The seventeenth century witnessed the foundation of five of the six greatest Rñiṅ-ma monasteries, Rdo-rje-brag (1610), Ka'-thog (1656), Dpal-yul (1665), Smin-grol-gliṅ (1676), and Rdzogs-chen (1685). Each played a significant role in the development of Rñiṅ-ma thought.

The Modern Era. Among the intellectual giants of the eighteenth century, Ka'-thog Rig-'dzin Tshe-dbaṅ-nor-bu (1698–1755) must be mentioned. He was not content with merely repeating what secondary sources claimed to be authoritative, but attempted to go back to the original sources, often reaching startling conclusions. His main interests were history and geography. No less important is 'Jigs-med-gliṅ-pa (1730–1798) whose major contributions are the *Kloṅ chen sñiṅ thig* practices, which he developed after having had a vision of Kloṅ-chen Rab-'byams-pa. Despite his wide interests, profoundness of thought, and remarkable scholarship, 'Jigs-med-gliṅ-pa never attained the brilliant organization and beauty of style that mark the writings of his model, Kloṅ-chen Rab-'byams-pa. Another important figure of this period was Gźan-phan-mtha'-yas (b. 1740), who stressed the importance of monastic rules (which he considered indispensable for education) and held that monks had an obligation to society. In this sense he was the first social reformer in Tibet.

The sense of a newly awakened social conscience in the spirit of Gźan-phan-mtha'-yas, together with the essence of *Kloṅ chen sñiṅ thig* teachings and practices, define the character of Rdza-sprul O-rgyan 'Jigs-med-chos-kyi-dbaṅ-po (b. 1808), better known to Tibetan tradition as Rdza Dpal-sprul or, as he liked to call himself, A-bu-hral-po ("the tattered old man"), who spent most of his life among the nomads. He specialized in the *Bodhicaryāvatāra,* a text that had always been a favorite with the Rñiṅ-ma-pas; their interpretation of the ninth chapter had aroused the ire of the Dge-lugs-pas, who in turn lost no opportunity to attack and vilify the Rñiṅ-ma scholars. Rdza Dpal-sprul's most significant contribution is his *Kun bzaṅ bla ma'i zhal luṅ,* a unique rational-mystical blend designed to introduce the profound *Rdzogs chen* teachings to a simple audience. Here one sees the new trend in education, whereby the teacher selected a number of Indian texts in their Tibetan translation and then helped the student to fully comprehend the texts in all their implications. This reorientation, as well as the inherent attempt to rise above sectarianism, became known as the Ris-med movement. It originated in eastern Tibet at Sde-dge, perhaps brought about in part by events surrounding the tragedy that befell the royal house of Sde-dge.

The fame of 'Jigs-med-gliṅ-pa had reached the ears of the young queen of Sde-dge. When she met him, a deep faith in him was born in her. 'Jigs-med-gliṅ-pa and his disciple Rdo-ba-grub-chen rapidly became the most influential teachers at Sde-dge. The honors bestowed on these Rñiṅ-ma-pa followers aroused the jealousy of the Ngor-pa lamas and their patrons among the aristocracy. When in 1790 the young king of Sde-dge, Sa-dbang-bzaṅ-po (alias Kun-'grub Bde-dge'-bzaṅ-po) died at the age of twenty-two while on a pilgrimage, he left a son and daughter behind. Their mother, Tshe-dbaṅ-lha-mo of the Sga-rje family, became regent for her infant son. This princess was regarded as a reincarnation of Ngaṅ-tshul-byang-chub, the queen of Khri-sroṅ-lde'u-btsan and disciple of Padmasambhava. Her patronage of 'Jigs-med-gliṅ-pa and Rdo-ba-grub-chen led in 1798 to a rebellion in which the Rñiṅ-ma-pa faction was defeated. The queen and Rdo-ba-grub-chen, accused of having been the queen's lover, were first imprisoned and later exiled. A number of Rñiṅ-ma-pa partisans were executed or forced to flee. The twelve-year-old prince became the nominal ruler of Sde-dge and was placed under the tutelage of lamas who were hostile to the Rñiṅ-ma-pas. When he had secured his succession to the throne, he renounced the world to become a monk. While he restated the time-honored special relationship that existed between the ruling house of Sde-dge and the Sa-skya-pa school, he insisted that a commitment to tolerance and patronage of all schools should be the basis of the religious policy at Sde-dge.

The Ris-med movement counted among its members such illustrious persons as 'Jam-mgon Koṅ-sprul Blo-gros-mtha'-yas (1813–1899), a competent physician and the author of the encyclopedia *Śes bya kun khyab* and a unique nonsectarian collection of texts pertaining to spiritual training, the *Gdams ṅag mdzod;* 'Jam-dbyaṅs Mkhyen-brtse'i-dbaṅ-po (1820–1892), a master of Buddhist poetry; and, last but not least, 'Ju Mi-pham 'Jam-dbyaṅs-rnam-rgyal-rgya-mtsho (1841–1912), who wrote on every imaginable topic. There were, and still are, other figures of significance.

When the Chinese occupied Tibet in 1959, a move that probably was a preemptive strike against other aspirants, the initial policy was one of destruction. This policy has changed from time to time, however, and reports coming from Tibet are conflicting. What may be stated with assurance is that the political power that the monasteries once wielded is a matter of the past. In those monasteries where the lamas are permitted to continue to perform religious ceremonies, no other activities are allowed, which means that no intellectual support is forthcoming. While ceremonies play an important role in the life of a community, they are not the whole of religion; there is thus an intellectual vacuum. With the annexation of Tibet by China, a chapter in the history of Buddhism—although certainly not Buddhism itself—came to a close.

[*For further discussion of Tibetan Buddhist doctrine, see* Buddhism, schools of, *articles on* Tibetan Buddhism *and* Esoteric Buddhism. *The interactions between Buddhism and indigenous Tibetan religions are discussed in* Bon *and in* Himalayan Religions. *For an overview of the* siddha *ideal in Tibetan Buddhism, see* Mahāsiddhas. *The quests for "hidden treasures" are further discussed in* Pilgrimage, *article on* Tibetan Pilgrimage. *See also* Dge-lugs-pa *and* Dalai Lama.]

BIBLIOGRAPHY

The best readily available book on Buddhism in Tibet is Giuseppe Tucci's *The Religions of Tibet* (Berkeley, 1980), translated from the German and Italian by Geoffrey Samuel. This book also contains an exhaustive bibliography, although the Tibetan titles listed may be difficult to locate. Valuable material is also found in R. A. Stein's *Tibetan Civilization* (Stanford, Calif. 1972), translated by J. E. Stapleton Driver. In this book the Tibetan source material has been listed so as to be identifiable. Stein has also used Chinese sources. David Snellgrove and Hugh Richardson's *A Cultural History of Tibet* (New York, 1968) is very readable but is sketchy and politically oriented.

HERBERT GUENTHER

Buddhism in China

Both literary and archaeological evidence indicate that Buddhism reached China in the first century of the common era and that it entered the country from the northwest, after having spread through the oasis kingdoms that had sprung up along the Silk Road, the transcontinental caravan route that at that time linked two powerful empires. At its western extremity, Buddhism flourished in the Kushan, or Indo-Scythian, empire that from its base in northwestern India dominated the Indo-Iranian border lands from present-day Bukhara to Afghanistan. In the east, it had its terminal at the frontier town of Tun-huang, on the border of the Han empire that ruled over most of present-day China and at times also extended its military dominance far into Central Asia. Thus, the oasis kingdoms were exposed to cultural influences from both sides. They became the main stations in the developing commercial and diplomatic relations between Han China and the Middle East, and, at the same time, flourishing centers of Buddhism. There are some indications that Buddhism also reached China along the sea route as early as the second century CE, but those contacts cannot be compared to the constant influx of Buddhist missionaries, scriptures, and artistic impulses from what the Chinese vaguely called the Western Region: present-day Sinkiang and Soviet Central Asia, and the even more distant lands of Parthia, Kashmir, and northwestern India.

Consequences of the Geographical Setting. The geographical configuration has in various ways been a conditioning factor in the development of Chinese Buddhism, particularly in its formative phase. In the first place, it has led to a certain regionalization in Chinese Buddhism. In general, the centers in the north and northwest remained in direct contact with the Western Region. For many centuries, the most prominent foreign missionaries were active mainly in the north, and it was also there that most Chinese versions of Buddhist scriptures were produced. The greater awareness of the foreign origin of Buddhism no doubt enhanced its popularity among the non-Chinese conquerors who ruled the northern half of China from the early fourth century until 589 CE. In the southern parts of China, which in those centuries were ruled by a succession of indigenous Chinese dynasties and had no direct overland communications with the Western Region, a much more sinicized type of Buddhism developed, less concerned with translation and scriptural studies, and much more focused upon the interpretation of Buddhist ideas in terms of traditional Chinese philosophy and religion. After the reunification of the empire under the Sui (589 CE), these two main streams of Chinese Buddhism amalgamated; their mixture and integration heralded the golden age of Buddhism under the Sui and T'ang dynasties (589–906).

Another important consequence was that China for centuries absorbed Buddhism from many different centers representing various types of Buddhism. This diversity was due not only to regional differences, but also to the fact that Buddhism in India steadily evolved new schools and movements that spread over the continent and eventually reached China. Thus, right from the beginning, the Chinese were confronted with Buddhism not as one homogeneous and fairly consistent religious system, but rather as a bewildering mass of diverse teachings that occasionally contradicted each other on essential points: thousands of scriptures of both Theravāda and Mahāyāna origin; a great variety of scholastic treatises; monastic rules of many different schools; sectarian texts and tantric rituals—all of which claimed to be part of the Buddha's original message, and hence to be of impeccable orthodoxy. This ever-growing diversity stimulated the Chinese religious leaders to explore new ways in order to eliminate the contradictions and to reduce the Buddhist message to one basic truth, transcending all difference of expression. The Chinese reaction was twofold. On the one hand, attempts were made to integrate all Buddhist teachings into vast structures of "graded revelation," differentiated according to periods of preaching and the varying spiritual levels of the audience. On the other hand, we find the most radical rejection of diversity by the propagation of a "direct," intuitive way to enlightenment and the abandonment of all scriptural study. The first tendency eventually produced the great scholastic systems of medieval Chinese Buddhism; the second one is most clearly (though not exclusively) represented by Ch'an (Jpn., Zen) Buddhism.

Finally, the factor of sheer distance between China and India, and consequently the infrequency of direct contact between the monastic communities in China and religious centers in the homeland of Buddhism, had important consequences for the way in which Buddhism developed in China. Apart from the few pilgrims who were able to undertake the journey to India and to stay there for study, Chinese masters had no firsthand knowledge of Indian Buddhism; throughout the history of Chinese Buddhism, only a handful of Chinese are known to have mastered Sanskrit. On the other hand, the foreign missionaries who came to China (some from India, but as often from Buddhist centers in Central and Southeast Asia) seldom were fluent in Chinese. The production of Chinese versions of Buddhist texts typically was done by a translation team, the foreign master reciting the text and making, mostly with the help of a bilingual interpreter, a very crude translation, that was written down and afterward revised and polished by Chinese assistants. It is easy to see the hazards of misunderstanding inherent in such a procedure. Buddhist concepts lost much of their original flavor once they were expressed in Chinese terms; the linguistic barrier remained a formidable obstacle to a direct understanding of Buddhism as it had developed outside China, and direct communication with Indian centers of learning—or, indeed, with any Buddhist center outside China—was too incidental to change the overall picture. But it is also clear that these same factors contributed to the profound sinicization of Buddhism in China and to its absorption into Chinese culture. Once translated into a peculiar kind of semiliterary Chinese (that became standardized as a Chinese scriptural language around the fifth century CE), any scripture, because of the special nature of the Chinese ideographic script, could be read all over China, and be interpreted in a great variety of ways, without any external guidance. It is a pattern of independent diffusion that led to countless forms of hybridization with indigenous non-Buddhist forms of religious thought and practice. By the sixth century, Buddhism had already become fully "interiorized": when around that time the most influential schools of Chinese Buddhism took form, they owed their existence to the creative and independent thought of Chinese masters working in a purely Chinese environment, in which the foreign missionaries played only a marginal role.

Buddhism and Chinese Culture. Once it had entered China, Buddhism was confronted with formidable obstacles: a colossal empire and a civilization dominated by political and social ideas and norms that had crystallized in the course of centuries. Especially at the level of the cultural elite, these dominant ideas ran counter to some of the most fundamental notions of Buddhism, both as a doctrine and as an institution. As representatives of the orthodox Confucian tradition, the Chinese literati maintained a worldview that was essentially pragmatic and secular, despite their assent to certain religious ideas belonging to the sphere of "political theology." The Confucian worldview was based on the idea that the world of man forms a single organic whole with Heaven and earth, and that the ruler, sanctified by the mandate of Heaven, maintains the cosmic balance by the perfect administration of government. His sphere of activity is therefore, in principle, unlimited: the emperor, and, by extension, the scholar-official class through which he rules, form the single focus of power, prestige, and authority in all matters, secular as well as religious. The basic values are those of stability, hierarchical order, harmony in human relations, and painstaking observance of the ritual rules of behavior, notably those pertaining to the mutual obligations within the family, and in the relation between ruler and subject. The ideal state is an agrarian society with a productive, hard-working population that is subjected to the paternalistic but all-embracing rule of a bureaucratic elite of ideologically trained managers. This characteristic and deeply rooted combination of political, moralistic, and cosmological ideas formed the central tradition of Chinese thought; in spite of periodic ups and downs, it had maintained its primacy from the second century BCE to the beginning of the modern era. Thus, even at the time of its highest flowering, Buddhism always was subordinated to the claims of the secular order. It had to grow up in the shadow of the all-powerful central tradition.

As a doctrine, Buddhism was bound to meet with the disapproval of the Confucian elite, who maintained that the basic ideals of human existence are to be realized in this life, and that doctrines must be appreciated according to their practical applicability and sociopolitical effectiveness rather than for their metaphysical qualities. In general, the quest for purely individual salvation was rejected as narrow-minded and selfish: man can perfect himself only within society. To a large extent, these attitudes also characterize the major non-Confucian indigenous tradition of religious and philosophical thought in China, that of Taoism: there, too, the goals are concrete and tangible—harmony with the forces of nature and the prolongation of bodily existence. In view of these concepts and attitudes, it goes without saying that Buddhism, once it was transplanted into Chinese soil, was subjected to heavy pressures. Its rejection of all existence as illusory and its belief in ideas like rebirth, the retribution of all acts *(karman)*, and the pursuit of metaphysical aims, such as enlightenment and *nirvāṇa*, that in India had been universally accepted both within and outside Buddhist circles, in China became outlandish novelties that ran counter to the teachings of China's most revered sages. And the non-Chinese origin of the doctrine was in itself sufficient to condemn Buddhism as "barbarian," and therefore unfit to be propagated in the Middle Kingdom, the only region of true order and civilization.

At the institutional level, the tensions were even more evident. The monastic ideal, implying, among other things, the total rejection and abandonment of family life, was bound to come into conflict with the very basis of Confucian morality, according to which man's primary duty lies in fulfilling his obligations toward his family: the cult of his ancestors, the observance of filial piety toward his parents, and marriage and the engendering of male offspring in order to ensure the continuity of the family. If the monks' life was branded as immoral, it was also condemned as parasitical. Since every subject was supposed to be a useful, that is, productive, member of society, the Buddhist clergy easily became stigmatized as an antisocial body within the state—in the Confucian perspective, a natural reaction to the fact that monks were not allowed to perform manual labor, normally spent part of their lives wandering, and were supposed to beg for their food. And, finally, much ill will and suspicion was created by the traditional claim of the Buddhist clergy to be regarded as an unworldly body, not subject to any temporal obligations (including corvée labor, military service, and the payment of taxes), and exempt from any form of government supervision. The idea that "the monk does not bow before the king" was an ancient conception in Buddhism that had always been accepted as self-evident in its land of origin. In China, the very thought of such an alien body within the state was considered both subversive and sacrilegious; it became the subject of heated controversies and conflicts for centuries, until, in late imperial times, the Buddhist clergy had to abandon its claims, and lost even the semblance of independence.

In spite of all these inhibiting factors, Buddhism was able to take root in China and to become an important factor in Chinese civilization, both spiritually and materially. To some extent, this was owing to the fact that its formative phase largely coincided with a period of political disintegration, coupled with a temporary decline of Confucianism as a powerful ideology. It is no coincidence that when in 220 CE the Han empire fell, Buddhism had existed in China for more than one and a half centuries in almost complete obscurity, and thereafter rapidly developed into a prominent religious movement in the period of disunity (311–589 CE) when the empire had fallen asunder, and large parts of China were under the sway of "barbarian" dynasties. In those dark ages, Confucianism, the ideology of imperial unity and universal power, had lost much of its prestige, and Buddhism could profit from this, as it did from the general state of political chaos and polycentrism. When the empire was reunified, Buddhism had gained a position from which it could no longer be removed, in spite of all opposition from Confucian quarters.

However, Buddhism obviously never could have gained any foothold in China if the environment had been totally hostile. There also were positive factors stimulating its spread and assimilation. In the first place, the Confucian opposition in medieval times was limited to an extremely small elite. The mass of the population had not yet been confucianized, as it eventually came to be in late imperial times, and was therefore open to the influence of new and heterodox movements. In many fields there were points of convergence, where elements of Buddhist origin could be grafted onto traditional ideas and practices with which they had (or seemed to have) a certain affinity. Thus the monastic ideal became associated with the indigenous tradition of "retired scholarship"; Buddhist meditation with certain forms of Taoist mental techniques; the Mahāyāna concept of salvation of all beings with the cult of the ancestors; Buddhist lay congregations with traditional peasant associations, and so forth. In this way, through an extremely complicated process of convergence and hybridization, Buddhist ideas and practices were woven into the fabric of Chinese civilization. Another reason why Buddhism, in spite of all opposition from conservative quarters, was able to maintain its influence even among a part of the educated elite, lies in the fact that it could present itself not as a rival of Confucianism, but as an enrichment of it: precisely because Confucianism was almost exclusively directed toward the ordering of state and society, it could be argued that Buddhism would serve as a kind of metaphysical complement to the social and political teachings of the Sage, just as it could provide the Taoist Way with the higher (but complementary) goals of Enlightenment and *nirvāṇa*. Finally, in certain periods official patronage played an important role, not only for reasons of imperial piety, but also—or even primarily—because the Buddhist clergy by its prayers and rituals could provide a magical protection for the dynasty, the state, and society. In spite of these positive factors, however, it remains true that even when Buddhism reached its zenith in Sui and T'ang times, China never became a "Buddhist country" in the true sense of the word.

Main Periods. For the purpose of a short survey, a division into five main periods seems appropriate, though it must be kept in mind that this periodization scheme is primarily based on social and institutional developments, and that the dividing lines would be drawn somewhat differently if it were exclusively based on doctrinal criteria.

1. *The embryonic phase* (from the first appearance of

Buddhism in China in the mid-first century CE to c. 300 CE). This was a phase in which Buddhism played only a marginal role in religious and intellectual life. In Chinese dynastic terms it covers the Later Han (25–220 CE), the era of the Three Kingdoms (220–265), and the Western Chin (265–326).

2. *The formative phase* (c. 300–589 CE). Politically, the formative phase covers the period of division, during which northern China was occupied by a great number of "barbarian" dynasties of conquest, while the Yangtze basin and southern China were governed by a series of feeble Chinese dynasties. Intellectually, it marks the penetration of Buddhism into the educated minority, and within the clergy itself, the formation of an elite group of scholarly monks. During this period Buddhism spread to all regions of China and to all social levels, including the Chinese and "barbarian" courts. By the end of this period the stage was set for the rise of indigenous Chinese Buddhist schools.

3. *The phase of independent growth* (coinciding with the second era of imperial unification during the Sui and T'ang dynasties, 589–906 CE). The phase of independent growth was the "High Middle Ages" of Chinese history. On the one hand, indigenous Chinese sects or schools formed; on the other hand, some Indian forms of Buddhism were transplanted to China. During this period there was unprecedented material prosperity and economic activity in the large monasteries. In 845 a severe repression occurred that is commonly regarded as the beginning of the gradual decline of Buddhism in China.

4. *Buddhism in premodern China* (from the tenth to the nineteenth century). In the urbanized and bureaucratized "gentry" society, and under the pressure of a revived and expanded Confucianism, Buddhism gradually lost the support of the cultured elite and was more and more reduced to a despised popular religion. Ch'an (meditation) Buddhism alone continued to exert a limited appeal in intellectual circles.

5. *Buddhism in modern and contemporary China* (c. 1880–present). The attempt to revive Buddhism remains a small and rather elitist movement. In the twentieth century, and especially since the 1920s, Buddhism has been increasingly exposed to the combined pressure of nationalism, modernization, and Marxism-Leninism.

The embryonic phase. According to a famous story, the Han emperor Ming (reigned 58–75 CE) once had a dream in which he saw a "golden man." When one of his counselors informed him that this was a foreign god called Buddha, he sent envoys to northwestern India who returned three years later, accompanied by two Indian missionaries. For them the emperor founded the first monastery in China, the Pai-ma Ssu, or White Horse Monastery, in the capital, Loyang. The story is no more than a propagandistic tale that is probably not older than the late second century. It may, however, contain a memory of the existence of Buddhism in court circles at the time of the emperor Ming, as an early and reliable historical source refers to the presence of Buddhist monks and laymen in the entourage of an imperial prince in 65 CE. This is the first authentic—but, unfortunately, quite isolated—sign of the existence of Buddhism in China. It actually is not known precisely when Buddhism entered China. In the course of the first century CE, under the circumstances previously mentioned, it must have infiltrated from the northwest via the Kansu corridor to the Yellow River basin and the North China Plain. For a considerable time its devotees may have largely consisted of foreigners on Chinese soil.

The scene becomes clearer from the middle of the second century onward, when the first known foreign missionaries (Parthians, Kushans, Sogdians, and only a few Indians) started their translation activities in the Lo-yang area. Together they produced a considerable number of Chinese versions of Buddhist texts, about thirty of which have been preserved. This activity—proof that Buddhism had started to spread among the Chinese—marks the beginnings of an immense translation effort that was to remain one of the most impressive achievements of Buddhist culture in China. To judge from the works selected for translation, the scope of Buddhism in the last decades of the Han was rather limited. Much attention was given to short texts dealing with meditation or trance *(dhyāna)*, probably because of its resemblance to certain Taoist mental and physical techniques. After the fall of the Han (220 CE), the scope widened. Hundreds of texts were translated, including the first crude versions of some of the classics of Mahāyāna Buddhism such as the *Lotus Sutra* and the *Teachings of Vimalakīrti.* Apart from the activity of translation, not much is known about the spread and organization of Buddhism in China in the embryonic phase. Its role still was very modest—that of a new, "exotic" way of salvation that gained its adherents from the lower social ranks, as is proven by the fact that up to the end of the third century Buddhism is hardly mentioned in secular Chinese literature, the domain of the cultured upper class.

The formative phase. Early in the fourth century a political and cultural landslide took place, the effects of which were to last for almost four centuries. Making use of China's internal weakness, various non-Chinese tribes invaded the ancient homeland of Chinese culture from the northern frontier regions; in 311 the capital was sacked by the invaders, and the Chinese court had to flee in disgrace to the area south of the Yangtze. From

311 onward, China was divided into two halves: northern China, ruled by a great variety of non-Chinese in very unstable regimes, and southern China, governed by a series of equally short-lived Chinese dynasties. However, especially in southern China, political weakness was combined with cultural brilliance and an intense and many-sided activity in the field of thought. The decline of Confucianism had led to a new intellectual atmosphere, one more inclined to accept alternative ways of escape from the horrors of incessant warfare, chaos, and misery. Taoism, in both its religious and philosophical varieties, gained many adherents among the cultured elite, and there was a vivid interest in metaphysical problems based on the cryptic musings of the classical Taoist thinkers (notably Lao-tzu and Chuang-tzu), and on the even more mysterious *I ching* (Book of Changes). In this atmosphere, Buddhism was able to catch the attention of the cultured upper class; at the same time we see the formation of a clerical elite of scholarly monks—often themselves belonging to the educated class by birth—who were able to propagate the new creed in that milieu. Thus, in southern China we see the development of a particular type of "high-class Buddhism" characterized by extensive hybridization and a clear emphasis on Buddhism's more philosophical aspects, notably the Mahāyāna doctrine of universal emptiness *(śūnyatā)*. Scholar-monks like Chih Tun (314–366) and Hui-yüan (334–416) explained the doctrine to the cultured public in terms of traditional Chinese thought and thereby laid the foundation of Chinese Buddhist philosophy.

The influence of Buddhism and the material prosperity of the larger monasteries reached their zenith under the emperor Wu of the Liang dynasty (r. 502–549), who took the Buddhist vows of the layman, personally explained Buddhist scriptures in the palace, forbade the use of animals in sacrifice, and officially prohibited the Taoist religion. It was under his reign that Bodhidharma, the reputed founder of Ch'an (Zen) Buddhism, is said to have come to China. However, the spread of Buddhism was by no means restricted to the upper classes. To the masses of exploited peasants Buddhism was attractive for various reasons. On the one hand, they could find solace in the more elementary teachings and rituals of devotional Mahāyāna Buddhism: the invocation of saving Buddhas and *bodhisattvas*, the magic spells, and the colorful temple festivals. But in those difficult times the Buddhist monastery also offered a refuge from the burdens of military service, taxes, and forced labor. By 400 CE the southern territory counted already more than 1,700 monasteries and 80,000 monks and nuns—a sudden expansion that for the first time aroused the opposition of anti-Buddhist circles, who urged measures to restrict the growth of the "antisocial" clergy. In "barbarian"-occupied northern China, Buddhism was, for various reasons, generally patronized by the foreign rulers. At first they welcomed monks as a new type of shaman, able to ensure prosperity and military victory by magical means. Later they tended to employ monks at their courts, since Buddhism, as an alien doctrine, could be used to counterbalance Confucianism, and also because the monastic life prevented monks from having dangerous family connections.

Throughout this period, northern Buddhism was characterized by a close connection between church and state, with all its positive and negative side effects. The grandiose government patronage (of which the Yün-kang cave temples, founded by the proto-Mongolian Toba Wei rulers in the fifth century, represent the most impressive testimony) was reflected in the enormous growth of monastic institutions: in the early fifth century the Wei empire counted some thirty thousand monasteries and two million monks and nuns. On the other hand, there was close supervision of the church by state-appointed clerical officials, a government-sponsored system of temple serfdom that enabled large monasteries to expand their economic activities, and also, partly due to Buddhist-Taoist rivalry, occasional outbursts of anticlericalism culminating in ruthless persecutions (452–466 and 574–578). Doctrinally, the most important event was the arrival, in 402 CE, of the great missionary and translator Kumārajīva at Ch'ang-an (present-day Sian), then the capital of a fervently Buddhist proto-Tibetan ruler. Kumārajīva, who had already become a famous scholar in his native Kuchā in Central Asia, introduced to China the Mahāyāna philosophy of the Middle Path (Mādhyamika), in which the ultimate truth of nonreality transcends both being and nonbeing. He produced an enormous number of superior translations of Buddhist scripture with the help of the largest translation team known in history. At the end of this period, Buddhism had come to permeate Chinese society at all levels. The clergy had become a distinct social group with considerable spiritual and material influence. The most important texts had been translated, and Chinese masters had begun their own doctrinal systems on the basis of these works.

The phase of independent growth. Under the Sui and T'ang dynasties, Chinese Buddhism reached its apogee. There was great and creative activity in every field. Under various emperors Buddhism was patronized on a lavish scale, though not always for purely religious reasons. Under the notorious empress Wu (reigned 690–705), both state sponsorship and the political use of Buddhism reached excessive proportions. Official patronage was, however, always combined with attempts to place the clergy under bureaucratic control and to check its growth. Once more under Chinese control, Central Asia retained its function as a diffusion area and as a transit zone between China and India until the late seventh century. There was an upsurge of pilgrimage, the most famous pilgrim being Hsüan-tsang (c. 559–664), an exceptional figure in Chinese Buddhism not only for his remarkable journey (629–645) and the quality of his observations, but also for his mastery (then rare among Chinese) of Sanskrit and his work as a great scholar and translator. In the late seventh century, the Arab conquests obstructed the overland route to India. The last wave of pilgrimage took place by the sea route, from the southern coast of China to Tāmraliptī (near modern Calcutta) and Sri Lanka.

In the early T'ang, Buddhism was by far the most creative movement in the religious and intellectual life of the era. Some of the schools or sects that flourished from the late sixth to the ninth century were directly inspired by India: Hsüan-tsang founded the Chinese counterpart of Indian "idealistic" (Yogācāra) Buddhism, and somewhat later various types of esoteric (Tantric) Buddhism were introduced by Indian masters. The most prominent schools, however, were basically Chinese, and they independently developed theories of great originality. Some schools, such as the Ching-t'u (Pure Land) sect, were devotional, advocating faith, repentance of sins, and surrender to the saving grace of the Buddha Amitābha and the *bodhisattva* Kuan-yin (the Indian Avalokiteśvara, who in China assumed a female form) as a simple way to salvation. Other schools were scholastic in nature. Partly in reaction to the doctrinal diversity of Buddhism as it was presented to the Chinese, such schools of "graded revelation" concentrated upon one particular scripture held to contain the final and highest revelation; all other teachings were not rejected, but were regarded as preliminary instruments that served to prepare the minds of less advanced hearers. Thus, the prestigious T'ien-t'ai school (so called after a mountain in Chekiang) classified, in a stupendous scholastic structure, all known teachings according to a scheme of five phases of teaching, the whole culminating in the doctrine of the *Lotus Sutra* as the expression of ultimate Truth.

The Meditation School, known in China as Ch'an (a transcription of the Sanskrit term *dhyāna*, "meditation, trance") and in Japan as Zen, appeared in the seventh century as a unique blend of Chinese (notably Taoist) and Mahāyāna notions and practices. Starting from the basic idea that the highest Truth is inaccessible to speech and rational thought, it propagated a direct, intuitional approach to enlightenment without recourse to canonical texts or rational reflection. It held that all reasoning must be broken down, by means of exhausting meditation sessions, the use of bizarre themes for concentration, including paradoxes, and even deliberate forcible blows from the master. When the ultimate state of "no-mind" has been realized, not gradually but as a sudden explosion, all distinction between holy and profane is obliterated, so that "the Highest Truth is contained in carrying water and chopping firewood." Ch'an Buddhism exerted an enormous influence, especially in intellectual circles. It has had a great impact on art and literature in China and Korea, where it persisted after the disappearance of most other schools, and even more in Japan, where it has flourished up to the present time.

As long as the T'ang state prospered, it was able to tolerate the growing privileges of the innumerable monastic institutions and clerical domains. But when, in the second half of the T'ang, the state was undermined by political turmoil and economic crisis, anticlericalism gained force. Buddhism was also losing ground intellectually, for the ninth century witnesses the beginning of a revival of Confucianism and, consequently, an increasing aversion to Buddhism as a basically un-Chinese creed. In 845, the combined forces of economic considerations, Confucian anticlericalism, and the influence of Taoist masters at the court led to persecution of Buddhism on an unprecedented scale. More than 40,000 temples were destroyed, and 260,500 monks and nuns were forced to return to lay life. Later, the clergy was allowed to grow again, but its economic power had suffered a blow from which it never recovered.

The premodern period (c. 900–c. 1880). The beginning of the premodern period is marked by the great political, social, and economic processes of change that in the tenth and eleventh centuries transformed the agrarian-based, aristocratic society of the Chinese Middle Ages into that of late imperial China: an urbanized and bureaucratized society with a sophisticated urban civilization that was shared by an elite of gentry and rich merchants. Confucian values increasingly predominated. The eleventh and twelfth centuries witnessed a powerful "Neo-Confucian" revival, in which earlier Confucianism was expanded into a vast scholastic system including a metaphysical superstructure that incorporated certain Buddhist ideas. In the fourteenth century, one of these Neo-Confucian systems became the official orthodoxy, and the orthodox interpretation of the Confucian classics became the only one valid for the state examinations that opened the way to a career in public office. The family and clan system, with its typically Confucian code of behavior, was propagated throughout the population.

In late imperial times (Sung, 960–1279; Ming, 1368–1644; Ch'ing, 1644–1912) Chinese society had become thoroughly confucianized. Under such circumstances, Buddhism declined steadily, though not in quantitative terms. At the grass-roots level, the religion flourished in countless forms of popular devotion, and the size of the clergy remained impressive. The decline was mainly intellectual: the interest of the cultured minority shifted from Buddhism to Neo-Confucianism. This shift ultimately reduced Buddhism to a despised creed of the lower classes, with the exception of Ch'an, which in a much petrified form maintained its popularity in some intellectual circles. The doctrinal impoverishment of Chinese Buddhism is also shown by the disappearance of most of the schools of T'ang Buddhism. There was a general tendency toward syncretism and mutual borrowing, by which the earlier schools gradually lost their identity; in Ming times, only Ch'an and popular Pure Land devotionalism remained as recognizable trends of Buddhist thought and practice. Syncretism became the prevailing trend: the idea of the "basic unity of the Three Teachings" (Confucianism, Taoism, and Buddhism) gained great popularity. Another characteristic feature of this late Buddhism was the ever more important part played by the laity, whose role in religious life became more prominent as the status of the clergy declined. Between 1280 and 1368 China was part of the Mongol empire, a curious intermezzo in later Chinese history. The Mongol rulers of the Yüan dynasty were mainly interested in Tantric Buddhism in its Tibetan form, and the influence of Lamaism in China dates from that period. Under the last two dynasties, Tibetan and, somewhat later, Mongolian Lamaism were sponsored by the court, largely for political reasons. But at the same time religious life was more than ever subjected to dirigistic government control.

Buddhism in modern and contemporary China. The late nineteenth century witnessed the first attempts, undertaken by some cultured laymen, to revive Buddhism. It was part of a general tendency to overcome China's backwardness in the face of Western and Japanese dominance, and also, more specifically, a reaction to the impact of the Christian missions in China. After the revolution and the establishment of the republic (1912), various attempts were made to organize the Buddhist clergy on a national scale, to raise its cultural level through the founding of Buddhist seminars, and to establish contacts with Japan, India, and the Buddhist countries in South and Southeast Asia. From the late 1920s, the movement, or at least its more progressive wing, was led by the venerable abbot T'ai-hsü (1899–1947), who devoted his whole adult life to the regeneration of Chinese Buddhism. Not much came of it. The general intellectual climate left little room for a religious renaissance. Both a large part of the new educated elite and the Nationalist government itself tended to reject all religion as "feudal superstition," and even within the Buddhist community only a tiny minority was touched by the movement at all. The revivalist movement also suffered from the fact that in the years preceding World War II the Japanese government consciously used it to foster pro-Japanese sentiments.

Following the establishment in 1949 of the People's Republic, official Chinese policy toward the Buddhist clergy oscillated between political supervision (exercised through a completely politicized Buddhist Association) and violent suppression, notably during mass campaigns such as the Cultural Revolution (1966–1969). Where Buddhism is tolerated, it is clearly a truncated Buddhism, limited to devotional activities and divested of all the social and economic functions that the monasteries once had. The clergy itself, on which no reliable quantitative data are available, has no doubt been decimated by laicization and the lack of new ordinations. In general, prospects for Buddhism on the Chinese mainland are gloomy. Even if in the most recent years (since 1976) there are signs of a somewhat more liberal policy, the pressure of a hostile ideology, this time combined with an excessive emphasis on modernization, science, and technology, is not favorable to the existence, let alone the flourishing, of Buddhism as an organized religion.

[*See also* Buddhism, Schools of, *Article on* Chinese Buddhism, *and the biographies of the principal figures mentioned above. For a general discussion of Buddhism's role in Chinese religion, see* Chinese Religion, *overview article; for an overview of religious practice, see* Worship and Cultic Life, *article on* Buddhist Cultic Life in East Asia.]

BIBLIOGRAPHY

The best and most up-to-date monographic works dealing with the history of Chinese Buddhism as a whole are Kenneth Ch'en's *Buddhism in China* (Princeton, 1964) and *The Chinese Transformation of Buddhism* (Princeton, 1973). The best short presentation of the subject is to be found in Paul Demiéville's masterly survey *Le bouddhisme chinois* (Paris, 1970). A. F. Wright's *Buddhism in Chinese History* (1959; reprint, Stanford, Calif., 1965) is readable but somewhat superficial. The history of Indo-Chinese relations as illustrated by Chinese Buddhism is treated by Probodh C. Bagchi in *India and China: A Thousand Years of Cultural Relations*, 2d ed. (Bombay, 1950). The early period (until the early fifth century CE) is extensively covered in my book *The Buddhist Conquest of China*, 2 vols. (1959; reprint, Leiden, 1979). The social and economic aspects of the Buddhist clergy in the medieval period (fifth to ninth centuries) have been excellently treated by Jacques Gernet in *Les aspects économiques du bouddhisme* (Saigon, 1956). There is a voluminous Western-language literature on Ch'an (Zen) Buddhism, most of which is of mediocre quality. Positive exceptions are *The Secrets of Chinese Meditation* (London, 1964) by Charles Luk (K'uan Yü Lu) and *The Platform Sūtra of the Sixth Patriarch*, edited and translated by Philip B. Yampolsky (New York, 1967). On the tensions between state and church in premodern China the only overall study still is the now outmoded and rather partisan *Sectarianism and Religious Persecution in China*, 2 vols. (Amsterdam, 1903–1904), by J. J. M. de Groot. The best surveys of Chinese Buddhism in modern times can be found in the relevant parts of Wing-tsit Chan's *Religious Trends in Modern China* (New York, 1953) and of Yang Ch'ing-k'un's *Religion in Chinese Society* (Berkeley, 1961); for a more detailed treatment of Chinese Buddhism in the twentieth century, see Holmes Welch's *The Practice of Chinese Buddhism, 1900–1950* (Cambridge, Mass., 1967) and *The Buddhist Revival in China* (Cambridge, Mass., 1968). Welch has also described the fate of Buddhism in the People's Republic of China up to the late 1960s in *Buddhism under Mao* (Cambridge, Mass., 1972).

Erik Zürcher

Buddhism in Korea

In any examination of the Korean Buddhist tradition, it is essential to recall that in no way was Korea isolated from neighboring regions of Northeast Asia. During its prehistory, Korean culture was most closely akin to that of the seminomadic tribes of the Central and North Asian steppes. From the Warring States period (403–221 BCE) on, however, when refugees from the northern Chinese states of Yen, Ch'i, and Chao immigrated to the peninsula to escape the ravages of the mainland wars, Han civilization began to eclipse that indigenous culture at an ever-increasing pace. It is for this reason that Korean Buddhism must be treated as part and parcel of a larger East Asian Buddhist tradition. Indeed, Korea's later appellation as the "hermit kingdom" notwithstanding, there was in fact an almost organic relationship between the Korean, Chinese, and, during its incipient period, the Japanese Buddhist traditions. Admittedly, the Silk Route afforded China closer ties with the Buddhism of India and Central Asia, and China's overwhelming size, both in territory and population, inevitably led to its domination of the doctrinal trends within East Asian Buddhism. This does not deny, however, that Korean exegetes working on both the peninsula and the Chinese mainland made seminal contributions to the development of what are commonly considered to be distinctively "Chinese" schools of Buddhism, such as T'ien-t'ai, Hua-yen, and Ch'an. At the same time, many Chinese Buddhist theological insights were molded into new forms in Korea, innovations comparable to the Chinese syntheses of Indian and Central Asian Buddhist teachings. Hence, any appraisal of characteristically East Asian developments in the Buddhist tradition cannot neglect to take into account the contributions made by Koreans.

Three Kingdoms Buddhism (c. late fourth century–668 CE). According to such traditional Korean historical sources as *Samguk sagi* (Historical Record of the Three Kingdoms), *Haedong kosŭng chŏn* (Biographies of Eminent Korean Monks), and *Samguk yusa* (Memorabilia and Mirabilia of the Three Kingdoms), Buddhism was transmitted to Korea from the Chinese mainland during the (Korean) Three Kingdoms period. The introduction of Buddhism into Korea is presumed to have occurred in 372 CE, when King Fu Chien (r. 357–384) of the Former Ch'in dynasty (351–394) sent a monk-envoy, Shuntao (Kor., Sundo), to the Koguryŏ court with scriptures and images. Former Ch'in hegemony over the remarkably cosmopolitan region of eastern Turkistan had brought Chinese culture into intimate contact with Indian, Iranian, and Hellenistic civilizations, ultimately engendering a new, sinified form of Buddhism. Fu Chien's defeat, in 370, of the Former Yen state, which had for decades laid siege to Koguryŏ, initiated close ties between Fu Chien and his Koguryŏ contemporary, King Sosurim (r. 371–383). These contacts allowed this vibrant northern Chinese culture, which included the Buddhist religion, to be introduced into Korea. While a paucity of information remains by which we can evaluate the characteristics of the Buddhism of this early period, it is probable that it was characterized by thaumaturgic practices, a symbiotic relationship between the ecclesia and the state, Maitreya worship, and the study of scriptures affiliated with the Mahāyāna branch of Buddhism. A monastery is said to have been erected for Sundo in 376, the first reference to a formal Buddhist institution on Korean soil.

Sundo was followed in 384 by the Serindian monk Maranant'a (*Mālānanda; *Kumārānandin), who is reputed to have come via sea to Paekche from the Chinese state of Eastern Chin (317–420). His enthusiastic reception by the royal court initiated the rapid diffusion of Buddhism throughout the Paekche kingdom. Less than a year after his arrival a monastery had been founded on Mount Han for Maranant'a and the first Korean natives ordained as Buddhist monks. Studies on Buddhist monastic discipline (Vinaya) appear particularly to have flourished in Paekche. In both Koguryŏ and Paekche, there is evidence that such schools as Samnon (Mādhyamika), Sarvāstivādin Abhidharma, Nirvāṇa, Satyasiddhi, and Ch'ŏnt'ae (Chin., T'ien-t'ai) flourished, though few works from this period are now extant. [*These Chinese traditions are reviewed in* Buddhism, Schools of, *article on* Chinese Buddhism.] Of vital importance for the dissemination of Buddhism throughout East Asia, however, was Paekche's nautical skill, which made the kingdom the Phoenicia of medieval East Asia. Over its well-developed sea lanes, Paekche began in 554 to dispatch Buddhist doctrinal specialists, psalmodists, iconographers, and architects to Japan, thus transmitting to the Japanese the rudiments of sinified Buddhist culture and laying the foundation for the rich Buddhist culture of the Asuka and Nara periods. Silla expansion throughout southern Korea also prompted massive emigration of Koreans to Japan (where they were known as *kikajin*), and many of the cultural and technical achievements of early Japan—such as the development of paddy fields, the construction of palaces and temples, and town planning—were direct results of the expertise introduced by these successive waves of emigrants. These advancements ultimately paved the way for Japan's first constitution, purportedly written by Prince Shōtoku in 604, and led to the Taika reform of 646, which initiated a sinified bureaucracy in Japan. [*See also* Buddhism, *article on* Buddhism in Japan.]

It was not until 529, following the martyrdom of Ich'adon (Pak Yŏmch'ok), that Silla, the last of the three kingdoms to consolidate its power, officially embraced Buddhism. Political exigencies were probably the catalyst for the acceptance of Buddhism in Silla. The Silla nobility, who continued their drive for peninsular unification, found strong incentive to embrace Buddhism in an effort to accommodate the newly conquered Koguryŏ and Paekche aristocracy, which had embraced Buddhism long before. The vital role played by the Buddhist religion as a conduit through which Chinese civilization was introduced into Silla closely parallels the sinification of non-Chinese tribes that occurred throughout Chinese history.

Three Kingdoms Buddhism seems to have been a thoroughgoing amalgamation of the foreign religion and indigenous local cults. Autochthonous snake and dragon cults, for example, merged with the Mahāyāna belief in dragons as protectors of the Dharma, forming the unique variety of *hoguk pulgyo* ("state-protection Buddhism") that was thereafter to characterize Korean Buddhism. One of the earliest examples of this amalgamation was the vow of the Silla king Munmu (r. 661–681) to be reborn as a sea dragon after his death in order to guard his country and its new faith from foreign invasion. Buddhism and the state subsequently evolved a symbiotic relationship in which the monks entreated the Buddhas and *bodhisattva*s to protect the state and the state provided munificent support for the dissemination of the religion throughout the empire. Many of the most visible achievements of the Korean church throughout its history, such as the xylographic carvings of the Buddhist canon undertaken during the succeeding Koryŏ dynasty, were products of this concern with national protection. Buddhist monks also sought to demonstrate correspondences between Korean ancestral heroes and the new religion, thereby accelerating the assimilation of the religion among Koreans. Attempts were made, for example, to prove that Hwanin, the Celestial Emperor, was identical to Śakro Devāṇām Indra (Chesŏk-ch'ŏn), the Indian and Buddhist king of the gods, and that Tan'gun, the progenitor of the Korean race, was the theophany of Śrī Mahādevī (Kilsang-ch'ŏn). Vestiges of the dispensations of previous Buddhas were alleged to have been uncovered in Korea, and the advent of the future Buddha, Maitreya, was prophesied to occur in the south of the peninsula. Modern-day visitors to a Korean monastery will notice on the perimeter of the campus shrines devoted to the mountain god or to the seven stars of the Big Dipper, the presence of which is indicative of the synthesis of common sinified culture with Buddhism. [*For an overview of indigenous Korean religion, see* Korean Religion.]

One of the most prominent institutions of Three Kingdoms Buddhism that is commonly assumed to have been indicative of this interaction between Buddhism and indigenous Korean culture was the Hwarang (Flower Boy) movement. According to the *Samguk sagi*, this movement was instituted around 576 by the Silla king Chinhŭng (r. 540–575), and was patterned upon a more primitive association of shamanesses. The formation of the Hwarang movement is considered to have been part of the expansionist policies of the Silla court, and was intended to instill in the sons of nobility a regard for ethical virtues and an appreciation of refined culture. A later Silla writer relates that they were trained in Confucian filial piety and national loyalty, Taoist quietism, and Buddhist morality. The prominent religious orientation of the Hwarang as related in this and other accounts militates against the popular notion that it was a paramilitary organization. The group aesthetic celebrations—such as singing and dancing out in the open—that are commonly associated with the Hwarang has suggested to a number of scholars the shamanistic activities of initiation journeys and pilgrimages. While the Hwarang's Buddhist affinities are far from certain, their eventual identification with Maitreya assured that tradition would regard the movement as one intended to disseminate the Buddhist faith among Koreans.

Unified Silla Buddhism (668–935). After the unification of the peninsula under the Silla banner in 668, the fortunes of the new religion expanded on an unprecedented scale. It was during this period that the major schools of scholastic Buddhism that had developed in China were introduced into Korea. The doctrinal teachings that had begun to be imported during the Three

Kingdoms period were consolidated during the Unified Silla into five major ideological schools: the Kyeyul-chong, which stressed the study and training in Buddhist monastic discipline (Vinaya); the Yŏlban-chong, which promulgated the teachings of the *Mahāparinirvāṇa Sūtra;* the Pŏpsŏng-chong (Dharma Nature), a uniquely Korean school of Buddhism that stressed a syncretic outlook toward Buddhist doctrine; the Wŏnyung-chong, which was the early Korean branch of the Flower Garland (Kor., Hwaŏm; Chin., Hua-yen) school; and the Pŏpsang-chong, based on the "consciousness-only" *(vijñāptimātratā)* teachings of Yogācāra. Some of the greatest achievements of early Korean philosophy occurred during this period, and such important scholiasts as Wŏnhyo (617–686) and Ŭisang (625–702) forged approaches to Buddhist philosophy that would become the hallmarks of the Korean church from that time onward. Korean exegetes working in China also played major roles in the development of Chinese schools of Buddhism. Both Wŏnhyo and Ŭisang were important vaunt-couriers in the Hua-yen school, as reflected in their influence on the systematizer of the Chinese Hua-yen school, Fa-tsang (643–712). Wŏnch'ŭk (613–696), a close disciple of Hsüan-tsang (d. 664), was a prominent exegete in the Chinese Fa-hsiang school, whose commentaries on such texts as the *Saṃdhinirmocana Sūtra* exerted profound influence on early Tibetan Buddhism. [*See* Hua-yen *and the biographies of Wŏnhyo, Ŭisang, Fa-tsang, and Hsüan-tsang.*]

It was during this era of ardent scholarly activity that one of the most characteristic features of the mature Korean Buddhist tradition developed: that of syncretism. From the inception of Buddhism in East Asia, the religion had formed around a number of disparate scriptural and commentarial traditions that had developed first in India and later in Central Asia. For this reason, the Chinese church became characterized by a loosely-structured sectarianism. The various extremes each of these factional divisions took led to an attempt, begun first in China and considerably refined later in Korea, to see these various approaches, each ostensibly Buddhist yet each so different, in some common light, so as to find some means by which their discordant elements could be reconciled. Certain features of the Korean tradition contributed to the syncretic tendency of the religion. Owing to the smaller size of Korea and its monastic population, there was little hope that Buddhism could continue as a stable and influential force within the religious arena if it was divided into contentious factions. In addition, the constant threat of foreign invasion created the need for a unified, centrally organized ecclesiastical institution. The quest to discover the common denominators in all of these sectarian interpretations—and subsequently to use those unifying elements in order to establish an interdenominational approach *(t'ong pulgyo)* to the religion that could incorporate all elements of Buddhist philosophy and practice—was to inspire the efforts of all major Korean Buddhist philosophers. This attitude prompted the Koreans to evolve what remains one of the most ecumenical traditions of Buddhism to be found anywhere is Asia.

One of the most momentous developments in the history of Korean Buddhism occurred during the Unified Silla period: the introduction of the Ch'an teachings, known in Korea as Sŏn. The earliest transmission of Sŏn to the peninsula is attributed to the monk Pŏmnang (fl. 632–646), a Korean who is said to have trained with the fourth patriarch of the Chinese Ch'an school, Tao-hsin (580–646). While little is known of Pŏmnang's life or thought, there are indications that he attempted to combine the teachings of two distinct Chinese Ch'an lineages—that of Bodhidharma (c. fifth century), Hui-k'o (487–592), and Seng-ts'an (d. 606) and that of Tao-hsin and Hung-jen (688–761)—with the syncretic *tathāgatagarbha* theory of the *Ta-sheng ch'i-hsin lun* (Awakening of Faith). [*See* Tathāgata-garbha.] A successor in Pŏmnang's lineage eventually founded the Hŭiyang-san school, the oldest of the Korean Sŏn schools. During the eighth and ninth centuries, other Korean adepts returning from the mainland established eight other mountain Sŏn sites, forming what came to be known as the Nine Mountains school of Sŏn (Kusan Sŏnmun). Of these eight, seven were affiliated with the Hung-chou lineage of the Middle Ch'an period, which eventually evolved into the Lin-chi school of the mature Ch'an tradition; one, the Sumi-san school, was derived from the lineage of Ch'ing-yüan Hsing-ssu (d. 740), from which developed the Ts'ao-tung school. Korean masters on the mainland, however, also played major roles in the development of Chinese Ch'an. Perhaps the most prominent of these Koreans was the monk Musang, also known as Kim Ho-shang (694?–762), who was regarded as a patriarch of the Pao-t'ang school of the Szechwan region, and was the first Ch'an master known to the Tibetans. Despite the continued traffic of Sŏn adepts between China and Korea, the entrenched position of the scholastic schools within the Korean ecclesia thwarted the propagation of Nine Mountains Sŏn. Continued frustration at their inability to disseminate their message led such Sŏn adherents as Toŭi (d. 825) and Muyŏm (799–888) to attack the scholastic schools directly, leading ultimately to a bifurcation of the Korean Buddhist church into two vociferous factions. [*See also* Ch'an.]

Koryŏ Buddhism (937–1392). The principal contribution of Koryŏ Buddhists to the evolution of the Korean church was the reconciliation they effected between the Sŏn and scholastic schools. It was Ŭich'ŏn (1055–1101) who made the first such attempt, by seeking to combine both the Nine Mountains and scholastic schools into a revived Ch'ŏnt'ae school. [*See the biography of Ŭich'ŏn.*] Ch'ŏnt'ae teachings are known to have been present on the peninsula prior to Ŭich'ŏn's time. A century before, for example, Ch'egwan (d. 971), a renowned Korean Ch'ŏnt'ae adept, had been invited to T'ang China to reintroduce long-lost T'ien-t'ai manuals; during his expatriation Ch'egwan systematized the school's philosophies in his *T'ien-t'ai ssu-chiao i,* one of the most important of Chinese T'ien-t'ai exegetical writings. [*See* T'ien-t'ai.] Ŭich'ŏn's efforts to revitalize the school, however, have led to his being considered the effective founder of its Korean branch. It appears that Ŭich'ŏn regarded the meditative exphasis of the Ch'ŏnt'ae teachings as the ideal vehicle for accommodating the varying concerns of the Sŏn and scholastic schools. Unfortunately, his premature death at the age of forty-six brought a sudden end to his endeavor and left the sectarian scene still more unsettled.

Ŭich'ŏn's efforts were followed some three generations later by those of Chinul (1158–1210), a charismatic Sŏn master who was similarly motivated by a syncretic vision of the unity of Sŏn and the scholastic teachings. Unlike Ŭich'ŏn's scholastic orientation, however, Chinul sought to merge the various Buddhist schools of his time into a new Sŏn school that would synthesize a disparate variety of Buddhist soteriological approaches. Chinul introduced into Korean Sŏn practice the investigation of the "critical phrase" (Kor., *hwadu;* Chin., *hua-t'ou),* better known by the closely synonymous term *kongan* (Chin., *kung-an;* Jpn., *kōan*), as it had been developed in China by Ta-hui Tsung-kao (1089–1163). Chinul then sought to incorporate this investigation into the soteriological scheme of sudden awakening/gradual cultivation taught by Tsung-mi (780–841), and finally to amalgamate this approach to Sŏn with the interpretation of Hwaŏm thought given by Li T'ung-hsüan (635–730). Chinul's synthesis of Sŏn and the scholastic teachings came to be regarded as a distinctively Korean school of Sŏn, called the Chogye-chong. His efforts revitalized the enervated Koryŏ church, and marked the ascendancy of Sŏn thought in the Korean Buddhist tradition. [*See the biographies of Chinul and Tsung-mi.*]

It was Chinul's disciple, Chin'gak Hyesim (1178–1234), who assured the acceptance of *hwadu* practice as the principal meditative technique in Korean Sŏn Buddhism. Following the model of Chinese thinkers of the Sung dynasty (960–1279), Hyesim examined the points of convergence between the three religions of Buddhism, Confucianism, and Taoism. This attempt to extend the embrace of Chinul's syncretic outlook so as to accommodate still other religions was to inspire a series of such investigations by later Korean authors. A Sŏn master of the later Koryŏ period, T'aego Pou (1301–1382), worked prodigiously to merge the remnants of the Nine Mountains Sŏn schools with the new Chogye-chong, and sought to graft onto this ecumenical school the Chinese Lin-chi (Kor., Imje; Jpn., Rinzai) lineage, into which he had received transmission in Yüan-dynasty China. The efforts of these and other teachers assured that the Chogye-chong would remain the predominant school of Korean Buddhism, a position it has retained down to the present.

Yi Buddhism (1392–1910). With the advent of the Yi dynasty in 1392 the fortunes of Buddhism began to wane. While the official policies of the Yi dynasty are commonly considered to have been Confucian in orientation, many of the kings continued to give munificent personal support to Buddhism. For example, the founder of the dynasty, Yi T'aejo (r. 1392–1398), appointed the renowned monk, Muhak Chajo (1327–1398), to the official post of preceptor to the royal family *(wangsa),* and the account of T'aejo's reign in the *Yijo sillok* (Veritable Record of the Yi Dynasty) teems with references to his sponsorship of temple construction projects, maigre offerings to monks, and various Buddhist rites. Confucian bureaucrats, however, continued to pressure the throne for stricter selection procedures for Buddhist monks, limits on the number of temples and hermitages, reduction in the number of officially sanctioned sects, and reorganization of the ecclesiastical system, all in order to effect more centralized supervision of the religion. Such policies were formally adopted by T'aejong (r. 1400–1418), the third Yi sovereign, and carried out on a massive scale by his successor, King Sejong (r. 1418–1450). In Sejong's proclamation of 1424, the Chogye, Ch'ŏnt'ae, and Vinaya schools were amalgamated into a single Sŏn (Meditative) school, and the remaining scholastic schools were merged into the Kyo (Doctrinal) school. New regulations were adopted for obtaining monk's certificates, making ordination much more difficult, and many monks already ordained were defrocked. The official ranks of national master *(kuksa)* and royal master *(wangsa)* were abolished. Temple paddy lands and forest properties were confiscated by the state and the legions of serfs retained by the monasteries were drafted into the army. Buddhist temples were no longer permitted within the capital or major cities. It is not surprising that during this dire period, Buddhist activities were as much concerned with the very survival of the tradition as with novel scholarly and meditative endeavors.

During this extremely difficult period in Korean Buddhist history, it is Sŏsan Hyujŏng (1520–1604) who epitomizes the continued Sŏn orientation of the church. Drawing his inspiration from Chinul's earlier vision of the unity of the Sŏn and scholastic schools, Hyujŏng produced a succinct manual of practice, titled the *Sŏn'ga kugam* (Guide to the Sŏn School). His other guides to Confucianism and Taoism were intended to sustain the reconciliation between Buddhism and its rival religions that was begun during the mid-Koryŏ and to outline their many similarities of purpose. Despite all the attempts of Hyujŏng's lineage, however, Buddhism's creative drive continued to wane. [*See also* Confucianism in Korea *and the biography of Hyujŏng.*]

Buddhism during the Modern Era. Japanese inroads on the peninsula from the late nineteenth century onward presented both new opportunities and new pressures for the Korean Buddhist tradition. Following the ratification of the Korea-Japan treaty of 1876, Japanese Buddhist sects, beginning with the Higashi Honganji sect of Pure Land, began to proselytize among the increasing number of Japanese immigrants resident in Korea, an activity that soon spread to the native Korean populace as well. Remonstrations by Japanese Nichiren missionaries compelled the impotent Yi court in 1895 to lift the centuries-old prohibition against the presence of Buddhist monks in the capital of Seoul. During the same period, a resurgence of Sŏn practice was catalyzed by the Korean Sŏn master Kyŏnghŏ (1857–1912) and his disciples, and successors in his lineage continue to teach today.

After the annexation of Korea in 1910, some Korean monks felt that the fortunes of the religion were dependent upon arranging a merger with a major Japanese sect. Yi Hoe-gwang went so far as to negotiate a combination of the Korean church with the Japanese Sōtō sect, but most Korean Sŏn monks regarded the gradualistic teachings of the Sōtō sect as anathema to the subitist orientation of their own tradition, and managed to block the merger. Another movement threatened to further divide the Buddhist church. As early as 1913, Han Yong-un (1879–1944), the only Buddhist signatory to the 1919 Korean independence declaration and a major literary figure, had shocked his contemporaries by advocating that monks be allowed to marry, a move he felt was necessary if Buddhism were to maintain any viable role in modern secular society. While this position was diametrically opposed to the traditional celibate orientation of the Korean ecclesia, the Japanese colonial government ultimately sustained it in 1926 with its promulgation of new monastic regulations that legalized matrimony for monks. Within a decade, virtually all temple abbots were married, thereby producing a dramatic change in the traditional moral discipline of the Korean church. Other reform movements designed to present Buddhism in a way that would be more relevant to modern concerns arose with increasing frequency. Among the most prominent of these was Wŏn Buddhism, founded in 1916 by Pak Chung-bin (1891–1943), which combined Buddhist teachings with a disparate variety of elements drawn from Confucianism, Taoism, Tonghak, and even Christianity.

After independence in 1945, Korean Buddhism was badly split between two irreconcilable sects. The T'aego-chong, a liberal sect of married monks, had flourished under Japanese patronage and was based principally in the cities where it catered to the lay Buddhist population. The Chogye-chong was a smaller, religiously conservative faction of monks who had managed to maintain their celibacy during the long years of Japanese occupation; their concern was to restore the meditative, scholastic, and disciplinary orientations of traditional Korean Buddhism. Only after years of intense conflict did the Chogye-chong finally win government support for its position in 1954. While litigation continues between the two sects, all of the major monasteries have reverted to its control. Now the predominant sect of Buddhism in Korea, the Chogye-chong has had considerable success in attracting a new generation of lay believers and monastic postulants to the teachings and practices of Buddhism. [*See also* Worship and Cultic Life, *article on* Buddhist Cultic Life in East Asia.]

BIBLIOGRAPHY

It remains difficult for the nonspecialist to find reliable books on Korean Buddhism in Western languages. Some summaries of research by Korean and Japanese scholars have appeared in *Buddhist Culture in Korea*, "Korean Culture Series," vol. 3, edited by Chun Shin-yong (Seoul, 1974). J. H. Kamstra's *Encounter or Syncretism: The Initial Growth of Japanese Buddhism* (Leiden, 1967), part 3, includes a useful survey of Three Kingdoms Buddhism and its influence on early Japan. The biographies of several prominent monks of the early Three Kingdoms period are translated in Peter H. Lee's *Lives of Eminent Korean Monks: The Haedong Kosŭng Chŏn* (Cambridge, Mass., 1969). A liberal rendering of a major Korean hagiographical and doxographical collection dealing with Three Kingdoms Buddhism appears in *Samguk Yusa: Legends and History of the Three Kingdoms of Ancient Korea*, translated by Tae-hung Ha and Grafton K. Mintz (Seoul, 1972). The travelogue of a Korean monk's pilgrimage to India and central Asia has been newly translated by Han Sung Yang, Yün-hua Jan, and Shotarō Iida in *The Hye Ch'o Diary* (Berkeley, 1984). Korean Hwaŏm thought receives some coverage in Steve Odin's *Process Metaphysics and Hua-yen Buddhism: A Critical Study of Cumulative Penetration vs. Interpenetration* (Albany, N.Y., 1982); the appendix includes a translation of Ŭisang's outline of Hwaŏm philosophy. Ch'egwan's survey of Ch'ŏnt'ae philosophy has been translated in David W. Chappell and Masao Ichishima's *T'ien-t'ai Buddhism: An Outline of the Fourfold Teachings* (Honolulu, 1984).

Korean Sŏn Buddhism is covered in my own book *The Korean Approach to Zen: The Collected Works of Chinul* (Honolulu, 1983). My introduction there includes a rather extensive survey of the early history of Korean Buddhism, and particularly the Sŏn tradition, in order to trace the contexts of Chinul's life and thought; specialists may also consult the bibliography of works in Asian languages on Korean Buddhism that appears there. Chinul's contributions to Korean Buddhism have also been examined in Hee-sung Keel's *Chinul: Founder of the Korean Sŏn Tradition* (Berkeley, 1984). A provocative exposition of Korean Sŏn practice appears in Sung Bae Park's *Buddhist Faith and Sudden Enlightenment* (Albany, N.Y., 1983). The principal works of Wŏn Buddhism are translated in Chon Pal-khn's *The Canonical Textbook of Won Buddhism* (Seoul, 1971). A number of seminal literary compositions by Korean Buddhists from all periods are translated in Peter H. Lee's *Anthology of Korean Literature: From Early Times to the Nineteenth Century* (Honolulu, 1981). A representative selection of philosophical and hagiographical writings by Korean Buddhist authors will appear in *Sources of Korean Tradition*, edited by Peter H. Lee (New York, forthcoming). The few Western-language works on Korean Buddhism written up to 1979 are listed in *Studies on Korea: A Scholar's Guide*, edited by Han-Kyo Kim (Honolulu, 1980); see chapter 4, "Philosophy and Religion."

ROBERT EVANS BUSWELL, JR.

Buddhism in Japan

Buddhism, originating in India and journeying a long distance through Central Asia and China, reached the islands of Japan in the middle of the sixth century CE. At the time of inception, it was an essentially alien religion quite dissimilar in outlook to the unorganized complex of indigenous beliefs and cults that later came to be known by the name of Shintō. In the ensuing fifteen hundred years, however, it not only took firm root among the Japanese, but also played an important part in their social, cultural, and religious life. Indeed, its impact has been and remains so powerful that any attempt to comprehend these dimensions of Japanese life would be insufficient if it did not pay due attention to Buddhism. This is not to say, however, that Japan became a completely Buddhist country. At no point in Japanese history did Buddhism exercise a religious monopoly; rather, it coexisted with other religious and intellectual traditions such as Shintō, Confucianism, and, in modern times, Christianity. Furthermore, in the course of development on Japanese soil, Buddhism has itself been significantly modified under the influence of indigenous culture so as to exhibit peculiarly Japanese traits. Thus, the phenomenon of Japanese Buddhism may be viewed in two contrasting perspectives: how far and in what manner Buddhism has contributed to the formation of Japanese culture and, conversely, how the alien religion of Buddhism was transformed in the process of adaptation to the social and intellectual milieu of the nation.

Historical Setting and General Features. Before describing this twofold process of impact and modification through the ages, a few circumstances that determined Buddhism's general character may be pointed out. In the first place, it must be noted that the Buddhism brought to Japan was by no means uniform but comprised diverse elements derived from successive stages of its history. According to the *Nihonshoki* (720 CE), Japan's first official chronicle, Buddhism was introduced to Japan from Paekche, a kingdom in Korea, in 552 CE. (Another source gives the date as 538 CE.) Intermittently from the sixth to the seventeenth century, knowledge of Buddhism was acquired directly from China by official envoys and missionary monks. Inasmuch as Buddhism was transmitted to Japan by this northern route, Japanese Buddhism is usually classified as a branch of Mahāyāna, as opposed to Theravāda, which is found in several Southeast Asian countries. Such a characterization is not incorrect, for Japanese Buddhism, especially in its present form, is obviously quite different from Theravāda and other of the so-called Hīnayāna schools, of which the core is the monastic orders of the *saṃgha*. Yet it must be remembered that in Japan elements not only of Mahāyāna but also of Hīnayāna can be found. More concretely, the scriptures, teachings, disciplines, and rituals belonging to nearly every phase of Buddhist development have been transmitted, preserved, and studied here.

In a sense, Japanese Buddhism may be thought of as a kind of summary of the whole of Buddhist history from its Indian beginning to the manifestations of later days. Consideration of the location of Japan may render this fact readily intelligible. Since the Japanese archipelago is located near the eastern border of the Chinese mainland, it naturally formed a terminus of the Buddhist pilgrimage. The further transplantation of Buddhism from Japan to other parts of the world, notably to the American continents and Europe, is only of recent date. [*See also* Missions, *article on* Buddhist Missions.]

Second, Buddhism was accepted in Japan in close association with other elements of Chinese culture. This, again, can be accounted for by the historical circumstances in which the Japanese found themselves. Broadly speaking, Japan was one of the satellite societies surrounding the powerful center of highly developed civilization that was China. These societies, with China as their center, formed a sort of semiautonomous circle that may be dubbed "the East Asian world" and shared some common elements: the Chinese system of writing; political and legal organization based upon the Chinese model; broadly Confucian teachings; and Buddhism, which, although Indian in origin, took on Chinese attributes. Since China was by far superior, both politically and culturally, to these neighboring societies, it was only natural that for them China served as a source of new information and cultural skills. When, beginning in the fifth century, the Japanese came into contact with imperial China, they were politically in the process of building a new social order by uniting the previously autonomous clans under the centralized leadership of the imperial clan. Culturally, Japan was in a rather primitive stage of development and remained as yet preliterate. It is no wonder that in such a situation Buddhism was welcomed as an element of a highly refined culture. This applies especially to the initial period after its introduction, but this situation prevailed more or less until the advent of Western civilization in the modern age.

What attracts one's attention at this juncture is the fact that in Japanese history there seems to be a peculiar pattern of alternating periods: periods in which contact with the external world is eagerly sought and elements of foreign culture are diligently absorbed, and periods in which people are more intent upon digesting what they received and creating something of their own. These may be called periods of "outward orientation" and "inward orientation," respectively. In this respect, too, the insular position of Japan was of decisive importance, because it enabled the Japanese to be selective in importation and then to concentrate on naturalizing and refining the alien elements without being disturbed. Thus, the centuries following Buddhism's introduction were characterized by an enormous zeal to appropriate it as an integral part of continental culture, while the period after about the end of the eighth century was spent mostly in elaborating it to produce distinctively indigenized expressions. When, after a rather long period of internal maturation, Japan experienced another large-scale encounter with the external world, that is, during the sixteenth century and again more markedly after the middle of the nineteenth, it was no longer Buddhism but Christianity that figured as the chief agent of a new era.

The fact that Buddhism was first introduced as part and parcel of the superior culture of China was not unrelated to the patterns of development it experienced in Japan. In earlier times, in particular, those who readily accepted and aligned themselves with the newly arrived faith were recruited from the members of the imperial family and influential court nobles. This does not mean, to be sure, that Buddhism did not affect the lives of the common people at all. On the contrary, as early as during the Nara period (710–784) there are some signs of Buddhist influence on the lives of people of humble birth. Taken as a whole, however, it was not until the medieval age of the Kamakura (1185–1333) and the Muromachi (1338–1573) periods that Buddhism began to genuinely influence wider circles of population. Therefore, Buddhism spread geographically from the center to the periphery and sociologically from the upper strata of society to the lower. For this reason, Japanese Buddhism in its early stage is frequently called "aristocratic," while the later forms are regarded as mass movements.

The above statement of the overall characteristics should not be taken to mean that Japanese Buddhism has been uniform in terms of doctrine and/or practice. On the contrary, it has always encompassed a wide variety of positions that resulted partly from the complexity of the tradition prior to its entry into Japan and partly from the changes it underwent during the process of appropriation. On the organizational level, too, Japanese Buddhism has been and is classified into a number of "sects" (*shū*). Since in Japan there has never been a semblance of a Buddhist church with a universal claim, the term *sect* is a bit misleading; a more appropriate term is *school*. It is clear that this internal variety is an outcome of the historical development of Buddhism in Japanese history, of which a brief survey may be in order. In this attempt the conventional historiographical distinction of periods will be employed as the general framework, for the status of Buddhism in Japan has been affected, if not completely determined, by the events in the political, social, and cultural lives of the people.

From the Introduction to the End of the Nara Period. One of the most crucial periods in the history of Japanese Buddhism is no doubt that which started with its official introduction in the middle of the sixth century and came to its culmination in the Nara period. It is, as suggested earlier, the formative era of the unified Japanese state. During these centuries Buddhism was first accepted by influential clans and court nobles in central Japan and thence gradually gained ground in Japanese society, laying the foundation for all later developments.

Upon closer examination, however, one sees that acceptance of the new faith did not proceed without obstruction. For one thing, the position of the emperor was based on the Shintō-derived notion of theocracy that united religious and political functions in one person. For emperors to embrace an alien religion would have meant a threat to the very basis of their power. In addition, there was internal strife between two camps among the influential clans, one advocating and the other rejecting the new religion until, finally, the more liberal Soga clan succeeded in securing imperial permission to practice Buddhism in the form of a private cult. What seems remarkable about this conflict is that, to all appearances, neither the supporters nor the opponents possessed a proper understanding of the Buddhist teaching. For them, the Buddha was merely a kind of *kami* (numinous force, divinity) from abroad; they admired Buddha statues mainly for their exquisite beauty and accepted Buddhism only as superior magical means to achieve practical benefits such as healing from illness or prosperity.

Shōtoku Taishi. In this early stage, Prince Shōtoku (574–622) played a decisive role in furthering the cause of Buddhism and at the same time prepared the way for a deeper understanding of its ideas. As a statesman and thinker he pursued two complementary objectives: he sought, on the one hand, to establish a centralized state under the authority of the emperor and based on the model of Chinese bureaucracy and, on the other, to enrich the spiritual life of the nation by officially endorsing Buddhism. For this purpose, he sent a governmental envoy to the Chinese court in 607 that brought back valuable information about Chinese institutions and Buddhist *sūtras* and teachings. This contact he opened with China proved to be of utmost importance to the development of Japanese Buddhism for the next several centuries. At the same time, he initiated the construction of a number of great temples in the capital or its vicinity, of which Horyūji, the oldest Buddhist structure in Japan, may be mentioned. Considering these achievements, Shōtoku has been rightly admired as the father of Japanese Buddhism.

Shōtoku was influential not only in these activities, but also in his intellectual grasp of the essence of Buddhist teaching. The phrase attributed to him, "the world is illusory, the Buddha alone is true," reveals a knowledge of Buddhism far more deep than that of his contemporaries. The phrase is noteworthy as the first testimony to the idea of world negation, hitherto unknown in Japan. In addition, there are several documents traditionally accredited to his authorship: the so-called Seventeen-Article Constitution and the commentaries on three important Mahāyāna *sūtras* (the *Saddharmapuṇḍarīka Sūtra*, the *Vimalakīrtinirdeśa Sūtra*, and the *Śrīmālāsiṃhanāda Sūtra*). The Constitution consists of a set of moral and administrative injunctions, of which the contents are largely Confucian mingled with some Legalist elements, but it gives Buddhism a predominant role as the source of ultimate value. As for the commentaries, they show not only a surprisingly correct understanding of Buddhist principles but a singularly Japanese tendency to adapt Buddhist ideas to the needs of practical life. [*See the biography of Shōtoku Taishi.*]

The Nara schools. Generally speaking, the developments after the death of Shōtoku took place along the course envisioned by him. Measures like the Taika Reforms of 645 and the promulgation of the Taihō Code in 701 had as their aim the establishment of a centralized administration, the Ritsuryō system, coupled with the promotion of religion, most notably of Buddhism. After the completion of the first permanent capital of Heijōkyō (modern Nara), this policy of government support for Buddhism reached its climax. Of particular importance in this respect was the official decree issued by Emperor Shōmu in 741 to build a network of state-subsidized temples (*kokubunji*) in each province. Further, he had a gigantic bronze statue of Vairocana Buddha cast and erected at the main temple in Nara, Tōdaiji, in 749. Completed and consecrated with ceremonial pomp three years later, this Vairocana Buddha was at once a symbol of the magnificent universe and of the centralized state. Shōmu, in addition, was the first emperor to declare himself a servant of Buddhism, thus confessing his personal commitment to the faith and elevating it almost to the status of a national religion. [*See also* Mahāvairocana.]

Another feature of Nara Buddhism was that it comprehended diverse viewpoints within Buddhism. Each of the so-called six Nara schools represented a tradition of study of a particular text or textual cycle of Indian Buddhism that flourished in the T'ang capital, Ch'angan, during the eighth century:

1. Ritsu, named after the Chinese Lü, or Vinaya tradition, concerned itself with exegesis of the Vinaya (the Buddhist code of monastic discipline). Based principally on Tao-hsüan's Nan-shan branch of the tradition, this sect was also responsible in Japan for the ordination of the clergy. [*See the biography of Ganjin.*]
2. Jōjitsu refers to an exegetical tradition that takes its name from the *Satyasiddhi* (Chin., *Ch'eng-shih lun*; Jpn., *Jōjitsuron*), a text attributed to the Indian monk Harivarman.
3. Kusha is named for Vasubandhu's *Abhidharmakośa* (Chin., *Chü-she lun*; Jpn., *Kusharon*), a systematic treatise on the Abhidharma thought of the Sarvāstivāda-Sautrāntika tradition of Hīnayāna Buddhism.
4. Sanron (Mādhyamika) derives from the "three treatises" (*sanron*) that form the basis of the Mādhya-

mika tradition in East Asia: the *Madhyamakakārikā* (Chin., *Chung-lun*) and the *Dvādaśadvāra* (Chin., *Shih-erh-men lun*) of Nāgārjuna, and Āryadeva's *Śataśāstra* (Chin., *Po-lun*). [*See* Mādhyamika.]
5. Hossō (Yogācāra) is based on the Yogācāra tradition introduced into China by the famous pilgrim-monk Hsüan-tsang (596?–664) and called there Fa-hsiang (Jpn., Hossō; "*dharma* characteristic"). [*See* Yogācāra.]
6. Kegon is devoted to the study of the *Avataṃsaka Sūtra* (Chin., *Hua-yen ching*; Jpn., *Kegongyō*), a major Mahāyanā scripture. [*See* Hua-yen.]

Although commonly referred to as sects, these traditions were schools of thought rather than concrete sectarian institutions, and it was not unusual for a monk of those days to receive instruction in more than one of these "schools." The first three traditions shared a pronounced Hīnayāna orientation, the latter three were devoted to the study of Mahāyāna texts; together, they covered nearly the entire range of Buddhist thought as transmitted to China by the eighth century. It must be emphasized, however, that these distinctions obtained primarily in the academic study of Buddhist dogmatics. In the actual life of the nation the major function of Buddhists and Buddhist institutions was to conduct certain rites and services believed to be efficacious in securing the welfare of the state and to offer prayers for the achievement of mundane requests on behalf of their patrons. [*For further discussion of the antecedents of the Nara sects, see* Buddhism, Schools of, *article on* Chinese Buddhism.]

While geared mostly to the political objectives of the government and the ruling aristocracy, Nara Buddhism did not lack its popular aspect. This popular side was best exemplified by the semilegendary figure of Gyōgi (c. 670–749), a recluse monk living in the vicinity of the capital who allegedly was in possession of miraculous powers. Tradition maintains that he traveled through the countryside performing many beneficial deeds for the populace, and that Emperor Shōmu had to ask his cooperation for the successful accomplishment of the building of the great Buddha statue. These accounts seem to indicate that Buddhism had already begun to penetrate into wider circles of the population, associating itself with the native shamanistic beliefs. Here we notice the beginning of the undercurrent of folk Buddhism that increased in influence with the passage of time. [*See also* Hijiri *and the biography of Gyōgi.*]

Of the so-called six Nara schools, three have survived until this day: the Hossō school represented by Kōfukuji (Kōfuku Temple) and Yakushiji, the Kegon school with Tōdaiji as its center, and the Ritsu school based at Tōshōdaiji. To this group, the Shōtoku school with Hōryūji as its center may be added. Confined to the district of Nara and having few lay adherents, the social impact of these schools is rather limited compared with other later and more powerful organizations. However, they possess a certain symbolic value, as evocative of the heyday of Buddhism in ancient times and as the fountainhead from which all the later schools have sprung.

The Buddhist Synthesis of the Heian Period. With the move of the capital from Nara to Heiankyō (modern Kyoto) in 794, Japanese history entered the second half of its antiquity. During this period, known as the Heian era (794–1185), the centralized bureaucratic system partly realized in the preceding era slowly declined and eventually gave rise to the feudalism of the next age. Although nominal power continued to rest with the imperial court, actual political initiative gradually passed into the hands of a few aristocrats, the Fujiwara clan in particular, whose basis of power was in privately owned estates. In this general trend toward disintegration, Buddhist institutions gained a certain amount of autonomy in relation to the state but, on the other hand, had to associate themselves in some way or other with the interests of the ruling aristocrats. In addition, official contact with China was suspended at the end of the ninth century and the constant flow of religious influences from the continent came to a halt, a circumstance that favored indigenization.

In the earliest part of this period the two new schools of Tendai and Shingon were founded separately by two distinguished leaders: Saichō (767–822, generally known by his posthumous title of Dengyō Daishi) and Kūkai (774–835, commonly referred to as Kōbō Daishi). Although quite different in character and temperament, these monks nevertheless were similar in a number of respects. They both had as their aim the establishment of a new center for Japanese Buddhism, one free from the control of the orthodox Nara schools. For this purpose they both went to China to acquaint themselves with the latest forms of Buddhist doctrine and practice and upon returning erected their headquarters on sacred mountains outside the turmoil of the city. What is more important, however, is that their schools were quite comprehensive and synthetic in orientation: both sought to work out an all-encompassing framework in which different points of view, Buddhist and non-Buddhist alike, could be assigned a place. Because of this emphasis, Tendai and Shingon teachings offered an excellent theoretical basis for the fusion of indigenous beliefs and Buddhism that gradually took place.

Tendai. Tendai is a Japanese form of the Chinese T'ien-t'ai, the name of a mountain in China, the temple located on that mountain, and a school established there by the monk Chih-i (fl. sixth century). [*See* T'ien-t'ai.] Having studied in his youth at Tōdaiji in Nara and become somehow disillusioned by the formalism of the traditional schools, Saichō sought a new form of teaching capable of uniting different viewpoints into one, an orientation he was to find in T'ien-t'ai. Meanwhile, Saichō had managed to gain the personal favor of Emperor Kammu and was chosen as a student to be sent to China. The Chinese T'ien-t'ai attached particular value to the *Saddharmapuṇḍarīka* (Lotus) *Sūtra* and developed an elaborate philosophical system concerning the realization of the ultimate truth coupled with the practice of meditation. Saichō faithfully learned these teachings but, in contrast to the Chinese model, assigned equal importance to such other elements as moral discipline, Zen meditation, and Tantric (Esoteric) ritualism. In brief, Saichō's Tendai was more eclectic in nature than Chinese T'ien-t'ai. In addition, we can recognize a certain ethnocentric tendency in his thought, for he considered the pursuit of Buddhist teaching as part of the service for the protection of the nation.

Saichō returned home to Enryakuji, a monastery he had built a short distance northeast of the capital on Mount Hiei, and devoted the latter half of his life to establishing Tendai as an independent school. During his lifetime, however, this goal remained unrealized. In order for any Buddhist group to be officially acknowledged, it was necessary for it to have the right to ordain monks, which in those days was the sole prerogative of the Ritsu school. In spite of Saichō's eager requests the government withheld permission for some time, but finally granted it a few days after his death. Since that day, the Mount Hiei monastery has grown to become one of the most important centers in Japan for the study of and training in Buddhism. Its historical significance may be inferred from the fact that all the major schools emerging in the subsequent Kamakura period, that is, Pure Land, Zen, and Nichiren, were connected in one way or another with Mount Hiei. [*See also* Tendaishū *and the biography of Saichō.*]

Shingon. The term Shingon, derived from the Chinese term for *mantra, chen-yen,* means the word embodying a mysterious power that can bring about unusual effects, both spiritual and material. This form of Buddhism, introduced to Japan by Kūkai, stems from Tantrism, which arose during the last phase of Buddhist development in India. [*See* Buddhism, Schools of, *article on* Esoteric Buddhism.] It may be characterized as a mixture of highly sophisticated metaphysical ideas and elaborate rituals deeply imbued with magic. Kūkai, trained for a career in government service, at the age of eighteen suddenly abandoned his studies of Confucianism and Taoism to turn to Buddhism. Fortunate enough to be selected as a member of the mission sailing for China, he visited the Chinese capital of Ch'ang-an and devoted himself to the study of Esoteric Buddhism then in vogue. Over the next three years he successfully mastered the teaching and was appointed the eighth patriarch of the Esoteric transmission. [*See* Chen-yen.] On returning to Japan he established Kongōbuji on Mount Kōya, south of Nara, and Tōji in Kyoto in order to propagate his teaching.

As Kūkai was a versatile genius talented in the fields of art and literature as well, his influence was far-reaching. His most important achievement, however, was the systematic account of the teaching of Esoteric Buddhism. This he accomplished in his *Jūjūshinron* (Treatise on the Ten Stages of Spiritual Development) in which he classified Buddhist and non-Buddhist points of view on an ascending scale of stages that starts with the natural state of consciousness and culminates in the perfect state of being realized in Esoteric Buddhism. According to Esoteric Buddhism, ultimate truth is symbolically present in all phenomena, but above all exists in three forms: *mantra*s, mysterious formulas; *maṇḍala*s, the graphic representations of the orders of the universe; and *mudrā*s, ritual gestures symbolic of religious truth. Because of this symbolism, Esoteric Buddhism has exerted a remarkable influence on Buddhist iconography and fine arts. At the same time, there is no denying the fact that in subsequent eras Esoteric Buddhism was not infrequently exposed to the danger of degenerating into mere ritualism. [*See also* Shingonshū *and the biography of Kūkai.*]

Other trends. During this period, a series of trends that were to determine the future course of Buddhist history became increasingly conspicuous. One was a strong tendency toward syncretism with the native religion of Shintō. On the practical level, it led to the construction of many *jingūji* (shrine-temples) where Buddhist rituals were performed within the precincts of a Shintō shrine. On the ideological level the fusion was comprehended by the *honjisuijaku* theory, according to which the Shintō *kami* were secondary manifestations in Japan of certain Buddhas or *bodhisattvas*. This syncretism, which was primarily based on the synthetic Tendai and Shingon teachings, was a dominant feature of Japanese Buddhism until the beginning of the Meiji period (1868), when by governmental decree the fusion was somewhat violently broken. [*See* Honjisuijaku.] Another factor that came to the fore, especially in the late Heian period, was a keen sense of historical crisis and the accompanying search for new forms of teaching. The sense of crisis, no doubt exacerbated by the general instability of the contemporary social order, expressed itself in the theory of *mappō*. This theory held that the Buddhist religion was destined to decline in three successive stages, and, more ominously, that the last stage had already begun. [*See* Mappō.] In fact, one can observe in these centuries a gradual rise of belief in various savior figures, Amida (Skt., Amitābha) in particular, among both the aristocrats and the common people, thus preparing the way for the next age. [*See the biography of Kōya.*]

New Movements of the Kamakura Period. The establishment of the Kamakura shogunate (1185–1333) opened a new period in Japanese history. Political power passed from the hands of aristocrats living at the imperial court in Kyoto to the newly arisen military class, initiating an age of feudalism that would last until 1868. Almost parallel to this shift in the political sphere was the appearance of a series of new movements in Buddhism, of which three are especially worth mentioning: the Pure Land, Zen, and Nichiren schools.

Sometimes at variance with each other, these schools nevertheless shared a few common characteristics. To begin with, the three each derived from the Tendai tradition. Each chose from among the synthetic teachings of the previous era one particular teaching or practice and made it the focus of exclusive attention. Thus, Pure Land Buddhism selected the way of salvation through faith in Amida Buddha, Zen employed the way of meditation, and the Nichiren school concentrated on the path of devotion to the truth as revealed in the *Lotus Sutra*. In a word, all three, in marked contrast to the comprehensive approach of the Tendai and Shingon schools, were selective and sectarian in orientation. As a consequence of this one-sidedness, they often had to face conflicts with the long-established schools.

Historically, each of them had a different background. Among the three, Zen is somewhat exceptional in that it owed much to the direct influence of Sung China. The practice of meditation (Skt., *dhyāna;* Chin., *ch'an*; Jpn., *zen*) was of course an essential element of Buddhism from its inception. In the hands of the practical-minded Chinese, however, an independent "meditation" tradition (the Ch'an school) arose, which claimed to eschew metaphysical speculation in favor of direct insight gained through meditation. Pure Land Buddhism, whose origins date almost from the beginning of the Mahāyāna era, had both Indian and Chinese prototypes, although its increasing popularity during the late Heian and early Kamakura periods must be interpreted in the context of the historical situation at that time. The Nichiren school, finally, had no foreign antecedent. In this respect it differs from Zen and Pure Land Buddhism and may be regarded as most typically Japanese.

The Pure Land schools. As mentioned earlier, faith in the saving mercy of Amida and the idea of birth into his Pure Land *(jōdo)* named Sukhāvatī ("land of bliss") was not unfamiliar during the Heian period. [*See* Amitābha *and* Pure and Impure Lands.] However, it was Hōnen (1133–1212, also known as Genkū) who gave the trend the decisive turn that made it one of the most powerful streams in Japanese Buddhism. Hōnen studied at the Mount Hiei Tendai monastery but became dissatisfied with the prevailing scholasticism; he thus left to seek out a sort of Buddhism that would be more appropriate to the needs of the people. In 1175, after a long period of spiritual quest, Hōnen found this Buddhist practice in the teaching of the Nembutsu, the simple calling of the Buddha's name. [*See* Nien-fo.] In order to defend his view, he later composed his principal work *Senchaku hongan nembutsu shū* (Treatise on the Selection of Nembutsu of the Original Vow). In it, he divided all Buddhism into two types: one in which the goal of enlightenment is sought by means of disciplined self-endeavor, and one in which the goal is to be reborn into the Pure Land through a wholehearted reliance on the mercy of Amida, there to hear Amida preach and thus to gain enlightenment. Of the two, he favored the latter and declared all traditional exercises other than the Nembutsu merely auxiliary.

In this way, Hōnen introduced reliance on a single, easy practice, an idea that was completely new in the history of Japanese Buddhism. The choice of reliance on Amida was supported not only by confidence in his mercy but also by the conviction that people were so deeply enmeshed in sinfulness that they could not even attempt to make an effort to become enlightened. In a degenerate age such as his, Hōnen thought, it was simply not possible for men to achieve enlightenment by their own power *(jiriki)*; instead, they had to rely on the "power of another" *(tariki)*. No doubt such a pessimistic view of human nature and of history was related to the political and social instability of the age. What is most important about his teaching, however, is that by denouncing lofty speculation and elaborate, costly rituals and by replacing them with a simple act of faith, Hōnen opened a way of salvation to the common people. [*See* Jōdoshū *and the biography of Hōnen.*]

Hōnen had many an able disciple, but it was Shinran (1173–1262) who gave his master's teaching its most radical interpretation. He emphasized an idea in Hōnen's system that, while basic, remained for Hōnen only one among others, namely, the idea of the all-encompassing and absolute mercy of Amida. Firmly believing in the compassion and saving power of the Buddha, Shinran came to the conclusion that Amida Buddha had *already* completed his salvific scheme. Each person, regardless of his or her status and quality, was already saved, although he or she might not realize it. Accordingly, the Nembutsu was regarded by Shinran as an expression of gratitude to Amida rather than a practice leading to birth in his Pure Land. Out of this conviction, Shinran also dared to take an extraordinary step: calling himself "neither monk nor layman" *(hizō hizoku)*, he deliberately ignored the rules of monastic life by marrying and raising children. Through this act he established a new model for the integration of secular life and the religious quest. His Jōdo Shinshū (the True Pure Land school, as distinct from Hōnen's Jōdoshū or Pure Land school) grew in size and influence in the following centuries and remains one of the most powerful Buddhist institutions in Japan. [*See* Jōdo Shinshū *and the biography of Shinran.*]

Zen Buddhism. The establishment of Zen, which was the second of the major schools to appear during the Kamakura period, marked a departure from traditional Buddhism insofar as Zen put aside abstruse metaphysics and complicated rituals and tried instead to concentrate on the personal experience of enlightenment in the midst of daily life. This stance is best expressed in the famous Zen motto *kyōge betsuden* ("a special transmission outside the formal teaching"). In this search for simplicity Zen was in basic agreement with the Pure Land school; however, in contrast with members of this school, who in a pietistic manner taught salvation from without, Zen's proponents firmly retained the more traditional notion that enlightenment is gained through one's own endeavors.

Having enjoyed wide popularity in Sung China, Zen was transmitted to Japan by several figures. [*See* Ch'an.] One of the first was Eisai (1141–1214), originally a Tendai monk, who visited China twice. In 1191, after his second sojourn, Eisai introduced the Rinzai (Chin., Lin-chi) version of Zen, one of the so-called five houses then prevailing in China. With the aid of the Kamakura shogunate he was able to found two bases for his activities, Jufukuji in Kamakura and Kenninji in Kyoto. The fact that he turned to the rising warrior class for support is noteworthy, for in Kyoto he was liable to be exposed to severe criticisms from the Tendai establishment on Mount Hiei, and because the aristocrats living in Kyoto generally had a natural predilection for the traditional schools of Buddhism. Even though he thus made the first step in transplanting Zen, his was not a pure Zen inasmuch as it was still mingled with some elements of earlier schools, Esoteric ritualism in particular. In this respect, Eisai stood with one foot in the tradition of Heian Buddhism and one in the newer tradition of Zen. [*See the biography of Eisai.*]

Some thirty-six years later, Dōgen (1200–1253) introduced from China the Sōtō (Ts'ao-tung) school of Zen. The main difference between Rinzai and Sōtō consists in the approach to achieving enlightenment: while Rinzai employs a question-and-answer technique between master and disciple focusing on *kōan*, riddle-like topics taken mostly from the anecdotes of past masters, Sōtō concentrates almost exclusively on the practice of sitting meditation. This Dōgen called *shikantaza*, sitting straight without entertaining vain thoughts, for according to him enlightenment is not separate from practice and practice equals enlightenment. In contrast to Eisai, Dōgen held a stricter attitude toward other schools: he did not engage himself in ritualism and rejected Nembutsu practice as utterly useless. Such an austere spirit also led him to stay aloof from worldly affairs; during the latter half of his life he withdrew to a remote province in northern Japan and sequestered himself in Eiheiji, dedicating all his energy to the training of a few elect disciples. [*See the biography of Dōgen.*]

In their subsequent development, Rinzai and Sōtō, the two major schools of Zen in Japan, took markedly different courses. As is clear from the examples of Eisai and many of his successors, the Rinzai school flourished chiefly by the patronage of high-ranking samurai who were now in positions of power. Its headquarters, the so-called five temples *(gozan)*, were located in either Kyoto or Kamakura and served as centers of both Zen education and the study of newly introduced Chinese learning, including Neo-Confucianism. Thus Rinzai came to play an important role in the dissemination of refined culture. [*See* Gozan Zen.] The Sōtō school, on the contrary, sought its adherents mostly among provincial samurai and the peasantry. In order to win these people's support, the rigid and elitist stance of Dōgen had to be abandoned in favor of a more conciliatory attitude in relation to their religious needs. As a means of gaining their allegiance Sōtō assimilated a certain amount of popular beliefs and rituals but devised, above all, funeral and memorial services for the dead, a trait that was to become one of the characteristic features of almost all Buddhist schools in Japan. [*See also* Zen.]

Nichirenshū. The thirteenth century also witnessed the emergence of a unique movement that bears the name and the imprint of its founder, Nichiren (1222–1282). One of the most charismatic personalities in the religious history of Japan, Nichiren was deeply concerned with the material and spiritual state of the country and fought incessantly for its improvement. His aim was *risshō ankoku* ("restore the right teaching [and thereby] achieve the security of the nation"). In a sense, his was a sort of reform movement from within the Tendai school, but in its exclusive pursuit of its goal it went far beyond the traditional forms to become a new, independent school.

Troubled from his youth by doubts concerning the cause of natural and social calamities that plagued his day, Nichiren reached the conclusion that they were due to the disappearance of the "true (Buddhist) teaching" and that the country would never be safe before true Buddhism was restored. This "right teaching" he believed to have found in the *Lotus Sutra* as interpreted in the Tendai tradition. Accordingly, he urged people to praise the *Lotus Sutra* as the only true text, and harshly condemned all schools that depended on other scriptural sources (particularly Ritsu, Shingon, Zen, and above all Pure Land) as being false doctrines. Nichiren was not content with criticizing other schools, however; he made remonstrances to the Kamakura shogunate, demanding a reform of Buddhism and of the government in keeping with the spirit of the *sūtra*. Such drastic behavior naturally aroused the enmity of his opponents and met with repeated opposition on the part of the shogunate until finally he was exiled to the island of Sado in northern Japan. Although his efforts did not have any actual results during his lifetime, he attracted a dedicated following and inspired many an influential movement in later centuries.

Nichiren's teaching came to be embraced by members of the merchant class in Kyoto and other cities. During the fifteenth century, in the general collapse of political order, the adherents of the Nichiren school even equipped themselves with arms, and their uprising, called Hokke-ikki, had formidable effects. It is interesting to notice that the Nichiren school exhibits a strong propensity toward active political and social involvement; this prophetic vein is what distinguishes it from other branches of Buddhism in Japan and elsewhere. Nichiren's legacy is still very much alive, as may be readily seen in the contemporary new religious movements of Buddhist origin. The fact that many powerful organizations, such as Reiyūkai, Risshō Kōseikai, and Sōka Gakkai, are all related in a substantial way to his teaching testifies to the lasting influence of this school. [*See* Nichirenshū; Reiyūkai; Risshō Kōseikai; Sōka Gakkai; *and the biography of Nichiren.*]

Institutional Consolidation of the Tokugawa Period. In many expositions, the history of Japanese Buddhism is related as if Buddhism reached its apex during the Kamakura period. In a sense this holds true, for by the close of the period all the major schools in Japan had made their appearance, and what occurred thereafter constituted, by and large, merely internal developments within each group. For this reason it is possible to divide Japanese Buddhism roughly into Nara Buddhism, and the Tendai, Shingon, Pure Land, Zen, and Nichiren schools, a scheme that is adopted in contemporary official statistics as well. This does not imply, to be sure, that there were no developments of importance in subsequent eras. On the contrary, although no new doctrines or practices emerged during the Tokugawa period (1600–1867), Buddhism underwent a process of institutional consolidation hitherto unknown in its history. The changes that took place during this time bear directly upon the nature of Buddhism in the modern age.

On the whole, Buddhist schools enjoyed official recognition during this period, while at the same time they were made subservient to the political and administrative objectives of the Tokugawa regime. In the early part of the seventeenth century Buddhist temples, along with Shintō shrines, were brought under the control of commissioners (*jisha bugyō*) appointed both at the national and local level. In each school temples were organized to form a hierarchical system of head and branch temples. Furthermore, concurrent with the banishment of Christianity, then commonly known as Kirishitan, the shogunate ordered every Japanese to be affiliated with a particular temple, which issued certificates *(tera-uke)* attesting that the person in question was not a member of the forbidden religion. These measures resulted in the formation of a network of parish-like organizations in which every household was at least nominally affiliated with a Buddhist temple. This system, called *danka seido*, although legally abolished since the early years of the Meiji period (1868–1912), still continues to provide an important social basis for many Buddhist organizations.

It is clear that this policy of the Tokugawa regime contributed much to the stability of the various Buddhist schools. Since it demanded the presence of a temple in each locality the number of temples actually increased. However, it is equally clear that this stability was obtained at a high cost. The material well-being of many temples often led to the moral corruption of the clergy. Harsh criticisms resulted: inside Buddhist organizations, the distrust of priests sometimes gave rise to a kind of underground religious activity by devout members of the laity; critical voices from without also increased as time went on. In this context, too, there was a remarkable decline of intellectual creativity on the part of Buddhists, despite the seeming prosperity of scholarship in the many academies established by various groups. Since new teachings were not allowed to be propounded, effort was concentrated on elaborating and refining the details of traditional dogmatics. While

Buddhists were previously among the foremost thinkers of each period, now it was Confucian and, to some extent, Shintō scholars who addressed themselves to the real social and religious problems of the time. [*See also* Confucianism in Japan.]

Buddhism in Modern Japan. The modern period in Japanese history began with the Meiji restoration in 1868 and brought a series of radical changes in all spheres of life, including religion. Buddhism was deeply affected both in a positive and negative sense by the rapid process of modernization. One of the most pronounced changes took place on the institutional level, particularly in the relation of Buddhism to the state. In its attempt to mobilize the nation under the authority of the emperor, the Meiji government gave a definite priority to Shintō and thereby put an end to the age-old Shintō-Buddhist syncretism. Certainly, in the beliefs and practices of the common people the two traditions are still regarded as harmoniously united. Even today, many Japanese pay homage to Shintō shrines at the same time that they are associated with Buddhist temples. Yet it is clear that, at least legally, Buddhism is no longer in possession of the privileged status it formerly enjoyed and has become one tradition among others in a religiously pluralistic society.

These changes in the social milieu, combined with the influences from the Christian West that began to enter the country beginning in the latter half of the nineteenth century, elicited a number of responses from traditional Buddhist organizations on different levels and in various forms. One was a new and active engagement in educational and social work projects. Previously, many Buddhist temples had served as centers of education and of social welfare. Now they made it their task to promote these activities in conformity with modern institutional regulations. Parallel to this trend, one can also observe a renewal of missionary efforts, which in some cases even led to the establishment of overseas missions. These and similar efforts may be summarized under the rubric of organizational reform.

Side by side with these reforms, many Buddhist leaders felt the need to cope with the challenge of modernity. Thus, new academic studies of Buddhism, both philosophical and philological in nature, were initiated. When Buddhism first encountered Christianity during the sixteenth century, theoretical reflection on the basic premises of each religion had already begun in the form of disputations. In the modern period, however, Buddhism was confronted not only with Christianity but also with the modern scientific worldview. Out of this encounter emerged various attempts at reinterpreting the Buddhist teaching; these have continued until the present. On the other hand, the introduction of modern research techniques after the 1880s, coupled with the availability in Japan of materials from nearly all stages of Buddhist history, has led to the flowering of Buddhist studies in accordance with rigorous standards of modern scholarship. [*See* Buddhist Studies.]

Finally, a number of new movements appeared on the fringes of or outside the established groups. Insofar as they do not conform to the traditional clerical framework, they may be loosely characterized as lay Buddhist movements. Some of them remain rather small, consisting of only a handful of people dedicated to spiritual quest and the study of Buddhist ideas. The *seishinshugi* ("spiritualism") movement, initiated in 1900 by Kiyozawa Manshi (1863–1903) and, in the post–World War II period, Zaike Bukkyō Kyōkai (Buddhist Laymen's Association), founded by Katō Benzaburō (1899–1983), may be cited as examples. Others, such as Reiyūkai, Risshō Kōseikai, and Sōka Gakkai, have grown to nationwide organizations with membership in the tens of thousands. These latter occupy an important section of the so-called new religious movements *(shinkō shūkyō* or *shin shūkyō)* that have appeared in the course of the twentieth century. [*See* New Religions, *article on* New Religions in Japan.] Their presence, as well as various reform measures and intensive academic activities, seem to indicate the lasting relevance of Buddhism to Japanese life.

[*For an overview of the role of Buddhism in Japanese culture, see* Japanese Religion. *For further discussion of the history and development of the Japanese Buddhist schools, see* Buddhism, Schools of, *article on* Japanese Buddhism. *Buddhist syncretism with indigenous Japanese traditions is treated in* Shugendō *and* Shintō. *For Buddhist cultic life, see* Worship and Cultic Life, *article on* Buddhist Cultic Life in East Asia; Domestic Observances, *article on* Japanese Practices; *and* Pilgrimage, *article on* Buddhist Pilgrimage in East Asia.]

BIBLIOGRAPHY

Works in English. The number of Western-language materials dealing with this subject belies its importance. Among the few works now available, some treat Buddhism within the larger context of Japanese religion. A standard reference of this category remains Masaharu Anesaki's *History of Japanese Religion with Special Reference to the Social and Moral Life of the Nation* (1930; reprint, Rutland, Vt., and Tokyo, 1963), although some of its data and interpretations are naturally outdated. Fortunately we have an excellent successor to it in Joseph M. Kitagawa's *Religion in Japanese History* (New York, 1966). Intending to treat Japanese religion as a whole, the book traces the intricate relationship between various religious systems of Japan roughly from the third century to the post–World War II period. It also contains an extensive bibliography and glossary.

For the study of the position and role of Buddhism in Japan, the pertinent sections of H. Byron Earhart's *Japanese Religion: Unity and Diversity*, 3d rev. ed. (Belmont, Calif., 1982) as well as of *Japanese Religion* (Tokyo and Palo Alto, Calif., 1972), issued by the Agency for Cultural Affairs of the Japanese Government, may be consulted with profit. As for books addressing themselves specifically to Buddhism in Japan, Charles Eliot's *Japanese Buddhism* (1935; reprint, New York, 1959) deserves attention. While not exhaustive, it nevertheless gives important insights into some aspects of Buddhism in Japan. Very useful is Daigan Matsunaga and Alicia Matsunaga's *Foundation of Japanese Buddhism*, 2 vols. (Los Angeles and Tokyo, 1974–1976). These volumes contain detailed information about the historical transmission and the basic tenets of major schools together with a brief description of the social background, but their coverage is limited roughly to the end of the medieval period.

Generally, Buddhism after the medieval period is a subject that has so far been relatively neglected and publications in this area are scarce even in Japanese. In this sense, *Japanese Religion in the Meiji Era*, compiled and edited by Hideo Kishimoto and translated by John F. Howes (Tokyo, 1956), is noteworthy as it gives a succinct account of the situation of Buddhism from the Tokugawa through the Meiji era.

Specialized studies. In addition to works of a more general nature, there are materials dealing either with a particular period, a particular school, or personalities, of which the following represents only a tentative selection. About the ancient period, we have Marinus Willem de Visser's *Ancient Buddhism in Japan*, 2 vols. (Paris, 1928–1935). There have been relatively few titles on Esoteric Buddhism despite its popularity. Minoru Kiyota's *Shingon Buddhism: Theory and Practice* (Los Angeles, 1978) is one of the recent books to fill in this gap, together with E. Dale Saunders's *Mudrā: A Study of Symbolic Gestures in Japanese Buddhist Sculpture* (New York, 1960). Of the works on the life and thought of Hōnen, the founder of the Jōdoshū, Harper Coates and Ryūgaku Ishizuka's *Hōnen, the Buddhist Saint*, 5 vols. (1925; reprint, Kyoto, 1949) is most basic, being the translation of the authorized biography with a careful introduction. Nichiren, the founder of another influential school, is vividly portrayed in Masaharu Anesaki's *Nichiren the Buddhist Prophet* (1916; reprint, Gloucester, Mass., 1966). Heinrich Dumoulin's *A History of Zen Buddhism*, translated by Paul Peachey (New York, 1963), gives a good survey both of the historical background and of the development of Zen in Japan. The influence of Zen on Japanese culture is a topic that has enjoyed some popularity, for which D. T. Suzuki's *Zen and Japanese Culture*, 2d ed., rev. & enl. (1959; reprint, Princeton, 1970), may be regarded as classic, although the author tends to stress somewhat one-sidedly the impact of Zen. As for the new religious movements derived from Buddhism, basic information can be found in Clark B. Offner and Henry van Straelen's *Modern Japanese Religions* (Leiden, 1963) as well as in Harry Thomsen's *The New Religions of Japan* (Tokyo and Rutland, Vt., 1963).

Further references. Because of the nature of the subject, the bulk of source materials as well as of research results are published in Japanese. In order to supplement the perhaps uneven selection listed above, a few descriptive bibliographies in English on Japanese publications may be cited. These are *A Bibliography on Japanese Buddhism*, edited by Shōjun Bandō, Shōyū Hanayama, Ryōjun Satō, Shinkō Sayeki, and Keiryū Shima (Tokyo, 1958), and *K. B. S. Bibliography of Standard Reference Books for Japanese Studies, with Descriptive Notes*, vol. 4, *Religion*, edited by the Kokusai Bunka Shinkōkai (Tokyo, 1963). The former has about 1,660 entries and the latter, under the heading of Buddhism, 92 basic works. A successor to the latter is *An Introductory Bibliography for Japanese Studies* (Tokyo, 1975–), published by the Japan Foundation in two- to three-year intervals. It gives a brief report on the research works done in the area of Japanese Buddhism during the years under review.

Works in Japanese. Each of the major schools of Japanese Buddhism has collected its own textual corpus. See *Tendaishū zensho*, 25 vols., edited by the Tendai Shūten Kankōkai (Tokyo, 1935–1937); *Shingonshū zensho*, 42 vols., edited by the Shingonshū Zensho Kankōkai (Wakayama, 1933–1939); *Jōdoshū zensho*, 21 vols., edited by the Jōdoshū Shūten Kankōkai (Tokyo, 1929–1931), and its sequel, *Zoku Jōdoshū zensho*, 20 vols., edited by the Shūsho Hozonkai (Tokyo, 1940–1942); *Shinshū zensho*, 74 vols., edited by Tsumaki Naoyoshi (Tokyo, 1913–1916); *Kokuyaku Zengaku taisei*, 25 vols., edited by Miyauchi Sotai and Satō Kōyō (Tokyo, 1930–1931); and *Nichirenshū zensho*, 30 vols., edited by the Nichirenshū Zensho Shuppankai (Tokyo, 1910–1916). These sources provide fuller documentation for the sectarian traditions than is available in such standard canonical collections as the *Taishō shinshū daizōkyō*, 100 vols. (Tokyo, 1924–1932) or the *Dainihon zokuzōkyō*, 150 boxes (Kyoto, 1905–1912).

While Buddhist studies in the premodern period had been pursued mostly in the form of dogmatic exegesis, historical scholarship has flourished in this century. Among its many achievements, by far the most basic reference is Tsuji Zennosuke's *Nihon bukkyōshi*, 11 vols. (Tokyo, 1944–1953). Covering the whole of Buddhist history from its inception down to the dawn of the Meiji era, it gives a vivid picture of Buddhism in the context of the social, political, and intellectual situation of each period. While not as voluminous, Tamamuro Taijō's *Nihon bukkyōshi gaisetsu* (Tokyo, 1940) is very instructive. Written from the perspective of socioeconomic history, it successfully clarifies the position of Buddhist organizations throughout Japanese history. Representative of a different, intellectual history, approach are Ienaga Saburō's *Jōdai bukkyō shisōshi kenkyū* (Tokyo, 1948) and *Chūsei bukkyō shisōshi kenkyū* (Kyoto, 1947). In many essays collected in these two books, Ienaga tries to decipher the peculiarity of the Buddhist outlook and its impact on the Japanese mentality. On the history of Buddhism in modern Japan, a hitherto unexplored field, Yoshida Kyūichi's *Nihon kindai bukkyōshi kenkyū* (Tokyo, 1959) gives a succinct overview. Finally, *Bukkyōgaku kankei zasshi rombun bunrui mokuroku*, 2 vols., edited by the Ryūkoku Daigaku Toshokan (Kyoto, 1931–1961), serves as a useful guide to the research works undertaken from the beginning of the Meiji era to the late 1950s.

Tamaru Noriyoshi

Buddhism in the West

Encounters between Westerners and Buddhism began with Alexander's invasion of India in 326 BCE, little more than a century and a half after the Buddha's death. The first Western notice of the new Indic faith may appear in the *Indika*, a history of India composed around 300 BCE by Megasthenes, ambassador of Seleucus Nikator to the court of Candragupta. These reports, preserved in Strabo's *Geography*, carefully distinguished between *śramaṇa*s (ascetic monks), and brahmans at the court. In any event, it was not long before Greeks remaining in the East had established a striking Greco-Buddhist civilization, memorialized in the *Milindapañha* (first or second century CE), an influential text comprised of questions put to the monk Nāgasena by King Milinda, whom scholars have usually identified as the Greek ruler Menander (Menandros, c. 155–130 BCE), and answered by the monk Nāgasena. Commerce and information flowed between India and the Mediterranean world during the Hellenistic and Roman periods. But the Buddha and Buddhism received slight mention from classical authors, save a well-informed account by the Christian Clement of Alexandria, who referred to a missionary returned from India as his source.

During the Middle Ages, however, communication between the now-Christian West and the Eastern faith dwindled. Barbarian invaders and then the Islamic front occupied the region between Europe and the rest of Asia, and the Buddhist center of gravity itself moved away from India toward the continent's Eastern rim. Despite scattered notice by such intrepid travelers as Marco Polo and the Franciscan Willem van Ruysbroeck, and the popular story of Barlaam and Josaphat, in which the Buddha seems to appear as two Christian saints, the very existence of the world's third great international religion was barely known to even the most learned scholars in Christendom.

This situation was remarkably slow to change even after the age of European exploration, missionary effort, and imperialism had gotten underway. The Portuguese and others encountered Buddhism, of course, sometimes subjecting it to shameless persecution, as in Ceylon, sometimes engaging it in grudging dialogue, as did Francis Xavier and his followers in Japan. But rare is the account from the period between da Gama and the beginning of significant European Sanskrit studies at the end of the eighteenth century that shows much comprehension of Buddhism at all. Interestingly, it is from lay sources rather than clerical writers that we receive the best insights into the path of the Enlightened One. La Loubère, envoy of Louis XIV to the king of Siam, perceptively described *nirvāṇa* as "neither true annihilation nor the acquisition of any divine nature." Engelbert Kaempfer, a physician who visited Siam and who served the Dutch trading colony in Japan in the 1690s, left vivid and reasonably sympathetic portrayals of Zen and *yamabushi* practitioners, although he was uncertain whether the Buddha worshiped by the Siamese was the same as the "Siaka" (Shaka, i.e., Śākyamuni) honored in Japan (a question that remained unresolved until well into the nineteenth century).

Hinduism and Confucianism, at least in their major literary expressions, were introduced to the West considerably earlier than Buddhism. The transcultural character of the Buddha's path; the fact that such major strongholds of the faith as Japan and Tibet were opened late to extensive contact with Europeans; the tendency of Buddhism to syncretize with indigenous religions; and its puzzling disappearance from the land of its origin—all these factors combined to make that distant persuasion seem elusive to Western eyes, quite apart from the peculiar problems of comprehension offered by such paradoxical Buddhist concepts as *nirvāṇa*, "no self," and the nature of the Buddha, who was neither god nor man in any sense most Westerners could understand.

Thus the pioneering generation of Sanskritists of the late eighteenth century, including the brilliant linguists Sir William Jones, Charles Wilkins, and H. H. Wilson and the Indian scholar Ram Mohan Roy, turned into English the basic Hindu texts but few works of significance for Buddhism. Buddhist scholarship had to await the availability of Sanskrit and Tibetan texts, later collected in the Himalayas by such adventurous visitors as the Hungarian Sándor Csoma de Körös and the Englishman Richard Hodgson (both of whom also wrote on Buddhism). Collections of Pali writings were made at various places further south. A coherent picture of Buddhism finally began to emerge in the Western world when these texts were laboriously studied by the great French savant Eugène Burnouf (1801–1852), who published a Pali grammar, a translation of the *Lotus Sutra*, and, in 1844, his *Introduction à l'histoire du bouddhisme indien*. The work of Burnouf and that of a few others such as George Turnour, translator of the *Mahāvaṃsa*, a Buddhist-oriented Pali history of Sri Lanka, paved the way for the foundational studies of Buddhism, which by the second half of the nineteenth century was associated with such names as Senart, Minaev, Fausböll, Oldenberg, and Rhys Davids.

Buddhist scholarship was now making the religion known in the West, but what of the West's spiritual response to the fruits of those labors? In 1844 the *Dial*, the voice of New England Transcendentalism, published in English part of Burnouf's translation of the *Lo-*

tus Sutra. Still, the Buddha's faith made little impact in the world of Yankee Hindoos. Although the transcendentalists occasionally referred to the Buddha as an archetype of the spiritual seeker and sage, in their view Buddhism could not compete with the religion of the *brahman*-Oversoul. Emerson clearly regarded its nirvanic "nothingness" and its lack of even the most impersonal God with some distaste, speaking of Buddhism's "icy light"; he much preferred the warm, affirmative mysticism he found in the Upaniṣads and the *Bhagavadgītā.*

The 1870s brought the beginning of a more positive interpretation of Buddhism. The Theosophical Society was founded in New York in 1875 by H. P. Blavatsky, a Russian-born mystic, and H. S. Olcott, an American attorney and journalist. When the pair moved to India in 1879, they were initially drawn by the Hindu Ārya Samāj of Swami Dayananda Sarasvati. But it was not long before they had made contact with Ceylonese Buddhists, whose cause Olcott enthusiastically took up. Both he and Blavatsky took *pansil* in 1880, and were thus perhaps the first modern Westerners formally to become Buddhists. As Theosophists, they believed in the convergence of all religions and in the ancient wisdom behind them all, and so did not mean this act to imply an exclusive conversion: still, in the heyday of Western imperialism it was a gesture much appreciated by the Ceylonese. Olcott, in fact, went on to labor energetically on behalf of Buddhism, composing a Buddhist catechism, designing a Buddhist flag, representing Buddhist interests before colonial overlords, and traveling as far as Japan to promote an early Buddhist ecumenism. [*See* Theosophical Society.]

The year 1879 also saw the publication of *The Light of Asia,* Sir Edwin Arnold's epic poem on the life of the Buddha. Now half forgotten, this romantic depiction of the Enlightened One received a hearty response at the time and did much to implant in the mind of a generation a sympathetic image of the Buddha and his faith.

It was, in fact, the reading of *The Light of Asia* that led to the conversion of Allen Bennett, an Englishman who took the ocher robe in Burma in 1902 as Ananda Metteyya, the first known Buddhist monk of occidental extraction. In 1891, the Mahabodhi Society, later to do missionary work on behalf of Buddhism in Europe, was founded in Calcutta by Anagārika Dharmapāla, a Ceylonese who had associated with Blavatsky and Olcott. Not long after, in 1893, the celebrated World's Parliament of Religions brought Dharmapāla to Chicago; another visitor to the conference, the Japanese monk Shaku Sōen, was to establish Zen Buddhism in the United States.

At the turn of the century, Western, and especially European, Buddhist interest centered chiefly on the Theravāda tradition. In Great Britain, where interest was most active, colonialism had brought Englishmen into most intimate contact with Buddhism in Theravāda Ceylon and Burma. Moreover, Buddhist apologists then stressed the alleged rationalism of the religion, a quality best appreciated in the Pali canon. Finally, Theravāda was presumed to represent the oldest and simplest form of Buddhism, that closest to the Buddha's own teaching, a hypothesis that appealed to nineteenth-century scholars in their "quest for origins." Thus when the Buddhist Society of Great Britain and Ireland was founded in 1907, largely to prepare for a mission by Ananda Metteyya (Allen Bennett), then visiting from Burma, it was inevitable that its orientation should be almost entirely Theravāda. In 1909 the society founded a periodical, *The Buddhist Review,* later called *The Middle Way.*

A German Buddhist group was founded in Leipzig as early as 1903, under the leadership of Karl Seidenstücker; it began publishing *Der Buddhist* in 1904. A German, Anton Güth, was ordained as Nyanatiloka in 1904. German Buddhism was, in fact, to produce a generation of distinguished monks who lived in the East and wrote important books on Buddhism that did much to promote its popularity in the West. Among them were Nyanaponika Thera, author of *The Heart of Buddhist Meditation,* and Lama Anagarika Govinda, author of *The Foundations of Tibetan Mysticism* and many other works, who like the others began his monastic career in Theravāda Ceylon but later transferred his allegiance to the Vajrayāna of Tibet.

In England, the original Buddhist Society dissolved with the onset of World War I. It was succeeded in 1924 by the Buddhist Lodge of the Theosophical Society, whose first president was Christmas Humphreys. Destined to be the dominant figure in British Buddhism for more than half a century, Humphreys himself was both a Buddhist and a Theosophist. However, the theosophical connection proved untenable, and in 1926 the Lodge was re-formed as the independent Buddhist Society. In 1925 it had welcomed a visit by Anagārika Dharmapāla of the Mahabodhi Society, who established a London branch of that organization that often housed resident *bhikkus* (monks) from Ceylon. However, the dominance of Theravāda gradually weakened as interest rose in Mahāyāna, chiefly under the influence of the writings of D. T. Suzuki. Suzuki visited England in 1936, making a deep impression on the young Alan Watts, who had written *The Spirit of Zen* at the age of twenty; in 1938 Watts himself would embark on an American career of high visibility as a popular expounder of Zen and comparable spiritual paths.

In America, Mahāyāna has always been the most prominent expression of Buddhism. Just as colonialism gave Britain its most significant Buddhist contacts in Theravāda Burma and Ceylon, so relative proximity, trade, westward immigration, and historical destiny, including the postwar occupation of Japan, have brought Americans most in touch with Mahāyāna's East Asian strongholds.

North American Buddhism has long had two strands, ethnic and occidental. By the time of the 1980 census, somewhat over two million people in the United States were Asian-Americans from traditionally Buddhist countries. Older immigration was represented by some eight hundred thousand Chinese and seven hundred thousand Japanese; the remainder were newer immigrants, mostly since 1970, from Korea, Vietnam, and Theravāda Cambodia and Thailand, plus a sprinkling of Tibetans and others. Only a minority of the Asian-American population is actively Buddhist, but their numbers have been sufficient to maintain a visible Buddhist presence in the form of Buddhist temples and churches, particularly in the major immigration centers: the larger cities, the West Coast, and Hawaii.

The first wave of Asian immigration was made up of Chinese who came to California during the Gold Rush; by 1860 they numbered 60,000. The first Chinese temple was built in San Francisco in 1853, and there were eight by 1875. These were the characteristically syncretistic temples of Chinese popular religion, combining Buddhist, Taoist, and Confucian features. But Buddhist priests were early present among the population, and eventually more purely Buddhist centers were established. These include Buddha's Universal Church (San Francisco, 1963), a modern reconstruction of Buddhism, and the "orthodox" (largely T'ien-t'ai doctrine and Ch'an practice) Sino-American Buddhist Association (San Francisco, 1959), whose Gold Mountain Monastery and other establishments, despite their rigorous discipline, have drawn occidental as well as Asian adherents.

Although they traveled to Hawaii when it was not yet a U.S. possession, Japanese immigrants did not arrive on the mainland in large numbers until the end of the nineteenth century and the beginning of the twentieth century. As in its homeland, Japanese-American Buddhism took a much more structured form than Chinese. As the result of a Jōdo Shinshū mission, the Buddhist Church of America (BCA) was founded in San Francisco in 1899. Adapting its worship to a somewhat Protestant format and working diligently to serve the Japanese community, the BCA has been the preponderant Japanese Buddhist institution, with over one hundred churches and missions operating by the 1980s. But other forms of Japanese Buddhism are also present as largely ethnic churches, including Jōdoshū, the Higashi Honganji wing of Jōdo Shinshū (the BCA is related to the Honpa or Nishi Honganji), Zen, Nichiren, Shingon, and Buddhist-oriented "new religions" such as Gedatsukai and Risshō Kōseikai.

From time to time Americans of occidental background have joined Asian-American Buddhist groups, either because of marriage ties or through independent conversion. But for the most part the quite different needs of Western seekers have been met by another body of institutions, which despite occasional exchanges with ethnic groups has generally pursued a separate career. The roots of occidental Buddhism go almost as far back in American history as ethnic Buddhism. Apart from the generalized interests of Transcendentalists and Theosophists, it was the World's Parliament of Religions, held in Chicago in 1893, that gave the movement its impetus, largely in the person of the Japanese Zen monk Shaku Sōen. An American couple from San Francisco who met Sōen at the Parliament, Mr. and Mrs. Alexander Russell, visited Sōen in Japan in 1905 and invited him to return with them. He remained with the Russells in California for nine months, during which time Mrs. Russell became the first American of occidental background to do formal *zazen* and *kōan* work. Several disciples sent by Sōen to the United States—Shaku Sokatsu (in 1906), Senzaki Nyogen (in 1905), and D. T. Suzuki (in 1899)—in quite diverse ways laid the real foundations of American Zen, which has the longest history of continuous practice of any form of occidental Buddhism in the United States.

Shaku Sokatsu remained only a few years in the United States, but his disciple Sasaki Shigetsu (known as Sokei-an) left a lasting impact. After an interesting career that moved back and forth between American bohemianism and intensive Japanese Zen training, Sokei-an in 1931 founded the Buddhist Society of America (later the First Zen Institute) in New York, and guided this pioneer occidental Buddhist group until his death in 1945. In San Francisco (1928) and Los Angeles (1929), Senzaki Nyogen established *zendōs* (meditation halls) that were open to Westerners. The immense influence of the books of D. T. Suzuki, who resided in the United States from 1897 to 1909 and again in the 1950s, is well known. Suzuki was a student of Zen who came to work as translator and editor with Paul Carus's Open Court Publishing Company in LaSalle, Illinois, as a result of contacts made at the World's Parliament of Religions between Carus and Shaku Sōen.

The postwar years saw a considerable expansion of occidental Buddhism. Largely because of the work of D. T. Suzuki, Zen enjoyed a cultural vogue in the 1950s, when it was associated with (but not limited to) the

Beat movement in art, letters, and life-style. That interest led to the establishment of large Zen centers in such major cities as Los Angeles (1956), San Francisco (1959), and Rochester, New York (1966). By the early 1970s the first *rōshis* (masters) of occidental descent, including Richard Baker of San Francisco, Philip Kapleau of Rochester, and Robert Aitken of Honolulu, had received *dharma* transmission and headed the more important centers, a significant step in the coming of age of occidental Buddhism.

The 1960s saw the introduction, in no small part a response to the interest expressed by that decade's exuberant counterculture, of two new forms of occidental Buddhism: Japanese Nichiren, as presented by the powerful Sōka Gakkai movement, and Tibetan Vajrayāna. An American Sōka Gakkai headquarters was established in Los Angeles in 1963; in 1967 it became Nichiren Shōshū of America. Initially the movement was almost entirely Japanese in membership, but by 1970 over two-thirds of the then rapidly growing membership was occidental, mostly young people drawn by its vital spirit and the reported power of its simple central practice, chanting the Daimoku, a mantralike repetition of the name of the sect's principal scriptural warrant, the Lotus Sutra.

In the 1960s, Tibetan Buddhism began to acquire visibility in both Europe and the United States through the arrival of refugee lamas. One of them, Tarthang Tulku, in 1969 established the Nyingmapa Center in Berkeley, California; the following year another lama, Chögyam Trungpa, founded a center in Vermont, later moving his headquarters to Boulder, Colorado, where among other works he directs the Naropa Institute as a sort of Buddhist university. In 1971 Kalu Rinpoche was sent to Europe and the United States, where he founded a number of centers and trained the first regular classes of Western lamas by means of the difficult traditional three-year retreat; by the 1980s his students were directing centers of their own.

The 1970s also brought a certain revival of interest in Theravāda, but with a new emphasis on its meditation techniques. In 1976 Jack Kornfield and Joseph Goldstein, both of whom had studied Theravāda in Southeast Asia, founded the Insight Meditation Center in Barre, Massachusetts, to teach *vipassanā* meditation. Theravāda work is also done by the Stillpoint Institute of San Jose, California, and the Washington (D.C.) Vihāra.

In little more than a century since it was first coherently presented to the Western eye, Buddhism has inspired not only a library of scholarship, but also an institutional presence complete with occidental monks, *rōshis*, and lamas. Although that presence is miniscule compared to either traditional Western religions or modern secularism, Buddhism offers a spiritual option that has drawn a remarkable diversity of personalities and forms of expression. Western Buddhism may, as many of its adherents predict, ultimately evolve into a fresh vehicle of the Dharma.

[*See also* Buddhist Studies; World's Parliament of Religions; *and the biographies of Burnouf, Oldenberg, and Suzuki.*]

BIBLIOGRAPHY

On the Western discovery of Buddhism from classical times to the early twentieth century, with particular emphasis on scholarly sources and development, a standard work is Henri de Lubac's *La rencontre du bouddhisme et de l'Occident* (Paris, 1952). Guy R. Welbon's *The Buddhist Nirvana and Its Western Interpreters* (Chicago, 1968) is a history of Buddhist scholarship that focuses on a particular issue but sheds much light on Western Buddhist studies in general.

European Buddhist scholarship and practice alike are briefly surveyed in Yamamoto Kōshō's *Buddhism in Europe* (Ube, Japan, 1967). Christmas Humphreys's *Sixty Years of Buddhism in England, 1907–1967* (London, 1968) gives that story through the eyes of one of its key figures, and Brooks Wright's *Interpreter of Buddhism to the West: Sir Edwin Arnold* (New York, 1957) presents a man whose role in furthering Buddhism was equally pivotal, albeit very different. Wright's biography reveals much about the Victorian age's response to the Asian faith. On the American response to Buddhism in this period, see Carl T. Jackson's *The Oriental Religions and American Thought: Nineteenth-Century Explorations* (Westport, Conn., 1981).

On American Buddhism, Emma McCloy Layman's *Buddhism in America* (Chicago, 1976) and Charles S. Prebish's *American Buddhism* (North Scituate, Mass., 1979) provide complementary historical and descriptive accounts of this complex and rapidly changing scene. Rick Fields's *How the Swans Came to the Lake: A Narrative History of Buddhism in America* (Boulder, 1981) is more informal but is well researched and provides much additional information. Finally, Kashima Tetsuden's *Buddhism in America* (reprint, Westport, Conn., 1977) offers a perspective on ethnic Buddhist groups in America.

ROBERT S. ELLWOOD

BUDDHISM, SCHOOLS OF. [*This entry treats the division of the Buddhist community into schools, sects, orders, and traditions in various historical and regional contexts. It consists of seven articles:*

An Overview
Hīnayāna Buddhism
Mahāyāna Buddhism
Esoteric Buddhism
Chinese Buddhism
Japanese Buddhism
Tibetan Buddhism

The overview article introduces the various parameters by which the tradition has become differentiated; the succeeding articles focus on specific doctrinal or geographical divisions of the community.]

An Overview

Like all world religions, Buddhism presents a picture of bewildering variety: doctrinal, liturgical, linguistic, and organizational. This diversity was largely the combined result of geographical diffusion and cultural adaptation. Wherever it was introduced, over an area ranging from Afghanistan to Indonesia and Japan, Buddhism became an integral part of different cultures, partly coexisting with local beliefs and cults, and partly absorbing them into its own system. But diversity was also stimulated by certain features within Buddhism itself: the absence of a central doctrinal authority; social stratification within the clergy; the relation of the Buddhist order with the temporal powers; royal patronage; the influence of the laity; and, in some cases, competition between large monastic centers. However, in spite of all this diversity we must not lose sight of the basic and always recognizable identity of Buddhism: a doctrine of salvation, aimed at the acquisition of liberating insight and at the complete extinction of attachment, and, consequently, of continued rebirth in the world of suffering. In most cases, the way to achieve that goal is indissolubly connected with the monastic life (with a few exceptions, such as the Japanese Jōdo Shinshū with its married preachers, or Chinese lay Buddhism in Indonesia); the Buddhist order of monks, or *saṃgha,* has remained the very heart of religious life and the most important unifying element throughout the Buddhist world.

Movements, Monastic Traditions, Schools, and Sects. A clarification of terms is needed, for much confusion has been created by the indiscriminative use of these words.

Movements. In the course of its long history, Buddhism has seen the development of three huge complexes of religious doctrine and practice, each of which represents a well-defined "way leading to release"; these are characteristically called *yāna* ("vehicles"). We shall refer to them as "movements." They represent three basic orientations within Buddhism, each with its own doctrinal ideas, cultic practices, sacred scriptures, and iconographic traditions.

The first movement comprises the whole complex of ancient Buddhism, of which one type is still alive in Sri Lanka and most of continental Southeast Asia. Since the name *Hīnayāna,* the "Lesser Vehicle," sounds pejorative, its adherents now prefer their type of Buddhism to be called Theravāda, "the Doctrine of the Elders" (originally the name of one school). Theravāda Buddhism has, among other things, always been characterized by an extreme emphasis on monastic life; by the ideal of becoming an *arhat,* who has reached individual saintliness and is assured of his total extinction at the end of his life, and a conception of the Buddha as a sublime yet mortal teacher who, after having reached his final *nirvāṇa,* has ceased to be at whatever level of existence.

Since the beginning of the common era, Hīnayāna was challenged by a new movement that called itself the "Great Vehicle" (Mahāyāna). It claimed to be a more comprehensive and universal way toward liberation, with a more ambitious religious ideal (Buddhahood instead of arhatship); the belief in *bodhisattvas* as superhuman guides and saviors; the idea of a transcendental, all-pervading and eternal Buddha or "Buddha nature"; a philosophical reinterpretation (in many variations) of the most basic ontological concepts of ancient Buddhism, and a much higher estimate of the status of lay believers as potential "candidates for release."

In the sixth century, possibly even somewhat earlier, a third orientation emerged, the movement called the "Diamond Vehicle" (Vajrayāna), commonly referred to as Tantric or Esoteric Buddhism in the West. It was characterized by its use of spells, symbols, and very complicated rituals, and the acquisition of magic powers as a way toward enlightenment; by the development of psychophysical "techniques" (partly of a sexual nature); and by a system of esoteric transmission from master to disciple.

It is clear that in these three cases we cannot speak of "schools," let alone "sects." They were by no means localized: both Mahāyāna and Vajrayāna spread like waves throughout the Buddhist world. Above all, they were not mutually exclusive. In the Mahāyāna vision, the whole complex of Theravāda teachings is not rejected but incorporated as a kind of "simple revelation," intended by the Buddha to raise the minds of his "hearers" *(śrāvaka)* to a certain level of preliminary insight. In the same way, Tantric Buddhism claims to incorporate (and, of course, to transcend) the two previous Vehicles, without denying their limited applicability. In fact, Mahāyāna doctrinal literature freely quotes from Theravāda scriptures as teachings of the Buddha that are, at that level, both authentic and authoritative.

Monastic traditions. What we call monastic traditions are basically different from such large and many-sided movements. Their origin is closely related to the paramount role of the disciplinary code (Vinaya), and notably of the detailed set of rules governing the monk's daily life that had to be recited at every fortnightly Prātimokṣa confessional by all monks resident in a single self-governing "parish" or begging circuit *(sīmā)*. The early dissemination of Buddhism over the Indian subcontinent was a continuous process of expansion of contact: since any local center of population could only support a certain number of mendicants, the clerical surplus had to move out to establish new parishes elsewhere. The process was further stimulated by the itinerant life led by many monks outside the rainy season, and by the missionary ideal that has been characteristic of Buddhism from the very beginning. Thus, Buddhism spread in ever-widening circles, but without any central authority that could impose doctrinal and ritual uniformity. The only binding element was the Vinaya, and the frequent Prātimokṣa recitation in fact functioned as the only instrument to preserve the homogeneity of the Buddhist order.

However, as the territory covered by Buddhism widened, local variations in the disciplinary code started to develop, partly owing to lack of communication and probably also caused by the necessity to adapt the rules to local circumstances. If the Buddhist tradition speaks of the emergence of eighteen of such monastic traditions in the first two centuries after the Buddha's decease, we must realize that the difference that divided them mainly concerned details of discipline rather than doctrinal matters. No less than five different Vinayas of various early schools have been preserved in the Chinese Buddhist canon: extensive works that differ among themselves as to number of rules, prescriptions governing minute details of daily behavior, and the degree of elaboration of stories justifying each particular rule, but that as far as doctrine is concerned show very little variation.

Schools. Of quite another nature are the schools found in Theravāda and (to a much larger extent) in Mahāyāna Buddhism. Here the accent is on the interpretation of certain basic elements of the doctrine of release, issues such as the nature of the *arhat,* the nonexistence of a permanent self, the process of causation, and so forth. In Mahāyāna Buddhism we find a proliferation of such schools, ranging from the earliest propagation of the doctrine of universal "emptiness" *(śūnyavāda)* in India to Chinese and Japanese Ch'an (Zen) Buddhism, with its iconoclastic message of "no words" and "no mind."

In spite of their endless variety, such schools share some common features. In the first place, their field of activity is not discipline but scholastics: the various Abhidharma of Theravāda Buddhism and the many systematizing treatises of Mahāyāna scholars. A second feature shared by most schools is the prominent role of famous "masters of the Law," both as founding fathers and as transmitters of the teachings of a particular school: Kātyāyanīputra, Vasumitra, and other "patriarchs" of the Sarvāstivāda tradition that flourished in northwestern India and Kashmir; Nāgārjuna and Āryadeva, who systematized the doctrines of the School of Emptiness; Asaṅga and Vasubandhu, who, probably in the fifth century CE, founded the Yogācāra school, and, in East Asia, the great masters who founded and developed the major schools of Chinese Buddhism: the vast and complicated system of the T'ien-t'ai school founded by Chih-i (538–597), the Hua-yen doctrine of all-pervading totality of Fa-tsang (643–712); the Pure Land (Ching-t'u) devotionalism of T'an-luan (476–542) and Tao-ch'o (562–645), and the many "patriarchs" and branch founders of Ch'an (Zen) in China, Korea, and Japan.

Third, although such schools recognize the validity of all Buddhist scriptures (even if in some schools texts favored by other schools are considered "provisional teachings," as we have seen), many of them tend to be focused on one particular scripture or group of scriptures that are supposed to contain the final and supreme revelation of truth. Thus, the School of Emptiness largely relied on the class of Mahāyāna scriptures known as the Prajñāpāramitā ("perfection of wisdom") literature, just as the Yogācāra school appealed to the authority of the *Laṅkāvatāra Sūtra.* For the founder of the T'ien-t'ai school, the highest revelation was to be found in the message of universal salvation as expounded in the *Saddharmapuṇḍarīka Sūtra* (Scripture of the Lotus of the Good Law), whereas Fa-tsang found the expression of ultimate truth in the vast *Avataṃsaka Sūtra* (Chin., *Hua-yen;* Flower Garland Scripture). And even Ch'an, in spite of its rejection of written texts, in its first stage largely relied on the *Laṅkāvatāra Sūtra.* The scholastic and "learned" nature of all such schools also appears from the fact that they essentially remained a clerical phenomenon: the creation and exclusive domain of an elite of scholar-monks, in which the laity took no part. Their bastions were the large and richly endowed monasteries that all over the Buddhist world functioned as centers of Buddhist learning and doctrinal disputes. However, one of their most remarkable features is that they were by no means exclusive communities with a well-defined "membership." Monks would travel from one monastery to another irrespective of the school that dominated in each center; in many cases several scholastic interpretations could be studied successively or even simultaneously, and both eclecticism and syncretism flourished without any stigma of "unorthodoxy."

Sects. This, then, may be the dividing line between schools and sects, the latter being characterized by a high degree of exclusivity, a clear concept of "membership," and, in general, a very important role played by the laity. As a rule, sectarian movements are centered around a charismatic leader who in his own person exemplifies the religious message of the sect: in many cases he claims to be the incarnation or the manifestation of a Buddha (notably the future Buddha Maitreya) or a powerful *bodhisattva*. In contrast to the schools that are not confined to one area (the Representation-Only doctrine reached from India to Japan, and Ch'an/Zen was found all over East Asia), most sects are localized, and deeply rooted in local circumstances. As I shall show, sects generally belong to strata lower, both socially and intellectually, than the schools mentioned above; the latter may be said to represent the "great tradition" of Buddhism at its highest level of expression.

Parameters of Diversification. In the diffusion of Buddhism we can recognize a number of factors that contributed to the process of ongoing diversification. Only the most important ones can be treated within the limits of this article.

Distance from the center. As noted above, the spread of Buddhism over the Indian subcontinent mainly took the form of gradual expansion of contact, a process that offers the best chances for maintaining a fairly high degree of homogeneity. However, once outside its country of origin, the propagation of Buddhism assumed the character of long-distance diffusion in various directions: from northwestern India through the empty heart of the continent to China; along the sea routes from the east coast of India to continental Southeast Asia, Sumatra, and Java; from the Ganges Basin crossing the Himalayas into Tibet. In all those outlying regions, far from the center of expansion, Buddhism developed independently. As a result, both China and Tibet eventually became secondary centers of diffusion: Korean and Japanese Buddhists were inspired by Chinese examples and had hardly any contact with India; in all of East Asia, classical Chinese became the Buddhist scriptural language. In the same way, Tibetan Buddhism, especially in its lamaist form, developed into a unique system far removed from any Indian prototype. In the sixteenth century Tibet also became a secondary center of expansion, from which Lamaism was spread to Mongolia.

In Southeast Asia, Buddhism at first was introduced not independently but as one element in a general process of cultural borrowing; from the second to the fifth centuries, the spread of Indian culture in the whole area from Burma to Sumatra led to the formation of a whole series of more or less indianized states in which Buddhism (mainly in its Mahāyāna and Tantric forms) coexisted with Hinduism. This independent development of Buddhism in peripheral areas was naturally reinforced by its disappearance in India itself after the twelfth century. It may not be fortuitous that around that time Sri Lanka, where the Theravāda *sangha* had been restored and reorganized under the powerful king Parakkamabāhu II (1236–1271), became a strong center of diffusion. It was owing to Sinhala missionary efforts that Theravāda Buddhism became the state religion in Burma, Thailand, Laos, and Cambodia between the twelfth and fourteenth centuries.

Confrontation with local cultures. Wherever it arrived, Buddhism was in varying degrees influenced by local beliefs and practices, the incorporation of which led to further differentiation. In some areas, like the oasis kingdoms along the Silk Road and Southeast Asia, the cultural resistance against Buddhism appears to have been slight; there the Indian religion was taken over as an instrument of higher civilization, often together with other elements of Indian culture like statecraft, astronomy, representational arts, and the script. Elsewhere, notably in China, Buddhism had to compete with strong preexisting philosophical and social traditions that on many points were opposed to Buddhist ideals and practices. In China, it had to grow up in the shadow of the dominant Confucian ideology, and much that is characteristic in Chinese Buddhism is the result of "adaptation under pressure." However, everywhere, and especially at a popular level, Buddhism merged with and incorporated non-Buddhist traditions: Taoist eubiotics and Confucian morality in China; Shintō in Japan; elements borrowed from the indigenous Bon religion in Tibet; and from shamanism in Mongolia.

Social stratification. Since the earliest times, monastic Buddhism was for its very existence dependent on the patronage of the ruling elite; the close ties between the *saṃgha* and the temporal powers form a constant feature in the history of all countries where Buddhism penetrated. This cooperation (and in some areas, such as Sri Lanka, even complete interdependence) has produced both positive and negative results: on the one hand, corruption and abuse of power; on the other hand, the formation of a clerical elite within the *saṃgha*, associated with the largest monastic centers, to whom we owe the most sophisticated products of Buddhist thought, literature, and art. This articulate group only constituted a tiny minority—the thin top layer of the Buddhist establishment. In all Buddhist countries, we find a vertical differentiation between the cultured clerical elite residing in the major monasteries and the vast majority of "priests among the people," who perform their humble services in countless small temples and local shrines, at the grass-roots level, where they often are the only people who can boast of a modicum of literary training. If the world of court priests, learned doctors, and scholastic philosophy constitutes the "great tradition" of Buddhism, it is everywhere counterbalanced by an endless variety of popular Buddhist beliefs and cults that represent its "little traditions." It is at that level that we mostly find the traces of (generally not well documented) sectarian movements of the type mentioned above. In general, their message is extremely simple, centering around one or two basic ideas derived from the Buddhist scriptural tradition: the theme of the dark "final age" in which the doctrine will disappear and the world will be steeped in chaos and corruption, and the belief in the imminent appearance of the Buddha Maitreya, who will come to create a world of piety and justice. [*See also* Folk Religion, *article on* Folk Buddhism.]

Movements espousing such ideas have often been persecuted as "subversive," both by the temporal powers and by the representatives of the clerical establishment. These movements sometimes assumed a violent character. Examples of such sectarian activities can be found in many parts of the Buddhist world: the millenarian movements that have time and again appeared in continental Southeast Asia in times of crisis; the militant and protonationalist sect founded by the Japanese reformer Nichiren (1222–1282), who combined socioreligious activism and opposition against the established clergy with an extremely simple way to salvation, and, in China, the equally militant activities of the complex of Buddhist-inspired secret societies collectively known as the White Lotus, which harassed Chinese political authorities from the fourteenth century until modern times. But such violent activism and social protest have always been the exception rather than the rule—the vast majority of Buddhist religious life at the grass roots level presents the familiar and peaceful picture of local societies, fraternities, and associations devoted to mutual help, charitable activities, and collective ceremonies. [*See also* Millenarianism, *article on* Chinese Millenarian Movements.]

Linguistic differentiation. Unlike the Brahmanic tradition, which is based on Sanskrit as a scriptural medium, Buddhism never has known the concept of a "sacred language." Buddhist scriptures have for many centuries been translated in a great variety of regional languages, and even Pali, the written medium of Theravāda Buddhism, certainly does not represent the language of the original Buddhist sermons. However, in the course of time the diffusion of Buddhism from secondary centers led to the use of some languages, in petrified forms, as what we may call "clerical literary idioms": classical Chinese in Japan and Korea; Pali in continental Southeast Asia; and literary Tibetan. But here again, social stratification was at work, for in all these areas, popular tracts and other types of simplified religious literature (both written and oral) generally made use of the living language—in fact, Chinese vernacular literature owes its origin to simple Buddhist stories written in the metropolitan dialect and destined to be recited to a largely illiterate public of lay devotees. Thus, the linguistic aspect combines the two main features that we have observed in the spread of Buddhism as a whole: geographic diffusion coupled with ongoing regional differentiation, and internal stratification producing a great diversity of expression at various social levels, both within the Buddhist clergy and among the lay population.

[*For a review of the geographic dispersion of the tradition, see* Missions, *article on* Buddhist Missions.]

BIBLIOGRAPHY

The following works contain information on the main themes treated in this article: the diversity of Buddhism (monastic traditions, schools, sects), social stratification (elite versus popular Buddhism), and adaptation to cultural environments.

Anesaki Masaharu. *Nichiren: The Buddhist Prophet* (1916). Reprint, Gloucester, Mass., 1966.

Bareau, André. *Les sectes bouddhiques du petit véhicule.* Saigon, 1955.

Bechert, Heinz. *Buddhismus, Staat und Gesellschaft in den Ländern des Theravāda-Buddhismus.* 3 vols. Frankfurt, 1966–1973.

Bechert, Heinz, ed. *Buddhism in Ceylon and Studies in Religious Syncretism in Buddhist Countries.* Göttingen, 1978.

Chan, Wing-tsit. *Religious Trends in Modern China.* New York, 1953.

Ch'en, Kenneth. *Buddhism in China: A Historical Survey.* Princeton, 1964.

Dutt, Nalinaksha. *Early History of the Spread of Buddhism and the Buddhist Schools* (1925). Reprint, New Delhi, 1980.

Dutt, Nalinaksha. *Buddhist Sects in India.* Calcutta, 1970.

Groot, J. J. M. de. *Sectarianism and Religious Persecution in China.* 2 vols. Amsterdam, 1903–1904.

Hackmann, Heinrich Friedrich. *Laien-Buddhismus in China.* Stuttgart, 1924.

Hanayama Shinshō. *A History of Japanese Buddhism.* Tokyo, 1960.

Hoffmann, Helmut. *The Religions of Tibet.* Translated by Edward Fitzgerald. New York, 1961.

Lester, Robert C. *Theravada Buddhism in Southeast Asia.* Ann Arbor, 1973.

Malalgoda, Kitsiri. *Buddhism in Sinhalese Society, 1750–1900.* Berkeley, 1976.

Matsunaga, Alicia. *The Buddhist Philosophy of Assimilation.* Tokyo, 1969.

Miller, Robert J. *Monasteries and Culture Change in Inner Mongolia.* Wiesbaden, 1959.

Thomsen, Harry. *The New Religions of Japan.* Rutland, Vt., 1963.

ERIK ZÜRCHER

Hīnayāna Buddhism

The term *Hīnayāna* refers to the group of Buddhist schools or sects that appeared before the beginning of the common era and those directly derived from them. The word *Hīnayāna*, which means "small vehicle," that is, "lesser means of progress" toward liberation, is pejorative. It was applied disdainfully to these early forms of Buddhism by the followers of the great reformist movement that arose just at the beginning of the common era, which referred to itself as the Mahāyāna, or "large vehicle," that is, "greater means of progress" toward liberation. Indeed, the adherents of the Mahāyāna charged those of the Hīnayāna with selfishly pursuing only their own personal salvation, whereas they themselves claimed an interest in the liberation of all beings and vowed to postpone their own deliverance until the end of time. In other words, the ideal of the practitioners of the Hīnayāna was the *arhat* (Pali, *arahant*), the saint who has attained *nirvāṇa*, while that of the Mahāyāna was the *bodhisattva*, the all-compassionate hero who, resolving to become a Buddha in some far-distant future, dedicated the course of his innumerable lives to saving beings of all kinds. It would be more correct to give the name "early Buddhism" to what is called Hīnayāna, for the term denotes the whole collection of the most ancient forms of Buddhism: those earlier than the rise of the Mahāyāna and those that share the same inspiration as these and have the same ideal, namely the *arhat*. [*See* Arhat.]

Although it is directly descended from the earliest Buddhism—that originally preached by the Buddha himself—this early Buddhism is distinguished from it by the continual additions and reformulations of its adherents and teachers in their desire to deepen and perfect the interpretation of the ancient teaching. This constant, and quite legitimate, effort gave rise to many debates, controversies, and divisions that resulted in the appearance of a score of sects or schools. The actual, original teaching of the Buddha is accessible to us only through the canonic texts of these schools, texts that were set down in writing only about the beginning of the common era and reflect the divergences that already existed among these sects. Moreover, only a very small part of this vast canonic literature has survived, either in its original Indian language or in Chinese or Tibetan translation, and for this reason our knowledge of the doctrine taught by the Buddha himself still remains rather vague and conjectural. We do not possess all the documents necessary to recover it with certainty: even by compiling all the doctrinal and other elements common to the canonic texts we do have, we can reach, at best, only a stage of Buddhist doctrine immediately prior to the divergence of these schools. Their texts have been preserved for us by the mere chances of history.

The Indic word, both Sanskrit and Pali, that we translate here as "school" or "sect" is *nikāya*, meaning, properly, "group." In our context, it refers to a group of initiates, most likely monks *(bhikṣus)* rather than laymen, who sincerely profess to be faithful disciples of the Buddha but are distinguishable from other similar groups in that they base their beliefs on a body of canonic texts that differs from others to a greater or lesser extent. These differences between canonic texts involve not only their wording or written form but also a certain number of doctrinal elements and rules of monastic discipline. Despite the disaggregative pressures to which they were exposed (the same pressures, indeed, that created them), despite their geographical expansion and sometimes considerable dispersion, and notwithstanding the vicissitudes of history, which often posed new problems for them, most of these groups preserved a remarkable internal cohesiveness throughout several centuries. Still, schisms did occur within many of them, leading to the formation of new schools. Moreover, to judge from the documents we have—though these are unfortunately very scarce—it seems that relations among these various groups were generally good. Their disputes remained at the level of more or less lively discussion and degenerated into more serious conflicts only when involving questions of economics or politics.

Several factors account for these divisions and for the formation of these sects or schools. First of all, the Buddhist monastic community *(saṃgha)* never knew a supreme authority, imposing its unity by powerful and diverse methods, as was long the case in Christianity with its papacy. If we believe some canonic texts that seem to faithfully reflect reality, the Buddha himself was probably faced with several instances of insubordination on the part of certain groups of his monks and was not always able to overcome them. The oldest traditions, furthermore, agree that he did not designate a successor to head the community but only counseled his followers to remain faithful to his Doctrine (Dharma). This was a fragile defense against the forces that tried to break up the community once it was "orphaned" by the death of its founder.

For at least five centuries, the Buddha's teaching was actually preserved by oral transmission alone, very probably in different, though related, dialects. This, and the absence of an authoritative ecclesiastical hierarchy in the *saṃgha*, constitute two obvious sources of progressive distortion and alteration of the message left by the Blessed One to his immediate disciples. Furthermore, this message was not entirely clear or convincing to everyone it addressed, leading Buddhist preachers to furnish explanations and interpretations of the teaching. Finally, the teaching given by the Buddha was far from a complete system containing solutions to all the problems that might occur to the minds of people as diverse as those it was destined to reach. Thus, monks and lay disciples, as well as people outside Buddhism but curious and interested in its doctrine—brahman opponents, Jains, and others—easily found numerous flaws, errors, and contradictions in the teaching. These troubled the *saṃgha* but pleased those who were determined to refute or discredit it. Although the Buddhist preachers who improvised answers to these varied questions and objections were guided by what they knew and understood of the Buddha's teaching, their attempts expanded upon the original teaching and at the same time inevitably created new causes for differences and disputes within the heart of the community itself.

According to some eminent scholars, we must distinguish Buddhist "sects" from "schools." Sects, under this interpretation, were invariably born from serious dissent over issues of monastic discipline. Such dissent resulted in a fracturing of the community, a *saṃghabheda*, or schism, the participants in which ceased to live together or carry on a common religious life. By contrast, schools were differentiated by divergences of opinion on doctrinal points, but their dissension in these matters never gave rise to actual schisms or open hostility. This interpretation is certainly attractive, but it must be mitigated somewhat by the recognition that the actual situation prevailing between the various communities of the early church was somewhat more complex and variable than that indicated by the theory advanced here.

Origin and Relationship of the Sects and Schools. All the documents from which we can draw information about the origin of the early Buddhist groups were written after the beginning of the common era and are therefore unreliable. Nevertheless, since the oldest of these texts generally agree on the main points, we can attempt to restore with a certain amount of confidence the common tradition from which they derive. This should provide a fairly accurate reflection of the true interrelationships among the sects and schools.

The first division of the community probably occurred toward the middle of the fourth century BCE, some time after the council of Vaiśālī but having no direct connection with this event, the claims of the Sinhala (Theravāda) tradition notwithstanding. The schism was probably caused by a number of disagreements on the nature of the *arhat*s, who, according to some authorities, retained imperfections even though they had attained *nirvāṇa* in this world. Because they were more numerous, the supporters of these ideas formed a group called the Mahāsāṃghikas, "those of the larger community"; their opponents, who claimed to remain faithful to the teaching of the Buddha's first disciples and denied that the *arhat* could retain any imperfections, took the name Sthaviravādins, "those who speak as the elders" or "those who teach the doctrine of the old ones."

Each of these two groups were then, in turn, divided progressively into several sects or schools. Although we are in little doubt about their origins as Mahāsāṃghikas or Sthaviravādins, we often do not know precisely how these subsequent sects were linked with the first two groups, nor do we know the circumstances or time in which they appeared. We are particularly bereft of information about the sects and schools that arose directly or indirectly from the Mahāsāṃghika.

Among the groups that developed from the Mahāsāṃghika were the Ekavyāvahārika, then the Gokulika, and finally the Caitika schools. The Ekavyāvahārikas probably gave rise, in turn, to the Lokottaravādins, but it may be that the Lokottaravādins were simply a form taken by the Ekavyāvahārikas at a particular time because of the evolution of their doctrine. From the Gokulikas came the Bahuśrutīyas and the Prajñaptivādins. At least a part of the Caitika school settled in southern India, on the lower Krishna River, shortly before the beginning of the common era. From them two important sects soon arose: the Pūrvaśailas and the Aparaśailas, then a little later the Rājagirikas and the Siddhārthikas. Together, the four sects formed Andhraka group, which took its name from the area (Andhra) where they thrived during the first few centuries CE.

The Sthaviravāda group seems to have remained united until about the beginning of the third century BCE, when the Vātsīputrīyas, who maintained the existence of a quasi-autonomous "person" *(pudgala)*, split off. A half century later, probably during the reign of Aśoka (consecrated c. 268 BCE), the Sarvāstivādins also separated from the non-Vātsīputrīya Sthaviravādins and settled in northwest India. This time the dispute was over the Sarvāstivādin notion that "everything exists" *(sarvam asti)*. In the beginning of the second century, the remaining Sthaviravādins, who appear to have taken at this time the name Vibhajyavādins, "those who teach discrimination," to distinguish themselves from the Sarvāstivādins, found themselves divided once again. Out of this dispute were born the Mahīśāsakas and the Dharmaguptakas, who opposed each other over whether the Buddha, properly speaking, belonged to the monastic community and over the relative value of offerings made to the Blessed One and those made to the community. At an unknown date about the beginning of the common era four new groups sprang from the Vātsīputrīyas: the Dharmottarīyas, the Bhadrayānīyas, the Ṣaṇṇagarikas, and the Sammatīyas. The Sammatīyas, who were very important in Indian Buddhism, later gave rise to the Avantaka and the Kurukulla schools. One group broke from the Sarvāstivādins: the Sautrāntikas, who can be identified with the Dārṣṭāntikas and the Saṃkrāntivādins.

Some of the Vibhajyavādins settled in southern India and Lanka in the mid-third century BCE and seem to have maintained fairly close relations for some time with the Mahīśāsakas, whose presence is attested in the same area. Adopting Pali as a canonical language and energetically claiming their teaching to be the strict orthodoxy, they took the name Theravādins, a Pali form of the Sanskrit Sthaviravādins. Like the Sthaviravādins, they suffered from internal squabbles and divisions: some years before the common era, the Abhayagirivāsins split from the Mahāvihāras, founded at the time of the arrival of Buddhism in Lanka; later, in the fourth century, the Jetavanīyas appeared.

Finally, three sects derived from the Sthaviravādins present some problems regarding their precise relationship and identity. The Kāśyapīyas, whose basic position was a compromise between those of the Sarvāstivādins and the Vibhajyavādins, apparently broke from the latter shortly after the split that created the Sarvāstivāda and Vibhajyavāda *nikāyas*. More mysterious are the Haimavatas, about whom the facts are both scarce and contradictory. As for the Mūlasarvāstivādins, or "radical Sarvāstivādins," they appeared suddenly at the end of the seventh century with a huge "basket of discipline" (Vinaya Piṭaka) in Sanskrit, much different in many respects from that of the earlier Sarvāstivādins. It is impossible to determine exactly what connection the Mūlasarvāstivādins had with the Sarvāstivādins.

Except for a few of the more important of these sects and schools—such as the Theravādins, who left us the treasure of their celebrated Sinhala chronicles—we know nothing of the history of these different groups. Their existence is nevertheless assured, thanks to the testimony of a fair number of inscriptions and other substantial documents. To judge from the information given by Hsüan-tsang and I-ching, by the time they made their long visits to India in the seventh century, most of the sects had already disappeared. Of all the many groups descended from the original Mahāsāṃghikas, only the Lokottaravādins were still numerous and thriving, but only in a very specific location, Bamian (Bāmiyān, in present-day Afghanistan). (See figure 1.)

Here arises an important question, one whose answer is still uncertain: what connections existed between these early Buddhist sects and schools, known as Hīnayāna, and the groups formed by the followers of the Mahāyāna? Were any of them—in particular those of Mahāsāṃghika origin—converted in large numbers to the Mahāyāna, or did they perhaps give birth to it through the natural evolution of their doctrine? Should we interpret in this sense the expression Mahāyāna-Sthaviravādin, which Hsüan-tsang used to refer to numerous Buddhist communities he encountered throughout India, and deduce from it that their followers were Sthaviravādins converted to the Mahāyāna? Or did believers of both groups live together, without mingling, in the areas where they were found? This second interpretation strikes one as more satisfactory; nevertheless, the first cannot be rejected definitively.

Geographical Distribution. Two types of records inform us about the geographical distribution of the sects and schools: inscriptions and the reports of a number of Chinese pilgrims who came to India. Numbering only a few tens and ranging in time between the second century BCE and the sixth century CE, the inscriptions that mention early sects give us only spotty and very insufficient data. Although they may actually attest to the presence of a given group in a specific place at a particular date, they leave us completely ignorant about the presence or absence of this sect in other places and at other times. The information supplied by the Chinese travelers, principally Hsüan-tsang and to a lesser extent I-ching, is incomparably more complete, but it is valid only for the seventh century, when their journeys took place.

The study of these two kinds of sources—like that of the Sinhala chronicles, which are concerned mostly with Sri Lankan Buddhism—reveals some important general features about the early Buddhist schools. None of the groups was present everywhere throughout India and its neighboring countries; on the other hand, no area was the exclusive domain of any one group. For reasons that unfortunately nearly always escape us, certain groups were in the majority in some places, in the minority in others, and completely absent in still others but, as far as we can tell, coexisted in varying proportions with other groups wherever they were found. For example, in a number of places—especially those that history or legend made holy in the eyes of Buddhist devotees and were important places of pilgrimage—the monks of various sects lived together in neighboring monasteries and often venerated the same sacred ob-

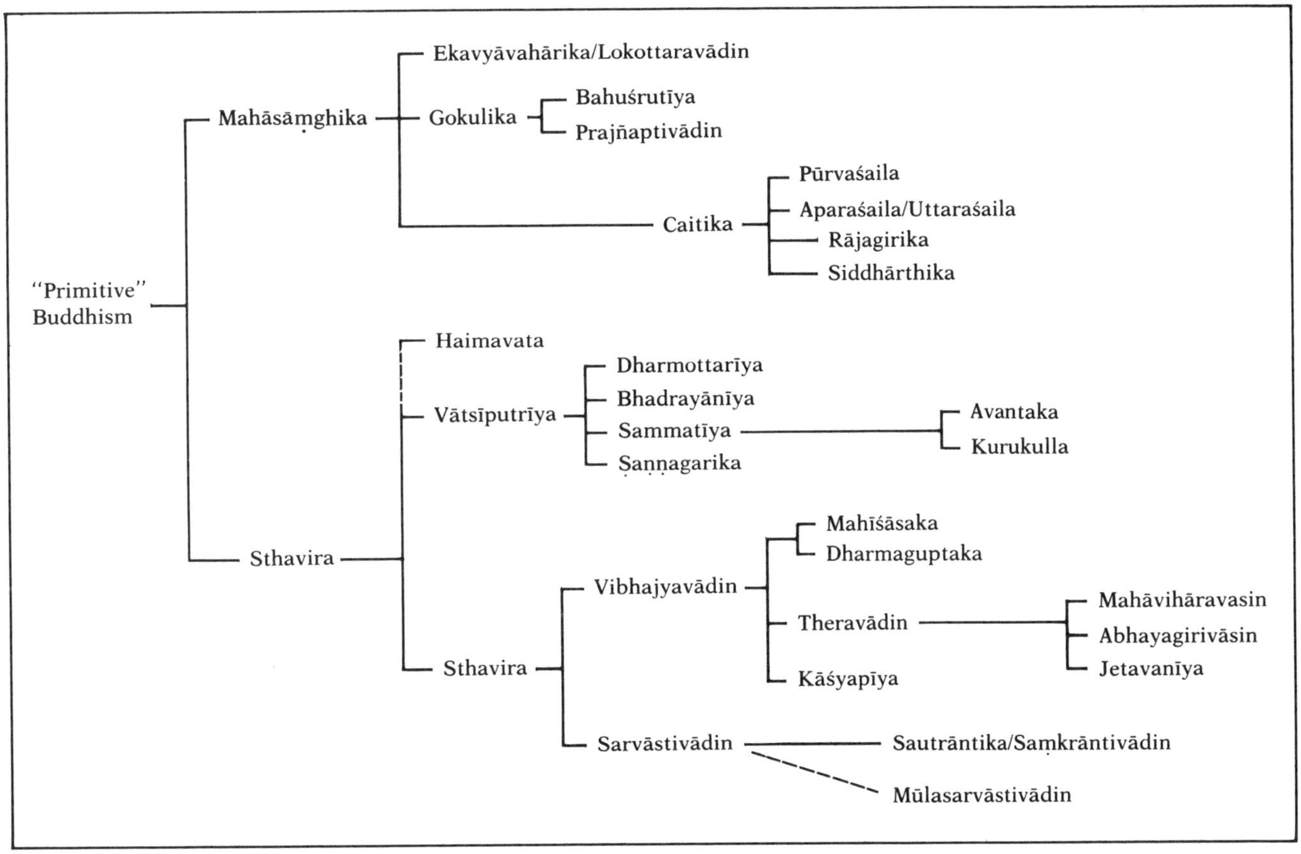

FIGURE 1. *Filiation of the Hīnayāna Sects*

jects—topes (*stūpas*), Bodhi trees, and others. This was the case not only in the holy places in the Ganges Basin, where the major events in the Buddha's life occurred, but also far from there, in Sāñchī, Karlī, Amarāvatī, Nāgārjunikoṇḍa, and elsewhere. In Sri Lanka, the three great monasteries that became the centers of the three subsects of the Theravāda, the Mahāvihāra, the Abhayagiri, and the Jetavana, were located on the outskirts of the island's ancient capital, Anurādhapura.

All of the sects and schools seem to have been present in the middle Ganges Basin, which is easily understandable since the principal places of pilgrimage were located there. The more important ones, which originated in both the Mahāsāṃghika and Sthaviravāda groups, also appear to have coexisted in eastern India, Bengal, and nearby areas, at least in the seventh century, as reported by both Hsüan-tsang and I-ching.

The Theravādins always dominated most of Sri Lanka and still do today. In the eleventh century, they also largely converted the Burmese, followed a little later by the people of Thailand, Cambodia, and Laos, where they continue to exercise religious dominion today. In the seventh century, the Vibhajyavāda Sthaviravādins, who were very close, if not identical, to the Theravādins, likewise controlled all the Tamil country, the part of India nearest to Sri Lanka, and were also extremely numerous in the coastal region north of Bombay and near Buddhist holy places on the Ganges from which people embarked on journeys to Lanka and southern India.

Very little is known about the location of the sects most closely related to these. The presence of the Mahīśāsakas is recorded both in the Indian northwest, on the banks of the Krishna, and in Sri Lanka; that of the Dharmaguptakas in the Indian northwest only; and that of the Kāśyapīyas mostly in the Indian northwest but also around Bombay. The Sarvāstivādins were clearly in a majority over all of northwest India, from the upper Ganges Basin to Kashmir, from the mid-third century BCE to at least the seventh century CE.

In the seventh century, the Sammatīyas formed the sect comprising the largest number of monks and generally controlled all of western India, from the middle Indus Valley to southeast of Bombay. They were also very numerous throughout the Ganges Basin and in eastern India. Several inscriptions testify to the presence, at the beginning of the common era, of Dharmottarīyas and Bhadrayānīyas in the area of Bombay.

Data concerning the Mahāsāṃghika proper, and most of the sects that developed from it, are rare and widely scattered. We know for certain that the Mahāsāṃghika existed in northwestern India, around Bombay and on the banks of the lower Krishna. Caitikas also inhabited these last two areas but primarily the second, where Bahuśrutīyas also resided. By the seventh century, the Lokottaravādins had made Bamian, in the heart of present-day Afghanistan, one of the main centers of Buddhism in the Indo-Iranian realms and were still very numerous there, as Hsüan-tsang reports. The Pūrvaśailas, Aparaśailas, Rājagirikas, and Siddhārtikas prospered during the first centuries of the common era in the lower Krishna Valley, which they covered with magnificent monuments, but by the beginning of the seventh century they had almost disappeared.

Major Doctrinal Differences. We are well acquainted with the principal doctrinal differences that gave rise to many of these schools, the basic ideas that distinguish them, and the reactions and rebuttals the various sects offered each other. In most cases, though, and particularly with regard to the apparently less important sects, our information is unfortunately too vague, and sometimes even contradictory or nonexistent, to tell us anything about the specifics of their doctrine.

Although many questions divided all or some of the schools, they did not provoke the formation of new sects. These debates were sometimes very important for the evolution of Buddhism as a whole. Often, various of the early sects that we might expect to hold similar views given their genesis in fact adopted doctrinal opinions at great variance with one another. Thus, there often came about, among schools with similar opinions on specific questions, entirely different regroupings from those one would expect in light of their traditional relationships. Let us first examine the fundamental ideas that appear to have brought about the formation of the principal sects.

The Mahāsāṃghikas probably separated from the Sthaviravādins over the belief that certain *arhat*s, although they had attained *nirvāṇa* in this world, could be subject to nocturnal defilements as a result of erotic dreams; that they still harbored vestiges of ignorance; that they had areas of doubt on matters outside Buddhist doctrine; that they could be informed, indeed saved, by other people; and, finally, that they utter certain words when they meditated on the Path of Liberation. The Sthaviravādins denied these five possibilities, arguing that the *arhat* is completely free of all imperfections.

The Vātsīputrīyas and the schools that later developed from them, the Sammatīyas and others, believed in the existence of a "person" *(pudgala)* who is neither identical to the five aggregates (*skandhas*) that make up the living being nor different from them; neither within these five aggregates nor outside them. Although differing from the Brahmanic "soul" *(ātman)*, denied unanimously by Buddhist doctrine, this "person" lives on from one existence to the next, thus ensuring the continuing identities of the agent of an act and of the being who suffers its effects in this life or the next. All the other schools rejected this hypothesis, maintaining the logical impossibility of conceptualizing this "person" and seeing in it simply a disguised form of the *ātman*.

The Sarvāstivādins claimed that "everything exists" *(sarvam asti)*, that is, that the past and the future have real and material existence. This belief enabled them to explain several phenomena that were very important to Buddhists: the act of consciousness, which is made up of several successive, individual mental actions; memory or consciousness of the past; foresight or consciousness of the future; and the "ripening" *(vipāka)* of "actions" *(karman)*, which takes place over a longer or shorter span of time, often exceeding the length of a single life. For the other sects, however, it was perfectly clear that what is past exists no longer and that what is to come does not yet exist.

The Kāśyapīyas, also called Suvarṣakas, maintained a position between these two, namely, that a past action that has not yet borne fruit exists, but the rest of the past does not. This approach, however, satisfied neither the Sarvāstivādins nor their critics.

The Sautrāntikas distinguished themselves from the Sarvāstivādins insofar as they considered the canonic "basket of sermons" (Sūtra Piṭaka) to be the only one to contain the authentic words of the Buddha, whereas the "basket of higher teaching" (Abhidharma Piṭaka) is the work of the Blessed One's disciples. According to some of our sources, the Sautrāntikas were also called Saṃkrāntivādins because they held that the five aggregates (*skandhas*) constituting the living being "transmigrate" *(saṃkrānti)* from one existence to the next; probably this should be understood to mean that, in their view, four of these aggregates were absorbed at the moment of death into the fifth, a subtle consciousness. It also seems that the Sautrāntikas can be identified with the Dārṣṭāntikas, who were often criticized in the Sarvāstivāda writings and apparently gained their name because of their frequent use of comparisons or parables (*dṛṣṭāntas*) in their discussions.

An important disagreement separated the Mahīśāsakas from the Dharmaguptakas. For the former, the Buddha is part of the monastic community *(saṃgha)*; hence a gift given to the community produces a "great fruit" *(mahāphalam),* but one directed specifically to the Buddha does not. The Dharmaguptakas, on the other hand, held that the Buddha is separate from the community, and as he is far superior to it—since it is composed only of his followers—only the gift given to the Buddha produces a great fruit. These two opposing views had considerable influence on the religious practices of early Buddhism.

The Lokottaravādins differed from other Mahāsāṃghika schools in holding that the Buddhas are "otherworldly" *(lokottara),* a word having several very different senses but which they employed loosely to attribute an extraordinary nature to the Buddhas. According to them, the Buddhas are otherworldly not only because their thought is always perfectly pure but also because they remain outside and above the world. Thus it would seem to be among the Lokottaravādins that we should seek the origin of Buddhist docetism, that is, the distinction between the real, transcendent, and infinite Buddha, the "body of doctrine" *(dharmakāya),* and the apparent Buddha, the "body of magical creation" *(nirmāṇakāya)*—a kind of phantom emanating from the real one. To rescue beings, the *nirmāṇakāya* becomes incarnate, taking on their form and thus seeming to be born, to grow up, to discover and preach the doctrine of enlightenment, and to finally die and become completely extinguished. The Lokottaravādins must have also extolled the extraordinary character of the *bodhisattva,* undoubtedly on account of their supernatural conception of the Buddhas. These singular notions lead one to believe that this sect played an important part in the formation of the Mahāyāna, whose teaching adopted and developed similar ideas.

As their name seems to indicate, the Prajñaptivādins were probably distinguished from the other schools that arose from the Mahāsāṃghika group because they taught that all things are mere products of linguistic convention *(prajñapti)* and, hence, are devoid of actual existence. One might see here the origin of the famous theory of the universal "void" *(śūnyatā),* which is one of the basic elements of the Mahāyāna doctrine and is the main theme, reiterated with the greatest insistence, of its oldest works, the first Prajñāpāramitā Sūtras.

Unfortunately, we do not know the basic premises of the other schools, whether they arose from the Sthaviravāda group or the Mahāsāṃghika. The data that have come down to us concerning a few of them, such as the Gokulikas (also called Kukkuṭikas), the Bahuśrutīyas, the Sammatīyas, and some others, are very doubtful, vague, or extremely obscure, even contradictory. For others, we possess no information at all.

As noted above, hundreds of controversies also set the various schools apart from one another without provoking new divisions of the community. Most of these debates apparently concerned only two or three sects and lasted for a short time—unless this impression is due solely to our lack of information. On the other hand, certain of these arguments affected, and even impassioned, a large number of schools for long periods, sometimes for centuries, as evidenced by the treatises and commentaries on canonic texts that have come down to us. In these more important controversies the distribution of the sects between the two opposing camps is often independent of their derivational connections. It may be that relations of good neighborliness and, hence, ties based on geographical distribution favored such doctrinal alliances. In any case, I will point out the most significant of these divergences of opinion, which are important features in the history of early Buddhist thought.

The Sarvāstivādins, the Sammatīyas, and the Pūrvaśailas firmly believed in an "intermediate existence" *(antarābhava)* that linked death and rebirth. This concept was rejected by the Theravādins and the Mahāsāṃghikas. The latter, along with the Andhakas and the Sarvāstivādins, maintained that the *bodhisattva* may be born in the so-called "evil existences" *(durgati),* even in the various hells, to lighten the sufferings of the beings who live in them. The Theravādins denied that this was possible because, in their view, of the automatic retribution consequent upon all actions, a retribution that completely determines the circumstances of rebirths. According to the Vātsīputrīyas, the Sammatīyas, the Sarvāstivādins, and the Pūrvaśailas, the *arhat*s could backslide in varying degrees and even lose *nirvāṇa,* but the Theravādins, Mahāsāṃghikas, and Sautrāntikas refused to accept this idea. The Theravādins, the Sarvāstivādins, and the Dharmaguptakas agreed that it was possible for the gods to practice the sexual abstinence *(brahmacarya)* of ascetics, whereas the Sammatīyas and the Mahīśāsakas judged this impossible. For the Theravādins and the Sarvāstivādins, there were only five fates (*gati*s), namely, those of gods, men, animals, starving ghosts (*preta*s), and the damned, but the Andhakas and the Vātsīputrīyas added another, that of the *asura*s, the superhuman beings who were adversaries of the gods (*deva*s) yet were not devils in the Christian sense.

The Mahāsāṃghikas, the Theravādins, and the Mahīśāsakas taught that the clear understanding *(abhisamaya)* of the Four Noble Truths *(catvāry āryasatyāni)* was instantaneous, whereas the Andhakas, the Sarvāstivādins, and the Sammatīyas believed that it happened gradually. So important was this dispute that it was still the central theme of the council of Lhasa (held in the eighth century), where Chinese and Tibetan Buddhist teachers opposed each other in doctrinal debate. The Sarvāstivādins seem to have been alone in denying that "thought" *(citta)* is inherently pure and contaminated only by accidental impurities, a belief held by the Mahāsāṃghikas, the Theravādins, and the neighboring schools.

The Theravādins, the Vātsīputrīyas, and the Sammatīyas recognized only one absolute, or "unconditioned" *(asaṃskṛta) dharma,* namely, *nirvāṇa,* but the majority of schools also considered empty space *(ākāśa)* an unconditioned *dharma.* Several of them taught that "dependent origination" *(pratītya-samutpāda),* the path *(mārga)* of enlightenment, and sometimes other entities as well, in particular the "suchness" *(tathatā)* or "permanence" *(sthitatā)* of things, were equally absolute and unconditioned. Thus, the ideas of these schools were quite close to those of the Mahāyāna.

Several important debates centered on the nature of the passions, more specifically, latent passions or tendencies *(anuśaya)* and active passions or obsessions *(paryavasthāna).* The Mahāsāṃghikas, the Andhakas, and the Mahīśāsakas set up a very precise distinction between them, while the Theravādins and Sarvāstivādins chose to see in them only two aspects of the same passions. For the Theravādins and the Sarvāstivadins, tendencies and obsessions alike were connected, or cofunctioned, with thought (*cittasaṃprayukta*), whereas for the Mahāsāṃghikas, the Vātsīputrīyas, the Sammatīyas, and the Mahīśāsakas, tendencies were unconnected, did not cofunction, with thought *(cittaviprayukta),* while obsessions were connected with it. As for the Andhakas, they held that obsessions and tendencies were equally separate from thought.

According to the Sarvāstivādins and the Vātsīputrīyas, ascetics of other, non-Buddhist beliefs *(tīrthika)* could, through their efforts, obtain the five lesser supernatural faculties *(abhijñā)* and thus work various miracles—perceiving the thoughts of others, recollecting their past lives, seeing the rebirths of creatures as conditioned by their past actions, and so forth. The Mahīśāsakas and the Dharmaguptakas, however, declared that the five supernatural faculties—like the sixth, the cleansing of impurities, that is, the attainment of *nirvāṇa*—could be acquired only by Buddhist ascetics treading the Path of Enlightenment.

The relation between "matter" *(rūpa)* and the mechanism of the ripening *(vipāka)* of actions *(karman)* also gave rise to disagreements. For the Theravādins, matter is independent of the ripening of actions, and it is not the fruit of this ripening. It is morally neither good nor bad but inherently neutral. In contrast, the Sarvāstivādins, Sammatīyas, and Mahīśāsakas taught that matter can be good or bad when it participates, through the body of man, in a good or bad act. Matter is also the fruit of ripening when it becomes the body—be it handsome or ugly, robust or sickly—received by a person at birth as a consequence of past deeds.

According to the Sarvāstivādins, the five forms of sensory perception are always associated with passionate desires (*rāgas*). The Mahāsāṃghikas and the Mahīśāsakas thought that they were sometimes associated and sometimes unassociated with them, while the Vātsīputrīyas rejected both these possibilities, declaring that the five forms of sensory perception are morally neutral by nature and thus can never be either good or bad.

Literature. The literature of early Buddhism must have been very important in extent and interest because what has been preserved for us, even though it represents only a small part of the whole, is considerable. The great majority of this literature vanished with the sects that produced it; let us recall that only one, the Theravāda, still flourishes today in Sri Lanka and Southeast Asia. Most of the schools have left us nothing, save perhaps a few fragments, isolated *sūtras*, and other brief works in the original Indian language or more often in Chinese translation. Which sects they belonged to nearly always remains undetermined.

Roughly half of what has been handed down to us is in the original Indian language, in a more or less "hybrid" Sanskrit, in various Middle Indic dialects, and above all in Pali. It is in Pali that the body of Theravāda literature, which we possess practically in its entirety, was written. The remainder, of approximately the same size, has come down to us only in Chinese or Tibetan translations. The scope of what was preserved in the Tibetan version, as far as the Hīnayāna in particular is concerned, is much more limited than that of the Chinese translation and, moreover, is confined almost solely to works of the Sarvāstivādins and Mūlasarvāstivādins. In Mahāyāna literature, in contrast, the enormous amount of material translated into Tibetan is virtually equal to what was translated into Chinese.

Thus, it seems that a greater proportion of the canonical literature—properly speaking, that which belonged to the Tripiṭaka ("three baskets")—than of the postcanonical literature has been passed on to us. It comprises, primarily, the complete Pali Tipiṭaka, made up of its Sutta Piṭaka ("basket of sermons"), its Vinaya Piṭaka ("basket of discipline"), and its Abhidhamma Piṭaka ("basket of higher teaching").

The Sutta Piṭaka, in turn, is composed of five Nikāyas, or "groupings," bringing together the "long" *(dīgha),* "medium" *(majjhima),* and "grouped" *(saṃyutta)* sermons; those arranged according to number of categories *(aṅguttara);* and, lastly, the "minor" *(khuddaka)* sermons, the longest and most varied section of all. The *Khuddaka Nikāya* assembles the legends of the former "births" *(jātaka)* of the Buddha, legends recounting the "deeds" *(apadāna*; Skt., *avadāna)* of the great disciples, didactic stanzas *(gāthā)* attributed to them, a famous but anonymous collection of other instructional stanzas called the *Dhammapada*, and ten or so other equally varied works.

Like the other Baskets of Discipline that have survived, the Pali Vinaya Piṭaka essentially contains three parts. These provide detailed definitions and explanations of the numerous rules of discipline imposed on monks (*bhikkus*), those to be observed by nuns (*bhikkunīs*), and specific rules concerning the material life of both: the correct use of objects they were allowed to own, ceremony, sentencing of offenders, settling of disputes, and so on.

The Pali Abhidhamma Piṭaka consists of seven different works, in which the doctrine set forth in no particular order in the sermons (*suttas*) is reorganized, classified systematically, and fleshed out at numerous points. One of these seven books, the *Kathāvatthu* (Points of Controversy), refutes more than two hundred opinions held by other Buddhist schools and in the process reveals the doctrines peculiar to the Theravāda.

Sadly, we do not possess a complete Tripiṭaka from any other early sect, but more or less significant parts of several of them have been preserved. Thus, five Vinaya Piṭakas have come to us intact: those of the Mahāsāṃghikas, Mahīśāsakas, Dharmaguptakas, Sarvāstivādins, and Mūlasarvāstivādins, all in Chinese translation, plus more or less extensive fragments of the last two in the original Sanskrit. We have an entire Tibetan translation of the Mūlasarvāstivādin Vinaya Piṭaka, which is much more voluminous and written later than the others. In addition, we have a detached portion of the Lokottaravāda Vinaya Piṭaka under the name *Mahāvastu* (Great Tale) in Hybrid Sanskrit. This is actually a traditional and partial biography of the Buddha, heavily encrusted with legendry.

The non-Theravāda sects used the term *āgama* ("tradition") for the four or five parts that made up their Sūtra Piṭakas, which correspond to the Pali Nikāyas. Five of these Āgamas, evidently complete, have survived in Chinese translation: the *Dīrghāgama* of the Dharmaguptakas; the *Madhyamāgama* of the Sarvāstivādins; the *Saṃyuktāgamas* of the Sarvāstivādins and the Kāśyapīyas; and, finally, an *Ekottarāgama* that most probably belongs to a sect derived from the Mahāsāṃghikas but different from the Lokottaravādins. There are also more than 150 isolated *sūtras*, nearly all preserved in Chinese and a few in their original Indian language, but it is generally impossible to determine what school they come from. No collection corresponding to the Pali *Khuddaka Nikāya* survives, but we do have the Chinese translations of some seventy works similar to those that make up the Theravāda collection, as well as the Indian originals of a number of others.

Two complete Abhidharma Piṭakas have survived in Chinese translation: that of the Sarvāstivādins (one part of this also exists in Tibetan) and one entitled *Śāriputra-abhidharma*, which seems to have belonged to the Dharmaguptakas but was perhaps also influenced by the Mahāsāṃghika. Like the Abhidharma Piṭaka of the Theravādins, that of the Sarvāstivādins comprises seven works, but its overall structure is very different, as is its doctrine, although there are notable similarities between some parts of the two works. The *Śāriputra-abhidharma*, which is made up of four main sections, differs even more from the Theravādin text. For the most part these three collections definitely postdate the first appearance of the sects that composed them and defended their own positions in them. The teaching given by the sermons in the various Nikāyas or Āgamas of the Sūtra Piṭakas, in contrast, presents a truly remarkable consistency, whatever their school of origin, and, thus, a great fidelity to the common early Buddhist base, predating the community's division into sects. The same is true for most of the monastic rules contained in the various Vinaya Piṭakas, which are distinguished mainly by details of secondary or minor aspects of the ascetic life.

The postcanonical literature was undoubtedly very important, but even less of it remains than of the canonic material, and it is more unevenly distributed. Luckily, we possess in Pali the greater part of what was written by the Theravādins—commentaries on the canonic texts, treatises on doctrine, collections of legends, and devotional poems. We have also the principal Sarvāstivāda treatises, several commentaries on these works and on the major portion of their Abhidharma Piṭaka, as well as a few other late works. Unfortunately, the postcanonic literature available to us from all the other schools is limited to a half-dozen works.

The whole series of commentaries in Pali on the Theravāda canonic texts was composed in the fourth and fifth centuries CE by Buddhadatta, Buddhaghosa, and Dhammapāla, who made use of ancient commentaries, now lost, in Old Sinhala. We also owe to Buddhaghosa, the wisest and most renowned of all the Theravāda masters, a substantial treatise entitled *Visuddhimagga* (The Path of Purity), in which the Mahāvihāra school's entire doctrine is set forth. Another famous treatise is the *Abhidhammatthasaṅgaha* (Collection of Interpretations of the Higher Doctrine), written by the Sinhala monk Anuruddha about the eleventh century. Other, less important treatises of the Mahāvihāra school were composed by various authors between the fourth and fifteenth centuries. Each of these works was the subject of one or more commentaries, most of which have not survived. Only one non-Mahāvihāra Theravāda work—strangely, in Chinese translation—is extant: a large treatise called *Vimuttimagga* (The Path of Liberation), attributed to Upatissa, who must have lived some time before Buddhaghosa and was probably a master of the Abhayagiri school.

To the treatises may be added the *Lokapaññatti* (Description of the World), a fourteenth-century adaptation by the Burmese monk Saddhammaghosa of a lost Sanskrit work, and especially the well-known *Milindapañha* (Questions of King Milinda), likewise inspired by a lost work. This seems to have been a little Buddhist propaganda manual aimed at the Greeks and Eurasians, such as King Menander (Milinda), who lived in northwestern India in the second century BCE. Besides the Pali version, there are two Chinese translations of the *Milindapañha* that rather differ from each other and even more so from the Theravāda text.

The postcanonic Theravāda literature also includes instructional poems and collections of legends in verse or prose. Among the instructional poems are the *Anāgatavaṃsa* (History of the Future), in which the monk Kassapa recounts the life of the next Buddha, named Metteyya, and the *Jinacarita* (Story of the Conqueror), Medhaṃkara's account of the miraculous life of the historical Buddha. The *Rasavāhinī* (Transportress of Flavors), translated into Pali by Vedeha from an Old Sinhala poem, is a collection of some one hundred legends meant to encourage a life of piety.

However, it is its famous chronicles, a genre almost entirely abandoned in ancient India, that make Theravāda literature stand apart from that of the other sects. The series of the *Dīpavaṃsa* (History of the Island), *Mahāvaṃsa* (Great History), and *Cūḷavaṃsa* (Lesser History) records in verse the whole history of Sri Lanka, from its beginning to the end of the eighteenth century, from the very specific point of view of the "elders" (*theras*) of the Mahāvihāra, the principal Sinhala Theravāda school. Other chronicles recount, in grandiose verse style, the stories of sacred relics: the *Bodhivaṃsa* tells the story of the Bodhi tree, the *Thūpavaṃsa* that of the principal mound of Anurādhapura, and the *Dāṭhāvaṃsa* that of the Buddha's tooth.

The main works of the Sarvāstivādin postcanonic literature have generally survived in Chinese or Tibetan translation. Complete or partial Sanskrit originals of several of them have also been found.

Only two commentaries on the postcanonic literature of the Sarvāstivādins have come down to us. One concerns the rules of monastic discipline and is entitled *Sarvāstivāda-vinaya-vibhāṣā*; the other, called *Abhidharma-mahāvibhāṣā*, comments on the *Jñānaprasthāna*, the principal work of the Abhidharma Piṭaka of this sect. This *Mahāvibhāṣā* (Great Commentary) is an immense summation of the doctrine of the Sarvāstivādins or, more precisely, of their most important school, known as the Vaibhāṣika, "supporter of the *(Mahā-) Vibhāṣā*." It is one of the most voluminous works in all Buddhist literature.

The Sarvāstivādins left several treatises written in Sanskrit during the first few centuries of the common era. The principal and best known is the *Abhidharmakośa* (Treasury of Higher Doctrine), written by Vasubandhu in the fifth century and the subject of numerous commentaries, many of which are extant in the Sanskrit original or in Chinese or Tibetan translation. Vasubandhu was accused of holding Sautrāntika views by his contemporary Saṃghabhadra, a strictly orthodox Sarvāstivādin. Saṃghabhadra refuted these views in a large treatise entitled *Abhidharma-nyāyānusāra* (Consistent with the Logic of the Further Doctrine) and in a long commentary on the didactic stanzas (*kārikās*) of the *Abhidharmakośa*. The Sarvāstivādins also composed a *Lokaprajñapti* (Description of the World) according to Buddhist ideas, which has survived in Chinese and Tibetan translations.

The other schools have left only Chinese translations of a few treatises and commentaries, often very short and of unknown origin. Among the commentaries, which all correspond to complete or partial Vinaya Piṭakas, we may mention the *Vinayasaṃgraha* (Collection of Discipline) by the Mūlasarvāstivādin Viśeṣamitra and the *Vinayamātṛkā* (Summary of Discipline), the sectarian affinity of which is uncertain.

All that remains of the literature of the Vātsīputrīyas and related schools, which must have been considerable, are the Chinese translations, sadly inferior and obscure, of two small treatises summarizing their teaching. The most important of these is entitled *Sammatīya-nikāya-śāstra* (Treatise of the Sammatīya Sect).

Two other works of the same type have also survived in Chinese translation, but although they are better translated and are much longer, their sectarian origin presents some difficulty. One, called *Satyasiddhi* (Realization of the Truths), written by Harivarman around the third century CE, teaches and defends the doctrine of a Mahāsāṃghika-derived school, probably the Bahuśrutīyas. The other is the *Vimuttimagga*, mentioned above, whose author, Upatissa, probably belonged to the Sinhala Abhayagiri school; its Pali original was recently rediscovered.

The literary genre of devotional legends in verse or prose was also a great inspiration to authors of all sects, most of whom remained as anonymous as those of the canonic texts. Some of these works recounted the life of the historical Buddha, embellishing it with numerous miracles for the sake of greater glory. Two of the three most famous were preserved by chance in their Indian originals. These were composed in Hybrid Sanskrit, which is to say greatly influenced by the Prakrit dialects: the *Mahāvastu* (Great Tale) and the *Lalitavistara* (Account of the Sport), both important sources for the development of the Buddha legend. The first is a detached portion of the Lokottaravāda Vinaya Piṭaka, but in scope, as well as in specific subject matter, it can be considered a distinct and, moreover, rather late work. The *Lalitavistara* was first compiled by the Sarvāstivādins but later revised by followers of the Mahāyāna. In contrast with these two, the *Buddhacarita* (Story of the Buddha) was written in classical Sanskrit by one of the greatest Indian poets, Aśvaghoṣa, who lived around the second century CE; only half of the Sanskrit text has been recovered, but the Chinese translation is complete.

The collections of legendary material recounting the edifying deeds of Buddhist saints, or the previous incarnations of these or the future Buddha, are numerous, whether in Hybrid Sanskrit originals or in Chinese versions. We shall mention here only the best known, the *Avadānaśataka* (Hundred Exploits) and the *Divyāvadana* (Divine Exploits).

Notable Personalities. Be they Buddhists, brahmans, or otherwise, the Indians of ancient times had practically no interest in history as we understand it, with its concern for the exact recording of events, dates, names, and biographies of important figures in order to preserve a precise record of them. This is especially true for the history of Indian Buddhism and the lives of its great masters. With very rare exceptions, to us the masters are only names attached to one or more literary works or, much less often, to an important item or event in the history of Buddhism—such as an idea that was declared heretical, a dispute, or a council. Nearly always, we know nothing whatever of the lives of these people, including the regions where they were born or lived and the centuries in which they were active. Moreover, the scant information that tradition has preserved about them is either vague, contradictory, or obviously distorted by legend, obliging us to make use of it with great skepticism. Even the biographies of the principal Sinhala elders (*theras*) of the Theravāda sect, whose history is told at length and in detail by the chronicles of Sri Lanka, are hardly better known to us than those of the masters of other groups and schools of early Indian Buddhism. In any case, we possess infinitely less detail about the lives of these *theras* than about those of the kings, princes, and generals who studded the history of Sri Lanka and protected the island's monastic community for two thousand years. Nonetheless, these chronicles permit us to know the names of a much larger number of these Sinhala Theravāda elders than of the masters of other sects, and thanks to them we are generally informed with some precision about the time and place in which many of them lived.

Among the most noteworthy figures of the Theravāda, we must first point out the three great scholars to whom all of the commentaries on the Pali canon and several important treatises on doctrine are attributed. The most famous is certainly Buddhaghosa, author of the *Visuddhimagga*. [*See the biography of Buddhaghosa.*] According to tradition, Buddhaghosa was an Indian brahman from Bihar who converted to Buddhism, then probably came to live in the Tamil country and afterward in the Sri Lankan capital, Anurādhapura, during the reign of Mahānāma (409–431). Buddhadatta, who was, it seems, a little older than Buddhaghosa, was probably born in the Tamil country, on the banks of the Kāverī, and spent most of his life there, but he probably sojourned in Anurādhapura as well. Finally, Dhammapāla was probably also a Tamil, born in Kāñcīpuram in the late fourth century, and most likely lived mainly in his native land but also journeyed to Lanka. Thus, it would seem that in the early fifth century, Tamil India was an important seat of Buddhist—or, more precisely, Theravāda—culture, on a par with Sri Lanka and perhaps even more active.

The reign of Parakkamabāhu (Parākramabāhu) I (1153–1186), an especially prosperous epoch for the Sinhala Theravādins, was made illustrious by a number of scholar-monks. The most famous was Sāriputta, a pupil of Kassapa of Udumbaragiri, who had played a pivotal role in the reform of the community ordered by the king and was himself a great scholar. Sāriputta turned his residence, the new monastery of Jetavana at Polonnaruwa, into the major center of knowledge and Buddhist learning of his time. Author of several authoritative subcommentaries on canonic texts, highly esteemed grammarian and poet, he was as well versed in Sanskrit as in Pali and composed his works in both languages. Several of his many students became learned monks and authors of valued literary works, notably Dhammakitti, Saṅgharakkhita, Sumaṅgala, Buddhanāga, Medaṅkara, and Vācissara.

In modern times, mention must be made of one first-rank figure whose influence on the evolution of Theravāda Buddhism was both decisive and extensive. Prince Mongkut, the youngest son of the Siamese king Rama II, became a monk and, during the quarter-century that he spent in yellow robes, undertook a great reform of the community in his country. In particular, he founded a new monastic order, the Thammayut, which observed the rules of discipline more strictly than did its contemporaries, but he also kept abreast of the social realities of Siam and enthusiastically studied the culture and religions of the West. Becoming king on the death of his elder brother, he ruled under the name Rama IV (1851–1868), completing his work and transforming his country into a modern state largely open to trade and external influence. He is one of the principal architects of the great reform of Theravāda Buddhism that took place after the mid-nineteenth century not only in Siam but also in the neighboring kingdoms and in Sri Lanka. This movement was characterized by a return to the sources of the religion, namely the Pali Tipiṭaka, and also by a necessary and rational adaptation to modern circumstances. [*See the biography of Mongkut.*]

The best-known figure of the Sarvāstivādins is certainly Vasubandhu, the author of the *Abhidharmakośa*. Unfortunately, our information about this great master is suspect and seemingly contradictory, so that his life remains a subject of debate. Is Vasubandhu the Sarvāstivādin identical with Vasubandhu the Yogācāra, the brother of Asaṅga? Did he live in the fourth or the fifth century of our era? Was he born at Puruṣapura (present-day Peshawar) into a brahman family? Did he live in Kashmir, and then Ayodhyā (present-day Fyzabad), where he probably died? No agreement has been reached on these or other, lesser points of his biography. [*See the biography of Vasubandhu.*]

We know even less about his principal adversary, Saṃghabhadra, except that he was Vasubandhu's contemporary, a Kashmiri, and a staunch defender of Vaibhāṣika Sarvāstivāda orthodoxy. As for other great teachers of this sect, to whom are attributed various interpretations of the notion of *sarvam asti* or the treatises that have come down to us in Chinese translation, they are hardly more than names to us: Vasumitra (one or several?), Kātyāyaniputra, Dharmaśrī, Ghoṣaka, Upaśānta, Dharmatrāta. . . . Indeed, the Sarvāstivāda's founder, Madhyāntika, who probably settled with his disciples in Kashmir during the reign of Aśoka, seems himself to belong more to legend than to history.

The founders of other schools are also nothing but names to us, and even these have been handed down: Mahādeva for the Mahāsāṃghikas, Vātsīputra for the Vātsīputrīyas, Uttara for the Sautrāntikas, and so on. We only know two or three other masters, whose names have been preserved by chance, such as Śrīlāta of the Sautrāntika and Harivarman, the author of the *Satyasiddhi*. Of Śrīlāta we know nothing more than his opinions, as these were criticized in Sarvāstivādin tracts. Harivarman was probably a brahman from the middle Ganges basin, who most likely lived around the third century CE and was converted to Buddhism as a follower of one of the Mahāsāṃghika sects, probably the Bahuśrutīya, to judge from the study of his long treatise.

Expansion of the Schools Outside of India. Owing to the pious zeal of the emperor Aśoka, from the mid-third century BCE Buddhism began to expand outside of India proper, southeastward into Sri Lanka and northwestward into what is now Afghanistan. Numerous important epigraphic and archaeological monuments show that it soon prospered in both these areas. From this evidence and from the Sinhala chronicles we know that the Theravādins very quickly became, and remained, the dominant group in Sri Lanka, but we do not know exactly which sects flourished at the same time—during the last three centuries BCE—in the mountainous areas of the northwest, then called Gandhāra and Kapiśa. It seems, however, that the Sarvāstivādins, traditionally believed to have originated in nearby Kashmir during the reign of Aśoka, began the conversion of these lands to Buddhism and were joined somewhat later by schools of the Mahāsāṃghika group.

A few very scarce inscriptions, but especially the reports of the famous Chinese pilgrims Hsüan-tsang and I-ching, as well as the numerous discoveries of Buddhist manuscripts in Central Asia, provide information on the presence of various early sects outside India. Sects were found in Southeast Asia, Indonesia, Central Asia, and China in the first few centuries of the common era, especially in the seventh century.

At this same time, the Theravādins had found their way into Indonesia, where the Sarvāstivādins or Mūlasarvāstivādins were a strong majority. These two groups were extremely numerous and nearly alone in all of Central Asia, and they also flourished in southern China, where the Mahīśāsakas, Dharmaguptakas, and Kāśyapīyas prospered as well. These last three sects thrived in Indonesia, and Dharmaguptakas were also found in eastern China as well as in Shensi Province. As for the Sammatīyas, they were in the majority in Champa, in the center of present-day Vietnam. Such is the information provided by I-ching.

The Chinese translations of three different works of early Indian Buddhist sects formed the basis of an equal number of distinctively Chinese schools, which were introduced shortly afterward into Japan. The oldest is known by the name Ch'eng-shih, which is the title of Kumārajīva's Chinese translation (411–412) of Harivarman's *Satyasiddhi*. The main doctrine of this treatise, which attracted and held the attention of its Chinese followers, distinguishes two truths: a mundane or relative truth and a supreme or absolute truth. It teaches that all things are empty of substance, not only the individual person made up of the five aggregates of phenomena, but also the whole of the external world. Thus, the teaching of this work would seem to lie between those of the Hīnayāna and the Mahāyāna or, more precisely, the Mādhyamika. The Ch'eng-shih school was in fact founded by two direct disciples of Kumārajīva, Seng-tao and Seng-sung, who each headed a different branch, one centered in An-hui and the other in Kiangsu. These two masters and some of their disciples composed many commentaries on the *Satyasiddhi* or, more exactly, on its Chinese translation, which helped make it widely known throughout southern China. The leaders of the Chinese Mahāyānist San-lun sect, who were faithful followers of the Mādhyamikas, vigorously combatted this teaching, insisting that its concept of the void was mistaken. Their attacks resulted in the decline of the Ch'eng-shih school in the mid-seventh century and in its disappearance shortly afterward. Still, in 625, a Korean monk introduced the Chinese translation of the *Satyasiddhi* and its teaching to Japan, but the sect, which received the name Jōjitsu (after the Japanese pronunciation of Ch'eng-shih), found less success there than in China and was quickly absorbed by the rival school of Sanron, the Japanese form of San-lun.

The second sect was called Chü-she, a transliteration of the Sanskrit *kośa*, because it was based on the famous *Abhidharmakośa* of Vasubandhu, translated into Chinese by Paramārtha in 563–567 and by Hsüan-tsang in 651–654. The Sarvāstivāda realism expounded in this treatise was not very successful in China, where Mahāyāna doctrines were then dominant; consequently, the Chü-she school died out in the late eighth century, when it was absorbed by the Chinese form of Yogācāra known as Fa-hsiang. Previously, as early as 658, two Japanese monks, Chitsu and Chitatsu, had introduced the sect to Japan, where it bacame known as the Kusha. There it had less success and longevity as an independent school than in China, for Chitsu and Chitatsu themselves were followers of Fa-hsiang, called Hossō in Japan. Hossō had already attained considerable importance, and it soon absorbed the Kusha school.

The third and final Chinese school derived from early Buddhism was quite different from the other two. Called Lü ("discipline"), it was established in the mid-seventh century by the eminent monk Tao-hsüan as a reaction against the doctrinal disputes that preoccupied Chinese Buddhists of the time. He maintained that moral uprightness and strict monastic discipline were much more necessary for the religious life than empty intellectual speculations. Consequently, he imposed on his followers the well-defined rules in the *Ssu-fen-lü*, a Chinese translation of the Vinaya Piṭaka of the Dharmaguptakas made by Buddhayaśas and Chu Fo-nien in 412. Although his school never had many adherents of its own, it had a clear and lasting influence on Chinese Buddhism. Thanks to the school's activities, the *Ssu-fen-lü* became, and remains, the sole collection of disciplinary rules to be followed by all Chinese Buddhist monks regardless of their school, including followers of the Mahāyāna. The school was introduced to Japan in 753 by the Chinese monk Chien-chen (Jpn., Ganjin), who was welcomed with open arms at the court of Nara. [*See the biography of Ganjin.*] Known by the name of Ritsu (not to be confused with a homophonous branch of the Shingon sect), it is still active in Japan today (it also existed in China early in this century) but no longer has many adherents.

However, the only early Buddhist sect to thrive after spreading outside of India is the Theravāda. Its lasting success (it still flourishes today) can be explained by the fact that it was established well before the common era in Sri Lanka, a relatively isolated region, and that it has almost always maintained a strongly preferential relationship with the island's political authorities and has known how best to profit from it. Much less certain was the extension of this phenomenon to a compact group of countries of mainland Southeast Asia from the eleventh century, a time when Buddhism, especially the early, so-called Hīnayāna Buddhism, was dying out throughout India itself. At that time, Hīnayāna Buddhism could claim only a very few followers, scattered among small and failing communities, in the whole vast territory of India. We can understand how the effect of such a happy chance could have seemed miraculous to Buddhist devotees.

This process began in Burma, in the mid-eleventh century, when Anorātha, who ruled the central and northern parts of the country, conquered the southern, maritime region, where Theravāda monks had recently converted the ruler. Anorātha, too, soon adopted the Buddhist faith of the Theravādins. Driven by religious zeal, he compelled all of his subjects to follow his example. From that time on, Theravāda has remained the religion of the majority of the Burmese people.

Two centuries later, when the Thai descended from the mountains to the north and took control of the entire country known today as Thailand, the same process took place. Their king converted to the Theravāda and exercised all his authority to promote its extension to the whole of the population.

In the following century, under circumstances that are still poorly known, neighboring Cambodia, where Mahāyāna Buddhism and Hinduism had flourished until then, became completely Theravadin in a short space of time and has remained so to the present day. The petty kingdoms of Laos, stretched out along the middle Mekong, were not long in following suit.

In contrast to what had happened in India, this distribution of Theravāda Buddhism among a number of different countries, which were (except for Sri Lanka) in close proximity to each other, helped ensure the sect's lasting prosperity. Indeed, when a monastic community in one of these countries found itself in difficulty or in decline, which happened a number of times here and there, the pious Buddhist king would ask for and receive help from another country's ruler, who would then send him a group of knowledgeable, respected monks to resolve the problems in question and restore the Theravāda to its full value and strength. Similarly, whatever reforms and progress were made in one country quickly spread to the Theravāda communities in others. Such was the case in the last century, when the prince-monk Mongkut, who became King Rama IV of Siam, instituted great transformations that allowed the Theravāda to adapt to the modern world at the same time that he carried out a return to its distant canonic sources.

[*For treatment of particular Hīnayāna schools, see* Mahāsāṃghika; Sarvāstivāda; Sautrāntika; *and* Theravāda. *Hīnayāna thought is treated in greater detail in* Four Noble Truths; Eightfold Path; Karman, *article on* Buddhist Concepts; Dharma, *article on* Buddhist Dharma and Dharmas; Pratītya-samutpāda; Nirvāṇa; Soteriology, *article on* Buddhist Soteriology; *and* Buddhist Philosophy. *For further discussion of Hīnayāna sectarianism, see* Councils, *article on* Buddhist Councils, *and* Saṃgha, *overview article. For the geographical distribution of Hīnayāna, see* Missions, *article on* Buddhist Missions; Buddhism, *articles on* Buddhism in India *and* Buddhism in Southeast Asia; Sinhala Religion; *and* Southeast Asian Religions, *overview article. For an overview of Hīnayāna literature, see* Buddhist Literature, *article on* Survey of Texts.]

BIBLIOGRAPHY

Aung, Schwe Zan, and C. A. F. Rhys Davids, trans. *Points of Controversy* (1915). London, 1969. A translation of the Pali *Kathāvatthu*, a text treating the doctrinal controversies between the various Hīnayāna sects from the Theravāda point of view.

Bareau, André. *Les sectes bouddhiques du Petit Véhicule*. Publications de l'École Français d'Extrême-Orient, vol. 38. Saigon, 1955. An exhaustive survey based on all available documents.

Bechert, Heinz, and Richard Gombrich. *The World of Buddhism*. London, 1984. This excellent work includes a discussion of schisms on page 82.

Ch'en, Kenneth. *Buddhism in China; a Historical Survey*. Princeton, 1964. See pages 129–131 and 301–303 for information on the Hīnayāna-derived Chinese sects.

Demiéville, Paul. "L'origine des sectes bouddhiques d'après Paramārtha." In *Mélanges chinois et bouddhiques*, vol. 1, pp. 15–64. Brussels, 1932. A masterfully annotated French translation of one of the principal documents on the subject.

Dube, S. N. *Cross Currents in Early Buddhism*. New Delhi, 1980. Interesting study of doctrinal disputes among early sects, but based primarily on the *Kathāvatthu*.

Dutt, Nalinaksha. *Buddhist Sects in India*. 2d ed. Calcutta, 1978. Good general description of the history and, especially, the doctrines of the Hīnayāna sects.

Fujishima Ryauon. *Les bouddhisme japonais: Doctrines et histoire de douze sectes bouddhiques du Japon* (1889). Reprint, Paris, 1983. This old book is the most complete description in a Western language of Japanese Buddhist sects, particularly the three derived from the Hīnayāna.

Hajime, Nakamura. *Indian Buddhism: A Survey with Bibliographical Notes*. Hirakata, 1980. This large work brings into focus our knowledge of the whole of Indian Buddhism and contains an extremely rich and up-to-date bibliography. A long chapter concerns the Hīnayāna sects (pp. 90–140).

Lamotte, Étienne. *Histoire du bouddhisme indien: Des origines à l'ère Śaka*. Louvain, 1958. A large part (pp. 571–705) of this excellent work discusses early sects, their origins and distribution, Buddhist languages, and the sects' doctrinal evolution.

La Vallée Poussin, Louis de, trans. *L'Abhidharmakośa de Vasubandhu* (1923–1931). 6 vols. Reprint, Brussels, 1971. This French translation of the famous treatise includes copious notes and a very long introduction by the great Belgian scholar. It is rich in information on the doctrinal controversies that concerned the Sarvāstivādins.

Law, Bimala Churn. *A History of Pāli Literature*. London, 1933. Complete, very detailed description of Theravāda literature.

Masuda Jiryō. "Origins and Doctrines of Early Indian Buddhist Schools." *Asia Major* 2 (1925); 1–78. English translation, with notes, of the *Samayabhedoparacanacakra*, an account of the Hīnayāna sects and their main tenets.

Renou, Louis, and Jean Filliozat. *L'Inde classique*. Paris, 1953. Volume 2, pages 315–608, deals especially with the Hīnayāna sects, their literature, and doctrines. The collaboration of the Sinologist Paul Demiéville and the Tibetologist Marcelle Lalou is invaluable.

Shizutani Masao. *Shōjō bukkyōshi no kenkyū; Buha bukkyō no seiritsu to hensen*. Kyoto, 1978. The most recent work on the origin and evolution of the Hīnayāna sects. Detailed and complete study of literary and epigraphic sources.

Takakusu Junjirō, trans. *A Record of the Buddhist Religion as Practiced in India and the Malay Archipelago (A.D. 671–695)* (1896). Reprint, Dehli, 1966. English translation of I-ching's account of his pilgrimage to South and Southeast Asia.

Warder, A. K. *Indian Buddhism*. 2d rev. ed. Dehli, 1980. Treats Hīnayāna sects at length, offering interesting solutions to the problems they pose.

Watters, Thomas, trans. *On Yuan Chwang's Travels in India, 629–645 A.D.* 2 vols. London, 1904–1905. English translation of numerous extracts from the accounts of Hsüan-tsang's journey, with excellent commentary correcting most of the many errors of earlier translations (those of Stanislas Julien, Samuel Beal, etc.), which are today unusable.

ANDRÉ BAREAU

Translated from French by David M. Weeks

Mahāyāna Buddhism

The Sanskrit term *mahāyāna* literally means "the great vehicle [to enlightenment]." It refers to a form of Buddhism that developed in northern India and Central Asia from about the first century before the advent of the common era, and that is prevalent today in Nepal, Sikkhim, Tibet, China, Mongolia, Vietnam, Korea, and Japan. Mahāyāna Buddhism was also transmitted to Sri Lanka and the Indo-Chinese peninsula, but it eventually vanished from South Asia.

The name *Mahāyāna* is rendered *theg pa chen po* in Tibetan, *ta-sheng* in Chinese, and *daijō* in Japanese. The meanings "greater, numerous," and "superior" are all reflected in the *ta* or *dai* of the Chinese and Japanese translations, for, according to Mahāyāna, its teachings are greater than those of the Hīnayāna tradition, and those delivered from suffering by Mahāyāna more numerous than those saved by the other, more conservative wing of the tradition. According to its devotees, the Mahāyāna is therefore superior to Hīnayāna. More objectively, it can be observed that when compared with Theravāda and other Hīnayāna forms, Mahāyāna is more speculatively ambitious, embraces a broader range of practices, some specifically intended to address the needs of lay practitioners, and is more frankly mythological in its conception of Buddhahood and the religious career that leads to it. Mahāyāna Buddhism also stresses altruistic attitudes and proclaims as its goal the universal enlightenment of all beings. Its scriptures were originally written in Sanskrit, but most of these have been lost; many, however, have been preserved in Tibetan and Chinese. (Works for which no attested Sanskrit title is available are identified here by the title of the translation.)

Origins

The origins of Mahāyāna are not yet entirely understood. Its first propounders seem to have been homeless ascetics who did not belong to orthodox *saṃghas* (Buddhist orders). Early Mahāyāna *sūtras* address among their audiences *kulaputras* and *kuladuhitṛs* ("good sons and daughters"), suggesting that lay men and women were also of some importance in the first Mahāyāna orders, which were probably entirely separate from the Hīnayāna orders. These Mahāyāna orders appeared in the second century CE in northwestern India, and the movement later spread to other areas. One such order, the Śiṣyagaṇa ("congregation of disciples"), seems to have devoted itself to altruistic activities.

The Mahāyāna movement probably began with groups of religious individuals whose activities centered around certain stupas. [*See* Stupa Worship.] These groups later became orders whose members, consisting of both clergy and laity, called themselves *bodhisattvas*, by which they designated as the goal of their practice nothing less than Buddhahood itself. They were led by preachers and reciters of scripture (called *dharmabhāṇakas*) and by practitioners of meditation. Thus, in time the early Mahāyāna orders moved away from the worship of stupas and the building of temples—activities stressed in the Hīnayāna *nikāyas* (what I have chosen to refer to here as Conservative Buddhism)—toward recitation of the *sūtras* (the sermons of the Buddha), an approach that had more appeal to (and was more practical for) the ordinary laity. The glorification of Buddhas and the magical character with which Mahāyāna endowed itself were also effective in the competition with the emerging *bhatki* movements of the contemporary Hindu tradition. [*See* Bhatki; Vaiṣṇavism; Kṛṣṇaism; Avatāra; *and* Śaivism.]

Epigraphic evidence and the dates of Chinese translations of Mahāyāna texts have been used by Shizutani Masao to distinguish between "Proto-Mahāyāna," a movement that did not use the appellation *Mahāyāna*, and the more self-conscious "Early Mahāyāna." (The first scripture to use the term *Mahāyāna* is the *Aṣṭasāhasrikā Sūtra*, dating in its earliest verses to perhaps the first century BCE but containing sections from later periods.) Shizutani designates the period 100 to 1 BCE as the incipient stage of Proto-Mahāyāna, 1 to 100 CE as its developed stage, 50 to 100 as the incipient stage of Early Mahāyāna, and 100 to 250 as the developed stage of Early Mahāyāna.

The development of the Mahāyāna *sūtras* began with the incipient Proto-Mahāyāna stage and culminated in about the seventh or eighth century. These *sūtras* as a group are often given the epithet *vaipulya* ("extensive, glorious"). Many are literary masterpieces, artfully created to produce their effects. They contain no information about when and where they were created, but they were probably produced not only in India and the northern part of what is now Pakistan but also in Central Asia, where the Buddhist orders were also sizable. Some *sūtra* manuscripts discovered in Central Asia are very early; those written on birch bark may date to the first century BCE or the following century. Some *sūtras* appeared first in Prakrit or in the languages of Central Asia (e.g., Tocharian and Uighur), but by the sixth century, when the *sūtras* were studied at the university at Nālandā, they had been rewritten in Sanskrit (with some lingering traces of Prakrit colloquialism). It was the adoption of Sanksrit as the official language of the Gupta dynasty in 320 CE that caused the shift from Prakrit. Nearly all the inscriptions on pre-Gupta monuments and tablets are in Prakrit, but almost all similar inscriptions made after the founding of the Gupta dynasty are in Sanskrit. Large numbers of Buddhist Sanskrit manuscripts have been discovered within the last hundred years at Gilgit (in Kashmir) and elsewhere in Central Asia. These, and others in Central Asian languages, are the basic material for modern study; their Chinese translations can be used for cross-reference. Significantly, the Sanskrit *sūtra* copies produced in Central Asia also differ from those discovered in Nepal.

Doctrinally, Mahāyāna Buddhism was not at first completely distinct from Conservative Buddhism. The *bodhisattva* doctrine, to which Mahāyāna owes its existence, can in fact be traced to pre-Mahāyāna Buddhist literature. The concept of the *bodhisattva* apparently emerged between the beginning of the first century BCE and the middle of the first century CE, after the carving of the Bhārhut sculptures and before the appearance of the early Mahāyāna scriptures. In fact, archaeological evidence from this period indicates that the *bodhisattva* idea preceded that of Mahāyāna itself: *bodhisattva* images have been found only in shrines of Conservative Buddhism that date from this time; none have been found at the sites of Mahāyāna structures. The various virtues emphasized in Hīnayāna (e.g., the *pāramitās*) were also appropriated by the Mahāyāna, but in their hands the virtues of benevolence *(maitrī)* and compassion *(karuṇā)* became central. [*See* Karuṇā.] Another, related notion that emerged as a major feature of Mahāyāna is the belief in multiple Buddhas; this too has its antecedents in pre-Mahāyāna belief.

Major Features

Mahāyāna Buddhism is characterized by a variety of doctrines, practices, and orientations that at once distinguish it from the Hīnayāna tradition.

Worship of Multiple Buddhas and Bodhisattvas. In early Buddhism the term *bodhisattva* referred to the Buddha (or, later, to *a* Buddha) prior to the time of his enlightenment, including all previous existences during which he had aspired to become a Buddha. In keeping with the soteriology and cosmology of these early teachings, it was assumed that there was only one *bodhisattva* in any one world cycle. Later, this idea was elaborated and integrated into the Jātaka stories, tales of Śākyamuni Buddha's previous lives. A few Conservative Buddhists embraced the belief that there were many Buddhas at any one time, but this belief was most highly developed in Mahāyāna, where myriads of Buddhas are said to inhabit myriads of world systems simultaneously. [*See* Buddha.]

Some Mahāyāna *sūtras* enjoin adoration of all Buddhas in an equal manner (e.g., *The Sutra Enumerating Buddha's Names*) and some twenty-one *sūtras* extol recitation of the names of many Buddhas. Repeated utterance of the names of Buddhas and *bodhisattvas* is also encouraged in the *Nāmasaṃgīti.* Another *sūtra* (T.D. no. 427) describes invocations of eight specific Buddhas; in the *Ratnacandraparipṛcchā Sūtra* Śākyamuni calls for worship of ten Buddhas who dwell in Pure Lands in each of the ten directions, while the *Bhadrakalpasamādhi Sūtra* (one of twelve similar *sūtras*) extols the thousand Buddhas that are said to live in the present age and calls for the practice of eighty-four thousand "perfections" (*pāramitās*). This text seems to have been composed between 200 and 250 CE.

But it is not simply in their profusion that the Buddhas of the Mahāyāna differ from their Hīnayāna counterparts. Mahāyāna Buddhas enjoy many more superhuman and divine traits than does the single Buddha of the Conservative tradition. Nonetheless, they retain many of the same physical and spiritual characteristics. Glorification of and speculation on the nature of Buddhas led Mahāyāna practitioners to develop the theory of the "triple body" *(trikāya)* of the Buddha, in which the Buddha is conceived as having three aspects or "bodies": a cosmic body *(dharmakāya),* the ineffable Absolute itself; an "enjoyment" body *(saṃbhogakāya),* a body of magical transformation that the Buddha "enjoys" as the fruit of the merit generated through aeons of religious practice (often conceived as surrounded by a supernal region, a Pure Land, similarly generated); and the body that appears in living form to save people from suffering *(nirmāṇakāya).* Śākyamuni, of course, is such a Buddha (i.e., *nirmāṇakāya*) for our age. [*See* Celestial Buddhas and Bodhisattvas.]

In Mahāyāna Buddhism, the common hope for rebirth in a heaven often took the form of yearning for the Pure Lands of various Buddhas, where, it was believed, the Law was preached for the benefit of the beings born there. [*See* Pure and Impure Lands.] Akṣobhya Buddha's Pure Land in the east and that of Amitābha in the west appear in contrast throughout Mahāyāna scripture. The *Karuṇāpuṇḍarīka* (Lotus of Mercy) *Sūtra* describes the Padma wonderland of the Buddha Padmottara, whose life lasted for thirty ages of the world, but the text also responds to those *sūtras* that praise Akṣobhya and Amitābha by praising the compassion that Śākyamuni exercises within this world. An important figure in this *sutra* is Mahākāruṇika Mahāśramaṇa, who saves living beings from suffering. A similar figure is the *bodhisattva* Vāyuviṣṇu, *avatāra* of the deity Viṣṇu.

The *bodhisattva* Mañjuśrī plays an important role in many *sūtras*. One *sūtra* (T.D. no. 463) describes the efficacy of worship of Mañjuśrī at the moment of death. In another (T.D. no. 464), Mañjuśrī explains enlightenment; and elsewhere (T.D. no. 843) he demonstrates *ānimitta* ("formlessness") through magical power. In the *Acintyabuddhaviṣayanirdeśa* he explains *bodhisattva* practices. Mañjuśrī often appears with a counterpart *bodhisattva*, Samantabhadra. The association of Mañjuśrī with Wu-t'ai Shan, a mountain in China, was established by the seventh century and was widely known even in India. The *bodhisattva* Samantabhadra is often mentioned in conjunction with Mañjuśrī. [*See* Mañjuśrī.]

As in Hīnayāna Buddhism, the *bodhisattva* Maitreya was worshiped as a Buddha of the future, one who, at some time to come, will leave his present abode in the Tuṣita Heaven and be born on earth for the benefit of sentient beings. Devotees of Maitreya thus focused their aspirations on rebirth in Tuṣita and eventual descent to earth in his company. Three Maitreya *sūtras* were especially esteemed in China and Korea: the *Mi-le ta-ch'eng-fo ching*, composed in the third century CE; the *Mi-le hsia-sheng ch'eng-fo ching (Maitreyavyākaraṇa* or *Maitreyasamiti)*, also composed in the third century; and the *Kuan-mi-le shang-tou-shuai-t'ien ching*, composed at the end of the fourth century. In the *Maitreyaparipṛcchā* the Buddha Śākyamuni explains *bodhisattva* practices to Maitreya. The *Adhyāśayasaṃcodana Sūtra* tells how sixty *bodhisattvas* who had fallen into distraction and laziness are led into the presence of the Buddha by Maitreya, who seeks advice on their behalf. This *sūtra* is well known for the phrase, "whatever is well spoken is spoken by the Buddha." [*See* Maitreya.]

But the *bodhisattva* most adored throughout Asia is Avalokiteśvara, the "Lord Who Looks Down [with infinite pity on all beings]." His name appears as Avalokitasvara in early manuscripts. Some of his features are those of the Vedic deity Aśvin. Avalokiteśvara is regarded as a savior of suffering beings and his response to petitions for aid is immediate. The best-known scripture concerning his virtues is the twenty-fourth chapter of the *Saddharmapuṇḍarīka* (Lotus Sutra), which emphasizes the rewards in this world that he grants to believers and the virtue of helpfulness to others that he represents. In the *Gaṇḍavyūha*, his homeland is called Potalaka. In Pure Land Buddhism, he is Amitābha's companion and attendant. [*See* Avalokiteśvara.]

Chapters 22 and 23 of the Chinese version of the *Lotus Sutra* shows how another *bodhisattva*, Bhaiṣajyarāja ("king of the art of healing") protects his worshipers and grants wishes. This idea was further developed in the figure of Bhaiṣajyaguru, who also became the object of intense adoration, and independent scriptures consecrated to him extolled his powers. One of these, the *Bhaiṣajyaguru-vaiḍūryaprabhāsa-pūrvapraṇidhāna-viśeṣavistara Sūtra*, is concerned with benefits in this world as well as the future and describes paradises in both east and west. [*See* Bhaiṣajyaguru.]

But if there is one feature of the Mahāyāna *bodhisattva* doctrine that truly separates it from that of other forms of Buddhism, it is the Mahāyāna insistence that the goal of all religious practice is Buddhahood itself, making all those whose conceive of the aspiration to be liberated *bodhisattvas*, or future Buddhas. Mahāyāna practice thus begins with the formulation of this aspiration (*bodhicitta*, the "mind set upon enlightenment") in a vow *(praṇidhāna)* to become a fully enlightened Buddha and is articulated in a series of "stages" (*bhūmis*) leading to the goal. The conspicuous feature of this vow and practice, however, is the resolve of the practitioner to delay final liberation, to remain "in the world," as it were, until all beings have been saved. The Mahāyāna *bodhisattva* is committed to work ceaselessly for the benefit of other beings and to transmit to them the merit generated by his or her own religious practice. While a few *bodhisattvas*, some mentioned above, are frankly mythological in their conception, they represent, ideally, spiritual attainments accessible to all practitioners. In the words of one Mahāyāna scripture, the Buddha nature (i.e., enlightenment) is the endowment of all beings without exception. [*See* Bodhisattva Path.]

Disciplines. There is no unanimously agreed upon code of discipline in Mahāyāna, reflecting the fact that it is institutionally less coherent than is Conservative Buddhism. But Mahāyāna distinguishes two ways of practice: the *śrāvakamārga* ("way of the disciples") for those who follow the Hīnayāna practices and the *bodhisattvamārga* ("way of *bodhisattvas*") for those who adhere to Mahāyāna values, particularly the intention to save other suffering beings. Those who practice the latter way are deemed worthy of worship and are relied upon because they have refrained from entering Buddhahood, preferring instead to dwell among the living in order to save them from their sufferings. The *bodhisattvamārga* was first described in pre-Mahāyāna works collectively called Avadānas. At first, these described *bodhisattvas* who resembled the person and character of the historical Buddha Śākyamuni, but later other qualifications for the *bodhisattva* were appended, namely, vows *(praṇidhāna)* and practice *(bhāvanā)*. All *bodhisattvas* make the same basic vows, but some (e.g.,

Amitābha) add certain others that are unique to them. The privilege of becoming a *bodhisattva* is open to all who seek enlightenment; hence the *bodhisattva* ideal is accessible to every human being.

The basic institutional structure of the Conservative Buddhist order (specifically, the Vinaya, or monastic rules) continued to be observed in Mahāyāna, but Mahāyāna ethics set its orders apart from its Hīnayāna counterparts. [*See* Vinaya.] When the Chinese pilgrim Hsüan-tsang visited India in the first half of the seventh century, he found that some monks were specifically called Mahāyāna-Sthaviras. Some Mahāyāna *sūtras* prescribe ethical practices for both monks and nuns, lay-men and lay women. In particular, practice of the "ten virtues" *(daśakuśala-śīlāni)* was encouraged. Compared to the ethics of Conservative Buddhism, Mahāyāna ethics were more flexible, and were altered in various environments. The ideal virtues were codified as six "perfections" (*pāramitā*s) incorporated within the *bodhisattva* ideal: liberality *(dāna)*, morality *(śīla)*, effort *(vīrya)*, forbearance *(kṣānti)*, meditation *(dhyāna)*, and transcendental insight *(prajñā)*. A seventh perfection, "expedient means" *(upāya)*, was added in some texts, and others expanded the concept to ten perfections. In general, *dāna*, or selfless giving (the rendering of help to others) was stressed. The *Āryasaṃgītigāthāśataka* is a collection of one hundred verses in praise of this perfection. The Buddha's great compassion was interpreted as his gift to sentient beings. The transference of merit to others *(pariṇāmanā)* was also encouraged as a form of giving. [*See* Pāramitās *and* Merit, *article on* Buddhist Concepts.]

Mahāyāna ethics were most explicitly set forth in the "Discipline Sūtras," the essence of which is altruism. Among the *sūtra*s that provided the theoretical basis for the Mahāyāna orders is the *Sarvadharmapravṛttinirdeśa*, which was highly esteemed by the Japanese monk Saichō (767–822). Others that explicated Mahāyāna discipline are the "Buddha Treasure Sutra" (T.D. no. 653), the "Enlightenment mind Sutra" (T.D. no. 837), and the *Dharmavinayasamādhi Sūtra*. Some texts reflect the Mahāyāna idea that discipline is to be practiced by both clergy and laity; one, the *Bodhisattvaprātimokṣa Sūtra*, sets forth the "Vinaya" of *bodhisattva*s, here referring to both clerics and lay practitioners. The precepts in the *Śrīmālādevī Sūtra* were well known in China and Japan.

The most famous and controversial of these texts is the *Brahmajāla Sūtra*. Greatly esteemed in China, it became the fundamental discipline text for Japanese monks. Scholars now believe that this text was produced in China, where there is evidence that it was in use in some form as early as the year 350. Another text bearing on the conduct of the *bodhisattva*, the *Bodhisattvabhūmi*, calls upon all aspirants to the Way of *Bodhisattvas*—both monks and laymen—to observe three kinds of *bodhisattva* practice: adherence to all the precepts *(saṃvaraśīla; prātimokṣa)*, practice of all virtuous deeds *(kuśaladharma-saṃgrāhakaṃ śīlam)*, and the granting of mercy to all sentient beings *(sattvārtha-kriyāśīlam)*. The first element in this code represents a retention of the traditional Vinayas of Conservative Buddhism, while the second and third are expressions of Mahāyāna ideals.

The *Śikṣāsamuccaya*, Śāntideva's eighth-century compendium of Mahāyāna literature, explains that the principle of compassion can even sanction physical love; according to Śāntideva, carnal desire is not nearly so sinful as anger. Eventually, married monks appeared among the Mahāyāna orders. In the fifth century, King Meghavāhana's consort built a monastery in Kashmir, half of which was occupied by *bhikṣus* (mendicants) whose conduct conformed to the precepts, and half of which was reserved for those who had wives, children, cattle, and property. Some later *sūtras* (e.g., the *Mahāsaṃnipāta Sūtra*), however, refer to the marriage of monks as evidence of decadence in the orders. Today, Nepalese monks are free to marry, and marriage is to some extent common among Tibetan and Buriat Mongolian monks as well. The Jōdo Shin sect was the first in Japan to sanction the marriage of monks; since the introduction of Western civilization, marriage of Japanese monks has become more common.

Repentance is the theme and object of several Mahāyāna *sūtras*. One of these *sūtras* (T.D. no. 1493) shows that repentance leads to delight in the deeds of others, moral admonition, and transference of merit. Another text teaches that a reaffirmation of the insight that all things are originally pure can dissolve the obstacles created by *karman* (T.D. no. 1491). Bondage in *karman (karmāvaraṇa)* can be destroyed by repentance, meditation, or by repeated application of magical formulas.

While some *sūtra*s describe and promote various meritorious deeds (T.D. no. 683, for example), others focus on specific practices such as circumambulation of stupas (T.D. no. 700) and the offering of votive lights at stupas and *caityas* (T.D. no. 702). Worship of both stupas and Buddhas was combined in others (T.D. no. 688). The merit attributed to the manufacture of images of Buddhas and *bodhisattvas* (T.D. nos. 692–694) suggests the fervor of image-making activity in Gandhāra and Mathurā. Another *sūtra* gives details of the rite of anointing Buddha images (T.D. no. 697). The use of rosaries, a practice adopted from the brahman priests, is extolled in yet another *sūtra* (T.D. no. 788). Originally, brahmans, not Buddhist monks, were officiants at South Asian funerals, but eventually Mahāyāna monks took their place. One *sūtra* encourages the observance of funeral rites as an affirmation of impermanence (T.D. no. 801). Later, officiating at funerals was to become a major duty of Japanese monks.

Lay Buddhism. The position of the layman was recognized and exalted by most Mahāyāna texts, although a few display a tendency to place the ascetic life of the monk above the lay life. However, the notion of emptiness *(śūnyatā)* that is the foundation of most Mahāyāna thought provides for the identity of liberation and mundane existence, *nirvāṇa* and *saṃsāra,* thus providing a rationale for the sanctity of lay life. This led many to the conclusion that the essence of religion should be sought in the life of householders rather than in the life of renunciants; hence, lay Buddhism came to be advocated in the Mahāyāna as a religious ideal. The grace of *bodhisattva*s was believed to extend to laymen; Mañjuśrī, for example, is said to save ordinary laymen and even nonbelievers.

To be sure, many Mahāyāna practitioners were *bhikṣu*s, and some were termed *bodhisattva bhikṣu*s (in the *Mahāyānasūtrālaṃkāra,* the *Śikṣāsamuccaya,* etc.). But the tendency toward lay Buddhism remained conspicuous. The *Ugradattaparipṛcchā,* an early Discipline Sūtra composed before Nāgārjuna (fl. 150–250), prescribes five conditions for the lay practice of the Mahāyāna. Later, codes of discipline intended specifically for laymen were composed. Among the disciplines required of laymen was observance of the regulations for *upoṣadha* days (when the fortnightly confessions were made).

The *Vimalakīrtinirdeśa Sūtra,* in which the pious layman Vimalakīrti gives a sermon to monks and denounces the homeless ascetic life they lead, is perhaps the best expression of the lay Buddhist ideal. This *sūtra* was composed no later than 150 or 200, and was studied and lectured upon frequently in China and Japan. Other *sūtra*s represent extensions of its teaching, and in some the central figures are laywomen. In the *Candrottarādārikā-vyākaraṇa Sūtra,* the central figure, Vimalakīrti's daughter, expresses views that meet with the Buddha's approval. The central figure of another *sūtra* (T.D. no. 818) is a prostitute who teaches Buddhist doctrine to her lover during a rendezvous in a forest. The *Śrīmālādevīsiṃhanāda Sūtra* (which became quite important in China and Japan) is delivered by a queen, with the Buddha's sanction. An eight-year-old girl, Sumati, delivers a sermon in the *Sumatidārikā-paripṛcchā.* These *sūtra*s defy the stereotypical view (otherwise common to most Mahāyāna texts) that women are mentally and physiologically inferior to men—assumptions that reflected the inequality of the sexes in Indian society.

The presence of the notion of filial piety, another lay ideal, in Buddhism represents an accommodation and syncretization of values that occurred under the stimulus of Chinese culture. Filial piety was the most important virtue in Confucian ethics, which required one-sided obedience from children toward their parents. [*See* Hsiao.] This idea was never more than a minor one in Indian Buddhism. There is no single term in the original Sanskrit and Prakrit texts that corresponds to the Chinese *hsiao* (filial piety), but the character is found frequently in Chinese versions of scripture. To reconcile the two traditions, Chinese Buddhists created such spurious *sūtras* as the *Fu-mu-en-chung ching* and the *Tai-pao-fu-mu-chung ching,* which teach filial piety in the guise of Buddhist morality. A Buddhist concept of filial piety also took shape in the *Ullambana Sūtra,* which extols a rite that centers on offerings to one's dead parents. The *sūtra* appears to have originated in part in India and was later expanded upon in China. The Ullambana rite itself became a very important one in China, Vietnam, Korea, and Japan (where it is called Obon). [*See* Worship and Cultic Life, *article on* Buddhist Cultic Life in East Asia.]

Major Scriptures

Unlike the various recensions of the Hīnayāna canon, which were virtually closed by the early centuries of the common era and which shared, at least ideally, a common structure (Vinaya, Sūtra, Abhidharma; i.e., the Tripiṭaka), the Mahāyāna scriptures were composed in a variety of disparate social and religious environments over the course of several centuries, diverge widely from each other in content and outlook, and were in many cases meant to stand as individual works representing (it has been conjectured) rivals to the entire Hīnayāna corpus. Thus, when treating this literature it is perhaps most fruitful to consider the various textual *classes* that constitute Mahāyāna Sūtra literature.

The Wisdom Sūtras. The earliest Mahāyāna *sūtra*s are those that deal with *prajñāpāramitā* ("perfection of wisdom"); they constitute the philosophical basis of much of later Buddhist thought as well. The earliest Prajñāpāramitā text is almost surely a version in eight-thousand *śloka*s, the *Aṣṭasāhasrikā-prajñāpāramitā Sūtra,* dating in the earliest of its verse portions to perhaps 100 BCE and probably completed in the first century CE. The Pūrvaśailas, a Hīnayāna sect, are said to have possessed the Prajñāpāramitā Sūtras in a Prakrit edition, but most Japanese scholars claim that these *sūtras* first came into existence in South India, perhaps in Andhra, among the Mahāsāṃghikas. Others maintain that the Prajñāpāramitā Sūtras were initially composed in Northwest India. The origins of the *Vajracchedikā-prajñāpāramitā Sūtra* (The Diamond Cutter Sutra) and the *Prajñāpāramitāhṛdaya Sūtra* (The Heart Sutra) should be placed between 150 and 200 CE. The *Diamond Cutter* is actually the ninth section of an extremely long text, the *Mahāprajñāpāramitā Sūtra;* the *Heart Sutra* is an even more condensed version. The *Mahāprajñāpāramitā Sūtra* is very early and was very enthusiastically transmitted, recited, explained, and commented upon in Central Asia, Tibet, China, Korea, and Japan, where interest in it is far greater than in India, the land of its origination. Other Prajñāpāramitā Sūtras, for instance, the *Pañcaviṃśatisāhasrikā, Daśasāhasrikā, Saptaśatikā, Śatasāhasrikā,* and *Adhyardhaśatikā,* followed the *Aṣṭasāhasrikā.* These generally represent either inflations or conflations of the basic text.

Most of the technical terms used in the Wisdom Sūtras were inherited from Conservative Buddhism, but the ideas presented here are very new indeed. The central theme of these texts is that the "perfection of wisdom"—recognition of the truth of human existence—can be attained only through the realization that nothing exists in and of itself, that all things are like dreams or are the creations of magical power *(māyā).* [*See* Māyā.] The ultimate truth of existence is comprehended by the term "emptiness" *(śūnyatā),* one of the subtlest and most sophisticated concepts in the philosophical armory of Mahāyāna Buddhism. Understanding of *śūnyatā* entails the awareness that all things rely for their existence on causal factors and as such are devoid of any permanent "own-being" *(svabhāva).* The purely relative existence of all *dharma*s taught by this doctrine entails the realization that the things of this world, the self *(ātman)* included, are merely the reifications of conceptual and linguistic distinctions formed under the productive influence of fundamental ignorance *(avidyā).* Insofar as the things of this world derive their reality solely from a nexus of causal conditions *(pratītya-samutpāda),* their nature, what they all share, is precisely a "lack" of self-nature. [*See* Śūnyam and Śūnyatā; Dharma, *article on* Buddhist Dharma and Dharmas; Avidyā; *and* Pratītya-samutpāda.]

In practical terms, the perfection of wisdom involves the cultivation of a nondual insight into this fundamental (non)nature, characterized in the Mahāyāna as *dharmatā* ("dharmaness") or *tathatā* ("suchness"), that is, things just as they are without the duality imposed by conceptual categories. Other synonyms for emptiness are *dharmadhātu, dharmakāya,* and *buddhadhātu.* The Wisdom Sūtras reinterpreted the traditional concepts of *nirvāṇa* and transmigration in this light: the goal of salvation is no longer *nirvāṇa* but an understanding of the reality of transmigration as emptiness. Ultimately, emptiness itself is eneffable, but the idea of emptiness can be taught in accordance with the mental ability of those who would learn about it. Thus, "expedient means" *(upāya)* are established in the Wisdom Sūtras as the link between emptiness and compassion. In order to be effective guides to the liberation of beings, the *sūtra*s teach, the Buddhas must make concessions to the understanding of their audience. While it may be that the self and all *dharma*s lack real existence, to baldly assert such without any preliminary preparation would engender lack of confidence in the Dharma and a nihilism that is far from what is meant by *śūnyatā.* Thus the Buddhas have recourse to a variety of "expedient" teachings by which they prepare the practitioner for the revelation of final truth. In literary terms, such devices are often couched as metaphors and parables (this is especially true of texts such as the *Lotus,* a *sūtra* from another Mahāyāna tradition) that offer the devotee a more simple (if imperfect) grasp of the teachings of the Buddhas. [*See* Prajñā; Tathatā; Upāya; *and* Nirvāṇa.]

All of the Wisdom Sūtras encourage an attitude of nonattachment. Devotees of Wisdom Sūtras held that the theory of emptiness is not nihilism but rather a basis for practice, and the wisdom literature does offer practical assistance: those who desire to diminish their personal cares may use these *sūtra*s as a guide to the practice of the disciplined contemplation of spiritual truths and the cultivation of the Six Perfections. Nor do the scriptures overlook the necessity for the gradual development of the mind of the aspirant to enlightenment: the texts proclaim a series of ten stages *(bhūmi)* through which the practitioner may approach enlightenment. Another important contribution of the Wisdom Sūtras is the concept of the "original purity of mind" *(cittasya prakṛtiprabhāsvaratā),* a concept fundamental to Mahāyāna soteriology.

Meditation Sūtras. The Meditation Sūtras of Mahāyāna may have originated among the Yogācāras, a Buddhist tradition that emphasized the practice of meditation. Of course, esteem for meditation characterized the Buddhist tradition from its inception and both early Buddhism and the Hīnayāna *nikāya*s had their own characteristic meditative disciplines. [*See* Meditation, *article on* Buddhist Meditation.] In Mahāyāna, meditation on various Buddhas and their "Pure Lands" became a means for calming the mind, eliminating mental defilements, and attaining awareness of emptiness. Meditation was also held to confer miraculous powers on the practitioner.

The *Yogācārabhūmi Sūtra* (for which the Sanskrit has been lost) sets forth a systematic scheme of the stages of meditation. It is, in essence, an anthology of passages relevant to meditation by Saṃgharakṣa. The *Dharmataradhyāna Sūtra* gives a systematic explanation of meditations as understood by Dharmatara and Buddhasena. It was important in the development of Ch'an (Zen)

Buddhism and the meditation on *maṇḍalas* of Vajrayāna Buddhism. The *Pratyutpanna-buddha-saṃmukhāvasthitasamādhi Sūtra* teaches a *samādhi* that makes all the Buddhas in the ten directions visible to and present with the practitioner. Other *sūtras* (e.g., the *Kuan-fo san-mei-hai ching*) teach a meditation on just one Buddha, Amitābha. The *Samādhirāja* or *Samādhirājacandrapradīpa Sūtra* explains how a *bodhisattva* can attain the highest knowledge by means of a series of meditations that culminate in the "king of meditations" *(samādhirāja).*

Transmigration Sūtras. Another group of *sūtras* describes aspects of the transmigration of living beings. Some depict sufferings in five spheres *(gati)* of transmigratory existence: the spheres of gods, men, beasts, ghosts *(preta)*, and denizens of the Buddhist hells. In the *Ṣaḍgatikārikā*, a sixth sphere, that of the *asuras* (warlike demons), is also depicted. Other *sūtras* analyze the patterns of karmic retribution that lead to rebirth in one sphere or another. In one, Maudgalyāyana responds to a *preta*'s questions about these causal patterns. The *Saddharmasmṛtyupasthāna Sūtra* and the *Dharmaśarīla Sūtra* place this analysis in the larger context of Buddhist cosmology, then turn to meditations upon the human body. The *Chan-cha-shan-e-pao ching*, which enumerates the forms of retribution for specific good and bad deeds, was probably composed in China.

Some of these *sūtras* treat in detail the theory of *pratītya-samutpāda*, or "dependent origination," the classic Buddhist explanation for the conditions that account for the genesis of sentient beings and their involvement in the cycles of samsaric existence. Some devote particular attention to the concept of ignorance *(avidyā)* as the first of the series of causal links *(aṅga)* that make up sentient existence. In the *Śālistamba Sūtra*, the theory of dependent origination in twelve links is metaphorically likened to the growth of a rice plant.

The Lotus Sūtra and Related Works. Probably the single most influential Mahāyāna *sūtra* is the *Saddharmapuṇḍarīka Sūtra* (The Lotus of the Superb Religion). Its central part was probably composed by the end of the first century CE, and the whole *sūtra* was most likely completed around the end of the second century in Gandhāra or perhaps in the area of Kapiśa. The *sūtra* as a whole is a narrative drama in which scenes change often and suddenly; Buddhas, *bodhisattvas*, and mortals interact in lively discourse. Some scholars believe that the character of the *sūtra* was influenced by Indian theatrical forms that may have been themselves influenced by the conventions of Greek drama.

The *Lotus* refers to all living beings as "children of Buddha," and its teachings are esteemed for their insistence that all those who have faith in the Buddha and his Dharma will become Buddhas. In the first half of the *sūtra* the traditional division of soteriological paths into those of the *śrāvaka* (the Hīnayāna devotee), the *pratyekabuddha* (those who are enlightened without having heard the Dharma preached), and the *bodhisattva* (the Mahāyāna practitioner) is declared a mere "expedient device" *(upāya)* conceived by the Buddha to lure to the Dharma beings of differing levels of spiritual attainment. In reality, the *sūtra* declares, the "three vehicles" are but one vehicle *(ekayāna):* the Buddha vehicle itself. Under this dispensation, the spiritual destiny of all beings is nothing less than Buddhahood.

The second half of the *sūtra* reveals that the Buddha's existence among beings in this world—his birth, renunciation, enlightenment, and death—are mere elements in a cosmic drama of salvation. In reality, the Buddha is eternal, and his apparent enlightenment at Bodh Gayā a mere device to provoke faith in his teachings. The Buddha has always (or so the text implies) been enlightened. These teachings, and the dramatic and moving way in which the text presents them, have made the *sūtra* enormously influential, especially in East Asia. In particular, the T'ien-t'ai tradition and its derivatives have looked to this text as the revelation of the Buddha's true message and the very justification for his appearance on earth. [*See* T'ien-t'ai *and* Tendaishū.]

Several *sūtras* present ideas related to those expounded in the *Lotus*. The "Sutra on the Immeasurable Meanings" (T.D. no. 276) presents the concept of emptiness as the theoretical basis of "one vehicle" thought and teaches the way to attain sudden enlightenment. Some scholars think that this *sūtra* was composed in China; the *Samantabhadra-bodhisattva-dhyānacaryādharma Sūtra* claims that it was taught by the Buddha at the end of his life. The *Mahāsatya-nirgranthaputravyākaraṇa Sūtra* and its prototype (T.D. no. 173) are scriptures that expand upon the conciliatory character of the *Lotus*. Here, the spirit of tolerance is personified in the figure of a Jain ascetic who preaches Buddhist teachings. The *Suvarṇaprabhāsa Sūtra* also has traits that are comparable to the *Lotus*. It elucidates the infinity of the life of the Buddha, addresses political ideas, and reflects Esoteric trends; it also describes worship of the (originally Hindu) goddess Sarasvatī. [*See* Sarasvatī.] Its magical qualities and the ritual for repentance appended to this text made it very popular in China and Japan.

The Buddhāvataṃsaka Sūtra. The *Buddhāvataṃsaka Sūtra* has been influential in many Buddhist cultures. The work is a composite of various smaller, independent texts and textual cycles that by about 350 CE had been redacted into a single work comprising in its first complete Chinese recension some sixty fascicles. References to China and Kashgar in the *Buddhāvataṃsaka Sūtra* suggest that its compilation took place somewhere in Central Asia. Some scholars believe that portions of the *sūtra* were extant prior to the second century CE. Its major components, the Sanskrit texts entitled the *Gaṇḍavyūha Sūtra* and the *Daśabhūmika Sūtra,* were both known to Nāgārjuna. The *Daśabhūmika Sūtra* was compiled between 50 and 150 CE, and linguistic evidence indicates that the *Gaṇḍavyūha* probably belongs to the same period; it may have been composed early in the Kuṣāṇa dynasty. Scenes and characters from it are represented in the eighth- and ninth-century reliefs at Borobudur. The influence of the text was felt most strongly in China, Korea, and Japan, where, in the Hua-yen, Hwaŏm, and Kegon traditions, respectively, its teachings were made the basis of perhaps the most subtle and doctrinally sophisticated systems of the tradition. The great Buddha image at the Tōdaiji in Nara, the Daibutsu, is a representation of the Buddha Vairocana, the cosmic figure who is the central focus of the text. [*See* Mahāvairocana *and* Hua-yen.]

Unlike most *sūtras*, in which it is Śākyamuni who preaches, this sermon is delivered by *bodhisattvas* and other divine beings as well as by mortals, who preach in eight assemblies in a variety of locales, including the Buddhist heavens. Their teachings are given religious sanction and authority insofar as the beings who preach them live in the period immediately following the Buddha's enlightenment. This text undertakes to sets forth the content of the Buddha's enlightenment exactly as it was, without concession to the spiritual capacities of its audience. This ultimate state of the Enlightened One is here characterized as the "ocean seal meditation" *(sāgaramudrā samādhiḥ),* symbolizing in its images of depth and boundlessness the ineffable and profound character of enlightenment itself.

In the *Daśabhūmika* portion of the text the doctrine of the ten *bodhisattva bhūmis* is systematically outlined, while the *Gaṇḍavyūha* relates the spiritual quest of the youth Sudhana, who seeks instruction from some fifty-two teachers in his search for enlightenment. His quest, a metaphor for our own, is itself a depiction of the *bodhisattva* career. The *sūtra* also stresses the interconnection between each individual being and the whole universe; it asserts that the altruistic spirit of benevolence or compassion is the fundamental principle of Mahāyāna. The Buddha's own great compassion toward living beings *(tathāgatagotra-saṃbhava)* is seen as the force that causes all manner of Buddha activities to arise from his cosmic body. The *Avataṃsaka* also holds that the essence of the Tathāgata exists "in embryo form" in all living beings, even though they are unaware of it.

Pure Land Texts. Pure Land Buddhism probably appeared first among early lay orders. It focuses on a Buddha who is known by two names: Amitāyus ("limitless life") and Amitābha ("limitless light"). The latter name appeared earlier, and later was associated with the Jātaka-like story of the monk Dharmākara, who is said to have made a series of vows (forty-eight in one recension of the text that recounts the story) to save living beings from suffering. The vows express Dharmākara's intention to establish a "Pure Land" where sentient beings, free from all manner of affliction, could hear the Dharma preached by a Buddha and hence win enlightenment. The text of each vow includes Dharmākara's resolution to refuse final enlightenment until the terms of the vow shall have been fulfilled. The *sūtra* goes on to relate that Dharmākara is now, aeons later, the Buddha Amitābha, and that he resides in a splendid land in the western quarter of our universe known as Sukhāvatī ("land of ease"). Beings who have faith in this Buddha, the *sūtra* relates, and who focus their mind upon him for up to ten successive moments can be reborn in this Pure Land, and can attain enlightenment easily from there. [*See* Amitābha.]

Because in the fully elaborated Buddhology of Mahāyāna Buddhism other Buddhas, residing in their own Pure Lands, were also acknowledged, it is not surprising that these figures should also become the focus of cultic activity. (Akṣobhya is conspicuous in this respect.) But the special quality of compassionate concern for suffering beings that pervades the Amitābha mythic cycle made this Buddha a figure of great popular appeal, especially in East Asia, where the various Pure Land traditions, Ching-t'u, Jōdoshū, Jōdo Shinshū, and others enjoy wide followings. [*See* Ching-t'u; Jōdoshū; *and* Jōdo Shinshū.]

Amitābha Buddha figures in many *sūtras*, but the teaching of the Pure Land as the Buddha land of Amitābha is based chiefly on three scriptures: the "smaller" *Sukhāvatīvyūha Sūtra,* the "larger" *Sukhāvatīvyūha Sūtra,* and the *Kuan wu-liang-shou-fo ching (Amitāyurbuddhadhyāna Sūtra).* The *Larger Sukhāvatīvyūha Sūtra* was compiled before 200 CE, during the Kuṣāṇa dynasty, by an order of the Mahīśāsaka *bhikṣus* of Gandhara. The *Amitāyurbuddhadhyāna Sūtra* is more advanced than the *Sukhāvatīvyūha Sūtra* in that it deals less with elaborate descriptions of the blessed land than with the practice of meditations *(dhyāna)* on Amitāyus and the Pure Land by means of which the meditator may reach it. Cultivation of the *bodhi* (enlightenment) mind, hearing the name of Amitābha, directing one's thoughts toward him, and planting roots of goodness are all described by this text as causes for birth in the Pure Land.

But meditation on Amitābha *(buddhānusmṛti)* is the essential practice espoused by all the Pure Land scriptures of India. These emphasize the attainment of a pure and tranquil state of mind *(prasāda)*. The original concept of faith in the Pure Land *sūtras* was not *bhakti,* devotional faith in the Buddha who preached them, but *śraddhā,* or faith in their teachings, a much different conception than that advocated by later Chinese and Japanese Pure Land Buddhists. The magical character of Amitābha worship was especially appreciated in China, where the inescapable resonances between worship of a divinity of "limitless life" and Taoist conceptions of immortality went far toward guaranteeing the popularity of Pure Land practices. In a reflection of this trend, the Chinese monk Shan-tao reinterpreted *buddhānusmṛti* (Chin., *nien-fo;* Jpn., *nembutsu*) as the oral recitation of the *name* of Amitābha. This remained the normative interpretation of *nien-fo* among subsequent Pure Land thinkers, especially in Japan. [*See* Nien-fo.] Later, in a more intellectual and sophisticated view of Amitābha as "principle" (Chin., *li*) rather than person, his essential body was interpreted as *dharma,* the universal law.

The Ratnakūṭa Sūtra. The *Mahāratnakūṭa-dharmaparyāya-śatasāhasrikā-grantha* took its present form sometime after the fifth century. Its core, now its forty-third part, is the *Kāśyapaparivarta*. The whole text consists of a long series of "questions" (*paripṛcchās*), the contents of many of which have not yet been fully analyzed.

The Mahāparinirvāṇa Sūtra. The Sanskrit original of the Mahāyāna version of the *Mahāparinirvāṇa Sūtra* (Sutra of the Great Decease [of the Buddha]) must have been compiled between 200 and 400 CE. (A text of Hīnayāna province of the same name is much earlier; both purport to record the final sermon of the Buddha.) One passage quotes Śākyamuni's prediction that "seven hundred years after my *nirvāṇa* Māra will gradually destroy the *saddharma*" ("true Dharma"). This and other passages seem to reflect the the deterioration and persecution of the order that was taking place at the time of the *sūtra*'s composition. [*See* Mappō.]

As the text claims to be the last sermon preached by Śākyamuni before his death, it allegedly reveals secret teachings that had not been preached before (i.e., that had not appeared in other *sūtras*). Basic Buddhist doctrine denies the existence of a permanent underlying element, an *ātman,* or "soul," in sentient beings; here, however, the Buddha teaches a theory of a "great *ātman*" and a view of *nirvāṇa* as "permanent, joyous, personal, and pure," assertions that were characteristically denied in other Buddhist texts. The *sūtra* emphatically maintains that the cosmic body of the Buddha is permanent and eternal, and that every human being is endowed with Buddhahood. The Buddhist order represented in the first part of the *sūtra* consists of homeless monks and nuns, like those of Conservative Buddhism, but in the latter half of the text the Buddhist order clearly is taken to include laymen, and faith is emphasized as the force that binds the order together. Harsh punishment, even execution, is prescribed for those who slander Mahāyāna teachings—an attitude that is rarely expressed in Buddhist literature.

Yogācāra Sūtras. The *sūtras* instrumental to the development of the Yogācāra tradition, that branch of Mahāyāna that sees consciousness as constituitive of all phenomena, include especially the *Mahāyāna-abhidharma Sūtra* (now lost but quoted in other works), the *Saṃdhinirmocana Sūtra,* and the *Laṅkāvatāra Sūtra.* The *Avataṃsaka,* another text with a pronounced idealistic orientation, is often mentioned as having influenced the tradition. The *Saṃdhinirmocana Sūtra* brings together for the first time the variety of terms and doctrines commonly associated with Yogācāra thought: "storehouse consciousness" *(ālaya-vijñāna),* the "three natures" and "triple unreality" of phenomena, and a detailed accounting of meditative practices *(śamatha* and *vipaśyanā)* enabling the practitioner to gain insight into the fundamental role of consciousness in constructing phenomenal existence. The *Laṅkāvatāra Sūtra,* a less than completely systematic work, also emphasizes that phenomena are the products of mind, lacking all independent reality *(svacitta-dṛśya bāhyabhāvābhāva);* it also asserts the identity of the *ālaya-vijñāna* with the *tathāgata-garbha* ("matrix [womb] of the Tathāgatas"), a concept expressive of the fundamental enlightenment present in all beings.

The Mahāsaṃnipāta and Other Sūtras. The various chapters of the *Mahāvaipulya-mahāsaṃnipāta Sūtra* seem to have been composed at different times. Some claim that the completed text dates from between 200 and 300 CE, but it probably did not achieve its present form until much later. This *sūtra* expresses the pessimistic belief that the Buddha's "True Religion" would last for a mere thousand years, after which the order would suffer gradual decay until its complete disappearance from the world. This notion may reflect the social tumult contemporary with the composition of the text caused by the invasion of India by the Ephthalites in the sixth century.

The *Lien-hsu-mien-ching* was probably produced in Kashmir in the first half of the sixth century. Its content appears to be influenced by the invasion of India by the Ephthalites and the destructive conquests of Mihirakula, which occurred between 502 and 542; the work was translated into Chinese in 584, so it must have been written between 542 and 584.

Worship of the *bodhisattva* Kṣitigarbha (Chin., Ti-tsang; Jpn., Jizō) may have originated in the belief in the Vedic earth goddess, Pṛthivī. Some scholars believe that when Iranian peoples immigrated to the southern region of the Tarim Basin in the fourth century, they introduced the idea of angels from Zoroastrianism; this may have led to worship of Kṣitigarbha as an independent *bodhisattva.* Ti-tsang was also worshiped in Chinese Manichaeism. In the many *sūtras* extolling him—the *Daśacakra-Kṣitigarbha Sūtra* and the *Kṣitigarbha-praṇidhāna Sūtra* are our principal scriptural sources—he is always represented as a monk. Passages of *sūtras* extolling him are also cited in Mahāyāna treatises. [*See* Kṣitigarbha.]

The *Ākāśagarbha Sūtra* describes the virtues of the *bodhisattva* Ākāśagarbha and the benefits he bestows on those who believe in him. The *sūtra* seems to have been written by Iranian Buddhists in Kashgar, and shows the influence of conceptions of Amitābha.

The Philosophical Schools

To what extent the rise of Mahāyāna *sūtra* literature represents the growth of philosophical "schools" is not at all clear. Like much of Indian social history, the institutional history of the *saṃgha* presents a puzzle that perhaps will never be entirely understood. Certainly, we can infer from the contents of specific works a group of practices or doctrines that characterized a given religious community; but beyond this bare inference, the origins of the texts and the life of the communities that produced them remains obscure. We know of course that the Mahāyāna first conceived of itself as an alternate soteriological path centered around the figure and career of the *bodhisattva.* At a certain point in the history of the movement nameable figures appear to whom doctrinal treatises (*śāstras*)—often commentaries on scripture—can be attributed. These figures produced works on a variety of subjects: meditation, logic, epistemology, liturgy, and so forth. Around such works clusters of commentaries, subcommentaries, rebuttals, and refinements developed, enabling us to speak in textual terms at least of various philosophical and practical traditions. But little information is available to us concerning the institutional profile of such traditions.

One of the earliest, and certainly the greatest, of the Mahāyāna *ācāryas* was Nāgārjuna (fl. 150–250), the *de facto* founder of the first doctrinal "school" of Mahāyāna, the Mādhyamika (Madhyamaka). Nāgārjuna was the first Mahāyāna thinker whose works survive to address the topics raised by the Mahāyāna *sūtras*, particularly the Prajñāpāramitā *corpus*, in a philosophically self-conscious and critical way.

Early Mādhyamika and Nāgārjuna. The origins of the Mādhyamika school are obscure. Some scholars assert that it was influenced by the Mahāsāṃghika school. [*See* Mahāsāṃghika.] Its central philosophy of emptiness *(śūnyatā)* was propounded by Nāgārjuna, whose influence in the Buddhist tradition is so great that he is regarded as a patriarchal figure of eight Mahāyāna schools by the Japanese. A great number of works are attributed to him, including the *Mūlamadhyamakakārikā*, the *Dvādaśadvāra Śāstra* (extant only in Chinese), the *Vigrahavyāvartanī* (a refutation of Nyāya thought), the *Vaidalyasūtra* and its autocommentary, the *Vaidalyaprakaraṇa* (both refutations of Nyāya thought), the *Yuktiṣaṣṭikā*, the *Śūnyatāsaptati* (extant only in Tibetan), the *Ratnāvalī* and the *Suhṛllekha* (both discourses on statecraft), the *Pratītyasamutpādahṛdaya*, the *Daśabhūmikavibhāṣā Śāstra*, and the *Mahāprajñāpāramitopadeśa* (extant only in Chinese). The authenticity of some of these works, however, is highly questionable.

Nāgārjuna strove not to establish a fixed dogma but to prove the fallacies of other doctrines; he sought to refute all dogmatic views *(dṛṣṭi)* by showing how their initial propositions lead to unwarranted conclusions. This method of refutation is called *prasaṅga (reductio ad absurdum)*, and Nāgārjuna's works were dominated by it. With it he eschews discussion of metaphysical problems, reduces the verbiage of speculative philosophy, and dismisses meaningless propositions. No substance can abide forever, he holds; all things are dependent upon causal conditions; nothing has independent existence.

The notion of *śūnyatā*, the core of Mādhyamika thought, is explained in many ways in Nāgārjuna's writings. In the *Madhyamakakārikā*, for example, it is identified with dependent origination *(pratītya-samutpāda):* since things arise dependently, he argues, they are without essence of their own; as they are without essence, they are void (i.e., devoid of the thing itself), and hence empty of "own-being." The "Middle Way" is a synonym in Nāgārjuna's writings for "voidness" and dependent origination; enlightenment, according to Mādhyamika thought, is the realization of the Middle Way. The term *nonself* was also here equated with voidness, explained here as substancelessness *(niḥsvabhāvatā)*, which was declared the true nature of reality itself. The Mādhyamika adoption of these ideas led to its theory of two kinds of truth, *saṃvṛti-satya* and *paramārtha-satya.* The former is our everyday, mundane, linguistically constructed truth; the latter is the ultimate, inexpressible truth, the truth of the lack of own-being of all *dharmas*. Under this doctrine, however, the two truths depend upon each other. Mundane and ultimate truths do not constitute separate "essences," for the distinction between mundane and ultimate, *saṃsāra* and *nirvāṇa*, is itself empty of reality. [*See* Mādhyamika *and the biography of Nāgārjuna.*]

Nāgārjuna's most famous disciple was Āryadeva (c. 170–270), whose harsh attacks on other schools made him an object of hatred and led to his assassination. His works include the *Śataśāstra, Catuḥśataka,* and *Akṣaraśataka;* others attributed to him are spurious but philosophically important. A set of twenty-one verses in praise of the *Prajñāpāramitā* by his follower Rāhula (or Rāhulabhadra, c. 200–300) is preserved in both Sanskrit and Chinese. Nāgārjuna's *Madhyamakakārikā* and *Dvādaśadvāra Śāstra* and Āryadeva's *Śataśāstra,* all translated into Chinese by Kumārajīva (d. 413), were highly esteemed in China and Japan, and formed the basis of the teachings of the San-lun (Jpn., Sanron), or Three Treatises, school there. [*See the biographies of Āryadeva and Kumārajīva.*]

Early Vijñānavāda. Mādhyamika thought, in its refusal to posit any "view" (proposition) whatsoever, was content to employ its critical philosophy against the views of others, views, the Mādhyamika thinkers contended, that were themselves the source of karmic suffering. Not content with this purely critical spirit, the Vijñānavādins (or Yogācāras, as they are also known) sought to systematically account for the origin of sentient existence and the relationship between mundane existence and enlightenment. As the name *Yogācāra* indicates, they advocated the practice of meditation as the means for attaining release from *saṃsāra.*

Mādhyamika analysis had gone beyond the assertions of early Buddhism, which declared the "self" *(ātman)* a poisonous fiction that was the source of suffering, to declare that the *dharma*s (elements of existence) themselves were empty of independent existence. Like the Mādhyamika, Yogācāra thought denies the reality of the phenomenal world, but it accepts the reality of the consciousness that produces it. It is from this doctrine that the school derives its alternate name, Vijñānavāda, the doctrine that all existences are the creation of consciousness.

For the Yogācāras, all phenomena are mere manifestations of "seeds" *(bīja)* deposited by past actions. These seeds are held in a "receptacle" or "storehouse" consciousness *(ālaya-vijñāna),* by which is designated, however, no substantial entity but merely the collectivity of the seeds themselves. The aggregation of the *bījas* is itself the *ālaya-vijñāna.* Under the appropriate conditions, these seeds manifest themselves as our psychophysical selves and as the contents of our everyday consciousnesses—the various sensory events that present themselves to us as an objective world. Thus, no object exists apart from the function of cognition by the subject; objects appear only on the basis of this cognitive function of the subject. Vijñānavāda incorporation of the concept of the Middle Way led to a description of all things as neither "decidedly existing" nor "decidedly nonexisting," and the claim that realization of the Middle Way is achieved through active insight into the fact that phenomenal existences are none other than "mere representations" *(vijñaptimātratā)* appearing in our consciousness. The *ālaya-vijñāna* was identified as the basis of the twelve links of dependent origination. [*See* Ālaya-vijñāna.]

The founder of this school of thought was Maitreya (Maitreyanātha, c. 270–350), sometimes identified with the *bodhisattva* of the same name. Maitreya's works include:

1. *Yogācārabhūmi,* the fundamental text of the Yogācāras. One of its sections, the *Bodhisattvabhūmi,* sets forth the *bodhisattva*'s discipline and describes his ideal life. The work is attributed to Maitreya's disciple Asaṅga (c. 310–390) by the Tibetans.
2. *Mahāyānasūtrālaṃkāra,* a systematic exposition of the stages of the *bodhisattva* that shares the same structure as the *Bodhisattvabhūmi* section of the aforementioned *Yogācārabhūmi.* The work is attributed to Asaṅga by the Chinese.
3. *Madhyāntavibhāga,* a discussion of the theories of *vijñaptimātratā,* the triple body of the Buddha, the three natures of reality, and other Yogācāra topics. The prose section is often attributed to Vasubandhu (c. 320–400), allegedly Asaṅga's younger brother.
4. *Abhisamayālaṃkāra,* a synopsis of the contents of the *Aṣṭasāhasrikā,* thus not specifically a Yogācāra work. The work was commented upon in the eighth century by Haribhadra.
5. *Dharmadharmatāvibhaṅga,* a short treatise on the function of "unreal imagination" *(abhūta-parikalpa)* in the production of phenomenal existence.
6. *Vajracchedikavyākhya,* a treatise on the *Diamond Cutter Sutra.*

The *tathāgata-garbha* theory is discussed in several of Maitreya's works and in the *Ratnagotravibhāga-mahāyānauttaratantra Śāstra,* attributed in the Tibetan tradition to Maitreya but probably composed by Sāramati (c. 350–450). All of the works of Maitreya and his followers hold that the Buddha nature underlies the existence of all living things.

Maitreya's disciple Asaṅga inherited and systematized Maitreya's teachings. In the *Mahāyānasaṃgraha* he presents a three-part classification of phenomena conceived by the human consciousness. Under this analysis, all phenomena have three "natures":

1. *Parikalpita-svabhāva:* as fictive creations of mind, things are in this sense devoid of original substance and are thus not real.
2. *Paratantra-svabhāva:* to the extent that things are the products of dependent origination they have a provisional or temporary existence, one dependent upon causes.
3. *Pariniṣpanna-svabhāva:* the nature of reality in and of itself as perfect suchness *(tathatā),* divested of all false imaginings that go toward the construction of images in our consciousness.

Paratantra-svabhāva is a mixture of pure and defiled aspects; it makes possible the turn from defilement toward purity. Realization of *pariniṣpanna-svabhāva* is tantamount to attainment of "representation only" awareness.

Other of Asaṅga's works include the *Abhidharmasamuccaya* and the *Hsien-yang-sheng-chiao lun (*Āryadeśanāvikhyāpana).* This latter work is an abridgement of the *Yogācārabhūmi.* [*See the biography of Asaṅga.*]

In his many works, Vasubandhu carried on the systematization of *vijñaptimātratā* philosophy and in the process became the tradition's greatest systematic thinker. His *Viṃśatikā* (Twenty Verses) refutes the belief in the objective world; the work betrays the influence of Sautrāntika thought. Vasubandhu is alleged to have been an exponent of the philosophy of Conservative Buddhism prior to his conversion to Mahāyāna by his brother, Asaṅga. His *Triṃśikā* (Thirty Verses) explains how *vijñānapariṇāma* ("modification of consciousness"), the process by which the various consciousnesses (the six sense consciousnesses of early Buddhism and an "I consciousness" called *manas*) arise from the *bījas,* takes place. This, perhaps the fundamental text of the Yogācāra tradition, was widely commented on by later thinkers. Other of Vasubandhu's works include a treatise on the Buddha nature known in China as the *Fo-hsing lun;* the *Karmasiddhiprakaraṇa,* treating the notion of *karman* from a Vijñānavāda standpoint; the *Trisvabhāvanirdeśa;* and the *Pañcaskandhaprakaraṇa,* a Hīnayāna-oriented work on the *skandhas.*

In Vasubandhu's works, the philosophical system of Vijñānavāda, which rests on the theory of *ālaya-vijñāna,* contains an idealistic or spiritualistic individualism: its description of *manas* and *ādāna* ("seizing") consciousnesses suggests Buddhist counterparts to the Western concept of "I" or "ego." This school also considered the problem of subjectivity, a fundamental element in Buddhist philosophy. The strict idealism espoused by Vasubandhu—his denial of the existence of objects in the external world—provoked severe criticism from other schools. [*See* Yogācāra *and the biography of Vasubandhu.*]

Later Developments in Vijñānavāda and Mādhyamika. After Vasubandhu, a number of philosophers made further developments in the ideas of their predecessors. Both Mādhyamika and Yogācāra developed as independent schools, side by side with the Sarvāstivāda, Sautrāntika, and other philosophical schools of Conservative Buddhism, and they exchanged ideas with one another. These schools conflated, diversified, and separated into distinct branches.

The Vijñānavādins. One branch, the Nirākāra-vijñānavāda, which held that consciousness is pure and possesses no forms, that is, that the forms of both object and subject are of fictive nature and hence unreal, was expounded by Sthiramati (c. 510–570) and others and introduced into China by Paramārtha (499–590). The Yogācāra teachings introduced to China by Paramārtha were called there the She-lun teachings, after Asaṅga's *Mahāyānasaṃgraha* (Chin., *She-lun*), the basic text of the school. Another branch of Yogācāra thought, the Sākāra-vijñānavāda, which maintained that consciousness is necessarily endowed with the forms of the subject and the object, originated with Dignāga (c. 400–480), was transmitted by Asvabhāva, and systematized by Dharmapāla (530–561). Dharmapāla's system was conveyed to China by Hsüan-tsang, where, as the Fa-hsiang ("dharma characteristic") school, it enjoyed a brief vogue. Thereafter, it was transmitted to Japan (where it was known as the Hossō school) and became one of the major scholastic traditions of the Nara period (710–785). Other exponents of the Sākāra-vijñānavāda tradition include Śīlabhādra and Śubhagupta (c. 650–750). [*See the biographies of Sthiramati, Paramārtha, Dignāga, Dharmapāla, Hsüan-tsang, and Śīlabhādra.*]

Dignāga's philosophical works led to innovations in Vijñānavāda thought. In his *Prajñāpāramitā-piṇḍārtha-saṃgraha* he discusses eighteen "emptinesses" and ten types of discriminative knowledge *(vikalpa).* The subject *(vijñāna)* is held to exist, but objects *(vijñeya),* as mere *parikalpita,* do not. However, in the undifferentiated, perfect form of knowledge *(prajñāpāramitā)* there is no confrontation of subject and object. Other of his works include the *Ālambanaparīkṣā,* the *Hastavalāprakaraṇa,* the *Sāmānyalakṣaṇaparīkṣā,* the *Yogāvatāra,* and the *Trikālaparīkṣā.* These analyze cognition and the theory of "representation only." Dignāga's studies of logic were also important for later philosophers.

Dharmapāla is best known for his *Vijñaptimātratāsiddhi,* a commentary on Vasubandhu's *Thirty Verses.*

Dharmapāla admitted the reality of objects of cognition *(parikalpita) in one sense.* He also drew a distinction between "that which changes" and "that which is changed" in consciousness. In addition to introducing the notion of eight consciousnesses, he distinguished four aspects of consciousness: its subjective aspect, objective aspect, self-conscious aspect, and self self-conscious aspects. The first three aspects may have been admitted by his predecessors, but Dharmapāla clearly was responsible for the addition of the fourth. Dharmapāla also taught that things may exist, in a relative sense, in the objective aspect of consciousness. It was Dharmapāla's unique understanding of Yogācāra thought that became normative in East Asian Vijñānavāda.

The scholar Śāntirakṣita (c. 680–740) and his disciple Kamalaśīla (c. 700–750) revived the ideas of the Nirākāra-vijñānavāda school. The former wrote a voluminous tract, the *Tattvasaṃgraha,* to which the latter produced commentaries. Śāntirakṣita knitted together the Mādhyamika and Yogācāra doctrines; Kalamaśīla established this combination as a synthesis superior to either of the two independent traditions. Śāntirakṣita's idealistic views deny the assertion of the existence of external objects and see self-cognition *(svasaṃvedana)* as the unity of all cognition. Śāntirakṣita held, however, that every cognition is devoid of both "the cognized" and the "cognizer." [*See the biographies of Śāntirakṣita and Kamalaśīla.*]

The Mādhyamikas. Disputes between two great scholars of Mādhyamika after Nāgārjuna, Buddhapālita (470–540) and Bhavya (or Bhāvaviveka, c. 490–570), led to the formation of two schools, known by the names given them in the Tibetan tradition: the Prāsaṅgika school of Buddhapālita and the Svātantrika school of Bhavya. The best known of Bhavya's works are the *Prajñāpradīpa,* a commentary to the *Madhyamakakārikā;* the *Madhyamakahṛdayakārikā* and its autocommentary, the *Tarkajvālā;* the *Madhyamārthasaṃgraha;* and the *Karatalaratna.* Bhavya's school admitted degrees of reality and levels of insight that are dependent on spiritual maturity and the degree of *samādhi* achieved, arguing therefore that it is possible to make assertions about the existence of things from the standpoint of conventional truth. Bhavya held that all the works of the Buddha as they appear in the *sūtra*s are *pramāṇa* (right knowledge) and do not require verification by reason *(yukti);* the function of *yukti* is a correct understanding of scripture *(āgama),* not a verification of it. Bhavya also tried to demonstrate *niḥsvabhāvatā,* or *śūnyatā,* by way of syllogism, a departure from the more common Mādhyamika view that all such assertions are ultimately self-contradictory *(prasaṅga).* His use of independent inference *(svatantra-anumāna)* in this respect gave his school of thought its name Svātantrika. Kamalaśīla inherited and developed this method and was instrumental in its transmission to Tibet. [*See the biography of Bhāvaviveka.*]

Buddhapālita, on the other hand, extended Nāgārjuna's use of the *prasaṅga* form of argumentation and denied the use of independent inference. His *Mūlamadhyamakavṛtti,* a commentary on the *Madhyamakakārikā,* is the sole extant treatise by his hand. Buddhapālita's thought was later championed by Candrakīrti (c. 600–650), who defended the *prasaṅga* method of reasoning against the attacks of Bhavya and hence is himself classed as a Prāsaṅgika by Tibetan sources. Candrakīrti is also known for his refutation of Yogācāra doctrines concerning the reality of consciousness and the Absolute. His major works include the *Prasannapadā,* a commentary on the *Madhyamakakārikā,* and the *Madhyamakāvatāra.* [*See the biographies of Buddhapālita and Candrakīrti.*]

Another important Mādhyamika thinker was Śāntideva (c. 650–750). In his *Bodhicaryāvatāra,* an introduction to the practices of the *bodhisattva,* he criticized the theory of self-consciousness *(svasaṃvid)* of mind *(vijñāna)* from an epistemological standpoint while admitting its temporary existence, a view he maintained without contradicting the notion of emptiness. An exponent of the Prāsaṅgika tradition, he also embraced the Nirākāravāda concept of mind. Other of Śāntideva's major works include the *Śikṣāsamuccaya* and the *Sūtrasamuccaya,* both anthologies of Mahāyāna scriptural passages. [*See the biography of Śāntideva.*]

Tathāgata-garbha Thought. The notion of the *tathāgata-garbha,* or "womb of the Tathāgata," represents the tendency of some Mahāyāna scriptures toward a more kataphatic way of regarding ultimate reality. In contrast to the assertions of the Śūnyavādins, who spoke of the Absolute solely in terms of absence or lack of independent existence, advocates of *tathāgata-garbha* tended to see in all sentient beings an indestructible core of Buddhahood that is productive of both mundane and transcendental reality. By emphasizing an ontological basis for both everyday existence and enlightenment, Tathāgata-garbha thinkers were able to speak fruitfully of the ultimate identity of the two realms and therefore to assert not only the potential for enlightenment in every being but also the sense in which all things are fundamentally and originally enlightened. In Japan, this *hongaku* ("original enlightenment") theory was transmitted and developed within the Tendai school, and became one of the dominant religious and philosophical motifs of Japanese Buddhism. Tathāgata-garbha thought shows, especially in its later phases, a relationship with Yogācāra thought founded principally on the integration of the notions of *tathāgata-garbha* and *ālaya-vijñāna*.

Tathāgata-garbha literature developed in three major phases. In the first phase, represented by the *Tathāgatagarbha Sūtra* and the *Śrīmālādevī Sūtra*, no mention is made of *ālaya-vijñāna*. Texts of the second period, including the *Mahāyānasūtrālaṃkāra* and the *Fo-hsing lun*, mention both but fail to elaborate on their relationship. In the third period, the *ālaya-vijñāna* doctrine was incorporated into that of the *tathāgata-garbha* to produce a *tathāgata-garbha* theory of dependent origination. Such is the work of the *Laṅkāvatāra Sūtra* and the *Ta-sheng ch'i-hsin lun* (**Mahāyāna śraddhotpāda Śāstra*, attributed to Aśvaghoṣa but according to some scholars, produced in Central Asia or China itself). Other major works treating this notion include the *Ratnagotravibhāga Śāstra* and the *Mahāyānāvatāra*, both perhaps the work of Sāramati, who is often credited as the systematizer of Tathātgata-garbha thought.

The *Ta-sheng ch'i-hsin lun* became particularly important in East Asia Buddhism, where it was widely read and commented upon, particularly in the Hua-yen tradition. This highly sophisticated and intricate text explores the nature of "original enlightenment" in its aspects as both "substance" *(t'i)* and "function" *(yung)*. By substance, the text refers to the underlying and unchanging enlightenment that is the nature of all sentient existence; by function it refers to the way in which this fundamental enlightenment is present in the world—the interplay between original enlightenment, nescience *(avidyā)*, and the experience of enlightenment as replacing ignorance in the consciousness of the religious practitioner. The text thus demonstrates the reliance of nescience, the source of our false imputation of independent reality to phenomena, on fundamental mind itself. [*See also* Tathāgata-garbha.]

The Logicians. Logical methods came to be emphasized in Buddhist thought as an outgrowth of the need to provide greater rigor for the epistemologies of the Mahāyāna tradition, particularly in defending their positions against proponents of non-Buddhist schools such as the Nyāya. [*See* Nyāya.] Incipient forms of Buddhist logic can be identified in the *Saṃdhinirmocana Sūtra*, in Maitreya's *Yogācārabhūmi*, and Asaṅga's *Abhidharmasamuccaya*. Vasubandhu is regarded as the progenitor of Buddhist logic, although the discipline was given its first full formulation by Dignāga. Vasubandhu's logical works include the *Vādaviddhi*, the *Vādavidhāna*, the *Vādakauśala*, and the *Tarkaśāstra* (although the provenance of this last work is disputed).

Working from this beginning, Dignāga created a new Buddhist logic. The "old" logic of the Nyāya school employed a five-step syllogism: (1) proposition *(pratijñā)*; (2) reason *(hetu)*; (3) example *(dṛṣṭānta)*; (4) application or recapitulation of the cause *(upanaya)*; and (5) conclusion *(nigamana)*. For example: (1) a word is impermanent; (2) it is impermanent because it is produced by causes; (3) a word is like a pot [for]; (4) a pot is produced by causes and is impermanent [just as words are]; (5) therefore, a word is impermanent. Another famous example is as follows: there is fire on the mountain for the mountain is smoking; wherever there is smoke there is fire, as is the case on a kitchen hearth; the mountain smokes, therefore, there is fire on the mountain. Dignāga omitted the fourth and fifth steps of this scheme, giving it a concision and simplicity comparable to the Aristotelian syllogism. He also set forth a theory of nine types of valid and invalid arguments. The fifth type corresponds to the fallacy of irrelevant conclusion, but Dignāga called it "inconclusive," on the basis of the Buddhist assumption of "neither being or nonbeing" as a logical mode different from "being" and "nonbeing." Dignāga's theories of knowledge appear in his *Pramāṇasamuccaya*, while his *Nyāyamukha* deals with the forms of argumentation. Also by Dignāga are the *Hetucakranirṇaya* and the *Hetucakraḍamaru*. Śaṃkarasvāmin's *Nyāyapraveśaka*, a brief introduction to Dignāga's logic, was widely studied by East Asian students of Buddhist logic.

Dignāga's fusion of logic and epistemology was elaborated upon by Dharmakīrti (c. 600–650), whose major works include the *Nyāyabindhu*, the *Pramāṇavārttika*, a treatise on Dignāga's *Pramāṇasamuccaya* in which he admits two kinds of valid knowledge, direct perception and inference (Dharmakīrti also regarded the Buddha as a source of valid knowledge), and the *Pramāṇaviniścaya*, an epitome of the *Pramāṇavārttika*. According to Dharmakīrti, every being is transitory; what is assumed to be the continuous existence of an individual is nothing but a sequence of moments; the person is merely a construct of our imagination and discriminative thinking *(vikalpa)*. Objects of inference are for Dharmakīrti universals, whereas objects of perception are individual, nothing but moments. [*See the biography of Dharmakīrti.*]

Later logicians include Śāntirakṣita and Kamalaśīla (both eighth century), Śubhakara (c. 650–750), Dharmottara (c. 730–800), Paṇḍita-Aśoka (ninth century), Jitāri (940–980), and Jñānaśrībhadra (fl. 925). Śāntirakṣita and Kamalaśīla adopted Dignāga's three-point syllogism, refuting the traditional five-point syllogism of the Nyāya school. Śāntirakṣita also defended Dharmakīrti's analysis of three characteristics of reason *(hetu)* against the attacks of Pātrakesari. Śubhakara, who was probably Dharmottara's teacher, composed the *Bāhyārthasiddhikārikā,* which attempted to prove the objective reality of external things, thus refuting Buddhist idealism *(vijñānavāda).* Major works of these later scholars include Dharmottara's *Apohaprakaraṇa,* Paṇḍita-Aśoka's *Avayavinirākaraṇa* and *Sāmānyadūṣaṇadikprasāritā,* Jñānaśrībhadra's *Laṅkāvatāravṛtti* and *Sūtrālaṃkāra-piṇḍārtha,* and Jitāri's *Jātinirākṛti* (in which he sets forth the controversy on universals between Buddhists and the Vaiśeṣikas, the Mīmāṃsākas, and the Jains) and *Hetutattvopadeśa.*

The eleventh-century scholar Jñānśrīmitra, a follower of the Dharmakīrti school at Vikramaśīla University, wrote twelve treatises on logic. Ratnakīrti, who flourished at about the same time, proved the existence of other minds from the standpoint of relative truth in his *Īśvarasādhanadūṣaṇa,* but denied it from the standpoint of highest truth in *Saṃtānāntaradūṣaṇa.* This latter work is particularly interesting because it unreservedly declares that solipsism is the final goal of idealism. Ratnakīrti's other works include *Apohasiddhi,* two works entitled *Kṣaṇabhaṅgasiddhi,* and *Sthirasiddhidūṣaṇa.* Ratnākaraśānti (fl. 1040), a scholar of the Nirākāra-vijñānavāda school, is the author of the *Antarvyāptisamarthana.* Mokṣākaragupta (c. 1050–1202) wrote an introductory work based on Dharmakīrti's *Nyāyabindu* entitled *Tarkabhāṣā.* Other noteworthy scholars of this period include Haribhadra (fl. 1120), author of the *Anekāntajayapatākā,* and Ravigupta, who advocated the theory of momentary flux *(kṣaṇikatva).*

Social and Political Thought

Expressions of political and social idealism are evident in a variety of Mahāyāna texts. Some appear in the form of letters from monks to kings. Mātṛceta's *Mahārājakanikalekha,* Nāgārjuna's *Ratnāvalī* and *Suhṛllekha,* the *Wang-fa cheng-li lun* (T.D. no. 1615), attributed to Maitreya, and the thirteenth chapter of the *Suvarṇaprabhāsa Sūtra* are among the important works that address rulers and proper rule. Other texts, such as the *Cittaviśuddhiprakaraṇa* by Āryadeva and the *Vajrasūcī,* advocate equality. The latter, a direct attack on the Brahmanic caste system, is attributed to Dharmakīrti by the Chinese.

Mahāyāna political and economic theories reflect the conditions in which they developed, when India consisted of many major and minor kingdoms. Some texts call upon subjects to overthrow kings who do not rule according to the ideals of *dharma.* Kings are directed to rule with clemency toward both men and other living things; they must also assure peace for their kingdoms (with military force, if necessary), increase national production, provide necessities in times of calamity, maintain social order, and promote education—all through their allegiance to and support of Buddhism. Āryadeva, on the other hand, asserted that the prestige and authority of kings is fictitious.

The spiritual leaders of Mahāyāna were monks who led otherworldly lives; they never engaged in the economic activities that they denounced. But some held that the worldly economic life was also of religious significance. Material charity was encouraged, and the abolition of poverty was espoused. However, certain vocations, such as cattle-raising, slave trading, and sales of liquor, were utterly condemned.

The problem of taxation also came under Mahāyāna scrutiny. Out of sympathy for the people, Mahāyānists called upon kings to minimize their exercise of the right to collect tribute and dispose of it at will. It was proposed that taxes be limited to one sixth of production, and it was argued that low taxes would stimulate production and fulfill this additional duty of the king. Kings were encouraged to distribute their treasures among their subjects to promote happiness, which would in turn increase the king's income. Thus, a rudimentary form of redistributive finance was proposed.

Advice was also offered on the use of force, the goal of which should be to protect the needy and to maintain tranquillity in the state. Although the guilty must be punished, clemency should be applied in the assignment of penalties. Capital and corporal punishments of all degrees were forbidden. If attacked, the king was obligated to protect his subjects and to repulse invaders. Hence, defensive war was recognized, but maintenance of pacificism was upheld as the ideal.

The king was also expected to be as virtuous in his private life as he was diligent in his administration of the state; sensual enjoyments and sexual dalliance were condemned. He was encouraged to choose advisors and subordinates wisely and to promote on the basis of merit. The state's goal should be to guide each subject to salvation. If the king administers the state according to divine law, he will bring benediction upon it and the state will flourish. Both he and his subjects will be happy, and his rebirth in heaven will be assured.

Above all, altruism was stressed, based on the virtue of compassion. A sense of human solidarity shaped Mahāyāna thought and governed its ethics: the refusal to give alms was regarded as the gravest of sins. Men were taught to help one another in the belief that no single man has the strength to sustain his own life, the highest sense of the idea of Buddhist solidarity.

[*See also* Buddhism, *article on* Buddhism in India; Soteriology, *article on* Buddhist Soteriology; *and* Buddhist Philosophy. *For further discussion of the development of Mahāyāna literature, see* Buddhist Literature, *article on* Survey of Texts.]

BIBLIOGRAPHY

Burtt, Edwin Arthur. *The Teachings of the Compassionate Buddha.* New York, 1955.

Conze, Edward. *Buddhist Thought in India: Three Phases of Buddhist Philosophy* (1962). Reprint, Ann Arbor, 1970.

Conze, Edward, ed. and trans. *Buddhist Scriptures.* Harmondsworth, 1959.

Conze, Edward, et al., eds. *Buddhist Texts through the Ages.* New York, 1954. A comprehensive collection of Indian Mahāyāna texts.

Cowell, E. B., et al., eds. *Buddhist Mahāyāna Texts.* Sacred Books of the East, edited by F. Max Müller, vol. 49. Oxford, 1894; reprint, New York, 1969.

Dayal, Har. *The Bodhisattva Doctrine in Buddhist Sanskrit Literature* (1932). Reprint, Delhi, 1975.

Dutt, Nalinaksha. *Aspects of Mahāyāna Buddhism and Its Relation to Hīnayāna.* London, 1930.

Frauwallner, Erich. *Die Philosophie des Buddhismus.* 3d rev. ed. Berlin, 1969.

Glasenapp, Helmuth von. *Der Buddhismus in Indien und im Fernen Osten.* Berlin, 1936.

Hamilton, Clarence H., ed. *Buddhism: A Religion of Infinite Compassion; Selections from Buddhist Literature.* New York, 1952.

Hirakawa Akira. "The Rise of Mahāyāna Buddhism and Its Relationship to the Worship of Stūpas." *Memoirs of the Research Department of the Tōyō Bunko* 22 (1963): 57–106. A well-documented analysis of a crucial topic in the history of Buddhism.

Hirakawa Akira. *Indo bukkyōshi.* 2 vols. Tokyo, 1974–1979. This comprehensive survey of Indian Buddhism contains extensive bibliographies of Japanese secondary sources.

Lamotte, Étienne. *Histoire du bouddhisme indien des origines à l'ère Śaka.* Louvain, 1958. Extensive footnotes and a comprehensive index make this work an invaluable reference tool.

Lamotte, Étienne, trans. *Le traité de la grande vertu de sagesse.* 5 vols. Louvain, 1944–1980. A translation from Kumārajīva's Chinese translation *(Ta chih-tu lun)* of the Sanskrit *Mahāprajñāparamitā Śāstra,* a commentary on the *Pañcaviṁśatisāhasrikā-prajñāparamitā.* the original Sanskrit commentary, sometimes attributed to Nāgārjuna, is no longer extant.

La Vallée Poussin, Louis de. *Bouddhisme.* Paris, 1909.

McGovern, William Mongomery. *An Introduction to Mahāyāna Buddhism.* New York, 1922.

Radhakrishnan, Sarvepalli. *Indian Philosophy,* vol. 1. 2d ed. London, 1927. A lucid introduction for the beginning student.

Schayer, Stanislaw. *Vorbereiten zur Geschichte der Mahāyānistischen Erlösungslehren.* Munich, 1921. Translated by R. T. Knight as *Mahāyāna Doctrines of Salvation* (London, 1921).

Stcherbatsky, Theodore. *Buddhist Logic* (1930–1932). 2 vols. Reprint, New York, 1962.

Suzuki, Beatrice Lane. *Mahāyāna Buddhism* (1938). 3d ed. New York, 1959.

Suzuki, D. T. *Outlines of Mahāyāna Buddhism* (1907). Reprint, New York, 1963.

Thomas, Edward J. *The History of Buddhist Thought.* 2d ed. New York, 1951.

Thomas, Edward J., trans. *The Quest of Enlightenment: A Selection of the Buddhist Scriptures.* London, 1950. A brief anthology of Mahāyāna texts in translation with particular reference to the career of the *bodhisattva.*

Wassiljew, W. *Der Buddhismus.* Saint Petersburg, 1860.

The Way of the Buddha. Delhi, 1957. Published by the Publications Division of the Ministry of Information and Broadcasting, Government of India.

Wayman, Alex. *The Buddhist Tantras: Light on Indo-Tibetan Esotericism.* New York, 1973.

Wayman, Alex, trans. *Calming the Mind and Discerning the Real: Buddhist Meditation and the Middle View, from the Lam rim chen mo of Tson-kha-pa.* New York, 1978.

Winternitz, Moriz. *Der Mahāyāna-Buddhismus, nach Sanskrit- und Prākrittexten.* 2 vols. Tübingen, 1930.

Winternitz, Moriz. *A History of Indian Literature,* vol. 2, *Buddhist Literature and Jaina Literature* (1933). Reprint, New York, 1971. Even now, this work remains probably the best introduction to the subject.

NAKAMURA HAJIME

Esoteric Buddhism

Buddhist esotericism is an Indian movement obscure in its beginnings. Combining yoga and ritual, it calls itself the Diamond Vehicle (Vajrayāna)—where *diamond* means "the unsplittable"—or the Mantra Vehicle (Mantrayāna)—where *mantra* means "magical speech." The revealed texts of the tradition are called *tantra,* in contrast to *sūtra* (the generic name of the non-Tantric Buddhist scriptures), but both these words have the implication "thread" or "continuous line." In the case of the Tantras, the "continuous line" can be understood in various ways: the lineage of master-disciple, the continuity of vows and pledges in the practitioner's stream of consciousness, or the continuity of practice leading to a religious goal.

Much of Tantric literature is ritualistic in nature, manifesting Brahmanic influence by the use of incantations *(mantra)* and the burnt offering *(homa),* both of which were employed for magical purposes as far back as Vedic times. [*See also* Mantra]. Similarly, the notion of the "five winds" found in certain of the Tantras dates back to some of the Upaniṣads. Many of the hand gestures and foot stances of Buddhist Tantric practice are also found in Indian dance. [*See also* Mudrā.] However, as specifically Buddhist Tantras, such texts are colored both by Buddhist theories and practices and by the typical terminology of Mahāyāna Buddhism. These texts regularly employ such ancient Buddhist formulations as the triad body, speech, and mind, and draw upon such common Mahāyāna notions as the pair "means" *(upāya)* and "insight" *(prajñā)*. [*See also* Upāya *and* Prajñā.] The Tantras accept the old Buddhist ontology of three worlds filled with deities and demons, and contribute the premise that one can relate to these forces by ritualistic manipulation of one's nature (body, speech, and mind), thereby attaining "success" *(siddhi)* in such mundane forms as appeasing the deities, or the supermundane success of winning complete enlightenment (Buddhahood), possibly in a single lifetime. The old Buddhist terminology "son or daughter of the family," here the Buddhist family, was extended to refer to Buddha families. Initially, the texts propose a triad of three Buddhas or Tathāgatas: Vairocana, Amitābha, and Akṣobhya. Later, Ratnasambhava and Amoghasiddhi are added to make up a family of five, and Vajrasattva to make a family of six. A supreme Buddha, referred to variously as Mahā-Vajradhara, Heruka, or Ādibuddha ("Primordial Buddha"), is also mentioned. But the texts do not use the term "Dhyāni Buddhas" that is sometimes found in Western books on the subject.

Influence in Time and Place. Buddhist Tantrism appears to have originated in eastern India and to have been transmitted orally in private circles from around the third century CE. When we speak of the period of the origination of the tradition, however, we refer only to that era in which Buddhist Tantras arose in syncretism with an already extant lore non-Buddhist in character, and not to some hypothetic origin of Tantrism per se. The first textual evidence of this current is found in chapters bearing the title *dhāraṇī* (a kind of *mantra*) within certain Mahāyāna scriptures. The ninth chapter of the *Laṅkāvatāra Sūtra* (fourth century CE), for example, is devoted to magical formulas of supposedly meaningless sounds, which, when recited for one hundred and eight times, are claimed to ward off demons. The earliest Tantras are those that still give a leading role to Śākyamuni, the historical founder of Buddhism, perhaps placing him at the center of a *maṇḍala*. By comparing the names of the five Buddhas in the *Durgatipariśodhana Tantra* (i.e., Vairocana, Durgatipariśodhana, Ratnaketu, Śākyamuni, and Saṃkusumita) with those of the five Buddhas of the Mahākaruṇāgarbha Maṇḍala, which is derived from the *Vairocanābhisaṃbodhi Tantra* (i.e., Mahāvairocana, Dundubhinirghoṣa, Ratnaketu, Amitāyus, and Samkusumitarāja) and with the five of the Vajradhātu Maṇḍala, derived from the *Tattvasaṃgraha Tantra* (i.e., Mahāvairocana, Akṣobhya, Ratnasambhava, Amitābha, and Amoghasiddhi), we can observe that the name Śākyamuni is still employed in the earliest Tantras but is later replaced by the name Amitāyus, and finally by Amitābha, resulting in the standard set of Buddha names of later times.

Between the third and the eighth centuries, these cults, with their "revealed" scriptures, were transmitted secretly from master to disciple, but by the eighth and ninth centuries a remarkable change had occurred in the fortunes of Buddhist Tantrism. Evidence of the growing influence of the movement may be seen in the fact that a king called Great Indrabhūti of Uḍḍiyāna is said to have been initiated into the Tantric mysteries at about this time. Other important evidence of the growth of the tradition is found in the texts of the period. Whereas the revealed Tantric works of earlier centuries were written in strict anonymity and attributed to divine authorship, now historical figures begin to attach their names to commentarial literature. Buddhaguhya (second half of the eighth century) wrote learned commentaries on the three Tantras mentioned above. A host of commentaries also arose on the *Guhyasamāja Tantra* and the *Śrī-Cakrasaṃvara Tantra* cycles by such celebrated writers as Saraha and the Tantric Nāgārjuna (author of the *Pañcakrama*). While some Tantric works had been translated in Chinese earlier, it was not until the eighth century that Tantrism would take hold in China, owing largely to the efforts of the monk Vajrabodhi and his disciple Amoghavajra. Their kind of Tantrism was transmitted to the talented Japanese monk Kūkai (posthumously called Kōbō Daishi, 774–835), who introduced to Japan an elaborate cult based on the "two Tantras," the *Vairocanābhisaṃbodhi* and the *Tattvasaṃgraha*. This cult, a fusion of art, mysterious rituals, colorful costumes, religious music, and handsome calligraphy, would have a great cultural impact on Japan.

In this period certain Tantras were also translated into Tibetan. Tibet eagerly embraced these cults, and in time would produce native works on the most popular Tantras. While a vast number of Tantric texts was translated into Tibetan, a lesser amount was preserved in Chinese translation. Chinese Buddhism generally disliked the Tantras, partly for their intricate ritualism, but more for the sexual symbolism, offensive to the Chinese mind, found in Tantras such as the *Guhyasamāja*. In Java, construction of the Borobaḍur monument, begun in the eighth century, shows Tantric influence in its use of *maṇḍalas* at its central stupa. It is also known that Atīśa, who arrived in Tibet in 1042 and became a towering figure in Tibetan Buddhism, had earlier studied for twelve years in the celebrated Tantric college of Śrīvijaya (now part of Indonesia). Thus it is clear that after the eighth century, Buddhist Tantrism was strongly entrenched in eastern India from Bengal north, had advanced to Nepal and Tibet, flourished for a time in China, became highly influential in Japan, and would establish a great school in the "Golden Isles" (Indonesia).

Tibet became an extraordinary center for Tantrism as well as the major storehouse of Tantric literature. The Indian *guru* Nā-ro-pa (956–1040?) was an important link in this development. It was Nā-ro-pa who transmitted Buddhist esotericism to the translator Mar-pa, who in turn taught it to the poet Mi-la-ras-pa. [*See the biographies of Nā-ro-pa, Mar-pa, and Mi-la-ras-pa.*] Thereafter, from this lineage arose the Bka'-brgyud-pa school, continuing the Great Seal *(mahāmudrā)* teachings and the six yoga doctrines that had been taught by Nā-ro-pa. In modern times, the Tibetan tragedy has resulted in a number of Tibetan monk refugees transplanting their Tantric lineages to Europe and the United States.

Buddhist Tantric Literature. The Tibetan canon classifies the Tantras into four groups, the Kriyā Tantras, the Caryā Tantras, the Yoga Tantras, and the Anuttarayoga Tantras. The translations of the revealed Tantras were included under the four headings in a section of the canon called the Bka'-'gyur (Kanjur); the commentaries are grouped in a section of exegetical works called the Bstan-'gyur (Tanjur). The Sino-Japanese canon does not so group them. In the Tibetan canon, the two chief works of the Japanese Tantric school (Shingonshū), the *Vairocanābhisaṃbodhi* and the *Tattvasaṃgraha,* are the principal works of the Caryā and Yoga Tantras, respectively. The *Hevajra Tantra* and the *Guhyasamāja Tantra,* works well known to Western scholars, belong to the Anuttarayoga Tantra class, and are respectively a "Mother" and a "Father" Tantra of this class. The status of the popular *Kālacakra Tantra,* definitely an Anuttarayoga class text, has been disputed. There is also a host of small works called *sādhana,* which set forth methods of evoking a given deity. The *Sādhanamālā* is a well-known collection of such works. Since in the Tantric tradition deities are arrayed in designs called *maṇḍalas,* there are also treatises devoted to *maṇḍalas* and their associated rituals. [*See also* Maṇḍalas.] The *Niṣpannayogāvalī* is a work on twenty-six of these *maṇḍalas.* During the last period of Buddhism in India the popularity of Tantrism gave rise to a group of Tantric heroes called *mahāsiddhas* ("great adepts"), and tales were compiled concerning their superhuman exploits. Their Tantric songs are collected in a work called the *Caryāgīti.* Other well-known Tantras include the *Mañjuśrī-mūla-kalpa* (a Kriyā Tantra), the *Sarvadurgatipariśodhana* (a Yoga Tantra), and the *Mañjuśrī-nāmasaṃgīti,* which was commented upon both as a Yoga Tantra and as an Anuttarayoga Tantra.

The editor of the Tibetan canon, Bu-ston (1290–1364), arranged the Tantras in their respective four classes according to a theory that in order for a Tantra to be a Buddhist one, it should be in some Buddhist family, headed by one of the Buddhas. In the case of the Anuttarayoga Tantras, the Mother Tantras were classified under one or another of seven Buddhas, in order: "Teacher" (Tib., *ston pa,* probably referring to Vajrasattva), Heruka (i.e., Akṣobhya), Vairocana, Vajraprabha (i.e., Ratnasambhava), Padmanarteśvara (i.e., Amitābha), Paramāśva (i.e., Amoghasiddhi), and Vajradhara. The *Śrī-Cakrasaṃvara* and the *Hevajra* were included under Heruka. The Father Tantras were classified under six Buddhas, identical to those used to classify the Mother Tantras except that the first, "Teacher," is omitted. The *Guhyasamāja Tantra* was classified under Akṣobhya and the *Yamāri* (or *Yamāntaka) Tantra* under Vairocana. The *Mañjuśrī-nāma-saṃgīti Tantra* and the *Kālacakra Tantra* were not included in this classification, presumably because they were classed under Ādibuddha, "Primordial Buddha."

In the case of the Yoga Tantras, the basic scripture, called *Tattvasaṃgraha,* is itself divided into four sections corresponding to four Buddha families. Explanatory Tantras of the Yoga Tantra class could thus be classed in one of those four sections or families, or could emphasize either "means" *(upāya)* or "insight" *(prajñā).* For example, the *Paramādya* is classed chiefly as an "insight" scripture.

The Caryā Tantras were classified under three Buddha families, the Tathāgata family (under Vairocana), the Padma family (under Amitābha), and the Vajra family (under Akṣobhya). The *Vairocanābhisaṃbodhi* is classed under the Tathāgata family; the *Vajrapāṇyabhiṣeka* is classed under the Vajra family; but the Padma family has no corresponding text among the Caryā Tantras.

The arrangement of the Kriyā Tantras is rather complicated. Using the same three families that govern the Caryā Tantras, the Kriyā Tantras make further subdivisions for the Lord of the Family, the Master, the Mother, Wrathful Deities, Messengers, and Obedient Ones. In addition, the Tathāgata family is subdivided into Uṣṇīṣa, Bodhisattvas, and Gods of the Pure Abode. For example, the *Suvarṇaprabhāsottama,* which was also quite popular as a Mahāyāna *sūtra,* is included under the Mother of the Tantras family. The Kriyā Tantras also include a category "Worldly Families" as well as "General" Kriyā Tantras, a category that includes the *Subāhuparipṛcchā.*

Naturally, there was always a considerable degree of arbitrariness in such categorizations; in fact, certain Tantras had a disputed status. The traditions carried to Tibet also classified the four divisions of Tantras according to their respective deities and according to the preferences of the human performers. When classed in terms of deities, the division reflects degrees of courtship: laughing for the Kriyā Tantras, mutual gazing for the Caryā Tantras, holding hands for the Yoga Tantras, and the pair united for the Anuttarayoga Tantras. When arranged according to human performers, the respective preference for outer ritual or inner *samādhi* is the determining factor. Kriyā Tantras appeal to those with a preference for ritual over *samādhi*. In the Caryā Tantras, ritual and *samādhi* are balanced; in the Yoga Tantras *samādhi* prevails over ritual; and in the Anuttarayoga Tantras *samādhi* alone is the requisite practice. An unorthodox explanation of these four classes is found in Smṛti's commentary on the *Vajravidāraṇā-nāma-dhāraṇī* (Kriyā Tantra, Master of the Family class). This author claims the four classes correspond to four kinds of Buddhist followers and the way in which they "cleanse with voidness." For the *śrāvaka*s (i.e., Hīnayāna monks) external cleansing purifies the body. For the *pratyekabuddha*s (*ṛṣi*s, "seers") inner cleansing purifies speech. For the Yogācāras (the Mind Only school) secret cleansing purifies the mind, and for the Mādhyamikas "reality cleansing" with a diamondlike *samādhi* unifies body, speech, and mind. [*See also* Samādhi.]

The Language of Buddhist Esotericism. Opponents of the Tantras have based their condemnations on what they read in such works. Since works of the Anuttarayoga Tantra class, the *Hevajra* and *Guhyasamāja Tantras* in particular, are still preserved in the original Sanskrit, modern scholars have consulted these for their conclusions about Tantrism and are usually unable to consult the Tibetan or Sino-Japanese versions of a wide range of Tantras. Some scholars accordingly have referred to Buddhist Tantrism by names such as the Vāmācāra ("left-handed path") or the Sahajayāna ("together-born path"), but the Tantras themselves do not use such terms, and in fact such designations fail to throw light on their contents. It should be recognized that the followers of the Tantric cults, including many Tibetan monks, would *never* presume to interpret a Tantra from the language of the revealed text alone. These invariably require the assistance of a commentary, perhaps one written by their *guru*. On such grounds a number of Tantras translated into Tibetan have traditionally been considered "off-limits" precisely because they were not transmitted with their "lineage," the authoritative explanation, or with "permission" *(anujñā)* to evoke the deity of the Tantra. Commenting on the *Guhyagarbha Tantra*, the Tantric Līlavajra observes that the literal interpretation of Tantric texts is the basis for misunderstanding them and practically admits that some of his contemporaries not only misunderstand the texts but also appeal to them in order to justify their own corrupt practices. In the same way, modern authors who are outsiders to the cult assume that the literal meaning is the only meaning, and thus wrongly explain fragments of Tantras available to them.

A commentary on the *Guhyasamāja Tantra* by the Tantric Candrakīrti sets forth four kinds of explanation of the sense of a given passage (cf. Wayman, 1977, pp. 116–117): (1) the invariant sense *(akṣarārtha)*, or literal meaning; (2) the shared sense *(samastāṅgārtha)*, or sense of the text that is shared either with non-Tantric traditions or with Tantras of the three lower classes; (3) the pregnant sense *(garbhyartha)*, by which is meant a meaning that either clarifies the doctrine of lust *(rāgadharma)*, reveals conventional truth *(saṃvṛtisatya)*, or considers the three gnoses *(jñānatraya;* i.e., Light, Spread of Light, Culmination of Light); and (4) the ultimate sense *(kolikārtha)*, or the one that clarifies the Clear Light *(prabhāsvara)* or reveals the paired union *(yuganaddha)*.

Equally important, the Tantras frequently use language that is deliberately obscure. In the Anuttarayoga Tantras this kind of arcane language is called *sandhyābhāṣā*, frequently rendered "twilight language" or "intentional language." In this highly metaphoric idiom the term "Diamond Body" *(vajrakāya)* is used to refer to menstrual blood, "Diamond Speech" *(vajravāk)* to refer to semen, and "Diamond Mind" *(vajracitta)* to refer to scented water. Clearly, Tantric language does not conform to our expectations of ordinary expository writing, where the clearer text is considered "better." In no other Buddhist tradition do the texts strive deliberately to conceal their meaning. But the Tantras have a synthetic character that combines such standard, and nonesoteric, practices as the contemplation of voidness *(śūnyatā)* with special secret practices all their own. The most basic meaning of "secret" in the Tantric tradition is that its theories and practices should be kept secret from those who are not fellow initiates, that is, from those who have not obtained initiation *(abhiṣeka)* or taken vows *(saṃvara)* and pledges *(samaya)*. When these works explain the term "secret" (usually *guhya* in Sanskrit), they apply it to certain things that owe their secrecy to being inward or hidden, like the secret of female sexuality. A list of secret topics in this literature would comprise states of yoga, the circle of deities, and other experiences that are not accessible to ordinary consciousness and cannot be appreciated by the thoroughly mundane mind. Accordingly, it was never maintained that a person with initiation into a Tantric cult had thereby experienced such esoteric matters. Rather, it continues to be held that someone who had gone through such a ritual establishes a bond with a *guru* who will supply the lore of the particular Tantra and guide the disciple in its practice. Tantric language shares with many other Indian works a difficulty of interpretation. The compact style of Indian philosophical treatises, for example, is the cause for much dispute over their meaning. The Tantras compound this difficulty by the very nature of their contents, making interpretation of the texts all the more difficult. [*See also* Language, *article on* Buddhist Views of Language.]

Tantric Practice and Analogical Thinking. Tantric practice aims at relating man to supramundane forces or deities. In so doing, it makes use of two widely disparate systems of analogy. One procedure associates man and the divine by means of rules applicable to all practitioners. The other procedure assigns persons to one or another Buddha family according to the dominant personality traits of the individual practitioner. In terms of the four divisions of the Tantras, the first two, the Kriyā and Caryā, make use of the first system. The latter two, the Yoga and Anuttarayoga, generally employ the second. Each approach has its supporters who claim that it provides a way to become a *saṃbuddha* ("complete Buddha").

A preeminent Tantra of the first kind is the *Vairocanābhisaṃbodhi.* This Tantra stresses the basic triad Body, Speech, and Mind—the "three mysteries" of the Buddha—and the prescribed practices by which certain attainments may be generated. Here, the human performer affiliates with the Body by means of hand gestures *(mudrā);* with the Speech by means of incantations *(mantra);* and with the Mind by means of deep concentration *(samādhi),* especially on the *maṇḍala.* In this Tantra, the transcendental Buddha is Mahāvairocana, and the human Buddha is Śākyamuni. This correspondence agrees with the division of the bodies of the Buddha into *dharmakāya* and *rūpakāya* that is found in early Mahāyāna Buddhism. In the same light, Kūkai, the founder of the Japanese Shingon school, explicitly identifies Mahāvairocana with the *dharmakāya.* It is noteworthy that the practice in the Caryā Tantra, in fact the practice based on the *Vairocanābhisaṃbodhi,* has a twofold basis: "yoga with images" and "yoga without images." In the former, one contemplates the inseparability of "self reality" *(ātmatattva)* from "deity reality" *(devatātattva),* and in sequence the performer meditatively generates himself into Vairocana with one face and two hands, making the *samāpatti mudrā* ("seal of equipoise"). The process is called the "subjective ground." The performer then contemplates the Buddha Vairocana, like himself, in front of himself. This step is termed the "objective ground."

In the "yoga without images" the mind is understood to have two sides, one mundane-directed (the *manas* face), the other supramundane-directed (the *buddhi* face). Upon reaching the limit of "yoga with images" one perceives as though before the eyes a configuration of the body of the deity on the mundane-directed side of the mind. The practitioner then follows this with a contemplation in which the deity body appears as a bright illusion on the supramundane-directed side of the mind. Through this process one achieves the same result as do practitioners of the early Buddhist meditations on "calming the mind" *(śamatha)* and "discerning the real" *(vipaśyanā).* This approach is directed to an ultimate goal indicated by the term "arising of the Tathāgata," and chapters bearing this title are found both in the *Vairocanābhisaṃbodhi* and in the Mahāyāna scripture collection called the *Avataṃsaka Sūtra.* The multiple Buddhas in this tradition of Tantric analogies are on the mental level; they may also be understood to refer indiscriminately to "all Buddhas" rather than to particular Buddha families.

The fasting cult of Avalokiteśvara, which uses the *mantra* "Oṃ mani padme hūṃ," employs a similar system of analogies. [*See also* Avalokiteśvara.] The famous six-syllabled formula is correlated with six Buddhas, six colors, and six realms of sentient beings. It is also recited during six times of the day and the night. The individual performer must pass ritually through the six syllables. The situation is comparable to the youth Sudhana's tenure of study under many different teachers in sequence, as portrayed in the *Gaṇḍavyūha Sūtra* (part of the *Avataṃsaka*).

The second analogical system is formulated in the Yoga Tantra *Tattvasaṃgraha.* It consists of four sections. Persons of different predominant vices in their stream of consciousness are affiliated respectively with these sections, each presided over by a Buddha, as shown in table 1. The commentator Buddhaguhya explains that the fourth of these sections results from a merger of the Ratna family (as agent) and the Karman family (as the fulfilling action), but for convenience, the *Tattvasaṃgraha* usually mentions only Ratnasambhava as the presiding Buddha here. The correlation of persons with particular Buddha families indicates which of the predominant mind-based vices is to be eliminated by the "purification path" of the particular Buddha family. Each of the four paths in turn requires four kinds of *mudrā* ("seal"), but each path emphasizes one of the four and subordinates the other three. The first path emphasizes the Great Seal *(mahāmudrā);* the second, the Symbolic or Linkage Seal *(samayamudrā);* the third, the Dharma Seal *(dharmamudrā);* and the fourth,

TABLE 1. *Analogical Correspondences according to the* Tattvasaṃgraha

Section of Fundamental Tantra	Buddha Family	Presiding Buddha	Predominant Consciousness
1. Diamond Realm	Tathāgata	Vairocana	lust
2. Victory over the Three Worlds	Vajra	Akṣobhya	hatred
3. Training the Living Beings	Padma	Amitābha	delusion
4. Achieving the Objective	Ratna Karma	Ratnasambhava Amoghasiddhi	avarice

the Action Seal *(karmamudrā)*. The paths have been expanded by the addition of four corresponding *maṇḍalas*, as shown in table 2.

According to Mkhas-grub-rje's *Fundamentals of the Buddhist Tantras* the practice of these purificatory paths commences with an effort by the practitioner to generate the Symbolic Being, the practitioner's own symbolization of the deity with whom he has established a link or bond. One then draws in (usually through the crown of the head) the Knowledge Being *(jñānasattva)*, the deity in the absolute sense, who is usually said to emanate "from the sky." Mkhas-grub-rje explains: "The purpose of executing the seals of the Four Seals is to merge and unify the body, speech, mind, and acts of the Knowledge Being with the body, speech, mind, and acts of the Symbolic Being. There would be no foundation for merger if either were present by itself."

The Japanese school of Tantra called Shingon is based on the *Vairocana* scripture (mainly its first chapter) and the *Tattvasaṃgraha* (mainly its first section, "The Diamond Realm"). Thus, this school ignores the real clash between these two scriptures. Shingon employs two *maṇḍala* realms, that of the Vajradhātu Maṇḍala (Jpn., Kongōkai), an unchanging "diamond" knowledge realm derived from the *Tattvasaṃgraha*, and that of the Mahākaruṇāgarbha Maṇḍala (Jpn., Taizōkai), the changing realm of becoming that makes possible the "arising of the Tathāgata." This latter *maṇḍala* is derived from the *Vairocana* scripture. In the terminology of Tibetan Tantrism, this theory and practice of becoming a Buddha is classified as Caryā Tantra because the scripture from which the Mahākaruṇāgarbha Maṇḍala derives is so classified. This is so because there is no attempt here to relate performers to particular Buddha families according to dominant fault as is the case in the Yoga Tantras. The Yoga Tantra *Tattvasaṃgraha* serves here to add a further dimension of knowledge in the form of commentarial additions and related practices, so as to preserve consistency between the two *maṇḍala* (Jpn., *mandara*) cycles.

The Anuttarayoga Tantras continue the procedure of the Yoga Tantras, and, in the Father Tantras, allot dis-

TABLE 2. *Correspondence of the Four Maṇḍalas according to the* Tattvasaṃgraha

Maṇḍala	Seal *(mudrā)*	Object Symbolized	External Symbolizer	Internal Symbolizer
1. Great *(mahā)*	Great Seal of Body	Form of the deity's body	Hand gesture[1]	Identification of oneself and the deity
2. Memory *(dhāraṇī)* or Linkage *(samaya)*	Symbolic Seal of Mind	Knowledge of deity's mind	Hand symbol[2]	Identification with deity and his knowledge
3. Doctrinal Syllables *(dharma)*	Dharma Seal of Speech	Elegancies of deity's voice	Syllables imagined in deity's body	Identification with deity and with an array of interior syllables
4. Action *(karman)*	Action Seal of Wondrous Action	[not stated]	[not stated]	[not stated]

[1]Hand gesture refers to such well-known gestures as "giving confidence" or "meditative equipoise."
[2]Hand symbol refers to material emblems (e.g., the lotus [*padma*] or arrow) held in the hand.

tinct character to the five Buddhas for the purpose of a fivefold correspondence with five different kinds of persons. The Mother Tantras of this class raise the correspondences to six. The Anuttarayoga Tantras also have a basic division into two stages, a stage of generation *(utpattikrama)* and a stage of completion or consummation *(saṃpannakrama)*. Indeed, the stage of generation overlaps the Yoga Tantra by way of what it calls the "three *samādhis*," named "preliminary praxis," "triumphant *maṇḍala*," and "victory of the rite." Tsoṅ-kha-pa's *Sṅags rim chen mo* (Great Treatise on the Mantra Path) elucidates the stage of generation in terms of six consecutive members, each of which corresponds to one of the three *samādhis*, as shown in table 3. These three *samādhis* can be used as a classification in Yoga Tantra practice as well. In fact, when generalized, the three are the three parts of every Buddhist Tantric ritual: the preliminaries, the main part, and the concluding acts.

The second stage of the Anuttarayoga Tantra, the "stage of completion," deals with more concrete matters like the centers in the body *(cakras)* and five mysterious winds (first mentioned centuries earlier in the *Chāndogya* and other Upaniṣads). This stage comprises a six-membered yoga *(ṣaḍaṅgayoga)*, also classified in five steps *(pañcakrama)*. The five steps are accomplished in members three through six, while the first and second members represent a link with the stage of generation. Table 4 shows the six members and how they were identified with goddesses (*ḍākinīs*) in the *Tantra Śrīḍākārṇava-mahāyoginī-tantra-rāja* (Ocean of Ḍākinīs).

The Anuttarayoga Tantras also contain passages on the "higher initiations," the practice of which includes elements often referred to by modern writers as "sexo-yogic." Briefly speaking, these have to do with worship of the female, and, perhaps, a rite of sexual union in which the male performer does not emit semen. Before attempting any explanation of this topic, it would be well to mention that historically there were lay as well as renunciant Tantrics, just as there were lay as well as renunciant *bodhisattvas* in the Mahāyāna tradition. Among the Tibetan sects that practice Tantrism, it is only the Dge-lugs-pa that observes the Vinaya code of monastic morality. This does not mean, however, that the Dge-lugs-pa practices a "cleaned-up" Tantrism with the objectionable passages expurgated from the texts. As we have noted before, it is not necessary to read the Tantras in the literal manner without benefit of commentaries, as some modern scholars are wont to do.

The four initiations *(abhiṣeka)* of the Anuttarayoga Tantras begin with the "initiations of the flask," rites taken in common with the three lower classes of Tantras. To this is added a "secret initiation," an "insight-knowedge initiation," and an initiation known as the "fourth" (also called *akṣara*, denoting "syllable" or "the incessant"). The secret initiation involves a mysterious "red and white element," an experience of "bliss-void," and the implication that the initiation takes place in the *cakras* of the body (those centers ranged along the spine but said to exist as well in a subtle body). Treatises such as that by Mkhas-grub-rje distinguish between a *kar-*

TABLE 3. *The Stages of Generation according to Tsoṅ-kha-pa's* Sṅags rim chen mo

MEMBERS	SAMĀDHI	BUDDHA FAMILY	ACTIVITY	REASON FOR THE FAMILY
1.	Preliminary Praxis	Vairocana	Contemplation of the palace that is the Buddha's dwelling place	Because Vairocana is the nature of the material aggregate *(rūpa-skandha)*
2.	Preliminary Praxis	Vajrasattva	Generation of the symbolic circle *(samayacakra)* and the knowledge circle *(jñānacakra)*, followed by the generation of passion via the divine Father-Mother	Because Vajrasattva uses passion to "materialize" the *maṇḍala* deities from the *bodhicitta* ("thought of enlightenment") of the Father-Mother pairs
3.	Triumphant *Maṇḍala*	Akṣobhya	Initiation *(abhiṣeka)* conferred by the *vidyā* ("wisdom") goddesses	Because Akṣobhya is the essence of the water initiation
4.	Victory of the Rite	Amitābha	Enjoyment of the ambrosia *(amṛta)*	Because Amitābha is the "diamond of speech" that satiates the devotee
5.	Victory of the Rite	Amoghasiddhi	Making offerings	Because Amoghasiddhi is the progenitor of the Karma family, with power over offerings made to the Buddha and over acts on behalf of sentient beings
6.	Victory of the Rite	Ratnasambhava	Praise of the Buddhas[1]	Because praise extols merits, and Ratnasambhava ("arising of jewels") is the arising merits of Body, Speech, and Mind

[1]Some other formulations conclude the "victory of the rite" with the acts of dismissing the deities, along with a burnt offering *(homa)*.

TABLE 4. *Correspondence of the Six Yogic Stages with Goddesses (Ḍākinīs) according to the* Ocean of Ḍākinīs

MEMBER	NAME OF MEMBER	ḌĀKINĪ	THE FIVE STEPS	COMMENT
1.	*pratyāhāra* ("withdrawal")	She the Crow-faced		Withdrawal, i.e., interiorization of the ten sense bases (five subjective and five objective)
2.	*dhyāna* ("meditation")	She the Owl-faced		Meditation on the nature of the five Tathāgatas
3.	*prāṇāyāma* ("control of the winds")	She the Dog-faced	Diamond Muttering	Control of the winds in five colors by means of "diamond muttering" *(vajrajāpa)*
4.	*dhāraṇā* ("retention")	She the Boar-faced	Purification of Mind Personal Blessings	Manifestation of the five signs by means of purification of mind *(cittaviśuddhi)* and personal blessings *(svādhiṣṭhāna)*. Movement to the Clear Light via the Three Gnoses
5.	*anusmṛti* ("recollection")	She, Yama's Messenger	Revelation-Enlightenment	Recollection, so as to proceed in the reverse order, by means of revelation-enlightenment *(abhisaṃbodhi)*. Movement from the Clear Light via the Three Gnoses
6.	*samādhi* ("consummation")	She, Yama's Cremation Ground	Pair United	The consummation of knowledge by means of *yuganaddha*, "the pair united"

mamudrā (the female partner) and a *jñānamudrā* ("seal of knowledge"). The insight-knowledge initiation involves a sequence of four joys *(ānanda)* associated with the downward progress of the "melted white element": descending from the forehead to the neck there is joy; descending to the heart there is "super joy" *(paramānanda)*; descending to the navel there is the "joy of exhaustion" *(viramānanda)*; and upon reaching the sex center there is "together-born joy" *(sahajānanda)*, on which occasion the element is not to be emitted. If we are to assume that the element in question is indeed semen, how was it able to descend from the forehead?

There is also an Anuttarayoga Tantra explanation of the "four seals," but it differs from that found in the Yoga Tantras. In the Anuttarayoga Tantra, two separate sequences of *mudrā* are employed, one for the stage of generation, the other for the stage of completion. These are discussed in chapter 36 of the Mother Tantra *Śrīcakrasaṃvara* and in Tsoṅ-kha-pa's commentary to this text, the *Sbas don*. For the stage of generation the sequence is as follows:

1. *Karmamudrā:* one imagines the external *prajñā* woman in the form of an attractive goddess.
2. *Dharmamudrā:* sacred seed syllables such as *hūṃ* are imagined in that body.
3. *Samayamudrā:* the radiation from the seed syllables is drawn back together in the circle of the completed *maṇḍala*.
4. *Mahāmudrā:* one imagines oneself as having the body of the principal deity.

The version for the stage of completion reverses the position of the *samayamudrā* and the *mahāmudrā*, as shown in table 5.

Particularly worthy of note in conjunction with table 5 is the difference in the description of the *prajñā* woman in the stage of generation and in the stage of completion. In the former, the practitioner approaches

TABLE 5. *Correspondence of the Four Seals according to the Anuttarayoga Tantras*

MUDRĀ ("SEAL")	PATH	BUDDHA BODY
karmamudrā	The external *prajñā* woman, because by the four acts of courtship she confers joy.	*nirmāṇakāya*
dharmamudrā	The central channel *(avadhūtī)* and its inner *prajñā* woman	*dharmakāya*
mahāmudrā	The *bodhicitta* of great bliss *(mahāsukha)*, which is the fruit of those two *mudrās* (above)	*saṃbhogakāya*
samayamudrā	Manifestation of a variety of divine images	*mahāsukhakāya*, with *bodhicitta* of bliss-void

the *prajñā* woman only through his imagination, that is, he imagines that she is a goddess with radiating germ syllables in her body. He imagines drawing back the radiation into his own body as a *maṇḍala,* and finally imagines himself as the chief deity. In the stage of completion this woman can confer concrete joy in the four degrees of courtship previously mentioned in correlation with the four classes of Tantras (laughing, mutual gazing, holding hands, the two united). But there is also another *prajñā* woman, the one of the central channel (among the three said to be in the position of the spine). When the texts speak of a *prajñā* consort, which one is intended? Nā-ro-pa has some important information about this in his commentary on the *Hevajra Tantra.* He cites a verse from the *Mañjuśrī-nāma-saṃgīti* (10.14) referring to the four *mudrās*, and gives their order in agreement with the stage of completion described above, substituting *jñānamudrā* for *dharmamudrā.* He then makes this revealing statement:

> The *karmamudrā* [i.e., the external woman] is the causal one, being initial, from which there is the together-born [*sahaja*] non-transiting joy. While this is indeed a truth [*satya*], there are two truths [conventional and ultimate], and [the *prajñā* woman of the *karmamudrā*] is true in a conventional sense, like a reflection in a mirror, but is not true in the absolute sense. Thus, one of keen intelligence should not embrace the *karmamudrā.* One should cultivate the *jñānamudrā* by such means as purifying the personal aggregates [*skandhas*], elements [*dhātus*], and sense bases [*āyatanas*] into images of deities, as the ritual of the *maṇḍala* reveals. By working them with continual friction one ignites the fire of wisdom [*jñāna*]. What is to be attained is the Great Seal [*mahāmudra*]. How is it attained? Through that fire when the *haṃ* syllable is burnt [as is stated in the final verse of chapter 1 of the *Hevajra Tantra*]. The Great Seal is like a dream, a hallucination, and the nature of mind. One should embrace this [the Great Seal] until one realizes directly the Symbolic Seal [*samayamudrā*], which is not a perishing thing.
>
> (*Vajrapada-sāra-saṃgraha-pañjikā,* Peking Tanjur, Jpn. photo ed., vol. 54, p. 2-4-8 to 2-5-5)

Nā-ro-pa thus acknowledges that some male Tantrics (presumably laymen) resort to the concrete woman as both "initial" (mother) and "together" (wife) in this part of the stage of completion. But he goes on to insist that one of keen faculty, striving for the high goal, will skip this *mudrā* and go directly to the inner *prajñā* consort, the ignited "fire of wisdom" that brings on the Great Seal. Staying on this Great Seal, which introspects mental processes as a hallucination, one realizes directly the *samayamudrā,* the *mahāsukhakāya,* or "body of great bliss."

The above remarks should lend a more benign interpretation to the Tantras than has been the case in the past, when judgments such as "ghastly" were often passed on this literature. The style, of course, is quite unlike that of the older Buddhist scriptures.

Ritual in the Tantras. The *maṇḍala* rites of the *Guhyasamāja Tantra* cycle may be seen in outline form in the following sequence:

1. Rites of the Site: clearing the site; seizing (contemplatively) the site; elimination of the obstructing demons
2. Preparatory Acts: pitching the (initial) lines (in the *maṇḍala*) with chalk; preparing the flask (i.e., placement of the flask by the *maṇḍala*); beseeching the gods; preparation of the disciple
3. The Main Rite, beginning with *maṇḍala* construction: placement of the five colored threads (representing the five Buddhas); putting in the colors (in the colored areas of the *maṇḍala*); invitation of the gods (to take residence in the *maṇḍala*)
4. Initiations of the Flask: drawing the disciple into the *maṇḍala;* diadem initiation; diamond initiation; mirror initiation (=water initiation); name initiation; emblem initiation (=bell initiation)
5. Offerings: offerings to the gods; offerings to the guru
6. Permission and Drawing Together: conferral of permission on the disciple to invoke the deity; drawing together of the deities who are in the *maṇḍala*
7. Concluding Acts: release of the magic nail, that is, dismissal of the deities along with a burnt offering *(homa)*

In order to work, each of these rituals must be accompanied by an intense awareness, referred to as *samādhi,* that could also be termed *yoga.* By "working" is meant that at all times the performer maintains a connection with the divine, as is confirmed by the *mantra* "Samayas tvam" ("You are the symbol").

These rituals are replete with details that would take much space to set forth properly. A few details can be given about one that is especially interesting, the disciple's entrance into the *maṇḍala.* The first phase is divided into "entrance outside of the screen" and "entrance inside of the screen." While outside the screen, the disciple ties on a red or yellow blindfold. This is not removed until later in the ceremony, when the initiate receives a superintending deity by throwing a flower into the *maṇḍala,* after which it will be proper to view the complete *maṇḍala.* The preceptor tells the disciple to imagine in his heart a *vajra,* thereon a sun, and on this a black *hūṃ* syllable. He is then to imagine in his throat a lotus, thereon a sun, and on this a red *āḥ* syllable; and in his head a wheel, thereon a moon, and on this a white *oṃ* syllable. He should also imagine that rays from those syllables make his body full of light. The preceptor guides the disciple to the east gate of the *maṇḍala*. Now, in the phase inside the screen, the disciple recites *mantras*. He begins with the east gate, reciting to both the deity of the center and the deity of the east gate. The east gate deity is addressed in order to empower oneself; the south gate deity, to confer initiation on oneself; the west gate deity, to turn the wheel of the Dharma for oneself; and the north gate deity, to make the ritual acts effective. He also bows at each gate: for the east, he bows with all the limbs, the diamond palms (i.e., adamantine and thus unassailable by demons) advanced; for the south, he bows with the forehead, the palms joined at the heart; for the west, he bows with the mouth, the diamond palms joined at the top of the head; for the north, he touches the earth with the head, the diamond palms having been lowered from the top of the head and placed at the heart. Then at the east gate, the preceptor sets forth the pledge(s), contacting the disciple by taking his hand, or else by touching the disciple on the head with the *vajra*, and saying, "Today you may enter the family of all the Tathāgatas," in recognition of the fact that entrance into the *maṇḍala* makes one their progeny; and that having seen the *maṇḍala* means the deities are revealed to the initiate.

The disciple is not to disclose the rituals he has undergone to others who have not entered the *maṇḍala*. Dire consequences are threatened for violating the pledge; guarding it yields magical success. Among the pledges is one requiring that the initiate avoid the fourteen transgressions, especially the first one, disparaging one's master, and the seventh one, revealing the secrets to immature persons (that is, persons who have not been initiated). Both are transgressions of Dharma. After taking the pledge, the officiant goes through an imaginative process, the aim of which is to have the gnosis deity *(jñana-sattva)* descend from the sky into the disciple. It begins with the officiant imagining the disciple in voidness, then generating him into a Buddha from a germ syllable, and then going through a sequence of *sādhanas* (evocations) in which he imagines the disciple's body filled with light. The disciple is induced to circumambulate the *maṇḍala* carrying a *vajra* in his right hand and doing a dance. The second phase is entering, in the sense of viewing, the *maṇḍala*. Still wearing the blindfold, the disciple is directed to throw a flower onto an area with five pictures representing Buddha families. The throwing of the flower constitutes entrance into the *maṇḍala*. The deity on whom the flower then falls is the superintendent deity *(adhideva)* for the disciple. The preceptor imagines that the Diamond Being is opening the Diamond Eye of the disciple; the disciple performs the same act of imagination and removes the blindfold, reciting the *mantra* "Oṃ jñānacaksuḥ Hūṃ Āḥ Svāhā," where *jñānacakṣuḥ* denotes the eye of knowledge. Then the preceptor says, "Now, by virtue of faith, may you see the reality of this *maṇḍala!* May you be born in the family of the Buddha, be empowered by *mudrā* and *mantra*, be endowed with all *siddhis* (magical success), be the best pledge *(samaya)!* May you realize the *mantras* with the sport of the *vajra* and lotus!" Thus the disciple is given the "initiation of the flower wreath," a process that establishes whether the disciple should receive other initiations. When it is the case of conferring permission on the disciple to evoke a particular deity, a different procedure is followed. Such evocations are undertaken after examining dreams and other omens.

The burnt offering is among the concluding acts of the ritual. There are four kinds of burnt offering, each corresponding to a different type of magical art: the worldly aims of appeasing the deities *(śāntika)*, winning material prosperity *(pauṣṭika)*, subduing demons *(vaśīkaraṇa)*, and overpowering enemies *(abhicāruka)*.

Judging from these various indications, one may conclude that Buddhist esotericism has considerable appeal to Buddhists who find fulfillment in ritual participation, who prefer a secret life that is religiously motivated, and who believe that by exercising all avenues of one's being (body, speech, and mind) one is speeding up the progress to enlightenment. The performer must be strong in imagination of images and in belief, and resolute in daily service to the presiding or tutelary deity.

[*For the place of Esoteric Buddhism within the larger Tibetan context, see* Buddhism, *article on* Buddhism in Tibet. *The Tantric lineages of Tibet are discussed in* Mahāsiddhas. *Tantric literature is treated in* Buddhist Literature, *article on* Survey of Texts. *For Esoteric Buddhism in China, see* Chen-yen, *and in Japan, see* Shingonshū.]

BIBLIOGRAPHY

Bhattacharyya, Benoytosh. *The Indian Buddhist Iconography.* 2d ed., rev. & enl. Calcutta, 1958.

Chou, Yi-liang. "Tantrism in China." *Harvard Journal of Asiatic Studies* 8 (March 1945): 241–332.

Eliade, Mircea. "Yoga and Tantrism." In his *Yoga: Immortality and Freedom*, pp. 200–273. New York, 1958.

Evans-Wentz, W. Y. *Tibetan Yoga and Secret Doctrines.* 2d ed. London, 1967.

First Panchen Lama. *The Great Seal of Voidness.* Prepared by the Translation Bureau of the Library of Tibetan Works and Archives. Dharamsala, 1976.

George, Christopher S., ed. and trans. *The Caṇḍamahāroṣaṇa Tantra, Chapters 1–8.* American Oriental Series, vol. 56. New Haven, 1974. In English and Sanskrit.

Guenther, Herbert V., ed. and trans. *The Life and Teachings of Nāropa.* Oxford, 1963.

Guenther, Herbert V., ed. and trans. *Yuganaddha: The Tantric View of Life.* Chowkhamba Sanskrit Studies, vol. 3. 2d rev. ed. Varanasi, 1969.

Hakeda, Yoshito S., ed. and trans. *Kūkai: Major Works.* New York, 1972. With an account of his life and study of his thought.

Kvaerne, Per. "On the Concepts of Sahaja in Indian Buddhist Tantric Literature." *Temenos* (Helsinki) 11 (1975): 88–135.

Kvaerne, Per. *An Anthology of Buddhist Tantric Songs.* New York, 1977.

Lessing, Ferdinand D. *Yung-ho-kung: An Iconography of the Lamaist Cathedral in Peking.* Stockholm, 1942.

Lessing, Ferdinand D. and Alex Wayman, eds. and trans. *Fundamentals of the Buddhist Tantras.* Indo-Iranian Monographs, vol. 8. The Hague, 1968. A translation of Mkhas-grub-rje's *Rgyud sde spyi'i rnam par bźag pa rgyas par bśad pa.*

Snellgrove, David L., ed. and trans. *The Hevajra Tantra: A Critical Study.* 2 vols. London Oriental Series, vol. 6. London, 1959.

Tajima, Ryūjun. *Étude sur le Mahāvairocana-sūtra.* Paris, 1936.

Tajima, Ryūjun. *Les deux grands maṇḍalas et la doctrine de l'esoterisme Shingon.* Paris, 1959.

Tsuda, Shin'ichi. *The Saṁvarodaya-tantra: Selected Chapters.* Tokyo, 1974.

Tsuda, Shin'ichi. "A Critical Tantrism." *Memoirs of the Research Department of the Tōyō Bunkō* 36 (1978): 167–231.

Tucci, Giuseppe. "The Religious Ideas: Vajrayāna." In *Tibetan Painted Scrolls,* vol. 1, pp. 209–249. Translated by Virginia Vacca. Rome, 1949.

Wayman, Alex. *The Buddhist Tantras: Light on Indo-Tibetan Esotericism.* New York, 1973.

Wayman, Alex. "The Ritual in Tantric Buddhism of the Disciple's Entrance into the Maṇḍala." *Studia Missionalia* 23 (1974): 41–57.

Wayman, Alex. *Yoga of the Guhyasamājatantra: The Arcane Lore of Forty Verses.* Delhi, 1977.

Wayman, Alex. "Reflections on the Theory of Barabuḍur as a Maṇḍala." In *Barabuḍur: History and Significance of a Buddhist Monument,* edited by Hiram W. Woodward, pp. 139–172. Berkeley, 1981.

Wayman, Alex. "The Title and Textual Affiliation of the Guhyagarbhatantra." In *Daijō Bukkyō kara Mikkyō e* [From Mahāyāna Buddhism to Tantra: Honorary Volume for Dr. Katsumata Shunkyō], pp. 1320–1334 (Japanese order), pp. 1–15 (English order). Tokyo, 1981.

Wayman, Alex, ed. and trans. *Chanting the Names of Mañjuśrī: The Mañjuśrī-nāma-saṁgīti (Sanskrit and Tibetan Texts).* Boston, 1985.

Alex Wayman

Chinese Buddhism

In any discussion of the schools of Chinese Buddhism it is important to bear in mind that the widely used English term *school* is simply the conventional translation of the Chinese word *tsung.* As we shall see, the practice of equating *school* and *tsung* has resulted in some persistent misconceptions about what actually constitutes a school in Chinese Buddhism. The root of the problem lies in the word *tsung,* for which dictionaries list as many as twenty-three separate definitions. In Buddhist texts, however, it is used primarily in three different senses: (1) it may indicate a specific doctrine or thesis, or a particular interpretation of a doctrine; (2) it may refer to the underlying theme, message, or teaching of a text; and (3) it may signify a religious or philosophical school.

Tsung as Doctrine. *Tsung* in the sense of doctrine or thesis is frequently encountered in fifth-century texts in such phrases as *k'ai-tsung,* "to explain the [basic] thesis," or *hsü-tsung,* "the doctrine of emptiness." Especially common was the use of the term *tsung* to categorize doctrinal interpretations of theses enumerated in a series. In the 470s, for example, the monk T'an-chi wrote the *Ch'i-tsung lun* (Essays on the Seven Interpretations), which presented the views of seven different monks on the meaning of nonsubstantiality as found in the *Po-jo ching* (*Prajñāpāramitā Sūtra;* Sutra on the Perfection of Wisdom). A few years later the renowned Buddhist lay scholar Chou Yung wrote an influential tract entitled *San-tsung lun* (Essays on the Three Theses), which examined the complementary Buddhist concepts of absolute truth and empirical truth from three perspectives. In neither case should *tsung* be understood as denoting an institutionalized school.

The term *tsung* was also used to designate the major categories of Buddhist doctrines, particularly when they were arranged in a scheme commonly known as *p'an-chiao* (classification of teachings), in which the doctrines were ranked in relation to each other. Although there were classifications that reduced the Buddhist teachings to two, three, four, five, six, and ten types of doctrine *(tsung),* the most influential were the four-doctrine classification devised by Hui-kuang (468–537) and the ten-doctrine classification established by Fa-tsang (643–712). Hui-kuang divided the Buddhist teachings into four essential doctrines *(tsung),* none of which refers to an institutionalized Buddhist school: (1) the doctrine that phenomena arise in accordance with preexisting causes and conditions *(yin-yüan tsung),* the basic teaching of the Abhidharma, advanced in refutation of the non-Buddhist view of spontaneous production; (2) the doctrine of the *Ch'eng-shih lun* that phenomena were no more than empirical names *(chia-ming tsung)* insofar as they could not exist independently of the causes and conditions that produced them; (3) the doctrine proclaimed in the *Po-jo ching* and the *San-lun* (Three Treatises) that even empirical names are deceptive *(k'uang-hsiang tsung)* insofar as there are no real or substantial phenomena underlying them; and (4) the doctrine taught in the *Nieh-p'an ching (Mahāparinirvāṇa Sūtra), Hua-yen ching* (*Avataṃsaka Sūtra;* Flower Garland Sutra), and other such *sūtras* that the Buddha nature is ever abiding *(ch'ang tsung)* and constitutes the ultimate reality.

The doctrinal classification devised by Fa-tsang was far more ambitious in that it delineated ten types of Buddhist doctrines *(tsung),* of which the first six corresponded to the teachings of specific schools of Indian Hīnayāna. Of the remaining four types of doctrines, each of which represented a different variety of Mahāyāna teaching, only the last, the Hua-yen, can be identified with a specific school of Chinese Buddhism. [*See the biography of Fa-tsang.*]

The Emergence of the Exegetical Traditions. The arrival of the translator Kumārajīva (d. 409) in Ch'ang-an from Kucha in 401 marked a turning point in the development of Chinese Buddhism. [*See the biography of Kumārajīva.*] Well versed in Chinese and Indic languages, Kumārajīva created an extensive terminology that made it possible to transmit Buddhist ideas with a degree of accuracy and clarity that had not been achieved by his predecessors, who had often used Taoist terms to express Buddhist concepts. But Kumārajīva's contribution to the development of Chinese Buddhism was not simply that of a translator. He involved large numbers of native Chinese monks in the translation process, generally lecturing on the text he was translating before audiences numbering in the hundreds or even thousands. His leading disciples wrote prefaces or postfaces for the newly translated texts or produced commentaries on them. It was around these disciples that the first exegetical traditions developed.

The approximately thirty-five texts selected for translation by Kumārajīva belong to the three major categories of Chinese Buddhist scriptural writings: Sūtra (purported discourses of the Buddha), Vinaya (the disciplinary codes covering the clergy), and scholastic discourses, which include both treatises and commentaries on the *sūtras*. Although not all the texts translated by Kumārajīva were of equal importance or had equal appeal, a surprisingly large number came to be regarded as basic scriptures of East Asian Buddhism. Of the ten texts most commonly studied during the fifth century in South China, seven had been translated by Kumārajīva. These included four *sūtras*, *Fa-hua ching* (*Saddharmapuṇḍarīka;* Lotus of the Good Law), *Wei-mo ching* (*Vimalakīrtinirdeśa;* Teaching of Vimalakīrti), *Po-jo ching* (in two versions), and *Shih-chu ching* (*Daśabhūmika;* Ten Stages [of the Bodhisattva]); the recension of the Vinaya called in Chinese *Shih-sung lü,* which was used by the Sarvāstivāda school; and two works belonging to the category of scholastic discourses, *Ch'eng-shih lun* (Treatise on the Perfection of Truth) and *San-lun* (Three Treatises), which, as the name indicates, actually refers to three distinct, but closely related treatises that are usually studied together. The three other major texts studied in South China during the fifth century were the *Nieh-p'an ching,* translated by Dharmakṣema in 421, the *Tsa o-p'i-t'an hsin lun* (Treatise on the Essence of the Abhidharma; popularly referred to as *P'i-t'an*), translated by Saṃghavarman around 435, and the *Sheng-man ching* (*Śrīmālāsiṃhanāda Sūtra;* Sutra on the Lion's Roar of Śrīmālā), translated by Guṇabhadra in 436.

Dynastic wars in the 420s and 430s, followed by a harsh suppression of the Buddhist religion in the 440s, led to a precipitous decline in Buddhist scholarship in the North during much of the fifth century. When the traditional scholarly activities of the clergy—lecturing on scripture and writing commentaries—were finally resumed in the North in the last decades of the fifth century, monks for the most part focused their attention on texts that were different from those that were the mainstays of southern Buddhism. Although northern monks of the sixth century did occasionally lecture on the texts popular in the South (the *Nieh-p'an ching* is a conspicuous example), their main focus was on texts that had either been ignored in the South or were newly translated. In the former category were the *Hua-yen ching,* translated by Buddhabhadra in 420, the *P'u-sa-ti-ch'ih ching* (*Bodhisattvabhūmi Sūtra,* Sutra on the Bodhisattva Stages), translated by Dharmakṣema in 418, and the *Ssu-fen lü* (Four Part Disciplinary Code), the Vinaya recension used by the Dharmaguptaka school of Indian Hīnayāna.

Of the many new translations appearing in the North during the first half of the sixth century, the one that excited the most interest was the *Shih-ti ching lun* (Commentary on the Sutra of the Ten Stages; commonly called *Ti-lun*), translated by Bodhiruci and others in 511. Similarly, two new translations caught the attention of learned monks in South China in the second half of the sixth century: the *She ta-sheng lun* (*Mahāyānasaṃgraha,* Compendium of Mahāyāna; commonly called *She-lun*) and the *O-p'i-ta-mo chü-she shih lun* (*Abhidharmakośa,* Treasury of the Abhidharma), both translated by Paramārtha in 563. Finally, to complete the list of the major scriptural texts of Chinese Buddhism used during the fifth and sixth centuries, mention should be made of the *Ta chih-tu lun* (Commentary of the Sutra on the Perfection of Wisdom; popularly called *Ta-lun*), translated by Kumārajīva in 405. This work was largely ignored until the second half of the sixth century, when its study was taken up by scholars in the San-lun tradition.

Unlike most monks of the fourth century, who tended to interpret Buddhism through Taoist concepts, the learned clergy of the fifth and sixth centuries were aware that Buddhism and Taoism were two distinct systems that differed fundamentally from each other and hence sought to understand Buddhism on its own terms. Although monks during this period were generally well versed in a number of scriptures, there was a growing tendency to specialize in a specific text, which was often viewed as representing the highest teaching within Buddhism. We might cite as typical examples of such monks Pao-liang (444–509), who during the course of his life is said to have lectured on the *Nieh-p'an ching* eighty-four times, the *Sheng-man ching* twenty-four times, the *Wei-mo ching* twenty times, the *Ch'eng-shih lun* fourteen times, and the *Po-jo ching* ten times, and Chih-tsang (458–522), who lectured and commented on the *Po-jo ching, Nieh-p'an ching, Fa-hua ching, Shih-ti ching,* and *P'i-t'an,* among others. Yet despite their familiarity with such a broad range of scripture, each was recognized by his contemporaries as being a specialist in a particular text: for Pao-liang it was the *Nieh-p'an ching;* for Chih-tsang, the *Ch'eng-shih lun.*

Tsung as the Underlying Theme of a Text. When commenting on a particular text, the exegetical scholars of the fifth and sixth centuries were of course interested in the definition of terms and the explanation of difficult passages. But their principal concern was to identify and expound the text's *tsung,* that is, its underlying theme or essential doctrine. Scholars who devoted themselves to the comparative study of the Sūtra literature as well as those who became expert in a single *sūtra* were known by the broad designation *ching-shih* ("*sūtra* masters"), whereas monks specializing in a particular treatise were generally referred to by the name of the treatise that they expounded. Thus, an exponent of the *Ch'eng-shih lun* was called a *Ch'eng-shih shih* (*Ch'eng-shih* master); an exponent of the *Ti-lun* became a *Ti-lun shih* (*Ti-lun* master). In addition to these two types of treatise masters, we also find references to *San-lun shih* (or *Chung-lun shih,* the *Chung-lun* being the most important treatise of the *San-lun* group), *P'i-t'an shih, She-lun shih,* and *Ta-lun shih.* Since the *Ta-lun,* which attracted scholarly attention only in the latter half of the sixth century, was closely related in doctrine to the *San-lun,* we can speak of five basic exegetical traditions centered on the treatise literature, those of the *Ch'eng-shih lun, Ti-lun, San-lun, Pi-t'an,* and *She-lun.*

It is highly questionable whether these exegetical traditions can properly be termed "schools" as is done in much of the contemporary scholarly writing on Chinese Buddhism. That the *Nieh-p'an ching,* the two recensions of the Vinaya, and the five treatises (or groups of treatises) mentioned above were studied intensively by several generations of scholars and had their staunch partisans cannot be disputed. But a school, as we shall explain below, implies something more than a group of scholars who study a particular text, even if they exalt that text above all others. While we do encounter in fifth- and sixth-century primary sources occasional references to *Ch'eng-shih tsung, Nieh-p'an tsung, P'i-t'an tsung,* and others, a careful reading of these sources shows that the term *tsung* when following the title of a text does not mean "school," as it has often been mechanically interpreted, but rather the "underlying theme" or "essential doctrine" of the text in question.

Although it is misleading to refer to the various exegetical traditions as schools, it is clear that by the end of the sixth century "study groups" *(chung)* specializing in particular texts were accorded formal recognition by the government. We note, for example, that in the years 596 and 597 Emperor Wen of the Sui dynasty appointed eminent monks to head the *Ti-lun, Vinaya, Ta-lun, Nieh-p'an* and *Treatise* (i.e., the *Ta-lun*) study groups at the Ta-hsing-shan Ssu, the main state temple in Ch'ang-an.

Tsung as a Full-fledged School. The term *tsung* should be translated "school" only when it refers to a tradition that traces its origin back to a founder, usually designated "first patriarch," who is believed to have provided the basic spiritual insights that were then transmitted through a unbroken line of successors or "*dharma* heirs". This definition is derived from the original meaning of *tsung,* which signified a clan that was descended from a common ancestor. Although later patriarchs often expanded the insights of the founder in response to new challenges from rival traditions, they viewed themselves essentially as guardians of an exclusive orthodoxy to which no other tradition could lay claim. Competing traditions were thought to have only varying degrees of validity compared to one's own school–hence the need to engage in *p'an-chiao,* the relative ranking of the different teachings within Buddhism.

Judged by these criteria, none of the exegetical traditions of the fifth and sixth centuries, with the possible exception of the San-lun tradition, can be regarded as a school in the proper sense of the word. Although the *Nieh-p'an, P'i-t'an, Ch'eng-shih, Ti-lun, She-lun,* and the two recensions of the Vinaya were studied by generations of scholars, no founder's name is associated with any of these traditions, nor were these traditions transmitted through an exclusive lineage. A careful examination of the master-disciple lineages that have been reconstructed for the fifth and sixth centuries reveals that there was no consistent transmission of specific interpretations of texts, nor indeed was the disciple necessarily expected to specialize in the same text as his master.

San-lun stands midway between the exegetical traditions of the sixth century and the full-fledged schools of the T'ang dynasty (618-907). The notion that the San-lun tradition constituted an orthodox transmission that passed through a clearly defined lineage seems to have been first espoused by Chi-tsang (549–623), its *de facto* systematizer, who repeatedly cited the "succession on Mount She" *(She-ling hsiang-ch'eng)* as the source of his authority. [*See the biography of Chi-tsang.*] According to Chi-tsang, the San-lun teaching was transmitted from India to China by Kumārajīva, whose Chinese spiritual heir, Seng-lang, settled in the Ch'i-hsia Monastery on Mount She in Kiangsu Province. From Seng-lang the San-lun *dharma* was passed in an unbroken line to Chi-tsang, who was the third generation successor to Seng-lang. It is difficult, however, to view San-lun as a genuine school because the lineage to which Chi-tsang belonged became extinct around 650 with the death of Yüan-k'ang, his successor in the second generation. If the San-lun is to be considered a school, it is one that barely survived its founder.

It is only in the eighth century that we encounter full-fledged schools with founders, lineages, supposedly orthodox transmissions of doctrine, and large numbers of followers. Three such schools made their appearance during the second half of the T'ang dynasty: Ch'an, T'ien-t'ai, and Hua-yen. The early history of Ch'an is too complex to be dealt with here; I shall simply mention that by the late eighth century there were five or six competing Ch'an lineages, almost all claiming descent through a mutually recognized line of patriarchs. The pivotal position in this line of patriarchal descent was held by Bodhidharma, a semilegendary figure who was believed by Ch'an Buddhists to be the twenty-eighth, and last, patriarch of Indian Buddhism in a line that extended back to Śākyamuni Buddha himself. By proclaiming in China the "true law," the Ch'an teaching, to which he alone was the rightful heir, Bodhidharma became the first patriarch of Chinese Ch'an and the ultimate source of legitimacy. It is of little consequence that the historical reality concerning the origins of Ch'an in China are at variance with the Bodhidharma legend; what matters is the perception that all Ch'an orthodoxy must pass through Bodhidharma. [*See the biography of Bodhidharma.*]

Historical evidence indicates that the first true Ch'an monastic community was the one founded by Tao-hsin (580–651), who in later Ch'an legend was counted as the fourth patriarch in a direct line from Bodhidharma. Moreover, the designation *Ch'an-tsung* ("Ch'an school") was not in fact used until the ninth century, when it replaced the earlier designations *Tung-shan tsung* ("East Mountain school") and *Tung-shan fa-men* ("East Mountain doctrine") Tung-shan being the site of Tao-hsin's monastic establishment in Hupei.

A similar discrepancy between legend and fact is also found in T'ien-t'ai. The *de facto* founder and systematizer of this school, Chih-i (538–597), did not see himself as the creator of a new tradition but rather as the inheritor of a doctrine that had been transmitted through a lineage that extended from Śākyamuni Buddha to Nāgārjuna in an unbroken succession of Indian masters. [*See the biography of Chih-i.*] Chih-i believed that the Chinese spiritual heir of Nāgārjuna was the relatively obscure monk Hui-wen, whose disciple, Hui-ssu, had been Chih-i's teacher. Believing that his teachings were an outgrowth of this transmission and nothing less than *the* true Buddhism, Chih-i did not give a specific name to the elaborate doctrinal system that he fashioned.

The designation *T'ien-t'ai tsung* ("T'ien-t'ai school") was first used by Chan-jan (711–782), a successor to Chih-i in the fifth generation, who wrote lengthy commentaries on Chih-i's major works. Active in the latter half of the eighth century, when other schools of Buddhism, notably Ch'an and Hua-yen, had already appeared, Chan-jan was forced to take note of their doctrines, particularly when they were in conflict with the position of T'ien-t'ai. He asserted the superiority of his own school over the rival Ch'an, arguing that the T'ien-t'ai lineage counted the eminent scholiast, Nāgārjuna as its first patriarch, whereas the first patriarch of Ch'an, Bodhidharma, was merely one of many Indian masters who settled in China.

The third major school of Chinese Buddhism to appear under the T'ang dynasty was the Hua-yen, which, according to traditional accounts, was founded by Fa-shun (557–640). In fact, however, as in the case of the T'ien-t'ai school, its real founder/systematizer was not the so-called first patriarch but the monk who was subsequently designated third patriarach, Fa-tsang (643–712). Like his T'ien-t'ai counterpart, Fa-tsang did not apply a sectarian name to the elaborate doctrinal system that he formulated, although he was keenly conscious of his spiritual debt to his predecessors in the study of the *Hua-yen ching*. The designation *Hua-yen-tsung* ("Hua-yen school") occurs for the first time in the writings of Fa-tsang's third generation disciple Ch'eng-kuan (738–839). The orthodox Hua-yen lineage was, in turn, fixed by Ch'eng-kuan's disciple Tsung-mi (780–841), who drew up a list of patriarchs in which Fa-tsang figured as the third. Later Hua-yen sources designated

Ch'eng-kuan and Tsung-mi the fourth and fifth patriarchs respectively.

Buddhist Schools as Reflected in the Sung Chronicles. The frequent polemics in the eleventh century between Ch'an and T'ien-t'ai, in which each side attacked the legitimacy of the other's lineage, led scholars of these two schools to produce chronicles that sought to establish the validity of their own traditions. The two surviving T'ien-t'ai chronicles from the Sung dynasty (960–1279), the *Shih-men cheng-t'ung* (1237) and the encyclopedic *Fo-tsu t'ung-chi* (1269), offer us valuable information regarding how the schools of Buddhism were actually viewed in the thirteenth century.

Both works recognized five schools under the heading *tsung:* Ch'an, Hua-yen, Tz'u-en, Mi (or Yü-ch'ieh Mi), and Lü (or Nan-shan Lü). In addition, the two chronicles also provided a lengthy account of the T'ien-t'ai lineage, which, however, was not included among the *tsung* but followed immediately after the biography of Śākyamuni Buddha, thus showing that T'ien-t'ai was not merely one among several schools but rather a unique lineage that stemmed from the Buddha himself.

Whether the Tz'u-en, Mi, and Lü actually constituted full-fledged schools during the T'ang period is open to question. Tz'u-en (commonly called Fa-hsiang in modern times after its Japanese counterpart, Hossō) was an important doctrinal system based on Hsüan-tsang's translations of Yogācāra texts and the commentaries and treatises on these by his disciple Chi (632–682), later known as K'uei-chi or Tz'u-en (hence the name of this doctrinal system. [*See the biography of K'uei-chi.*] The Yogācāra teachings transmitted by Hsüan-tsang and systematized by Chi were intensively studied during the eighth and ninth centuries and exerted some influence on the development of T'ien-t'ai and Hua-yen thought. Nevertheless, these teachings did not evolve into a truly independent school because their premise that enlightenment was reserved for a predestined elite ran counter to the ideals of Chinese Buddhism. It is not surprising, therefore, that the Sung chronicles listed only two Chinese "patriarchs": the translator Hsüan-tsang and his disciple Chi. Unlike T'ien-t'ai, Hua-yen, and Nan-shan Lü, which all had their eminent exponents in the Sung and later periods, the Tz'u-en teachings were virtually ignored until the twentieth century, when its long lost treatises and commentaries were retrieved from Japan.

Equally dubious is the classification of the Mi (Esoteric) teaching as a school. The *Fo-tsu t'ung-chi* lists three patriarchs, but two of these, Vajrabodhi (671–741) and Amoghavajra (705–774), are simply translators of Esoteric (i.e., Vajrayāna) texts. The third, Hui-lang, who was a disciple of Amoghavajra, had already become a totally obscure figure by the time the *Fo-tsu t'ung-chi* was compiled. Virtually nothing is known about him, nor do any of his writings survive. Although a large number of Vajrayāna texts were translated into Chinese and many Esoteric practices eventually incorporated into Chinese Buddhist ritual, no attempt was made in China to develop a comprehensive system of Esoteric Buddhism, as had been done in Japan.

The Nan-shan Lü school has its origins in the exegetical traditions of the fifth and sixth centuries that focused on two Chinese recensions of the Vinaya, the *Shih-sung lü* and the *Ssu-fen lü.* By the beginning of the T'ang dynasty the *Ssu-fen lü* had effectively displaced the *Shih-sung lü,* gaining universal acceptance by the clergy, which recognized it as the supreme authority in ecclesiastical matters. Of the three outstanding seventh century scholars who wrote commentaries on the *Ssu-fen lü,* the most influential was Tao-hsüan (596–667), also known by his sobriquet Nan-shan, who, in addition to being the author of what are now regarded as the definitive treatises and commentaries on the *Ssu-fen lü,* was also a church historian and bibliographer of the first rank.

Although Tao-hsüan was the systematizer of the *Ssu-fen lü* tradition, he did not regard himself as the founder of a new school. This role was assigned to him by his successor in the fourteenth generation, Yüan-chao (1048–1116), who was the leading *Ssu-fen lü* scholar of the Sung period and the author of numerous commentaries on Tao-hsüan's major writings. While it is doubtful that a Nan-shan Lü school existed under the T'ang dynasty in any meaningful sense, it is clear that such a school had taken shape in Sung times. The *Fo-tsu t'ung-chi,* in its account of the Nan-shan Lü, counts Tao-hsüan as the ninth patriarch in a lineage that begins in India with Dharmagupta, the reputed compiler of the *Ssu-fen lü.* The Nan-shan Lü lineage has been perpetuated down to our own day by the monks who staff the large monasteries where most ordinations are conducted.

It is important to note that neither of the Sung dynasty chronicles cited above included Pure Land among the Buddhist schools. Although an entire section of the *Fo-tsu t'ung-chi* consists of biographies of Pure Land devotees, the Pure Land faith was not recognized as a distinct school; rather, it was considered a type of devotional practice that pervaded all segments of the Buddhist community. The *Fo-tsu t'ung-chi* lists among its devotees patriarchs of the various schools, eminent monks and nuns, members of Pure Land societies *(she),* and devout laymen and laywomen.

Buddhist Schools in Modern China. Although a number of independent schools arose under the T'ang dynasty, occasionally quarreling with each other about points of doctrine or wrangling over the legitimacy of their respective lineages, it should be remembered that some monks sought to reconcile the seeming differences between the schools in the hope of preserving what they considered to be the essential unity of Buddhism. Since a monk often studied with several masters, each belonging to a different school, it was not uncommon for a single monk to appear in lineages of different schools. Just as the independent sectarian lineages of the T'ang dynasty tended to crisscross under the Sung, so too were many of the finer points of doctrine lost on monks of later periods because of the interruption of oral transmissions and the destruction of much of the commentarial literature in the wars that attended the collapse of the T'ang. Although T'ien-t'ai, Hua-yen, and to a lesser extent Fa-hsiang, have survived into the modern period as doctrinal systems *(fa-men)*, they no longer command the exclusive allegiance of groups of monks nor maintain even a fictive lineage that goes back to T'ang or even Sung times. By the Ming period (1368–1644) the pre-eminence of Ch'an had been so firmly established that almost the entire Buddhist clergy were affiliated with either its Lin-chi or Ts'ao-tung lineages, both of which claimed descent from Bodhidharma.

It has been customary since the Sung dynasty to divide Buddhism into three major traditions (*men*, "gateways"): lineal traditions *(tsung-men)*, doctrinal traditions *(chiao-men)*, and the disciplinary tradition *(lü-men)*. The term *lineal traditions* refers to the two previously mentioned Ch'an lineages that have come down to the present. Virtually every monk in China today belongs to one of these two lineages. A monk's formal affiliation with a lineage is established when he is tonsured and granted a religious name by his master at the latter's temple. The designation *doctrinal traditions* is applied to the T'ien-t'ai, Hua-yen, Fa-hsiang, and other formal systems of Buddhist thought, any one (or several) of which would be studied by a monk with scholarly interests, regardless of his lineal school affiliation. The teacher who instructs a monk in a particular doctrinal system is usually different from the master who tonsured or ordained him. *Disciplinary school* is another name for the Nan-shan Lü school, to whose lineage belong the monks who carry out most ordinations. Thus, the present-day Chinese monk typically will belong to a Ch'an lineage *(tsung-men)*, will probably have studied in some detail a particular doctrinal system *(chiao-men)*, and will have been ordained by a master who stands in the lineage of one of the branches of the Nan-shan Lü school *(lü-men)*. In addition, his daily devotions are likely to be derived from the Pure Land teaching.

[*For discussion of some of the traditions discussed in this article, see* T'ien-t'ai; Hua-yen; Chen-yen; *and* Ch'an. *San-lun and Fa-hsiang doctrines are treated in* Mādhyamika *and* Yogācāra, *respectively.*]

BIBLIOGRAPHY

The single most important study of the concept of school in Chinese Buddhism is T'ang Yung-t'ung's "Lun Chung-kuo fo-chiao wu shih tsung," *Hsien-tai fo-hsüeh* 4 (1962): 15-23. Also of value, although in some ways superseded by the preceding study, is the same scholar's *Sui T'ang fo-chiao shih kao* (Peking), which was written in the late 1920s but not published until 1962. The treatment of the schools in post-T'ang Buddhist literature is surveyed in detail in Yamanouchi Shinkei's *Shina bukkyōshi no kenkyū* (Kyoto, 1921). For a comparative study of the rise of schools in India, China, and Japan, see Mano Shōjun's *Bukkyō ni okeru shū kannen no seiritsu* (Tokyo, 1964). Hirai Shun'ei's *Chūgoku hannya shisōshi kenkyū* (Tokyo, 1976) is primarily a study of the San-lun tradition, but it also contains a valuable discussion of the definition of school in Chinese Buddhism (pp. 25–57). A traditional account in English of the doctrines of the various schools is given in Takakusu Junjirō's *The Essentials of Buddhist Philosophy*, edited by Wing-tsit Chan and Charles A. Moore (Honolulu, 1947). The most reliable account of the role of schools in twentieth-century China is found in Holmes Welch's *The Practice of Chinese Buddhism, 1990–1950* (Cambridge, Mass. 1967).

STANLEY WEINSTEIN

Japanese Buddhism

Prior to its official introduction into the court in 552 CE, Buddhism had been brought to Japan by Chinese and Korean immigrants and was presumably practiced widely among their descendants. According to the *Nihongi*, an envoy of the king of Paekche presented Buddhist statues, *sūtras*, and other artifacts to the Japanese court in 552 (other sources give 538). The official introduction of Buddhism exacerbated the antagonism that had been developing between the internationalist Soga clan, which supported the court's recognition of Buddhism, and the more parochial clans, which considered the Buddha a *banshin* (foreign deity). To avoid further dissension, the court entrusted the administration of Buddhism to the Soga clan. The Buddhism promulgated by the Soga was primarily magical. However, aristocrats and court nobles were initially attracted to Buddhism as an intrinsic part of the highly advanced continental (i.e., Chinese and Korean) culture and civilization, which also encompassed Confucianism, Taoism, medicine, astronomy, and various technological skills. As it developed on the continent, Buddhism was not exclusively a religion, for it was also associated with a new, esoteric culture that included colorful paintings, statues, buildings, dance, and music.

Although Japanese understanding of Buddhism was superficial and fragmented in the early stages of assimilation, it gained religious depth through the course of history. The rise of Japanese Buddhism and the growth of schools or sects were closely related to and influenced by the structure of the state bureaucracy, which was itself in the initial stages of development. Yōmei (r. 585–587) was the first emperor officially to accept Buddhism, but it was his son, the prince regent Shōtoku (574–622), who was responsible for creating Japan's first great age of Buddhism. Although the sources provide very little precise information about his activities, Shōtoku is said to have been a great patron of Buddhism. In addition to building many Buddhist temples and sending students and monks to study in China, he wrote commentaries on three texts—the *Saddharmapuṇḍarīka* (Lotus) *Sūtra,* the *Vimalakīrti Sūtra,* and the *Śrīmala Sūtra*—and is supposed to have promulgated the famous "Seventeen-Article Constitution" based on Buddhist and Confucian ideas. Later, Shōtoku was worshiped as the incarnation of the *bodhisattva* Avalokiteśvara. His promotion of Buddhism fell strictly within the bounds of the existing religio-political framework of Japanese sacral kingship: he upheld the imperial throne as the central authority and envisioned a "multireligious system" in which Shintō, Confucianism, and Buddhism would maintain a proper balance under the divine authority of the emperor as the "son of Heaven." Shōtoku's religious policies, his indifference to the doctrinal and ecclesiastical divisions of Buddhism, his dependence on the universalistic soteriology of the *Lotus Sutra,* and his emphasis on the path of the lay devotee significantly influenced the later development of Japanese Buddhism. [*See the biography of Shōtoku Taishi.*]

Buddhism in the Nara Period. During the Nara period (710–784) the Ritsuryō state, based upon the principle of the mutual dependence of imperial law *(ōbō)* and Buddhist law *(buppō),* recognized Buddhism as a state religion and incorporated it into the bureaucratic system of the central government. Under these conditions Buddhism enjoyed royal favor, and temples and monks became wealthy. However, the state's sponsorship of Buddhism was not entirely altruistic. Throughout the Nara period the government was concerned with the political power held by the Buddhists. The state promoted Buddhism as a religion that could civilize, solidify, and protect the nation. Monks were encouraged to engage in the academic study of Buddhist texts, probably in the hope that they would settle in the government-controlled temples. These temples were presumably subordinate to the state and functioned as an intrinsic part of the state bureaucracy: priests were expected to perform rites and ceremonies to ensure the peace and order of the state, and monks and nuns were ordained under the state authority and thus were considered bureaucrats. The Ritsuryō government prohibited monks from concerning themselves with the needs and activities of the masses. However, those who were not granted official status as monks became associated with folk Buddhist activities. Movements of *ubasoku* (Skt., *upāsaka;* laymen), *hijiri* (holy men), and *yamabushi* (mountain ascetics) emerged spontaneously, integrating indigenous Shintō, Buddhist, and other religious and cultural elements. At the center of these movements were unordained magician-priests who lived in mountainous regions and who had acquired, through ascetic practices, shamanistic techniques and the art of healing. Later, these groups were to inspire powerful popular movements and would influence the development of Japanese Buddhism. [*See* Hijiri.]

Prior to the Nara period Buddhism had remained nonsectarian. However, as the study of texts and commentaries on the *sūtras* became more intense and sophisticated, groups of scholar-monks organized themselves into schools or sects. Here, the term "sect" *(shū)* does not refer to an organized school but, rather, to a philosophical position based on the various *sūtras.* Differences between the sects were based solely on the particular text chosen as the focus of study: the ecclesiastical, doctrinal, or religious orientations of the individual sects were not mutually exclusive. Often, these sects were housed in a single temple and, under the restrictions imposed by the Ritsuryō government, they remained dependent on both the state and each other.

Of the six most noteworthy sects of Nara Buddhism, two were affiliated with the Hīnayāna tradition and four with the Mahāyāna tradition. In the first category were the Kusha, based on Vasubandhu's *Abhidharmakośa* (Jpn., *Kusharon;* Treasury of Higher Law), and the Jōjitsu, based on Harivarman's *Satyasiddhi* (Jpn., *Jōjitsuron;* Completion of Truth). The Mahāyāna-affiliated sects included Sanron (Chin., *San-lun*), based on the *Mādhyamika Śāstra* (Jpn., *Chūron;* Treatise on the Middle Way) and on the *Dvādaśadvāra* (Jpn., *Jūnimon;* Treatise on Twelve Gates), both of which were written by Nāgārjūna, as well as on the *Śataśāstra* (Jpn., *Hyakuron;* One Hundred Verse Treatise), written by Āryadeva; the Hossō sect (Skt., Yogācāra), principally based on the *Vijñaptimātratāsiddhi* (Jpn., *Jōyushikiron;* Completion of Mere Ideation) by Dharmapāla; the Kegon sect, based on the *Avataṃsaka Sūtra* (Jpn., *Kegongyō;* Flower Garland Sutra); and the Ritsu sect (Vinaya), based on the so-called Southern Mountain tradition of Chinese Vinaya studies, represented chiefly by the work of Tao-hsüan (596–667). In the early years of the Nara, the most prominent and prestigious of these sects was the Hossō, which was transmitted by Dōshō, a Japanese monk who had studied in China. The prestige of the Hossō gradually waned, to be replaced by the Kegon sect under the leadership of Rōben. The Ritsu sect provided the codes and external formalities of monastic discipline. The remaining three sects represented, for the most part, academic and political alternatives to the more powerful temples. [*See also* Mādhyamika; Yogācāra; *and* Hua-yen.]

Schools of the Heian: Tendai and Shingon. The government's decision to move the capital from Nara to Kyoto was motivated in part by the need to regain the power held by the large, wealthy Buddhist temples. Toward the end of the Nara period, the effort to integrate Buddhism and temporal politics resulted in the accumulation of wealth and the acquisition of large tracts of private land by the Buddhist temples and the involvement in state politics by the more ambitious monks. This trend culminated in the so-called Dōkyō incident, which was, in effect, an attempt to make the religious authority of Buddhism supreme. Under the sponsorship of Empress Kōken (later, Shōtoku), Dōkyō, a monk in the Hossō sect, was promoted rapidly through the ranks of the state bureaucracy. In 766 Dōkyō was appointed "king of the Law" *(hō-ō),* and several years later he attempted to usurp the throne, an action that was quickly crushed by the court aristocracy. The government responded to this affair by once again affirming Buddhism's subordination to the state and enforcing traditional Buddhist discipline. Throughout the Heian period (794–1185), Buddhism continued to be promoted as the religion that would ensure the safety of the state *(chingo kokka).* The sects that arose in the Heian, however, were considerably different from the six Nara sects. Like their predecessors, the Heian sects depended on teachings recently brought back from China as a source of their religious authority. But rather than relying on Japanese and Chinese commentaries, as had their Nara counterparts, Heian-period monks began to focus their study on the actual *sūtras*, allegedly the words of the Buddha himself. In addition, the schools of the Heian were established by individuals who were considered de-facto "founders" of sectarian lineages. They also tended to be centered in the mountains, that is, at a symbolic distance from political authority, and had their own systems of ordination. The two most important schools of this period were Tendai (Chin., T'ien-t'ai) and Shingon (Chin., Chen-yen). Both stressed the importance of learning, meditation, and esoteric cults and mysteries. Most significantly, however, both schools attempted to establish a united center for Buddhism that would encompass all sects and unite Buddhism and the state.

Tendaishū. The founder of this sect, Saichō (767–822, also known by his posthumous title, Dengyō Daishi), was a descendant of Chinese immigrants. In his youth, Saichō was trained in the Hossō, Kegon, and Sanron traditions; at the age of nineteen he was ordained at Tōdaiji in Nara. Thereafter, he withdrew from the capital city and opened a hermitage on Mount Hiei. Here, he began to study the writings of Chih-i, the systemaizer of Chinese T'ien-t'ai. [*See* T'ien-t'ai *and the biography of Chih-i.*] During his travels in China, Saichō received the *bodhisattva* ordination *(bosatsukai)* from Tao-sui, was initiated into *mantra* practices *(mikkyō)* by Shun-hsiao, studied Zen (Chin., Ch'an) meditation under Hsiao-jan, and trained in the Chinese Vinaya traditions. Upon his return to Japan, Saichō established a Tendai school that synthesized these four traditions within the framework of the *Lotus Sutra.* Saichō adhered to the T'ien-t'ai doctrine that recognized universal salvation, that is, the existence of the absolute nature of Buddhahood in all beings, and stressed the meaning and value of the phenomenal world. These teachings stood in opposition to the standard philosophical position of the Nara schools, best represented by the Hossō doctrine that claimed that Buddhahood was accessible only to the religious elite.

Saichō's ecumenical approach won the approval of the court. With the death of his patron, Emperor Kammu, and the rise of Kūkai and the Shingon sect, Saichō's influence at court diminished. One of his dreams—that the court approve the establishment of an independent center for Tendai ordination—was granted only after Saichō's death. The Tendai sect continued to exercise a profound influence on Japanese Buddhist life for centuries after the death of its founder. Under Ennin (794–864), a disciple of Saichō, the full flowering of Tendai Esotericism (Taimitsu) took place. Ennin was also responsible for the transmission of the Nembutsu cult (i.e, the practice of invoking the name of Amida Buddha) from China. Enchin (814–891), another prominent Tendai monk, also propagated the Taimitsu tradition and was responsible for the formation of the so-called Jimon subsect of Tendai, a group that vied for ecclesiastical power with Ennin's Sanmon subsect. Additionally, many of the most prominent Buddhist figures of the Kamakura period studied at the Tendai monastic center on Mount Hiei, including Hōnen of the Pure Land sect, Shinran of True Pure Land, Eisai of Rinzai, Dōgen of Sōtō Zen, and Nichiren, whose school bears his name. Through them the Tendai legacy was firmly, if subtly, maintained in Japanese Buddhism. [*See also* Tendaishū *and the biographies of Saichō, Ennin, and Enchin.*]

Shingonshū. Kūkai (774–835, also known by his posthumous title, Kōbō Daishi), the founder of the Shingon school, was originally a student of Confucianism and hoped to enter government service. According to various legends, he experienced a compelling desire to leave the capital and live in the mountains, where, it is said, he trained with shamanistic Buddhist priests. He was inspired by the *Mahāvairocana Sūtra* (Jpn., *Dainichikyō;* Sutra of the Great Sun Buddha), which eventually led him to the tradition of Esoteric Buddhism (Vajrayāna). Between 804 and 806 he traveled in China, where he studied under Hui-kuo, the direct disciple of the Tantric master Amoghavajra. [*See the biography of Amoghavajra.*] On his return to Japan he began to promote Shingon (i.e., Tantric) doctrine. At this time he wrote the *Jūjūshinron* (Ten Stages of Religious Consciousness), in which he systematized the doctrines of Esoteric Buddhism and critically appraised the existing Buddhist teachings and literature. Under the patronage of Emperor Saga, Kūkai established a monastic center of Mount Kōya and was appointed abbot of Toji (Eastern Temple) in Kyoto, which was granted the title Kyōō Gokokuji (Temple for the Protection of the Nation). In return for these favors, Kūkai performed various rites for the court and aristocracy.

According to the Shingon teachings, all the doctrines of Śākyamuni, the historical, manifested Buddha, are temporal and relative. Absolute truth is personified in the figure of Mahāvairocana (Jpn., Dainichi), the Great Sun Buddha, through the "three secrets"—the body, speech, and thought—of the Buddha. To become a Buddha—that is, to bring one's own activities of body, speech, and thought into accord with those of Mahāvairocana—one depends on *mudrās* (devotional gestures), *dhāraṇī* (mystical verse), and *yoga* (concentration). The Shingon school developed a system rich in symbolism and ritual, employing *maṇḍala*s and icons to meet the needs of people on all levels of society. Like the Tendai sect, Shingon produced many outstanding monks in subsequent generations. [*See* Chen-yen, Shingonshū *and the biography of Kūkai.*]

Owing to the support of the court and aristocracy, the Esoteric Buddhism of Tendai (Taimitsu) and Shingon (also called Tōmitsu; "Eastern Esotericism," after its chief monastery, Tōji) prospered. While each school had its own principle of organization and its own doctrinal position, both sought the official authorization and support of the court. Therefore, as the power of the state declined, Tendai and Shingon evolved into religions associated solely with the elite, for whom they offered various magico-religious rites.

Buddhist Schools in the Kamakura Period. The decline of the Ritsuryō system and the rise of military feudalism brought many changes to the organization and practice of Buddhism, although the basic ideology of the Ritsuryō persisted until the Ōnin War (1467–1477). It has been argued that the new Buddhist schools that emerged in the Kamakura period (1185–1333) transformed Buddhism in Japan into Japanese Buddhism. Unlike the schools of the Nara and Heian, which identified the religious sphere with the national community, the schools of the Kamakura attempted to establish specifically religious societies. The earlier schools had never seriously questioned the soteriological dualism that divided the path of monks from that of the laity, nor had they developed an independent community governed by normative principles other than the precepts. In spite of its otherworldly beliefs, Buddhism, as practiced in Nara and Heian Japan, was a religion grounded firmly in this world. The founders of the new schools in the Kamakura period had all studied at the Tendai center on Mount Hiei but had become dissatisfied with the emphasis on ceremonies and dogma, the perceived corruption of monastic life, and the rigid transmission of ecclesiastical office. In their stead, these religious leaders stressed personal religious experience, simple piety, spiritual exercise, intuition, and charisma. In many respects the practices and doctrines of the new schools reflect the eschatological atmosphere that had emerged toward the end of the Heian, when the country had experienced a series of crises, including famine, epidemics, war, and a deadlock of economy and politics. This sense of apocalypse found its expression in the widespread belief in *mappō,* the notion that Buddhism and society as a whole had entered an era of irreversible decline, and in the resultant popularity of the cult of Amida, which offered a religious path expressly intended to provide for beings living during *mappō.* In one way or another, these popular beliefs were incorporated into the most representative schools of the Kamakura period—Jōdoshū (Pure Land school), Jōdo Shinshū (True Prue Land school), Nichirenshū, and the Rinzai and Sōtō schools of Zen. [*See* Mappō.]

Jōdoshū. Prior to Hōnen (1133–1212), the founder of the Jōdo sect, most Buddhist schools incorporated the belief in the Pure Land and the practice of Nembutsu as adjuncts to their other practices. It was only with Hōnen, however, that absolute faith in Amida (Skt., Amitābha) Buddha became a criterion for sectarian affiliation. [*See* Amitābha *and* Nien-fo.] Like many of his contemporaries, Hōnen had become disillusioned with his early training in the Nara and Tendai schools. He turned to the charismatic teachings of such masters as Eikū, who promoted the belief in *mappō* and the efficacy of the cult of Amida. Under their tutelage, Hōnen came to realize the impossibility of attaining salvation and sanctification through the practice of precepts, meditation, and knowledge. Instead, Hōnen held that one must seek the path to salvation in the Pure Land and the saving grace of Amida. In this, Hōnen was much influenced by Genshin's *Ōjōyōshū* (The Essentials of Rebirth, tenth century), a work that provides the theoretical basis for faith in the Pure Land. [*See the biography of Genshin.*] However, in his own work *Senchaku hongan nembutsushū* (Collection of Passages on the Original Vow in which Nembutsu Is Chosen Above All), Hōnen clearly departs from earlier forms of the cult of Amida. Here, Hōnen claims that one's salvation depends exclusively on one's "choice" (i.e., one's willingness) to place absolute faith in the salvific power of Amida Buddha. The community Hōnen established in the capital city was structured on the notions of egalitarianism and faith and, thus, was able to transcend the social distinctions of kinship and class. Such organizing principles made Hōnen's school a paradigm for the later development of Buddhism. [*See also* Jōdoshū *and the biography of Hōnen.*]

Jōdo Shinshū. Little is known of the formative influences in the life of Shinran (1173–1262), the founder of the Jōdo Shin school, except that he entered the Tendai monastery on Mount Hiei at the age of eight. When he was twenty-nine, Shinran met Hōnen, with whom he studied for six years. Shinran's notion of Amida Buddha's salvific power went far beyond that of his master. In holding that one's faith in Amida must be absolute, Shinran denied the efficacy of relying on one's own capacity to bring about redemption. His teachings went to the extreme of claiming that the recitation of the Nembutsu was an expression of gratitude to Amida rather than a cause of one's salvation. Shinran further stated that it is not man who "chooses" to have faith in Amida, but that it is Amida's Original Vow that "chooses" all beings to be saved. Therefore, even those who lead lives of crime and sin are saved.

Shinran's teachings represent a radical departure from traditional Buddhist doctrine. He reduced the Three Treasures (i.e., Buddha, Dharma, and Sangha) to one (i.e., Amida's Original Vow) and rejected the accepted methods of spiritual exercises and meditation as paths to enlightenment. He was critical of the government's persecution of Hōnen and argued that the secular authority of the state was subordinate to the eternal law of the Dharma. In the religious communities that surrounded Shinran, distinctions between the clergy and laity were eliminated; Shinran himself was married and had children. Although Shinran never formally established an independent sect, his daughter began to build a True Pure Land sectarian organization. This was the first time in the history of Buddhism in Japan that the continuity of a school was based on heredity. [*See* Jōdo Shinshū *and the biography of Shinran.*]

Nichirenshū. Nichiren (1222–1282), eponymous founder of the sect, is perhaps one of the most charismatic and prophetic personalities in Japanese history. In the time he spent on Mount Hiei between 1242 and 1253, Nichiren came to believe that the *Saddharmapuṇḍarīka Sūtra* (Lotus Sutra) contained the ultimate and complete teaching of the Buddha. In many respects, Nichiren's thought is based on Tendai doctrine: he upheld the notion of *ichinen sanzen* (all three thousand spheres of reality are embraced in a single moment of consciousness) and advocated universal salvation, urging the nation to return to the teachings of the *Lotus Sutra.* However, Nichiren was also a reformer. Rather than accept the traditional concept of the transmission of the *Lotus Sutra* through ecclesiastical offices, Nichiren argued that it was transmitted through "spiritual succession." Thus, he saw himself as the successor to the transmission that began with Śākyamuni and passed to Chih-i and Saichō. He also identified himself as the incarnation of Viśiṣṭacāritra (Jpn., Jōgyō), the *bodhisattva* to whom the Buddha is said to have entrusted the *Lotus Sutra.* Other of his reforms included the attempt to discredit the established Buddhist sects, in particular, Pure Land and Zen. At the same time, however, Nichiren incorporated many of their key notions and practices. With Shingon he shared the use of the *maṇḍala* and the concept of *sokushin jōbutsu* ("becoming a Buddha in this very body"), and with Pure Land he shared the practice of chanting (in this case, the title of the *Lotus Sutra*) and the concept of the salvation of women and people whose natures are evil. Although Nichiren promoted the doctrine of universal salvation, his school developed into the most exclusivist and often militant group in Japanese religious history. Several modern Japanese movements trace their inspiration to Nichiren. [*See* Nichirenshū; New Religions, *article on* New Religions in Japan; *and the biography of Nichiren.*]

Zen Buddhism. In the Nara and Heian periods, Zen (Chin., Ch'an) meditation was a spiritual and mental discipline practiced in conjunction with other disciplines by all Buddhist sects. It was not until the Kamakura period, when the Lin-chi (Jpn., Rinzai) and Ts'ao-tung (Jpn., Sōtō) schools of Ch'an were brought from Sung-dynasty China, that Zen emerged as a distinct movement.

Rinzaishū. The establishment of Rinzai Zen in Japan is associated with Eisai (1141–1215). Discouraged by the corruption of Buddhism in the late Heian, Eisai was initially concerned with the restoration of the Tendai tradition. He traveled to China, first in 1168 and again between 1187 and 1191, hoping to study the true Tendai tradition. In China, Eisai was introduced to the Lin-chi school of Chinese Ch'an. At that time Ch'an was noted for its purist approach—its emphasis on a transmission that stood outside the classical Buddhist scriptures and what is termed the "direct pointing to the mind and perceiving one's own nature." In addition, the Ch'an monks in Sung China refused to pay obeisance to the secular authorities. Eisai, however, was more conciliatory. He studied the practices, ceremonies, and texts of other schools and willingly paid obeisance to the Kamakura regime, which in return favored him with its patronage. Eisai strongly believed that one of the central tasks of Buddhism was to protect the nation and that Zen was a state religion. Far from approaching the common people, Eisai's form of Zen was elitist. Rinzai was established by Eisai's followers as an independent school, and while it remained an elitist group throughout the Kamakura period, its contributions to the cultural life of Japan were significant. [*See* Zen *and the biography of Eisai.*]

Sōtōshū. Dōgen (1200–1253), the transmitter of the Ts'ao-tung school of Chinese Ch'an to Japan, entered the Tendai monastery on Mount Hiei when he was thirteen years old. His intense search for the certainty of attaining Buddhahood drove him from Mount Hiei, first to a Pure Land teacher and later to Myōzen, a disciple of Eisai. Finally, in 1223, Dōgen traveled to China, where he attained enlightenment under the guidance of Ju-ching, a Ch'an master of the Ts'ao-tung school. In 1227 Dōgen returned to Japan and began to expound Sōtō doctrine, eventually establishing an independent sect. As a student of the Ts'ao-tung sect, Dōgen emphasized the gradual attainment of enlightenment through the practice of *zazen* (sitting in meditation), a meditative discipline that entailed sitting without any thought or any effort to achieve enlightenment. Dōgen's notion of *zazen* (also called *shikantaza*) stood in marked contrast to Eisai's use of the *kōan* as a means to attaining sudden enlightenment.

In spite of his adherence to Ts'ao-tung tradition, Dōgen is known for his independence and self-reliance. He was convinced that the truth of Buddhism is applicable to everyone—regardless of sex, intelligence, or social status—and that enlightenment could be attained even in secular life. This doctrine is best expressed in Dōgen's dictum that all beings *are* the Buddha nature. Dōgen also rejected the theory of *mappō* popular among other Kamakura Buddhists. He held that the "perfect law" of the Buddha was always present and could be attained by a true practitioner at any time. Dogen's emphasis on faith in the Buddha represents yet another departure from traditional Zen teachings that stress self-realization. Because he claimed that the Zen practitioner must have faith not only in the Buddha but also in scriptures and one's masters, Dōgen's school is often characterized as sacerdotal and authoritarian. However, after his death, Dōgen's school was institutionalized and grew to be one of the most politically and socially powerful movements in later periods. [*See the biography of Dōgen.*]

Buddhism in the Modern Era. As a result of the Ōnin War and the Sengoku period (a period of incessant wars among feudal lords), the political system was destined to undergo formal changes. Oda Nobunaga (1534–1582), Toyotomi Hideyoshi (1536–1598), and Tokugawa Ieyasu (1542–1616), the three men who unified the nation, rejected the Ritsuryō system's principle of the mutual dependence of imperial and Buddhist law. The Tokugawa regime (1600–1868) instead adopted Neo-Confucianism as the guiding principle of the nation, manipulating Buddhist institutions to strengthen its systems and policies. It maintained strict control over the development, organization, and activities of religious sects. The Tokugawa government continued to recognize and support all the Buddhist schools including those that the Muromachi government had deemed official religions. However, many of its policies toward Buddhism were stimulated by its persecutions of Christianity and its adoption of Confucianism as the state ideology. New sects and doctrinal developments were prohibited, forcing new movements, such as folk Nembutsu to go underground or suffer suppression. Existing schools forfeited their autonomy, and temples, monks, and nuns were institutionalized and routinized within the political structure. In many temples and local temple schools, particularly those associated with Zen, monks studied and taught the Confucian classics.

Along with political and economic modernizations, the Meiji restoration of 1868 brought significant changes to religious institutions. The Meiji government (1868–1912), which attempted to restore the actual rule of the emperor in a modern context, rejected some aspects of the religious policies of the feudal Tokugawa. It rejected the religious institution of Buddhism as a state religion and devised the hitherto nonexistent State Shintō as a "nonreligious" national cult. The loss of government patronage and the decline in prestige, power, and security experienced by institutionalized sects of Buddhism forced them to cooperate with the government. The various sects worked within the structure of the imperial regime by performing ancestral and life-cycle rituals. However, the absence of government favor also brought about a spiritual awakening within Buddhism. Buddhist intellectuals attempted to integrate Buddhist thought and tradition into the newly acquired Western culture and technology. Throughout the Meiji and into the Shōwa period (1912–), popular Buddhism continued to thrive. [*See* New Religions, *article on* New Religions in Japan.] Such movements as Kokuchūkai (Nation's Pillar Society), led by the ex-Nichiren priest Tanaka Chigaku, gained popularity in the nationalist fervor of the 1890s. Another folk movement to grow out of Nichiren was the Honmon Butsuryūkō (Association to Exalt the Buddha), founded by the former monk Ōji Nissen and concerned primarily with faith healing. The increased popularity of new religions and lay Buddhist associations such as Sōka Gakkai, Reiyūkai, and Risshō Kōseikai continues in post–World War II Japan.

[*See also* Japanese Religions, *overview article, and* Buddhism, *article on* Buddhism in Japan.]

BIBLIOGRAPHY

Anesaki Masaharu. *History of Japanese Religion* (1935). Reprint, Tokyo and Rutland, Vt., 1963.

Ienaga Saburō, Akamatsu Toshihide, and Tamamura Taijō, eds. *Nihon bukkyōshi.* Kyoto, 1972.

Kitagawa, Joseph M. *Religion in Japanese History.* New York, 1966.

Saunders, E. Dale. *Buddhism in Japan.* Philadelphia, 1964.

Takakusu Junjirō. *The Essentials of Buddhist Philosophy.* Edited by Wing-tsit Chan and Charles A. Moore. Honolulu, 1947.

Tsuji Zennosuke. *Nihon bukkyōshi.* 10 vols. Tokyo, 1944–1955.

ARAKI MICHIO

Tibetan Buddhism

The various sects or schools of Buddhism in Tibet are probably best referred to as "religious orders" in that most of them are in many ways analogous to Christian monastic orders in the West, namely Benedictines, Dominicans, and so forth. Thus, not only do they accept as fundamental the same Tibetan Buddhist canon (finally compiled in the thirteenth century and consisting almost entirely of works translated from Buddhist Sanskrit originals), but many of them were founded by outstanding men of religion, just as the various Christian orders were established, and so far as doctrine and religious practice is concerned there are no considerable differences between them. Conversely, the various sects or schools of Indian Buddhism were clearly distinguishable at two levels: first, they began to separate according to their various diverging versions of the traditional "monastic rule" (Vinaya), attributed by all of them to Śākyamuni Buddha himself; second, ever greater divergences developed from the early centuries CE onward as some communities adopted philosophical views and religious cults typical of the Mahāyāna, while other communities held to the earlier traditions.

Distinctions of these kinds do not exist in Tibetan Buddhism, since all Tibetan religious orders have accepted unquestioningly the monastic rule of one particular Indian Buddhist order, namely that of the Mūlasarvāstivādins, who happened to be particularly strong in Central Asia and in northern India, and it was in these circles that the Tibetans found their first Indian teachers. Moreover, the form of Buddhism which became established in Tibet represents Indian Buddhism in its late Mahāyāna and Vajrayāna form, with the result that the earlier sects, known collectively as Hīnayāna, have left no impression on Tibetan Buddhism and are known in Tibet only in a historical and doctrinal context. These considerations inevitably lent an overall unity to Tibetan Buddhism that was lacking in India. It follows, however, that such divergences as do exist between the various Tibetan orders are special to Tibet, being largely the result of the many historical vicissitudes which have conditioned the gradual introduction of Buddhism into Tibet—a long process which lasted from the seventh until the thirteenth century. Thus their differences, which from the Tibetan point of view may appear appreciable, can only be explained against a historical context. Moreover, having compared Buddhist religious orders with Christian ones, one must emphasize that whereas monastic orders are in a sense accidental to Christianity, which can operate quite well without them, monastic orders are fundamental to Buddhism in all its traditional forms. Once the monasteries have been destroyed or "laicized," it ceases to exist as a effective cultural and religious force.

Yet another distinction must be drawn, one which is important for an understanding of Tibetan religious life in general and which affects profoundly the relationships between one Tibetan religious order and another. The idea of a religious lineage, that is to say, of a particular religious tradition, usually involving special kinds of religious practice, which is passed in succession from master to pupil, is not altogether unknown in the West, but it is absolutely fundamental in Tibetan thought, and it is precisely this idea which gives coherence to their various religious orders and explains the many links which may exist between them. As distinct from a "lineage," which is bound up with the personal relationships of those involved in the various lines of transmission, who may often belong to different religious orders, we may define a "religious order" (or sect) as one which is to outward appearances a separate corporate body distinguished by its own hierarchy and administrative machinery, by the existence of its various monastic houses, and by its recognized membership. It is precisely in these respects, as well as in the manner of its foundation, that some Tibetan orders may be said to resemble Christian ones. However, religious lineage remains so important in Tibetan Buddhism that some supposed religious orders exist rather as a group of lineages than as an order in any understandable Western sense. This can be made clear only by dealing with them in a historical sequence.

From the time of the foundation of the first monastery in Tibet (Bsam-yas) toward the end of the eighth century until the mid-eleventh century there was no separately named religious order in the country. It had been ordained by royal decree that the Vinaya of the Mūlasarvāstivādins should be followed, and as more monasteries were founded there was no need in the early period for distinctions of any other kind to be made. However, the breakup of the Tibetan kingdom in 842 and the disappearance of any central control resulted in a kind of free-for-all in the matter of maintaining or winning the support of people in Tibet for the new religion, and the conditions of proselytization varied greatly from one part of the country to another. Contacts were certainly maintained with the Tun-huang region in eastern Central Asia, whence Chinese Buddhist influences had already made themselves felt during the royal period, while Indian teachers and Tantric yogins continued to remain easily available across the western and southern borders of the land. Through lack of aristocratic patronage many temples and monasteries fell into decay, but religious lineages were maintained and new ones initiated, and as circumstances became more favorable old monastic sites were brought to life again and fresh ones were founded. According to later Tibetan accounts, this period was one of almost total disruption; but if one judges by what emerged later, this is certainly not the whole truth.

Toward the end of the tenth century, a new royal dynasty began to assert its authority in western Tibet, and the rest of the country gradually became stabilized under the rule of local chieftains. There is now no sign of opposition to the new religion, which certainly made itself felt during the earlier period, and thanks to the royal and aristocratic support which became available once more, religious life began to be organized again under some semblance of control. The vast work of translating Sanskrit Buddhist literature into Tibetan was a continuing priority, and monasteries and literary centers began to flourish. It was in this context that the famous Indian scholar Atīśa (more properly, Atiśa) was invited to Tibet in 1042, remaining there until his death in 1054. He was one of many such teachers, but is especially important in the present context, because his chief Tibetan disciple, 'Brom-ston (1008–1064), established with his master's support the first distinctive Tibetan religious order with the founding of Rwa-sgreṅ Monastery in 1056. Known as the Bka'-gdams-pa ("bound to the [sacred] word"), this new order was intended to bring a proper measure of organized monastic discipline into the professed religious life. A few years later, in 1073, another monastery was founded in the principality of Sa-skya by Dkon-mchog Rgyal-po of the 'Khon family, who was one of the disciples of a remarkable scholar-traveler known as 'Brog-mi (a name meaning simply "the nomad," 992–1072).

This later period, from the later tenth century onward, is known as the "second diffusion" of Buddhism in Tibet; it differed from the earlier period in that the influences were now exclusively Indian, earlier contacts with Central Asia and China having been very largely forgotten. While the same level of scholarly activity, which typified the earlier royal period, was encouraged primarily by the religious rulers of western Tibet, much the same kind of free enterprise which had characterized the hundred years and more of the politically unstable period which had followed continued to account for much of the progress which was now made.

Another successful entrepreneur, who seems to have had no aristocratic support at all, was Mar-pa (1012–1096), who made several journeys to eastern India, studying with various Tantric yogins and especially with his chosen master, Nā-ro-pa (956–1040). The most famous of Mar-pa's pupils is Mi-la-ras-pa ("the cotton-clad Mila"), renowned for his life of extreme asceticism. It is interesting to note how the practice of sexual yoga, in which Mar-pa was adept, could be associated in this particular lineage with the strictest abstinence. Mi-la-ras-pa transmitted Mar-pa's teachings, derived from those of famous Indian sages and yogins, to Sgam-po-pa (1079–1153), who founded the monastery of Dwags-lha-sgam-po, where the teachings continued to be passed on, although it never became the center of a distinct religious order. However, Sgam-po-pa's direct disciples established six famous schools, which developed subsequently into the various branches of the now well-known Bka'-brgyud order, all of whom trace their traditions back through Sgam-po-pa, Mi-la-ras-pa, and Mar-pa, to the Indian yogin Nā-ro-pa and his master Ti-lo-pa, who are placed in immediate succession beneath the supreme Buddha Vajradhara. The so-called Bka'-brgyud order therefore represents an interrelated group of suborders, which are effectively religious orders in their own right, in that they have developed from the start separate hierarchies and administrative organizations with some quite distinct traditions. [*See the bio-*

graphies of Mi-la-ras-pa, Mar-pa, Nā-ro-pa, and Ti-lo-pa.]

The greatest of Sgam-po-pa's disciples was probably the lama Phag-mo-gru (1110–1170), who founded the first important Bka'-brgyud monastery, that of Gdan-sa-mthil. It is interesting to record that he started this later-flourishing establishment as a simple hut in which he lived, while disciples gathered around building huts of their own. It was soon transformed into a wealthy monastery, however, thanks to the patronage of the wealthy Rlaṅs family, which thereafter provided the religious head as well as the chief administrative officer. This close relationship between an important religious hierarchy and a local ruling family also has characterized the Sa-skya order. As may be expected, both of these religious orders have been involved in national politics, and they may be said to foreshadow in their organization the later religious form of government which became the Tibetan norm.

Special mention must also be made of the Karma-pa order, established by another of Sgam-po-pa's disciples, namely Dus-gsum-mkhyen-pa (1110–1193), who founded the monastery of Mtshur-phu in 1185. This order is probably named after the monastery of Karma Gdan-sa, which he had earlier founded in eastern Tibet, whence he had come. This order has the distinction of being one of the first to use the reincarnation system for the discovery and identification of successive head lamas, and its hierarchy has continued right down to the present day. Other Bka'-brgyud-pa orders adopted the same system, especially those that were not subject to aristocratic patronage, in which cases the controlling family would normally keep the succession within its own ranks. The practice was presumably adopted by these early Bka'-brgyud-pas from the circles of Indian Tantric yogins, with whom they were so closely connected in their origins and where such reincarnations were traditionally believed to occur. Gradually, the practice was adopted in other religious orders, of which the best-known examples are the reincarnating heads of the Dge-lugs-pa order, the Dalai and Panchen lamas (see below), but they are but two of many later hundreds.

It should be added that the name *Karma-pa* is explained traditionally in another way. According to this interpretation, an assembly of gods and *ḍākinīs* is believed to have bestowed upon the founder of the order knowledge of the past, present, and future (viz., the whole chain of karmic effects) as well as a magical black miter, woven from the hair of a myriad of *ḍākinīs*. This has resulted in the nickname "Black Hats" for this order as distinct from the later "Red Hat" lineage, which branched off after a certain Grags-pat-seṅge received special honors, including a fine red hat from one of the Mongol emperors of China. We shall refer to such political involvements briefly below.

Returning to Sgam-po-pa's disciples, one recalls a third important one, Sgom-pa (1116–1169), who founded the suborder known as Mtshal-pa from the name of the district where his first monastery, Guṅ-thaṅ, was established. Three other Bka'-brgyud orders are second-generation foundations, in that they were started by disciples of the great lama Phag-mo-gru. These are the 'Bri-guṅ-pa, named after 'Bri-guṅ Monastery, which was founded by 'Jig-rten-mgon-po (1143–1212); the Stag-luṅ-pa, also named after its chief monastery; and the 'Brug-pa, named after the monastery of 'Brug in central Tibet, although it was Rwa-luṅ which became in effect its chief monastery. Whether one refers to these various Bka'-brgyud-pa branches as orders or suborders is a matter for choice, depending upon their later historical vicissitudes. Important ones surviving to this day are the Karma-pa, which is well established now in exile, the 'Bri-guṅ-pa, which survives in Ladakh, and the 'Brug-pa, which has been all-powerful in Bhutan since the seventeenth century and which is also well represented in Ladakh.

Noting that Bka'-brgyud (Śaṅs-pa-bka'-brgyud) has the more general meaning of "lineage of the (sacred) word," one may draw attention to the Śaṅs-pa-bka'-brgyud, a separate order founded by Khyuṅ-po-rnal-'byor around 1100 (dates uncertain). Having begun his religious life studying Bon and Rñiṅ-ma doctrines, this remarkable scholar later traveled in northern India, where his chief teacher was the extraordinary *yoginī* Ni-gu-ma, the sister of Nā-ro-pa. Having studied with her and other Tantric teachers, he established himself at Źaṅ-źuṅ in Śaṅs, after which his school was named. The lineage of his teachings has continued to the present, but internal dissensions later brought his school to an end as a separate order.

These various Bka'-brgyud traditions, whether linked as most were with Mar-pa's line of transmission or not, and also the traditions of the Sa-skya order, all have related origins in the late Mahāyāna and Tantric Buddhism of northeast India from the tenth to the early thirteenth century. It is exactly the same form of developed Indian Buddhism, which varies only insofar as their original Indian masters preferred slightly varying Tantric traditions. The Bka'-gdams-pa order differed only in its far stricter adherence to the monastic rule, while the others permitted noncelibate as well as monastic religious life. However, wherever there were monasteries, it was always the same ancient Indian Buddhist monastic rule, namely that of the Mūlasarvāstivādins, that was followed. High standards of scholarship were of the order of the day, for it was precisely during this period that the great enterprise of transferring all that remained of Indian Buddhism onto Tibetan soil was achieved. One should mention in particular the considerable works of translation of the great Rin-chen-bzaṅ-po (958–1055) of western Tibet and of his collaborators and successors, who may be associated with the Bka'-gdams-pa order from the time of its foundation, and later the impressive scholarship of the great Sa-skya lamas during the twelfth and thirteenth centuries. Scholars of all orders contributed in their various ways to the eventual formation of the Tibetan Buddhist canon, consisting of well over a hundred volumes of doctrine attributed to Śākyamuni Buddha himself or his accredited representatives and over twice as many volumes of commentaries and exegetical works by Indian masters.

The Rñiṅ-ma-pa and Bon Traditions. All the various orders so far discussed were founded during the eleventh and twelfth centuries in a country where Buddhist traditions had been more or less active since the eighth century, if not before. In the earlier period there had been religious lineages of the kind described above, but no religious orders with separate hierarchies and distinctive traditions as already defined. However, it is quite understandable that those who continued to represent the earlier teachings, which were still being transmitted, should begin to band together in order to protect them, the more so as the new orders tended more and more to challenge their orthodoxy. Thus, the "Old Order" (Rñiṅ-ma) and Bon as another clearly constituted order gradually appear on the scene from the twelfth century onward. The latest to achieve recognized existence, they preserve the oldest Buddhist as well as pre-Buddhist traditions, while at the same time benefiting from the teachings accumulated during the later period.

Neither the Rñiṅ-ma-pas nor the Bon-pos are religious orders in the precise sense defined above, but rather groupings of related lineages, where certain high lamas (like many other orders, they came to adopt the reincarnation system) have achieved particular eminence. By their very nature they have no clearly distinguishable historical founder, as do the later orders, although the Rñiṅ-ma-pas claim in retrospect the yogin-magician Padmasambhava, who visited Tibet in the later eighth century, as their founder, while the Bon-pos attribute their teachings to the mythical teacher Gśen-rab, who came from the country of Ta-źig, a vague region beyond western Tibet (the same name occurs in Tadzhik S.S.R.) in the remote past. While they hold many religious teachings in common, there is one fundamental difference between them. Although the later orders rejected some of the teachings of the Rñiṅ-ma-pas as unorthodox (thus inducing them to make their own special collection of Rñiṅ-ma Tantras), they have never doubted their credibility as reliable Buddhist teachers; thus, they unquestioningly form part of the whole Tibetan Buddhist tradition.

On the other hand, the Bon-pos have put themselves beyond the acknowledged Buddhist pale by insisting that their teachings, very largely Buddhist in content as they undoubtedly are, have come not from India but from Ta-źig or Shambhala, a totally mythical land, and maintaining that while Gśen-rab is a genuine Buddha, Śākyamuni is a counterfeit one. I suspect that their earliest Buddhist traditions go back to the period before the seventh century, when Indian religious teachings were already penetrating ancient western Tibet from the far northwest of India and from Central Asia, and that subsequently they would never have accepted the undoubted historical origin of similar teachings when they were later imported into Tibet under royal patronage. Much pre-Buddhist Tibetan religion has been formally incorporated into their teachings, but their whole way of life from the time they appear in Tibet as an organized body from the twelfth century onward has been modeled on that of the recognized Buddhist orders and, in recent centuries, especially on the Dge-lugs-pa, in whose great monastic schools they had no hesitation in studying. Since the recognized Buddhist orders have also adopted many non-Buddhist cults at a popular level of practice, the Bon-pos have lost even that separate distinction. Seemingly unaware of the overwhelmingly Buddhist content of Bon-po teachings, orthodox Tibetan writers have identified them retrospectively with all those who opposed the introduction of the new religion into Tibet during the seventh and eighth centuries. All in all, the Bon-pos are a most curious religious phenomenon. They survive now in exile together with the other Tibetan religious orders that have succeeded in rebuilding their fortunes abroad after the organized destruction of religion in Tibet from 1959 onward.

In their transmitted teachings the Rñiṅ-ma-pas have much in common with the Bon-pos because they have preserved teachings which were developed in Tibet under Central Asian and Chinese Buddhist influence from the eighth century onward. Most distinctive of these is the Rdzogs-chen ("great fulfillment") tradition, which can be traced back through eighth-century Tibetan teachers to Central Asian and Chinese masters. The loss of contact with the Indian originals, inevitably involved in such long lines of transmission, led scholars of the later orders, who could so easily obtain Indian originals directly from Nepal and northern India, to challenge in good faith many Rñiṅ-ma-pa teachings, although it must be added that in some cases the Rñiṅ-ma claim has since been vindicated by the discovery of Sanskrit originals. At the same time, none of the later schools deny the great importance of Padmasambhava, often incorporating rituals that center upon him as a recognized Buddha emanation.

Both Rñiṅ-ma-pas and Bon-pos have resorted to the practice of rediscovering "hidden treasure" *(gter ma)*, namely religious books, really or supposedly deposited in some secret place by an earlier renowned teacher, often in times of persecution, real or imagined, so that they might be rediscovered at an appropriate later date by those who are skilled in the task. Some of these works are in a prophetic form and (like the *Book of Daniel*) can be dated more or less by the later events to which they refer. The Rñiṅ-ma and the Bon traditions represent the most complex and interesting of Tibetan religious orders.

Other Later Religious Orders. We may refer briefly to later Tibetan orders of the fourteenth and fifteenth centuries, which were constituted after the completion of the formative period of Tibetan Buddhism described above and which are therefore more or less relatable to the already existing orders, although their leaders often appealed directly to Indian Buddhist sources in justification of their teachings. The Jo-naṅ-pas emerge as a distinct school in the fourteenth century as the result of the precise form given certain teachings on the nature of the absolute by a renowned scholar, Śes-rab-rgyal-mtshan of Dol-po (1292–1361), although similar views can be traced back to earlier teachers, certainly to the Indian Yogācārins to whom this Tibetan school appeals. It was named after the monastery of Jo-mo-naṅ, founded by Śes-rab-rgyal-mtshan's own teacher. It would seem to be a rare example of a Tibetan order of which the distinctive characteristic was a particular philosophical doctrine, namely the real existence of Buddhahood in an ontological sense. Like some of their Yogācārin forebears, they were accused of being "Buddhist brahmans," and the order was formally proscribed by the fifth Dalai Lama after he came to power in 1642, but probably more for political than philosophical motives.

Yet another totally innocuous order was started by the disciples of the great scholar Bu-ston (1290–1364), who had been largely responsible for bringing the work on the Tibetan canon to a successful conclusion. Named Źwa-lu-pa after his monastery Źwa-lu, this small order had close associations with the then powerful Sa-skya order. [*See the biography of Bu-ston.*] In the fifteenth century a great Sa-skya scholar, Kun-dga'-bzaṅ-po (1382–1444), founded the monastery of Nor E-vam-chos-ldan, and based on this foundation there developed a new Sa-skya suborder known as Nor-pa, which, like other surviving Tibetan schools, exists nowadays in exile in India.

Left for final consideration is the very important order of the Dge-lugs-pa, nicknamed the "Yellow Hats," founded by the great scholar-reformer Tsoṅ-kha-pa (1357–1419). Having studied with teachers belonging to several of the already established orders, Mtshal, Sa-skya, Phag-mo-gru, Źwa-lu, and Jo-naṅ, he joined the great Bka'-gdams-pa monastery of Rwa-sgreṅ, founded by Atīśa's disciple 'Brom-ston. After he founded his first monastery of Dga'-ldan near Lhasa in 1409, his school was referred to as the "New Bka'-gdams-pa," since he insisted on the same strict monastic discipline as had his great predecessor Atīśa. His flourishing order certainly won early esteem on account of its superior moral virtues, but to the detriment of such qualities it eventually achieved political power during the reign of the fifth Dalai Lama by the same method of calling upon foreign aid as had been used earlier by other religious orders.

Political Involvements. The history of Tibet is so bound up with its religious orders and, prior to 1959, its form of government was so peculiarly religious in structure, that some brief summary of these political involvements is required. Tibet was strong and independent as a self-constituted united country of Tibetan-speaking peoples from approximately 600 CE until the fall of the last of the line of Yar-kluṅs kings in 842. Thereafter, although disunited it remained free from foreign interference until the Mongols, united under Chinggis Khan, took possession of it during the first half of the thirteenth century. Looking for a notable local representative whom they could hold responsible for Tibetan submissiveness, they lighted upon the grand lamas of Sa-skya as the most suitable in the absence of any obvious nonreligious choice. The Sa-skya order began to benefit greatly from this connection, especially when Khubilai Khan became the first Mongol emperor of China and established Peking as his capital (1263). Jealous of the wealth and power that Sa-skya enjoyed, other orders, the Karma-pa, the Mtshal-pa, and the 'Bri-guṅ-pa, also sought for Mongol patrons. Thus from 1267 until 1290 the monasteries of Sa-skya and 'Bri-guṅ waged war with one another, resulting in the destruction and burning of 'Bri-guṅ. However, the Karma-pas maintained a profitable interest at the Chinese court, lasting beyond the Mongol (Yüan) dynasty into the Ming without such untoward results.

Sa-skya preeminence was brought to an end by one of its own monks, Byaṅ-chub-rgyal-mtshan of the Rlaṅs family, which was affiliated with the Phag-mo-gru order, and for one hundred thirty years Tibet was ruled by him and his successors as an effectively independent country. Their rule was then replaced by that of their powerful ministers, the princes of Rin-spuṅ, and they in turn by the rulers of Gtsaṅ, both of these families being supporters of the Karma-pa order, which duly benefited. With the destruction of the supremacy of Gtsaṅ by the fifth Dalai Lama and his new Mongol supporters, the Karma-pas suffered most from his displeasure. It was probably as much due to the patronage which the Jo-naṅ-pas had also previously enjoyed as a result of their good relations with the Karma-pas, which led to their proscription by the fifth Dalai Lama, as to any unorthodox views which they may have held.

Scarcely any country throughout its history has been as tolerant in the religious sphere as Tibet, but vengeance has been terrible wherever political interests were involved. It is significant that the Rñiṅ-ma order, which might well be judged even more unorthodox, has survived more or less unscathed throughout the centuries, thanks to its lack of political involvement; the same is true of the Bon-pos, whose views must surely be interpreted as totally heretical so far as the person of Śākyamuni Buddha himself is concerned. The Karma-pas survived the displeasure of the fifth Dalai Lama and have since lived gentle lives remote from the political scene. However, their "Red Hat" incarnation came to a sad end in 1792 as a result of his treacherous involvement with the newly established Gorkha regime in Nepal. Largely at his personal instigation, the Gorkhas invaded Tibet in 1788 and sacked Bkra-śis-lhun-po, against which he harbored a particular grudge. When the Gorkhas were later defeated by a Chinese army he committed suicide and was duly forbidden by the Tibetan government to reincarnate in future.

The last victim of Tibetan political intrigue was the Incarnate Lama of Rwa-sgreṅ Monastery (the original Bka'-gdams-pa foundation) in 1947, an event that was surely disastrous for the whole country, just when it was threatened with foreign Communist occupation. Whatever benefits the Tibetans have gained in spiritual well-being from their religious orders, they have suffered correspondingly politically as a result of the built-in weaknesses of such a religious form of government. Quite apart from sectarian jealousies, the reincarnation system leaves long periods of interregnum between the decease of one ruling lama and the time when his successor becomes old enough to attempt to regain power from the regents who have been operating in his stead.

[*See also* Buddhism, *article on* Buddhism in Tibet; Tibetan Religions, *overview article*; Bon; Dge-lugs-pa; Mādhyamika; *and* Yogācāra.]

BIBLIOGRAPHY

Kapstein, Matthew. "The Shangs-pa bKa'-brgyud: An Unknown Tradition of Tibetan Buddhism." In *Tibetan Studies in Honour of Hugh Richardson*, edited by Michael Aris and Aung San Suu Kyi, pp. 136–143. Warminster, 1979.

Kvaerne, Per. "The Canon of the Bonpos." *Indo-Iranian Journal* 16 (1974): 18–56, 96–144.

Kvaerne, Per. "Who are the Bonpos?" *Tibetan Review* 11 (September 1976): 30–33.

Li An-che. "Rñin-ma-pa: The Early Form of Lamaism." *Journal of the Royal Asiatic Society* (1948): 142–163.

Li An-che. "The bKa'-brgyud-pa Sect of Lamaism." *Journal of the American Oriental Society* 69 (1949): 51–59.

Petech, Luciano. "The *'Bri-guṅ-pa* Sect in Western Tibet and Ladakh." In *Proceedings of the Csoma de Kőrös* Memorial Symposium, edited by Louis Ligeti. Budapest, 1978, pp. 313–325.

Richardson, Hugh E. "The Karma-pa Sect: A Historical Note." *Journal of the Royal Asiatic Society* (1958): 139–165 and (1959): 1–18.

Richardson, Hugh E. "The Rva-sgreng Conspiracy of 1947." In *Tibetan Studies in Honour of Hugh Richardson*, edited by Michael Aris and Aung San Suu Kyi. Warminster, 1979.

Ruegg, David S. "The Jo-naṅ-pas: A School of Buddhist Ontologists According to the *Grub-mtha' śel-gyi-me-loṅ*." *Journal of the American Oriental Society* 83 (1963): 73–91.

Sperling, Elliot. "The Fifth Karma-pa and Some Aspects of the Relationship between Tibet and the Early Ming." In *Tibetan Studies in Honour of Hugh Richardson*, edited by Michael Aris and Aung San Suu Kyi, pp. 280–287. Warminster, 1979.

Snellgrove, David L., and Hugh E. Richardson. *A Cultural History of Tibet* (1968). Reprint, Boulder, 1980.

Tarthang Tulku. *A History of the Buddhist Dharma*. Crystal Mirror, no. 5. Berkeley, 1977.

Tucci, Giuseppe. *The Religions of Tibet*. Translated by Geoffrey Samuel. Berkeley, 1980.

DAVID L. SNELLGROVE

BUDDHIST ETHICS is a term of convenience, uniting under one rubric what in fact has been a quite diverse set of beliefs practiced in cultures that have spanned much of the globe for two and a half millennia. Hence most of this discussion will trace the salient divergences of ethical discourse through the Theravāda, Mahāyāna, and Vajrayāna traditions and into the modern era. Yet amid this historical diversity, it is nevertheless possible to identify certain broad foci of attention, certain patterns and tensions that have more or less consistently characterized ethics in the Buddhist tradition as a whole. It is to these that we first turn.

Overall Patterns. One way of characterizing the Buddhist ethical tradition is to note the close association between the central Buddhist insight into reality as "selfless" *(anātmān)* or "empty" *(śūnya)* on the one hand, and authentic moral activity on the other. In most Buddhist traditions the two are considered to be complementary and reciprocal. Insight into selflessness or emptiness informs moral activity, while moral activity supports the cultivation of insight.

A second general characteristic of Buddhist ethics is that the moral character of human action is closely associated with the intention that constitutes it. It is simply presumed that actions constituted by good intentions will, by virtue of the universal order that structures reality, lead to good and pleasant results for the individual and for society; and that actions constituted by bad intentions will, by virtue of that same universal order, lead to bad and unpleasant results for the individual and for society.

A third broad characteristic of Buddhist ethics is that it combines an adherence to precepts and responsibilities with an emphasis on the rooting out of vices and the cultivation of virtues. These rule-oriented and vice/virtue-oriented modes of ethical activity are occasionally seen to be in tension, but Buddhists have largely assumed that they mesh together in a manner that is mutually supportive.

Finally, Buddhist communities have differentiated among levels of ethical responsibility and attainment. These levels are often associated with various stages of soteriological achievement. They are also commonly correlated with the institutional and social hierarchies that have traditionally characterized Buddhist societies.

Early Buddhist and Theravāda Ethics. The fourth noble truth taught by Gautama Buddha is that of the path that leads to the cessation of suffering. This Middle Path (or Noble Eightfold Path) consists of eight components that are usually subsumed under three headings: moral conduct (Pali, *sīla;* Skt., *śīla*), mental discipline *(samādhi),* and wisdom (Pali, *paññā;* Skt., *prajñā*). *Sīla* includes three of these eight components, namely: right conduct, right speech, and right livelihood. The Buddha taught *sīla* to laity and his own wandering followers *(bhikkhu); sīla* was therefore a primary basis for the moral and spiritual development of both the lay and the elite segments of the Buddhist community. [*See* Eightfold Path.]

A primary basis of lay ethics is the following hallowed list of five precepts, to which lay persons sometimes subscribe after ritually taking the Three Refuges: not to take life; not to steal; not to speak falsely; not to engage in sexual misconduct; and not to take intoxicating liquor. Three or five more rules were sometimes added to this list: these were the supererogatory rules followed by the *upāsaka,* lay persons who tried to attain the standard of monkhood by taking upon themselves extra renunciations. The expanded list of ten precepts was also followed by novice candidates for monkhood.

These precepts were not understood as commandments in the sense that certain Western traditions consider ethical prescriptions to be commandments. Rather, they were guidelines set forth by the Buddha for the social and personal well-being of his followers, and were intended to be followed in that spirit. Their disregard, however, clearly brought on negative sanctions. The Buddhist tradition is filled with accounts of the horrible results that accrue, in accordance with the law of *kamma* (Skt., *karman;* the law that establishes a direct connection between a deed and its effects in this life and in future lives), to those who ignore these basic moral prescriptions.

A second kind of ethical activity prescribed for the laity in early and Theravāda Buddhism was the giving of alms to monks (*bhikkhus*). Giving alms to the monastic order (Pali, *sangha;* Skt., *saṃgha*) was presented as the most efficacious kind of offering through which the laity could both express and cultivate the primary Buddhist virtue of giving. At the same time almsgiving constituted the laity's role in what has continued to be the social relationship *par excellence* in Theravāda Buddhism, namely, the reciprocal interaction between the laity and the *sangha.*

Like the failure to adhere to the five basic precepts, the failure to give alms (or, perhaps more accurately, the stinginess that led to the failure) was considered to be a source of negative *kamma* that would lead to various forms of exceptional suffering in the human world and in the various hells within the Buddhist cosmos. But in the case of almsgiving, the emphasis in the teaching was placed on the positive karmic results that it generated. For almsgivers who desired an increase in sensual pleasures, rebirth in a better condition in this world, or in a heavenly realm, was promised. The cultivation of self-giving that true almsgiving involved was also considered to prepare one for the higher levels of religious and ethical attainment.

Within the early and Theravāda tradition, the monastic order constituted a segment of the community with its own distinctive ethos. The *bhikkhus* who composed this segment of the community were expected to adhere to the same precepts that had been set down for the laity; but many other precepts were added, including regulations dealing with daily habits, matters of dress and decorum, and proper organization of the order itself. In the fully developed Theravāda tradition the normative collection of these regulations, called the Paṭimokkha, contained 227 separate rules. [*See* Vinaya.]

For the individual *bhikkhu* the monastic rules were

justified by their crucial role in spiritual training. According to the early and Theravāda traditions, adherence to these rules constituted a discipline necessary for the practice of the higher path. This discipline played a crucial role in uprooting the core vices of delusion, hatred, and greed—vices that, because they fueled the accumulation of *kamma,* had to be eliminated if salvation was to be attained. But justification of the monastic rules was offered on the communal level as well. The monk's adherence to the rules was considered both a cause and a sign of the religious and ethical purity that made the *sangha* worthy of the support and alms offered by the laity.

The obligations of the monastic community to the laity extended well beyond the maintenance of its own purity and its availability as an efficacious field of merit. The monks were also responsible for preserving and studying the *dhamma* taught by the Buddha, and for teaching it to others. In the later phases of the tradition, the monks' obligation to attend to "the welfare of the many" was extended to include more secular community services as well.

While adherence to precepts and the performance of reciprocal acts of giving were the most frequently commended modes of ethical activity in the early and Theravāda traditions, other kinds of ethical action were prescribed as well. For example, both the monks and the laity were called upon to show sympathy *(anukampā)* to their fellow human beings. Both monks and laity were also encouraged to cultivate, through meditation, the mental attitudes of love *(mettā),* compassion *(karuṇā),* sympathetic joy *(muditā),* and equanimity *(upekkhā).* It was generally presumed that laymen and laywomen would practice these morally efficacious meditations at a lower level than the monks. But the basic character of the practice was the same, and some laypersons reached higher levels of attainment than many of the monks.

Scholars have debated whether the ethical activities enjoined by the early Buddhists and the Theravādins had as their end primarily the well-being of the practitioner (in which case their designation as ethical is often held to be suspect), or whether they were oriented primarily to the benefit of others; that is, whether moral action was undertaken for self-regarding or for other-regarding reasons. Clearly, both emphases can be discerned in the texts, and there were certainly tensions between the two. However, the key point is that for the mainstream of the tradition the dichotomy does not exist; on the contrary, a constant theme of the Pali (Theravāda) texts is that the world is so ordered that "he who protects himself protects others; he who protects others protects himself." This flows directly from the central insights of Theravāda doctrine, the insights of no-self *(anattā)* and the dependent co-origination of all reality *(paṭicca-samuppāda,* Skt., *pratītya-samutpāda).* For the doctrine of no-self entails that there is no ultimate distinction between good accruing to one agent and to another, and the doctrine of dependent co-origination stresses the mutual interdependence of all beings. [*See* Soul, *article on* Buddhist Concepts; *and* Pratītya-samutpāda.]

Scholars have also debated whether the moral activities and virtues enjoined by the early Buddhists and Theravādins constituted a mere means to the goal of enlightenment, or an end in themselves. Perhaps it is more accurate to say that for the *arahant* ("perfected being," Skt., *arhat*) who has reached the level of *asekha* ("requires no further training in *sīla*"), religious realization and ethical action were utterly inseparable. [*See* Arhat.] It was not the case that for the *arahant* ethical actions became irrelevant and were therefore abandoned; nor was it true on the other hand that the perfection of the *arahant* was exclusively moral in content. The perfected one, by virtue of his uprooting of all the *āsavas* ("hindrances" or "cankers," such as the canker of sensual pleasures, the canker of becoming, the canker of false views, and the canker of ignorance), realized a purity of intention that was immediately manifest in right action. The action of the *arahant,* while absolutely spontaneous, was at the same time by its very nature fully in accord with the *dhamma* ("truth, law") as the Theravādins understood it. [*See also* Worship and Cultic Life, *article on* Buddhist Cultic Life in Southeast Asia.]

Mahāyāna and Vajrayāna Ethics. The basic elements of Buddhist ethics present in the early and Theravāda traditions persisted in the Mahāyāna and Vajrayāna traditions as well. These latter traditions maintained the basic precepts and obligations imposed by the former on both laity and monks. But proponents of the Mahāyāna and Vajrayāna selectively highlighted certain features of the Buddhist ethical tradition and developed these features to a far greater extent than had the Theravādins. This set of Mahāyāna and Vajrayāna emphases, combined with genuinely new elements introduced as Buddhism spread north and east into non-Indian cultures, constituted new understandings of ethics within the Buddhist tradition.

Theravāda writings already contained references to *bodhisattvas* (those who were practicing the path that leads to Buddhahood), but the Mahāyānists developed the *bodhisattva* ideal to such an extent that it became the single most important element in Mahāyāna ethics. The *bodhisattva* ideal was developed in response to what were identified by its proponents as the inferior, "Hināyāna" ("smaller vehicle" that includes the Theravāda) ideals of the *śrāvaka,* the *arhat,* and the *pratyekabuddha.* The chief defect of all these "inferior" practitioners was their supposed failure, despite having achieved some insight, to proclaim to the world the truth they had discovered and thus to aid others. As an alternative to the *arhat's nirvāṇa,* these Mahāyāna proponents advanced a notion of enlightenment that emphatically included the desire to succor fellow beings in the samsaric world of impermanence. The hierarchy of ethical ideals thus established put the *bodhisattvas* in the highest position both because of their higher levels of cognitive and religious insight and because of the supposedly broader reach of their moral practice. [*See* Bodhisattva Path.]

The *bodhisattva's* salient trait is altruistic compassion for all sentient beings. He or she helps all beings not only to achieve spiritual release *(nirvāṇa)* but also to attain material advantages and welfare *(artha)* in the world. To do this the *bodhisattva* must refuse to enter *nirvāṇa* himself, since after *nirvāṇa* he cannot be of help to beings still in *saṃsāra;* he must sacrifice his own final attainment for the sake of others. In order to strengthen himself in this resolve he takes a vow such as the following: "I shall not enter into final *nirvāṇa* before all beings have been liberated." Then follows a course of disciplined development lasting for eons, during which the maturing *bodhisattva,* through successive rebirths, cultivates a large array of cognitive and physical powers and moral virtues (the thirty-seven *dharmas,* ten powers, five *balas,* six or ten *pāramitās,* etc.), and progressively rises through a series of stages (*bhūmis*) toward perfection.

In this hierarchical scheme of development all earlier Buddhist virtues, including *śīla,* were encompassed yet transmuted to a "higher" stage of practice. For instance, the first six *pāramitās* (to which four were added only later) were *dāna* ("giving, generosity"), *śīla* ("virtuous conduct, righteousness"), *kṣānti* ("forbearance, patience"), *vīrya* ("energy"), *dhyāna* ("rapt musings"), and *prajñā* ("wisdom"). *Dāna* and *śīla* were regarded as the laity's special duties, leading to better rebirth. Hence, their inclusion in the *bodhisattva's* positive scheme of moral development through the *pāramitās* ("perfections") was a deliberate effort by Mahāyāna proponents to formulate an ethical ideal that transcended those of the *śrāvaka,* the *arhat,* and the *pratyekabuddha.* It was an ideal that combined the social virtues of a righteous householder with the ascetic ideals of a meditating monk, bridging what was perceived by its proponents as a gap between monastic and popular Buddhism. [*See* Pāramitās.]

Similarly, the practice of *dhyāna* encompassed Theravāda's four cardinal virtuous attitudes of love, compassion, sympathetic joy, and equanimity; only now the Mahāyānists stressed compassion *(karuṇā)* above the others as the one thing needful for *bodhisattvas.* They summed up this key virtue in a simile: the *bodhisattva* loves all beings as a mother loves her children. As an attitude, compassion consisted in realizing the ultimate nondifferentiation of oneself and others, and hence in mentally substituting others for oneself. It was put into practice chiefly by generosity *(dāna)* in accordance with two principles: (1) do to others as you would do to yourself; (2) do to others as they wish you to do to them. In early texts the motives given for this kind of compassion were both self-regarding and altruistic: that is, in this practice *bodhisattvas* were said both to advance themselves on the ladder of perfection and to help other beings. Later texts, however, dropped all reference to self-regarding motives, and altruism remained the sole acceptable reason for compassion. [*See* Karuṇā.]

Aside from the *bodhisattva* ideal, another distinctive feature of Mahāyāna ethics requires mention. Mahāyāna Buddhism encompassed several currents of thought whose collective tendency was to relativize ethical distinctions and bridge dualities. Like the doctrine that the *bodhisattva* may violate *śīla* precepts if moved to do so by compassion, these currents of thought were soteriologically motivated. Yet they went beyond the mere recognition that virtues take precedence over formal ethical rules. From the Mādhyamika school's dialectical use of the concept of emptiness *(śūnyatā)* to the Yogācāra school's doctrine of absolute "suchness" *(bhūtatathatā),* the net effect of these various teachings was strikingly similar. The experience of enlightenment, interpreted by some Mahāyāna schools as the recognition of an identity with the Absolute or "unproduced," transported one to a higher plane of awareness. From this plane of awareness ethical distinctions (e.g., good/bad, right/wrong) and moral rules and precepts all were seen to be not so much irrelevant as relative. For such an awakened one, right conduct became no longer a matter of discipline but instead the spontaneous expression of his awareness. One became so closely identified with suchness that one's words and deeds inevitably expressed the moral order of the universe. Although one subjected oneself to the discipline of relative morality at earlier stages of development, after enlightenment (whether gradual or sudden) one was in a position to use morality as an instrument of free spontaneous living. Grounded in the realization of emptiness, suchness, or the primordial Buddha nature of reality, one continued to exhibit compassion; one might even live by the precepts, but not any longer as a discipline. [*See* Śūnyam and Śūnyatā.]

The Indian Mahāyāna tradition provided the basis for

two further developments in Buddhist ethics. First of all, it provided a basis for distinctive Mahāyāna traditions that developed in eastern Asia. For example, it set the stage for the subtle but important shift toward a more "this-worldly" emphasis in teaching and practice. East Asian Mahāyānists maintained their adherence to the classic Indian Mahāyāna identification of *saṃsāra* (the phenomenal world) with *nirvāṇa,* but they modified the renunciatory tonality that had characterized the interpretation of that teaching in India. They interpreted the doctrine so as to emphasize the positive presence of the void or the Buddha nature in every phenomenal entity. Thus they placed an affirmative religious and ethical value on the natural world and on ordinary human activities. Moreover, East Asian Mahāyānists placed special emphasis on moral attitudes and obligations—notably those associated with loyalty to the family and the state—that were highly valued by the indigenous traditions that coexisted and competed with Buddhism in China and later in Korea and Japan.

Second, within India itself the Mahāyāna tradition provided the matrix for the emergence of the Vajrayāna tradition and Vajrayāna ethics. The Vajrayāna tradition was eventually established in Tibet, enjoyed a brief success in China, and flourished in Japan, where it came to be known as Shingon. The most important innovations of the Vajrayānists were a concentration of the image of the religiously and ethically perfected individual (the *mahāsiddha*) and the closely correlated emphasis on the transcendence of all dualities. [*See* Mahāsiddhas.] Maintaining that the Mahāyānists' *bodhisattva* ideal represented an inordinately slow path to salvation, the Vajrayānists advocated the practice of a "fast path" through which religious virtuosos could become, in this very life, living Buddhas who could exercise the full powers of Buddhahood, including particularly the magical powers. This fast path involved the transcendence of all duality, including the duality of good and evil; it therefore insisted very strongly on the relativity of moral rules for those dedicated to its practice. Thus the Vajrayānists were far more willing than other Buddhists to de-emphasize the preceptive elements of *dharma* in favor of the paradoxical and liberating elements.

Buddhist Ethics and Social Order. The earliest redactors of canonical literature already ascribe to the Buddha a clear interest in matters of social order. At one level his intention was to relativize ordinary socio-ethical bonds and to affirm that the individual must transcend these if salvation were to be attained. At the same time, the Buddha's teachings, as these are recorded in the early scriptures, presented a normative conception of social organization and activity.

The ancient canonical teaching set the Buddhist notion of the good society in definite contrast to preexisting Brahmanic views on caste and sacrifice. For example, in the Pali *Aggañña Sutta* the Buddha described the devolution of the present world system and human society in such a way that the Brahmanic grounding of the social hierarchy in ontological and hereditary distinctions was definitively undercut. Or to cite another example, in the famous *Sigālovāda Sutta* the Buddha commended the suspension of traditional Brahmanic rituals for the maintenance of proper order in the world, and urged their replacement by the cultivation of proper relationships between parents and children, teachers and students, husbands and their dependents, friends and companions, masters and workers, and religious teachers and ordinary practitioners.

The ancient canon also established the basis for Buddhist ideals of morally regulated sacral kingship that came to play a crucial role in the Buddhist tradition. In the *Aggañña Sutta* the primordial devolution of human society was checked by the decision of the people to appoint a king (*mahāsammata,* "the great elect"), who was given responsibility for establishing justice and adjudicating quarrels. Other *suttas* presented similar religio-ethical figures, such as the *cakravartin* (the mythical monarch who set in motion the wheel of the *dharma* and went on to establish his royal dominion over all the earth) and the *dharmarājā* (the *dharma*-king who established prosperity, justice, and peace in his realm).

A major turning point in the development of the Buddhist social ethic came several centuries after the Buddha's death, when an important Indian monarch named Aśoka became a Buddhist convert and a sponsor and interpreter of the *dharma.* From his inscriptions we know that he took upon himself the responsibility for assuring the integrity and well-being of the monastic community. His inscriptions also display his conception of the "true *dharma,*" consisting of basic social morality supported by ritual celebrations and simple forms of meditational practice. After Aśoka's death the community's memories of him crystallized into a new, more fully developed model of the Buddhist king who fulfilled an obligation to support and practice the Buddhist religion. Across the Buddhist world Aśoka came to be pictured as a *dharmarājā* or *cakravartin* monarch who, in addition, was a devoted Buddhist layman. [*See* Cakravartin.]

As Buddhism developed and spread, its ideal of a society regulated in accordance with *dharma* was realized in a variety of forms. In Theravāda societies, dharmic social order took the form of an emphasis on maintenance of the purity and hence spiritual authority of the *sangha;* on the king as a unique *bodhisattva* figure responsible for protecting the *sangha* and for maintaining dharmic order and justice within his realm; and on the responsibility of the laity to follow the five basic precepts and to cultivate the virtue of giving. In Mahāyāna and Vajrayāna societies, the relations between Buddhist ideals and actual social structures were more problematic. Generally, however, dharmic order in these situations took form around a single figure, usually a monarch but occasionally (as in Tibet) a monk. This figure, because of his status as a preeminent *bodhisattva* or living Buddha, tended to be the primary locus of concentrated religious authority.

The way in which Buddhist social ideals were articulated varied greatly across the cultural traditions and sociopolitical positions of those who espoused them. In India, Sri Lanka, and Southeast Asia, Buddhist notions of social ethics and law were heavily supplemented by borrowings from the Brahmanic tradition. In China and Japan, Buddhist social ideals were modified by such indigenous traditions as filiality, pervasive social and moral hierarchy, and unitary political authority. In Tibet, certain indigenous traditions combined with Buddhist influence to produce uniquely Tibetan sociopolitical conceptions, for example, of ruling lines of lamas (Tib., *bla-mas*) who were thought to be the successive incarnations of great Buddhas and *bodhisattvas*.

Finally, Buddhist social ideals were articulated in one way by those who were integrated into the established regimes, in quite another way by those who sought to overthrow established authorities. Conservative social visions that legitimated and guided the exercise of authority by those already in power have been the norm in Buddhist history. But revolutionary versions of the Buddhist social ethic were also developed in countries all across Asia. Many of these antiestablishment expressions of Buddhist social ideals were connected with expectations of the imminent coming of the future Buddha Maitreya. This *bodhisattva,* often identified with the leaders of revolutionary groups espousing political change, was expected to establish on earth a new social dispensation in which prosperity, justice, and soteriological opportunity would abound for all classes of people.

Recent Trends in Buddhist Ethics. Over the past two centuries Buddhism has confronted and assimilated many of the ideas associated with "modernity." In many Buddhist communities confidence in the *dharma* as a cósmic-social reality that could be maintained through adherence to traditional patterns of monastic, royal, and lay activity has been seriously eroded. This erosion has evoked different and sometimes conflicting responses.

One major type of response in the nineteenth and twentieth centuries has been a rationalist, scripturally oriented reform. This kind of reform movement, particularly evident in Theravāda countries, has emphasized the purification of the monastic order through strict adherence to the rules set forth in the canonical Vinaya. In some cases this call for monastic reform has been accompanied by the encouragement of a regimen of "this-worldly asceticism" among the laity. For example, one influential Sinhala reformer known as Anagārika Dharmapāla promulgated a set of two hundred rules for the laity that combined elements of Buddhist asceticism with newly introduced forms of bourgeois morality.

A second important trend in modern Buddhist ethics has been the emergence of a new emphasis on immediately practical forms of social activism. Monks have been encouraged to give up many traditional forms of Buddhist piety in favor of supposedly more efficacious modes of educational and social service. Similarly, Buddhist laymen and laywomen have been encouraged to forgo their traditional patterns of almsgiving and instead to support the establishment of schools, hospitals, and other social service agencies. As a result, the ethical status of the monastic vocation has been depreciated, and the role of the laity and of lay associations has been greatly enhanced. This trend has reached an extreme form in the Buddhist "new religions" in Japan, in which monks and monastic virtues play virtually no role.

A third important trend in Buddhist ethics has been the attempt to forge Buddhist forms of contemporary political and social ideologies. Buddhist interpretations of nationalism and national responsibility, Buddhist conceptions and justifications of democracy, and Buddhist versions and justifications of socialism have been developed. Perhaps the most concerted effort in this direction came in Burma in the 1950s and early 1960s, when a number of Burmese Buddhists worked toward a theoretical and practical synthesis between Buddhism and Marxist social theory. [*See* Saṃgha, *article on* Saṃgha and Society.]

Finally, Buddhists have attempted to organize themselves internationally, and in that context to formulate statements that address such contemporary ethical issues as nuclear disarmament, international justice, and human rights. Unfortunately, however, the international congresses that have convened (primarily those sponsored by the World Federation of Buddhists) have been so deeply split along national and ideological lines that positive results have been very difficult to achieve. In almost every instance the delegates have found it impossible to unite in endorsing Buddhist ethical positions that seriously address the issues at hand.

Buddhism today confronts many ethical challenges both within particular countries and in its role as one of the great world religions. Buddhist scholars and practitioners have a rich body of ethically relevant scriptures and a variety of ethical traditions upon which they can draw as they seek to meet these challenges. The results of their efforts will have a crucial impact on the lives of Buddhist individuals, on the structure of the societies in which Buddhists live, and on the entire world community.

[*See also* Soteriology, *article on* Buddhist Soteriology, *and* Dharma, *article on* Buddhist Dharma and Dharmas. *For a discussion of ethics in a broader religious context, see* Morality and Religion.]

BIBLIOGRAPHY

The great majority of serious works that have been written on Buddhist ethics have focused on the Theravāda tradition. Two solid texts are Shundo Tachibana's *The Ethics of Buddhism* (1926; reprint, Delhi, 1975) and the more recent effort by H. Saddhatissa, *Buddhist Ethics: Essence of Buddhism* (London, 1970). Other more interesting interpretations are provided in Winston L. King's *In the Hope of Nibbana* (LaSalle, Ill., 1964) and by a group of authors in the Spring 1979 issue (vol. 7) of the *Journal of Religious Ethics*. Important studies of particular aspects of Theravāda ethics are available in John C. Holt's *Discipline: The Canonical Buddhism of the Vinayapiṭaka* (Delhi, 1981), in Emanuel Sarkisyanz's *Buddhist Backgrounds of the Burmese Revolution* (The Hague, 1965), and in Richard F. Gombrich's *Precept and Practice: Traditional Buddhism in the Rural Highlands of Ceylon* (Oxford, 1971).

Among the books specifically devoted to Mahāyāna ethics the most significant is clearly Har Dayal's *The Bodhisattva Doctrine in Buddhist Literature* (1932; reprint, Delhi, 1975). Also relevant are chapters 4 and 5 (on monasticism, culture, and ethics) in Lal Mani Joshi's *Studies in the Buddhistic Culture of India* (1967; 2d rev. ed., Delhi, 1977), chapter 5 on "Ethical Life," in Kenneth Ch'en's *The Chinese Transformation of Buddhism* (Princeton, 1973), and Wolfram Eberhard's *Guilt and Sin in Traditional China* (Berkeley, 1967). For two short but interesting discussions of particular aspects of Buddhist ethics in Japan, see Douglas A. Fox's "Zen and Ethics: Dōgen's Synthesis," *Philosophy East and West* 21 (January 1971): 33–41, and Hajime Nakamura's "Suzuki Shōsan, 1579–1655, and the Spirit of Capitalism in Japanese Buddhism," *Monumenta Nipponica* (Tokyo) 22 (1967): 1–14.

Additional references can be located by consulting Frank E. Reynolds's "Buddhist Ethics: A Bibliographical Essay," in *Religious Studies Review* 5 (January 1979): 40–48.

FRANK E. REYNOLDS and ROBERT CAMPANY

BUDDHIST LITERATURE. [*This entry consists of three articles.* Canonization *treats the redaction of the scriptures into various collections disseminated throughout Buddhist Asia;* Survey of Texts *catalogs the extensive literatures of the tradition;* Exegesis and Hermeneutics *surveys the various interpretive stances developed by Buddhist thinkers with respect to their canonical literature.*]

Canonization

The canonical literature of Buddhism has a number of characteristics that make it unique among the religious scriptures of the world. First, the literature is not all contained within a single canon: various regional, linguistic, and sectarian divisions have brought about the compilation of a number of separate canons. The scriptural collections vary from one another in significant ways, and there are few texts that can be found in every tradition. In addition to the multiplicity of canons, the various versions are marked by their size. Each contains a large number of texts and some of these works are of great length. The Chinese canon alone covers nearly one hundred thousand pages in its printed form. The Buddhist sacred texts are perhaps more adequately described as a library, and bear little resemblance to the single volumes that make up the canons of the religions of western Asia.

Since Buddhism in India was diversified by its expansion into regions far separated from one another, and since there was never any proscription against the use of local languages for transmitting the discourses of the Buddha, identification of the texts to be included in the canon remained unfixed. In the beginning, the texts were preserved orally and were recited for the followers by monks called *bhāṇakas*. These recitations were probably of two types. The first was the recitation of Dharma, the remembered words of the Buddha, identified by the preamble, "Thus have I heard." The hearer referred to in this case was the disciple Ānanda, who was asked to give the first recitation of the remembered teachings at an assembly of *arhat*s immediately following the *parinirvāṇa*, or death, of the Buddha. Ānanda is held by tradition to have delivered his memorized teaching at the First Council held at Rājagṛha in the company of five hundred *arhat*s. [*See* Councils, *article on* Buddhist Councils.] In addition to these types of teachings, later codified as the Sūtra literature, there was a second division that related to the rules of conduct (Vinaya) for the followers, in particular for those who lived in a monastic setting. Eventually, the canon was expanded to include a third category called Abhidharma, a special exegetic literature that organized the teaching found in the Sūtras into numerical categories. These lists were originally referred to as *mātṛkā* ("mother").

Although taken from the recitation of Dharma recounted at the First Council, the masters of this tradition held that the full explication of the teaching through these categories was the "high" *(abhi) dharma.* Given this tripartite division, the Buddhists referred to the canon as a whole as the Tripiṭaka ("three baskets").

There was another early grouping based on twelve different textual genres: *sūtra, geya, vyākaraṇa, gāthā, udāna, nidāna, itivṛttaka, jātaka, vaipulya, adbhūtadharma, avadāna, and upadeśa.* We are no longer able to identify the exact definition of each of these types.

As Buddhism grew, it developed a number of sectarian groups, recognized in the histories as the "Eighteen Schools." These schools contended with one another for support and argued over the question of which texts were canonical. Since most of these groups have disappeared, leaving behind no full description of their canons, it is not possible to have a full inventory of the variety of texts that were held to be scriptural by all of them.

It was some centuries before the canon was preserved in written form. In the Theravāda tradition of South and Southeast Asia, it is alleged that the canon was kept in its oral form until 29 BCE, when the Fourth Council was held in Sri Lanka under the aegis of King Vaṭṭagāmaṇī. At that council, similar to the First, a single monk was called to recite the entire teaching; in this case it was a monk called Mahendra, who had been sent to Sri Lanka by King Aśoka. King Vaṭṭagāmaṇī had five hundred scribes and reciters set to work to commit the canon to written form. While this is the traditional view, it should be noted that it was not until the fifth century CE that the final list of texts for the Theravāda canon could be agreed upon, and even then the material to be included in the *Khuddaka Nikāya* remained unsettled.

The Pali-language canon of the Theravāda tradition has been preserved and maintained in areas such as Burma, Sri Lanka, Thailand, and Cambodia. These areas faithfully preserved the Indic form, but seldom attempted to put the texts into the vernacular. This was also the pattern followed in Korea and Japan, where the Chinese version was accepted as the standard and for centuries was the only one available.

The Pali canon has been preserved in several forms. In Burma, the so-called Fifth Council was held in 1871 under the patronage of King Mindon Min. During that council, the canon was reedited by comparison of text variants and at the end of the process was engraved on 729 stones that have been placed in a monastery near Mandalay. A "Sixth Council" was opened in Rangoon in 1954 and the canon was chanted by an assembly of twenty-five hundred monks. After two years the council was concluded and a printed version of the Pali canon, approved by the gathering, appeared in Burmese script.

While Theravāda Buddhists have held that Pali is the official canonical language, they have been willing to transcribe the canon in various local scripts, reproducing the Pali sounds without translating. In Cambodia, the court ordered that the Khmer edition of the canon be published; work on it was begun in 1929 and was not completed until 1969. In this case, the Cambodians broke with the older tradition and not only put the Pali into Khmer script but added a vernacular translation that paralleled it. In Europe, a major effort was mounted, under the direction of the Pali Text Society, to preserve and translate the Pali canon. The preparation of a modern critical edition was started in 1882 and to date eighty-nine volumes have been edited and printed in roman transliteration. While this version has no official support from the *sangha* (Skt., *saṃgha;* the Buddhist religious community), as do the Burmese and Khmer editions, it is a major contribution to the study of the Pali canon. The Thai Buddhists have also been active in the work of editing and preserving the canon. In the eighteenth century, King Rama I convened a council of several hundred monks to restore the canon that had been destroyed when the capital at Ayutthayā had been pillaged by the Burmese. The group prepared a palm leaf edition that was presented to King Rama in 1788. His grandson, Rama III, had seven additional copies made of the leaves. It was much later that their descendant King Chulalongkorn set in motion the project of having the canon printed in Thai script, an activity that was completed in 1893.

The emergence of the Mahāyāna tradition around the beginning of the common era brought about a burst of creative literary energy within Buddhism. Based on the premise that "whatever is well-spoken is the word of the Buddha," Mahāyāna communities began to produce new works that they called *sūtras*, to which they came to affix the preamble "Thus have I heard," indicating that these texts, like their counterparts in the Eighteen Schools, were originally spoken by the Buddha. The Mahāyāna texts severely attacked the other schools and called them the "Lesser Vehicle" (Hīnayāna), thereby claiming that they had understood only a portion of the higher teaching.

The Mahāyāna, along with the other schools, added to the canon commentaries on the *sūtras* called *śāstra, vyākhya,* and *ṭīkā.* Such commentaries kept the canon open and made it possible for later teachings that developed over the centuries to be incorporated into it.

Today, the extant Sanskrit manuscripts are few in

number compared to other Buddhist canonical collections. There are a few palm leaf manuscripts that survive in India, some from the ninth-century Pāla dynasty. The Nepalese manuscripts are greater in number than those preserved in India, since through the centuries an active scribal tradition there continued to ensure the preservation of the materials. These Nepalese copies date mostly from the eighteenth or nineteenth centuries and show all the marks of the many scribes, including a large number of errors that have accumulated over the years. Some Sanskrit documents were kept in Tibet, and it is reported that the Potala in Lhasa still houses forty thousand leaves of such texts in its archives.

As Buddhism began to spread outside of the Indian cultural sphere, canonical texts were carried along in both written form and in the memories of the missionary monks. Because there was no restriction regarding the language to be used for the texts, many of them were eventually translated. The most important development in this regard took place in China, where the task of translating was indeed a formidable one. The Sanskrit and other Indic texts presented the Chinese with a complex grammatical configuration of nouns in three numbers and three genders, verbs in three persons and numbers, along with designations for such inflections as present, imperfect, imperative, optative, and the like. How difficult for the Chinese, who had to render these texts into their own language using characters rather than a syllabary, with a written language that lacked inflections for case, number, tense, mood, or voice, and where the relationship between characters established—by position, stress, or particles—the nature of syntax. Not withstanding all of these problems, for over a thousand years the Chinese devoted themselves to the translation of the canon and in the process preserved hundreds of texts that have disappeared in every other area. Ironically, some of these Chinese versions of the texts (a number of which were translated as early as the second century CE) may be closer in content to the ur-text than the extant Sanskrit manuscripts of India and Nepal, which date from a late period in Buddhist history. The translated canons played a major role in the promulgation of Buddhism. From Sanskrit came the Chinese as well as a major portion of the Tibetan canon, and from the Chinese came the Manchu and Tangut canons. The Tibetan canon was used for the later Mongolian canon.

The preservation of the Chinese canon followed a different course than that of India or Southeast Asia, where, as we have seen, the manuscript form was the only one used until modern printed versions were completed and published. At first, the Chinese made manuscripts on silk or paper and rolled them into scrolls. Canonicity was established largely through the compilation of catalogs of various monastic libraries, and occasionally through the direct intervention of the emperor, who might order a particularly treasured text added to the canon. Biographies of eminent Chinese monks, travelogues, church histories, and apologetic literature were also included. As the canon continued to grow in magnitude, the problem of recopying became severe. Unlike the Pali canon (which, although large, was still of a size that could be copied with support from devoted laity), the Chinese canon, with its thousands of rolls, was too unwieldy to copy without massive effort. It was in fact not produced in its entirety until the Sung dynasty undertook a project that was to revolutionize the distribution of the canon. In the year 972 a commission was given by the court to carve the entire canon onto wooden printing blocks in the city of Ch'eng-tu (in Szechuan), the wood-carving center for China. This work went forward until 983, during which time 130,000 blocks were carved, containing the material of more than five thousand rolls of manuscripts.

When this printed edition was made available manuscript copying was no longer necessary, and many copies of the xylographic version were made and spread throughout China. One copy of the printed edition was taken to Korea, where the court immediately ordered that a similar set of printing blocks be prepared in the hope that it would secure help and good fortune for the nation. This first Korean edition, thought to be a virtual copy of the Sung xylographs, was completed during the period from 1010 to 1030. It remained in use and continued to expand until the invasion of Korea by the Mongols in the thirteenth century. The troops of the occupation force burned the Hungwang Monastery where the wooden plates were stored. During this difficult period the court was forced to flee to exile on the island of Kanghwa. King Kojong ordered a second set of blocks to be made and the assignment of overseeing this enterprise was given to a monk named Sugi.

From 1236 to 1251 Sugi and his staff labored on the new version and did not content themselves with merely reproducing a facsimile of the first set of blocks. Sugi tells us in his account of the work that he used a number of sources to check the readings and in the process made many editorial changes in the new set of blocks. At the conclusion of the work more than eighty-one thousand blocks had been carved with the new Sugi edition, an edition that had relied upon the canon prepared earlier by the Khitan people of the Liao dynasty in China. The Korean blocks are now housed in Hae-in Monastery; rubbings of them have been distributed all over the world. As the oldest complete set of the Chinese canon, they have been the basis for the modern printed editions made in Japan.

The Sung edition was not the only one to be made in China, for once the idea of printing had been introduced great prestige accrued to those who made sets of blocks. The first Sung edition is now called the Kai-pao edition, but there are also others, which have been identified by the location of the blocks or by the period in which they were made.

1. Ch'ung-ning edition (eleventh to twelfth century): Tung-ch'an Monastery in Fu-chou.
2. P'i-lu edition (twelfth century): K'ai-yüan Monastery in Fu-chou.
3. Ssu-hsi edition (1126–1132): Yüan-chüeh Monastery in Hu-chou. This is the so-called Sung edition.
4. Tzu-fu edition (1237–1252): from Hu-chou; thought to be a copy of the Ssu-hsi edition.
5. Chi-sha edition (thirteenth to fourteenth century): prepared in P'ing-chiang-fu in Kiangsu. A copy of the major portions of this edition was discovered in Shansi Province in 1929 and was published in facsimile in 1932 in Shanghai using the Yung-lo edition to supply the missing portions.
6. P'u-ning edition (thirteenth century): P'u-ning Monastery in Hang-chou. This is the so-called Yüan edition. There are a handful of volumes from a fourteenth-century Yüan version discovered in Yunnan in 1979.
7. Hung-wu edition (1368–1398): the first version of the canon done in Southern Ming in Nanking. The blocks were destroyed in 1408.
8. Yung-lo edition (completed 1419): the second version prepared in Nanking, usually referred to as the Southern Ming edition.
9. Yung-lo edition (fifteenth century; supplement in 1584): prepared in Peking and called the Northern Ming edition.
10. Wu-lin edition (fifteenth century): portions recovered in 1982 of this Hang-chou edition.
11. Wan-li edition (sixteenth century): recovered in 1983. This is a recarving of number 8 above.
12. Chia-hsing/Ching-shan edition (sixteenth to eighteenth century): notable for its format of sewn volumes rather than folded ones.
13. Ch'ing edition (1733–1738): a court project, often referred to as the Dragon edition.
14. P'in-chia edition (1909–1914): a movable type edition done in Shanghai. Based on the Shukusatsu edition of Japan, this version is sometimes called the Hardoon canon because of the support of the Hardoon family.

There were some important editions of the Chinese canon prepared by the non-Chinese people of the northeast, the Khitan and the Chin. The Khitan canon has been a mystery because so little of it has been preserved for study. Recently, twelve rolls from this version were discovered in Shansi province, giving scholars material by which to judge the readings and approach used by the Khitan redactors. Previously, our only knowledge of the collection was through the discussions and quotations of Sugi, the editor of the second set of Korean blocks. Included in the Korean xylographs is a text written by Sugi under the title *Koryŏ-kuk sinjo taejang kyojŏng pyŏllok,* in which the author describes his use of the Kai-pao edition from Sung as well as the canon of the Khitan. This thirteenth-century document is one of the few descriptions of editorial procedure and gives evidence that the scholars of China and Korea were not just scribal copiers in their labors connected to the canon, but felt free to make corrections and to pick alternate readings when the text witness appeared to be in error.

A second canon was produced outside Chinese borders by the Jurchen people, who were for a time in confederation with the Khitan. When the Jurchen defeated the Liao dynasty of the Khitans they followed the practice of having a xylograph set made for the canon. Fortunately, a sizable portion of rubbings from this set have been found in Shensi Province and are being published in a facsimile edition in Peking. Since the readings and format of this canon are very close to the Korean version, the Peking printed edition uses the Korean to fill in any missing sections.

There is one other major source for our knowledge of the Chinese canon, the engraved stones found in the caves of the Fang-shan district. Here are housed more than fifteen thousand milled stone slabs that have been incised on both sides with the Buddhist texts. It is misleading in one sense to call this collection a *version* of the canon because it has been made by copying a variety of sources over a period of six centuries. Started in the seventh century of the common era by a monk named Ching-wan, just before the founding of the T'ang dynasty, the project continued until the last days of the Chin dynasty. Since many of the stones carry inscriptions regarding the donors and the dates, it has been possible to reconstruct the process by which the carving was accomplished. The stones dated 631 to 863 are a direct copy of T'ang manuscripts, the largest extant collection of this type of document.

When the Khitan people established their reign over the Fang-shan area, they continued the work of their T'ang predecessors and, in 1042, started the second phase of the carving. By 1110, the dated stones indicate that work had come to a virtual halt as the Liao dynasty began to wane and the Jurchen people were coming to power under the name of the Chin. The Khitan picked up the work in 1132 and continued with it until 1182 when, once again, the project came to a halt. Not until 1957 did the Chinese Buddhist Association undertake the task of removing the stones from the caves; in the process, they discovered that the Chin stones were buried underneath the pagoda in a nearby monastery. The first publication of facsimiles from the rubbings of these stones will include all of the Liao stones, representing a copy of the Khitan version of the texts. All in all, the Liao stones contain the equivalent of some twelve hundred rolls of the canon, a collection that far surpasses the meager extant scrolls taken from the printing blocks of the Khitan. Fang-shan may be the most important source for a study of the Chinese Buddhist canon, since its stones are, in many cases, the oldest dated textual witness.

The Yüan dynasty of the Mongols turned its attention away from the Chinese canon and supported efforts to make the scripture available to non-Chinese. They had a canon prepared in the Hsi-hsia, or Tangut, script in the fourteenth century. Because of their support of the Tibetan form of Buddhism, there was also much attention given to the preservation and dissemination of a Tibetan translation of the Sanskrit and Chinese texts.

The Tibetans had several problems to overcome in the construction of a canon in their own language. When Buddhism was introduced onto the plateau there was neither an alphabet nor a written form of the language that could be easily used for the work of translation. In the seventh century, King Sroṅ-btsan-sgam-po (d. 649) had set in motion the creation of a Tibetan alphabet, and tradition says that by the eighth century, with the help of such Indian masters as Śāntirakṣita and Padmasambhava, the work of translation was started. It was not until the thirteenth century that we have an indication that the translations were collected together and classified into a set that could be called a canon. The monastery at Snar-thaṅ undertook this task and made the first catalog, dividing the texts into the Bka'-'gyur (Kanjur), which included all of the *sūtras* (the words attributed to the Buddha), and the Bstan-'gyur (Tanjur), or commentaries. It was the Yüan court that undertook to make a printing block set for the Tibetan translations. In 1410, in Peking, the Bka'-'gyur was put on blocks shaped in the long, narrow format used by the Tibetans, which copied the style of the palm leaf manuscripts of India. A second set of blocks, added as a supplement to the earlier ones, was produced in the seventeenth century. In the latter part of the same century another carving was done, and this was followed in 1724 by a set of Bstan-'gyur blocks. Today, the set of rubbings taken from the blocks made during the reign of the K'ang-hsi emperor and from the 1724 set are known collectively as the "Peking edition." In the eighteenth century there were blocks being carved in Tibet itself: sets were made at Snar-thaṅ, Co-ne and Sde-dge. Of these the Sde-dge (Derge) is the favorite among scholars because of its careful editing. The last major editing task was commissioned by the thirteenth Dalai Lama, which resulted in the production of the "Lhasa edition" of the Bka'-'gyur in 1931. This later edition is a comparison of the Sde-dge and Snar-thaṅ editions.

The Mongolian canon was started in the Yüan dynasty when, by imperial command, Buddhist texts were translated into Mongolian. Ligdan Khan supported the project, which resulted in the translation of the Bstan-'gyur using the Tibetan rather than the Chinese form of the canon. The 113 volumes that resulted from this effort were written in gold and silver. The K'ang-hsi emperor decided to have the translations revised and edited and then carved on printing blocks. The first rubbings were made from the blocks in 1720 and, since red ink was used, the 108 volumes of the set became known as the "Imperial Red edition."

Japanese versions of the (Chinese) canon have come to play an important role in Buddhist scholarship, and today most scholars use printed editions from Japan as the standard text for the Chinese canon. Prior to the modern printed versions woodblock editions were made in Japan. One was made by Tenkai (1633–1645) and another, based on the Ming editions, by Tetsugen in 1681. In the nineteenth century, the "Tokyo canon" was printed (1800–1885) and punctuation was introduced. A "Kyōto canon" appeared between 1902 and 1905, based on the Korean as well as some of the Ming readings from the Tetsugen edition. A critically edited version was printed in 1922–1933 and is known as the "Taishō canon." It is this latter edition that is used by most scholars when making footnote references.

In addition to these "received" versions of the canons, there are from time to time some important archaeological finds, especially in regions of Central Asia. The discoveries of documents in Cave 17 at Tun-huang, the cache of birchbark manuscripts found in the stupa at Gilgit, and the texts written on wood in the ruins of the Tarim Basin have all contributed to our knowledge of the way in which the Buddhist canon has been spread throughout Asia.

The translation of the canons is still an ongoing process: in the twentieth century there has been an increase in the efforts to have vernacular versions available in printed form. Continued interest in the Buddhist scripture is indicated by the 1969 Cambodian translation of the Pali canon, the modern Korean translation of the Chinese into *hangul* script, and the translation of the Chinese into classical Japanese. Perhaps the most active translation projects have involved the English language. The Pali Text Society has completed a major portion of the Pali canon translation into English, along with critical editions and aids such as dictionaries and studies. More recently, with funding from the Yehan Numata Foundation, a translation bureau has been established for the purpose of translating the Chinese canon into English. Plans call for 139 texts to be translated and published by the year 2000.

From this survey of the history of the Buddhist canons it should be clear that, long before such activities were prevalent in the West, the Buddhists were editing, translating, and printing their scriptures. Because the canons remained open for such a long period (in a sense, the Chinese canon is still open), the size and nature of the collections of texts were unique among the religions of the world. No one group has ever controlled the development of the canons nor exercised dominion over the decision about the inventory of texts to be included. In China especially, the canon was lengthened because of a willingness to accept a great variety of texts into it. Some of these texts were written and compiled in China itself, although they claimed to be of Indian origin. It is this variety of texts that makes the canon so important for a study of religious developments wherever Buddhism exists.

Printing has also played an important role in the development and dissemination of the canons. Whenever blocks were carved for xylograph copying, the canons tended to be standardized, and in some cases it appears that the printing of the canon was the time of closure.

A major problem for the editor or translator of a Buddhist text is that of making decisions based on a multiplicity of versions, sometimes in several languages and dating from different periods. The usual object of the editor is to achieve a reading that is as close as possible to the Ur-text. For the Buddhist materials this is especially difficult, because the texts have been in a fluid state for centuries. Some of the *sūtra*s are compilations of a series of set pieces of teaching that could remain available for use in a variety of texts. These pieces, put together in a number of arrangements, could be altered from one time or place to another. Thus, the collating of various codices from a number of stemmas does not lead to an autograph from which all the witnesses have emerged. If one could reconstruct the edition in such a fashion as to remove all the conflations, the additions, and the expansion of doctrine for the sake of showing the matrix from which it all started, the results would be misleading in terms of Buddhism. Since the texts exhibit the changing modes of the tradition, it is important to preserve all of the changes and rearrangements because these reflect the more complete picture of textual development.

Since the Buddhist canons represent the written part of a religion that teaches the constant availability of the insights of enlightenment and holds that the teaching of its founder, Śākyamuni, was not the only expression of the highest teaching, it is not surprising to find the vast array of texts that make up the scriptures. The Buddhist canons provide us with a source for the study of religion because they have allowed for the constant inclusion of those ideas and concepts that arose in all the parts of Asia where Buddhism has spread.

BIBLIOGRAPHY

Goodrich, L. Carrington. "Earliest Printed Editions of the Tripiṭaka." *Visva Bharati Quarterly* 19 (Winter 1953–1954): 215–220.

Jong, J. W. de. "Notes à propos des colophons du Kanjur." *Zentralasiatische Studien* 6 (1972): 505–559.

Lancaster, Lewis R. "Editing of Buddhist Texts." In *Buddhist Thought and Asian Civilization,* edited by Leslie Kawamura and Keith Scott, pp. 145–151. Emeryville, Calif., 1977.

Lancaster, Lewis R. "Buddhist Literature: Its Canons, Scribes, and Editors." In *The Critical Study of Sacred Texts,* edited by Wendy Doniger O'Flaherty, pp. 215–229. Berkeley Buddhist Studies Series, vol. 2. Berkeley, 1978.

Mitra, Rājendralāla. *The Sanskrit Buddhist Literature of Nepal.* Calcutta, 1971.

Ray, A. K., ed. *Sacred Texts of Buddhism: A Catalogue of Works Held in the Australian National University Library.* Canberra, 1981.

Simonsson, Nils. *Indo-tibetische Studien: Die Methoden der tibetischen Übersetzer, untersucht im Hinblick auf die Bedeutung ihrer Übersetzung für die Sanskritphilologie,* vol. 1. Uppsala, 1957.

LEWIS R. LANCASTER

Survey of Texts

[*This article surveys principally the religious literature of the Indian Buddhist tradition. For the Buddhist literatures of Tibet, China, Inner Asia, Korea, and Japan, see the relevant articles in the entries on* Buddhism *and* Buddhism, Schools of. *Works associated with specific schools or attributed to major historical figures within these schools can be found in the individual entries on these schools and in the biographical entries for these figures.*]

Of the major religions of the world, Buddhism has one of the most extensive and diverse literary traditions. With an extant literature dispersed among four principal canonical collections and several more derivative canons, and with an attitude toward text and tradition that for over two millennia has conferred religious authority on documents from diverse sources, Buddhist literature presents the student of the tradition with formidable philological, historical, and hermeneutical problems. The modern historical study of Buddhism began with the discovery of Buddhist texts in a multitude of cultural and linguistic settings, and with the attempt by scholars to account for the astonishing number and diversity of doctrines and practices that they found in these texts. The study of Buddhism and of Buddhist texts is thus predicated on a comparative review of a variety of literary sources—Sanskrit, Pali, Tibetan, Chinese, Mongolian, and Japanese, to name only the more important sources of our knowledge of the tradition. [*See also* Buddhist Studies.]

The intersection of doctrinal, geographical, and cultural diversity is another factor that makes a survey of Buddhist literatures so very difficult. In its twenty-five-hundred-year history Buddhists have embraced a broad spectrum of philosophical views, meditative and devotional practices, rites, and forms of social organization. Most of these are sanctioned by texts that claim, historically or not, the authority either of the Buddha himself or of those who, like the Buddha, have attained a religious insight that enables them to speak authoritatively about *dharma*. This dispersal of religious authority was a powerful tool in the hands of those who wished to introduce new insights into the tradition, but for the student of the tradition it presents serious problems of categorization and classification. Then too, the social and historical background of many of these texts and of the communities that produced them are, particularly in the case of India, still imperfectly unknown. As a result, basic issues of textual filiation and historical sequence remain to be explored for many of these collections. In light of this profusion of diverse documents, and the space that would be needed to do justice to even a small number of them, in the article that follows I propose to limit my discussion to an examination of some of the root texts of the tradition, the literary production of Indian Buddhism. Where appropriate, I shall make use of the insights into the provenance of these texts afforded by a comparative study of other canons, principally that of the Chinese.

Early Buddhism. Tradition has it that immediately after the *parinirvāṇa* (i.e., death) of the Buddha his followers gathered at Rājagṛha, the capital of Magadha, to recite the words of the Buddha *(buddhavacana)* as they remembered them. In the absence of a designated successor to the Buddha, such an assembly, later referred to as the "First Council" *(paṭhama-saṅgīti)*, provided the fledgling community with a corpus of doctrinal and disciplinary dicta that could be used to define the teachings of the Buddha and settle disputes in the communal life of the monks. For the three months of the rainy season *(varṣa)* these monks collected the teachings that the Buddha had preached during the forty-five years since his enlightenment. In order to ascertain that the monks all remembered the teachings in the same way, they chanted *(saṅgīti)* them together. The elder Mahākāśyapa presided over the council. Ānanda, renowned for his memory, recited the *dharma* (Pali, *dhamma*), with the other monks joining him. Upāli, a monk knowledgeable about monastic discipline, was in charge of reciting the Vinaya. Pious legend to the contrary, however, the precise contents of this rehearsal of the teachings are not known to us. [*See* Councils, *article on* Buddhist Councils.]

During the last twenty-five years of the Buddha's life, Ānanda served as his personal secretary and had been present at most of the discourses he had preached. When Ānanda recited the sermons of his master, he therefore prefaced his recitation with the words, "Thus have I heard on one occasion" *(evaṃ mayā śrutam ekasmin samaye)*, indicating that what followed he had heard directly from the Buddha. Because of the authority conferred on the scriptures by this device, the words *evaṃ mayā śrutam ekasmin samaye* became a formulaic introduction to all texts calling themselves *sūtras*, or discourses of the Buddha, including even those composed centuries after his death.

Shortly after the Buddha's death, his teachings were collected into two groups, Dharma and Vinaya, and were transmitted to later generations. The Dharma is thus called the *āgama* (literally, "that which has been transmitted"). As the teachings were orally transmitted from teacher to disciple, they were organized and collected into *sūtras* and *gāthās* (verses). The root meaning of the term *sūtra* denotes the warp of a woven cloth and thus refers metaphorically to the manner in which Buddhist teachings were condensed into phrases that could be easily memorized. Verses were used because they too could be readily memorized and recited. Since the terse words of the *sūtras* could be interpreted in a variety of ways, comments were often incorporated directly into the texts, yielding longer *sūtras*. In this manner, both prose and verse were used in the transmission of the Buddha's teachings.

Similarly, the rules of monastic discipline were collected and put into the form of a legal code. A collection of rules, the Prātimokṣa (Pali, Pātimokkha), was compiled and commentaries on each rule in the Prātimokṣa appended. Finally, the procedures *(karman)* for monastic assemblies (e.g., ordinations), the use of the monastery, and the distribution of alms were formulated.

Gradually, the words of the Buddha were transformed into a canon; however, the teachings were still transmitted orally.

The Second Council and the Early Divisions of the Canon. Approximately one hundred years after the death of the Buddha, differences in the interpretation of the rules concerning monastic discipline arose between several orders of monks. On the one side were the monks of Magadha and Vaiśālī, on the other were the monks of Avanti and the "Southern Road" (Dakkhiṇāpatha). As a result of this dispute, involving principally the handling of money given as alms (handling money was forbidden the monks by the Vinaya), a council of seven hundred monks, representing both factions, was convened to determine the orthodoxy of this and other practices allegedly common among the monks of the Vaiśālī faction. In the aftermath of this "Second Council" the Buddhist community, the *saṃgha,* was divided into opposing camps—the Sthaviras (Pali, Theravāda, from which derives the Theravāda order that flourishes today in Southeast Asia), or Order of the Elders, and the Mahāsāṃghikas, or Order of the Majority. (Some argue that the schism in the community took place sometime after the Second Council and was precipitated by other issues altogether.) From this point on the texts of the two traditions (still not committed to writing) began to diverge, and in the centuries to follow, as further divisions in the community occurred—some precipitated by disagreements on matters of monastic discipline, some on points of doctrine, and some reflecting merely geographical diffusion—a variety of "canons" emerged. It is important to remember that no text remaining to us today predates the original schism in the community; all the extant documents are the product of sectarian redaction.

The contents of these early canons are difficult to ascertain; however, we know that the Dharma was probably divided into nine categories or textual genres *(navaṅga-buddha-sāsana):* (1) *sūtra* (Pali, *sutta*); (2) *geya (geyya);* (3) *vyākaraṇa (veyyākaraṇa);* (4) *gāthā;* (5) *udāna;* (6) *ityuktaka* or *itivṛttaka (itivuttaka);* (7) *jātaka;* (8) *vaipulya (vedalla);* and (9) *adbhutadharma (abbhutadhamma).* The ninefold classification is mentioned in both the Mahāsāṃghika and Theravāda Vinayas, indicating that it was formulated before the schism.

Some of the schools that later split off from the Sthaviras, the Sarvāstivāda, Mahīśāsaka, and Dharmaguptaka, for instance, added three more categories of literature to their canons. This twelvefold system *(dvādaśāṅga-dharma-pravacana)* is probably later than the ninefold classification; it contains, in addition to the nine listed above, stories of edification *(avadāna),* tales about the causes of events *(nidāna),* and commentaries *(upadeśa).* These systems of classifying the Buddha's teachings according to literary genre reflect the organization of scripture approximately one century after the death of the Buddha.

Beginning with the second century after the Buddha's death and the advent of the schisms in the community, Buddhism entered a new phase often referred to as Sectarian *(nikāya)* Buddhism, or, to use the nomenclature of the Mahāyāna community, Hīnayāna Buddhism. This Buddhism is characterized by the profusion of many sectarian traditions (the number eighteen is widely attested but there were probably others), each with their own version of the texts recited at the First Council. While the sources remaining to us indicate that a basic congruency of content and organization probably prevailed among these canons, modifications were introduced into each to reflect the particular position of the school in question. The basic organization of the canon in two sections, Sūtra (Sutta) Piṭaka and Vinaya Piṭaka, was retained by all the schools, indicating that these sections antedate the period of the first schism. With the advent of Sectarian Buddhism, however, some of the schools compiled an Abhidharma (Pali, Abhidhamma) Piṭaka, containing more systematically conceived scholastic discourses on Dharma. With the addition of this third "basket" *(piṭaka),* the canon came to be referred to as the Tripiṭaka ("three baskets"). This tripartite canon was largely complete by the first century before the beginning of the common era, indicating that it must have been formed during the third and second centuries BCE. [*See* Buddhism, Schools of, *article on* Hīnayāna Buddhism.]

Organization of the Vinaya Piṭaka. Seven full Vinayas are extant today. Besides the Vinaya of the Theravāda school (in Pali) and the Tibetan translation of the Vinaya of the Mūlasarvāstivādins, five Chinese translations of complete Vinayas are extant. In addition, some Sanskrit Vinaya literature has survived.

The Theravāda Vinaya is divided into three parts: *Suttavibhaṅga, Khandhaka* (consisting of two sections, *Mahāvagga* and *Cullavagga*), and *Parivāra.* The first part, the *Suttavibhaṅga,* is a commentary on the *sutta,* or Pātimokkha. In the Theravāda Vinaya, the monks are expected to follow 227 precepts; the nuns, 311 precepts. The precepts for monks are divided into the following categories, which vary as to the severity of the infraction: four *pārājika* offenses, thirteen *saṃghādisesa* offenses, two *aniyata* offenses, thirty *nisaggiya-pācittiya* offenses, ninety-two *pācittiya* offenses, four *pāṭidesanīya* offenses, and seventy-five *sekhiyā dhammā* offenses. With the exception of the categories of the *pācittiya* and *sekhiyā-dhammā*, the numbers of the precepts in the various Vinaya Piṭakas are the same. Only slight differences are found in the number of *pācittiya* precepts, with figures ranging from ninety to ninety-two. However, the number of *sekhiyā-dhammā (śaikṣā-dharmā)* ranges from sixty-six to one hundred thirteen, indicating major differences in this category. Consequently, with the exception of the *sekhiyā-dhammā*, the monastic precepts must have been fixed before the schism between the Sthaviravāda and Mahāsāṃghika schools.

The *Suttavibhaṅga* is a explanation of the precepts listed in the Pātimokkha. The Vinayas of the various schools have a similar format. The second division of the Vinaya, the *Khandhaka* (literally, "chapters"), is divided into two parts; the *Mahāvagga* consists of ten chapters, the *Cullavagga*, twelve. These contain the rules by which the order is to be managed. Sections corresponding to it are found in the Vinayas of other schools. The third major division in the Pali Vinaya is the *Parivāra*. Since no corresponding division is found in the Vinayas of other schools, it must have been added at a later date to the Theravāda text. Because the organization and contents of the *Suttavibhaṅga* and *Khandaka* are found in the Vinayas of other schools, these sections must have been established before the first schism.

The Vinaya Piṭakas of five other schools are extant in Chinese translation:

1. *Shih-sung lü* (T.D. no. 1435; *Daśabhāṇavāravinaya*). The Sarvāstivāda Vinaya translated by Kumārajīva between 404 and 409.
2. *Ssu-fen lü* (T.D. no. 1428; *Caturvargikavinaya*). The Dharmaguptaka Vinaya, translated by Buddhayaśas between the years 410 and 412. This detailed and clearly written text was highly popular in East Asia, where it was used in the Lü-tsung (Vinaya school), and remains the Vinaya adhered to by the Chinese.
3. *Mo-ho-seng-ch'i lü* (T.D. no. 1425; *Mahāsāṃghikavinaya*). Fa-hsien obtained this text in Pāṭaliputra at the beginning of the fifth century. After he returned to China, he translated it with the help of Buddhabhadra between 416 and 418.
4. *Wu-fen lü* (T.D. no. 1421; *Pañcavargikavinaya*). This is the Vinaya of the Mahīśāsaka school. Fa-hsien obtained the text in Sri Lanka, but died before he could translate it. It was translated by the Mahīśāsaka monk Buddhajīva in 423.
5. *Ken-pen shuo-i-ch'ieh-pu pu lü* (T.D. nos. 1442–1459; *Mūlasarvāstivādavinaya*). I-ching found this text in India and translated it from 695 to 713. Because many Avadānas were added to it, it is four times longer than any of the other Vinayas. The Tibetan translation of the *Mūlasarvāstivādavinaya* corresponds closely to the Chinese.

With the exception of the *Mahāsāṃghikavinaya*, the other extant Vinayas all belong to schools of Sthaviravāda lineage. Substantial differences exist between the organization of the *Mahāsāṃghikavinaya* and the Vinayas of Sthaviravāda lineage because the split between the two traditions occurred early in Buddhist history. The organization of the *Khandaka* in particular differs; however, the contents are similar with the exception, naturally enough, of the account of the "Council of the Seven Hundred," the Second Council.

Chinese translations of the *Prātimokṣa Sūtra* and other parts of the Vinayas also exist; among them is the *Prātimokṣa Sūtra* of the Kaśyapīya school (T.D. no. 1460). A large number of Sanskrit manuscripts from the *Mūlasarvāstivādavinaya* were discovered at Gilgit. Parts of the *Mahāsāṃhikavinaya*, including the Lokottaravādin *Bhikṣunīvinaya*, were found in Tibet. Finally, Sanskrit fragments of the Vinaya of the Sarvāstivādas were discovered in Central Asia. All of these have been published. By comparing the extant Vinayas it has been possible to plausibly reconstruct the Vinaya as it must have existed prior to the schisms. [*See* Saṃgha, *overview article, and* Vinaya.]

Organization of the Sūtra Piṭaka. The sources for the study of the Sūtra Piṭaka are not as plentiful as for the Vinaya Piṭaka. Only the Theravāda Sutta Piṭaka and the Chinese translations of the Āgamas survive. Besides these, a few Sanskrit texts and several Tibetan translations are also extant. The Pali Sutta Piṭaka is divided into the following five collections:

1. *Dīgha Nikāya*. 34 longer *suttas*
2. *Majjhima Nikāya*. 152 *suttas* of medium length
3. *Saṃyutta Nikāya*. 2875 (or 7762, according to Buddhaghosa) *suttas* arranged according to 56 topics
4. *Aṅguttara Nikāya*. 2198 (or 9557 according to Buddhaghosa) *suttas* arranged by numerical categories
5. *Khuddaka Nikāya*. 15 *suttas*: (1) *Khuddakapāṭha;* (2) *Dhammapada;* (3) *Udāna;* (4) *Itivuttaka;* (5) *Suttanipāta;* (6) *Vimānavatthu;* (7) *Petavatthu;* (8) *Theragāthā;* (9) *Therīgāthā;* (10) *Jātaka;* (11) *Niddesa;* (12) *Paṭisambhidāmagga;* (13) *Apadāna;* (14) *Buddhavaṃsa;* (15) *Cariyāpiṭaka*

The discrepancies between Buddhaghosa's count of the *suttas* in the *Saṃyutta* and *Aṅguttara Nikāyas* occurs because Buddhaghosa counted even abbreviated *suttas*.

The term *nikāya* is not used in northern Buddhist sources, which instead refer to these collections as Āgamas. Only the *Dīrgha, Madhyama, Saṃyutta*, and *Ekottara Āgamas* are found in the Chinese translations of these texts. No fifth Āgama was mentioned; however, a Kṣudraka Piṭaka was included in some canons. According to the section of the *Mahāsāṃghikavinaya* on the councils, four Āgamas and a Kṣudraka Piṭaka were collected in that school. The Dharmaguptaka, Mahīśāsaka, and Mūlasarvāstivāda Vinayas have similar entries. However, the Sarvāstivāda school apparently did not have a Kṣudraka Piṭaka.

All four Āgamas were translated into Chinese; these, however, derive from different schools. No complete *sūtra* collection similar to that of the Theravāda school is extant, although taken as a whole, the Āgama collection in Chinese is roughly coextensive with the Pali Nikāyas. The following five major Āgama texts are included in the Chinese canon:

1. *Dīrghāgama* (T.D. no. 1): 30 *sūtras*
2. *Madhyamāgama* (T.D. no. 26): 222 *sūtras*
3. *Saṃyuktāgama* (T.D. no. 99): 136 *sūtras*
4. *Saṃyuktāgama* (T.D. no. 100): 364 *sūtras*
5. *Ekottarāgama* (T.D. no. 125): 473 *sūtras*

The *Dīrghāgama* corresponds to the Pali *Dīgha Nikāya;* it probably belonged to the Dharmaguptaka school, as it was translated (in 413) by Buddhayaśas, the translator of the Dharmaguptaka Vinaya. The *Madhyamāgama* corresponds to the Pali *Majjhima Nikāya;* it belonged to the Sarvāstivāda school and was first translated in 384 by Dharmanandin of Tukhāra and the Chinese monk Chu Fo-nien. Because the translation had many omissions and mistranslations. Saṃghadeva of Kashmir revised it in 397. The extant text is Saṃghadeva's revision. The first of the two Saṃyuktāgamas (T.D. no. 99) corresponds to the Pali *Saṃyutta Nikāya* and belongs to the Mūlasarvāstivāda school. Guṇabhadra, who came to China by sea from South India, translated it sometime between 424 and 453. The second (T.D. no. 100) also corresponds to the *Saṃyutta Nikāya*. However, the sectarian affiliation of the work, which was translated sometime before the sixth century, has not been determined. The *Ekottarāgama* corresponds to the Pali *Aṅguttara Nikāya.* It was translated by Dharmanandin, the translator of the *Madhyamāgama,* from 384 to 385. Unlike the *Madhyamāgama*, it was not revised by Saṃghadeva; however, since the translation is well written, it may have been emended by someone. The work is usually considered to be a Mahāsāṃghika text, but as many of its doctrinal positions differ from those found in the *Mahāsāṃghikavinaya,* this attribution must be questioned. The preface contains such Mahāyāna terms as *"tathāgata-garbha,"* indicating that it may have been used by Mahāyānists.

Although the Āgamas translated into Chinese belong to a variety of schools, they provide a valuable source for comparisons with the Pali Nikāyas, enabling us to discern pre-schism textual strata. Individual *sūtras* contained in the Āgamas were also translated into Chinese. In addition, many Sanskrit fragments of the Āgamas have been recently discovered, most often in Central Asia, and have been published. These too have enhanced our understanding of the formation of the canon.

Both the Dharmaguptaka and Mahāsāṃghika schools apparently had Kṣudraka Piṭakas, but these were never translated into Chinese. Several individual texts that correspond to those in the Pali *Khuddaka Nikāya* exist in Sanskrit or Chinese. For example, three Chinese translations corresponding to the *Dharmapada* are found in the canon: *Fa-chü ching* (T.D. no. 210), *Fa-chü p'i-yü ching* (T.D. no. 211), and *Fa-chi yao-sung ching* (T.D. no. 213). The first of these was translated around 220 by the Indian monk Wei-ch'i-nan and preserves the early format of the text.

The *Ch'u-yao ching* (T.D. no. 212) corresponds to the *Udānavarga*, (the Sanskrit recension of the *Dhammapada*). The *Sheng ching* (T.D. no. 154) and the *Liu-tu chi ching* (T.D. no. 152) are important examples of Chinese translations of the *Jātaka.* Mahāyāna influence is evident in the latter. In Sanskrit, Āryaśūra's *Jātakamāla* is also extant.

Biographies of the Buddha developed out of the Jātaka literature. The Pali text of the *Nidānakathā*, a preface to the *Jātaka*, and Sanskrit texts of the *Mahāvastu* and Aśvaghoṣa's *Buddhacarita*, all treating the biography of the Buddha, survive. Among the biographies translated into Chinese are the following:

1. *Fo pen-hsing chi ching* (T.D. no. 190; a Dharmaguptaka text)
2. *Kuo-ch'u hsien-tsai yin-kuo ching* (T.D. no. 189; a Sarvāstivāda text)
3. *Fo so-hsing tsan ching* (T.D. no. 192; *Buddhacarita)*
4. *P'u-yao ching* (T. D. no. 186, *Lalitavistara)*
5. *T'ai-tzu jui-ying pen-ch'i ching* (T.D. no. 185; a Mahīśāsaka text)

Many of the Avadānas are extant in Sanskrit, including the *Avadānaśataka* and the *Divyāvadāna.* Many Avadānas were also translated into Chinese. A number of passages in the *Mūlasarvāstivādavinaya* correspond to Avadānas in the *Divyāvadāna.* Three representative Avadāna texts in the Chinese canon are the *Chuan-chi po-yüan ching* (T.D. no. 200; *Avadānaśataka), Ta chuang-yen lun ching* (T.D. no. 201; *Kalpanāmaṇḍitikā)* and *Hsü-mo-t'i-nü ching* (T.D. no. 128; *Sumāgadhāvadāna*).

Abhidharma Buddhism

Inevitably, with the passage of but a few centuries following the death of the Buddha, doctrinal elaboration and scholastic codification of the master's insights came to play an ever greater role in the Buddhist community. The early teachings of the Buddha were subjected to a process of redaction that quite naturally attempted to supply systematic rigor to a corpus of discourses that originally made no pretense to philosophy, and to expand upon the early teachings in accordance with the *saṃgha*'s own understanding of *dharma.* This transformation of the tradition is reflected in the canon, where, in addition to the various textual genres mentioned above, the need to systematically classify the teachings gave rise at an early period to texts known as *mātṛkās* ("matrices"), lists or outlines of *dharmas.* These lists, greatly elaborated upon and expanded, probably formed the basis for a new direction in Buddhist exegesis and practice and for a new type of Buddhist literature: inquiries into the "higher" Dharma *(abhidharma).* Collected in a third *piṭaka* (in most schools), Abhidharma literature explored the material and mental constituents of reality with a systematic rigor unknown to the Sūtra literature, providing the scholar-monks who conceived of these texts with a highly detailed map of the path to liberation through the systematic review of *dharmas.* [*See* Dharma, *article on* Buddhist Dharma and Dharmas.]

The Establishment of the Abhidharma Piṭaka. The earlier Abhidharma texts were composed around the second century BCE. These were collected into Abhidharma Piṭakas by the first century BCE.

The Abhidhamma Piṭaka of the Theravāda school is composed of seven texts: (1) *Dhammasaṅgaṇi,* (2) *Vibhaṅga,* (3) *Dhātukathā,* (4) *Puggalapaññati,* (5) *Kathāvatthu,* (6) *Yamaka,* and (7) *Paṭṭhāna.* Of these seven, the *Puggalapaññati* is early, as are parts of the *Vibhaṅga* and the *Dhammasaṅgaṇi.* The remaining portions of the *Vibhaṅga* and *Dhammasaṅgaṇi* were probably compiled next. The *Dhātukathā, Yamaka,* and *Paṭṭhāna* were compiled at a later date, probably around the first century BCE. The *Kathāvatthu,* a polemical collection of the doctrinal positions held by various Buddhist schools, was the last text of Abhidhamma Piṭaka to be compiled, also in the first century BCE. The treatises of the Theravāda Abhidhamma Piṭaka are primarily concerned with ordering and explaining the doctrines presented in the Nikāyas. Consequently, they break little new doctrinal ground.

The Sarvāstivāda Abhidharma Piṭaka is extant in Chinese. It too is composed of seven texts:

1. *Jñānaprasthāna* (T.D. nos. 1543–1544)
2. *Prakaraṇapāda* (T.D. nos. 1541–1542)
3. *Vijñānakāya* (T.D. no. 1539)
4. *Dharmaskandha* (T.D. no.1537)
5. *Prajñaptiśāstra* (T.D. no. 1538)
6. *Dhātukāya* (T.D. no. 1540)
7. *Saṃgītiparyāya* (T.D. no. 1536)

The establishment of the doctrinal independence of the Sarvāstivāda school can be dated from Kātyāyanīputra's composition of the *Jñānaprasthāna.* Since this treatise is the most important work in the Sarvāstivāda Abhidharma Piṭaka, it is often referred to as "the body" (of the Abhidharma), while the remaining six works are called "the feet" *(pāda).* Vasumitra's *Prakaraṇapāda* was written after the *Jñānaprasthāna,* further developing Sarvāstivāda doctrine.

Both the *Jñānaprasthāna* and the *Prakaraṇapāda* were composed around 50 BCE. The remaining five treatises are all older, with the *Dharmaskandha* and the *Saṃgītiparyāya* being the earliest, dating from around the second century BCE. The Chinese translation of the *Prajñaptiśāstra* is incomplete, but a full Tibetan translation does exist. Six of the seven treatises of the Abhidharma Piṭaka were translated by Hsüan-tsang (600–664) from Sanskrit texts he brought back from India. The *Jñānaprasthāna* (T.D. no. 1543) was translated by the Saṃghadeva in 383; the *Prakaraṇapāda* (T.D. 1541) was translated by Guṇabhadra. [*See* Sarvāstivāda.]

Complete Abhidharma Piṭakas exist for both the Theravāda and Sarvāstivāda schools. The Three Baskets (Tripiṭaka) of their canons were probably complete by the first century BCE. Around this same time, written copies of the Pali canon were made in Sri Lanka, largely because the gradually increasing size of the canon had made memorization difficult.

In addition to the Theravāda and Sarvāstivāda collections, the *Śāriputrābhidharma* should also be recognized as a part of an Abhidharma Piṭaka, probably from the Dharmaguptaka school. Although a wide variety of teachings are discussed in the work, few doctrinal advances are found in it, possibly because it is an early treatise. The *Śāriputrābhidharma* was translated into Chinese (T.D. no. 1548) around 415 by Dharmayaśas of Kashmir with the help of Dharmagupta.

Postcanonical Literature. The *Milindapañha* (Questions of King Milinda) was compiled in North India around the third century of the common era. The text was translated into both Pali and Chinese (T.D. no. 1670). Although the name of the person who translated the text into Chinese is not known, the translation was probably done around 400, and preserves an earlier version of the work than the Pali text. Other Pali postcanonical texts that deserve mention are the *Nettippakaraṇa, Peṭakopadesa,* and *Dīpavaṃsa.*

Vinaya Commentaries. Once the Tripiṭaka had been established, monks began to write commentaries on it. Today, Theravāda commentaries, written in Pali, and Sarvāstivāda commentaries, translated into Chinese, survive. In addition, a few commentaries from other schools are extant. Overall, commentaries on the Vinaya are particularly well represented.

At the beginning of the fifth century, a South Indian by the name of Buddhaghosa went to Sri Lanka and, on the basis of earlier Sinhala commentaries, composed a series of commentarial works on the Pali canon. Among them were two commentaries on the Vinaya: the *Samantapāsādikā* and the *Kaṅkhāvitaraṅī*. The *Samantapāsādikā* was translated into Chinese by Saṃghabhadra in 489 as the *Shan-chien-lü p'i-po-sha* (T.D. no. 1462). (An English translation of the Chinese version is now available.) The *Kaṅkhāvitaraṇī* is a commentary on the Pātimokkha. [*See the biography of Buddhaghosa.*]

Besides the *Samantapāsādikā*, the following commentaries on the Vinaya were translated into Chinese:

1. *Sarvāstivāda-vinaya-vibhāṣā* (T.D. no. 1440)
2. *Sarvāstivāda-vinaya-mātṛkā* (T.D. no. 1441)
3. *Mūlasarvāstivāda-vinaya-saṃgraha* (T.D. no. 1458)
4. *Lü erh-shih-erh ming-liao lun* (T.D. no. 1461)
5. *Vinaya-mātṛkā* (T.D. no. 1463)

The contents of the first two works closely agree with that of the *Shih-sung lü*, the Chinese translation of the Sarvāstivāda Vinaya. The translator of the former is not known, but the work was probably translated around the middle of the fifth century. The latter of the two was translated by Saṃghavarman, who was in China from about 424 to 453. The third text, a commentary on the *Mūlasarvāstivādavinaya*, was compiled by Viśeṣamitra and translated by I-ching. A Tibetan translation also exists. The fourth text was composed by Buddhatrāta of the Sammatīya school. Here, the teachings of the Vinaya are related through twenty-two verses with prose explanations. Buddhatrāta's commentary was translated into Chinese in 568 by Paramārtha. The school to which the last of these commentaries belonged is not known; however, since the contents agree with the Dharmaguptaka *Caturvargikavinaya*, it may be considered a Dharmaguptaka work. In addition, Chinese translations of commentaries on the deportment of *śramaṇas* (renunciants, monks) are also extant (T.D. nos. 1470–1476).

Theravāda Commentaries on Sutta and Abhidhamma. As was the case with the Vinaya, once the Sutta Piṭaka had been established, a number of commentaries on its various texts came to be written. When Buddhaghosa came to Sri Lanka he consolidated these works and composed the following five commentaries on the Nikāyas:

1. *Sumaṅgalavilāsinī*, a commentary on *Dīgha Nikāya*
2. *Papañcasūdanī*, a commentary on *Majjhima Nikāya*
3. *Sāratthappakāsinī*, a commentary on *Saṃyutta Nikāya*
4. *Manorathapūraṇī*, a commentary on *Aṅguttara Nikāya*
5. *Paramatthajotikā*, a commentary on *Khuddaka Nikāya*

In addition, Buddhaghosa may have composed other works on the *suttas*, including the *Dhammapadaṭṭhakathā* and the *Jātakaṭṭhakathā*.

Buddhaghosa also wrote several works on the Abhidhamma: the *Atthasālinī*, a commentary on *Dhammasaṅgaṇi*; the *Sammohavinodanī*, a commentary on *Vibhaṅga*; and the *Pañcappakaraṇaṭṭhakathā*, a commentary on other works in the Abhidhamma Piṭaka. Buddhaghosa's *Visuddhimagga* is a systematic explanation of the doctrine of the Nikāyas, and, along with the *Atthasālinī*, is a key text for the study of Theravāda doctrine.

A number of influential scholars wrote works after Buddhaghosa's time. Among them were Buddhadatta, Dhammapāla, Cūla-Dhammapāla, Upasena, and Vajirabuddhi. Later, in the twelfth century, Anuruddha composed the *Abhidhammatthasaṅgaha*, an important introductory text that summarizes Theravāda doctrine. [*See also* Theravāda.]

Chinese Translations of Sūtra- and Abhidharma-related Texts. Among the few commentaries on the Āgamas found in the Chinese canon are the *Fen-pieh kung-te lun* (T.D. no. 1507), the *Ssu-o-han mu ch'ao chieh* (T.D. no. 1505), the *San fa tu lun* (T.D. no. 1506), and the *O-han k'ou-chieh shih-erh yin-yüan ching* (T.D. no. 1508). The first of these is a Chinese translation of a partial commentary on the *Ekottarāgama*, focusing on its first chapter. Although the name of the translator is not known, it was probably translated by the fifth century. The next two works (T.D. nos. 1505 and 1506) are translations of a text by Vasubhadra that analyzes the doctrines of the Āgamas under three classification systems: (1) the Three Refuges (Buddha, Dharma, Saṃgha), (2) the Three Poisons (lust, hatred, ignorance), and (3) the categories of the aggregates *(skandha)*, sense-fields *(āyatana)*, and elements *(dhātu)*. The former was translated by Kumārabuddha in 382, the latter, by Saṃghadeva in 391. The *O-han ching* is a commentary explaining the twelve links of dependent origination *(pratītya-samutpāda)*; it was translated (T.D. no. 1508) in 181 by the Chinese An-hsüan and Yen Fo-t'iao.

Abhidharma Commentaries. Many Abhidharma commentaries are included in the Chinese canon, most of them translations of Hsüan-tsang. The most important are commentaries on the *Jñānaprasthāna.* Among them are the following:

1. *Abhidharma-mahāvibhāṣā* (T.D. nos. 1545–1546)
2. *Abhidharmahṛdaya* (T.D. no. 1550)
3. *Abhidharmahṛdaya Sūtra* (T.D. no. 1551)
4. *Saṃyuktābhidharmahṛdaya* (T.D. no. 1552)

The *Mahāvibhāṣā* is a commentary of 100,000 verses on the *Jñānaprasthāna.* After the *Jñānaprasthāna* had been compiled, Sarvāstivāda research in Abhidharma naturally centered on the explication of this comprehensive text. The results of this centuries-long intensive study were collected into the *Mahāvibhāṣa* at a council of five hundred *arhats* held in Kashmir at the order of King Kaniṣka (r. 132–152). However, the actual text was probably put into its final form around 200 CE. The title *Mahāvibhāṣā* means "great commentary." Besides the *Jñānaprasthāna,* the *Prakaraṇapāda* was also studied by the Sarvāstivādins.

The *Mahāvibhāṣā* was translated into Chinese twice. From 396 to 418, the Chinese monk Tao-t'ai and Buddhavarman collaborated in Liang-chou on the first translation (T.D. no. 1546) of this text. Although the original translation was one hundred fascicles long, only sixty remain. The second translation (T.D. no. 1545) was made by Hsüan-tsang between the years 656 and 659. At two hundred fascicles, it is one of the longest texts in the Chinese canon.

Because the *Mahāvibhāṣā* was so long, shorter guides to the Abhidharma were required. The *Abhidharmahṛdaya, Abhidharmahṛdaya Sūtra,* and *Saṃyuktābhidharmahṛdaya,* compiled in the third and fourth centuries, are examples of such guides. The *Abhidharmakośa* (hereafter referred to as *Kośa*) by the eminent scholiast Vasubandhu (c. 400–480) was compiled next. This text is a skillful presentation of the teachings of the *Mahāvibhāṣā;* however, in it many Sarvāstivāda doctrinal positions are criticized from the viewpoint of the Sautrāntika school. The *Kośa* was translated into Chinese twice, first by Paramārtha (T.D. no. 1559) and later by Hsüan-tsang (T.D. no. 1558). The *Kośa* had an immense influence on Buddhism. Its detailed presentation of Sarvāstivāda positions is necessary for a thorough understanding of Mahāyāna doctrine, especially of the Vijñānavāda tradition. In addition, the *Kośa* served as the doctrinal basis for much of Chinese and Japanese Buddhism.

Because the *Kośa* is such a difficult text, it was inevitable that it be read with detailed commentaries. Of these, Yaśomitra's *Abhidharmakośavyākhyā* is extant in Sanskrit. Although Yaśomitra's text is a valuable reference, the following three commentaries by Chinese monks are also vital for a correct understanding of *Kośa* doctrine:

1. *Chü-she-lun chi,* by P'u-kuang (T.D. no. 1821)
2. *Chü-she-lun shu,* by Fa-pao (T.D. no. 1822)
3. *Chü-she-lun sung shu,* by Yüan-hui (T.D. no. 1823)

P'u-kuang, Fa-pao, and Yüan-hui were all disciples of Hsüan-tsang and each helped in the translation of *Kośa;* thus their commentaries reflect Hsüan-tsang's understanding of the text. In the *Kośa,* Vasubandhu had criticized Sarvāstivāda tenets from the Sautrāntika point of view. In rebuttal, Saṃghabhadra defended Sarvāstivāda doctrines and attacked the *Kośa* in his *Abhidharma-nyāyānusāra Śāstra* (T.D. no. 1562). This work, also translated by Hsüan-tsang, is particularly useful for determining which doctrines of those presented in the *Kośa* are uniquely Sarvāstivāda.

The Chinese translations of Vasubandhu's *Pañcaskandhaprakaraṇa* (T.D. no. 1612, *Ta-sheng wu-yün lun*) and *Karmasiddhaprakaraṇa* (T.D. no. 1609; *Ta-sheng ch'eng-yeh lun*) both have the term Mahāyāna *(ta-sheng)* in their Chinese title. Principally Hīnayāna works, however, they are based on Sarvāstivāda and Sautrāntika doctrines that are treated in terms of the Yogācāra teaching concerning the "store-consciousness" *(ālaya-vijñāna).* They are thus representative of the period when Vasubandhu was moving from a Sarvāstivāda position toward a commitment to Yogācāra thought. These texts exist in both Chinese (by Hsüan-tsang) and Tibetan translation.

Several texts that reflect teachings from other schools are also preserved in Chinese translation. The *Satyasiddhi* (T.D. no. 1646, *Ch'eng-shih lun*) was composed by Harivarman and translated by Kumārajīva around 410. It contains either Sautrāntika or Mahāsāṃghika doctrines. In the *Sammatīya Śāstra* (T.D. no. 1649, *San-mi-ti-pu lun*), Sammatīya teachings are related. The *Vimuttimagga* (T.D. no. 1648, *Chieh-t'o-tao lun*) was composed by the Sinhala monk Upatissa and translated into Chinese by Saṃghavarman in 515. It is a Theravāda text that reflects the influence of the Abhayagirivihāra. A comparative study of the *Vimuttimagga* and the *Visuddhimagga* would be a valuable contribution to Theravāda studies. Many other Abhidharma texts survive in Chinese translation.

Sanskrit and Tibetan Sources for Abhidharma. Little Abhidharma literature has survived in Sanskrit. Fragments of the *Saṃgītiparyāya* and *Dharmaskandha,* two of the works in the Sarvāstivāda Abhidharma Piṭaka, have been discovered. In addition, the following three texts are extant in Sanskrit: the *Abhidharmakośabhāṣya*, the *Abhidharmakośavyākhyā*, and the *Abhidharmadīpa* with its *Vibhāṣāprabhāvṛtti*. The discovery of the Sanskrit text of Vasubandhu's *Abhidharmakośa* has led to significant advances in the scholarly study of the text, as well as of the history of Abhidharma. By beginning with the *Kośa*, earlier sources such as the *Mahāvibhāṣā* can be more profitably studied. The *Abhidharmadīpa*, is an important work for the study of the development of Abhidharma after the *Kośa;* unfortunately, neither a Tibetan nor a Chinese translation of the *Abhidharmadīpa* exists.

Few Abhidharma texts exist in Tibetan translation. In addition to one volume of the *Abhidharma Piṭaka*—the *Prajñapti*—the *Kośa;* with several commentaries, and the *Abhidharmāvatāraprakaraṇa*, also with several commentaries, survive in Tibetan. These texts are valuable not only for *Kośa* studies but also for their new explanations of certain doctrinal points and for their abundant quotations from canonical sources.

Issues in Abhidharma. The Eighteen Schools are each traditionally said to have had a canon (Tripiṭaka). According to I-ching's travel diary the *Nan-hai chi-kuei nei-fa chuan* (T.D. no. 2125), the Mahāsāṁghika, Sthaviravāda, Mūlasarvāstivāda, and Sammatīya schools each had a canon of 300,000 verses. However, today only the Theravāda canon in the Pali language and (partially) the Sarvāstivāda canon in Chinese translation survive. In addition to these two canons, the Vinaya Piṭakas of several schools are extant. In Abhidharma literature, the *Śāriputrābhidharma* of the Dharmaguptaka school, the *Sammatīya Śāstra* of the Sammatīya school, and the *Satyasiddhi* of the Sautrāntika (or Mahāsaṃghika) survive in Chinese translation. In addition, texts such as the *Kathāvatthu* of the Theravāda school and the *Mahāvibhāṣā* of the Sarvāstivāda school cite and criticize the doctrines of a variety of other traditions. In the *Samayabhedoparacanacakra* (T.D. nos. 2031–2033; a Tibetan translation of T.D. no. 2031 also exists) the schisms and the distinctive doctrines of the various Hīnayāna schools are discussed.

Hīnayāna Buddhism continued to flourish after the rise of Mahāyāna. The travel diaries of Fa-hsien, Hsüan-tsang, and I-ching (635–713) all reveal that Hīnayāna orders were generally more powerful than those that followed the Mahāyāna tradition. These texts should be compared with Tibetan sources such as the translation of the *Samayabhedoparacanacakra* and Bhavya's *Nikāyabhedavibhaṅgavyākhyāna*, as well as the church histories of Bu-ston and Tāranātha. [*See the biographies of Fa-hsien, Hsüan-tsang, and I-ching.*]

Mahāyāna Buddhism

The rise of Mahāyāna Buddhism in the first century of the common era signals the development of a newly conceived path to liberation centered around the figure of the *bodhisattva*. This divergence from the soteriology of Nikāya Buddhism, and the accompanying shifts in doctrine, practice, and even social organization it entailed, required a new scriptural dispensation, a new set of sacred texts, to legitimize and sanctify the movement. These texts, like their Hīnayāna counterparts, claim the authority of the Buddha, who is alleged in many of them to have preached these scriptures to assemblies that include *bodhisattva*s and "sons and daughters of good families," a reference to the lay orientation of the early Mahāyāna community. While the Mahāyāna represents a fairly radical departure from the doctrines and practices of Hīnayāna Buddhism, it must be emphasized that after the rise of Mahāyāna, monks of both dispensations sometimes continued to live together in monastic compounds and almost always observed a common Vinaya. Mahāyāna often sees itself as a continuation, not a rejection, of the teachings found in the Hīnayāna canon. [*See* Buddhism, Schools of, *article on* Mahāyāna Buddhism.]

The Emergence of Bodhisattva Orders. Mahāyāna Buddhism appeared in the first century of the common era. The people who propagated the new teachings of the Mahāyāna referred to themselves as *bodhisattva*s and to their organization as a *bodhisattva-gaṇa* ("*bodhisattva* group"), in contrast to the *bhikṣu-saṃgha* ("orders of monks") of Nikāya (Hīnayāna) Buddhism. The term *bodhisattva-gaṇa* was often contrasted with *śravaka-saṃgha* in Mahāyāna *sūtras*.

The term *bodhisattva* originally referred to Śākyamuni Buddha during the period of practice before he realized Buddhahood. Since early and sectarian (Hīnayāna) Buddhists took the *arhat* as their model and goal when they practiced, they did not refer to themselves as *bodhisattvas*. However, early Mahāyānists took the Buddha as their model as they practiced the six "perfections" (*pāramitās*). Striving to realize Buddhahood, they consequently called themselves *bodhisattva*s in imitation of Śākyamuni during the period of his austerities. The practices of the Buddha, including the Six Perfections, had been described in the Jātaka tales and in the biographies of the Buddha. Mahāyāna Buddhists utilized this literature in the formulation of their own practice. Besides striving to realize enlightenment for themselves, they endeavored to perfect their efforts in order to save others. They called their practices the Bodhisattvayāna ("*bodhisattva* vehicle") or Mahāyāna ("great vehicle") in order to emphasize that their view of practice included the salvation of others (hence the term "great") in contrast to those who followed the "self-centered" practices of the Hīnayāna ("lesser vehicle") or Śrāvakayāna ("vehicle of the hearers"). [*See* Bodhisattva Path.]

The early *bodhisattva* orders were located at stupas (Skt., *stūpas*) or at quiet places in the forests *(āraṇyāyatana)*. As the practitioners paid homage at the stupa they probably imitated the Buddha's practices and vowed that they too would become Buddhas. They were able to live from the offerings made by the pious pilgrims who visited the stupa. [*See* Stupa Worship.] The *bodhisattva* practitioners formulated teachings that honored the magnificence of the power of the Buddha to save sentient beings. In quiet retreats in the forests they performed meditations that led to visualizations of the Buddha *(pratyutpannasamādhi)* and developed a variety of new meditations that stressed the resolve required of a *bodhisattva*, meditations such as the *śūraṃgamasamādhi*. At the same time, they incorporated teachings from both Early and Abhidharma Buddhism into their systematization of Mahāyāna doctrine.

Mahāyāna doctrine was based on stupa worship and had as its focus beliefs concerning the Buddha. Behind the human Buddha, they discovered and theorized about the Buddha as absolute principle *(dharmakāya)*. In contrast, Nikāya (Hīnayāna) Buddhism respected Śākyamuni as a human being and based its practice on his teachings *(dharma)*.

Early Mahāyāna Literature. Mahāyāna texts may be divided into two major groups: "early texts" compiled before the time of Nāgārjuna (c. 150–250) and "later texts" composed after Nāgārjuna.

Perfection of Wisdom literature. The Prajñapāramitā texts constitute the earliest type of Mahāyāna literature. These first appeared in South India, were later transmitted to western India, and finally to the North. The number of important scriptures were probably compiled in northern India.

Perfection of Wisdom scriptures developed out of the descriptions of the Six Perfections found in biographies of the Buddha. But here the Six Perfections were systematized on the basis of the Perfection of Wisdom teachings. In particular, the practice of the "perfection of wisdom" *(prajñāpāramitā)*, the realization of the nonsubstantiality *(śūnyatā)* of phenomena, was said to lead to Buddhahood. [*See* Prajña *and* Śūnyam and Śūnyatā.]

The beginnings of Prajñāpāramitā thought date from the first century BCE, but these ideas were not collected into scriptures until the first century CE. By 150, the *Aṣṭasāhasrikā-prajñāpāramitā Sūtra* (Perfection of Wisdom in Eight Thousand Verses) had been translated into Chinese (T.D. no. 224). This text is made up of thirty chapters; by determining which chapters are the earliest, scholars have been able to identify those teachings that date back to before the beginning of the common era.

The *Pañcaviṃśatisāhasrikā-prajñāpāramitā Sūtra* (Perfection of Wisdom in Twenty-five Thousand Lines) was compiled later than the *Perfection of Wisdom in Eight Thousand Lines* and is divided into ninety chapters containing many doctrinal innovations not found in the shorter text. The work was translated into Chinese in the third century (T.D. no. 221), indicating that it was compiled before 250 CE in India. Since the *Prajñāpāramitā Sūtra in Eight Thousand Lines* was translated into Chinese six times and the text in twenty-five thousand lines was translated four times, the comparative study of these translations can be used to reveal much about the historical development of Perfection of Wisdom literature.

A commentary on the *Aṣṭa* by Haribhadra (fl. 800), the *Abhisamayālaṃkārālokā*, is extant in both Sanskrit and Tibetan, but was not translated into Chinese. A commentary on the *Pañca*, the *Mahāprajñāpāramitopadeśa Śāstra*, attributed to Nāgārjuna, is extant in a Chinese translation (T.D. no. 1509), but is not attested in either Sanskrit or Tibetan.

While the *Aṣṭa* and the *Pañca* are the most important Perfection of Wisdom scriptures, several others also deserve mention. The *Vajracchedikā* (T.D. nos. 235–239) is an early text. The *Daśasāhasrikā* exists in Tibetan translation, but not in Chinese. The *Ratnaguṇasaṃuccayagāthā* (T.D. no. 229) is extant in Sanskrit, Tibetan, and Chinese. Other texts are the *Saptaśatikā* (T.D. nos. 232–233), *Adhyardhaśatikā* (T.D. nos. 241–244), *Suvikrāntavikrāmiparipṛcchā*, and the *Prajñāpāramitāhṛdaya Sūtra* (T.D. nos. 250–257). Many of these were included in the *Mahāprajñāpāramitā Sūtra* (T.D. no. 220; Prajñāpāramitā Sūtra in Two Hundred Thousand Lines) translated by Hsüan-tsang in 663. A Tibetan translation corresponding to this immense work exists. The first half is extant in Sanskrit as the *Śatasāhasrikā*. In addition, several brief commentaries on the *Aṣṭa* are extant—these include the *Piṇḍārtha* (T.D. no. 1518) and the *Navaślokī* (T.D. no. 1516).

Several Prajñāpāramitā texts are closely associated with Akṣobhya Buddha. Akṣobhya is mentioned in the nineteenth chapter of the *Aṣṭa*, the *Gaṅgādevī-bhaginī-parivarta*, which relates how Gaṅgādevī was born in Akṣobhya's Pure Land and realized Buddhahood there. Thus, texts concerning Akṣobhya Buddha must have predated this chapter of the *Aṣṭa*. In addition, Akṣobhya is mentioned again in the twenty-seventh and twenty-eighth chapters of the *sūtra*. Since the *Akṣobhyatathā-*

gatasyavyūha (T.D. no. 313) was translated into Chinese around the year 150, texts concerning Akṣobhya must have existed by the first century CE. According to this text, when Akṣobhya was still performing religious practices as a *bodhisattva* in order to realize Buddhahood in the land of Abhirati, he undertook various vows, including one never to be moved by anger. When his vows had been fulfilled, he attained Buddhahood as Akṣobhya and established a Buddha land in order to save sentient beings.

The *Vimalakīrtinirdeśa Sūtra,* a text concerned with nonsubstantiality, is closely related to Prajñāpāramitā literature. According to the twelfth chapter, Vimalakīrti originally lived in Akṣobhya's land of Abhirati. He came to this realm of suffering (Sahā) in order to save its sentient beings. The *Vimalakīrti* was first translated into Chinese between 222 and 253 by Chih Ch'ien (T.D. no. 474), but is much older than the date of translation indicates. Akṣobhya is mentioned in many other texts. The Perfection of Wisdom and belief in Akṣobhya Buddha are major themes of a large group of early Mahāyāna texts.

Nāgārjuna systematized the Perfection of Wisdom literature in his *Mūlamadhyamakakārikā* (T.D. no. 1564). Later, the Mādhayamika tradition carried on Nāgārjuna's thought.

The Buddhāvataṃsaka Sūtra. Among the texts translated by Chih Lou-chia-ch'an (Lokakṣema?) around 150 was the *Tou-sha ching* (T.D. no. 280). This text corresponds to two chapters of the prefatory part of the *Buddhāvataṃsaka Sūtra* (T.D. nos. 278–279; Tibetan translation). Many of the major themes of the *Buddhāvataṃsaka* are found in it, proving that an early version of the important sections of the *sūtra* existed by 150. Although the text claims to reveal the content of the Buddha's enlightenment, it could not do so directly. Instead, enlightenment is indirectly explained in this text by describing the Buddha's religious practices and the stages that led to his enlightenment. Consequently, before the actual contents of the Buddha's enlightenment are discussed (in chapters such as the "Appearance of the Buddha"), the practices of the *bodhisattva*—his leaving home and progressing through the ten abodes, ten degrees of practice, ten degrees of dedication of merit, and ten lands—were explained. Descriptions of the path to enlightenment were thus formulated in Buddhist literature at an early date. For example, the classification of the *bodhisattva*'s practice into ten stages found in the Mahāsāṃghika biography of the Buddha, the *Mahāvastu,* might have provided the basis for the discussion of the stages in the *Buddhāvataṃsaka.*

After Chih Lou-chia-ch'an, some of the separate chapters of the *Buddhāvataṃsaka* were translated by Chih Ch'ien (fl. c. 222) and Chu Fa-hu (Dharmarakṣita?, fl. c. 266). These texts seem to have circulated and to have been translated as independent works. They were collected and incorporated into a larger work, the *Buddhāvataṃsaka-nāma-mahāvaipulya Sūtra,* in the fourth century. This larger text was translated by Buddhabhadra (T.D. no. 278) from 418 to 421. His version consisted of thirty-six chapters, the last being the *Gaṇḍavyūha,* which relates the spiritual quest of the youth Sudhana. Sudhana visits fifty-three people in search of the teaching, and gradually realizes ever higher degrees of enlightenment, culminating in Buddhahood. The chapter thus demonstrated the correspondence between the *bodhisattva*'s practices and the Buddha's enlightenment. Since many of Sudhana's teachers are said to have lived in South India, we may infer that the text was probably compiled in that region.

From 695 to 699, the Khotanese monk Śikṣānanda translated an eighty-fascicle version of the *Buddhāvataṃsaka* in thirty-nine chapters. A Tibetan translation of the *sūtra* with even more chapters was completed later. In addition, a number of independent texts containing *Buddhāvataṃsaka* teachings exist in Chinese translation (T.D. nos. 281–304).

Sanskrit versions exist of the *Daśabhūmika* (describing the ten stage stages to Buddhahood) and the *Gaṇḍavyūha* (both are chapters in the *Avataṃsaka Sūtra*). In addition, the Sanskrit text of the *Bhadracarī-praṇidhānarāja* is extant, and quotations from the *Buddhāvataṃsaka* exist in the *Śikṣāsamuccaya.*

The *Buddhāvataṃsaka* explains enlightenment through the preaching of the Buddha Mahāvairocana. This theme later became an important influence on Esoteric Buddhism. In fact, the *Buddhāvataṃsaka* has many elements in common with Esoteric Buddhism, including the southern origin of both traditions. [*See also* Hua-yen.]

Pure Land literature. Texts that describe Amitābha's power to save sentient beings date back to the first century of the common era. The name of this Buddha refers to his qualities, namely, unlimited life *(amita-āyus)* or unlimited light *(amita-ābha).* The attribute of light has led many scholars to hypothesize Zoroastrian influence, but the doctrines expounded in Buddhist texts on Amitābha are based entirely on Buddhist doctrine. Before attaining Buddhahood, these texts relate, Amitābha had been known as the *bodhisattva* Dharmākara. After seeing the suffering of sentient beings, Dharmākara compassionately vowed to create an ideal land for the salvation of sentient beings who were unable to perform strenuous religious austerities. There, conditions would be ideal for sentient beings to realize Buddhahood. In order to fulfill his vows *(praṇidhāna),* Dharmākara fulfilled the Six Perfections and other austerities over aeons of time, accumulating many merits until finally he realized Buddhahood as Amitābha and established his Pure Land, Sukhāvatī. According to Amitābha's primordial vow *(pūrva-praṇidhāna),* any person who believes in Amitābha's saving power and wishes to be reborn in the Pure Land is in accord with Amitābha's intention and will achieve rebirth. These teachings are fully congruent with Mahāyāna doctrines on compassion and wisdom.

The earliest text to focus on Amitābha was probably the *O-mi-t'o-fo ching* (T.D. no. 362, *Mahāmitābha Sūtra?*). Since it was translated into Chinese by Chih Ch'ien, it was probably composed before 200 CE. The *Wu-liang ch'ing-ching p'ing-teng chiao ching* (T.D. no. 361, *Amitaprabha-buddha Sūtra?*) was probably composed next. It is said to have been translated by Chih Lou-chia-ch'an, but this has been questioned by some scholars. If Chih Lou-chia-ch'an did in fact translate it, its composition would predate 100 CE. The contents of both of these texts are similar. The *Wu-liang-shou ching* (T.D. no. 360, *Amitayuḥ Sūtra*) was translated into Chinese at the beginning of the fifth century and played an important role in China, where it was often read and chanted. Fascicle 5 of the *Ratnakūṭa Sūtra* (T.D. no. 310) is also an Amitābha text; it was translated at the beginning of the eighth century. The Sanskrit version and Tibetan translation of the "larger" *Sukhāvatīvyūha* contain forty-eight vows and more advanced doctrinal positions than the other texts. *The Wu-liang-shou chuang-yen ching* (T.D. no. 363) was translated into Chinese in 991; it had only thirty-six vows.

The texts mentioned above are related to the *Larger Sukhāvatīvyūha.* A "smaller" *Sukhāvatīvyūha* also exists; it was translated into Chinese twice, first by Kumārajīva (T.D. no. 366) and later by Hsüan-tsang (T.D. no. 367). A Sanskrit version and Tibetan translation are extant. This text is concerned with the description of the Pure Land; no mention is made of Dharmākara's vows or the origins of Sukhāvatī. The *Smaller Sukhāvatīvyūha* is an earlier work than the *Larger Sukhāvatīvyūha.*

In the *Kuan wu-liang-shou ching* (T.D. no. 365, *Amitāyur-nidhyāna Sūtra?*), meditations *(vipaśyanā)* on the attributes of the Pure Land, Amitābha, and the *bodhisattvas* Avalokiteśvara and Mahāsthāmaprāpta are discussed. The text was translated into Chinese in the fifth century. Although no Tibetan or Sanskrit versions exist, the text has played an important role in the East Asian Pure Land tradition.

The abovementioned scriptures are all primarily concerned with Amitābha's power to save sentient beings, but Amitābha is mentioned in passing in more than three hundred other Mahāyāna *sūtras*, indicating that rebirth in Pure Land was the aspiration of many Mahāyāna believers. Among these texts are the *Pan-chou san-mei ching* (T.D. no. 418, *Pratyutpannasamādhi Sūtra*) and the *Hui-yin san-mei ching* (T.D. no. 632).

According to the *Shih-chu p'i-p'o-sha lun* (T.D. no. 1521, *Daśabhūmika-vibhāṣā*), attributed to Nāgārjuna, Amitābha's Pure Land is intended to provide an easy path for those who lack the will to perform strenuous religious austerities. Vasubandhu is credited with a commentary on the *Larger Sukhāvatīvyūha,* the *Wu-liang-shou-ching yu-po-t'i-she* (T.D. no. 1524, *Amitāyuḥ-sūtropadeśa*), a work that became a major influence on East Asian Pure Land Buddhism. [*See also* Amitābha.]

The Lotus Sutra. The first Chinese translation of the *Saddharmapuṇḍarīka Sūtra* (Lotus Sutra) was done in the year 286 by Dharmarakṣa (T.D. no. 263), indicating that early versions of the text must have been compiled in northern India before 250 CE. The *Lotus* was next translated by Kumārajīva (T.D. no. 262) in 406. However, Kumārajīva's translation was based on an earlier version than that of Dharmarakṣa, suggesting that the composition of the *Lotus* can be moved back to before 200. Kumārajīva's translation was composed of twenty-seven chapters. The last six chapters are later than the first twenty-one. Moreover, the first twenty-one were not composed at the same time. The earliest chapters are those thematically associated with the second chapter, the *Upāyakauśalya.* They were probably compiled between 100 and 150 CE. The fifteenth chapter, the *Tathāgatāyuṣpramāṇa,* consists of earlier teachings that were incorporated into the *Lotus;* it too is an early part of the text.

The theme of the second chapter is the "one vehicle" *(ekayāna);* the fifteenth is concerned with the unlimited lifespan of the Buddha (and how he realized Buddhahood in the distant past). These are the two main themes of the text. According to the doctrine of the One Vehicle, all the multitudinous Buddhist doctrines can be resolved into one ultimate teaching and all sentient beings are said to possess the essential quality necessary for the realization of Buddhahood (Buddha nature). The object of the Buddha's teaching is to lead people to the realization of their own essential nature, to the attainment of Buddhahood. The teaching of the "three vehicles" *(śrāvakayāna, pratyekabuddhayāna,* and *bodhisattvayāna)* that preceded the *Lotus* is said in that text to be merely an expedient to lead people to the ultimate teaching of the One Vehicle. Thus, the *Lotus* was compiled in order to criticize the early Mahāyāna teaching of a distinct *bodhisattva* vehicle.

The *Lotus* was translated into Chinese again in 601 (T.D. no. 264). This translation includes the *Devadatta-parivarta,* a chapter not found in Kumārajīva's original translation. Today, three Chinese translations, a Tibetan translation, and various Sanskrit texts exist. Because in early Mahāyāna cults of the book *(pustaka),* in which believers were encouraged to copy texts such as the *Lotus* or the Prajñāpāramitā literature, were common, many manuscripts of the *Lotus* have been preserved until modern times. Also extant is a commentary on the *Lotus* by Vasubandhu, the *Saddharmapuṇḍarīka-sūtropadeśa* (T.D. nos. 1519–1520). Although short, the text was studied by many Chinese followers of the *Lotus.* [*See also* T'ien-t'ai.]

Other early Mahāyāna texts. Because many other Mahāyāna texts compiled before Nāgārjuna's time are extant, only a few of them can be mentioned. Mañjuśrī Kumārabhūta's power to save sentient beings is discussed in many *sūtras.* The *bodhisattva* Mañjuśrī is the personification of Mahāyāna wisdom. In the *Buddhāvataṃsaka,* the Buddha Mahāvairocana's wisdom is demonstrated through the actions of Mañjuśrī and Samantabhadra. The *bodhisattva* Samantabhadra is a personification of the religious practices that enabled Śākyamuni to realize Buddhahood. Samantabhadra and Mañjuśrī are the protagonists of many Mahāyāna texts. [*See* Mañjuśrī.]

The *Śūraṃgamasamādhi Sūtra* (T.D. no. 642) is representative of the many Mahāyāna *sūtras* in which Mañjuśrī is the main character. According to this text, Mañjuśrī completed the practices necessary to realize Buddhahood long ago, but remained a *bodhisattva* in order to save sentient beings. He underwent countless rebirths without tiring in his efforts to benefit others. According to the *Ajātaśatru-kaukṛtya-vinodana* (T.D. nos. 626–629), when King Ajātaśatru realized that he had committed a grave sin by killing his father, Mañjuśrī taught him how to meditate on nonsubstantiality *(śūnyatā),* freeing him from his fear of wrongdoing. In addition, Mañjuśrī is said to have led Śākyamuni into the Buddhist path aeons ago, and is thus called the mother and father of the Buddhist path. A variety of other texts (T.D. nos. 458–473) are also concerned with Mañjuśrī.

Maitreya *bodhisattva* is discussed in six *sūtras* (T.D. nos. 452–457). According to popular Buddhist belief, Maitreya currently resides in Tuṣita Heaven, where he awaits rebirth in his next life in this world, here to realize Buddhahood and save sentient beings by preaching in three assemblies. Such teachings attracted many believers, especially in China and Japan, who hoped to be present at such assemblies and to be saved by Maitreya. [*See* Maitreya.] Bhaiṣajyaguru-vaiḍūryaprabha, the healing Buddha, is also the subject of several texts (T.D. nos. 449–451). [*See* Bhaiṣajyaguru.]

The *Mahāratnakūṭa* (T.D. no. 310) is a large collection of Mahāyāna *sūtras.* A variety of Mahāyāna doctrines are found in the collection, but several texts are early. In particular, the *Kāśyapaparivarta* (T.D. no. 310.43; also T.D. nos. 350–353) was probably composed very early and is the central text in the collection. In it, nonsubstantiality, the Middle Way *(madhyama-pratipad),* and Mahāyāna practice are expounded.

The *Mahāsaṃnipāta Sūtra* (T.D. no. 397) is a collection of seventeen Mahāyāna texts. It is important because it includes *tathagāta-garbha* teachings. In addition, the work contains many *dhāraṇīs* (short mantric spells), and thus is a significant text for research on the origins of Esoteric Buddhism. Other texts reflect Mahāyāna practices such as meditation (e.g., T.D. nos. 602–620) and the chanting of the Buddha's name in order to vanquish wrongdoing (e.g., T.D. nos. 425–448 and 1492–1496).

Later Mahāyāna Literature. By "later Mahāyāna literature" we mean texts compiled after Nāgārjuna (c. 150–250). A large number of Mahāyāna texts are quoted in the *Mahāprajñāpāramitopadeśa* (T.D. no. 1509), attributed to Nāgārjuna, but technical terms peculiar to the Tathāgata-garbha and Vijnāptimātra traditions do not appear. Kumārajīva (active in Ch'ang-an from 402 to 413), translator of the *Mahāprajñāpāramitopadeśa,* translated texts by Nāgārjuna, but not by Asaṅga and Vasubandhu. Texts by Asaṅga and Vasubandhu were translated by Bodhiruci (arrived in China in 508) and Ratnamati. However, even earlier, Dharmakṣema (arrived in China in 412) and Bodhiruci (arrived in China in 424) had translated the *Bodhisattvabhūmi* (T.D. nos. 1581–1582), a section of the *Yogācārabhūmi.* Consequently, texts concerning Yogācāra or Tathāgata-garbha thought are believed to have been compiled after Nāgārjuna's time.

Tathāgata-garbha literature. The earliest scripture to use the term *tathāgata-garbha* was the *Tathāgatagarbha-nāma-mahāvaipulya Sūtra* (T.D. no. 666), translated in 418 by Buddhabhadra. However, as early as 311, Fa-chü had translated a text entitled the *Ju-lai-tsang ching.* Fa-chü's translation is not extant and its contents are unknown; however, if the contents were the same as the *Tathāgatagarbha Sūtra* then the term *tathāgata-garbha* would be attested prior to the year 300. Amoghavajra (705–774) also translated the *Tathāgatagarbha-nāma-mahāvaipulya Sūtra* (T.D. no. 667).

Guṇabhadra (arrived in China in 420) translated the *Śrīmālādevīsiṃhanāda Sūtra* (T.D. no. 353, variant translation, T.D. no. 310, fascicle 48) and Bodhiruci translated the *Anūnatvāpūrṇatvanirdeśa Sutra* (T.D. no. 668). These *sūtra*s are typical of Tathāgata-garbha literature; others worthy of mention are the following:

1. *Aṅgulimālīya Sūtra* (T.D. no. 120), translated by Guṇabhadra
2. The Mahāyāna version of the *Mahāparinirvāṇa Sūtra* (T.D. no. 374), translated in approximately 424 by Dharmakṣema
3. *Mahābherīhāraka Sūtra* (T.D. no. 270), translated by Guṇabhadra
4. *Laṅkāvatāra Sūtra* (T.D. no. 670), translated by Guṇabhadra (T.D. nos. 671–672 are other translations of this text.)
5. *Suvarṇaprabhāsottama Sūtra* (T.D. no. 663), translated by Dharmakṣema (T.D. no. 664–665 are additional translations of this text.)

The term *tathāgata-garbha* was used to express the idea that an ordinary person *(pṛthagjana)* possesses the essence of the *tathāgata (dharmakāya)* but that it is hidden by defilements. Explaining the relationship between the seemingly opposed spiritual qualities of ordinary people and the Buddha was the central theme of this literature. In the *Tathāgatagarbha-nāma-mahāvaipulya Sūtra* (T. D. no. 666), the manner in which the *dharmakāya* is hidden within the body of a person is described through the use of nine metaphors. In the *Anūnatvāpūrṇatvanirdeśa Sūtra* the realms of the Tathāgata and sentient beings *(bahujana-dhātu)* are said to be identical, without gain or loss. The *Śrīmālādevī Sūtra* is particularly detailed and systematic about the relationship between the *dharmakāya* and the defilements of sentient beings.

These scriptures were composed between 250 and 400. The *Ratnagotravibhāgo-mahāyānottaratantra Śāstra* (T.D. no. 1611) is a later text that systematically explains Tathāgata-garbha thought; it is extant in Sanskrit, Tibetan, and Chinese. The *Ta-sheng ch'i-hsin lun* (*Mahāyāna-śraddhotpāda Śāstra*, T.D. nos. 1666–1667) is probably even later. Although some modern scholars have argued that it was written in China, the contents of the text are clearly based on Indian, rather than Chinese ideas.

Tathāgata-garbha thought has its origins in earlier technical terms such as "the element of the Buddha" *(tathāgata-dhātu)*, "the clan of the Buddha" *(tathāgata-gotra)*, and "the originally pure mind" *(prakṛtiprabhāsvaraṃ cittam)*. Such terms were found in scriptures such as the *Buddhāvataṃsaka, Prajñāpāramitā, Saddharmapuṇḍarīka, Vimalakīrtinirdeśa, Ratnakūṭa*, and the *Mahāsaṃnipāta*. [*See* Tathāgata-garbha.]

Yogācāra literature. The *Abhidharma-mahāyāna Sūtra* and the *Saṃdhinirmocana Sūtra* are particularly important Yogācāra scriptures. The *Abhidharma-mahāyāna Sūtra* was quoted in the *Mahāyānasaṃgraha* and other Yogācāra texts, thereby enabling us to gain some sense of its contents. However, since it was never translated into Chinese or Tibetan, its overall structure is unknown. There are two full Chinese translations of the *Saṃdhinirmocana Sūtra* (T.D. no. 675 by Bodhiruci in 514, and T.D. no. 676 by Hsüan-tsang in 647). In addition, a partial translation by Paramārtha (T.D. no. 677) exists; this corresponds to the first five of the eight chapters of Hsüan-tsang's translation, the sections of the text that contain the important Yogācāra doctrines. In 435 Guṇabhadra translated parts of the text (T.D. nos. 678–679) that correspond to the last two chapters of Hsüan-tsang's translation; however, none of the important Yogācāra doctrines are found in these chapters. Consequently, the composition of the *Saṃdhinirmocana* should probably be dated around 400. The Tibetan translation of the text is similar to the texts translated by Bodhiruci and Hsüan-tsang. No Sanskrit version of the work has been discovered.

Yogācāra doctrine is composed of three major elements. The first is the yogic practice through which self-awareness is gained. Meditative practices such as the visualization of the Buddha led to the doctrinal position that the three realms are exclusively products of mind *(cittamātram traidhātukam)*. This position is found in texts such as the *Pratyutpannasamādhi Sūtra* (T.D. no. 418) and the *Buddhāvataṃsaka* (T.D. no. 278). The second element consists of teachings concerning the "store-consciousness" *(ālaya-vijñāna)*. The description of the relationship between the store-consciousness, roughly analogous to a subconsciousness, and the seven active levels of consciousness *(vijñāna)* was a major Yogācāra theme. The store-consciousness played an important role in explanations of *karman* and rebirth. The third element of Yogācāra doctrine is the "three natures" *(trisvabhāva)* teaching. Through this teaching, Yogācāra thinkers were able to criticize both Abhidharma views on innate existence *(svabhāva)* and Mādhyamika positions on nonsubstantiality *(śūnya)*.

Mahāyāna Schools. Below we shall consider the literature of the "schools" of Mahāyāna, the Madhyāmika and Yogācāra traditions, and the works of the logicians.

Mādhyamika. The teaching of the Mādhyamika school is based on Nāgārjuna's *Madhyamaka Śāstra* (*Mūlamadhyamakakārikā;* T.D. no. 1564). Biographies of Nāgārjuna (T.D. no. 2047) and his disciple Āryadeva (T.D. no. 2048) were translated into Chinese by Kumārajīva. The *Madhyamaka Śāstra*, along with commentaries, exists in Sanskrit, Tibetan, and Chinese. In Sanskrit, Nāgārjuna's *Mūlamadhyamakakārikā* and Candrakīrti's commentary, the *Prasannapadā*, are extant.

Three commentaries on the *Madhyamaka Śāstra* exist in Tibetan translation: a commentary by Buddhapālita, Bhāvaviveka's *Prajñādīpa-mūlamadhyamaka-vṛtti,* and Candrakīrti's *Prasannapadā.* Kumārajīva's translation of the *Madhyamaka Śāstra,* with Ching-mu's (Piṅgala?) commentary, is also extant. In addition, Bhāvaviveka's *Prajñāpradīpa* (T.D. no. 1566) and Sthiramati's *Ta-sheng chung-kuan shih lun* (T.D. no. 1567) were also translated into Chinese.

Nāgārjuna is credited with the authorship of many works besides the *Madhyamaka Śāstra.* Among them are the following:

1. *Vigrahavyāvartanī* (Skt., Tib., and Chin.; T.D. no. 1631)
2. *Yuktiṣaṣṭikā* (Tib., Chin.; T.D. no. 1575)
3. *Śūnyatāsaptati* (Tib.)
4. *Mahāyāna-viṃśatikā* (Skt., Tib., Chin.; T.D. no. 1576)
5. *Daśabhūmikavibhāṣā* (Chin.; T.D. no. 1521)
6. *Mahaprajñāpāramitopadeśa Śāstra* (Chin.; T.D. no. 1509).

Many other works besides these are attributed to Nāgārjuna. The *Madhyamaka Śāstra* influenced both Indian and Tibetan Buddhism. The *Mahāprajñāpāramitopadeśa* played a major role in Chinese Buddhism; however, its authenticity has been questioned by some modern scholars. [*See the biography of Nāgārjuna.*]

Nāgārjuna's disciple, Āryadeva (c. 170–270), is said to have been a native of South India or Sri Lanka. He was the author of the *Catuḥśataka* (Skt. and Tib; a Chinese translation of the last half of the text exists, T.D. no. 1570). A commentary on the text by Dharmapāla (T.D. no. 1571) is extant. Āryadeva also wrote the *Śataka* (T.D. no. 1569) and the *Śatakṣara Śāstra* (T.D. no. 1572). [*See the biography of Āryadeva.*]

Rāhulabhadra (c. 200–300) was active after Āryadeva. He is the author of stanzas in praise of both the Perfection of Wisdom *(Prajñāpāramitāstuti)* and the *Lotus Sutra (Saddharmapuṇḍarīkastava).* Since Rāhulabhadra's works are quoted in Asaṅga's *Shun-chung lun* (T.D. no. 1565), Rāhulabhadra must antedate Asaṅga.

The names of Rāhulabhadra's immediate successors are not known. After Buddhapālita (c. 470–540) wrote a commentary on the *Mūlamadhyamakakārikā* entitled *Mūlamadhyamakavṛtti,* explaining Nāgārjuna's thought from the Prāsaṅgika position, the tradition flourished again. Later, Bhāvaviveka (c. 490–570) explained the Svātantrika stand in the *Prajñāpradīpa,* and attacked Buddhapālita's position. According to Prāsaṅga thought, the Mādhyamika adherent should point out the errors in an opponent's views but not advance positive views of his own. In contrast, according to the theory of *svatantrānumāna* (independent inference), Mādhyamika views could be formulated as propositions valid at least on a mundane level. Candrakīrti (c. 600–650) criticized Bhāvaviveka's use of inference *(anumāna)* and defended Buddhapālita's position. As a result, the Mādhyamika tradition was divided into Svātantrika and Prāsaṅgika factions in later accounts. [*See the biographies of Buddhapālita, Bhāvaviveka, and Candrakīrti.*]

Besides the *Prajñāpradīpa,* Bhāvaviveka is the author of the *Madhyamakahṛdayakārikā,* its autocommentary (*Vṛtti-tarkajvālā,* extant in Tibetan translation), and the *Ta-sheng chang-chen lun* (extant in Chinese; T.D. no. 1578). Avalokitavrata (c. 700) wrote a commentary on the *Prajñāpradīpa,* the *Prajñāpradīpaṭīkā* (extant in Tibetan); this very large text cites the positions of many Mādhyamika scholars. Unfortunately, the development of the Svātantrika after Avalokitavrata is not clear.

In addition to the *Prasannapadā,* a number of works by Candrakīrti have survived in Tibetan translation, including the *Madhymakāvatāra, Śūnyatāsaptativṛtti, Yuktiṣaṣṭikāvṛtti,* and *Pañcaskandhaprakaraṇa.* Although Candrakīrti's views are regarded as authoritative within Tibetan Buddhism, his works were never translated into Chinese. Śāntideva (c. 650–700) was active after Candrakīrti. Among his works are the *Bodhicaryāvatāra* (T.D. no. 1662), a description of Mādhyamika practice, and the *Śikṣāsamuccaya* (T.D. no. 1636), which concerns the Mahāyāna path; both survive in Sanskrit, Tibetan, and Chinese. An important commentary on the *Bodhicaryāvatāra,* the *Bodhicaryāvatārapañjikā* by Prajñākaramati (c. 950–1030), survives in Sanskrit and Tibetan. [*See the biography of Śāntideva.*] Jñānagarbha (c. eighth century) is the author of the influential *Satyadvayavibhaṅga,* its autocommentary *(Satyadvayavibhaṅga-vṛtti),* and the *Yogabhāvanāmārga.* These survive in Tibetan translation.

Śāntirakṣita (c. 725–790) was a scholar at Nālandā and a disciple of Jñānagarbha. He is the author of the *Tattvasaṃgraha,* a large work of twenty-six chapters in which other schools are criticized from the Mādhyamika position. Both the *Tattvasaṃgraha* and a detailed commentary *(pañjikā)* by Kamalaśīla survive in Sanskrit and Tibetan. Śāntirakṣita also wrote the *Madhyamakālaṃkāra,* an autocommentary *(vṛtti)* on it, and a commentary on Jñānagarbha's *Satyadavayavibhaṅga.* These exist in Tibetan translation.

Kamalaśīla (c. 740–795) was a disciple of Śāntirakṣita. Both men were invited to Tibet by King Khri-sroṅ-lde-brtsan and played vital roles in the establishment of Tibetan Buddhism. Kamalaśīla is the author of the *Madhyamakāloka, Tattvāloka,* and *Sarvadharmaniḥsvabhāvasiddhi,* as well as commentaries on the *Tattvasaṃgraha* and *Madhyamakālaṃkāra.* He also wrote three works entitled *Bhāvanākrama,* a discussion of the stages of Mahāyāna practice. These texts are all extant in Tibetan translation. A Sanskrit text of the *Bhāvanākrama* also survives, and *Bhāvanākrama* I was translated into Chinese (T.D. no. 1664). The works of Śāntirakṣita and Kamalaśīla are vital for an understanding of the later history of Mādhyamika. Śāntirakṣita is noteworthy for his synthesis of Mādhyamika and Yogācāra thought and the establishment of a Yogācāra-Mādhyamika tradition. [*See the biographies of Śāntirakṣita and Kamalaśīla.*]

Also extant are texts by a number of later Mādhyamika scholars. Vimuktisena (eighth century) wrote a commentary *(vṛtti)* on Maitreyanātha's *Abhisamayālaṃkāra* that survives in Tibetan. His disciple Haribhadra (fl. 800) was the author of the large work, *Aṣṭasāhasrikā-vyākhyā-abhisamayālaṃkārālokā* based on the *Abhisamayālaṃkāra.* Maitreya's Yogācāra works were commented upon by Mādhyamika scholars such as Vimuktisena and Haribhadra. Later Mādhyamika scholars include Bodhibhadra, author of the *Jñānasārasamuccayanibandhana* (Tib.), and Advayavajra, author of the *Tattvaratnāvalī* (Skt. and Tib.). In the eleventh century, Ratnākaraśānti of the Vikramaśīla Monastery wrote the *Antarvyāptisamarthana,* a logic text, and the *Prajñāpāramitopadeśa,* a Mādhyamika-Yogācāra work. Later, Atīśa (982–1054) served as head of the Vikramaśīla monastery. [*See the biography of Atīśa.*] He subsequently went to Tibet, where he reformed Buddhism. Atīśa was the author of many works, including the *Bodhipathapradīpa,* and is usually considered to be a Prāsaṅgika scholar. [*See also* Mādhyamika.]

Yogācāra. The Yogācāra or Vijñānavādin school was based on the *Abhidharma-mahāyāna Sūtra* and the *Saṃdhinirmocana Sūtra.* The founder of the tradition was Maitreyanātha (c. 350–430). He was followed by Asaṅga (ca. 395–470), who systematized Yogācāra thought, and by Asaṅga's younger brother and disciple Vasubandhu (c. 400–480), who completed the system. Some scholars, however, have questioned the historicity of Maitreyanātha, arguing that he has been confused with the future Buddha, Maitreya.

If Maitreyanātha is recognized as a historical person, then among the works attributed to him are: *Yogācārabhūmi* (T.D. no. 1579), *Mahāyānasūtrālaṃkārakārikā* T.D. no. 1604), *Madhyāntavibhāgakārikā* (T.D. nos. 1599–1601), *Dharmadharmatāvibhaṅga,* and the *Abhisamayālaṃkārakārikā.* The *Mahāyānasaṃgraha* is considered to be the work of Asaṅga because its contents differ from the verses of the *Mahāyānasūtrālaṃkāra* and the *Madhyāntavibhāga.* In the Tibetan tradition, Asaṅga is considered the author of the *Yogācārabhūmi;* however, since the text is large and probably includes the thought of a number of monks, it should not be attributed to any single author. Tibetan translations of all five works attributed to Maitreya are extant, as are Sanskrit versions of all but the *Dharmadharmatāvibhaṅga.*

The biographies of Asaṅga and Vasubandhu were translated into Chinese by Paramārtha (T.D. no. 2049) and recorded by Hsüan-tsang in his travel diary (T.D. no. 2087). Asaṅga's *Mahāyānasaṃgraha* (T.D. nos. 1592–1594), which exists in both Tibetan and Chinese translation, was commented on by both Vasubandhu (T.D. nos. 1596–1597) and Asvabhāva (T. D. no. 1598). Asaṅga was also the author of *Hsien-yang sheng-chiao lun* (T.D. no. 1602), *Abhidharmasamuccaya* (T.D. 1605), *Vajracchedikā-saptārthaṭīkā* (T.D. no. 1510), *Liu-men chiao-shou hsi-ting lun* (T.D. no. 1607), and *Shun-chung lun* (T.D. no. 1565). The first, fourth, and fifth of these (T.D. nos. 1602, 1607, and 1565) exist only in Chinese translation. The existence of several Chinese translations of the *Mahāyānasaṃgraha* indicates its importance. This text was a systematization of Yogācāra thought based on the *Abhidharma-mahāyāna Sūtra* and the *Saṃdhinirmocana Sūtra.* The *Mahāyānasaṃgraha* and *Abhidharmasamuccaya* are the two most important sources for Asaṅga's thought. [*See the biography of Asaṅga.*]

Vasubandhu wrote several Yogācāra texts, including the *Triṃśikā-vijñaptimātratāsiddhi* (T.D. no. 1586) and the *Viṃśatikā-vijñaptimātratāsiddhi* (T.D. no. 1590). Both texts exist in Sanskrit, Tibetan, and several Chinese versions. The *Viṃśatikā* is both a refutation of attacks on Yogācāra thought and a presentation of proofs of the Yogācāra position. The *Triṃśikā* is a systematic presentation of Yogācāra thought. Sthiramati's commentary on the *Viṃśatika* is extant in both Sanskrit and Tibetan. Comments on it by Dharmapāla and nine other scholars have been combined in the *Ch'eng wei-shih lun* (T.D. no. 1585, *Vijñaptimātratāsiddhi*), the text that has traditionally served as the basic source for Yogācāra study in East Asia.

Vasubandhu also wrote the *Trisvabhāvanirdeśa,* extant in Sanskrit and Tibetan, and commented on a number of Yogācāra texts, including the *Mahāyānasaṃgraha* (T.D. no. 1597) and *Madhyāntavibhāga* (T.D. no. 1599). In addition, Vasubandhu is credited with commentaries on *sūtras* that clarified several important Mahāyāna traditions outside the Yogācāra tradition. The following three commentaries discuss the ten stages of the path to Buddhahood, the *Lotus Sutra* and the *Sukhāvatīvyūha* (Pure Land) *Sūtra,* respectively: (1) *Daśabhūmikavyākhyāna* (T.D. no. 1522), (2) *Saddharmapuṇḍarīkopadeśa* (T.D. no. 1519), and (3) *Sukhāvatīvyūhopadeśa* (T.D. no. 1524). The *Fo-hsing lun* (T.D. no.

1610, *Buddhadhātu Śāstra*) is said to have been written by Vasubandhu, but so closely resembles the *Ratnagotravibhāga* that this attribution is questionable. [*See the biography of Vasubandhu.*]

After Vasubandhu, the Yogācāra tradition split into two factions: the Nirākāra-vijñānavādins, beginning with Guṇamati (c. 490) and Sthiramati (c. 510–570), and the Sākāra-vijñānavādins, beginning with Dignāga (c. 480–540) and Dharmapāla (530–561). Guṇamati and Sthiramati were active in Valabhī in western India. Guṇamati was the author of the *Sui-hsiang lun* (T.D. no. 1641). He is also credited with commentaries on the *Abhidharmakośa* and *Triṃśikā*, but neither of these has survived. Sthiramati wrote the *Tattvārtha* (a commentary on the *Abhidharmakośa* that survives in Tibetan translation), a commentary on the *Triṃśikā*, and the *Pañcaskandhaprakaraṇa-vaibhāṣya* (T.D. no. 1613). [*See the biography of Sthiramati.*]

Dignāga is famous principally for his systematization of Buddhist logic. His major text on logic, the *Pramāṇasamuccaya*, is extant only in Tibetan. In this book he discusses the requirements for causal relations to be valid and establishes new views on Buddhist logic (*hetuvidyā*). Dignāga's *Nyāyamukha* (T.D. nos. 1628–1629) is famous as an introductory text on logic. Dignāga was also the author of a number of texts on Yogācāra, including the *Ālambanaparīkṣā* (T.D. nos. 1619, 1624), *Upādāyaprajñaptiprakaraṇa* (T.D. no. 1622), *Chieh chüan lun* (*Hastavālaprakaraṇa*; T.D. nos. 1620–1621), and the *Sāmānyalakṣaṇaparīkṣā* (T.D. no. 1623). Tibetan translations of two of these (T.D. nos. 1619–1620) exist. In addition, the *Yogāvatāra*, *Marmadīpa* (commentary on the *Kośa*), *Trikālaparīkṣā*, and others are extant only in Tibetan translation. [*See the biography of Dignāga.*]

Dignāga's disciple, Asvabhāva (c. 500), was the author of a commentary on the *Mahāyānasaṃgraha* (T.D. no. 1598). His disciple Dharmapāla (530–561), a native of South India, became the head of the monastic university at Nālandā at an early age. Dharmapāla was the author of a commentary on the *Triṃśikā* that formed the basis of the *Ch'eng wei-shih lun* (T.D. no. 1585). Other texts by him include the *Ta-sheng kuang pai-lun shih-lun* (T.D. no. 1571), *Ch'eng wei-shih pao-sheng lun* (T.D. no. 1591), and the *Kuan so-yüan lun-shih* (T.D. no. 1625). [*See the biography of Dharmapāla.*]

Dignāga and his successor, Dharmakīrti, were scholars of both Yogācāra and Buddhist logic. As a result, Yogācāra gradually developed into a logical tradition. As I have noted, Yogācāra thought was gradually imported into Mādhyamika doctrine, yielding a tradition called Yogācāra-Mādhyamika. Thus, Yogācāra was absorbed into Mādhyamika and Buddhist logic and disappeared as an independent tradition. [*See also* Yogācāra.]

Buddhist logic. Logic has been used by Buddhists since Śākyamuni's time. However, many early Buddhists also believed that the true nature of reality could not be understood through logical means. In the Mahāyāna tradition, Nāgārjuna, Asaṅga, and Vasubandhu are all credited with works that concern logic.. The rivalry between the Svātantrika and Prāsaṅgika factions was due, in part, to their evaluation of logical methods. The first text to have Buddhist logic as its primary topic was Dignāga's *Pramāṇasamuccaya*. After Dignāga, Śaṃkarasvāmin (fl. 570) wrote the *Nyāyapraveśa* (T.D. no. 1630). This text was translated into Chinese by Hsüan-tsang, and the Chinese text was later rendered into Tibetan. A Sanskrit version has also been discovered. The *Nyāyapraveśa* was widely studied and commented upon by Chinese and Japanese monks.

Dharmakīrti (c. 600–670) further developed Dignāga's studies in logic. Although his works were never translated into Chinese, many are extant in Tibetan translation and Sanskrit. Among them are (1) *Nyāyabindu*, (2) *Pramāṇaviniścaya*, (3) *Pramāṇavārttika*, (4) *Hetubindu*, (5) *Sambandhaparīkṣā*, (6) *Vādanyāya*, and (7) *Saṃtānāntarasiddhi*. The *Nyāyabindu* is a summary of Dharmakīrti's views on logic. Sanskrit commentaries such as Dharmottara's *Nyāyabinduṭīkā* and Durvekamiśra's *Dharmottarapradīpa* are extant. A Tibetan translation of a commentary by Vinītadeva also exists. Dharmakīrti's major work, the *Pramāṇavārttika*, is in four chapters. Dharmakīrti wrote his own commentary on the first (*Svārthānumāna*) chapter. Prajñākaragupta's commentary on the other three chapters, the *Pramāṇavārttikālaṃkāra*, is also extant. Commentaries by Manorathanandin and Vibhūticandra also survive. The *Pramāṇavārttika* and these commentaries survive in Sanskrit; others are preserved in Tibetan translation. Because the source material on the *Pramāṇavārttika* is so abundant, many modern scholars have studied it. [*See the biography of Dharmakīrti.*]

The study of logic developed by Dignāga and Dharmakīrti influenced scholars from other religious traditions, including Uddyotakara, Vācaspatimiśra, and Udayana from the Nyāya school, Kumārila of the Mīmāṃsā school, and several Jain thinkers. Among the Buddhist monks who advanced Dharmakīrti's views on logic were Devendrabuddhi (c. 630–690), Vinītadeva, Dharmottara (c. 800), and Prajñākaragupta (c. tenth century). Jñānaśrīmitra (fl. eleventh century) was known for both his logical and Esoteric Buddhist studies. A collection of twelve of his works on logic entitled *Jñānaśrīmitranibandhāvalī* has survived. The *Ratnakīrti-*

nibandhāvali, a collection of ten texts by his disciple Ratnakīrti (fl. eleventh century), is also extant. These were followed by such men as Ratnākaraśānti, Mokṣākaragupta, and Jitāli.

Esoteric Buddhism

Esoteric, or Tantric, Buddhism, claims to offer its devotees a path to enlightenment based on meditation and ritual action that speeds the accomplishment of the goal, taking as its aim the realization of Buddhahood "in this very body." Although based firmly on the doctrines of the Mahāyāna, Esoteric practices diverge widely from the norm in that tradition, and emphasize a magico-ritual orientation to religious practice that is indeed present but not prominent in other forms of Buddhism. Tantric Buddhists find scriptural warrant for their practices in texts known as *tantras,* a term that, like *sūtra,* refers to the warp of a fabric. In these texts a variety of meditative and ritual practices are revealed for the sake of initiates (hence the term *esoteric*) of the tradition, who undergo a series of consecrations in which successively more sophisticated practices and teachings are made known to them. [*See also* Buddhism, Schools of, *article on* Esoteric Buddhism.]

Early Esoteric Buddhism. Followers of Esoteric Buddhism consider Mahāyāna Buddhism to be a tradition distinct from their own and refer to it as the Pāramitāyāna (Perfection Vehicle). In contrast, Esoteric Buddhism is referred to by such terms as Mantrayāna and Vajrayāna (Adamantine Vehicle). Esoteric Buddhism did not arise suddenly; Esoteric elements are found in Early and Mahāyāna Buddhism. Over the centuries, the Esoteric tradition gradually gained strength until it was an independent tradition.

Esoteric scriptures are called *tantras* and are classified into four categories: (1) Kriyā Tantra, (2) Caryā Tantra, (3) Yoga Tantra, and (4) Anuttarayoga Tantra. [*See the biography of Bu-ston.*] The first category, Kriyā Tantra, contains Mahāyāna texts with Esoteric elements and is typical of the stage when Esoteric Buddhism had not developed sufficiently to be an independent tradition. Examples of the many Kriyā Tantras are the *Suvarṇaprabhāsottama Sūtra* (T.D. no. 664), *Mahāmāyūrīvidyārājñī* (T.D. no. 982), *Bhaiṣajyaguruvaiḍūryapūrvapraṇidhāna* (T.D. no. 450), *Tathāgatoṣṇīṣasitātapatrā* (T.D. no. 976), and the *Subahūparipṛcchā* (T.D. no. 895).

Few texts are included in the second category, the Caryā Tantras. The *Mahāvairocanābhisaṃbodhivikurvitādhiṣṭhāna* (T.D. no. 848) is particularly important. It is known to have existed in northern India around 670 and was translated into Chinese in 724; consequently, it was probably composed during the first half of the sixth century. It exists in Tibetan and Chinese translation; Sanskrit fragments have also been discovered. In contrast to the *Buddhāvataṃsaka,* which is preached by Vairocana, this text is preached by Mahāvairocana (Great Vairocana), who is presented in a *maṇḍala.* The appearance of Mahāvairocana as protagonist suggests that Esoteric practitioners considered themselves independent of Mahāyāna Buddhism [*See* Mahāvairocana.] The text is particularly important in the Japanese Esoteric tradition. [*See* Shingonshū.] A Chinese commentary by I-ching, the *Ta-p'i-lu-che-na ch'eng-fo ching su* (T.D. no. 1796), exists. Tibetan translations of both an extensive and a shorter commentary by Buddhaguhya (eighth or ninth century) survive. Among the other texts in the Caryā Tantra class are the *Nīlāmbaradharavajrapāṇikalpa* and the *Mañjuśrīmūlakalpa* (T.D. no. 1191).

The *Sarvatathāgatatattvasaṃgraha* (T.D. nos. 865–866, 882) is representative of the third category, the Yoga Tantras. This text was composed around 680. It exists in Sanskrit, as well as in one Tibetan and three Chinese translations. A number of Tibetan translations of commentaries to it also survive, including Buddhaguhya's *Tantrārthāvatāra,* Śākyamitra's *Kosālālaṃkāra,* and Ānandagarbha's *Tantratattvālokakarī.*

According to Amoghavajra's *Chin-kang-ting-ching yü-ch'ieh shih-pa-hui chih-kuei* (T.D. no. 869), the *Chin-kang-ting ching (Vajraśekhara Sūtra?)* was composed of eighteen sections, of which the *Tattvasaṃgraha* was the first. [*See the biography of Amoghavajra.*] However, all eighteen sections of the *Chin-kang-ting ching* probably never existed in written form. In the *Tattvasaṃgraha,* Mahāvairocana's realization of Buddhahood is described in terms of five stages. Since even the first stage is said to surpass the realization of Buddhahood in the "exoteric" tradition, the text can be viewed as demonstrating the superiority of Esoteric over Exoteric Buddhism. A description of the Vajradhātu Maṇḍala, which includes female *bodhisattvas* in the *maṇḍala* of the thirty-seven deities, is included in the *Tattvasaṃgraha,* indicating that its doctrinal positions had advanced beyond those of the Caryā Tantras.

The *Prajñāpāramitā-naya-śatapañśatikā* (T.D. no. 241) is also an example of a Yoga Tantra. This text reflects the transition from Perfection of Wisdom to Esoteric Buddhism. The use of erotic representations of *śakti* to represent enlightenment is suggestive of the fourth category of Esoteric texts, Anuttarayoga Tantra. Six Chinese and four Tibetan translations of the *Prajñāpāramitā-naya* survive. A commentary on the text by Amoghavajra, the *Pan-jo po-lo-mi-to li-ch'ü shih* (T.D. no. 1003), is extant.

Later Esoteric Texts. The culmination of Esoteric Buddhism was embodied in the fourth category of *tantras*, Anuttarayoga ("Supreme *yoga*") Tantra. This type of *tantra* is characterized by the inclusion of *śakti* (sexual energy) in its yogic practices, a characteristic that already had appeared in an incipient form in Yoga Tantra. In addition, various types of meat and drink (proscribed in ordinary monastic practice), were imbibed in Anuttarayoga Tantra practices.

Anuttarayoga Tantra is divided into two major categories: "father" and "mother" *tantras*. In the Father Tantras the nonsubstantiality of expedient means *(upāya-śūnya)* is emphasized and the practitioner meditates on the process by which the *dharmakāya* is present in the phenomenal world. In Mother Tantras the great bliss of wisdom *(prajñā-mahāsukha)* is emphasized and the practitioner aims at absorption into the *dharmakāya*. The Father Tantra tradition flourished in Koṅkana in South India, while the Mother Tantras were followed by people in Uḍḍiyāna in northwest India.

The *Guhyasamāja Tantra* is representative of the Father Tantras. It survives in Sanskrit, Tibetan, and Chinese (T.D. no. 885). Because the work is closely related to the *Tattvasaṃgraha*, a Yoga Tantra work, and was translated into Chinese by Dānapāla (fl. 990), its composition can be placed around the end of the eighth century. Two sects follow the *Guhyasamāja*, the Jñānapāda sect founded by Jñānapāda (late eighth century) and the 'Phags-lugs sect founded by the Esoteric Buddhist Nāgārjuna. Many of the texts of the Jñānapāda sect survive in Tibetan translation. Many of the texts of the 'Phags-lugs sect were attributed to major figures in the Mādhyamika school such as Nāgārjuna, Āryadeva, and Candrakīrti. The 'Phags-lugs sect probably dates from the tenth century. *Maṇḍalas* and commentaries on the *Guhyasamāja Tantra* by Jñānagarbha, a member of the sect, are preserved in the Tibetan canon.

Numerous Mother Tantra texts survive, including the *Hevajra Tantra, Saṃvarodaya Tantra, Abhidānottara, Vajraḍāka, Dākārṇava, Vajravarāhī, Cakrasaṃvara, Buddhakapāla*, and the *Mahāmāyā*. Texts are found in Sanskrit, Tibetan, and Chinese. Among the famous practitioners of this type of Esoteric Buddhism were Advayavajra, Ratnākaraśānti, and Nā-ro-pa.

As Esoteric Buddhism was being destroyed in India, Kālacakra ("wheel of time") Tantras were composed. These texts were written during the six decades following 1027.

Issues in Chinese and Tibetan Translations

Because Chinese translations of Buddhist texts began appearing around 150 CE, many translations of early Buddhist texts are included in the Chinese canon. In contrast, since translations into Tibetan began much later, the Tibetan canon is particularly rich in medieval and later Buddhist texts, especially those concerned with Esoteric Buddhism.

Among the early works included in the Chinese canon were Āgama, Vinaya, and Abhidharma texts. Four of the Āgamas were translated, as well as five Vinaya Piṭakas including those of the Sarvāstivāda, Dharmaguptaka, and Mahāsāṃghika schools. In contrast, the Tibetan canon includes few of the Āgamas and only the Mūlasarvāstivāda Vinaya. The Chinese canon is also richer in Abhidharma literature than the Tibetan.

The Chinese canon also includes many translations of early Mahāyāna *sūtras*. The existence of several translations of the same scripture is particularly noteworthy, since by comparing the various translations, the historical development of a text can be investigated. In contrast, the Tibetan canon usually includes only one version of each scripture, enabling the researcher to examine only the finished version of the text.

Buddhist texts were translated into Chinese from 150 to about 800. A resurgence of translating activity occurred around 980, but ended within seventy years. By 800, Chinese Buddhism had been formulated in such a way that the Chinese no longer depended upon new translations of Indian texts. Consequently, the works of later Mādhyamika scholars such as Bhāvaviveka and Candrakīrti were not translated into Chinese. However, around 980, works by Śāntideva and Kamalaśīla appeared, but few Chinese monks studied the newly translated texts.

Many Esoteric Buddhist works were translated into Chinese by Amoghavajra (705–774). The Chinese Esoteric tradition was based on the *Mahāvairocana Sūtra*, a Caryā Tantra text, and on the *Tattvasaṃgraha*, a Yoga Tantra text. [*See* Chen-yen.] Between 980 and 1050 many Anuttarayoga Tantra works were translated into Chinese; however, those texts were not studied by the Chinese and they had no influence on Chinese Buddhism. [*For prominent translators, see the biographies of Kumārajīva; Paramārtha; I-ching; Hsüan-tsang; and Amoghavajra.*]

In Tibet, the translation of Buddhist texts began in the seventh century and continued until the decline of Indian Buddhism. In 1203, when the Vikramaśīla Monastery was destroyed by Muslims, many Buddhists fled to Tibet. As a result, later Indian Buddhism was transmitted to Tibet. Later Mādhyamika and Yogācāra literature, as well as Buddhist logic and Esoteric Buddhist texts have been especially well preserved; these are the areas in which the Chinese canon is deficient. Consequently, the strengths of both the Tibetan and Chinese canons must be employed in the study of Indian Buddhism.

[*See also* Buddhism, *article on* Buddhism in India, *and* Language, *article on* Buddhist Views of Language. *For the diffusion of the tradition geographically, see also* Missions, *article on* Buddhist Missions.]

BIBLIOGRAPHY

The sheer size of the corpus of Buddhist literature makes a comprehensive bibliography impossible in a context such as this. Below I have listed a few studies on the formation of Buddhist literature and some Western-language translations of various of the more important texts mentioned in the article above.

Akanuma Chizen. *Kan-Pa shibu shiagon goshōroku.* Tokyo, 1929. A comparative study of the Pali Nikāyas and the Chinese Āgamas.

Akanuma Chizen. *Bukkyō kyōten shiron.* Tokyo, 1939.

Anacker, Stefan. *Seven Works of Vasubandhu.* Dehli, 1984. Includes translations of Vasubandhu's *Vādavidhi, Pañcaskandhaprakaraṇa, Karmasiddhiprakaraṇa, Viṃśatikā, Triṃśikā, Madhyāntavibhāgabhāṣya,* and *Trisvabhāvanirdeśa.*

Aung, Shwe Zan, and C. A. F. Rhys Davids, trans. *Points of Controversy.* London, 1915. A translation of the *Kathāvatthu.*

Bagchi, Prabodh Chandra. *Le canon bouddhique en chine.* 2 vols. Paris, 1927–1928.

Banerjee, Anukul Chandra. *Sarvāstivāda Literature.* Calcutta, 1957.

Beautrix, Pierre. *Bibliographie du bouddhisme,* vol. 1, *Editions de textes.* Brussels, 1970. A complete listing of various editions of Buddhist texts; does not include translations.

Bendall, Cecil, and W. H. D. Rouse, trans. *Sikshasamuccaya: A Compendium of Buddhist Doctrine* (1922). Dehli, 1971.

Bhattacharya, Kamaleswar, trans. *The Dialectical Method of Nāgārjuna.* New Delhi, 1978. A translation of Nāgārjuna's *Vigrahavyāvartanī.*

Cleary, Thomas, trans. *The Flower Ornament Scripture.* Boulder, 1984. The first volume of a multivolume translation of the *Avataṃsaka Sūtra* from the eighty-fascicle Chinese translation by Sikṣānanda.

Conze, Edward, et al., eds. *Buddhist Texts through the Ages.* New York, 1954.

Conze, Edward, ed. and trans. *Buddhist Scriptures.* Harmondsworth, 1959.

Conze, Edward. *The Prajñāpāramitā Literature.* The Hague, 1960.

Conze, Edward, trans. *The Perfection of Wisdom in Eight Thousand Lines and Its Verse Summary.* Salinas, Calif. 1973.

Cowell, E. B., et. al., eds. *Buddhist Mahāyāna Texts.* Sacred Books of the East, edited by F. Max Müller, vol. 49. Oxford, 1894; reprint, New York, 1979. Translations of several major Mahāyāna texts, including the three principal Pure Land scriptures.

Demiéville, Paul. "Le Yogācārabhūmi de Saṅgharakṣa." *Bulletin de l'École Française d'Extrême-Orient* 44 (1954): 340–436.

Filliozat, Jean. "Le bouddhisme: Les sources." In *L'Inde classique: Manuel des études indiennes,* edited by Louis Renou and Jean Filliozat, vol. 2, pp. 361–388. Paris, 1953. A descriptive survey of the whole of Sanskrit Buddhist literature.

Frauwallner, Erich. *The Earliest Vinaya and the Beginnings of Buddhist Literature.* Rome, 1956.

Fujita Kōtatsu. *Genshi jōdo shisō no kenkyū.* Tokyo, 1970. The standard work on early Pure Land Buddhism.

Geiger, Wilhelm. *Pāli Literature and Language.* 2d ed. Translated by Batakrishna Ghosh. Delhi, 1943. A concise survey of both canonical and noncanonical Pali literature.

Hanayama Shōyū. "A Summary of Various Research on the Prajñāpāramitā Literature by Japanese Scholars." *Acta Asiatica* 10 (1966): 16–93.

Hirakawa Akira. *Ritsuzō no kenkyū.* Tokyo, 1960. Treats the development of the Vinaya.

Hirakawa Akira. *Shoki daijō bukkyō no kenkyū.* Tokyo, 1969.

Hirakawa Akira. *Indo bukkyōshi.* 2 vols. Tokyo, 1974–1979. A valuable survey of Indian Buddhism, with excellent bibliographical materials.

Hopkins, Jeffrey, trans. *The Kālacakra Tantra.* London, 1985.

Horner, I. B., trans. *Milinda's Questions.* London, 1964. A translation of the *Milindapañha.*

Hurvitz, Leon N., trans. *Scripture of the Lotus Blossom of the Fine Dharma.* New York, 1976. A translation of Kumārajīva's fifty-century Chinese translation.

Iida Shotarō. *Reason and Emptiness: A Study in Logic and Mysticism.* Tokyo, 1980. A study of Bhāvaviveka's philosophy; includes partial translations.

Jacobi, Hermann, trans. *Triṃśikāvijñapti des Vasubandhu, mit bhāṣya des ācārya Sthiramati.* Stuttgart, 1932.

Kern, Hendrik, trans. *The Saddharma-puṇḍarīka; or, the Lotus of the True Law* (1884). Reprint, Dehli, 1965. A translation from the Sanskrit.

Kimura Taiken. *Abidammaron no kenkyū.* Tokyo, 1937. Surveys Sarvāstivāda Abhidharma.

Lamotte, Étienne, trans. *Saṃdhinirmocana Sūtra: L'explication des mystères.* Louvain, 1935.

Lamotte, Étienne, trans. *La somme du Grand Véhicule d'Asaṅga (Mahāyānasaṃgraha).* 2 vols. Louvain, 1938–1939.

Lamotte, Étienne. *Histoire du bouddhisme indien des origines à l'ère Śaka.* Louvain, 1958. Extensive footnotes and a comprehensive index make this work an invaluable reference tool.

Lamotte, Étienne, trans. *L'enseignement de Vimalakīrti.* Louvain, 1962.

Lamotte, Étienne, trans. *Le traité de la grande vertu de sagesse.* 5 vols. Louvain, 1944–1980. A translation from Kumārajīva's Chinese translation (*Ta chih-tu lun*) of the Sanskrit *Mahāprajñāpāramitā Śāstra,* a commentary on the *Pañcaviṃśatisāhasrikā-prajñāpāramitā.* The original Sanskrit commentary, sometimes attributed to Nāgārjuna, is no longer extant.

La Vallée Poussin, Louis de, trans. *Vijñaptimātratāsiddhi, La Siddhi de Hiuan-tsang.* 2 vols. Paris, 1928–1929.

La Vallée Poussin, Louis de, trans. *L'Abhidharmakośa de Vasubandhu* (1923–1931). 6 vols. Reprint, Brussels, 1971.

Lévi, Sylvain, ed. and trans. *Asaṅga: Mahāyāna-sūtrālaṃkāra,* vol. 2, *Exposé de la doctrine du Grand Véhicule selon le système Yogācāra.* Paris, 1911.

Lévi, Sylvain. *Un système de philosophie bouddhique: Materiaux pour l'étude du système Vijñaptimātra.* Paris, 1932.

Malalasekera, G. P. *The Pāli Literature of Ceylon.* London, 1928. Treats only those works composed in Sri Lanka; a valuable literary history of Sri Lankan Buddhism.

Masuda Jiryō. "Origins and Doctrines of Early Indian Buddhist Schools." *Asia Major* 2 (1925): 1–78.

Matics, Marion L., trans. *Entering the Path of Enlightenment.* New York, 1970. A translation of Śāntideva's *Bodhicaryāvatāra.*

Mayeda Sengaku. *Genshi bukkyō seiten no seiritsushi kenkyū.* Tokyo, 1964.

Mizuno Kōgen. "Abhidharma Literature." In *Encyclopaedia of Buddhism,* edited by G. P. Malalasekera, vol. 1, fasc. 1, pp. 64–80. Colombo, 1963.

Mizuno Kōgen, ed. *Shin butten kaidai jiten.* 2d ed. Tokyo, 1977.

Mochizuki Shinkō. *Bukkyō kyōten seiritsushiron.* Tokyo, 1946.

Norman, K. R. *Pāli Literature.* In *History of Indian Literature,* edited by Jan Gonda, vol 7., fasc. 2. Weisbaden, 1983.

Ñyāṇamoli, Bhikkhu, trans. *The Path of Purification.* 2d ed. Colombo, 1964. A translation of Buddhaghosa's *Visuddhimagga.*

Obermiller, Eugene, trans. *History of Buddhism.* 2 vols. Heidelberg, 1931–1932. A translation of Bu-ston's *Chos 'byuṅ.*

Ono Gemmyō, ed. *Busshō kaisetsu daijiten.* 14 vols. Tokyo, 1933–1978. A comprehensive survey of Buddhist literature available in Chinese and Japanese, including translations of Indic texts. Each entry is copiously annotated.

Potter, Karl H., comp. *Bibliography of Indian Philosophies.* Dehli, 1970. Invaluable bibliographic material on the writings of Indian Buddhist thinkers.

Renou, Louis, and Jean Filliozat. *L'Inde classique: Manuel des études indiennes.* 2 vols. Paris, 1947–1953. Concise and scholarly survey of Indology.

Reynolds, Frank E. *Guide to Buddhist Religion.* Boston, 1981. A critical bibliographic survey of Buddhism.

Ruegg, David S. *The Literature of the Madhyamaka School of Philosophy in India.* In *History of Indian Literature,* edited by Jan Gonda, vol. 7, fasc. 1. Wiesbaden, 1971.

Shiio Benkyō. *Bukkyō kyōten gaisetsu.* Tokyo, 1933.

Skorupski, Tadeusz. *The Sarvadurgatipariśodhana Tantra: Elimination of All Evil Destinies.* Delhi, 1983.

Snellgrove, David L., ed. and trans. *The Hevajra Tantra: A Critical Study.* 2 vols. London, 1959. Includes a translation of this major Tantric work.

Stcherbatsky, Theodore. *Buddhist Logic* (1930–1932). 2 vols. Reprint, New York, 1962. Volume 2 includes a translation of Dharmakīrti's *Nyāyabindu.*

Stcherbatsky, Theodore, trans. *Madhyānta-vibhaṅga: Discourse on Discrimination between Middle and Extremes, Ascribed to Maitreyanātha and Commented by Vasubandhu and Sthiramati.* Moscow, 1936.

Streng, Frederick J. *Emptiness: A Study in Religious Meaning.* Nashville, 1967. Includes a translation of the *Madhyamakakārikā.*

Suzuki, D. T., trans. *The Laṅkāvatāra Sūtra.* London, 1932.

Tajima Ryūjun. *Étude sur le Mahāvairocana-Sūtra (Dainichikyō).* Paris, 1936.

Takakusu Junjirō. "On the Abhidharma Literature of the Sarvāstivādins." *Journal of the Pāli Text Society* (1904–1905): 67–146.

Takasaki Jikidō. *A Study on the Ratnagotravibhāga (Uttaratantra): Being a Treatise on the Tathāgatagarbha Theory of Mahāyāna Buddhism.* Rome, 1966.

Ui Hakuju. *Indo tetsugakushi.* Tokyo, 1932.

Ui Hakuju. *Bukkyō kyōtenshi.* Tokyo, 1957.

Wayman, Alex, trans. *Analysis of the Śrāvakabhūmi Manuscript.* Berkeley, 1961. Includes a partial translation of Asaṅga's *Yogācārabhūmi Śāstra.*

Wayman, Alex. *The Buddhist Tantras: Light on Indo-Tibetan Esotericism.* New York, 1973.

Wayman, Alex, and Hideko Wayman, trans. *The Lion's Roar of Queen Śrīmālā: A Buddhist Scripture on the Tathāgatagarbha Theory.* New York, 1974.

Wayman, Alex. *Yoga of the Guhyasamājatantra: The Arcane Lore of Forty Verses; A Buddhist Tantra Commentary.* Delhi, 1977.

Winternitz, Moriz. *Der Mahāyāna-Buddhismus, nach Sanskrit- und Prākrittexten.* 2 vols. Tübingen, 1930.

Winternitz, Moriz. *A History of Indian Literature,* vol. 2, *Buddhist Literature and Jaina Literature* (1933). Translated by Silavati Ketkar and Helen Kohn. Reprint, Delhi, 1983.

Yamada Ryūjō. *Bongo butten no shobunken.* Kyoto, 1959.

Yamada Ryūjō. *Daijō bukkyō seiritsuron josetsu.* Kyoto, 1959.

The Theravāda (Pali) canon has been translated in its entirety and published, variously, by the Pāli Text Society and in the Sacred Books of the Buddhists and Sacred Books of the East series. See Reynolds (1981) for full publication data and for a more comprehensive listing of Buddhist literature in translation.

HIRAKAWA AKIRA
Translated from Japanese by Paul Groner

Exegesis and Hermeneutics

The fundamental problems of Buddhist hermeneutics are the coexistence of conflicting sources and concepts of authority, a voluminous canon of relatively late compilation, and a complex history of interpretations that may be described as "hermeneutic pluralism." Furthermore, the emphasis on *dharma* (the eternal truths discovered by the Buddha) rather than on *buddhavacana* (the literal content of his message) reduce the significance of textual and historical constraints as part of a method of interpretation. [*See also* Dharma, *article on* Buddhist Dharma and Dharmas.]

According to tradition, the Buddha was not the sole preacher of Dharma. Even during the Buddha's life his disciples acted as missionaries, and their words were considered part of the "original" message of Buddhism. The texts affirm that at the Buddha's own behest the disciples began each sermon with the words "Evaṃ mayā śrutam ekasmin samaye" ("Thus have I heard on one occasion"). This formula presumably served as a guarantee of authenticity, or rather, of faithfulness to the teaching of the Master. Yet, the same introductory formula was used indistinctly for sermons attributed to the Master, to his disciples, or to mythical sages and deities.

There had also been previous Buddhas, and they had their own disciples, all of whom could have preached the Dharma. These "Buddhists" from the mythical past could speak to human beings. Their words, as well as the "inspired speech" *(pratibhāṇa)* of ancient and contemporary *ṛṣis*, gods, and spirits, could be regarded as Dharma, and thus be prefaced by the famous formula.

Even traditions that believe that the canon was redacted and closed during the First Council at Rājagṛha, shortly after the Buddha's death (c. 483 BCE), concede that not all Buddhist elders were present at that gathering, and that at least one group of "five hundred monks" insisted in keeping their own version of the teachings as they remembered them. All available evidence indicates that most of the canons were never closed. The Theravāda school, proud of its conservatism in scriptural matters, was still debating the content of its canon at least as late as the fifth century CE. Even today there is no complete agreement among Therāvadins regarding the *Khuddaka Nikāya* section of their canon. Thus, it is not always possible to distinguish clearly between canonical, postcanonical, and paracanonical Buddhist literature.

All schools believe that at least some texts have been lost, truncated, or altered, and that a number of false or late texts have been incorporated into the canons of various schools. Even if occasionally these statements are used to bolster the position of one school or another, they probably represent an accurate description of the general state of things by the time the first scriptural collections were formally constituted. It is not difficult to see the impact that such a perception, combined with the mythology of revelation outlined above, would have on the tradition's view of the meaning of the scripture and on the principles that should guide its interpretation.

Buddhist Exegesis: Methods of Interpretation

The Buddhist canons were the result of a long process of compilation and redaction that we can no longer reconstruct. For many centuries the task of interpretation was complicated by a shifting definition of canonicity. The first steps in understanding scriptural traditions—identifying the limits and forms of scripture—were slow and hesitant.

It took roughly three centuries before the oral texts of specialized schools of reciters (*bhāṇakas*) were brought together into collections (*piṭakas*). Another century went by before the first canons were committed to writing (an early Theravāda canon was written down under King Vaṭṭagāmaṇī of Sri Lanka, c. 32 BCE). Even then the canons were not closed; some of the extant collections (i.e., the Tibetan and Chinese "canons"), were not compiled until more than a millenium had passed since the life of the founder, and they have remained open to the introduction of new literature until recent times.

The Canon. Most Buddhists came to accept the theoretical division of scripture into three sections (metaphorically called "baskets" *(piṭaka)*—Sūtra (Pali, Sutta), Vinaya, Abhidharma (Pali, Abhidhamma)—hence the name *Tripiṭaka* (Pali, *Tipiṭaka*), or Three Baskets. But in practice the corpus of authoritative Buddhist texts is not always divided into these three categories. This division is in itself of secondary importance for the history of Buddhist exegesis, whereas the variety of canons that seem to have existed in ancient India, and their flexibility, are important factors in the development of Buddhist attitudes toward canonical authority and interpretation.

The earliest system of this type was the classification of Buddhist teachings (and texts) into two main divisions: Dharma (instruction on doctrine and meditation) and Vinaya (monastic rules and discipline). This classification probably was followed closely by a division, attested in some of the latter parts of canonical literature, that recognizes the existence of a third type of sacred text—the *mātṛkā*, or numerical list.

Also ancient, and obviously precanonical, is a system of "genres" *(aṅga)*. The Theravāda tradition distinguishes nine such genres, whereas the Sanskrit tradition counts twelve *(sūtra, geya, vyākaraṇa, gāthā, udāna, nidāna, ityukta, jātaka, vaipulya, adbhutadharma, avadāna,* and *upadeśa)*. Although some of these terms are well known as words for literary genres or forms of canonical literature, the exact meaning of the items in these lists is not always transparent. The list clearly shows, however, an early interest in analyzing scripture by literary forms.

By the time Buddhists began compiling their "canons," several forms of exegesis had developed within the body of literature transmitted as sacred scripture. Beyond the implicit exegetical work of the redactors, which is more obvious in Buddhist scripture than it is in the Bible, important sections of the canons are composed of exegetical material. Some works considered to derive directly from the Master's mouth are, in structure and reference, major acts of interpretation or statements on the nature of interpretation. Such, for instance, are the *Mahāpadesa Suttanta,* on forms of appealing to authority, the *Kālāma Sutta,* a critique of authority and an affirmation of the hermeneutical value of meditation, the *Alagaddūpama Sutta,* on the instrumental value of doctrine, and the *Pratisaraṇa Sūtra,* on the criteria of interpretation. These texts reflect a precanonical concern with the problems of transmission and interpretation. Other texts included in the Tripiṭakas are frankly exegetical in character (although they may be of more recent vintage). These include two commentaries (the *Niddesas*) incorporated into the Sutta Piṭaka of the Theravādins, two works of theoretical hermeneutics included in the Sutta sections of the Burmese Tipiṭaka, and of course the totality of the Abhidharma Piṭaka and the *Sūtravibhaṅga* section of the Vinaya Piṭaka (an exegesis of the Prātimokṣa).

The Abhidharma as Exegesis. The Abhidharma played a central role in the development of the practice and theory of exegesis in all schools of Buddhism. The hermeneutical strategy of the Abhidharma is itself derived from a practice attested frequently by the *sūtras*: dogmatic lists known as "matrices" *(mātṛkā).* These may appear to be mere catechistic or numerical lists; but more than topical indices or lists defining the limits of canonicity, they are digests or exegetical guides. Some, evidently the oldest, are preserved in the Sūtra Piṭaka (e.g., *Saṅgīti Suttanta, Daśottara Sūtra*), and were the object of commentaries (e.g., Mahākauṣṭhila's *Saṅgītiparyāya*).

The role of *mātṛkās* as early canons of orthodoxy and interpretation is revealed by a legend, according to which the Buddha's disciple Śāriputra composed the *Saṅgīti Suttanta* in order to prevent a division in the Buddhist order similar to the one he had seen in the Jain community. The basic list, however, is not only a model for a definition of orthodoxy, it is also a pattern for exegetical coherence. The *mātṛkās* provide the structure for abhidharmic exegesis; each text must fit one or more of the categories contained in the traditional "matrix." The "matrices" provided a simple logic of classification; all items of doctrine can be understood by opposites (the *dukas* of Pali Abhidhamma: anything is *a* or not *a*) or by contraries (the *tika: x* is *a,* or *x* is *b,* or *x* is neither *a* nor *b*). Some of the earliest works of Abhidharma, organized on this model (for instance the Pali *Dhammasaṅganī*), purport to reveal the underlying logic and structure of the *suttas.*

Non-Mahāyāna Exegetical Literature. The Abhidharma can be understood as a series of attempts at an exegesis of *the whole body* of Buddhist teachings (texts and practices). Some books, therefore, tried to preserve an explicit connection with the *sūtras.* But the Abhidharma was more a work of philosophical hermeneutics than of exegesis. Accordingly, a different genre of literature was developed to carry out the difficult task of preserving, recovering, or eliciting the meaning of individual texts.

Two of the earliest Buddhist works of conscious exegesis have been incorporated into the canon in the Sutta Piṭaka. These are the *Mahāniddesa* and the *Cullaniddesa,* commentaries on the fourth and fifth books of the *Suttanipāta.* They date from approximately the third century CE. However, two other works of early, but uncertain date occupy a much more important position in the development of Buddhist exegetical theories: the *Nettippakaraṇa* and the *Peṭakopadesa,* both attributed to a (Mahā) Kaccāyana.

The *Nettippakaraṇa* formulates the principles of interpretation *(netti)* common to both works on the basis of twelve techniques classified under the headings of "interpretation as to sense" *(byañjana)* and "interpretation as to meaning" *(attha).*

Earlier, at the beginning of the common era, the compilation of canonical collections and the explosion of Abhidharma literature had created great works of synthesis on the Indian peninsula. The most famous and influential of these was the *Mahāvibhāṣā* (c. 150–200 CE), a work of collective scholarship that attempted to make sense of the complex Abhidharma literature of the Sarvāstivādins, in particular the *Jñānaprasthāna* of Kātyāyanīputra (or Kātyāyana; c. first century CE). Although it resulted in an equally abstruse production, the *Mahāvibhāṣā* became an important source for doctrinal and interpretive categories, even for those who criticized it—especially the Mahāyāna.

Mahayana Exegetical Literature. In addition to playing the more obvious roles of criticism, reform, and systematic construction, the Mahāyāna *sūtras* fulfilled an exegetical role as well. It is common for a Mahāyāna *sūtra* to attempt a redefinition or reinterpretation of a classical formula from pre-Mahāyāna literature. The *Vajracchedikā-prajñāpāramitā,* for instance, presents the Mahāyāna reinterpretation of the "Parable of the Raft." The same text, in fact, the entire body of Prajñāpāramitā literature, is devoted to what amounts to an all-out criticism of pre-Mahāyāna Abhidharma. The traditional order established by orthodox exegesis is deconstructed in a search for the "ultimate meaning" behind the words of the older scriptures. The *Laṅkāvatāra Sūtra* and the *Tathāgataguhya Sūtra*—to quote another example—radically change the meaning of a classical passage by identifying truth with "holy silence." The earlier, canonical passage stated that "from the night of his Enlightenment to the night of his *parinirvāṇa,* . . . every word uttered by the Buddha was true." The two Mahāyāna *sūtras* changed the phrase to read "from the night of his Enlightenment, to the night of his *nirvāṇa,* the Blessed One did not utter a single word."

These new departures, however, are not wholly the creation of Mahāyāna, for some of them are found in the literature of the Mahāsāṃghikas, a Hīnayāna sect. Some members of this sect held that Buddhas never pronounce a single word, yet living beings hear them preach. It was also claimed by some Mahāsāṃghikas that the Buddha can preach all things with a single word. [*See* Mahāsāṃghikas.]

Another form of continuity within innovation occurs in Mahāyāna texts that follow the pattern of the Abhidharma *mātṛkās* as a way of redefining or expanding on earlier doctrine. Some of these *sūtras* may be rightly called "abhidharmic" Mahāyāna *sūtras*. Such are, for instance, the *Dharmasaṅgīti* and the *Akṣayamatinirdeśa*.

Some texts make explicit pronouncements on the principles of interpretation or evaluation of Buddhist scripture in general. For instance, the *Laṅkāvatāra Sūtra*'s statement on the silence of the Buddha is extended to mean that all words of the Buddha have only a provisional value. They are pronounced only in response to the needs of living beings who cannot penetrate directly into the mystery of the Tathāgata's silence. The *Mahāyāna-mahāparinirvāṇa Sūtra* offers a model for a hierarchy in scriptural study and understanding. At the first level, one becomes "learned" in scriptural study by studying all of the twelve genres *(aṅga)* of scripture. Subsequently, one may study only one *aṅga*—the *vaipulya* (here equivalent to Mahāyāna) *sūtras*. Then one may study only the most subtle passages of the *vaipulya* section. But one may also study only one stanza of two lines from these *sūtras* and still be learned. Last, one becomes learned in scripture by understanding "that the Buddha never taught anything." The last of these is clearly, by implication, the most "learned."

Other statements with obvious implications for the interpretation of texts are those dealing with the relative value of various transmissions. Perhaps the best known of these formulations are those of the *Saddharmapuṇḍarīka Sūtra* (Lotus Sutra), which asserts that the Buddha has been in *nirvāṇa* eternally and denies that the Buddha ever "entered *nirvāṇa*," as claimed by earlier scriptural tradition. The *Lotus* also reduces the meaning of the human lives of the Buddha to a mere teaching device, developing the theory of "skillful means" *(upāya)* as an explanation for the competing claims of its own brand of Mahāyāna and those of non-Mahāyāna Buddhists. Other texts establish criteria for authenticity that open doors to the new creative efforts of the Mahāyāna. The *Adhyāśayasaṃcodana Sūtra*, for example, establishes the well-known principle that "whatever has been well said has been said by the Buddha." Such statements are evident signs of a break with tradition and became seeds for further, perhaps dangerously limitless innovation.

Śāstras and Commentaries. In India the methodology used in the composition of technical treatises (*śāstras*) was modeled on the commentarial tradition of Indian linguistics, heavily influenced by Patañjali's *Mahābhāṣya*. But the disciplines of poetics and logic also played an important role in the creation of standards for the composition of commentaries. [*See the biography of Patañjali the grammarian.*]

As Indian technical literature evolved through commentaries, continuity was preserved by reference to a common "root" text, which could be a scriptural text *(sūtra)* or the conscious work of an individual *(śāstra)*. A certain latitude for variation was allowed in the commentaries of each school of thought, but the root text was authoritative. That is, the commentary had to be verbally faithful to the root text and had to recognize its authoritative status. But the *śāstras* themselves required commentaries, and some of the *śāstras* that became the object of commentaries acquired quasicanonical status almost equivalent to that of the *sūtras*.

The system of authoritative texts followed by authoritative commentaries also produced a plethora of subcommentaries. The hierarchy was not always well-defined and the terminology not always consistent, but it was normally assumed that a *sūtra* would be the object of a commentary called a *bhāṣya*, or a more detailed gloss known as *vyākhyā* or *ṭīkā*. The root text of a *śāstra*, on the other hand, was often a versified treatise written in *kārikās* or mnemonic verses (parallel to the Hindu *sūtras* or prose aphorisms), and explicated in a *bhāṣya* or *vṛtti* (sometimes by the author of the root text).

The beginnings of the Mahāyāna commentarial literature seem to be coterminous with the development of independent philosophical or dogmatic treatises (*śāstras*). But the exact dates of these events cannot be fixed with any certainty as an exact chronology depends in part on establishing the authorship of what may be the earliest major work in the genre, the commentary on the *Pañcaviṃśatisāhasrikā-prajñāpāramitā Sūtra* (Perfection of Wisdom in Twenty-five Thousand Lines), traditionally attributed to Nāgārjuna, whose dates are equally uncertain. This work, the *Mahāprajñāpāramitā-upadeśa Śāstra* (preserved only in Chinese translation under the title *Ta-chih-tu lun*), set the tone for Chinese exegesis, and defined some of the most important issues of Buddhist exegetical and hermeneutical theory for the Far East.

The genres of commentary and treatise flourished in India beginning in the fourth century of the common era with Asaṅga and Vasubandhu. Although the tendency was to force the text into established scholastic molds, or to use it as a pretext for the formulation of independent philosophical dogmatics, commentators sometimes showed unusual sensitivity to the forms and structures of the text (e.g., Kamalaśīla's commentary on the *Avikalpapraveśa*). There was also room for the development of independent criteria and exegetical guides. A valuable example of this type of work is Vasubandhu's extensive treatise on the mechanics of the commentary, *Vyākhyayukti* (preserved only in Tibetan translation).

Exegetical Categories. Outside of India the exegetical issue became even more critical, since there was no sense of a living tradition that could justify any apparent deviation from the texts or suggest an integral explanation of the canon. The need for exegetical and hermeneutical principles was especially acute in China. An exegetical schema attributed to an early scholar of Chinese Buddhism, Tao-an (312–385), was based on three categories that supposedly reflected accurately the structure of all *sūtras*: the setting *(nidāna)*, the doctrinal and narrative core, and the transmission *(parīndanā)*. This basic schema was widely used in China (where it was known as the *san-fen k'e-ching*) and was adopted by Chih-i in his classical analysis of the *Lotus Sutra*, the *Miao-fa lien-hua ching wen-chu*. The schema is not attested in India until later, as, for example, in Bandhuprabha's (sixth century CE) *Buddhabhūmi Śāstra*, a commentary on the *Buddhabhūmi Sūtra*. In practice, each of the three parts was itself subdivided to account for obvious and important elements of style, narrative development, and so forth. For instance, the text was expected to satisfy the traditional requirements for a definition of the audience (in the *nidāna* section) and for a positive assessment of the value of the faith and practice inspired by it (usually in the transmission section). Other schemas, some evidently inspired by a similar conception, developed one or more of the three parts. For instance, the sixfold division of the introductory formula of the *sūtras (evaṃ mayā śrutam . . .)* according to the manner proposed in the *Mahāprajñāpāramitā-upadeśa Śāstra* was extremely popular among Far Eastern exegetes. This led to multiple variations in the division of the text of the *sūtras*, such as Shan-tao's threefold introduction and Chih-i's five parts of the introduction.

The most fruitful, though perhaps less rigorous, strategies were those that tried to discover metaphysical meanings in the structure of texts. Such was Chih-i's "twofold approach"—by way of the deep structure and by way of the surface structure *(pen-chi erh men)*—to a text. This doctrine was part of a more complex exegetical plan, the four exegetical methods of the T'ien-t'ai tradition *(T'ien-t'ai ta-ssu-shih)*, which brings us closer to broader hermeneutical issues. According to this doctrine, any scriptural passage can be treated from four perspectives: (1) the passage as expression of a particular relationship between the audience and the Buddha (the circumstances determining the intention); (2) the passage as embodying one of four methods of teaching; (3) classification of the passage into absolute or relative statements; and (4) the introspective method *(kuan-hsin)*. In this methodological schema one can see in outline some of the salient features of Mahāyāna hermeneutics: contextual meaning, levels of meaning, and meditation as a tool of understanding. [*See also* T'ien-t'ai.]

Buddhist Hermeneutics: Theories of Interpretation and Canonicity

In traditional terms the fundamental questions of Buddhist hermeneutics can be classified into three broad categories:

1. If enlightenment *(bodhi)* is at least theoretically open to all (or most) sentient beings, what is the role of sacred words and authoritative texts? How does one distinguish the exegesis of sacred texts from the actual transmission or realization of the Dharma?
2. Since the Buddha preached in so many different ways, adapting his language, style, and even doctrine to the spiritual disposition and maturity of his audience, did he have a plurality of messages or did he have a single truth to offer? If the latter, what was it and how is one to choose among his many teachings?
3. If Buddhism rejects conventional concepts of substance, self, possession, and property, so fundamental to our conception of the world, is there a "higher language" that can be used to describe accurately reality as seen from the point of view of enlightenment?

From a modern perspective, one could characterize these three problems as defining the main subfields of Buddhist hermeneutics: the first statement addresses issues of Buddhist soteriology—the conflict between the ascetic-contemplative ideal and the institutional realities of Buddhism, between orthopraxy and orthodoxy. The second problem is that of Buddhist exegetical hermeneutics. Awareness of the late date and the diversity of "canonical" sources generates a "hermeneutical pluralism" that compounds the problem of determining the meaning of diversity and unity in tradition. The third item summarizes the problems of Buddhist philosophical hermeneutics: what are the relative positions and meanings of conventional language, its Buddhist critique, and "the silence of the sages"?

A better perception of the tone underlying the discussion of these issues can be derived from representative traditional responses to the problems:

1. The Buddhist Dharma is not dependent on the historical event of Śākyamuni's enlightenment, ministry, and *nirvāṇa*. Whether a Tathāgata arises in the world or not, the basic teachings of Buddhism—impermanence, suffering, no-self, and liberation—remain facts of existence. Although the tradition initiated by Śākyamuni is a necessary aid to enlightenment, it is (in the metaphor of the *Laṅkāvatāra Sūtra*) only a finger pointing at the moon. The moon is always there, waiting to be seen (whether there is a finger to point at it or not); the finger is not the moon. Nevertheless, some Buddhists, the Theravādins, for instance, would insist on the historical significance of Śākyamuni's life and ministry, and on the close connection between exact literal meaning of doctrinal statements and effective practice.
2. The diversity of teachings is not due to confusion or weakness in the transmission. On the contrary, it is proof of Śākyamuni's wisdom and compassion, of his ability to adapt to the needs, capacities, and dispositions of living beings. According to the *Mahāprajñāpāramitā-upadeśa Śāstra,* his teachings were of four types, according to their definite purport *(siddhānta)*: worldly *(laukika),* or surface meaning; therapeutic *(prātipakṣika),* or meaning intended as an antidote to mental afflictions and passion; personal *(prātipauruṣika),* or meaning intended for particular individuals; and absolute *(pāramārthika),* or ultimate meaning. This second point is further complicated by the Mahāyāna belief in multiple Buddhas and in the timeless *saṃbhogakāya* ("body of bliss") of the Buddhas, which eternally preaches in the heavens and is seen and heard in the visions of *bodhisattvas* and sages. Other Buddhists, however, (the Theravādins, for instance) emphasize canonical integrity, rejecting both the doctrine of multiple meanings and the doctrine of multiple Buddhas. The Mahāsāṃghikas seem to have wanted to forestall exegetical pluralism and protect the integrity of scripture by claiming that all *sūtras* have only one explicit meaning.
3. The above attitudes toward the sacred word are inseparable from Buddhist views on levels of meaning, whatever the historical or causal connections between these three problems may have been. The creation of abhidharmic technical language was the first step in separating two orders of truth and expression. Speculation about the nature of the Path and the state of perfect freedom of Buddhas further contributed to a theory of levels of meaning, since a progression in spiritual insight was taken to imply an increased capacity to penetrate behind the words of the doctrine.

The Mahāyāna insists that the higher sphere is only embodied in the silence of the *āryas*. The highest stage in the Path, and, therefore, the highest order of meaning, can only be expressed in apophatic statements such as "appeasing all discursive thinking" *(sarvaprapañcopaśama)* and "cutting out all doctrines and practices" *(sarvavādacaryoccheda)*. Still, all traditions, including the Mahāyāna, develop a language of the sacred (whether or not it is directly inspired by abhidharmic Path theories), for it is necessary to explain holy silence in order to lead living beings to it. Thus, the culmination of this sort of speculation comes with the recognition that language, with all its limitations, is an important vehicle for salvation: language is *upāya* (e.g., in the Mādhyamika treatises, the *Laṅkāvatāra,* and the Tantras). [*See also* Language, *article on* Buddhist Views of Language.]

Criteria of Authenticity. Early concepts of orthodoxy were based on doctrines of confirmation or inspiration, rather than on a literal definition of "the word of Buddha" *(buddhavacana)*. A disciple could preach, then receive the Buddha's approval, or the authority of his words could be implicit in the Buddha's request or inspiration. Although it may seem difficult to have maintained this fiction when the Buddha was no longer living among his followers, Buddhists did not always see things this way. Since the Dharma is, after all, the Buddha's true body, and since it exists whether or not there is a human Buddha to preach it, one could assume that the preaching of Dharma would continue after his death. This justification formed part of the context for the proliferation of texts and the elasticity of concepts of canonical authenticity. It may also explain in part why the Abhidharma and, later, the commentarial literature achieved such a prominent role in the development of Buddhist doctrine.

Such flexibility does not mean, however, that no attempt was made to establish criteria or rules for determining the genuineness of any particular statement of doctrine. The *Mahāpadesa Suttanta* of the *Dīgha Nikāya* (and its parallel in the *Aṅguttara Nikāya* and in the Āgamas) recognizes four possible ways of appealing to or arguing on the basis of authority: one may appeal to the authority of the Buddha, a community of monks, several elders, or a single elder. The validity of these appeals and their potential sources of authority, however, must be confirmed by comparing the doctrinal statements attributed to these persons against the "Sūtra" and the "Vinaya."

The Sanskrit recensions of the *Mahāpadeśa Sūtra* add a third criterion: statements of doctrine must conform "to the reality or nature of things" *(dharmatā)*. The same expansion is found in Pali literature in the *Nettippakaraṇa*, where the principles are actually applied to the analysis and evaluation of texts, and the three criteria are summarized in very suggestive language: "Which is the *sūtra* with whose approach [phrases and words] must agree? The Four Noble Truths. Which is the Vinaya in which they must be seen? The Vinaya restraining covetousness, aversion, and delusion. Which is the *dharma* with which they must conform? The *dharma* of conditioned arising" (paras. 122–124).

The principle implies, of course, that whatever agrees with Sūtra, Vinaya, and Dharma (i.e., conditioned arising) carries authority for the Buddhist. If applied to texts this could mean that any new creation that is perceived as a continuation of the tradition (*secundum evangelium*, as it were) could have canonical authority. Indeed, the Mahāyāna used it in just this way to justify the development and expansion of earlier teachings. Theravādins, on the other hand, would understand the broad definitions of the *Nettippakaraṇa* as references to the letter of the canon, not to its spirit. Ultimately, then, the issue remained one of setting the limits of the interpretability of scriptural tradition.

What then is *buddhavacana*? The *Nettippakaraṇa* passage epitomizes the Buddhist tendency to use philosophical rather than historical arguments for authority. But the three tests do not form a complete system of criteria of textual authenticity. In the canonical versions they seem to refer to statements of doctrine and appeals to authority, not to texts. Most certainly if they were meant to constitute a system for establishing canonical authenticity their value would be limited, if not totally inexistent, for as tests of canonical authority the first (and original) two criteria clearly would be tautological. One must accept that the teaching on the "four appeals to authority" was originally a method for determining orthodoxy, not a criterion of authenticity. Still, since Buddhist notions of the "word of Buddha" were elastic, the principle must have been ambiguous. That is to say, the circularity of the argument "a genuine *sūtra* is one that agrees with the Sūtra," may not be so obvious in the context of Buddhist notions of canonicity—at least in the early stages in the formation of the corpus of scriptures.

Some Buddhists, the Mahāyānists in particular, came to consider "agreement with the *sūtras*," rather than "inclusion in the Sūtra Piṭaka," the ultimate test of authority. Thus, in China a distinction is made between, on the one hand, pseudepigrapha, or "spurious *sūtras*" *(wei-ching)* that are nevertheless "canonical" (that is, in agreement with the spirit of the Dharma and therefore to be accepted in the canon) and, on the other, those *sūtras* that are "false" (that is, in conflict with established Buddhist teaching) and therefore to be excluded from the canon. Both types of *sūtra* are not "genuine" only when contrasted to the "original" *sūtras* composed in India (which were themselves obviously much later than the time of the Buddha). Thus, given the history of the canon and the broad definition of "authoritative *sūtra*" current among all Buddhists, it must have been difficult to find any good reason for excluding a text only on historical grounds—to say nothing of establishing those grounds.

Interpretation. Three major sets of principles become central to the latter development of Buddhist hermeneutics. These are: the "four reliances," or strategies for understanding a text, the "four types of intentional and metaphoric language," and the "four modes of reasoning." Since the last of these three doctrines falls more under the rubric of philosophy, we shall omit it from this discussion.

Authority and interpretation. The problem of establishing criteria of interpretation cannot be completely separated from that of the hierarchy of authority. The interaction of both spheres of hermeneutics is seen clearly in the doctrine of the four "points of reliance" *(pratisaraṇa)*. This doctrine is found in several Mahāyāna versions, the most popular of which is the *Pratisaraṇa Sūtra*, a text no longer preserved in the original Sanskrit except in quotations. According to this text there are four criteria of interpretation: (1) relying on the nature of things *(dharma)*, not on the opinion of a person; (2) relying on the meaning or purport *(artha)* of a text, not its letter; (3) relying on those passages that explicitly express the higher doctrine *(nītārtha)*, not on those that do not express it explicitly; and (4) understanding by intuitive realization *(jñāna)*, not by conceptual thought *(vijñāna)*. [*See* Jñāna.]

Some of these principles are restatements of the Buddhist tendency to emphasize personal realization as the ultimate source of understanding. But this tendency is not without significant implications for a theory of shared or communicable meaning. A *sūtra* now lost in the original Sanskrit but preserved in Chinese and Tibetan translations, the *Adhyāśayasaṃcodana Sūtra*, says, "whatever is well spoken *(subhāṣita)*, has been spoken by the Buddha." This is perhaps the most extreme formulation of the Mahāyāna's historical view of the roots of its traditions. The system, nevertheless, is not totally open, for implicit in it are the earlier notions of the meaningfulness and appropriateness of the words of the Buddha (and by extension, of scripture). Conversely, then, "whatever is spoken by the Buddha has been well spoken" (as stated, for instance, by King Aśoka in his Bhābrā Rock Edict). Therefore, all passages of scripture must be meaningful—as well as agreeing with the Dharma, and leading to liberation. But it is not always apparent that scripture meets these standards. It is not evident that scripture speaks with one voice. The interpreter must therefore explain the hidden meanings that reveal the underlying unity of intention in scripture, whatever may be the grounds for its authenticity.

Types of intention. In his major works, Asaṅga mentions several methods of understanding that can be applied to scripture. Among these, the four types of explicit intentions and the four types of implicit intention suggest the outlines of a hermeneutical theory. Implicit or contextual meanings *(abhiprāya)* appear to be alternatives for decoding a passage—words intending an analogy, words intending another time frame, words intending a shift in referent, and words intended only for a specific individual. The four types of hidden intention *(abhisaṃdhi)* show another aspect of the process of decoding the sacred text: introductory hidden intention (where the meaning is relevant only for the beginner), metaphysical hidden intention (where the meaning is a statement on the nature of reality), therapeutic hidden intention (where the meaning is realized by following the instructions in combating unhealthy actions or states of mind), and metaphorical intention (where the meaning is not the literal meaning, and often is paradoxical in character; e.g., referring to a virtue as a vice).

The concept of intentional speech brings to mind the third of the four points of reliance and the third principle of T'ien-t'ai exegesis. The common problem in these doctrines is best expressed by the theory of the two levels of meaning: the implicit or interpretable meaning *(neyārtha)* and the explicit or self-evident meaning *(nītārtha)*. This is perhaps the most important doctrine of Buddhist hermeneutics. Under this doctrine, passages or complete texts can be taken at face value as statements of the "ultimate" teaching of the Buddha or they can be understood as teachings preached in response to provisional or individual needs. If a passage is considered to be of the first type, then it is in no need of further elucidation. Its meaning *(artha)* has already been brought out *(nīta)* by the text itself. If a passage belongs to the second group, then the higher meaning can be found only through interpretation. It must be brought out *(neya)* from underneath the surface meaning, so to speak.

Only the Mahāsāṃghikas seem to have rejected this distinction, claiming that all words of the Buddha mean what they literally mean, and therefore need no interpretation. But this extreme position was rejected by other schools, including the more conservative Sthaviras (Theravādins, Sarvāstivādins, etc.).

This hermeneutical schema is closely related to the doctrine of the two levels of truth, the relative or conventional *saṃvṛtti* and the absolute or ultimate *paramārtha*, originally developed in the Mādhyamika school. But the fundamental distinction in the case of implicit and explicit meaning is between modes of intention and meaning, rather than between levels of reality. The point at issue is not whether the words of the text are the ultimate truth (they are not), but whether or not they point directly and unambiguously to it.

Upāya. Also central to Mahāyāna understanding of the religious text is the concept that all forms of discourse are ultimately *saṃvṛtti-satya* (or at best a lower level of *paramārtha*). This is based on both a radical critique of language (as in the Mādhyamika doctrine of "emptiness") and a revaluation of language as a means to an end. In the case of religious language, the end is liberation—the ultimate purpose and the ultimate meaning of all religious discourse. On the lips of the enlightened speaker, language becomes a "skillful means" *(upāya)*, pointing at or eliciting *(udbhāvanā)* realization of the goal. The doctrine finds mythological expression when it is stated that the Buddha's preaching always conforms to the aspirations and maturity of his audience and that his pronouncements are instruments to guide sentient beings, not propositions expressing absolute truth. The religious text is *upāya* in at least three ways: it is a compassionate concession to the diversity, aspirations, and faculties of sentient beings; it is an instrument to be used in attaining the goal; and it is the expression of the liberating techniques of the Buddha. [*See* Upāya.]

Hermeneutics in the Tantras. Tantric hermeneutics presupposes Mahāyāna hermeneutics. Among other Mahāyāna principles, it accepts the four reliances and Asaṅga's eight types of intention. Of course, Tantric theories of interpretation also retain the fundamental distinction between implicit and explicit meaning. However, the intention is now clearly determined by the context of Esoteric practices. Thus we find again the close connection between interpretation and religious practice that characterizes much of Buddhist hermeneutics and that is also evident in scholastic speculations on the Path (as in the Abhidharma); but here orthopraxy becomes central to textual interpretation. Here too, the traditions consider that the "root" text *(mūlatantra)* requires an explanation *(ākhyānatantra)*, but as each text and school has specific practical contexts it is never assumed that a given hermeneutical scheme can be applied to all texts.

The Tantric Candrakīrti (c. 850 CE) explains in his *Pradīpoddyotanā* the basic principles of his school's hermeneutical system as applied to the *Guhyasamāja Tantra*. He explains this "root" text by means of seven analytic procedures called "ornaments" or "preparations" *(sapta-alaṃkāra)*. All seven are used directly or indirectly to bring out the meaning of the text in interpretation or practice, but only two sets appear to bear directly on the issue of interpretation, being at the same time exegetical topics, hermeneutical tools, and levels of meaning. These are the six alternative interpretations of the meaning of words in a passage *(ṣaṭkoṭikaṃ vyākhyānam*; Tib., *mtha' drug* or *rgyas bshad mtha' rnam pa drug)*, and the "fourfold explanation" *(caturvidham ākhyānam*; Tib. *tshul bzhi* or *bshad pa rnam pa bzhi)*.

The six alternatives (with slight alterations to the order of the original) are (1) standard terms used in literal sense *(yathāruta)*, (2) nonstandard or nonnatural terms (*aruta* or *na yathāruta*; i.e. Esoteric jargon), (3) implicit meaning requiring interpretation *(neyārtha)*, (4) explicit or evident meaning *(nītārtha)*, (5) intentional or metaphoric language *(saṃdhyāya bhāṣitam, saṃdhyā bhāṣā)*, and (6) non-intentional language *(no saṃdhyā)*. Western scholars are not in agreement as to the hermeneutical function of this "ornament," but the Tibetan tradition considers the six alternatives an integral part of the interpretation theory unique to Tantra.

The "fourfold explanation," on the other hand, is generally accepted as a hermeneutical schema. In this case Candrakīrti makes an explicit connection between levels of meaning and the stages of spiritual growth *(utpattikrama*, and *sampannakrama*, the latter being divided into five stages or *pañcakrama)*. The four explanations are (1) literal, surface, or secular meaning *(akṣarārtha)*; (2) common meaning *(samastāṅgam)*; (3) hidden *(garbhī)* meaning; and (4) ultimate *(kolikam)* meaning. The first type of meaning is shared by those on the Path and those who have not entered it. The second type is shared by the Mahāyāna and the Tantra (specifically those in the "initial" or *utpatti* stage). The third type is open only to those in the first three stages of the fivefold higher path. The last level of meaning is open only to those who have advanced to the fourth and fifth stages.

This schema is clearly a subtle application of the basic principle of the explicit and the intepretable meanings. One must note, however, that in Tantric exegesis a single text or passage can be both *nīta* and *neya*, depending on the receptor of the message. This entails not only a complex hermeneutics, but also the possibility that the so-called direct meaning *(nīta)* of one level requires interpretation (i.e., is *neyārtha*) for those who are at another level of the path.

Progressive Revelation. The Tantric hermeneutical schema manifests, even more transparently than earlier theories, one of the basic assumptions of Buddhist views of meaning: meanings (and "truths") are a function of the audience as much as, or more than, a function of the intention of the author. If this principle is extended into the cosmic or historical dimension, then new hermeneutical concepts can be derived from the doctrine that the Buddha can preach simultaneously to various assemblies of celestial *bodhisattvas*, adapt his teaching to the needs and faculties of diverse living beings, or preach only one message (in words or silence) yet be understood in different ways. This doctrine, applied to the historical reality of the conflict of authorities, transmissions, and interpretations, provides reasons, albeit *ex post facto*, for choosing and justifying any particular version of the many "teachings of the Buddha."

The turnings of the wheel. In context, statements about relative teaching and ultimate teaching are more sectarian and polemical in spirit than their mere abstract formulations suggest. When a text states that all teachings of the Buddha are only skillful means or empty sounds there is always a conflicting claim to the ultimate validity of the text's own interpretation of the "one true teaching" underlying the "provisional teachings." This is evident in all the classical statements—the *Lotus Sutra*, the *Laṅkāvatāra Sūtra*, the *Saṃdhinirmocana Sūtra*, and others. In some of these texts we see attempts to formulate a historical argument in favor of doctrinal claims. The Buddha, the argument goes, preached in two (or three) major periods that divide his ministry as to location, audience, and depth of the teaching. These major divisions in the Buddha's ministry are called "turnings of the wheel of Dharma." According to the most widely accepted doctrine (as presented in the *Saṃdhinirmocana Sūtra*), there were three "turnings": the Buddha first preached the Hīnayāna teachings in the Deer Park in Banaras. Then he preached the doctrine of "emptiness" (i.e., the Mādhyamika teachings) at the Vulture Peak in Rājagṛha. Last, he preached, in the same place, but when his disciples were more mature, the doctrine of "mind-only" (i.e., the Yogācāra doctrines).

There is, of course, a Mādhyamika version of this story, in which the third turning is in fact that of emptiness and the second the "idealistic" doctrine of the *Saṃdhinirmocana Sūtra*. There is also a late Tantric version that adds a fourth turning: the revelation of Mantrayāna at Dhānyakaṭaka. Nevertheless, the scriptural weight of the *Saṃdhinirmocana* was such that the scholastics could not ignore its clear statement. Thus, Tsoṅ-kha-pa (1357–1419), in his *Legs bshad sñiṅ po,* goes through the most subtle arguments to show that the *sūtra*'s ordering of the turnings does not imply a privileged position for the doctrine of mind-only.

The formulation of pseudohistorical apologetic and hermeneutical strategies became very popular in China. The Indian schema of the Three Turnings was adopted in the schools of San-lun and Fa-hsiang, while others developed autonomous systems: Hua-yen and Nieh-p'an (The Teachings of the Five Periods) and T'ien-t'ai (The Eight Teachings in Five Periods). The last of these, a synthesis created by the T'ien-t'ai monk Chan-jan (711–782), divided and interpreted the scriptures according to the four types of doctrine used in the Buddha's preaching (*hua-fa*: the doctrines of the Tripiṭaka, the common doctrines, the special doctrines, and the perfect or complete doctrine) and his four teaching styles (*hua-i*: direct, gradual, secret, and indeterminate or variable). These eight forms of teaching were used in different proportions and combinations during five periods (*wu-shih*) in the Buddha's ministry: the Buddhāvataṃsaka cycle, the Deer Park cycle, the Vaipulya cycle, the Prajñāpāramitā cycle, and the cycle of the *Lotus* and *Nirvāṇa sūtras*.

This is traditionally taken to imply that a given passage or statement can have multiple levels of meaning. But the function of these "classifications of the teachings" (*chiao-p'an*) was apologetic as well as hermeneutic. The method served as much to establish the preeminence of a particular school as to make sense of the diversity of teachings.

The ages of the Dharma. A parallel development, based on Indian scriptures but characteristic of East Asian Buddhism, is the doctrine of the "Latter Age of the Dharma" (Chin., *mo-fa*; Jpn., *mappō*). The use of this doctrine as a hermeneutical device consists in proposing that changes in historical circumstances require a different interpretation of the tradition or a new definition of orthopraxy. This doctrine developed in China during the turbulent sixth century CE, which culminated in the persecutions of 574 and 578 and led many Buddhists to believe they were living in the last days of the Buddhist Dharma.

Tao-ch'o, for instance, believed the "difficult" practices that were at the heart of traditional Buddhist ascetic and contemplative discipline had become meaningless in the "Latter Age." He therefore proposed that the scriptures prophesying this age justified a new dispensation that would only require the "easier" practices of Pure Land devotion. Matching Indian prophecies on the future of the Buddhist religion with his historical circumstances, he felt he could indirectly derive the authority for doctrinal change from the changed circumstances themselves. [*See* Mappō.]

Zen Demythologization. A different form of adaptation, responding nevertheless occasionally to the issue of the "decay" of Dharma, was the Ch'an (Zen) emphasis on a "return" to orthopraxy. Here the general four principles of the *Adhyāśayasaṃcodana* are used in their most extreme forms. Partially inspired by Chinese interpretations of the Mādhyamika critique of language, partially moved by Taoist rhetoric, this was a movement that emphasized "ultimate meaning," "direct experience," and "freedom from words" to the point of appearing—if not becoming—iconoclastic. One can understand the movement as a process of adaptation of foreign ideas by demythologization, assisted by the deconstructive tendencies built into Buddhist hermeneutical doctrines.

The basic object of meditation, the *kung-an* (Jpn., *kōan*), stands for the sacred utterance of enlightened beings, an *upāya*, a finger pointing at the moon, and the embodiment of different aspects of the single realization common to all Buddhas. This is, after all, a tradition that claims "a transmission outside the scriptures, not relying on words." Nevertheless, the Ch'an (Zen) tradition continues, in its *kōan* collections, the Buddhist predilection for the classification and collection of words "well spoken." Furthermore, these collections, like the ancient *sūtras*, require commentaries, and in them Ch'an also revives, albeit in a new form, the tendency to develop numerical frames of reference. The *Jen-t'ien yen-mu* (compiled by Chih-chao, 1188 CE) contains a number of classificatory systems that can be understood as either guides to meditation or hermeneutical grids to interpret the student's progress in practice. Many of these "matrices" remain in use today. For instance, the elusive teachings of Lin-chi I-hsüan (d. 867 CE) are presented in formulas such as "Lin-chi's Three Phrases," extrapolated from his *Recorded Sayings (Lin-chi lu)*. Modern Zen masters still study the "Eighteen Questions of Fen-yang" *(Feng-yang shih-pa wen)*, a terse guide to the various ways one can "handle" (treat, investigate, and answer) a *kōan*. These questions were devised by the Sung Dynasty master Fen-yang Shan-chiao (947–1024). Also central to modern day practice, and outlined in the *Jen-t'ien yen-mu*, are the "Five Ranks" *(wu-wei)* of Tung-shan (910–990) and Ts'ao-shan (840–901). One can see in these schemas a certain parallel to the techniques of Abhidharma.

However, Zen also preserves the opposite Buddhist tendency, best represented by the teachings of the Japanese master Dōgen Kigen (1200–1253). Dōgen echoes a particularly novel interpretation of the doctrine of "whatever is well spoken" in his writings on *sūtra* (*Shōbōgenzō*; "Okyō" and "Dōtoku"): all things are *sūtras*, in all things is manifested the enlightenment of the Buddhas of all times. This vision, inspired by the *Buddhāvataṃsaka Sūtra*, also raises the question of how this "*sūtra*" which is found in all things can be opened, read, and understood. Zen tradition of course would find the answer in silent meditation.

Dōgen also summarizes much of what is characteristic of the Zen view on intepreting the tradition in a few terse lines in his *Gakudōyōshinshū*: reliance on scripture only leads to confusion, to projecting one's own preferences on the text. The only way to correct understanding is by divesting oneself of the self.

Other approaches to Zen practice are not necessarily as distant as they seem from Dōgen's deceptively simple recommendation. Traditional Chinese and Japanese classifications and methods of "handling" or "studying" *kōan* were systematized by Hakuin Ekaku (1658–1768) and his disciples. The resulting system of *kōans* (five levels of miscellaneous *kōans*, plus the five *goi kōans*, and the Ten Precepts) has all the marks of Buddhist catechistic instincts; Hakuin himself, in his essay *Goi kōketsu* in the *Keisō dokuzui*, established exact correlations between some of these stages and Indian scholastic categories. Still, the system also emphasizes the quest for meaning in practice and a gradual detachment from doctrinal conceptions, as well as from meditation experiences. The crowning piece of the system, the last *kōan (matsugo no rōkan)* asks the disciple to reflect on the meaning of "completing" a system of *kōans*–that is, what should be the last question, once the adept has answered all questions? [*See* Ch'an *and* Zen.]

Hermeneutics and Apologetics. All Buddhists tend, even today, to claim a certain immunity from history, partly justified by the emphasis on the presence of Dharma in all things and all times, by the plurality of Buddhas, and by the obvious diversity and plasticity of the tradition. When first faced with historical criticism, coming from non-Buddhists such as Tominaga Nakamoto (1715–1746) in his *Shutsujō kōgo* (1745), some Japanese Buddhists (e.g., Murakami Senshō, 1851–1929, in *Bukkyō tōitsu ron*) readily admitted that the Mahāyāna scriptures could not be the *ipsissima verba* of the Master. They based the orthodoxy of their tradition on concepts outlined above: the unity of the spirit, consistency in the goal, the development of "skillful means." Some, for instance, Maeda Eun (1855–1930), also appealed to the doctrine that all teachings are implicit in the one, original, and ineffable teaching. The concept of levels of meaning is also used to preserve some form of religious discourse while claiming that the ultimate is beyond language and history. Mahāyāna Buddhists continue to appeal to these principles, relying fundamentally on the ancient apologetic and hermeneutic strategies outlined in this article. The Theravāda tradition, on the other hand, tends to build its hermeneutics on the reaffirmation of its conviction that its canon contains the words of the Buddha.

[*See also* Buddhist Philosophy *and* Hermeneutics.]

BIBLIOGRAPHY

Bharati, Agehananda. "Intentional Language in the Tantras." *Journal of the American Oriental Society* 81(1961): 261–270. Interpretation of the meaning of *saṃdhā-bhāṣā*.

Bond, George D. *"Word of the Buddha": The Tipiṭaka and its Interpretation in Theravāda Buddhism*. Colombo, 1982. This is a survey of Theravāda theories of exegesis, based primarily, but not exclusively on the *Nettippakaraṇa*.

Buddhadāsa. "Everyday Language and Dhamma Language." In *Toward the Truth*, edited by Donald K. Swearer, pp. 56–86. Philadelphia, 1971. A modern Theravāda view on levels of language.

Cabezon, Jose I. "The Concepts of Truth and Meaning in the Buddhist Scriptures." *Journal of the International Association of Buddhist Studies* 4 (1981): 7–23. Deals mostly with Mahāyāna views of levels of truth and meaning.

Chappell, David W. "Introduction to the 'T'ien-t'ai ssu-chiao-i'." *Eastern Buddhist*, n.s. 9 (May 1976): 72–86. Although this paper is a survey of the content and history of a T'ien-t'ai scholastic manual, much of the discussion centers on the nature of T'ien-t'ai hermeneutical schemata.

Doherty, Gerald. "Form is Emptiness: Reading the Diamond Sutra." *Eastern Buddhist*, n.s. 16 (Autumn 1983): 114–123. A bold analysis of this famous *sūtra* from the point of view of deconstructive theory.

Gregory, Peter N. "Chinese Buddhist Hermeneutics: The Case of Hua-yen." *Journal of the American Academy of Religion* 51 (1983): 231–49. On the philosophical presuppositions of Hua-yen hermeneutics.

Ishizu Teruji. "Communication of Religious Inwardness and a Hermeneutic Interpretation of Buddhist Dogma." In *Religious Studies in Japan*, edited by the Nihon Shūkyō Gakkai, pp. 3–21. Tokyo, 1959. This paper is a good example of an extreme ahistorical view on the meaning of Buddhist doctrines.

Lamotte, Étienne. *Saṃdhinirmocana Sūtra: L'explication des mystères*. Louvain, 1935. Translation of one of the most important sources for the doctrine of the Three Turnings and the distinction of explicit and implicit meanings. Lamotte also translated the first and most important half of the *Mahā-prajñāpāramitā-upadeśa-śāstra* as *Le traité de la grande vertu de sagesse*, 5 vols. (Louvain, 1944–1980). This work is attributed to a Mahāyānist Nāgārjuna, who was evidently trained in the Sarvāstivāda tradition. Lamotte also has two studies on questions in Buddhist hermeneutics: "La critique d'authenticité dans le bouddhisme," in *Indian Antiqua*, edited by F. D. K. Bosch (Leiden, 1947), pp. 213–222; and "La critique d'interprétation dans le bouddhisme." *Annuaire de l'Institut de Philologie et d'Histoire Orientales et Slaves*, vol. 9, *Mélanges Henri Grégoire* (Brussels, 1949), pp. 341–361.

MacQueen, Graeme. "Inspired Speech in Early Mahāyāna Buddhism." *Religion* 11 (October, 1981): 303–319 and 12 (January 1982): 49–65. An exploration of the importance of *pratibhāṇa* for Mahāyāna notions of canonical authenticity.

Ñāṇamoli, trans. *The Guide*. London, 1962. A translation of Kaccāyana's *Nettippakaraṇa*, the classical Theravāda manual of exegesis. The attribution of this work to Kaccāyana, the Buddha's disciple, has been questioned by modern scholarship.

Pye, Michael, and Robert Morgan, eds. *The Cardinal Meaning: Essays in Comparative Hermeneutics; Buddhism and Christianity*. The Hague, 1973.

Steinkellner, Ernst. "Remarks on Tantristic Hermeneutics." *Proceedings of the Csoma de Kőrös* Memorial Symposium, edited by Louis Ligeti, pp. 445–458. Budapest, 1978. Outline of some aspects of Candrakīrti's exegetical and hermeneutical theory.

Thurman, Robert A. F. "Buddhist Hermeneutics." *Journal of the American Academy of Religion* 46 (1978): 19–39. This is an outline of the principles of Buddhist hermeneutics based on the *Legs bhsad sñiṅ po*, a work translated by Thurman as *Tsong Khapa's Speech of Gold in the Essence of True Eloquence* (Princeton, 1984).

Wayman, Alex. "Concerning *saṃdhā-bhāṣā/saṃdhi-bhāṣā/saṃdhyā bhāṣā*." In *Mélanges d'indianisme à la mémoire de Louis Renou*, pp. 789–796. Paris, 1968. Summarizes much of the debate on this technical term. Wayman's own thesis was developed further in "Twilight Language and a Tantric Song," in his *The Buddhist Tantra* (London, 1973), pp. 128–135.

LUIS O. GÓMEZ

BUDDHIST PHILOSOPHY. Scholars are generally agreed that the beginnings of Buddhist thought as propounded by Siddhārtha Gautama, the Buddha, comprised no more than a collection of ethico-religious principles, lacking the form or content of what could be called a philosophy. It was only with the appearance of Abhidharma (Pali, Abhidhamma) scholarship that Buddhism began to face philosophical questions and take up apologetic problems through the exegesis of canonical texts. Yet, true though this be, we should not forget Max Weber's statement that "like Jainism, but even more clearly, Buddhism presents itself as a product of the time of urban development, of urban kingship, and the city nobles" (*The Religion of India: The Sociology of Hinduism and Buddhism*. Glencoe, Ill., 1962, p. 204). It would have been impossible for the Buddha to appeal to the people of his time, many of whom were deeply interested in philosophical issues inherited from the Upaniṣadic philosophy (such as Yajñavalkya's lofty speculations on *ātman* mysticism), had he not raised his new message to the revolutionary heights of a spiritual philosophy able to hold sway over the numerous traditional and contemporary trends of religious thought in India.

The notorious silence of the Buddha regarding metaphysical problems—in particular, (1) whether or not the universe is eternal; (2) whether or not the universe is finite; (3) whether or not the *jīva* (spirit or principle of life) belongs to the body; and (4) whether or not a *tathāgata* (i.e., a Buddha), once released from worldly life, continues to exist, exists and does not exist at the same time, or is neither existent nor nonexistent—does not mean that he was either indifferent to philosophical problems or ignorant of them. Quite the contrary, his teaching presupposes a critical standpoint vis-à-vis metaphysical reasoning that enabled him to comprehend and analyze the antinomies implicit in the assertions of the various contemporary traditions. We find the Buddha forging a "middle path" between the antinomic extremes of theoretical and practical reason by shifting the focus to the question of the efficacy of ideas to deliver the self from the ceaseless transmigratory repetition of karmic misery through death and sin.

It is in this context that the Buddha offers his teaching on the Four Noble Truths (Skt., *catvāry āryasatyāni*; Pali, *cattāri ariyasaccāni*). It was from a similar focus on soteriological efficacy that in early Buddhism there sprang the main doctrinal themes of the five aggregates (Skt., *skandhas*; Pali, *khandhas*) or existential components of being human, of the dependent co-arising (Skt., *pratītya-samutpāda*; Pali, *paṭicca-samuppāda*) of all being-in-the-world, or in later Mahāyāna Buddhism the notion of emptiness *(śūnyatā)*, the philosophic implications of which were worked out in Mādhyamika and Yogācāra thinking. In turn, the Mādhyamika and Yogācāra schools in India provided the framework for later philosophical syntheses of doctrine in China, Tibet, Japan, and elsewhere.

Early Buddhist Thought: The Four Noble Truths. It is recorded that in his first sermon after his enlightenment, directed to the five men who had shared his ascetic practices, the Buddha proclaimed a Middle Path toward absolute truth that avoided the extremes of hedonism on the one hand and asceticism on the other. In their stead he proclaimed the Four Noble Truths as the only effective way to purify insight and terminate suffering. Here we find the simplest statement on the content of enlightenment and the means to attain it. The early scriptures depict the Buddha as constantly preaching these truths. During his last journey and in the face of death, the eighty-year-old Buddha repeats the same doctrine to the people of a village he passes through.

We cannot now share the certitude of early believers that the extant texts (the Pali Nikāyas and Chinese Āgamas) on the Four Noble Truths represent the actual content of the Buddha's first sermon. It is impossible to distinguish clearly his own words from those of later disciples. Yet the tradition witnesses to the fact that from the time he started preaching until the end of his life, the Buddha himself took the Four Truths as the central core and axis of his doctrine.

The Four Noble Truths express the content of the Buddha's religious experience of conversion and enlightenment. They are the Truth about Suffering (illness), the Truth about the Origin of Suffering (its cause), the Truth about the Surcease of Suffering (its annihilation), and the Truth about the Way to End Suffering (the Noble Eightfold Path).

Recently, some scholars have begun to question whether the doctrine of the Four Noble Truths can in fact be attributed to the Buddha himself. They argue that the medical format in which these truths are expressed first appears in Buddhist and other writings only around the beginning of the common era. But Greek philosophy can shed some unexpected light on the question, for it has been ascertained that Greek medicine of the time of Plato and Aristotle, or even as much as a century before them, was heavily influenced by Indian medical science. The section on mental illness in Plato's *Timaeus* describes the pathological elements as the illness, the cause of illness, the removal of that cause, and the method of treatment. In Aristotle's *Metaphysics* (Z, 1032b15–30), specific mention is made and detailed explanations are offered on the technique of treating cases according to the four elements of the illness, its cause, the removal of that cause, and the method of so doing.

Nowhere in Buddhist writings, or in any other Indian sources, is it made clear just how the Four Truths relate to one another as categories of medical science or how they constitute an effective method of treatment. Yet all of this appears very clearly in Plato and Aristotle. If one can conclude that these Greek ideas come from an earlier Indian source, it becomes credible that they may have been known and respected by the Buddha and his disciples. Moreover, there seems to be a connection between medical science and skepticism, particularly in Greek antiquity. If we can assume the same connection in the Buddha's India, then the fact that some of the most intellectual followers of the Buddha, Sāriputta and Mogallāna, before becoming followers of the Buddha were disciples of the famous skeptic Sanjaya Belatthiputta suggests the possibility that medical terminology was prevalent in the group surrounding the young Gautama. This may be quite significant in that Sāriputta played a central role in the formative history of Buddhist thinking.

One must, however, note that the medical usage of these terms differs from their soteriological use. The concern with "suffering" in primitive Buddhism points to the basic problem of human finitude, not simply to dissatisfaction resulting from frustrated passions or unpleasantness involved with sensations of pain. Any modern interpretation of the truths of suffering, its cause, the removal of that cause, and the path leading to such must begin in an awareness of the radical existential thrust of these concepts. Suffering must be seen against the background of impermanence, for Buddhism describes suffering as: "All things are impermanent [*anitya*], all things are suffering and sorrow [*duḥkha*], all the elements of being are no-self [*anātman*]."

Here impermanence does not simply indicate the objective fact of the perpetual change and disappearance of external things. First and foremost, impermanence signifies the problem of my own existence, my being-unto-death. Deep insight into and resignation to my own impermanence does not mean that I have accepted any particular fact about external conditions, but that I am resigned in all things and all circumstances to my own existence as impermanent. It is the turning around of the outward-looking eye of the self carried along by everyday desires to focus upon that self as it really is. The self and its feelings undergo a crystallization in the process, for everything previously experienced congeals within an awareness of that self as impermanent. It is within the framework of this experience that suffering comes to awareness.

Thus the suffering signified by the phrase "All things are impermanent, all things are suffering" is not the psycho-physical sensation of pain or dissatisfaction with the course of events. These are instances of suffering defined by some object whereby one is inflicted. For this kind of suffering the fundamental issue is how to dispose of this object through the proper technical means.

Likewise, to look for "the origin of suffering" does not mean to investigate the cause of an illness from its symptoms. Rather it means that the self crystallizes in suffering, congealing into a definite structure with suffering as its focus. In that crystallization the opposition between subject and object tends to be clarified in its true nature as the attachment of the subject to objects. This is what the commentaries mean when they take the origin of suffering to be the self-regenerating, unquenchable thirst of desire.

One must completely understand suffering and annihilate its origin. It is like the suffering that appears in a dream: once one realizes that one has been dreaming, the suffering is completely understood and one is brought to a new awareness that the dream was the cause of the suffering. Indeed, the awareness of the dream as dream entails an awakening from the dream.

The Buddha is the awakened one, and through his awakening he must rouse and awaken those who still go on sleeping.

From the above we can summarize the Four Noble Truths in the propositions that (1) the arising of suffering is itself the surcease of suffering and (2) the noble truths involve a communication of I and Thou on the way to awakening, whereby that surcease implies that one's own awakening awakens others. Often the path is conceived as simply the means or method to reach the goal of surcease or awakening. But while that is appropriate when speaking in medical or technical terms, it does not express the dynamic structure of the existential categories proper to religion.

It is reported that the skeptical Sāriputta, before he became a follower of the Buddha, once met Assaji, one of the five original disciples of the Buddha, and asked him about the essentials of the Buddha's doctrine. The disciple, however, excused himself, saying that he was not yet sufficiently versed in the doctrine. But he added, "Those things that arise from a cause, of these the Buddha had told the cause and that which is their surcease—the great recluse has such a doctrine." Upon hearing these words, Sāriputta immediately attained the insight that "the arising of suffering turns into the surcease of suffering." In other words, he realized that the condensation of all suffering into its cause or ground triggers an immediate turnabout into its annihilation.

There is one radical difference between the skepticism of ancient Greece or India and modern skepticism. In the former, the suspension of all judgment provoked by the awareness of the relativity of all human knowing is accompanied by a decision to abandon all attachment. It is in this abandonment that the heart is brought to the peace of detachment. Here skepticism is a doctrine of religious liberation through renunciation, although for Sāriputta it lacked an ultimate foundation on which to ground this liberation and peace. It was not until Sāriputta met Assaji that he recognized in this lack of foundation the final bondage to be overcome in order to arrive at true liberation. Thus a single phrase was sufficient to lead him to grasp the promise of conversion: "The darkness of ignorance turns around and light is born." It should, however, be remembered that this conversion was only the first step on Sāriputta's road to complete awakening, which was to be realized later in his continued master-disciple relationship with the Buddha.

By understanding the doctrine of the Four Noble Truths as an existential path wherein one's own awakening awakens others, we gain access to the fundamental spirit of early Buddhism. Undoubtedly, through the religious community they shared the Buddha and his disciples went on to deepen their insight into the meaning of the identity of the arising of suffering with the surcease of suffering. The more philosophical speculations of the Abhidharma scholars also stemmed from their insight into the communal aspects of the Four Truths. Certainly, many Buddhist tenets trace their origin back to that spiritual communion. Such early doctrines as the five aggregates and the six sense organs, as well as such central philosophical notions as dependent co-arising, were first taken up as religious symbols within the community, developing in Buddhist doctrinal history from that beginning.

In the later enfolding of Buddhism within its various historical circumstances and in its various communities, we find the same emergence of the Buddha's original thrust recurring again and again. Both the cognitive and the ethical value of each of the Buddha's teachings derive from their overall religious significance. The interrelationships between the individual teachings are like the various constellations of the evening sky brightening before our view. Just as the whole configuration of the stars gently revolves as one star after the other rises up from the horizon of space, so the different teachings throughout the history of Buddhism present themselves to our awareness. Although it remains the same from beginning to end, yet it is always giving rise to something new, for this is how the teaching that one's own awakening awakens others developed and deepened within the Buddhist community. Since Dharma-teaching is a work of compassion (love), we can see how it must always be concretized in the world, for it evinces a cosmic love that embraces all equally and reaches to the totality of being in all its dimensions and configurations.

This existential thrust of early Buddhism did not then exclude philosophical understanding. Rather, it led directly to the Abhidharma schools and their attempts to express its content in a clear and consistent philosophy. [*See also* Four Noble Truths *and* Eightfold Path.]

Abhidharma Philosophy. The rise of the Abhidharma schools some centuries before the beginning of the common era signaled a shift from the popular style of the earlier scriptures to a more systematic and theoretical understanding of the content of the Buddha's teaching, deemed necessary in order to preserve its meaning against misinterpretations. Although at first the term *abhi-dharma,* which literally meant "in regard to the doctrine," referred to commentarial explanations of the scriptures, in time the Abhidharma masters began to rearrange the teachings systematically and offer their own interpretations of their meaning. The Abhidharma then became known as the "superior *(abhi)* doctrine *(dharma)*" and constituted a separate, third collection of the canon, along with the Scripture (Sūtra) and Discipline (Vinaya) collections.

The Abhidharma thinkers began by composing lists of technical terms *(mātṛkā)* aimed at defining the basic truths of Buddhism. They sought to identify the "essences" *(svabhāva)* of all things, which then were regarded as absolutely real and true, since they were incapable of any further analysis. For example, the belief in selfhood was rejected because no self *(ātman)* could be identified underlying the continuity of human living. But the five constituent factors *(dharma)* or aggregates *(skandha)*—material form *(rūpa)*, sensation *(vedanā)*, conceptualization *(saṃjñā)*, karmic impulse *(saṃskāra)*, and consciousness *(vijñāna)*—were detected as being the real factors behind the mistaken belief in self and were accordingly pronounced to be real and true. Abhidharma is a philosophy of realism and conceptualism, for its principal thinkers, by and large, held that such real factors were correctly and truly expressed in well-analyzed concepts. [*See also* Dharma, *article on* Buddhist Dharma and Dharmas *and* Soul, *article on* Buddhist Concepts.]

The Abhidharma thinkers, however, did not undertake their theoretical task from a mere desire for logical consistency or academic learning. Their main interest was soteriological, for they thought that detachment from passion *(kleśa)* resulted from the attainment of the correct view *(samagdṛṣṭi)*. They discoursed at length on the sixteen aspects of the Four Noble Truths and on the many stages of meditation necessary to reach cessation *(nirvāṇa)*. The tradition they initiated continues in the Theravāda tradition today.

Yet, in the eyes of the founders of the Mahāyāna tradition, the Abhidharma thinkers' basically intellectualist approach tended to substitute conceptual and propositional truth in place of the existential thrust of the primitive Buddhist teachings. The basic doctrine of dependent co-arising was shunted to the periphery and treated under the heading of karmic maturation, for in a world of absolutely true and real *dharma* factors the stress is upon the ontological status of things, not upon their interdependence.

It was in direct response to this Abhidharma realism and conceptualism, particularly that of the Sarvāstivāda school, that the Prajñāpāramitā scriptures were composed from 50 BCE to 150 CE. These scriptures, written in an anti-intellectual and paradoxical style, recommended as "the perfection of wisdom" a nondiscriminative understanding *(prajñā)* that rejected all Abhidharma "attachment" to views and declared all things to be empty of essence. [*See* Prajñā.] These scriptures declared that the truth of wisdom is found not in correct views, but in the embodiment of wisdom in practices of compassion. [*See* Karuṇā.]

But these Prajñāpāramitā scriptures were composed in a direct and paradoxical style and did not deign to engage the Abhidharma masters in philosophical dialogue. Indeed, it is probable that the Prajñāpāramitā adherents were not trained monks like the Abhidharma masters but rather laymen committed to the Buddha's doctrine. It was the Mādhyamika philosophy of Nāgārjuna (fl. c. 200) that took these wisdom insights and expressed them in philosophic terms. [*See also* Sarvāstivāda *and* Sautrāntika.]

Mādhyamika Philosophy. Nāgārjuna's Mādhyamika philosophy laid the foundation for all subsequent Mahāyāna thinking. He took over and continued the Prajñāpāramitā theme of emptiness *(śūnyatā)* and argued consistently against the Abhidharma ideas of real essences (*dharmas*). [*See* Śūnyam and Śūnyatā.]

However, the main feature of Mādhyamika philosophy is not simply its insistence upon emptiness. Rather, the unique achievement of Nāgārjuna lies in his identification of emptiness with dependent co-arising. The primitive teaching of dependent co-arising *(pratītya-samutpāda)* had fallen into a rigid formulation within the Abhidharma ontology as the operation of *karman*. Nāgārjuna reclaimed it as expressing the dependent co-arising of all essenceless reality. Things co-arise dependently because they are empty of any fixed essence and that which is empty is precisely the essenceless being of dependent co-arising. All being is empty of essence, for emptiness is embodied in dependently co-arising being. [*See* Pratītya-samutpāda.]

Although Mādhyamika is permeated with "a hundred negations and a thousand denials," it is not nihilism *(nāstivāda)*. Rather, it thematizes the essenceless being of dependent co-arising. Nāgārjuna aimed not only at a deconstruction of Abhidharma realism, but also at a construction of a dialectic of dependently co-arising being that might embody awareness of emptiness. His insistence on emptiness is not the nihilistic ravings of a madman but an attempt to think being within the context of emptiness and emptiness within the context of being. In Mādhyamika, reality *(dharmatā)* and suchness *(tathatā)* signify dependently co-arising being understood through the negation of emptiness. Stated conversely, they signify emptiness embodied in essenceless being. The Middle Path is this understanding of emptiness as concretized in the empty, concrete being of dependent co-arising. [*See also* Tathatā.]

The identity of emptiness and dependent co-arising flows into the complementary Mādhyamika theme of the double truth *(satya-dvaya)*, a teaching the Nāgārjuna was probably the first to treat as central. The truth of ultimate meaning *(paramārtha-satya)* is always ineffable and beyond any conceptual knowing, and yet it must be expressed in the truth of worldly convention *(saṃvṛti-satya)* in order to be understandable to common worldlings. Conventional truth is language attempting, but always failing, to express the ineffable. It is thus described as a clouding over and occluding of truth. When recognized as such, it can point beyond to that ultimate meaning that it clouds and occludes.

Mādhyamika takes its stand upon the identity of emptiness and dependent co-arising and weaves the theme of the double truth within that context. Ultimate meaning is the truth of emptiness, while conventional meaning is the truth of dependent co-arising, appearing to the awakened as totally inadequate and false, but to the unawakened as propositional truth in the world.

Yet, although the Prajñāpāramitā scriptures and the Mādhyamika philosophy are in no sense nihilistic, they did occasion distress among Buddhists who could not follow their initial deconstructionist mode of thinking. Not all practitioners were concerned with the dangers of Abhidharma realism, for most had probably never had the inclination to engage themselves in its intricate scholasticism. It is thus not surprising that the more affirmative Tathāgatagarbha mystic trend of thought should have arisen to counter the perceived negativism of Prajñāpāramitā and Mādhyamika. The notion of emptiness was found to be unacceptable (or at least, incomplete), for the Buddha declared that "the Buddha nature exists in every sentient being." In contrast to the supposed negativism of Mādhyamika, the Tathāgatagarbha texts all present the Buddha nature, the realm of the seed *(garbha)* of awakening (becoming a *tathāgata*), as the only truly existent being. [*See* Tathāgatagarbha.]

Rather than Nāgārjuna's identification of emptiness and dependent co-arising, the reality of empirical, everyday being *(sat-tva)* is identified with the ultimately true Dharma Realm *(dharmadhātu)*. All things are not empty, for the Buddha nature is really real and existent, as evidenced in the attribution to it of the four perfect qualities of eternity, constancy, purity, and immutability, attributes that Nāgārjuna would have immediately rejected as illusory fabrications. The one real reality is this Buddha nature. This really existent seed of Buddha nature is empty of all defilements, which are unreal and illusory, but not empty of the Buddha attributes, which are not really distinct from it. All defilements are adventitious *(āgantuka)* and do not pertain to the original essence of that seed. The scope of emptiness and nonbeing is restricted to the defiled coverings over that underlying seed and its intrinsic attributes. Emptiness is no longer all-inclusive, for after negating all the defilements as illusions, there remains left over *(avaśiṣṭa)* the eternal, immutable, already pure reality of the Buddha nature. The Tathāgatagarbha tradition represents a Buddhist philosophy of original being and stands in sharp contrast to Prajñāpāramitā and Mādhyamika thought.

However, the Tathāgatagarbha tradition in India was not a fully articulated philosophical alternative to Mādhyamika. It is represented by only one *śāstra* (treatise) and was never criticized by Mādhyamika thinkers. But its presentations of the theme of the original, really existent Buddha nature served as a basis for much philosophical thinking in later developments, especially in China, where it was reinterpreted in terms of the dependent co-arising of the awakening in the world.

In the Indian context, however, the Tathāgatagarbha tradition failed to account for the genesis of defilement, for all defilement was swept away by it as unreal and illusory. Even Mādhyamika in its thematization of dependent co-arising had not focused upon the genesis of illusion, being content to demonstrate the logical falsity of all views. But without some explanation of the genesis of illusion it was difficult to ground doctrinal discourse within the dependent co-arising world of ignorance and illusion. The rejection of Abhidharma theory by Mādhyamika and the bypassing of any theory by Tathāgatagarbha left scant room for any rational presentation of doctrine and seemed to undermine even the possibility of doctrinal discourse. [*See also* Mādhyamika *and the biography of Nāgārjuna*.]

Yogācāra Philosophy. The critical Yogācāra philosophy of Asaṅga and Vasubandhu (fourth century) attempted to ground Nāgārjuna's teaching of emptiness within a critical understanding of the consciousness that generates all meaning. [*See* Vijñāna.] Their intent was not only to maintain the teachings of the Prajñāpāramitā scriptures and the basic themes of Mādhyamika, but also to allow scope for theoretical thinking within the context of the identity of emptiness with dependent co-arising. The contribution of Asaṅga and Vasubandhu to Buddhist philosophy lies principally in their understanding of emptiness and dependent co-arising within a critical understanding of consciousness. They carried out their project under the themes of the development of consciousness into illusion *(vijñāna-pariṇāma)* and the three patterns of consciousness *(tri-lakṣaṇa)*.

Asaṅga summarizes his thinking in three points. The first is his presentation of dependent co-arising, which grounds the meaning of emptiness within consciousness by identifying the imagined pattern of clinging to unreal essences as empty. This illusory, imagined pattern *(parikalpita-lakṣaṇa)* results from the development of words and images clung to as if they represented real essences. It is a grasping at such imagined essences *(svabhāva)*, as if a named image signified the reality of a corresponding essence over against the knower.

The second point is the presentation of the character of that which is dependently co-arisen, that is, the basic other-dependent pattern of consciousness *(paratantra-lakṣaṇa)*, which identifies within consciousness the ground of dependent co-arising. Consciousness is a synergy of different operations and functions. The storehouse consciousness *(ālaya-vijñāna)* functions as a store of conceptually and verbally unmediated karmic experience acting in tandem with the active consciousnesses *(pravṛtti-vijñāna)* that do mediate those experiences in words and ideas. [*See* Ālaya-vijñāna.] Thus, there is a mutual dependency between base experience and thinking upon that experience, for each depends on the other. Furthermore, consciousness is other-dependent because it appears as image *(nimitta)* and insight *(darśana)*. Images are presented by the senses but do not of themselves issue in meaning, for imagination is not constructive of meaning. It is only insight into those images that constructs meaning.

In the absence of such insight, images remain uninterpreted pictures imagined to depict of themselves the essences of things seen and imagined. But without the image no insight can occur. Here the notion of dependent co-arising is understood as the basic structure of all consciousness and grounded critically within an understanding of conscious understanding as other-dependent. In virtue of this other-dependent pattern, consciousness not only devolves into its illusory, imagined pattern but also is open to and capable of being converted into wisdom, into the fully perfected pattern *(pariniṣpanna-lakṣaṇa)* of consciousness, which is precisely the absence of the imagined pattern within the other-dependent pattern. It is the absence of imputing essences to things presented in images. It is the realization that all dependently co-arising things are empty of essence.

In these first two points Asaṅga has reinterpreted and critically grounded the notions of emptiness and dependent co-arising within consciousness. But he does not stop with this, for his third point is a presentation of the meaning of what has been declared in the scriptures. Here Asaṅga makes a unique contribution to Buddhist philosophy in presenting a hermeneutic based on the theme of the three patterns of consciousness, for once consciousness has been converted *(āśraya-parāvṛtti)* from the imagined pattern to that of full perfection, it becomes capable of skillfully embodying the wisdom of ultimate meaning within worldly and conventional language. The validity of such conventional truth is found then in its faithfulness to the scriptures and its logical consistency. Thus, both Asaṅga and Vasubandhu composed works on logic, explicating the genesis and validity of conventional truth.

All words and ideas are dependent on others, for they are nothing but constructs of consciousness *(vijñapti-mātra)*. But once recognized as such, once they no longer threaten to usurp the place of silent realization, they have a valid, if limited truth. Thus, in evolving their critical theory of consciousness Asaṅga and Vasubandhu allow scope for valid doctrinal discourse and meaningful theoretical thinking within an understanding of the other-dependent and empty structure of consciousness [*See* Yogācāra *and the biographies of Asaṅga and Vasubandhu.*]

Epistemology and Logic. Epistemological and logical issues had not been neglected in Buddhist thought. Within the Abhidharma circle such questions had indeed been discussed. Nāgārjuna, Asaṅga, and Vasubandhu all dealt with logic and treated the question of the valid means of knowing *(pramāṇa)*. These endeavors were brought to the fore by the Yogācāra affirmation of a critical understanding of consciousness. If thinking is valid as other-dependent, if conventional truth is indeed truth, then questions of epistemology and logic become crucial prolegomena for all philosophical discussion. Thus such thinkers as Dignāga (480–540) and Dharmakīrti (seventh century) developed a "Buddhist" epistemology and logic.

Inasmuch as these thinkers inherited the Yogācāra affirmation of the validity of other-dependent knowing and the synergistic structure of understanding, they are also known as Yogācārins. But inasmuch as they do not employ either scriptural authorities or the Yogācāra doctrinal language, never mentioning such central terms as the storehouse consciousness or the three patterns of understanding, they are distinguished as Vijñaptimātra thinkers of the logical tradition *(nyāyānusārino vijñānavādinaḥ)*. Yet, although they avoid such terminology, they do reflect the basic Yogācāra teachings on consciousness.

The interdependent, synergistic functioning of consciousness is described by Dignāga in terms of the two means of knowing: direct perception and inference. Direct perception *(pratyakṣa)* is unmediated, pure sensation, prior to words and before any imagining. It presents the "own mark" *(svalakṣaṇa)* of the sensed thing. Since the Yogācārins had identified the source of illusion as imagining through verbal fabrication, so Dignāga identified true and sure knowing as the pure perception that precedes such fabrication. By contrast, inference *(anumāna)* is the verbal mental construction that by naming things establishes their classes and gains insight into their relationships, presenting their "common mark" *(sāmānya-lakṣaṇa)*. Logic is developed as the correct procedure for such inference and serves to safeguard the constructed truth of reasoning about the "common marks" of things. Just as for Asaṅga and Vasubandhu consciousness was structured as the synergistic interplay between preverbal experience stored in the container consciousness and the mental constructs of the active consciousnesses of thinking and imagining, so here consciousness is a synergy between preverbal, pure experience and verbal thinking.

The same epistemological understanding is seen in Dignāga's understanding of the structure of consciousness. The image aspect *(nimitta-bhāga)* is the presence of sensed images as objects for understanding. The insight aspect *(darśana-bhāga)* is the understanding of the meaning of those images. The awareness aspect *(svasaṃvitti-bhāga)* is the awareness of the knower implicit in such acts of insight into image. Later, the Yogācārin Dharmapāla (530–561) added a fourth aspect of reflexive awareness *(svasaṃvitti-saṃvitti-bhāga)* as the critical understanding that one is indeed understanding through insight into image.

Dharmakīrti furthered Dignāga's pioneering work and constructed a vast epistemological system that was transmitted to and studied in Tibet. However, the Chinese, although they translated some of Dignāga's works, showed scant interest in epistemological and logical questions and did not devote much attention to this aspect of Buddhist thinking. [*See the biographies of Dignāga, Dharmakīrti, and Dharmapāla.*]

Later Buddhist Thought. The themes of emptiness, dependent co-arising, and double truth, and of their interpretation through the Yogācāra notion of the three patterns of consciousness and the Tathāgatagarbha notion of the original Buddha nature, form the bedrock philosophical themes that reappear throughout the subsequent centuries in Mahāyāna Buddhist thinking.

The identity of emptiness and dependent co-arising appears clearly in the philosophy of the Chinese T'ien-t'ai school. Its principal thinker Chih-i (538–597 CE) describes the "middle" *(chung)* path as including within itself an awareness of emptiness *(k'ung)* and of the temporary and provisional *(chia)*, thus repeating Nāgārjuna's notion of the Middle Path as the identity of emptiness and dependent co-arising. Chih-i also seems to have been influenced by the Yogācāra notion of the three patterns of consciousness, where the other-dependent pattern includes both the perfected pattern of emptiness and the imagined pattern of transient being. [*See* T'ien-t'ai *and the biography of Chih-i.*]

Chinese Hua-yen philosophy begins its analysis with the distinction between truth *(li)* and phenomena *(shih)*, reflecting the notion of the double truth. It then moves to a third step, which gains insight into the interpenetration of truth and phenomena, reflecting Nāgārjuna's identification of emptiness and dependent co-arising. The fourth Hua-yen step, the interpenetration of phenomena and phenomena, seems to hark back to the Yogācāra theme that to the awakened one all things are merely conscious constructs infused with the wisdom of perfection. [*See* Hua-yen.]

The Tantric schools in both Tibet and China were direct outgrowths of the Mādhyamika and, especially in China and Japan, were also heavily influenced by Yogācāra. The basic theme of the two *maṇḍalas* of the womb *(garbha)* as truth and the lightning bolt *(vajra)* as the seeker after truth reflects the structure of the double truth as the attempt to embody the ineffable within worldly experience. [*See* Buddhism, Schools of, *article on* Esoteric Buddhism.]

Of course, the Mādhyamika school itself continued into China in the San-lun school, although this school seems to have concentrated its attention on refutation and emptiness. The entire Tibetan tradition takes its stand upon Mādhyamika thinking and develops it within its Tantric thrust. Yogācāra also had its successor in the Fa-hsiang school in China, but in the absence of the Indian concerns over the value of theory and its critical grounding within consciousness, it seems to have followed along more narrow scholastic channels.

Chinese Ch'an and Japanese Zen were heavily influenced not only by the Prajñāpāramitā teaching of emptiness, but also by the notion of the Buddha nature, especially Rinzai Zen, with its paradoxical invitation to discover "one's original face." This theme was also treated by Chinese and Japanese Buddhists of many schools and reinterpreted to indicate the dependent co-arising of the already existing potential for awakening within all sentient beings. It influenced the teaching of the One Vehicle *(ekayāna)* for all beings, which was common to most Chinese schools. [*See* Ch'an *and* Zen.]

The same themes continue into the present, as seen in the philosophy of the Kyoto school founded on the work of Nishida Kitarō (1870–1945). Nishida, Nishitani Keiji, and Takeuchi Yoshinori attempt in their philosophizing to synthesize modern Western philosophical understandings within the Mahāyāna theme of emptiness or "nothingness." [*See the biography of Nishida Kitarō.*]

These various developments in Buddhist thinking each attempted to bring the Buddha Dharma to speech and relate it to contemporary concerns and issues. Later Buddhists did not merely repeat Indian themes but evolved creative understandings of Buddhism for their times. Yet the basic themes remained as the parameters for Buddhist thinking

[*See also* Indian Philosophies; Nirvāṇa; Soul; *article*

on Buddhist Concepts; Buddhist Ethics; *and* Soteriology, *article on* Buddhist Soteriology. *For further discussion of the notion of "two truths" in Buddhist thought, see* Language, *article on* Buddhist Views of Language, *and* Buddhist Literature, *article on* Exegesis and Hermeneutics.]

BIBLIOGRAPHY

The best single source for works by both Eastern and Western scholars on the basic philosophic themes of Indian Buddhism is Nakamura Hajime's *Indian Buddhism: A Survey with Bibliographical Notes* (Hirakata, 1980). On pre-Mahāyāna Buddhism the standard study is Étienne Lamotte's *Histoire du bouddhisme indien: Des origines à l'ère Śaka* (Louvain, 1976). The entire history of Indian Buddhism is covered in A. K. Warder's *Indian Buddhism* (Delhi, 1970). More popular in style is the often reprinted *The History of Buddhist Thought* (1933; 2d ed., New York, 1951) by Edward J. Thomas and *Buddhism: Its Essence and Development* (1951; reprint, New York, 1959) by Edward Conze, although this last work reflects the strong preference of its author for the Prajñāpāramitā negation of all philosophic theory.

Walpola Rahula's *What the Buddha Taught* (1959; 2d ed., Bedford, 1967) is a concise and clear statement of the early teaching. For a scholarly Abhidharma translation, see Louis de La Vallée Poussin's six-volume translation, *L'Abhidharmakośa de Vasubandhu* (1923–1931; reprint, Brussels, 1971). Herbert V. Guenther's *Philosophy and Psychology in the Abhidharma* (Lucknow, 1957) is a readable and informative introduction to Abhidharma. Kimura Taiken's, *Abhidatsumaron no kenkyū* (Tokyo, 1937) is a pioneering study on the developmental stages of Abhidharma thinking.

An excellent study of Mādhyamika thought is Frederick J. Streng's *Emptiness: A Study in Religious Meaning* (New York, 1967), which examines the meaning of Nāgārjuna's use of the theme of emptiness. Richard H. Robinson's *Early Mādhyamika in India and China* (Delhi, 1976) focuses attention upon the transmission of Mādhyamika in China. Mervyn Sprung's *Lucid Exposition of the Middle Way* (Boulder, 1979) not only presents an exceptionally good translation of the main sections from Candrakīrti's *Prasannapadā*, but also offers a particularly insightful introduction to Mādhyamika thinking. Nagao Gadjin's *Chūkan tetsugaku no komponteki tachiba* (Tokyo, 1976; English translation in preparation), is a classic work on the philosophical issues in both Mādhyamika and Yogācāra and has served as the source for much of the above treatment of these schools.

The most comprehensive work on the Tathāgatagarbha tradition is Takasaki Jikidō's *Nyoraizō shisō no keisei* (Tokyo, 1974), which traces the development of Tathāgatagarbha thought from its beginning in the *Tathāgatagarbha Sūtra* to the *Ratnagotravibhāga Śāstra*. David Seyfort Ruegg's *La théorie de Tathāgatagarbha et du Gotra* (Paris, 1969) examines the same tradition as it moves from the *Ratnagotravibhāga Śāstra* to later Tibetan texts. Also to be noted is *The Lion's Roar of Queen Śrīmālā*, translated by Alex Wayman and Hideko Wayman (New York, 1974), which presents a clear introductory essay on Tathāgatagarbha and a translation of the above scripture.

There are no comprehensive studies on Yogācāra in any Western language, although Japanese scholars have long studied this foundational school of Mahāyāna. Of particular note is Nagao Gadjin's *Chūkan to yuishiki* (Tokyo, 1978). However, translations and studies of particular texts have been made by Louis de La Vallée Poussin, *Vijñaptimātratāsiddhi: La Siddhi de Hiuan-tsang* (Paris, 1928–1929); Étienne Lamotte, *Saṃdhinirmocana Sūtra: L'explication des mystères* (Louvain, 1935); John P. Keenan, *The Scripture on Explicating Underlying Meaning* (Tokyo, 1986); Étienne Lamotte, *La somme du Grand Véhicule d'Asaṅga (Mahāyānasaṃgraha)* (1938–1939; Louvain, 1973); John P. Keenan, *The Interpretation of the Buddha Land* (Tokyo, forthcoming); and Janice Dean Willis, *On Knowing Reality: The Tattvārtha Chapter of Asaṅga's Bodhisattvabhūmi* (New York, 1979), which also contains valuable notes and interpretations.

On Buddhist epistemology and logic Theodore Stcherbatsky's *Buddhist Logic* (1930–1932; reprint, New York, 1962), although now dated, is still the only comprehensive treatment. Hattori Masaaki's *Dignāga on Perception* (Cambridge, Mass., 1968) sets the standard for scholarship on these difficult issues. Also see Kajiyama Yūichi's "Later Madhyamikans," in *Mahāyāna Buddhist Meditation: Theory and Practice*, edited by Minoru Kiyota (Honolulu, 1978), for a treatment of later controversies on the need for images in understanding.

On the overall Chinese domestication of Indian Buddhist thought, Erik Zürcher's *The Buddhist Conquest of China* (1959; reprint, Leiden, 1972) remains a classic study of the early period up until 400 CE. There are many excellent studies of the individual schools, but to date no satisfactory doctrinal history of Chinese Buddhism has appeared. For Japanese Buddhism, the two-volume *Foundations of Japanese Buddhism* (Los Angeles and Tokyo, 1974–1976) by Daigan and Alicia Matsunaga is the standard resource. Tibetan Buddhism is discussed in Giuseppe Tucci's *The Religions of Tibet*, translated by Geoffrey Samuel (Berkeley, 1980).

On the Kyoto School, the works of Nishida Kitarō still available in English are *Art and Morality*, translated by David A. Dilworth and Valdo H. Viglielmo (Honolulu, 1973), and *Fundamental Problems of Philosophy: The World of Action and the Dialectical World*, translated by David A. Dilworth (Tokyo, 1970). See also Nishitani Keiji's *Religion and Nothingness*, translated by Jan van Bragt (Berkeley, 1982); Takeuchi Yoshinori's *The Heart of Buddhism* (New York, 1983); Hans Waldenfels' *Absolute Nothingness: Foundations for a Buddhist-Christian Dialogue*, translated by James W. Heisig (New York, 1980); *The Buddha Eye*, edited by Frederick Franck (New York, 1982); and Tanabe Hajime's *Philosophy as Metanoetics* (Berkeley, 1986).

TAKEUCHI YOSHINORI and JOHN P. KEENAN

BUDDHIST RELIGIOUS YEAR. The Buddhist religious year celebrates seminal events in the life of the founder and the early religious community and sanctifies the annual changes of the seasons and the cyclical passage of time in which the life of the community is embedded. Particular cultural traditions adjust and amplify both dimensions of the Buddhist calendar according to their own histories and circumstances.

Each Buddhist culture developed its own religious calendar punctuated by particular ceremonies, rituals, and festivals. Chinese Buddhists, for example, celebrated the life of the Buddha and various *bodhisattvas*, the death anniversaries of certain figures in Chinese Buddhist history, various celestial beings *(t'ien-kung)*, the emperor's birthday, and such seasonal events as the celebration of the new year and the end of summer. In Tibet, the religious year included not only celebrations for the Buddha and major religious figures such as Padmasambhava, but also monthly commemorations of a wide variety of deities and saints and the celebration of the new year. Within any given cultural tradition the specifically Buddhist events of the year—the life of the Buddha, the observance of the rains retreat *(vassa)*, and so forth—are likely to be articulated with the agricultural cycle. Thus, in much of Southeast Asia, Buddha's Day occurs at the onset of the monsoon rains in May; the *kaṭhina* ceremonies, in which gifts are presented to the monks, comes at the end of *vassa*, the end of the planting season; and the merit-making ceremony in honor of the Buddha's appearance as Prince Vessantara comes in February–March, after the rice harvest. In short, the Buddhist religious year is closely integrated with the cycle of rice cultivation and its accompanying economic activities.

For the purposes of this article we shall not divide the Buddhist religious year chronologically, in part because of the variance among Buddhist calendars from culture to culture. Rather, we shall first examine the major observances of the Buddhist year as defined by the events in the life of the Buddha and the founding of his religion *(sāsana)*, and then seasonal celebrations, in particular, the New Year. Although these two dimensions of the Buddhist religious year are separable for analytical purposes, within the lives of Chinese, Tibetan, Japanese, Thai, Sri Lankan and Burmese Buddhists the distinction is, at best, moot. From the perspective of the individual, furthermore, the religious year is also marked by life-transition ceremonies of an annual (e.g., birth and death anniversaries) or occasional nature, for instance, house consecrations. In traditional Buddhist societies, then, the religion essentially sanctified and made meaningful all aspects of life, whether cosmic, communal, or individual.

In short, the experience of the tradition calibrates the religious year, its founding, the major events within its early history, its most significant turning points. The major annual observances of the Buddhist year include, but are not limited to, the life of the Buddha, the proclamation of the Buddha's teaching, or *dharma*, the founding of the monastic order, the beginning and end of the monsoon rains retreat *(vassa)*, founder's celebrations, and saint's anniversaries. Observances celebrated more frequently, monthly or bimonthly, weekly or daily, include sabbath ceremonies, the fortnightly monastic confessional, or Prātimokṣa, and daily monastic rituals.

Celebrating the Buddha. Buddhist doctrine traditionally divides the Buddha's life into eight or twelve acts, many of which are commemorated in various ways in particular Buddhist cultures. These acts include the Buddha's birth, enlightenment, first discourse, entry into *nirvāṇa*, descent from Trāyastriṃśa Heaven, where he had instructed his mother in the Abhidharma, the simultaneous appearance of the 1,250 *arhat*s at Veḷuvana monastery in Rājagṛha, and the miracle of Śrāvastī, where the Buddha miraculously multiplied himself into an infinite number of flaming manifestations, thereby vanquishing the heretics who had challenged him to a magical competition.

Buddha's Day. Buddha's Day, or Visākhā Pūjā in the Theravāda tradition, is considered by many to be the most holy day in the Buddhist year, as it commemorates the birth, Enlightenment, and death (i.e., *parinirvāṇa*) of the Buddha, believed by Theravāda Buddhists to have occurred miraculously on the same day of the week. In Theravāda countries this celebration, known as Vesak in Sri Lanka, occurs on the full-moon day of Visākha (Skt., Vaiśākha; April–May). Vesak celebrations in Southeast Asia focus on the monastery. Devotees observe the precepts and listen to sermons on the life of the Buddha. In Thailand, the traditional Vesak sermon, the *pathama-sambodhi*, continues throughout the entire night. It begins with the wedding of Suddhodana and Mahāmāyā, the Buddha's parents, and concludes with the distribution of the Buddha's relics and an accounting of the reasons for the decline of Buddhism in India. The text is a composite of scripture and popular commentary in which the Buddha is depicted as a teacher and miracle worker. In addition to attendance at monastery services, other common Vesak practices include watering Bodhi trees within monastery compounds, circumambulation of the *cetiya* reliquary at night with incense and candles, acts of social service such as feeding the poor and treating the sick in hospitals, pilgrimage to sacred sites, and the bathing of Buddha images.

The celebration of Buddha's Day is both ancient and widespread. The seminal events of the Buddha's career coalesced into Vesak by the Theravādins are acknowledged independently in other Buddhist cultures. In Tibet, for example, the traditional religious year included celebration of the Buddha's conception or incarnation on the fifteenth day of the first lunar month, the attainment of Buddhahood on the eighth day of the fourth month, the Buddha's death, or *parinirvāṇa*, on the fifteenth day of the fourth month, and the Buddha's birth on the fourth day of the sixth month of the Tibetan year. The first of these events, the Buddha's incarnation, occupied a preeminent place in the Tibetan religious year, in part because of its assimilation into the New Year carnival. It was a day when special respects were paid to the Dalai Lāma, and the Buddha's mother, Mahādevī, was solicited for special boons. In China, Korea, and Japan, the Buddha's birthday has been marked, in particular, by a procession of Buddha images and the bathing of these images. These traditions associated with Buddha's Day or Buddha's Birthday appear to be of early origin.

The Mahāvaṃsa mentions a procession of Buddha images during the reign of Duṭṭhagāmaṇī (Sinhala, Duṭugämunu; r. 101–77 BCE), for which the prototype may well have been a ceremony described in Aśoka's Fourth Rock Edict. Fa-hsien observed a similar procession in India during his visit in the fifth century of the common era. The tradition of bathing Buddha images appears to be symbolized by the *Lalitavistara* episode of the two *nāga* serpents, Nanda and Upananda, bathing the *bodhisattva* after his birth, an episode depicted at such far-flung sites as Tun-huang and Borobudur. The *Mahāsattva Sūtra* describes a similar event where the Buddha is bathed by Indra and the four *deva* kings. It designates the eighth day of the fourth lunar month as the time when all devotees should wash his images in respect of the Buddha's power to grant boons.

Buddha's Day ceremonies and festivities embody both normative and popular dimensions of the Buddhist tradition, as do other celebrations marking the Buddhist religious year. Although relatively free of non-Buddhist elements, the focus on the Buddha image—whether through consecration, procession, or lustration—has primarily a mythic and/or magical significance. The Buddha is honored as a being greater than any other deity, and as a granter of boons. On the popular level, this aspect of Buddha's Day has assumed a greater importance than remembrance of the Buddha as the Enlightened One and great teacher.

The commemoration of Buddha relics. According to the *Mahāparinibbāna Sutta*, after the Buddha's death his relics were divided among the eight *cakkavatti* (Skt., *cakravartin*) rulers of India, who enshrined them in *cetiya* (Skt., *caitya*, reliquary mounds) at eight locations throughout India. While the obvious symbolic nature of this story belies its historicity, by the Mauryan period in India (fourth to second century BCE) *caitya* the likes of Sāñcī and Bhārhut had become important centers of pilgrimage and popular piety. The early association of Buddha relics with kingship in India points to a pattern perpetuated throughout much of Buddhist Asia: the enshrinement of a major Buddha relic as a monarch's attempt to legitimate his rule through the appropriation of the *buddhasāsana* (the Buddhist religion), and, even more importantly, to base his realm around a center of magical, sacred power. Buddhist chronicles often make no clear distinction between the sacred boundary of a Buddhist sanctuary housing a major Buddhist relic and jurisdictional limits of towns or larger political units. Both temple and kingdom, in one sense, derive their identity from the Buddha relic. Consequently, ceremonies commemorating the enshrinement of a Buddha relic are often major annual celebrations honoring the person of the Buddha that empower both the religion and the state. An outstanding example of such an annual celebration is found in Sri Lanka. [*See also* Kingship, *article on* Kingship in Southeast Asia, *and* Stupa Worship.]

In Sri Lanka, the most elaborate national festival celebrates the arrival of the eyetooth relic of the Buddha, which is enshrined as the palladium of the kingdom in the Daladā Māligāwa (Temple of the Tooth) in Kandy. The *Dhātuvaṃsa* (Chronicle of the Tooth Relic) states that the relic was brought to Sri Lanka from Kaliṅga in India during the reign of King Kitsirimeghavaṇṇa (352–377). The king enshrined the relic in the capital, Anurādhapura, ordered that a grand festival celebrate its arrival, and dedicated the whole of Sri Lanka to it. Fa-hsien, who visited Sri Lanka in the ninth century, gives us a record of the annual festival celebrating the tooth relic, reputed to have been brought to Sri Lanka only ten days after the Buddha's *parinirvāṇa*. He reports that the procession of the relic around the precincts of the capital occurred in the middle of the third lunar month. The procession he witnessed passed between five hundred people costumed to represent the five hundred lives *(jātaka)* of the *bodhisattva* according to the Theravāda tradition. The *Daladāsirita* (History of the Tooth Relic), written in the fourteenth century, describes in great detail the annual circumambulation of the tooth relic around the capital. The procession was marked by the sprinkling of holy water throughout the city sanctified by the chanting of the *paritta*. Today, the festival takes place during the month of Āsāḷha (Skt., Āṣādha; the lunar month of July–August) in the town of Kandy. The festival, which has taken on a carnival atmosphere, goes on for eleven nights, culminating in the twelfth day with a water cutting ceremony.

Similar festivals occurred in East Asia, as well. During the T'ang dynasty (618–907) the festival that attracted the largest crowds in the capital, Ch'ang-an, centered around Buddha relics. During the second or third lunar month, tooth relics from four temples and a finger-bone relic from the Fa-men Ssu were put on display for a week. The Fa-men Ssu relic was, on occasion, put on public view inside the royal palace. A ninth-century memorial by Han Yü claimed that the display of the relic produced such a frenzy on the part of the viewers that they burned their heads, roasted their fingers, and threw away their clothes and money. Such annual festivals honoring Buddha relics calibrate the religious year not so much in terms of the life of the Buddha but in terms of the magical power of his bodily presence, a presence fraught with political as well as religious significance.

Honoring the Buddha's Dharma. The Buddha's teaching, or more narrowly conceived, particular Buddhist texts, are often honored in annual ceremonies and ritual celebrations. In Tibet, the feast of the First Discourse was traditionally held on the fourth day of the sixth lunar month. In modern Thailand, the commemoration of the *Dhammacakkappavattana Sutta* occurs on the full moon of Āsāḷha, the eighth lunar month, at the beginning of the monsoon rains retreat *(vassa).* In addition to the first discourse, the tradition also celebrates the Buddha's preaching of the Abhidharma to his mother and the teaching of the Prātimokṣa, the core of the monastic discipline (Vinaya), which the tradition holds took place three months before the Buddha's *parinirvāṇa.* These celebrations may be assimilated into other parts of the Buddhist year, as, for example, in Tibet, where the Buddha's descent from Trāyastriṃśa Heaven marks the end of the monsoon rains retreat.

As an example of an annual popular ceremony celebrating a particular text we look to the preaching of the *Vessantara Jātaka* in the Theravāda countries of Southeast Asia. This ceremony is known in Thailand as Thet Mahāchāt. To be sure, the occasion focuses on the Buddha's perfection of the virtue of *dāna* (generosity) and on the efficacy of *puñña* (religious merit), but it also clearly demonstrates the power of the *dharma* as a text, not only as a teaching or narrative, but as something with special potency in both its written and oral form. Thus, as with the annual celebrations focusing on the Buddha, which remember not only the seminal events of his life but also the magical power of his physical presence, annual celebrations remembering the *dharma* refer not simply to the Buddha's teaching of Dharma, Abhidharma, and Vinaya but to the power of the text, especially as chanted.

In northeastern Thailand the preaching of the *Vessantara Jātaka,* which recounts a former life of the Buddha as Prince Vessantara, occurs in February–March after the rice harvest. While the ceremony includes various animistic and Brahmanic elements, the celebration focuses on the preaching of the thirteen chapters of the Thai version of the story. Monks famed for preaching particular chapters may be invited by sponsors whose donations to the *sangha* (Skt., *saṃgha;* the monastic order) are thought to be particularly meritorious. Prior to the recitation of the text the laity may enact the journey of Vessantara from the kingdom of Sivi and back again, having passed the tests to his generosity arranged by the god Indra. When the entire story is preached the ceremony, which begins in the morning, lasts well into the night.

In China, Korea, and Japan texts such as the *Saddharmapuṇḍarīka Sūtra* (Lotus Sutra) were the objects of major ceremonies. In Japan the *Ninnōkyō,* or *Sutra of the Benevolent Kings,* was from the seventh to the thirteenth century one of the most important scriptures in Japanese Buddhism. It became the object of a public cult *(ninnō-e),* and ceremonies celebrating it were frequent at the Japanese court in order to ensure the maintenance of the dynasty and the welfare of the state. In Tibet, the fifteenth day of the third lunar month commemorated the preaching of the *Kālacakra Tantra;* each monastery also annually celebrated the particular *tantra* to which its school ascribed special importance.

Thus, while the Buddhist year celebrated the Tripiṭaka in terms of three events in the Buddha's legendary life, other texts, which often dealt with such popular topics as the *bodhisattva,* miracles, and, more specifically, magical protection of the state, were often the occasion of annual ceremonies. In short, on the level at which the *dharma* enters into the popular perception of sacred time, it too, like the figure of the Buddha, takes on magical significance that protects the individual and guarantees social and political wellbeing.

Celebrating the Religion. The religious year not only celebrates the person and life of the Buddha and his teaching, but the founding of the Buddha's community or monastic order, the establishment of the Buddha's religion in various parts of Asia, the monastic year as focused on the period of the monsoon rains retreat, and particularly important religious figures such as holy founders and reformers of the tradition.

The founding of the Saṃgha. The founding of the *saṃgha* is tied to the miraculous event of the Buddha's appearance before the 1,250 *arhats* at Veḷuvana Mahāvihāra in Rājagṛha. All had received ordination from the Buddha with the words "Ehi bhikkhu" ("Come, O monk"); according to tradition, the Buddha used this occasion to hand down the Prātimokṣa to his assembled followers. In short, the unannounced, miraculously simultaneous gathering of over a thousand monks ordained by the Buddha himself became the occasion for establishing the rule of order for the Buddhist monastic life.

In Thailand this event in the religious year is celebrated on the full moon sabbath of the third lunar month (Māgha) and is known as Māgha Pūjā. The celebration follows a relatively simple pattern. At about dusk crowds of laity gather in temple compounds to circumambulate the temple *cetiya* before entering the preaching hall for an evening of chanting and a sermon. The traditional text used for the occasion is a *gāthā* on the Pratimokṣa composed in the early nineteenth century by King Rama IV when he was a monk. It encourages the *sangha* to be a field of merit through constant attention and heedfulness, a teaching similar to the Buddha's instructions to the monks at Veḷuvana to do no evil of any kind, be established in the good, and to maintain a clear mind.

Establishing the tradition. Various types of annual events celebrate the establishment of Buddhism in a particular location or cultural area. These events range from commemorations of the arrival of Buddhist missionaries to the founding of particular temples or monasteries, often with royal support, for instance, the Shōmusai festival of the Tōdaiji in Nara held in May in commemoration of the death of the Japanese emperor Shōmu (701–756) and his patronage of Buddhism.

Temple or pagoda festivals and holy days commemorating events in the life of the Buddha are the most often observed Buddhist ceremonies in Burma. Nearly every Burman will attend at least one pagoda festival annually. Unlike observances connected with the life of the Buddha, Burmese temple and pagoda anniversaries are much more in the nature of a country fair. At larger temples the event may last a week with a temporary bazaar featuring commercial goods for sale, games of chance, and of course, numerous makeshift restaurants. Evenings will be filled with various kinds of dramatic performances, including traditional plays and dances and the showing of films. Temple anniversary celebrations also provide an opportunity to solicit donations, often as part of merit-making ceremonies. As in the case of the annual festival at Wat Cedī Luang in Chiangmai, northern Thailand, ceremonies may also include significant non-Buddhist elements such as propitiation of the guardian spirits of the area or region. In the case of Wat Cedī Luang, the anniversary celebration in May includes propitiation of the foundation pillar of the city (identified with the Hindu god Indra) as well as offerings to the autochonous guardian spirits of Chiangmai, a ceremony performed somewhat surreptitiously outside of the city.

In Sri Lanka the establishment of Buddhism on the island is celebrated about a month after Vesak with the Poson festival. The major activities take place at Anurādhapura and Mahintale, where thousands of people come to honor Mahinda, the patron saint of Sri Lanka, who is reputed to have brought the *dharma* to the island at the request of his father, King Aśoka. Later, Mahinda's sister, Sanghamitta, came to the island to establish a Buddhist order of nuns. She brought a branch of the sacred Bodhi Tree with her, which was planted in the capital. Paying homage to the sacred Bodhi Tree is an important part of the festivities that take place.

The rains retreat. The earliest form of Buddhist monastic organization seems to have been mendicancy. In the *Mahāvagga* of the Vinaya Piṭaka monks are encouraged to adopt a peripatetic existence. During the monsoon rains, however, the Buddha's disciples gathered in more stable communities. Indeed, assuming that mendicancy characterized the earliest Buddhist monastic practice, cenobitism may well have grown out of the tradition of rains-retreat residence *(vassāvasa).*

Practical explanations for the origin of the observance of a rains retreat fail to take account of its more archaic, magical nature, which is associated with ascetic practice. Various aspects of early Buddhist monastic life and discipline can be interpreted as contrasting the sexual continence of the monk with its polar opposite, the feminine principle of life, gestation, and generation. This principle is embodied not only by women, whose contact with celibate monks is highly circumscribed, but by mother earth, who gives birth to life-sustaining crops. Monastic confinement during the monsoon rains-retreat period might be interpreted as protecting the life-generating power of the earth from the ascetic power of the monk and, correspondingly, defending the monk from the potencies of the earth during the most crucial gestation period of the cycle of plant life. Such an interpretation of the symbolic-magical significance of the origin of the rains-retreat period provides insight into one of the most important annual calendric rituals in Theravāda Buddhist countries, celebrations at the onset and, in particular, at the conclusion of the rains retreat, or Buddhist lenten period.

Both the beginning and end of the rains-retreat period are marked by auspicious rituals held on the full-moon sabbaths of July and October. The onset of *vassa* often witnesses many ordination ceremonies, for in Burma, Thailand, Cambodia, and Laos many young men observed the custom of accepting ordination for one lenten period only. On the July full-moon sabbath the laity will process to the monastery bearing gifts *(dāna)* for the monks. During the sabbath service monks and laity will be exhorted to observe an austere lent, thereby emphasizing the primary theme of the rains-retreat period. Especially for monks, the lenten period is a religiously observant time. More time is spent inside the monastery in study, meditation, and monastic devotions. In short, *vassa* epitomizes the lifestyle of the monk as an ascetic, *nirvāṇa*-seeking follower of the Buddha. On a magical level, his more rigorous practice during this period charges the monk with power, to which the laity gain access through the rituals marking the end of the rains retreat.

In Theravāda countries the end of the Buddhist lenten period provides the occasion for the most significant merit-making ceremonies. In Burma, the full-moon day of October marks the reemergence of the Buddha himself from Trāyastriṃśa Heaven. Oil lamps ringing monastery pagodas represent the mythic heavenly torches that lit his descent to earth. During the ceremonies that take place over the month following the October full-moon sabbath the laity give generously to the *sangha*, especially gifts of new robes *(kaṭhina)*. In Burma, Thailand, Laos, and Cambodia *kaṭhina* ceremonies were and are often marked by processions to the monastery compound highlighted by the gift of a "wishing tree" *(padesa)* reminiscent of the trees in the Southern Island of the Buddhist cosmology that supplied the populace with all their needs simply for the asking. Symbolically, this annual celebration provides a ritual mechanism whereby the laity can gain access to the magical-spiritual power of the monks generated during the rains retreat. Thus, even this most exemplary period of the monastic life has a parochialized, magical significance that serves the immediate needs of the laity.

Celebrating the saints. The Buddhist year not only commemorates the Buddha and his teaching, the monastic order and its institutionalization at various times and in various places, but also the lives of saints. In Mahāyāna and Tantrayāna cultures *bodhisattva* days honor popular mythic savior figures, for instance, Kuan-yin (Avalokiteśvara), as well as legendary patriarchs (e.g., Bodhidharma) and historic reformers such as Hakuin. Some Buddhist figures are celebrated at the national level (e.g., Padmasambhava in Tibet) while others are of regional or more local significance.

Traditionally, the Chinese celebrated Kuan-yin's birthday on the nineteenth day of the second lunar month. In addition, her enlightenment and entry into *nirvāṇa* were also celebrated on the nineteenth day of the sixth month, and nineteenth day of the ninth month, respectively. Kuan-yin is celebrated as a merciful savior, the granter of intelligent sons and virtuous daughters, and the dispeller of natural catastrophies. In popular Chinese accounts of Kuan-yin's origins she is depicted as having been a royal princess from Szechwan Province by the name of Miao-shan who, as a consequence of her ascetic piety, was reborn as a *bodhisattva* destined to return to the human realm as the merciful Kuan-yin. [*See also* Avalokiteśvara.]

Bodhidharma is looked upon as the founder of the Ch'an (Jpn., Zen) school of Buddhism in China and the first of six traditional Ch'an patriarchs. His death anniversary is celebrated on the fifth day of the tenth lunar month. Other annual celebrations commemorating founders of Buddhist schools honor, among others, Pai-chang, a noted Ch'an master of the T'ang dynasty (nineteenth day of the first month) and Chih-i, founder of the T'ien-t'ai school (the twenty-fourth day of the eleventh lunar month).

In Tibet saint-founders were the object of annual celebrations. The Rñiṅ-ma-pa school, for instance, established a sequence of monthly ceremonies commemorating various aspects of Padmasambhava's life; the tenth day of the first month celebrates his flight from the world; the tenth day of the second month, his taking religious vows; the tenth day of the third month, his changing fire into water having been consigned to the flames by the king of Zahor, taking the name Padmasambhava, and so on.

In short, the lives of saints, founders, patriarchs, and reformers, whether deified in myth or valorized in legend, provide a special definition to the year in various Buddhist cultures. In the case of Padmasambhava episodes from the guru's biography provide a narrative structure of sacred time to the religious year. In other Buddhist traditions, death anniversaries commemorating key figures in patriarchial lineages integrate the year into a sacral continuum that includes the Buddha, the originator of the sect or school, the father of the subtradition, and so on down to the founder of the local monastery.

Seasonal Celebrations. The Buddhist religious year celebrates the seasonal changes, the agricultural calendar, and the seasons of human life and death. In Japan, for example, seasonal celebrations include New Year's Eve Day (Joya-e) and New Year's Day (Oshōgatsu), 31 December and 1 January; the heralding of spring (Setsubun-e), 3 February; spring and fall equinox (Higan-e), 21 March and 21 September; Festival of the Dead (Obon), 15 July; and Buddhist Thanksgiving Day (Segaki-e), sometime in the summer. Seasonal celebrations tend to be highly syncretic, with the Buddhist dimension competing with various non-Buddhist elements.

In Tibet, the New Year festival (Lo-gsar) incorporated a Buddhist element, the great miracle of Śrāvastī, but its fundamental meaning is the exorcism of evil influences from the old year and the calling up of good fortune for the year to come. The elaborate ritual performances held during the New Year festival aimed not only at the welfare of the individual, but, even more so, at the good of the community. In Japan, New Year may be celebrated by visiting well-known Buddhist temples and shrines, but the traditional custom of eating pounded rice cakes *(mochi)* and drinking sweetened wine *(toso)* symbolized the hope for good health and longevity.

In Thailand, the New Year celebration (Songkrān) falls in the middle of April at the end of the dry season just prior to the coming of the monsoon rains. Although Buddhist temples and monasteries are the site of many New Year ceremonies, the New Year festival, as in Tibet and Japan, seems to have more to do with good luck and a healthy life in the year to come than with specifically Buddhist concerns. In the Thai case, elements of the New Year celebration are obviously intended as acts of sympathetic magic to abet the onset of the monsoon rains, necessary for the planting of the rice crop.

Seasons in the agricultural year are demarcated in various ways in the Buddhist religious calendar. In some cases, agricultural transition may be subsumed into specifically Buddhist events, such as the close relationship between Buddha's Day in monsoon, Theravāda countries, and the planting of rice. In other instances, however, these transitions may simply be made more meaningful by the Buddhist dimension of the culture in which they are embedded. For example, in Sri Lanka the seed-sowing festival (Vap Magula) traditionally held for the prosperity of the nation, is given Buddhist legitimation through the legend of Siddhārtha's presence at the plowing ceremony held by the future Buddha's father, King Suddhodana. In the modern period, all-night *pirit* (Pali, *paritta*) ceremonies will be held before the festival, attended by ministers of state who play the role of traditional Buddhist kings. The harvest festival in Sri Lanka (Aluth Sahal Maṅgalya) and Theravāda Southeast Asia focuses on the offering of first fruits in gratitude to the Buddha and the gods. In Sri Lanka, the contemporary harvest ceremony is held in Anurādhapura under the leadership of the minister of agriculture and development. Both the seed festival and the harvest festival undoubtedly represent Buddhist transformations of Brahmanic ceremonies.

Although individual life-transitions ordinarily do not define a community's religious year unless the person occupies a position of signal importance in China, Korea, and Japan, annual festivals for the deceased achieved national significance. While the festival represents the pervasive significance of the propitiation of ancestral spirits in these cultures, the Buddhist tradition provided its own distinctive validation. According to legend, the Buddha's disciple Maudgalyāyana descended to the deepest hell to rescue his mother from its torments. The Buddha advised Maudgalyāyana that by making offerings of food, clothing, and other necessities to the monks on behalf of the denizens of hell they would be relieved of their suffering. In China it became the custom that offerings made at the Ullambana All Soul's Feast held during the seventh lunar month were believed to rescue ancestors for seven preceding generations. In Japan the Obon festival takes place over three days, 13–15 July. Activities will include special services at the home altar, visits to temple graveyards in order to welcome the ancestral spirits back to their home, and special vegetarian feasts. On the last day of the celebration the spirits will be sent off in miniature boats *(shōryōbune)* filled with food and lighted lanterns.

Concluding Remark. The Buddhist religious year sanctifies the life of the individual and the community in all of its aspects. Through annual ritual ceremonials and festivals mundane life is transfigured and the seemingly chaotic nature of existence finds meaning in an ordered sequence of paradigmatic events. While the life of the founder and the events of the early Buddhist community provide the central focus of the Buddhist religious year, its comprehensive scope incorporates all aspects of life from the beginning (the New Year festival) to the end (the All Soul's Feast).

[*See also* Worship and Cultic Life, *articles on* Buddhist Cultic Life in Southeast Asia; Buddhist Cultic Life in Tibet; *and* Buddhist Cultic Life in East Asia.]

BIBLIOGRAPHY

Information on the Buddhist religious year or on Buddhist calendric rituals and festivals can be found in numerous books treating Buddhism in particular cultural contexts. Material on this subject in Theravāda Buddhist cultures is somewhat more recent than that for Central and East Asia. For Sri Lanka, Lynn de Silva's *Buddhism, Beliefs and Practices in Sri Lanka*, 2d rev. ed. (Colombo, 1980), provides an extensive, concise description of major calendric festivals. H. L. Seneviratne's "The Äsala Perahära in Kandy," *Ceylon Journal of Historical and Social Studies* 6 (1963): 169–180, is a detailed treatment of the major annual Buddhist festival in Sri Lanka. James G. Scott (Shway Yoe) discusses various calendric festivals (e.g., pagoda, harvest, and end of the rains retreat) in *The Burman, His Life and Notions*, 3d ed. (London, 1910). Melford E. Spiro has a brief section on annual ceremonies in *Buddhism and Society: A Great Tradition and Its Burmese Vicissitudes*, 2d ed. (Berkeley, 1982). Many studies of Thai Buddhism touch on the ceremonies of the Buddhist religious year. Stanley J. Tambiah's *Buddhism and the Spirit Cults in North-East Thailand* (Cambridge, 1970) is a gold mine of information, as is Kenneth E. Wells's earlier study, *Thai Buddhism: Its Rites and Activities* (Bangkok, 1939).

More specialized contributions include my *Wat Haripuñjaya: A Study of the Royal Temple of the Buddha's Relic, Lamphun, Thailand* (Missoula, Mont., 1976), which has a chapter on calendric ceremonies, and Charles F. Keyes's "Buddhist Pilgrimage Centers and the Twelve Year Cycle: Northern Thai Moral Orders in Space and Time," *History of Religions* 15 (1975): 71–89. For Laos, Henri Deydier's *Introduction à la connaissance du Laos* (Saigon, 1952) provides a concise introductory survey to the Laotian calendar and religious festivals. A more focused and interpretative work is Frank E. Reynolds's "Ritual and Social Hierarchy: An Aspect of Traditional Religion in Buddhist Laos," *History of Religions* 9 (August 1969): 78–89. For Cambodia, Adhémard Leclère's *Le bouddhisme au Cambodge* (Paris, 1899) contains a section that concisely surveys the annual festivals in Cambodia.

For China, Joseph Edkins's *Chinese Buddhism,* 2d rev. ed. (London, 1893), provides a brief sketch of the Buddhist calendar. Kenneth Ch'en's *Buddhism in China: A Historical Survey* (Princeton, 1964) is also a useful introduction to annual festivals. Wolfram Eberhard's *Chinese Festivals* (New York, 1952) does little more than list the festivals of the Buddhist calendar. Other important studies include C. K. Yang's *Religion in Chinese Society* (Berkeley, 1961) and Emily Ahern's *The Cult of the Dead in a Chinese Village* (Stanford, Calif., 1973). All Souls' festivals are treated in J. J. L. Duyvendak's "The Buddhistic Festival of All-Souls in China and Japan," *Acta Orientalia* 5 (1926): 39–48; J. J. M. de Groot's "Buddhist Masses for the Dead in Amoy," in *Actes du Sixième Congrès International des Orientalistes* (Leiden, 1885), sec. 4, pp. 1–120; and Karl Ludvig Reichelt's *Truth and Tradition in Chinese Buddhism,* 4th ed. (Shanghai, 1934), pp. 77–126. See also Marinus Willem de Visser's *Ancient Buddhism in Japan,* 2 vols. (Leiden, 1928–1935), which treats a variety of Japanese Buddhist festivals, including Obon. For Korea, see Roger L. Janelli and Dawnhee Yim Janelli's *Ancestor Worship and Korean Society* (Stanford, Calif., 1982).

For Central Asia, three classic studies on Tibet provide brief descriptions of the religious calendar and annual festivals: L. Austine Waddell's *The Buddhism of Tibet,* 2d ed. (Cambridge, 1934); Giuseppe Tucci's *The Religions of Tibet,* translated by Geoffrey Samuel (Berkeley, 1980); and Rolf A. Stein's *Tibetan Civilization,* translated by J. E. Stapleton Driver (Stanford, Calif., 1972). Mary M. Anderson's *The Festivals of Nepal* (London, 1971) treats thirty-six annual festivals. For Mongolia, see Walther Heissig's *The Religions of Mongolia,* translated by Geoffrey Samuel (Berkeley, 1970).

DONALD K. SWEARER

BUDDHIST STUDIES. The first group to engage in Buddhist studies was the community of monastic dwellers who followed the practices and teachings attributed to the Buddha. Beginning in perhaps the second century BCE, these religious scholastics dedicated themselves to the study, analysis, and systematization of the doctrines preserved in the Sūtras, and their work was considered of such importance that it became a part of the canon under the name Abhidharma Piṭaka. Throughout history Buddhists have maintained this tradition of study, and it continued when the religion expanded outside of India. For example, in China, scholars not only translated the Indian texts, they also honored the treatises written by their own masters by including these works in the canon. The result of these centuries of scholarly endeavors has been the creation of a large corpus of documents that allow scholars to study intellectual developments within Buddhism. Little, however, was recorded about the history of the movement as a social institution, and the only documents we possess that describe the activities of believers in specific locations are the few accounts left by Chinese and Korean pilgrims who made the difficult journey from East Asia to India.

An entirely new approach to the study of Buddhism emerged when Europeans started to collect, translate, and interpret the texts still extant in the nineteenth and twentieth centuries. It is this study of Buddhism, developed outside of the monastic centers in Asia, which is to be considered here.

Early Accounts. Reports of Buddhism appear in European texts as early as the *Stromateis* of Clement of Alexandria (200 CE), in which the Buddha is mentioned as one of the deities of India. Some two centuries later, Hieronymus (fourth–fifth century) stated that the Buddha was born from the side of a virgin. Nothing indicates the Europeans' lack of information more than the fact that the story of the life of Śākyamuni found its way into Europe and West Asia and became the basis for the biographies of two Christian saints, Barlaam and Josaphat, with no one challenging the identifications. These popular medieval saints were not seen in their true light—as thinly disguised Buddhist figures—until the work of Édouard Laboulaye (1859).

Contact between Asia and Europe increased during the time of the Mongols, when small groups of travelers began to visit the eastern regions of Asia for trade and Christian missionary activity. Following his trip to Asia (1275–1291), Marco Polo commented on the practice of Buddhism among the Tibetans and the Sinhalese. Prior to Polo's visit, the pope had sent envoys to the Mongol court (1245), and they sometimes included a few sentences about Buddhism, primarily the Tibetan form favored by the ruling khans, in their letters home. In the seventeenth century Tibet once again came to the attention of the Vatican when it was visited by priests who hoped to prove the rumor that Christians were living there. Little came of these missions, but in the following century Francesco Orazio della Penna (1680–1745), a Capuchin missionary, began to study Tibet's language and culture in earnest. He was followed by a Jesuit, Ippolito Desideri (1684–1733), who learned to read and speak Tibetan and prepared a manuscript that describes, in surprising detail and accuracy, the nature of Mahāyāna and its interpretation by Tibetan masters. Although his document can be called the first true study of Buddhist thought by a European, it received little attention and was not published until 1904.

Nineteenth-Century Canonical Studies. The nineteenth century marks the beginning of the era of Buddhist academic study. It was then that a small group of scholars in European universities became involved in research on the materials brought back from Asia by missionaries, diplomats, and merchants. The most important of these early pioneers in Asian studies are Eugène Burnouf (1801–1852) and his collaborator Charles Lassen (1800–1876). These two produced a systematic study of Pali (1826), which they understood to be the sacred language of the Buddhists. They were not aware that Benjamin Clough had completed a similar study in 1824 because no copies of his work were available in Europe until 1836. At about this time, other scholars interested in language research began to collect and work on manuscripts, mainly Buddhist in nature, found in Ceylon (present-day Sri Lanka). In the decades following Burnouf's initial efforts, new discoveries about Buddhism began to appear in print. In part, the interest in Asia and its religions was fueled by the growing economic and political involvement of European nations in the East. Some of the officials sent out from Europe made contributions to scholarly study. For example, Brian Hodgson (1800–1894), the British consul in Katmandu, found that Sanskrit Buddhist texts were still preserved in the temples and libraries of the city and hired scribes to copy these documents, which had in many cases been long lost in India. When Burnouf read some of these Sanskrit texts, he saw the necessity of working with both Pali and Sanskrit materials to understand how Buddhism had developed. At the same time, he became aware of the Tibetan translations of the Buddhist canon and recognized that they were equally important in the study of doctrinal history. Thus, it was in the middle of the nineteenth century that the full significance of the task of the Buddhist researcher became known. Within a few decades the discovery of Buddhist canons in Sanskrit, Pali, Tibetan, Mongolian, and Chinese established that Buddhism was unique among religions in that it possessed a variety of canons in different regions. Thus, the study of tradition was not possible without doing a comparative review of these multiple scriptures.

For a time in the first half of the nineteenth century, the Tibetan canon received more attention than other aspects of Buddhism. Russian scholars, for example, were studying the languages and customs of the peoples living in the eastern part of their empire. An important figure in this growing field was Isaak Jakob Schmidt (1799–1847), who published translations of Buddhist texts from the Tibetan sources. The most colorful figure, however, and in many ways the founder of Tibetan studies, was the Hungarian Alexander Csoma de Kőrös (1784–1842), who in 1819 set out on foot in search of his ancestral roots in Central Asia. He managed to walk from Hungary as far as India. In Ladakh he studied Tibetan and later produced a Tibetan grammar and dictionary (1834), as well as an analysis of the Bka'-'gyur (Kanjur, or "*sūtra* translation") section of the Buddhist canon.

During the last half of the nineteenth century Buddhist studies continued at an increased rate. British and German scholars turned their attention to the Pali literature, and they made many contributions that still form the basis for the scholarly study of this material. T. W. Rhys Davids (1843–1922) founded the Pali Text Society in 1831, and almost all Pali editions since then have appeared under the imprint of the society.

As more of the Buddhist canons became available for study, the content of these texts came under closer scrutiny. One of the first debates about textual content concerned the nature of the Buddha and the problem of his historicity. Current trends of scholarship in Europe influenced the debate. Émile Senart's essays on the legend of the Buddha (1873–1875)—in which he pointed out that the story of the Buddha contained many legendary elements, in particular the depiction of the Buddha as a solar mythic figure—set the tone. Hendrik Kern (1833–1904) took Senart's solar concept even further, leaving little room for any historical basis for the life of the Buddha. Since these two leading scholars explained the legend of the Buddha so plausibly, and since India itself had preserved no records that could be used to prove the existence of Śākyamuni, little attention was paid to the historical figure of the Buddha. It was not until archaeologists began to discover inscriptions and commemorative pillars (1895–1896, 1911) at the sites of the major events of Śākyamuni's life that more credence was given to the concept of a historical figure and that Kern and Senart's ideas were put aside.

European Expeditions. At the end of the nineteenth century and the beginning of the twentieth, a new element was added to the Buddhist scholarly enterprise. At this time European nations began to organize expeditions to Central Asia. Russian representatives in the area of Khotan and Kuchā sent home fragments of ancient manuscripts, some recognized as the oldest extant copies of Buddhist texts. These finds led to a number of other expeditions into the area, led by distinguished scholars of the time: from England, Aurel Stein (1862–

1943); from Germany, Albert Grunwedel (1856–1935) and Von le Coq (1860–1930); from France, Paul Pelliot (1878–1945); and from Russia, Serge Oldenburg. Chief among their finds was the cave at Tun-huang, which contained thousands of manuscripts covering a wide range of topics, both religious and secular, in a number of languages. The expeditions also cast new light on the spread of Buddhism and the route that it had followed from India to China.

Japanese Scholarship. The last part of the nineteenth century and the early decades of the twentieth brought about significant developments in Buddhist studies in Europe as well as in Asia. As European scholarship increased in scope and more volumes were published, these efforts attracted the attention of scholars in Buddhist areas, especially Japan. After the Meiji reformation, Japanese scholars and officials began to travel to Europe and students were encouraged to study abroad. Nanjō Bunyū, for example, went to Oxford University and studied with F. Max Müller. It was Nanjō who produced a catalog of the Chinese Buddhist canon that made reference to the Sanskrit and Tibetan counterparts. Once this research volume became available to Western scholars the importance of the Chinese version of the canon became apparent. Nanjō did not limit his contribution to his work for Europeans; he returned to Japan and founded the study of Sanskrit there. A whole group of young Japanese scholars followed Nanjō's example and sought more training in Western universities. Among these was Fujishima Ryōen, who studied with French scholars and wrote the first history of Japanese Buddhism to appear in European publications. The list of Japanese studying abroad during the last decade of the nineteenth century is nothing less than a roster of the names of those who created the environment in which Buddhist studies in Japan has thrived—Tokiwa Daijō, Takakusu Junjirō, Wogihara Unrai, Ui Hakuju, Yamaguchi Susumu, and Anesaki Masaharu.

Contemporary Buddhist studies could never be described adequately without looking at the developments in Japan. In contrast to other East Asian nations, Japan has maintained its Buddhist heritage, and its centers of higher education have included Buddhist studies *(bukkyōgaku)* as an integral part of their curriculum. Combining European techniques with more traditional scholasticism, Japanese scholars have produced works that are still unsurpassed in many areas of study. Philosophical and philological research have flourished in a number of universities, both public and private, under scholars such as Nagao Gadjin, Kajiyama Yūichi, Takasaki Jikidō, Hattori Masaaki, Kamata Shigeo, and many others. Of all the nations that can be called Buddhist, only Japan has produced a major academic approach to the study of the religious tradition, that of focusing carefully on one sect or school with little effort at comparative research. A number of the best Japanese scholars combine their academic life with a position as a priest of one of the Buddhist communities.

European Buddhist Studies. During the period when Japanese scholars first turned to the universities of Europe to pursue their training, some of the greatest European scholars of Buddhist studies were active in the field. Among these giants was Sylvain Lévi (1863–1935), who produced new editions, translations, and studies that helped shape the whole future of Buddhist studies. In his travels to Asia, Lévi found many texts of Mahāyāna in Nepal that had not been available in Europe. For example, he discovered and edited the *Viṃśatikā* and *Triṃśikā* of Vasubandhu (1922), two texts that form the basis of the Yogācāra school, and made a comparative study of the translations of the Tibetans and the Chinese. Lévi's work was carried on by his pupil Louis de La Vallée Poussin (1869–1938), who became the foremost scholar of his time in Buddhist philosophy. His work on the Abhidharma Piṭaka still stands as the outstanding achievement in his field during his era. Another of Lévi's pupils, Jean Przyluski (1885–1944), joined Marcelle Lalou (1890–1967) in founding the *Bibliographie bouddhique* (1930–1967), which provided an annotated reference to all important Buddhist studies published between 1928 and 1958. Étienne Lamotte (1903–1983), who studied under La Vallée Poussin, continued his teacher's great scholarly tradition and provided translations from the Chinese and other canons for works found within Mahāyāna. His copious, annotated five-volume translation of the *Ta chih-tu lun*, Kumārajīva's translation of a massive commentary on the *Prajñāpāramitā Sūtra* in twenty-five thousand *ślokas*, was published between 1944 and 1980 under the title *Le traité de la grande vertu de sagesse*; it constitutes a masterpiece of modern Buddhist scholarship. One more link on the chain has been added by Lamotte's pupils, especially Hubert Durt, who is director of the *Hōbōgirin* encyclopedia project of the École Française d'Extrême Orient, located in Kyoto.

Among the other great centers of Buddhist studies in Europe was Russia, where scholars such as J. Minaev, Fedor Shcherbatskii, Hermann Oldenberg, and Eugène Obermiller made major contributions to the understanding of the philosophical aspects of the religion. Oldenberg (1897) started the *Bibliotheca Buddhica* series, which published many volumes and translations of Buddhist texts and remains a major source for crucial texts in the study of Buddhist philosophy. Shcherbatskii (1866–1942), a pupil of Minaev's, began the study of logic and epistemology of Buddhism, and his pupil Eugène Obermiller (1901–1935) continued work on the Yogācāra school.

The study of Chinese Buddhism has differed somewhat from the study of Buddhism in South Asia or Tibet. Since work on Chinese culture and religions started during Mongol rule, the Tibetan form of the religion was first to receive attention, rather than the monastic and lay traditions of the Han Chinese believers. By the end of the nineteenth century, China was the object of intensive missionary activity from both Europe and North America, and much of the early information on the Han Buddhist community came from the observations of missionaries such as the Reverend Samuel Beal. Beal's work revealed to the scholarly world that many important Sanskrit and Tibetan Buddhist texts had one or more Chinese counterparts. At this time the Danish architect J. Prip-Møller, who was interested in the monastery buildings of China, produced work that went far beyond architectural drawings of the monastic layouts; he sought to understand the activities and teachings of those who used the buildings for ritual and meditation purposes.

The scholarly efforts of these pioneer investigators have become the basis for much of contemporary Buddhist studies. While new fields of endeavor have been undertaken by the growing group of researchers who come from a variety of disciplines, many of the problems and discoveries of the pioneers are still relevant.

Philosophical Studies after World War II. One area in which scholars have made great progress in the decades following World War II has been philosophical studies of Buddhist texts. The availability of printed editions and translations has made possible studies with a greater awareness of the scope of Buddhist thought. Because Buddhist scholars have been so prolific throughout the centuries, the work of understanding the complexities of their systems has required more than a century of effort, and many texts have not yet been touched. Among those who have focused on philosophical study are German and Austrian scholars, especially those who have made use of Central Asian fragments as well as the received texts within India and Tibet. Active in this field has been Heinrich Lüders, who edited many fragments from early expeditions into Central Asia; his student Ernest Waldschmidt has also worked on these ancient manuscripts. In Austria, Erich Frauwallner has made new discoveries about the nature of the Vinaya Piṭaka and the development of Buddhist philosophy, and Ernst Steinkellner has turned his attention to the epistemological texts and to some of the lesser figures in the later philosophical schools.

The philosophical study of Mahāyāna Buddhism has depended in no small way on the Tibetan materials, especially the noncanonic writings of some of the great systematizers of the Buddhist schools in that culture. David Seyfort Ruegg, whose monumental work on the Tathāgatagarbha tradition stands as a model of research for this type of study, has shown how important it is to combine the insights of the Tibetan tradition with the doctrinal discussions found in the Sanskrit texts. Herbert Guenther has also approached the problem, but he has adopted a somewhat different method. Using Tibetan sources with reference to the Sanskrit, Guenther has attempted to explicate Buddhist thought by using philosophical concepts and terms from the West as possible equivalents. Alex Wayman has involved himself in the same enterprise, making use of the Sanskrit and Tibetan treatises as descriptions of the normative positions held by the diverse schools of Buddhism.

On the South Asian side, scholars continue to explore the Sanskrit and Pali traditions for evidence of the developments that occurred in India and Ceylon without showing much concern about how individuals outside of this cultural sphere dealt with these doctrinal matters. Edward Conze dedicated his life to the translation and study of the Prajñāpāramitā literature, in some ways continuing the type of work that Burnouf had been doing with the Hodgson manuscripts. Padmanabh S. Jaini has explored the Sanskrit treatises dealing with Abhidharma and has added new dimensions to the value and importance of these doctrinal treatises in Buddhist studies. Other South Asian scholars, influenced by philosophical study in the West, have explored Buddhist tradition against the backdrop of this non-Indian approach. T. R. V. Murti took the Mādhyamika system of Mahāyāna and compared it to such philosophical traditions as that of Kant. K. N. Jayatilleka produced a masterpiece on Buddhist philosophical thought (*Early Buddhist Theory of Knowledge*, 1963), using the Theravāda texts as a source for philosophical insight comparable to similar discussions found in the writings of Western philosophers. A younger generation of scholars such as Luis Gómez, Steve Collins, and Douglas Daye have turned their attention to the Sanskrit and Pali texts, attempting to provide a new view from the perspective of the philosophical developments in contemporary Western academic circles.

Textual Studies after World War II. A number of scholars involved in textual work—translation as well as editing—have also traveled to Asia to study active Buddhist communities. David Snellgrove, who spent much time doing fieldwork in Nepal, reported on current practices there and at the same time translated important texts such as the *Hevajra Tantra*. Giuseppi Tucci taught for a time at Calcutta and Santiniketana universities and later became the president of the Istituto Italiano per il Medio ed Estremo Oriente (IsMEO). He traveled extensively in Nepal and Tibet, and his work has set the pace for many other scholars who deal with the breadth of Tibetan tradition. S. McDonald, an anthropologist, has investigated the spread of Buddhism in Nepal, and Michael Aris has used his years of living and studying in Bhutan as a basis for works that deal with the religion and history of the area. Per Kvaerne dedicates much of his research to the little-studied Bon tradition of the Tibetans. From these traveler-scholars and their students has emerged a much enlarged and more accurate description of the texts in current use and the practices associated with them.

Contemporary Tibetan Buddhist Studies. After the unsuccessful revolt against Chinese occupation in 1959, a large number of Buddhists, including many important religious leaders, left Tibet and settled in India, Sikkim, Nepal, and Bhutan. This major exodus has had a great impact on current Buddhist studies. Having lost much of their base of support and fearing that events would prevent the Tibetan Buddhist tradition from ever recovering its former base of power, the lamas set up centers of teaching outside of Tibet and included Western scholars among their students. From this contact with Tibetans outside of Tibet itself, a group of scholars, including Robert A. F. Thurman, Per Kvaerne, and Jeffrey Hopkins, began to give time and effort to providing descriptions of the teachings held to be normative by these religious leaders. The study of the tradition among refugees is especially important for Buddhist research, not only because the lamas have allowed access to heretofore unavailable texts but because it provides us with a case study of how a cultural pattern is preserved when it is removed from its homeland and must survive in a foreign environment. With the removal of many of the restrictions on travel into Tibet proper and the revival of Buddhism that has taken place in the last ten years, future studies will also center on the Buddhists in Tibet as well as those in India.

One important scholarly development that resulted from the Tibetan movement to India has been a Library of Congress publication program headed by Gene Smith. With money provided under U.S. Public Law 480, thousands of Tibetan Buddhist works have been photographed and reproduced for distribution to major university libraries in the United States. Scholars with access to these collections now have at their disposal more materials than any scholars have ever had. The effort needed to study and evaluate all of these texts will be enormous and will take many years.

Contemporary Study of Chinese Buddhism. The study of Chinese Buddhism has become more sophisticated as materials have become available and scholars have been exposed to the complexities of the Chinese situation. The work of Kenneth Ch'en brought to the English reader an outline of the history of Chinese Buddhism, relying primarily on Japanese scholarly studies. Recent works by Western scholars have taken a quite different approach to the study of China. In the north and west of China, Tibetan culture came into contact with the Han, and Buddhism has played a role throughout the history of this interchange between the two cultures. Thus, Paul Demiéville's studies of Buddhist Chinese tradition not only make use of documents from Chinese writers but also of Tibetan materials that relate to the interaction. His volume on the Ch'an school (*Entretiens de Lin-tsi,* 1972), along with his work on the controversy in Tibet over the relative merits of Indian and Chinese Buddhist approaches, has given a new understanding to the nature of the contact between these cultures. Rolf Stein has also turned his talents to the Chinese situation, comparing the Taoist tradition with that of the Buddhists, especially the Tantric elements in the Chinese monastic and folk situations. His Tibetan work has also made a considerable contribution to Buddhist studies in that setting, and the translations of the works of the yogin 'Bras-pa Kun-legs (1972) is similar to the work of Demiéville in that it provides a new vision of the traditions within China and Tibet.

In the 1960s and 1970s the study of Chinese Buddhism was severely hampered by the limited access to China, as well as by the proscriptions that were placed on Buddhist practice there. Much of the work on contemporary activities had to be based on reports in the newspapers and on interviews with refugee informants. This type of reporting is best exemplified by the work of Holmes Welch, who used twentieth-century documents as well as informants for his study of Buddhism in China. Other scholars studied practices among the Chinese in Taiwan and Hong Kong in an attempt to determine the traditions present in China before the troubled times of the recent past. The discoveries made by these scholars, who explored the Taoist and folk religions of China, have been of great import in current scholarship. For example, Eric Zürcher, author of the most detailed study of early Chinese Buddhism, found that doctrinal terms are used in totally different senses in the Taoist canon and in the *sūtras*. He suggests that the meaning of a term in Taoism may be closer to the use made by the majority of the Chinese, in contrast to the understanding of such terms within Buddhist monastic centers. Zürcher's study of the apocalyptic visions among the various communities in China and the role of this type of thinking for the Buddhist as well as other Chinese is in the forefront of the current comparative study of Taoism and Buddhism. Daniel Overmyer and Michel Strickmann, who focused on folk traditions and Taoist developments, attempted to show how these non-Buddhist elements have played a major part in the Buddhist community.

American Buddhist Studies. Buddhist studies in the United States began much later than in Europe, but by the mid- to late twentieth century it had already developed its own approaches. Early pioneers in the United States were Franklin Edgerton (1885–1963), Ferdinand Lessing, Henry Clark Warren (1854–1899), and W. Y. Evans-Wentz (1878–1965). Edgerton's companion volumes of Buddhist Hybrid Sanskrit grammar and dictionary (1953), considered a major reference work for Buddhist scholars, presented the controversial idea that Buddhist texts contain a type of language that has undergone three phases of hybridization. Some scholars, such as John Brough of England, agreed with Edgerton's thesis in part but challenged his method of dealing with readings. These, they felt, were often easily explained within the scribal tradition of Nepal, and they opposed Edgerton's postulations of linguistic rules to cover the differences between these texts and the classical Sanskrit. Edgerton's work aroused disagreement, but his impact has clearly been far-reaching, calling into question many editorial decisions that had once judged nonstandard forms of words in the manuscripts to be either errors or of no consequence.

Ferdinand Lessing, who became interested in the Tibetan and Mongolian traditions of Buddhism after travels in Mongolia and northern China, instituted the first classes in Tibetan in the United States. He also collected a number of Tibetan xylographs, which are now housed at the East Asiatic Library of the University of California at Berkeley. Two of his students went on to make major contributions to Buddhist studies: Arthur Link, who concentrated on the Chinese materials of Tao-an and the *Kao-seng chuan,* and Alex Wayman, who focuses on Tibetan and Sanskrit sources.

World War II also had an effect on Buddhist studies. Many European-sponsored programs of Buddhist studies in Asia lost the type of support they enjoyed during the colonial period, and such studies have also declined in centers throughout Europe. For the United States the war brought about an involvement with Asia, which created a new American interest in the study of the area. In particular, many young Americans who took part in government language-study programs were assigned the task of learning Japanese and Chinese, and a number of them became teachers in the universities and colleges of the United States. The Japanese language-study group was taken to Japan when the war ended, and many stayed on or returned later to study there. For example, Leon Hurvitz of British Columbia worked with Tsukamoto Zenryū of Kyoto and translated his history of Chinese Buddhism into English. Stanley Weinstein at Yale University has focused his research and teaching on Japanese methods and sources, stressing that the number of scholars in Japan who are engaged in Buddhist studies far exceeds all of those in the rest of the world, making the detail of information available in Japanese crucial for adequate study. Philip Yampolsky at Columbia University is yet another scholar who looks to Japan for training and inspiration. His work on the *Platform Sutra,* which combines both Western and Japanese scholarly approaches, gives a detailed account of the research that has been done in Japan on this text. This same focus on the Japanese tradition can be seen in the work of Carl Bielefeldt, who has given a new view of the role of the Zen master Dōgen.

In 1961, Richard Robinson instituted the United States' first Ph.D. program in Buddhist studies at the University of Wisconsin. His attempt was to bring to one program the range of approaches and types of study that have characterized the development of the discipline in European universities as well as those in Japan and India. Other programs based on this approach were established at centers such as the University of California at Berkeley. Many institutions with programs in religious studies also added the Buddhist tradition to their curriculum: Harvard, Chicago, Virginia, Princeton, British Columbia, and others. From these programs has come a new generation of scholars, many trained by those involved in the events during and subsequent to World War II. This generation has tended to follow the example of their mentors and study in Japan or in Taiwan: Frank Cook, Whalen Lai, Robert Gimello, and David Chappell are among those who have taken up the detailed study of the development of the Chinese Buddhist scholastic tradition.

Interdisciplinary Methods in Buddhist Studies. The social sciences—sociology, ethnology, and anthropology—have become more popular in both European and North American universities. In particular, these disciplines have focused their study on Buddhism in South and Southeast Asia, places that have been easily accessible for fieldwork. In some ways the anthropological study of Theravāda has been more dominant than the more traditional textual studies characteristic of the time of T. W. Rhys Davids and the Pali Text Society. Melford Spiro, an anthropologist whose research dealt with Burmese religious life, distinguished between Buddhists who search for the enlightened state of *nirvāṇa* and those who wish only to accumulate good *karman* in the hopes of success and fortunate rebirths. Since Burma had been closed to long-term visitors for the past two decades, anthropologists researching the Buddhist impact on society have tended to focus on Sri Lanka. Richard Gombrich, Stanley Tambiah, and Gananath Obeyasekara have all investigated the various practices found in the Buddhist movement in Sri Lanka, and each has debated how the Buddhist monastic community has adapted to society's needs.

Anthropologists have also studied Chinese Buddhism. David K. Jordon and Emily Ahern have studied the ways in which Taiwanese folk practice and funereal cults have absorbed Buddhist elements and how local traditions have in turn been incorporated into the monastery.

Interdisciplinary study and related efforts have added much to the knowledge about Buddhism and its development. For example, art historians in regions where Buddhist traditions once flourished or still thrive have made significant contributions to the understanding of Buddhist thought and history. Ananda Coomaraswamy, René Grousset, Alexander Soper, and Jan Fontein are all scholars who have examined Buddhist artifacts and made valuable studies that advance our knowledge of the movement. From the other perspective, Buddhist specialists have also contributed to the field of art history, as in the case of Stephan Beyer, whose *Cult of Tārā: Magic and Ritual in Tibet* (1973) analyzes art forms in terms of textual sources.

Study of Korean Buddhism. There are still some regions in the Buddhist world, most particularly Korea, where few scholars have turned their attention. An exception is Rhi Ki-young, who has been a major figure in the Buddhist academic life of Korea for some decades. Seeking training outside of his own country, Rhi went to Belgium after World War II and studied under the renowned Étienne Lamotte. Some Korean studies by American-trained specialists such as Robert Buswell, Hee-sung Keel, and myself have also begun to appear. A number of anthropologists in Korea have also explored Buddhist development within the community; Barbara Young and Laurel Kendall, for example, have reported extensively on the role of Buddhism in the practices of the *mudang* (shamans).

Conclusion. The Buddhist tradition continues to offer the student of religion and culture a major challenge. Possessing the largest collection of scriptures of any of the world's religions and practiced all over Asia, with small communities beginning to emerge in Europe and North America, Buddhism has always defied the talents of any one scholar to master it in all its forms. It is possible that Buddhist studies will develop into a truly comparative discipline to adequately comprehend the complexities of this religious community and its variety of sectarian and regional differences; only after such a comparative approach is taken can scholars begin to describe the Buddhist tradition as a whole.

[*See also* Indian Religions, *article on* History of Study; Tibetan Religions, *article on* History of Study; *and* Chinese Religion, *article on* History of Study.]

BIBLIOGRAPHY

Conze, Edward. *Buddhist Scriptures.* Edited and revised by Lewis R. Lancaster. New York, 1982. A bibliography of translations and editions of the major Buddhist texts.

Hanayama Shinshō. *Bibliography of Buddhism.* Tokyo, 1961. A bibliography of works in European languages up to 1932.

Jong, J. W. de. "A Brief History of Buddhist Studies in Europe and America." *Eastern Buddhist,* n.s. 7, no. 1 (May 1974): 55–106, and no. 2 (October 1974): 49–82. Reprinted independently (Varanasi, 1976). The most complete description of the formation and development of Buddhist studies in the West.

Nakamura Hajime. *Indian Buddhism: A Survey with Bibliographical Notes.* Inter-cultural Research Institute Monograph, no. 9. Hirakata, Japan, 1980. A comprehensive look at the scholarly material available for the study of Indian Buddhism.

Peiris, William. *The Western Contribution to Buddhism.* Delhi, 1973. Short biographical sketches of Buddhist scholars.

Przyluski, Jean, et al. *Bibliographie bouddhique.* Buddhica: Documents et travaux pour l'étude du bouddhisme, vols. 1–31. Paris, 1929–1961. An annotated listing of all major articles and books on Buddhism up to 1958. These volumes cover both European- and Asian-language works.

Winternitz, Maurice. *A History of Indian Literature* (1933). Rev. ed. Delhi, 1972.

LEWIS R. LANCASTER

BUGIS RELIGION. The Bugis, sometimes referred to as the Buginese, are an Indonesian people numbering about three million, most of whom live in their homeland of Celebes (South Sulawesi). *Bugis* is an archaic form of their name retained by the Malay/Indonesian language; in fact they call themselves Ugi' or ToUgi'. Bugis emigrants have also established significant, mostly coastal, settlements throughout the Indonesian archipelago. They speak a language of the Western Austronesian family, the same family as their national language (Malay or Indonesian). [*See map accompanying* Southeast Asian Religions, *article on* Insular Cultures.]

After a long period of contact with Muslim, mainly Malay, traders who had settled in their main trading harbors, and after some spontaneous but aborted attempts to adopt Christianity during the middle of the sixteenth century, the Bugis officially became Muslims between 1605 and 1610 under the initiative and pressure of the neighboring kingdom of Goa. But although they soon came to be considered among the most devout Muslims in the archipelago, they have retained in their traditions many pre-Islamic elements. These include the *bissu,* transvestite priests in charge of the regalia of the ruling house and of princely rituals; popular practitioners called *sanro;* sacred places, to which offerings are regularly brought; and the psalmody, on certain ceremonial occasions, of the sacred epic *La galigo,* which provides an interesting if incomplete view of pre-Islamic Bugis culture.

The Myth of Origin. The Bugis creation myth has been somewhat mixed with Islamic mysticism, but as far as it can be reconstituted, the early Bugis believed in a supreme deity called To Papunna ("the owner of everything") or Déwata Sisiné, later Déwata Séuwaé ("the one God"). From this deity emanated a male and a female being, linked to some extent to the sun and the moon. From their separated seed were born a number of beings who were not clearly identified; then from their sexual union were born the main gods of the upper-world and the underworld, said to number either seven, fourteen, or nineteen, according to various versions of the myth. Of these gods, six married couples are described in *La galigo* as playing a significant role, and two couples are mentioned as being more important than the others: one at the depths of the Abyss, whose male partner was known as Guru ri Selle'; and the other at the summit of Heaven, whose male entity, Datu Patoto' ("the prince who fixes destinies") or Datu Palanro ("the princely smith"), was considered the highest god of all. These two couples had nine children each, seven of whom reigned over various strata of Heaven or the Abyss. The eldest son of Datu Patoto', La Toge'langi' (also known as Batara Guru), and Guru ri Selle's daughter were sent to the Middle World to establish there, in Luwu', the first human settlement. However, they are not the primeval ancestors of mankind, which rather descends from the servants who followed them from Heaven and the Abyss, as well as from the servants of other divine rulers, the children of the secondary heavenly and abyssal couples, who came later to establish other kingdoms in and around Sulawesi (Celebes).

The Political Myths. The *La galigo* epic tells of the life and deeds of six generations of earthly descendants to these first divine rulers, and especially of Sawérigading, the Bugis cultural hero, a grandson of Batara Guru. Still considered sacred by a small group of non-Muslim Bugis, *La galigo* is a repository of princely rituals, performed by the *bissu,* and of princely conduct. The epic tells that after the sixth generation of rulers descended from Batara Guru and other children of the gods, all princes of divine origin had to leave this world to go back to Heaven or the Abyss, except for the princely couple in Luwu'. All Bugis nobility is said to be descended either from that Luwu' couple, or from other divine princes sent either from Heaven (Tomanurung) or from the Abyss (Totompo'). Most of the Bugis lordships and kingdoms claim to have been founded by a divine couple, and they keep as regalia various articles such as swords, banners, and ploughs, which are said to have been brought by these ancestors of their rulers.

The Cult and Its Objects. Two kinds of closely related Bugis rituals can be distinguished. One was performed by the *bissu* at princely courts; now, however, the number of *bissu* is rapidly declining and their activity is becoming more and more limited. The other ritual is enacted by the popular practitioners called *sanro,* who are still very active in Bugis country. Both kinds of rituals include sacrifices (of buffalo, goats, or chickens) and offerings of glutinous rice, usually presented in four (or, sometimes, two, seven, or eight) colors. The rituals are performed during rites of passage, house or boat building, first-use rites, anniversaries, and during certain phases of the rice cycle, as well as at community celebrations in order to obtain the welfare or protection of the people, of the lordship, or of the state, especially in case of bad crops, epidemics, or wars.

In *La galigo,* the objects of the cult are expressly said to be the gods of Heaven and the Abyss; they decided, in turn, to people the Middle World just because "one is no god when there is no one to pay homage to you." Nowadays, the average Bugis knows very little of pre-Islamic theology, which, moreover, was never recorded systematically but was only implicit in the tradition. Still, many Bugis continue to believe that besides Allāh, whom they call Puang Allataala or Déwata Séuwaé, there are many spiritual beings to whom one must pay homage and who, in turn, act as intercessors between humans and the supreme being, who is too far above mankind to be contacted directly. Sawérigading is sometimes named as one such intervening figure, but he seems to have been the object of a cult maintained more by the *bissu* than by laity. Likewise, a deity named Déwata Mattanru' Kati ("the god with golden horns"), to whom a special cult is rendered by the *bissu,* may be one of the heavenly gods of *La galigo.* Other divine beings who are, still today, the object of a general cult among all categories of Bugis include the rice goddess, Sangiang Serri. According to *La galigo* she was the first child born on earth to Batara Guru, but she died after seven days, whereupon her body, once buried, transformed itself into the rice plant. Another revered being is Taddampali, an aquatic being who may be the same as La Punna Liung, the messenger of the Abyss in *La galigo*. Included here also are the local *tomanurung* ("descended [from heaven] beings"). Many Bugis still keep in their homes wooden tabernacles or miniature beds where the divine beings are said to descend during ceremonies.

Other kinds of spiritual or invisible beings *(totenrita)* also appear as divine-human intercessors. Among these are house and boat spirit guardians and local spirits dwelling in large stones, trees, or springs. Other spirits may be dangerous, as for example the *paddengngeng* ("hunters"), invisible horsemen who capture people's souls with their lassos, thereby provoking unexpected illness and death. Their kingdom, described in some of the oral traditions, seems to recall the Land of the Dead as described in *La galigo*.

The Afterworld. In *La galigo*, the afterworld is described as a distant island somewhere in the western seas. The dead come first to a land where they must wait until all the funerary rituals and required offerings have been accomplished by their living relatives; otherwise they cannot proceed further. In that place, sinners must also undergo various punishments. The dead must then take a ritual bath, pay their entrance to the keeper of the heartland, and cross a golden bridge. In the inner Land of the Dead, everything is the reverse of life among the living.

With islamicization, most of these observances have been obliterated, and Muslim funerals have now replaced traditional ones. However, an ancestor cult still exists that features pilgrimages to sacred, non-Islamic graves and offerings brought to family ancestors in a special place in the home.

BIBLIOGRAPHY

Hamonic, Gilbert. "Pour une étude comparée des cosmogonies de Célèbes-Sud: À propos d'un manuscrit inédit sur l'origine des dieux bugis." *Archipel* 25 (1983): 35–62. The first translated edition, with commentary, of a hitherto secret text on creation and the genesis of the gods according to a Bugis view.

Hamonic, Gilbert. *Le langage des dieux: Cultes et rituels préislamiques du pays bugis (Célèbes-Sud, Indonésie).* Forthcoming. An important work containing a corpus of about two thousand verses of *bissu* ritual chants, with translation and commentary.

Kern, Rudolph A. *Catalogus van de Boegineesche, tot den I La Galigo-cyclus behoorende handschriften der Leidsche Universiteits Bibliotheek, alsmede van die in andere Europeesche bibliotheken.* Leiden, 1939.

Kern, Rudolph A. *Catalogus van de Boeginese, tot de I La Galigo-cyclus behorende handschriften van Jajasan Matthes (Matthesstichting) te Makassar (Indonesië).* Makassar, Indonesia, 1954. A complete compilation in two books of all manuscripts containing episodes of the *La galigo* epic. Includes lists of gods and heros appearing in the cycle.

Matthes, Benjamin F. *Boeginesche chresthomathie: Oorspronkelijke Boeginesche geschriften in proza en poëzij, uitgegeven, van aanteekeningen voorzien en ten deele vertaald.* 3 vols. Vol. 1, Makassar, Indonesia, 1864; vols. 2 and 3, Amsterdam, 1872. The only anthology thus far available of Bugis texts, including the beginning of the *La galigo* epic. Liberally annotated.

Matthes, Benjamin F. *Over de bissoe's of heidensche priesters en priesteessen der Boeginezen.* Amsterdam, 1872. An extremely valuable account of the *bissu* priests and their rituals.

Pelras, Christian. " 'Herbe divine': Le riz chez les Bugis (Indonésie)." *Études rurales* 53–56 (1974): 357–374. A description of rice cultivation among the Bugis, including associated rituals.

Pelras, Christian. "Le panthéon des anciens Bugis, à travers les textes de *La galigo*." *Archipel* 25 (1983): 65–97. A reconstitution of the Bugis pantheon and worldview, according to the *La galigo* epic and other texts.

Pelras, Christian. Les éléments du rituel dans la religion populaire bugis." *Ethnologica Helvetica.* Forthcoming. An analysis of the constituents of Bugis ritual.

Pelras, Christian. "Religion, Tradition, and the Dynamics of Islamization in South Celebes." *Archipel* (In press). Discusses the transition from paganism to Islam in South Celebes.

CHRISTIAN PELRAS

BUKHĀRĪ, AL- (AH 194–256/810–870 CE), more fully Muḥammad ibn Ismāʿīl al-Bukhārī; a great scholar of Islam who devoted his career to the collection, transmission, and classification of *ḥadīth*. He was an Iranian, born in Bukhara, an outstanding center of Islamic scholarship in Central Asia. His attraction to the study of *ḥadīth* manifested itself early: from the age of ten he began to learn the reports of the life and words of the prophet Muḥammad as transmitted by scholars in Bukhara. At sixteen he made the pilgrimage to Mecca with his mother and brother, and from then on he traveled extensively to Balkh, Baghdad, Mecca, Medina, Basra, Egypt, Damascus, Homs, and other localities in search of *ḥadīth*. Before reaching maturity he had established a reputation for the thoroughness and exactitude with which he collected and learned *ḥadīth*.

Upon the suggestion of an older colleague, Ibn Rāhwayh of Nishapur (d. 853), al-Bukhārī undertook to prepare a compendium of *ḥadīth* carefully selected from the mass of material that he had at his disposal. This task is said to have taken sixteen years, and the resulting collection constitutes the enduring monument to al-Bukhārī's science. Entitled *Al-jāmiʿ al-ṣaḥīḥ* (The Sound Epitome), it is the result of the compiler's rigorous sifting of a fund of *ḥadīth* reported to have numbered 600,000.

The *Ṣaḥīḥ* of al-Bukhārī represents a major development in the science of *ḥadīth* criticism. Where earlier compilers tended to include material from all possible sources, without regard for the degree of reliability of their chains of transmission, al-Bukhārī designated the 2,602 different texts in the *Ṣaḥīḥ* as authentic *(saḥīḥ)* on the basis of the competence and integrity of their narrators. After many centuries of scrutiny by Muslim scholars, the authenticity of only 110 texts in his collection has been questioned, and *Al-jāmiʿ al-ṣaḥīḥ* remains the most respected collection of *ḥadīth* in the Islamic world.

Al-Bukhārī considered his *Ṣaḥīḥ* to be a work of religious devotion, and it is said that he never included a text in the compilation without first bathing and engaging in prayer. It was also intended to be a tool for the study of jurisprudence, with many of the texts arranged according to the categories of Islamic law; the headings of the different sections reveal the compiler's competence in jurisprudence. Although all four schools of Sunnī law consider him to be one of their basic sources, he never identified with any particular school. The *Ṣaḥīḥ* also contains much material on Qur'ān interpretation, morals and religious life, and the early history of Islam. Because many texts are repeated under several subject headings, the total number of *ḥadīth* in the *Ṣaḥīḥ*, including repetitions, is 9,082.

In his later life al-Bukhārī returned to his home city but was not able to stay because of a dispute with the local governor. He died in the village of Khartank, near Samarkand.

BIBLIOGRAPHY

A summary of the somewhat meager information on al-Bukhārī's life available in the ancient Arabic sources is found in *The Encyclopaedia of Islam*, new ed. (Leiden, 1960–). Muhammad Z. Siddiqi, an Indian scholar, gives a slightly fuller sketch of the traditionist and adds a useful description of his methods of compiling *ḥadīth* in *Hadith Literature: Its Origin, Development, Special Features and Criticism* (Calcutta, 1961), pp. 88–97. Ignácz Goldziher's *Muslim Studies*, vol. 2, edited by S. M. Stern, translated by Stern and C. R. Barber (Chicago, 1973), includes remarks on al-Bukhārī's method and his contribution to the science of Islamic jurisprudence *(fiqh)*. A thorough and reliable monograph in Arabic is al-Ḥusaynī ʿAbd al-Majīd Hāshim's *Al-Imām al-Bukhārī muḥaddithan wa-faqīhan* (Cairo, 1966). *Al-jāmiʿ al-ṣaḥīḥ* has been translated into English by Muhammad Muhsin Khan as *The Translation of the Meanings of Ṣaḥīḥ al-Bukhārī*, 9 vols., 4th ed. (Chicago, 1977–1979). This edition is intended for general reading by the Muslim public, so it lacks many features of interest to scholars.

R. Marston Speight

BULGAKOV, SERGEI (1871–1944), Russian economist, philosopher, theologian, and Russian Orthodox priest. Sergei Nikolaevich was born in Livny, province of Orel, less than fifty years before the revolutions of 1917. The son of a Russian Orthodox priest, Bulgakov was raised in a pious Orthodox home. Following his early formal education, he was enrolled in the theological seminary in Orel Province, which he left shortly thereafter for secular studies. A convinced atheist, at age nineteen he enrolled in the law school of the University of Moscow. By the time of his graduation in 1894 he was a committed and enthusiastic Marxist, with a special interest in political economy. His master's thesis on the relationship of capitalism and agriculture was published in 1900.

In 1901 Bulgakov was appointed to the faculty of the Polytechnic Institute of Kiev as a political economist. During his tenure there he began to have doubts about Marxism both as a philosophy and as an economic theory. The publication in 1903 of his *Ot Marksizma k idealizmu* (From Marxism to Idealism) signaled his definitive break with Marxism. In 1906 he was elected to the Second Duma and appointed to the faculty of the Institute of Commerce of Moscow. At this time, along with other members of the Russian intelligentsia, he began to turn from economics to philosophy, theology, and religion. He joined with thinkers such as Pavel Florenskii, Nikolai Berdiaev, and Vladimir Solov'ev in founding and writing for such periodicals as *Novyi put'* (New Path) and *Voprosy zhizni* (Problems of Life). Their movement, which developed in the direction of Eastern Orthodox Christianity, began as an angry attack on the radical intelligentsia through the journal *Vekhi*. Later, the movement took on a more positive orientation. Bulgakov expressed these emerging views in his works *Filosofiia khoziaistva* (Philosophy of Economics; 1912); *Svet nevechernii* (The Unending Light; 1917); and *Tikhie dumy* (Quiet Meditations; 1918).

Bulgakov became fully identified with the Russian Orthodox church after 1917 and was ordained a priest on 11 June 1918. He was elected to the newly formed Supreme Ecclesiastical Council, under the reconstituted patriarchate of Moscow. Because he was a clergyman, he lost the position that he held at the University of Simferopol. In 1922 he was expelled from the Soviet Union.

After a short stay in Prague, Bulgakov moved to Paris, where he spent the rest of his life as dean and professor of dogmatics at the Saint Sergius Theological Institute. He proved a creative and prolific author of theological works, many of which have a controversial and polemical character. Between 1926 and 1938 he produced seventeen major works. Six additional works were published posthumously, including *Die Tragödie der Philosophie* (The Tragedy of Philosophy; 1927), *The Social Teaching of Modern Russian Orthodox Theology* (1934), *Agnets Bozhii* (The Lamb of God; 1933), and *Nevesta Agntsa* (The Bride of the Lamb; 1945). There remains a significant corpus of unpublished writings. In striving to present the basic doctrines of Eastern Orthodox Christianity in a contemporary light, Bulgakov provoked more conventional thinkers and became the center of theological controversy.

Bulgakov is remembered particularly for his controversial sophiological teachings, for which *The Unending Light* is a major early source. In 1936 and 1937 he published additional works on sophiology, which was the theological vehicle for his cosmology. In his formulation, Wisdom (*sophia*) is the all-inclusive concept of creation. It is the eternal female reality, the maternal womb of being, the "fourth hypostasis," the "world of ideas, the idealist basis of the created world." In Bulgakov's analysis, Wisdom is the pattern for divine creation. His sophiological teachings, which attempt to bring together the cosmological understandings of modern science and traditional theological understandings of creation, were accepted neither by the patriarchate of Moscow nor by the Karlovskii Synod, which represented Russian Orthodoxy outside the Soviet Union. The official Orthodox church condemned Bulgakov's sophiology, especially its conceptualization of the "fourth hypostasis," which was seen as a distortion of the received doctrine of the Holy Trinity. However, he was never excommunicated for this teaching. One of the most powerful and creative theological minds of his era, at his death Bulgakov was buried with full ecclesiastical honors.

BIBLIOGRAPHY

For a general understanding of Bulgakov's place in the theological climate of Russian Orthodoxy in Paris, see Donald A. Lowrie's *Saint Sergius in Paris: The Orthodox Theological Institute* (New York, 1951). For his general place in the range and dynamics of Russian intellectual history, see Nicolas Zernov's *The Russian Religious Renaissance of the Twentieth Century* (London, 1963) and N. O. Lossky's *History of Russian Philosophy* (New York, 1951). A full bibliography of his works is found in L. A. Zander's *Bog i mir: Mirosozertsanie Ottsa Sergiia Bulgakova*, 2 vols. (Paris, 1948).

The most helpful of his own writings in understanding his intellectual history is his autobiography, *Avtobiograficheskie zametki* (Paris, 1947). The following are representative writings in English translation: *A Bulgakov Anthology*, edited by Nicolas Zernov and James Pain (Philadelphia, 1976); *The Wisdom of God: A Brief Summary of Sophiology* (New York, 1937); and *Karl Marx as a Religious Type*, edited by Virgil Lang and translated by Luba Barna (Belmont, Mass., 1980).

STANLEY SAMUEL HARAKAS

BULL-ROARERS have been used as cult objects by various peoples from ancient times to the present day, usually in the context of male initiation ceremonies. They are generally made of wood (or ceramics, as in ancient Greece) and are generally flat, most commonly measuring sixty centimeters long and eight centimeters wide. Either through the whirring sound they make when swung or through the carved or painted marks they bear, they symbolize generalized powers of fertility, in particular those of male generative powers, of wind, and of rain.

In the mythology of ancient Greece, a bull-roarer was one of the toys with which the Titans distracted the child Dionysos before they slew him. As a cult object, the bull-roarer was used in rainmaking ceremonies, symbolizing Kronos as rainmaker, and in the Eleusinian mysteries, where the connection between Dionysos and Demeter as fertility deities was emphasized (Frazer, vol. 7, 1912). In present-day Europe the bull-roarer is still used among the Basques by boys to frighten women and girls during and after the Mass on Good Friday.

Through comparison with South American myths and rituals, where the bull-roarer's sound is associated with a giant snake, with the generative power of the phallus, and also with the period of food depletion and hunger, Lévi-Strauss (relying on the work of Otto Zerries and Geneviève Massignon) develops the following correlation: as the instrument is used during the absence of food and of fire (connected to European customs of extinguishing the fire before Easter), and thus with fasting, it indicates symbolically a time when man and nature are in close contact, a primordial time before the invention of fire, when food had to be consumed raw or warmed by the sun. The use of the bull-roarer's sound to separate women (nature-bound) from men (culture-bearers) seems to be corroborated by Australian Aboriginal usage of bull-roarers for fertility rituals or "increase-ceremonies" with secret-sacred character (Lévi-Strauss, 1966, pp. 354–357). However, there are also exceptions, as the Ungarinyin know of "female" bull-roarers. [*See* Ungarinyin Religion.] In general, Aboriginal devices of this sort are described under the Aranda term *tjurunga*, and in all tribal regions they embody the spirit, the essence, and the vital forces of the heroes and creator-spirits of the Dreaming. [*See* Tjurungas.] The spiritual power of these beings can be activated through ritual use of bull-roarers to affect procreation. Some tribal groups maintain that bull-roarers already exist in specific trees and have only to be "set free" through the ritual act of carving. Certain specific acts, such as shaving particles from a *tjurunga* and blowing them over the landscape or reciting and singing stories of the Dreaming featuring the totemic ancestors represented in and through a *tjurunga,* have the effect of continuing procreation of all nature (Petri and Worms, 1968).

Relying on New Guinean materials wherein bull-roarers symbolize phallic power, van Baal (1963) suggests that the secrecy surrounding the bull-roarer rituals in Australia points to the sacredness of the meaning of the sexual act. Without such rituals, sexual intercourse is too sacred to be practiced. As bull-roarer rituals take over the sacred meaning, intercourse can be performed as a profane act of pleasure.

BIBLIOGRAPHY

Baal, Jan van. "The Cult of the Bull-Roarer in Australia." *Bijdragen tot de Taal-, Land- en Volkenkunde* 119 (1963): 201–214. Provides an original interpretative framework for bull-roarer cults, relying on field experience in New Guinea and using Australian data for comparative purposes.

Frazer, James G. *The Golden Bough.* 3d ed., rev. & enl. London, 1911–1912. See especially part 1 (vols. 1–2), *The Magic Art and the Evolution of Kings,* an indispensable classic on means for the magical control of rain with primary sources on a global scale, and part 5 (vols. 7–8), *Spirits of the Corn and of the Wild,* an extensive discussion of fertility rituals in ancient Greece with cross-cultural comparisons.

Lévi-Strauss, Claude. *Mythologiques,* vol. 2, *Du miel aux cendres.* Paris, 1966. Translated as *From Honey to Ashes* (New York, 1973). An extensive structural analysis of myths and rituals of South American tribes in regard to culinary and musical coding.

Massignon, Geneviève. "La crécelle et les instruments des ténèbres en Corse." *Arts et traditions populaires* 7 (July–December, 1959): 274–280. The major European source of Lévi-Strauss's deductive hypothesis concerning aerophones and their symbolic connection with times of fasting, absence of fire, and male procreative powers.

Petri, Helmut, and Ernest A. Worms. *Australische Eingeborenen-Religionen.* Stuttgart, 1968. A comprehensive survey of Australian Aboriginal religious systems with a great amount of original data.

Zerries, Otto. "The Bull-Roarer among South American Indians." *Revista do Museo Paulista* 7 (1953). The main empirical data with which Lévi-Strauss supports his deductive theory that bull-roarers are instruments of darkness.

KLAUS-PETER KOEPPING

BULTMANN, RUDOLF (1884–1976), Christian theologian and New Testament scholar. Born in Wiefelstede, in what was then the grand duchy of Oldenburg, Bultmann was the son of a Lutheran pastor, himself the son of a missionary to Africa, and also the grandson on the maternal side of a pastor in Baden. He attended the humanistic *Gymnasium* in Oldenburg before studying theology in Tübingen, Berlin, and Marburg. After receiving a scholarship to Marburg in 1907, he took his doctoral degree there in 1910 and qualified as university lecturer in 1912. He taught as instructor in Marburg until 1916, when he was appointed assistant professor in Breslau. In 1920 he was called to Giessen as full professor, only to return after one year to Marburg, where he taught as full professor until becoming professor emeritus in 1951, and where he continued to live until his death.

Bultmann's special field of competence as a theologian was the New Testament, and it is quite possible that he is the most influential scholar in this field in the twentieth century. His first major work, *Die Geschichte der synoptischen Tradition* (1921; The History of the Synoptic Tradition, 1963), established him as one of the cofounders of form criticism of the synoptic Gospels. Together with his book *Jesus* (1926; Jesus and the Word, 1934), it has been decisive for the ongoing quest of the historical Jesus as well as for subsequent critical study of the tradition redacted in the Gospels. Hardly less significant for research in the field are his studies of the Fourth Gospel, epitomized by the commentary that is perhaps his masterwork, *Das Evangelium des Johannes* (1941; The Gospel of John: A Commentary, 1971), and his interpretation of the theology of Paul, especially in his other major work, *Theologie des Neuen Testaments* (1948–1953; Theology of the New Testament, 1951, 1955). In any number of other respects as well, from the general problem of biblical hermeneutics to the special question of gnosticism and the New Testament, his work and the critical discussion of it continue to be determinative for serious study of the New Testament.

Yet it is not only or even primarily as a New Testament scholar that Bultmann is significant for theology and religious studies. In his own mind, certainly, he was, first and last, a Christian theologian, who did all of his historical work in service of the church and its witness, and it is in this capacity that he is now also widely regarded as one of the two or three Protestant theologians of this century whose impact on theology promises to be lasting. The warrants for this promise in his case are many, but two features of his thought in particular are basic to its significance.

First of all, Bultmann was distinctive among his contemporaries in clearly distinguishing and resourcefully addressing both of the essential tasks of Christian theology. Thus, as much as he agreed with Karl Barth that theology's first task is to interpret the Christian witness appropriately, in accordance with the normative witness to Jesus Christ attested by scripture, he differed from Barth in insisting that theology also has the task of interpreting this witness understandably, in terms that men and women today can understand and find credible. On the other hand, if his efforts to deal with this second, apologetic task brought him into close proximity to Paul Tillich, his deep concern with the first, dogmatic task gave his thought a very different character from the more speculative, unhistorical cast of Tillich's kind of philosophical theology.

The other equally fundamental feature of Bultmann's thought was his thoroughgoing interpretation of Christian faith, as of religion generally, in existentialist terms. In this respect, there is no question of the formative influence on his theology of the existentialist philosophy of the early Martin Heidegger, who was his close colleague in Marburg from 1923 to 1928. But if Heidegger provided the conceptuality for Bultmann's existentialist theology, he had already learned from the Lutheran pietism out of which he came and, above all, from his teacher Wilhelm Herrmann, that faith can be understood only as an existential phenomenon. Consequently, while he never doubted that faith does indeed have to do with the strictly ultimate reality called God, he was convinced that faith always has to do with this reality, not in its being in itself, but in its meaning for us, and hence as authorizing our own authentic existence.

The first of the four volumes of Bultmann's collected essays, *Glauben und Verstehen* (1933; Faith and Understanding, 1969), shows that the theology defined by these two basic features had already taken shape during the 1920s. But it is also clear from the three later volumes (1952, 1960, 1965; Eng. trans. of vol. 2, 1955) as well as from his other writings during the so-called demythologizing debate, all of which appeared in the series edited by H. W. Bartsch, *Kerygma und Mythos* (1948–1955; Kerygma and Myth, partial Eng. trans., 1953, 1962), that the same theology found its classic expression in 1941 in his programmatic essay "New Testament and Mythology," which provoked this famous debate. If Bultmann was insistent in this essay that theology has no alternative but to demythologize the New Testament, he was also clear that the demand for demythologizing is not merely apologetic but, as he later formulated it, is also "a demand of faith itself." And when he explained the demythologizing he called for positively, as a procedure for interpreting rather than for eliminating myth, it proved to be nothing other than thoroughgoing existentialist interpretation now applied to the mythological formulations of the New Testament.

Even today, Bultmann's theology remains the most controversial of the century, and it is still uncertain whether he will be reckoned among the fathers of the modern church or among its arch heretics. But there seems little question now that this is the level at which his work must be judged, and its impact already confirms that the history of theology, no less than the history of philosophy, is never quite the same after the shock of a great thinker.

BIBLIOGRAPHY

Works by Bultmann in English in addition to those cited above include his Gifford Lectures, *History and Eschatology* (Edinburgh, 1957), and the selection of his shorter writings I edited and translated in *Existence and Faith* (New York, 1960). His most important contributions to the demythologizing debate are all available in my edition and translation of *New Testament and Mythology and Other Basic Writings* (Philadelphia, 1984). Among works on his theology, the volume edited by Charles W. Kegley, *The Theology of Rudolf Bultmann* (New York, 1966), provides a useful orientation to the extensive critical discussion, while the best general introduction is Walter Schmithals's *An Introduction to the Theology of Rudolf Bultmann* (London, 1968).

SCHUBERT M. OGDEN

BUNYAN, JOHN (1628–1688), English Nonconformist and author of *The Pilgrim's Progress.* The son of a brazier, John Bunyan was born in the village of Elstow, near Bedford, and may have attended a local grammar school. During the Civil War he served with the parliamentary forces at Newport Pagnell, Buckinghamshire, where he came into contact with various religious sects. In the early 1650s he underwent prolonged spiritual turmoil, at the nadir of which he was convinced that he had betrayed Christ by allying himself with the devil. About 1655 Bunyan joined the open-communion Baptist church at Bedford, whose pastor was John Gifford, a former royalist officer. Some members of the congregation were sympathetic to the tenets of the Fifth Monarchists, a radical millenarian group to which Bunyan himself was apparently attracted for a time.

Bunyan launched his career as a preacher and prolific author before the monarchy and the Church of England were restored in 1660. For preaching illegally, he was arrested in November 1660 and imprisoned for twelve years in the county jail at Bedford. While imprisoned, he spent much of his time making laces to support his family and writing new books, but near the end of his incarceration he also worked closely with representatives of four other churches to organize a network of preachers and teachers in northern Bedfordshire and contiguous areas in order to resist the uniformity imposed by the Church of England and thus help to ensure the survival of Nonconformity during future periods of persecution. In January 1672 Bunyan was chosen pastor of the Bedford church, although he was not released from prison until the following September. The period of intense ministerial activity that ensued was threatened when a warrant for his arrest was issued in March 1675. Although Bunyan eluded this warrant by temporarily fleeing Bedford, he was rearrested late in 1676, only to be freed the following June. The last dozen years of his life were devoted to preaching in the Midlands and London, as well as to further writing. When the Roman Catholic monarch, James II, tried to win support by granting toleration to Nonconformists, Bunyan was cautious, although some members of his congregation accepted positions in the reorganized Bedford Corporation. Bunyan did not live to see James deposed in the Glorious Revolution, for he died in London on 31 August 1688.

Of Bunyan's approximately sixty works, the most popular is *The Pilgrim's Progress,* the first part of which was composed during his long imprisonment but not published until 1678. A virtual epic of the Christian life couched in Puritan ideals, the story of Christian's struggles from the Slough of Despond to the Eternal City draws heavily on Bunyan's own religious experience. The dramatic power of the narrative is enhanced by vivid symbolism, homely colloquialisms, and myriad human touches. The same ground is traversed in more quiescent fashion by Christiana and her children in the second part, published in 1684, in which Bunyan paid more attention to women. Both parts depend extensively on Bunyan's spiritual autobiography, *Grace Abounding to the Chief of Sinners* (1666), a *sine qua non* for understanding all his works. In its pages such psychologists as William James and Josiah Royce have sought the key to Bunyan's personality. Whether he was in fact troubled by psychotic disorders is difficult to ascertain, for *Grace Abounding,* like other works of this genre, follows a rather commonplace thematic pattern: the path to sainthood commences with denunciations of one's utter depravity.

Bunyan's attempt to repeat the success of *The Pilgrim's Progress* with *The Holy War* (1682), a ponderous albeit technically superior allegory, produced a sophisticated but less personal work. Its complex allegorical levels embrace world history, recent English events, the experience of the individual soul, and probably an apocalyptic vision. Bunyan abandoned allegory to depict the wayward reprobate in *The Life and Death of Mr. Badman* (1680), which, although it lacks the emotional intensity and dramatic tension of *The Pilgrim's Progress,* has captured the interest of both literary specialists, as a possible forerunner of the novel, and historians, for its incisive comments on English society.

Bunyan's theological views were substantially shaped by the Bible, John Foxe's *Book of Martyrs,* Martin Luther's commentary on *Galatians,* and works of two early seventeenth-century Puritans, Arthur Dent's *The Plaine Mans Pathway to Heaven* (1601) and Lewis Bayly's *The Practice of Piety* (1612). Bunyan's views were essentially compatible with those of other strict Calvinists of his period, such as the Nonconformists John Owen and Thomas Goodwin. This is notably manifest in his exposition of the key concept of the covenants, particularly as expounded in his major theological treatise, *The Doctrine of the Law and Grace Unfolded* (1659). Bunyan's emphasis on God's role in establishing the covenant of grace set him apart from such moderate Calvinists as Richard Baxter, who gave greater prominence to human responsibility, but Bunyan stopped short of the antinomians by insisting that the moral law has a valid and significant place in the covenant of grace. Unlike most strict Calvinists, however, Bunyan repudiated the idea of a baptismal covenant, for in his judgment water baptism was necessary neither for admission to the Lord's Supper nor for church membership. Bunyan hotly debated this subject with such traditional Baptists as Henry Danvers, Thomas Paul, and John Denne. As a controversialist he also engaged in literary debates with the Quakers Edward Burrough and William Penn and with the latitudinarian Edward Fowler. Another prominent theme in Bunyan's theology was millenarianism, the *loci classici* of which are *The Holy City* (1665) and *Of Antichrist and His Ruin* (1692, posthumous).

Although Bunyan achieved virtually instantaneous recognition with the publication of *The Pilgrim's Progress,* especially in lay Protestant religious circles, critical acclaim was slow to follow. Alexander Pope and Jonathan Swift referred kindly to his masterpiece, but Edmund Burke and David Hume sneered. With the onset of romanticism and the evangelical revivals, interest in Bunyan soared, and by the Victorian period he was commonly referred to in evangelical circles as a genius. Copies of *The Pilgrim's Progress* poured from the press—more than thirteen hundred editions by 1938—accompanied by numerous popular commentaries, nearly all from evangelicals. Predictions at the turn of the twentieth century of Bunyan's theological and literary obsolescence proved premature when the atrocities of World War I brought new relevance to his works. Although religious interest in him has waned in the late twentieth century, his reputation is now firmly established among students of religion, history, literature, and psychology.

BIBLIOGRAPHY

The standard critical edition of Bunyan's works includes *The Pilgrim's Progress,* edited by James Blanton Wharey and revised by Roger Sharrock (Oxford, 1960); *Grace Abounding to the Chief of Sinners,* edited by Roger Sharrock (Oxford, 1962); *The Holy War,* edited by Roger Sharrock and James Forrest (Oxford, 1980); *The Life and Death of Mr. Badman*, edited by Roger Sharrock and James Forrest (forthcoming); and thirteen volumes of *The Miscellaneous Works of John Bunyan* under the general editorship of Roger Sharrock (Oxford, 1976–). The best biography is still John Brown's enthusiastic *John Bunyan, 1628–1688: His Life, Times, and Work*, revised by Frank Mott Harrison (London, 1928). For Bunyan's thought and its antecedents, the standard account is Richard L. Greaves's *John Bunyan* (Abingdon, England, and Grand Rapids, Mich., 1969). A provocative analysis of Bunyan's relationship to his contemporaries is provided in William York Tindall's *John Bunyan: Mechanick Preacher* (New York, 1934). For a full bibliography of Bunyan studies, see James Forrest and Richard L. Greaves's *John Bunyan: A Reference Guide* (Boston, 1982).

RICHARD L. GREAVES

BUREAUCRACY. [*This entry is limited to a discussion of bureaucratization of leadership within Christian denominations, chiefly American, during the twentieth century. For discussion of the process of rationalization in broader perspective, see* Modernity *and the biography of* Weber.]

The emergence of large church organizations, marked by complexity of internal structure and multi-tiered staffs of paid professional employees, has been a prominent feature of American religious life in the twentieth century. This enlargement of ecclesiastical bureaucracy is apparent on every front and far exceeds the fairly modest rate of growth in overall church membership among the mainline denominations, both Catholic and Protestant. In Roman Catholicism, the number of dioceses in the United States increased some 70 percent from 1900 to 1960, from 82 to 139. Yet, more remarkable by far was the expansion of diocesan staffing over the same period: chancel functionaries per diocese in urban areas grew sixfold, from 2.7 positions in 1900 to 15.5 in 1960 (Winter, 1968, p. 137). In addition, there has been a major increase in Catholic agency personnel at the diocesan level (Catholic Youth Organization directors, Council of Catholic Men secretaries, and so forth). In this category the typical diocese had no official charged with such an assignment in 1900, whereas by 1960, after a long, steady growth, the average per diocese was 7.7 in urban areas and 3.6 in rural areas (ibid., p. 136). And these figures do not take into account the major Catholic bureaucracies that have emerged at the national level, none of which even existed in 1900.

Expansion in professional staff has been a no less prominent feature of American Protestantism. At the local and state levels there have been substantial enlargements in professional cadres in denominational judicatory offices and interdenominational church federations. One must look to the national level, however, to observe the most dramatic changes. One typical denomination, the Disciples of Christ, can serve as an example. Here, the number of technical and executive personnel (excluding all clerical staff) expanded tenfold, from 16 to 162, between 1900 and 1962, and this in a period when the total number of disciples grew only about 50 percent, or from 1.1 million to 1.7 million members (ibid., p. 123). The nation's leading interchurch organization, the National Council of the Churches of Christ (before 1950 the Federal Council of Churches) functioned with just two executive and technical personnel during its first ten years, from 1908 to 1918, whereas by the 1960s it employed in excess of two hundred such individuals.

These developments can best be interpreted in light of the classic writings of Max Weber (1867–1921). Weber's sociology is united by one overarching thematic element: the constant refrain of the nature, causes, and effects of rationalization, which he looked upon as the distinguishing feature of the modern era in the West. The concept *Rationalität* includes not only the development of technical-instrumental processes based upon empirically grounded and efficiently directed reason (*Zweckrationalität*), but also rationalization of values (*Wertrationalität*). The opposite side of the rationalization process is the "disenchantment of the world" (*Entzauberung der Welt*), so that the extent and direction of rationalization are measured negatively in terms of the extent to which magical elements of thought are displaced (Swatos, 1981). It is a condition of survival for established institutions to confront these fundamental changes and adjust to their requirements.

Within this larger pattern the growth of modern, rational-legal bureaucracy was seen by Weber as a key element. Indeed, Weber hinted that bureaucracy is perhaps the characteristic structural feature of the modern age, since its presence is so tenacious. He wrote:

> History shows that whenever bureaucracy gained the upper hand as in [some ancient civilizations], it did not disappear again unless in the course of the total collapse of the supporting culture. . . . In contrast to these older forms, modern bureaucracy has one characteristic which makes its 'escape proof' nature much more definite: rational specialization and training. (Weber, 1978, p. 1401)

Weber saw the power of bureaucrats as resting on knowledge of two kinds: their technical know-how, acquired through specialized training, and their monopoly of official information, which provides the bureaucrat with the facts on which decisions can be based (ibid., pp. 1417–1418).

Although bureaucracy achieves its fullest expression in the administrative apparatus of the state, Weber broke new ground in recognizing that the same basic process is at work in all major structures of society—the mass political party, the business firm, the trade union, and, not least important, the church. In the particular case of the church, however, he noted that in addition to rational and pragmatic considerations, there is a second major source of bureaucratic authority. Bureaucrats are validated in part by their indirect relation to the charismatic power of an individual, one who was set apart from ordinary men and treated as endowed with superhuman, or at least specifically exceptional, powers or qualities. Ecclesiastical structures are created in the first place out of a desire to "routinize" this charisma, once the founding leader is no longer physically present. Bureaucracy, then, is a further extension of this "routinization."

While one can find examples of religious bureaucracy at all periods of history, including ancient times (ibid., pp. 476–477), such structures took on new significance under the impact of forces associated with modernism, especially ones coming to the fore in the nineteenth century. In discussing this, Weber laid special stress on the spread of democratic values and behavior, involving the democratic emphasis on equal rights, universal accessibility of office, and a general leveling of the governed by the governing group. He viewed such changes as exerting a major pressure on the Roman Catholic church, tending there to undercut the power of mediating structures that had long existed between the leadership group in Rome and the mass of the faithful. The rise of bureaucracy in the Catholic church, even though underway for centuries, thus reached its zenith in the mid-nineteenth century under Pius IX and, especially, following the Vatican Council of 1867 (ibid., p. 986).

Weber's thought on these topics is marked by contextual richness and suggestiveness, and it is not surprising that more recent analysts of religious organization (e.g., Cox, 1967) in many cases have adopted an essentially Weberian approach. In the course of their efforts, Weber's original insights have been extended and, to a degree, modified. His writings have been accepted as a prelude, not a coda, to scientific understanding.

One issue that has attracted a good deal of attention is whether Weber's notions of authority are adequate to account for the great prevalence of bureaucracy in American church life. Analysts tend to agree that Weber's typology of authority is useful without serious modification in assessing the Roman Catholic, Episcopal, and Lutheran churches, in all of which the position of the church executive is validated in both canon law and accepted principles of hierarchy. Nevertheless, problems arise in attempting to apply Weber's constructs to the "free church" tradition, including the Baptist, Congregational (United Church of Christ), Reformed, and several other denominations. Here the principle of hierarchy is rejected, and claims to legitimacy on the part of all appointive officers above the local congregational level are fragile and vulnerable to challenge. Ever present for national officials is the grim prospect that their position may be attacked from within the church on the basis of pervasive antibureaucratic norms and, in the limiting case, that their office may be abolished outright. Yet, surprisingly, Paul M. Harrison (1959) found that the position of staff executives at the national level in one such church, the American Baptist Convention, is typically quite secure. In accounting for this strength, Harrison emphasized that "free church bureaucrats" may survive indefinitely insofar as they can acquire a "quasi-charismatic" authority. To achieve this they shrewdly manipulate the "informal system of power in the church, thereby acting in accordance with the standard procedures of rational organization without admitting or even recognizing that they are doing so" (Harrison, 1959, p. 212).

Conclusions broadly in line with Harrison's were arrived at by James R. Wood (1981) on the basis of a study of several Protestant denominations during the civil rights era of the 1960s. Wood was interested in finding out how church executives managed to legitimize their role under conditions of uncertain support by the rank and file and of outright opposition from some quarters. Seeking to win compliance for civil rights actions that were quite radical from the standpoint of traditional doctrine and social teaching, the executives were found to manipulate symbols that derived from the more prophetic elements of the Christian faith. Rank-and-file church members in most cases were aware of these tenets in an abstract sense but were inclined to "forget" their potential applicability, especially during the long periods of relative social peace in the United States. Although initially quite distressed by and apprehensive about the actions of church executives in behalf of racial justice, church members did not in most cases elect to quit the church, and so provided the executives time to play a critical "reminding" role. The members' attention was held "long enough for reflection on the core values of the organization to change their evaluation" (Wood, 1981, p. 92). Thus, it was not any intrinsic belief in the legality of the executives' pronouncements and actions that brought about the ultimate compliance among the rank and file; instead, it was a consequence of changes that occurred in the members' own perceptions and attitudes.

Another theme found in the literature is the potential for bureaucrats to exert a pronounced conservatizing influence on internal church affairs and also on the wider society in the name of church practice and moral views. Harrison made this potential a kind of leitmotif in his treatment of the American Baptist Convention. As he pictures it, the bureaucracy is not particularly interested in "real achievement" as long as objective and impressive results are continuously presented to the constituency. In the process, original goals become displaced by the methods of bureaucratic procedure. Similarly, John Wilson (1978), in a survey of several American church bodies, concluded that the very nature of bureaucracy, with its emphasis on routine, predictability, and set procedures, tends to inhibit the desire to change and instead encourages a moderate position on all issues. (It should be noted, however, that this is only a tendency, and one that can be offset to a large degree, as will be suggested later in this discussion.)

The literature also contains evidence of a fairly conservative, status-conscious response on the part of some elective and appointive church executives in their behavior vis-à-vis the wider external environment. I have examined the behavior of the Protestant Council of New York City during the 1950s and early 1960s—a critical period for Protestantism in that city (Pratt, 1970). Beginning around 1900 New York experienced a long, steady slide in church membership and an apparent loss of Protestant "presence" in the city's social, cultural, and political affairs. By the 1950s Protestant leaders—especially those of the mainly white, "old stock" denominations that largely comprised the Protestant Council's constituency—were beginning to experience feelings of status anxiety and threat. Applying the distinction between manifest and latent function drawn from the work of Robert K. Merton (1957), I suggested that the council's manifest role in these years remained that of assisting its constituent churches toward the fulfillment of their essentially "religious" functions (religious education, evangelism, social education and action, chaplaincy programs, and so forth). In the 1950s, however, council executives began as well to act in ways supportive of a major latent function, namely, to arrest the long slide in Protestant political and social status. This aim was pursued by a vigorous program of political intervention (a "Protestant quota" was demanded of city officials in making appointments to high-level city offices and judgeships) and by a well-publicized campaign of moral uplift (featuring sponsorship of annual "Family of Man" dinners at which prominent government officials, including U.S. presidents, were invited to speak).

A traditional bureaucracy, such as that in the Roman Catholic church, may have special reasons for feeling threatened when developments associated with the modern age impinge on its sphere of action. A classic instance of bureaucratic defensiveness, documented in the works of Gibson Winter (1968), Louis J. Putz (1956), and John Tracy Ellis (1969), was the behavior of the Vatican and of certain elements in the American Catholic hierarchy in connection with the decision to form the National Catholic Conference. This organization was successor to the National Catholic War Council (NCWC), which had been organized in 1917, when the United States entered World War I. The NCWC's work won wide approval at all levels in the American church, and at the war's end a number of Catholic leaders saw an opportunity to extend these successes into the postwar era. Cardinal Gibbons, the special delegate of the Holy See in the United States, won the Vatican's initial approval to establish the council on a regular, permanent basis, and at a meeting in September 1919 the American bishops met and voted the new organization into existence. Yet, by its very nature the NCWC had represented a significant form of centralization, and its work came to be viewed in some quarters as a threat to established patterns of local jurisdiction and authority. A few dissident American bishops protested to Rome, and in 1922 the newly installed pontiff, Pius XI, proved to be highly receptive to their complaints. The pope nearly dissolved the whole structure, and was dissuaded from doing so only on the basis of urgent pleas from other members of the American hierarchy who dispatched representatives to Rome to counter the work of their colleagues. The pope did finally allow the fledgling organization to endure, but decreed that its role must be drastically modified: as a means of preventing the growth of a permanent bureaucracy its agents could hold office only from meeting to meeting, and the word *Council* in the original name was changed to the less ominous *Conference*. The organization has long since weathered these early storms and secured a place for itself in the American Catholic church. Yet, its early trials illustrate the kinds of problems that can occur, and more recent examples would not be difficult to find.

It would be misleading, however, to suggest that religious bureaucracy inevitably works to foster a defensive, status-preserving posture in the church. In fact, such bureaucracies can promote a variety of policy tendencies, ranging from left to right on the political spectrum, depending on situational factors. Weber nowhere in his writing gave systematic attention to the possibility of a radicalizing bureaucracy (Swatos, 1981), yet his writings are replete with hints that such a structure may emerge given the right circumstances. He pointed out that a central value system—and in the case of a church this would include the authority of scripture and of church tradition and doctrine—may evoke varying degrees of commitment among church participants;

this makes it possible for charismatic sensitivity to slumber within the rational-legal and traditional legitimations of authority. Such charismatic elements may exist in segregated form within a church polity or in a diffuse half-life within the larger body of believers, there awaiting the proper constellation of external events to be "transformed into incandescence" (Shils, 1975, pp. 122, 130). The work of Wood (1981) in this connection has already been noted.

Just such a set of events occurred during the civil rights era of the 1960s. I have presented evidence (Pratt, 1972) that by the 1950s a church bureaucracy with pronounced liberal-to-radical tendencies existed in a kind of segregated place within American Protestantism, namely, at the headquarters of the National Council of Churches in New York. In "normal" times the impact of whatever radical tendencies might have existed at this level were effectively insulated from the local level in American Protestantism, where real authority tends to be centered. These normal expectations were shattered, however, as the civil rights revolution gained momentum, especially following the arrest in Birmingham, Alabama, of Martin Luther King, Jr., after civil rights demonstrations there in 1963. Appointive executives of the council together with one or two elective denominational leaders took the lead in forcing through to adoption a dramatic series of civil rights resolutions and then in mobilizing substantial resources in behalf of further initiatives. Without these efforts, support for civil rights among the mainly white Protestant church bodies of the United States would scarcely have been so forceful or sustained as it was.

From these and other writings reported on in the literature on organized religion one sees that the Weberian tradition remains a vital stream. Although Weber has often been interpreted as presenting a fairly mechanistic, machine-model view of bureaucracy and a monistic view of its wider societal impact, the present discussion should help to dispel any such impressions. Weber's thought on bureaucracy in fact contains much nuance and suggestive power. Clearly, bureaucracy has had major significance for religious bodies in the twentieth century, with consequences both direct and indirect, concrete as well as subtle. At the same time, however, no single model or construct seems entirely adequate to convey the complex patterns of behavior that tend to ensue when a bureaucratic dynamic is introduced into established religious structures.

BIBLIOGRAPHY

Cox, Harvey G. "The 'New Breed' in American Churches: Sources of Social Activism in American Religion." *Daedalus* 96 (Winter 1967): 135–150.

Ellis, John Tracy. *American Catholicism.* 2d ed. Chicago, 1969.

Harrison, Paul M. *Authority and Power in the Free Church Tradition.* Princeton, 1959.

Merton, Robert K. *Social Theory and Social Structure.* Rev. ed. 1957. Reprint, New York, 1968.

Pratt, Henry J. "Politics, Status and the Organization of Ethnic Minority Group Interests: The Case of the New York Protestants." *Polity: The Journal of the Northeastern Political Science Association* 3 (Winter 1970): 222–246.

Pratt, Henry J. *The Liberalization of American Protestantism: A Case Study in Complex Organizations.* Detroit, 1972.

Putz, Louis J., ed. *The Catholic Church, U.S.A.* Chicago, 1956.

Shils, Edward. *Center and Periphery: Essays in Macrosociology.* Chicago, 1975.

Swatos, William H. "The Disenchantment of Charisma: A Weberian Assessment of Revolution in a Rationalized World." *Sociological Analysis* 42 (Summer 1981): 119–136.

Weber, Max. *Economy and Society.* Edited by Guenther Ross and Claus Wittich; translated by Ephraim Fischoff et al. Berkeley, 1978.

Wilson, John. *Religion in American Society: The Effective Presence.* Englewood Cliffs, N.J., 1978.

Winter, Gibson. *Religious Identity: A Study of Religious Organization.* New York. 1968.

Wood, James R. *Leadership in Voluntary Organizations: The Controversy over Social Action in Protestant Churches.* New Brunswick, N.J., 1981.

HENRY J. PRATT

BURIAL. *See* Funeral Rites.

BURIAT RELIGION. The Buriats, northern Mongols, are the most significant minority native to eastern Siberia (353,000 in 1979; in 1970, 179,000 were living in the Buriat Autonomous Socialist Republic, the others are located primarily in the Buriat National Districts). They are not a homogeneous body; there are two cultural extremes, between which exists a range of intermediate groups.

The western or Cisbaikalian extreme is represented by the Ekhirit-Bulagat tribe, forest dwellers who are engaged in hunting and fishing. Although they were isolated from the Mongolian empire, they had begun to practice livestock breeding through the influence of Mongolian émigrées at the time of the arrival of Russian cossacks in the mid-seventeenth century. After colonization and sedentarization, their segmentary clan structure survived more ideologically than practically. Shamanism has remained strong there up to the present, successfully resisting the assaults of lamaist propaganda and affected only superficially by Orthodox Christianity.

The eastern or Transbaikalian extreme is represented

by the Khori, who, as a result of Mongolian civil wars during the sixteenth and seventeenth centuries, settled with their herds in the steppes. They were treated favorably by the rulers of the Russian empire because of their strategic position in relation to the Chinese empire. Beginning in the eighteenth century, lamaism, which had come from Mongolia, spread rapidly. While lamaism favored the ideals of nomadic pastoralism and developed the tendency toward a centralizing hierarchy, it was forced to adapt its practice to traditional shamanic forms and to fight the power of the shamans themselves.

Shamanism is a constituent element of traditional Buriat society. Within the framework of the clan institution, due to its control of the spirits (which originate from souls), it assures a mediation between man and the supernatural concerning access to natural resources, thereby assuring a general regulation of societal life, transcending by far the individual shaman and his activity. Many authors have tended to exaggerate the role of the shaman's personality and to construct an independent and rigid pantheon of spirits fundamentally linked with daily tribal life. The shamanic institution and its practice varies according to the modes of subsistence and society and associated exterior influences. Three kinds can be distinguished, the second being the only well-documented one.

The Hunter's Shamanism. The first type of shamanism is associated with hunting. Animals, conceived as being organized in exogamic clans maintain relations of alliance and vengeance that are analogous to those that obtain between humans. Hunter and shaman are each in his own way similar to the son-in-law who takes a wife and gives a sister: in return for the game meat taken from the forest spirits, the hunter feeds the animal spirits (*ongons*); in return for the living human and animal souls obtained from the corresponding spirits, the shaman restores the souls of the deceased to their world, whence his role in birth and death. [*See* Ongon.]

Any misbehavior or infraction entails sanctions that always affect biological life, resulting in such occurrences as intemperate weather, absence of game, sickness, and death. Because the soul is indispensable to bodily life, it is the shaman's lot to conduct preventative and restorative mediations. With the help of the personal allies he has made among human and animal spirits, he symbolically travels and meets the trouble-making spirits in order to negotiate a return to order. Invested to serve his clan, the shaman may be led to act against other clans (by diverting game away from them, afflicting them with sickness) and become the symbolic architect of wars.

The Cattle Breeder's Shamanism. The second and best-documented type of shamanism is found among those of the Ekhirit-Bulagat tribe who breed cattle. The essential part of relations between the human and spirit worlds consists of relations between the living and the dead. Subsistence is dependent upon one's ancestors *(übged)*, who are "masters" *(ezen)* of the mountains dominating the clan territory. These ancestors legitimize and protect the economic life of their descendants and punish them with biological harm for every breach of clan ethics. In the *tailghan* sacrifices (of mares or sheep) offered by each clan to its ancestors, the shaman participates as a member of the clan.

The principal causes for recourse to shamanic mediation are accidents in the realm of filiation ties and rules, that is, anything that affects patrilineal continuity: sterility, difficult childbirth, childhood illness, and even conjugal disputes and women's flights or escapades that entail the risk, for a man, not to have any descendants. (According to legend, shamanism originated from a wife who ran off.) Those involved must both be cured during their lifetime and spared frustration that would incite them to inflict harm after their death. Private sacrifices *(khereg)* are offered to their souls after death, first to neutralize and soothe them and then to transform them into *zayaan*. These spirits are the exceptional dead (of which the positive examples are the great shamans, warriors, or hunters), who govern the fate of men and are of prime importance in the religious practice. The ordinary dead support their descendants in wars against other clans; a clan without a shaman to intervene by mediating with its dead takes recourse to flight rather than expose itself to combat. In the pastoral setting, however, the restorative activities of the shaman generally prevail over the offensive ones.

The shaman. Among the Ekhirit-Bulagats, in order to become a shaman *(böö)* one must have a shaman "essence" *(udkha)*, that is, a genetically transmitted right, which is evidenced by the existence of shamans among one's ancestors. It is imperative for one of the descendants of a shamanic line to become a shaman so that the ancestor shamans can have a representative on earth. Equally important is that the candidate demonstrate his capability in order to be supported and invested by his people. Finally, although gender is proclaimed irrelevant, male shamans are much more numerous than female shamans (*udaghans*); patrilineal rule is compulsory.

A shaman's career generally is decided at adolescence, under a certain amount of pressure from the boy's relatives. Fainting fits, visions, flights or escapades, and anorexia called *khüdkhe* ("disordered state") are interpreted as signs that the shaman is familiarizing himself with the spirits under the aegis of his ancestors. He trains in the shamanic manner of singing and gesticulating (in a lugubrious voice with animal-like cries, sighs and gasping fits, leaping, swaying, etc., representing the voyage to the spirit world) and imitates or assists experienced shamans for several years. At the end of this apprenticeship, he is invested by his community through a rite (called *ughaalgha*) in which he receives his accoutrements (costume, drum, etc). This rite consists of symbolically "reanimating" the shaman, making him both spirit and human, dead and alive. It is this amalgamation of the two modes of being that permits him to ensure mediation. He then takes an oath to serve his people, who will monitor him closely in this work and who will not hesitate to replace or do away with him should they become dissatisfied.

Without an "essence" one still can become a shaman if one has numerous deceased relatives, particularly if one relative was struck dead by lightning, a process that energizes a new essence. His ability would then have to be demonstrated. Should the obligation to become a shaman be perceived as unbearable by the sole descendant of a line, the shamanic role nevertheless provides an excellent opportunity for an individual to emerge, especially for women. Female shamans whose vocations are thwarted become the most formidable "fates" *(zayaan)* upon death. In addition, those who are not shamans occasionally shamanize, either for their own psychic needs or within the framework of collective peregrinations *(böölööšen* or *naĭguur)* while trying to face natural disasters or pressures of acculturation.

The principal moments of the shamanic séance are (1) the censing of the area with the smoke of burning spruce bark (the spruce, known to the Buriats as *žodoo,* is the symbol of the shaman's function) in order to effect the shaman's entrance into sacred space-time; (2) the incorporation of auxiliary spirits; (3) the transcendent vision, in which the shaman identifies the spirit responsible for the disturbance; (4) the journey of the soul to the realm of the spirit in question in order to negotiate with him; (5) a sacrifice in accordance with his wishes; and (6) general divination. Following the séance, the shaman resumes his normal life.

The sky creators and their founding sons. If the spirits of the deceased rule over daily life, the *tengeris* (or *tengris*; "skies," a class of supernatural beings) creators and predestinators of humans, appear in the background. They are divided into opposite camps, the fifty-five White Tengeris of the West (or Right), whose leader is considered older, and the forty-four Black Tengeris of the East (or Left), whose leader is considered younger. This division, which illustrates the conflict between the Elder and the Younger, on the one hand denotes the principle of clan segmentation (and perhaps an ancient organization by moieties); on the other hand, it denotes the principle of dualistic power, viewed as a conflict between the established authority (symbolized by the elder) and the challenge to that authority (symbolized by the younger). The elder represents the clan institution, which has inherited legitimate authority but no real power; the younger represents the shamanic institution, which has real power but must subordinate the exercise of its function to the interests of the clan and which has a social position, resting on ability, that is always susceptible to being challenged (whence the fact that the shaman is both indispensable to the clan and feared by it at the same time on account of his ability to manipulate the powers of the spirits).

The first legendary shaman carried the adjective *khara* ("black") in his name. It seems that the notion of a white shaman is an artificial creation that resulted from religious acculturation or was a reaction against it: an examination of the facts reveals the nonexistence of white shamans as such. While the *tengeris* remain in the sky, expressing themselves through atmospheric phenomena, their sons descend to the earth, as did Buxa Noyon the Bull Lord, founder of the Ekhirit-Bulagat tribe; the epic hero Geser, founder of the rules of marriage; and the various "kings" *(khad)* of mountains and waters. [*See* Geser *and* Tengri.]

Marginalized Shamanism. The third kind of Buriat shamanism is that which survived in the lamaist regions in spite of persecution (which occurred at the beginning of the nineteenth century, primarily in the regions of Barguzin and Tunka). There the shaman is no longer a sort of "clan property." His role and status is marginalized; personal desire is the key motivator for becoming a shaman, and the door is open to women. Occasionally a family may have both a son who is a lama and a daughter who is a shaman. It is not unusual for one to contact a shaman to "call back the soul" *(hünehe kharyuulkha)* robbed from a sick person by a spirit after a lama's attempt has failed, for the shaman is still considered the more capable of succeeding.

The biggest changes affect the conception of the supernatural world (which continues to expand and develop as a hierarchy) and the social significance of rituals. The faces of the celestial *tengeris* are becoming more individualistic, borrowing traits from lamaist deities and occasionally becoming merged with them. It is to them and no longer to ancestral spirits that milk offerings and prayers are directed in order to obtain an increase in offspring and livestock. Some new faces appear, such as that of Erlik, master of the world of the dead. Some are transformed, like the spirit of the hearth fire, represented west of Lake Baikal by a couple worshiped by all hearths of the same clan; in the east this couple becomes an independent woman, *tengeri* or khan of the fire, worshiped separately by each family. [*See* Erlik.]

To compete with the clan sacrifices *(tailghan)*, the lamas organize great bloodless rituals *(oboo)*, which are open to a large parochial community and are held on a mountain summit. The lamaist practice threatens to eliminate or at least to overtake the shamanic practice on all levels (through control over pastoral space and daily life, divination, medicine, and magical demonstrations). Judging from the actual relics, it is clear that the lamas have succeeded only superficially. The establishment of an actual Buriat Lamaist church in Transbaikalia was encouraged by the Russian Empire in order to avoid dependence on Mongolia and hence on China; in fact, lamaism obtained a strong sociopolitical position but was nearly emptied of all Buddhist content. Comparatively, in the agricultural regions of Cisbaikalia, Orthodox Christianity has had only a superficial influence over the ritual seasons (for example, the cults of Saint Nicholas and other saints). Along with the official existence of the lamaist monastery at Ivolga, the cult of Maydar (Maitreya), the future Buddha, seems to be the only living practice today; it is supported by a kind of nationalistic prophesying, but it is very limited geographically.

The Adaptation of Shamanism. Organically linked with a noncentralized type of society, pragmatic in its own principle, deriving its power from simple spirits, turning each shaman into a rival of others, shamanism is vulnerable to every centralizing influence and to the penetration of any dogma that implies transcendental entities and is represented by a constituent clerical body. This weakness is at the same time a strength: shamanism can adapt. The spirits are brought into line with current tastes (for example, the souls of revolutionaries who died tragically, victims of the Second World War), whereas in the sky, such a figure as Lenin deliberates with the *tengeris* concerning world affairs. Despite these innovations, illness, especially children's illness, remains the principal occasion for true shamanic intervention. Free from all liturgy and cultural servitude, based on flexibility and individual innovation, the shaman's practice is all but formalist and may take place in secrecy. Communication with the dead plays a role in the awareness of ethnic identity; certain ritualistic details, like the drops of alcohol poured at the inauguration of all feasts, or like the ribbons hung on trees growing through a hill or near a thermal spring, have become true cultural traits of the Buriats.

[*See also* Southern Siberian Religions *and* Shamanism, *article on* Siberian and Inner Asian Shamanism.]

BIBLIOGRAPHY

Eliade, Mircea. *Shamanism: Archaic Techniques of Ecstasy* (1951). Princeton, 1964. The only general overview on shamanism covering a wide range of peoples. Includes extensive data on the Buriats.

Khangalov, M. N. *Sobranie sochinenii.* 3 vols. Ulan-Ude, 1958–1960. A remarkable compendium of data gathered at the end of the nineteenth and beginning of the twentieth century in the regions to the west of Lake Baikal by a highly learned Buriat authority on shamanism.

Lamaizm v Buriatii XVIII–nachala XX veka: Struktura i sotsial'naia rol' kul'tovoi sistemy. Novosibirsk, 1983. An excellent study of the conflicts and accommodations between lamaism and shamanism in Transbaikalia during the eighteenth, nineteenth, and twentieth centuries.

Manzhigeev, I. A. *Buriatskie shamanisticheskie i doshamanisticheskie terminy.* Moscow, 1978. Presents, in the form of a glossary, the notable personalities and concepts of Buriat shamanism and mythology.

Mikhailov, T. M. *Iz istorii buriatskogo shamanizma (s drevneishikh vremen po XVIII v.).* Novosibirsk, 1980. A history of Buriat shamanism, treated as a discrete religious system. Balances both critical and theoretical approaches.

Sandschejew, Garma. "Weltanschauung und Schamanismus der Alaren-Burjaten," *Anthropos* 22 (1927): 576–613, 933–955; 23 (1928): 538–560, 967–986. A richly informative panorama of the shamanism of the Alar Buriats (west of Lake Baikal) based on the personal observations of the author.

ROBERTE HAMAYON
Translated from French by Sherri L. Granka

BURMESE RELIGION. The Burmese people, for the purpose of this article, are the majority population of the Socialist Republic of the Union of Burma, the westernmost country of mainland Southeast Asia. The language they speak is Burmese (or Arakanese, its most important dialect variant), and they are often called Burmans. The word *Burmese* is reserved for the total population of this country, including "tribal" minority peoples (chiefly residing in the mountains and practicing religions other than those of the Burmans), the Tai-speaking Shan of the eastern plateau (the Shan State), and the Austroasiatic-speaking Mon of southern Burma. The traditional religion of the Shan and Mon is the same Theravāda Buddhism as that of the Burmans, although with some variation peculiar to themselves. The Burmese made their first appearance in history about the tenth century of the common era.

Any Burman will tell you that this traditional religion is Theravāda Buddhism, although a small minority of Burmese are not themselves Buddhists. It is sometimes alleged that to be Burmese is to be a Buddhist. What is really at issue is the fact that the traditional social and cultural institutions of the Burmese, now and historically, are found in large measure in the social, political, and ideological fabric of Buddhist doctrine, so that even non-Buddhist Burmese recognize the centrality of Buddhism to their social cultural identity.

There is a good deal about Burmese Buddhism that is distinctive. In the first place, there is a specifically Burmese tradition in the way Buddhism is interpreted and practiced. Burmese Buddhism is no more deviant from a supposed pristine scriptural norm than any past or present form of the religion. In addition, the Burmese also practice a cult of service to various spirits (Spiro, 1967). This cult exists both at the national level as a formal institution of the former Burmese monarchy (the cult of the Thirty-seven Lords (*nats*), the spirit guardians of the kingdom) and locally with regard to spirits associated with features of the landscape and with family lines and administrative jurisdictions as their proper domains *(nat)*, as well as homeless ghosts, demons, and so on. Not only are the details of belief and practice of these cults (sometimes including the serving of killed animals and alcoholic spirits to these beings) not to be found in the Buddhist scriptures or commentaries, but it is also the case that the practices of this cult are often at odds with the Buddhist behavioral precepts. Burmese themselves, while insisting that they are committed Buddhists, see a contradiction between what some authors have therefore called these two different religions. It will be a major task of this article to try to resolve this issue.

Such facts have led many to speak of a syncretic Burmese religion rather than of Buddhism, some of them purporting to see Buddhism as a mere veneer. However, while Burmese religion consists of the two "cults," careful consideration of the full range of canonical Buddhism shows that the religion of the Burmese is simply Buddhism, and that the conflict between the two cults has a basis in paradoxes within canonical Buddhism itself. Nor is it sufficient to say that Buddhism, being ultimately concerned with long-term, transcendental goals, provides no means of immediately quelling one's fears and anxieties about wordly suffering, which the cult of spirits serves specifically to alleviate.

There is ample scriptural basis for the idea that it is the positive duty of authority, in particular of a proper Buddhist monarch, to subdue, by conversion, subversion, or other means, whatever spirit forces may be thought to exist as a threat to the conditions in which Buddhism, its doctrine, practice, and monastic order (Skt., *saṃgha;* Pali, *sangha*) may flourish in society. It is therefore the king's duty, and, by extension of his authority, that of all secular persons in his jurisdiction, to protect religion by dealing with potentially harmful spirit agencies. Buddhism presupposes the existence of various classes of spiritural beings, including, of course, gods (*devas*, *devatas*), in its brahmanically derived cosmology, so that it has no need to specify completely either their natures or how to deal with them. That is left to local tradition, and it is unsurprising that, consequently—since beliefs have to come from somewhere—there is in Burma a close relationship between the leading ideas of the spirit cult within Buddhism and the leading ideas of pre-Buddhist animism as evidenced in the traditional religions of neighboring non-Buddhist tribal peoples. Syncretism that may well be, but it is nevertheless canonically motivated, even positively enjoined. Here arises the first paradox.

The means for dealing with whatever spirit agencies may exist are to be arrived at according to what local tradition says of these various spirits. In fact, these demands often require one to act contrary to Buddhist precepts of Right Action. This is no more problematical than the inherent tension (Tambiah, 1976, pp. 22–23) in the role of a Buddhist monarch, who, creating and maintaining the conditions wherein religion can flourish, must be responsible for acts of violence, as in war and the punishment of crime. The consequence, in both cases, is ambivalence, defining Buddhism as the Middle Way.

In traditional Burma the king was expected ideally to conform to the Theravāda version of the *bodhisattva* idea. Yet the king was also one of the "five evils," along with war, pestilence, spirit *nats*, and the like; indeed, as a peremptory, if not arbitrary, "lord," a king was himself, not altogether metaphorically, a *nat*. Although he had to have earned enormous previous merit in order to now have the entire order as his field of merit (a field so productive that he might look forward to future Buddhahood), it was also incumbent upon him, as the *bodhisattva (hpaya:laun)* ideal might suggest, to take on a burden of demerit in the course of carrying out his obligations. This is so for the *cakravartin* (Pali, *cakkavatti*), the Wheel-turning World Conqueror, that ideal *min:laung* (immanent king) or *hpaya:laung*, who serves as the model not so much for the general run of Buddhist kings as for what may be called a major Buddhist throne or monarchical lineage and for the *ekarāja*, the "sovereign king" who rules righteously, the actual model for the ordinary Buddhist monarch depicted in such Burmese court manuals as *Hywei Nan: Thoun: Wohara Abhidān* (Maung Maung Tin, 1979).

The cult of spirits is also at once enjoined and disparaged by Buddhism. On the one hand there are the aforementioned canonical precedents and injunctions. On the other hand, just as regional *nat* cults and messianic forms of Buddhism tend to be suppressed by the state because they imply the need to redress social disorder and constitute a challenge to a state and its moral legitimacy, so also from the point of view of an orthodox *sangha,* the need for extracanonical cult practices addressed to spirits is held to imply that religion is not flourishing, so that the world of spirits is not properly under control and religion is not, of itself, adequate for protection against them. This is not canonically unthinkable, but the order quite reasonably wishes to see itself as pure and vigorous, just as, indeed, government desires its own legitimacy to be upheld by the view that religion is in good order.

Then too, there is the positive injunction, fully canonical, to bring about the end of wrong action. Since much of what constitutes wrong action has to do with causing suffering to other beings (and the spirits are often cast in such a role), it is not only proper to try to get agents of suffering to desist, it is positively enjoined to do so. Thus, both the existence of spirit cults and the ambivalence with which Burmese Buddhists view these cults is well within the scope of canonical Buddhist motivation and rationalization.

The Nats. The chief object of the cult of spirits in Burma are the *nat*s, of which there are numerous kinds. The first distinction is that between the *upapāti nat* and the *mei?hsa nat,* that is, between the *deva* and *devata:* respectively, denizens of the heavens atop Mount Meru, essentially of Brahmanic origin, and the many kinds of local spirits. The words *upapāti* and *mei?hsa* derive from Pali terms meaning "well born" and "[born owing to] evildoing." This distinction does not indicate that all of the second kind are of purely indigenous origin. In fact, many of the *mei?hsa nat*s belong to Indian-derived categories of tree spirits (*you?hka-zou;* from Pali, *rukkha,* "tree," and Burmese *sou:,* "to rule or govern," equivalent to Indian *yakkhas*) and demons (e.g., Burmese *goun-ban,* from Pali, *kumbhaṇḍa*), although technically, demons and ogres, being without fixed abodes or at least without proper domains, are not *nat*s. Nor should it be thought that all *mei?hsa nat*s are inherently malevolent, in the sense of being anti-Buddhist. The potential malevolence of proper *nat*s comes from two facts: the manner of their creation and/or the fact that they are lords of their perspective domains, either by nature or by royal appointment *(amein.do).* Indeed, most of the appointed *nat*s, at least, are guardian spirits of the whole country, of regions, villages, families, households, and individuals. As such, they are expected to protect these various levels of jurisdiction of the nation as a Buddhist (originally monarchical) entity, and so they serve as guardians of religion. This is so to the extent that some *nat*s, speaking through mediums, will take their "subjects" to task for not living according to Buddhist precepts.

The *nat*s that are above all the objects of a formally organized cult are the Thirty-seven Lords. There are more than thirty-seven of these, but the number thirty-seven is dictated by the consideration that ideally a Buddhist kingdom should be organized as a microcosm of a proper portion of the Buddhist view of the universe as a whole in order that the proportion between merit and status-power characteristic of the universe as a whole be mirrored in the political and social hierarchies of a Buddhist kingdom. The reason for this organization appears to be that only thus will the economy of merit-seeking necessary to an orderly Buddhist society be effected. Viewed secularly, the king is to his domain as the god Indra (Pali, Sakka; Skt., Śakra; from which Burm. Thagya: [Min:]) is to his heaven, Tāvatiṃsa (Tawadeintha). Moreover, as Indra is ultimate secular ruler in the world at large, so a king aspiring to the state of *cakkavatti,* the ideal occupant of a Buddhist throne, should have kingdoms under him, on the same galactic principle of merit hierarchy. Hence, the hypothetical ideal organization of the kingdom, in the Burmese (and Mon) view, is a center surrounded by thirty-two subordinate realms, just as Indra at his ultimate cosmic center has thirty-two *devata*s and their realms as his subordinates. This makes thirty-three; to these are added the Four Kings (*cātummahārājā,* or *lokapāla,* Quarter Guardians) of the heaven immediately between Indra's and the world of men, yielding thirty-seven.

However, from the reign of Kyanzittha (fl. 1084–1113) the kings of Burma were *dhammarājika* monarchs. That is, while not entirely eschewing various sorts of symbolic identification with one or other Brahmanic god (Kyanzittha himself with Viṣṇu), as Buddhist kings they took as their ideal symbolic model a *cakkavatti* not after the fashion of a conquering king who (re)turns to the center of the cosmic wheel having reached to its rim *(cakkavāla),* but rather after the fashion of the Buddha, who, in preaching his doctrine to men, is said to have turned, or set in motion, the "Wheel of Dhamma" (ultimate principle or law). Nevertheless, the god-centered model for kingship had somehow to be realized. This was done by having a sort of spirit kingship of royally appointed guardians in parallel, so to speak, with human kingship, the system of Thirty-seven Lords.

It is Sakka himself who is chief among these thirty-seven, but, as he is in his paradise atop Mount Meru (Burm., Myin:mou Taun), the more immediate head of this group is Min: Maha-giri, the king or lord of the great mountain, who resides atop Mount Poppa, a prominent and sacred hill in the neighborhood of Pagan, the first Burmese capital (tenth to thirteenth century). Mount Poppa served as the local analog of Meru and its placement relative to the capital/center of the kingdom was in the sacred southeastern direction, the directional corner most proper, for instance, to Buddhist and *nat* shrines in a house. In spite of a great deal of literature suggesting that in the indianized kingdoms of Southeast Asia the symbolic sacred mountain was located in the center of the capitals, in Burma at least, the mountain's symbolic effectiveness required that it be outside, at the center of some even larger domain properly containing the kingdom. Min: Maha-giri serves as guardian of the kingdom as a whole, more particularly as the guardian of the palace, and, by extension, of every house in the kingdom, where, as Ein-hte: Min: Maha-giri ("lord of the great mountain within the house"), he is represented at a shrine in the form of a coconut (representing a head) bound with a red scarf.

The Maha-giri *nat* seems to have had an indigenous origin, perhaps overlain by brahmanic (specifically, Śaiva) influences during the time of the Pyu, the people whose kingdom preceded that of the Burmans in central and upper Burma. All thirty-seven, save Thagya: min:, are filled by a set of royal appointees, mostly male. Each of these was given a fief, each has an elaborate mythological history recording his or her origin, characteristics, and manner of being served. These *nat*s have various functions as guardian spirits, and most serve several of these. One at least has jurisdiction over certain fields in connection with her primary jurisdiction (shared with another) over Aungpinlei, the great artificial lake and former irrigation tank in the vicinity of present-day Mandalay, although generally, nature *nat*s, including *nat*s owning fields, local hills, trees, and the like, are not among the Thirty-seven Lords. Each town and its administrative jurisdiction (*myou.* refers to both without distinguishing between them) and each village has its official guardian *nat,* and every person has what is called a *mizainhpa-zain nat,* that is, a guardian inherited from parents (*mihpa,* "mother-father"). This should not be interpreted as one from the "side" of each parent; there ought to be only one for each person. Indeed, the parental *nat*s derive their jurisdiction, as such, from their primary township charges.

In the time of the Burmese kingdom (until the final British conquest of 1885), virtually all persons belonged to one or other of three sumptuary classes: *kyun* (slaves, or rather, persons fully bound and without civil status), *athi* (persons whose duty of service to the king was essentially commutable by a head tax), and *ahmu.dan:* (persons hereditarily bound to specific civil or military state services—the so-called service classes, organized into "regiments"). *Athi* were generally under the civil jurisdiction of the place where they happened to live, hence under the jurisdiction of that place's guardian *nat. Ahmu.dan:* were supposed to be under the civil jurisdiction of the place where their regimental headquarters was located, a place where the lands assigned for their maintenance was also to be found. For the latter in particular, intermarriage with persons from different service groups was discouraged because it resulted in mixed civil and spirit jurisdictions, and of course, created difficulties in the proper keeping of the rolls of the service groups. For these reasons, for service people and even for *athi,* who were also subject to some service requirements, taxes, and census controls, there was a strong tendency toward local endogamy supported by numerous royal orders. These orders made it clear that part of what was intended was clear jurisdiction, and that unambiguous *nat* jurisdiction was included in this. The system of *mizainhpa-zain nat*s has its origins in this set of considerations. Many people also have a wholly individual guardian *nat* (and in fact six *deva*s and six other guardians who may or may not be of the Thirty-seven), but almost nothing is known about these *kou-zaun.* (self-protection) *nat*s.

In order to understand how the Thirty-seven Lords were created, it is necessary to explain the concept of *asein-thei,* a "green" (i.e., unprepared) death, a widespread concept throughout both literate and tribal Southeast Asia. In ordinary circumstances, when someone is about to die he or she is expected to fix the mind upon his or her accumulated store of merit and demerit, and upon the teachings of religion. Friends, relatives and neighbors will, especially right after the funeral, read religious sermons aloud both to fix the minds of the bereaved so that their spirits will not wander from the body out of grief and shock, and so that the spirit of the deceased, if still about, may listen to *dhamma* (Skt., *dharma*) and so pass to a new birth according to his or her *kamma* (Skt., *karman*). When, however, someone dies violently, the spirit of the deceased will fly off in shock and anger and will be so unprepared that attention to merit, demerit, and *dhamma* will not be likely. In such a case, the deceased becomes a ghost, indeed a lost dissatisfied one, preying upon the living in its frustration (the most virulent perhaps are the women dying in childbirth).

When the person killed has been a person of great physical and/or charismatic power, and especially when he or she has been killed because of someone's deliberate treachery, the ghost created is especially dangerous. This type of ghost can, however, be dealt with if the king, who is in any event often the cause of the killing, issues a royal order *(amein.do)* appointing the spirit to an official position (in particular, one among the Thirty-seven Lords). The idea is no doubt related to the tribal notion that the virulent ghost created by the taking of an enemy's head can be converted to a servant of great power by the rites celebrating the head so taken. In any event, such was the origin of the Thirty-seven Lords; they were powerful guardian spirits of the kingdom and of religion, converted or subverted to the latter interests by royal appointment. They remain, however, a potential danger to the community, especially as lords, so that it remains necessary to placate them. It is to this end that the formal *nat* cult exists.

An additional function of this system of Thirty-seven Lords is that it replaces strictly local spirits that have regional jurisdiction with centrally appointed ones, thus replacing symbolic motivations to divisive regional loyalties with symbolic motivations to a sense of nationality for all Burmans. This is true not only because the lords are royal appointees, but also because the cult organization of all these *nat*s is nationwide and because it replaces strictly local cults (understood as going back to pacts made with local spirits by the ancestors of the local inhabitants, hereditarily binding upon these descendents and open to no one else).

The cult consists essentially of a system of mediums, *nat kado* (wives—but see Lehman, 1984, for male *nat*-wives), who, for various reasons, psychological for the most part, enjoy a relationship with one or more of the lords that obligates the mediums to serve them by dancing for them periodically in offering rituals. Such behavior occurs especially at one of the several annual *nat* celebrations of national importance (e.g., the Taunbyoun festival devoted to the two Taunbyoun brothers among the Thirty-seven—they were Muslims, so even Buddhists who have them as their *mizainhpa-zain nat* must abstain from pork), pilgrimage to which tends to create a sense of Burmese national self-identification. This sense parallels that resulting from pilgrimage to such nationally important Buddhist shrines as the Shwei Dagon pagoda at Rangoon and the Mahā Muni shrine, the shrine of the palladial Buddha image of the last several kings of Burma. These occasions, which, the great fairs aside, are often local and locally sponsored on an unscheduled basis, are known as *nat pwe:* (where *pwe:* refers to any show, display, or demonstration) or, especially in upper Burma, *nat kana:* (*kana:* refers to the temporary openwork bamboo shed in which these rites are held—*nat sin* in other places). The rituals consist of dances symbolic of the mythology of the lord in question, and of obeisances and offerings of fruits and other things at the altars upon which the figurines of various lords are ranged. It is common to speak of "worshiping" *nat* (*nat pu-zo,* from Pali, *pūjā; nat hyi.hkou:,* to bow down in adoration or homage). Technically, such terms are supposed to be reserved for the veneration of the Buddha, his order, and his relics, and obeisance to those persons (parents, elders, monks, teachers, and king and government as patron of religion) from whom one gets merit by example and by the act of merit sharing that follows all Buddhist rituals. This veneration is undertaken in order to validate their greater merit and apologize for possible offences *(gado)*. But the act is also performed (at least in its modified form of salutation by raising hands, palms together, to the forehead) toward any powerful or exalted persons (*nat*s included). The veneration is undertaken sometimes in flattery and out of fear of their power, but sometimes because all officials can be looked upon as extensions of government and because of the implicit correlation between charisma (*hpoun:,* from Pali, *puñña,* "merit-quality"), distinction *(goun),* and influence and authority *(o-za a-na),* on the one hand, and merit *(kuthou;* Pali, *kusala),* on the other. Properly speaking, *nat* are said to be "served" *(pa.tha.)* or "offered to" *(tin).* No Burmese Buddhist will ever talk of his involvement in *nat* service as *nat ba-tha* (from Pali, *bhāsa,* "doctrine").

Millenarianism. Yet another strand in Burmese religion is millenarian Buddhism. It combines magical-alchemical practices with meditational exercises and has a strong association with the aforementioned notion of the *min:laun-hpaya:laun* as a messianic Buddhist figure heralding the coming of the future Buddha (Skt., Maitraya; Pali, Metteya). Devotees of one or other of these millenarian figures (sometimes appearing as royal pretenders replete with imitation royal courts and retinues, more often held to exist in some mystical state or realms) are frequently organized into *gain: (Pali, gaṇa).* *Gain:* is often rendered in the literature as "sect," but means "congregation" in this usage. (Within the *sangha,* Burmese usage maintains a blurred distinction between *gain:,* with their separate monasteries, ordination traditions, and Vinaya interpretations, and *nikāya,* sects, which may, in addition, refuse commensality and monastic coresidence with other groups of monks.

These *gain:* are semisecret congregations, no doubt partly owing to their millenarianism being perceived as defiance of constituted government, but also because of the nature of their practices. These practices, including the attempt to compound alchemical substances (*dat-loun:,* "lumps of power"—the essential ingredient is mercury) that are expected to make one invincible and to prolong one's existence indefinitely, are intended to ensure that the devotees will attain what amount to the fruits of the higher absorptions or meditation stages (Pali, *jhāna;* Burm., *zān,* colloquially understood as the possession of supernormal powers). In this way, the practitioners expect to be preserved until the arrival of Metteya, in order that they may hear him preach his dispensation and so be able "at once" to attain *nibbāna* (Skt., *nirvāṇa;* Burm., *nei?pan*). The importance of the idea of congregation here is that the conjoint practice of these acts and rites will generate conjoint powers (rather on the analogy of a battery), a notion also employed in the chanting of the protective *paritta* (Burm. *payei?*) texts.

The supreme adept in *gain:* practices is said to obtain *wei?za* (Pali, *vijjā,* "wisdom"), or to be, more correctly *wei?zadou* (Pali, *vijjādhara;* a knower of charms, a sorcerer). Technically, the point of becoming a *wei?zadou* is to attain the highest *zān,* in which case one is said to exist in a sort of suspended state. This state, condition, or realm is known to the Burmese as *htwe? ya? pau?,* which may be translated perhaps as "the point of going out." It seems not unlikely that there are connections here with the idea of "going beyond" in wisdom characteristic of the *prajñāpāramitā* view in Mahāyāna Buddhism. This is not impossible in view of the long history of mutual influences between the various schools of Buddhism and the complex history of pre-Pagan Mon Buddhism. It was from this latter that the Burmese supposedly got their Theravāda and earliest Pagan Buddhism in Burma, which, far from being pure Theravāda, was largely Sanskritic, partly Tantric, partly Sarvāstivāda, and partly other, less clearly known things.

Another reason for the semiclandestine nature of millenarian Buddhism and the *gain:* is the profound ambivalence that in Theravāda countries has always attended emphasis on meditation practices and the associated study of *Abhidhamma,* owing to the suspicion that such adepts and students may be chiefly interested not in salvation but rather in securing and using the supernormal powers attendant upon such practices. The deliberate pursuit of such powers as an end in itself, and the overt claim to such powers, is prohibited by the Buddha for monks, and by implication at least, for Buddhists in general. Furthermore, the rise in popularity of both monastic and lay-oriented meditation movements and centers, and perhaps even the prominence in Burma of Abhidhamma *pariyatti* (scholarship), given the close canonical relationship between the two, may reflect a sort of domestication of millenarian tendencies in a country, and nowadays in an age, marked by a considerable amount of political instability, social change, and cultural malaise. Its popularity among Burma's westernized classes as part of an attempt to make it compatible with their notion of a modern worldview makes this likely. In particular, it may be significant that, as in most aspects of millenarian Buddhism, the organizations are lay only, so there also exists a considerable proliferation of purely lay meditation organizations; the absence of monks in these cases seems to represent a development distinct from traditional notions of Theravāda orthodoxy.

It would be a mistake to equate all aspects of magical Buddhism, however, with millenarian Buddhism. For, as ambivalent as orthodoxy, represented in particular by the Vinaya, is toward the practice by monks of the apotropaic use of Buddhist symbols in astrology, the casting of horoscopes, the provision of amulets, and the preparation of charms, and as common as it is for practitioners of these arts to be laymen, there are plenty of otherwise perfectly orthodox monks who practice them, too. Furthermore, those laymen who possess ability in this area tend overwhelmingly to learn their craft during periods of relatively prolonged monastic residence as monks or novices, presumably from monks.

One final matter requires an account, and that is the question why it is that millenarian movements, the intense and pervasive concern with acquiring merit, and all other attempts to be reborn as a male human being with wealth and status characterize so much of Burmese Buddhism. Is this an indication of a failure of the capacity to believe in the goal of *nibbāna,* of a noncanonical (if not positively unorthodox) tendency in Burmese religion? Is the fact, common in many Theravāda countries, that merit-making activities are occasions of public display of one's giving *(dāna)* unambiguously contrary to the scriptural adjuration that unpublicized giving is the most, if not the only, meritorious form? It seems not.

Consider some ambiguities connected with merit. First, there is the economic principle that it takes the fruits of previously earned merit to make greater merit, and that merit is to some extent proportional to the fruits of previous merit—because only then does one have the good fortune to be born into the position from which the greater merit may be made. Translated into practical action, this principle leads to the notion that the meritoriousness of any act is arguable. In particular, a person in a position of social or personal obligation with respect to any act of giving earns little merit from it, since only free, unobligated acts really earn merit for the actor. Consider also the principle that one rarely if ever knows where one stands in one's samsaric trajectory; one does not know, for instance, how much demerit may still have to be expiated or how much merit must still be made in order that one may be in the position to make a serious attempt towards transcendental goals, *nibbāna* above all.

Since the merit from an act is relative to the act's being done freely, and since a consequence of the uncertainty about one's overall store of merit and demerit is a pervasive uncertainty about relative social status and one's sumptuary obligations toward others, the only way one can be reasonably certain about one's *dāna* is to have its meritoriousness publicly acknowledged, hence publicly displayed. In the same vein, it must often seem canonically justifiable that one finds oneself psychologically incapable of giving serious positive commitment to purely religious goals. In such cases, it may seem perhaps wiser to aspire to a future human birth in which one's store of merit will be sufficient to motivate one toward transcendental objectives, or even to have such objectives taught to one by Metteya. The devotee hopes for greater personal, social, and economic stability at some future time as a better basis for ultimate accomplishments, and invests one's present resources in merit making accordingly. The measure of the practitioner's commitment to nibbanic soteriology is clearly the embarrassment people admit to when they shy away from trying for nibbanic extinction and the fervency with which they pray that they may in a better future life be able to try and attain *nibbāna*.

[*See also* Buddhism, *article on* Buddhism in Southeast Asia; Theravāda; Saṃgha, *article on* Saṃgha and Society; Kingship, *article on* Kingship in Southeast Asia; Cakravartin; Merit, *article on* Buddhist Concepts; Folk Religion, *article on* Folk Buddhism; Worship and Cultic Life, *article on* Buddhist Cultic Life in Southeast Asia; Buddhist Religious Year; *and* Nats.]

BIBLIOGRAPHY

Aung-Thwin, Michael. *Pagan: The Foundations of Modern Burma.* Honolulu, 1985. A trenchant analysis of the political economy of royal merit making.

Bizot, François. *Le figuier à cinq branches: Recherche sur le bouddhisme khmer.* Paris, 1976. Fine analysis of non-Theravāda aspects of Southeast Asian Buddhism and monasticism.

Ferguson, John P. "The Symbolic Dimensions of the Burmese Sangha." Ph.D. diss., Cornell University, 1975. The major study of monastic sectarianism and its history.

Ferguson, John P., and E. Michael Mendelson. "Masters of the Buddhist Occult: The Burmese Weikzas." *Contributions to Asian Studies* 16 (1981): 62–80. The one easy introduction to Burmese millenarian Buddhism.

Htin Aung, Maung. *Folk Elements in Burmese Buddhism.* London, 1962.

Lehman, Frederic K. "On the Vocabulary and Semantics of 'Field' in Theravada Buddhist Society." *Contributions to Asian Studies* 16 (1981): 101–111.

Lehman, Frederic K. "Remarks on Freedom and Bondage in Traditional Burma and Thailand." *Journal of Southeast Asian Studies* 15 (September 1984): 233–244.

Luce, Gordon H. *Old Burma, Early Pagán.* 3 vols. Locust Valley, N.Y., 1969. A great Burma scholar's monumental work; the standard source on earliest Burmese history.

Mendelson, E. Michael. *Sangha and State in Burma.* Ithaca, N.Y., 1975. To date, the definitive work on its subject.

Nash, Manning. *The Golden Road to Modernity.* New York, 1965. Probably the best modern village ethnography of Burma.

Ray, Nihar-Ranjan. *Sanskrit Buddhism in Burma.* Calcutta, 1936.

Schober, Juliane. "On Burmese Horoscopes." *South East Asian Review* 5 (1980): 43–56. The latest and most acute treatment of Burmese astrological concepts in a Western language.

Scott, James George. *The Burman: His Life and Notions* (1882). 3d ed. London, 1910. The standard general introduction to Burmese social and cultural life.

Shorto, H. L. "The Planets, the Days of the Week and the Points of the Compass: Orientation Symbolism in 'Burma.' " In *Natural Symbols in South East Asia*, edited by G. B. Milner, pp. 152–164. London, 1978. A unique and insightful treatment of Burmese ideas of temporality and directionality.

Spiro, Melford E. *Buddhism and Society: A Great Tradition and Its Burmese Vicissitudes.* New York, 1970. Spiro's books are the most thorough descriptions and analyses of Burmese religion, combining fine ethnography and fine anthropological analysis with sound use of philosophical and textual knowledge, although the author's psychoanalytical emphasis has been often criticized.

Spiro, Melford E. *Burmese Supernaturalism.* Exp. ed. Philadelphia, 1978.

Steinberg, David I. *Burma: A Socialist Nation of Southeast Asia.* Boulder, 1982. A fine popular introduction to modern Burma, its peoples, history, politics, economics.

Temple, R. C. *The Thirty-seven Nats: A Phase of Spirit-Worship Prevailing in Burma.* London, 1906. The standard description of these figures, illustrated.

FREDERIC K. LEHMAN (CHIT HLAING)

BURNOUF, EUGÈNE (1801–1852), French Sanskritist, Buddhologist, and Indologist. Son of the classicist Jean-Louis Burnouf, Eugène Burnouf was born in Paris on 8 April 1801. After distinguishing himself at the Lycée Louis-le-Grand and the École de Chartes, Eugène began the study of Sanskrit with his father and Leonard de Chézy in 1824, only one year after de Chézy's appointment to Europe's first Sanskrit chair. Just two years later, Burnouf, together with Christian Lassen, published *Essai sur le Pali* (1826) which identified and analyzed the sacred language of Theravāda Buddhism of Ceylon (Sri Lanka) and mainland Southeast Asia.

If a single person can be credited with inaugurating the West's serious study of Buddhism according to primary sources, he is Eugène Burnouf. In less than three decades prior to the middle of the nineteenth century, Burnouf succeeded in establishing European Buddhist studies on solid footing through his own research and preparation of young scholars, and also in contributing significantly to the foundation of studies in the Veda and the Purānas, and to Avestan studies as well.

In 1833, a year that also saw publication of *Commen-*

taire sur le Yaçna, a landmark in modern Avestan studies, Eugène succeeded de Chézy as professor of Sanskrit at the Collège de France. About the same time, he began work on the Buddhist texts sent by Brian H. Hodgson, an East India Company resident in Katmandu, to the French Asiatic Society in Paris. By 1837, Burnouf had resolved to translate the *Saddharmapuṇḍarīka Sūtra* (Lotus Sutra of the True Dharma), a text that he felt was most representative of the materials sent by Hodgson.

About 1840, Burnouf decided that the annotations needed to make a translation of the *Lotus Sutra* intelligible to European audiences threatened to overwhelm the text. He thus set as a preliminary task the writing of an "introduction to Buddhism" that would provide the necessary context. His *Introduction à l'histoire du bouddhisme indien* was published in 1844. His *Lotus de la bonne loi*, the translation of the *Lotus Sutra*, appeared posthumously in 1852.

Although Burnouf is deservedly celebrated for his own pathbreaking scholarship on Buddhism and the Avestan tradition, his importance to the history of religions does not end there. Among his students in Paris in the 1840s was the young Sanskritist F. Max Müller. "Went to Burnouf, [who is] spiritual, amiable, thoroughly French," Müller wrote in his journal in 1845, and continued,

> He received me in the most friendly way, talked a great deal, and all that he said was valuable, not on ordinary topics but on special [ones]. "I am a Brahman, a Buddhist, a Zoroastrian; I hate the Jesuits"—that is the sort of man [he is]. His lectures were on the *Rig-veda*, and they opened a new world to me. He explained to us his own research, he showed us new manuscripts that he had received from India, in fact he did all he could to make us his fellow-workers.

It was at Burnouf's urging that Müller undertook his own critical edition of the *Ṛgveda Saṃhitā* (1849–1873).

In addition to Burnouf's teaching and his continuing research in Buddhist, Sanskrit, and Tibetan sources, he also worked on materials directly significant for the study of Hinduism, seeing a translation of the first nine books (in three volumes) of the *Bhāgavata Purāṇa* (1840–1847) into print before his death.

To his pioneering Buddhist studies Burnouf brought a calm and imperturbable attitude generally unruffled by the new and often puzzling ideas his research disclosed. Patient and thorough, this scholar, whose genius effectively introduced in Europe the scientific study of Hīnāyana and Mahāyāna Buddhist traditions, remained open throughout his lamentably brief career to information from all Buddhist sources. He set standards for Buddhist studies that few of his successors would match.

BIBLIOGRAPHY

Although by no means of merely antiquarian interest, Eugène Burnouf's scholarly writings have remained untranslated into English. *L'introduction à l'histoire du bouddhisme indien* (Paris, 1844) and the translations *Le Lotus de la bonne loi* (Paris, 1852) and *Le Bhāgavata Purāṇa*, 5 vols. (Paris, 1840–1898) are still important and provide the reader of French with eloquent testimony to the spirit and grace of Burnouf's judicious scholarship.

Appreciations of Burnouf's life and work are numerous. Among the more helpful are Sylvain Lévi's preface to the 1925 edition of *Le Lotus;* Raymond Schwab's *La renaissance orientale* (Paris, 1950), esp. pp. 309–316; and Ernst Windisch's *Geschichte der Sanskrit-Philologie und indischen Altertumskunde*, 2 vols. (Strasbourg, 1917–1920), pp. 123–140.

G. R. WELBON

BUSHIDŌ, the Japanese warrior's code, cannot be defined by a single neat formula. Every age can be said to have had notions of acceptable warrior behavior, but apart from certain core values—of which the most obvious were skill at arms, courage, hardihood, and a serious demeanor—the criteria varied substantially. It was until recent times an unwritten code, in the sense that no one document contained a complete formulation; rather, the code was reflected in literature, regulations, and decrees. Even when it was committed to writing, it was subject to periodic change.

Origin and Development. The *bushi* emerged as a class during the tenth century, when a militia system controlled by the central government broke down in the provinces. Local bands brought together by blood ties and geographic propinquity were formed under the leadership of a provincial governor or large holder of land rights, with few exceptions sprung from the lower echelons of the aristocracy. A bond of mutual loyalty, heavily weighted in the leader's favor, emerged: unspecified protection in exchange for unlimited military service.

It has been plausibly suggested that these warriors inherited their fighting spirit from the continental immigrants who had established themselves as the dominant racial strain centuries earlier. These had been mounted fighting men, whose ethos may well have survived on the frontier during the sinicization of the Japanese heartland. Certainly, the indomitable warrior spirit is portrayed in Japan's earliest surviving literature, which dates from the eighth century. During the eleventh century, however, although the silken aristocrats of the capital used them to settle their power contests, they looked down on them as inferior relations, rebels, or uneducated rustics. But by the end of the twelfth century, the *bushi* had become indispensable in keeping order in the capital. Eventually they took over the effective administration of the whole country, with a consequent enhancement of status.

Thenceforth, terms attesting the existence of a concept of Bushidō began to appear, although the word itself is not noted in literature until 1604. Phrases signifying "the warrior's charisma" and emphasizing the special fighting qualities of the warriors of the eastern provinces proliferated. These extolled their physical strength, superb skill at arms and daring horsemanship, resourcefulness, fearlessness, ferocity, readiness to die, and generosity of mind.

Not all *bushi* could have equaled the paragons depicted in the medieval war tales, but they all shared a clearly defined ideal. Most prominent was their obsession with the honor of the family name. This gave rise to the pre-battle ritual of self-identification, recital of ancestors' exploits, and boasts of personal valor. Expectation of personal reward earned in individual combat, attested by eyewitnesses or by trophies of severed enemy heads, was a concomitant phenomenon. Bestowal of rewards nurtured the notion of loyalty between lord and vassal that became the essence of Bushidō. But an attempt was made to separate the ethic of loyalty from material considerations by generous recognition of high-minded conduct, whether displayed by friend or by foe.

Inevitably, the age of civil war (1467–1568) led to an eclipse of the loyalty central to the unwritten code. A morally and financially bankrupt central government changed gradually to a system of decentralized administration, dangerously lacking in check or balance, and accompanied by gross disorder. The military prestige *(iegara)* of a family—its ability to afford protection—rather than possession of an ancient name became all-important. Traitors and turncoats abounded, for some *bushi* did not scruple to desert or oust an incompetent or unfortunate lord. The hereditary military classes were also diluted by the recruitment of peasants as infantry and by the rise of men of low birth to the ranks of feudal lords. Within a century most of the old leadership had been replaced by new blood.

To survive, a warlord had to mold his followers into an efficient, reliable fighting force. Discipline was upgraded and regulations issued enjoining frugality, vigilance, conscientiousness, and other useful virtues. An ideal of unremitting and self-sacrificing service was created, and the bond between lord and vassal was formalized by oaths of allegiance. New weapons and defense measures leading to the building of fortresses and castles made it necessary for the feudal lord to keep his vassals near at hand rather than domiciled on scattered holdings. The process of the separation of the *bushi* from the soil and his development into a full-time fighting man was under way.

This new spirit had been generally discernible from about 1500. From then on, the struggle for the acquisition of land gradually came to be motivated more by considerations of power politics than mere greed. National hegemony became a general dream.

The Tokugawa Bushi: New Functions, New Ideals. When unification was finally attained and peace firmly established, the function of the *bushi* changed. The Confucian scholar Yamaga Sokō (1622–1685) set out specifically to define an appropriate role for the *bushi* in peacetime. Concerned that they should earn their keep not only as a standing army and police force but as administrators, he urged the raising of their educational standard. Additionally, he saw them as eminently qualified to fulfill the function of political and intellectual leaders. Ingeniously, Yamaga grafted onto the traditional feudal virtues of self-sacrifice and readiness to die a selection of Confucian qualities: moral and intellectual superiority, prudence and good judgment, a cultivated mind and a humane heart. He thus produced a blend of the Confucian "superior man" with the traditional Japanese warrior temperament—what has been called "the heroic man." He did not merely codify hitherto unwritten notions of chivalrous conduct; he created a new ideal.

Of a more hectic temper was the thinking of Yamamoto Tsunetomo's manual for *bushi*, *Hagakure* (1716), which emphasized total self-dedication and constant preparedness. Because it was written during an age of peace, this work has been inappropriately labeled "escapist"; it was, in fact, essentially revivalist. Yamamoto's aim was the moral rearmament of the *bushi* by the cultivation of a resolute will to right action regardless of the consequences. The dangers inherent in such a fundamentalist attitude are obvious, but clearly it supplies a powerful stimulus to purposeful conduct.

An important aspect of Bushidō that now received special emphasis was its elitism. This had early emerged. During the twelfth century, the warrior's obsession with protecting the honor of his name had distinguished him sharply from the court nobles who hankered after high rank and title. Further, that canny general Minamoto Yoritomo (1147–1199) sought to burnish the warrior image by setting up criteria for the recruitment of vassals. Very early also, the *bushi* attempted to distance themselves from the populace by acquiring refinement. Devotion to aesthetic pursuits was particularly prominent during the period of the civil wars. A sword hunt in 1588, by disarming the populace, greatly strengthened the self-image of the "two-sworded" *bushi* as a superior caste. Similarly, the codification of Bushidō during the Tokugawa period (1603–1868) gave the warrior a sense of separation from the emerging commercial classes. The combination of the concept of *bun* (learning) with that of *bu* (martial arts) as the new Tokugawa ideal emphasized Confucian education as the monopoly of the military classes, and reinforced the cachet of elitism. Inevitably, arrogance was nurtured along with self-pride.

The central government and local lords employed Confucian scholars to lecture to the *bushi* on the ethic, and subsidized popular preachers to carry the same message to other classes in a form suitable to their station. *Bushi* values were thus widely disseminated throughout the whole Japanese people, so that the *bushi* ideal drew strength from its congruence with the core values of society.

Through such constant exhortation, the *bushi* were in some measure preserved from becoming parasites. They did not produce, but they provided essential services with a high degree of efficiency. For two and a half centuries they supplied administrators, magistrates, judges, police, firechiefs, supervisors of public works, and so on—functions they had been trained to perform since at least the thirteenth century. They also became doctors, teachers, researchers, advisers, theorists, and advocates of new ideas.

The recent wholesale denigration of the Tokugawa *bushi* as urbanized and emasculated, mere hirelings, is not supported by fact: they engineered the Meiji restoration and the dismantling of feudalism, and, as the bulk of the educated class, they contributed substantially to the modernization of the state. That a class comprising 6 percent of the population provided 23 percent of the Meiji entrepreneurs is significant.

Modern Bushidō: An Enduring Ideal. Debate on the relative positions of emperor and shogun in the body politic has been aroused by the application to the Japanese situation of the Confucian tenet that function should fit title. Also, Tokugawa encouragement of learning revived the study of ancient emperor-centered literature. The result was a movement honoring the emperor as the ultimate focus of loyalty. The amalgamation of this idea with the newly formulated bureaucratic *bushi* ethic penetrated the Japanese mind and prepared the way for Meiji Bushidō (after 1868).

This "new" Bushidō was created by the deliberate utilization of traditional values to strengthen the modern state. Though the *bushi* as a class were abolished, a Meiji statesman, Itō Hirobumi, described Bushidō as "our ancient feudal chivalry," which defined the conduct of "man as he ought to be" and constituted "moral education of the highest type." The discarding of the identification of Bushidō with the warrior made clear the intention to transform it into a mass religion.

By 1937 *Kokutai no hongi* (Fundamentals of Our National Polity), published by the Ministry of Education as the bible of nationalism, apotheosized Bushidō as the central tenet of morality and the mainstay of society, transcending Confucianism and Buddhism. This form of Bushidō enjoined total suppression of self-interest, with death as its supreme expression. It implied the shift of unquestioning loyalty from an immediate superior to the sovereign, substituting unconditional service to the state for a bond depending on personal gratitude, and Shintō mythology for Confucian rationalism. There were available exemplars of devotion to the legitimate imperial court in exile during its unsuccessful struggle (1336–1390) against a puppet court supported by the presiding military power. Of these, the general Kusunoki Masashige (1294–1336) was the most illustrious. Inevitably, he became the focus of a new cult.

Although loyalty to a superior had always been central to Bushidō, it had never been blind loyalty. Confucianism emphasized the necessity of thinking things out for oneself. This implied the duty of remonstrance if the conduct of superiors was considered culpable. Earlier ages had provided notable illustrations, but when this obligation was democratized during Meiji, it led to admonitory assassinations anticipating the horrors of modern terrorism.

The *bushi*'s contempt for death, strongly reinforced by his predilection for Zen, had been constant throughout. Trained to kill or be killed, he made indifference to it a point of honor, giving the attitude its most succinct expression in the saying "Bushidō lies in dying." Translated into practical peacetime terms, this simply meant total and selfless dedication. Coincidentally, since death was always regarded as the final proof of sincerity, it gave rise to a cult of suicide. This could take the form of self-disembowelment to accompany one's lord in death or, when faced with defeat, the throwing away of life by a feat of reckless daring. Modern extreme extensions of this view were the hopeless charges of the so-called human bullets in the Russo-Japanese War (1904–1905) and the kamikaze pilots in World War II.

World War II imparted a sinister meaning to the idea of Bushidō. The code was identified with war atrocities, many of which arose from a fanatically held conviction that death was preferable to surrender. This engendered contempt for, and hence ill treatment of, prisoners of war. On the other hand, it also triggered gruesome mass suicides by captured Japanese soldiers.

Some say Bushidō expired with Japan's defeat in 1945. Yet not long after the war, historical novels elucidating the viewpoint of the *bushi* of the civil war period became best-sellers among businessmen. They saw the magnates of that competitive age as excellent models for successful leadership in the world of modern international commerce. The stage-managed suicide of the modern novelist Mishima Yukio (1925–1970) was a lurid example of how susceptible even a modern Japanese mind is to Bushidō's perennial glamour.

From the seventeenth century to modern times, Bushidō has come under sharp criticism as illogical, irrelevant, and morbid. It is true that excesses have been committed in its name through adherence to its anachronistic aspects. Yet it has by and large been a dynamic concept. To the original core values, others were added from time to time in a continuous process of merging and synthesizing. But always Bushidō carried the implication of some kind of sinewy superiority, of effort beyond the capabilities of the ordinary man. And the durability of its appeal surely furnishes some justification for the Meiji scholar Inazo Nitobe's claim in his famous essay of 1905: "Bushidō is the soul of Japan."

[*See also* War and Warriors, *overview article, and the biography of Yamaga Sokō.*]

BIBLIOGRAPHY

Three small books provide a simple historical background and a succinct introduction to the study of Bushidō: Peter Duus's *Feudalism in Japan* (New York, 1969); H. Paul Varley, Ivan Morris, and Nobuko Morris's *The Samurai* (London, 1970); and Conrad Totman's *Japan before Perry: A Short History* (Berkeley, 1982). Three large and lavishly illustrated volumes give detailed expositions of *bushi* lifestyle and way of thought: George Richard Storry's *The Way of the Samurai* (New York, 1978), Stephen R. Turnbull's *The Samurai: A Military History* (New York, 1977), and Oscar Ratti and Adele Westbrook's *Secrets of the Samurai* (Tokyo and Rutland, Vt., 1973). *Sources of the Japanese Tradition*, 2 vols. (New York, 1958), compiled by Ryūsaku Tsunoda, Wm. Theodore de Bary, and Donald Keene, presents valuable source material on the formulation of Bushidō.

Finally, three essays throw additional light on significant aspects of the topic: Yamamoto Tsunetomo's *Hagakure: A Code of the Way of Samurai*, translated by Takao Mutoh (Tokyo, 1980); Mishima Yukio's *The Samurai Ethic in Modern Japan*, translated by Kathryn Sparling (Tokyo, 1978); and Inazo Nitobe's *Bushidō: The Soul of Japan* (Tokyo, 1980).

JOYCE ACKROYD

BUSHMEN. *See* Khoi and San Religion.

BUSHNELL, HORACE (1802–1876), Congregational minister and theologian. Born in Bantam, Connecticut, and reared in nearby New Preston, Bushnell attended Yale College and the Law School in New Haven. Stirred by a revival that swept the college in 1831, he decided to enter Yale Divinity School. In 1833 he was ordained pastor of the North Church of Hartford. He experienced an extraordinary spiritual illumination in 1848, a year in which he was also invited to lecture at Harvard, Andover, and Yale. The books resulting from these lectures and from Bushnell's attempts to clarify and refine their content in the face of criticism (*God in Christ*, 1849, and *Christ in Theology*, 1851) stirred up a hornet's nest of controversy and brought charges of heresy from conservative churchmen. In 1858 Bushnell's *Nature and the Supernatural* was published, and *Christian Nurture*, probably his best-known work, appeared in 1861 (an earlier version had come out in 1847). Persistent health problems forced him to resign his North Church pastorate in April 1861, but he continued to be active during the last fifteen years of his life, preaching, lecturing, and producing such additional books as *Work and Play* (1864), *Christ and His Salvation* (1864), *The Vicarious Sacrifice* (1866), *Moral Uses of Dark Things* (1868), *Forgiveness and Law* (1874), and *Building Eras in Religion* (published posthumously in 1881).

Four traits of Bushnell's theological thought suggest something of the distinctive contribution he made to his times. The first is its high degree of originality. Bushnell did not prize originality for its own sake; he saw it as necessary for penetrating to the enduring heart of Christian teaching and rediscovering its relevance to the needs and concerns of human beings in a time of rapid change. Second, his theology was intended to be a mediating theology, one seeking grounds of consensus that could allay the spirit of divisiveness and contumely that marked so much of the theological debate of his day. Third, Bushnell held that religious doctrines are not meant to satisfy speculative curiosity. The decisive test of any doctrine is an experiential one, that is, the contributions it can make to the transformation of life and character. He insisted that divine revelation itself has this "instrumental" function (as he termed it), and that its import can be grasped only when it is approached with its practical end clearly in mind. Fourth, Bushnell tried to put theological discourse and method on a new footing by arguing that the language of religion, including that of the Bible, is the language of analogy, metaphor, and symbol, and that its function is to suggest and evoke truths and modes of awareness that cannot be literally expressed. Hence, its proper use and interpretation requires the imaginative skill of the poet or orator, not that of the abstract speculative reasoner. These ideas about theological language and method went much against the grain of the prevailing concept of theology in Bushnell's time, which was that theology should be an exact rational science, with precise definitions, finely drawn distinctions, and strict logical deductions.

Bushnell was one of the two most creative Protestant theologians in America prior to the present century; the other was Jonathan Edwards (1703–1758). Bushnell's book on Christian nurture has exerted more influence on theories of Christian education among Protestants than any other work of recent times. His ideas on religious language anticipated much that is now being said about the crucial role of myth, symbol, story, and paradox in the discourse of the religions of the world. His fresh approaches sounded the death knell of the Edwardian Calvinism that was dominant in his day and had been so since the time of Jonathan Edwards, and they provided the point of departure for what came to be called the "new theology" of American Protestant liberalism. His critique of biblical literalism helped to pave the way for theological acceptance of the results of biblical criticism and for easier rapprochement between religion and science.

BIBLIOGRAPHY

Cherry, Conrad. *Nature and Religious Imagination: From Edwards to Bushnell.* Philadelphia, 1980. Explores Jonathan Edwards's symbolic vision of nature and its religious meanings, shows how this vision suffered sharp decline among religious thinkers in New England after Edwards's death, and then exhibits the resurgence of a similar vision in the thought of Bushnell.

Crosby, Donald A. *Horace Bushnell's Theory of Language.* The Hague, 1975. Investigates Bushnell's theory of language and religious language in the context of other philosophies of language in nineteenth-century America, discussing its implications for theological content and method. Examines and evaluates reactions to Bushnell's language theory from his theological peers.

Cross, Barbara M. *Horace Bushnell: Minister to a Changing America.* Chicago, 1958. Occasionally misinterprets Bushnell's thought but is a very useful placing of his ideas and the events of his life in the context of his time.

Smith, David L. *Symbolism and Growth: The Religious Thought of Horace Bushnell.* Chico, Calif., 1981. Argues that the principal focus of Bushnell's thought is his theory of how human beings influence each other through their social and linguistic interactions. Seeks to show how Bushnell used this theory to explain God's communications of himself for the purpose of nurturing and redeeming human character.

Smith, H. Shelton, ed. *Horace Bushnell.* New York, 1965. Valuable collection of some of Bushnell's most important writings, with informative general introduction and introductions to each selection. Includes an extensive bibliography of works by and about Bushnell.

DONALD A. CROSBY

BU-STON (1290–1364), also known as Bu-ston Rin-po-che and Bu Lo-tsā-ba; properly, Rin-chen-grub-pa; Tibetan Buddhist monk-scholar, translator, redactor, historian, and architect. In the annals of Tibetan Buddhism, Bu-ston holds a singular position. He is renowned as the codifier of the Tibetan Buddhist canon and as the last great translator and systematizer prior to the fourteenth-century reformer Tsoṅ-kha-pa. Considered to have been an incarnation of the Kashmiri saint Śākyaśrī-bhadra (Tib., Kha-che-paṇ-chen), Bu-ston showed a precocious and prodigious talent for translation. Furthermore, he mastered certain aspects of the Tantras and became known as a chief authority on the Yoga Tantra cycles and on the Kālacakra system in particular.

Bu-ston wrote one of the earliest authoritative histories of Buddhism, covering its development both in India and Tibet up to the fourteenth century. He also compiled and produced detailed catalogs of all Buddhist scriptures translated into Tibetan up until his time, retranslating many and editing out of the official canon texts deemed spurious. It was Bu-ston who first organized the Tibetan canon into the now famed subdivisions of "Sūtra translations" (Tib., Bka'-'gyur) and "Śāstra translations" (Tib., Bstan-'gyur). Although the texts constituting the Bka'-'gyur were fairly well established by his time, it was due exclusively to Bu-ston's incredible zeal and effort that the Bstan-'gyur came to assume its present shape.

Bu-ston was born into an illustrious line of Tantric practitioners. From age seven onward, he studied the Tantras under the guidance of both his grandfather and the renowned Bka'-brgyud-pa master Khro-phu-ba. (Bu-ston's biography claims that he came to possess such mastery of Tantric ritual that even as a child people sought him out in preference to his grandfather.)

At the age of eighteen Bu-ston left home and became a novice monk. For the next several years he studied under learned masters from all traditions; his teachers are said to have numbered some twenty-eight. In 1312 he took full ordination. Thereafter, he devoted himself to mastering Candragomin's works on grammar, and subsequently, the various languages of east and west India, including Kashmiri and Sanskrit. Henceforth, he became famed as an unparalleled translator of Indian Buddhist scripture. During this period he also made an intensive study of the Kālacakra, later earning the reputation of being a master of this particular Tantric cycle.

At age thirty Bu-ston was invited to assume the see of the Źwa-lu Monastery of the Sa-skya order. This monastery remained his main seat throughout the rest of his life. From it he expounded the Kālacakra and other Tantric cycles along with numerous exoteric scriptures; he gave innumerable initiations and composed commentaries on the Sūtras and Tantras. It was during his tenure at Źwa-lu that Bu-ston wrote his famous *Chos-'byuṅ* (History of Buddhism), completed about 1322. It was also a Źwa-lu that Bu-ston began to organize the first definitive Tibetan Buddhist canon. Applying his genius to systematizing the canon, Bu-ston established a new method of classifying the scriptures. With regard to the Sūtra collection he introduced a threefold schema. He divided the collection philosophically and historically into what he called the "three *dharmacakras*," or "turnings of the wheel of the Law." Above all, he is revered for having given to the Tantra collection a fourfold schema, classifying these works into four distinct *rgyuds*, or classes: Kriya, Carya, Yoga, and Anuttarayoga. This method of treating the Tantra literature was later adopted and preserved by Tsoṅ-kha-pa and his disciple Mkhas-grub-rje.

In addition to writing and teaching, Bu-ston was an accomplished architect. In 1352 he composed a classic work on the construction of Buddhist stupas (reliquary mounds) called the *Shape and Dimensions of the Mahābodhi Stūpa,* and at the age of sixty-three he oversaw the construction at Źwa-lu Ri-phug of a stupa measuring almost thirty meters in height. This Ri-phug stupa later served as the primary model for the great stupa raised at Rgyal-rtse.

On reaching his sixty-seventh year, Bu-ston handed on the see of Źwa-lu. Still, for the next seven years he zealously continued to carry out the three chief activities performed by a true *bla ma* ("superior teacher")—namely, to study, to teach, and to write. He died peacefully in 1364.

[*See also* Tibetan Religions, *overview article;* Buddhism, *article on* Buddhism in Tibet; *and* Buddhism, Schools of, *article on* Tibetan Buddhism.]

BIBLIOGRAPHY

Bu-ston. *Chos-'byuṅ.* Translated by Eugene Obermiller as *History of Buddhism,* 2 vols. (Heidelberg, 1931–1932). An invaluable resource for both Buddhist history and literature to the fourteenth century.

Ruegg, David S. *The Life of Bu-ston Rinpoche.* Rome, 1966. A fine translation of the "liberative life story" (Tib., *rnam-thar*) of Bu-ston.

JANICE D. WILLIS

BUTLER, JOSEPH (1692–1752), English theologian and moral philosopher. Butler was born into a Presbyterian family in Berkshire. He began his studies at a dissenting academy, but changed his allegiance to the Church of England and entered Oriel College, Oxford University. After ordination, he held a succession of charges, including clerk of the closet to Queen Caroline, clerk of the closet to King George II, bishop of Bristol, and bishop of Durham. He died at Bath and is buried in the cathedral at Bristol.

The first part of Butler's only systematic work, *Analogy of Religion* (1736), argued against those deists of his day who, although rejecting the Christian scriptures, believed that God had created the universe and that a rational religion could be found in nature. These deists denied special revelation on the grounds of alleged rational difficulties. Butler attempted to show that the difficulties found in special revelation, rejected by deists, were analogous to the difficulties found in natural revelation, which deists accepted. To be consistent, deists should accept special revelation. Butler was aware—but did not think it probable—that one who accepts this analogy may reject both revelations. The second part of his *Analogy* is one of the classic defenses of Christian theism.

Butler's ethical theory is based on an analysis of the component parts of human nature. There are three levels operating harmoniously: the several passions, each directed at a particular desire; the rational principles of self-love and benevolence, concerned with the individual's general welfare; and conscience, the moral standard and decision maker. Butler considered ethics to be a subdivision of theology, presenting his theories in *Fifteen Sermons* (1726). Philosophers, however, generally treat his ethics independently of his theology. Butler is also known for his refutation of psychological egoism, based on his analysis of benevolence, a natural component of human nature.

[*See also* Deism.]

BIBLIOGRAPHY

There have been many editions of Butler's two books: *Fifteen Sermons Preached at the Rolls Chapel* (1726) and *The Analogy of Religion, Natural and Revealed, to the Constitution and Course of Nature* (1736). The most readily available complete editions of his works (which also include a few additional sermons) are *The Works of Joseph Butler, D.C.L.,* 2 vols., edited by W. E. Gladstone (Oxford, 1896–1897), and *The Works of Bishop Butler,* 2 vols., edited by J. H. Bernard (London, 1900). Both texts have informative introductions.

The best general work on Butler is Ernest C. Mossner's *Bishop Butler and the Age of Reason* (New York, 1936), while the most penetrating analysis of Butler's ethics is Austin Duncan-Jones's *Butler's Moral Philosophy* (Harmondsworth, 1952). Recommended as a work integrating his natural theology and ethics is my own *Butler's Ethics* (The Hague, 1964).

P. ALLAN CARLSSON